Ayurvedic Materia Medica
for
Domestic Use

VOLUME - ONE

Ayurvedic Materia Medica for Domestic Use

A Guide for Every Home

VOLUME - ONE

By

Thomas J. Graham

LOGOS PRESS, NEW DELHI-110002

Cataloging in Publication Data—DK
Courtesy: D.K. Agencies (P) Ltd. <docinfo@dkagencies.com>
Graham, Thomas J.
Ayurvedic materia medica for domestic use : a guide for every home/ by Thomas J. Graham.
2 v. cm.
Includes index.
ISBN 8172680848 (set)
ISBN 8172680856 (v. 1)
ISBN 8172680864 (v. 2)

1. Materia medica, Vegetable. 2. Medicine, Ayurvedic. I. Title.

DDC 615.53. 21

ISBN : 81-7268-085-6....(Vol. I)
ISBN : 81-7268-086-4.......(Vol. II)
ISBN : 81-7268-084-8....(Set)

Edition : Published in this form 2006

Printed & Published by
LOGOS PRESS
Building No. 4788-90, Street No. 23, Ansari Road,
Darya Ganj, New Delhi-110 002 (India)
Phone : 23272187

PREFACE

My object in the composition of the following Treatise has been to present the unprofessional reader with a clear and correct description of the nature, symptoms, causes, distinction, and most approved treatment of the diseases to which the human frame is liable; knowing that such a work is in constant requisition by clergymen in their endeavours to help their poor parishioners, and also by the heads of families in the absence of their medical friend; and that to travellers, emigrants, and persons proceeding to a foreign climate, it must prove of frequent, and sometimes of signal, service. The chief design of the writer of a work of this description should be, I conceive, to lay before his readers a just and clear view of the nature of the different maladies treated of, and the best and most manageable remedies for the relief of pain and irritation, and the cure of disease; and these are the objects which I have constantly kept in view throughout the volume, and to the accomplishment of which every consideration of minor importance has been sacrificed. In every instance, the HEAD OF TREATMENT has received the greatest attention, because it is the most important; and under this division the plan or plans of management which are generally applicable to the particular malady treated of, and which are the most certain of success, in the majority of cases, have in general been first laid down, and afterwards almost every other useful remedy has been described separately. So that the reader will, I hope, find a determinate mode of treatment, of general and superior efficacy, detailed under each complaint for which he may be desirous of prescribing, and thus be preserved from doubt and anxiety as to those remedies which merit his first and chief regard.

So far as my experience and observation extend, the soothing plan of treating diseases will be found almost invariably the best and most successful, and this conviction has constantly influenced me in the advice and instructions now offered. On this point, no higher general principles can be presented for the reader's consideration and guidance than these, —THE FORMATION OF HEALTHY BLOOD AND THE RELIEF OF IRRITATION ARE THE GREAT OBJECTS OF MEDICINE. These truths it is of immense importance he should bear in mind, whenever he wishes to alleviate bodily sufferings in himself of others; for he will uniformly find, that those means which are the most powerful in promoting the life and purity of the blood, and in allaying irritation, are the most speedy and effectual in the relief and cure of disease. These facts have stimulated me to oppose, to the best of my ability, in these volumes, as well as in my other publications, the frequent and excessive use of mercury, and all other debilitating means,—a practice far more general and destructive than is commonly apprehended. Mercurial preparations, especially calomel, are of inestimable value; but it must never be overlooked, that the quentity administered ought to be very small. Mercury, taken in minute doses, soothes and tranquillizes the disordered system, and sometimes proves the most certain and powerful means of recovery; but when given in large doses it breaks down the integrity of the blood, becomes highly irritating to all the organs, and, for the most part, permanently deleterious.

The human body often falls quickly into a state of debility and disease, but from such a condition, the progress towards recovery is generally slow, (although it may be certain), even under the use of the most efficient means of cure; consequently, when any advantage is gained in the beginning, from the administration of medicine, together with a good diet and regimen, we have much reason to be satisfied, and both our wisdom and strength will lie in following up this advantage by perseverance in nearly the same measures. In the practice of medicine, small beginnings frequently ripen into grand results, and it is too often from a disregard of this truth, and a foolish desire to try new plans of treatment, that persons afflicted with severe diseases fail to get well.

In the original composition of these volumes, and in its subsequent revision, I have uniformly and earnestly endeavoured to exhibit the real value of different professional opinions and modes of medical practice; being desirous throughout to divest myself of all undue partiality, either to the one side or the other, so that my readers may be enabled to recognize here a fair statement, and an unbiassed opinion of the real value, both of prevailing and conflicting sentiments, so far as my ability enables me to exhibit them. In all the affairs of human life, it is, unhappily, too frequently found that prepossession, prejudice, of interested motives, exert a powerful sway, as well over the judgment as the affections of mankind; and hence partly have arisen the error, misrepresentation, and conflict, so remarkably conspicuous in medical writings and opinion. Of course, I cannot hope that the present sheets will be found free from imperfection and error; but if I have erred, I enjoy the sweet satisfaction of knowing that it has not only not been wilful, but also that it has not been without a most sincere and resolute endeavour to state the *real truth.* In no case, to my knowledge, have I delivered an opinion, more especially if relating to practical matters, which has not been verified by personsl experience, or sanctioned by the authority of distinguished professional men, whose veracity and ability are undoubted.

I do not desire or expect to make unprofessional people skilful physicians, but the diseases to which flesh is heir are so many, so painful, and so complicated; the circumstances of the sufferers are so various and changeable; the difficulty of procuring immediately efficient medical assistance is sometimes so great, and the influence of medicines and other means, that may always be safely used, is so salutary, —that we possess herein multiplied and sufficient reasons for diffusing among the public minute descriptions of diseases, and the most precise directions, that can be embodied in a moderate space, for the use of efficient medical means of relief and cure. Accordingly, from medical men in the army and navy, from retired professional men, and also from some of high standing in active practice, the author has received the most flattering testimonies to the value and usefulness of this work. I shall only add in the words of one of the most illustrious of physicians : — "I have always thought it a greater happiness to discover a certain method of curing even the slightest disease, than to accumulate the largest fortune; and whoever compasses the former, I esteem not only happier, but also better and wiser. For can a person give a stronger proof of his benevolence and wisdom than by endeavouring always to promote the public good, rather than his private interest, as he makes so small and inconsiderable a part of the whole? and, in reality, as it is the part of a wicked man to destroy his fellow-creatures, so it is the duty of a good man to preserve them, and instruct others how to save them from death, even after his own decease. Nor can anything be more inhuman and detestable than to insinuate a disregard and unconcern for whatever misfortunes may happen to mankind after our death." — *Sydenham's Works*, vol.ii. p. 384.

I beg leave to recommend to the female part of my readers my TREATISE OR THE DISEASES OF FEMALES, and to the clergh and heads of families my volume. ON INFANCY AND CHILDHOOD.The first describes the proper manngement of women before and after delivery, with an ample consideration of their peculiar maladies, and of many points of uncommon consequence, especially to persons living in the country, or embarking for foreign lands. It contains also engravings of the different regions of the body and the situation of the viscera, with a Glassary of Medical terms, additional prescriptions, etc.. The volume on *Infancy and childhood* embraces the subjects of nursing, food, weaning, choice of wet nurses, exercises of children, bathing, clothing, moral management of children, hints for the mother's management of herself, approved prescriptions in children's disorders, and a consideration of the complaints peculiar to Infants and Children, etc. Both these works should invariably accompany the *Domestic Medicine*, to which they are designed to be supplementary and companions.

N.B. The reader's attention is requested to the following remarks, and also to those on the anatomy and physiology of the intestines at page 696.

1. By the term *disorder of function* is here meant, a derangement of the natural of healthy functions of the organ or part affected. For example, a disordered liver, or a disorder of the stomach, indicates a derangement of the biliary secretion, or a derangement in the secretions and general functions of the stomach.

2. By *organic disease* or *organic injury* is meant, actual disease in the structure of the part affected. A diseased liver or stomach, therefore, means an actual alteration in the structure of the liver or stomach; which, for the most part, is incurable, except in the incipient stage, but commonly admits of great relief. Persons with organic disease may live and enjoy a large measure of comfort for many years, provided their method of living is well regulated.

3. As disorders or diseases of the lungs form so large a proportion of our bodily maladies, the reader will find it necessary to have some clear ideas of the structure of the lungs, in order to understand what is said of the nature and causes of *asthma, cough*, etc. I would, therefore, remark, that the most accurate investigations seem to prove that the pulmonary organs are principally composed of the windpipe, and its terminations called *bronchia*, which, at their extremities, are subdivided into a multitude of small canals, terminated by culs-de-sac of a globular form, grouped somewhat in the manner of the terminal branchlets of the cauliflower. So that we may say, that the parenchyma, or substance of the lungs, is formed by the aggregation of a multitude of small vesicles (called air cells), of an irregularly spheroid or ovoid figure, full of air, and separated from each other by opaque white partitions.

Thomas J. Graham

CONTENTS

VOLUME - TWO

VOLUME - ONE

AYURVEDIC MATERIA MEDICA
FOR
DOMESTIC USE
Containing an Account of the Principal Medicine

Materia Medica is that department of the science of medicine, that treats of the nature and properties of the substances which are employed as remedies to restore health to diseased bodies. It constitutes the first part of the present work, and contains an account of the medical virtues, doses, and different preparations, of all such medicines as are used in domestic practice and with the use of which it is advisable for every one to be in some measure acquainted. Appended to it is a copious collection of approved prescriptions adapted to family use; and a description of the properties, virtues, and correct manner of using the different mineral waters of Europe, and the warm, cold, and vapour baths.

ACONITE

Or monkswood, is a powerful poison, not fit for internal use in any case; but externally applied, in the form of ointment mixed with lard, it is often efficacious in relieving nervous and rheumatic pains. It is better adapted to nervous pain (*neuralgia*) than to rheumatic pains, and should always be cautiously used under the direction of a skilful medical man.

ALOES

Aloes is a bitter, warm, stimulating purgative, of slow solution, and which acts chiefly on the lower intestines. It empties the large intestines without making the stools thin, and is a very useful purgative, especially in the habitual costiveness of the sedentary and hypochondriacal, or in that arising in *jaundice*, *green-sickness* and *scropheula*. It likewise promotes the monthly flow in women, and the discharge from piles in men, and, therefore, when a stoppage of these discharges has been followed by injurious effects, it should always form a part of the opening medicine administered; on the contrary, when these fluxes are already too profuse, or apt to recur on the operation of slight causes, aloes should never be given.

The dose is from five to fifteen grains, made into a pill with a little soap and mucilage of gum arabic; but it is almost always best given in combination with colocynth and myrrh, etc. as in the compound colocynth pill. Aloes forms the basis of most of the aperient pills in common use, such as Dixon's, Hooper's, and Fothergill's Antibilious Pills. Lady Webster's, or Lady Crespigny's dinner pill, is made by mixing three drachms of the best aloes with one drachm of mastic and one of red roses, which are to be beat into a mass with a sufficient quantity of syrup of wormwood, and divided into one hundred pills. One, two, or three of them are taken every day an hour before dinner. They produce a copious and bulky evacuation, and, when they agree, increase the appetite.

The *beaume de vie*, or compound decoction of aloes, presents an excellent form of taking aloes. In this way it does not at all injuriously affect the *rectum.*

There are several kinds of aloes, the best of which are the socotorine, which is in small pieces of a reddish brown colour.

ALKALINE SOLUTION

This medicine is a solution of lime, the ashes of the ash tree, etc. in water, and was first recommended to public attention as a valuable remedy in king's evil and general debility. It certainly is sometimes of great utility in *indigestion, bilious complaints, and red gravel*; also in general weakness accompanied with a sense of fluttering about the heart. Under the head of *Indigestion*, I have noticed the description of cases in which it is more especially useful. An elderly lady was some time since complaining much of languor, weakness, drowsiness, and an uncomfortable sensation of fluttering about the region of the heart, occasionally accompanied with deficient appetite, to whom I recommended a trial of this alkali, in doses of half a tea-spoonful twice a day, in a tea-cupful of milk and water. After taking it for three or four weeks, she found her spirits much enlivened, and her appetite and strength greatly increased; and by continuing it a short time longer, the sense of fluttering entirely left her, and she became quite well, after having tried in vain various tonic medicines recommended to her by several able professional men whom she had previously consulted. Its powers of neutralizing morbid acidity in the stomach, and thus curing heart-burn, are scarcely to be equalled by any other medicine, excepting the water of ammonia; and so great has been its value from possessing this effect, and the power of increasing the appetite and general strength, that many persons, after taking a first quantity, have sought eagerly for a second. A skilful surgeon at Cheltenham, who had administered it to several respectable patients there, told me that his supply was unavoidably exhausted for some days, during which short period the applications from his patients for fresh supplies were numerous and pressing. In *red* gravel and in stone, it is an appropriate and most efficacious remedy.

Its administration is attended with good effects both in chronic and acute gout, during the intervals of the fits. It is also very beneficially employed in the decline of gouty attacks, when the critical evacuations cease too soon from want of constitutional energy, or when they, on the other hand, continue too long and occasion debility; in the complaints of the stomach, as heart-burn, loss of appetite, etc. so distressing to the victims of chronic gout; and in the langour and debility succeeding or accompanying gouty attacks. For the relief of these symptoms, it is good practice to give it in decoction of bark, as we thus use an effectual antacid and tonic.

Several cases of spasmodic asthma have been cured by it; and in the habitual asthma also, and old coughs of aged persons, it is useful. It is likewise of much service in some eruptions of the skin, particularly those which are connected with acidity, and other disorders in the stomach.

Its obvious qualities are those of a tonic and antacid, strengthening the stomach, and promoting the appetite. Sometimes great advantage is derived from putting two or three drachms of coarsely powdered rhubarb, into a small six-ounce bottle of the alkali. In this state it is called *the alkaline tincture of rhubarb*, and is more aperient than in its simple state, and perhaps more tonic. The proper dose is half a tea-spoonful, gradually increased to a tea-spoonful, twice or thrice a day, in water, milk and water, linseed tea, or any other agreeable vehicle; but it requires to be taken in a good deal of liquid, not less than half a tea-cupful, and all acid and subacid fruit must be avoided while taking it. It is prepared by Mr. G. F. Watts, *Chemist, No.* 68, *Strand, London, from whom it may always be obtained of excellent quality.*

AMMONIA

This is one of our most valuable saline alteratives, stimulants, antacids, diaphoretics, and antiseptics. It is generally employed as a stimulant, but its operation is really that of a mild and yet most efficient *blood-medicine*, that is, a medicine whick quickly improves the quality of that vital fluid, neutralizing poisonous matter in it, gently determining to the surface of the body, and improving the cutaneous secretion. Ammonia is carried directly into the blood, and beneficially affects the nerves through the circulation, of which we have clear and abundant proof. It is a diffusible sustaining saline alterative, and antiseptic; but from the crude notions usually advanced by writers on Materia Media, professional men have contracted the opinion that it is merely a stimulants although a valuable one, and therefore not to be depended on in formidable complaints. This is assuredly an erroneous opinion, from which many have severely suffered. Dr. Chapman, who was at the head of the profession in America, has an important remark in point. "In one respect", he says, "this medicine differs from every article of the class to which it is attached, and, it would seem, from all other medicines. The peculiarity to which I allude is this, that the excitement it raises approaches more nearly to that of healthy action."[1] No doubt it does, because it does not properly belong to the class of stimulants, but to that of restorative blood medicines, which counteract a septic tendency in the organic fluids.

The principal preparations of this medicine are, 1. The *Sesqui-Carbonate of Ammonia,* and 2. The *Water of Ammonia.*

Sesqui-Carbonate of Ammonia (formerly called *subcarbonate*) is beneficially given in *hoarseness, scarlet fever, measles, gout, hysterics, indigestion*, and *erysipelas*. It is highly useful in those stomach affections which follow habits of irregularity and debauchery, and in cases of muscular debility so frequently witnessed as the consequence of chronic rheumatism. In the latter instance it should be given in large doses, as twelve or fifteen grains, or more, thrice a day, in spearmint water, or camphor mixture. It possesses specific powers in *scarlet fever, measles* and *diphtheria*.

Sesqui-Carbonate of Ammonia does not act on the nerves but on the blood, and is one of the mildest and yet most powerful and salutary *blood medicines* we possess. If it is not natural to the blood, yet it is a *vital antidote*, possessing the specific property in *scarlet fevers, measles*, and erysipelas, of counteracting and destroying the morbid material by which these diseases are induced. Instead of being temporary in its action, as it has been too much the fashion to regard it, it is permanent; effecting in a marked manner lasting relief and cure, partly by counteracting the putrescence of the fluids, and partly by expelling the offending matter. It does not directly exalt nervous force, but it is most evident that it supplies vital force, and thus increases nervous energy. It invigorates the capillary vessels, accelerates the movement of the blood in them, and effectually controls the strong tendency in scarlet fever and diphtheria to fibrinous deposition. It aids materially in the change of venous into arterial blood. Hence its singular efficacy, in combination with squills, in the chronic bronchitis of old people; and, when combined with tartar emetic, in acute bronchitis and

1. Eberle's *Materia Medica*, vol. ii. p. 164.

pneumonia at all ages. Both in acute and chronic bronchitis, when we see the signs of venous blood mingling in the general circulation, the complexion being dusky, and the lips bluish, ammonia is a valuable remedy in combination with emetic tartar. The latter medicine checks and reduces the inflammation present, and the ammonia sustains the strength and promotes expectoration, by invigorating the capillary circulation and assisting in arterializing the blood.

In indigestion and bilious affections, this medicine will often be found very efficacious, in correcting acidity, relieving languor and chilliness, and exhilarating the spirits; indeed, for the relief of these symptoms it has scarcely any equal; and an important advantage attending its use is, that the benefit bestowed by it is more or less permanent. The cases most benefited by it, are those in which the pulse is feeble, and in which the patient complains of great depression, hangs over the fire, and says, that no exercise he can take has the effect of warming him.

The ordinary dose is from five to eight grains, twice or thrice daily, dissolved in some aqueous vehicle. The dose may be dissolved in three table-spoonfuls of spearmint water, or camphor mixture, to which a tea-spoonful of compound tincture of cinnamon may be added. *See* mixture No. 79. In some cases larger quantities are taken. Those who prefer it may take it in pills, by mixing a drachm with a little extract of chamomile, and dividing the mass into twelve pills, of which one or two may be taken, thrice a day.

With the addition of a little scent, it forms the common smelling salts of the shops, and thus applied as a local stimulant to the nostrils, is useful in fainting, hysterics and languor.

Water of Ammonia, (Liquor Ammonia. This is a very valuable stimulant, diaphoretic, antacid and antiseptic, being speedily absorbed, and operating in a very salutary manner on the blood of every part. Thus, it will often speedily cure head-ache and heart-burn, and is the most efficacious remedy known for the bites of serpents, and all other venomous animals, and of insects. *The usual dose* is from ten to twenty drops, *largely diluted* with water, say in half a tumblerful of water. Ten or twelve drops in a wine-glassful of water are given on ordinary occasions; but in the bites of venomous serpents, or insects, it ought to be given in doses of twenty drops, or even half a tea-spoonful, in half a tumblerful of water, every hour or two.

Rubbed over the throat and chest it is of great service in sore-throat, cough, and pains of the chest, and it gives some instant relief. It is one of those articles which should be kept in all houses at all times, in a stopper bottle.

ANTIMONIAL WINE

Antimonial wine is made by dissolving a scruple of emetic tartar in eight ounces of boiling distilled water, to which, after filtering, two ounces of rectified spirit of wine must be added.

This preparation is a useful diaphoretic and emetic. In feverish states of the constitution it is usually combined with Mindererus's spirit, and the sweet spirit of nitre, which, with water, forms the common diaphoretic draught. In acute rheumatism it is sometimes of great utility, when in combination with laudanum, especially in the commencement of the disease. A valuable anodyne sudorific is formed of six drachms of antimonial wine and a drachm of laudanum, of which mixture eighteen drops may be taken in water every four or six hours. In this state it determines to the surface, produces perspiration and relieves pain. Half a tea-spoonful of this mixture at bed-time is a very convenient and proper medicine for promoting perspiration, and carrying off cold, in ordinary cases, plenty of warm slop being drunk at the same time.

An excellent medicine for eruptions on the skin is made by mixing together four drachms of antimonial wine, one of laudanum, and one of the solution of bi-chloride of mercury; of which from twenty to thirty drops may be taken night and morning, in water, or any other agreeable vehicle.

ARSENIC

The greater part of the white oxyde of arsenic of commerce is obtained in Bohemia and Saxony, in roasting the cobalt ores, in making zaffre, and sometimes by sublimation from arsenical pyrites.

This substance has been long known as the most virulent of the mineral poisons. In a very small quantity it occasions vomiting, purging, tremors, and palsy; in a quantity a little larger, it excites some pain in the stomach, with a sense of heat extending from the gullet, extreme thirst, violent vomiting, with anxiety and depression. Notwithstanding, when properly administered, it is occasionally a medicine of great efficacy, and is employed internally as a tonic, and externally as a caustic.

It is used internally with the beat effects in *ague* and *periodic head-ache*; and is sometimes of great service in *leprosy* and other *cutaneous eruptions, chronic rheumatism, seirrhus* and *cancer*. It has long been used in Lincolnshire as an empirical medicine, under the name of the "ague drop", with unusual success in the cure of intermittent fever; and Dr. Fowler, of Stafford, has established its reputation as a powerful remedy for periodic head-ache. It sometimes proves of greater benefit in leprous affections and chronic rheumatism, than any other medicine; and is now and then used, with similar advantage, in scirrhus tumours, and open cancer. In some forms of tic doloureux and epilepsy, it has likewise been administered with success; and also in some anomalous cases of severe nervous disorder. The solution of arsenic was given to a man who had been for four or five years afflicted with trembling of the hands, great irritability, and other severe nervous symptoms, and perfectly cured him.

The internal use of arsenic is improper in all cases attended with strong arterial action, and where there are any pulmonary symptoms; and should a cough even intervene during its use, it should be instantly discontinued. When it is exhibited in proper cases and with necessary precaution, the effect it produces must be carefully watched : the feeling of swelling and stiffness of the eye-lids and face, heat, soreness and itching of the edges of the eye-lids, or tenderness of the mouth, are indications that the dose of the remedy has been carried to its full extent, and should then be diminished. It should be altogether abandoned if pain of the stomach, nausea, vomiting, head-ache, vertigo or cough be induced.

The best mode of giving this active substance is in solution, in the form of the arsenical solution of the shops, which may be given in a dose of four drops, twice a day, in any agreeable vehicle, and gradually increased, if necessary, to double or *treble* that quantity, twice a day.

As an external applications arsenic has been long employed in cases of cancer; and will certainly do much to improve the ulceration, and give it a disposition to contract and heal. But in this point of view it is a less safe and efficacious remedy than preparations of iron. It has been sprinkled in the form of a powder upon the sores : but the most violent pain follows this mode of applying it; and, in some instances, probably from its absorption, the general system has been dangerously affected.

The more usual mode of using it is in the form of a lotion, composed of eight grains of white arsenic, and the same quantity of subcarbonate of potash, dissolved in four fluid ounces of water; or as an ointment, formed by rubbing together one drachm of arsenic, and twelve drachms of spermaceti ointment. These applications produce less pain and irritation, cause the diseased parts to slough off, and amend the fetid discharge.

ARTIFICIAL ASSES' MILK

The value of asses' milk as an article of diet for the consumptive, is well known and where it cannot be procured, an excellent substitute for it may be made by pouring half a pint of water of super-carbonate of soda upon two ounces of boiling milk. Or it may be made in the following way :—Take of eryngo root and pearl barley, of each, half an ounce; liquorice root, three ounces; water, a quart; boil it down on a gentle fire to one pint, then strain it, and add an equal quantity of new cow's milk warm. If eight or ten fine garden snails are bruised together, and boiled in the mills for a quarter of an hour, strained, and then added to the other ingredients, the value of the substitute, as a restorative, will be much increased.

AROMATIC CONFECTION

Take of cinnamon bark and nutmegs, two ounces of each; cloves, an ounce; cardamom seeds, half an ounce; dried saffron, two ounces; prepared shells, sixteen ounces; refined sugar, powdered, two pounds; water, a pint. Rub the dry substances, mixed together, into a very fine powder; then add the water gradually, and mix until the whole be thoroughly incorporated. This forms the Aromatic Confection of the shops, which is a useful combination of various aromatics, given with advantage in nervous languors, and gout in the stomach. It is a common and valuable addition to the chalk, and other mixtures, administered for the purpose of moderating looseness. The dose is from ten grains to a drachm or more.

ASSAFOETIDA

This article is a gum resin, obtained from the roots of a tree which is a native of the south of Persia. It is brought into this country packed in cases, mats and casks. The best is clear, and of a pale reddish colour, contains many of the white tears, and has the odour very strong.

It is powerfully antispasmodic, and expectorant, and is given with advantage in *hysterics, low spirits, flatulent colic*, and in the *coughs* of the aged and the nervous. The dose is from five grains to a scruple; it is best taken in the form of pills, on account of its nauseous taste. In hysterics a drachm of assafoetida may be mixed with an ounce and a half of peppermint water, two drachms of ammoniated tincture of valerian, and two drachms of sulphuric ether, of which mixture the dose is a table-spoonful every second hour. When given in a clyster for the cure of flatulent colic, it often operates like a charm. For this purpose two drachma may be mixed with a pint of warm gruel.

Its internal use is improper in inflammatory habits.

BALSAM OF CAPIVI OR COPAIVA

This balsam has of late years got much into use in a variety of disorders. The tree from which it is obtained by excision is a native of South America, and the Spanish West India islands, where it grows in great plenty. The capivi balsam is stimulant, diuretic and laxative, and seems to act most powerfully on the urinary passages, and on the internal or mucous membrane of the bowels and windpipe. It is, therefore, useful in *the whites*, and in that state of the womb sometimes occurring on the final cessation of the menses, which is accompanied with a thin unhealthy discharge, great bearing down, and many of the symptoms of incipient *cancer*.[1] It affords considerable relief in *piles* from relaxation, and in *old coughs*. It has been recommended in *consumption*, but in the majority of these cases its heating and irritating qualities will certainly render it injurious. Elderly persons are often troubled with weakness and irritation in the larger bowels, in which case it may prove of much service.

The dose is from twenty drops to a drachm or two, twice or thrice a day, either dropped on sugar, or mixed with soft water by means of mucilage of gum arabic. Its taste is nauseous, and it may be taken in the form of pills, by rubbing together two parts of copaiva and one part of carbonate of magnesia, and leaving the mixture for some time at rest, until it becomes solid, when it may be rolled and divided into pills. If the copaiva be genuine, this mass remains diaphonous. But the most agreeable and best mode of taking copaiba and cubebs is in the *saccharated capsules*, sold by Jozeau, 49, Haymarket. Thus, the nauseous taste is covered.

A considerable quantity of the copaiva sold in England is entirely *factitious*, and I am afraid it is not an easy matter to get it pure. As above remarked, this balsam is a natural production, obtained from trees growing in South America; yet a curious trial took place some times since between the owner of certain premises that were burnt down, and the Governors of the Sun Fire Office, in consequence of the latter refusing to indemnify the proprietor for his loss, because the fire had been occasioned by his *making* Balsam of Capivi.

1. *See* the author's *Treatise on the Diseases of Females.*

BALSAM OF PERU

The tree producing this medicine is a native of the warmest provinces of South America. The balsam is stimulant and tonic, and is of use in *chronic coughs, whites, palsy* and *chronic rheumatism;* but it is improper wherever any inflammatory action is present. As an external application, it is employed with advantage in cleansing and stimulating foul and indolent *ulcers*. Dr. Ainslie recommends it as a very efficacious application in *incipient mortification* of the limbs occurring in tropical climates. A piece of lint, large enough to cover the whole of the affected part, is dipped into the balsam, and laid on immediately that the gangrene is perceived, and renewed night and morning.

The dose is from ten drops to a drachm, twice a day, in milk.

BALSAM OF TOLU

This is obtained from the same tree as the preceding, and may be considered as the white balsam of Peru, hardened by exposure to the air. Its virtues and dose are similar to the Peruvian balsam, but it is less stimulating.

The Tolu lozenges are made by mixing together eight ounces of fine sugar, one ounce of cream of tartar, two drachms of starch, and a drachm of the tincture of balsam of Tolu of the Edinburgh Dispensatory, which are brought to a proper consistence, and formed into lozenges, by means of a sufficient quantity of mucilage of gum tragacanth.

BARK

This heroic medicine, which was formerly called the Peruvian or Jesuit's bark, is now almost always by distinction called the Bark. The Latin name for it is *Cinchona*, and there are three varieties in common use, *viz*. the yellow, pale and red bark. The yellow bark is that which is now most frequently used by medical men in this country.

It is well known that the tree producing this medicine is a native of South America, whence the bark was first introduced into Europe about the year 1640, by the Countess of Cinchon, who, it is asserted, was cured by it of a severe ague, and who was the wife of the Count of Cinchon, Viceroy of Peru. It was sold at first by the Jesuits for its weight in silver, and was consequently very little used; till Talbot, an Englishman, brought it into vogue by the many cures he performed by it in France, under the name of the *English Remedy*. This remedy was an infusion of the bark in Port wine; and so successful was Talbot's practice, that Louis XIV. was induced to purchase at a large price the secret of his specific; and Charles the Second afterwards appointed him one of his physicians. Long since this period, however, warm controversies have at different times been carried on respecting its virtues; and the most injurious consequences have been attributed to its employment, even by respectable physicians! And it is not a little singular and lamentable, that, according to Baron Humboldt, the present people of South America have the most inveterate prejudices against the employment of the different kinds of *cinchona*; and in the very country where this invaluable remedy grows, they try to cut off the fever by infusions of scoparia *dulcis*, and hot lemonades prepared with sugar and the small wild lime, the rind of which is equally oily and aromatic.

In England, the bark is now universally allowed to be a powerful and permanent tonic, superior to all other remedies in counteracting the diseased actions of *intermittent fever*, and of eminent utility in restoring strength and vigour to the human frame, when weakened by *hectic, remittent or typhus fever, periodical pains* and *acute rheumatism*. A striking circumstance with respect to its operation is, that those diseases are most benefited by it, the exacerbation, or increase of which returns at stated periods; among which we find ague and hectic fever, and often head-ache and other pains, hysterics, epilepsy, and acute rheumatism. In the lower stage of remittent and typhus fevers, (particularly when these are attended with symptoms of putridity, as in jail-fever, putrid sore throat, malignant scarlet fever, confluent small pox, and in putrid measles) the bark must be regarded as often a valuable remedy; and the best adjuncts in these cases are the diluted sulphuric, or the muriatic acid, or the tincture of cayenne pepper. It is likewise useful in some cases of gout, and in the termination of acute diseases, when the patient is certainly recovering. Should it fail in the cure of ague when used alone; it will often perfectly succeed if infused in Port wine, or mixed with strong brandy and water. The compound tincture of bark is also a useful addition to the decoction and powder.

In indigestion it is not of so much service, being generally in that complaint inferior to the purer bitters, as the chamomile, gentian and calumba.

It is given in the form of powder, decoction, infusion or tincture. The form of powder is that which is in general the most efficacious, but the compound tincture is without doubt an elegant and effectual preparation, being the same as the celebrated tincture of Huxham, who generally gave it in agues and low nervous fevers, in diluted wine or water, with ten drops of the elixir of vitriol in each dose. The dose of the powder is from ten grains to two drachms. In ague, large doses are required even at the commencement; but in other diseases, fifteen grains are sufficient to begin with, which may be repeated every two, three or four hours, and gradually increased to a drachm. Its taste is best covered by milk, or a strong solution of liquorice, and the dose should be taken directly after it is mixed. The dose of the decoction and infusion is from two to three ounces, and of the compound tincture from one to three or four tea-spoonfuls in water.

There is a concentrated preparation of bark lately brought into notice, called *sulphate of quinine*, which is of great service, and which I have noticed m alphabetical order.

BATTLEY'S SEDATIVE LIQUOR OF OPIUM

This medicine is similar in its nature and effects to the "*Black Drop*. It is, perhaps, a still milder and more valuable preparation of opium than the *Black Drop*. The dose is from twenty to forty drops, in any agreeable liquid.

BEAR'S WHORTLE-BERRY

This medicine is also called *bearberry* and *trailing arbutus*. It is astringent and tonic, and is sometimes of much service in *gravel, ulceration of the bladder*, and urinary passages, and when there is an inability of retaining the urine, in consequence of relaxation and weakness in the parts concerned. It has likewise been usefully employed in *diabetes* and in *consumption*. Dr. Bourne, of Oxford, has spoken very highly of its virtues in the latter disease. His prescription was ten grains of whortle-berry powder, fifteen grains of powder of cinchona bark, and half a grain of opium, in any aromatic or simple water, thrice a day.

The dose of the powder is from a scruple to a drachm, two or three times a day, in any agreeable vehicle; but it often disappoints the expectations of the medical practitioner from the difficulty of procuring it of a good quality. It ought to have a dark green colour, whereas that usually sold by druggists looks more like dark sand than the powder of a green herb. In this state there can be no doubt of its being quite worthless.

BELLADONNA

Or Deadly Nightshade, is an active poison, and wholly unfit for domestic practice. It has been extolled as a remedy in hooping-cough, but a combination of rhubarb and ipecacuanha is a better medicine. I have a mean opinion of its medicinal virtues, but a belladonna plaster is sometimes useful in relieving pains in the chest and other parts. It has been praised by homoeopaths as a preventive of the infection of scarlet fever, but there is no solid foundation for such an opinion. In this respect, it is as worthless as powder of post.

BI-CHLORIDE OF MERCURY

Contains twice the proportion of chlorine that calomel does. In large doses, this very active medicine is a violent poison; but in small portions it may be used with safety, and often with the greatest advantage in the cure of diseases. The illustrious Boerhaave has remarked that in the hands of those who know how to employ it, it will sometimes cure obstinate diseases which are not curable by and other remedy, and this I fully believe. In small doses it is a powerful tonic and alterative, and is frequently very beneficial in severe *cutaneous affections, chronic rheumatism, swelling of the bones, scrophula,* and various local indurations and ulcerations which depend upon a deranged state of the general health. Sir Astley Cooper strongly recommends it in *scrophulous enlargement of the mesenteric glands* and glands of the neck, indolent enlargements of the joints, and scrophulous inflammation of the eyes of a chronic character. His mode of administering it, is to rub two grains of the bi-chloride of mercury in a mortar, with a table-spoonful of distilled water, then adding seven ounces and a half of compound tincture of bark; of which mixture two tea-spoonfuls are given twice or thrice a day, in a little water. In this way it has not the specific effect of mercury, but acts merely as a tonic. The best way, however, to exhibit it is, to give from half a tea-spoonful to a tea-spoonful of the solution of bi-chloride of mercury, according to the London Pharmacopoeia, either in water, or a tea-cupful of the compound decoction of sarsaparilla. This dose may be repeated twice or thrice a day, and the sarsaparilla very much increases its efficacy in diseases of the skin, chronic rheumatism, or disorders of the general health. Whatever way it is exhibited, it should be at all times taken on a full stomach, and its successful operation is much increased by drinking plentifully of diluting fluids through the day, such as barley-water, toast-water, etc. Immediately after breakfast and tea, is a very proper time for taking it.

If it should occasion nausea, griping, or purging, the dose should be lessened, and given in conjunction with laudanum.

When bi-chloride of mercury is taken in over-doses, either by mistake, or designedly as a poison, the beat antidote is white of egg *diluted* with water, which should be given in large frequently repeated doses.

Gowland's Lotion is a solution of *sublimate* in an emulsion of bitter almonds; and it is the active ingredient in *Spilsbury's*

Anti-scorbutic Drops, Solomon's Anti-impetigines, Green's Drops, Ward's White Drops and other celebrated empirical nostrums.

BISMUTH

The subnitrate or oxyde of bismuth, (formerly called *Magistery of Bismuth* is a tonic and antispasmodic medicine of uncommon efficacy in many cases of *indigestion*, where pain in the stomach is a prominent symptom. It is also of peculiar efficacy in that disorder when accompanied with frequent rejection of water from the stomach; and in spasmodic affections, such as *epilepsy, palpitation of the heart* and *spasm of the limbs*. The extract of hop affords an excellent means of making it into pills, as in the form No. 103A. The dose of bismuth is from two to six or ten grains, twice or thrice a day. I have usually found four grains, as a dose, quite sufficient.

It has lately been recommended on the continent as a valuable remedy in *Cholera*.

The *subcarbonate of bismuth* is strongly recommended as a substitute for the nitrate, but I cannot say that I have yet found it superior to the old preparation. It is a valuable new remedy; is soluble in the gastric juice; its action is rapid; it produces no sensation of weight at the stomach; it rarely constipates, colours the stools less than the nitrate, and may be employed for a long time without oppressing the stomach. The subcarbonate appears to act as a sedative during the first days of its employment and subsequently as a tonic. All cases of gastralgia, or chronic inflammation of the digestive organs, cases m which the tongue is red and pointed, and cases in which the digestion is laborious and accompanied with putrid or acid eructations, or in which there is a tendency to diarrhoea, or spasmodic vomiting, are benefited by the employment of the subcarbonate of bismuth. It is also valuable in the vomiting of children, whether caused by dentition, or succeeding frequent fits of indigestion, and in the diarrhoea of weak children, especially when occurring at the time of weaning. One great advantage possessed by the subcarbonate of bismuth is, that it neutralises the acids in excess which are found in the stomach.

The *subcarbonate of bismuth* is perfectly insipid, and excites no repugnance. It is best taken before meals in a little water, or milk, or milk and water. The dose for adults is from fifteen to forty-five grains, taken twice or thrice a day. The dose for infants is from one to five grains.

BLACK DROP

This is a preparation of opium, which has long been sold as a *nostrum*. It is powerfully anodyne, and antispasmodic, producing the ordinary effects of opium, without affecting the head, or confining the bowels. For general use it is certainly preferable to laudanum or solid opium, but is not superior to *Battley's Solution of Opium*. The secret of its preparation has never been discovered till lately, when the manuscripts of the late Edward Walton of Sunderland, one of the near relations, it is said, of the original proprietor, fell into the hands of the late Dr. Armstrong, who has published the manner in which it is prepared, which is as follows: take half a pound of opium sliced, three pints of good verjuice, (juice of the wild crab), one and a half ounce of nutmegs and half an ounce of sffaron. Boil them to a proper thickness, then add a quarter of a pound of sugar, and two table-spoonfuls of yeast. Set the whole in a warm place near the fire, for six or eight weeks; then place it in the open air till it becomes a syrup; lastly, decant, filter, and bottle it up, adding a little sugar to each bottle.

The ordinary dose of the Black Drop is twelve or fifteen drops, one drop being equal to three of laudanum. But it is often given to the extent of twenty or thirty drops at a dose.

BLUE PILL

The mercurial pill, usually called Blue Pill, is a mild and valuable alterative of great service in *disorders of the digestive organs*, and also in many severe diseases, both external and internal, which originate in congestion or obstruction. It was the favourite remedy of that celebrated but eccentric man, Mr. Abernethy, whose recommendation of it has been the principal cause of its high repute in the present day. He employed it in almost all cases of disease, whatever were the character, stage, or peculiar circumstances of the malady; but he was far more cautious in its exhibition than the generality of his followers, for under his directions it was always taken in small doses, and never became injurious. It is, however, a mistaken notion to suppose that it is generally applicable to the stomach and bilius complaints, which are so frequently met with in medical practice. Many of such cases are of recent origin, accompanied with a considerable share of remaining strength of stomach, and often with some local malady, and then the good effects of the blue pill are frequently, very striking; but a great number, perhaps the majority of them, are of some continuance, the stomach being in a very weak, as well as disordered state, when this medicine will often fail to procure any advantage, and if persisted in, will prove very detrimental. According to my experience, if that sensible and important organ the stomach is much enervated, and rendered very irritable from some primary affection of its coats, the blue pill will very generally fail of affording relief; but when its disorder is secondary, and dependant chiefly on previous disease in the bowels, liver, or other abdominal organ, it will frequently work wonders, if judiciously exhibited. It ought to be observed, however, that, as a general remedy, for the correction of internal chronic disorder, or the care of external disease, it is by no means so eligible and efficacious as a combination of calomel, antimony, and guaiacum. *See* the prescription No. 98.

The ordinary dose is five grains every night at bed time; but it is often advisable to limit it to three grains every night, or four grains every other night. Mr, Abernethy frequently did not advance beyond two grains and a half, or three grains every second night. Some physicians think, that a grain, or a grain and a half, combined with the same quantity of extract of hemlock, repeated twice or thrice a day, is in general preferable to administering the same quantity in a single dose, at night, and, no doubt, there are instances in which this plan ought to be preferred.

In all instances, its efficacy is greatly a augmented by combining with it small closes of tartarized antimony. The form

No. 99, (*Collection of Prescriptions*). I have found of uncommon service in numerous instances.

BLUE VITRIOL

Blue vitriol or sulphate of copper, is powerfully emetic in the dose of five or six grains in water; and astringent in the dose of a quarter of a grain, combined with extract of logwood. In doses of from two to twelve grains, dissolved in two ounces of water, it operates almost instantly as on emetic, and is, therefore, an eligible medicine to excite vomiting when laudanum has been swallowed as a poison. A solution of it in water is a very beneficial application to indolent and foul ulcers, which it stimulates and cleanses, and thus promotes their healing. In the *dose* of a quarter of a grain, or even half a grain, mixed with extract of logwood, it is efficacious in diarrhoea and dysentery.

BORAX

This is a sub-borate of soda. The natural salt is found chiefly in Persia and Thibet. The preparation commonly in use is the *Honey of Barax*. This is a cooling, cleansing application to the tongue and fauces in thrush. Dissolved in water, in any agreeable proportion, it proves an excellent gargle in those affections.

BROMIDE OF POTASSIUM

Resembles in its effects the iodide of potassium, and is given in scrophula, enlarged liver and spleen, fibrous tumours and some skin diseases. It acts as an alterative, lessens irritation in the mucous membranes of the digestive organs, promoting healthy secretions from the skin. The *dose* is four or five grains in distilled water, twice or thrice a day.

BROOM ASHES AND TOPS

Broom tops are a powerful diuretic, and they likewise often act at the same time by stool, and are, therefore, of much service in *dropsy*. The best form of administering them is in decoction, made by boiling an ounce of the green tops in a pint of water, down to half a pint. The proper dose of this decoction is two table-spoonfuls, which, with twenty drops of sweet spirits of nitre put into it, may be taken every second or third hour till it operates freely. It is a convenient as well as useful medicine for the poor afflicted with *dropsy*. Dr. Cullen says it seldom fails to operate both by stool and urine, and by repeated exhibition every day, or every second day, some dropsies have been cured. Dr. Paris also strongly recommends it, having frequently exhibited it in the Westminster Hospital with very great success.

Sydenham, and other old writers, were in the habit of recommending the broom ashes, and they are no doubt useful, but are neither so convenient nor efficacious as the decoction of the tops. A quotation from Sydenham will be found under the head of *Dropsy*.

BUCHU LEAVES

The buchu is a plant whose leaves much resemble senna, and is a native of the Cape of Good Hope. Its leaves have long been considered by the natives of the Cape a sovereign remedy for chronic disorders of the bladder, and have recently enjoyed much confidence among British practitioners.

They are warm, aromatic, diuretic and sudorific, giving tone to the stomach and constitution in general, at the same time that they prevent the formation of *red* gravel. The usual mode of prescribing them is in the form of infusion; but the tincture of the leaves may be used. The dose of the infusion is an ounce and a half or two ounces; and of the tincture, from one to four drachms, in water, twice or thrice a day. The infusion is made by pouring half a pint of boiling water on half an ounce of the buchu leaves, and, after allowing them to stand four hours, straining it through a linen rag.

BURNT SPONGE

This article is prepared by cutting sponge into small pieces, then burning it in a covered vessel until it becomes black and friable, when it is rubbed to a very fine powder. In this state burnt sponge is beneficially employed in the cure of *bronchocede*, or *Derbyshire neck*, and other *scrophulous swellings*. If persevered in, it will almost always reduce the size of such enlargements, and will sometimes perfectly cure them; but it is liable to produce a considerable degree of debility, and emaciation, and should therefore, when practicable, be combined with Peruvian bark. In such a combination, it is often of great service in reducing the size and mitigating the pain of enlarged and diseased testes. It seems to derive its efficacy from the iodine it contains.

The dose is from one to two drachms, twice a day, mixed into the form of an electuary, with powdered cinnamon, Peruvian bark, and honey or treacle.

The purchaser should be careful in procuring this article, as some druggists have been known to substitute for it charcoal powder.

CADMIUM

The *Iodide of Cadmium* is a new preparation possessing all the advantages of iodine, iodide of potassium, or iodide of lead, without any of the inconveniences attending the use of these preparations. One drachm mixed with an ounce of lard, forms a perfectly white and soft ointment, which produces but little local action upon the skin, and appears to be readily absorbed when properly applied with friction. The size of a nut rubbed into enlarged glandular swellings, or swelled joints, night and morning, is soon found to relieve pain and inflammation, and reduce the swelling.

CALOMEL

This celebrated article is prepared from a mixture, made, according to certain rules, from purified quicksilver, sulphuric acid, common salt, and muriate of ammonia. It was formerly considered to be a muriate of mercury, that is, muriatic acid united with mercury, but is now ascertained to be a chloride of that metal, that is, chlorine, combined with mercury. It has been known in pharmacy for upwards of two centuries, is the most useful of the preparations of mercury and is more generally employed than almost any other remedy in the whole range of the materia medica. It is purgative and antispasmodic, but its most useful properties are those of an alterative and deobstruent, in which, as well as in its influence in checking the progress of *acute inflammation*, its powers are commonly of the highest value, and are almost unrivalled. As an alterative and deobstruent, (or remover of obstructions), it is employed with great advantage in *indolent inflammation of the liver, eruptions on the skin, glandular enlargements, diseased joints*, and in very many other complaints; when it is generally combined with guaiacum and some antimonial preparation, by which its efficacy is much increased. Indeed; so great is its power of altering a diseased condition of action in the smaller vessels of the circulating system, in which morbid action very many diseases originate, and really consist, that there are few chronic complaints in which this mineral may not, at some time or other, either singly, or in combination, be exhibited with much benefit.

In almost all acute inflammations, it is of eminent utility after bleeding, and is, perhaps, more to be relied on than any other remedy, (except tartar emetic), particularly in *inflammation of the brain*, in children, vulgarly called water in the head. In all the acute inflammations of tropical climates it is, perhaps, unrivalled in efficacy, both on account of the certainty and quickness of its operation.

As a purgative, in doses of three or four grains, mixed with double the quantity of powdered jalap, and repeated twice a week, it is a valuable remedy for worms in children.

But, notwithstanding its admirable properties, there is no medicine which is so much abused both in and out of the profession; for it is daily given in disorders to which it is not, at the time, applicable, and in doses which are highly detrimental. As commonly employed, it has been a minute instrument of mighty mischief, and has shaken to their very foundations thousands of excellent constitutions. Too many of the profession have a vast deal to answer for in their unwarrantable employment of this mineral. Indigestion, and what are called *bilious* complaints, are now extremely common in Great Britain, and for these calomel is considered a sovereign remedy. When the seat of the disorder is chiefly in the liver and bowels, very small doses of it are often employed with great advantage, but in large quantities it rarely fails to be injurious. When, however, the stomach is principally affected, neither calomel nor any other mercurial preparation is either a suitable or safe medicine; yet nothing in medical practice is more common, than for both calomel and the blue pill to be given in considerable doses to patients labouring under severe stomach complaints. In such cases its usual effects are greater loss of appetite, emaciation, debility, lowness of spirits, and general nervous irritability.

It has been fashionable for mothers to give their children calomel, even on common and trifling occasions a very mischievous practice, which—cannot be too forcibly condemned. It is, undoubtedly, of great benefit in the disorders of infancy and childhood, but it is too active a substance for a mother to administer upon her own opinion, especially beyond the dose of a quarter of a rain. It should never be forgotten by mothers, that when skilfully employed it is capable of accomplishing the most desirable purposes; but in the hands of the unskilful it quickly becomes a deadly weapon, producing great weakness of the whole digestive tube, general irritation, and emaciation, with other alarming symptoms, which are, for the most part, more or less permanent, on account of the peculiar activity of this mineral.

As an alterative in chronic disorders, the dose is from the. twelfth of a grain to a quarter of a grain every other day, or once a day, in conjunction with antimony, etc., as in the pill No. 98, or 98A. Under the heads of INDIGESTION and LIVER COMPLAINTS, and in other places, I have remarked on the proper mode of administering calomel, and therefore shall here only lay it down as a very important rule, that IN ITS USE IT IS A GREAT OBJECT TO PRODUCE AS LITTLE IRRITATION AS POSSIBLE. Should it irritate the bowels, a little opium or Dover's powder must be added; should it occasion general restlessness and nervousness, the dose ought to be lessened, and if these effects continue several days notwithstanding the attempts to relieve them, it is a clear indication that it is injurious. I have shown in a note, under LIVER COMPLAINTS, the extraordinary susceptibility of some constitutions to the action of mercury.

In acute inflammations, it should be given in doses of a grain or two every second, third, or fourth hour, combined with the same quantity of Dover's powder, to prevent its running off by the bowels. In hot climates six grains, at a dose, are said to be frequently required, but I do not believe it. If it is likely to succeed in the acute diseases of warm climates, it will work salutary changes in the smaller doses of two or three grains. Thousands of constitutions have been irrecoverably ruined by it in those climates. As a purgative, the dose is from two to six grains, united with rhubarb and jalap, or compound extract of colocynth. When used for general purposes in the disorders of children, any quantity beyond a a quarter of a grain is a large dose, and all quantities above two grains may be considered large in adult cases. Many respectable medical men use it freely, and commonly in doses of three, four and five grains in children's complaints, as well as in those of adults; but, in my opinion, this is a practice unscientific unnecessary, and injurious.

CALUMBA

Calumba or Columba root comes from the eastern part of southern Africa, and is one of the most valuable bitter tonics and stomachics we possess. It possesses little stimulus or astringency, and is, therefore, particularly adapted as a tonic to cases of *pulmonary consumption, hectic fever,* and *indigestion.* It is often of great service in the latter stage of diarrhoea, bilious remittent fever, cholera morbus, and childbed-fever. It also allays the nausea and vomiting which accompany pregnancy. Some eminent physicians of the present day hold it in high esteem.

The dose of the powdered root is from fifteen grains to half a drachm, repeated three or four times a day. The infusion of columba is also frequently given, but it soon spoils; the dose is an ounce and a half, to two ounces.

CAMPHOR

The greater part of the camphor brought to Europe is obtained in Sumatra, and is produced by many plants of different kinds. It is a stimulant, disposes to sleep, and determines to the surface of the body. In moderate dose it operates as a cordial, increases the heat of the body, exhilarates, and softens the pulse: in larger doses, it allays irritation and spasm, abates pain, and induces sleep. As a stimulant, it is beneficially employed in *typhus fever, putrid sore throat, malignant measles,* and *confluent small pox.* It is sometimes useful in spasmodic affections, as *hysterics, epilepsy, St. Vitus's dance,* and also in *painful menstruation,* and *worms.* If sleep is required by a patient, and opium disagrees, or is improper on account of the existence of inflammation, camphor may often be given with with advantage, in doses of six or eight grains.

It is used with considerable effect, dissolved in oil or spirit of wine, for allaying rheumatic and muscular pains; and with the addition of laudanum, as in No. 39, it is occasionally of great efficacy, when rubbed on the abdomen, in flatulent colic, dysentery, and looseness. Two drachms of camphor dissolved in an ounce of oil of turpentine, form a remedy in high repute in tooth-ache, which, put into the hollow of a carious tooth by means of lint, will afford almost immediate relief.

The dose of camphor is from three grains to a scruple, which should be repeated, in general, at short intervals, as its effects are apt to be transient. The bad effects of an over-dose are most effectually obviated by opium.

CASCARILLA

The tree producing the cascarilla bark is a native of the Bahama Islands, and is found also in Jamaica. It is a valuable tonic, possessing aromatic qualities, and is of much service in *indigestion,* the latter stages of *dysentery,* and *looseness,* and in general debility, from whatever cause arising. Its aromatic qualities render it an excellent adjunct to the bark, in *intermittent* and *remittent fevers,* making it to sit easier on the stomach, and increasing its efficacy. Dr. Underwood recommends it in the *gangrenous* or *black thrush,* peculiar to children.

The dose of the powder is from twelve grains to half a drachm, two or three times a day. The infusion of cascarilla is a convenient preparation, of which the proper dose is three or four table-spoonfuls.

CASTOR

This substance is secreted by the beaver, in bags near the rectum. It is antispasmodic, and seems to act more particularly on the womb and its connections. It is supposed to be given with advantage in *hysterics, epilepsy, low fevers,* and spasmodic affections generally. Some medical men appear to have considerable confidence in its powers, but they seem to me doubtful. It is a scarce and high priced article, and is with difficulty obtained unadulterated.

The dose of the powder is from ten grains to a scruple, made into a bolus with conserve of roses. The dose of the tincture is from one to two drachms.

CASTOR OIL

The plant which yields this oil is a native of the East and West Indies, South America and Africa. When good, it is thick, viscid, transparent and colourless, or of a very pale straw colour.

It is a mild purgative, operating very quickly, and with so little irritation as to render it peculiarly fitted for cases in which the stimulating purgatives would prove hurtful, as *piles, Devonshire colic, inflammation of the bowels,* and all-states of *costiveness* connected with great weakness and irritability of the bowels. It is an excellent purgative for infants and children, and for women in child-bed. But in obstinate constipation, where copious evacuations are required, it is not to be trusted, as it will insinuate itself through the intestinal canal, bringing with it a small portion of the more fluid contents, but leaving behind it the collection of indurated faeces.

The dose is from three tea-spoonfuls to two table-spoonfuls, either floated on a little water, and covered with a small quantity of any ardent spirit; or diffused in a cup of coffee; or in water, by adding to it mucilage of gum arabic, or the yolk of an egg. The addition of one or two tea-spoonfuls of some aromatic tincture, as tincture of cardamoms, occasions it to sit easier on the stomach. One of the most agreeable ways of taking it is to rub the dose of castor oil in a mortar with the yolk of an egg, and then add two or three table-spoonfuls of cinnamon or peppermint water.

CATECHU

The tree which yields this article grows plentifully in Hindostan. The catechu which is commonly in use, is in the form of an extract, and was formerly called Terra Japoniha, from the supposition that it came from Japan, and was an earth. The dark coloured is the best. It is one of the most valuable astringents, and is used with the best effects in *bleeding from the anus or womb, whites, obstinate coughs,* which depend on weakness and relaxation, and in *dysentery* and *looseness* when the employment of astringents is admissible. The slow solution of a small piece of it in the mouth, is a certain remedy for' relaxation of the uvula and fauces It is an excellent astringent in sponginess of the gums, and equal parts of it and Peruvian bark, with one-fourth the quantity of powdered myrrh, form a valuable dentifrice in such cases. It should not be used in combination with any alkaline or metallic salt, nor with a solution of isinglass.

An ointment composed of four ounces of extract of catechu, five drachms of alum, four ounces of white resin, and ten ounces of olive oil, with a little water to bring it to a proper consistence, is in great repute in India as an application to ulcers.

The dose of catechu may be from ten grains to a drachm. The tincture is a very good preparation; the dose from one to three drachms.

CARBONATE OF SODA

This medicine is antacid, diuretic and sedative. It is efficacious in the removal of obstructions of the digestive organs. In disordered states of the digestive functions, it frequently acts with good effect, by neutralizing the morbid acidity present. There is scarcely any medicine in such common use in indigestion, and general debility, in which cases it is usually combined with bitters and tonics, as infusion of gentian, columba, or cascarilla, etc. Indeed, if we may judge from the frequency with which we witness professional men prescribe the carbonate of soda, we must regard it as a most valuable remedy; and of general utility in the circumstances just adverted to, and also in other eases. But there are few medicines frequently employed which are more debilitating to the stomach, and through it to the whole frame. Therefore, instead of being a medicine which may be safely prescribed; and taken frequently, it is one requiring great discernment for its safe prescription, and which should scarcely ever be employed largely and freely. It certainly often affords great present relief in disorders of the stomach, by neutralizing the acidity, but this should not deceive the patient, for if he takes it frequently, he will find his stomach weakened, and the intervals between his attacks shortened. I have known it extremely injurious to many persons. It has great palliative effect in *red gravel,* and sometimes in *gout.* When used in conjunction with tartaric acid and water, it forms soda water, which is a cooling, grateful, and very useful draught in all acute fevers.

The *dose* is from six grains to half a drachm, once or twice a day, in water, or infusion of calumba : the addition of ten drops of tincture of ginger to each dose is sometimes advisable. When we wish to give it in pills, the dried carbonate must be used.

CARBONATE AND BI-CARBONATE OF POTASH

The virtues of these salts are similar to those of the carbonate of soda; but the salts of potash act more especially on the kidney, and the salts of soda on the liver. In the formation of saline draughts, the potash has the superiority. The effervescing saline draught, of so much service in all fevers, is made by mixing a scruple of carbonate of potash with a table-spoonful of lemon juice, or fifteen grains of citric acid, and three or four ounces of water, which may be sweetened with syrup or sugar. This effervescing draught is very useful in great irritability of the stomach. Bi-carbonate of potash is considered one of the best remedies in acute rheumatism. The ordinary *dose is* from ten grains to one drachm, in a large wine-glassful, or, what is better, two wine-glassfuls of water, two or three times a day.

CHAMOMILE FLOWERS

Are tonic and carminative, and are useful in indigestion, gout, green-sickness, flatulent colic, and chronic weakness of the stomach and bowels. In such cases they are best given in the form of a cold infusion, or tea, in combination with ginger and carbonate of soda. The warm strong infusion is emetic. The extract of chamomile flowers is an excellent stomachic, possessing little stimulus, and favouring the natural action of the bowels, and is, therefore, a convenient and useful addition to other tonics which we wish to give in the form of pills, as preparations of iron, ipecacuanha, carbonate of soda, etc.

The dose of the powder is from half a drachm to a drachm, twice or thrice a day; of the infusion, from one to two ounces; and of the extract, from ten grains to a scruple.

CHELTENHAM SALTS

The Cheltenham salts usually sold are little else than common *Glauber's salt.* This fact has been confirmed by the experiments of Mr. Richard Phillips, an eminent chemist in London.[1] Good Glauber's salt may be bought for a penny an ounce. The best factitious compound which is vended under the name of Cheltenham salts, is made by rubbing together the following articles :

1. See *Annals of Philosophy*, No. 61.

Best Glauber's Salt	120 grains.*
Best Epsom Salt......................	66 grains.
Best Common Salt....................	10 grains.
Best Sulphate of Iron	½ grain.

This compound may be kept in a stopper bottle for use, provided the salts are first deprived of their water of cryst-allization, and in doses of two, three or four drachms, dissolved in water, will prove an efficacious purgative. The majority of physicians consider it superior to the salt actually obtained by the evaporation of the Cheltenham water itself. Two drachms of this mixture, dissolved in a pint of lukewarm water, and taken regularly every morning before breakfast, will be nearly as efficacious as a pint of the Cheltenham water drunk at the spa, if we except the influence of the *medicina mentis,* or the auxiliary power arising from the change of air and scene, early rising, and more correct habits, which most persons participate in who visit that delightful watering place. Both the real and artificial Cheltenham water are often of the greatest benefit in *bilious and liver complaints, costiveness, gall-stones,* and other complaints originating in disorder of the bowels, stomach and liver.

CHIRETTA

This is an intensely bitter substance, lately introduced into medical practice in England, and in its operation and effects is closely allied to gentian, but is perhaps not so constipating. It is a native of India : and is very useful as a stomachic, being especially serviceable in the dyspepsia of gouty subjects.

It is usually given in infusion; the dose being two or three table-spoonfuls, twice a day. The infusion is prepared by pouring a pint of boiling water upon half an ounce of chiretta, which is allowed to stand for two hours, and then strained through linen or calico.

CHLORIC ETHER

Is a solution of one part of chloroform in five parts of rectified spirit of wine, and is stimulant and antispasmodic. Being a new preparation, it is a good deal employed by medical practitioners as a stimulant in spasmodic complaints, but I question whether it is equal to the old remedy, sulphuric ether. Mankind love novelty, and in the rage for it often forsake an old friend, tried and very valuable, for a new one of which they know little, and which when fully tried is found wanting.

The usual *dose* of chloric ether is from twenty drops to half a drachm, or a drachm, in water.

CHLORIDE OF SODA

The chlorides of soda and lime are of the highest value in preventing the generation and checking the progress of all malignant fevers, and in destroying the offensive odour arising in sick rooms, and from cancerous and other ill-conditioned ulcers. The uses of these articles demand the attention of masters who keep extensive workshops, of coroners, undertakers, etc. and the heads of every family, more especially where the family is large. *See* the articles on *Contagion* and on *Measles.*

The chloride of soda, largely diluted with water, forms also an excellent lotion for ulcers, particularly for those which are offensive and ill-conditioned.

CHLORODYNE

This is a proprietary medicine, discovered by Dr. Browne, which appears to possess very valuable anodyne, sedative and antispasmodic properties. It is given when opium and henbane disagree, as anodyne and sedative in consumption, asthma, cholera, diarrhoea, pains in the joints and many other complaints. Some practitioners declare that it induces a feeling of comfort and quietude not obtainable by any other remedy. The ordinary dose is about twelve drops in water, repeated as the pain may require; and the sole manufacturer is Mr. Davenport, 33, Great Russell Street.

CHLOROFORM

This is a colourless heavy liquid, prepared by a certain process from chloriated lime, rectified spirit, water and chloride of calcium. It has a peculiarly agreeable, fruity, ethereal odour. When rubbed on the skin it quickly evaporates, and, if pure, leaves no odour.

Its action when taken internally is narcotic and antispasmodic, like that of ether; but it has a more distinctly marked sedative effect, and in large doses it diminishes sensorial power, and produces drowsiness, without exhilaration or acceleration of the pulse. It has been employed in spasmodic affections, such as spasmodic coughs, asthma, and cholera, and also in insanity; but we do not yet know enough of its powers to say much in favour of them.

Its chief employment is in the form of vapour, for the production of insensibility during severe labour, or surgical operations; and also during the passage of gall-stones, and in violent attacks of colic, in which its use has been sometimes followed by great relief. But it requires to be used with extreme caution, and is not at all suitable or safe in domestic practice. Indeed, it cannot be safely administered even by a practised professional man; no one can say whether the patient will survive its administration or not. A young woman in this town has just been killed by it, to whom it was cautiously administered before the extraction of a tooth.

It is in truth a very dangerous thing. A friend of mine who had it employed on himself in the extraction of teeth, began to suffer immediately after from terrific noises in his head, which stuck by him for two or three years, or longer, and which he could not trace to anything but this use of chloroform.

To recover a person from an over-dose, the best treatment is to sprinkle a little cold water on the face, to rub the limbs in the direction of the veins towards the heart,—to open all the windows and let in as much fresh air as possible,—to turn the patient over on his right side, and fan fresh air with a fan on his chest and neck, and to place a tea-spoonful of brandy now and then on the tongue. The machinery of the heart is at a standstill, and if we once excite that all is right. Attempts at recovery ought not to be given over for at least two hours.

CINNAMON

Cinnamon bark is an agreeable astringent and cordial, and as such is used with advantage in dysentery and looseness, proceeding from a weakened and languid state of the bowels, and in indigestion and chronic nervous debility. It is of service in discharges of blood from the uterus. It is principally used, however, as an agreeable aromatic adjunct to more powerful articles, as Peruvian bark, etc., which it causes to sit easier on the stomach. The compound powder of cinnamon is a valuable cordial and aromatic's and is given in doses of from eight to twenty grains.

Oil of cinnamon is a powerful stimulant and stomachic, and is used as such in cramps of the stomach, flatulent colic and nervous languor. The dose is from one to three or four drops, on a lump of sugar.

CITRATE OF IRON

This is a new, highly efficacious and very agreeable preparation of iron. It is very much in use among the profession, many of whom prefer it to any of the old preparations. The ordinary dose is from four to eight grains, two or three times a day; which may be dissolved in infusion of orange peel. It has almost superseded the steel wine formerly in use.

CITRATE OF QUININE AND IRON

This salt is now employed very extensively as a general tonic, and is found efficacious in all cases where quinine and its salts, and especially in combination with iron, are applicable. It will be found invariably to agree with the stomach. The energy of the respective bases, quinine and iron, is greatly increased by their union in this compound, and this salt seems to exercise a specific action upon the economy. It is admirably adapted to most cases of debility, to ague, and neuralgic pains; and generally where a combination of iron and quinine is required, this is the most efficient preparation. Mr. Bullock's citrate of quinine and iron contains more than double the amount of quinine than many salts now prepared, which therefore can be sold at a lower price; it also differs in chemical constitution, and consequently in its effects on the economy. Dose, two to five grains. The syrup of citrate of quinine and iron is the most agreeable form in which it can be prescribed for children. The dose of the syrup is from half a drachm to a drachm, in plain or spiced water.

CITRIC ACID

Is crystallized lemon, or lime, juice, and may be used dissolved in water for all the purposes for which lemon juice is employed. A scruple of citric acid dissolved in a pint of water, and a little grated lemon peel, and sweetened with sugar, forms *a good lemonade,* and is a cooling refreshing drink. Fifteen grains dissolved in a large wine-glassful, or ale-glassful of water, with a little sugar, and a scruple of bi-carbonate of potash, make an effervescing draught. These acidulated drinks are exceedingly useful for allaying thirst, and as refrigerants in feverish and inflammatory complaints, and in haemorrhages. When our object is to determine to the skin, an effervescing draught composed of citric acid (or lemon juice) and sesqui-carbonate of ammonia is to be preferred.

In the formation of effervescing draughts, the relative proportions of the alkalies, and of citric acid, or lemon juice, is as follows :

Citric Acid Lemon Juice.	A scruple of
15 grains, or a table-spoonful	Bi-carbonate of potash.
17 grains, or a table-spoonful	Carbonate of potash.
24 grains, or a table-spoonful and a half, dissolved in water	Sesqui-carbonate of ammonia.

Lemon juice, or citric acid, has long been regarded as a valuable antiscorbutic.

COD'S-LIVER AND NEAT'S-FOOT OIL

Are valuable remedies in *Consumption*, *Rheumatism*, and many other maladies. They both nourish the blood, and increase the weight of the body; and are sometimes exceedingly beneficial in scrophula. The dose of cod oil is a dessert, or table-spoonful, or two, repeated twice or thrice daily. It may be taken on a little ginger wine, or peppermint water, or milk, or spread on toast with pepper and salt, like anchovies. The dose of neat's-foot oil is rather less, about three or four tea-spoonfuls, thrice a day, floated on ginger wine, or sound table beer, water or milk.

When, about seventy-five years since, cod-liver oil was largely used at the Manchester Infirmary, chiefly in the treatment of rheumatism, the medicine was ordinarily given combined with an alkali. The favourite prescription there was twelve drops of solution of potash (liquor potassae), an ounce of cod oil, and half an ounce of peppermint water. Sometimes a little lemon juice was given afterwards.

By improving the general health these oils tend indirectly to restore a natural condition of the bowels. In consumption they expand the pulse, lessen the cough and expectoration, moderate the night perspirations, and frequently supersede the necessity for the use of any other remedy. By securing a healthy nutrition of the whole system, they assist nature to recover from the effects of tubercles in the lungs. *Chronic rheumatism* is the malady for the treatment of which cod-liver oil was first introduced into this country, and for which it has been largely and successfully employed on the continent. The variety of rheumatism in which the oil is most effectual is that in which an impoverished condition of the blood is most visible.

The clearest oil is the best, and the most agreeable, because it is purified from extraneous dirt. I do not recommend the brown oil. The clear scentless oil is easily assimilated, and thus becomes a directly life-giving article; and it being a necessary material for the renewal of the body, "we have a satisfactory explanation of the instinctive desire shown by all nations for an oleaginous diet". "Hence", says Dr. Chambers, "under its use, beneficial influences are exerted throughout the whole body; old wounds and sores heal up; the harsh, wrinkled skin regains the beauty of youth; debilitating discharges cease, at the same time that the healthy secretions are more copious; the mucuous membranes become clear and moist, and no longer loaded with sticky epithelium; the pulse, too, becomes firmer and slower—that is to say, more powerful, for unnatural quickness is always a proof of deficient vitality".

Dr. Percival, (see *Works Literary, Moral, and Medical, by* Dr. Thomas Percival, vol. 4, p. 354.) observes,

> "Men and women advanced in years, whose fibres may be supposed to have acquired a degree of rigidity, find surprising effects from it (cod oil). Some who have been cripples for many years, and not able to move from their seats, have after a few weeks' use of it been able to go with the assistance of a stick, and, by a longer continuance, have enjoyed the pleasing satisfaction of being restored to the natural use of their limbs, which for a long time before had been a burden to them. Two cases occurred lately in which the oil had an extraordinary effect, even on young persons, whose ages did not exceed ten years. Guaiacum, calomel, blisters, etc. were tried on both these patients, but with so little benefit that opiates were given merely to procure temporary relief. Their lower limbs seemed to be a burden to them, and they had such an appearance of distortion, that no hopes of relief could be well entertained. In compliance with the particular request of their parents, the cod oil was given. The one obtained a perfect cure, the other nearly so; the latter having a little distortion in his back, it prevented the use of his legs. So general (adds Dr. Percival) has been the use of the oil with us, that we dispense fifty or sixty gallons annually; and the good effects of it are so well known amongst the poorer sort, that it is particularly requested by them for almost every lameness. Except bark, opium, and mercury, I believe no medicine in the materia medica is likely to be of more service, and I should wish for a more general use of it, in order to prove that the above account of its good effects is no exaggeration."

I can, from personal experience, state that the preceding account is no exaggeration. On the contrary, it falls short of the virtues of this oil, which, in my opinion, is a more efficient article of the Materia Medica than bark, opium, or mercury. I have repeatedly found it to be of the greatest service both to the young and old, in almost all chronic complaints, attended with great debility.

Dr. Theophilus Thompson, the able physician to the Consumptive Hospital at Brompton, has related a well marked case of great improvement in consumption from the use of neat's-foot oil, which will be interesting to the reader.—*Clinical Lectures, in Lancet,* October, 11, 1851—

> J. K., a tailor, aged thirty-four, unmarried, square built, of middle stature and dark complexion, was admitted as an in-patient on November 20, 1849; was born in Cork, but had been for fifteen years in London; accustomed to sleep in a close room, and to work in a confined apartment with from forty to sixty companions; always feeling faint and weak in the evening, and occasionally indulging in drinking bouts, which much impaired his appetite; for three years unemployed during the winter months. His brother, who was accustomed to work with him, lately died in this hospital. He lost a sister, aged sixteen, from phthisis, and probably his mother, at the age of thirty-eight. His father is living, aged sixty-one, and a sister, aged thirty-six, with a family of five children.
>
> *Treatment*—Ordinary diet with eggs, and an extra allowance of milk; cod-liver oil externally and internally. For the cough, blisters were applied, and he took in succession hydrocyanic acid, four minim doses of tincture of aconite in spermaceti mixture, and afterwards morphia, with which gallic acid was combined, with a view to moderate the perspirations; acetate of potash and decoction of broom were also given on account of the oedema.
>
> On the 29th of December he was still unable to leave his bed, and as the symptoms were aggravated, and his weakness increasing, I determined to give a trial to neat's-foot oil, thus combined: two ounces of neat's-foot oil, a drachm of solution of potash, six ounces of peppermint water: of this mixture, an ounce thrice a day. Under this treatment, the pulse, which on the 29th of December was 100, gradually improved, being on January the 9th, 1884, and fuller, and

on the 4th of February, 1880. At this latter date he was sufficiently improved in strength to go down stairs to be weighed, and was found to be seven stone five pounds and three-quarters. The weight steadily increased, being on February 13th, seven stone six pounds; March 1, seven atone six pounds and a half; March 16, seven stone seven pounds and three-quarters; April 16, seven stone nine pounds and a half. Three grains of tannic acid in infusion of cascarilla were given twice or thrice daily with apparent advantage; the expectoration gradually diminished to half the previous quantity. In the third week of April lie left the hospital, so much improved as to be able to resume his work.

Pale cod-liver oil may be purchased at Keating's, 79, St. Paul's Church Yard, and probably at the other wholesale druggists, at ten shillings and six pence a gallon.

COLCHICUM

This is the meadow-saffron, and is an indigenous perennial plant, (the *Hermodactylus of* the ancients), generally found growing in moist rich meadow grounds, and flowering in September. Its official name is *colchicum autumnale,* and it is well known to be poisonous to animals of all classes. That admirable principle of preservation, called *instinct,* implanted in animals by the All-wise and Beneficent Creator, leads them to avoid the foliage in the fields.

It operates chiefly on the *duodenum,* or first intestine; and its action is that of a purgative, diuretic, and sedative or narcotic. Hence it stimulates the excretory ducts of the liver and pancreas, and the mucous membrane of the intestines, producing copious bilious stools, and diminishing febrile action; but it is a violent medicine, often dreadfully depressing, and therefore unfit for domestic use. Indeed, I have a mean opinion of its remedial powers, and advise it never to be used in a larger dose than fifteen minims of either the vinegar or tincture of colchicum, thrice a day, with fifteen grains of magnesia, half a drachm of sulphate of magnesia, and three table-spoonfuls of cinnamon or peppermint water. It has been strongly recommended in *gout* and *rheumatism;* but in order to its being of much permanent benefit in these maladies, it requires to be administered with caution and judgment, or otherwise it will prove detrimental instead of being useful. In gout and rheumatism, its powers, when directed and regulated by a judicious mind, are often valuable as an anodyne, since it allays the tormenting pain of those cruel disorders more speedily and effectually than any other remedy, and in combination with other suitable medicines, may shorten the period of the disease. As just remarked, in such attacks it should not be given alone, and never in large or frequent doses. *See* the prescription No. 80, and the article *Gout.* It operates on the bowels chiefly, and the nerves; and, when taken in excess, it enervates the digestive organs, and has a terrible effect of a depressing nature on the whole nervous system, which is apt to be permanent. *White's Pill,* No. 114A, is one of the best modes of taking colchicum in a fit of the gout.

The dose of the extract is from half a grain to one grain. The wine *(see the Collection of Prescriptions)* is the best mode of administering it; but the tincture may also be given in the dose of fifteen drops, combined with a little magnesia and water.

COLLODION AND CASTOR OIL

Is a mixture used with great success, as an artificial cuticle, in burns and abrasions of the skin, from whatever cause arising. Wherever painful excoriations are produced from the dribbling of urine, or any other cause, this composition will be found of the utmost service, as it forms a smooth elastic coating or varnish, which resists the action of the urine for many hours, and effectually protects the excoriated skin.

The General Apothecaries' Company, 49, Berners Street, prepare a perfectly neutral collodion and castor oil mixture that always succeeds in forming an artificial skin.

COLTSFOOT

This is a well-known indigenous plant, which has been used for centuries as an expectorant in coughs and consumption. It has undoubted expectorant and demulcent qualities, and I think the decoction is tonic, and a valuable remedy. It is made by boiling six or eight ounces of the plant in a quart of water down to a pint, of which the dose is two or three ounces, or more, (a tea-cupful), thrice a day. It is very useful in scrophulous swellings and sores.

COMMON SALT

This invaluable article is one of the most abundant productions of nature, being found in almost every country of every quarter of the globe; either existing in mineral springs, or lakes, spread in strata under the surface of the ground, or rising from it into mountains: and to its presence, also, the ocean owes its saltness.[1] The effects of salt upon the animal and vegetable kingdoms are striking and important. It is a natural stimulant to the digestive organs, and seems absolutely necessary to the health of the animal body; for those who neglect it as an article of diet, have a weak and depraved digestion, and engender worms often with a frightful rapidity.[2]

Carnivorous animals are instinctively led to immense distances in pursuit of it; and in the 39th vol. of the *London Medical Journal*, the case of a lady is published who had a natural antipathy to salt, and was, in consequence, most dreadfully infested with worms; during the whole of her life. The principal cause of children being so generally troubled with worms, seems to lie in the pernicious custom of feeding them with a great deal of sweetened food, to the neglect of a daily use of salt.

It is tonic and stimulant. Taken in moderate quantities, it promotes digestion, strengthens the stomach and bowels, assists

1. The salt mines of Williska, near, Cracow, in Poland, are 6691 feet long, 1115 feet broad, and 743 feet deep. Near Cordova, in Spain, is a mountain of common salt, 500 feet high, and nearly three miles in circumference.
2. A mode of punishment formerly existed in Holland, which places the effects resulting from a total disuse of salt, more especially in moist climates, in a striking point of view. The ancient laws of the country enacted that certain convicted men should be kept on bread alone, *unmixed with salt,* as the *severest* punishment that could be inflicted upon them in their moist climate; the effect was horrible, these wretched criminals are said to have been devoured by worms, engendered in their own stomachs.

the natural action of the intestines, and corrects that weakened condition of them which favors the propagation of *worms*. *See* a valuable case related under the article on *Worms*. The celebrated Dr. Rush, of America, used to employ it largely and successfully to destroy worms. A saturated solution of it in water, forms a powerful local stimulant, of great service in *tooth-ache,* in reducing the size of *scrophulous* and other *tumours,* and in allaying symptoms of heat, irritation, and pain, attendant on various local maladies. For the relief of such symptoms it is a remedy which will be found of unusual advantage in domestic practice; and being very cheap, and always readily to be procured, I have much pleasure in strongly recommending it to the attention of the public. This solution, when kept constantly applied to the part is, in some instances, equal to the cure of very large or hard swellings.

To act as a tonic the dose of salt may be from twelve to forty grains, two or three times a day.

COMPOUND COLOCYNTH PILL

This pill is a combination of socotorine aloes, scammony, colocynth pulp, sulphate of potash, and oil of cloves, and is one of the most valuable aperients in cases of *habitual costiveness, head-ache, sickness at the stomach,* and other disorders depending upon a deranged and confined state of the bowels. It acts mildly and effectually in doses of three, four, or five grains, taken every night, or every second night; and is still more valuable when united with equal quantities of the compound rhubarb pill, or with a little calomel and James's powder.

COMPOUND POWDER OF IPECACUANHA

This medicine is popularly known by the name of *Dover's powder.* It is frequently referred to in that part of this work which describes the proper treatment of diseases, for it is invaluable in its effects as a remedy to allay pain, determine to the surface of the body, and alter the diseased action of the vessels, in many obstinate complaints. From such operation, it is often of the greatest service in *chronic rheumatism,* and all complaints originating in, or connected with, suppressed perspiration, in *old coughs*, and *spasmodic asthma,* and in *dysentery* and *looseness.* In small doses of three or four grains, it operates mildly, safely, and for the most part insensibly; but in doses of eight and ten grains it acts as a powerful sudorific, occasioning profuse perspiration. Where opium is indicated to relieve pain, or procure sleep, it may often be used with still greater advantage than either laudanum or solid opium; since it does not affect the head, or produce such uncomfortable feelings as are frequently the consequence the day after using those medicines. When given in chronic rheumatism, flying anomalous pains, dysentery, or looseness, etc., the best way of administering it is in doses of three grains, three or four times a day, made into a pill with a little conserve of hips; but if the object is to excite a speedy and profuse perspiration, ten grains is the proper dose.

COMPOUND POWDER OF JALAP

Is jalap combined with cream of tartar, and is much milder in its operation than simple jalap powder. It is very serviceable as a purgative, and is particularly useful to children with tumid bellies, in worm cases, and in dropsy. The dose is from one to two scruples for adults, and about half that dose for children, taken in thick gruel or jelly. The cream of tartar mixed with jalap proves alterative to the blood, improving its quality.

COMPOUND RHUBARB PILL

Is composed of rhubarb powder, socotorine aloes, myrrh, and oil of peppermint. It is a warm stomachic, laxative pill, very useful for obviating costiveness, and at the same time giving tone to the bowels in *indigestion, gout,* and *hypochondriasis or* low spirits. The dose is from five to ten grains formed into pill and taken once a day. Those who have very weaks bowels, and find a difficulty in procuring any aperient medicine sufficiently mild, will find this pill of great value.

COMPOUND SQUILL PILL

This pill is diuretic and expectorant, and is given with much benefit in *old coughs, difficulty of breathing,* and *asthma.* It is likewise useful in *dropsy,* in which case its efficacy is almost always increased by being combined with a little calomel. The dose is from five to ten grains, repeated thrice a day.

COMPOUND TINCTURE OF BENJAMIN

This medicine was formerly called Friar's Balsam, and was much used as a stimulating expectorant in *old coughs, asthma,* and *shortness of breath,* and as a healing application to *recent wounds* and *indolent ulcers.* It is, however, an improper dressing for recent wounds, because of its stimulating qualities, and of the separation of the resinous ingredients which takes place on its intermixture with the blood; but it is often efficacious in the case of indolent ulcers, and in chronic coughs and asthma. In the latter cases, its warm balsamic properties render it very grateful and useful to the stomachs of the weakly and aged; and it is not so much employed by medical men as it deserves.

The dose is from thirty drops to a drachm, twice or thrice a day, on a lump of sugar, or in mucilage.

COWHAGE

This medicine is sometimes very efficacious in the expulsion of *worms*, particularly the *round worm.* The best mode of preparing the remedy, is to dip the pods in syrup or treacle, and then with a knife to scrape off the hairs along with the syrup. When the mixture attains the thickness of honey, it is sufficiently impregnated with the hairs, and is fit for use.

The dose of this mixture for a child of three or four years old, is two tea-spoonfuls, given in the morning for three days, and then followed by a brisk cathartic.

CREAM OF TARTAR

Is a bi-tartrate of potash. It is a valuable purgative, diuretic, and refrigerant. It exerts a marked and salutary influence on the blood, and is-thereby often found to be of the most signal service in *passive* haemorrhages from the lungs, bowels, womb and kidneys. It acts mildly in the dose of half a drachm, twice or thrice a day, in barley water, and is a cooling alterative, especially if combined with half the quantity of sulphate of potash and six grains of nitre.

In combination with sulphate of potash it is an efficacious purgative in dropsy, the ordinary dose being about a drachm, three times a day, dissolved in barley water.

CROTON OIL

The plant yielding the seed from which this oil is expressed, is a native of the Molucca islands, and of the greater part of the Peninsula of India. It is a powerful purgative, which produces watery stools, and operates in a very short time after it is taken. Indeed so active a substance is it, that merely applying the cork of the bottle containing it to the tongue, is sufficient directly to purge some people. It has been given with great advantage in *obstinate costiveness, madness, apoplexy,* and a few other cases in which it is desirable to purge the bowels quickly, and to lessen the quantity of the circulating fluids. But as small doses produce great effects, the utmost caution is necessary in its administration; and it is scarcely ever applicable to the disorders of the aged and weakly. If the oil is genuine, it will usually operate powerfully in doses of one or two drops, but sometimes it is necessary to carry it as far as four or five drops. It may be made into pills with crumb of bread, or combined with thin mucilage of gum arabic and sugar, in the form of emulsion.

CUBEBS

Cubebs is a species of Java pepper. It is diuretic, and slightly purgative, and certainly possesses considerable effect in allaying irritation in the urethra, and mucous membrane of the bowels. It has been much and successfully used of late in the cure of gonorrhoea; but my reason for noticing it here is the belief that it will be found of great service in many cases of *weakness, relaxation,* or deficient action in the larger bowels, in which it acts as a mild stimulant and corroborant, that improves the secretion of the parts, and gives a cool sensation to the rectum, in passing the faeces. It will be found useful in piles and whites, and in the chronic affections of other mucous membranes, as in chronic disorder of the bladder, etc.

The best mode of taking it is in powder; in doses of from a scruple to a drachm and a half, four times a day, in water. It is frequently adulterated.

CURTIS'S PASMA, OR HEALING POWDER

Is also an excellent remedy for excoriations, burns, ulcers, and eruptions, and as a prophylactic of abrasions in tender and irritable skins. It is prepared by Messrs. Curtis, 15, Crawford Street, London.

DAFFY'S ELIXIR

This well-known nostrum is made in a manner very similar to the tincture of seena of the London Pharmacopoeia, by macerating senna leaves, carraway and cardamom seeds, and raisins, in proof spirit of wine or brandy. The tincture of senna of the shops will be found quite as efficacious. It is a useful stomachic and purgative, being sometimes very serviceable in *flatulent cholic, chronic gout,* and as an opening medicine for those whose bowels have been weakened by intemperance. In such cases, its virtues are greatly improved by combining it with tincture of rhubarb, in the proportion of one-third of this tincture to two-thirds of the tincture of senna. The combination is often very useful in correcting a confined and disordered state of the bowels in weakly- habits; and, for general use, I consider it more valuable than the true Daffy's Elixir.

The dose of the tincture of senna alone, or combined with the tincture of rhubarb, is from one to two table-spoonfuls, in water.

DANDELION

Dandelion is aperient, diuretic and alterative. Boerhaave was partial to its employment, and the German physicians appear to have great confidence in its powers in the cure of *jaundice, dropsy, obstructions of the liver,* and *cutaneous eruptions* depending upon disorder of the digestive organs. It is now much used in England, and certainly proves an efficacious remedy in some cases of chronic derangement of the functions of the stomach, bowels, liver and kidnies. The best way of preparing it is to boil half a pound of the sliced root in about one pint and a half of water, down to three-fourths of a pint, of which the dose is four ounces, (a tea-cupful) twice or thrice a day. If a wine glassful of the juice of cliver be added to the decoction of dandelion, its alterative and curative powers are increased.

The recent root is to be preferred, and in the summer the decoction should be made fresh every day. It may also be given in the form of an extract, of which the dose is from ten grains to a drachm, in water, thrice a day. When the medicine is obtained from the druggist, I advise ten grains of the extract to be added to each dose of the decoction. I have known it of extraordinary service in some disorders of the stomach and liver.

In the case of a man at Croydon who suffered for several months from severe pain in the stomach, attended with a puffy swelling at the pit of the stomach, it proved curative. He had received a violent blow on that part, which immediately laid him aside, and its effects, which were loss of appetite and strength, low spirits and pain, drove him into a London hospital, whence he returned almost as bad as lie went, and was subsequently cured by drinking a strong decoction of dandelion which he prepared himself, of which he took a tea-cupful twice a day. *See* another case detailed under *Liver Complaint.*

Since the publication of the earlier editions of this book, I have prescribed the dandelion still more extensively, and have found it to be one of the most valuable resources of physic. Sarsaparilla I have also found an invaluable remedy; but dandelion has succeeded in several cases of severe chronic disorder, (especially where the liver was concerned,) after the sarsaparilla had failed to produce any good effect. Soda ought not to be joined with it.

DOVER'S POWDER

See **Compound Powder of Ipecacuanha**

ELIXIR OF VITRIOL

Elixir of vitriol is the aromatic sulphuric acid of the Edinburgh Pharmacopoeia. It is a grateful medicine, and is tonic, antiseptic and refrigerant. Its tonic and antiseptic powers render it extremely serviceable in *low fevers,* of a typhus type, *indigestion, diabetes,* and *cutaneous eruptions*. From its astringent properties it is often of great use in *profuse sweating,* and *internal bleedings,* as from the lungs, bladder, bowels or nose.

Dr. Huxham was fond of its use in low fevers, and it was Sydenham's favourite remedy in *spitting of blood*. In the first mentioned cases, as typhus fever etc., it is usually combined with infusion of bark, gentian, cascarilla, or other vegetable bitters; and in the latter, as internal bleedings etc., with infusion of roses, or mucilage.

It was at one time extolled as a valuable medicine in pulmonary consumption, but is too often injurious in such cases, from the want of information as to the proper time for its administration. In the first and inflammatory stage, it is certainly hurtful; but in the more advanced periods, when an open ulcer exists in the lungs, it may frequently promote its healing, and from its tonic qualities may become otherwise useful.

The dose is from twenty to forty drops, three or four times a day, in any convenient fluid vehicle. To prevent it from injuring the enamel of the teeth, it may be sucked through a quill, and the mouth should be carefully washed after each dose.

EMETIC TARTAR

This is the tartarized antimony, of the shops. It is emetic, diaphoretic, expectorant, alterative, rubefacient, and sometimes purgative, according to the dose and manner in which it is administered. It is generally considered to be the most important of the antimonial preparations; and some physicians think that, by proper management, it may be made to supersede the use of all the others, a sentiment in which I cordially unite.

It is given as an emetic in the commencement of *fevers,* in doses of from one to two grains, dissolved in distilled water; but the best mode of giving it is in divided doses, three or four grains being dissolved in four ounces of water, and an ounce of this solution given every quarter of an hour till it operates. It generally excites full vomiting, and is liable to be more harsh in its operation than the milder emetics, such as ipecacuhana, etc. In fever, croup, and many other cases, however, this is an advantage; and in such maladies, as well as in all morbid affections where the stomach is not easily affected, it is the emetic, properly employed; while when the stomach is irritable, where its contents are merely to be evacuated, or where the system is in a debilitated state, the milder emetics, the best of which is ipecacuanha, should he preferred. It is of great efficacy in procuring sleep in fever.

Assisted in its operation by tepid diluting drinks, it may be brought to operate as a diaphoretic, and to produce the effects of antimonials on the general system; relaxing the skin, promoting perspiration, and relieving fever. For this purpose the dose is from one-sixteenth to one-fourth of a grain, every three or four hours; but the most manageable preparation in this case is antimonial wine, (which is emetic tartar dissolved in white wine), the dose being from half a drachm to a drachm, taken in a little warm slop, every four hours.

In the quantity of one-tenth of a grain, it will likewise; operate as an expectorant, when combined with squill, gum ammoniac and camphor. In the same minute doses, united with calomel, it is a powerful alterative in many *cutaneous eruptions, internal obstructions,* and other severe *chronic maladies.*

It is an invaluable remedy in *acute inflammations,* especially acute bronchitis, and inflammation of the brain, and the lungs, or other parts within the chest; and so suitable and efficacious a medicine does it often prove in these cases, that it should never be neglected, and will often be found a more powerful remedy in subduing the inflammation than calomel, blood-letting, or any other means usually resorted to in such maladies. The Italian physicians trust to it alone for the cure of pleurisy and inflammation of the lungs, and give it in doses of a quarter or half a grain, dissolved in water, and repeated every second or third hour. In croup it is a medicine of incomparable power, as I have remarked under that head. In fact, it is one of the most valuable resources of the physician.

Being one of the most powerful medicines in exciting the action of the skin, it is found of great service in many cases of *indigestion* and *bilious complaints,* when the skin is dry or harsh, and the tendency to feverish attacks considerable. If, in such cases, this state is associated with a determination of blood to the head, it often proves of signal advantage; and it has nearly an equally good effect in severe nervous agitation arising in protracted cases of indigestion, not depending on any local irritation, the seat of which the patient can point out, but on the state induced by long continued irritation of the brain. In these instances of nervous agitation, about the seventh part of a grain of emetic tartar is the proper dose, combined with twenty or thirty drops of tincture of henbane, and an ounce and a half of rose water, which may be repeated thrice a day. But in the preceding affections, from the tenth to the eighth part of a grain is a sufficient dose.

In all these chronic disorders, it may require to be continued for some time, in order to insure all the effect it is capable of producing. *See* the prescription, No. 98A.

One or two drachms of emetic tartar rubbed in a mortar with au ounce of hog's lard, forms an ointment which, when rubbed on the skin, occasions a pustular eruption, that has proved very serviceable in pulmonary consumption, severe cough, hooping cough, white swellings, obstinate chronic pains, and other diseases in which eternal irritation and a discharge from the neighbouring skin are likely to be beneficial. The attention of medical men was first excited to the value of this external application, by the recommendation of the celebrated Dr. Jenner.

Norris's Drops are a solution of emetic tartar in spirit of wine, and disguised by the addition of some vegetable colouring matter. As a remedy in colds and fever, they are in no degree superior to well made antimonial wine.

When taken in large closes, emetic tartar acts as a corrosive poison, producing violent vomiting, hiccough, pain in the stomach, fainting, difficult respiration, convulsions and death. The treatment consists in evacuating the poison by bland, oily liquids freely taken; after which, decoction of yellow Peruvian bark should be immediately administered, with opium.

EPSOM SALT

This salt is a valuable purgative and diuretic, and in general use among medical men for these purposes on all common occasions. It operates readily, without griping; and, notwith-standing its nauseous taste, is generally retained by the stomach when almost all other things are rejected; especially when it is administered in small repeated doses of a drachm, largely diluted with half a pint of water, or united with half the quantity of acidulated infusion of roses. In these forms it is a useful purgative in some cases of *low spirits, costiveness* with internal obstruction, *Devonshire colic*, and in all acute diseases. Its mildness and efficiency of operation are always increased by the addition of an equal quantity of Glauber's salt, when, of course, half the usual quantity of Epsom salt is sufficient; and should the state of the stomach, or the general weakness require its coldness to be obviated, it may be taken dissolved in lukewarm water, with or without the addition of two drachms of tincture of senna. Thus combined, it is often of great service in bilious and liver complaints; indeed, half a drachm or a drachm of each of these salts dissolved in a pint of lukewarm water, and taken every morning, or every second morning, before breakfast, is almost as efficacious in these and other disorders, as the celebrated waters of Cheltenham and Leamington, and as those of Epsom once were.

By moderate exercise in the open air, while taking thin salt, the purgative effect is diminished, and its diuretic property increased. It is invariably more pleasant and certain in its operation when largely diluted with water.

It is also an efficacious alterative when taken in the small dose of half a drachm every morning in water, but it is not so much employed in this way as it merits. The alterative powder recommended in my volume ON THE DISEASES OF FEMALES, p. 268, in which Epsom salt is combined with cream of tartar and sulphur, is of superior efficacy.

The ordinary dose is from a drachm to half an once, dissolved in tepid water, or in compound infusion of orange-peel or cloves, or any other convenient fluid vehicle. About five or six drops of diluted sulphuric acid added to each dose renders it less nauseous, and sometimes more efficacious. When it is taken to overcome some internal obstruction or disease, it is, in general, best to take it in doses of a drachm or two in three-fourths of a pint of water, which may be repeated every morning, in the same way that the Cheltenham waters are administered. Combined with infusion and tincture of senna, it forms the common black purging draft so much in use on ordinary occasions.

ERGOT OF RYE

Spurred rye, commonly called by professional men ergot of rye, is a diseased production which grows on the ear of rye, barley, and wheat, but most frequently on that of rye. The diseased grain varies mach in length, sometimes being perfectly concealed within its husk, at others growing to near an inch and a half; its usual length is about an inch, and its general appearance resembles much the *spur* of the cock.

This substance has been known to possess deleterious and poisonous qualities for more than seven hundred years. If taken in considerable quantity, mixed with the healthy grain, as food, it produces giddiness, spasms, and convulsions, on which gangrene and sloughing of the lower limbs supervene. From this cause, an epidemic raged in the Kingdom of Hesse in 1596, and in both

Saxony and Sweden in 1648-1649, and twenty years after in Blois and Montarges, in France. In 1777, a similar epidemic from the same cause ravaged Cologne, and its neighbourhood and since that time, in different years, its baneful influence has been more or less remarked in France. Some persons thought the deaths might be owing to great vicissitudes in the weather and temperature, but the various experiments of a M. Tessier, on animals, removed out of the influence of such exciting causes, fully prove the accidents were attributable to the grain itself.

This substance has, nevertheless; been employed on the Continent by female midwives, as a promoter of labour pains for 150 years; and it first attracted the attention of professional men, in consequence of a brief letter of Parmentier to the Editor of the *Journal Physique,* in 1774, wherein he made known that it was frequently used by Madame Depille, a midwife at Chamont, as a child-bed remedy. Its great influence over the uterine system is undoubted, and it now enjoys the utmost confidence amongst French, English and American practitioners. Indeed its action on the womb is specific, and it is almost the only medicine now employed as an excitant of the womb, that is, to rouse the energies of that organ in cases of lingering labour, dependant on its inefficient action.

It is likewise useful in some cases of *leucorrhoea*, or whites, probably in those instances in which the complaint is owing chiefly to a relaxed and disordered condition of the internal surface of the *uterus.* I do not, however, consider it by any means commonly necessary in this complaint—the most powerful remedy here is, in my opinion, the cantharides in large doses. *See* my *Treatise on the Diseases of Females.*

Thus, we see that the Divine Author *of* all good brings good out of evil, and causes that to be of the most essential service to mankind, when *skilfully* employed as a remedy, which is even poisonous in large quantities, and under improper management. The dose of the *ergot* of *rye* in powder (which is of a perfect ash colour), is from five to twenty or twenty-five grains. The ordinary dose is fifteen grains, which may be repeated in a quarter of an hour, if the uterine action has not become apparent. It may be given in infusion—two drachms of the ergot may be infused in six ounces of boiling water for twenty minutes, and then strained; of which the proper dose is two or three table-spoonfuls. Of course it should never be used but in cases of decided inefficient action of the womb, in lingering labours, and where there is no rigidity of the parts, nor malposition of the head; and it is rarely admissible in first children.

The cases in which this valuable medicine is useful are well pointed out in the following example, related *by* Dr. Beatty, in *Dublin Medical Journal,* No. xii. (1834).

> Mrs. K— aged thirty-five, pregnant of her fourth child, fell in labour. The pains were slight, the membranes gave way, and the waters drained off. The same state continued next day. In the afternoon the pains increased, and Dr. Beatty was summoned. The pains, however, had now entirely subsided—the head of the child presented, and almost touched the perineum—the month of the womb was dilated, and the parts relaxed. Hour after hour passed, but no recurrence of the pains took place. After six hours absence of the labour pains, he determined to exhibit the ergot of rye. One drachm of the powder was infused in four ounces of boiling water for five minutes. The fluid was then strained through muslin, and a third part of the powder caught on the strainer was mixed with half the fluid, and exhibited to the patient. She had not swallowed it five minutes when the pains came on, with considerable force, and continued to increase in severity and duration, so that at last there was no intermission. In less than twenty minutes the labour was terminated by the expulsion of a living child, followed by the after-birth— the mother did very well.

ETHER

Sulphuric ether is stimulant, narcotic, and antispasmodic, and is sometimes beneficially employed as a cordial in typhus and low fevers, and as an antispasmodic in *spasmodic asthma, hysterics* and *fainting*. It is also employed with advantage in *cholera morbus,* to check the vomiting; and it allays the violence of sea-sickness.

But its effects are transitory, and, therefore, in all cases the dose must be repeated at short intervals, of an hour or two, to produce the full effect of the remedy.

The usual dose is from half a drachm to two drachms, but it may be given to the extent of half an ounce, in any agreeable vehicle. All ethers must be kept in closely-stopped bottles.

FOXGLOVE

Foxglove (*digitalis*) is an indigenous biennial plant, found growing generally at the sides of hills, or where the soil is dry, sandy or gravelly. It flowers in July, which is the proper time for obtaining a supply of the leaves of this plant, and those only which are fresh should be selected. In its medical qualities, it is sedative and diuretic. It has a considerable influence over the action of the heart, and of the extreme vessels of the circulating system, and is, therefore, often very beneficially employed in *palpitation; dropsy, aneurism,* and *delirium tremens.* It weakens the force of all the vital functions, diminishes the frequency of the pulse, and the general irritability of the system. In palpitation of the heart, accompanied with great nervous irritability, it may be combined with camphor mixture and tincture of columba, and is often very useful.

In *dropsy of the chest,* it is considered by some able physicians to be superior to every other remedy. It is frequently of great service in other kinds of dropsy, especially in the dropsy supervening scarlet fever; and its beneficial effects are more certainly obtained in those constitutions in which there is laxity of fibre, pale complexion, feeble intermitting pulse, cold skin, and where the swelling easily pits. It has also been found of great value, when conjoined with nitric acid, in the dropsy which occurs in broken-down constitutions that have been long harassed by mercury.

It has been much praised for its virtues in pulmonary consumption, but they have been greatly overrated; and those physicians who have chanced to find it beneficial in this disease, have neglected to observe the species and particular state of the constitution in which it is most useful. It is of service in some cases, and may have proved curative; but it is probably rarely applicable to any other than the florid species of consumption.

It cannot be advantageously exhibited under the pressure of high arterial action. This is owing to its primary effect as a stimulant. Its subsequent or secondary effects are, indeed, sedative and depressing. Thus, in all cases the inflammatory condition must be reduced by blood-letting, purging, etc. before we can administer foxglove with certain and good effect. Hence in paroxysms of insanity it will act as a valuable narcotic and sedative, provided the inflammatory symptoms be first controlled by the usual means; and hence also it appears fitted lather for the advanced than the early stages of consumption.

It may be given in substance, in watery infusion, or in tincture. When given in substance it is always proper to begin with a dose not exceeding a grain of the powdered leaves, made into a pill, twice a day, it being gradually increased till its effects are apparent either on the kidneys, the stomach, the pulse, or the bowels; the medicine then must be discontinued. But in dropsy it may be repeated after an interval, if the whole of the water be not evacuated. The infusion is made by macerating for four hours a drachm of the dried leaves in half a pint of boiling water, to which is then added, half an ounce of spirit of cinnamon. The dose is from two to six drachms given twice or thrice a day. The tincture contains all the virtues of the plant, and may be given in doses of ten or fifteen drops thrice a day. If foxglove occasions vomiting or purging, it almost certainly fails as a diuretic, and should, therefore, in such cases, be united with a small quantity of opium or opiate confection. In dropsy its efficacy is increased by being combined with calomel; and an occasional dose of sweet spirit of nitre is useful in counteracting nausea and flatulence. During its employment, under any farm, diluting drinks are useful and necessary; and immediately it is discontinued, the strength should be recruited by generous food, steel and cordial tonics.

The deleterious effects of an over-dose are best counteracted by laudanum in brandy and water, and by the application of a blister to the pit of the stomach.

GAMBOGE

Gamboge is a powerful and active cathartic, and frequently excites vomiting, even in moderate doses. It is sometimes useful in obstinate *costiveness* and *dropsy*, especially in the latter complaint. When given in dropsy, it should be combined with squill and cream of tartar. Used as an occasional medicine for the removal of costiveness, and at the same time to promote a free discharge of urine, the best form is the compound gamboge pill of the shops, the dose of which is from ten to fifteen grains at bed-time.

GINGER

The ginger plant is a native of the East Indies, and is particularly abundant in the mountainous district of *Gingi*, to the east of Pondicherry, whence it derives its name. It is now naturalised to the West Indies.

It is stimulant and carminative, and is useful in *flatulent* colic, and *indigestion,* also in *gout* when it attacks the stomach. Though it has a hot biting taste, it rarely heats the body, though taken to a considerable extent. It is less frequently used alone than as an adjunct to other remedies, to promote their efficacy, and give them warmth. The dose of the powder is from ten to fifteen grains. The tincture of ginger, taken in doses of from one to two tea-spoonfuls in warm water, and sweetened with sugar, is sometimes a useful medicine in weakness of the stomach, to afford relief from a sense of oppression or pain after eating.

GOULARD OINTMENT

See **Collection of Prescriptions**

GLAUBER'S SALT

This is a *sulphate of soda,* and is a very common and useful purgative, whose virtues are the same as those of the Epsom salt. It is given in doses of from one to six drachms, in the same way as the Epsom salt; but a combination of these salts, in equal proportions, is, as I have before remarked, more certain and pleasant in operation, than either of them used singly.

It is called Glauber's salt from Glauber, a German chemist, who first prepared it, and who named it *sal mirabile.* The *tartarized soda* was formerly called *sal polycrest,* or salt of many virtues, and these names are not unappropriate, so very efficacious are these mild saline purgatives often found in many complaints.

GLYCERINE

Is the sweet principle of oils produced during the making of soaps. It has been recommended internally in consumption, but I have there no confidence in it. It is usefully employed as an external application in scaly diseases of the skin, and to ulcers, and it has been recommended in deafness.

GREY POWDER

Is a combination of mercury with chalk. It merits attention as a mild alterative for children; the dose being from two to four grains, given at night, mixed in jelly, or thick gruel. It is particularly applicable to affections of the skin.

GUAIACUM

The guaiacum tree is a native of Jamaica, Hispaniola, and the warmer parts of America. Both the wood and the gum guaiacum are stimulant, diaphoretic, and alterative, and these qualities render them of great service in *chronic rheumatism gout, cutaneous eruptions,* and *scrophulous offections* of the membranes and ligaments. Its power of curing chronic rheumatism is well known even to the common people. When the gum is united with antimony or calomel, it very much increases their alterative powers; indeed, a combination of this gum with emetic tartar and calomel, forms one of the most powerful alterative medicines we possess. *See* prescriptions, No. 98.

The guaiacum wood forms a principal ingredient in the decoction of the woods, which is often a very useful medicine in cutaneous eruptions, rheumatism, and secondary symptoms of syphilis.

The Chelsea Pensioner, a nostrum by which Lord Amherst was cured of rheumatism, is composed of guaiacum, one drachm; rhubarb in powder, two drachms; cream of tartar, an ounce; flowers of sulphur, two ounces; one nutmeg finely powdered; which are to be made into an electuary with one pound of clarified honey. Two large spoonfuls to be taken night and morning.

The dose of gum guaiacum is from ten grains to half a drachm made into pills, or a bolus, with a little conserve of roses, and taken every night, or night and morning. But the *ammoniated tincture of guaiacum is* preferable for general use, of which the dose is from thirty drops to two drachms, or more, repeated three times a day. It had better not be mixed with water as that decomposes it, but should be taken rubbed with any viscid solution, as thin mucilage of gum arabic, on tragacanth. This tincture is sometimes very useful in a stoppage of the menstrual discharge, and is frequently of superior efficacy in outer female complaints, particularly *dysmenorrhoea,* or painful menstruation. In the author's book *On the Diseases of Females*, a case is related, under Painful Menstruation, of a lady who had been married nineteen years without issue, but who was cared of a female obstruction by the guaiacum, and a few months after was delivered of a fine girl. She took twenty four ounces of the tincture.

The guaiacum mixture *(mistura guaiaci* of the paharma-copaeia), not much used, but is of great service both in acute and chronic rheumatism. It merits notice when the other preparations of this substance fail to be serviceable. *See* RHEUMATISM.

GUM AMMONIAC

Ammoniac or ammoniacum is a stimulating expectorant, and is sometimes useful in obstructions in the bowels. It is prescribed with advantage in *asthma* and *chronic cough,* but is seldom used alone, being, for the most part, combined with emetic tartar, squill and ipecacuanha, when given for the relief and cure of these diseases. It forms a valuable ingredient in the compound squill pill of the shops. On account of its stimulating properties, its use must be avoided where any inflammatory action of the chest is going on. After the exhibition of smart purgatives, if given in combination with rhubarb, it is said to have proved valuable in mesenteric affections, by correcting the viscid secretions of the intestines. Dr. A. T. Thompson observes, that the same combination of ammoniac and rhubarb is singularly efficacious in that peculiar state of the bowels often accompanying hypochondriasis and indigestion, in which there is an almost constant degree of colic, particularly after taking food, and which appears to arise from a viscid mucus lodged in the intestines. The German physicians have great confidence in it in obstruction of the glandular viscera of the abdomen. In incipient scrophulous consumption, attended with a languid and irritable state of the system, this gum has been employed, in conjunction with tartarized antimony, with marked advantage.

It is particularly serviceable in those cases where the expectoration is deficient, from a want of power to throw up the viscid mucus accumulated in the bronchia, and where the skin is cold, and the pulse weak and sluggish.

The dose of ammoniacum is from ten to thirty grains made into pills with mucilage. In abdominal obstructions it is usually combined with small doses of rhubarb, and sometimes of tartar emetic also; in affections of the chest with squill, and perhaps ipecacuanha. The form of emulsion is an agreeable way of taking it—two drachms may be rubbed with the yoke of an egg, or half a drachm of gum arabic, and eight ounces of water gradually added—the close is one or two table-spoonfuls every two or three hours; with or without an equal quantity of almond mixture.

Externally, it is applied under the form of a plaster to reduce the size of indurated tumours, and white swellings of the joints. The plaster of ammoniac and mercury is often vary valuable for this purpose.

GUM ARABIC

The tree which yields this article is found in almost every part of Africa. This gum is a simple demulcent, serving to lubricate abraded surfaces, and involve acrid matters in the stomach and bowels. It is chiefly used in the state of mucilage, but is sometimes taken in the solid form, to sheath the fauces, and allay the tickling irritation which occasions the cough in catarrh and pulmonary consumption; in which cases, a piece of it is allowed to dissolve slowly in the mouth.

The mucilage of gum arabic is made by dissolving four ounces of gum arabic in powder, in half a pint of boiling water. This, in the dose of half an ounce or an ounce, is a useful demul cent in looseness, dysentery, gravel, and scalding of urine, or as a vehicle for opium, and other medicines in these complaints.

Gum water, made by pouring a pint of boiling water on two or three ounces of gum arabic, is a very useful and agreeable diluent in many disorders, both acute and chronic. Thus in fever, in cough, consumption, stomach, and other chronic complaints, it cools the mouth, and sheaths the throat and alimentary canal, and likewise affords some support.

HARTSHORN SHAVINGS

These shavings are nourishing, and when dissolved in boiling water and united with orange juice and sugar, with or without a little wine, as circumstances may indicate, form a good article of diet for the sick and convalescent. Four ounces of the shavings, boiled in two pints of water, until one pint be dissipated, and the remainder strained, affords a clear transparent jelly.

HELLEBORE

Black hellebore root is a powerful cathartic, and was formerly much celebrated for the cure of *insanity*, *dropsy*, and *worms*; but its curative powers are much doubted by medical men of the present day, and, therefore, it is rarely employed. It is, however, sometimes of service in suppression of the menstrual discharge in full plethoric habits, when preparations of iron are inadmissible. In such cases Dr. Mead thought highly of it. The tincture is the best form of administering it, which may be given in doses of from thirty drops to a drachm, two or three times a day, in any agreeable vehicle.

HONEY

This well known substance is laxative, and, externally applied, detergent and stimulant. It is seldom ordered alone as an internal medicine, but applied to sores and cracks in the skin it proves a cleansing and grateful application, which promotes their healing. When mixed with a little water, it forms the best wash which can be obtained for the skin when chapped and excoriated by cold. It is an excellent adjunct to gargles in sore throat and ulcerations of the mouth.

Honey of borax is made by mixing a drachm of sub-borate of soda with an ounce of clarified honey, and is a cooling application of excellent use in thrush, excoriations, and ulcerations of the mouth.

HEMLOCK

Hemlock is a biennial, indigenous plant, growing under hedges, by road sides, and among rubbish, flowering in June and July. It is distinguished from other umbelliferous plants with which it may be confounded by *its large and spotted stem,* the dark and *shining colour of its lower leaves,* and their *disagreeable smell,* when fresh and bruised, resembling in some degree the urine of a cat.

It is a powerful narcotic and sedative, and is used as such, both internally and externally. Its present extensive use among professional men is a sufficient proof of its efficacy. When the plant is gathered at the right time, and properly prepared, it is of much service in extensive *ulcerations,* whether of a *scrophulous, cancerous,* or *syphilitic* character, and in *glandular tumours* : it allays their irritability, alleviates the pain, and corrects and improves the discharge. Dr. Fothergill thought highly of its virtues in some forms of *scrophula*, and many practitioners have found it of great value in cancerous diseases. It is also of much advantage in the latter stage of *hooping coughs* and *pulmonary consumption.* The extract of hemlock and henbane combined in equal proportions, and adapted, by means of mucilage and syrup, to the form of a mixture, affords an effectual palliative in coughs and pulmonary irritation, but the more agreeable and not less efficacious way, is to take this combination in pills.

Hemlock is of much service in many other cases where pain, uneasiness, or irritation are present; for example, in palsy complicated with rheumatism, in which the deficiency of motion is attended with acute pain,—in chronic rheumatism, in female complaints, and in periodical head-aches. In the latter case, it may be advantageously united with quinine in some instances, and with arsenic in others.[1]

The recent leaves are applied externally, and often with great advantage, to painful or ill-conditioned ulcers, or a poultice for the same purpose may be formed from the dried powder mixed with crumbs of bread.

The powder of the dried leaves, and the extract, are the forms in which it is given. The powder ought to have a fine lively green colour, without which it is useless; the dose is three grains, twice or thrice a day, gradually increased to five or eight grains. The extract *prepared in vacuo* is that only which can be depended upon; it may be given in doses of from three to twenty grains, twice or thrice a day. The extract of hemlock prepared by Mr. Allen, of Plough Court, and that at Apothecaries' Hall, is worthy of every dependance.

An over-dose of hemlock produces sickness, giddiness, great anxiety, stupor and convulsions. The best antidote is vinegar, after the stomach has been evacuated by an emetic of twenty grains of sulphate of zinc, and the excitement in the brain reduced by bleeding and purging.

---

1. It is thought by some to be an aphrodisiac. Bergins, a foreign author of credit, says, "Impotentiam virilem sub usu conii curatam observavi".

HENBANE

Henbane (in technical language *hyoscyamus*) is well known to be an indigenous plant, growing on waste grounds and at the sides of roads.

It possesses a very considerable narcotic and anodyne[1] power, and in large doses is poisonous. In medicine it is chiefly employed as a substitute for opium, to alleviate pain or procure sleep, in cases where the latter disagrees with the constitution, or it is desirable to avoid its constipating effects. It is also peculiarly indicated in complaints which call for the constant use of some anodyne for a considerable time, as, when properly managed, it produces its anodyne effects without distressing the general system. Like hemlock it favours the natural action of the bowels. It is thought to be peculiarly adapted for insanity occurring in child-bed; and is much employed in red gravel and stone, to allay pain and irritation.

It is generally considered by the profession to be a more effectual narcotic than hemlock, and, therefore, more commonly employed; but in my opinion it does not possess so much of an alterative quality as the latter, that is, it does not afford us so much assistance in our endeavours to alter the condition of diseased parts, and, consequently, is not so suitable and valuable a remedy, where we wish, at the same time, to alleviate pain, induce sleep, and remove disease. Hence we find hemlock to be the better medicine in cancerous and scrophulous swellings and ulcerations, and in many other indurations and ulcers attended with pain.

Henbane is administered either in the form of extract, or tincture. The dose of the extract is from four to twenty grains made into pills, with a little tragacanth or gum arabic powder and repeated twice or thrice in the twenty-four hours, if necessary. The dose of the tincture is from half a drachm to one or two drachms. Dr. A. T. Thompson says, *Elements of Materia Medica,* vol. i, p. 584, "In my own practice I have seen more good derived (in mania) from

1. Anodynes are medicines which relieve pain.

eight or ten grains, combined with ten grains of camphor, and given at bed time, than from the repetition of smaller doses".

Alkalies and lime water are inadmissible in combination with henbane, since they destroy its narcotic power.

The means of counteracting the injurious effects of an excessive dose, are the same as are pointed out above; in the case of taking too large a quantity of hemlock.

HIERA PICRA

The words signify, Holy *Bitter,* from *τεροζ*, holy, and *τιχροζ*, bitter. It is a well known domestic remedy, chiefly used in female obstructions, and is prepared by mixing together a pound of hepatic alĩes, and three ounces of white canella bark. These are to be rubbed separately into powder before they are mixed together. It is usually taken in wine or spirits; and the dose is from ten to twenty grains; but it is also taken in pills, mixed together with a little oil of cloves and castile soap, a mode which I much prefer.

The canella bark is a valuable aromatic, and it both covers the taste, and modifies the operation of the alĩes, lessening its tendency to griping.

Hiera Picra is undoubtedly useful in some cases of female obstruction, and likewise in that form of bleeding from the womb which is liable to occur on the final cessation of the menses; and its success proves the importance of gentle purging in these complaints. A striking and successful case of this kind of haemorrhage may be seen in the author's *Treatise on Female Diseases,* under the head of *Final Cessation* : The lady was forty-two years of age, and almost all the known remedies for haemorrhage had been prescribed without effect—the *hiera picra* cured her speedily.

HOFFMAN'S ANODYNE LIQUOR

This is the compound spirit of sulphuric ether of the shops, and is stimulant, narcotic, and antispasmodic. It is used for the same purposes as the common sulphuric ether, and is sometimes useful in allaying irritability, and disposing to sleep, in the latter stages of typhus and other malignant fevers. It is less exciting than simple ether. When united to opium for the purpose of procuring sleep, it renders the operation of the opiate more pleasant, and counteracts its deleterious properties. The dose is from half a drachm to a drachm, in any simple fluid vehicle.

All ethers should be kept in closely-stopped phials.

JALAP

The jalap root comes from South America, and is said to take its name from Xalappa, a city of Mexico. It is a stimulant cathartic, acting briskly on the bowels, especially the larger bowels, and although occasionally griping severely, yet safe and efficacious. It is a good purgative in the torpid state of the intestines, in *low spirits, melancholy,* and other forms of *insanity;* in *worm cases,* and the slimy state of the bowels to which children are subject; and to carry off the water by stool in *dropsy*. In worms and insanity it should be combined with calomel, and in dropsy with cream of tartar, as compound powder of jalap, since these additions quicken its operation, and render it more effectual. A drop or two of some essential oil, as the oil of carraway or anniseed, should be added to each dose of jalap, to prevent griping. The watery extract purges moderately without griping, and is therefore well adapted for children; but the *compound powder of jalap* is by far the best preparation, of which the ordinary dose for an adult is a scruple, or half a drachm.

The dose of simple jalap powder is from ten grains to half a drachm, given in the form of powder, pills or bolus.

JAMES'S POWDER

This celebrated and valuable medicine is a *nostrum,* the original proprietor of which was Dr. James, a respectable physician in London, from whose prescription it is still prepared by Messrs. Newberry, of St. Paul's Church Yard. It operates as a diaphoretic and alterative, and is often of excellent use in *colds, coughs,* the commencement of, *fevers,* and all *inflammatory diseases,* as it changes, in a very gentle and frequently insensible manner; the diseased condition of action in the minute vessels of the circulating system, and thus conducts the existing malady to a favourable termination. If it be administered early, after the stomach and bowels have been previously evacuated by purgatives and an emetic, fevers of the most threatening aspect are often cut short by it. Its good effects may sometimes be increased by the addition of a small quantity of calomel, such as quarter of a grain to each dose. It is advantageously given in acute rheumatism, measles, small pox, colds, and recent coughs; and in obstinate eruptions of the skin it should be united with guaiacum as well as calomel. A gain and a half of James's powder, the eighth of a grain of calomel, and two grains of gum guaiacum in powder, made into a pill, and given every other night, forms one of the most efficient alteratives we possess, and is of the greatest service in almost all chronic diseases. In fever, inflammation, and other acute complaints, it must be given in larger doses, more frequently repeated, as three, four or five grains, with half a grain of calomel, every four or five hours; and its operation is assisted by the patient's drinking freely of some warm diluting fluid during the day.

As it is insoluble in water, the best manner of taking it is made into pills with conserve of hips. *Mewberry's James's Powder* is always to by preferred.

ICELAND MOSS

Iceland moss, called also Iceland Liverwort, is tonic and demulcent. It unites a strong bitter principle with demulcent properties, on which its medicinal effects are supposed to depend. Its virtues for the cure of *pulmonary consumption*, have been very highly extolled; but it does not appear of much service, except in that particular species called catarrhal consumption, whose more immediate seat is in the windpipe and its terminations. This species of *phthisis* frequently follows hopping cough, measles, and common cold, and is sometimes certainly much benefited by it. It allays the tickling cough, relieves the oppressed breathing, mitigates the hectic fever, invigorates the digestive organs, and seems in this way to have the power of exciting a salutary action in the internal membrane of the windpipe. This plant is a native of Iceland, where it still possesses a high reputation as a remedy for cough and *consumption.*—*Mackenzie's Travels,* 4 to. *Appendix,* p. 411.

It is generally given in the form of decoction, which is prepared by boiling one ounce of the picked moss in a quart of water down to a pint, and then straining it while hot. The dose is from half an ounce to two ounces, three times a day, either alone or mixed with milk. In this state the decoction is very bitter, but although not the most pleasant, it is probably the most efficacious way in which it can be taken. If, however, the patient will not take it in this way, it may be freed from a considerable portion of its, bitterness by being steeped in hot water for two or three hours, previous to its being used to make the decoction. This water is, of course, thrown away, and then the ounce of moss is boiled in two pints of water, as above directed.

IODINE

This is a peculiar substance procured from sponge, and other species of *fucus*. It is a very active medicine, and in all its forms is sometimes used with advantage in relieving the acute pain attendant upon hard and *malignant swellings*, whether of a scrophulous or cancerous nature, and in reducing their size, or preventing their increase. It will often speedily mitigate the most agonizing pain in these complaints, and is applicable to solid tumours of almost every description. It has been highly praised for its virtues in scrophula,—too highly certainly,—for here its use is limited, and its efficacy in curing the disease seldom considerable. For iodine being a remedy of great activity, it cannot under any circumstances be used unremittingly for more than a very short time, and even when employed with regular intervals, its continued use is apt to induce much emaciation and debility, and thus to aggravate the scrophulous symptoms, rather than relieve them; since they originate in debility, and are never permanently benefited by any means which lessen the tone of the general system. Notwithstanding, I think it worthy of much notice as an auxiliary, in the management of scrophula,[1] In indolent enlargement of the testes in men, accompanied with severe pain, it is a valuable medicine, giving more speedy and effectual relief than any other substance; and it is reportèd to have been of great service in reducing enlargement of the liver, even when dropsy has supervened.

It has proved of uncommon service in some female complaints, which I have fully noticed in my publication on those diseases, especially in tumours of the breast and womb, and in diseases of the *ovaria*.

Much caution is required in its administration. In delicate nervous habits, it is liable to bring on palpitations, dry cough, tremors, and other disagreeable symptoms. Many medical men employ it in complaints to which it is not at all applicable, and to an extent which sets all sound medical principles, and common sense, too, at defiance; and I warn my readers to be sparing in its employment.

Internally it may be given in the form of tincture of iodine, or solution of iodide of potassium. The dose of each is at first ten drops for adults, thrice a day, in a wine-glassful of barley water, or common water, gradually increased to half a drachm, if the patient can bear it. It should not be taken constantly, the safest and most effectual mode of administering this medicine being for the patient to take it for thirty days, then to lay it aside for a few days, and afterwards to resume and discontinue it alternately, at similar intervals. The *solution of iodide of potassium* is generally and deservedly preferred, on account of its mildness. It is made by dissolving half a drachm of the salt in one ounce of water. The *iodide of potassium* itself may be taken in the dose of three grains, twice or thrice a day, in a wine-glassful of water, barley water, or decoction of bark.

Iodide of iron is a tonic form of taking iodine, and may be

1. It is worthy of remembrance that the Genevese and Swiss physicians, who were the first to bring this substance into notice, anal to extol it, were also the first to abandon their original confidence in it.

used with confidence when debility is present, in the dose of two, three, or four grains, made into a pill, thrice a day.

For external use, a drachm of the iodide of potassium is mixed with an ounce of recent hog's lard, and about the size of a nut rubbed into the scrophulous and cancerous tumour, night and morning, for ten or twenty days; and then laid aside and resumed in the same manner as I have directed above for the use of the tincture. When this remedy is employed for alleviating the pain and reducing the size of hard and painful swellings, it is often not necessary for a patient to take it internally, the external use, in the form of ointment, having as much effect as its internal exhibition, with the advantage of greater safety, and direct application to the diseased parts.

IPECACUANHA ROOT

This plant comes from Bahia, Rio Janeiro and other provinces of the Brazils. There are three varieties of the root, the brown, the grey, and the white, of which the first is by far the best.

Ipecacuanha, when administered in large doses of ten or fifteen grains, is emetic; in smaller ones of two or three grains, diaphoretic and expectorant; and in still smaller doses it acts as a stomachic, stimulating and giving energy to the digestive organs. As an emetic, it is mild, safe and certain in its operation; it evacuates completely the contents of the stomach, and does not so much weaken it as antimonial emetics. It is the emetic best adapted for children, It is an established fact, that an emetic given at the commencement of continued fevers, will sometimes cut short their progress, or if it fail in accomplishing this object, will give to the subsequent symptoms a milder aspect, and with this view, fifteen or twenty grains of ipecacuanha powder may be used with great advantage. In doses of two or three grains repeated every three or four hours, till it operates by vomiting, sweating, or purging, it is found of eminent utility in dysentery and chronic looseness; indeed its effects in these severe complaints are often invaluable, and it is, perhaps, the most beneficial aperient in dysentery; for when we can bring it to act in this way, it produces a steady determination of the peristaltic motion of the bowels downwards, at the same time that it strengthens their internal surface, and relaxes the skin. Helvetius first made known its use in *dysentery,* and was rewarded by Louis XIV, with 1000 *l* sterling for the discovery. In the same doses it is of excellent use in *spitting of blood, hooping cough, difficulty of breathing* and *spasmodic asthma.* In spitting of blood it is particularly worthy of confidence, both to stop its progress and prevent its return.

In still smaller quantities of a grain, or half a grain, three or four times a day, it strengthens the digestive organs, and is very beneficially employed as a remedy for indigestion, bilious and liver complaints. In such cases it may either be used alone, made into pills with a little hard soap, or be combined with steel or any bitter extract.

When combined with opium, it forms the compound ipecacuanha powder, and proves a valuable anodyne, sudorific, and alterative, of great service in acute and chronic rheumatism, and, in other complaints in which we wish to relieve pain, procure sleep, and at the same time relax the skin.

IRON

Preparations of iron or steel, as they are sometimes called, are of all metals the most salutary to the animal system, from being the only metal having any sensible activity which hay no poisonous quality. When given medicinally, the effects obtained from it are those of a tonic; it increases the vigour of the circulation, causes, the blood to assume a more florid hue, promotes digestion, excites the secretions, or restrains them when they have been morbidly increased from debility and by its astringency, checks profuse evacuations, and counteracts the tendency to haemorrhage. The diseases in which it is used are those which are dependant on; or attended with, a weak, languid habit of body, as *green-sickness, indigestion* and its consequences, *hysterics, whites, palsy, scrophula, rickets,* and *consumption.* It is also extremely beneficial in *cancerous ulceration,* and other ill-conditioned sores. The use of iron is improper where there is a considerable tendency to inflammatory action, or any particular fulness of the vessels. In these states of the system it occasions heat, thirst, head-ache, laborious breathing, and many other unpleasant symptoms, when its administration ought to be suspended. But when given in a proper state of the body, few medicines are capable of producing more beneficial effects, as I have repeatedly proved in my practice.

Numerous preparations of this metal are medicinally employed, the chief of which are the sesqui-carbonate of iron, citrate of iron, the sulphate, and tartarized iron, and the *tincture of muriate of iron.*

The *sequi-carbonate of iron* and the *citrate of iron* are two of the most valuable of its preparations, and are in common use. They are tonic, and useful in indigestion, head-ache, scrophula, green-sickness, worms, and in all cases in which preparations of iron are indicated. Mr. Carmichael, of Dublin, used the sesqui-carbonate of iron as a remedy in cancerous ulceration, both internally, administered in large doses, and eternally applied, sprinkled on the sore. Cases have been reported in which this practice has proved successful; and no doubt it relieves pain, promotes a healthy discharge, and strengthens the general habit. The dose is from five to twenty grains, repeated twice or thrice a day, made into pills, with a little mucilage of gum arabic, or extract of liquorice. A small quantity of aromatic powder causes it to sit easier on the stomach.

The *sulphate of iron is* one of the most active preparations of the metal, and may be advantageously employed in all the complaints above enumerated. The dose is from one to five grains, combined with extract of gentian, and a little aloes.

Tartarized iron possesses the same medicinal powers as the other preparations of iron; but from its mildness, slight taste, and ready solubility, it is a more convenient form for the administration of iron to children, and in those cases in which the other saline, preparations of it prove nauseating, and sit uneasy on the stomach. It has been extolled as a remedy in dropsy, in which it is supposed to exert both a diuretic and a tonic power. The dose is from ten grains to half a drachm, given in the form of powder or bolus, combined with four or five brains of aromatic powder. It may be repeated twice or thrice a day.

Tincture of muriate of iron (now called *tincture* of *sesqui-chloride of iron)* is a tonic of great power. It is also diuretic. It has been found of signal service in *erysipelas* and *diphtheria,* and likewise in *scrophula*, and all cases where a blood tonic is required. The *dose is* from fifteen minims or drops to thirty or forty, in a glass of water, twice a clay.

Wine of iron is a very useful tonic, especially adapted for children. The dose is about a tea-spoonful, or two, in water.

JUNIPER BERRIES

The common juniper is indigenous, growing on heaths and chalky hills, and flowering in May. But the great majority of juniper berries which are used in Britain, are brought from Germany, Holland and Italy.

They are diuretic and cordial. They have been long known as a remedy in *dropsy*, but cannot be depended on alone, although they form an excellent adjunct to foxglove and squill. The tops are also used, and as the virtues of the berries depend on the essential oil, which is found in the woody part also of the plant, they must be equally efficacious. They have been recommended in scorbutic and cutaneous affections. The best form of using the berries is that of infusion, made by pouring a pint of boiling water on three ounces of the berries bruised, of which the dose is a tea-cupful every four hours. The proper dose of the oil of juniper is from three to twelve drops, combined with water by means of sugar or mucilage.

KINO

Kino is a powerful astringent. Like catechu, it is employed in obstinate *chronic looseness, whites,* and *internal haemorrhages;* but it is thought to be less certain in its effects than catechu, and is, therefore, less used. Dr. Watson, however, seems to think highly of it, and to be much in the habit of employing it. The alkalies, solutions of isinglass, and strong acids are incompatible in prescriptions with kino.

The dose in substance is from ten grains to half a drachm, and of the tincture from one to two drachms.

KOUSSO

The Kousso is the flowers and unripe seeds of the *Hagenia Abyssinica* of Bruce, and subsequent travellers, and which has been lately very strongly recommended as an efficacious remedy for tape worm. It is called *Brayera Anthelmintica,* and is obtained from *Abyssinia.* Some writers assert it to be pre-eminent in its operations as a vermifuge.

The dose of kousso for an adult is half an ounce, reduced to a fine powder, and infused for a quarter of an hour in a pint of boiling water; the whole to be well stirred together and drank, early in the morning on an empty stomach. The mixture is almost tasteless, and consequently does not require any addition for the purpose of making it palatable; but the Abyssinian method of mixing honey with it, is a good practice. The French physicians give a dose of castor oil twenty-four hours before exhibiting the kousso, but this is not necessary. It is advisable that the bowels should be in an empty state when it is taken, but not relaxed; therefore, a small quantity only of simple food should be taken, both before and after the dose for twenty-four hours.

The immediate result of the medicine is generally two or more evacuations of the bowels during the day; these should be carefully examined, to ascertain if the whole of the worm is expelled, and the head of the animal should be particularly sought for, if possible, by the aid of a microscope. Should it not be found, or should the bowels not act sufficiently within twenty-four hours, a dose of castor oil must be given, and the same attention be directed to the evacuations. It is said to be very seldom that a second dose of the kousso is required, and some little time should be allowed for the action of the first dose, before it is resorted to; it may, when necessary, be repeated with perfect safety.

The effect of kousso upon the worm appears to be very severe and distinctive. When discharged it is generally found completely saturated, as it were, with the powdered kousso; its joints are filled with it, its various mouths choked up by 'it; and it is even found to have penetrated the alimentary canal. Such being its effects, I recommend the kousso to be taken in a tolerably fine powder.

KREOSOTE

Kreosote or Creosote signifies meat-preserver, and is a compound term derived from the Greek *κρεαζ*, flesh, and *σωζει* to preserve. This name was given by Dr. Reichenbach, of Blencko, in Moravia, to a peculiar proximate principle, discovered by him in 1832; and found to exist in the tar resulting from the destructive distillation of wood.

In its pure state it is a colourless, transparent, oily liquid, having the fluidity of thin almond oil. One of its most remarkable properties, is the decisive power with which it is endowed of effecting tile rapid coagulation of all the albuminous and serous fluid's existing in the living, as well as the dead animal tissues. When brought in contact with white of egg, coagulation instantly ensues. Kreosote, in its concentrated state, and in consequence probably of its coagulating power, exerts all the decisive and rapid effects of a strong poison on man and animals; small animals, as wasps; beetles, etc. when moistened with it, dying under long and violent convulsions, and fish ceasing to exist in water impregnated with one-hundredth part of it.

Where two or three drops of *very dilute* kreosote are taken into the stomach, a sensation of warmth is experienced. The greatest circumspection is required in the administration of this medicine. Internally administered, it is chiefly useful in a few peculiar cases of indigestion, where a good deal of torpor exists; externally it is used with uncommon advantage in ringworm of the scalp, in itch, and in tooth-ache. In tooth-ache from decayed teeth, it is only necessary to moisten the point of a wooden spill with the kreosote, and introduce it into the hollow of the tooth.

LACTUCARIUM OR JUICE OF LETTUCE

The soporific properties of the garden lettuce were known in the earliest ages. Galen used to eat the lettuce in the evening as a remedy for wakefulness at night; and most persons find it induces sleep.

Lactucarium is the inspissated juice of the garden lettuce, and has the colour, and in some measure, the taste and odour of opium; but no morphia has yet been obtained from it, and its narcotic principle is, therefore, still undiscovered. Its analysis is said to prove it to contain a large proportion of caoutchouc, (or India rubber), as much as twenty-two parts in fifty.

Its medicinal effects are very nearly the same as those of opium, but it is undoubtedly much milder in its operation, and may consequently be used in *cough* and *consumption,* and in other cases, where opium, from its stimulating effects, cannot be borne. Lactucarium may be advantageously taken by persons who cannot take opium in any shape. Dr. Duncan, Sen of Edinburgh, first suggested its use in his *Observations on Pulmonary Consumption, Appendix,* p. 162. The dose is from one to six grains or more, in the form of a pill.

LAUDANUM

What is generally termed laudanum is the tincture of opium of the shops, which is made by pouring two pints of proof spirit of wine on two ounces and a half of powdered opium. These articles are allowed to digest for a week or two, and then strained, when they are fit for use. Nineteen minims, or about thirty-five drops, of laudanum contain one grain of solid opium.

This tincture is used in all cases in which opium is indicated, and is a very convenient and elegant form of giving the remedy. In general it operates more speedily than the solid opium. The usual dose is from twenty drops to a drachm; but in case of violent and continued pain, and in some particular diseases, very large doses can be borne, and are even necessary. It is not, however, so eligible a remedy for general purposes as the "Black Drop", or "Battley's Solution", since both these preparations are more powerfully anodyne than laudanum, and do not affect the head or confine the bowels so much.

It is worthy of notice, that the vehicle in which laudanum is exhibited is often of much consequence, from its effect on the stomach; thus if given in lemon juice or vinegar, or in some a greeable aromatic water, or in a cordial draught, (*see* No. 79), or, in other cases, in a little brandy and water, it may be rendered both less irritating to the system, and more useful to the patient, than when merely taken in water.

As an external application, this tincture rubbed on the skin produces its usual anodyne effects in a smaller degree, allaying pain, and relaxing spasm.—Under the head of OPIUM I have considered the various uses of laudanum, and its modification by combination, age, sex, etc.

LAVENDER DROPS

These are the compound spirit of lavender of the shops, and are composed of the simple spirit of lavender, spirit of rosemary, cinnamon bark bruised, nutmegs bruised, and red saunders-wood. They are an elegant and grateful cordial and stimulant, useful in *languors* and *faintings*. But it should be recollected, that they are merely a palliative, and their use should not be allowed to supersede that of tonics, and other medicines capable of acting beneficially and permanently on the cause of these symptoms. It is a useful adjunct to stomachic infusions, as infusion of gentian, cascarilla, etc.

The dose is from thirty drops to two tea-spoonfuls, in any agreeable vehicle.

LEECHES

As these little animals are very serviceable, and frequently used in domestic practice, it is necessary that I should say a little about applying and cleaning them, etc. They are at times applied in all cases where local blood-letting is necessary, and particularly to places where cupping-glasses cannot be applied. In acute inflammation of vital organs, their use should never be neglected; for however important general bleeding is in these instances, the drawing of blood from the immediate vicinity of the inflamed part, by means of leeches, is of great consequence.

It is sometimes extremely difficult to make them bite, which they never will do when they are sick. The best mode of applying them seems to be, to take them out of the water for some minutes before they are to be used, and to dry them well with a very soft cloth directly before they are applied. The part should also be well cleaned with soap and water, then washed with a little pure water, and made very dry. If there be any hairs on the spot, these must be close shaved. When they, nevertheless, will not readily fix, or where it is wished to apply them very exactly on one particular spot, putting them into a large quill cut at both ends, and applying the end at which the head of the animal lies to the part, with the finger on the other end, is an excellent mode of making them bite. The quill is withdrawn after they are firmly fixed. Another excellent mode of making them fix directly on any particular spot, is said to be by touching the part with the bloody spongy point of a quill recently taken from a pigeon's wing. Putting them into some porter for a few minutes before applying them, is likewise a good way to make them bite. They drop off spontaneously, whenever they have gorged themselves with blood; and they may be separated at any time by placing a minute quantity of salt on the head. Few leeches can draw more than half a fluid ounce of blood; and therefore it is necessary, in order to increase the quantity, to keep the orifices bleeding by bathing them with hot water. After the leeches drop off, the application of a very minute quantity of salt makes them disgorge all the blood they have sucked; and if they be imediately thrown into clean water, and this repeatedly changed for three or four times, they soon recover their health and vigour. Dr. Johnson, who has written a treatise on the economy of the medicinal leech, advises the use of vinegar instead of salt, which is not apt to blister the lips of the leech, as salt does, preventing it from sucking for some considerable time.

Broth made with the fattest part of tripe is an admirable wash for leech bites, soothing and healing them very rapidly.

LENITIVE ELECTUARY

Lenitive electuary is made in the following manner. Take of best senna leaves, in very fine powder, four ounces; pulp of prunes, a pound; pulp of cassia, a quarter of a pound; pulp of tamarinds, three ounces; treacle or simple syrup, a pint and a half; essential oil of carraway, two drachms. Boil the pulps with the syrup or treacle, to the thickness of honey; then add the senna, and, when the mixture is nearly cold, the oil of carraway; finally, mix the whole thoroughly together.

When properly prepared this electuary is a mild and pleasant aperient, and may be used as such in all cases of costiveness. It is well adapted to regulate the bowels of children, pregnant women, and all delicate persons; and may be used either alone, or combined with a small portion of sulphur and cream of tartar. When united with an equal quantity of flowers of sulphur and cream of tartar, it forms one of the best remedies for piles now known. Employed alone, the dose is from one to three tea-spoonfuls taken at bedtime.

But it is very rarely properly prepared, the wholesale druggists too frequently employing apples, jalap and other cheap ingredients, instead of the articles ordered by the pharmacopoeia. The electuary from Apothecaries' Hall is excellent.

LETTUCE JUICE

See **Lactucarium**

LIME WATER

Lime water is made by pouring six pints of boiling water upon a quarter of a pound of fresh burnt lime. They are to be agitated together, and the vessel covered directly and set apart for three hours; afterwards the solution is to be preserved upon the undissolved lime, in well stopped glass bottles, and the clear fluid poured off when it is wanted for use.

It is tonic, antacid, destroys worms, and is externally detergent. It proves very useful in *indigestion,* attended with much acidity on the stomach, in *chronic looseness, diabetes* and *whites*. It destroys intestinal worms, and is serviceable in slimy bowels. Mixed with an equal quantity of milk, it furnishes an excellent remedy in the bowel complaints of children, and is very useful in consumption and fever. Sometimes it is used with advantage in *red* gravel, and in stone.

Dr. Hutchinson of Dublin, has strongly recommended an infusion of Peruvian bark in lime water as a very valuable tonic in *scrophula, rickets* and *extreme general debility.* He asserts, that it has cured several desperate cases of debility which had been pronounced hopeless; and it appears to me to be a remedy, worthy of great confidence. A pint of lime water may be allowed to digest for six hours, upon an ounce of Peruvian bark, coarsely powdered, then strained off, and taken in doses of a wine-glassful or more, three times a day.

Milk disguises the flavour of lime-water without impairing its virtues. The dose is from half an ounce to half a pint, once or twice a day.

LIQUOR POTASSAE

This is a medicine much employed by professional men as an antacid, and to remove or lessen certain tumours and other swellings. In urinary calculi, in leprosy, and those disorders of the skin which are symptomatic of derangement in the digestive functions, its remedial powers are well ascertained.

In the reduction of glandular and other tumours its efficacy is often great, and I have known it of uncommon service in certain anomalous swellings. It perfectly relieved a lady who had suffered for twelve years from an enlargement of the brain, attended with a fixed pain on the top of the head, total inability to take exercise, and who, at uncertain intervals of a few months, was repeatedly attacked, through the whole period of the twelve years, with acute inflammation of the brain, in which her life was again and again despaired of. This lady had tried iodine, sarsaparilla, digitalis, calomel, and other means almost without number, and certainly without much benefit, and was at length cured by taking a tea-spoonful of the *liquor potassoe,* twice a day, in barley water.—*See* my *Treatise on Indigestion.*

The dose is from a quarter of a tea-spoonful to a tea-spoonful, twice or thrice a day, in half a tea-cupful of barley water. Its long continued use weakens the stomach.

LOBELIA INFLATA

The *lobelia inflata,* or Indian tobacco, is a medicine which has been lately introduced into medical practice, especially for the relief and cure of spasmodic asthma, and spasmodic cough. It is a biennial plant, growing almost throughout the United States, and is much employed, I believe, in America. It is an emetic, and also possesses expectorant and sedative properties. It is with this plant as with the ordinary tobacco, some people can bear it well, while in other cases the smallest dose produces giddiness and vomiting. It should, therefore, be always commenced in small doses, as twenty or thirty drops of the tincture, and gradually increased if it agrees.

It is praised for its efficacy in spasmodic asthma in *Bigelow's American Medical Botany,* a respectable work; and a case is therein related of a physician (Dr. Cutler), who suffered from asthma for ten years, and during the paroxysm, resorted to many medicines for relief, without experiencing much benefit from any, until he took the tincture of *lobelia inflata,* which immediately relieved him, and subsequently improved his general health. It is undoubtedly sometimes of uncommon efficacy in this complaint, and if persons have tried other means without effect, I advise this medicine not to be disregarded; but I question whether it be in general superior, or even equal, to many other remedies for asthma, and would therefore guard my readers against being imposed upon by the strong (which are indeed too often interested and airy), representations of some persons of the present day.

The tincture is the form in which it is used, which is made by digesting, for a few hours, two ounces of the dried plant in a pint of diluted spirit of wine; of which a tea-spoonful is the ordinary dose, taken in water, and repeated thrice a day.

LOGWOOD

Logwood is a valuable astringent in chronic dysentery and diarrhoea. It checks the frequent action of the bowels in these complaints without producing constipation and feverishness, and is therefore well adapted to check the diarrhoea of consumption.

The *dose* of the extract is from ten to twenty grains made into pills, and of the decoction from two to four tablespoonfuls, repeated after every loose motion. The decoction is the beat form of using it, but the pill is the most agreeable.

MAGNESIA

Magnesia is antacid, and when acidity in the stomach prevails, purgative; but if no acid be present, it does not appear to increase the peristaltic motion of the bowels. It is a useful remedy in *acidity of the stomach* and bowels, particularly of children, and proves to them a suitable and efficient purgative, when combined with a little rhubarb powder. It is preferable to chalk and other absorbents in heart-burn, when the bowels are costive. In *red* gravel it is very useful; and when the concretions are formed in the kidney, no remedy is so efficacious. When gout and gravel are combined, and magnesia can be brought to act gently on the bowels, the symptoms of the former disease, as well as those of the latter, are often much relieved by it. There are two preparations of this article—the calcined magnesia and the carbonate. When much flatus exists in the stomach, the former is preferable. The dose of the calcined magnesia is from ten grains to half a drachm, taken in water or milk; of the carbonate of magnesia, from half a drachm to a drachm or more.

Henry's Magnesia appears to differ from the best calcined magnesia of the shops, only in being prepared so as to form a more impalpable powder, which causes it to act more pleasantly and effectually.

MANNA

Manna is the produce of the flowering ash, a tree which is a native of the South of Europe, growing abundantly in Calabria, Apulia, Sicily, and on the loftier mountains of Greece.

It is a very gentle laxative, fit only for children, and persons of very weak habits. Indeed, even to such patients it is not in general a useful medicine alone, and is advantageously combined with senna tea, or rhubarb. The dose for children is from one to four drachms.

MARSH-MALLOWS

Both the marsh and common mallow are useful demulcents in cough, gravel and stone, in which cases they are given in the form of decoction, a pint or two being drank in the course of the twenty-four hours. The roots and leaves, well boiled together, are sometimes used as an emollient poultice to promote suppuration, in other words, to bring any inflammatory swelling to what is vulgarly called a head, when that course is considered desirable.

Warm fomentations of the leaves and roots of the mallow, boiled in water, are of great service in many severe *contusions* and wounds, both in man and animals, in which cases they have considerable effect in reducing the inflammation and swelling, and promoting a favourable termination of the injury. An animal most severely gored in the belly, soon recovered by fomenting the part very frequently with the above decoction.

MAY APPLE OR MANDRAKE

This is one of the new American remedies lately introduced into this country, and which are highly extolled by some persons; but we as yet know little of their virtues. Time and experience are needful to enable us to speak of them with well-grounded confidence. *Podophyllin* is the active principle of the may apple, and is extolled as an efficient purgative and alterative, operating chiefly on the liver; and very useful in torpid states of that organ. The dose is one or two grains in a pill. But I do not believe that *podophyllin* will be found so efficacious in torpid liver and goat as dandelion, mild mercurials, and our ordinary purgatives and alteratives, such as No. 97 or 98A, or No. 104 or No. 74D.

The mercantile spirit of the age is now deluging this country with new American medicines, but they are untried, and the value of most of them as yet unknown. What we require is not a multiplication of new medicines, but a more exact knowledge of the virtues and mode of administration of the old.

MEZEREON BARK

This is a stimulating diaphoretic and alterative, of considerable efficacy in *chronic rheumatism, cutaneous eruptions,* and some cases of *scroplaula.* It is likewise a useful remedy for the secondary symptoms of syphilis, and forms an active ingredient in the celebrated decoction of sarsaparilla. Dr. Withering employed it successfully as a local stimulant in a case of difficulty of swallowing, occasioned by Palsy. *See* Palsy.

An ointment of the expressed juice of the bark is valuable for dressing issues—it is said to have advantages over the savine or any other ointment for this purpose.

It is generally given in the form of decoction, made by boiling two drachms of the bark of mezereon root, with half an ounce of liquorice root, in three pints of water, down to two pints; of which the dose is from four to six ounces, three times a day.

MORPHIA

See **Opium**

MUSK

Musk is obtained from an animal resembling the deer, inhabiting the Alpine Mountains of the East of Asia, particularly of the Himala Mountains, which divide Thibet from India. It is a solitary animal, living among the rocks, and frequenting the highest tops of the snowy peak; very timid, and difficult to be taken.

This article is stimulant, and antispasmodic, possessing much power in resolving spasm, and increasing the energy of the brain and nerves. Hence it is sometimes efficaciously given in *typhus fever*, when *low delirium,* twitching of the tendons, and hiccough supervene. It has also been praised for its virtues in arresting the progress of *gangrene,* when combined with ammonia. Dr. Cullen considered it one of the most powerful antispasmodics we are acquainted with, and many other eminent practitioners are of the same opinion. I think it much inferior to assafoetida. It is sometimes advantageously exhibited in spasmodic diseases, especially in *epilepsy, hysterics,* and *cholera morbus*. In large doses it is of great service when gout suddenly leaves the extremities, and fixes on the stomach, or some other vital organ. It is a very high priced article, and is with great difficulty obtained genuine.

It is given in substance, in the form of a bolus, of which the dose may be from eight grains to a drachm, repeated at intervals of three and six hours.

MUSTARD SEED

Mustard seeds are slightly stimulant, diuretic, and aperient, and have been found useful in costiveness, indigestion, dropsy, and the torpid state of the bowels which accompanies palsy. They have become of late a very popular remedy for *indigestion, costiveness,* and some other complaints, and much has been deservedly said of their good effects. I was formerly inclined to look upon them as frequently objectionable, on account of their supposed stimulant properties, and that when they did agree their efficacy was not so great as was represented; but a closer attention to the subject has convinced me that they form a remedy of no mean power, more especially in costiveness, indigestion, and some anomalous affections of the general health. They act very mildly and yet effectually as an aperient, but have little stimulating power, and afford a voluminous stool of a proper consistence. It is very evident that they exert a considerable alterative effect on the constitution when persevered in, which seems to be owing to their containing sulphur, (a minute portion of that valuable alterative substance having been detected in their envelope), and also to their regular laxative operation. For whatever substance acts regularly and mildly as an aperient, is at the same time alternative and invigorating, an effect which results no doubt from the marked influence which a regularly healthy action of the bowels has on the whole system. In the above disorders, these seeds may be taken (swallowed whole) in doses of two or three tea-spoonfuls, or a table-spoonful, twice or thrice a day.

The powder of mustard seed, mixed with water, in doses of three or four tea-spoonfuls, is emetic, and, as such, is used in paralytic cases, and will often operate quickly and fully when other emetics fail. Mustard poultices, made by mixing the flower with water, are powerfully stimulant when applied to the skin, and put on the soles of the feet, are often of much service in the delirium of typhus, and in comatose affections.

MINDERERUS'S SPIRIT

This is the solution of acetate of ammonia of the shops, and is made by mixing together two ounces of sub-carbonate, or, as it is now called, sesqui-carbonate of ammonia, and four pints of diluted acetic acid. It is a very useful cooling diaphoretic, and is in common use in all *fevers,* for the purpose of relieving heat, relaxing the skin, said promoting a gentle perspiration. Its operation in this way is much assisted by the patient drinking freely of some warm slop, and by his keeping the body moderately warm. It is of signal service in painful menstruation, probably from its solvent powers on the blood. It forms a principal ingredient in the common saline draughts, and is generally given in combination with camphor mixture, antimonial wine, and purified nitre. The ordinary dose is from half an ounce to an ounce, given every three or four hours, in water or camphor mixture.

Diluted with water, it is externally applied as a lotion to inflamed surfaces.

MURIATIC ACID

This acid is now called hydrochloric, and is tonic and antiseptic, and is efficaciously used in *typhus* and *typhoid fevers, malignant sore throat,* and *cutaneous eruptions.* The good effects of this acid in malignant typhus fever are sometimes remarkable; and Dr. Reich, Professor of Medicine in the University of Erling' in Franconia, was rewarded with a considerable pension from the King of Prussia, for the success with which he employed it in such cases. I have proved its value in my own practice. Sir William Fordyce also strongly recommends it in the same class of diseases; and Dr. Paris, of London, says, that he has uniformly exhibited it, with success, in the most malignant cases of typhus and scarlet fever, during several years extensive practice in the Westminster Hospital. It is likewise useful in some cases of *indigestion* accompanied with general debility, in the secondary symptoms of syphilis, and in *white* gravel. The dose is from ten to twenty drops, in a tea-cupful of barley water, or infusion of barb. In desperate cases of typhus, half a drachm, may be given at a dose, every four hours, properly diluted.

In typhus and typhoid fevers, Dr. Chambers says (*Clinical Lect.* p. 59) "It is so large a constituent of the body, that it might almost be called a food instead of a medicine, and it is a powerful arrester of the decomosition of animal matter". He has employed it with gratifying results, having adopted it from the description given him by another practitioner, of the advantageous use of it by Dr. Mackenzie.

In the proportion of a drachm or two in six or eight ounces of infusion of roses, or decoction of bark, it forms a very useful gargle in ulcerated sore throat.

It should never be measured in a leaden or pewter spoon—one

of wood is best. Diluted muriatic acid is made by mixing one part of the acid with four of water, say, one drachm of the acid with four drachms of water.

Its antiseptic properties have been long known. Sir William Fordyce relates, that a drysalter acquired a large fortune from possessing a secret that enabled him to send out provisions to India in a better state of preservation than any other of the trade; his secret consisted in adding a small quantity of muriatic acid to the contents of each cask.

By pouring a little sulphuric acid on common salt, muriatic acid gas is disengaged, which has the important property of destroying the infection in sick rooms and hospitals, where putrid fever exists.

When this acid is taken as a poison, the best antidotes are soap and calcined magnesia, suspended in water, the patient taking care to drink copiously of warm water, milk or broth.

MYRRH

Myrrh is the produce of Arabia and Abyssinia.[1] It is a stimulant and slight tonic, promoting expectoration, and is, therefore, serviceable in some cases of *indigestion,* accompanied with *cough,* in *green-sickness, old coughs, habitual asthma,* and the latter stages of *pulmonary consumption.* In indigestion, old cough, and habitual asthma, it should be united with a small quantity of sulphate of zinc, in the proportion of six or eight grains of powdered myrrh to half or three-fourths of a grain of sulphate of zinc, made into one or two pills with conserve of roses, and repeated twice a day. Thus combined, it has been found extremely useful in the peculiar cough

1. Myrrh is frequently mentioned in the writings of Moses. We find it noticed in the very touching narrative of the selling of Joseph, by his brethren, to the Ishmaelites, in *Genesis, chap.* xxxvii. *v. 25. "And they sat down to eat bread: and they lifted up their eyes, and looked, and behold, a company* of *Ishmaelites came from Gilead with their camels bearing spicery and balm and Myrrh, going to carry it down, to Egypt".* Notwithstanding its being noticed so early, it is remarkable that to this day the plant from which it is procured, and how it is procured, whether by spontaneous exudation, or artificially, is wholly unknown.

which sometimes accompanies pregnancy, and continues after abortion. In the commencement of pulmonary consumption, it proves too great a stimulant, and is generally injurious; but in the advanced periods it may frequently be given with advantage, when it should be united with sulphate of iron, or zinc. It seems most beneficial in pulmonary ulceration following acute inflammation of the lungs, and other advanced cases of the florid species of consumption. The ordinary dose is eight or ten grains twice or thrice a day, but it may be increased to half a drachm. If there is much hectic fever present, it may be advisable to unite it with a little nitre, or cream of tartar.

The tincture of myrrh diffused in water is an efficacious lotion to the gums when in a spongy and diseased state, and it forms a valuable stimulant application to old fetid ulcers. It is likewise a very useful gargle in putrid sore throat.

MOXA

The term Moxa is given to a cone, or cylinder, composed of a certain quantity of cotton wool, over which a piece of fine linen is rolled, and fastened at the side by a few stitches, the base of which is placed on or near the diseased part to be operated on, the top being set fire to and allowed to burn until the whole is consumed. This conical cylinder should be about an inch long, and of a proportionate thickness. The moxa has been used in the eastern parts of the world many centuries, and among the Chinese it consists of the tomentum of the leaves of the *artemesia latifolia*.

A porte-moxa is intended to fix the cylinder upon the precise spot where the application is to be made. The metallic ring of this instrument is kept from touching the skin by means of three small supports of ebony, which is a bad conductor of heat. After the extremity of the cone has been set fire to, the combustion is kept up by means of a blow pipe, still allowing it to proceed slowly. The precise spot to which the moxa is to be applied ought to be first marked with a little ink, and all the surrounding surface covered with a wet rag, that has a hole in the middle, so as to leave the part bare which has been marked. After the whole has been consumed, in order to prevent the subsequent inflammation and suppuration from being too considerable, the water of ammonia should be immediately applied to the burnt part.

The diseases in which the moxa has been most efficacious, are *gutta serena,* obstinate pain fixed in a particular part, *tic doulourex, partial palsy, diseased joints,* and *incipient cataract.* In some examples of these maladies, it has occasionally succeeded beyond expectation, and in others it has given an impulse or new action to the part affected, which has been of decided benefit. It enjoys more confidence among professional men on the continent than with those in this country; but several English physicians and surgeons think highly of it, and when other remedies fail, it ought not to be neglected.[1]

NITRE

Nitre is refrigerant and diuretic. Taken in repeated small doses of six or eight grains, it abates heat and thirst in fevers and inflammations, diminishes the force and frequency of the pulse, and increases the secretion of urine. It is, therefore, efficaciously given in rheumatic fever, and all inflammatory diseases, and generally forms a part in saline draughts. But it is improper in hectic fevers. In the foregoing diseases, it is best given in doses of six or eight grains, every three or four hours, dissolved in water, and in combination with the solution of acetate of ammonia, and antimonial wine. In some kinds of *dropsy*, it may be given to the extent of a drachm every morning, dissolved in ale, and in this manner it has cured several cases.

It frequently affords relief in the advanced stages of indigestion, and what are too often called liver complaints. It is most useful in allaying the general increase of heat, and burning in the hands and feet, which are so apt to come on in these disorders towards night; but it likewise seems to add to the good effects of the other alterative

1. *In Thornton's Family Herbal,* p. 692, there is a valuable letter on the use of moxa, from Sir W. Temple, who found it very useful in his own case of gout. Baron Larrey is a strenuous advocate for its employment; and in the two volumes of *Boyle* on *Moxa*, and *Wallace on Moxa*, its uses are fully described.

means employed, whenever there is a considerable hardness in the pulse. It is not at all adapted to recent cases of indigestion, nor to those of some standing if there is no evident tightness in the pulse. The dose most extensively useful in the former description of case, is five or six grains, which may be made into a draught with twelve drops of tincture of henbane, half an ounce of Mindererus's spirit, and an ounce of water, and taken thrice in the twenty-four hours. If the languor of the circulation be considerable, it will often be better to substitute a drachm of the tincture of orange-peel for the henbane.

A small portion of it allowed to dissolve slowly in the mouth, often removes incipient inflammatory sore throat; and it is a useful adjunct to gargles in that complaint.

In very large quantities, which have sometimes been given by mistake for other salts, it excites vomiting, bloody stools, convulsions, and even death. The best antidotes are opium and aromatics. Copious draughts of a decoction of linseed or barley, or sugar and water, should be taken, and the poison extracted from the stomach by the stomach pump.

NITRIC ACID

Diluted nitric acid is made by mixing one fluid ounce of nitric acid with nine ounces of distilled water. This acid is tonic and antiseptic, and is of much service in *indigestion, liver complaints,* frequent-sickness accompanied with general debility, *old ulcers* depending upon the same cause, and in cases of gravel where *white* sand is deposited. It is also of great benefit in *syphilis* and its *secondary symptoms,* and as a tonic to restore the constitution to a measure of its former health, when it has been injured by the excessive use of mercury. It is often employed with great advantage in those cases of indigestion, and chronic affection of the liver, in which the skin has contracted a yellowish tinge, the bowels being costive, the appetite deficient, and the palms of the hands and the soles of the feet being frequently affected with a distressing sensation of heat and burning. In such instances, it is sometimes of more value than any mercurial preparation whatever. But many of those cases in which it is so beneficial are not truly liver complaints, but examples of severe indigestion, which this acid cures from its salutary influence on the stomach. In aggravated cases of syphilis, and secondary symptoms, which resist the powers of mercury, it will be found a valuable remedy, even when dropsy bas supervened.

This acid is indicated in those cases of gravel in which the urine is alkaline, the water turning turmeric paper inserted in it of a brown colour. In such examples, there are generally symptoms of great debility present.

The late Dr. Scott, of Russell Square, strongly recommended a bath, composed of strong nitric and muriatic acid mixed with water, for diseases of the liver; and I have known it of striking and permanent benefit in extensive ulceration of the internal surface of the bowels, in which the most efficient mercurial alteratives were of no service, and which appeared to me quite hopeless. I am persuaded that this bath is invaluable in many cases of disease affecting the stomach and bowels, as well as the liver. The bath is made in the following way; three parts in measure of strong muriatic acid are to be mixed with two of nitric acid, and a pint of this mixture is to have an equal quantity of water added to it. The acid bath is to consist of an ounce and a half of this diluted acid to half a gallon of water, in a wooden tub, which is in general sufficient to form the bath.[1] This quantity may be put into a deep narrow tub, into which the feet are to be immersed for twenty minutes, or half an hour, every night, the legs, thighs, and abdomen, being in the meantime frequently sponged with the same. In the winter, the water may be made warm by the addition of a little hot water; but this is not necessary in the summer. The bath may be employed at first daily, for a fortnight or three weeks, and afterwards, every other day, or only twice a week.

Nitric acid, in the form of lotion, is of great service to foul and indolent ulcers. To form the lotion, one or two drachms may be mixed with a pint of water, with a little of which mixture the whole surface of the ulcer may be touched twice or thrice a day.

1. Mr. Garden, Chemist, in Oxford Street, manufactures a nitro-muriatic acid, which answers extremely well ; about half an ounce of it, when mixed with half a gallon of water, forming a bath of proper strength.

The dose of *diluted* nitric acid is from fifteen to thirty drops in two or three ounces of water, or decoction of sarsaparilla, three times a day, sweetened with syrup of orange peel.

The dose of *nitro-muriatic acid is* three or four drops in four or five table-spoonfuls of water.

NUT-GALLS

Are obtained from a species of oak indigenous to Asia Minor. This oak is also found growing in the southern countries of Europe; and the galls are excrescences from the young shoots of this tree, and are produced by the puncture of an insect to deposit its egg. Nut-galls were analyzed by Sir Humphrey Davy, who obtained from five hundred grains of Aleppo galls—

> Tannin or tannic acid, 130 grains; mucilage and other matters, 12 grains; gallic acid, with a little extractive, 31 grains; calcareous earth and saline matter, 12 grains.

Nut-galls are a very powerful astringent; and the infusion, prepared by pouring 6 oz. of water upon 4 drachms of nut-galls, is a very useful injection in *whites* and *gleet*. It forms also an excellent astringent gargle in relaxation of the uvula, and is undoubtedly of great service as an astringent in *prolapsus of the anus* and *womb.*

Gallic acid is one of the most efficacious remedies in bleeding from the bladder, and other parts, in doses of 5 grains in mucilage of gum arabic, repeated as occasion may require.

OIL OF TURPENTINE

See **Turpentine**

OPIUM

The white poppy is a native of the warmer regions of Europe and Asia, but it also grows in colder climates with little diminution of its powers. The larger capsule which it bears, affords, by incision in its cortical part, a milky juice, which, by exposure to the sun and air, becomes concrete, and of a brown colour. This is named opium, and is the product of the plant that is chiefly medicinally employed.

The medicinal virtues of opium are very great, and often of the first importance in the treatment of disease. It operates as a powerful and very diffusible stimulus, but its primary operation is followed by narcotic and sedative effects in a degree much greater than could be expected from the previous excitement it produces. It acts directly on the nervous system, and when taken into the stomach destroys irritability, and allays pain in the most distant parts of the body, independent of the circulation, and without inducing any change on the composition of the blood. As the principle, therefore, on which opium acts is the same over all the body, the topical application of it is capable of producing similar effects, only in a diminished degree, to those resulting from it when it is taken into the stomach. In moderate doses it increases the fulness, force, and frequency of the pulse, augments the heat of the body, quickens respiration, and invigorates both the corporeal and mental functions, exhilarating even to intoxication; but, by degrees, these effects are succeeded by languor, lassitude, and sleep; and in many instances, head-ache, sickness, thirst, tremors, and other symptoms of debility, such as follow the excessive use of ardent spirits, supervene. Even in small doses it commonly impairs the appetite and digestion, and produces costiveness; yet there are cases of depraved digestion which are benefited by it, which are those where much pain is felt in the stomach, especially soon after eating or drinking.

The principal indications which opium is capable of fulfilling, are supporting the actions of the system, in the advanced stages of *typhus* and *typhoid fever and gangrene;* allaying pain and irritation, in *acute rheumatism, small pox,* and many other diseases; relieving spasmodic action, in *hysterics, epilepsy, Saint Vitus's dance,* etc.*;* inducing sleep; and checking morbidly increased evacuations, as in *dysentery, diarrhoea, hoemorrhage* after delivery, *cough,* etc.

In *typhus* and *typhoid fever,* when given in small doses, frequently repeated, it is sometimes a useful assistant to wine and tonics in supporting the actions of the system; and, at the same time, allaying irritation, and obtunding the susceptibility of those morbid impressions which occasion watchfulness, delirium, tremors, and twitching of the muscles. Some caution, however, is required in its exhibition; for if the heat of the body be much above the natural standard, and the skin dry, opium increases these symptoms, augments thirst, and occasions restlessness; but if moisture be coming on, opium accelerates it, and tranquillity and sleep follow. It is hurtful also when there is any disposition to local inflammation, particularly of the chest; and where there is much determination to the head, and when the pupils of the eye are contracted. It very materially assists the bark in curing ague, and prevents it from running off by the bowels. When given at the approach of the cold fit, it sometimes checks its attack, or shortens and renders it milder, and abates the violence of the hot stage by determining to the surface and inducing sleep.

In *spasmodic* and *convulsive diseases,* it is of the greatest service, especially in tetanus, Saint Vitus's dance, hysterics, colic and cholera morbus. In spasmodic cough it is very useful. It is used with the same benefit in all bleedings which are called passive, and which arise from an increased degree of irritability, where the pulse, instead of being strong and full, is small, quick, and intermitting. In the hoemorrhage of pregnant women it is often of signal service.

The action of opium is much modified by *age, sex, temperament, custom,*[1] and *climate,* as well as by combination with other articles. The younger the patient, the more energetic is its action on the system; hence extreme caution is necessary in its administration to infants and childern. Its very energetic action upon infants and children is probably owing to their higher degree of nervous susceptibility; hence in them narcotics generally produce rather irritating than calming effects, and palpitations of the heart and convulsions not unfrequently follow. Women are more susceptible of its action than men, and therefore, a smaller dose

1. Persons long accustomed to its use may sometimes take very large doses with at least a present exhilarating effect. Dr. Russell, in his History of Aleppo, remarks that a Turk, named Mustapha Shatar, on opium-eater in Smyrna, took daily three drachms of solid opium, and even then found a necessity for increasing the dose. M. Dhere, a French writer, mentions the case of a French officer who took a drachm of pure opium daily. Such persons may sometimes appear in tolerable health, but in general they are pale and emaciated.

produces in them a greater effect, and we more frequently fend among them than among men, those who cannot bear it in any dose. It produces more decided effects in the *sanguine* than in the melancholic temperament,—in the full than in the spare habit of body; and those individuals who- are easily affected by wine, are likewise easily influenced by opium.

In *combination* with aromatics the stimulant effect of opium is increased, and its sedative and narcotic influence lessened; hence the Turks and Persians combine it with confections of aromatics and syrups, and use it as wine for promoting hilarity. When combined with antimonial, it determines more certainly to the surface of the body, and is rendered less likely to impede the other secretions (see *Dover's powder).* With acids, a much smaller dose will produce a full effects and is less likely to affect the head or confine the bowels.[1]

The influence also of peculiarity of habit, called *idiosyncrasy,* must not be overlooked. Some persons cannot take opium at all, without its producing the most distressing effects, or operating in a very singular manner; thus in some it produces restlessness delirium, and convulsions, in others a miliary eruption on the skin. Dr. A. T. Thomson states, *(Elem. of Materia Medica*, vol. i, p. 506,*)* that he has met with one lady in whom 66 it never produces its soporific effects until the day following that on which she takes it; and an instance of the same peculiarity in a man is mentioned by Lorry, who also details the case of a woman who was thrown into furious delirium, spasms, and convulsions, even by the external application of opium".

The use of opium is contra-indicated in all morbid states of the body where a strong inflammatory action exists, at least until blood-letting, tartarized antimony, and other active measures have subdued the inflammation; then it may be given with excellent effects. It is injurious in pulmonary affections, when the cough is

1. In combination, the medical powers of opium are wonderfully extended, so that there is scarcely a disease in which it may not, during some of its stages, be rendered useful. United with ipecacuanha, it forms the compound ipecacuanha powder, which is of eminent utility in acute and chronic rheumatism, dysentery, diarrhoea, and some other complaints.

dry and hard, and the expectoration difficult and scanty. In insanity it must be given with great caution, and in the mildest forms, such as acetate of morphia.

Externally employed, opium alleviates pain and spasmodic action. Applied by friction, it relieves the pain of cramp, and even of tetanus, and when rubbed over the abdomen, it alleviates spasmodic pain of the stomach and intestines. This made of employing it will also succeed in reducing the violence of the paroxysms of mania, and of a furious fit of epilepsy, and in relieving the delirium of typhus fever, by removing irritation and inducing sleep. Opiate friction is also used with great advantage in cholera-morbus, hysterics, and hooping-cough.

In exhibiting opium in a *liquid* form, it must not be given in conjunction with oxymuriate of mercury, acetate of lead, sulphate of zinc, iron and copper, carbonates of alkalies, lime water, infusion of galls, and infusion of yellow Peruvian bark, as all these substances decompose it. In combination, however, with vinegar and the vegetable acids, its narcotic power is much increased, while its constipating properties are lessened, and it does not affect the head. The celebrated *Black Drop,* and the *Sedative Liquor of Opium* of Mr. Battley are preparations of opium, which owe their strength and mildness of operation to the manner in which they are prepared with vinegar, or some other vegetable acid.

The dose of this narcotic is very various, according to the state of disease, and the intention with which it is administered. If we wish to obtain its stimulant effect, we give small doses at short intervals; if its sedative influence be required, we administer a large dose at once. It is material to observe, that *in all cases of fever or inflammation, when pain or restlessness calls for the use of a narcotic, the dose must be large enough to induce at once its anodyne effect, without the previous excitement.* One grain of solid opium, or twenty-five drops of the tincture, is the medium quantity to a person unaccustomed to its use; but to remove the symptoms of irritation, or relieve pain, it often requires to be given in a larger quantity. Thus, Dr. Chapman of America, says, that in a case of cancer in the womb he has given the tincture to the extent of three ounces, or more, in twenty-four hours, without any other effect than that of relieving pain. In all highly painful and spasmodic affections, the extent of the dose is to be limited only by its effects; thus, in tetanus, one hundred drops of the tincture have been given every hour with admirable effects, and Dr. A. T. Thomson states, *(Cyclopaedia of Practical Medicine, part xv.* p. 150*)*, "in cases of gall-stones and calculi of the kidneys, he has given upwards of eight hundred drops of the officinal tincture of opium in less than twelve hours, without any effect but that of relieving pain and aiding the passage of the concretions".[1]

A quarter of a grain, or eight or ten drops, frequently repeated, is in general sufficient to keep up its stimulant effect; and from ono to two or three grains act as a sedative, and produce sleep : while in tetanus, hydrophobia, and some other alarming diseases, much larger doses are required, and in the last disease, it has been taken, in the solid form, to the extent of two drachms in twelve hours, without abating the violence of the symptoms. It is employed either in the solid or liquid form; being used in the solid state when we wish it to act slowly, or on the stomach or intestinal canal; otherwise it is more convenient in the liquid form.

Morphia or *morphine* is a peculiar saline substance existing in opium, in combination with an acid called the *meconic*. It is to this *meconate of morphia* that opium owes its soporific and narcotic properties; and it is, therefore, the most important of its constituents. Morphia, separated from opium, is now combined with various acids for medicinal purposes, and extensively used in practice in all cases calling for the use of opium. This is considered one of the

1. Robert Hall, the baptist minister, so well known for his eloquence and acuteness, suffered intensely for many years from a pain in his back, for the relief of which he took " in 1812 from fifty to one hundred drops of laudanum every night. Before 1826 the quantity had increased to one thousand drops every night"—Works of *R. Hall, by Gregory,* vol. vi. page 95, *edition* 1832. He never lessened, but rather increased this quantity. In his last sickness his medical attendant says (p. 109), "The pain in his back had been uncommonly severe during the whole night, and compelled him to multiply, at very short intervals, the dose of his anodyne, until he had taken no less than one hundred and twenty-five grains of solid opium, equal to more than three thousand drops, or nearly four ounces of laudanum!!".

most valuable achievements of modern medical chemistry, the *muriate* and *acetate* of *morphia* especially being esteemed of superior value, as displaying the most powerful soporific and narcotic properties while they affect the head but little, and possess little exciting power. This is true more especially of the *muriate of morphia,* the, best of all the salts of morphia. Its dose is from one quarter to three quarters of a grain, in a pill.

The means of counteracting the bad effects of an over-dose of opium are detailed under the head of *Poisons*.

Opium is the quack's sheet anchor. The various nostrums advertised as "*Cough Drops* for the cure of colds, asthmas, catarrhs, etc." are preparations of opium, very similar to paregoric elixir. *Pectoral Balsam of Liquorice, Essence of Coltsfoot, Grindle's Cough Drops, Squire's Elixir,* and many others are combinations of this kind; and it behaves the patient to be very cautious in their use, for, as Dr. Fothergill has observed, the mischief that has proceeded from the *healing* anodynes of quacks can be scarcely imagined, since opiates generally do much harm in coughs, arising from suppressed perspiration, or an inflammatory state of the system.

OLIVE OIL

The olive tree is a native of the south of Europe, and the north of Africa, but it is cultivated in France, Spain and Italy. The best oil is made in Provence, its excellence arising from the olives being carefully cleaned and garbled; but what we receive in this country comes from Lucca and Florence.

Olive oil is demulcent, relaxing and laxative. It is used internally as a demulcent in cough, and other pulmonary affections, diffused in water by means of mucilage; and is also given internally, in large quantities, to mitigate the action of acrid substances, as some poisons, taken into the stomach. Externally applied, it is a very useful relaxant to the skin; but is generally used as a vehicle for more active substances, in the form of embrocation ; thus it is an excellent solvent of opium, which can, through its means only, be used in frictions, with any advantage. It is also used as an adjunct to glysters in dysentery and intestinal abrasions.

OXYDE OF ZINC

Oxyde of zinc is sometimes called the flowers of zinc, and is tonic and antispasmodic. It has been praised for its virtues in *epilepsy, St. Vitus's dance, hooping cough, asthma* and other *spasmodic affections,* in which it is frequently of much service. Gaubius, a foreign physician of great judgment and celebrity, used to recommend it as a remedy for these diseases, in the strongest terms. It may be given in doses of from two to eight grains, twice or thrice a day, made into pills, with extract of gentian or chamomile.

The zinc ointment of the shops is a useful application to sore eyes, chronic inflammation of the eye-lids, and all ulcers which require a stimulating application.

OXYMURIATE OF MERCURY

See **Bi-chloride of Mercury**

PAREIRA BRAVA

This is a perennial plant, growing in the West India islands, and in South America. The root, which is the part employed, is brought to us from Brazil; it is long; thick, and covered with a furrowed brown bark.[1] It has little or no smell; the taste is bitterish, blended with a sweetness like that of liquorice.

It has been for many years in high repute among the Brazilians as a remedy in all obstructions of the urinary organs. The common people of Jamaica use a decoction of it for pains and weakness of the stomach proceeding from relaxation, and it is probable that its

1. "It is woody, fibrous, hard, twisted, of the size of a child's arm, brown externally, of a yellowish grey colour internally, and marked with concentric circles." *Edwards's Materia Modica,* p. 222.

effects in urinary disorders are due chiefly to its tonic influence on the bladder. Geoffry, in a paper inserted in the *Memoirs of the Royal Academy of Sciences* for the year 1710, reports very favourably of it in ulceration of the kidneys and bladder; and Sir B. Brodie also speaks strongly in its favour. See his *Lectures on Diseases of the Urinary Organs,* p. 170. One of the most prominent symptoms of chronic inflammation of the bladder is an abundant discharge of a ropy adhesive alkaline mucus, and we have Sir B. Brodie's testimony to the fact, that the use of the decoction of the root of the *pareira brava* is here frequently productive of excellent effects.

The decoction is prepared by simmering four ounces of the root in three pints of water, until it is reduced to two pints, and then strained; the dose of this decoction is a small tea-cupful (about four ounces) twice or thrice a day. A little tincture of henbane may sometimes be advantageously combined with it.

PAREGORIC ELIXIR

This is very similar to the *compound tincture of camphor* of the shops, and is made by mixing together two scruples of camphor, one drachm of hard opium in powder, one drachm of acid of benzoin, and two pints of proof spirit; which are allowed to digest for fourteen days and afterwards filtered.

It is advantageously employed to allay irritation and procure rest in habitual cough, *chronic asthma,* and the latter periods of *hooping-cough.* It is most appropriate in *dry coughs.* It may also be employed with effect, for the same purposes, in recent cold and cough, after the inflammatory symptoms have abated; but it is highly improper in all cases of cough attended with much fever, pain in the chest, and full quick pulse. Half a fluid ounce of this elixir contains nearly a grain of opium. The dose to procure ease in cough is from one to two tea-spoonfuls occasionally; and three tea-spoonfuls where quiet rather than sleep, is required.

PEPSINE

Is a preparation of *gastric juice*, chiefly obtained from the stomachs of sheep, and is usually given in the form of powder. It is recommended as a powerful digestive agent, in cases of want of appetite, of sluggish and painful digestion; of vomiting, water brash, consumption, and in the weakness of stomach found at the commencement of the convalescence from severe fever. It is an *artificial*, and therefore *partial* substitute for a *natural* process. Gastric juice prepared by a healthy animal is by means of this powder mixed with the food, instead of that which the patient's stomach ought to prepare. It acts in the body very much as it would out of the body, under the same circumstances of heat and motion. The chewed meat is dissolved by it in the stomach, and the putrefactive process is arrested by it in the intestinal canal. It is, therefore, a substitute for the natural secretion of the stomach, and to a certain extent supplies its place.

It is best to begin with five grains of pepsine given with the meal, or before it, and repeat it twice or thrice a day, gradually increasing the dose to ten or twelve grains. If regular meals are eaten, then it is best taken spread as a sandwich between two thin slices of bread at the commencement of the dinner. If the patient is so ill that the food is obliged to be administered more frequently and in small quantities, so as to keep up a continuous supply, five grains of pepsine powder may be given in a little syrup of orange or lemon, after meals.

Dr. Chambers has prescribed pepsine with great advantage in consumption, hysterical vomiting and nausea, and pain in the stomach after meals. He says "Give half a mutton chop with pepsine the first day or two; and if that is digested well, try a whole chop the next; but remember, that then you have got to the end of your tether, and that the digestion of a larger quantity will not be at all assisted by artificial means". He adds, "In a case of diarrhoea and mucous vomiting, occurring in an old victim of atonic gout, the stools became more natural and less frequent, and strength was regained, on taking pepsine and mutton chops instead of opium and acetate of lead".

Pepsine is now given in good white wine, and *pepsine wine,* and *pepsine,* may be procured of excellent quality from Mr. Squire, 277, Oxford Street, and from Morson and Son, 19, Southampton Row, Russell Square.

Rennet Wine is prepared by Mr. Twinberrow, 2, Edwards Street, Portman Square, which merits confidence as an assistant to digestion. Good *rennet wine* may be procured also from Squire, 277, Oxford Street, and from Morson and Son, 19, Southampton Row.

PHOSPHATE OF ZINC

Is a new medicine, and has been found of great benefit in epilepsy by Dr. Barnes. The dose of the phosphate of zinc in powder is from two to five grains, two or three times a day; made into pills with extract of liquorice.

PHOSPHOROUS ACID

Dr. Rowbotham strongly recommends this acid as an efficacious remedy in asthma. He says it has given marked relief when all other remedies had failed. The *dose* is from ten to twenty minims, twice or thrice a day in water.

PILE-WORT OINTMENT

The Pile-wort or *Ranunculus Ficaria,* usually flowers in March and April. It should be gathered when full blown, *chopped as fine as possible,* (after the dirt has been removed from the roots, and the plant washed and dried with a clean cloth). The chopped herb is then to be boiled in lard for about two hours, constantly stirring it, and then strained. About *double* the quantity by *weight* of the fine chopped pile-wort is to be boiled with half the quantity of lard, say six pounds of the herb to three pounds of lard or "fresh liquor". "Fresh liquor", or lard without salt, is best. Strain it off through a small hair sieve, and keep the ointment in a cool place.

This is an excellent ointment for piles, prolapsus of the anus, and all discharges from that part.

POMEGRANATE BARK

This bark comes from Asia and the West Indies. It is a mild ringent, and was formerly much used in *chronic diarrhoea* and *dysentery.* The decoction is now much esteemed as gargle in sore throats, and as an injection. The ordinary way of making the decoction is to boil four drachms of the bark with six ounces of water, of which six drachms may be taken every three hours; or it may be taken in the form of powder, in doses of from half a drachm to a drachm, in water. The powder is useful to check diarrhoea in the last stage of consumption.

It is likewise employed as a remedy for tape-worm in the form of a strong decoction, prepared by boiling two ounces of the bark in a pint and a half of water, until it is reduced to nine ounces, of which a wine-glassful is given when cold, and repeated every half hour to the fourth time. It generally produces nausea. in this mode of taking it.

POPPY-HEADS

Poppy-heads, or the dried capsules of the poppy, possess anodyne properties, and their active matter is extracted by decoction with water. They are chiefly employed either alone, or in conjunction with chamomile flowers, boiled in water, as fomentations to inflamed and ulcerated surfaces, in which manner they are often of great service in allaying pain and irritation. The decoction is made by boiling for a quarter of an hour four ounces of the white poppy-heads bruised, in four pints of water, and then straining. The seeds should not be rejected in making this decoction, as they contain a considerable portion of bland oil, which increases the emollient quality of the decoction.

PRUSSIC ACID

This peculiar acid, commonly called *hydrocyanic acid,* exists in a great variety of native combinations in the vegetable kingdom, the principal of which are *bitter almonds,* the *cherry laurel,* the leaves of the *peach tree,* the kernels of fruit, pips of apples, etc. The prussic acid appears to be the most abundant in the thin pellicle that envelopes the kernel; the fleshy parts of these fruits do not contain it, and even the berries of the *cherry laurel* may be eaten with impunity; yet the distilled water, and oil of this plant, is the most destructive of all narcotic poisons.

In a sufficient dose, it instantly destroys life, by extinguishing the nervous energy of the body, and the quantity necessary to produce these fatal effects is very small. It is said that a very few drops let fall on the eye, will speedily kill small animals, as dogs, cats, etc., and smelling the vapours sometimes occasions vertigo, spasmodic constriction of the lower part of the windpipe and other deleterious effects.

But skilfully employed in small doses, it is sometimes very useful in pulmonary *consumption,* and *spasmodic coughs* of every description, particularly *asthma, chronic cough* and *hooping-cough.* Linnaeus informs us that it was frequently used in Holland in pulmonary consumption, and some eminent medical men of our own country appear to have thought highly of it as a remedy in this complaint, and especially in spasmodic coughs. It would seem to be most beneficial in coughs and consumption originating in great irritation and disease in the windpipe. It is also useful in those instances of indigestion which are attended with pain and acidity of the stomach, and accompanied with heat and soreness of the tongue; but, upon the whole, it is much inferior to many other remedies for this disorder. The dose is from two to eight drops, which may be taken in distilled water, almond emulsion, or infusion of Peruvian bark, and repeated twice a day.

It has lately been very much praised as a remedy in various spasmodic disorders, especially in *asthma, St. Vitus's dance, epilepsy,* and *hooping-cough.* The very strong opinion given by some physicians respecting its wonderful efficacy is not worthy of confidence.

As a local application, it is very efficacious in allaying the *itching* and *tingling* which are so distressing in *tetters,* and other *cutaneous eruptions,* which appear on the face, head, hand, etc., and it nut only allays the itching of these pustules, but will often be of much service in promoting their cure. The lotion for external use, is made by mixing a drachm of the by drocyanie acid with an ounce and a half of rose-water, with which the part affected may be washed three times a day. It may be used advantageously in the following combination, two drachms of the prussic acid, sixteen grains of the acetate of lead, half an ounce of spirit of wine, and eight ounces of distilled water, which are to be mixed together for a lotion. This soothes the irritability of the diseased surface, and disposes the skin to renew its healthy action.

The cherry laurel water *(aqua lauro-cerasi)* acts in the same way as the medicinal prussic acid, but is less energetic. The dose is from six drops to half a drachm. It is much used on the Continent.

QUASSIA

Quassia wood comes from Jamaica and the Caribbean islands, where it is called the bitter ash. It is said to owe its name to Quassia, a negro slave, who discovered to Polander the wood of this tree, as that which he had employed with success as a secret remedy in the malignant endemic fevers of Surinam. It is a powerful bitter tonic, which is used with much advantage in debility of the stomach and intestinal canal, nervous irritability, intermittent and bilious remittent fevers, looseness, and irregular and atonic gout. It has been said to be highly useful in that combination of debility and hysterics to which the female sex is so prone. Here it is reported to afford more vigour and relief to the system than the Peruvian bark, especially when combined with a small portion of sulphate of zinc. In typhus or remittent fevers, (says Murray in his *Apparatus Medicam*) it may be administered in every stage of the disease, as it neither quickens the pulse, nor augments the animal heat, nor operates on the bowels.

Infusion is the best form of administering quassia, which is made by pouring a pint of boiling water on a drachm of the wood, which must be strained when cold. The dose is from one to two ounces, repeated twice or thrice a day.

RHATANY ROOT

Is a powerful astringent and tonic, and may be used as such in most diseases of debility and relaxation. It has been long known to the manufacturers of Port Wine, who use it to impart the astringency which that wine always contains. It is particularly useful in some cases of chronic diarrhoea and dysentery.

It is most frequently administered in infusion, decoction, or extract. The infusion is made with half an ounce of the bruised root to six ounces of boiling water, poured on it; of which the dose is from one to two ounces. The decoction is made by boiling two ounces of the bruised root in a pint of distilled water; the close is the same as of the infusion. A tea-spoonful or two of the tincture in water, two or three times a day, is a convenient mode of taking it, and also an efficacious one.

RHUBARB

The plant which yields this invaluable root is a native of China and Tartary, and arrives at considerable perfection when cultivated in this country. Many individuals have reared large quantities of it in Great Britain, and some of it extremely good; yet so powerful and unreasonable is prejudice, that very little of it can be sold. There are two principal varieties of rhubarb known in the shops, *Turkey* rhubarb, and *East Indian* rhubarb. The *Russian* or *Turkey* rhubarb is in roundish pieces, perforated with a large hole, of a yellow or reddish colour on the outside, somewhat soft and friable, and, when broken, exhibiting many diverging streaks of a beautiful bright red colour.

It is stomachic and astringent, or purgative, according to the extent of the dose in which it' is administered. In the dose of one, two or three grains, twice or thrice a day, it acts as a valuable stomachic, stimulating the stomach, increasing the appetite, and promoting a healthy flow of bile; and is of much service in *indigestion, low spirits, jaundice*, and a weakened relaxed state of the bowels. It acts chiefly on the stomach and first intestines, and in these complaints may be advantageously combined with soap, dried sub-carbonate of soda, ipecacuanha, or extract of gentian. A pill of two grains of rhubarb, one of ipecacuanha powder, and one of soap, repeated three or four times a day, is sometimes of superior benefit in indigestion and bilious complaints, especially of elderly persons.

In doses of from twelve grains to a scruple it opens the bowels freely. Its purgative operation is mild, and it may be given to the youngest infants. It is particularly adapted for the majority of cases of diarrhoea, as it evacuates any acrid matter that may be offending the bowels, before it acts as an astringent; and from its power of strengthening the intestinal canal, it forms a suitable and valuable purgative for children, in whom that canal generally possesses a great deal of relaxation and morbid irritability. As a common purgative in the disorders of childhood, it is far preferable to calomel, being equally effectual in its operation, without possessing any deleterious principle. When it is intended to act on the bowels, it should be administered in conjunction with about fifteen grains of super-sulphate of potash, which covers its taste, and causes it to act more readily and with greater certainty. This combination has been praised by physicians of great ability as very efficacious in curing the costiveness, bilious affections, enlarged bellies, and other disorders of children, in which it is now a fashionable but pernicious custom to administer calomel.

The powder of rhubarb sprinkled on foul indolent ulcers is sometimes of great use in exciting in them a healthy action.

SAL AMMONIAC

This salt is a compound of muriatic acid and ammonia. It is found as a product of volcanoes, and the eruption of Etna in 1811, afforded as much sal ammoniac as supplied all the manufactories and apothecaries' shops in Sicily; but the greater part of that which is employed in medicine and the arts, is artificially prepared in the north of England.

It was formerly considered a powerful aperient and attenuant of viscid humours, but is now not so much used as an internal medicine as it deserves to be. It is, however, frequently employed, dissolved in water, *as a lotion to indolent tumours* and *chilblains,* and from its stimulus is very efficacious in allaying the irritation, and reducing the size of such swellings. It is the active ingredient in the following plaster, which is one of the best local applications to the chest in severe coughs and pulmonary consumption. Take of soap, one ounce; lead plaster, two drachms; which are to be liquefied together, and when nearly cold, half a drachm of sal ammoniac, finely powdered, is to be added. It is then to be spread on leather, and directly applied to the chest, being renewed every twenty-four hours, otherwise the intention is lost.

One ounce of this salt dissolved in nine ounces of water, an once of spirit of wine being afterwards added; forms an excellent lotion for indolent tumours, scrophulous swellings, etc., but, on account of its stimulus, it is not proper where there is active inflammation in the part.

SAL VOLATILE

This is the aromatic spirit of ammonia of the shops, and is a useful stimulant cordial in languors, fainting and flatulent colic. The dose is from half a tea-spoonful to a tea-spoonful, in any agreeable vehicle. It is a grateful medicine to the stomach; and forms an adjunct to many mixtures which are prescribed for the relief of nervous complaints and debility.

SAL POLYCHREST

This is a *tartrate of soda and potash;* it is very similar in its operation to the sulphate of potash, and is a very useful adjunct to rhubarb, the operation of which it quickens and renders more certain. Ten grains of *sal polychrest* and nine or ten of powdered rhubarb, is an efficacious purgative for children, pregnant women, and other persons in delicate health. It is a cooling aperient that beneficially influences the blood.

SALT OF WORMWOOD

Salt of wormwood and salt of tartar are the same substance—the carbonate of potash. In small doses of eight or ten grains, dissolved in a little rose-water, and repeaded twice or thrice a day, it is considered to be of great service in indigestion and bilious complaints, especially where there is a good deal of morbid acidity in the stomach. A bitter infusion, such as infusion of calumba or gentian, should always be added to it; but it should not be much indulged in, so as to be habitually resorted to.

It may be used for all the purpose for which the carbonate of soda is generally employed, but is not so pleasant a medicine. One scruple of this salt, and four drachms of lemon juice, with two or three ounces of water, form the common saline effervescing draught, which is so grateful and very serviceable in relieving heat, and quenching thirst, in fever.

SARSAPARILLA

The Sarsaparilla plant is a native of youth America and Virginia. The best sarsaparilla grows on the borders of a lake on the north of the Cerra Unturan, not far from Esmeralda; and is celebrated all over South America by the name of *Zarza del Rio Negro.* Baron Humboldt states, that nearly five thousand quintals are annually exported from Vera Cruz.

It is demulcent and alterative, and may often be given with great advantage in various *obstinate internal chronic diseases,* and in *swellings, ulcerations,* and other local maladies *depending upon constitutional indisposition.* I have found it of inestimable value in cases of extreme irritation and debility of the mucous membrane of the digestive organs. Some physicians seem to doubt its medicinal powers !—a doubt at which indeed we may wonder, and which proves how soon some men contract doubts, and how ready they are to express them. Unquestionably, it is frequently of incomparable utility in chronic diseases even when used alone, and certainly of great assistance in promoting and establishing the curative effects of an alterative course of mercury in many different complaints. Maps eminent practitioners of the present day are very partial to its employment. It was first introduced as a medicine of greet efficacy in the cure of *lues venerea;* and I firmly believe that, given in conjunction with five grains of blue pill, or Plummer's pill, every night, or every second night, it is equal to the perfect cure of the majority of these cases, and in whatever form they may appear : from such treatment the constitution cannot suffer, while the diseased ulcerations and swellings will be effectually removed. In *nocturnal pains* in the limbs, *painful enlargements* of the knee and elbow joints, *nodes,* and *cutaneous ulcerations,* arising from a *syphilitic taint,* it is superior to any other remedy. Some time since I had a patient who had taken a vast deal of mercury for a syphilitic complaint, with little benefit to the disease for which it was taken, but to the great injury of his general health and strength; his pains were constant and severe, accompanied with loss of appetite, strength and flesh, numerous swellings and ulcers in different parts of the body, and a quick small pulse; indeed, the poor fellow was reduced to so extreme a state of disease and pain, that he was attacked with severe fits of epilepsy for some days in succession, and we had little hope of his recovery. Notwithstanding; the decoction of sarsaparilla restored him.

Since the preceding remarks were first written, another very remarkable case has come under my care, establishing the uncommon efficacy of this remedy. It occurred in the person of an officer in the India Company's Service, whose life was despaired of from the deplorable condition of his general health and appearance, but who from close medical attention, and especially from the efficient use of sarsaparilla, is now quite equal to all his military duties. Numerous other cases have proved to me the extraordinary virtues of this celebrated medicine, and my opinion that it will often effect the most salutary changes, and such as, perhaps, no other medicine will secure, is one of personal experience.

This remedy is best given in powder or pills. The compound decoction is likewise a form in which it is commonly given, and the addition of twenty drops of antimonial wine to each dose augments its alterative effects. The manner of making this decoction is stated in the *Collection of Prescriptions.*

The powder of sarsaparilla is an invaluable alterative, and is commonly far more efficacious than the decoctions. The dose of the powder is from one to two drachma, twice or thrice a day, in water; and the patient should be careful to procure it fresh, and of the best quality.

The hydro-alcoholic Compound fluid Extract of Sarsaparilla. Water does not take up all the active principles of sarsaparilla root, but they are soluble in weak alcohol, which forms this preparation of *The General Apothecaries' Company,* 49, Berners Street, and by which the full virtues of sarsaparilla may be secured. The dose is from two to four tea-spoonfuls, in water, twice a day.

Still in some irritable states of the stomach the powder of sarsaparilla will be found to agree better, because it is thus taken in water, and in the simplest state. On the whole, the powder of sarsaparilla is the most efficacious form in which that valuable alterative can be taken.

SALACINE

See **Willow Bark**

SCARIMONY

This purgative substance is usually imported from Smyrna. In its operation it is closely allied to jalap, but is more active and irritating, although not so nauseous. It is inadmissible in inflammatory conditions of the alimentary canal. It is principally used as a smart purgative for children, on account of the smallness of the dose necessary to produce the effect, the slight taste, and the energy of its operation. One of the best modes of administering it is in the compound scammony powder of the shops; of which the dose for an adult is from ten to twenty grains, and for children from six to twelve years of age half that quantity, and a quarter of a grain of calomel may be added to it with advantage; the whole being taken in some thick vehicle, such as jam or jelly.

SENEKA

Seneka or Senega, is a native of the United States of America. It is a stimulant to the mucous membranes and skin, and is expectorant, acting especially on the bronchial tubes—the air passages; and is therefore, useful in chronic cough and humoral asthma. It is a very valuable remedy in some cases in the latter stages of *bronchitis,* in aged and debilitated constitutions; and its efficacy is greatly increased in combination with sesqui-carbonate of ammonia

It is best given in decoction. Ten drachms of seneka root is mixed with two pints of water, and boiled down to one pint, of which the *dose* is from two to four table-spoonfuls, three times a day.

SENNA LEAVES

The plant which yields the senna leaves, is a native of Upper Egypt, and is imported from Alexandria. The best Alexandrian grows in the Vallies of Nubia; but senna is also cultivated at Tinivelly, on the Malabar Coast, and is imported in large quantities into this country under the name of East Indian senna. It is milder in its operation than the Alexandrian species. In this country it is usually sold at about six pence per ounce; yet Burckhardt, the traveller, states, that the Bedonin Arabs, who are the chief collectors of senna, sell it to the merchants of Esne, at about one pound sterling per camel load (from 400 to 500 weight.)

Senna is a purgative very frequently employed, having a considerable degree of activity, without being liable to be harsh in its operation. The best form of administering it is that of watery infusion, two drachms being infused in four or five ounces of tepid water, to which three or four drachms of compound tincture of cardamoms should be added to prevent griping. Sugar or manna covers its taste, and is a suitable addition when it is given to children. The dose of the above infusion is from one to three or four ounces.

Senna may be advantageously given in combination with any of the purgative neutral salts, as Epsom salt, Glauber's salt, or soluble tartar. Two or three drachms of Epsom salt, an ounce and a half of infusion of senna, and a drachm of tincture of senna, form the common black draught in so general use among apothecaries.

The tincture of senna of the shops is similar in composition to the famous *Daffy's Elixir;* and, when good, is very little inferior to it.

SERPENTARIA

This (the *Aristolochia Serpentaria)* is a plant usually rising eight or ten inches in height, a native of Virginia and Carolina, having a slender, flexuous stem. It has an aromatic smell and a warm, bitter, pungent taste.

It was probably first used in America as a remedy against the bites of serpents, whence its name. It is a warm cordial aromatic tonic, and acts as a diaphoretic. It has been much employed as a cordial medicine to support the powers of life, and promote a free perspiration in low and *putrid fevers.*

It is a very appropriate and useful medicine in the *advanced stages of malignant ,fevers,* when the powers of life are greatly reduced, and yet the skin is hot and dry; hence it is of excellent use in confluent small-pox, especially when there is a receding of the eruption.

When joined with bark it often proves of great service, since it makes the bark more cordial, and to sit easier on the stomach. *Agues* yield sooner to the bark mixed with serpentaria than without it, and it forms properly one of the ingredients in the compound tincture of bark.[1]

In some cases of *indigestion,* the circulation being very languid, the pulse feeble, and the skin dry and harsh, the serpentaria is useful.

Dr. Robert Thornion says *(Family Herbal,* p. 744*)*—

---

1. I have given it in cases of protracted intermittents, especially when these have been combined with cough; and it bas removed the disease after quinine and arsenic had faild. Thomson's *Materia Medica.* vol. i. p. 193.

> "The editor of this work has frequently employed the serpentaria in the low stages of small-pox, and has often found it to do wonders in stopping mortification, joined with opium and other cordials; a remarkable instance of which occurred in the case of Mr. Cossart. From a bad fracture mortification came on, and it advanced so rapidly, attended with delirium, that Mr. Astley Cooper and Mr. Luxmore, eminent surgeons, declared all hopes to have vanished, when I ordered serpentaria, which was given, two drachms of the tincture with ten grains of powder, and five drops of laudanum, every three hours, which calmed all the outrageous symptoms, stopped the mortification, and enabled an operation to be performed, by which this gentleman's life was preserved."

It is usually given in the form of infusion, made by pouring twelve ounces of boiling water on an ounce of the bruised root, of which, after straining, an ounce and a half, or three table-spoonfuls, may be taken twice or thrice a day, with or without a little of the tincture. The dose of the tincture alone is one, two or three tea-spoonfuls in water; and of the powder from six to thirty grains.

BLACK SNAKE ROOT

This is a new American remedy for rheumatism, and some cases of neuralgia. The officinal name is *Actaea Racemosa.* It is narcotic and antispasmodic, and seems to have a special influence on the womb. Dr. Simpson, of Edinburgh, has strongly recommended it in rheumatism, and in that peculiar state of hypochondriasis sometimes found in women after their confinement. He says, "I have found it in my own case repeatedly cure an attack of lumbago with wonderful rapidity". It is rather agreeable to the taste, and acceptable to the stomach. It is best taken in the form of tincture, of which the dose is from twenty to thirty or forty drops, thrice a day, in water.

SOAP

Castile or hard soap is an article often employed medicinally, both internally and externally. Given internally, it corrects morbid acidity in the stomach, and favours the natural action of the bowels. It is, therefore, of service in indigestion, bilious complaints, jaundice, gravel, and stone; but in all these diseases it may be advantageously united with rhubarb, ipecacuanha, or extract of gentian. As an external remedy, it is efficaciously used, dissolved in spirit of wine, in frictions to sprains and bruises, and it forms a valuable ingredient in the soap liniment. Dr. A. T. Thomson states, that he has seen much benefit derived from rubbing the tumid bellies of children labouring under mesenteric or worm fever, with a strong lather of soap every morning and evening.

The dose internally is from three to twenty grains made into pills, and repeated twice or thrice daily.

SOLUTION OF ACETATE OF AMMONIA

See **Mindereus's Spirit**

SPIDER'S WEB

It is the fashion of these days for medical men to recommend medicines of the most active and even poisonous properties, many of which can be obtained only by the exercise of sound chemical knowledge, and very careful manipulations, and it is equally the fashion for people to take them freely;— practice both unnecessary and dangerous. It is invincibly repugnant to reason and experience frequently to employ *poisons* in order to restore health and strength; there are many simple remedies which are at least equally beneficial with those opcrose and dangerous medicines, and I would now introduce one to the confidence of my readers. The cob-web of cellars, barns, and stables, is a valuable remedy for ague, (*see* AGUE); and it also allays diseased irritability, and calms irritation, both of body and mind, often in a surprising manner. If it operates well, when the pulse is quick, frequent, irregular, and irritated, it becomes by its influence, slow, calm and regular. Some American physicians who have taken it, say it produces a calm and delightful state of feeling, succeeded by a disposition to sleep. It will thus often tranquillize much better than opium or henbane, and its soothing properties point it out as a valuable palliative in the advanced stage of consumption—in—asthma in chronic hysterics, and in other spasmodic complaints.

Dr. Robert Jackson details a remarkable case of asthma, in which the tranquillizing effects of this substance were conspicuously evinced. The complaint was hereditary, and connected with malformation of the chest. The patient was unable to lie down in bed from a sense of suffocation, and was obliged to take the little sleep he could get in a half-sitting posture, being supported by pillows. In this distressing condition he one night took twenty grains of the spider's web, and obtained from it a sound and uninterrupted sleep all night, "a blessing to which he had been an entire stranger above six years".

The dose is from five to ten or twenty grains at bed-time, rolled into a pill. To cure ague it must be given thrice a day.

SPIRIT OF HARTSHORN

This spirit is stimulant and antacid, and is a useful cordial in lowness of spirits, fainting, and languor; for which purpose it may be taken internally, in doses of fifteen or twenty drops, in any agreeable vehicle. It should not be taken in less than half a tea-cupful of liquid. Twenty drops of this spirit, taken in a tea-cupful of water, and repeated five or six times in each intermission, has sometimes succeeded in curing ague after the Peruvian bark has failed; and it is of great service in the bites of serpents and other venomous creatures.

Externally, it is used as a grateful stimulant to the nostrils in case of fainting and languor; and united with two-thirds, or one-half the quantity of olive oil, it forms the common domestic stimulating liniment for sore throat, and relaxation of the throat. This liniment, when rubbed freely over the external part of the throat, is very useful in these complaints.

SQUILL

Squill is the bulbous root of a plant which grows on the sandy shores of Spain and Italy. It is a stimulating expectorant and diuretic; and is of great service in chronic cough and asthma, and in dropsy from disease of the heart. In large doses it vomits and purges, but is scarcely ever given with either of these intentions.

Its medicinal powers in *cough* and *dropsy* were very early known, and it still retains its character as a remedy of great efficacy, when judiciously exhibited. It is principally adapted to the *coughs, asthma* and *difficulty of breathing of* old people, in which there is an accumulation of mucus within the chest; and in all cases combining it with ipecacuanha, or tartarized antimony, increases its expectorant effect. Plentiful dilution also with warm mucilaginous liquors, contributes in no small degree to its successful operation. It deserves particular attention, that it can never be employed when the skin is hot and dry, with a hard pulse, or where other marks of inflammation are present; as it then checks instead of promoting expectoration. It is sometimes useful in the latter stages of hooping-cough. The compound squill pill is a combination of squill with ginger, hard soap and gum ammoniac, and is a valuable expectorant; the dose of this compound pill is from five to eight grains, twice or thrice a day.

As a diuretic, it is always given in substance, under the form of either the recent or the dried root. The dose of the former is from five to fifteen, of the latter from one to three grains; the smaller dose being given at first every six hours, in the form of a pill, and this increased slowly until the diuretic effect is obtained. Its nauseating operation ought to be avoided by the due regulation of the dose. Its efficacy in dropsy is well ascertained, and is promoted by combination with calomel; indeed it is more frequently employed in this combination than alone. A little opium should be added to prevent its running off by the bowels. The union of squill with calomel is well adapted to the treatment of dropsy, connected, as it frequently is, with obstruction or chronic inflammation in the heart or liver, and is more successful in this case than any other diuretic. Two grains of dried squill, with a grain of calomel, and a grain of extract of henbane, forms a valuable pill in many dropsical cases, which may be administered every six hours till it takes effect.

There is a syrup and an oxymel of squills sold by druggists, which are frequently used in doses of one or two tea-spoonfuls; to relieve old coughs.

STEEL *See* Iron

N.B.—All preparations of iron should be taken immediately after a meal.

STRYCHNIA or STRYCHNINE

This is the active alkaline principle of *nux vomica*. The nux vomica tree is large, a native of the East Indies, found on the coast of Coromandel, Cochin China, and in other places, and called there by the name of *Caniram* The nut is flat, round, about an inch broad, and near a quarter of an inch thick, with a prominence of a grey colour, covered externally with a velvety down, being internally hard and horny. It is intensely bitter.

Strychnine is a powerful stimulant to the spinal cord, and is in large doses a virulent poison. It is scarcely adapted to domestic use. Notwithstanding, it is said to have been employed medicinally with good effects, especially in waterbrash, costiveness, and paralysis of the throat and lower limbs, or of one side. Dr. Chambers, physician to St. Mary's Hospital, thinks highly of the use of strychnine as a tonic in some cases of dyspepsia, and even of dilatation and want of power in the heart. He says (*Clinical Lect.* p. 207) "I often join with iron small doses (from 1/20 to 1/14 of a grain) of strychnine. If the pulse intermits, this remedy sometimes exhibits its tonic powers over muscular fibre by restoring regularity of beat, and thus gives you the satisfaction of feeling the good you do with it". He believes (p. 328) that strychnine has great power in imparting tone and invigoration to the involuntary muscles of the stomach, and he prescribes it in the sense of oppression found in indigestion, especially where bark, iron or other tonics in any way disagree. I am, nevertheless, fearful that medical men are getting too fond of prescribing this active poison. The dose of the *alcoholic extract of nux vomica* is a quarter of a grain, given night and morning at first, and afterwards three or four times a day : it may be increased to a grain at a dose.

But it is best to give it in the form of *strychnine.* One grain of pure strychnia may be dissolved in one drachm of distilled vinegar, of which solution six minims or drops may be given in half a wine-glassful of water, thrice a day, the dose being cautiously increased to twelve or twenty minims. Should the remedy display its influence on the system by exciting involuntary tetanic movements or convulsions of the limbs, then the medicine must be either discontinued or much lessened in the dose.

If charcoal is swallowed immediately after strychnia it will be the proper antidote, as it will decompose the strychnia; but when the poisonous effect of strychnine has been manifested, camphor is the most likely stimulus to destroy that poisonous effect. Charcoal is the chemical, and camphor the vital, antidote to the poison of strychnia.

SUGAR OF LEAD

This is a very powerful astringent and sedative, of marked advantage in restraining *profuse bleeding* from the lungs, womb, bowels, nose and almost all other internal parts; but from its activity it must be exhibited with caution. The alkalies, alkaline earths, most of the acids, alum, borax, all sulphates and muriates, soaps, ammoniated and tartarized iron, tartarized antimony, and distilled water decompose it, and should, therefore, never be given with it. It is not uncommon to administer with it Epsom salt dissolved in rose water, which decomposes it, and renders it useless. Physicians generally consider this salt to be one of the most valuable resources of physic, in case of alarming bleedings from any internal organ. Some think it of greater efficacy in stopping haemorrhage from the lungs and womb, than any other known remedy, and believe its application to be equally safe and manageable, an opinion in which I cordially agree. It should be invariably united with opium. Two grains of the acetate of lead, united with one-fourth of a grain of opium, and made into a pill with a little conserve of hips, may be given every six hours; in any urgent case of haemorrhage it may be exhibited every hour, until the bleeding is restrained, and not only so, but the dose of the acetate of lead may be increased to three grains.

Ten or fifteen grains of this salt, dissolved in half a pint of distilled water, or in the same quantity of common water, with the addition of half an ounce of distilled vinegar, forms an excellent lotion for inflamed surfaces.

SULPHATE OF QUININE

This is an invaluable preparation of Peruvian bark, which concentrates, in a small compass, all the virtues of the powder of that celebrated substance, at least in the majority of cases; and is, therefore, generally resorted to by medical men on account of the smallness of the dose necessary, acid the great ease with which it sits on the stomach.

M. M. Pelletier and Caventou, eminent Parisian chemists, first procured *quinine* or *quinia,* from the *yellow* bark of the shops. It is an alkaline salt, which in conjunction with sulphuric acid, forms the *sulphate* of *quinine* or *quinia.* This appears as a pure white powder, in silky needles, scarcely soluble in cold water, more so in boiling water and completely so in dilute sulphuric acid. It is also very soluble in spirit of wine.

Eight grains of it are equal to about an ounce of the bark in substance; so that the ordinary dose is from one to three grains, twice or thrice a day, or oftener, made into a pill with extract of gentian, or combined with cinnamon water and gyrup and tincture of orange peel.—See the *Prescriptions.* Where it is necessary to administer larger doses at short intervals, as much as five grains have been given every three hours. It is very successfully employed for the cure of ague, brow-ague and as a tonic and febrifuge in indigestion, general debility and all other complaints for which the bark itself is recommended.—*See Bark.*

I have remarked under the article Bark, that those diseases are most benefited by it which assume a regular intermittent type and would here add that this obtains even in local affections. A curious case recorded by Sir B. Brodie illustrates this in an instructive manner. A gentleman, who had lived many years in a warm climate, became affected with *spasmodic* stricture of the urethra, *which recurred every alternate night* about twelve o'clock and continued until five or six O'clock in the morning. Sir B. Brodie was consulted and cured the disease by anticipating the paroxysm, as we do in the treatment of ague and administering sulphate of quinine in large doses, at short intervals of time.

Mr. Annesley states, in his book on *the Diseases of India,* that although the bark is the grand remedy in the fevers of India during the cold season, yet it fails *in the rainy season,* in which calomel and antimony only prove beneficial. This is a fact worthy of remembrance. Probably calomel and antimony given then at night and bark in the day, is the best practice.

SULPHATE OF ZINC OR WHITE VITRIOL

Sulphate of zinc, called formerly white vitriol, is tonic and astringent. It is sometimes very useful in *indigestion, whites,* old *chronic cough, hooping-cough* and *pulmonary consumption,* as it stimulates the digestive functions, strengthens the pulmonary organs and whole system and represses inordinate secretions from these and other parts. As a tonic, it is less heating and stimulant than preparations of iron and hence is often preferable in consumption, hooping-cough, indigestion and other diseases attended with great irritability and general weakness. In indigestion, it may be advantageously combined *with some* bitter extract, as extract of gentian, etc., in whites, chronic cough, asthma and pulmonary consumption, with gum myrrh, or hemlock; and in hooping-cough, with extract of gentian or hemlock. When combined with opium, it is of great service in removing the weakness and frequent motions, unaccompanied with pain, that take place in the protracted stages of dysentery and diarrhoea. As a tonic, the dose is from half a grain to a grain and a half, thrice a day.

In large doses, of from fifteen to twenty-five grains, it operates *instantaneously* as an emetic and offers, therefore, a prompt resource in case of poison, or where an immediate discharge from the stomach is required.

As an external application, this salt dissolved in rose-water, in the proportion of ten grains to half a pint of rose-water, forms an excellent collyrium in the latter stage of ophthalmia, after the inflammatory action has subsided. About sixteen grains dissolved in half a pint of water, is a useful injection for the whites; and if twenty grains be dissolved in the same quantity of rose-water, it forms one of the best lotions that can be used to scrophulous tumours, after they have suppurated and the abscess has been discharged.

SULPHUR

Sulphur is found native in the neighbourhood of volcanoes and is imported into this country chiefly from Sicily and Naples.

The sublimed sulphur, commonly called the flowers of sulphur, is laxative and diaphoretic, acting in a very mild manner, principally on the large intestines and at the same time determining to the surface of the body. In consequence of the mildness of its operation as a laxative, it is one of the best remedies for *piles,* a disease which generally arises from weakness and irritation of the bowels, of such a description as is always touch increased by costiveness, but will not allow of the use of active purgatives. In this complaint, it is best given in conjunction with a little lenitive electuary and cream of tartar.

Its alterative and diaphoretic effects render it serviceable in *chronic rheumatism* and *cough,* in *atonic gout, cutaneous eruptions, rickets, asthma* and other *pulmonary affections* not attended with acute inflammation; and it is probable, that its beneficial operation in these complaints is, in some measure, owing to its laxative effects. Its power of curing itch is universally admitted.

Precipitated sulphur, or the milk of sulphur, is whiter than the flowers of sulphur and is procured by receiving the vapours of common sulphur into a vessel filled with steam.

The ordinary dose is one or two drachms taken in milk. An

electuary, made by mixing together three drachms of sulphur, one drachm of cream of tartar and four drachms of lenitive electuary, is a very useful form for administering this substance and adapted to all the cases to which the remedy is applicable, in the dose of a tea-spoonful, once or twice a day.

SULPHURIC ACID

This is the oil of vitriol and vitriolic acid of commerce and is usually prepared by the combustion of sulphur.

It is always employed medicinally under the form of the diluted sulphuric acid, which is made by mixing a fluid ounce and a half of the strong acid with fourteen fluid ounces and a half of distilled water. The usual dose of this diluted acid is from twenty to forty drops, twice or thrice a day, in a wine-glassful of water. As it is injurious to the teeth, it should be sucked through a quill. It is tonic, antiseptic and refrigerant and is found of great service in *haemorrhages, indigestion, diabetes, cutaneous eruptions* and in *typhus* or *typhoid fever*. It is also a grateful and useful medicine to restrain the colliquative sweats which attend hectic fever. In the first-mentioned cases, the diluted acid is generally combined with infusion of bark, gentian or other bitters. It covers the taste of bark and causes it to sit easier on the stomach than when given alone. *See Elixir* of *Vitriol.*

SWEET SPIRIT OF NITRE

This medicine is a pleasant refrigerant and diuretic and is used with much advantage in all *febrile affections,* to allay heat and quench thirst and in dropsy as an adjunct to other diuretic remedies. Its operation is greatly increased by dilation with water, or some other aqueous vehicle. In fevers, thirty or forty drops of it may be given every three hours, united with two drachms of the solution of acetate of ammonia and an ounce and a half of water. In dropsy it may be administered to the extent of a drachm at a dose, combined with other and more powerful diuretics.

It appears that when added in a small proportion to malt spirits, it communicates to them a flavour resembling that of French brandy.

TAR WATER

Tar water is made by pouring a gallon of water on two pints of the best Norway tar, which is to be stirred with a wooden rod for a quarter of an hour; then, after the tar has subsided, the liquor should be strained and preserved in well corked bottles for use.

It is stimulant and alterative; and, when its operation is aided by bodily exercise, will frequently prove diuretic. It is certainly useful in some cases of *indigestion, scurvy, cutaneous eruptions* and other *chronic diseases.* The celebrated Dr. Cullen, of Edinburgh, thought highly of it and states that he has found it to strengthen the tone of the stomach, to excite appetite, promote digestion and cure all the symptoms of indigestion. Berkeley, the excellent and learned Bishop of Cloyne, through whose strong recommendation the drinking of this water was once so much in vogue, says, "When right, it is not paler than French, nor deeper coloured than Spanish white wine and full as clear and that if there be not a spirit very sensibly perceived in drinking it, you may conclude the water is not good. It may be drank cold or warm. As to the quantity, in common chronical indispositions, a pint a day may suffice, taken on an empty stomach, at two or four times, *viz.* night and morning and about two hours after dinner or breakfast; more may be taken by stronger stomachs. But those who labour under great and inveterate maladies, must drink a greater quantity, at least a quart every twenty-four hours. In acute cases, for example, fevers of all kinds, it must be drank in bed warm and in great quantity, perhaps a pint every hour, which I have known to work surprising cures".

We must not, however, forget that the *surprising cures* of former days would not appear such to us now, but many of our present cures would have been, indeed, surprising cures to our forefathers—and I have not so much faith in the efficacy of tar water as the Bishop of Cloyne had.

THORN APPLE

The officinal name of this article is *stromonium.* The plant is a native of America, but is now common in this country. It is stimulant, powerfully narcotic and in over-doses poisonous. It was first recommended as a powerful remedy in *insanity;* but its virtues in this disease are not considerable. It is occasionally of great service in quieting the mind and procuring rest in violent paroxysms of *insanity,* but beyond this seems rarely of much advantage. It has lately been considered almost specific in severe chronic pains of the head, or other parts of the body; but it is with this as with other very energetic substances, what does one person much good, may be either hurtful or of no service to another. This very active substance requires to be exhibited with caution. It is given either in the form of tincture or extract of the former, the dose is ten or twelve, or even twenty minims or drops, twice a day, in water; of the latter, one quarter or half a grain, which may be gradually increased to three or four grains or more, in the twenty-four hours.

Smoking the herb in the manner of tobacco sometimes affords relief in the paroxysm of *spasmodic asthma* and has lately become a common practice; but it produces violent effects on some persons. It has, from time immemorial, been smoked in Ceylon to relieve asthma and the poorer Turks use it instead of opium.[1]

TORMENTIAL ROOT

This is a mild yet powerful astringent, of great service in *looseness* and *dysentery.* It is mild because it operates without producing

1. The following are judicious remarks respecting the probable operation of the stramonium in smoking it—"It seems to act in two ways: in the first place, it is applied to the mucous membrane in a state of great irritability and, by operating as a sedative and allaying this state, it permits the secretion of the mucous follicles to be effected more slowly and perfectly : so that the mucus, being formed in a more natural state, is easily separated and excreted. In the second place, by influencing generally the nervous system, the spasmodic symptoms attendant on the paroxysm of asthma are allayed and respiration proceeds in a calm and undisturbed manner".—Thomson's *Elements of Materia Medica,* vol. ii. p. 155.

any stimulant effect and is, therefore, well adapted to check the diarrhea attendant upon pulmonary consumption and in other cases of that complaint where the general excitement is considerable. For this purpose, its union with small doses of ipecacuanha powder forms a very eligible medicine, which was highly spoken of by that distinguished physician Dr. George Fordyce.

It is also beneficial in old ulcers and in those cases of weak bowels where the patient is liable to frequent relaxations, although they may be of short duration.

Its astringency is so powerful, that it has been substituted for oak bark in the tanning of skims for leather.

It may be given in the form of a strong decoction, made by boiling one ounce of the bruised root in a pint of water, of which the dose is from one to two ounces, twice or thrice daily. It is likewise given in substance, the dose of the powder being from half a drachm to a drachm, in dill or simple water, which may be repeated twice or thrice daily, or oftener.[1]

TURPENTINE

There are several varieties of turpentine, but the Venice and Canada turpentine and the oil of turpentine, are those which are chiefly employed internally in the cure of disease. They are all stimulant, diuretic and cathartic. All turpentines seem to derive their virtues from the oil they contain. If the dose be small, they act chiefly on the kidneys; but when large, some degree of nausea is excited,

1. I witnessed once most extraordinary cures performed by this root. A poor man, fond of botanical excursions, either by tradition or accident knew the powers of this root; and by making a strong decoction of it, sweetened with honey, he cured agues which had resisted the bark, long-standing diarrheas, ulcers of the legs turned out of hospitals as incurable, the worst scorbutic ulcers, fluxes, etc., so as to excite the attention of Lord William Russell, who allowed him a piece of ground out of his park to cultivate his plant, which he kept as a secret; and in fluxes of blood I have found a drachm, given four times a day, in an infusion of hops, do wonders. The danger of suddenly checking discharges should be guarded against, of which this old man knew nothing; and occasional purges should be used, or an issue made in the thigh"—Dr. Thornton's *Family Herbal,* p. 504.

with slight giddiness and soon a copious discharge from the bowels. In moderate doses, they produce a sensation of warmth in the stomach, raise the pulse and impart additional excitement to the whole vascular system. They are sometimes beneficially employed in *gleet, whites, habitual coughs a*nd mucous discharges from the urinary passages. Formerly, it was no uncommon practice to give them as a remedy for pulmonary consumption; but in that complaint their heating and irritating qualities never fail to render them injurious. In *old chronic coughs* they are often beneficial. The oil is justly regarded as a useful remedy in *lumbago*; *sciatica a*nd other varieties of *chronic rheumatism,* in which complaints its efficacy seems to be often increased by the addition of Peruvian bark. It is likewise of great service in some cases of epilepsy, especially when originating from worms; in infantile convulsions, arising from a disordered state of the stomach and bowels; and in tape worm.

For internal use, the dose of Venice or Canada turpentine is from ten grains to a drachm, made into pills with powdered liquorice root and repeated three or four times a day. As a diuretic, or stimulant, the oil of turpentine may be taken in doses of from twenty drops to a drachm, thrice daily. By means of a little yolk of egg and mucilage of gum arabic, it may be uniformly mixed with water. When taken to expel the tape-worm, the quantity must be from three to four drachms or more, repeated every eight hours till the worm is ejected. In these large doses, it is more easily taken when exhibited merely floating upon water, with the addition of a drop or two of oil of cinnamon or anniseed. If it does not operate by stool in four or five hours after it has been taken, a dose of castor oil should be exhibited.

Applied externally, the turpentines increase the tone of the part, counteract indolence of action and cleanse ill-conditioned ulcers. As local stimulants, they have been efficaciously exhibited in the form of injection, in cases of colic, obstinate costiveness and the small thread-worm. The oil is the most useful in such instances. It proves also an excellent addition to stimulating embrocations in chilblains, indolent swellings, palsy, etc.

VALERIAN

Valerian root is antispasmodic and tonic; and is sometimes highly beneficial in those diseases which appear to be connected with a morbid susceptibility of the nervous system, as in *hysterics,* pain of one side of the head and in some species of epilepsy. It is of service in some instances of *hypochondriasis,* or low spirit and it may (in powder) often be advantageously combined with Peruvian bark; but its very nauseous taste is a great obstacle to its frequent employment. Dr. Cullen thought highly of it as a remedy for nervous disorders and lie remarks, that it should be given in large doses. It is best given in substance, united with a small portion of mace or cinnamon, which in some degree disguises the flavour. The dose is from a scruple to a drachm, given three or four times a day.

The ammoniated tincture of valerian is an clegant and efficacious cordial and antispasmodic, of great benefit to the nervous and low-spirited. The dose is from one to two or three tea-spoonfuls, with a tea-spoonful of tincture of cinnamon, thrice a day, in water; but it should not be given in any bitter infusion.

VERATRIA

This is the poisonous principle found in colchicum and other plants. It is a white, very acrid, inodorous substance, scarcely soluble in water and not very soluble even in boiling water. It is quite soluble in alcohol, ether and the vegetable acids. It is little used in medical practice; but from having sometime since been highly extolled by certain persons for its curative powers, as an external remedy, it is necessary to notice it here. It is employed only externally and chiefly in the relief of rheumatic and other chronic pains, rubbed into the parts in the form of an ointment, being mixed with hog's-lard. From ten to twenty grains of *veratria* mixed with an ounce of hog'slard is the safe proportion,—about the size of a large nutmeg being rubbed into the part night and morning. The proof of its taking effect is the sensation of sharp pricking which is usually felt on the part subject to its operation. After it has been used for three or four days, it will sometimes occasion sickness and vomiting. I have known it of great service in rheumatism and sciatica.

But my readers must be very cautious in the use of all remedies of this class. They are *poisonous* and should be used only under the superintendence of an able professional man. I do not believe the glowing reports of the marvellous powers of this medicine which have been published. Interested medical adventurers swarm throughout the land and especially in London and my readers should be upon their guard.

VINEGAR

Vinegar is a weak vegetable acid, produced by exciting the acetous fermentation in substances which have undergone, or are susceptible of the vinous fermentation. Sugar and water, the saccharine vegetable juices, infusions of malt, malt liquors, cyder and wine, may be converted into vinegar, by adding to them yeast, or any other ferment and exposing them in vessels to which the air has access, in a temperature between seventy-five and ninety degrees.

Distilled vinegar is sometimes employed as a cooling medicine in fevers, being added to any common diluting drink. When taken into the stomach it is cooling, promotes a gentle breathing perspiration and the discharge of urine. It allays thirst and diminishes excessive heat. In inflammatory fevers, it may be used to acidulate barley-water, or any other ordinary beverage of the patient. It is also an efficacious remedy for the scurvy and one of the best means of counteracting the fatal effects of over-doses of opium, hemlock and other narcotic poisons. For this last purpose, it should be administered in doses of a table-spoonful, frequently repeated, after the stomach has been freely emptied by a proper emetic.

Diluted with water and applied externally as a lotion, it is sometimes of much service in burns, bruises, sprains and chronic inflammation of the eye and for clearing the eye of small particles of lime, when they adhere to any part of the ball, or the lids. Its odour is grateful when it is sprinkled on the floor of the chamber of the sick in malignant fevers, though it has little efficacy as a fumigation.

WATER

Common water is an agent of great importance in the prevention, relief and cure of diseases; and it is, therefore, necessary that its qualities and effects should be made known in the present work.

Water retains its fluidity under the ordinary pressure of the atmosphere, at any degree of temperature between thirty-two and two hundred and twelve degrees of Fahrenheit's thermometer; but under thirty-two degrees it crystallizes and becomes solid, or is changed into ice; and above two hundred and twelve degrees assumes an aëriform character, or becomes steam, expanding to 1698 times its ordinary bulk.

Although water is almost universally diffused over the surface of the earth, it never occurs in a state of absolute purity, which is owing to its extensive powers as a solvent. It is generally found holding earthy matter in a state of mechanical suspension, or saline and other bodies in chemical solution, but the nature and degree of its contamination must necessarily vary according to circumstances and situation. These impregnations, however, are not sufficient in general to give it any very sensible taste or odour, or to render it unfit for the ordinary purposes of life. All the varieties of common water may be arranged under the three following heads :

1. Rain Water.
2. Spring Water.
3. River Water.

Rain Water, when collected in the open fields, is certainly the purest natural water and consequently of the least specific gravity; but when collected in towns, or from the roofs of houses, it contains a small portion of sulphate of lime, soot and other impurities and requires to be boiled and strained previous to internal use. Hippocrates gave this advice and the precaution has been strongly advised by modern chemists and physicians of eminence.

Snow water, when newly melted, is destitute of air, which is the reason that fish cannot live in it; but when allowed to remain for some time exposed to the atmosphere, it does not differ in its qualities from rain water.

Spring Water, in addition to the substances detected in rain water, generally contains a small portion of common salt and frequently other salts. The larger springs are purer than smaller ones and those which occur in siliceous rocks, or beds of gravel, contain the least impregnation. If it has not filtered through a very soluble soil, it is often almost as pure as rain water.

Well or pump water, which is spring water obtained by digging to a considerable depth, is by no means so pure. It is commonly distinguished by a property named hardness, implying an incapability of dissolving soap; which is owing to its containing many earthy salts, the principal of which is sulphate of lime. *Soft Water* is a more powerful solvent of all vegetable matters than hard water and is consequently to be preferred for domestic as well as for medicinal purposes; the brewer knows well from experience, how much more readily and copiously soft water will dissolve the extractive matter of his malt. The great superiority in point of wholesomeness which soft water has over that which is hard, is proved by many striking facts. Horses, by an instinctive sagacity, always prefer the former and when, by necessity or inattention, they are confined to the latter, their coats become rough and ill-conditioned and they are frequently attacked with the gripes. Hard water has a tendency to produce disease in the spleen of certain animals, especially sheep; and pigeons refuse it when they have been accustomed to that which is soft. Some very eminent and discerning physicians have ascribed the scrophulous swellings and complaints of gravel, so common in certain districts, to the hardness of the water there and there is often much to countenance the opinion. The best mode of freeing hard water of its earthy salts, is first to boil it; then, after it has cooled, to drop into it an alkaline carbonate, or a little carbonate of soda, etc., and lastly, to filter it.

Probably the purest *spring water* in this kingdom is found at St. Winifred's Well, at Holywell, in Flintshire; at Bridgend, Glamorganshire; at Malvern and at Matlock; at least, these are well known as very pure waters. All these have acquired much celebrity in the cure of affections of the skin, kidneys and bladder, owing no doubt to the diluting and diuretic effects resulting from their greater purity.

River Water, when the stream is rapid and runs over a pebbly or siliceous channel, is as pure as the softer spring water; but when the current is slow and the bed clayey, it approaches nearer, to the nature of well water and frequently contains putrified vegetable and animal matter, as is generally the case in the water of lakes and marshes.

The medicinal properties of water as a diluent are considerable and were well known to the ancients; and cold water used as a drink in fevers, was the principal remedy of Hippocrates, the father of physic, in these complaints.[1] The temperature of sixty degrees is the proper degree where it is intended that water should produce its diluent effects without the aid of heat. Under forty-five degrees it produces a sedative and astringent effect; above sixty degrees and under a hundred, it relaxes the fibres of the stomach and is apt to induce nausea; but at a higher temperature, the stimulus of heat prevents that effect. Simple water may supersede the use of all other diluents; but animal and vegetable infusions are generally employed, or toast and water, which is more agreeable to most palates and is an excellent diluent in fevers and inflammatory diseases. The temperature of water as a diluent should be regulated by the nature of the disease; in internal bleedings, tile temperature should not exceed forty-five degrees, but it may be sixty degrees

1. A physician now "leaves the quantity to be regulated, in a degree, by the desires of the patient. This is undoubtedly the best guide; and it has been remarked by every writer on diseases, that, in acute fevers, the desire for watery fluids is so striking as to be almost a measure of the degree of fever which rages. As simple water contains nothing in itself noxious, the attention of the physician is required to be directed only to quantity and temperature. And with regard to both these circumstances, the measure of both may, in truth, be left to the desires of the patient".—(Thomson's *Elem. of Mat. Med.* vol. ii. p. 671.)—He means in ordinary cases.

in fevers; unless in the cold stage of the paroxysm of fever, when thirst should be allayed by tepid or warm water, or other bland fluids; and the same precaution is necessary when the sweat has become general and profuse. In cases in which there exists a morbid increase of bile, or of the secretions of the stomach and bowels, disturbing the functions of these organs, the temperature of the water used as drink may be from ninety to one hundred and fourteen degrees; and in some cases of indigestion, which are attended with the sensation of coldness at the stomach and with cold extremities, a cupful of water, taken hot, affords very considerable relief. Some medicines, as sudorifics, diuretics, emetics and refrigerants, scarcely produce their effects, unless their operation be assisted by copious dilutions with water or watery fluids.

Distilled water is transparent, colourless, wholly void of taste and smell, lighter than any other water and feels softer to the touch when the fingers are wetted with it,—the purest is obtained from rain water once distilled. It possesses powerful solvent properties, in respect both to animal and vegetable matter and is capable of pervading the minutest vessels of the body; hence it is of great value as a diluent in most chronic disorders, more especially in urinary, scrophulous and cutaneous affections. In some cases of such diseases, especially when combined with a spare animal, or a vegetable diet, it has proved of uncommon service. Some curious facts relating to the subject may be found in Dr. Lambe's publications *on the Cure of Constitutional Diseases.*

WILD CUCUMBER

The expressed juice of the fruit of this plant deposits a fecula, which, when dried, has been known by the name of *Elaterium.* It is a very powerful cathartic and is supposed by some physicians, to be the best hydragogue purgative we possess. It is frequently employed in *dropsies,* when purgatives are admissible and other milder remedies fail in evacuating the water; and it appears that ancient, as well as modern, physicians administered it with much confidence and success. Dr. Ferriar, of Manchester, is said to have found it an efcacious remedy for dropsy of the chest. But it is often very violent in its action and requires to be given with caution, more especially in elderly or debilitated subjects. Its dose is a quarter of a grain, made into a pill and repeated every second or third hour, until it *begins* to operate, when no more should be given until the extent of its operation is ascertained. It is frequently advisable to unite the half grain of elaterium with the same quantity of calomel. The late Dr. Alexander Buchan has observed, that he has known this combination evacuate gallons of water, in numerous instances of dropsy. The patient must always be supported with strong beef tea and bread, etc. during its operation.

WILD CHERRY BARK

This is a large and handsome tree indigenous to the United States. The bark of the tree *(Prunus Virginiana)* is tonic, expectorant and sedative and is employed by American physicians in the cure of ague, dyspepsia and consumption. It is said to leave considerable effect in controlling an inordinate action of the heart and arteries. Infusion is the best mode of taking it. An ounce of this bark should be infused in a pint of cold water for twenty hours, of which the dose is a wine-glassful, every four or six hours. It is said to relieve more effectually than any other remedy that peculiar sense of sinking in the pit of the stomach, complained of by the consumptive. The bark is supposed to owe its virtues chiefly to a small portion of prussic acid which it contains.

WILLOW BARK

The bark of the common willow is tonic and alterative and is useful in ague, indigestion and some chronic eruptions on the skin. In fact, it may be efficaciously employed in all the complaints for which Peruvian bark or quinine, is ordinarily administered. The *dose* of the powder is from half a drachm to a drachm, twice a day, in water. The *decoction is* an eligible mode of taking it, made by simmering together for half an hour one ounce of the bark in a pint of water, of which the dose is from two to four table-spoonfuls twice a day.

Salıcine is the crystalline active principle obtained from willow bark and is a mild bitter tonic, similar to quinine. Should quinine irritate the stomach, probably salicine would not do so. The *dose* is from ten to twenty grains, in a wine-glassful of infusion of orange peel, twice a day.

WINE

The term wine is more strictly and specially applied to express the fermented juice of the *grape,* although it is generally used to denote that of *any* sub-acid fruit. The presence of tartar, is, perhaps, the circumstance by which the grape is most strongly distinguished from all the other sub-acid fruits, that have been applied to the purpose of wine making. The juice of the grape, moreover, contains within itself all the principles essential to vinification, in such a proportion and state of balance, as to enable it at once to undergo a regular and complete fermentation, whereas the juices of other fruits require artificial additions for this purpose; and the scientific application and due adjustment of these means, constitute the art of making wines. It has been remarked, that all those wines that contain an excess of malic acid are of a bad quality, hence the grand defect that is necessarily inherent in the wines of this country and which leads them to partake of the properties of cider; for in the place of *tartaric,* the *malic* acid always predominates in our native fruits.

Various circumstances, such as climate, soil and the mode of conducting the fermentation, modify the flavour and taste of wine. Wines may be arranged into four classes, *viz.,* (1) *Sweet Wines,* as Malaga, Frontignac, Tokay, Vino Tinto, Montefiascore, Schiras and the Malmsey wines of the Greek islands, (2) *Sparkling or Effervescine Wines,* as Champagne, Gooseberry, etc., (3) *Dry and Light Wines,* as Hock, Rhenish, Mayne, Moselle, Barsac, Burgundy, Claret and Hermitage; and (4) *Dry and Strong Wines,* as Marsala, Madeira, Port and Sherry. But notwithstanding these differences, the essential components of all wines are the following: one or more *acids,* especially the malic and tartaric; *extractive matter,* which in old wines is deposited with the tartar; *a volatile oil,* on which the flavour depends; *colouring matter* and *alcohol, or spirit of wine,* the most important of their ingredients and that one on which their dietetic and medical properties depend.

Wine, when good and of a proper age, is cordial and tonic; but when new, it is flatulent, debilitating and purgative and intoxicates sooner than old wine. In a dietetical point of view, the temperate use of it promotes digestion and gives additional energy to the action of the heart and arteries, strengthens the animal functions, exhilarates the spirits, sharpens the wit and calls into action all the intellectual powers; but when taken in excess, it intoxicates, producing sickness, head-ache giddiness and looseness, with nervous tremors, which continue for two or three days; and, like ardent spirits, its habitual excessive use, extinguishes the faculties of both body and mind, producing indigestion, emaciation and debility, inflammation of the lungs and liver, palsy, gout, dropsy and a long train of diseases and wretchedness. In almost all cases of indigestion, bilious complaints and other disorders in which there exists great weakness of the stomach, the white wines will be found preferable to the red; they sit easier on the stomach and do not tend to confine the bowels as the latter do, which are material points, worthy of much attention. For the use of wine as an article of *Diet,* see that head.

As a remedy, wine is stimulant, tonic and antispasmodic. Its chief medicinal application is in the treatment of fevers of a malignant type, to support the strength of the system in the advanced stages and to obviate the symptoms arising from debility. With these views, it is given sometimes with more advantage than any other tonic,—a superiority derived from its stimulating power being obtained with more certainty and being more easily regulated by due administration, from its being more grateful and probably not requiring to be assimilated by the digestive organs to produce its effects. The quantity in which it is given, is dependent on the state of the disease; the object to be obtained, is that of supporting the strength of the system, until the fever has run its course; the danger to be avoided, is that of giving it so largely as to occasion any degree of exhaustion. The administration is regulated, therefore, by the effects it produces; advantage being always derived from it, when it renders the pulse more slow and firm; when the recurrence of delirium is prevented; when irritation is lessened and sleep induced. If the pulse be quickened and the countenance become flushed; if it excite thirst, increase the heat of the body and occasion restlessness or delirium, it is obviously injurious and the dose must either be diminished, or its use suspended. In typhus, the proper rule is to give it till the pulse fills, the delirium abates and the extremities warm; and it should be repeated on the smallest appearance of stupor, quick and sinking pulse or tremor. A few glasses, given in the space of twenty-four hours, will often produce all that is required from wine; but sometimes very large quantities are necessary. In malignant sore throat, a woman, unaccustomed to the use of wine, has taken three bottles of Madeira every day for some time, with marked advantage.

In extensive ulceration or gangrene, wine is not only the best addition to Peruvian bark and ammonia, but is a remedy on which alone there is much reliance; and in the convalescencies from all severe diseases, it is an efficacious means of restoring the exhausted strength and vigour.

When wine is prescribed as a cordial in a state of recovery from any acute disease, or in a weakened state of the habit, it should not be taken with dinner or any other meal, but at noon, on an empty stomach. In such a case, it is an excellent practice to get a crust of good bread, dip it piece by piece, into a glass of very old rich wine, as Canary, Tent, Madeira, Sherry or Port and take it every day about twelve; it is a valuable cordial. Sometimes in convalescence from a severe disease, the nerves are so irritable as to produce a feverishness in the system on the application of stimulants, when the quantity of wine used must be small and Claret, Moselle or Hock, will be found the best sort.

I ought not to dismiss this article without observing, that the adulteration of wines is a frequent practice among wine merchants and one which is fraught with much mischief; for so iniquitous are the means made use of by some dealers, to enable them to pass bad wine off as that which is good, that such adulterated wines often operate like slow poisons. They occasion head-ache, pain of the stomach, uneasiness, cough and difficulty of breathing and afterwards colic, constipation, palsy and consumption. Some of the adulterations of wine are rather harmless, others extremely dangerous. The common red wines are frequently made of new, tart and half-spoiled white wines, by tinging them with red sumach, or other woods or berries. In order to make the wine stronger and more pungent, a variety of spices are employed, such as galangal, cardamom, mace and the like; or an unfermented mash, wort, or the mash for distilling spirits, are occasionally added and allowed to ferment together with inferior wines. But the most deleterious of all adulterations of wine, is that with sugar of lead and other preparations of that mineral. This infamous practice was carried on, some years ago, in Paris to such an extent, that the Excise Office could not account for the prodigious increase of vinegar, entered at the city gates. But it was at length discovered, that this vinegar consisted only of tart and adulterated wines, imported under the pretended character of vinegar, in order to avoid the high duty imposed upon wines, on their entrance into Paris; and sugar of lead, joined to some absorbent earth, was employed to change these vinegars into sweet wines, which destroyed the lives of many thousand persons. This secret of the utmost importance to health and life, was confessed by a rich old wine merchant, on his death bed, to relieve in some degree his tortured conscience.

To detect adulterated wines, we must attend to the following particulars: every white or straw-coloured wine, of a sweetish taste, afterwards astringent and at the same time new; every wine that has an unusually high colour, not in proportion to its strength. and age, or the flavour of brandy, penetrating the tongue; or lastly, an uncommon strong flavour, may be justly suspected of adulteration. Red wines, either of a very deep or of a very faint colour ; of a woody or tart taste; and those which cover the inside of the glass as well as the bottom of the bottles, with a red sediment, are generally tinged with some colouring substances.

In order to discover whether suspected wine contains any metallic adulteration, we are possessed of an excellent chemical test, discovered by Professor Hahnemann of Germany and known by the name of *Liquor Vini Probatorius*. It is prepared as follows: one drachm of the dry liver of sulphur and two drachms of cream of tartar, are shaken together in two ounces of distilled water, till it be completely saturated with hepatic gas; the liquor is then filtered through blotting paper and kept in a closely-stopped phial. From sixteen to twenty drops of this liquid are dropped into a small glass, filled with wine that is suspected to have been adulterated. If the wine turn only thick with white clouds and deposit only a white sediment, we may be certain that it contains no metallic ingredients whatever; but if it turn black, or even muddy, if its colour approach to that of a dark red, if it have first a sweet and then an astringent taste, it is certainly impregnated with sugar of lead, or some other impregnation of that metal, equally destructive. If, however, the dark colour be of a blue cast, not unlike that of pale ink, we may suspect the wine to contain iron in its composition. Lastly, if the wine be impregnated with copper or verdigris, it will deposit a sediment of a blackish grey colour. This experiment ought to be made with a fresh-prepared test and in the open air.

COMMON WINTER CHERRY

This is a perennial plant, common in our shrubberies. Boerhaave asserts that it is useful in fevers and disorders of the kidneys and some medical men of the present day say that it is of great service in gout and much safer than colchicum. Of the last opinion there can be no doubt. The *dose* is from six to twelve of the berries, or half an ounce or more of their expressed juice, twice a day. Or from half a tea-spoonful to a tea-spoonful of the tincture may be taken, thrice a day, in water.

WORMWOOD

Wormwood is a bitter tonic, of considerable service in indigestion and low spirits; and it has also been used with advantage in ague, gout and scurvy. Reports have been recently circulated of its having been found of great service in epilepsy. Notwithstanding, it is now seldom employed by British practitioners in these complaints. Its powers in expelling worms are well ascertained and have bestowed upon it the name of *wormwood.* It will frequently bring away the smaller sorts of worms in great quantities. The dose in powder is from one to two scruples, twice or thrice a day. The infusion is made by pouring a pint of boiling water on an ounce of the plant, of which from an ounce to an ounce and a half may be taken twice or thrice in twenty-four hours.

Infused in ale it forms the beverage known by the name of *purl.*

ZINC

I have noticed the *oxyde and sulphate of zinc* at pages 96 and 118. Three preparations of zinc remain to be noticed, namely, *the valerianate of zinc, the acetate and chloride.*

The *valerianate of zinc* is used internally as a tonic antispasmodic, of great service in neuralgic complaints, depending on a loss of tone in the system. It is therefore, taken with advantage in neuralgic pains of the face and head and in St. Vitus's dance. The *dose* is a grain twice or thrice a day, made into a pill with a little extract of dandelion or gentian.

The *acetate of zinc* is rarely used internally, but as a *topical* remedy it is employed with very great effect, on account of its astringent qualities, in chronic inflammation of the eye, vagina and womb. It seems to be more successful than the sulphate of zinc. An injection composed of six grains of sulphate of zine and four ounces of the diluted solution of the sub-acetate of lead *(liquor plumbi sub-acetatis dilutus)* is an efficacious remedy in the advanced stage of whites.

The *chloride of zinc* is a powerful and valuable caustic. As such it penetrates deeper in its action than the nitrate of silver and besides corroding the parts to which it is applied, it exercises an influence over the vital actions of neighbouring parts; and it possesses this superiority over the arsenical caustics, that there is no danger of any constitutional disorder from its absorption. As an application to parts affected with malignant disease, such as cancer, or other intractable forms of local malady, it is of great value.

COLLECTION
OF
APPROVED PRESCRIPTIONS
AND
MEDICINAL PREPARATIONS
Adapted to Family and Domestic use

BALSAMS

The subject of this section is not the natural balsams, but certain compositions, which, from their being supposed to possess balsamic qualities, generally go by that name. In strict medical language, however, only those compositions are called balsams which contain benzoic acid.

Friar's Balsam **No. 1**

Is composed of benzoin, purified storax, balsam of tolu, socotorine aloes and rectified spirit of wine.

It is sometimes very useful in *old coughs* and *asthamas,* as it stimulates the stomach and pulmonary organs and thus increases the tone of those parts and promotes expectoration. But it is not proper in recent coughs. It is an excellent application to languid ulcers, which require stimulating. The dose is from twenty to sixty drops, twice or thrice a day, on sugar or rubbed with mucilage.

It has been celebrated under the name of *Commander's Balsam, Jesuits Drops, Wade's Drops, Turlington's Balsam,* etc.; and is sold at all druggists' shops under the name of Compound Tincture of Benjamin.

Balsam of Honey **No 2.**

Take of Balsam of tolu 1ounce;
Gum storax 1drachm;
Purified opium 15grains;
Best honey 4ounces;
Rectified spirit of wine .... 1pint.
Let them digest together for five or six days and strain.

This is a pectoral balsam, serviceable in *coughs* and *colds*, in doses of one, two, or three tea-spoonfuls occasionally, when no fever is present. It is most applicable to habitual coughs. It is the same medicine as is puffed off under the title of *Sir John Hill's Balsam of Honey.*

CATAPLASMS OR POULTICES

Cataplasms, or poultices, are frequently made too thin, by which means the least pressure or their own gravity, remove them from the part; they should always be thick enough to support a certain form when applied.

The best way of making a common bread poultice, is to scald out a basin, then to put into it a sufficient quantity of bread crumb and cover it with boiling water and after the bread flax absorbed as much of the water as it will contain, the remainder should be poured off, when the poultice is fit for use.

Yeast Cataplasm **No. 3**

Take of Flour .... 1 pound;
Yeast of beer .... half a pint.

Mix and expose the mixture to a gentle heat, until it begins to swell, when it is fit for use.

This cataplasm is of excellent use when applied to painful, foul or gangrenous ulcers. It affords a gentle yet valuable stimulus to such ulcerations, correcting any existing tendency to mortification, cleansing the wound and removing the factor of the discharge.

Mustard Poultice **No. 4**

Take of Mustard seed, in powder .... half a pound;
Linseed, in powder .... half a pound;
Hot vinegar.......................... a sufficient
.... quantity.

Mix them to the thickness of a poultice and they are fit for use.

It is a powerful local stimulant and rubeficient, of great service in obviating a determination to the head in the low stage of typhus or remittent fever, particularly when stupor or delirium is present and in apoplexy and many other cases. It is spread on cloth to the thickness of about half an inch and when applied to the soles of the feet, its rubefacient effects are very quickly produced and often so powerfully as to raise blisters on the part. It is rendered still more decidedly stimulant by the addition of one or two table-spoonfuls of oil of turpentine.

Charcoal Cataplasm **No. 5**

Take of Linseed meal .... half a pound;
Charcoal powder .... 2 ounces;
Hot water, a sufficient quantity to make a poultice.

This is a useful antiseptic cataplasm, which has the power of cleansing foul ulcers and correcting a tendency to mortification and is applicable to all cases in which these objects are to be fulfilled.

Goulard's Poultice **No. 6**

Take of Extract of lead, (the liquor plumbi acetatis of the shops)................. 1½drachm;
Rectified spirit of wine 2ounces;
Common water 12ounces;

Crumb of bread, a sufficient quantity to make the whole into a proper consistence.

It is beneficially applied to inflamed surfaces, to allay irritation and reduce inflammation and swelling in any part of the body.

Hemlock Cataplasm **No. 7**

Pour 2 pints of water on 2 ounces of hemlock leaves and boil it till only a pint remains, when as much linseed meal as necessary is to be added.

The hemlock poultice is an excellent application to many cancerous and scrophulous ulcers and other malignant sores; frequently producing a great diminution of the pain of such diseases and improving their appearance. The fresh herb bruised, when it can be obtained forms the best hemlock poultice.

French Poultice **No. 7A**

Take of Olive oil	4 ounces;
Pork fat, fresh butter, mutton suet, yellow wax and litharge, of each	2 ounces;
Black pitch	half an ounce.

Mix them together; warm them in a pipkin, then add a quarter of a pound of linseed-meal poultice, or more if necessary and apply the poultice warm.

This is the celebrated *onguent de la mere* of the French physicians and is an emollient poultice very useful in inflamed surfaces and in hastening suppuration.

N.B.—Of course, less than the quantity above specified may be used if the swelling is of such a size as to require less.

Suppurative Poultice **No. 7B**

Take of barley-meal and linseed-meal, of each a sufficient quantity,—say two or thee ounces; put it into a sufficient quantity of decoction of marsh-mallows and cook it to a suitable consistence, frequently stirring it.

This is an excellent emollient poultice, suited to inflamed parts. If it is desirable to hasten the suppuration of an abscess, then add one ounce and a half of basilicon or of *French Poultice,* No. 7A; or, instead of basilicon, two ounces of the pulp of the bulb of white lily may be added, which very decidedly hastens the suppuration of an abscess.

CLYSTERS OR ENEMAS

Purging Clyster **No. 8**

Dissolve an ounce of Epsom salt in a pint of barley-water, or thin gruel, or lukewarm water and then add two ounces of olive oil or castor oil.

This is a useful purging clyster, of great service in all cases in which it is desirable to procure a speedy evacuation of the bowels.

One of the best, if not the very best, clyster or enema apparatus is *Twinberrow's, of No. 2, Edwards Street, Portman Square.* It seems to be at once the *most simple and perfect* yet produced.

The *piston* or *pump,* which so *frequently gets out of order*, is *not introduced* into this *apparatus;* there is therefore, an absence OF OILY OR GREASY MATTER AND BLACK LEAD, (which are absolutely necessary to lubricate the piston in the usual syringes), which soon become *rancid* and *green,* some portion of which inevitably *passes* with the fluid *injected* from an *ordinary syringe.*

One hand only is required to work this instrument and it is done *without any exertion.* No. *AIR can possibly Pass with the injection.*

From the description thus given, the *superiority* of this instrument is apparent. It requires no *adaptation of parts,* no *screwing* or *unscrewing of conduit pipes* or *tubes.* It is *extremely portable,* the conduit pipe moving on the hinge-joint allows it to fold back upon the reservoir; it is thus reduced to the smallest possible compass. In this way it can be taken to the closet and there used without the *least delay* or *annoyance.*

Anodyne Clyster **No. 9**

> Add thirty, forty, or sixty drops of laudanum to three ounces of olive oil. Or add forty or sixty drops of laudanum to three ounces of thin starch, warm.

These clysters are particularly useful in cases in which there is great irritation about the rectum, bladder, or urinary passage; and in dysentery and diarrhoea, after the bowels have been cleared. They have great effect in relieving pain and diminishing spasm, in all the organs contained within the lower belly. Anodyne clysters are always administered in the small quantity now ordered.

Clyster for the Colic **No. 10**

> Mix two drachms of assafoetida gum with a drachm and a half of sal volatile, half a drachm of laudanum and ten or twelve ounces of warm gruel, or barley water.

This clyster will frequently operate like a charm in the cure of flatulent colic and be of much service in other varieties of this complaint when unattended with inflammation.

COLLYRIA OR EYE-WATERS

Astringent Collyrium **No. 11**

> Mix 10 drops of extract of lead, that is, the liquor plumbi acetatis of the shops and 2 drachms of distilled vinegar, with 4 ounces of distilled water.

This is a good application to inflamed eyes, especially when one of a gently astringent cooling quality is indicated.

Another **No. 12**

> Dissolve 5 or 6 grains of sulphate, or of acetate of zinc, in 4 ounces of distilled or of rose water.

This is the most common of all eye-waters, for the relief of inflammation of the eyes and in the advanced stages of this complaint it is often advantageously increased in strength.

Anodyne Collyrium **No. 13**

Take of Solution of acetate of ammonia	2	ounces;
Distilled water, hot........................	6	ounces;
Soft extract of opium	10	grains.

Dissolve the soft extract of opium in the hot water, strain through fine linen and add the solution of acetate of ammonia.

In inflammation of the eye, where the pain and irritation are very considerable, this is often productive of great relief.

Soothing Collyrium **No. 14**

Take of Acetate of lead	12	grains;
Wine of opium.........................	1	drachm;
Distilled water	6	ounces.

Mix them together.

This is another excellent application when there is much pain and swelling, or chronic inflammation in the eyes. I prescribe it with satisfactory effect on all ordinary occasions.

Collyrium for Specks on the Cornea **No. 15**

Dissolve half a grain of bi-chloride of mercury in 4 ounces of the best rose water.

This eye-water is of great service in removing the redness and indolent inflammation and the white specks, left after an acute inflammation of the eye—that is, when the inflamed state has become chronic.

DECOCTIONS

These are aqueous solutions of the active principles of vegetables, obtained by boiling. They-are intended to afford more powerful remedies than can be obtained by the simple infusion of the same substances in cold, or even in boiling water. For making decoctions, the substances to be employed must be divided, if in the dry state, by pulverization, or if fresh, by slicing, so as to expose an extended surface to the action of the water; which is thus enabled to take up their soluble principles in a shorter space of time, a circumstance of much importance in the preparation of decoctions. Decoctions should invariably be quickly made, because by long decoction in water, even in covered vessels, the constituents of many vegetable bodies are liable to re-act upon one another and produce entirely new compounds, possessed of properties different from those which they previously constituted. They should be strained while hot and prepared in small quantities only, as they are apt to ferment and spoil soon. In summer they ought seldom to be used after they have been made forty-eight hours.

Compound Decoction of Aloes **No. 16**

Take of Extract of liquorice	half an ounce;
Carbonate of potash	2 scruples;
Extract of spiked aloes	1 drachm;
Powdered myrrh	1 drachm;
Pondered saffron	1 drachm;
Water	1 pint.

Boil down to 12 fluid ounces and strain; then add of compound tincture of cardamoms, 4 fluid ounces.

This is a very mild purgative medicine, of great service in costiveness, bilious and nervous disorders, jaundice, low spirits, accompanied with constipation of the bowels and female irregularities connected with this state of the intestinal canal. The dose is from half an ounce to four ounces taken in the morning. In order to obtain its full effect in severe cases, it should be taken every other morning, for two or three months, in such a quantity as just to keep the bowels free, without being purged.

It is very similar to the celebrated *Beaume de Vie* and may be kept a much longer time than any other decoction without spoiling; indeed it is more efficacious after being kept a week than when fresh made.

Compound Decoction of Sarsaparilla **No. 17**

Take of Sarsaparilla root, sliced .... 4 ounces;
Boiling water .... 4 pints.

Macerate for four hours in a vessel lightly covered and placed near the fire; then take out the sarsaparila and bruise it. Return it again to the liquor and macerate in a similar manner for four hours more, first adding of raspings of guaiacum wood, bark of sassafras root, liquorice root, bruised, of each, an ounce ; bark of mezereon root, 3 drachms. Finally strain.

This decoction is a successful imitation of the once celebrated *Lisbon Diet-drink.* It operates as a diaphoretic and alterative and is often of the greatest service in the treatment of chronic rheu-matism, cutaneous eruptions, the advanced stages of indigestion and many very severe local diseases originating in disorder of the constitution. It is of eminent utility in the secondary forms of syphilis. If it agrees, it generally occasions a pleasant moisture in the mouth, cleans the tongue and promotes a lax state of the bowels. Should a gentle looseness come on during its employment, it must on no account be checked. It is commonly given in conjunction with some mild mercurial pill. The dose is a quarter of a pint, repeated three times a day, or half a pint twice a day.

The *alkaline infusion of sarsaparilla* proves sometimes a more powerful alterative and restorative than the preceding decoction. It appears to have more of a strengthening quality and to be generally more eligible than the latter, when the patient is troubled with much acidity and other symptoms of great weakness in the stomach. It is taken in the same doses as the decoction and is made in the following manner.

Take of sarsaparilla root, sliced and bruised, four or six ounces; liquorice root, sliced, an ounce; fresh made lime water, four pints. Let them digest together in a covered vessel for twelve hours, during which time they should be frequently stirred and shaken. After being strained it is fit for use. *See Sarsaparilla,* page 110. Still of all modes of taking sarsaparilla, the powder is the most efficacious.

Decoction of Bark **No. 18**

Take of Lance-leaved Peruvian bark, bruised .	1 ounce;
Water	1 pint.

Boil for 10 minutes in a lightly covered vessel and strain the liquor while it is hot.

Peruvian bark in this form agrees better with most stomachs than when in powder; but its powers are necessarily diminished. It is given in all cases in which the bark in substance is useful. The dose is from two to five table-spoonfuls, twice a day.

Barley-Water **No. 19**

Take of Pearl barley	2 ounces;
Water	5 pints.

First wash away any extraneous substance that may adhere to the barley; then, having poured on it half a pint of water, boil for a few minutes. This water being thrown away, let the remainder be added boiling, then boil down to two pints and strain.

This is a simple decoction of barley, commonly called barley-water and is of much service in all fevers and other acute diseases attended with much thirst and irritation, in which it is taken as freely as the patient pleases. The following is a compound decoction of barley, which is a still more effectual demulcent in cases of pulmonary consumption, strangury, gravel and other diseases accompanied with fever.

Compound Barley-Water **No. 20**

Take of the above simple decoction of barley .	2 pints;
Figs, sliced	2 ounces;
Liquoric root, sliced and bruised	half an ounce;

Raisins, stoned .... 2 ounces;
Water .... 1 pint.

Boil down to two pints and strain.

Two or three tea-spoonfuls of syrup of poppies may be added to this decoction, to obviate its laxative effect, where this might prove hurtful; but, generally speaking, this effect will be an advantage rather than otherwise.

Astringent Decoction **No. 21**

Take of Oak bark .... 1 ounce;
Water .... 2 pints.

Boil down to a pint and strain.

This is a very astringent decoction, of considerable use in whites and the thin whitish discharge which often remains after miscarriage; and in piles and prolapsus of the anus. In the former cases, it is injected up the passage by means of a common syringe and in the latter, it is used as a lotion. It is also employed as a gargle in sore throat and relaxation of the uvula, in which complaints it may be either used alone, or three drachms of tincture of myrrh or capsicum may be added to every half pint of the decoction.

It is also an excellent internal medicine in the advanced stages of the snuffles in infants, to give tone to the vessels of the head and to the constitution at large.

DRAUGHTS

This is a proper form for exhibiting those liquid medicines in the dose of which it is necessary to be exact and such other remedies as are intended to operate immediately and do not need to be frequently repeated, as narcotics purges and vomits.

Anodyne and Sleeping Draught **No. 22**

Take of Bi-carbonate of potash .... half a drachm;
Lemon juice, half an ounce, or citric acid .... 20 grains;

Spearmint, or common water . . . . a wine-glassful;
Battley's solution of opium, or Laudanum, 20, 30 or 40 drops;
Syrup of tolut . . . . 1 drachm.[1]
Mix.

This is a very useful draught to procure sleep and ease pain, in the majority of diseases. I have already said, in noticing separately the different articles in the Domestic Materia Medica, that *Battley's Solution of Opium,* or the *Black Drop,* are far preferable to laudanum, or any of the common preparations of opium, for procuring sleep and alleviating pain, since they accomplish these objects without occasioning subsequent head-ache, feverishness, or any other unpleasant symptom. This is a point requiring particular attention when we wish to procure sleep, or ease pain, in diseases attended with inflammatory or febrile symptoms; but it is not so much attended to by some professional men as it ought to be.

Another Anodyne Draught **No. 23**

Take of Camphor mixture, ... 1 ounce;
Nitrate of potash . . . . 4 grains;
Hoffman's liquor, that is, the compound
spirit of sulphuric ether, ... 1 drachm;
Battley's solution of opium . . . . 10 drops, or more;
Syrup of poppies . . . . 1½ drachm.
Mix them together for a draught, to be taken at bed time to procure sleep, or allay irritation.

Refrigerant Draught for Fevers **No. 24**

Take of Bi-carbonate of potash, ... 1 scruple;
Cinnamon water . . . . 2 drachms;

---

1. Many persons cannot bear either laudanum or Battley's solution and yet they require an opiate, or some anodyne. in which case I recommend a trial of ten drop: of the solution of muriate of morphia; in a large table-spoonful of lemon juice or vinegar. Or a quarter of a grain of the muriate of morphia made into a pill and taken with the lemon juice, will answer quite as well.

Common water .... a wine-glassful;
Syrup of orange peel .... 1 drachm.

Mix them and, when taken add a table-spoonful of lemon juice, or 15 grains of citric acid, powdered and drink it immediately.

This is the effervescing saline draught which is usually given in fevers and inflammatory diseases, to allay heat, quench thirst and determine to the surface of the body, for which purposes it is often used with great and immediate effect. It may be repeated every three hours. When the heat and thirst are very considerable, it is frequntly advisable to add six or eight grains of purified nitre to each draught, by which its efficacy is much increased.

Carminative Draught **No. 25**

Take of Sesquicarbonate of magnesia	1 drachm;
Rhubarb, in powder	6 or 8 grains;
Oil of aniseed	3 drops;
Liquor potassae	12 drops;
Water of ammonia	8 drops;
Dill or pimento water	2 ounces.

Mix them together.

This is valuable in neutralizing acidity in the stomach and bowels, relieving depressed spirits and imparting a comfortable warmth internally. It is aperient and is very useful in heart-burn and indigestion; and, in the dose of a dessert-spoonful, may be given with great advantage in the gripings and flatulency of infants or young children.

Draught for Diarrhoea **No. 25A**

Take of Compound powder of chalk	10 grains;
Timcture of catechu	1 drachm;
Cinnamon water	9 drachms.

Mix for a draught, which is an astringent very useful in checking diarrhoea in fever and on ordinary occasions. It may be repeated twice a day, if necessary and is well adapted for ordinary domestic use.

Diaphoretic Cooling Draught **No. 26**

Take of Solution of acetate of ammonia	3	drachms;
Camphor mixture	10	drachms;
Ipecacuanha wine	30	drops;
Syrup of tolu	1	drachm.

Mix. To be repeated every four hours.

This is very useful and is in common use, in fevers and inflammations. It promotes a gentle perspiration, relieves heat, quenches thirst and tends to lower tire pulse.

Purging Draught **No. 27**

Take of Epsom salt, Glauber's salt, of each ..	2	drachms;
Spearmint water, ...	1½	ounce;
Antimonial wine, ...	40	drops;
Tincture of senna, ...	3	drachms.

Mix.

This is a very valuable and effectual purgative for all acute diseases and most common purposes. If a purgative be required which will operate very quickly and powerfully, the draught may be repeated at the end of an hour, or half an hour.

Aperient Draught **No. 27A**

Take of Sulphate of potash	1½	drachm;
Carbonate of potash	10	grains;
Powder of jalap	6	grains;
Manna	2	drachms;
Infusion of senna, pimento water, of each, ...	6	drachms.

Mix them together.

This is a mild and yet effectual aperient, suitable for domestic purposes.

Excellent Draught For Acute Rheumatism — No. 27B

Take of Bicarbonate of potash	1	drachm;
Acetate of potash		half a drachm;
Solution of acetate of ammonia	2	table-spoonfuls;
Water,	2	wine-glassfuls.

Mix them in a tumbler and take this draught every four hours, in a state of effervescence, by adding to each draught, at the time of taking, one scruple of citric acid.

This is one of the safest and most *effectual* remedies now known for acute rheumatism, whenever the urine is acid and the fever high. Half a tumbler of plain water, or barley water, should be taken directly after every draught.

Common Black Draught — No. 28

Take of Compound infusion of senna	1½	ounce;
Pimento water	2	drachms;
Manna	1	drachm;
Epsom salt	2	drachms or more.

Mix.

This is the common purging draught so much in use with apothecaries on all ordinary occasions.

Emetic Draught — No. 29

Take of Emetic tartar	1	grain;
Powder of ipecacuanha	15	grains;
Common water	1½	ounce.

Mix.

This is commonly employed for unloading the stomach on the accession of fevers and in ordinary cases.

Another **No. 30**

Take of Blue vitrol, (sulphate of copper).....	10	grains;
Distilled water	2	ounces.

Mix.

This operates instantaneously and is very proper when laudanum, or any other deleterious substance, has been taken as a poison.

Another Emetic Draught **No. 31**

Take of Sesqui-carbonate of ammonia	1	scruple;
Ipecacuanha, in powder..................		half a drachm;
Peppermint water.......................	3	ounces;
Tincture of cayenne pepper	2	drachms.

Mix for a draught, to be taken directly.

In case of poisoning, this is said to be more certain and effectual in arousing the action of the stomach, than either of the preceding draughts.

Antispasmodic Draught **No. 32**

Take of Ammoniated tincture of valerian	2	drachma;
Tincture of castor......................	1	drachm;
Battley's sedative liquor of opium..........	20	drops;
Camphor mixture.......................	1	ounce;
Syrup of tolu	1	drachm.

Mix.

This is a valuable antispasmodic in spasm of the stomach arising from flatulence or weakness and in the hysterics and convulsive disorders, of the weakly and delicate.

Tonic Draught for the Nervous **No. 33**

Take of Compound tincture of bark,		
ammoniated tincture of valerian, of each	1	drachm;

Compound tincture of aloes...............	10 or 12 drops;
Camphor mixture.........................	1½ ounce.

Mix.

This is a strengthening draught, of great service to the weakly and nervous. It may be repeated two or three times a day.

Draught for Heartburn **No. 34**

Drop fifteen drops of water of ammonia (not the strongest preparation) into two ounces of almond mixture, or of common water.

This is a powerful remedy for heartburn and other cases of morbid acidity of the stomach. Stir it before drinking.

Febrifuge Tonic Draught **No. 35**

Take of Solution of acetate of ammonia	2 or 3 drachms;
Decoction of bark	1½ ounce;
Tincture of bark........................	1½ drachm;
Aromatic confection	half a drachm.

Mix.

This is a mild tonic draught, combined with a diaphoretic, to make it suitable to those cases of disease which call for a strengthening medicine, but which, from the existence of a hot and dry skin, or other symptoms of fever, require us to unite the tonic with a medicine which relaxes the skin and tends to abate fever.

Soothing or Sedative Effervescing Draught **No. 35 A**

Take of Sesqui-carbonate of ammonia	1 scruple;
Water...................................	1½ ounce;
Syrup of orange peel	1 drachm.

Mix them together and take it with a table-spoonful and a half of lemon juice, or twenty-four grains of citric acid, added. It may be repeated two or three times a day.

This is very soothing and useful in all cases of great irritability or nervous excitement. It is very refreshing when tired or ill, and may be used with great advantage in colds, fevers and inflammation of the lungs, or bronchia and in acute rheumatism. It is at once sustaining and soothing.

Draught for Spasm and Depression **No. 35B**

Take of Compound spirit of either,
sal volatile, of each .... half a drachm;
Camphor mixture .... 10 drachms.

Mix them and repeat the draught every three or four hours if necessary. It is useful in most cases of difficulty of breathing, spasm and depression of spirits.

ELECTUARIES

Electuaries are mixtures of vegetable and light earthy powders, combined by means of honey or syrup, so as to form masses of a moderate consistence. All substances of this description may, therefore, be made into electuaries; but as the intention of this form of preparation is to render remedies as palatable as possible, those matters only can be employed to form electuaries, the taste of which is not too ungrateful to be covered with syrup or honey.

Astringent Electuary **No. 36**

Take of Extract of catechu................ 1 ounce;
Kino .... 6 drachms;
Cinnamon bark, nutmegs, of each, ... 2 drachms;
Opium, diffused in a sufficient
quantity of white wine.................. 20 grains;
Syrup of red roses, boiled to the
thickness of honey .... 9 ounces.

Reduce the solid ingredients to powder; then mix them with the opium and syrup, so as to form an electuary.

This is a valuable combination of astringents and aromatics and is often of great service in looseness and bloody flux, especially in the chronical form of these complaints and in their advanced stages. The dose is from a scruple to two drachms, which may be taken in the form of a bolus, or diffused in cinnamon or dill water and repeated twice or thrice a day.

Aperient Electuary **No. 37**

Take of Cream of tartar .... 1 ounce;
Milk of sulphur .... 1 ounce;
Sub-borate of soda .... 2½ drachms;
Syrup of ginger, a sufficient quantity to form an electuary.

The dose is one or two tea-spoonfuls at bed-time, or twice a day, according to its action on the bowels, which ought to be moderate.

This acts very mildly as an aperient and is sometimes particularly useful in aiding the other means employed to remove the uterine obstructions of females.

Electuary for the Piles **No. 38**

Take of Flowers of brimstone .... half an ounce;
Lenitive electuary .... 2 ounces;
Cream of tartar .... 3 drachms;
Oil of cinnamon .... 3 drops;
Syrup of orange peel, a sufficient quantity to make the whole of a proper consistence.

Mix.

A tea-spoonful or two, should be taken once or twice a day, so as to keep the bowels gently open. It is a very effectual aperient and alterative for the piles and will rarely fail in affording great relief.

The manner of preparing the Lenitive Electuary is described under that article at page 79.

EMBROCATIONS AND LINIMENTS

These are compositions which have the consistence of oil or balsam; so as to allow them to be easily rubbed upon the skin. They are in general more active remedies than cerates or ointments; and act as local stimulants, relieving deep-seated inflammation and pains.

Embrocations for Sprains and Bruises — No. 39

Take of Compound liniment of camphor .... 1½ ounce;
Tincture of opium .... half an ounce.
Mix.

This is a very useful application to sprains and bruises, after all inflammation has disappeared and for rheumatic pains. Warmed and rubbed over the surface of the abdomen, it is of much service in allaying the pain of colic unattended by inflammation.

Exbrocation for Bruises, when Inflamed — No. 40

Take of Solution of acetate of ammonia and
soap liniment, of each .... 1 ounce.
Mix.

This is useful when bruises and sprains are accompanied with inflammation.

Guestonian Application for Rheumatism — No. 41

Take of Olive oil, of turpentine, of each ..... 1½ ounce;
Spirit of vitriol .... 3 drachms.
Mix.

This is an excellent stimulant embrocation for rheumatism, sprains, chilblains and other cases in which an active application is necessary.

Sir Astley Cooper's Chilblain Liniment No. 42

Take of Camphorated spirit of wine .... 1 ounce;
Liquor of subacetate of lead .... half an ounce.

Mix and apply in the usual way three or four times a day. It is very efficacious.

Roche's Embrocation for Hoofing-Cough No. 43

Take of Olive oil .... 8 ounces;
Oil of amber............................ 4 ounces;
Oil of cloven, a sufficient quantity to scent it strongly.

Mix.

This is the same as the famous embrocation of Roche. When rubbed on the chest, it stimulates the skin gently and is sometimes serviceable in pooping-cough and the other coughs, of children; but in pooping-cough it ought not to be used for the first three days of the disease.

Valuable Lotion for Hoofing-Cough, Etc. No. 44

Dissolve one drachm of emetic tartar into two ounces of common water, then add half an ounce of tincture of Spanish fly.

This is a very valuable lotion in the advanced stages of pooping-cough and is likewise of much service in all other coughs, as well of adults as children. It is often of singular utility in removing the distressing cough and oppression of the chest, left after the hoop has quitted the patient. After it has been rubbed into the chest night and morning for about a week, it will create a redness and bring out some small pustules, when the lotion should be applied only once a day; and if the part becomes very sore, it may be laid aside altogether and the pustules anointed, twice a day, with simple white ointment.

In very severe cases it will be necessary to continue the use of this lotion until a large crop of pustules appear; and if they are kept discharging freely, for a week or fortnight, by an occasional use of it the relief will be more striking and permanent.

Strong Liniment of Ammonia **No. 45**

Take of Water of ammonia, or spirit of hartshorn	1	ounce;
Olive oil	2	ounces.

Shake them together till they unite.

This is an excellent rubefacient liniment and is efficaciously employed in inflammatory sore-throat, spread on a piece of flannel and applied round the throat, or rubbed in.

Strong Stimulating Liniment **No. 46**

Take of Strong liniment of ammonia (No. 45)	1½	ounce;
Oil of turpentine	1	ounce;
Spirits of camphor	1	ounce;
Hard soap	4	drachms.

Mix them well together.

This is a strong application, suitable for spasms, palsied limbs and severe cases of chronic rheumatism, where there is no inflammation; also for sprains bruises, coughs and oppression in the stomach or chest.

Anodyne Liniment **No. 46B**

Take of Compound soap liniment	2	ounce;
Tincture of cantharides		half an ounce;
Tincture of opium	1½	ounce.

Mix them.

This is useful in sprains, bruises; and rheumatism attended with great pain: to be rubbed in four or five times a day.

EMULSIONS

Emulsions are mixtures of bland mucilaginous substances with water and are used to allay irritation in the lungs, alimentary canal and other parts and likewise as vehicles for certain substances, which could not otherwise be so conveniently taken in a liquid form.

Emulsion of Gum Arabic **No. 47**

Take of Gum arabic, in powder .... 2 drachms;
Sweet almonds, blanched, white
sugar, of each .... half an ounce
Barley water, warm .... 1 pint.

Dissolve the gum in the warm barley water and when it is almost cold pour it gradually upon the almonds, previously beaten to a powder with the sugar, rubbing them at the same time so as form a milky mixture; then strain.

This is a useful demulcent in common colds and coughs and in strangury and general irritation about the urinary organs; and as a pleasant vehicle for the exhibition of more active remedies in these and other complaints.

Almond Emulsion **No. 48**

Take of Almond confection .... 2 ounces;
Common water .... 1 pint.

Add the water gradually to the almond confection whilst rubbing and then strain.

Emulsion for Recent Coughs **No. 49**

Take of Oil of sweet almonds .... 1 ounce;
The yolk of one egg,
Orange flower water .... 5 ounces;
Mucilage of gum arabic .... half an ounce;
Ipecacuanhia wine .... 1½ drachm;

Syrup of marsh-mallows .... half an ounce.

Mix them. The dose is a table-spoonful when the couch is troublesome. This in half the dose may be given to young children for the relief of cough.

Emulsion for Old Coughs No. 50

Take of Gum ammoniac .... 2 drachms;

Water .... half a pint.

Rub the ammoniac well, gradually adding the water until they are thoroughly mixed and then strain through linen.

This is a useful expectorant in old coughs and asthmas, when no inflammatory symptoms are present. The dose is from one to two table-spoonfuls, united with an equal quantity of almond emulsion.

Egg Emulsion No. 51

Rub the yolks of three new laid eggs and a little white sugar, with a pint of cold water, adding to it afterwards a glass of the best sherry, Madeira, or Rhenish wine, 2 drops of oil of cinnamon and a little lemon juice, to give it a flavour.

This forms a very nourishing restorative drink, of great benefit in cases of debility and when a patient is recovering from an attack of some severe disease. This emulsion, if a wine-glassful is taken at a time, is a good remedy in coughs, hoarseness, spitting of blood and costiveness.

Cough Linctus No. 51A

Take of Oil of almonds, syrup of lemons, of each 1 ounce;

Powder of ipecacuanha .... 6 grains;

Conserve of hips (confectio rosa canin) ..... 1 ounce;

Compound powder of tragacanth .... 3 drachms.

Mix them and swallow slowly a tea-spoonful now and then, when the cough is troublesome.

This is a useful linctus in case of cough or hoarseness.

ENEMAS.—*See* Clysters, p. 146

EXTRACTS

These are preparations obtained by evaporating aqueous and spirituous solutions of vegetable substances, until a mass of a somewhat firm tenacious consistency remains. By this means the active principles of many plants are procured in a small compass and in a state very favourable for the formation of pills, whirl: is a mode of administering medicines far more agreeable to the generality of patients and, in many instances, the most eligible, as being less offensive to the stomach.

A method of preparing extracts in *vacuo* has been introduced by Mr. Barry, of Plough Court, which is far superior to the former method of conducting the process, especially in preparing the extracts of hemlock, henbane and other narcotic plants. Indeed, there are no extracts of such plants meriting so much dependence as those prepared *in vacuo*. They may be purchased also at Apothecaries' Hall.

The *Compound Extract of Colocynth* of the shops, when good, is a valuable combination of colocynth and other purgative medicines, which operates much more mildly and effectually than either of them singly and is an aperient combination of great repute for its efficacy in obviating and removing costiveness and relieving all those complaints which depend upon, or are aggravated constipation. The ordinary dose is five grains, which may be taken either alone, or combined with half a grain or a grain of calomel. *See* page 191-192.

The *Extract of Gentian* is a useful bitter tonic, containing all the virtues of the plant. The dose is ten grains, twice or thrice a day. It is also a convenient vehicle for the exhibition of preparations of steel, zinc and other metallic tonics.

The *Extract of Garden Lettuce* and the *Extract of Poppies*, are mild narcotics, which are beneficially employed to relieve lain and procure sleep, in delicate habits, and where there is an objection to the use of opium arising from the presence of inflammation, or from other causes.

The *Extracts of Hemlock, of Henbane* and of *Sarsaparilla*, are excellent forms for administering those medicines, which are of great service in cancerons, scrophulous, rheumatic and several other severe diseases.

Extract of Dandelion is very useful in stomach and liver complaints, in the dose of ton or twenty grain, mixed with a wine-glassful of water or more. Its proper taste is bitter and aromatic, not sweet.

The *Extracts of Bark* and of *Rhubarb,* are not unfrequently prescribed by professional men, but are not much to be depended upon.

FOMENTATIONS

Warm fomentations are well known to ease pain, relieve irritation and tension, relax spasm and induce slight perspiration from the surface to which they are applied; while cold fomentations tend to brace and invigorate relaxed and debilitated parts. They are a simple remedy, but often prove of considerable service.

Anodyne Fomentation — No. 52

Take of White poppy heads .... 3 ounces;
Elder flowers .... half an ounce;
Water .... 3 pints.

Boil till one pint is evaporated, then strain out the liquor.

This fomentation is used to relax spasm and relieve acute pain. Sometimes it may be advisable to add three tea-spoonfuls of tincture of opium to it.

Common Fomentation — No. 53

Take of Common mallows, or marsh mallows 1 ounce;
Chamomile flower, dried .... half an ounce;

Water . . . . 1 pint.

Boil for a quarter of an hour and strain.

This is a very good fomentation for all common occasions.

Strengthening Fomentation **No. 54**

Take of Decoction of oak bark . . . . 2 pints;

Alum, ... 3 drachms.

Mix.

This is an astringent liquor, which is employed with considerable effect as a fomentation to weak parts.

GARGLES

These preparations, as well as those last noticed, are simple remedies, but are of no mean efficacy in allaying irritation and inflammation, in promoting a favourable suppuration, or in astringing and invigorating the membrane lining the throat and mouth, according to the nature of the ingredients of which their are composed and the object to be accomplished in their employment.

Gargles may be divided into four classes, according to the different objects we have in view in employing them: (1) Those employed for the purpose of procuring a subsidence of the irritation or inflammation, without the formation of an abscess— what surgeons call resolution; (2) Those proper when suppuration and abscess are unavoidable; (3) Those employed when the abscess has burst spontaneously, or been laid open; and (4) Those which are necessary when a tendency to gangrene or mortification has supervened.

When the inflammation is slight, it is of little consequence whether gargles be cold or lukewarm; but when it is more severe, they should be of the same temperature as the body. If we are endeavouring to promote suppuration, their temperature should be higher.

Gargle for Irritation and Inflammation No.55

Take of Purified nitre.................... 2 drachms;
Barley water.......................... 7 ounces;
Acetate of honey .... 7 drachms.
Mix. To be used frequently.

Another No. 56

Take of Muriatic acid .... half a drachm;
Decoction of black currant leaves,
or barley water........................ 7 ounces.
Mix.

These gargles are proper when the object is to reduce the inflammation in the throat without its proceeding to suppuration. They are likewise proper in relaxed sore-throat. The second possesses cleansing qualities and is proper when the fauces are clogged with viscid mucus. It may be made still more detergent, if necessary, by increasing a little the quantity of acid.

Excellent Domestic Gargle No. 57

Mix together, in a half-pint tumbler, three tea-spoonfuls of vinegar, two tea-spoonfuls of tincture of myrrh, two of honey and about one-fourth of a tumbler of Port wine; then fill up the tumbler with lukewarm water and the gargle is fit for use.

It is both a pleasant and efficacious gargle in all cases of sore-throat. If a decoction of black currant leaves is used instead of lukewarm water, it much improves the gargle.

Mucilaginous Gargle for Inflammation No 58

Take of Tincture of myrrh .... 3 drachms;
Emulsion or mucilage of gum arabic........ 7 ounces.
Mix.

This is useful to defend the parts when the saliva is thin and acrid.

Gargle to Promote Suppuration **No. 59**

Mix together equal parts of compound barley water and compound infusion of linseed. To be used warm.

When we wish to promote suppuration the gargle must be mild and be used warm and in large quantity, that its temperature may not lie suddenly reduced, since nothing for this purpose is more powerful than warmth.

After the abscess is burst, our view is to dispose the parts to heal; emollient and gently astringent gargles are the best for this purpose and in No. 57, or by adding three drachms of tincture of myrrh to half a pint of compound decoction of barley, we shall have a gargle of this description.

Gargle For Threatened Gangrene **No. 60**

Take of Tincture of capsicum	6 drachms;
Honey of roses	3 drachms;
Infusion of roses, or thin yeast	half a pint.

Mix.

Another **No. 61**

Take of Tincture of capsicum	6drachma;
Infusion of Peruvian bark	5ounces;
Port wine	3ounces.

Mix.

These are proper when a tendency to gangrene or mortification appears.

INFUSIONS

Infusions are solutions of vegetable matter, obtained by maceration, either in cold or boiling water. The strength and quality of infusions are varied by the degree of temperature of the water; those made with hot water being necessarily stronger, but particularly in the case of bitters; cold infusions are more grateful.

In making infusions, when heat is required, the vessel is to be placed near the fire, so that the temperature of the water may be kept up to the necessary point for a sufficient length of time to produce the effect intended.

Infusion of Peruvian Bark **No. 62**

Take of Lance-leaved Peruvian bark, bruised .	half an ounce;
Boiling water	half a pint.

Macerate for two hours in a lightly covered vessel and strain.

This infusion contains a considerable portion of the febrifuge and strengthening matter of the bark. It is very useful in convalescencies from acute diseases.

Bitter Tonic Infusion **No. 63**

Take of Gentian root, sliced		half an ounce;
Dried orange feel, bruised	1	drachm;
Coriander sees, bruised	1	drachm;
Boiling water	12	ounces.

Macerate for an hour in a lightly covered vessel and strain. This compound infusion of gentian is an elegant and efficacious tonic and stomachic, which is beneficially employed in indigestion, general debility, chronic gout and other diseases. The dose is from an ounce to two ounces, two or three times a day.

Diuretic Infusion **No. 64**

Take of Dried foxglove leaves	1	drachm;
Boiling water		half a pint.

Macerate for four hours in a light covered vessel and strain; then add of spirit of cinnamon, half an ounce.

This is a form of exhibiting foxglove well calculated to obtain speedily the diuretic effects of the remedy, in dropsical affections.

The dose is from one to two table-spoonfuls, given twice a day, or every eight hours, if the patient be strong and the symptoms very urgent.

Infusion of Calumba or Cascarilla **No. 65**

Is made in the same way as the last infusion, taking Calumba or Cascarilla root instead of foxglove leaves.

Demulcent Infusion **No. 66**

Take of Linseed, braised	1	ounce;
Liquorice root, sliced		half an ounce;
Boiling water	2	pints.

Macerate for four hours near the fire, in a covered vessel and strain.

Compound infusion of linseed is a particularly useful demulcent and is efficaciously used as such in inflammation and irritation in the urinary organs, in recent coughs and other disorders and as a vehicle for other remedies.

Compound Infusion of Senna **No. 67**

Take of Senna leaves	1½	ounce;
Ginger root, sliced	1	drachm;
Boiling water	1	pint.

Macerate for an hour in a lightly covered vessel and strain the liquor.

This is a useful purging infusion, in common use among medical men. It is usually given in conjunction with a little Epsom or Glauber's salt, which forms a purging mixture of great service in all acute disease.

LINCTUS

Linctus for Chronic Cough and Bronchitis No. 67A

Take of Tartarized antimony	2	grains;
Distilled water	½	ounce.
Oxymel of squills.......................	2½	onces;

Mix and take a tea-spoonful or two, three or four times a day.

This is very efficacious in promoting expectoration, unloading the congested vessels of the bronchia and lungs in severe hoarseness and cough and in chronic hooping cough. I have speedily and permanently relieved patients suffering from chronic bronchitis and difficulty of breathing by means of this linetus; after they had been discharged from hospitals as incurable and almost without any relief.

LOTIONS

Lotions Cooling Discutient Lotion No. 68

Take of Sal ammoniac	2	drachms;
Water	5	ounces;
Rectified spirit of wine	1	ounce.

Mix.

This is an excellent cooling lotion for all inflammatory tumours.

Superior Goulard Water No. 69

Take of Extract of lead (liquor plumbs acetatis)	1	drachm;
Distilled vinegar	2	ounces;
Proof spirit of wine		half an ounce;
Water	1	pent.

Mix

Lotion for Inflammation and Humours **No. 69 A**

Take of Spirit of wine	2 ounces;
vinegar	4 ounces;
Water	6 ounces.

Mix together first the spirit of wine and vinegar, then add the water.

This is an excellent application for inflammation, swelling and watery humour in the limbs, brought on by violent exertion, or from any other cause. Apply the lotion by wetting short pieces of calico or linen and laying them on the limb over the part affected.

Nitric Acid Lotion **No. 70**

Mix together 2 drachms of diluted nitric acid and a pint of water.

The nitric acid lotion is stimulating and detergent and is very serviceable when applied to foul foetid ulcers, attended with a thin ichorous discharge, from whatever cause arising. It is also useful in caries of the bone and when there is an impending mortification. It was a favourite lotion of Sir Astley Cooper in numerous instances of unhealthy ulceration, which require the application of a mild yet effectual stimulant.

Anodyne Lotion **No. 71**

Take of Crude opium	2 drachms;
Warm water	1 pint.

Rub the opium in a mortar with a little of the warm water, for a few minutes, then pour the remaining quantity of water upon it and mix them well together.

This is beneficially applied to painful irritable ulcers and to all painful swellings in which the use of opium is proper.

Astringent Lotion **No. 72**

Take of Sulphate of zinc	2 drachms;

Water	1	pint;
Camphorated spirit of wine	2	drachms.

Mix.

This is a very valuable lotion for piles and relaxation about the anus. It should be used night and morning.

Soothing Lotion **No. 72A**

Take of. Oxymuriate (bichloride) of mercury .	8	grains;
Rectified spirit of wine		half an ounce;
Distilled water	7½	ounces.

Mix them for a lotion.

This is very soothing and effectual in itching and painful eruptions on the scalp or anus or elsewhere.

Strong Astringent Lotion **No. 72 B**

Mix together a pint of decoction of oak bark (No. 21) and 2 ounces of alum.

This is very valuable as a lotion for piles and prolapsus of the anus, for which purpose the parts should be washed with it thrice a day.

MIXTURES

Valuable Guaiacum Mixture **No. 72 C**

Take of Guaiacum	3	drachms;
Sugar		half an ounce;
Mucilage of gum arabic		half an ounce;
Cinnamon water.	19	ounces.

Rub the guaiacum with the sugar, then with the mucilage and to these, while rubbing, add gradually the cinnamon water.

This is an admirable remedy for rheumatism, particularly for the chronic kind, operating both by stool and perspiration. It is strongly recommended in this work. The dose is from two to four table-spoonfuls, twice or thrice a day, according to its action on the bowels, which should be moderate in chronic cases. Rheumatic pains are much benefited by it.

Purging Mixture **No. 73**

Take of Epsom salt, Glauber's salt, of each ..		half an ounce;
Spearmint water	5½	ounces;
Antimonial wine	2	drachms;
Tincture of senna		half an ounce.

Mix.

Useful on all ordinary occasions as a purging medicine. Two, three or four table-spoonfuls may be taken for a dose and repeated, if necessary, every three hours till it operates.

Abernethy's Aperient Mixture **No. 74**

Take of Epsom salt		half an ounce;
Infusion of senna	6	drachms;
Tincture of senna	2	drachms;
Spearmint water	1	ounce;
Distilled water	2	ounces;
Best manna	2	drachms.

Mix and take three, four or five table-spoonfuls every morning or every other morning.

This was a favourite prescription with Abernethy; and I have known it extremely useful in chronic disorders of the stomach and bowels, when two or three grains of blue pill were taken every second night during the same period.

Tonic Aperient Mixture **No. 74A**

Take of Decoction of bark, infusion of senna, of each	3½	ounces;

Sulphate of potash	3	drachma;
Compound tincture of bark		half an ounce.

Mix them together and take three table-spoonfuls, once or twice a day, so as to keep the bowels regular or it may be used only occasionally, when an aperient is required.

Another Tonic Aperient Mixture — No. 74B

Take of Infusion of cascarilla or calumba and compound decoction of aloes, of each.	3½	ounces;
Sulphate of potash	4	drachms;
Tincture of calumba.		half an ounce.

Mix them and take the same dose and in the same way, as prescribed in the last prescription.

The combination of direct tonics with aperients is a form of prescription likely to be of great service in numerous instances and much called for. Weakness in the bowels is very often the chief cause of costiveness and in seeking to remove the effect, solely by means of aperients or purgatives, which act through irritation only, we do but add to the mischief. Tonics should, therefore, be combined with aperients, whereby we shall often at once strengthen the bowels and effect a more certain and comfortable exoneration of them.

Jephson's Tunic Aperient Mixture — No. 74C

Take of Epsom salt	1 or 2	drachms;
Sulphate of iron	6	grains;
Battley's liquid dandelion		half an ounce;
Dilated sulphuric acid	1	drachm;
Water,. or infusion of orange peel	5½	ounces.

Mix them and take three table-spoonfuls twice a day, so as just to keep the bowels regular.

This is similar to the favourite aperient mixture of Dr. Jephson of Leamington, which he was so much in the practice of prescribing and which acts on the bowels without debilitating. It is an excellent alterative and tonic.

Dr. Budd's Remedy for Jaundice — No. 74D

Take of Epsom salts	3 or 4 drachms;
Carbonate of magnesia	1 drachms;
Aromatic opirit of amonia	2 drachms;
Pure water	5½ ounces.

Mix and take one-fourth once or twice a day.

Emetic Mixture — No. 75

Take of Emetic tartar	4 grains;
Water	3 ounces
Syrup of mulberries	2 drachms.

Mix.

This emetic may be given with great advantage in the commencement of fevers and in all cases where emetic tartar is proper. It should never be given to infants, nor to very young children, unless under the direction of a medical man, ipecacuanha wine being preferable in such subjects. The dose of this mixture is two table-spoonfuls every ten or twelve minutes till it begins to operate.

Mixture for Recent Cough — No. 76

Take of Honey	5 ounces;
Treacle	quarter pound;
Best vinegar	7 ounces.

Mix them and simmer in a common pipkin over the fire for fifteen minutes; after removing it from the fire and the mixture has become lukewarm, add three drachms of ipecacuanha wine. The dose is a table-spoonful every four hours for adults.

In the opinion of the present author this is one of the best mixtures now known for recent cough. On account of its pleasant taste, it is particularly eligible in the coughs of children and infants...

Mild Cough Mixture **No. 76A**

Take of Camphor mixture	4 ounces;
Solution of acctate of ammonia	8 drachms;
Nitre	2 scruples;
Antinonial wine	1 drachm;
Syrup of tolu	4 drachms.

Mix them and take one-fourth thrice a day.

This is especially adapted to couch accompanied with fever.

Toxic Cough Mixture **No. 77**

Take of Myrrh, in powder	1½ drachm
Decoction of liquorice (warm)	5½ ounces.

Rub them together and strain it. Then add one drachm of arometic sulphuric acid. The dose is two table-spoonfuls two, three or four times a day.

This is an excellent. strengthening cough mixture, applicable in all coughs where debility and languor are present, provided much inflammatory action does not exist.

Mixture for Chronic and Habitual Cough **No. 78**

Take of Mixture of gum ammoniac, cinnamon water, of each	24 ounces;
Ipecacuhana wine	2 drachms;
Paregoric elixir	half a drachm;
Syrup of tolu	6 drachms.

Mix.

The dose of this composition is a table-spoonful every four hours, or when the cough is troublesome. It is well adapted to all cases of asthma and chronic cough.

Mixture for Chronic Cough and Bronchitis **No. 78A**

Take of Sesqui carbonate of ammonia....... 36 grains;
Tincture of squills .... 3 drachms;
Camphor mixture, to complete,............ 6 ounces.
Mix them and take two table-spoonfuls thrice a day.

This promotes a free expectoration and is of signal service in all the coughs of old people. It is very sustaining and improves the duality of the blood and the respiration.

Mixture for Acute Bronchitis **No. 78B**

Take of Antimonial wine, fresh prepared .... 3 drachms;
Sweet spirits of nitre .... 1 drachm;
Tincture of henbane....................... 1 drachm;
Mixture of gum arabic, syrup of
orange peel, of each...................... half an ounce;
Solution of acetate of ammonia............ 1½ ounce;
Camphor misture, sufficient to complete a six ounce
mixture; of which take a fourth part every three hours.

This is very efficacious in subduing inflammation in the bronchia, and promoting a free expectoration, in the acute stage of bronchitis, particularly when much difficulty of breathing is present, with lividity in the complexion and a pulse small and quick and the patient expectorates a glairy transparent mucus.

In children under two years of age, ipecacuanha wine should be substituted for the antimonial wine; and at that age a tenth part of the mixture is sufficient for a dose.

Mixture for Recent Cough **No. 78C**

Take of Almond mixture, sufficient to make.. 6 ounces;
Ipecacuanha wine .... 1½ drachm;
Bicarbonate of potash .... 2 drachms;
Syrup of tolu .... half an ounce.

Mix them and take three table-spoonfuls, with a table-spoonful of lemon juice, or 24 grains of citric acid, when the cough is troublesome.

This is very useful in all coughs and is pleasant to the taste.

Sustaining Remedy in Cough and Bronchitis **No. 78D**

Take of Sesqui carbonate of ammonia.......	1½	drachm;
Solution of acetate of ammonia,		
fresh prepared........................	4½	ounces;
Antimonial wine		half an ounce;
Camphor mixture......................	6	ounces;
Syrup of tolu	1	ounce.

Mix them and take two table-spoonfuls, in one or two table-spoonfuls of water, every four hours.

This is sustaining, diaphoretic and expectorant and is of eminent utility in cough and bronchitis and inflammation of the lungs, especially in elderly people and where symptoms of debility and sinking show themselves. It improves the quality of the blood, restrains inordinate secretions and prevents the deposition of fibrine from the blood. It thus proves useful also in female complaints.

Valuable Cordial Mixture **No. 79**

Take of Camphor mixture	5½	ounces;
Distilled water	1½	ounce;
Sesqui carbonate of ammonia	2	scruples;
Compound tincture of cinnamon	1½	drachm;
Spirits of lavender	2	drachms;
Syrup of ginger	3	drachms.

Mix them and take three table-spoonfuls twice or thrice a day.

This is useful in low spirits, debility and as a cordial tonic in some cases of indigestion attended with acidity and flatulence, or uneasiness in the bowels.

Valuable Gout Mixture **No. 80**

Take of Calcined magnesia	4 scruples;
Epsom salt	6 drachms;
Spearmint water	5 ounces;
Vinegar of colchicum	2 drachms;
Syrup of common saffron	half an ounce.

Mix.

This is an excellent mixture for opening the bowels and mitigating the severity of pain, in gout and acute rheumatism. It was first proposed by Sir C. Scudamore and is usually administered at the commencement of the attack of gout and rheumatism, a fourth part of it to be taken every six or eight hours until the bowels are freely moved; after which it may be continued, in doses of three or four table-spoonfuls every morning, or every second morning, to keep the bowels in a lax condition, through the whole continuance of these diseases.

Mixture for Stomachic Irritation **No. 80 A**

Take of Prussic acid	25 drops;
Ipecacuanha wine	30 drops;
Tincture of henbane	60 drops;
Tincture of orange peel	half an ounce;

Infusion of orange peel, sufficient to make up six ounces.

Mix them and take two table-spoonfuls twice or thrice a day.

This mixture will be found very efficacious in the relief of some cases of stomachic irritation. It is very soothing to the stomach and is especially indicated under circumstances of long-continued irritability of that important organ.

Mixture for Diarrhoea **No. 80B**

Take of Aromatic confection	2½ drachms;
Tincture of catechu	7 drachms;

Tincture of opium . . . . 1 drachm;
Chalk mixture cinnamon water, of each, ... 3½ ounces.

Mix. Excellent for ordinary occasions. The dose is a wine-glassful, after each liquid motion.

Fever Mixture **No. 81**

Take of Bi-carbonate of potash . . . . 2 drachms;
Purified nitre . . . . 30 grains;
Camphor mixture. . . . . 2 ounces;
Water to make a six ounce mixture,
Antimonial wine, recently prepared . . . . 1½ drachm;
Syrup of saffron . . . . 3 drachms.

Mix and for a dose take two table-spoonfuls, which should be mixed with a wine-glassful of water and a table-spoonful of lemon juice, or twenty-five grains of citric or tartaric acid and drank immediately. This may be repeated every three or four hours.

This is a cooling mixture of much service in all inflammatory fevers and acute inflammations.

Tonic Mixture for Indigestion **No. 82**

Take of Infusion of calumba . . . . 5½ ounces;
Compound tincture of cinnamon . . . . 2 drachms:
Sesqui-carbonate of ammonia . . . . 2 scruples;
Syrup of orange peel . . . . 2 drachms.

Mix.

This is an appropriate tonic in indigestion and bilious complaints; and it is useful in checking the severe vomiting which often occurs during pregnancy. The dose is two table-spoonfuls every four hours or twice a day.

Cinnamon Mixture for lose of Blood **No. 82A.**

Take of Compound tincture of cinnamon . . . . 6 drachms;

Cinnamon water........................ 5 ounces and 2 drachms;

Mix them and take two table-spoonfuls, thrice a day.

This is a very pleasant and efficacious remedy for discharge of blood from the nose, womb, bowels and other parts when the blood is dark coloured, when the loss of blood is not of an active, but of a passive nature. That is, when the blood, instead of being bright and arterial is dark-coloured and venous.

Tonic Mixture **No. 83**

Take of Compound infusion of gentian...... 5½ ounces;
Sesqui-carbonate of ammonia............. half a drachm;
Tincture of cascarilla.................... half an ounce.
Mix.

This is particularly useful as a tonic is gout, indigestion and general weakness, whether or not accompanied with morbid acidity in the stomach and symptoms of red gravel. The dose is three table-spoonfuls, repeated twice a day.

Tonic Mixture **No. 84**

Take of Decoction of Peruvian bark........ 6 ounces;
Tincture of bark......................... 2 drachms;
Muriatic acid........................... 40 drops.
Mix.

An excellent tonic in typhus and the low stages of all fevers, in doses of three table-spoonfuls every two, three or four hours.

An Excellent Steel Mixture **No. 84A**

Take of Citrate of iron, sesquicarbonate of ammonia, of each...................... 2 scruples;
Water, to make eight ounces,
Tincture of orange peel.................. 2 drachms.
Mix them.

The dose is two table-spoonfuls twice a day, in two table-spoonfuls of water. It is an admirable warm tonic, very useful when the patient has a blanched complexion, denoting a deficiency of good blood. It is one of the most pleasant, effectual and blood producing medicines that can be taken.

Tonic Ammonia Mixture **No. 84B**

Take of Sesqui carbonate of ammonia	2½	scruples;
Decoction of Peruvian bark	7½	ounces;
Compound tincture of bark		half an ounce.

Mix them and take three table-spoonfuls three or four times a day.

In putrid sore throat, diphtheria and general debility, this is an admirable remedy; also in rheumatism.

An Excellent Tonic Mixture **No. 85**

Take of Sulphate of quinine...............	8	grains;
Cinnamon and common water, of each	2½	ounces;
Syrup of orange peel	6	drachms;
Tincture of orange peel	2	drachms.

Mix.

This is a most agreeable and useful way of administering quinine. The dose is two table-spoonfuls, twice or thrice a day.

Tonic and Astringent Mixture **No. 85A**

Take of Muriatic acid and nitric acid, of each .	12	drops;
Infusion of rhatany or gentian root	5	ounces;
Tincture of orange peel, syrup of orange peel, of each.........................		half an ounce.

Mix them.

This is a tonic mixture almost equally pleasant and efficacious. It possesses considerable power as an astringent and will be found useful in diarrhoeas and chronic dysentery, when a tonic is admissible. It is beneficial in dyspepsia, and is particularly appropriate if white gravel be a concomitant symptom. The dose of the acids may often be increased to twenty drops. The dose is three table-spoonfuls twice a day.

Mixture for Dysentery and Diarrhoea **No. 85B**

Take of Pomegranate bark................ 2½ ounces;
Water.............................. 1½ pints.

Boil to a pint and strain, then add an ounce of syrup of morphia. Give a wine-glassful every four hours, in dysentery and diarrhoea.

Mixture Foil Dropsy **No. 86**

Take of Acetate of potash .... 5 drachms;
Infusion of digitalis .... 1½ ounces ;
Sweet spirits of nitre .... 3 drachms
Syrup of tolu .... half an ounce.
Water, sufficient to make up an eight ounce mixture.
Mix them and tale three table-spounfnfs thrice a day.

This is an excellent diuretic in dropsy, especially in dropsy arising from liver obstruction, pleurisy, or any other affection in the chest. It may he given at the same time with a pill of calomel and squills at bed-time.

Diuretic Mixture **No. 87**

Take of Purified nitre...................... 2 drachms;
Mixture of gum ammoniac .... 6 ounces;
Compound spirit of juniper berries .... 1½ ounce;
Vinegar of squill .... 6 drachms.
Mix.

The dose is a table-spoonful in water, every four hours. It is worthy of a trial in most cases of dropsy from disease in the chest.

Soothing Diaphoretic Mixture — No. 87A

Take of Solution of acetate of ammonia	2 ounces;
Antimonial wine, fresh prepared	2 drachms;
Syrup of orange peel	half an ounce;

Water to complete eight ounces.

Mix and take three or four table-spoonfuls thrice a day.

Dr. Graves's Fever Mixture — No. 87B

Take of Tartarized antimony	3 grains
Tincture of opium	half a drachm;
Mucilage of bum arabic	1 ounce;
Water	5 ounces.

Mix and take a table-spoonful every hour in the beginning, until relieved, then every second hours and after the patient is very sensibly relieved, four or five times in the twenty-four hours.

Dr. Graves, of Dublin, found this combination of eminent and superior efficacy in the delirium of fever and I believe it worthy of all confidence, not only for that particular symptom, but as capable of materially assisting to conduct the disease to a favourable issue. Sometimes the first doses of this mixture will vomit the patient, but that will do no harm and such an effect will soon cease to take place; and in many cases it purges and causes the discharge of a considerable quantity of bilious yellow fluid, affording great relief. Dr. Graves relates cases of its remarkably soothing power in his *Clinical Medicine,* p. 130, 135. One is an example of the worst form of typhus fever, in which there was intense mental excitement, total want of sleep, continued delirium and excessive disturbance of the nerves. This man manifested "continued mental wandering, incessant talking and raving and frequent attempts to get out of bed. He hurl terrific ocular spectra and alarming sounds, which threw him into a state of intense agitation; his eye was red and watchful and he never slept". Yet he was calmed and benefited by this mixture and gradually and completely recovered. It is very efficacious in *delirium tremens.*

OINTMENTS AND CERATES

Ointments and *Cerates* are compositions of fatty matters, either animal or vegetable, or both, employed as external dressings. They both possess a certain degree of firmness, but ointments are much less firm than cerates. The latter commonly contain a considerable proportion of wax, whence they derive their name.

Spermaceti Ointment — No. 88

Take of Spermaceti .... 6 drachms;
White wax .... 2 drachms;
Olive oil .... 3 ounces.

Melt them together over a slow fire and stir them constantly until they are cold.

Ointment of Nitrate or Mercury — No. 89

Take of Ointment of nitrate of mercury...... 1 drachm;
Spermaceti cerate........................ 2 drachms.

Mix them.

This is an invaluable composition. It is stimulant and cleansing and is used with the greatest advantage in scald head and other eruptions on that part, in chronic inflammation of the eye and specks on the cornea and in ulcers. In such cases it stimulates the part to a healthy action and will often cure very obstinate examples of these different affections, after other powerful remedies have failed. In scald head and ulcerations, it is either rubbed over the part affected with the finger, or applied spread on linen: and in chronic diseases of the eye, a little is taken on the end of the finger, or on a camel's hair brush, liquefied by the fire and applied along the inner part of the eyelid.

Sulphur Ointment — No. 90

Take of Sublimed sulphur .... 3 ounces;
Prepared lard .... half a pound;

Essential oil of bergamot . . . . 20 drops.
Mix them.

This is specific in itch. It should be rubbed on the body every night till the disease be cured, but not more than one-fourth part of the body should be covered with it at a time.

Ointment of Galls **No. 91**

Take of Galls, in fine powder . . . . 2 drachms;
Camphor . . . . half a drachms;
Lard . . . . 1 ounce.
Mix them.

This is a very useful application to piles, after their inflammatory state has been diminished by the use of Goulard water and leeches.

Very Excellent Lye Ointment **No. 92**

Take of Ointment of nitric oxyde of mercury,
spermaceti ointment, of each . . . . 1 drachm;
Mix them.

A little should be applied to the eyelids, night and morning, by means of a feather or camel's hair pencil, as advised for No. 89. It is excellent in all redness and chronic inflammations of the eyes or eyelids; and is similar to the celebrated Singleton's Golden Ointment.

Tartar Emetic Ointment **No. 93**

Take of Tartar emetic, in fine powder . . . . 1 drachm;
Spermaccti ointment . . . . 7 drachms.
Mix them together.

About the size of a large nut rubbed over any part night and morning, will speedily bring out a crop of pustules, which should be kept discharging by an occasional use of the ointment for a fortnight. If the irritation thus excited should be at any time great, it may be allayed by applying a warms bread and water poultice and renewing it, often as agreeable.

Goulard Ointment **No. 94**

Take of Acetate of lead, in powder	2 drachms;
White wax	2 ounces;
Olive oil	half a pint.

Melt the wax in seven fluid ounces of the oil; then add gradually the acetate of lead, separately rubbed down with the remaining oil and stir with a wooden spatula, until they be thoroughly incorporated.

This is an excellent cooling cerate for burns, excoriations and other inflamed sores and for all common purposes. It should be renewed night and morning. It is similar to *Goulard's Cerate a*nd under that name, or that of *cerate of acetate of lead,* may be purchased at all druggists.

Turner's Cerate **No. 95**

Take of Prepared Calamine, yellow wax, of each....	half a pound;
Olive oil	1 pint.

Mix the oil with the melted wax; then remove the mixture from the fire and as soon as ii begins to thicken, add the calamine, stirring constantly until it be cold.

This is a cooling drying cerate, very useful in excoriations, simple ulcers and burns after the inflammation has abated. *Goulard's Ointment* and *Turner's* Cerate mixed, in equal proportions, form a very efficacious soothing ointment, applicable to most cases of excoriations, ulcerations and erysipelas, met with in domestic practice.

Black Wash **No. 96**

Add one drachm of calomel to a pint of lime water; and shake the bottle every time it is used.

This is a soothing and favourite application to bad sores and to foul ulcerations of every kind. A piece of fine lint should be dipped in the lotion, laid over the sore and renewed night and morning.

PILLS

Pills are masses of a consistence sufficient to preserve a round form, yet not so hard as to be of too difficult solution in the stomach. This form of preparation is particularly adapted for medicines which have a very nauseous taste or flavour and such as operate in minute doses. Extracts, when not too hard, may be formed into pills without any addition; but more generally, pills are composed of either vegetable, or earthy, or metallic powders, combined by means of syrup, mucilage, or gum arabic, or some bitter extract, into a coherent mass. Pills should never weigh more than five grains each.

Purgative Pills — No. 97

Take of Compound extract of colocynth,
compound rhubarb pill, of each .... half a drachm;
Calomel .... 6 grains;
Oil of carraway .... 5 drops;
Syrup, a sufficient quantity to form the whole into a mass.
Divide it into sixteen pills.

These are excellent purgative pills, of great service in fevers, inflammation and all cases in which such a purgative is required. They evacuate the intestines through their whole extent and in doses of two or three at bed-time, are pretty certain of procuring some copious evacuations the next day.

One pill, or even half a one, generally operates as a very mild yet effectual aperient, of much benefit in costiveness, low spirits and on all ordinary occasions.

Alterative Pills — No. 98

Take of Calomel .... 7 grains;

Emetic tartar, two grains at first, gradually increased to two grains and a half;

Precipitated sulphuret of antimony .... 1 scruple;

Guaiacum, in powder.................... 2 scruples.

Rub them well together in a mortar for ten minutes, then, with a little conserve of hips, make them into a mass and divide it into twenty pills.

Alterative Pills **No. 98A**

Tale of Calomel .... 1 grain;

Emetic tartar .... 1 grain;

Precipitated Sulphuret of antimony .... 10 grains;

Guaiacum, in powder .... 1 scruple.

Rub them well together and, with a little confection of hips, divide them into ten pills; one to be taken every other night, or every night.

Alterative Pills **No. 99**

Take of Blue pill .... 30 grains;

Tartar emetic .... 2 grains;

Extract of hemlock .... 3 scruples.

Mix them well together and divide the mass into twenty pills; one of which should be taken every night, or every other night, or under urgent circumstances, twice a day.

These are excellent forms of alterative pills and are of eminent service in almost all chronic disorder. They operate mildly yet effectually in altering the diseased condition of action in the smaller vessels of the circulating system and thus are employed with superior advantage in numerous severe, obstinate and apparently dissimilar complaints. They enjoy the confidence of the majority of the most distinguished members of the medical profession in this country and are prescribed by them, as well to correct a derangement of function, as to check the progress of organic injury. They are of great service in bilious and liver complaints, diseased joints, scrophulous and other tumours; chronic diseases of the eye and skin and, indeed, in many other obstinate and protracted maladies. I consider them, without exception, the most valuable mineral alteratives known, being more generally applicable to the relief and cure of chronic disease than any other mineral medicine or combination with which we are at present acquainted. No. 98A is a very mild form and such as I commonly prefer, particularly in the case of delicate persons and in domestic practice.

One pill is given every night, or every other night for several days. If the disease is of an aggravated character, and it is necessary to employ means to check its progress directly, a pill may be administered night and morning, until that object is accomplished and then the quantity should be reduced to one every night, discontinuing the pills for three days occasionally. In very severe diseases, this plan may be perserved in for many consecutive days, or even weeks.

Mild Aperient Pills[1] **No. 100**

Take of Compound extract of colocynth		half a drachm;
Compound rhubarb pill	1	scruple;
Castile soap	10	grains;
Oil of juniper	3	drops.

Beat them into a mass and divide into twelve pills.

These are excellent aperient pills for occasional use in costiveness, bilious affections and on all ordinary occasions. They are suited to the relief and removal of these complaints in children as well as in adults. One pill taken at bed-time is generally sufficient, but some persons may require two.

Mild Aperient Pills **No. 100A**

Take of Blue pill	12	grains;
Precipitated sulphuret of antimony	6	grains;

1. The following is another form of aperient pill at once mild and efficient, and may be useful where neither No. 97 or No. 100 are found suitable:

Tarter emetic .... 1 grain;
Compound extract of colocynth .... 24 grains;
Extract of henbane...................... 12 grains;
Oil of cloves .... 1 drop.

Mix them together and divide the mass into twelve pills.

The dose is one, two or three every night, or every other night. We have numbered these 100 A. *One pill is usually sufficient, especially in delicate habits.*

Digestive Aperient Pills **No. 101**

Take of socotorine aloes, thirty-six or forty grains; rub it well with eighteen grains of gum mastic; and add of compound extract of gentian, and compound galbanum pill, of each, twenty-four grains; oil of aniseed, a sufficient quantity to make twenty pills.

Take, when costive, two or three of these pills an hour before dinner, or at night. These are stomachic aperient pills, containing an antispasmodic and producing usually a full feculent evacuation. They are very suitable to persons who have no vital energy to spare and require a medicine which will operate mildly, surely and safely.

Stomachic Aperient Pills **No. 101A**

Take of Compound rhubarb pill, (or
compound extract of colocynth) .... 1 drachm:
Ipecacuanha powder .... 8 grains;
Extract of chamomile.................... 26 grains;
Extract of henbane...................... 24 grains.

Mix them well together and divide the mass into twenty-four pills; of which one, two or three may be taken as a dose, when costive.

Tonic Aperient Pills **No. 101B**

Take of Sulphate of quinine............... 30 grains;

Compound rhubarb pill .... 1 drachm;

Compound extract of colocynth .... 30 grains;

Oil of aniseed, a sufficient quantity.

Mix them together and divide the whole into thirty pills, of which one or two may be taken as a dose, when costive.

These pills, containing a direct tonic, are often employed with much better effect on the action of the bowels than those which have no invigorating influence. I am quite of opinion, that a tonic should in every case, where it is practicable, be combined with an aperient; more especially when the pills are frequently used.

Deobstruent Aperient Pills **No. 101C**

Take of Powdered gum guaiacum .... 1 scruple;

Gum ammoniacum, in powder .... 1 drachm;

Carbonate of ammonia.................. 15 grains;

Pill aloes with myrrh .... 2½ scruples;

Compound tincture of aloes, a sufficient quantity.

Mix them and divide into forty pills. Take three of them, once or twice a day, with or without a little infusion of chamomile.

These pills will be-found of superior utility to many persons who suffer from internal obstruction associated with constipation. Those who are troubled with griping or colicky pains and costiveness, will experience relief from this combination.

Deorstruent Aperient Pills **No. 101D**

Takeof Gum myrrh, gum ammoniacum, of each half a drachm;

Benzoin,............................ half a drachm;

Extract of gentian, ... 1 scruple;

Venice turpentine, ... 2 scruples;

Pill aloes with myrrh,.................... half a drachm;

Compound tincture of aloes, a sufficient quantity.

Mix them well together and divide the mass into forty pills. The dose is two pills, once or twice a day.

I recommend these pills as useful to such invalids as suffer from costiveness and urinary affection, or cough.

Mild Aperient Pills **No. 101E**

Take of Watery extract of aloes............	1	drachm;
Leaves of red roses		half a drachm;
Gum mastic		half a drachm;

Simple syrup, a sufficient quantity.

Beat them well together and divide into forty pills,

This is a mild useful aperient pill, operating also as a tonic to the stomach. The dose is two or three pills at bed-time.

Strengthening Pills **No. 102**

Take of Subcarbonate of iron	1½	drachm;
Ipecacuanha, in powder..................	8	grains;
Aromatic powder........................	8	grains;
Extract of gentian		half a drachm;
Socotorine aloes, in powder...............	2	or 3 grains;

Simple syrup, or mucilage of gum arabic, a sufficient quantity to form the whole into a mass of a proper consistence.

Divide it into thirty pills.

Two or three of these pills are to be taken twice a day. They are of great value as a tonic in indigestion, bilious complaints, general weakness, head-ache depending upon a nervous or debilitated state of the constitution, green-sickness and many other complaints where a mild yet effectual strengthening medicine is required.

Strengthening Pills **No. 103**

Take of Sulphate of iron		half a drachm;
Carbonate of potash.....................	10	grains;
Myrrh, in powder.......................	1	drachm;
Compound powder of aloes...............		half a drachm.

Beat them together and divide the mass into thirty pills.

These pills are often of the greatest service in green-sickness and retention or suppression of the menses, accompanied with a languid pulse; and also in indigestion, general debility and the advanced stages of pulmonary consumption. Two of them may be taken three times a day.

Bismuth Pills, for Indigestion **No. 103 A**

Take of Oxyde of bismuth . . . . 3½ scruples;
Powdered rhubarb . . . . 6 grains;
Aromatic powder . . . . 1 scruple;
Extract of hips, a sufficient quantity to make them into twenty pills; one to be taken twice a day.

These pills are very efficacious in removing pain *and weight in the stomach,* connected with indigestion.

Stomachic Pills **No. 104**

Take of Rhubarb, in powder . . . . 2 scruples;
Ipecacuanha, in powder . . . . 10 grains;
Castile soap . . . . 2 scruples;
Mucilage of gum arabic, a sufficient quantity to make the whole into a mass.

Divide into twenty-four pills; one to be taken twice or thrice a day.

These are very valuable stomachic pills in indigestion and bilious affections and many complaints which depend on derangement of the important organs of digestion, such as sick headache, frequent nausea, deficient appetite and stomach cough. Their principal operation is on the stomach and first intestine (duodenum) and by exciting a new and healthy action in these organs, they frequently secure a healthy flow of bile and are productive of the most beneficial consequences to the constitution generally.

Another Form of Stomachic Pills **No. 104A**

Take of Powdered rhubarb, powdered ginger,
of each . . . . half a drachm;

Extract of gentian, extract of chamo-
mile, of each .... half a drachm;

Oil of cloves, or aniseed, a sufficient quantity to form the mass.

Divide it into thirty pills, of which one or two may be taken an hour before dinner every day and again in the evening.

Pills Foil Chronic Cough and Asthma **No. 105**

Take of Compound squill pill .... 1 drachm;

Ipecacuanha, in powder .... 7 grains.

Mix them well together with a little syrup and divide the mass into twenty pills. One to be taken three, four or five times in the twenty-four hours.

This is a useful stimulating expectorant in all cases of indolent habitual cough and in asthma.

Another Form **No. 106**

Take of Myrrh, in powder .... 1½ drachm;

Sulphate of zinc .... 12 grains.

Mix them well together in a mortar and with a sufficient quantity of conserve of roses, make them into a mass. Divide it into twenty-four pills.

This is a stimulating tonic pill, which is sometimes very serviceable in chronic cough and asthma. One or two pills may be taken three times a day.

Pills for Chronic Bronchitis **No. 106A**

Take of Sulphate of zinc .... 1 scruple;

Extract of hemlock .... 2 scruples.

Mix them and divide into twenty pills. One to be taken thrice a day.

They are tonic and expectorant and are not liable to produce heat or head-ache as iron sometimes does.

Pills for Recent Cough — No. 107

Take of Extract of hemlock, prepared in vacuo	2	scruples;
Ipecacuanha, in powder	10	grains;

Hemlock, in powder, a sufficient quantity to make the whole into a mass.

Divide it into twenty pills. One to be taken twice or thrice a day.

These pills are sometimes of the greatest service in recent cough of almost every description. They promote expectoration, allay fever and relieve irritation and pain in the organs of the chest. They are useful in the hooping-cough, both of children and adults.

Another Form — No. 108

Take of Extract of hemlock, extract of white poppies, of each	2	scruples;
Ipecacuanha, in powder	10	grains.

Mix them well and divide into thirty pills. One to be taken thrice a day.

This prescription is applicable to the same cases as the last.

Anodyne Diaphoretic Pill — No. 109

Take of Muriate of morphia...............	1/6	or ½ of a grain;
Camphor	2	grains;
James's powder	2	grains;

Conserve of hips, a sufficient quantity to form a pill.

This is a very useful pill to procure sleep and ease pain, in the majority of diseases. It tends to relax the skin at the same time that it relieves pain. It may be given at bed-time, or twice in the day, according to circumstances.

Anodyne Pills — No. 110

Take of Compound ipecacuanha powder	2	scruples;

Extract of hemlock, prepared in vacuo ......
(page 147) .... 1 drachm.

Mix them together and divide into twenty pills.

These pills have in general great power in alleviating pain and irritation in most local complaints. There are very few painful maladies in which they are not both appropriate and useful. Where some anodyne is frequently called for, they are far better than the usual preparations of opium, because they do not affect the head, or distress the constitution, while they often exert more than a palliative effect. One or two pills, twice or thrice a day, is the proper dose.

Sometimes the extract of henbane may be advantageously substituted for the extract of hemlock, if the above combination is not sufficiently anodyne.

Pills to Procure Sleep **No. 111**

Take of Camphor .... 4 grains;
Nitrate of potash .... 5 grains;

Extract of henbane, prepare in vacuo, 4 grains, (or more);

Syrup of poppies, a sufficient quantity to form the mass into three pills, which may be taken at bed-time.

These are valuable pills for procuring sleep when opium cannot be given with propriety and especially when the patient complains of heat or feverishness at night.

Pills to Acute Inflammation **No. 112**

Take of Calomel .... 10 grains;
James's powder .... 15 grains;
Turkey opium, in powder .... 10 grains;

Conserve a of hips a sufficient quantity to form the ingredients into a mass, which is to be divided into ten pills.

One of these pills may be given in acute inflammation of the lungs, bowels, or any other part, every second, third or fourth hour, according to the severity of the symptoms and the urgency of the case. They are of the greatest service in such cases, when joined with the use of the lancet and other proper means and ought never to be neglected when the existing disease is dangerous.

Pills for Acute Bronchitis **No. 112A**

Take of Calomel .... 10 grains;
Tartarized antimony...................... 1 grain;
Dover's powder .... half a drachm;
Extract of hemlock, a sufficient quantity to mix them.

Divide into ten pills, of which one should be taken every night, or twice or thrice a day.

This is a valuable alterative soothing pill in acute bronchitis and also in dysentery and liver complaints.

Pills for Jaundice **No. 113**

Take of Socotorine aloes, rhubarb, in powder,
and Castile soap, of each .... 1 drachm;
Oil of juniper .... 15 drops.
Make them into a mass with a little syrup, or mucilage of gum arabic and divide it into forty pills.

Two of these pills may be taken twice or thrice a day. They are sometimes of great service in jaundice, bilious affections, costiveness and obstructions in the digestive organs.

Pills for Red Gravel **No. 114**

Take of Dried subcarbonate of soda .... 1´ drachm;
Compound powder of cinnamon .... half a drachm;
Castile soap .... half a drachm;
Balsam of Peru, a sufficient quantity to form the whole into a mass, to be divided into thirty pills.

Three of these pills may be taken thrice a day, *in red* gravel and stone, with much advantage.

Anthony White's Gout Pill **No. 114A**

Take of Calomel, acetic extract of colchicum, purified extract of aloes, ipecacuanha powder, of each .... 6 grains.

Mix them and by means of mucilage of gum arabic, or confection of roses, divide the mass into six pills, of which take one every four or six hours, until they act freely on the bowel and relief of pain is obtained.

This is a suitable and useful pill to take when threatened with gout, or at the commencement of a fit of it. But when it has operated well and relief of pain is obtained, then it should be discontinued and Scudamore's draught of magnesia, Epsom salt, etc., No. 80, p. 182, recommended under Gout, be taken every other morning. This pill of White's is designed to unload the bowels, improve the intestinal and biliary secretions and at the same time to relieve pain and determine to the skin. In all cases, when the pain has been relieved, this hill should be discontinued.

Pills for Ague **No. 115**

Take of sulphate of quinine 1drachm;

Extract of gentian, sufficient to divide it into thirty pills.

One of these pills taken every third, fourth or fifth hour, will prove in general a certain cure for the ague, unless some internal obstruction prevent it. They are also a valuable tonic in many cases of general debility.

Pills for Cardiac Dropsy **No. 116**

Take of Calomel .... 20 or 30 grains;

Tartar emetic .... 2 grains;

Compound squill pill .... 1 drachm;

Opium, in powder .... 3 grains;

Oil of juniper, a sufficient quantity to make the whole into a mass, which is to be divided into twenty pills.

The ingredients must be well rubbed together in a mortar before the oil is added.

One pill may be taken in dropsy thrice a day, until the symptoms permanently give way, when they should be taken less frequently. They form an invaluable remedy in every variety of dropsy, not arising from disease of the kidneys.

Plummer's Pills No. 117

Take of Calomel	20	grains;
Precipitated sulphuret of antimony	20	grains;
Gum guaiacum, in powder	2	scruples.

Rub them well together in a mortar for ten minutes and, with a little conserve of hips, divide them into twenty pills.

These are valuable alterative pills, first recommended by Dr. Plummer, a respectable physician in Scotland, for the cure of diseased joints, bilious complaints and many other chronic maladies, in which they are certainly an appropriate and efficacious remedy. The dose is one every night.

Diuretic Pills No. 118

Take of Blue pill		half a drachm;
Squill, in powder	1	scruple;

Conserve of roses, a sufficient quantity to divide them into twenty pills.

One of these pills may be taken every sip hours in dropsy of the belly; and general dropsy, not owing to kidney disease.

Sir H. Halford's Aperient Pills No. 119

Take of Blue pill	20	grains;
Compound extract of colocynth	30	grains;
Oil of cloves	2	drops.

Mix and divide into one dozen pills.

One or two of these pills taken for a dose, every second or third night, or as occasion requires, will act as a mild and effectual aperient. If taken regularly three times a week, for three or four weeks, in such, quantities as keep the bowels gently open without purging, they will frequently prove a valuable alterative medicine of great service in indigestion, bilious and nervous disorders and other chronic maladies.

Pills for Hooping-Cough **No. 119A**

Take of Ipecacuanha powder, rhubarb powder,
of each . . . . 12 grains
Extract of hemlock, sufficient to make them into twelve pills.

Take one of them three or four times a day, or the powders may be made into twelve powders and given in jelly.

This is a very useful pill in hooping cough and may be used at all stages of this complaint and in all ages. For infants give only one-fourth the quantity in powder.

POWDERS

This is the simplest form of administering medicines; but those remedies which are very unpleasant to the taste; those which deliquesce rapidly when exposed to the air, or are very volatile and those which require to be given in large doses, or which are not diffused readily in water, cannot with propriety be administered in the form of powder.

Generally speaking, a fine impalpable powder, is preferred for those substances which are exhibited in this form; but Peruvian bark, rhubarb, ipecacuanha and guaiacum, operate more powerfully in the state of coarse powder.

As powders are generally affected by the action of the air and light, they should be kept in opaque or green glass bottles; a practice not sufficiently adhered to either by druggists or apothecaries.

The lighter powders, such as powder of bark, rhubarb, etc. may be taken in any agreeable thin liquor, as tea, or watergruel.

The more ponderous, such as calomel, antimony and other mineral preparations, will require a more consistent vehicle, as thick syrup, jelly or honey.

Purgative Powder **No. 120**

Take of Calomel	2	grains;
Compound powder of jalap	1	scruple.

Mix them.

This may be taken in gruel or barley water, or treacle. It is a useful purgative for ordinary purposes.

Aperient Powder for Children **No. 121**

Take of Rhubarb, in powder	6	or 8 grains
Super-sulphate of potash	10	grains.

Mix them and give it in a little water.

This is a mild and efficacious aperient for children and adults. It is of great service in the enlarged bellies and bilious disorders of children, to whom it may be given in such cases every other morning, until the disease be overcome. Sir William Fordyce was very partial to its use in the disorders of children and infants; and it would be well if mothers, who are fond of administering calomel to their tender offspring on all ordinary occasions, were to lay it aside for this more mild and suitable formula. *Gregory's Powder* is an excellent aperient for children, given in water.

Gregory's Powder **No. 121A**

Take of Turkey rhubarb, in powder.........	2	drachms;
Calcined magnesia.......................	2	drachms;
Ginger, in powder	7	grains;
Cinnamon powder	15	grains.

Mix them well together.

This is very similar to the celebrated Gregory's Powder and is a composition which I would strongly recommend, in the dose of half a tea-spoonful, as a useful aperient for ordinary domestic purposes. It is also an excellent aperient in gout.

Worm Powder **No. 122**

Take of Calomel .... 2 or 3 grains;
Compound powder of scammony .... 10 grains.
Rub them well together and take it in treacle.

This is an efficacious powder for the expulsion of worms from children and adults and it may be repeated twice a week, or oftener, till the object be accomplished.

Emetic Powder **No. 123**

Take of Ipecacuanha, in powder .... 15 grains;
Emetic tartar .... 1 grain.
Mix them.

Proper for adults on ordinary occasions, taken in Water.

Fever Powder **No. 124**

Take of James's powder .... 4 grains;
Calomel .... ¼ of a grain;
Compound powder of tragacanth .... 6 grains.
Mix them.

This is a valuable diaphoretic cooling powder in the commencement of inflammatory and typhus fever, measles, smallpox and other febrile affections, after the stomach and bowels have been emptied by an emetic and purgative.

Diaphoretic Camphor Powder **No. 124A**

The prescription for an excellent diaphoretic powder, which is extensively used in the York County Hospital, is the following :

Take of Nitrate of potash . . . . 4 drachms;
Dover's powder . . . . 2 drachms;
Camphor . . . . 1 drachm;

The camphor, pounded in the usual manner, is mixed with the other ingredients. The dose is from ten grains to a scruple taken at bed-time in gruel, to produce perspiration and about eight grains to relieve pain.

This powder has long been a favorite remedy with Dr. Simpson, of York; and I would recommend it as a valuable diaphoretic in all cases to which Dover's powder is applicable. In many cases of diarrhoea, dysentery and fever, it will be found more efficacious than even Dover's powder. Whenever pain and irritation in the chest, abdomen, head, or limbs are severe, especially if accompanied with fever, ten grains of this powder in gruel is an admirable remedy. It may be repeated once or twice a day, according to the severity of the pain.

Powder for Rheumatism **No. 125**

Take of Peruvian bark, in powder . . . . half a drachm;
Sesqui-carbonate of ammonia . . . . 7 grains.

Mix them; to be taken in a wane-glassful of water.

This is often of eminent utility in acute rheumatism, after the exhibition of alkalies and purgatives. It is also sometimes very beneficially employed in chronic rheumatic pains and swellings. It may be repeated thrice a day.

Diuretic Powder **No. 126**

Take of Cream of tartar 1drachm;
Dried squill, in powder 1grains;
Ginger powder . . . . 4grains.

Mix then.

Proper in dropsy of the belly and also in general dropsy.

Astringent Powder **No. 127**

Take of Tormentil rout, in powder	half a drachm, or more.
Ipecacuanha, in powder	1 grain.

Mix them.

This is a mild and effectual astringent, which is beneficially employed in diarrhoea and dysentery and may be repeated after every liquid stool. Unlike the ordinary astringents, it does not prove stimulant; and is, therefore, particularly indicated in the looseness attendant on pulmonary consumption and wherever fever is present. Mix it in a little cinnamon or common water.

Chalk Powder for Diarrhoea **No. 128**

Take of Compound powder of ipecacuanha ..	3 grains;
Compound powder of chalk	1 scruple.

Mix them.

Another astringent powder of great value in looseness and flux. it tends to relax the skin at the same time that it astringes the bowels and is effectually employed to allay pain in such diseases. Take it in cinnamon water, or common water and repeat it after every liquid stool.

Anodyne Diaphoretic Powder **No. 129**

Take of James's powder	3 grains;
Sesqui-carbonate of ammonia	5 grains;
Compound powder of ipecacuanha	8 grains.

Mix them.

This is very useful to allay pain and procure sleep, in gout, rheumatism and in the majority of diseases. It may be taken, in a little jelly and be repeated every four hours, if necessary.

Tonic Powder **No. 130**

Take of peruvian bark, in powder	2 scruples;

Ipecacuanha, in powder		half a grain;
Compound powder of ciunamon	8	grains.

Mix them.

A useful strengthening powder in all cases in which bark is admissible. It is an eligible mode of taking that remedy for the cure of ague.

Saline Soothing Powder **No. 130A**

Take of Cream of tartar	2	scruples;
Sulphate of potash	2	scruples ;
Nitrate of potash	6	grains;
Camphor	3	grains.

Mix theta and take it twice a day, in half a tumblerful of water. It is extremely valuable as a common domestic remedy in feverishness with irritability and costiveness.

Powder for Impurities in the Blood **No. 130B**

Take of Epsom, salt, cream of tartar, precipitated sulphur, of each .... 1 ounce.

Mix them and put them into a wine-bottle, fill it with warm water and shake them well together. Take a wine-glassful every morning fasting.

This is a valuable alterative, of eminent service in all bloody discharges from the stomach, intestines or lungs and also in every kind of eruption on the shin.

PLASTERS

These are solid tenacious compounds, adhesive in the ordinary heat of the body. The base of the majority of plasters is a chemical combination of the semi-vitreous oxide of lead and oil; but some of them owe their consistence to wax and resin and others contain no oily nor fatty matter whatsoever.

Warm Plaster **No. 131**

Take of Blistering plaster.................	1	part;
Burgundy pitch	14	parts.

Melt them together with a moderate heat and mix them so as to form a plaster.

This plaster is stimulant and creates a slight, irritation on that part of the skin to which it is applied. It is used with advantage in common cough, hooping-cough, sciatica and local pain.

Resolvent Plaster **No. 132**

Take of Purified ammoniac	1	pound;
Purified mercury	3	ounces;
Sulphureted oil, ...	1	fluid drachm.

Rub the mercury with the sulphureted oil until the globules disappear; then add gradually the ammonite previously melted, and mix the whole together.

This is one of the most powerful plasters now known for promoting the absorption of glandular and other herd swellings. It is applicable to almost all hard indolent tumours; but perseverance in its use is absolutely necessary in order to obtain its full effect. It is a useful application to corns and bunion and is sold in the shops ready mixed, under the title of plaster of ammoniac with mercury.

Cumin Plaster **No. 133**

Take of Cumin seeds, carraway seeds, laurel
berries, of each........................ 3ounces;
Dried pitch 3pounds;
Yellow wax .... 3ounces.

Melt the pitch and the wax together; then add the ether ingredients in powder and mix.

This is a stimulant and discutient plaster, frequently applied to the lower part of the abdomen in flatulence and a cold feeling of the bowels and likewise to indolent tumours.

Adhesive Plaster **No 134**

Take of Yellow resin	half a pound;
Lead plaster	3 pounds;

Melt the lead plaster by a gentle heat, then add the resin in powder and mid.

This is the plaster commonly applied to cuts and to retain together the lips of recent wounds. It is also of very great service in old and indolent ulcers, to which it affords a proper support and thus relieves the sensations of weakness and pain and promotes their healing. In these cases, the plaster spread on calico should be cut into strips of two inches wide and fifteen or sixteen inches long, which are to go completely round the limb and such a number of strips applied as will cover the ulcer or ulcers and an inch or two of the surface both above and below them. They must be applied rather tightly and should be renewed every four or five days. It is sold in the shops ready spread.

Tarratt's Bandage and Strengthening Plaster **No. 134A**

This plaster from the nature of the composition and the material on which it is spread, is adapted for a permanent bandage, as it neither produces irritation of the skin, nor, when applied, does heat cause it to lose its adaptation to the part. Having these qualities, it is peculiarly valuable in the treatment of ulcerated legs, varicose veins, etc., where equal and constant support is required. Several of the most eminent surgeons continue to use this plaster in their practice, preferring it in certain cases to any other. It is well suited for exportation and use in warm climates, the high temperature having less effect on it than on any other plaster.

At Messrs. Westwoods and Hopkins, Wholesale Druggists, New gate-street, the plaster may be had in packets containing three yards, for 2s. 6d., or spread upon skins of chamois leather, at 3s. 6d.

Anodyne Plaster No. 135

Take of hard opium, powdered		half an ounce;
Resin of spruce fir, powdered	3	ounces;
Lead plaster	1	pound.

Melt the plaster and the resin together, then add the opium and mix the whole.

This plaster has some effect in relieving rheumatic and other local pains, in different parts of the body.

Plaster for Cough No. 136

Take of Castile soap	1	ounce ;
Lead plaster	2	drachms;
Sal ammoniac, finely powdered, ...		

half a drachm or a drachm.

Melt the soap and lead plaster together and when the mixture is nearly cold, add the sal ammoniac.

This is to be spread on leather and applied to the chest immediately after it is spread. It must be renewed every twenty-four hours, otherwise the intention is lost.

It is sometimes of much service in hooping-cough, asthmatic; and consumptive coughs, etc., and is certainly superior to a plaster of Burgundy pitch.

Blistering Plaster No. 137

A blistering plaster requires to remain applied for eight hours at least and sometimes longer, to raise a perfect blister; it is then to be removed, the vesicles are to be cut at the most depending part and without removing the skin, the blistered part is to be dressed with simple cerate, or spermaceti ointment, spread on lint; and the whole skin allowed to remain until a new one is formed under it, when it peels off and the whole is healed in the course of a few days. The application of blisters, however, is sometimes attended with strangury and bloody urine, which arises from the active principles of the insect being absorbed and irritating the kidneys and urinary passage. This effect is very much increased if the blister be applied over an abraded surface; and it also occurs if the plaster remain too long applied. These unpleasant effects are most effectually obviated by the patient drinking freely of diluting drinks, such as compound barley water, linseed tea and emulsion of gum arabic and by fomenting the blistered part with warm milk and water, after the removal of the plaster. When we intend to blister the head, it should be shaved ten or twelve hours before the plaster is applied.

Mr. Garden, of Oxford Street, prepares an *Acetum Lyttoe,* which is a liquid, a little of which, laid on the part to be blistered by means of a camel-hair pencil, readily raises a blister. This is a very clean and convenient method of blistering.

In some diseases of irritation, particularly in children, the blistered part, instead of healing kindly, becomes a spreading sore; the true skin is destroyed and the part cannot be healed until the irritability of habit which induced this unpleasant state is allayed. In such cases, a warm bread and milk poultice should be applied, the denuded surface being frequently bathed with tepid milk and water; while at the same time Peruvian bark is internally administered.

In children, especially if young, let the blister remain on only four hours; then cover it with thin tissue paper and it will subsequently rise without any risk being incurred of excessive irritation, or use one of the next blisters.

Albespeyres' Blister **No. 137A**

Albespeyres' Blister, applied with the black side, which is adhesive, to the skin, produces a blister in six or eight hours whilst the usual blaster frequently requires twenty-four hours.

It is sold by Warrick Brothers, 3, Garlick-hill, London.

Brown's Blistering Tissue **No. 137B**

Brown's Blistering Tissue, prepared from pure cantharides, is an elegant preparation, vesicating in much less time than the common blistering plaster, easily applied and removed and will not produce strangury or troublesome after-sores. It has received the sanction and commendation of many of the most eminent practitioners in the kingdom.

Brown's Tissue Dressing is an elegant, economical and cleanly substitute for all ointments as a dressing for blisters, burns, etc. and may be called a companion to the above.

It is sold by all Wholesale and Retail Druggists and Medicine Agents throughout the British Empire.

Strengthening Plaster **No. 138**

Take of Litharge plaster	24	parts;
White resin	6	parts;
Yellow wax, olive oil, of each	3	parts;
Red oxide of iron	8	parts.

Rub the red oxide of iron with the oil and adding the other ingredients melted, mix the whole well together.

This plaster is applied with advantage in cases of muscular relaxation and weakness of the joints from sprains, bruises or other causes.

Corn Plaster **No. 139**

Take of Purified ammoniac, yellow wax, of each	2	ounces;
Acetate of copper	6	drachms.

Melt the two first ingredients together and after removing them from the fire, add the verdigris just before they grow cold.

Spread the plaster on some soft leather, or a piece of linen; very carefully pare away as much of the corn with a knife as may be done, before the plaster is applied, which must be renewed in a fortnight, if the corn be not at that time gone. Mr. Samuel Cooper, in his Surgical *Dictionary,* states this to be "infallible."

SYRUPS

Syrups seldom possess much activity as medicines and are chiefly employed to render more active remedies palatable. I shall, therefore, notice only three or four that are most useful in domestic practice.

Simple Syrup is made by boiling two pounds and a half of refined sugar in a pint of water, until the sugar is perfectly dissolved, when it should be set aside for twenty-four hours, the scum then removed and the clear syrup poured off. It is used to sweeten various remedies.

Syrup of Opium, of a superior kind, may be made by mixing twenty drops of Battley's Sedative Liquor of Opium with an ounce of simple syrup. This is a useful anodyne for allaying the irritation which keeps up the cough in recent cold, after the inflammatory symptoms are abated and for easing pain and procuring sleep, in the diseases of children and delicate women. It is also of great service in some forms of chronic asthma and habitual cough. To allay the irritation of coughing in adults, the dose is one or two tea-spoonfuls taken occasionally; and to procure sleep or ease pain, one or two table-spoonfuls, or more. One third or fourth of these quantities is sufficient for children.

Syrup of Senna is made by allowing two ounces of senna leaves, and an ounce of fennel seeds bruised, to digest in a pint of boiling water for twelve hours; then strain the liquor, mix with it three ounces of manna and a pound of refined sugar and boil them to a proper consistence.

This is a useful and convenient purgative for children, in doses of three tea-spoonfuls. A still more valuable aperient, both for adults and children, is *Smith's Essence of Senna,* sold by all druggists.

Cough Syrup — No. 139A

Take of Oxymel of squills	1 ounce;
Ipecacuanha wine	1 drachm;
Syrup of roses	half an ounce.

Mix. One or two tea-spoonfuls when cough is troublesome.

TINCTURES

Tinctures are spirituous solutions of such of the principles of vegetable and animal substances as are soluble in rectified or proof spirit of wine. Rectified spirit is required in a very few instances only for the formation of tinctures, proof spirit, which is rectified spirit reduced in strength by the addition of water, being adequate for almost every purpose. They are prepared by macerating the ingredients in the spirit in a temperature not exceeding 80 degrees, at which degree, by allowing the menstruum to remain on the ingredients for a sufficient length of time, all the principles that can prove useful in the tincture are extracted and the solvent saturated. The ingredients must be dried and reduced to a coarse powder and the maceration made in close vessels and assisted by frequent agitation. When completely made, tinctures should not be allowed to remain upon the ingredients, but be filtered through bibulous paper and kept in this state in well-corked bottles.

Ethereal Tincture of Aloes — No. 140

Take of Socotorine aloes, myrrh, of each
in powder .... 1½ ounce;
English saffron, cut .... 1 ounce;
Sulphuric ether, with alcohol .... 1 pint.

Digest the myrrh with the ether for four days in a closed bottle; then add the saffron and the aloes. Digest again for four days and when the dregs have subsided, pour off the tincture.

This is a warm and grateful stomachic and purgative and is beneficially employed in indigestion, bilious affections, jaundice, gout, green-sickness and other cases in which aloes are indicated. The ethereal spirit with which it is made renders it very grateful and peculiarly useful in the above disorders when attended with spasm. In doses of a drachm twice or thrice a day, in any agreeable vehicle, it acts chiefly as a stomachic and mild aperient; but purges briskly in larger doses.

COMPOUND TINCTURE OF BENJAMIN

See **Friar's Balsam**

Compound Tincture of Bark — No. 141

Take of Lance-leaved Peruvian bark, powdered	2	ounces;
Dried orange peel	1½	ounce;
Virginian snake-root, bruised	3	drachms;
Saffron	1	drachm ;
Cochineal, in powder	2	scruples;
Proof spirit	20	flind ounces.

Macerate for fourteen days and filter.

This is the same as the celebrated tincture of Dr. Huxham and is a grateful stomachic and febrifuge. It is of great service in ague and low nervous fever. The dose is from one to three drachms, every two, three or four hours. It may be taken in water, or any other convenient vehicle.

Aromatic Tincture — No. 142

Is composed of cinnamon bark, cardamom seeds, long pepper, ginger root and proof spirit.

It is a warm aromatic tincture, which is beneficially employed in flatulencies, languor and gout when it attacks the stomach or chest and as an adjunct to bitter and tonic mixtures. The dose is from one to two tea-spoonfuls, taken in any agreeable vehicle. It is sold in the shops under the name *of Compound Tincture of Cinnamon.*

Bitter Tincture — No. 143

Take of Gentian root, cut	2	ounces;
Orange peel, dried	1	ounce;
Cardamom seeds, bruised		half an ounce;
Proof spirit	2	pints.

Macerate for fourteen days and filter.

This is a valuable stomachic bitter acid cordial, of great use in indigestion, bilious complaints and general weakness. The dose is the same as that of the last tincture. It is the *Compound Tincture of Gentian* of the London Pharmacopoeia.

Tincture for Rheumatism **No. 144**

Take of Guaiacum, in powder	4 ounces;
Aromatic spirit of ammonia	1½ pint.

Macerate for fourteen days and filter.

This is a stimulating sudorific and alterative and is of service in chronic rheumatism and at the termination of the acute species of this disease. It is also of much use in some cases of retention of the menses and difficult and painful menstruation. In all these complaints, it is given in doses of one or two tea-spoonfuls, twice or thrice a day, taken in the form of draught, when it must be first rubbed with a little yolk of egg, or mucilage of gum arabic and the necessary quantity of water afterwards added. It is tile Ammoniuted Tincture of Guaiacum of the shops.

Nervous Tincture **No. 145**

Take of Valerian root....................	4 ounces:
Aromatic spirit of ammonia...............	2 pints.

Macerate for fourteen days and filter.

This is the *Amoniated Tincture of Valerian* of the Pharmacopoeia, and is a very useful medicine in all nervous complaints, as languor, depression of spirits and hysterics. The dose is one or two tea-spoonfuls occasionally, taken in milk and water.

Warm Purgative Tincture **No. 146**

Take of Senna leaves	3 ounce;
Carraway seeds, bruised	3 drachms;
Cardamom seeds, bruised	1 drachm;

Raisins, stoned	4 ounces;
Best brandy	2 pints.

Macerate for fourteen mays in a gentle heat and filter.

This is quite equal to the celebrated *Daffy's Elixir* and is similar to the tincture of senna of the shops. It is stomachic and purgative and is very beneficially employed in flatulency, pains in the bowels, gouty habits, and as an opening medicine for those whose bowels have been weakened by intemperance.

The dose is from one to two or three tea-spoonfuls in water, or any agreeable vehicle.

Astringent Tincture **No. 147**

Take of Extract of catechu	3 ounces;
Cinnamon bark, bruised	2 ounces;
Proof spirit	2 pints.

Macerate for fourteen days and filter through paper.

This is a grateful warm astringent, useful in chronic looseness and flux and all cases in which astringents are indicated.

The dose is from one to two tea-spoonfuls, taken in water, or the chalk mixture of the Pharmacopoeia.

Tincture of Rhubarb **No. 148**

Take of Rhubarb root, sliced	2 ounces;
Cardamom seeds, bruised	1½ ounce;
Saffron	2 drachms;
Proof spirit	2 pints.

Macerate for fourteen days in a gentle heat and filter.

Equal quantities of this tincture and that of senna, or the ethereal tincture of aloes, in the dose of a table-spoonful in water, form a warm stomachic and aperient of great service in indigestion and lowness of spirits, in delicate and enervated habits. This combination is far better than the tincture of rhubarb alone.

Strengthening Tincture for the Weak and Nervous No. 149

Take of Compound tincture of bark .... 2 ounces;
Ammoniated tincture of valerian .... 1 ounce;
Ethereal tincture, or compound
tineture of aloes .... half an ounce.
Mix them.

This is a valuable stomachic and strengthening medicine for general debility, lowness of spirits and nervous irritability. One or two tea-spoonfuls should be taken twice or thrice a day, in milk and water.

Tincture for the Tooth-Ache No. 150

Take of Compound tincture of Benjamin and
Battley's solution of opium, of each .... half an ounce.
Mix them.

A little of this mixture dropped on cotton and applied to the hollow and along the hum, of a decayed and painful tooth, will afford great and sometimes effectual, relief.

WATERS BY INFUSION

Compound Alum Water No. 151

Take of Alum, sulphate of zinc, of each ..... half an ounce;
Boiling water .... 2 pints.
Dissolve the alum and sulphate of zinc together in the water, then filter the solution.

This is an astringent cleansing solution, which is beneficially employed as an injection in whites and as a lotion for cleansing ulcers and strengthening parts that are relaxed.

GOULARD WATER

See **page 173**

DISTILLED WATERS

Distilled waters have not much power as remedies, but are generally employed as elegant vehicles only for the exhibition of more active substances.

Cinnamon Water **No. 152**

Steep one pound of cinnamon bark, bruised, in a gallon and a half of water and one pint of brandy, for two days; and then distil off one gallon.

This is an agreeable aromatic water, possessing much of the fragrance and cordial virtues of the spice.

Peppermint Water **No. 153**

Take of Peppermint leaves .... 1½ pound;
Water, from a gallon and a half to two gallons.
Draw off by distillation one gallon.

WINES

Wine has long been used as a menstruum for extracting the active parts of medicinal vegetables; and the solutions thus formed have been denominated *Medicated Wines.* They should be kept in very well corked bottles and in a cool situation.

Wine of Colchicum **No. 154**

Digest two ounces of the unbruised seeds of colchicum in two pints of sherry wine, for eight days, then filter through blotting paper.

This is one of the best modes of exhibiting colchicum in goat, rheumatism and other inflammatory diseases. See page 39. The dose is from four to ten or even fifteen drops, taken in any agreeable vehicle; but colchicum is of little value except to relieve pain and then it should be combined with a little Epsom salt.

A table-spoonful is equal to half an ounce, by measure.

A dessert-spoonful is equal to two fluid drachms.

A ten-spoonful is equal to one fluid drachm.

A large wine-glassful is equal to two fluid ounces; and a small wine-glassful to one fluid ounce and a half.

Every household should contain a graduated four-ounce glass measure and a graduated minim, or drop, glass measure; and also a box of scales and weights.

MINERAL WATERS

It has been already noticed, that although no natural water is found in a state of absolute purity, yet in general the quantity of foreign matters is not sufficient to give it any, very sensible taste or odour. In some instances, however, these are so considerable and of such a nature as to prevent the water forming a part of the nourishment of animals; in which case it is denominated a *Mineral Water* and can be useful to mankind only in a medicinal point of view.

In the present day, mineral waters are generally arranged into the four following classes. 1. *Saline Purging Waters*; 2. *Chalybeate Waters*; 3. *Sulphureous Waters;* 4. *Acidulous Waters.*

Saline Mineral Waters

The *Saline Mineral Waters* owe their properties altogether to saline compounds; and as they are in the opinion of the present author, more extensively useful than any other land of mineral water, he consider them worthy of the first and chief notice. The saline ingredients which predominate and give their characters to the waters of this class, are chiefly Epsom or Glauber's salt, common salt, muriate of magnesia and carbonate of soda.

The most celebrated saline purging springs are those of Cheltenham and Leamington, in England; Landrindod Wells, in Wales; Pitcaithly, in Scotland; and Seidlitz, on the Continent. They are employed in diseases which require continued and moderate intestinal evacuations; such as indigestion, bilious and liver complaints, low spirits, jaundice, scrophulous swellings and many anomalous cases of internal obstruction. The bowers of the salts they contain are very much increased and modified by the large quantity of water in which they are exhibited and they, therefore, operate mildly and effectually on the bowels, promoting a considerable discharge from their internal surface and stimulating the whole of the digestive organs to a more healthy action, without inducing debility. At least, though they may purge briskly, yet they never occasion debility, even in constitutions enervated by previous disease, if they are suited to the case; and should their use weapon the patient, that circumstance is a sufficient proof that they are unsuitable and ought to be discontinued. In those instances of indigestion and bilious complaints accompanied with constipation and where the stomach retains a good measure of strength, these waters will often be of more service than almost any other remedy; but if there be real and primary debility of the stomach, they will generally do more harm than good. Cutaneous eruptions and nervous disorders frequently originate in disorder and obstruction of the digestive organs, in which case they are also taken with great and sometimes surprising, advantage.

The Cheltenham and Leamington waters require no preparation; but the proper quantity differs in different cases and can, for the most part, be known only by experience. The physicians practising in those towns almost invariably recommend a pint or two of the water to be taken every morning at two draughts, with an interval of half an hour between each, which time the patient is to spend in walking. This is to be continued for a fortnight or three weeks, when the water is directed to be discontinued for about a fortnight and then resumed in the same manner and for the same period as before. This plan will answer in many instances, but some patients will find greater advantage from taking half a pint, or even less, for a month or two without intermission, as in this dose it may be sufficiently active as an aperient, will frequently agree better with the stomach and bowels and prove a more certain and effectual alterative than when taken in larger quantities, with a long interval, as in the first plan. The best time for drinking these waters is in the summer; but there is no reason why a sick man should not take them at any season, if they promise him benefit.

It should never be forgotten by those suffering from obstinate chronic complaints, that diseases slow in their progress go off also very slowly; and that, according to the judicious remark of *celsus,* time is necessary to remove the deep-rooted evils which time has occasioned. Many individuals fail to receive from these waters all the benefit which they are able to afford them, from want of patience and perseverance.

The waters of *Llandrindod Wells,* near *Builth,* in *Radnorshire,* are of eminent utility in the treatment of chronic disease. They have been found of singular efficacy in liver complaints, paralysis, deranged general health and many other disorders. They are worthy of my strongest recommendation.

The water of Pitcaithly and Seidlitz has very nearly the same effect as that at Cheltenham and Leamington and is consequently useful in the same diseases.

Chalybeate Waters

Chalybeate Waters are so called from a Greek word, signifying iron, the taste of which is very perceptible in them when fresh from the spring, though they lose it on being exposed for solve time to the atmosphere. The reason of this is that the small portion of iron which they contain being kept in solution by *fixed air, or carbonic acid gas,* when this evaporates, the iron sinks to the bottom, forming the fine ochre that lines the channel or water-course. If the iron be in the state of sulphate, however, no sediment falls; and the black colour following the addition of the tincture of nut-galls is produced, even after the water has been boiled and filtered. Iron abounds in almost every part of the earth and there are, therefore, many clralybeates in Great Britain; but the most celebrated are Tunbridge, Brighton and Peterhead. The Spa springs also belong to this class. If I mistake not, the Brighton chalybeate is the strongest in this kingdom, but that of Tunbridge is the most celebrated. There is also a spring of this kind at Cheltenham and at Hartfell, near Moffat, in North Britain.

The water of Tunbridge Wells is found, upon analysis, to differ from that of common springs only by containing in every gallon a grain of iron, suspended by about three table-spoonfuls of fixed air, or carbonic acid gas. Yet its medicinal effects are sometimes very considerable. Through its operation oil the stomach, it gives a gentle stimulus to the relaxed nerves and muscles and contributes to restore their proper tone. It affords great relief in indigestion and other complaints of the stomach, especially when there is real debility of that organ; in flatulencies, bilious vomitings, scrophula and other consequences either of debility or intem-perance. It promotes the circulation of the blood and the various secretions, but more particularly that of urine; and this latter circumstance is one of the best proofs of its agreeing with the habit of the patient. In short, its natural tendency in the cases to which its stimulant and tonic powers are adapted, is to raise the spirits and increase the general vigour of the functions.

The Tunbridge waters are eminently serviceable in the disorders peculiar to females, arising from great weakness or derangement of the uterine system; such as an immoderate flow of the *menses,* green sickness, whites and other similar indispo-sitions, which are not only relaxing and painful in themselves, but are often the causes of abortion, or of sterility. If, however, the profuse flow of the *menses* occur in strong, full habits and is accompanied by feverish symptoms, pain in the back and local irritation, the stimulus of the waters will most likely prove injurious. Indeed, in all cases of disease, chalybeate waters, are for the most part, adapted to the care only of such as occur in delicate persons, of a thin habit and pale complexion, they being very generally improper in all inflammatory cases.

In all obstructions of the urinary passages and other complaints of that region, as seminal weakness, mucous discharges, etc., these waters are frequently found of singular efficacy; and they may he prescribed with great probability of success in such chronic disorders as arise from slow beginnings and are attended with great laxity and weakness of the solids, but without much organic disease.

Some caution is necessary in using these waters. Persons of rather a full habit should take one or two active purges before commencing with the chalybeate water; and when the stomach is foul, either a purgative or an emetic should be previously exhibited. What the immediate effect of the waters may be, can only be known by a trial. They often purge very briskly at first, but this effect soon ceases; and as their continued use has some tendency to occasion costiveness, gentle opening medicines from time to time are necessary. Sometimes giddiness, a heaviness of the head, nausea, vomiting, or a sense of fulness over the whole body, will be felt on beginning the course; but they will disappear after a short time. It is only when they stubbornly continue, that they should be regarded as a proof that the waters are not suited to the nature of the complaint, or to the patient's constitution. The nausea, or sickness being often occasioned by the coldness of the fresh-drawn water, acting on an empty, or a very weak and irritable stomach, it is advisable, in the first instance, not to drink it fasting, till the stomach becomes gradually reconciled to it; and in case of extreme irritability, it is a common and judicious practice at Tunbridge, to immerse in hot water a bottle filled with the chalybeate and well corked, that the chilliness may be diminished with as little evaporation of the fixed air as possible.

As all the spa waters are chalybeate, they are of coarse useful in the same diseases as those at Tunbridge and should be taken in the same manner.

Sulphureous Waters

Sulphureous Waters derive their character chiefly from sulphureted hydrogen gas; which in some of them is uncombined, while is others it is united with lime or an alkali. They are transparent, when newly drawn from the spring and have the foetid odour of rotten eggs, which is gradually lost from exposure to the air and the water becomes turbid. They generally contain muriate of magnesia, or other saline matters, which modify their powers as a remedy.

The most important sulphureous springs in this island are those of Harrowgate Kilburn and Moffat; on the Continent, Aix-la-Chapelle and Barege.

They are resorted to chiefly for the cure of cutaneous eruptions, chronic rheumatism, scrophulous obstructions, hypo-chondriasis or low spirits, costiveness and piles. But being a powerful, yet mild alterative, they are frequently of the greatest service in every kind of internal obstruction and chronic disease, since they gently move the bowels, determine to the surface of the body, promote the excretion of urine and strengthen the digestive organs. They operate more mildly than the best mercurial alteratives and will frequently cure obstinate chronic maladies, which have resisted the use of mercury.

Those who wish for the cure of any obstinate disease from the use of the Harrowgate, or any other sulphureous water, ought to take it in such a manner as to produce a daily exoneration of the bowelș without purging. With this view, a half-pint glass may be drank at bed-time and the same quantity an hour before breakfast and dinner. The dose, however, must vary according to circumstances. Even the quantity just mentioned will purge some persons, in which case it should be lessened, while others will drink twice as much without being in the least moved by it. Its operation on the bowels is the only standard for using the water as an alterative. In those few cases where the water is intended to purge, in consequence of the patient's complaint requiring a strong determination to the bowels, it may be necessary to drink a pint or two before breakfast.

When they purge, they do not irritate the nerves, or weaken the patient so much as other purgatives. At first, they are very nauseous to the taste, but after a little use they, at least to many persons, become much less so.

During the course of these waters, full, heavy meals and especially hearty suppers, must be carefully avoided. The stimulus of water impregnated with sulphur and salts often increases the desire for food, arid in some pleasure creates a false appetite; but this craving appetite cannot be satisfied without great injury and inconvenience to the patient. The proper diet in these cases is one of a light, nourishing and rather diluting description. Gentle exercise should be taken at the same time, either on foot, or horseback and agreeable company and conversation are highly advisable. Exercise promotes the operation of the waters and carries them through the system; and every thing that tends to exhilarate the spirits, not only increases the efficacy of the waters, but acts as a medicine.

The Harrowgate waters are used externally as well as internally and in this manner are considered a powerful auxiliary in many of the disorders for which they are resorted to, particularly in cutaneous eruptions. There are proper baths for this purpose, for the supply of which three springs out of four are devoted; that which is reserved for drinking being more strongly impregnated with salt and sulphur than the rest.

The sulphureous waters at Moffat, in North Britain, are almost as much resorted to as those of Harrowgate, but are not so strongly impregnated. Both these waters are cold, but those of Aix-la-Chapelle and Barege are hot, which in some instances gives them a preference over those of Great Britain. The temperature of the waters of Aix-la-Chapelle is about 130 degrees and their celebrity is Very great and of ancient date. It appears that Charlemagne resided for a long time at Aix and took so much delight in the use of the waters, as frequently to hold lyis levee in the bath, with all his attendants.

Acidulous Waters

Acidulous Waters owe their properties chiefly to carbonic acid. They sparkle when drawn from the spring or when poured into a glass; have an acidulous taste and become vapid when exposed to the air. Besides free carbonic acid, on the presence of which these qualities depend, acidulous waters generally contain also carbonate of soda, of lime, of magnesia and of iron; and sometimes common salt. There are *warm acidulous waters* and *cold acidulous waters;* the temperature of the former, however, does not generally exceed 72 degrees, while that of the latter is about 55 degrees. There is one great exception to this rule, *viz.* the Carlsbad water, which has a temperature of about 160 degrees.

The most celebrated springs of this class are Pyrmont, Seltzer, Spa and Carlsbad. They are tonic and diuretic; and in large doses produce a sensible degree of exhilaration. They all afford a grateful and moderate stimulus to the stomach but the Pyrmont, Spa and Carlsbad, containing carbonate of iron, are especially useful in all cases of impaired digestion; while those which contain alkaline carbonates, as the Carlshbad and Seltzer are more particularly employed as palliatives in red gravel and stone.

There are other mineral waters in this kingdom which enjoy a considerable share of popularity, such as Bath, Bristol, Matlock and Buxton; but as their virtues depend almost entirely on temperature and they are as much used externally as internally and some of them more so, I shall defer adverting to their internal use till I come to detail their virtues and uses as baths.

MINERAL WATERS *are now so much resorted to, both in our own country and on the continent and are likewise so efficacious in the treatment of diseases, as to render a more extended account of them unnecessary; and since I cannot make every desirable addition to this volume, already sufficiently large, a further consideration of the subject, including a description of the* GERMAN WATERS, *will be found in my book* ON THE DISEASES OF REMALES, *third edition —and of course to all subsequent editions.*

Thwaites's (of Dublin) Mineral Waters are excellent. His Soda Water is unequalled. His town address is 147, Regent Street.

Mineral Waters may now be obtained in a portable and most agreeable form. Savory and Moore, 143, New Bond Street, have prepared in a granular and effervescent condition the constituents of the following mineral springs: Vichy Salt, granulated and effervescent; Carlsbad Salt, granulated and effervescent; Pullna Salt, granulated and effervescent; Seltzer Salt, granulated and effervescent; Fachingen Salt, granulated and effervescent; Kissengen Salt, granulated and effervescent; Marienbad Salt, granulated and effervescent; Cheltenham Salt, granulated and effervescent.

COLD AND WARM BATHING

This important branch of physic is of excellent use and efficacy, both in the prevention and cure of diseases. Though the ancients could less dispense with the use of the bath, an account of the frequency of their athletic exercises, as well as from the want of linen, which was then much less in use than at present, yet in our times it would be of great service if the use of baths was more general and frequent and this beneficial practice not confined to particular places or seasons as a mere matter of fashion. Considered as a species of universal domestic remedy, as one which forms the basis of cleanliness, bathing, in its different forms, may be pronounced one of the most extensive and beneficial restorers of health and vigour. And they are often of the greatest service in the cure, as well as in the prevention of diseases. But their utility much depends on a clear and accurate knowledge of the properties and effects of the different baths and on their correct application to the state of the patient's constitution and the nature of his disease; and it will therefore, be necessary for me to notice the two principal classes, *viz.* the *cold* and the *warm* bath, separately.

The sick and valetudinary should remember, that the effects of bathing are not the same in all condition, of the system, but derive their character more from the varying circumstances of the patient, than from any intrinsic properties they may possess, of universal activity. Heat and cold are neither strengthening nor debilitating in themselves, but become so; merely in consequence of certain states of the body at the time of their application. The same application which in a strong person produces increase of strength, may tend immediately to debilitate the feeble; and that which is a stimulant when used with moderation, becomes rapidly destructive to vital power in an excessive dose. The uniformity of temperature in the human body is sustained entirely by the vital powers and the process appears to be carried on with the least expenditure of force, when the atmospheric air indicates sixty degrees. Every material deviation from this point, whether by increase or diminution of temperature, *if long continued,* draws equally upon the constitution and produces relaxation proportionate to the extent and duration of the cause, so that, *in this sense,* both heat and cold are directly debilitating powers to the human constitution. These facts prove that neither the cold nor warm bath should ever be resorted to by those who are in ill health, without the advice of some considerate and able professional man.

Cold Bathing

The sensible properties of the cold bath in general, consist in its power of contracting the solid parts of the body, which contraction is followed by a general reaction, indicated by a salutary glow of the whole surface. Any part of the body which is exposed to the sudden contact of cold water, experiences at the same instant a degree of tension and contraction and becomes narrower and smaller. Not only the larger blood-vessels, but likewise the small capillary tubes, are liable to this contraction and subsequent relaxation. The application of cold, when made to suitable habits and proper states of the constitution, is evidently attended with an immediate tonic effect, from the general glow which takes place through the whole body and the accompanying feeling of renewed strength, which indicates an increase of action, of a salutary nature, in all the vessels of the system; and this increased vigour of action is a test of the propriety of the application of cold and explains the manner in which it is beneficial. It shows that the nerves, blood-vessels and all the organs of the body, are excited to a more healthy and energetic performance of their functions; and when this re-action does not take place, the failure is a sufficient proof of such a weakness, or other state of body existing, as precludes the further employment of the cold bath.

Cold bathing is of the greatest service in most disorders originating in, or connected with, simple weakness and relaxation, that is, in debility unaccompanied with any disease of structure or positive injury in any important organ. In the scrophulous complaints and general weakness of children, in the debility and languor following fever, intense study, sedentary occupation, grief, or debauchery, it is often employed with the best effects, since the debility in those cases directly arises, for the most part, from unhealthy habits, depression passions, or the long continuance of a feverish action, when the cautious application of cold proves bracing and very salutary. But in case of positive injury to the structure of some important organ, the employment of cold water is sometimes improper; it may be too great a shock to the system and the diseased part and the patient be then benefited only by the use of warm bathing. Indeed, in complaints which call for the use of the cold bath, it is generally an excellent practice for the patient to commence with tepid bathing, at about 90 or 93 degrees, which he may resort to three or four times or more for the first week or two and then try the cold bath. This is particularly advisable where the weakness of the patient is extreme, or the causes of the debility have been a long time in operation.

Whatever may be the disease for which it is resorted to, every cold bath applied to the whole body ought to be of short duration, since all depends upon the first impression the cold makes on the skin and nerves. The head should be always first wetted, either by immersion or by pouring water upon it. The immersion ought always to be sudden, not only because it is less felt than when we enter the water slowly and timorously, but likewise because the effect of the first impression is uniform all over the body and the blood in this manner is not propelled from the lower to the upper parts. Hence the shower bath possesses greater advantages, as it pours the water suddenly upon the whole body and thus in the most perfect manner fulfils the three rules above specified. Gentle exercise ought to precede the cold bath, to produce some re-action of the vascular system on coming out of it, for neither complete rest nor violent exercise are proper, previous to the use of this remedy.

The morning or forenoon is the most proper time for cold bathing; and while in the water the bather should not remain inactive but move about in order to promote the circulation of the blood from the centre of the body to the extremities. After immersion the whole body ought to be wiped quickly with a dry and rough towel and moderate exercise in the open air is proper and indeed necessary.

In the following cases the cold bath is altogether inadmissible : 1. In a general plethora, or full habit of body and in the febrile disposition which attends it. 2. In active haemorrhages, or fluxes of blood, that is, bleedings, attended with a quick, hard, full pulse. and other signs of an inflammatory tendency. 3. In every kind of acute inflammation. 4. In diseases of the breast, difficult breathing and short and dry coughs. 5. In gouty and rheumatic paroxysms. 6. In most diseases of the skin. 7. In a state of pregnancy. 8. In palsy. In liver complaint also it may prove hurtful, if its effects are not carefully watched; and wherever it occasions chilliness, loss of appetite, languor, pain of the breast or bowels, or violent head-aches it ought to be discontinued. These unpleasant sensations are the surest proofs, that the actual state of the patient's habit is unfit to bear the shock; and that either the re-action of the heart and arteries is too weak to overcome the cold pressure on the surface, or that tire determination to the head, or some other vital part, is too rapidly increased.

The common method of cold bathing is in the sea, or a river; but in many instances the shower bath, or a free ablution with a sponge, or the roughest towel dipped in the water, merits a decided preference and this is especially the case where there is a determination of the fluids to the head. Although the shower bath does not cover the surface of the body so universally as the usual cold baths, this circumstance is rather favourable than otherwise, for those parts which the water has not touched, feel the impression by sympathy, almost as much as those in actual contact with it. Every drop of water becomes a partial cold bath in miniature and thus a stronger impression is excited than by any other mode of bathing. The shower bath, for the following reasons, possesses advantages superior to most others : 1. The sudden contact of the water, which in the common bath is only momentary, may here be prolonged, repented and modified at pleasure. 2. The head and breast, which are exposed to some inconvenience and danger in the common bath, are here effectually secured, by receiving the first shock of the water; the blood is consequently impelled to the lower parts of the body and the patient feels no obstruction in breathin, or undulations of blood towards the head. 3. The heavy pressure on the body, occasioned by the weight of the water and the free circulation of the blood in the parts touched by it, being, for some tine at least, interrupted, is an unfavourable circumstance in certain instances. The shower bath, on the contrary, descends in single drops, which are at once more stimulating and pleasant than the immersion into cold water and it can be more readily procured and more easily modified and adapted to the circumstances of the patient.

A proper apparatus for giving the shower bath is to be had at the tin shops, but where a saving of expense is an object, it may be effectually supplied by the following easy expedient: Fill a common watering pot with cold water, let the patient sit down undressed upon a stool, which may be placed m a large tub; and let the hair, if not cut short, be spread over the shoulders as loosely as possible; then pour the water from the pot over the patient's head, face, neck and shoulders and all parts of the body down to the feet, till the whole has been thoroughly bathed. Let him next be rubbed dry and take exercise, as has been already recom-mended, till the sensation of cold be succeeded by a gentle glow all over him.

When this kind of bath is first resorted to, it may be used gently and with water having some degree of warmth, so as not to make tire shock too great; but as the patient becomes accustomed to it, tire degree of cold may be increased and the water may be allowed to fall from a greater height, so as to make the shower heavier.

A new portable shower bath, called *ombrosome,* has lately been invented, which is extremely convenient and answers well. It may be procured from Howard and Co., of London and is worthy the attention of travellers.

The external use of cold water is often of singular benefit in tire commencement of fever,, in sprains, old swellings and rigidity of particular parts, in which cases it may be applied directly to the affected part and its employment continued for almost any length of time. This subject—*the use of cold water as a remedy .for disease*—has lately attracted the attention of our countrymen and cold water is in my opinion so valuable an auxiliary as to merit a distinct notice at the end of this volume.

Before quitting this subject, I would make a few remarks upon the impropriety of plunging into the cold bath after the body has been greatly heated by exercise. In the earlier stages of exercise, before profuse perspiration has dissipated the heat and fatigue debilitated the living power, the cold bath is generally safe and useful; on the contrary, nothing is more dangerous than for a person to go into the cold bath some time after exercise has produced great perspiration and terminated in languor and fatigue. The reason of this is sufficiently obvious. In the first case, the exercise is short of fatigue, being just such as produces an increased action of the vascular system, with some increase of heat and thus secures a force of re-action under the shock with corresponding benefit. In the second instance, where the person waits till he is perfectly cooled and some degree of languor follows as a necessary consequence, the heat is not only sinking rapidly, but the system parts more easily with the portion that remains and on plunging into cold water, a sudden chilliness is felt which is alarming and extremely dangerous. So that were an individual compelled to go into cold water after very active exercise, he had far better go in *when hot* than *when cooling after having been heated.*

Warm Bathing

The cold bath is water at a temperature below 85 degrees; from 85 to 95 degrees is usually called the *tepid* bath and from 95 to 98 degrees it is a warm bath. When the temperature of the water exceeds 98 degrees it is a *hot* bath, which is seldom used above 105 degrees. From 100 to 130 degrees is the *vapour* bath, which degree could not be endured in the condensed state of water.

The tepid and warm baths are sedative. They excite the sensation of heat, lessen the frequency of the pulse, relax powerfully the skin and simple solids, diminish increased excitement and prove very refreshing. The hot bath is stimulant; it augments the action of the heart and arteries, renders the skin red, quickens respiration and produces a copious flow of sweat. The effects of the vapour bath are nearly similar, but it acts with much greater power than water in the liquid form. These effects prove that a *hot* bath would be very improper in any case of acute inflammation; though a *warm* bath might then be very serviceable.

The Tepid Bath

Is applicable to all the diseases to which the cold affusion may be applied and is generally preferred when there is any doubt of the strength being sufficient to re-at, after a cold immersion. It possesses very considerable efficacy in reducing the general excitement and in lowering and lessening the frequency of the pulse in fever; it is safe, in a high degree grateful and may be extended to almost the whole class of febrile diseases, such as typhus, scarlet fever; small pox, etc. It is of great service in pregnancy and infancy. In the former case, it induces a pliability of fibre, which by diminishing resistance; lessens the pains and danger and shortens the period of actual parturition. To those women who are liable to tedious and painful labours, it presents a resource equally efficacious and grateful, which should be resorted to for four or five months before the expiration of their time. During the time of puberty, that is, for about two years at that period, sea bathing should be avoided, both in the case of boys and girls' but the tepid bath may then be used with great advantage.

It is often of eminent utility in indigestion, bilious and liver complaints, in the debility brought on by a long residence in a hot climate, in languor and extreme weakness occurring in persons of a delicate habit, for the pains and stiffness accompanying chronic gout or rheumatism and in all cutaneous eruptions. It is likewise usefully employed as an introduction to the use of the cold bath.

The practice of pouring cold water upon the head while the body of the patient is immersed in the tepid bath, is frequently resorted to with manifest benefit in insanity and threatened apoplexy. In the latter disease, cupping and the exhibition of purgative medicine may be beneficially employed with it.

Tepid bathing is particularly indicated in old age, the chilliness, stiffness and debility of which state, it is well calculated to lessen and remove. Franklin, Darwin and other eminent philosophers, speak in high terms of the benefit they received in their advancing years, from the frequent use of the tepid bath.

The best time of using it is in the morning, any time between ten and one o'clock and gentle exercise should be taken afterwards. In general, the period of immersion should not be less than twenty minutes, nor exceed one hour.

The Warm Bath

Is efficaciously employed in acute rheumatism, inflammation of the abdominal viscera, of the kidneys, bladder and womb; in suppression of urine and in the convulsions and other spasmodic diseases of infants, arising from teething and other irritations. It may also be applied with safety and efficacy in most diseases of the skin; in green-sickness; in slight cases of palsy; in Saint Vitus's dance and other spasmodic and convulsive affections, where the cold bath might prove too violent; in costiveness, intestinal obstruction and other complaints of the bowels that seem to depend on an irregular or diminished action of any part of the alimentary canal; and in cases of debility attended with nervous irritation. In all cases in which the constitution is injured and a general state of debility induced either by mercury, previous illness, intemperance, late hours, irregularity in diet or exercise, warm bathing is found to produce considerable advantage, when pursued under proper restrictions; and sometimes, in such instances, it is continued for a considerable time with great benefit; at other times, it is properly employed as a preparation for the cold bath. Delicate, weakly and nervous women, who may have suffered from miscarriages and the long train of complaints consequent to such accidents, as sexual weakness, attended with pain in the back and loins, etc., will sometimes fully realize their expectations of relief from warm bathing.

When the warm bath is intended to produce increased perspiration, it is best employed in the evening, when the immersion should not exceed ten minutes and the patient be removed from the bath to a warm bed. When it is not intended to excite perspiration, any time from an hour after breakfast till dinner, will be proper: in these cases, the bathing may be protracted to fifteen or twenty minutes, according to the feelings of the patient. Gentle exercise in the open air should afterwards be employed.

The Vapour Bath

Is recommended in the same diseases as the warm bath and will sometimes succeed in producing the effects wished for, after warm bathing has failed. In using the vapour bath, the power of heat is modified and tempered by the moisture diffused through the air;

and as the elastic vapour, like air, is a less powerful conductor of heat than a watery fluid, the effect of vapour in raising the temperature of the body is much less than that of the hot bath. Its immediate effects are to excite or increase the action of the superficial arteries, by which the determination of blood to the deeper seated parts is diminished. Therefore, the utility of this application is obvious in all cases of internal inflammation, since it draws a great quantity of blood to the surface and relieves the internal parts by the secretion of the skin, which is one mode nature takes to resolve inflammations and fevers. These effects render it of great advantage in inflammatory fevers, inflammation of the bowels stomach, etc., liver complaints, dropsy, obstinate rheumatic attacks, scrophulous and glandular swellings, gravel, palsy and gout. The vapour bath may be applied to the whole body, or to any part of it.

The best time for using it is the morning, or before dinner. From ten to fifteen minutes is generally sufficient time for the patient to be exposed to the vapour; but there may be cases where half an hour or an hour will be necessary. After the body is properly dried and rubbed, the cool air is perfectly safe. *A portable vapour bath.* I have described in my appendix on the cold water system, at the end of this volume.

The Air-pump Vapour Bath

Must not be lost sight of in this place. It consists of an apparatus capable of conveying vapour to a diseased limb, to which apparatus an air-pump is firmly attached for the purpose of exhausting the machine, when the fumigation has continued the proper time. This air-pump vapour bath has been found of signal service in gout, rheumatism, palsy, contractions of the muscles, cutaneous diseases and other complaints of a chronic kind, in many instances of which it evinces a remarkable power in altering the condition of action in the vessels and nerves of the affected part and in so arousing its impaired energies as to prove of great assistance in restoring it to a healthy state. That it must possess a very considerable power in many obstinate diseases, is, I think, evident from the fact that it combines the effect of the most efficacious fomentation and dry cupping; for it conveys the soothing vapour to the diseased part and retains it there, of a uniform temperature, as long as is necessary and then, by exhausting the air, removes all pressure from the surface, so as to occasion a temporary expansion of the vessels, thus affordin an apportunity and assistance to the resolution of obstructions. This will appear more clear, when we consider that the pressure of the air on the body is very great, being equal to about fifteen pounds weight on every square inch of surface[1] and the temporary removal of this enormous pressure from a diseased limb, cannot but prove an effectual means in numerous instances, of promoting a renewed and vigorous circulation, of resolving obstructions, loosening contractions and relieving pain in the part to which the apparatus is applied.

The Turkish Bath

Is now puffed off by some people, but it is a violent and, consequently, sometimes a dangerous thing and only fit for those who have a strong pulse and considerable vigour. Those who are most benefited by cold bathing will not find it agree with them and it should never be taken but under the sanction of an experienced medical man.

The Hot Baths and the Tepid Baths of Bristol, Matlock and Buxton

The *Bath Waters* are very efficacious in strengthening the bowels

1. It is a generally received opinion among philosophers, that the total amount of pressure on the whole surface of an ordinary man's body is equal to 32,000 pounds. This enormous pressure would crush us instantly, were it not exactly counter-balanced by the spring of the air, or other elastic fluid from within, diffused through every part of our bodies; just as the pressure on the surface of a shrivelled apple, is accurately counterpoised by the elasticity of the air contained in its pores. Now this is proved by experiment, for if a shrivelled apple be placed under the receiver of an air pump, we find that as the air is exhausted, the wrinkles on the apple gradually disappear and its surface becomes plump and turgid. These facts serve to illustrate the mode of operation and the utility of the air-pump vapour bath.

and stomach, bracing the related fibres and invigorating the circulation. In bilious disorders they are by some persons considered specific; and certainly prove serviceable in many nervous, paralytic, rheumatic and gouty complaints. They are attended with good effects in the green-sickness, particularly before any considerable affection of the stomach takes place, or any feverish symptoms appear; in obstructions of the viscera, when the consequences of ague or of long residence in hot climates, if the disorder in these instances has not advanced too far; in colic, especially the painter's or Devonshire colic; in jaundice, when arising from simple obstruction of the biliary ducts; in spasmodic affections of the womb and painful menstruation and in many cutaneous, but more especially leprous eruptions. In gouty cases, they are most useful in that stage of the complaint, when the inflammatory symptoms, if any have preceded, have in a good measure abated and a degree of weakness and want of tone in the system begins to take place. They are said to be also serviceable in morbus coxarius, or the hip disease and in white swelling of the knee. Upon the whole, these waters are often a powerful; but, in many instances, a nice remedy and should, therefore, seldom be resorted to without the advice of an able physician; and certainly they are by no means so efficacious a remedy as the MALVERN WATER.

They are unquestionably prejudicial in all scirrhous and other positive diseases in the lungs and abdominal visceras : and they do not appear suited to cases of palsy occurring in persons of a full habit.

The Bath water, when drank fresh from the spring, has, in most persons, the effect of raising and rather accelerating the pulse, increasing the heat and exciting the secretions. The action on the nervous system is felt at the same time, so that the stimulating properties of the water are very diffusive; and what is further remarkable, though these symptoms come on suddenly, yet they often continue much longer than we can suppose them to be excited by the actual presence of the water in the body.

This account of the primary and immediate effects of the water used internally, will enable any patient to judge from his own feelings, whether it agree with his constitution or not. If it excite, on being first taken, a pleasant glow in the stomach, followed by an increase of spirits and of appetite, particularly for breakfast and above all, a rapid determination to the kidneys, there is the greatest probability of its proving serviceable. But if it occasion head-ache, thirst and dryness of the tongue; if it sit heavy on the stomach, or produce sickness and do not pass off by urine, or perspiration, it may be fairly concluded that its continuance would do injury, unless these symptoms can be removed.

In their external application, these waters unite all the medicinal advantages of warm baths from about 160 degrees of heat to any inferior degree that may be desired and the permanence and uniformity of their warmth are no unimportant recom-mendations. Some physicians seem to consider that they possess some further powers and specific qualities superior to those of common water of the same temperature and certainly there are many facts to countenance such an opinion. They observe that their action on the nervous system is more stimulating than a common warm bath; that they raise the pulse and heat the body to a higher degree, yet are much less apt to produce a violent perspiration; that they remarkably increase the urinary discharge; and that so far from causing any relaxation or weakness, the bathers are observed to be in general more alert and vigorous and to have a better appetite on the days of bathing than in the interval.

In drinking this water, the safest method is to begin with a glass containing about a quarter of a pint, before breakfast; and to judge from its effects how often it may be repeated, or the quantity increased. If it feel easy, warm and cordial, to the stomach and spirits and excites no pain or sense of fulness in the head or eyes, a second glass of the same size may be taken the same day at noon and this quantity gradually increased to a pint in the day taken at two or three times, as convenience may suit. This is deemed a proper medium for the generality of people, though, in some cases, where the habit is not very irritable, the daily allowance may be augmented to a pint and a half, with safety and benefit. The Cross Bath Water, the temperature of which, when fresh from the spring, is 112 degrees, is usually recom-mended at the commencement of a course, especially when there is any affection, of the head, or when any tendency to plethora appears in the system. After some time, the more powerful water of the King's or the hot bath, which is four degrees higher in temperature, may be used; and this change will prevent, in some measure, the disgust which is apt to come on after a long trial of the Bath waters.

No less regard should be paid to the proper use of the bath. A short stay of five or six minutes is most advisable at first; and if this trial produce no symptoms that are disagreeable, but, on the contrary, seem to improve the health, spirits and strength, a longer stay may be gradually indulged in, till it comes to half an hour, but never so long as to cause lassitude, faintness, or disgust. The choice of the baths is often a matter of importance, as there is still a greater variation in the temperature of the waters when in the baths than at the pumps, the waters in the King's or the Hot Bath, being from eight to twelve degrees warmer than those in the Cross Bath. There are also private baths of any temperature, to suit the peculiarities of every patient's habit or complaint. The best time in general for bathing is the morning; and it may be repeated twice or thrice a week.

The Hot-well Water, near Bristol. Of the four principal warm waters naturally produced in England, this is the least so, excepting that of Matlock, the temperature not exceeding 74 degrees. As the Bath waters are proper where the secretions are defective, so the Bristol water is of service were they exceed the requirements of health. The Bath water warms; the Bristol cools. The former helps the stomach, intestines and nerves; the latter favours the lungs, kidney and bladder. The diseases in which this water is useful, are internal bleedings, immoderate flow of the menses, spitting of blood, dysentery, consumption, gravel and stone, scrophula and diabetes, in the last of which it is sometimes of eminent utility and may be drank as freely as the thirst requires it. It is well adapted to relieve the various symptoms of diabetes; such as the constant thirst, the impeded respiration, the dryness and frequent desquamation of the skin, the feverish quickness of the pulse and the preternatural discharge of urine. A regular course of the Hot-well water has been found to moderate this almost unquenchable thirst; to keep the skin moist and perspirable; to allay the fever; and to render the urinary organs fitter to receive benefit from the medicines usually prescribed to remove their debility and that of the system in general. In many cases, a little gentle aperient medicine may be used at the same time, if the bowels are not moved without.

A few years since this water was in high reputation for curing the incipient symptoms of consumption and affording considerable relief in the more advanced stages of this malady; but latterly it has been much less thought of. It is, however, agreeable to the palate and the effects it produces are very gradual and somewhat pleasant and, therefore, it will sometimes be of use to the consumptive and is not likely ever to be injurious.

This water is not made use of to bathe in, only being used internally. The hotter months are the best for taking it; and the full dose is half a pint, which is to be drank early in the morning and repeated before breakfast, at the interval of at least half an hour, spent in gentle exercise. Two more doses of the like quantity and with the like interposition of active amusement, are to be taken between breakfast and dinner, at the longest distance from each of these meals. But particular habits and complaints require variations in the quantity to be taken of this, as well as of any other mineral water. This water is also used at table and for domestic purposes, but in consequence of its altered temperature and of the loss of the fixed air it contained, it cannot be in so high a state of medicinal perfection as when drunk fresh from the spring.

The Bristol and Matlock waters are nearly of the same qualities.

The Buxton Water has a temperature of about 82 degrees and is highly and justly esteemed for its excellent effects in indigestion, low spirits and every kind of weakness and disorder in the digestive organs; and in many complaints which originate in the derangement of the functions of these very important parts, such as gravel and stone, flatulency, what are called bilious disorders, gout, chronic rheumatism and some cutaneous eruptions. It is also beneficially employed in diabetes, bloody urine, contractions of the vessels and limbs, especially from rheumatism and old age and painful affections of the kidneys and bladder. In all these maladies, it is employed both internally and externally.

This water has a sweet and pleasant taste; and contains calcareous earth, together with a small quantity of sea salt and no inconsiderable portion of a purging salt. It warms the stomach and intestines, relieves the sensations of pain, sinking and oppression, so common in deranged states of these organs, determines to the surface of the body and creates a comfortable glow through the whole frame. Whatever may be the disease for which it is used, it is generally advisable to keep the bowels regularly open by means of some gentle medicine, if the water does not produce a laxative effect, which it sometimes will without the aid of medicine and which is always salutary. The dose is about a pint taken at two or three draughts, before breakfast and the like quantity before dinner in the same manner.

The Buxton bath is well suited to languid, enfeebled and irritable habits, as the slight shock which follows immersion is almost immediately succeeded by a pleasant glow all over the body. It may be used in the morning, three or four times a week.

DIET[1]

All food is either of animal or vegetable origin. The former is, no doubt, more allied to our nature and most easily assimilated to our nourishment; the latter, though digested with more difficulty, is the foundation of the former, as vegetables are the nourishment of animals and all food is, therefore, properly derived from this source. In many respects, however, vegetable and animal food differ and this difference it is proper to remark, according to the various effects it displays on different parts of the human system. The first

1. The subject of Diet and Regimen is a very important one and therefore, I have been desirous of compressing into these pages as much valuable information relating thereto as possible; but as the space here allowed for these articles is necessarily limited, I beg to refer the reader, who is seeking for a more detailed account of the subject, to my small Treatise, entitled *"Best Methods of Improving Health by Regulating the Diet anal Regimen."*

difference to be observed between vegetable and animal food, is with respect to their effects on the stomach and bowels. In the stomach, vegetable food always displays a tendency to acescency, while animal food, on the contrary, tends towards putrefaction. Hence the former is apt to produce symptoms of uneasiness, while the latter, in moderate quantity, is almost never felt. In the same way, facility of solution belongs to vegetable food; while from greater firmness of texture and viscidity, animal food is a much longer time under the action of the digestive organs. The latter does not always mix easily in the stomach with other matter; while vegetables unite readily, but frequently continue long on the stomach for want of a proper stimulus. Effects sitnilar to what take place in the stomach are also produced in the bowels by these different kinds of food. The acescency of vegetable food is at all times apt to induce looseness; while the same effect is never known to arise from animal food, except in a very advanced state of putrefaction.

° The combination of a vegetable and animal diet appears to me best suited to preserve a perfect state of health and strength. There are few who subsist entirely on vegetables and of these few, the constitutions have generally inferior stamina. In hot climates, a vegetable diet may be carried to a great extent without injury; while, on the other hand, some northern nations live almost entirely on animal food and in very cold atmosphere, this may be indulged beyond what would otherwise be safe for the health of the body, So that a mixture of vegetable and animal nourishment appears best fitted for the health of mankind in general.

In the consumption of food we are liable to commit errors, both as to its quantity and quality. The error in the quantity, however, is generally the most detrimental. A small portion of food can be better digested and more easily changed into chyle, or that alimentary fluid from which the blood derives its origin, than a large portion, which injures the coats of the stomach and prevents them from exerting their full force. Hence, every excess is injurious. It is in infancy and early age, that the foundation is laid of many diseases arising from indigestion, which are now found in every family. If children are fed immoderately and beyond the real wants of nature, the digestive organs become too much distended and the stomach by degrees acquires an unnatural craving for food, which must be satisfied whatever be the consequence. These excessive supplies are not only unnecessary, but produce the most serious and fatal disorders. It should never be forgotten, that we are not nourished, as Mr. Abernethy was wont to say, by what we eat, but by what we digest. Nature is easily satisfied and is usually best provided when we do not intrude upon her more than a small and moderate quantity of the most digestible animal and vegetable food, at regular intervals of four hours through the day.

In regard to the quantity of food to be actually taken, it should be observed that this must be regulated entirely by the appetite, the supply required and the state of health of the individual. The appetite is, in general, the great indication of health; and where the stomach is in a healthy state, it relishes almost every kind of ordinary nourishment that is presented. This being the case, we are to be regulated in a great measure in the quantity taken, by the appetite, a due regard being paid to the supply necessary and the state of the system as it respects health or disease. Satiety is the natural consequence of repletion and before this takes place, the stomach itself gives the alarm. The strong, robust and active, require a larger quantity of food than the weakly, delicate and sedentary; infants need less than children and children than adults; and the aged ought to lessen their quantity of solid aliment in proportion to their age and the strength of their digestive functions. Women, in general, call for much less food than men; and all persons should take a smaller quantity in the relaxing days of summer, than during the cold of winter. It may be remarked, also, as a general rule, liable but to few exceptions, that the quantity of food taken should be much less in a state of disease than in health and this applies equally to acute and chronic diseases. Disease and weakness are necessary and invariable concomitants and it is a common and dangerous error among patients to suppose, that by increasing the quantity of their food, they shall augment their strength and become better able to throw off their diseases; for the reverse is the truth. In all bodily complaints the digestive organs are much affected and in the majority they are chiefly and primarily concerned; they are, therefore, fur the most part, in a state of considerable irritation and debility and by increasing the quantity of food, beyond the small supply which they can bear with ease, this irritation is strengthened and with it the existing malady. On the contrary, by carefully regulating our supplies of aliment under such circumstances, we adopt a principal means of lessening irritation in the stomach and intestines and likewise in the particular part of the body diseased; and thus nature is assisted in her efforts to restore the frame to health and the medicines made use of are capable of exerting their full effect. This is a fact worthy of great attention from patients, convalescent from any severe disease; since a small excess in the quantity of food taken at this period, will often bring back the disease with an aggravated force and is, perhaps, the most frequent cause of relapse.

There are three kinds of appetite; 1st : The *natural* or *healthy* appetite, which is stimulated and satisfied with the most simple dish, as certainly as with the most palatable, 2nd. The *artificial* appetite, or that excited by stomachic elixirs, liqueurs, pickles, high-seasoned dishes, wine, etc. and which remains only, so long as the operation of these stimulants continues, 3rd. The *habitual* appetite, or that by which persons enjoying no considerable stamina accustom themselves to take food at stated hours, but frequently without relishing it. The *true* and *healthy* appetite alone can ascertain the quantity of aliment proper for the individual. If we were seldom to trespass on the due limits of temperance, our natural appetite would be able accurately to determine how much food we may consume with satisfaction and benefit; but the usual physical education of children is now so careless and bad, that we rarely meet with a natural and healthy appetite either among them or adults. If after a meal we feel ourselves refreshed and as cheerful as before it, or more so, we may be assured that we have taken no more than a proper quantity; for, if the right measure be exceeded, torpor, heaviness and relaxation are the necessary consequences, our faculty of digestion will be irepaired and a variety of complaints gradually induced. The celebrated *Louis Cornaro* used to speak with delight of the cheerfulness and screnity he felt, after partaking of the small portion of food which he was accustomed to enjoy.

Before he determined on adopting a spare diet, he was much afflicted with lowness of spirits, heaviness and debility and severe bowel complaints were the torment of his life; but his careful and abstemious diet perfectly cured him of these and other evils. There can be no doubt that the majority of the more respectable inhabitants of Great Britain eat and drink twice as much as is necessary and beneficial; and this is nearly equally true of the same class of persons in most of the other nations of Europe. It is a remarkable fact, that almost all who have lived to a great age, have uniformly observed a very temperate diet and in numerous instances of longevity it has been scanty and coarse.

With respect to the quality of our food, if may be safely said that the flesh of full grown animals is much more digestible and nutritious than that of their young and, as it respects the larger animals, this rule is without an exception. Beef and mutton, for example, are more easily digested and more whole some than veal or lamb; yet it may be proper sometimes to give the preference to the latter in the case of patients who are convalescent from acute diseases, because they are less likely directly to excite heat or feverishness. Even here, however, it will be found, that where the stomach of the patient is very delicate and irritable, a little tender beef oh mutton will produce much less heat and general uneasiness than either veal or lamb, particularly the former. It may also be assumed as a general rule in chronic diseases and in health, that a solid diet is more digestible and better than a fluid one. In acute diseases it is the reverse. All salted meats are with difficulty digested and unwholesome. Generally, speaking, the flesh of tame animals is more wholesome than that of wild animals, the flesh of quadrupeds than birds and that of birds than fishes.

As the quantity of our food ought to vary according to the appetite, the supply required and the state of the health of the individual, so ought the quality. A keen and healthy appetite, calls for a daily supply of animal and other solid food, while the patient with a deficient and capricious appetite will often find a vegetable diet of most advantage. The sedentary and inactive and those whose constitutions ere naturally delicate, do not require such nourishing food as those of a strong robust habit and others who are daily engaged in laborious occupations in the open air. Infants need less animal food than children, children than adults, women than men.

It should be remarked that the nourishment conveyed by both animal and vegetable food is much the same, but the animal product is in greater quantity and more easily digested, while the vegetable retains its more watery nature, with a portion of unassimilating saline matter, which though introduced is again expelled by some of the secretions. The animal blood is then richer, more elaborated and stimulating and excites a stronger action of the system, than that produced from vegetables. Both products, however, equally take on an alkalescent nature in the circulation; for the acescency of the vegetable is confined entirely to its action on the stomach and bowels. Thus, from animal food a greater supply of nourishment is received for the wants of the system, depending on its greater quantity of oil, and its longer retention in the body than vegetable food.

It is obvious from these facts, and other considerations which will present themselves to every thinking mind, that in regulating the proportion of animal and vegetable food proper in any given case, attention must be paid to the season, way of life and climate. In summer, the quantity of vegetable food should be always increased, whatever our habits may be; the propriety of this is evidently pointed out by nature, from its abundance at this period. This increase of vegetable food is also the more necessary if the appetite is naturally keen and healthy, as a more strongly nourishing aliment would at this time expose to all the effects of putrescency, which the increase of the vegetable diet will, on the contrary, counteract.

The way of life must also regulate a good deal the proportion of vegetable nourishment. An essential circumstance in the use of all diet is, the production of such a distention of the stomach and bowels as may enable them to act properly on their contents. In the sedentary and inactive, it is particularly desirable that this distention should be produced by food of a less nourishing kind, and that no more nourishment be received than what the wants of the system require. Hence, in these cases, a vegetable diet is often to be preferred, while in the active and laborious the plan should be reversed.

The quality and nature of our food should be in a great measure determined by climate, and there is no doubt that the mortality of warm climates is aggravated by the use of too much animal food and strong drink. It is a common practice among Europeans in sultry climes to eat plentifully of either fresh or salt meat, at breakfast, tiffin, and dinner; this practice is followed day after day, and my surprise is, that such a dangerous course of living does not produce a much greater mortality among our countrymen in tropical countries than what actually takes place. A diet of a vegetable and acescent nature, with a large proportion of condiment, such as we find used by the natives of those countries, is best suited to the preservation of health; for by this excess of condiment, the morbid effects on the stomach and bowels, natural to vegetable food, are counteracted, and the chyle formed from it passes into the circulation in a proper state for supporting the body in such a situation. On the other hand, in a colder region, a permanence of nourishment is required, which animal food particularly conveys; and as this nourishment is less apt to disorder the stomach and bowels, no great portion of condiment is necessary, either as a stimulus to the organ, or in order to avoid any hurtful consequences that may arise. The proportion, therefore, of vegetable food is clearly pointed out to be small, and chiefly of the farinaceous or least acescent kind.

After these general observations on diet, we shall take a brief survey of the principal articles employed as food.

ANIMAL FOOD

The animals most commonly killed for the purpose of food are *the common bull and cow, the sheep, the calf, the lamb, the common stag the fallow deer, the domestic boar and sow, the hare and rabbit*, the amphibious animals, *the turtle and frog* and various kinds of birds and fishes.

The Flesh of the bull

The *flesh of the bull* has a strong disagreeable smell, and is dry, tough, and difficult of solution in the stomach. Bull-beef is rarely eaten. But the flesh of the ox, or castrated animal, called *ox-beef*, is a highly nourishing and wholesome food, readily digested when fresh by healthy persons, and constituting a principal part of the common diet of the inhabitants of this and many other countries. It is the most strengthening of all kinds of animal food, and is almost the only species of such food that is in season throughout the year. ow-beef is not so tender, nor so nourishing, nor so digestible as ox-beef.

Mutton

Mutton is well known to be a highly nutritious and wholesome meat. It appears to be the most digestible of all animal food, and is perhaps more universally used than any other. The flesh of rams has so strong and disagreeable a taste, and is, besides, so exceedingly tough and difficult of digestion, that it is never eaten but by those who cannot afford to purchase mutton of a better quality. *Ewe-mutton*, if it is more than between three or four years old, is likewise tough and coarse. *Wether-mutton,* or the flesh of the castrated animal, is most esteemed, and is by far the sweetest and most digestible.

Veal

Veal is usually considered not at all of a heating nature, and is therefore allowed, perhaps generally by the profession, to patients convalescent from an attack of fever, and to those who have a disposition to bleeding from the lungs or elsewhere, especially with the addition of some acid; but it is in my opinion so very indigestible an article, and has uniformly so strong a tendency to irritate the stomach and intestines, that I wholly prescribe its use wherever persons are not strong and healthy. In all stomach complaints it is peculiarly injurious. The flesh of calves which have been robbed of their blood by repeated bleedings, or reared by the hand with milk adulterated with chalk, and confinement in small dark places, so as prevent motion, is unusually depraved.

Lamb

Lamb, being less heating and less dense than mutton, is better suited to persons convalescent from acute diseases, but by the majority of patients labouring under indigestion, or any other severe affection of the stomach, it is not found so digestible as wether-mutton. It is, however, a wholesome food, especially when the lamb is not killed too young, and the fat is rejected. A lamb that has been allowed to suck five or six months is fatter and more muscular, and in every respect better, than one which has been killed when two months old, and before it has had time to attain its proper consistency. *House-lamb* is a dish esteemed chiefly because it is unseasonable. Like all animals raised in an unnatural manner, its flesh is depraved and unwholesome.

The flesh of the *common-stag,* and *fallow-deer,* is well known under the name of *venison,* and is very digestible, wholesome, and nutritious. The common stag should not be killed till he is above four years old, and the flesh is fattest and best flavoured in the month of August.

The flesh of the sow is strong, and makes bad bacon. It is the flesh of the castrated animal that is in common use, and that is known by the name of *pork.* It is a very savoury food, and affords a strong nourishment, suited to persons who lead an active or laborious life; but is not easily digested, nor can it be considered wholesome. The too frequent and long continued use of this meat favours obesity, produces foulness of the stomach and bowels, and occasions disorders of the skin. The flesh of the *sucking pig* is reckoned a great delicacy, and is nourishing, but I cannot think it more wholesome than that of the full grown animal; it is not readily dissolved in the stomach. Bacon is a coarse, heavy, and very indigestible food, only fit to be eaten by the robust, and by labouring people. Those who have an impure state of the fluids, wounds or ulcers, or a tendency to cutaneous eruptions, as well as those who are afflicted with indigestion, cough, or consumption, should abstain from the use of pork.

The flesh of the *wild hog* is dense, but sufficiently tender, very nourishing, and more savoury and digestible than that of the domestic hog. It is in season in the month of October. The head is esteemed the finest part, and the flesh of the young animal is reckoned a great delicacy.

The hare and rabbit

The *hare* and *rabbit* are sufficiently wholesome and nutritious. The flesh of the rabbit is softer, more digestible, and less heating than that of the hare; but it is not so nourishing. Wild rabbits are both more digestible and more palatable than such as are domesticated.

The Turtle

The *turtle* is a most nourishing and palatable food, and the esculent frog, though not very nutritious, tastes much like chicken.

BIRDS

Birds, the following species afford excellent nourishment, and are for the most part easily digested, *viz.* the common *fowl pheasant,* and *partridge,* the *turkey, Guinea hen,* and *quail,* the *common pigeon, lark, thrush, blackbird,* and *fieldfare.* The flesh of the young; *rook* is very similar to the *pigeon,* but is rather inferior in flavour and digestibility. The *woodcock,* the *snipe,* the *great plover,* and the *lapwing,* furnish very good and savoury food. The *swan,* the *goose,* the *wigeon,* the *teal,* and the *wild* and *tame duck,* are nourishing and wholesome for occasional food, but they are not very easy of digestion; the *barnacle,* the *puffin,* the *soland goose,* and the *black-backed gull,* are very fat, heavy, and have generally a fishy taste.

It is very probable that the eggs of all the birds now mentioned, and perhaps of most others, might be employed as food, but custom and convenience have given the preference to those of the common hen, the Guinea hen and the duck. The fluid contents of an egg consist of the white and the yolk. The former very much resembles the lymph of the blood, or the coagulable part of milk. The latter, *viz.* the yolk, is an animal mucilage, composed of oil, coagulable lymph and water. It is miscible with cold water, so as to form an emulsion. The ergs of all granivorous birds, and especially of the domestic fowl, yield a mild, demulcent, and strengthening aliment, well suited to consumptive and delicate persons, and such as are exhausted by immoderate evacuations. When lightly boiled, that is, for not more than three minutes, they are very easily digested; but when boiled hard or fried, they sit heavy on the stomach, and are unwholesome. Raw eggs are gently laxative, and are found to be serviceable in cases of jaundice and obstructions in the digestive organs.

I would here remark, that all broths and soups, and more particularly beef tea, and animal jellies, should invariably be taken with biscuit or bread, which renders them more easily digested, and much more nutritious. No man can subsist on even the strongest beef tea; because the *gelatine,* or jelly, thus taken, is not so nutritious as is generally supposed. If confined to it *alone,* he rapidly emaciates, and would die in a very short time; but if it be mixed with bread, he finds it nourishing.[1]

The wholesomeness of ***fish*** in diet has been much disputed. According to some, it is the most delicious food of any; and, according to others, it is without strength or substance. In the opinion of the present author, it affords, upon the whole, but little nourishment, and is, for the most part. of difficult digestion, and this appears to be the general sentiment of in telligent medical men.[2] Being of all animal substances the most putrescible, it is

1. The reason of this is fully described in my little work before alluded to entitled *Beat Methods of Improving Health.*
2. As a proof how little nutritive substance is to be found in fish, it may be observed that the jockies who, to reduce their weight, *waste themselves* at New market, are not allowed meat, nor even pudding, when fish can be got.

much inferior in quality to birds, and quadrupeds, and on this account, it seems questionable whether it ought to be allowed to febrile patients, or convalescents from acute diseases. The fat of fish is still more insoluble and indigestible than that of other animals, and readily turns rancid Acid sauces and pickles, calculated to resist putrefaction, render fish somewhat better, and more wholesome for the stomach, while butter has a tendency to impede digestion, and to promote the corruption of its flesh. On the contrary, spice and salt, used in moderate quantities, stimulate the fibres of the stomach, and facilitate the digestive process.[1]

Salt-water fish are the best of any, as their flesh is more solid, more agreeable, and healthy, less exposed to putrescency, and less viscid. They possess these excellent qualities, when fresh; when salted, they have all the properties of salt flesh, and consequently its disadvantages. Those fish which have scales are, in general, the most easily digested, and the best; and of all these the fresh herring appears to deserve the preference. The *herring,* the *whiting,* the *sole*, the *cod-fish*, the *dory,* the *turbot,* and the *flounder,* are perhaps the most digestible and best of fish. *Salmon, mackerel, lobster,* and most other kinds of shell-fish, are very difficult of digestion and unwholesome.

Oysters

Oysters are eaten both raw and dressed; when raw, they are in every respect preferable; for by cooking they are hardened, and deprived of the salt water which promotes their digestion in the stomach. Eaten raw they are nourishing and easily digested, and may be taken with great advantage by the robust as well as by the weak and consumptive. They are also generally attended with a laxative effect, if eaten in any quantity, and are, therefore, well suited as an article of diet for those liable to costiveness. Stewed oysters are particularly indigestible and unwholesome, and should never be eaten by the sick or delicate. They are extremely pernicious

1. Fish and milk ought never to be taken at the same meal, being a particularly indigestible combination.

to lying-in women, indeed, so much so as to have occasioned death, in more than one or two instances, when given to women in such a situation.

Oysters being a mild and cooling article of food, are of the utmost benefit to those who are troubled with warm flushings of the face, and other feverish symptoms, usually felt in declines, and in nervous and irritable constitutions. It is quite possible, by making them the principal part of a meal, to prevent in a great measure the irritation and heat which produces the hacking and distressing cough, in the more advanced stages of consumption. The great object to be kept in view in the prevention of consumption, is to maintain and increase the tone of the general system, and oysters, and other such mild nourishing food, will lend us powerful assistance in preventing consumption in those who are disposed to it, either from family or personal causes. Only a very small quantity of vinegar should be used by those who eat oysters to prevent consumption; those who take them to cure that disease may advantageously take it more freely, since this, and most other acids, have a favourable effect in subduing hectic fever, and in assisting the efforts of nature to overcome the disease.

As occupying a middle rank between animal and vegetable food, I shall here notice milk and its various products.

MILK

Milk holds a conspicuous place among the articles of nourishment. It is the type of all food. It is the proper and natural food of the young of all animals of the mammalia class; and cow's milk makes a principal part of the daily diet of a great proportion of the human race, both in the infant and adult state. On account of the abundance of oily and cheesy matter which it contains, cow's milk is by no means so well suited to infants as human milk; but as the mode of living in civilized society often depraves the quality of women's milk, or prevents its secretion, cow's milk, in too many instances, becomes a necessary substitute. On such occasions, as it is too heavy to be given alone, it should be diluted with water; and as it is disposed to become more acescent than human milk, and from that cause to produce gripings and other disorders of the bowels in young children, it will often be useful to mix with it decoctions of animal substances, such as chicken or veal broth, or decoction of hartshorn shavings; of which last, two ounces should be boiled in a quart of water, over a gentle fire, till the whole is reduced to a pint; when, after it has become cold, it will be of the consistence of a light jelly. This, mixed with about twice its quantity of cow's milk, with the addition of a little sugar, forms for young subjects a proper aliment, approaching nearly to the nature of human milk. Milk-porridge, as well as those puddings composed chiefly of milk and flour, are rather heavy, and difficult of digestion, and therefore not so wholesome as some others. Further information respecting milk will be found in the author's book *On Infancy and Childhood.*

Of course, the quality of milk varies greatly according to the season of the year, the pasture upon which the animal is fed, and the degree of exercise and free air allowed to it. In spring and summer the milk is peculiarly good and wholesome, on account of the salubrious nourishment of the herbs. In winter it is much inferior. Good cow's milk ought to be white, without smell, and so fat, that a drop being allowed to fall on the nail, will not run down in divisions. It is lighter, but contains more watery parts than the milk of sheep and goats; while on the other hand, it is more thick and heavy than the milk of asses and mares, which approaches neares the consistence of human milk.

It is an excellent article of diet both for children and adults, being for the most part easy of digestion and very nutritious. It is used medicinally in consumptions, especially in their early. stage; in gouty affections, after the paroxysm is gone off; in small-pox and measles, especially the malignant kind, diluted with water as the common drink; in cases of strangury and dysury from the absorption of cantharides, etc. ; and in many spasmodic and nervous affections, and disorders of the general health.

When milk is used medicinally, it is often serviceable to dilute it with Pyrmont, Seltzer, soda or lime-water. The two last, especially the soda-water, prevent acidity, and make it sit easier on the stomach. To obviate costiveness, which milk is apt to induce, it is often proper to mix brown sugar, or magnesia with it, or to boil it with oatmeal or veal broth.

In general, it is improper in inflammatory fevers, unattended with pustular eruptions; in bilious fevers; in scrophulous cases; and in rickets. It seldom agrees with hypochrondriacs, with the plethoric, the phlegmatic, or the corpulent, and disagrees particularly with tipplers, or those addicted to strong liquors.

The following are the principal products and preparations of milk in dietetic and medicinal use, viz., *cream, butter, curds, cheese, whey* and *butter-milk.*

Cream is exceedingly nourishing, and in small quantities sufficiently digestible and wholesome.

Butter, when taken in moderate quantity, spread cold on bread, is very nutritious, and, in general, not difficult of digestion. Melted butter and salt butter are unwholesome.

Curds are not to be recommended. In considerable quantity they are highly oppressive to the stomach.

Cheese may not be, in general, easily digested, though by producing a temporary stimulus in the stomach, it sometimes assists in the digestion of other food. When rich and good, it is nutritious, but is an aliment best suited to such persons as use great and constant exercise. It is sometimes of a constipating nature, and should be sparingly used by those of a costive habit of body. With some persons it disagrees very sensibly, while others find very good cheese as easy of digestion as it is delicious, so that no rule with respect to its use can be given as of universal application; and people must endeavour to find out for themselves whether it agrees, or not. Toasted cheese, though more agreeable to most palates than raw, is very indigestible and unwholesome.

Whey is the watery saccharine part of milk, freed in a great measure from the butyrace and Gaseous matters. It is diluent, and slightly aperient, and diuretic; and is given in consumptions, dysenteries, jaundice, etc. alone or mixed with mineral waters, and sometimes impregnated with the juices of medicinal herbs.

Butter-milk is milk deprived of its oily matter by churning or agitation. It is nourishing, cooling, and diluent, and is used sometimes with great, advantage in wasting, or a bad habit of body, hectic fever, and consumption. Good butter-milk is frequently of much service, both as an article of diet, and a remedy in pulmonary consumption, particularly in the early states of the florid species, so often met with in the young and blooming.

Milk, cream, butter, oil and cheese belong to the class of heat-forming food, and are unquestionably of importance in maintaining a due temperature of the body, and in promoting its health and strength.

Blanc mange is by no means so proper for patients and delicate persons as is generally supposed. Unless well made, it is apt to disorder the stomach.

VEGETABLE FOOD

The various articles of nourishment we derive from the vegetable kingdom, may with propriety be divided into five orders, *viz.* 1. The different species of farina, or grain, such as *wheat, rye, barley, oats* and *rice;* 2. The legumes, or pulse, such as *peas, beans,* etc.; 3. The various kinds of *salads* and *pot herbs;* 4. Alt the different kinds of *roots;* and 5. *fruits.*

Farinaceous Vegetables

The *farinaceous vegetables* are, of all others, the most wholesome and nourishing, and of these the preference is justly given to wheat. Bread is with much propriety called *the staff of life.* Home-made leavened bread, of a day or two old is extremely easy of digestion, wholesome and nutritious; but we cannot speak in terms so favourable of baker's bread, and new bread of any sort is difficult of digestion and unwholesome. Bread made with good new flour is more palatable than that made with old, but is not so digestible. Rye-flour makes very good bread, and is in common use on the continent.

Puddings made with flour are, for the most part, wholesome, when taken in moderate quantity, but are not so easy of digestion as bread, or animal food. Perhaps the most indigestible are the hasty, batter and Yorkshire puddings. The *vermicelli* and *macaroni* of the Italians, as well as all the dishes made of flour mixed up into paste, and either boiled in water or stewed in butter are indigestible, and ill calculated for patients and convalescents, to whom they are frequently administered. All unfermented pastry is exceedingly pernicious.

Barley is a very useful and wholesome vegetable. Pearl-barley, well boiled in water, forms a diluting, nutritive drink, of much service to all sick persons.

Oats, when boiled or deprived of the husk, and reduced to groats or meal, are used as a common article of diet for the infirm and sick, in Great Britain, France and Germany. When boiled in water, they impart a thick mucilage, which is very nourishing, wholesome, and digestible. This refers only to the mucilage obtained from genuine groats, or oatmeal, procured from a mealman who can be depended upon; as the oatmeal in common use is too often an impure article, and I fear all *patent prepared groats* and *meal,* as they are called, are adulterated.

Rice is a nutritious and wholesome vegetable. It is easy of digestion when taken in conjunction with some condiment, as cinnamon, nutmeg, all spice, and the like; these additions make it more palatable as well as more wholesome, and obviate its tendency to confine the bowels. It is almost the only food of the, native inhabitants of India—a sufficient proof of its mild, nutritive and wholesome qualities.[1]

All vegetables of the ***pulse*** kind are liable to strong objections, as articles of diet for civilized man. They are very indigestible, heating, productive of great flatulency, and contain little nourishment. Both peas and beans, whether green or dried, oppress the stomach, and are fit to be eaten only by the strong and laborious. Pea-soup is particularly indigestible and unwholesome.

---

1. Ale should never be drank after rice and milk, as it is almost certain of producing colic, or some other disorder in the bowels.

French beans, however, are among the most digestible vegetables our gardens produce. I mean the young, green pod, eaten as it usually is in England.

The best pot-herbs are ***asparagus*** and ***artichokes***, more especially to those troubled with gravel. Young spring greens and cabbages are very wholesome, but after the spring season they become less digestible. Young brocoli, cauliflower, and spinage, are also nutritious and easy of digestion.

Salads, lettuce, and all undressed vegetables of this kind, contain little nourishment, and are not much to be recommended. Blanched lettuce, being soporific, may sometimes be advantageously used at supper, by those who are frequently distressed by restless nights.

The fourth order of vegetables consists of all the esculent roots, of which the *potatoe,* the *turnip* and the *onion,* are the most wholesome and digestible. We may consider it as an unerring rule, that any kind of aliment for which we feel a natural and permanent appetite is salutary, and conformable to our nature. Of this kind is that valuable root the potatoe, which in the most simple preparation, and without any addition but salt, affords an agreeable and wholesome food to almost every person. It is a light alimentary substance, and can be hurtful only when immoderately used, when not mealy, or when severe indigestion is present. It is very nutritious, and sufficiently easy of digestion; although to a certain class of dyspeptics it is very irritating and pernicious. The arrow-root prepared from potatoes is very good; indeed, it seems that the greater part of that powder sold in England is extracted from the potatoe. The dry mealy sort is the most easy of digestion, and the simplest way of preparing them for the table is the best; mashed potatoes are not so easy of digestion.[1] Turnips are nutritious and wholesome.

1. The history of the potatoe conveys to us a most instructive lesson, forcibly reminding us of the extraordinary lengths to which prejudice will carry mankind, and showing us by what apparently trivial circumstances this prejudice is often removed, when the most powerful and influential arguments have failed to weaken it. The introduction of this valuable root to the gardens and tables of the people, received, for more than two centuries, an unexampled opposition from vulgar prejudice, which all the philosophy of the age was

(Contd. next page)

Onions assist digestion, although they cannot be considered very nourishing. They are best suited to persons of a cold and phlegmatic habit, and those whose stomachs require a stimulus. *Parsnips,* when well boiled, are nourishing and wholesome, and so is *Celery.*

Carrots, and especially all kinds of radishes, are rather difficult of digestion and unwholesome.

The best kind of fruits are *apples, pears, gooseberries, raspberries, red and white currants, grapes, peaches, apricots, strawberries,* and *oranges.* Of course they are wholesome only when quite ripe, and of apples and pears the more mellow and tender the fruit the better. *Cherries, plums, olives, cucumbers, melons,* and all kinds of *nuts,* are in general difficult of digestion, and fit only for the strong and active. *Black currants* have a strong tendency to affect the bowels, and are not very wholesome.

DRINK

Drink is indispensable to the solution and digestion of food, and to repair the waste which our fluids are incessantly suffering. Though the season, the state of the weather, cold, heat, the nature of our food, and the greater or less degree of our exercise, require more or less drink at one time than at another, yet we ought to drink only when we are thirsty, and to desist when the thirst is quenched. The

---

(Contd.)

unable to dissipate, until Louis XV of France wore a bunch of the flower of the potatoe in the midst of his court, on a day of festivity : the people then for the first time obsequiously acknowledged its usefulness, and its cultivation as an article of food soon became universal. Now, its stalk, considered as a textile plant, produces in Austria a cottony flax,—in Sweden, sugar is extracted from its root,—by combustion, its different parts yield a very considerable quantity of potass,—its apples, when ripe, ferment and yield vinegar by exposure, or spirit by distillation,—its tubercles, made into a pulp, are a substitute for soap in bleaching,—cooked by steam, the potatoe is one of the most wholesome and nutritious, and, at the same time, the most economical of all vegetable aliments,—by different manipulations, it furnishes two kinds of flour, a gruel, and a parenchyma, which in times of scarcity may be made into bread, or applied to increase the bulk of bread made from grain,—and its starch is little, if at all, inferior to the Indian arrow-root. Such are the numerous resources which this invaluable plant is calculated to furnish.—*See Paris's Pharmacologia,* vol. 1, page 54.

more we eat, and the drier our food is, the more we ought to drink in moderation.

The phlegmatic require less drink than the sanguine and choleric, the sedentary than the laborious, and all persons need less in winter than in summer.

To drink immediately before a meal is improper, because the stomach is thereby distended, and the gastric juice diluted, and digestion, consequently, cannot proceed in so favourable and perfect a manner. Hence, to avoid the necessity of drinking, it is advisable not to take violent exercise immediately before dinner. It is also somewhat objectionable to drink much during the time of taking food; as the same consequences *ensue* as from drinking directly before a meal. To take a small quantity of drink at the time of meals is natural and proper, but a large proportion of fluid swallowed at this period renders the stomach incapable of receiving the due portion of aliment, and impedes the digestive process.

Drinks may be divided into common water, animal fluids, animal infusions or decoctions, vegetable infusions or decoctions, and fermented liquors. The first three have been already spoken of, and I shall here only make a few observations on the last heads.

The vegetables employed for infusions or decoctions used as drink, are chiefly tea, coffee, and chocolate.

The annual consumption of *tea* in this kingdom is enormous, being about 80,000,000 lbs. The active principle in tea is called *theine,* and this with a volatile oil and tannic acid are the most important constituents of tea. Physicians now consider that the *theine* and *aromatic oil* of tea not only act as sedatives generally on the nervous system, but also exert a conservative action on the different structures of the body, checking any disposition to too rapid a change in them, and consequent exhaustion. Not only so; but as the daily removal of worn-out materials from the body, through the kidneys and other channels, is essential to health, tea and coffee are regarded as helpful to this process, when taken in moderate quantity.

Tea contains likewise potash, peroxide of iron, soda, and several other salts, which are most important to the human system.

Liebig, the German chemist, says, "We have, therefore, in tea a beverage contains the active constituents of the most powerful mineral springs".

The great proportion of *theine* and *aromatic oil* will be taken up by the water *first* poured on the tea, and it is of consequence, in order to make good tea that the water should be *boiling* and the teapot of silver, or other metal, first heated with boiling water.

Warm drinks once or twice a day are considered economical and useful to the people generally, and particularly so to the feeble and the aged, as saving an expenditure or loss of heat to the stomach in raising the temperature of the liquid to that of the human body.

Persons occasionally become alarmingly ill from taking *green* tea, then a wine-glassful of brandy, with or without water, is a powerful remedy. *Sal volatile,* or liquid ammonia, in water, may also be given with advantage.

One of the most promising substitutes for tea seems to be *coffee-leaves.* In Sumatra, and other islands of the Eastern Archipelago, the leaves of the coffee-plant are dried and prepared in the same way as those of tea, and used for drink and some of our own countrymen state that their effects are very similar to those of tea.

Tea is well known to have a very marked and irritating effect on the nervous system in some persons, and it is drank in this country far too often and too strong. It forms a refreshing antispasmodic beverage, but should not be taken either strong or very hot; the addition of milk renders it more wholesome, that of sugar less so. Individuals of a rigid and solid fibre are more benefited by it, than those of an opposite habit; but none should take more than two tea-cupfuls morning and evening. I cannot think it equal to cocoa or thin chocolate for common use; and it is very probable that some of our indigenous plants would yield a more wholesome and equally as palatable an infusion as the tea-leaf of China. With some persons no kind of China tea agrees, and then an infusion of agrimony, or some other native plant, should be substituted for it. I may state on very respectable authority, that the first leaves of whortleberry, properly gathered and dried in the shade, cannot be distinguished from real teas. *Sage,* (the *Tomentosa* or *Balsamic Sage),* and balm *(Melissa Hortensis* or *Garden Balm),* are likewise excellent substitutes for tea, more particularly in the case of debility in the stomach and nervous system.[1] It is certain that all *green* tea is exceedingly pernicious, having a strong tendency to injure the stomach and bowels, and the whole nervous system. Medicinally, tea is of much service in typhus and bilious fever, cramp of the stomach, flatulency, and to relieve the sensations of oppression and weight at the pit of the stomach, so frequently accompanying indigestion and bilious complaints. It is, however, worthy of particular notice from the dyspeptic, that few things will injure him more than an immoderate indulgence in this or any other warm slop.

Tea being an article of diet of daily and universal consumption, I would beg the reader's attention to the following rules in using it : 1. Carefully avoid the high-priced and high-flavoured teas, more especially if *green,* which generally owe their flavour to pernicious ingredients, and abound most with those active principles, whence the noxious effects of the article arise. 2. Take with it a good proportion of milk, as a corrective to any possible noxious qualities present. 3. Let the quantity of tea used at each infusion be very moderate. 4. Make the infusion properly, with water soft and otherwise of a good quality, and in a boiling state. 5. Tea is a beverage better adapted for the evening than the morning, and therefore less of it should be taken at the latter than the former period. The first meal we take in the morning to recruit the body, after the loss it has sustained during a long fast through the night, and to prepare it for the labours of the succeeding hours of the day, should be in some measure substantial, consisting of a large proportion of solid aliment. Indeed, except when drank soon after a hearty dinner, bread and biscuit should always be taken with tea.

The active principle in *coffee* is called *caffeine,* and it is identical with the *theine* of tea; and since coffee also contains oil, and useful saline matters, we may infer that, like tea, it is beneficial in retarding

1. John Hussey, of Sydenham, in Kent, who lived to 116, took nothing for his breakfast for fifty years, but balm tea, sweetened with honey.

the waste of the body, and therefore in husbanding the general strength. Those who drink coffee are said to be not liable to gout, and this is attributed to the beneficial influence of the saline constituents of the berry. To many *cofee* is heating, and does not sit so easy on the stomach as tea. The weakly and delicate often find it difficult of digestion, and it is not proper for those troubled with indigestion; yet it is sufficiently wholesome for occasional use. It is most wholesome when made of a moderate strength. Strong Mocha coffee sometimes affords considerable relief in the paroxysm of spasmodic asthma.

Chicory is extensively used in Great Britain as an admixture to coffee, and on the continent of Europe is used verb extensively alone. It contains an oil and bitter principle similar to coffee, and I believe is quite as wholesome.

Chocolate is more nourishing, more wholesome, and less heating than coffee. It is commonly made much too thick, and with too much milk, which renders it oppressive and cloying to the stomach. It is far better when made with water, and rather thin, the milk being added to it when poured out, in the same way that we add it to tea. In this form it is a light, nutritive, and wholesome beverage, well adapted to the nervous, the delicate, and those of a costive habit of body. It is improper for the corpulent, and those disposed to inflammatory diseases or apoplexy.

Cocoa is in fact only a, weak chocolate. It is a light, nutritious, and wholesome drink.

The principal fermented liquors are malt liquors, wine and ardent spirits.

Well fermented malt liquors, whether from barley or other grain, provided they are not too strong, are wholesome, refreshing and strengthening drinks. Formerly, medical men generally dissuaded their patients from taking malt liquor, but since the introduction of the bitter ales of Bass and Allsopp, a revolution of opinion is very evident. Good home-brewed beer,— I do not say public-house beer,—is much more suitable to the condition of people in general, than either wine, or brandy and water. Malt liquors are very nutritious, and are the most useful species of fermented liquors to the weak, the lean, and the laborious, provided they are not very subject to flatulency, nor troubled with diseases of the breast. With some sedentary and bilious persons they do not agree so well; and they are improper for the corpulent and asthmatic, and those who are liable to giddiness and other complaints of the head. They are better when of a middle age than when kept very long; and ale, with all the stronger malt liquors, although more nourishing, is also more difficult of digestion, than beer of a middling strength. Beer made from an infusion of malted groats, or malted rye, is lighter and more diuretic than the common barley beer. Spruce beer is a powerful diuretic and antiscorbutic, and is a wholesome beverage for the summer; in winter, it is too cold for some constitutions. Bottled beer is, on account of the fixed air which it contains, more refreshing than the barrelled, but it is not so wholesome. It is frequently prescribed as an antiseptic and restorative in low fevers and convalescencies; but care must be taken during the use of it, that it does not operate too freely by stool. London porter, with the common properties of malt liquor, possesses stomachic and diuretic qualities; but being strongly impregnated with bitters of a narcotic kind, it is by no means so wholesome for daily use as good and pure beer. Owing to this narcotic impregnation, it is very apt to induce drowsiness, and conse quently is improper whenever there is a tendency to head-ache, apoplexy, or other affections of the head. Bass and Allsopp's mild bitter ales are of excellent quality.

Of the use of foreign wine as a medicine; I have already spoken at pages 136-140, and shall now confine the few observations to be made respecting it, to its use as an article of diet. The sweet wines are nourishing, and may sometimes be useful to the weak and convalescent, but they are not so wholesome as the wines in more common use. The acid wines, as the Rhenish and Hock, are the least heating, and the most diuretic, and well calculated for consumption in hot weather. They pass freely by the kidneys, and are gently laxative; but all thin or weak wines, though of an agreeable flavour, yet from their containing little spirit, are readily disposed to become acid in the stomach, and to occasion or increase gravelly complaints, except in cases of *white* gravel, (see the article *Greavel),* in which they are in general more useful than any other sort of wine. It ought to be observed, however, that with some delicate persons, the best Rhenish wines agree very well, and are less liable to ferment than many of the stronger wines. The dry and strong wines, such as Sherry, Madeira, and Marsala, and the dry and light, as Burgundy, Claret, and Hermitage, are the most wholesome; they are snore cordial than the acid ones, and can be taken with safety in greater quantities than the sweet. The gentle stypticity, or astringency in genuine claret, renders it in the opinion of many, on the whole, the most wholesome of any strong liquor whatsoever, to be drank plentifully. Port is a strong astringent wine, and, when not mixed with more than a very small portion of brandy, is generous and stomachic, and well suited to the generality of British constitutions, in tolerable health. It is well calculated for cold and moist weather; but, like other red wines is apt to occasion costiveness, which renders it very objectionable to those who are habitually costive, and makes a change to white wine frequently advisable even to those who are not.

Sparkling brisk wines, as Champagne, inebriate more speedily than the stiller wines, but the morbid excitement is of short duration, and the subsequent exhaustion, is comparatively trifling. In feverish habits, Burgundy, Port, and the stronger white wines are to be avoided. To those who have a disposition to corpulence, Claret, Hock or Moselle, on account of their diuretic properties, are preferable to every other kind of wine for daily use.

The moderate use of wine is safe, and often highly beneficial to those who have passed the meridian of life, but to young persons it is almost invariably pernicious. Children in tolerable health are never strengthened, but always injured by it.[1] As a tonic and stomachic to the aged, three or four moderate sized glasses of good wine after dinner ought to be sufficient to most men. Now and then, perhaps, on very particular occasions, in the case of strong persons, half a bottle may be occasionally permitted to persons in

1. For further information respecting the qualities and use of wine, as well as of other points relating to diet in general, see my Treatise entitled "*Best Methods of Improving Health*". A striking proof is there related of the injurious effects attending the use of wine in children in tolerable health.

health, but to go frequently to that *utmost limit* of rational indulgence cannot fail to shorten life, at least in most instances.

Taken medicinally, in small quantities, *ardent spirits* are a powerful cordial and corroborant, and sometimes prove of much service in cramp or gout of the stomach, chronic spasmodic pains of the bowels, and flatulency. But in their nature, and ordinary effects, they are extremely unfriendly to the human constitution, and should never be taken by those who are desirous of preserving their health, except occasionally as a medicine. When used in any other manner, they stimulate the stomach and neighbouring viscera to an excessive and unnatural action, impair the appetite, impede digestion, and lay the foundation of organic mischief in the most important of the digestive organs; and these effects are as certainly produced by the frequent use of spirits, diluted with water, as when taken pure. A capricious and deficient appetite, head-ache, emaciation of body, lowness of spirits, and disease in the stomach, intestines, or liver, are the common effects of an indulgence in the use of ardent spirits.[1] They are much less detrimental in very cold countries, than in hot or temperate climates. French brandy appears to be the least pernicious; it is the most bracing and stomachic; gin and rum the most diuretic and sudorific. Their qualities are much improved by long keeping.

CONDIMENTS

Condiments are those substances which are taken with our food to promote digestion, or to correct some hurtful property in the food taken. They are usually divided into the saline, saccharine, oleaginous and aromatic.

Of the saline condiments, the principal are common salt and vinegar.

1. The celebrated John Hunter, on dissecting a man who had been much addicted to the use of spirits, found the blood converted into a kind of oily matter. And it has been proved by experiment, that the pernicious effects of spirits upon horses. are as great as those produced by giving them various well known poisons.

Common Salt is an article of the first importance to the health and vigour of the body. All animals require it. It facilitates the absorption of water into the system, and, being a compound of chlorine and sodium, it appears to supply to the body a certain quantity of chlorine necessary to the perfection of some of the vital processes. By its stimulant action on the throat, gullet, and stomach, it promotes the secretion of saliva and of the gastric juice, and thereby facilitates digestion. It is a natural and necessary stimulant to the digestive functions, and its daily use conduces much to the preservation of health and strength. It is not generally taken so freely as it ought to be by infants and children, for its use is essential to a healthy condition of the blood.

Vinegar, in small quantities, is a grateful and salutary stimulus to the stomach, correcting the putrescency of animal food, and the flatulency of vegetable. Its use is improper in many valetudinary cases, especially for gouty persons, and those troubled with red gravel, or costiveness; in green-sickness; and for rickety patients and young children. It is very useful to those troubled with white gravel.

Pickles are merely vegetable receptacles for vinegar, but the vegetable being hardened by the acid, renders it somewhat difficult of digestion, and, therefore, pickles are not much to be recommended. The pickled onion seems to be among the most wholesome of this sort of condiment.

Sugar is nutritious, antiseptic, and laxative. In moderate quantities, it is wholesome, but being very fermentable, is apt in some constitutions, to produce flatulency, heat and thirst. Rickety children, chlorotic girls, hysterical women, and all who are troubled with acidity and weakness in the stomach and bowels, should use it sparingly; and those who are anxious to preserve their teeth white and sound, should not make free with it.

The oleaginous condiments consist merely of olive oil and butter.

Oil, when used as a seasoning to raw vegetables, checks their fermentation in the stomach, and thereby prevents them from proving too flatulent. Used in this manner, in small quantities, it proves a help to digestion; and is certainly very nutritious. It seldom, however, agrees with weak stomachs for in such cases, even in its mildest state, it easily generates a rancid acrimony, extremely injurious to digestion. In consumptive cases it should be taken freely.

Of ***butter*** I have already spoken at page 243.

The aromatic condiments consist chiefly of the foreign spices, as pepper, Cayenne pepper, cinnamon, nutmeg, cloves, ginger, and of a few garden roots and seeds, such as garlic, union, horse-radish and mustard.

Most of these are wholesome, when taken in small quantities, with food of a flatulent or cold nature, and by persons who require a gentle stimulus. All the varieties of pepper as well as cloves, garlic and onions, are heating and stimulating, and should, therefore, be used sparingly, especially by persons of a full habit, and those disposed to inflammatory diseases. The best aromatic: condiments for frequent use are cinnamon, carraway, ginger, and mustard. Ginger is one of the most agreeable and wholesome spices.

I shall now make a few brief remarks on *Cookery*.

It is certain that simple cookery is a useful art. By it our food is rendered more palatable and digestible, and more conducive to health. It includes the following modes of dressing meat : 1. Roasting 2. Broiling 3. Boiling 4. Stewing 5. Frying 6. Baking.

Roasting was certainly the first mode invented to prepare animal food; for boiling is a more complicated process, and required the art of manufacturing vessels that could withstand the effect of heat. It is an excellent method of rendering food wholesome and nourishing, as, without greatly changing the chemical properties of meat, it renders it more tender, sapid, and highly flavoured, whilst there is not so much dissipation of its nutritive juices as in baking, boiling and some other processes. It is important to observe, that unless meat be kept after it is killed till the fibres begin to lose their firmness and tension, it will not become tender by roasting. The perfection of roasting consists in *doing* the meat neither too slowly, so as to wither it, nor too rapidly, so as to burn it. A small joint is best roasted on a string, by means of the bottle-jack; a large joint requires the spit. Our meat in England is generally overdone, and particularly over-roasted. In regard to over-roasting, the action of fire, if continued too long, has a tendency to change mild animal flesh into something of another quality: the fat, in particular, becomes bitter and rancid. The process is carried far enough when the steam of the meat puffs out in jets towards the fire, as this steam comes from the interior of the joint, and makes its way through the brown crust.

Broiling is an excellent mode of dressing animal food. It is a slight variation of the process of roasting, and though it may appear to differ but little, there is a very considerable difference of effect. In roasting and baking, it requires some time to form an incrustation on the surface of meat; but in broiling, the quick application of a brisk heat very speedily frees the outside fibres from their watery juices, and a crisp coating of fibre and fat is soon produced. This crust produces a strong barrier against the escape of the juices from the interior, which are more suddenly expanded than in the slower process of roasting, and, of course, must produce a more vioent separation of the small fibres from their several bundles. These effects, however, are chiefly mechanical, for there does not appear to be the same chemical union of the several substances as is observed in roasting; and it is found, that broiled meat contains more uncoagulated albumen, gelatine, and other uncombined chemical principles, than if it had been either roasted or boiled. It is this that renders broiled meat more juicy, and sapid than when roasted, and it must also make it more wholesome and nutritious. For restoring the strength of invalids it is the best mode in which animal food can be dressed, both from its nutritive qualities, and from its being easily digested, as the juices are so slightly altered, that they require little preparation to convert them into good chyle and healthy blood.

Boiling is also a useful mode of preparing some kinds of animal food, rendering it more soluble, without destroying, if properly done, its nutritive qualities. Some professional men seem to consider it a method of cooking peculiarly calculated for weak stomachs, but this certainly is a mistake; for, in general, boiled meat is neither so easy of digestion, nor so nutritious, as that prepared by either of the two foregoing processes. Boiled beef is inferior to roast, in every point of view, and boiled mutton, though a milder food, especially for invalids, cannot be considered so wholesome as when roasted. Boiling is not at all calculated for game, turkey, nor for any young and tender meat.

Boiling is, however, particularly applicable to vegetables, rendering them more soluble in the stomach, and depriving them of a considerable quantity of air, so injurious to those of weak digestive powers. Very striking and unexpected effects are sometimes produced from the boiling of vegetables, as in the case of several plants which are very acrid, and even poisonous, in a raw state, becoming bland, sweet and wholesome, by simply boiling them in water. The potatoe is a familiar example, being, in its raw state, nauseous and unpalatable, perhaps even in a slight degree poisonous, as it is one of the night shades *(solanum tuberosum)*, but, when dressed, it is rendered farinaceous, digestible, and wholesome. A more striking instance still is the cassava, *(jatropha manihot)* of America, which is strongly poisonous before it is boiled, and afterwards so highly nutritious. The prepared cassava is well known in this country under the name of tapioca, and forms the basis of an excellent and nutritive farinaceous pudding.

Stewing has a similar effect to boiling, in depriving the meat of much of its best juices, and other nourishing properties, which are washed out of the fibres by the constant entrance and recess of the water during the process. Stowed meat is also still less easy of digestion than that which is boiled, and, therefore, it is a mode of cooking that cannot be recommended as fit for frequent use, although it may be useful on certain occasions.

Frying is one of the worst modes of cookery, as it cannot be performed without the use of fat or oil, two things which are highly objectionable, and because it renders the meat very indigestible. It injures the digestible and nutritive qualities of vegetables as well as those of animal food. Potatoes when fried become waxy in texture, and will often produce derangement, even in healthy and vigorous stomachs.

Baking is a process to lie preferred to frying, but is not so excellent as either broiling or roasting. It differs from roasting in not permitting the escape of the vapour exhaled from the meat. There is a greater retention of the oleaginous juices of the meat, which are generally in a burnt empyreumatic state, rendering the food less digestible and nutritious. Yet baked meat, when carefully done, is sufficiently wholesome for occasional use.

Beside these various simple modes of preparing animal food, there is another, which it may here be proper to take notice of namely, when animal food is dissolved in water, and formed into a gelatinous solution or jelly. This substance is of a viscid nature, and though it contains much nourishment, yet is not easy of digestion, and of course less calculated for diseased or weak stomachs than is commonly imagined. Nor are those *jellies* which are the mucilaginous extracts of certain parts of animals, as hartshorn, very digestible. They should be taken sparingly, and can only be recommended for the sick, accompanied with a quantity of stale bread.

The above are the principal modes of simple cookery; but the ingenuity of man has been exerted to discover a number of other preparations, which may with great propriety be arranged under the head of refined or compound cookery, a system more flattering to the palate than favourable to the health. As it is impossible to speak of this system with any degree of approbation, I shall merely observe, that the generality of ragouts, made dishes, and the like, are difficult of digestion, and very liable to derange the functions of the stomach and intestines, and, therefore, cannot be too sedulously avoided by those who entertain any anxiety for the preservation of their health.

REGIMEN

The term *Regimen,* strictly speaking, signifies any rule, but in the present work I mean by it chiefly, a proper regulation of the following means of promoting health, *viz.,* 1. Air; 2. Exercise; 3. Sleep; 4. Clothing; and 5. The government of the Passions each of which will be briefly considered.

AIR

It is an undoubted fact, that though man may live without food even for several days, he can hardly exist for a few moments without breathing atmospheric air, a sufficient proof of its pre-eminent importance, not only to life, but also to health. For breathing does not merely preserve life, but likewise restores the florid colour, stimulus, and, so to speak, the life of the blood, thereby rendering it fit to maintain and increase the general energies of the body, and to repair all its most essential parts. By the same means the natural heat or temperature of the body is kept up, and the substances destructive to health and life are got rid of. These considerations prove that persons who are much confined to the house, must have poorer blood than those who are in the habit of being abroad in the open air; and will, therefore, *coeteris paribus,* be universally found to be weaker in body and mind, more liable to the accession of chronic or acute disease, and less able to struggle effectually under such attacks.

In health, nothing is more essential than for a person to breathe the fresh air at least twice a day, for two or three hours at each time. In large towns or cities, in particular, no day should be suffered to pass over, without enjoying the pure air beyond its boundaries, and that neighbourhood where the air is dry and moderately cold ought to be most frequently visited. Such exposure is the only way of guarding against too much sensibility in regard to the impressions and variations of the weather, one of the most abundant sources of disease, and an evil which is now very generally felt in this country. Invalids should not go abroad too late nor too early. In the winter after eight in the morning, and before four in the afternoon, is the best time; in the summer after six and before eight.

Night air is very unwholesome; and often about sun-set it is particularly injurious, on account of a greater quantity of dew falling at that time than at midnight. In hot countries those who wish to save their life cannot too sedulously avoid the evening and night air.

Infants and young children are much injured by being confined within doors, and it is well known that the mortality among them in large towns and cities, owing to the deteriorated state of the atmosphere, is much greater than in the open country. If freely exposed to the outward air, they are found to be little more sensible to the injuries of the weather than young cattle. All school-rooms and nurseries should be spacious, and well ventilated throughout the day. To cover children's faces when they are asleep is a very bad-custom.

In sickness a constant supply of fresh air is extremely valuable. Whatever the nature of the complaint may be, and whether of an acute or chronic character, the patient's apartment should be spacious and freely ventilated. In all fevers it is of the first importance, and in protracted maladies will be found a powerful auxiliary to the other means used for the patient's restoration. In its absence, all other cordials often have but a very partial effect. No sick person should ever sleep with the bed curtains drawn; indeed, this is a most pernicious custom to all delicate persons, and one that, cannot be too soon banished from the houses of all those who value the preservation of health.[1]

Some of the most salubrious and invigorating places in England for invalids are Scarborough, Malvern, Brighton, Llandrindod, the Mumbles, near Swansea, and a little place called Southern Down, near Bridgend. Near London, no place, probably, is equal to Epsom and Banstead for the dryness and invigorating quality of the air. Dorking and Reigate suit some people suffering from chest complaints, who require a mild air.

EXERCISE

Of the means of preserving and promoting health, exercise is, perhaps, that which has hitherto had the least justice done to it by

1. A correct idea may be formed of the injury likely to follow this habit by the following facts. Eighteen charity children, and a servant, slept in an apartment of a house in King Street, Golden Square, when, to render the room warmer, they shut up the chimney, and used every other means to exclude the fresh air; the consequence of which was, that the servant and ten of the children were seized with various alarming symptoms of a disorder nearly similar, accompanied with excruciating pains, convulsions, etc.

any individual author. Within the last five or six years, indeed, gymnastic exercises have come into frequent use, and have been found very useful, and most people are in a measure aware of some of the advantages of exercise; but the public at large are still far from having attained to any correct and adequate knowledge of its uncommon power, both in preserving health, and assisting in the cure of disease.

The body of man is evidently formed for activity and exertion. By labour or exercise man preserves his health, augments his strength, and improves his mental faculties, besides procuring the means of his subsistence, and the conveniences of life. In regard to health, none of the various processes connected with the important function of digestion could be properly or adequately performed, unless the body were stimulated for that purpose by labour or exercise. The health of all the parts, and the soundness of their structure, depend on perpetual absorption, and perpetual renovation; and exercise, by promoting at once absorption and secretion, invigorates life, without hurrying it; renovates all the parts and organs, and reserves them apt and fit for every office they have to perform. It also mainly contributes to the circulation and purification of the blood, and to the increase of strength.

By this means disease may often be prevented, and not unfrequently cured, even when it has taken a very strong hold of the constitution. It has been justly said, that IF ONLY SOME OF THE MANY ADVANTAGES RESULTING FROM EXERCISE WERE TO BE PROCURED BY ANY ONE MEDICINE, NOTHING IN THE WORLD WOULD BE IN MORE ESTEEM, OR MORE ANXIOUSLY SOUGHT AFTER. Generally speaking a sedentary life is the source of all those diseases which physicians call cachectic or chronic, the number of which is now very considerable. Among these scrophula, indigestion, bilious and liver complaints, lowness of spirits, nervous irritability, and pulmonary consumption, stand foremost, and there may be added to them jaundice, growing out of the shoulder and curved spine, palsy, apoplexy, etc. For these, exercise is one of the most effectual, as well as most agreeable, remedies; it strengthens the vessels, preserves the fluids in a healthy state, augments the appetite, facilitates the secretions and excretions, exhilarates the spirits, and, excites pleasing sensations throughout the whole system. I would, therefore, earnestly recommend exercise to the notice of my readers, both as a means of preserving health, and curing disease and deformity.

Exercise is of various kinds, but the principal are *gymnastic exercises, walking, riding, and friction.*

The most useful gymnastic exercises are leaping, throwing the discus or quoit, playing with the foot-ball, and fencing; and it is highly desirable that they should be frequently practised and encouraged to the utmost extent.

There is no exercise so natural to us, or in every respect so conducive to health, as walking. It is the most perfect in which the human body can be employed; for by it every limb is put in motion, and the circulation of the blood is effectually carried on throughout the minutest veins and arteries of the system. The most proper time for walking, and indeed for all exercises, is between breakfast and dinner, and it should then be continued for two or three hours, supposing we rest for a few minutes during that period, so as not to become over-fatigued.

Riding on horseback also is a most useful exercise, more especially for invalids. It has been laid down as a rule, that *riding is the best exercise for regaining health, and walking for retaining it;* and it is a very good one. This rule, however, does not prohibit the invalid from walking daily; but only inculcates that to him horse exercise is preferable in the beginning, as the chief mode of exercising the body.

Friction is a mode of exercise of great value, and highly worthy the attention of all persons, whether in health or labouring under disease; because when more active exercise can be freely taken, it augments its good effects, and may be used locally so as to act beneficially on particular parts, and when active exercise cannot be resorted to friction will be found the best substitute for it, and that which often most effectually paves the way for it. It has great power in strengthening the digestive organs, promoting a free perspiration, resolving obstructions, loosening contractions, and imparting a comfortable glove with an increase of energy to the whole system. Thus, it is uniformly of remarkable service to the gouty and rheumatic, to the paralytic, the weakly, and the nervous, in short, to all persons afflicted with any chronic disease, or suffering under a state of general debility. I have known it of great service in promoting sleep; especially in persons enfeebled by literary labours, or close confinement to the house from any cause. If sleep forsakes the invalid, he should rise from bed, and use friction actively all over the body fifteen or twenty minutes, or more.

Friction may be applied to the body by the hand, or with flannel, rough woollen gloves, or the flesh brush. The latter is by far the best instrument, and the proper time for using it is in the morning and evening, continuing it from fifteen to thirty minutes at each time.

Besides the preceding modes of exercise, the use of the shuttlecock anal dumb bells is deserving of much regard. The shuttlecock is a most excellent species of exercise, more particularly for ladies, both young and old, because it can be used almost at all times, and when females may not be able to ride or walk so much as is necessary for health.

SLEEP

Refreshing sleep is universally known to be a powerful restorative, and it should, therefore, be studiously cultivated by all persons. The advantages of sleep are, that by it the exhausted constitution is repaired, and the vital energies restored; the process of assimilation or nourishment goes on more perfectly; perspiration is promoted, and thus much acrid matter is expelled; the vigour of the mental faculties is renewed, and the body attains its proper growth. Such being the salutary effects of this "sweet restorer", we immediately perceive the propriety and value of the late Lord Mansfield's advice to *cultivate sleep;* advice that I wood strongly urge upon every individual, and especially on those who have much bodily or mental labour to undergo.

The number of hours necessary for sleep, varies from six to

eight in the twenty-four; many strong persons finding six hours sufficient, while the weakly, and the invalid, generally require seven hours and a half or eight hours. It is worthy of particular remark, that even the weakly very seldom require more than nine hours sleep at the utmost, and a longer indulgence will scarcely ever fail to injure them. Half-past ten is the best time to retire to rest at night, and six or half-past six the best hour, in general, for rising in the morning.

In order to insure comfortable sleep, it is necessary that sufficient exercise be taken in the day; the food, particularly in the evening, be moderate in quantity, and easily digested; the bed chamber freely ventilated; the bed clothes moderately light; and the mind free from much disturbance. It is a most pernicious practice to endeavour to stop every crevice in a bed room, so as to exclude the external air; and an this account the curtains of a bedstead ought never to be drawn around it. When persons have their sleep much disturbed, it is often owing to improper management and from being ignorant of the means to be used to promote sleep. These means are various, but it being necessary to confine this volume within a certain size, I am prevented noticing them particularly; the reader will, however, find them fully described in the *"Best Methods of Improving Health, by Diet and Regimen"*. The use of the flesh brush on going to bed, and keeping the body cool, and the feet warm, are grand means of promoting sleep.

Thick heavy quilts should always be avoided, especially by the invalid, as they irritate delicate frames, and prevent sleep. I strongly recommend *Booth and Foxes Patent Down Quilts,* (of 80, Hatton Garden), as excellent coverings for beds.

CLOTHING

Some of the principal rules regarding the use of clothing are : 1. That our garments should be made of soft and pliable materials, so as not to obstruct the free and easy motion of the limbs. 2. They should be made of such a shape as to be comfortable from their ease. 3. They should note warmer than is necessary to preserve the body in a proper degree of temperature. 4. The clothes we wear, more especially those next the skin, should be made of substances easily cleaned when necessary. 5. They should be suited to the constitution and age of each individual. Robust and young persons need only a small quantity of clothes, and those of a lighter sort; but the delicate, and especially those who are far advanced in age, require warm clothing. 6. A variety in regard to clothing is necessary, so that it may be adapted to the great difference of temperature in summer and winter. But the weakly ought to be careful not to make too great a change in the summer, more particularly in the evening. Invalids should rarely make such change in this respect till May is out.

The articles used for clothing are chiefly linen, cotton and woollen goods. The different uses of linen and cotton are now generally known; but the proper age and circumstances in which flannel, and other fabrics of wool, ought to be used, are not so well understood by the public. The majority of the most able professional men believe that childhood and old age are the proper periods for the use of this valuable species of clothing; and that to persons of all ages who are afflicted with consumption, or any complaint in the chest, or rheumatism, severe indigestion, diarrhoea, dysentery, colic, or diabetes, it is of essential service. In regard to age, flannel is well adapted to infants and very young children, but of course all extremes in point of quantity must be avoided. The celebrated John Hunter's receipt for rearing healthy children, was, "Plenty of milk, plenty of sleep, and *plenty of flannel*". In later years, the *flannel age* may be said to commence at forty-five or fifty, and after that period, the use of flannel becomes still more and more necessary as age advances. To all aged persons it is of eminent utility.

It is, however, certain that the frequent use of cold water daily to every part of the body, has a very great and sensible effect in so fortifying the skin as to render flannel much less necessary than it otherwise would be. *See* the appendix on COLD WATER.

In respect of disease, or tendency to disease, it is of great value to those afflicted with consumption and severe cough, or asthma, or a tendency thereto, and likewise to those who have weak stomachs, or are subject to rheumatism, or are naturally of a delicate constitution. All such persons should wear a flannel shirt or waistcoat, either next the akin, or immediately above the shirt. In the winter, it ought to be worn almost invariably next the skin; but it should generally be thrown off in bed.

The great use of flannel next the skin is, that it promotes the insensible perspiration, and defends the skin against the injuries likely to arise in our climate, from the frequent, great, and sudden changes in the weather.

THE PASSIONS

It is certainly of immense importance, as respects the health of the body, to possess a command over the passions of the mind—those strong emotions occasioned by the view of apprehended good or evil. All physicians agree that the passions, if given way to, have a strong tendency to exhaust the finest of the vital powers; to destroy, in particular, digestion and assimilation; to weaken the vigour of the heart, and the whole nervous system; and, by these means, to impede the important business of renovation. All that I have to say on this subject here, is to put my readers in remembrance of this fact, and to assure them, that a perfect command over the passions may always be gained by due reflection, resolute exertion and earnest prayer. God alone, by His Divine Spirit, can enable us to moderate and govern them perfectly. Fervent prayer and resolute effort, through Jesus Christ, are the ordained means of cure for *"the wild chase of false felicities"*, and the sure road to *"the composed possession of the truth"*; and we may safely assert, with an eminent clergyman of former days, who well understood the way to self command, and to present and future happiness, that *prayer and pains will* here accomplish all things necessary. Let every one earnestly try this prescription, and they will find it infallible.

We cannot be virtuous and possess self-command but in proportion as we become humble, disinterested, trusting everything to God, without any unquiet concern about ourselves. A Revelation from the upper world—from the Infinite and Eternal God, demands a deeply reverential hearing, and obedience is always highly productive to *us*. *"He that is slow to anger is better than the mighty; and he that ruleth his spirit than he that taketh a city"*. Prov. xvi. 32.

"On piety, humanity is built;
An on humanity, much happiness;
And yet still more on piety itself.
A soul in commerce with her God, is heaven;
Feels not the tumults and the shocks of life;
The whirls of passion, and the strokes of heart."

BLOOD-LETTING

Blood is in many respects the most important fluid of the animal frame. From it all the solids are derived and nourished, and all the fluids are secreted; and it is hence the basis or common pabulum of every part. These facts are quite sufficient to convince us, that the abstraction of this important, and, as it ought to be called, living fluid, can never be a matter of indifference to the welfare of the system from which it is taken; whether the system be strong or weak, healthy or diseased, the loss must either be beneficial or injurious, and, therefore, bleeding should not be resorted to on trifling occasions, and never without the advice and sanction of an able professional man. It is far too common a practice for individuals to submit to the loss of blood from the advice of a neighbour, or other ignorant persons, or from some crude notion of their own as to its usefulness and necéssity; and even some medical men are much too fond of the use of the lancet, and too indiscriminate in its employment, especially in chronical diseases.

Blood-letting is often proper at the beginning of all acute inflammations, as inflammation of the stomachs lungs, intestines, pleura, kidneys, throat, etc., but it is by no means so much resorted to now as formerly. It may also be necessary when there is too great a quantity of blood in the body: and when some cause supervenes, or is threatened in the constitution, which would speedily produce an inflammation, or some other dangerous symptom, if the system was not relieved by this means. It is upon the latter principle that patients are bled after wounds and bruises; that it is directed for a pregnant woman, if she has a violent cough with much feverishness; and, by way of precaution, in several other cases.

Occasionally, acute inflammation supervenes in diseases of debility, or in habits debilitated by grief or previous diseases, when the employment of the lancet is commonly highly injurious; but with the exception of these cases, to determine the presence of inflammation in vital organs, such as the lungs, heart, etc., and the propriety of both general and local blood-letting, is the same thing, at least, in the country. In such cases, the repetition of the bleeding must be regulated by the effects of that which has been employed.

With respect to the quantity of blood taken at each bleeding, in an adult of ordinary vigour, labouring under inflammation of an important organ, fourteen ounces is a moderate general blood-letting; a moderate local blood-letting by leeches or cupping, is from four or six ounces; and both will be the more effectual the earlier they are employed, and the more quickly the blood is taken.

On the contrary, in all cases of debility, bleeding is improper and injurious. Generally speaking, bleeding should never be practised in the following circumstances, unless for some peculiar and very strong reasons, of the due force of which none but skilful medical men can judge: *viz.*

1. In very advanced age, or very early infancy;
2. In persons naturally of a weakly constitution, or who have been rendered delicate by sickness, or some other accident;
3. When the pulse is small, soft, feeble, and intermitting, and the skin pale;
4. When the limbs, and the extreme parts of the body are often cold, puffed up; and soft;
5. When the appetite has been very small for a long time, and the food, consequently, only slightly nourishing;

6. When the stomach has long been disordered and the digestion bad, whence little blood could be spared;
7. When the patient has been considerably reduced, whether by haemorrhage, looseness, profuse urine or sweat;
8. When the patient has long been afflicted with some depressing disease. In all these cases, and in some others less frequent, a single bleeding often precipitates the patient into an extreme state of debility, and a condition absolutely incurable.

To the consumptive patient, bleeding always proves injurious, by the weakness which it aggravates or occasions.

It was formerly a very common practice to bleed insane patients freely; but all skilful persons are now aware of its injurious tendency. In madness bleeding lowers the physical force, without in general, correcting the mental error. It weakens the external expression, without impairing the internal strength of the disease. It converts the fury of madness into the passive sullenness of melancholy.

Persons so constituted as to make much blood, should carefully avoid all those causes which tend to augment it, especially an indulgence in animal food, wine, and strong malt liquors; and when they are sensible of a considerable increase in the quantity, they should confine themselves to a light frugal diet, on pulse, fruits, bread and water, sleep but very moderately, and take much active exercise. Nothing can be more opposed to reason and experience, than far such individuals to have recourse occasionally to the abstraction of blood by the use of the lancet, or cupping-glasses, in order to prevent too considerable a formation and flow of this fluid; for habitual blood-letting invariably begets, under such circumstances, habitual plethora, which calls incessantly for a repetition of the same supposed remedy. Some persons are in the habit of being bled every spring or fall, or at both these seasons; but, however, robust the constitution, this is not a practice to be recommended, since, like all other continued bleedings at stated periods, it proves only a palliative remedy, which sooner or later greatly enervates the whole body, deranges its functions, induces a premature old age, and calls for a more frequent recourse to the operation.

Blood-letting is either *general* or *local*. General blood-letting is performed by a lancet, and consists in opening a vein or the temporaral artery, with a view of lessening the whole mass of circulating blood; local or topical blood-letting is performed either by means of a cupping-glass and scarificator, or leeches, applied in the vicinity of the disease, for the express purpose of lessening the quantity of blood in a particular part.

The mode of bleeding most frequently practised, is that of opening a vein; and it may be done in the arm, ancle, jugular vein, frontal vein, veins under the tongue, or the back of the hand, etc. In whatever part, however, venesection is performed, it is always necessary to compress the vein, between the place where the puncture is made and the heart. Thus the return of blood through the vein is stopped, the vessel swells, becomes conspicuous, and, when opened, bleeds much more freely than would otherwise happen. Consequently, in bleeding from the arm, leg, hand or foot, the bandage is applied above the puncture; while in bleeding from the jugular or frontal vein, the means for making the necessary pressure is applied below it. When the external jugular vein is to be opened, the surgeon generally makes the necessary pressure with his thumb.

All the apparatus essential for blood-letting on the part of the patient, is a bandage or fillet, two or more small pieces of folded linen for compresses; a basin to receive the blood, and a little clean water and a towel. On the part of the surgeon, it is necessary to have a good lancet of proper shape. He should never bleed with lancets with which he has been in the habit of opening any kind of abscesses, as very troublesome complaints have been the consequence of doing so.

In bleeding in the arm, the bandage is to be tied round the limb, a little above the elbow, with a sufficient tightness to intercept the passage of the blood through all the superficial veins; but never so as to stop the flow of blood through the arteries, which would tend to prevent the veins from rising at all. The veins being thus rendered turgid, the operator should choose the one which seems most conveniently situated for being opened, and large enough to furnish as much blood as it may be proper to take away. Before applying the bandage round the arm, however, the operator should always feel where the pulsation of the artery is situated, and he should not open the vein immediately over this part.

With respect to the choice of a vein in the arm, the most experienced surgeons give the preference to one which rolls least under the skin. Such a vessel, though sometimes less superficial than another, may commonly be opened with greater facility. The vein, however, is always to be fixed as much as possible, by the operator placing the thumb of his left hand a little below the place where he intends to introduce the lancet.

In fat subjects, the large veins at the bend of the arm are sometimes totally imperceptible, notwithstanding the fillet is tightly applied, the limb is put into warm water, and every thing done to make those vessels as turgid as possible. In this circumstance, if the operator has not had much experience in the practice of venesection, he will do well to be content with opening one of the veins on the back of the hand, after putting the member for some time into warm water, and applying a ligature round the wrist.

Now and then it will happen, that an inflamed and swollen state of the parts in the neighbourhood of the puncture will take place even when the operation has been skilfully performed, and with a clean lancet, and occasionally the inflamation will extend a considerable distance down the arm; when it will be necessary to keep the limb perfectly quiet in a sling to dress the puncture of the vein with some mild simple salve, as the Goulard ointment, page 190, to cover the whole surface of the inflammation with linen, wet with the cooling lotion, No. 68, page 173, or with cold spring water, and administer some gentle aperient medicine, as No. 73, page 176. These means are generally sufficient to remove such inflammation, but if not, skilful medical advice should be obtained without delay.

SUSPENDED ANIMATION

A total suspension of all the mental and corporeal functions may arise :

1. From suffocation produced by hanging or drowning;
2. From the inhalation of carbonic acid, or some other noxious and irrespirable exhalation;
3. From a stroke of lightning or electricity; and
4. From intense cold.

In death, from hanging or drowning, the face is turgid and suffused with livid blood, especially in the former case; when it arises from the inhalation of irrespirable gases, the countenance is pallid; when from a stroke of lightning or electricity; it is also pale, the limbs being flexible, and the blood incoagulable; and when produced by intense cold, it is pale and shrivelled, and the limbs rigid.

In the first variety, or *asphyxia from hanging* or *drowning,* the chief immediate cause is suffocation, or a total obstruction to the respiration. The great majority of professional men of the present day do not consider there is any dislocation of the vertebrae of the neck, but regard the obstruction to respiration to be, in all instances, the chief, and in very many examples, the only cause of death, both in hanging and drowning. In hanging, the aperture of the windpipe is closed against the entrance of air by the pressure of the cord round the throat, and in drowning by a rigid spasm of its muscles. In drowning, it vasu formerly supposed that the suffocation was produced by a rush of water into the cavity of the lungs, but it is now well ascertained, that in many cases of death from submersion, not a drop of water enters into the lungs; and where it does enter, the quantity is, for the most part, very small; and that, whether small or large; it passes the windpipe after death instead of before it, and consequently cannot be a cause of death.

In the second variety of suspended animation, or *that from an inhalation of noxious vapours,* death in many cases takes place instantaneously, and from an utter destruction of the irritability and sensibility of the nervous system. In this case, there is not only a cessation of the action of the heart from the want of the necessary stimulus of the blood afforded by the lungs, but there seems a total abstraction of the nervous power, and this as completely in one part of the frame as in another.

The most fatal gases of the description before us, are the carbonic acid, hydrogen, nitrogen, and several of a more compound kind, which are thrown forth from putrefying animal and vegetable substances, and especially from cemeteries on opening fresh graves. The most common of these gases is the carbonic acid, which is chiefly found as a suffocating vapour in close rooms where charcoal has been burnt, at the bottom of large beer casks or wells, in cellars where a large quantity of wine or other liquors are in a state of fermentation, and in many natural caverns in the earth's surface. As it will not support flame, the common and easiest test, where it is suspected to exist, is that of a lighted candle, which is well known to be extinguished immediately, if this gas be present in a quantity sufficient to be injurious to respiration.

In the third variety, the whole system appears not so much rendered insensible to stimulants, as to be suddenly exhausted of its entire stock of nervous power, like a Leyden phial upon an application of the discharging rod; in consequence of which the limbs are flexible, and the blood does not coagulate.

Asphyxia from intense cold is always preceded by an insurmountable desire to sleep, which the utmost exertion of the will is unable to overpower. The sleep is, in most cases, fatal, and becomes the sleep of death. Extreme cold being one of the most formidable sedatives, carrying off the heat of the body far more rapidly than it can be recruited, it exhausts it of its irritable and sensible power, and death thus insensibly takes place.

Treatment; of suffocation by drowning—Here the two grand means by which we are to operate are the *restoration of breathing,* and the *promotion of warmth and circulation.* Dr. H. Silvester's method is now considered the beat, and his directions are—Place the patient on his back, with the shoulders raised and supported on a folded article of dress, and secure the feet, in a spacious room with a very good fire. Send immediately for medical assistance and blankets.

To maintain a free entrance of air into the windpipe. Wipe the mouth and nostrils. Draw forward the patient's tongue, and keep it projecting beyond the lips. *If the lower jaw be gently raised, the teeth may, be made to hold the tongue in the required position. Should it be found necessary, the tongue may be retained in that position by passing a handkerchief under the chin and fastening it over the head.*

To imitate the movements of deep respiration—Raise the patient's arms upwards by the sides of his head, and then keep them stretched steadily but gently upwards and forwards for two seconds. This action enlarges the capacity of the chest by drawing up the ribs, and induces an *inspiration.* Next, turn down the patient's arms and press them gently and firmly for two seconds against the sides of the chest. This action diminishes the cavity of the thorax, by pressing down the ribs, and produces a forcible *expiration.* Repeat these measures alternately, deliberately, and perseveringly fifteen times in a minute.

To induce circulation and warmth, and to excite inspiration—Rub the limbs from the extremities towards the heart. Replace wet clothing by warm and dry covering. Occasionally dash cold water in the patient's face. These measures are perfectly compatible with the systematic performance of the imitation of the movements of respiration. A similar remark applies to the use of the warm water bath, or hot air bath, if required. Should a warm bath be procurable, the body may be placed in it upto the neck, continuing "to imitate the movements of breathing". Raise the body in twenty seconds from the bath, and dash cold water against the chest and face, and occasionally pass ammonia under the nose.

To excite inspiration—During the employment of the above method excite the nostrils with snuff, smelling salts, or tickle the throat with a feather. Rub the chest and face warm, and dash cold and hot (temperature 120° Fahr.) water alternately on them.

These measures of imitating the movements of respiration,

rubbing the limbs, and applying warmth to every part of the body should be unremittingly continued for many hours. For this purpose relays of rubbers should be provided, each relay waiting outside the room till their services are required, so as not to render the air impure by their breathing. Mr. South refers to a case in which no sign of revival appeared until the rubbing, etc. had been continued for eight hours and a half from the time of the accident. A full expiration of warm air from the lips of a bystander should be repeatedly forced into the patient's mouth, and his nostrils held close to prevent its escape by that channel. Inflation may also be attempted by a pair of common bellows; or which is far better, if it can be readily procured, by a pair of bellows communicating with a pipe introduced through the nose or mouth into the windpipe, or as some have judiciously recommended, into an aperture made between the rings of the windpipe. If the lungs cannot be fully inflated by the other means advised, this aperture in the windpipe should invariably be made, and without much loss of time, since effectual inflation is more certainly secured by it than any other method, and the operation; if skilfully performed, is quite safe. Injections of assafoetida and oil of turpentine, or other stimulants, mixed with warm water, should at the same time be thrown into the rectum; and, if it be possible, some warm and cordial stimulant, as volatile tincture of valerian, volatile alkali, brandy, or the compound spirit of lavender, should be conveyed into the stomach by means of a canula or catheter.

Blood-letting was formerly recommended, but is now never employed.

Tobacco injections are altogether improper.

Returning life is first usually discoverable by the symptoms of sighing, gasping, twitching, slight palpitation, or pulsation of the heart; in effect, by a weak action of most of the organs. Our efforts should here be redoubled, for the feeble spark still requires to be solicited and nourished into a permanent flame, and has often disappeared from a relaxation of labour. A spoonful or two of warm wine, or wine or brandy and water, should now be given by the mouth, as soon as the power of swallowing is sufficiently restored;

which should be shortly succeeded by light, warm, and nourishing food of any kind, with a well-heated bed, and perfect tranquillity.

In attempting the recovery of *those who have hung themselves,* the same means are to be resorted to. Here bleeding from the jugular vein may be more frequently found necessary than in attending the drowned, since in hanging there is a greater tendency to apoplectic symptoms than in drowning; yet even here the quantity extracted need not be large, and should rarely exceed six or eight ounces.

How long the living principle may, under the foregoing circumstances, remain attached to the animal frame, and afford a chance of recovery, is not ascertained with any degree of accuracy, but I believe it exists in many instances longer than is generally supposed; and there are some undoubted cases of recovery, both from drowning and hanging, after such a lapse of time as ought to teach us the useful lesson of the necessity of not despairing too early. If the submersion has not exceeded five minutes, persons will be usually found to recover without much difficulty. After a quarter of an hour or twenty minutes, recovery is not common; and after half an hour it is nearly hopeless. Yet of twenty-three instances of the recovery of drowned persons at Paris, one was restored to life after having been three-quarters of an hour under water, four after having been half an hour, and three after a quarter of an hour. Mr. Glover, a surgeon in London, relates the case of a man who was restored to life after twenty-nine minutes hanging, and continued in good health for many years after; but his exertions for the recovery of this person were continued unremittingly for four hours and a half, before any signs of returning life were visible.

In a suspension of animation arising from the inhalation of Noxious Airs, the patient, if any degree of sensibility remain, should be freely exposed to the open air, instead of to a heated atmosphere, as in the preceding variety; and if he can swallow, acidulous liquids, as lemonade, etc. should be given him. If insensible, cold water should be largely dashed on his face; strong vinegar, and especially aromatic vinegar, be rubbed about his nostrils, and held under them, and stimulating clysters of assafoetida, or oil of turpentine, etc. mixed with water be injected. The lungs should be inflated with the warm breath of a healthy man, as advised under the preceding variety, or with oxygen gas. The inflation with oxygen gas is highly to be recommended.

But it appears that the use of the concentrated solution of chloride of soda or lime, is the most speedy and certain means of restoring persons who have been suffocated with carbonic acid gas, in any shape or combination, as it arises, for example, from burning charcoal, or from accumulated filth, or is encountered in descending into wells or cellars, or in opening extensive public sewers; etc. The patient should be brought into the open air, and a bottle of the solution of chloride of soda or lime, held close to his nostrils, so as to cause him to inspire it, which should be continued until the patient has fully regained his consciousness and the power of walking, which he should be kept doing for some time in the open air. Acidulated liquors may with propriety be given at the same time.[1]

1. The relation of the following case will be interesting to all my readers; and may serve to impress upon their minds the value of the above *chlorides* in asphyxia, from inhaling carbonic acid gas. A workman of a vermicelli maker was exposed to a current of deleterious gas, which proceeded from an accumulation of filth and rubbish heaped together from a pit of night soil which was undergoing repair. He fell without consciousness. M. Labarraque was called to the patient soon after the accident; the symptoms were, pulse strong, but furtive on pressure; excessive rigidity of the limbs; arms stretched, stiff and almost cold; head thrown backwards; veins of the neck turgid; face and lips violet-coloured; eyes closed, dull and insensible; respiration appeared extinct; the danger seemed imminent; vinegar, aether, and strong ammonia, placed under the patient's nostrils, produced no effect. The sensibility could not be recalled. A napkin moistened in the solution was placed under the patient's nostrils, and in less than one minute he uttered an acute and plaintive cry or groan; the rigidity ceased; his eyes opened to shut again in a few seconds; the tetanic rigidity had re-appeared with its frightful train. M. Labarraque had withdrawn the *chloride* too soon. The usual stimulants again tried produced no effect. The *chloride* was re-applied; in less than a minute the rigidity of the limbs ceased, and the patient sent forth a piercing cry, which was stopped by the linen impregnated with the *chloride.* A full inspiration took place, the air necessarily passing through the moistened linen, was therefore charged with *chloride* saturated with water. The disinfection of the gas contained in the chest was no doubt complete, since the symptoms ceased. He was made to walk in the street; keeping the *chloride* under his nostrils. Repose and the open air were afterwards prescribed, and the patient recovered his health, as perfectly as before the accident. Another case of asphyxia, from a similar cause, is related by M. Labarraque, in which the patient immediately recovered from adopting the same means after forty-eight house had elapsed since the commencement of the symptoms. In this instance the patient was not altogether insensible, though in a most deplorable condition.

A proper use of electricity is also, in many instances, found very serviceable. The fluid should be transmitted along the channel of the nerve, from the seat of the phrenic nerve in the neck, to the seat of the diaphragm, or that of the par vagum and great sympathetic nerve immediately under the sterno-mastoid muscle. Little advantage is likely to accrue from passing the electric aura across the chest, directly through the heart and lungs, which is a common practice.

The general plan of medical treatment proper when *animation has been suspended from a stroke of lightning,* has been detailed under the first variety. Stimulants of the most active kind should be resorted to without loss of time, as volatile alkali, and the stimulating liniments at page 161, externally; and phosphorus, brandy, and volatile tincture of valerian, internally. But of all stimulants, that of electricity seems to be especially called for in the present case.

In the treatment of a person who has been so long exposed to *extreme cold,* as to be in a torpid and apparently lifeless state, great caution is necessary in the employment of warmth, since its too quick and free application will undoubtedly produce mortification, and endanger life. The body should be first rubbed all over with snow or very cold water, and after active friction of this kind has been continued for a quarter of an hour, it should be wiped perfectly dry, and submitted to the friction of warm hands, several persons being engaged in the process simult-aneously. The body ought not, in the first instance, to be brought into a warm room; but after the friction with cold water has been continued for the period specified, and the body been wiped dry, then removal will be very proper and necessary, and it should be laid in flannel. Warm air may then be breathed into the lungs, and a little lukewarm wine and water conveyed into the stomach. Persons who have been buried in snow for a considerable time, or so exposed to intense cold, as to be deprived of animation for some hours, have been perfectly restored by these means; and it would be highly criminal in any professional man to relax his exertions to recover such persons, until his efforts have been strenuously exerted without effect for several hours. I have reason to fear, that many lives have been lost under such circumstances, from want of information and perseverance on the part of those medical practitioners who have been called upon for assistance.

In the treatment of infants who have been overlayed, or otherwise suffocated by the carelessness or inattention of their nurses, and of persons who suddenly expire in convulsions, or fainting fits, precisely the same plan should be pursued as is laid down under the first variety, or suspended animation from drowning. Here, as in suffocation from drowning, the two grand agents of restoration are warmth, and inflation of the lungs; and if these means are resorted to with *judgment* and *perseverance,* many of such cases will terminate favourably, which would be lost under a less vigorous and patient treatment.

Of the treatment of poisoning by CHLOROFORM, I have already treated at pages 33-34.

INTOXICATION

Few persons are fully aware of the injurious effects resulting from a daily use of spirituous and other fermented liquors in large quantities; yet their destructive tendency is proved to a demonstration, by the visible effects produced on the minds and bodies of the unhappy victims of this base and demoralizing practice, and on animals who feed on the refuse of distilleries and breweries. Those persons who exceed a moderate quantity of such drink, in a few years grow heavy and awkward in their gait; and bloated in their countenance; their complexion becomes bilious and sallow; their breath fetid; their eyes inflamed; their nose red and swollen; their appetite deficient and capricious, and their bowels irregular; and it is a remarkable fact, that hogs, fowls, and other domestic animals, when allowed to feed at pleasure on the refuse left after distillation and fermentation in distilleries and brewers' yards, soon become diseased, their intestines and livers exhibiting a state of great enlargement and hardness. By a large quantity of these liquors is here meant, any portion that sensibly affects the head or stomach, and which renders the individual taking it uncomfortable, either soon after or on the succeeding morning. If a man, after partaking of strong liquors, is less able to transact any important and difficult business than he was before, he may be assured of having not only exceeded the bounds of prudence and moderation, but of having taken such a quantity as cannot fail to be more or less injurious to the stomach, bowels, and heart, the healthy action of which are of the first importance to our bodily comfort and happiness.

It is fully ascertained, that drinking freely of strong liquors, especially of ardent spirits, immediately deranges the stomach, intestines, and liver, three of the most important organs in the human frame; and, in many instances, a short continuance of this practice brings on indurations and positive disease in the structure of those parts. Such effects are more frequently induced by the daily indulgence in what is too often considered a small quantity of such drink than is generally imagined. This practice affects the teeth also very visibly, giving them a stained and foul appearance. General Norton, the Mohawk chief, who was in this country a few years ago, was asked by a professional gentleman concerning the state of the teeth among the Indians. His reply was decisive upon this subject. "When the Indians (says he) are in their own settlements, living upon the produce of the chase, and drinking water, their teeth always look clean and white; but when they go into the United States, and get spirituous liquors, their teeth look dirty and yellow; and I have often heard that they were frequently afflicted with the tooth-ache, and obliged to have their teeth drawn".

The state of intoxication is similar to that of incipient apoplexy, or palsy. Drunken men stagger, their tongue loses its power of speech, they stammer and see things double, and moving circularly. The mind is equally affected, and imbecility is the concomitant effect. All these symptoms of partial palsy arise chiefly from the pressure of the blood-vessels on the brain, which are then surcharged with blood. If the intoxication has arrived at its utmost height, there is no longer any difference between this and the true appolexy, and the powers of sensation and motion are greatly impaired, if not entirely suspended. If, in this state, one of the smaller blood-vessels that press on the brain with unusual weight should accidentally burst, he is in danger of instant death.

A person much intoxicated ought to be carried without delay into a room of moderate temperature, and placed in bed between the blankets, with his head raised, particular care being taken that his neck is no way twisted, or has anything tight about it. Indeed, all close bandages on the body should be loosed; and if the individual is desirous of drink, to quench his thirst, the simplest beverages will be the best, such as tea, or toast and water. A gentle emetic of ipecacuanha powder is alwas useful.

When however, a man is found in a state of deep and alarming intoxication, with laborious breathing, cold extremities, and other threatening symptoms, he should be immediately cupped in the back of the neck, or a few ounces of blood taken from the arm, his feet and legs put into warm water, and a sharp purgative clyster, as No. 8, page 146, administered without delay. The clyster may be repeated, if necessary, three or four times within a short period.

Baron Cramer and a German physician of the name of Roth, have highly praised the following medicine as a valuable remedy for tippling and drunkenness. Dr. Roth says that he has succeeded with this medicine in completely curing many poor creatures, both men and women, who were actually killing themselves by this practice. I hope that many in this country addicted to this baneful habit will try it and find it effectual.

Take of Tincture of calumba	1 tea-spoonful;
Tincture of cascarilla	1 tea-spoonful;
Compound tincture of gentian, ...	1 tea-spoonful;
Infusion of quassia	1 wine-glassful;
Diluted sulphuric acid	20 drops.

Mix, and take it twice or thrice a day; and have a jug of cold water dashed over the head every morning on coming out of bed, and the feet bathed in warm water every night. Continue this for six or eight weeks.

Sometimes persons unaccustomed to drink strong liquors exceed the bounds of moderation, and become tipsy from the use of a small quantity of some fermented or spirituous liquor. Those of sober habits may, in an unguarded moment, be overcome in this manner, and such persons will find that the WATER OF AMMONIA often affords effectual and speedy relief in tipsiness. Twelve drops of the *pure water of ammonia* may be taken in a large wine-glassful of milk and water, or. water and if not effectual, it may be repeated in ten minutes after, and again in half an hour.

Dr. Plet relates the case of a young man of nervous and irritable constitution, who on the 15th of January, 1822, became so violently drunk, that he did the most indecent things, and broke every thing he could get at. When Dr. Plet saw him, he was armed with a knife, and running at his parents, with his eyes glaring and his mouth foaming. Twelve drops of the water of ammonia were given him in a glass of sugar and water, and he was calmed immediately, ashamed and confused at his conduct.

THE MEANS OF PREVENTING THE GENERATION, AND CHECKING THE PROGRESS OF TYPHUS, AND OTHER MALIGNANT FEVERS

In order to prevent the generation of malignant fevers, it is necessary to be acquainted with the sources of their contagion, and to avoid them.

Concerning the source of typhus and other contagious diseases, the most probable conjecture is that each, though afterwards propagated by its peculiar contagion, is at first produced independently of contagion, by a concurrence of causes which rarely takes place. And when at any period it happens that no person labours under the disease, it cannot be reproduced unless a sufficient quantity of the contagion is preserved in fomites, (substances impregnated with contagion), or till the same causes which first gave rise to it again conspire. Thus, contagious diseases may for a long time disappear, while a different combination of causes may give rise to others, which in like manner spread by their contagions.

The combination of a very few circumstances, and those of frequent occurrence, is sufficient to produce typhus fever. The most powerful of these are confinement in ill-ventilated and crowded places; uncleanliness of all kinds; the putrid effluvia of animal and vegetable substances; and innutritious and unwholesome food. Hence we find, that typhus frequently arises in hospitals, jails, transport ships, and the close and crowded habitations of the poor, where free ventilation has been little attended to; and it is evident, therefore, that the effluvia of the living body become putrid by stagnation, and are capable of producing it.

The confinement of the putrid effluvia is not always necessary for the production of typhus, for when the cause is sufficiently powerful, the whole air of a neighbourhood may be so loaded as to be capable of producing it. A malignant fever has been occasioned by the offal of a city being accumulated without the walls; and it has often happened tat typhus has spread over the adjacent country, when the dead were left unburied on the field of battle.

Contagious diseases may spread,

1. By actual contact;
2. Through the medium of the air;
3. By means of substances which have been in contact with or near the sick.

Concerning the first of these little need be said. It is probable, that the larger the surface which has been in contact with the sick, and the longer it has been so, the less will be the chance of escaping infection.

The air appears to be the medium through which contagion, in most instances, is applied to the body. It is common for people to be infected in consequence of approaching the sick, without touching them, or any thing which has been in contact with them. It appears from a variety of observations, however, that the contagious atmosphere, that is, the air sufficiently impregnated with the contagion to produce the disease, extends only for a short distance around the sick, not only in typhus, but in scarlet fever, and all other contagious diseases; certainly not above a few yards probably not above a few feet.

Contagion, however, may be conveyed from place to place by the wind, and thus the disease may be communicated at a considerable distance. In proof of this, many facts may be adduced; one of the most striking on record happened on the 12th of May, 1750, at the Old Bailey. The prisoners were kept for nearly a whole day, is a small, ill-ventilated, and crowded apartment; some of them laboured under the jail fever. When they were brought into court, the windows at the end of the hall opposite to the place where the judges sat, were thrown open; the people on the left of the court, whom the wind blew were infected with the fever, while those on the opposite side escaped. The lord chief justice and the recorder, who sat on the lord mayor's right hand, escaped; while the lord mayor and the rest of the bench, who sat on his left, were seized with the distemper. Many of the Middlesex jury on the left side of the court, died of it, while the London jury, who sat opposite to them, received no injury.

Generally speaking, hot weather, and damp foggy weather, is favourable, and cold weather unfavourable, to the spreading of contagious diseases.

The stools, especially if unusually fetid, are most apt to communicate the contagion to the air; next to these, the patient's breath; and then the effluvia from his body.

The last of the ways by which a contagious disease may spread, is by *fomites*, substances impregnated with contagion. Fomites often retain contagion for a great length of time, and may convey it to any distance. It is a general opinion, that fomites more readily communicate the disease, and communicate it in a worse form, than the sick themselves. Dr. Lind remarks, "I am convinced, from very extensive experience, that the body of the sick is not so apt to communicate the infection, as the dirty linen, etc. which has been about him". Contagion adheres to the furniture and utensils employed about the sick, as well as to all kinds of clothes, and even lurks in the walls of the apartments where the sick have lain. Woollen materials and wood are thought most apt to retain it.

On the foregoing facts respecting the sources of the contagion of typhus and other malignant fevers, and the different ways in which they spread, are founded the means of preventing their generation, and many of the precautions employed for checking their progress; and it is obvious, that a careful consideration, and proper use of these facts, will lead to the employment of many of the most powerful means for accomplishing these most desirable purposes. Communication, and especially actual contact with the sick, must be avoided; the patient should be lightly covered with bed-clothes; his chamber should be freed from all unnecessary furniture, and kept perfectly clean; his sheets and body-linen be frequently changed, and instantly taken out of the room; as should also the stools and urine.

Above all things, the chamber and adjoining apartments should be freely ventilated, by opening the opposite windows, or the windows and doors; for it should be constantly remembered, that contagion sufficiently diffused becomes inert, and that without a free circulation of air in the apartments of persons ill with malignant fevers, even fumigation is useless. Next to the free admission of pure air, fumigation with the mineral acids is one of the most effectual means of checking the progress of contagious fevers. The nitric and muriatic acids appear to possess equal power; but the former is preferable where persons are unavoidably obliged to be present, as it is breathed with the least inconvenience. The late Dr. Johnstone, of Worcester, and Dr. Carmichael Smyth, of London, are the physicians to whom we are chiefly indebted for the knowledge of the efficacy of fumigation, with the mineral acids, in destroying the contagion of malignant fevers. Dr. Smith used the nitric acid vapour as a fumigation, with the greatest success, in the typhus fever which broke out in the year 1780, among the Spanish prisoners confined in Winchester Castle, and also in 1798, in checking the further progress of a very malignant fever which had made great ravages among the crews of the Russian ships of war at Sheerness. From the great value of the fumigation, Parliament voted Dr. Smyth 5000(L) as a reward for the discovery.

The mode of obtaining the nitric acid vapour is by decomposing nitre by means of heated sulphuric acid, which may be done as follows : Put half an ounce of sulphuric acid, or best oil of vitriol, into a crucible, glass, or china cup, and warm it over a lamp, or in heated sand, adding to it, from time to time, a little nitre. Several of these vessels are to be placed in the patient's chamber, and the neighbouring apartments and passages, at twenty or thirty feet distance from each other, according to the height of the ceiling, and the virulence of the contagion.

The muriatic acid gas is obtained in the following manner. Put one pound of common salt into an earthern vessel, and pour over it from time to time a small quantity of sulphuric acid, till the whole salt is moistened. If the air is foul and peculiarly offensive, apply a gentle heat under the vessel, to extricate a larger quantity of vapour; but, in general, the simple addition of the acid to the salt will be found sufficient, unless the apartment be very large.

The most simple means of purifying houses and goods, is washing and exposing them to the air, and these are generally sufficient. It is common to wash, or, what is better, to lime-white the walls of houses where the sick have lain; and to procure a free circulation of air, by opening the windows, and making fires in the house. The clothes, and other articles which have been in contact with the sick, should be sprinkled with Condy's Fluid, and washed, then exposed to the air for a considerable time. In the different lazarettos of Europe, exposure to the air for a certain length of time, is generally thought sufficient to purify merchandise, even from cities where the plague rages.

A most valuable discovery was made some years since of substances which have greater power in destroying putrid and offensive effluvia arising from animal and vegetable matter, than any means previously known, and these substances being of very extensive use, and capable of being applied with equal facility, economy and success, they demand some notice in this place. The substances referred to are the chloride of soda and the chloride of lime, and to M. Labarraque, an apothecary in Paris, the honour is due of having discovered their inestimable value, and of having freely communicated their composition, and the mode of applying them, to the public authorities of France, for the general benefit of mankind. M. Labarraque's experiments have been of the most public and decisive nature, and have been carried on under the immediate inspection of some of the most scientific and distinguished physicians, surgeons and chemists, at the *Morgue,*[1] and in all the great hospitals at Paris; in the extensive workshops where catgut and other strings are manufactured from the intestines of animals, in a state of putrefaction; in the filthy and offensive public sewers, and in the lazaretto at Marseilles; from which it clearly appears, that the chlorides of soda and lime are highly efficacious in the destruction of noxious effluvia and that they may be used with equal success in destroying the infection of putrid fevers, in purifying the wards of hospitals and sick rooms, in the disinfection of crowded ships and foul stables, in the prevention of putrefaction in bodies previously to interment, and in the disinfection of reservoirs of urine, in the purification of putrid water, in short, in the total destruction of every species of infectious effluvia, and offensive odour. It has been used with excellent effects in correcting the fetid discharges from foul ulcers, cancer, hospital gangrene, carbuncle, etc.

In typhus, putrid sore throat, measles, small-pox, and other infectious fevers, the apartment of the patient is to be freely sprinkled with diluted chloride of lime, twice a day or oftener, if the disease be very malignant, or the apartment unusually confined. Sometimes it is advisable also to leave a small quantity, as a pint or two, exposed on a dish, or in a bason, in the sick chamber. And where many persons are living in the same house, or the disease is particularly rife, it is highly desirable to sprinkle the adjoining apartments and passages with the same liquid.

Medical men and others, attending patients labouring under contagious diseases, should have a bottle of the diluted liquid always at hand, which they ought to take with them and respire whenever they approach the bed-side of the patient, at the same time sprinkling some on the floor, and around the bed.

Ships which have been impregnated with contagious matter, are to be disinfected in the same manner, *viz.* by sprinkling their

1. The place where all the dead bodies found in the Seine, or in Paris, or its environs, are deposited for inspection, that they may be claimed or identified previously to interment.

whole interior with the diluted chloride of lime twice or thrice a day.

In no case ought the use of any disinfecting fluid to supersede strict attention to cleanliness, and a free ventilation of the apartments of the sick.

BURNETT'S PATENT DISINFECTING FLUID and CONDY'S DISINFECTING FLUID seem to be more efficacious in purifying than the chlorides of lime or soda; and they possess the peculiar advantage of having in themselves *no smell.* They are sold by all druggists, with full directions for use. *Condy's fluid* is the permanganate of potash, and is thought very highly of by professional men generally.

POISONS

Poisons are naturally divided into three classes, *viz.* mineral, vegetable and animal.

Mineral Poisons

The chief of the mineral poisons are the strong acids, as oil of vitriol, muriatic, nitric, and oxalic acids; the concentrated alkalies, as potash, soda, and ammonia; and the, preparations of arsenic, copper, antimony, mercury, silvery nitre, and sal ammoniac.

Strong Acids.—The symptoms which quickly follow the swallowing of oil of vitriol, or any other strong acid, are acid burning, and excessive disagreeable taste; acute pain in the throat, stomach and bowels; insuperable fetid smell from the breath; frequent eructations, vomiting of various coloured matters, sometimes mixed with blood, producing in the mouth a great sensation of bitterness, effervescing when mixed with chalk, and reddening the tincture of turnsole or litmus; in general, copious evacuations, more or less bloody; colic, and pains so acute, that even the weight of any clothing becomes insupportable; difficulty of breathing; frequent and irregular pulse; excessive thirst, yet drink augments the pain, and is shortly after vomited; the skin, particularly of the lower extremities, appears frozen; cold and clammy sweats;

vain and repeated efforts to make water; impossibility of maintaining the same position; convulsions of the face and limbs. The intellectual faculties are rarely disordered. Al1 these symptoms, however, are not always found in the same person, and their severity will in every instance, much depend upon the strength and nature of the acid. The nitric acid produces yellow spots upon the lips and skin.

In the treatment of these cases, the most efficient antidote is *calcined magnesia;* next to this *soap*, and then *chalk and water.* An ounce of calcined magnesia should be mixed with a pint of water, and a glassful taken every two minutes, so as to promote vomiting, and prevent the acid from acting. Should this not be at hand, dissolve half an ounce of soap in a pint of water and give a glassful every few minutes. Or chalk and water in any dose will be found very useful. If neither of these can be directly procured, decoction of linseed, marshmallows, gum arabic, or any other mucilaginous liquor may be taken in the mean time; for the success of the treatment depends entirely upon the activity with which aid is given. Clysters prepared with magnesia, soap, or chalk, should also he given.

The use of emetics, or other means of exciting sickness, as the finger, etc., is not advisable here, but the speedy employment of *Read's Stomach Pump*, with the view to extract its contents, is highly proper in this and every other case of poison taken into the stomach.

The acid being neutralized by the foregoing means, the in-, flammation caused by its action is next to occupy our attention. To reduce this, the patient should be placed in a warm bath at about 95 degrees, and the region of the stomach and bowels fomented with cloths rung out of lukewarm water. If relief be not speedily obtained by these measures, fourteen or sixteen leeches should be applied to the surface of the abdomen, and blood must also be taken from the arm. If there be a difficulty of swallowing, and the inflammation be great, twelve or fifteen leeches should be applied to the neck. The repetition and extent of the blood-letting, both by leeches and the lancet, must be entirely regulated by the severity of the pain, and the urgency of the other symptoms denoting inflammation; for the safety of the patient henceforth depends upon the copious evacuation of blood; and the debility caused thereby is to be considered merely as a slight inconvenience. These energetic measures will be assisted by the administration of a drink made with linseed, mallows, or gum arabic boiled in water. Every sort of food, not excepting broth, is to be forbidden.

Should the convulsive movements continue after the inflammation has subsided, thirty drops of compound spirit of sulphuric ether, twenty drops of laudanum, and three ounces of distilled water, may be mixed together, and a table-spoonful be given every fifteen minutes. The patient must return to his usual solid diet by very slow degrees.

Strong Alkalies—The effects of these are nearly similar to those caused by acids, except that the taste of the alkalies is not sour, but acrid and urinous. The matter vomited does not effervesce when mixed with chalk, but turns the blue colour of violets green.

Vinegar and lemon-juice are the best antidotes to the concentrated volatile alkali, potash, and all other alkaline poisons. A glassful of water, mixed with a table-spoonful of vinegar, or lemon juice, should be given frequently, and in defect of these, simple water, in such quantities as to cause vomiting. Emetics, and other irritating means, are to be avoided. If this be not sufficient, the treatment by leeches, the lancet, warm bathing, etc. as above recommended, must be followed.

Corrosive Sublimate, Calomel, Etc.— When large quantities, either of corrosive sublimate, arsenic, copper, or any of the preparations of antimony, tin, silver, etc. are taken, the patient complains, in general, of a severe constriction in the throat, pain in the back part of the mouth, stomach, and intestines, and a desire to vomit, vomiting follows with more or less violence. The matter vomited is of various colours, often mixed with blood, it does not effervesce when thrown on the ground, or mired with chalk; it never changes the colour of violets green, and when it reddens the tincture of litmus or red cabbage, it is in a very slight degree. To these alarming symptoms are joined frequent and fetid eructations; hiccup; difficulty of respiration, and almost suffocation; the polse becomes small, hard and accelerated, and in certain cases, it may said to vibrate under the finger like catgut.

An inextinguishable thirst, difficulty of making water, cramp, the extremities of an icy coldness, horrible convulsions, general decay of strength, the features of the face changed, and delirium, are the symptoms which announce approaching death, unless energetic measures for relief are speedily put in practice.

The *white of egg* beat up with cold water, is the best counter-poison to corrosive sublimate, and all other mercurial preparations. In defect of this, milk may be used with great success. The whites of twelve or fifteen fresh eggs should be beat up and mixed with two pints of cold water, and a glassful taken every two or three minutes, so as to favour vomiting. If the number indicated be not at hand, as many as are should be used, and others immediately sought after. The yolks may also be used with some advantage. In defect of eggs altogether, milk, gum-water, decoction of linseed, mallows, barley, or sugared water, should be taken in abundance. If, after taking the number of eggs prescribed, the symptoms be not removed, the same should be repeated, these should be prepared before hand, so that we may act with the greater promptitude. The patient is then to be treated by bleeding with leeches and the lancet, etc. as ordered under the head of strong acids, the abstraction of blood being proportioned to the severity of the symptoms denoting inflammation.

Arsenic.— Though this article is not unfrequently administered in small doses, for the cure of ague, and other diseases, it should never be forgotten that, even in extremely minute quantities, it is an energetic poison, which is readily absorbed into the circulation, and has a strung tendency to promote disease in the heart.

In cases of poison by arsenic, medical practitioners universally agree, that the first indication is to empty the stomach as quickly as possible. If Mr. Read's syringes invented for this purpose, be at hand, it is by far the best contrivance, and serves to empty the stomach more certainly and speedily than any kind of emetics. In case this syringe cannot be procured directly, the patient should drink large quantities of sugar and water, of warm or cold water, of linseed tea, and other mucilaginous fluids; by this means the stomach is filled, and vomiting effected. A drink composed of equal quantities of lime water, and sugar and water, may also be given, and sometimes with great advantage. At the same time, the throat ought to be tickled with a feather or the finger. Some practitioners are in the habit of giving emetics in the present case, while others refrain from them, on account of their tendency to increase the irritation created by this poison. If ever they are resorted to sulphate of zinc, in a dose of twenty-five grains, is the most proper.

When inflammation of the abdomen, and alarming nervous symptoms prevail, the means of relief are blood-letting, the warm bath, fomentations, emollient clysters, and antispasmodic medicines, as advised under strong acids.

When the poison has been evacuated from the stomach, it should never be forgotten, that the success of the treatment will depend, in a great measure, upon the regimen observed during the patient's convalescence, which is almost always tedious, and he should be chiefly nourished with milk, gruel, rice, and beverages of a softening mucilaginous nature. This advice is applicable to convalescencies after swallowing any mineral poison.

Copper—The white of eggs is the best antidote to all the preparations of copper when taken in poisonous quantities. A person who has swallowed verdigris, blue vitriol, or any salt of copper, is to be treated after the manner directed for corrosive sublimate.

Tartar Emetic— When large and poisonous doses of tartar emetic, or any other antimonial medicine, have been swallowed, should there be severe vomiting with cramp in the stomach, abundant supplies of sugar and water, or simple water, must be administered. If the vomiting continue after the poison may be supposed to have been rejected, and the pain be augmented, give a grain of opium, or thirty drops of laudanum, or of the solution of acetate of morphia, and repeat it at an interval of a quarter of an hour, for two or three times, if the symptoms are not calmed. In cases where the symptoms continue or increase, twelve or fifteen leeches should be applied to the abdomen, and to the throat also, if there be a great difficulty of swallowing.

If the individual who has taken the antimonial preparation does not vomit, and yet suffers from the other symptoms, several glasses of sugar and water should be taken; and if, in spite of this, vomiting does not occur, a decoction of gall-nuts, or of Peruvian bark, should be administered directly. Four or five gall-nuts may be boiled for ten minutes in two quarts of water, and then strained; of which a tumblerful should be taken every five or Six minutes. If tire gall-nuts are not at hand, two ounces of yellow bark may be boiled for the same time in the same quantity of water, and liven in the same manner. Emetics ought not to be given. If, notwithstanding the use of these means, the symptoms continue, the proper treatment will consist in the use of leeches to the region of the stomach, the warm bath, fomentations, etc. as already recommended under the head of strong acids, at page 305-06.

Tin—Milk is the best counter-poison to the salts of tin, of which several glassfuls should be given; or, in defect of milk, warm or cold water, to excite vomiting; as, for the rest, if the symptoms increase, the means of relief are bleeding, fomentations, emollient clysters, and other means for subduing inflammation recommended at page 306-07.

Lunar Caustic, or Nitrate of Silver—*Common kitchen salt* is the most effectual antidote to lunar caustic. A solution of a large spoonful in two pints of water should be made, and several glasses of this salt-water taken directly; vomiting will take place, and the symptoms diminish. If they should continue, the treatment calculated to allay irritation and inflammation, as pointed out at page 306-07, must be followed.

Poisoning from *bismuth* and *zinc*, is to be treated in the same manner as that produced by arsenic.

Nitre— When nitre has been swallowed in an excessive dose, the treatment should be the same as that advised for arsenic, except that the lime water must be suppressed. *See* page 306-07.

Lead—Sugar of lead, extract of lead, and the other poisonous preparations of this mineral, when taken in a large dose, give rise to a sweet, astringent, metallic taste, constriction of the throat, pain in the stomach, desire to vomit, or vomiting, and that often mixed with blood, fetid eructations, hiccup, difficulty of respiration, and other alarming symptoms.

Glauber's salt, Epsom salt, and hard water, are the best antidotes here. Several glasses of a solution of one of these salts should be given. The proportion may be half an ounce of the salt to a wine quart of water. When we have by this means occasioned vomiting, and expelled or decomposed the poison, and the principal symptoms are relieved, sugar and water, or gum water may be taken; but should the pain and other indications of inflammation' make progress, the treatment by leeching indicated at page 247, must be followed.

Vegetable Poisons

The principal vegetable poisons are opium, hemlock, foxglove, thorn-apple, deadly nightshade, henbane, poisonous mushrooms and prussic acid.

The general effect of these poisons, when introduced into the stomach, in a large quantity, are stupor; numbness; heaviness in the head; desire to vomit, slight at first, but afterwards insupportable; a sort of intoxication; pupil of the eye dilated; furious or lively delirium; sometimes pain; convulsions more or less violent of different parts of the body; palsy of the limbs; pulse variable, but in general strong and full at the commencement of the disease; respiration somewhat accelerated. Quickly the convulsions and dejection increase, and death ensues if relief be not speedily afforded.

Opium, Hemlock, Nightshad, and Henbane—In poisoning from either of these articles, and indeed from any vegetable or mineral substance, the first indication is to evacuate the stomach and I repeat, that if Mr. Read's syringe or stomach pump be at hand, it is far the most certain and the best way of accomplishing this evacuation. In defect of it, a scruple, or half a drachm, of sulphate of zinc should be given directly, in water, and repeated after an interval of a quarter of an hour, if necessary. It should rarely or never be repeated a third time. The success of the emetic will be favoured by irritating the throat with the finger or a feather, and especially by freely sprinkling and dashing cold water over the face, neck and breast of the patient. The free application of cold water to the surface of the body, under the present circumstances, has often a greater and more immediate effect in rousing the sufferer than any other expedient, and should never be neglected. Much liquid should not be given with the view of hastening the vomiting; as, far from being useful, the malady is thereby aggravated. If it be supposed that the poison has been taken long enough to reach the intestines, the purgative clyster, No. 8, page 146, ought to be administered.

Vinegar and lemon-juice are the best antidotes to these narcotic poisons; but they must not be given till the stomach has been evacuated. After the poison has been altogether ejected, or nearly so, a cup of water, strongly acidulated with vinegar or lemon juice, should be given every five minutes, which may be alternated with a strong cup of coffee, or green tea; and the limbs be rubbed with a piece of flannel or a flesh-brush. The use of the coffee and acidulated water must be continued until the patient is out of danger. The dashing of cold water on the surface of the upper part of the body should likewise be continued till recovery is insured. The powers of the system must also be supported by giving ammonia, brandy, and other cordials. Half a tea-spoonful of the pure water of ammonia mixed in a small tea-cupful of water, has sometimes great effect in rousing the sufferer, and may be repeated frequently, according to the degree of stupor present.

When the drowsiness is extreme, and the disease resembles an attack of apoplexy, bleeding from the arm or jugular vein must be had recourse to.

Foxglove—Here vomiting should be excited by the exhibition of sulphate of zinc, as just advised for poisoning by opium, and after the poison has been evacuated, the vinegar and water recommended under opium should be given. Twenty or thirty drops of laudanum in a glass of brandy and water may also be administered frequently, or a little of the water of ammonia, as above recommended.

Poisonous Mushrooms—The same treatment as advised under opium is proper here.

Prussic Acid—This is the most energetic of all known poisons, and when strong prussic acid is taken it destroys life before any succour whatever can be given. But when à large dose of the diluted acid has given rise to the symptoms detailed above, vomiting must be directly excited by the administration of a scruple of sulphate of zinc, as recommended for poisoning from opium. After the evacuation of the stomach, frequent draughts of strong coffee must be taken, and then, at intervals of half an hour, three or four table-spoonfuls of oil of turpentine mixed with the coffee. Brandy, water of ammonia, and other cordials, are also proper, to support the vital powers.

Animal Poisons

The venomous animals whose bite or sting is accompanied by symptoms more or less poisonous, are the viper, the rattle-snake, the Cobra di Capello, and other serpents found in hot climates. Some kinds of fish also occasionally prove poisonous, when eaten, particularly in tropical climates.

***Viper, Rattle-snake,* etc.**—The effects which follow the sting of these animals, are a sharp pain in the wounded part, which quickly spreads to all the members, and even to the interior of the body; great swelling, at first hard and pale, then reddish, livid, which appears gangrenous, and gradually augments; fainting, vomiting, and convulsive movements; the stomach is so sensible that it can retain nothing; a frequent, small, concentrated and irregular pulse; difficult respiration; copious cold sweats; disturbed sight; and the intellectual faculties are deranged. When the swelling is much increased, the small vessels no longer suffer the blood to circulate; and the pulse becomes hardly perceptible. When all the symptoms enumerated have acquired a degree of intensity, the patient dies.

The first thing to be done in these cases, if called early, is to give twenty or thirty drops of *pure water of ammonia* in a wine-glassful or a tea-cupful of water, or of water and white wine or brandy; then place a ligature rather tightly; immediately above the wound, and pour ammonia into the wound. Repeat the ammonia in half an hour. The ligature should not be so narrow as to irritate the skin; nor should it be continued too long a time, as it favours, if long continued, the development of gangrene. But the most direct and efficient means of counteracting the absorption of the poison is suction, and this is most effectually done by exhausting a cupping glass over the wound. The cupping glass must be applied as soon after the injury as possible, and kept exhausted until all danger is passed. It has been proved lately in France, that the bite of vipers, both on man and inferior animals, were rendered entirely harmless by the application of cupping glasses. Even the juice of the deadly Upas tree of Java, and prussic acid, have been inserted into wounds made in small animals, and the application of the cupping glasses has counteracted any deleterious effects. Dr. Barry, an English physician residing at Paris, has the honour of this valuable discovery.

If the cupping glass be not at hand, a mixture of equal parts of volatile alkali (pure water of ammonia) and oil, or strong ammonia itself, should be applied to the wound, and the swelled parts which surround it. When the principal symptoms are diminished, remove this, cover the wound with a rag dipped in sweet oil, and rub the limb from time to time with the same oil mixed with a small quantity of volatile alkali, in the proportion of an ounce of the oil to a tea-spoonful of alkali. If the swelling be very considerable, and the pain acute, remove the ligature. Scarifications should not be made. Hartshorn may be taken, and brandy, if the water of ammonia, is not at hand.

At the same time, the volatile alkali, (water of ammonia) must be given internally, in a dose of twenty or thirty drops in a glassful of water, every half hour in the beginning, if necessary, and afterwards every two hours.

If the case be urgent, as in the bite of the Cobra di Capello, or rattle-snake, the utmost dependence may be placed on a free use of the caustic volatile alkali (pure water of ammonia) both internally and externally, together with sound wine and brandy and water. Ammonia should be applied undiluted to the wound, and twenty, or even thirty drops taken in water every quarter of an hour, or as circumstances indicate. Free doses of the alkali are required. A tea-spoonful in water has sometimes been taken.

A glass of Madeira or Sherry wine, or brandy, may also be given frequently; and the patient is to be placed in bed; well covered, and perspiration promoted as much as possible. An emetic of twenty grains of ipecacuhana powder, or of sulphate of zinc, may sometimes be useful. If there be much bilious vomiting or jaundice, and gangrene continues to make progress, the decoction of bark should be given; a large wine-glassful of this decoction may be exhibited every three hours, mixed with twenty drops of volatile alkali. If, on the contrary, the symptoms diminish, and the individual enters into a state of convalescence, no solid food must be allowed during the first few days; but only a small quantity of light thin broth, with bread and light pudding.

The internal use of arsenic is also sometimes of eminent service in the bites of venomous serpents, but nothing is equal to ammonia. Twenty or thirty drops of the arsenical solution may be taken in water, or lemon-juice, every half-hour, during four successive hours; the purgative clyster, No. 8, page 146, being administered without delay, and the painful limb, or part, rubbed with a liniment, composed of half an ounce of, oil of turpentine, half an ounce of volatile alkali, and an ounce and a half of oil.

The guacho plant of America is very efficacious in counteracting the injurious effects of these poisons. The Indians make great use of it for this purpose, and it is invariably successful. They swallow one or two table-spoonfuls of the juice of this plant, and inoculate themselves with it in five or six wounds, which they make principally in the side of the chest; and between the fingers.

Scorpion and Centipede.—The sting of the European scorpion. is not very dangerous. It occasions serious danger only in those climates where the heat is excessive; it then produces a red spot of the size of a man's little finger nail, which gradually increases and becomes very black in the centre. This black spot is where the sting entered. The part swells and is painful, the inflammation is more or less considerable, and to these symptoms succeed alternate chills and fever, numbness, vomiting, hiccup and great trembling.

The internal treatment should be that directed when speaking of the viper. The caustic volatile alkali in water *(aqua ammonia pura),* or spirits of hartshorn, twenty drops to a wine-glassful of water, will probably be the best internal medicine, and the same article pure, or mixed with oil, may be applied to the wound; of a poultice of linseed meal; or bread and milk, moistened with a tea-spoonful of the volatile alkali, may be laid over it, and renewed twice or thrice a day. Wine or brandy and water should also by given.

When the sting of the centipede proves very troublesome, it may be treated in the same way.

The sting of the *Wasp, Bee, Tarantula,* etc. occasions, in our climate, only a slight degree of pain and swelling. It is sufficient to rub the parts with a, mixture of one part of olive oil, and one part of volatile alkali. The same application is of great service in the stinging of the *Mosquito*. If the symptoms should, from any cause, run extremely high, it will be advisable to apply the caustic volatile alkali to the wound, and adopt the internal treatment advised for the bite of the viper.

Whenever the sting of the insect has been left, it is advisable to extract it.

Poisonous Fish.—Muscles, the dolphin, the congor eel, the king fish, and the yellow-bill sprat, and some other fish, may, under certain circumstances, occasion symptoms more or less serious, and even death has been known to be the consequence of their ingestion.

If experience proves that the fish we have named are sometimes poisonous, it also demonstrates that they are far from being so at all times, and to all persons. The individual who can eat them with impunity in our climate, and in all seasons, may be greatly incommoded by them in hot climates, and especially during the summer season.

The usual effects of such fish, when they disagree, are acute pain in the stomach and head, nausea, difficulty of breathing, general uneasiness, intolerable itching of every part of the body, a crimson eruption on the skin, fainting fits, sometimes convulsions, with a coppery taste in the mouth, and a burning sensation in the throat.

The yellow-bill sprat (*clupoea thrysa*), has caused horrible convulsions, inflammation of the stomach, and death at the end of half an hour.

In the treatment of such cases, the first object should be to evacuate the stomach by the administration of an emetic of twenty grains of sulphate of zinc, or half a drachm of powdered ipecacuanha, dissolved in a little water; and should the poison have been some time swallowed, so as to have passed into the bowels, administer the clyster No. 8, page 146, after the emetic has operated. Immediately after these remedies have taken effect, mix together two drachms of ether, a drachm of laudanum, and four ounces of mint water, or any fluid at hand, of which the patient should take a table-spoonful every quarter of an hour, or ammonia may be given. Besides which, mix two table spoonfuls of vinegar or lemon juice, in half a pint of water, and let this be taken as a common drink. If the symptoms grow alarming, the use of a little strong brandy and water, or good Madeira wine, with a few drops of volatile alkali in each draught, would be necessary. If there are violent and continued pains of the stomach, apply twelve leeches to the upper part of the belly.

DISLOCATIONS

When a bone is forced out of its proper situation, so as to impede or destroy its natural functions, it is said to be *luxated* or *dislocated.*

As this often happens to persons in situations where no medical assistance can be obtained directly, by which means limbs, and even lives, are frequently lost, I shall lay down a few of the most useful principles applicable to these injuries, and endeavour to point out the method of reducing the most common dislocations, and those which require immediate assistance. Any person of common sense and resolution, who is present when a dislocation happens, may often be of more service to the patient than the most expert surgeon can after swelling and inflammation have come on, or after the bone has been out of its place for several days or weeks. When swelling and inflammation are present, it is difficult to know the state of the joint, and improper to attempt a reduction; and by waiting till they are gone off, the soft parts, and the bone itself, acquire a certain position, the muscles adapt themselves in length to the altered situation of the bone to which they are attached, and often cannot be lengthened sufficiently for it to be reduced.

The absolute immobility of a limb, or at least the inability of performing certain motions, is amongst the most characteristic symptoms of a dislocation. Sometimes, however, a considerable degree of motion continues for a short time after dislocation.

There are several important differences in dislocations, and the difference is immense, in regard to the danger of the case, arising from the circumstance of a dislocation being attended or unattended with a wound, communicating internally with the joint, and externally with the air. When there is no wound of this kind, the danger is generally trivial, and the dislocation is termed *a simple one;* when there is such a wound, together with the dislocation, the case is denominated *compound,* and is frequently accompanied with the most imminent peril. Some joints are much more disposed than others to compound dislocations. The accident is rare at the hip, shoulder, and knee, but is frequent at the ankle, elbow and wrist.

The following are some of the chief principles relative to the present subject, laid down by the late skilful Mr. Pott, formerly surgeon to Bartholomew's Hospital; and they merit great attention :

1. Although a joint may have been dislocated by means of considerable violence, it does by no means follow that the same decree of violence is necessary for its reduction.
2. That all the force used in reducing a luxated bone, be it more or less, be it by hands, towels, ligatures, or machines, ought always to be applied to the other extremity of the said bone, and as much as possible to that only.
3. That in the reduction of such joints as are composed of a round head, received into a socket, such as those of the

shoulder and hip, the whole body should be kept as steady as possible.

4. That in order to make use of an extending force, with all possible advantage, and to excite thereby the least pain and inconvenience, it is necessary that all parts serving to the motion of the dislocated joint, or in any degree connected with it, be put into such a state as to give the smallest possible degree of resistance.
5. That in the reduction of such joints as consist of a round head, moving in a socket, for example, the shoulder and hip, no attempt ought to be made for replacing the said head, until it has by extension been brought forth from the place where it is, and nearly to a level with the said socket. All that the operator has to do in these instances is to bring the bone to this level; the muscles attached to it will, for the most part, do the rest for him.
6. That whatever kind or degree of force may be found necessary for the reduction of a luxated joint, such force should be employed gradually; the lesser degree being always first tried, and it being increased little by little.

With respect to the second maxim here laid down, I would remark, that Sir Astley Cooper states, that so far as he has had an opportunity of observing, it is generally best to apply the extension to the bone which is dislocated; but that dislocations of the shoulder are exceptions, in which he mostly prefers to reduce the head of the bone by placing his heel to the arm-pit, and drawing the arm at the wrist, in a line with the side of the body.

Extension may either be made by means of assistants, who are to take hold of napkins, or sheets, put round the part, at which it is judged proper to make the extension; or else a multiplied pulley may be used. In cases of difficulty, Sir Astley cooper thinks the pulley should always be preferred.

When the attempts at reduction fail in consequence of the muscular strength of the patient, which counteracts all efforts to replace the bone, or from several days having elapsed since the receipt of the injury, constitutional means should be employed in conjunction with those that are mechanical. The constitutional means here referred to are those which produce a tendency to fainting, such as bleeding, the hot bath at 100 or 103 degrees, and small quantities of emetic tartar to produce nausea, but not vomiting.

All that is necessary after the reduction of a simple dislocation, is to apply to the part cloths dipped in Goulard water, or spirit of wine and water, with a proper bandage, and to keep the limb perfectly easy.

In compound dislocation, the reduction must be effected without delay, and with as little violence and disturbance as possible, and then the wound is to be treated in all respects as any other wound in the same part. *See* page 328.

Dislocation of the Lower Jaw

The lower jaw can only be luxated in one direction, that is, forwards. When both sides are dislocated, the mouth is wide open and cannot be shut; and an empty apace is felt before the ear. When only one side is dislocated, the mouth is distorted, and turned towards the opposite side, while the fellow teeth of the jaws do not correspond.

These dislocations may be reduced in the following manner: The operator is first to wrap some linen round his thumbs, to keep them from being hurt by the patient's teeth, and then introduce them into the mouth, as far as possible along the grinding teeth. At the same time he is to place his fingers under the chin and base of the jaw, and while he depresses the grinding teeth with his thumbs, he raises the chin with his fingers, by which means the condyles become disengaged from their situation; at which instant the muscles draw those parts so rapidly back into the articular cavities again, that the operator's thumbs might sometimes be hurt, did he not immediately move them outward between the cheek and the jaw.

The patient must for some time avoid much speaking, and such food as requires much mastication.

Dislocation of the Neck

Complete luxations of the first bone of the neck from the second are almost. inevitably and immediately fatal. Such a partial dislocation of some of the bones of the neck, however, sometimes occurs, as may be successfully treated. In this case the neck is bent, and the head generally falls forward on the breast.

Here the head should be gradually drawn up, whilst the shoulders are carefully pressed downwards by an assistant, until the bones are brought into their proper place; when the patient, if the injury has not been fatal, gradually recovers his senses.

The head may require to be retained in an elevated position by instruments contrived for that purpose.

Dislocation of the Collar-bone

The collar-bone may he dislocated either at its junction with the fore-part of the shoulder blade, or with the sternum or breast-bone.

In its junction with the breast-bone, it is rarely dislocated in any other way than forwards, when a hard circumscribed tumour is felt, or even seen, on the front and upper part of the breast-bone.

In the dislocation of this bone at its junction with the shoulder-blade, the nature of the injury is pointed out by pain at the top of the shoulder; a projection of the end of the collar-bone, under the skin covering the anterior point of the shoulder-blade; and a depression of the shoulder.

When reducing either of these luxations, the arms and shoulders of the patient are to be firmly drawn backwards and outwards, by an assistant, whilst the operator replaces the protruded end of the bone. A linen compress should then be placed on the point of dislocation, and a bandage applied, which is to go over each shoulder, and under each arm-pit. The patient's elbow should be kept close to his side, and the arm be supported in a sling.

Dislocation of the Arm

The humerus, or upper bone of the arm, may be dislocated in three different directions; *viz.* downwards, into the armpit; forwards, under the collar-bone; and backwards, on the shoulder-blade.

In every kind of dislocation of this bone, there is always a manifest depression under the anterior point of the shoulder; all the motions of the arm are painful, and limited; and the arm cannot move without the shoulder moving also.

In attempting the reduction of this luxation, the following plan of Sir Astley Cooper's should be resorted to, which he states to be the best, and generally successful, in three-fourths of such injuries, when recent. The patient should be placed in the recumbent posture, upon a table or sofa, and near its edge. The operator then binds a wetted roller round the arm immediately, above the elbow, upon which he ties a handkerchief. Then, with one foot resting upon the floor, he separates the patient's elbow from his side, and places the heel of his other foot in the arm-pit. The arm is then steadily drawn with the handkerchiefs for three or four minutes, at the end of which the bone in common cases is easily replaced. If more force be required, a long towel can be used, with which several persons may pull. The above distinguished surgeon generally bent the fore-arm nearly to a right angle with the upper arm (*os humeri*), because this position relaxes the large muscle (*biceps*) on the fore-part of the arm, and lessens its resistance; in many cases, however, he made the extension at the wrist, a plan in which he found more force requisite, but the bandage is less apt to slip.

Dislocation of the Elbow

The fore-arm consists of two bones, which may be dislocated together, back-wards or laterally. The radius, or upper bone, may also be alone dislocated, forwards, or backwards. The luxation of the fore-arm backwards is by far the most frequent. In this accident, the fore-arm is in a state of half-flexion, and every attempt to extend it produces acute pain; the point of the elbow, called olecranon, projects, and is higher than usual; and the extremity of the upper bone of the arm cannot be felt in the bend of the elbow.

It may be reduced by the following. method: the patient is to sit in a chair, and the operator placing his knee on the inner side of the elbow joint, in the bend of the arm, and taking hold of the patient's wrist, bends the arm. At the same time, he presses on the fore-arm with his knee, so as to separate them from the upper bone of the arm (the humerus); and whilst the pressure is kept up with the knee, the arm is to be forcibly, but slowly bent, and the reduction is soon effected.

When the bones are dislocated laterally, forcible extension of the fore-arm will in general be sufficient to reduce it.

Dislocation of the Hip

The head of the thigh-bone may be dislocated in four different directions, *viz.* upwards and backwards on the *ilium*; downwards into the *foramen ovule;* forwards on the *pubes;* and backwards on the *ischiatic notch.*

Dislocation Upwards and Backwards—In this case, the limb is from one inch and a half to two inches and a half shorter than its fellow; the thigh a little bent and carried inwards; the knee inclines more forwards and inwards than the opposite one; the leg and thigh are turned inwards; the foot cannot be turned outwards; and the natural roundness of the hip has disappeared.

In the treatment, the body of the patient must be first fixed by passing a strong belt or roller, etc. round the pelvis or hip, the ends being carried over the hip of the sound side, where they are either to be firmly held by assistants, or confined to some immovable body. A second belt is to encircle the dislocated thigh-bone, immediately above the knee, and with this extension is to be made in the direction of the line made by the limb, when it is brought across the other thigh a little above the knee. As soon as the head of the bone has been brought on a level with the cavity into which it is to be returned, by the assistants who are making the extension, the surgeon is to force it into the cavity by pressing on the large protuberance of the bone, called trochanter, which every one feels on putting their hand on the side of the hip; or the knee and foot may at this period be gently rotated outwards.

Dislocation Downwards—This is next in frequency to the preceding dislocation. Here the injured limb is two inches longer than its fellow; the thigh is flattened; a hard, round tumour, formed by the head of the thigh-bone, is felt at the inner and superior part of the thigh; and the knees are widely separated from each other.

This kind of luxation is very easy of reduction. The pelvis having been fixed as above described, the necessary extension is to be made downwards, and outwards, so as to dislodge the head of the bone. The muscles then generally draw it into its natural cavity, on the extending force being gradually relaxed, if the upper part of the bone be pulled outward with a bandage, and an assistant at the same instant inclines the ancle inwards. Then the limb is used as a lever, with very considerable power.

Dislocation Forwards—The thigh-bone is occasionally dislocated forwards, or upwards and forwards on the pubes, when the whole limb is turned outwards, and cannot be rotated inwards; it is shortened by one inch; the head of the bone forms a tumour high in the groin; and the knee is generally carried backwards.

The treatment of this injury only differs from that just described, in the extension being made in a line behind the axis of the body, so as to draw the thigh bone backwards, and when such extension has been continued for some time, a napkin is to be put under the upper part of the bone, and its head lifted over the edge of the cavity into which it is to go.

Dislocation Backwards—In this case, the head of the thigh-bone is placed behind its natural cavity, and a little above its middle; the limb is generally not more than half an inch shorter than its fellow; the knee and foot are turned inwards, but not nearly in so great a degree as in the first kind of dislocation; the thigh inclines a little forward; the knee is slightly bent; and the limb is so fixed, that flexion and rotation are in a great measure prevented.

The pelvis being fixed, the extension is to be made downwards and forwards, across the middle of the other thigh, so as to dislodge the head of the bone, while the operator, with a napkin placed under the upper part of the thigh, just below the trochanter minor, pulls the upper part of the thigh-bone towards its proper cavity. In this case, pulleys are preferable for waking the extension.

In dislocations at the knee, the situation of the displaced bone is obvious to the sight, and extension is to be made upwards by the thigh-bone, and downw aids by the fore-leg, while the bones are replaced by pressure with the hand.

Compound dislocations of the knee are serious accidents, but patience and cold wet bandages will work wonders.

FRACTURES OR BROKEN BONES

This subject is in many points an important one, but in a work like the present, little can be said respecting it, on account of the restricted size of the volume, and the more pressing nature of other matter. I shall, therefore, simply state those facts respecting the nature and treatment of fractures, which, from being of the greatest importance, will be the most useful to such persons as are desirous of assisting in the reduction and cure of a broken limb, when a skilful surgeon is not at hand.

Fractures are divided into *simple* and *compound.* By a simple fracture, surgeons mean a breach in the continuity of a bone, without any external wound. By a compound fractures they signify the division of a bone, where there is a corresponding wound in the soft parts, by which the fractured extremity of the bone becomes exposed. Of course, the danger attending a compound fracture is immeasurably greater than that of a simple one.

In the treatment of broken bones, the whole business of the operator consists in putting the displaced extremities of the bone into their natural situation again; in keeping them in this situation by means of a suitable apparatus; in endeavouring to avert unfavourable symptoms, and in adopting measures for their removal when they have actually occurred. The consolidation of a broken bone is, strictly speaking, the work of nature, and is effected by a process, to which a state of perfect health (humanly speaking) is above all things propitious.

The means employed for the reduction of fractures in general, are chiefly three, *viz.* extension; counter-extension; and setting. Extension signifies the act of pulling the broken part in a direction from the trunk, with a view of bringing the ends of the fracture into their natural situation. By counter-extension is implied the act of making extension in the opposite direction, in order to hinder the limb, or even the whole body, from being drawn along by the extending powers, which would then be unavailable. In all cases where the broken ends of the bone are displaced, as soon as the necessary extension has been made, the operator is to endeavour to place the broken ends of the bone in their natural situation, which is termed setting. One of the first principles to be attended to in the reduction of fractures, is to put the limb in such a position as will relax the most powerful muscles connected with the broken bone; because these muscles principally impede the reduction and disturb the ends of the fracture. The limb is, therefore, either to be bent or straightened, or turned a little to either side, as the nature of the case may point out.

After the bones have been put into their natural situation, time alone would complete their cure, were there not in the muscles a continual propensity to displace the ends of the fracture again. Hence the necessity of employing means for fixing the broken limb so effectually, that it may continue perfectly motionless during the whole time requisite for the union of the fracture. This indication is sometimes troublesome and difficult. The means employed for its fulfilment, are, an advantageous position; quietude; bandages; splints, etc. Whenever the case is a fracture of the lower limbs, the patient should lie strictly in bed until the union is complete; and the bed should be narrow, and consist of a horse hair mattress, or some other article that will not sink. A half-bent position of the limbs is the most natural and easy, and consequently, the best for fractures (excepting the broken thigh); and care must be taken that the broken limb is placed so that it may bear throughout its whole length, equally and perpendicularly upon the surface on which it lies, and not be only partially supported. It would appear, that the best pillows for the support of broken limbs, are those stuffed with chaff of oats; and in whatever position the limb is placed, it must be kept perfectly quiet.

A piece of soap plaster is the best application to the seat of injury in simple fractures, and over this an eighteen-tailed bandage may be applied rather loosely. This is a bandage consisting of several narrow strips of linen, long enough to encircle the limb, which are stitched to a long piece of linen running lengthways; and will, therefore, permit the limb to be examined without being removed. All tight bandages do harm.

But splints are the most efficient of all the applications made to a broken limb, with a view of keeping the ends of the fracture steady, and in a proper state of contact. They are usually made of wood, or strong pasteboard. In using them the object should be to preserve steadiness in the whole limb, without compressing the fracture at all. In the case of a broken leg, two splints only should be employed; they must reach above the knee, and below the ankle, and be so guarded with tow, rag, or cotton, as to press only on the joints. In the case of a fractured thigh-bone, the limb is now generally laid in a straight posture, when one splint should reach from the hip to the outer ankle, and another (somewhat shorter) from the groin to the inner ankle.

After having reduced the fracture, and applied a suitable apparatus for maintaining the reduction, means must be employed to prevent and remove any unfavourable symptoms. It is proper, therefore, in most cases, to allow for the first few days only very low diet, as broths, tea and bread. When the patient is young and strong, and the swelling and inflammation are considerable, bleeding from the arm to the extent of ten or twelve ounces should, perhaps, be practiced. In other circumstances, the cooling mixture, No. 81, page 183, will be sufficient. The patient may be permitted to drink as often, and as much as he likes, of any cooling acid beverage, as lemonade, etc. A very low diet is only to be continued for the first few days, unless great inflammation arise; for experience proves that this method when too much prolonged, has bad effects. Constiveness is to be averted by the use of the clyster, No. 8, page 146, or the mild aperient, No. 27A, page 155. When the bowels are relieved, a bed-pan should be carefully introduced under the patient, and a disturbance of the limb avoided as much as possible. The fracture-bed, invented by Mr. Earle, of London, is of much value in the present instances, as it enables the patient to void his faeces without the slightest change of position.

It is an excellent plan for the first few days, to wet the bandages freely and frequently with cold water; for in this way, the tendency to inflammation and swelling may be considerably lessened, and the pain is relieved.

Compound fractures are to be treated much in the same way as simple fractures, except that the wound will require a treatment similar to what is proper for other wounds in the same part. If the wound is but slightly lacerated, its edges should be gently drawn together with a few short strips of adhesive plaster, after the fracture has been set. This will give it a chance of uniting without suppuration. But when the wound is so bruised and lacerated, as to leave no room for the hope of its uniting without the formation and discharge of matter, a small piece of soft lint should be placed lightly between its edges, and over this a pledget of lint spread with the ointment, No. 94, page 190, or some other mild digestive. In order to allay irritation and inflammation in the part, linen cloths, wet with the cooling lotion, No. 68, page 173, may be applied over them; or should great swelling or tension take possession of the limb, a warm bread and water poultice may be substituted. Should high inflammation, attended with pain, irritation, and fever, supervene, it may be necessary to bleed the patient, and certainly to keep the bowels open, and administer the fever mixture, No. 81, page 183, with or without the solution of acetate of morphia, or laudanum, as the severity of the pain points out. After the matter has been formed and let out, and the pain and fever subside, the lowering plan of treatment must be dropped, and the patient be supported with food of a light and nourishing quality, a little of the decoction of bark being, given twice or thrice a day, and the relaxing poultice changed for some mild strengthening lotion or ointment, as No. 72, page 174, or No. 95, page 190.

The practice of applying rags wet with cold water to *fractures and dislocations,* especially when accompanied with a wound, is now universally regarded by our best surgeons as excellent, and of the greatest importance to the relief and recovery of the patient. The rags should cover the whole wound, or, swollen part of the limb, and be re-dipped in the coldest water as often as they become dry. This is a simple expedient for reducing inflammation and swelling, but a very effectual one. It cannot be urged too strongly on the attention of all sufferers and their friends. In gun-shot wounds, indeed, in large wounds of every description, its soothing efficacy is great and immediate, and it assists materially in the favourable recovery of the sufferer. Many severe wounds will require no other treatment, provided the patient has at the same time perfect rest and a pure air. It is generally supposed that gunshot and other severe wounds require the use of elaborate medicaments, but nothing can be more unfounded. Rags kept constantly wet with cold water are alone sufficient, the edges of the wound being supported and kept in contact by strips of adhesive plaster. Stitching wounds is now rarely practised by skilful surgeons. Stitches are unnecessary and painful, and strapping with adhesive plaster retains the lips of a wound in contact much better; and the whole may be kept cool by frequently squeezing a sponge filled with cold water over the bandage or plaster.

SUBSTANCES LODGED IN THE GULLET OR IN THE WINDPIPER

The gullet is the tube which conveys the food from the mouth into the stomach. Foreign bodies frequently lodge in it, and by pressing on the windpipe, and thus impeding respiration, or by exciting great irritation in the gullet itself, are often attended with bad, and even fatal, symptoms. Hence, an immediate attempt must be always made to extract them. For this purpose, the fingers may be employed, and if they will not reach far enough, a pair of long carved forceps should be used. A bunch of thread with a multitude of nooses, fastened upon the end of a probang, or piece of whalebone, is well calculated for catching hold of small substances, like fish-bones, needles, etc. If this resource fail, a piece of dry sponge may be fixed on the extremity of a probang, or piece of whalebone, and passed into the stomach, and when expanded with moisture and withdrawn, will sometimes bring up articles, which, on its introduction, it had passed in its dry and diminished state. When the stomach is full, the excitement to vomiting has sometimes answered; but if the foreign body be sharp and pointed, it is rarely advisable.

When the substances are not of a sharp, or otherwise very hurtful kind, and cannot be extracted, they must be pushed down into the stomach with a large bougie, or a long whale bone probang having a piece of fine sponge securely fastened to the end. But such practice is rarely advisable, when the foreign bodies have a sharp pointed form, like nails, pins, needles, etc. When surgeons have not ventured, or not been able to force such substances down into the stomach they have often made their way, after a time, to the surface of the body, where an abscess has been formed, out of which they have been discharged.

When the substances lodged in the gullet, can neither be extracted, nor pushed down into the stomach, if the breathing be not dangerously obstructed, and liquids can yet be swallowed, the wisest plan is to avoid irritating the passage with the further use of instruments, and leave the case to nature, that is to say, as far as manual interference is concerned; fur bleeding and the administration of mucilaginous oily draughts, may be often useful. But should the foreign body dangerously obstruct the breathing, and the substance itself cannot be felt externally, the patient would perish, if some means of facilitating the breathing, were not immediately adopted; and, under these circumstances, the most prudent plan would be to make an opening into the windpipe. This operation is neither difficult nor dangerous, and it is to be feared, that not a few persons have lost their lives under such circumstances, from its not having been performed. In those cases where the size of the foreign body is so large, as to indicate its situation by any hardness, or prominence in the neck, it might be more proper to make an incision in the gullet itself, for the purpose of its extraction.

The great art of passing any instrument down the gullet, for surgical purposes, consists in putting its extremity at office directly against the back part of the mouth, and, in passing it down, keeping it closely against the part it touches. The knowledge of this circumstance is extremely useful in passing probangs and bougies, etc.

It should be remarked, that after a sharp, hard substance has been either ejected, or propelled into the stomach by nature, or art, the same painful sensations in the throat frequently continue a certain time afterwards, which were experienced while the foreign body was actually lodged in the passage. These sensations, however, are only owing to the manner in which the bullet has been irritated, and, consequently, would be seriously aggravated by the further unnecessary introduction of instruments.

But pebbles, beans, or other small substances, may fall into the windpipe, as well as stick in the gullet, and this is far the worse accident of the two. The symptoms usually resulting from such a body getting into the windpipe, are immediate difficulty of breathing, severe convulsive cough, and a painful sensation in some part of the passage. In some cases, the violent cough produces convulsions in the limbs, and the difficulty of breathing is also attended with a rattling in the throat. Sometimes a perfect calm, at intervals, will follow the afflicting cough, during which time the patient will sit up, and appear cheerful and comparatively easy; which seems to arise from the foreign body's getting into a less sensible part of the canal. But this calm is deceitful, and should not allow us to delay having recourse to an operation, which is the only thing that can permanently and effectually relieve the patient in the present case. An incision must be carefully made, by a skilful surgeon, first, through the skin and muscles on the anterior part of the neck, and then through the rings of the windpipe, an opening being thereby made into some part of this canal, of such a size as to allow the offending body to pass out, which it then usually will by the simple efforts of the patient in coughing. Many children, who have let pebbles, or beans; fall into the windpipe, have been rescued from certain death by this operation; while others, in the same circumstances, on whom it has not been performed, have fallen victims to the ignorance and inattention of the medical attendant, or to the groundless fears of the parents. An *early* recourse should be had to the operation, for though the patient may live for several days with a foreign body in the windpipes, yet it must not be forgotten, that its presence there necessarily excites inflammation, and if the operation be too long delayed, the patient will often die of convulsions if very young, or of a consumption if older, at no long time after the extraction, of the foreign substance. The most skilful surgeon within reach should be obtained for the performance of this operation.

MANAGEMENT OF INFANTS AND YOUNG CHILDREN

DENTITION OR TEETHING

The time of teething is a most important period of the infant state, and subjects it to manifold complaints and dangers, more especially in a sedentary mode of rearing children.

This period usually commences between the fifth and tenth months, and the process of the first teething commonly continues to the sixteenth at the least, and sometimes much longer. It almost invariably begins with the incisores, or front teeth of the lower jaw. Usually two of those are cut, and then the corresponding ones in the upper jaw. After two teeth in each jaw have appeared, it is, in some instances, a considerable time before the contiguous ones come out; but now and then six or eight are cut in hasty succession. The incisores are succeeded by the four molares, or grinders; then the canine, and the last of all of an infant's first teeth, their antagonists, or the eye-teeth; making in all sixteen. This is the ordinary number of children's first teeth, though it is sometimes exceeded.

In children who are strong and healthy, this process goes on pretty much as above described, and the teeth are cut both easily and soon; but in unhealthy and weakly infants, the process is slow and uncertain. Accordingly, children sometimes cut their teeth irregularly or cross, as it is called, both by the teeth appearing first in the upper jaw, and also at a distance, instead of being contiguous to each other, this is accounted an indication of difficult, or painful dentition: The ease or difficulty of teething may likewise be guessed at, by the circumstances under which the two first teeth shall happen, to be cut; the succeeding ones frequently working their way in a corresponding manner.

Dentition is commonly preceded and accompanied with various symptoms: the child drivels; the gums swell, spread, and become hot; there is often a circumscribed redness in the cheek, and eruptions on the skin, especially on the face and scalp; looseness; gripings; stools, green or pale, or otherwise discoloured; watchings, startings in the sleep, and spasms of particular parts; a diminution, or increased secretion of the urine, which is often of an unnatural colour; now and then a discharge of matter, with pain in making water; in almost all cases the child shrieks often, and thrusts its fingers into its mouth. Less common symptoms are a swelling of the tops of the feet and hands; the tumifying of one or more of the glands of the neck; and cough, difficult breathing and fits.

Hippocrates, the father of physic, has correctly remarked, "that infants cut their teeth more readily in winter than in summer; that such as are rather inclined to be lean cut them more readily than those that are very fat; and children who are loose in the belly most safely of all".

In the *treatment* of difficult teething, the last remark of Hippocrates is worthy of special attention, *the successful management of the process mainly depending on preserving a free state of the bowels.* This must never be lost sight of; and it is surprising how great and perfect a change will often be wrought in the case of fever, convulsions, and other alarming symptoms arising from teething, by procuring an open belly and improving the secretions by the use of minute doses of calomel and jalap. Whenever, therefore, the teething of a child is difficult or painful, give immediately a little rhubarb and magnesia, or four grains of compound jalap powder, in water or beer, and afterwards a tea-spoonful of castor oil daily, so that the bowels may be freely moved every day; to which add great attention to diet, which should be very simple, smaller in quantity than usual, and of the most digestible nature, with plenty of pure air, and exercise.

A very excellent medicine for children during teething is the *liquor potassae,* or *alkaline solution,* with rhubarb, as prescribed in this form :—

Take of Liquor potassae, or alkaline solution .	1 drachm;
Infusion of rhubarb	6 drachms;
Dill water	7 drachms;
Simple syrup	2 drachms.

Give the child one tea-spoonful twice or thrice a day.

If the fever be considerable, saline medicines, as in No. 24, page 153, will be of much service; and in case the symptoms are alarming, a little discharge should be obtained and kept up from behind the ears, by rubbing the parts with Spanish flies, or putting on a small blister. In all severe cases, the gams should be freely lanced, down to the top of the rising teeth. Some persons object to the lancing of gums, but the general opinion among the best informed of the profession is, that when much fever, or other constitutional affection, is present, together with swollen and inflamed gums, the imprisoned tooth should at once be set at liberty.

If a child, during painful dentition; is at the breast, the nurse's diet and bowels must be particularly attended to. Her diet should be very mild and diluting, and small in quantity. Ample directions will be found in the author's book on "INFANCY AND CHILDHOOD".

When a looseness comes on during this process, it must on no account be hastily checked. Unless it be excessive, it ought not to be interfered with; and even when excessive, it must not be stopped, but only moderated by the use of some simple thing, as three grains of the compound powder of chalk in a table-spoonful of dill water.

FOOD AND FEEDING

Ever keep in mind, that it is generally right to be sparing in the quantity of food; for over-feeding, as well as feeding improperly, are highly injurious.

A child in health will require only breast milk for the first four months, unless there is not a sufficiently early provision made by the breast of the mother for this purpose; then the child must have something given it, as near in composition as possible to the mother's milk, and we can scarcely recommend any thing better than a mixture of cow's milk, water, and loaf sugar, in the proportion of two-thirds milk, one-third water and a very small quantity of loaf sugar. For the fifth month nothing but this should be given, and very little, if any thing else, for the sixth month; afterwards it may stand in need of a small cup of beef tea and crumb of bread daily. At the end of eight months it should be fed twice a day, once with bread and milk, or biscuit powder and milk, and once with light broth and bread, arrow-root, or rice. At twelve months, it should be fed three times in twenty-four hours; and then more solid food should be likewise given daily, as a bread or rice pudding, or a boiled egg. For an infant taken early from the breast, the diet should principally consist of cow's milk warmed, water and loaf sugar, afterwards of bread, first soaked in water and of light broth with bread. If the child has a purging, the milk should be boiled.

After the first year, animal food in substance may be given twice a week to children. To those four or five years old, animal food may be allowed daily, and bread and milk night and morning. Particular care is, however, necessary, not to give nutriment in large quantities to children who take but little exercise, or to those who are weakly, for in such, an excess, or even a great variety of food, is apt to produce worms, convulsions, rickets, slow fever, scrofula and purging.

The generation of acid in the stomach and bowels is a common cause of disease in children. If a child at the breast be repeatedly attacked with the gripes, and falls away, the diet ought to be changed from milk to one consisting of broths, and sago or baked flour with milk; and to aid in preventing a return of the gripes, the chill should be exercised well in the open air, and the mother's health must be attended to. In this case, it will be proper also for the mother to live chiefly upon animal food. If this should not be effectual, apply for medical assistance. In general, the use of spice in children's food is to be reprobated; and, in illness, the diet of all children should be as light as possible. In fever, drinks containing nourishment, such as barley-water, toast and water, thin tapioca, and rice-water, will be proper, taken cold in summer and warm in winter. In obstinate purgings, children must have rice, arrow-root, and also hartshorn shavings boiled in beef tea, or beef tea thickened with baked flour, or sago and thick milk; and much good has been derived from putting a flannel roller round the body, when the purging resists these means.

DRESS AND DRESSING

It should be particularly noticed, that over-clothing, or clothing improperly makes a child tender and subject to cold.

A child requires fewer clothes than an adult: a short shift, and flannel waistcoat tied behind, with a short petticoat sewed to it, and a short gown, rather stouter in winter than in summer, is all the body-dress a child requires; more clothes only make it tender, chilly, and subject to colds, unless it is weakly, and then a flannel shirt is sometimes useful. Until an infant reaches the seventh or eighth month, it is best without stockings; neither can its petticoats be too short. The whole of the dress of children, whatever may be their age, should be perfectly loose and easy, so as to allow of free motion to the limbs. It is highly beneficial to expose the legs, arms, and breasts of healthy children to the open air.

EXERCISE AND SLEEP

Generally speaking, it is a good rule never to prevent a child from attempting to walk, however young it may be. When a child seeks to put its feet on the ground, let it do so, but do not force it to walk. This effort at exercise is both pleasant and serviceable to a child; it is proper to encourage it in this, and, as it grows up, regularly to exercise, but to avoid fatiguing it. Amuse and employ a child, but never suffer it to be still when it is right for it to be in motion and actively employed. In exercising any child, however, avoid fatiguing it, and particularly a sickly one; a weakly child ought not to be allowed to stand or walk long together; therefore, it should be alternately carried in the arms, drawn in a vehicle, and invited to walk. The practice of placing children in the damp ground, after fatiguing them with long walks, cannot be too much reprobated.

Until the third year, most children require an hour's sleep in the middle of the day, after which they should be invariably exercised till they begin to be tired, and may be put to rest at seven O'clock. In summer let them rise at six, and in the winter at seven.

AIR

It is indispensably requisite for children to bear, without inconvenience, the vicissitudes of the atmosphere. A free and countinued exposure to the open air is of the utmost consequence to children's health; the sooner infants are taken into it the faster they will thrive; in the open air they grow up strong, less subject to colds, disordered bowels, convulsions, and tickets; complaints so frequent among those children who are reared in nurseries. Not only the face, but the legs, thighs, and arms, should be freely exposed to the air. Even in confined streets, in the populous district of the metropolis, it is of infinite service to keep the children out of doors; and the poor should set open the bed-room windows and doors of their habitations. Those children who have been properly exposed to the air from birth, may be safely exercised in it, if healthy, at all seasons.

COLD BATHING

Frequent bathing is conducive to cleanliness, it imparts vigour to the muscles and nerves, and promotes alacrity and cheerfulness of mind. In a striking manner does the cold bath preserve and promote the health of the infant race. It is proper to begin the practice of dipping in warm weather, and to continue it through every season after. The cold bath is not only a serviceable appli-cation to children in health, but to those that are sickly also, especially the rickety; it may be resorted to thrice a week. A sudden dip, twice repeated each time of using the bath, will be sufficient. The more delicate and weakly require the chill to be taken off the water the first three or four times of going into it. If the shock of a cold bath appears too powerful for the constitution, partial bathing with salt water, or sponging the body with it, may be substituted, and is often highly useful. Sea bathing is preferred for those having the king's evil.

Immediately after bathing lot the child be wrapped in a blanket, and well dried, and if it be disposed to sleep, allow it to do so; if not, it may be dressed and suffered to run about. Weakly children using the cold bath may wear a flannel shirt. Excoriations are effectually obviated by frequently washing the parts of the body subject to them with cold water.

What I have further to say respecting the management of infants and young children, will be best compressed into short rules, which it is highly advisable that every nurse should attend to.

Rules for the Mother and for the General Management of the Child during the First Month

1. Let her not permit herself to be persuaded from having her child put to the breast, so soon as she herself may be able to bear the fatigue.
2. Let her not delegate to another the sacred duty of nursing her own child, unless the reasons for so doing are insurmountable.
3. She must most scrupulously attend to the dressing and undressing, or even performing this herself, when her health and strength will permit this delightful task.
4. She should never, under any pretest of convenience, permit her child to be fed, so long as she can supply it with sufficient nourishment herself; and to secure to herself this important point, she should pay a scrupulous regard to her diet, and her exercise in the open air.
5. The dressing of the child should early engage the attention of the mother; it should always be made subservient to comfort instead of show.
6. This should consist in part of flannel; especially during cold, or even cool weather.
7. The dressings of the child should be changed as often as they become soiled, when this luxury can be indulged in.
8. Though it may be found that flannel is the most eligible substance as a general rule, there are cases in which it

may be improper; and these should be carefully distinguished.

9. The belly band is one of the most important parts of the child's dress; it should always be made of flannel, and should be always cut *bias*.
10. The greatest care should be taken to apply it properly; and too tight an application should be particularly avoided.
11. If this bandage be applied too tight, it may produce the evil it is intended to prevent.
12. The child should be carefully protected against all unnecessary wet; and when it is discovered to be in this situation, it should be changed as quickly as possible.
13. In dressing the child as few pins should be employed as possible; three are all that are necessary, if the clothes be properly arranged.
14. As a general rule, the child should never be fed at this period of its life; there may be exceptions, however, that may render this necessary.
15. When an exception to this rule exists, the food of the child should consist of milk, water and sugar; as advised at p. 271.
16. If the child be fed, it should have but small quantities at a time, and never be crammed to surfeit.
17. The woman should exercise in the open air, as soon as this is rendered safe, by the state of her health, the period after confinement and the state of the weather.
18. She should never subject herself to *partial* exposures, under the hope of hardening herself.
19. The re-application of a diaper, after it has been dried simply, should be prohibited; as several evils arise from the practice.
20. The mother may indulge in such diet as her experience has proved to be innocent—for it will seldom or never disagree with the child, when it perfectly suits the mother.
21. When the mother experiences any inconvenience from the

use of any substance or substances, she should not hesitate a moment to abandon them; for if they disagree with her, they will be sure to do so with the child.

22. Should there be a failure in the quantity of milk, the mother must not attempt to increase it by highly seasoned food and stimulating drinks.
23. She may, however, use, and sometimes with great advantage, the ordinary nutritious substances.

Rules Adapted to the Infant State

1. Use a child early to the boat or spoon—in case of illness, or of a failure of milk from the breast of the mother.
2. Keep an infant dry and warm—to preserve health, promote growth and obviate chafing.
3. Feed an infant in an upright posture—to give uniform distention to the stomach, and thus to obviate indigestion and gripes.
4. In the act of suckling it is proper to take a child frequently from the breast for a minute or two—to obviate too rapid a distention of the stomach, which occasions puking or acidities.
5. Expose an infant early in the air—to strengthen and enable it to withstand colds, and to obviate purging.
6. Attend invariably to cleanliness in an infant—to prevent diseases of the skin, slow fever, rickets and decline.
7. Let an infant's dress be loose and easy and free from pins—to avert accidents, glandular obstructions and impediments to growth.
8. Place an infant, when asleep, on the right side—to favour the descent of the food into the bowels, and to obviate indigestion.
9. Attend strictly to plaintive cries—by this means you may trace the first cause of illness; for an infant will never cry, if well and at ease.

10. Wash a *strong* child in cold water, and dip it thrice a week–wash *a weak* one in chilled water—to refresh, promote healthy perspiration, and prevent diseases of the skin.
11. Encourage a child to stretch and thrust out its limbs, and to crawl about—to teach it active habits early, to strengthen it and promote the circulation.
12. Rub a young child, night and morning, all over with the hand—this exercises it and promotes the circulation of the blood.
13. Comb a child's head and wash it frequently with soap and water—to prevent scald head, and painful eruptions behind the ears, and on the neck.
14. If a child has cut four teeth, if it is in good health, and its bowels are regular, wean it at nine months, without any previous preparation-do this to obviate numerous inconveniences both to the mother and child.
15. If a child has been lately weaned, and is attacked with hooping-cough, or any other severe disease, it may require the breast again—it will be thus supplied with the diluting nutriment, which it would then stand in need of; or should a weaned child, to which is offered suitable food, fall off in its health, decline and pine away, it may be prudent to procure for it a good breast of milk, and to let the child suck again–to obviate an exhausting fever, which will inevitably prove fatal.

    N.B.: This rule, however, must not be invariably adopted; and ought always first to have the sanction of an able professional man.

16. An infant should have three or four stools daily, of a bright orange colour—a deviation from this appearance denotes acidities and indigestion, requiring the prompt exhibition of a little rhubarb and magnesia, with or without a small quantity of the sulphate of potash. *See* the prescription, No. 121, page 205, and consult the author's book *On Infancy and Childhood.*

Rules Adapted to Childhood

17. If a young child takes but little exercise, give it but little solid food, increasing it in proportion to the exercise taken-to obviate thirst, fever, head-ache and glandular obstructions.
18. Should a child's breath smell, it is commonly a symptom of a disordered stomach, or of worms. Should its belly grow large, its complexion become pale, and flesh soft, disease has already commenced. In either of these cases the child will require a good free air, and not only domestic but medical management. The prescription No. 121 will be useful.
19. *In a fit*—untie the clothes, raise the head, wipe away all froth from the mouth and keep it open, pressing down the tongue and drawing it forward at the same time. Let the child be first quickly exposed to cool fresh air and its face sprinkled with cold water; then gently rub, with a warm hand, the belly, back and limbs; apply a succession of warm flannels to them or resort to a warm bath, and. put warm tiles under the arm-pits; strike the soles of the feet smartly with a piece of flat wood, tickle the nostril, and inside of the ear, with a feather or tooth-pick. To an infant give five drops of harts-horn or sal volatile, in a little water; to a child two years old, ten drops in a little water.

    N.B. :Remember, though no sign of life appears, it is necessary for two hours to act upto these directions. Do not suffer the head to hang back, nor to lean forward upon the chest.

Cautions Adapted to Infancy and Childhood

1. Never let an infant sleep alone at night in cold weather—for fear of suspending the breath and the circulation of the blood.
2. Never let an infant sleep the whole night on the mother's arm—for fear of suffocation.

3. Never wake an infant out of a sound sleep by rough means—for fear of producing fits or a purging.
4. Avoid the use of tight bandages, especially round the body—for fear of producing fits, obstruction of the bowels or decline.
5. Avoid giving Godfrey's Cordial, Daffy's Elixir, or any other warm anodyne—for fear of producing fits, fever or palsy, a common consequence of quack medicines, indiscreetly given.

   N.B.: Dalby's Carminative is a safer medicine than either of the foregoing, but it is objectionable from its containing laudanum, and a great deal of essential oil. In general, it is far inferior, as a remedy, to syrup of rhubarb, mixed with a little calcined magnesia and dill water. *See* recipe, pages 334.

6. Avoid giving any quack medicine—for fear of bringing on decline or sudden death.
7. Avoid feeding infants in the night—for fear of bringing on the gripes, and even worse complaints, from over distention of the stomach.

   I know a lady of rank who was so fond of feeding her infants, that she would have them taken up for this purpose, several times in the night. The consequence was that she lost all her children at the age of from twelve months to two years.

8. Avoid warm nurseries and close air—for fear of making a child delicate, weakly and susceptible of cold.
9. Avoid carrying a child always on the same arm—for fear of making it crooked.
10. Never confine a child's limbs by wrapping its clothes tightly round it, especially at night—by inaction of the muscles, and retention of moisture, the child will become weak and sickly.
11. Avoid exposing an infant to the open air, in a cold season, when its bowels are disordered or if it has shortness of breathing, with fever and cough—for fear of bringing on high inflammation.

12. Never allow a child's food to be chewed—it is not only a nasty practice, but if the nurse has a sore mouth or gums, she may communicate disease.
13. Never provoke violent laughter, nor disregard violent crying, for fear of a fit in either case.
14. Never wash a child with milk, with a view to heal a chafed part–milk will inflame, and cold water will heal it.

N.B. : In the author's volume ON INFANCY AND CHILDHOOD, that is THE MANAGEMENT AND DISORDERS OF CHILDREN, the present subject is fully considered.

The proper management of females in pregnancy, and immediately before, in, and after confinement, will be found in the author's TREATISE ON THE DISEASES OF FEMALES.

GENERAL PRINCIPLES
IN
THE TREATMENT OF DISEASE
Specially Worthy of the Attention of Heads of Families and also of Junior Medical Practitioners

1. Remember that the restorative powers of nature are great, very great; and consequently many disorders will be cured by time, mild diet, cheerful conversation, rest and pure air, without medicine. This is true of many medical disorders and equally so of many surgical complaints, such as affections of bones and joints.

2. Rest, joined with exercise, cheerful society, cleanliness, pure air, and a mild diet of easily digested food, are, therefore, among the most powerful means of cure.

3. In illness, it is in general a capital error to look chiefly to medicine for cure. A strong tendency exists in many diseases to a spontaneous favourable termination. Therefore, if we do not do wrong, they will get well under the use of rest, cleanliness, pure air, good diet and a little saline aperient.

4. On the other hand, some diseases are curable only by medicine. Here, in prescribing the appropriate medicine, in the right dose and manner, the skill of the physician is often strikingly displayed, and the patient certainly, and sometimes speedily recovers. An instance of this we have in giving ammonia in scarlet fever, measles and erysipelas, bark in ague, alkalies in rheumatism and muriatic acid in typhus fever.

5. Saline medicines are of great value in all *acute* diseases, such as fevers and inflammations. They should never be neglected. They relieve thirst, quiet the pulse, moderate fever, and obviate

the liability to obstruction in the minute vessels, that is, the minute arteries and veins, and improve the quality of the blood. For examples, refer to No. 27B, pore 156; No. 81, page 183 or No. 130A, page 209.

6. Ammonia, such as No. 78D, page 181, has a peculiarly favourable effect—a specific influence—in all cases of erysipelas, scarlet fever and measles. *See* also page 4.

7. In Fever, bleeding is not advisable when the pupils are dilated.

8. In Fever, never give opium when the pupils are contracted.

9. Never take a full dose of opium, so as to force sleep, when the *complexion is dusky, and the lips in any degree blue.* The cheeks and lips should remain florid in order to its being safe to take laudanum, solid opium or paregoric, in cough or any other complaint.

10. Except in fevers and acute inflammations, and diseases of the joints, Exercise is fever a powerful and principal remedy. I wish my readers always to bear this in remembrance, and to act upon it, although in some particular complaints I may not recommend it. Exercise acts on all the functions and processes; it is a natural means of freeing the skin, and promoting vital changes in the blood when passing through the lungs and liver; hence its remarkable power in almost all diseases not of an acute character. And it is of immense importance that sufficient daily exercise should be taken. More will be required in winter than in summer. Although some exercise may be taken daily, yet an *insufficient* quantity will not preserve from disorder or disease, neither will it assist in throwing it off. Therefore, the actual quantity of exercise taken daily is a matter of primary importance to every one.

11. At the onset of severe sore throat of every description, an emetic, or two, of antimony and ipecacuanha is followed by great relief. It unloads the vessels of the throat and chest, and determines to the surface of the body, and should never be neglected. *See* No. 123, page 206.

12. Calomel, blue pill, mercury with chalk, and other preparations of mercury, generally operate most beneficially in

small or minute doses. By small or minute doses, I mean about one-tenth of the ordinary dose, say of calomel, one-tenth of a grain; of blue pill, one or two grains.

13. In liberal doses mercury causes the destruction of the red globules of the blood–thus reducing its vitality. Hence in large doses calomel, blue pill, and other mercurial preparations, are irritating and destructive. In order to avoid or lessen the injury likely to follow on taking large doses of this destructive medicine—mercury—you must supply nutritive material, by giving good food freely. However, in small doses, they are often soothing, both to the membranes and whole body.

14. Calomel and other forms of mercury, are commonly given freely in all AFFECTIONS OF THE LIVER. Nothing can be more unsound and injurious, especially when feverishness is present. Saline remedies, such as No. 74D, page 178, or No. 130 A, page 209, are far safer and more efficacious.

15. The BLOOD is the common thoroughfare for distribution of good and evil to the whole body. An unhealthy state of the BLOOD is the most fruitful source of disease, both acute and chronic. It is the first element in fevers, and often also inflammation; and it produces congestion, degeneration, and other serious states in the lungs, kidneys, liver and other internal organs.

16. In all DISCHARGES OF BLOOD from the lungs, stomach, bowels, or any other internal part, saline medicines, and the neutral salts, are among the best remedies, and are frequently in the highest degree efficacious; and I particularly recommend a combination of cream of tartar, sulphate of potash, and nitre, as in the prescription No. 130A, page 209. This is a remedy admirably adapted to domestic practice, on account of its mildness and efficacy.

17. *Costiveness* is not to be conquered by aperient medicine; but by diet, exercise, and a regular patient solicitation of nature every morning.

18. The *general principles of treatment* are the same in all chronic complaints, whether they are organic diseases or only disorders of function; but weakening measures must be more cautiously guarded against in actual disease, than where the

functions only are deranged. *The general principles of treatment* are :

(a) That the secretions throughout—that is, all the natural discharges of the body,—are to be restored to as healthy a state as possible, by mild measures.

(b) That we are always to keep in view the relief of irritation, and the improvement of the quality of the blood, as two of the most important indications.

(c) That while we are aiming to fulfil these indications, the strength of the patient must be maintained and augmented to the utmost, by a generous diet, and by daily and sufficient exercise, as well as by tonic medicines.

It has certainly been too much the practice in all chronic maladies to overlook or disregard the *third* principle, while aiming to accomplish the objects described in the *first* and *second,* from which circumstance many patients lave necessarily suffered greatly for a time, and some permanently, as the mischief done by too low a diet, with bleeding, too strong purging, mercury or other active lowering measures, could not for a long time be perfectly surmounted, and in some instances never have been overcome.

19. Deficient vitality—imperfect nutrition of the body—lies at the basis of disease. That is, debility, either general or local or both, with impaired vital powers and impoverished blood, lie at the foundation of the existing malady, whatever may be its name, character, or seat. I 'therefore, in all diseases, except active inflammation, it is of the first consequence to increase the appetite, and strengthen the digestive powers. By this means a large majority of curable cases of disease will be cured, for the restorative power of the stomach is immense.

20. The more wear and tear the body or mind sustains, the more quickly do the various parts of the system melt down into fluids, or substances, which are quickly removed, as effete, by the excreting organs—the skin, kidneys, liver etc. Hence, this wear

and tear demand corresponding new supplies, in order to new material being formed.

21. In all diseases, both acute and chronic, the real immediate cause of a languishing state, and continued debility, is the non-renewal of the BLOOD by the supply of fresh matter. If the blood is dark coloured and half dead, it cannot properly fulfil the functions of life. You must therefore always attend to the supply of nutriment—not by over-stimulating and throwing in a large quantity of food, but by taking small quantities of food at regular intervals of about four hours in chronic complaints. In fevers and some inflammations, you must give food every two hours. This is a *general principle* of great moment, always to be acted upon, although I may not always insist upon it in every disease here treated of.

22. It is consequently of the first importance to attend to the living constituents of the BLOOD, especially to the *red globules,* the number and integrity of which are usually in direct measure to the bodily and mental vigour. The principal means of improving the quality of this precious fluid are exercise, pure air, nourishing food, sufficient sleep, iron, bark, cod-liver oil, and ammonia.

23. In the DELIRIUM OF FEVERS, whether mild or violent, few remedies are so suitable and efficacious as Dr. Graves's Mixture (No. 78B, page 180), of tartarized antimony.

24. Remember that MIND has much to do with producing many complaints—disappointnoent, vexation, losses, domestic affliction, are fruitful sources of debility and disease. Then moral treatment is absolutely necessary, and time and change of scene must be alloyed for the subsidence of the mental irritation.

25. SELF-GOVERNMENT possesses great power over disease. Fretfulness and impatience increase the action of the heart and arteries, and impair the action of the skin, and thus aggravate bodily diseases. While resignation to the Will of God, and a cheerful spirit, have effects of the very opposite kind, and we cannot suffer from any complaint which is not relieved by their salutary influence. "*A merry heart doeth good like a medicine; but a broken spirit drieth the bones*". Prov. xvii. ch. 22 verse.

NATURE, SYMPTOMS, CAUSES, DISTINCTION AND TREATMENT OF DISEASES

AGUE OR INTERMITTENT FEVER

AGUE, or intermittent fever, is a fever consisting of paroxysms, or periods of fever, between each of which there is a distinct and perfect intermission from febrile symptoms. There are several kinds or species of ague, but the *quotidian,* which returns every day; the *tertian,* which returns every other day; and the *quartan,* occurring on the first and fourth day, are the principal. It is likewise termed autumnal ague, when it happens in antumn and *vernal,* when in spring.

Every fit of ague, consists of three stages— a *cold,* a *hot* and a *sweating* stage. In the cold stage the face and limbs become pale, the features shrink, and sensibility is greatly impaired, the breathing short and anxious, and a sensation of a severe cold is felt over the whole body, succeeded by shivering and violent shaking. Afterwards, the heat of the body returns, and soon becomes dry, burning, and much above the natural standard; the countenance is now flushed and tumid; there is often acute pain of the head, sometimes slight delirium; the pulse is strong, full, and frequent, and the thirst urgent. These symptoms are followed, first, by moisture of the skin, and then by a universal and equable perspiration, which terminates the fit. The whole paroxysm generally occupies about eight hours.

In the intermission the countenance is apt to be pale and shrunk, and the constitution in general to be affected with languor and feebleness. In the commencement of agues, however, the patient is sometimes free from indisposition.

Spring agues are, in general, less severe and obstinate, and less liable to be followed by dangerous consequences, than the autumnal; they are also less liable to return. Quartan agues, which generally commence in autumn, often do not cease till spring. If quotidian agues lengthen their period, and change into tertian, it is a good sign; but the mutation of a disease of a long interval into a shorter one, denotes the increasing severity of the malady. Thus, a quart-an ague is not dangerous, but if it be converted into a quotidian, it is then very dangerous.

The chief predisposing *cause* is debility, however induced; but the grand exciting cause is *marsh miasma,* or the effluvia arising from stagnant water, or marshy ground, impregnated with vegetable matter in a state of putrefactive decomposition. Dampness, and the night air, are particularly favourable to the full operation of marsh miasma. Ague does arise, however, from other causes than marsh effluvia; and it may be produced by sympathy, or irritation in the stomach and intestines.

TREATMENT.–On the commencement of the actual fit, the patient should be placed in bed between the blankets, and partake freely of warm diluting, but not stimulating drinks, as water-gruel, barley-water, etc., and laudanum may be given in a little cinnamon or simple water. Laudanum is useful here, probably on account of its stimulant properties, and therefore a large dose should be given, not less than from forty to sixty drops. I think the best time to give it is an hour before the fit is expected, but it is often likewise useful after the commencement of the hot fit.[1]

1. "The mode of giving it (laudanum) just at the commencement of the cold stage, shortens this stage very much, and renders the whole paroxysm milder; facts of which patients are so conscious, that our soldiers in the Peninsular hospitals regularly applied for an ague-draught, (sixty drops of laudanum and a drachm of ether in water), when they saw their nails turning blue, which is generally the first sign of the commencement of a paroxysm."—*Cyclopoedia of Pract. Medicine, vol.* 1, p. 226.

One scruple of sesqui-carbonate of ammonia, with eight grains of compound powder of ipecacuanha, and an ounce and a half of mint water, form a draught of excellent service in moderating the attack, when given on the invasion of the cold fit, instead of laudanum.

In the intermission, the principal indications of treatment, are to cleanse and strengthen the stomach and bowels, and to invigorate the general habit. Peruvian bark is well known to be, in general, the most efficacious medicine in the cure of ague; but previous to its exhibition, the stomach must be cleansed by the use of an emetic, consisting of twenty grains of ipecacuanha powder, and after that has ceased to operate, the bowels should be evacuated by giving one of the pills, No. 97, page 191, washing it down with a full dose of the purging mixture, No. 73, page 176. The sooner the bark is commenced after these operations the better. It is most efficacious in the form of powder, and in large doses, administered at short intervals. An ounce of the best bark powder may be divided into eight doses, and a dose taken every hour or every second hour. When the interval between the fits is short, it must be administered immediately after the paroxysms, and continued till the return of the next; on the other hand, when the intermission is long, its exhibition should be delayed till within six or eight hours of the time at which the cold fit is expected. It must invariably be continued for some days after the attacks disappear.

If great debility prevail, the bark must be combined with wine and aromatics; each dose may be taken in a large wine-glassful of old port, with ten grains of sesqui-carbonate of ammonia or a scruple of aromatic powder. If it occasion purging, add three or four drops of laudanum to every dose; if costiveness, mix the dose with a scruple of powdered rhubarb occasionally. When nausea and oppression attend its use, twenty or thirty drops of the diluted vitriolic acid is an excellent addition to each draught.

In very obstinate agues, the bark will sometimes be more efficacious, if mixed with strong brandy and water, or combined with serpentaria. *See* page 114.

Quinine is the active principle of Peruvian bark, and is often still more valuable than bark itself, inasmuch as it operates more quickly, with greater certainty, and in a smaller compass than the latter. It is equal to the removal of the most inveterate cases, and will sometimes cure this disease after bark in substance has failed. Three or four grains of the sulphate of quinine, made into a pill with a small quantity of extract of gentian, may be taken in the same way as the powdered bark; and after the disease is removed, one of these pills should be continued twice a day, for a week or two, to prevent a relapse. This medicine is particularly useful in the ague of children, as it may be administered to them almost without their tasting it, and when they could not be prevailed upon to swallow bark in any other form. It is an article which enjoys the confidence of the whole medical profession.

Should the pulse be hard and strong, and other inflammatory symptoms be present, as pain in the side, etc., this state must be reduced, before giving the bark, by a low diet, and particularly by taking away eight or ten ounces of blood from the arm; since pounds of bark have been given, under such circumstances, without effect, when the disease has yielded readily after the loss of a little blood.

The two foregoing remedies are, in general, by far the best for intermittents of every kind; where they fail, arsenic or cob-web are the best substitutes. In Lincolnshire, and other counties where this fever is very prevalent, arsenic is much employed, and with great success; but it is a remedy of so active a nature, as to be fit to be taken only under the care of a medical practitioner, and then it ought never to be employed till other and less deleterious medicines have failed. Four drops of the arsenical solution, gradually increased, if necessary, to six or eight drops, twice or thrice a day, will speedily cure the most obstinate agues. It is seldom advisable, or requisite, to continue its use beyond ten days, or a fortnight.—See *Arsenic.*

Cob-web is an old and popular remedy for the present fever, and it is as efficacious as popular. Some writers speak of it as a mere dirty object of vulgar superstition; but they are much mistaken, for ten grains of cob-web given twice or thrice before the expected time of each paroxysm, and continued in this way for three or four days, or longer, as circumstances indicate, will be found a powerful mean of putting an immediate and permanent stop to the recurrence of the ague. The patient should, however, be prepared for its use by the previous employment of an emetic, and purgative, as prescribed before beginning the bark. The only valuable cob-web is that produced by the black spider, which inhabits cellars, barns and stables. It is sometimes very effectual in arresting the progress of the febrile symptoms in every other kind of fever. Dr. Jackson, a physician of acknowledged accuracy, and great experience in the treatment of fevers, observes that it is more abrupt and efficient in its operation than bark, or arsenic, or any other remedy employed for the purpose, with which he is acquainted.—*Dr. Jackson on Fever*, p. 241.

One of the reviewers (a physician) of the first edition of this work, although he was pleased to speak very favourably of it, expressed strong doubts of the utility of cob-web, and wished it to be expunged from the book, but I have too solid a foundation for the opinion given respecting it above, to change my sentiments on the subject. Indeed, so highly do I think of it that I hope it may be of service to insert here an extract from Dr. Jackson's observations on its value in remittent fever, and in typhus. Dr. Jackson was for fifty years in the medical department of the army, and during that period treated fevers of every kind and every grade, at home and abroad, equally under the burning sun of the West Indies, and on some of the most swampy plains of Europe. He was well known to the profession as one of the most attentive and accurate observers, as well as one of the most judicious practitioners. *See* also page 116. He says,—

> "I think I may venture to say that the cob-web prevents the recurrence of febrile paroxysms more abruptly, and more effectually than bark, or arsenic, or any other remedy employed for that purpose with which I am acquainted. The cob-web was rarely given before the subject was prepared by emetics, or purgatives; and given to a subject so prepared, it seldom failed to effect a cure comparatively permanent; relapse or conversion into another form of disease, being, upon the whole, a rare occurrence where the disease leas been suspended by

> this remedy. If it was not given until the paroxysm was advanced in progress, the symptoms of irritation, viz. tremors, startings spasms and delirium, if such existed as forms of febrile action, were usually reduced in violence, sometimes entirely removed. In this case, sleep, calm and refreshing, usually followed the sudden and perfect removal of pain and irritation. Vomiting, spasms and twitehings in the bowels, were also usually allayed by it, there was no effect from it where the vomiting or pain were connected with real inflamunation or progress to disorganization. In cases of febrile depression, deficient animation, and indifference to surrounding objects, the exhibition of eight or ten grains of cob-web was often followed by exhilaration; the eye sparkled; the countenance assumed a temporary animation; and though the course of the disease might not be changed, or the dangers averted, more respite was obtained from a pill of cob-web than what arises from or belongs to the action of wine, opium or ally thing else within my knowledge."

When this disease proves unusually obstinate a somewhat different plan may be pursued. In the case of a quatan, in St. Thomas's Hospital, which had lasted two years, Dr. Fordyce prescribed ten grains of the compound powder of ipecacuanha, with a scruple of carbonate of ammonia, (which may be taken in any aqueous vehicle), two hours before the paroxysm was expected. It succeeded perfectly. A profuse perspiration followed the use of this draught, and entirely prevented the cold fit; bark was next freely given, and this obstinate ague was cured in a few days.

Ten grains of sesqui-carbonate of ammonia, or fifteen grains of salt of tartar, with a scruple of chamomile flowers, in powder, and an ounee and a half of mint water, form a draught that has often been found of superior advantage in particular cases of ague which had resisted the employment of the bark. It may be given every fifth or sixth hour during the intermission.

When an ague is accompanied with a sallowness of the complexion and pain, tenderness or swelling about the region of the stomach or liver, indicating the existence of some internal obstruction or disease, the altertive pill, No. 98, page 191, should be taken every night for some time, in order to its removal. In very swampy situations; especially in hot climates, obstructions and disease of the bowels, liver or spleen, are very apt to arise in protracted agues; when the bark will often disagree, and it will be necessary to substitute some other bitter for it, as gentian, quassia, chamomile, or serpentaria. In such cases give ammonia with the bitter, as in No. 82 or 83, page 183-84. The compound powder of ipecacuanha will be found very serviceable as an adjunct to the bitters. Five grains may be taken every night or oftener, and the alterative pill, No. 98, at bed time must not be omitted.

With respect to diet, if, in the commencement, the pulse is hard and strong, and the face flushed, these inflammatory symptoms will require a spare mild diet; but debility generally prevails, and then it ought to be as full and generous as the stomach will easily bear, observing to take that food which affords the most nourishment with the least irritation, as roast mutton, chicken, eggs, bread and good wine.

All agues are very liable to return from the operation of slight causes, the patient will, therefore, find it necessary to avoid exposure to marsh miasma, and all other sources of debility. If he lives in a part of the country where swamps and fens are numerous, he should take a dose of the sulphate of quinine twice a day, for three or four weeks, occasionally, particularly in the spring and autumn, and carefully avoid exposure to the night air.

BROW-AGUE is a form of periodical pain affecting the upper part of the face and forehead, which is cured most certainly with bark and ammonia, and daily exercise. *See* 84B, page 185.

APOPLEXY

Apoplexy, or an apoplectic fit, is a sudden suspension of the powers of sense and motion, from some diseased affection of the brain, or nervous system, the respiration being generally laborious, and frequently attended with a stertorous noise. It is strictly a disease of the nervous system.

We are sometimes warned of the approach of apoplexy by a dull pain in the head, accompanied by a sense of heaviness;

giddiness; drowsiness; frequent fits of night-mare; fulness and redness of the face and eyes; obscurity of sight; bleeding from the nose; faltering in the speech; ringing in the ears, and loss of memory; but its attack is more frequently sudden, and the patient falls to the ground with scarcely any warning, and lies as if in a deep sleep, from which he cannot be roused.

In this state, his breathing is laborious, and generally accompanied by stertor, the face is red and puffed, the veins of the head and neck are distended, the head is hot, and often in a copious perspiration, the eyes are prominent, blood-shot, sometimes half open, but more frequently quite closed, the pupils dilated, and a frothy saliva is often excreted from the mouth. The pulse is at first regular, strong, full, and slow, but soon becomes weaker, frequent, irregular and intermitting. The pupils of the eye are commonly dilated, but they are now and then much contracted.

The duration of a fit of apoplexy is various; but it generally lasts from eight to twenty-four hours, and occasionally to thirty-six hours or still longer.

There are two varieties of apoplexy, which are in general clearly marked, the one attended with a hard full pulse, flushed countenance and generous breathing; the other with a feeble pulse and pale countenance. The former usually occurs in persons of a full plethoric habit, and considerable energy and strength; the latter, for the most part, in the cold, phlegmatic and feeble.

Generally speaking, the latter form of the disease is the most dangerous, since, from the general failure of the energies of life, nature has less ability to assist us in the use of our remedial measures. In other points of view, the degree of danger will be generally measured by the violence of the symptoms. In general, the shorter the fit the more favourable the prognosis.

It is very doubtful, whether the sudden deaths we so frequently hear of, ought to be ascribed, as is common, to apoplectic seizure, since genuine apoplexy very seldom destroys life in less than two hours. They appear to depend rather upon some violent affection of the heart or stomach or upon the rupture of some blood-vessel larger than those of the brain.

The most common immediate cause of apoplexy is pressure on the brain, either from an effusion of blood or serum, or from a distention of the vessels of the brain, by an accumulation of blood in them, independently of effusion.

Whatever operates in determining a great quantity of blood to the head, or in impeding a free return from it, may produce excessive distention or effusion within the cranium, and be, therefore, reckoned as exciting causes, such as violent passions of the mind, immoderate exercise, intense study, fits of intemperance, excessive straining, ligatures about the neck, the suppression of accustomed evacuations, as piles, etc., unrestrained indulgence of the appetite, and exposure to sudden and great heat, or to excessive cold. Some enlightened professional men think that fatty disease of the minute vessels of the brain is the immediate cause of sanguineous apoplexy.

This disease may happen at any age, but is most frequent about the middle, or in the decline of life, especially in persons of a plethoric habit, who have short necks, and who are indolent, and indulge much in eating and drinking.

Apoplexy is *distinguished* from epilepsy, or falling fits, by the presence of convulsions and contortions of the limbs in the latter, by the comparative shortness of the fit, and the greater facility with which the patient is roused.

In deep intoxication, the breath is in general tainted with the intoxicating liquor, and the patient may be in some degree roused by shouting in his ear, and by applying a strong stimulant to the nostrils.

TREATMENT.–Although, in systems of physic, it has been usual to divide this disease into the two varieties of *sanguineous* and *serous;* the former arising from the effusion of blood, the latter from the extravasation of serum; yet it is very doubtful whether these distinctions have any real foundation in experience or observation. But, in treating this disease, it is unquestionably proper and necessary to attend to the following modifications, namely :

1. *Apoplexy occurring in the vigorous and plethoric.*

2. *Apoplexy attacking a constitution infirm by nature or enfeebled by age, intemperance or excessive exertion.*

1. In the former case, blood-letting, both general and local, active purgatives by the mouth and in clysters, and the free application of cold to the head, form the best remedies; but in the apoplexy of the infirm, or enfeebled, it is better wholly to abstain from drawing blood in any way, and much purging is injurious.

In all cases of the disease, the patient should, if possible, be immediately carried into a spacious apartment, into which cool air may be freely admitted; his head and shoulders should be placed in an elevated position; all ligatures, especially those about the neck, must be speedily removed, and the legs and feet should be placed in warm water, or rubbed with the stimulating embrocation, No. 45, page 163.

When the disease occurs in a full habit, with a flushed face, and the pulse full and strong, a pint or two of blood should be immediately drawn from the arm, or jugular vein, and a dozen leeches may be applied to the temples, or the patient may be cupped on the back of the neck. Immediately subsequent to these operations, a copious purgative clyster, as No. 8, page 146, quickened by the addition of four ounces of infusion of senna, should be exhibited, which may be followed by active purgatives, administered by the mouth as soon as the patient is able to swallow. The powder, No. 120, page 205, washed down with a full dose of the mixture, No. 73. will be proper. The head may, at the same time, be covered with linen rags, wet with cold water, vinegar and water, or pounded ice. Should the patient not be able to swallow the ordinary purgatives, ten grains of calomel, and two of powdered gamboge, mixed with a little jelly or sweet butter, may be placed on the root of the tongue.

Unless the first clyster operates well, it ought to be quickly repeated, which may likewise be observed with regard to the purgative powder. In the commencement, the purgative medicine should be repeated every day, and afterwards every second or third day, for some time.

A mustard poultice, as No. 4, applied to the feet, is a proper measure in the beginning, and sometimes a useful one. Some practitioners recommend blisters, but they are of doubtful advantage.

An emetic is seldom advisable or safe, unless the fit has come on soon after a hearty meal, when it ought to be the first thing resorted to.

Dr. Watson's advice is sound. He says,—

> "If the pulse be full or hard or thrilling, or if there be obvious external signs of fulness about the head, yon must abstract blood. You are not to refrain from bleeding the apoplectic patient because he is pale, if the pulse warrants it, nor may you omit taking blood if the face be turgid, although the pulse be small, for that smallness may depend upon organic disease of the heart. On the contrary, if the skin is pale and cold, and the pulse flickering, you would probably insure your patient's death if you withdrew from the failing heart and blood-vessels a portion of their natural stimulus"–the blood.

Dr. Baillie, after recommending the treatment above laid down, says, "If the patient should recover by these means, the best plan of management, in order to escape from another attack, is to live almost entirely throughout future life upon vegetable food, and to abstain from wine, spirits and malt liquor. It will be of considerable advantage to avoid any strong, or long continued exertion of the mind. In a few instances, when the full state of the vessels of the brain had for some time subsided, I have derived considerable advantage from the moderate use of tonic medicines, and more especially of steel." —*Baillie's Posthumous Writings,* p. 168.

2. In the *second variety* of apoplexy, which is the disease of an enfeebled constitution, mild invigorating means alone should be employed. The system pursued should be restorative, and I would begin with the draught, No. 35A, page 158, keeping the bowels regular with a little of the mixture, No. 74 A, page 176, a dose of which may be taken daily, or as occasion may require. At the end of a week or ten days, a more decided tonic may be given, such as No. 35 page 158, or No. 82 or 83 page 183-84. When the patient is

recovering, a change of air and scene may be resorted to with the prospect of considerable advantage. Much of the treatment recommended for *Indigestion* will be useful here.

Numerous cases, both of apoplexy and paralysis, occur where the symptoms depend upon irritation alone, or on loss of nervous power or on a deficient circulation of blood through the brain, and in which the loss of the smallest quantity of blood is always injurious, and invigorating means are indicated. This fact ought never to be lost sight of.

There are many cases of apoplexy continually occurring, in which, at the time of seizure, there are present symptoms of deficient vital energy of the brain and constitution, although considerable corpulence may exist, or general appearance of strength; thus *in the commencement of the attack, and before reaction has supervened,* the countenance may be pallid or sunk, the pulse of the arteries of the neck weak or small, the temperature of the head not greatly increased,—and in such cases we must not bleed until reaction has followed, but administer gentle stimuli, as sal volatile and water internally, apply the volatile salts to the nose, and dash cold water freely over the head and face. After the patient has recovered a little, the face becomes flushed, and the arteries of the neck manifest an increased action, we may then order blood-letting with great safety and advantage. A useful case illustrative of this practice is found in Dr. Copland's, *Dictionary of Medicine,* p. 103. He says,—

> "Travelling in the summer, in one of the short stages, I sat opposite an aged and corpulent man who, very soon after our leaving town, suddenly lost his consciousness and power of motion. His countenance became first pale, then bloated and inexpressive, his breathing slow and slightly stertorous, all his muscles completely relaxed, and he fell in a few seconds upon those sitting around him. We were only a few doors from a chemist's shop; the coach was stopped, and he was carried thither. He was now profoundly, apoplectic; a copious perspiration flowed from his face and forehead, the veins of which were distended, and all his senses were completely abolished. There was no sign of hémiplegia,—but there was a general

> and complete loss of motion and sensation. His neckcloth having been removed, the pulsation of the carotids was found to be slow and of natural strength and fulness. Whilst he was held in a sitting posture in a chair, cold water was poured gently over his head from a sponge, and his head frequently sponged with it, volatile salts also were held for a short time, and at intervals to his nostrils. The power of deglutition was at this time abolished, so that it was impossible to administer a draught, chiefly consisting of a small quantity of spiritus ammoniae aromaticus, and camphor mixture, which was prescribed. In a very few minutes his consciousness returned, he took the draught, and, in a short time afterwards, he walked to a coach, in which I accompanied him home. He now complained only of a very slight confusion of ideas, with scarcely any head-ache, but his carotids beat more firmly. One full-blood-letting and an active purgative were now directed. The next day he was perfectly well, and has continued so. What would have been the result if he had been largely blooded previously to the reaction?"

After recovery, the diet may be a little more generous than what would be proper in the convalescence of a plethoric subject from an attack of this disease. The tonic pill, No. 102, page 196 or No. 104A, may be advantageously alternated with the strengthening draughts above noticed. It is a common practice also to recommend the external use of stimulants, as No. 45 or 46, which may be freely rubbed down the spine, over the arms, and on other parts of the body alternately.

As a preventive, the tartar emetic (*see* page 48-49) merits much confidence. Indeed, this medicine will often aid materially in the cure of the apoplectic patient.

Those who, from their constitutional robust make, are disposed to the present malady, ought to be very attentive in observing a mild spare diet, and regular habits; they should rise and retire early, take no strong drink, excepting, perhaps, sometimes, a little good home-brewed malt liquor; they should keep an open state of the bowels, and use a great deal of active exercise in the country. A seton in the nape of the neck, or between the shoulders, is often a valuable preventive, and highly merits the attention of those who have had one attack of apoplexy.

In recovering from an attack of apoplexy, strict attention to diet and regimen is of the utmost moment, and I shall, therefore, conclude this article with some of the most important rules relating to these points. It has been correctly remarked, that the recovery of health and strength, after the disorder has been in a measure subdued, requires, (and often for a long period of time), unceasing attention to minutiae.

1. Having the head shaved frequently, or at least washing it daily in cold water, are practices worthy of much regard. Frequently rubbing the head with a flesh-brush, dipped in cold water, is very beneficial. The scurf on the skin is thus votrid rid of a proper perspiration promoted, and the head can be ept much cooler.

2. As soon as it is practicable, it is highly expedient to use the shower bath, with cold or tepid water, at least occasionally, as the means of propelling blood from the head.

3. A strong flesh-brush ought to be applied for ten minutes, night and morning, to the feet and arms, with the view of giving, tone to the skin and muscles, and augmenting the *quantum* of daily exercise. Scarcely any thing is of such decided benefit in drawing the blood to the extremities as a cold foot-bath daily, about eleven o'clock—*See* the Appendix. A servant must rub the feet constantly while in the water. If the speech be affected, a very likely means of obtaining relief is by the application of a hard flesh-brush to the throat, as often in the day as may be convenient; and rubbing under the chin with the fingers. See what is said of *friction* at page 279.

4. The breathing of pure air is of the utmost importance to health; and for that purpose, the improved mode of ventilation, by pulling down the upper sashes, and having a wooden conductor, by which the air is made to strike against the ceiling, cannot be too strongly recommended. By this means the room occupied by the patient may be kept constantly cool in the summer, and in the winter an occasional recourse to it will prevent any stagnation of air in the apartment, and carry off superfluous heat.

5. The clothes should be kept loose (especially about the neck, the wrists and the knees), and light for the sake of easy conveyance. It is not difficult, by using Shetland stockings, etc., to combine warmth with lightness.

6. In regard to diet, at breakfast, a moderate quantity of milk may be taken, if it agrees with the patient, with hard baker's biscuit, or rusks or stale or toasted bread, which are both more agreeable to the stomach, and excite its digestive powers bettei, than common bread. If costive, toasted brown bread, especially with a little rye flour in its composition, will be preferable. Barley-meal porridge or gruel, might also be occasionally taken; or tea for a change. No coffee on any account.[1]

Luncheons ought to be entirely given up. For dinner, (about two o'clock), take a single plateful of light soup or broth, and then a moderate quantity of pudding, made of pearl barley, rice or bread. Pearl or pot-barley affords excellent nourishment. When ground into meal, it may be made into scones or cakes (prepared with milk), which are wholesomer than fermented bread. A little fowl or mutton or white sea-fish, in particular whitings and fresh herrings, is allowable once or twice a week for a change. The wholesomest fruits, as strawberries, gooseberries, grapes, currants, apples and oranges, may be taken, but never after the stomach is filled. Stone fruits are to be avoided, except perhaps peaches. Remember to eat slowly, and to masticate well what is eaten.

For drink whey, (more especially clarified, as the French *"petit lait")*, gum water or toast and water, carefully made, are to be preferred. Ginger or spruce beer, likewise may he taken; but no wine nor spirits, even with water. Spirits, in particular, are rank poison here. A very little mild *homebrewed* malt liquor may be tried.

A late *tea* or *cocoa* may be taken to prevent the necessity of supper, which ought to be given up, or indulged in very sparingly.

7. With respect to sleeping, a mattress is to be preferred; the head should be raised, and very lightly and thinly covered; the

1. "Coffee is decidedly injurious where there is an apoplectic tendency. Some eight years ago, a gentleman in this city (Philadelphia), of a strongly developed apoplectic habit, was seized with an attack of this affection. He was in the habit of taking large quantities of very strong coffee twice daily. I advised him to leave off taking this beverage enthely. He did so; and has not since experienced even the ordinary premonitory symptoms of the complaint."—Dr. Eberle's *Practice of Physic,* vol.2 p. 25, 1831.

pillow to be stuffed with horse-hair instead of feathers. A habit of retiring to bed early, and rising very early, ought to be studiously cultivated.

8. Daily exercise is of the first importance, more particularly if the patient be of a full habit. *Without,* walking much on level ground, surveying the beauties of Nature, and directing the operations, but not joining in the labours of gardening, are practices highly advisable. The management of a greenhouse, and attention to the culture of plants, are excellent means of occupation. These should be alternated with gentle horse exercise. In regard to *"in-door amusements"*, neither billiards nor cards are to be recommended, from the anxiety they occasion. Books of an amusing, instructive and religious nature are proper, and the company of the cheerful, serious and well informed, ought to be cultivated. Daily friction and percussion most not be forgotten.

Religious exercises ought not, by any means, to be omitted.The infallible pen of inspiration assures us, that *"Godliness is profitable for all things"*, it means that it is *pre-eminently* profitable, and these exercises will afford consolation and hope, when every other means of relief are sought for in vain.

9. Quit large towns and cities for the open elevated country.

On the whole, it is hardly possible, where the constitution is not gone, or the frame in a state of decay, that a careful attention to all these particulars, will not be productive of the most essential benefit.

ASTHMA

This disease consists in a difficulty of breathing, for the most part temporary, and occurring at uncertain periods, accompanied with a wheezing sound, and a sense of constriction in the chest, with cough and expectoration. At first view it seems to be a disease of the lungs, and these organs are, no doubt, often primarily and chiefly affected; but it is as certain, that in some instances there is no positive disease of the pulmonary organs; the difficulty of breathing, and other symptoms present, denoting deep-seated mischief in the lungs, arising secondarily and sympathetically from severe disorder in other important parts, as in the heart, and especially in the stomach and bowels. The late Dr. Heberden alluded to this in saying, "It is observable in pulmonary consumption where the whole lungs are diseased, and where a great part of them has been destroyed, that patients have indeed a shortness of breath upon motion, but not any of the violent fits of suffocation which belong to asthma; while in examining the lungs of asthmatic persons after death; there has sometimes appeared no hurt obvious to the senses which could account for the difficulty with which they had performed their office".–*Commentaries,* page 80. Asthma is a disease of the latter period of life, and is very difficult of cure.

The real nature of the difficulty of breathing, called *asthma,* is now much better known than it was even a few years ago. It is evident that there are three distinct and principal causes or sources of this disease, *viz.* 1. *Dry cough;* 2. *Organic disease of the heart, or large blood-vessels;* 3. *Disorder of the nervous influence simply.*

1. By *dry cough* is meant an habitual thickening or congestion in some part or other of the mucous membrane of the lungs. It is particularly remarkable in the smaller branches of the bronchia, or air passages, and it is reasonable to suppose that if this swelling and thickening takes place beyond a certain degree and extent, it will obstruct the passage of the air, more or less completely, and thus give rise to asthma.

2. Organic disease of the heart, or large blood-vessels, gives rise to asthma, by causing an extension of disease to the lungs, and by occasioning an irregularity in the transmission of blood through them.

3. In some instances of asthma there exists, as Dr. Heberden remarks in the above extract, no sign whatever of vascular congestion or thickening, or of any other organic lesion; and then we can attribute it only to disorder of the nervous influence simply.[1]

1. Many persons of a susceptible constitution cannot sustain a lively emotion, whether from physical or moral causes, without being immediately seized with a difficulty of breathing, and in some it is intense. This is what is meant here by disorder of the nervous influence simply. This is the chief or only form which a *nervous attack* assumes in many women—the circulation being

(*Contd. to next page*)

It is commonly divided into two species, the dry spasmodic, or nervous asthma; and the humid or habitual asthma. In the former, the fit is sudden, violent and of short duration; the constriction on the chest very hard and spasmodic; the cough alight, and the expectoration scanty, and only appearing towards the close of the fit. In the second species, or habitual asthma, the paroxysm is gradual and protracted; the constriction of the chest is heavy and laborious; the cough severe, and more or less constant; the expectoration commencing early, soon becoming copious, and affording great relief. The spasmodic asthma is comparatively a rare disease, not one case occurring for, perhaps, fifty cases of habitual asthma.

Asthmatic paroxysms are usually preceded by languor, flatulency head-ache, drowsiness, pale urine, disturbed rent, and pain in the head. Soon a sense of tightness and stricture is felt across the breast, with distressing straitness of the lungs, impeding respiration; the difficulty of breathing continues to increase; both inspiration and expiration are performed slowly, and with a wheezing noise; the speech becomes difficult and uneasy; a propensity to coughing succeeds, followed by the most anxious difficulty of breathing; the patient is threatened with immediate suffocation, and is obliged instantly to rise from a horizontal position. The face is sometimes turgid, and of a livid hue; at others it is morbidly pale and shrunk. These symptoms continue for a

---

(Contd.)

frequently not at all affected. Again, the difficulty of breathing which is so easily produced by the slightest exercise in very fat subjects, is also in great part nervous, and may be chiefly attributed to the great expenditure of nervous influence required to move a mass so disproportioned to the ordinary powers of motion.

In examples of impeded respiration, whatever was its cause, we have frequently seen its violence lessened by the patient merely shutting his eyes. We see the same thing is many other pains in different parts of the body, and particularly in pains of the stomach and intestines, (it may be so intense as to simulate those of inflammation,) which the patients could remove or induce at pleasure, by merely opening or closing the eyes, or by turning them to or from a bright light. In such cases it seems probable, that the effects can only depend on the stimulation com municated to or subtracted from the brain by the *light*; and, consequently, that disorder of the nervous influence simply, without any organic lesion, may give rise to diffculty of breathing, as well as other nervous affections.

longer or shorter period, when they gradually decline, the fit being generally terminated by an expectoration of mucus. Notwithstanding the violence of the assault, it is very seldom that asthma proves fatal at the time.

In spasmodic asthma, the patient frequently soon recovers from the fit, if we except the effects of weakness left behind, and when the weather is warm and favourable, may continue for weeks or months free from difficulty of breathing or cough; but in the humid habitual asthma, although weeks may be sometimes passed without a severe fit, yet the sufferer, for the most part, labours under a continual difficulty of breathing, accompanied with a wheezing noise and more or less cough.

The exciting *causes* are numerous, and among the chief of them we may reckon, hereditary predisposition,—cold and moist atmosphere,—sudden changes of temperature, removal from a healthy spot in the country to a crowded and populous city—suppression of long acustomed evacuations–mechanical constriction of the chest. Yet all these may be resolved into an irritation of some kind or other, existing within the cavity of the chest, and stimulating its moving powers to a convulsive constriction; or to speak with still more precision, in all cases the exciting cause is an irritant of some kind or other, acting on the too sensible membrane of the bronchia. In such instances, the asthma is a primary affection originating in the chest; but we have already remarked that this disease not unfrequently occurs secondarily, and as a mere symptom or result of some other complaint, or of a diseased state of some remote organ, as the stomach, bowels or liver, when it is only to be removed by removing the disorder on which it is dependent. Hence, it is of the utmost importance that we should trace out the actual cause, so as to determine whether it has its seat within the chest or in a more remote part.

The asthmatic attack itself, as above remarked, seems to be the immediate consequence of a spasmodic affection of the minute bronchia, that is the minute terminations of the windpipe. These terminations, though minute, are possessed of a set of completely circular muscular fibres, and it is very conceivable that the spasmodic contraction of these fibres may be carried so far, as to obstruct the air-passages to such a degree as to prevent the transmission of air to a great portion of the lungs.

When once asthma is established, a recurrence of the fit may be readily excited by any excess or imprudence in diet, or any unusual exertions of body or mind. The occasional causes of attacks of asthma are almost always of a kind to give occasion to an immediate and evident disturbance of the nervous influence. Whatever greatly deranges the functions of the stomach and bowels will prove a powerful cause of exciting the fits; and though this disease is not, generally speaking, immediately dangerous, frequent returns of it are liable gradually to induce incurable diseases of the heart or lungs and thus to occasion a fatal termination. These facts evince the importance of an unceasing attention in avoiding the constitutional or occasional causes of this affection.

TREATMENT.–I shall consider first the treatment proper during the paroxysm or fit; and then that which is suited to the intervals. The former is of course, only palliative, and adopted with the view to shorten the duration of the asthmatic fit, and render it less severe and painful during its continuance; while the latter is sometimes curative, and the object in resorting to it, should be to lessen or remove the diseased condition of the lungs, or other parts on which the malady depends, and thus to free the patient altogether from a subsequent repetition of the attacks, or to weaken their force, and lengthen the intervals between them.

When the fit is on, or felt to be coming on, the patient should be brought near a large fire, and the feet and legs be immediately immersed in warm water; he should drink frequently of some mild diluting liquor made warm, as barley-water, or very thin gruel, into a pint of which, two tea-spoonfuls of ether or of aromatic spirit of ammonia, may be put; and if there be much pain about the chest, the part may be fomented with hot flannels, or bladders of hot water. The draught of henbane and nitric acid, at page 371, will sometimes be very useful. Some recommend laudanum, or Battley's solution, but opiates do not usually agree. I think very highly of the mixture No. 78A, page 180, or two of the following pills may be taken every hour :

Take of James's powder, (Newberry's)......	10 grains;
Ipecacuanha powder	4 grains;
Camphor, scraped	12 grains;

Extract of henbane, a sufficient quantity to form the mass, which is to be divided into six pills.

Sir John Floyer and Sir John Pringle, both of whom were able physicians, confidently recommended coffee, and the latter eminent practitioner says, that it is the best abater of periodic asthma that he had seen. The best Mocha is to be preferred, which should be newly burnt, and prepared very strong immediately after grinding it. It may always be obtained in great perfection at Dakin and Co.'s, No. 1, St. Paul's Church Yard.

Most patients are aware of the approach of a fit of asthma, by certain premonitory signs, and whenever these signs present themselves, the immersion of the feet in warm water, drinking of warm slops, with the use of a mild aperient draught, as No. 27A, page 155, should *immediately* be resorted to, as the fit will thereby be frequently prevented.

An emetic, of twenty grains of ipecacuanha powder, is often attended with peculiar advantage on the accession of the fit, and may be beneficially employed afterwards, once in three or four weeks. The emetic determines to the surface of the body, promotes expectoration, greatly relieves the chest, and is a measure much approved by the generality of the most experienced physicians; but if the patient is averse to it, he may take instead three grains of compound ipecacuanha powder, made into a pill with conserve of roses, every second or third hour, till the fit abates.

See what is said of the value of spider's web in relieving the paroxysm of asthma, page 116.

The inhalation of ether will sometimes give perfect relief during the paroxysm, but it is a remedy not without danger, and should never be employed except under medical superintendence. It can be tried by heating a common tea-pot with boiling water, and, after pouring the water quite off, put a tea-spoonful or two of ether into the pot, shut the lid down close, and let the patient inhale the fumes by putting the spout into his mouth, and breathing in that way for several minutes. This may be repeated frequently if it agrees, and the severity of the disease makes it desirable; or the vapour may be inhaled from a pint of boiling water, poured upon half an ounce of camphor, balsam of tolu or extract of hops. This should be put into an inhaler. A simple and efficacious way of inhaling ether is to put two tea-spoonfuls in a saucer held in the lap; while a shawl is thrown over the shoulders, and brought round in front so as to envelope the upper part of the body. Thus, the ether can be inhaled so as to produce a delightfully soothing effect.

If the bowels are confined on the accession of the fit, they should be relieved by the exhibition of a laxative clyster, as No. 8, page 146, or by administering a dose of the aperient mixture, No. 73, page 176; but purging is almost invariably to be avoided.

I have known strong brandy and water afford more relief than any other thing during the fit. Dr. Dawson, of Bishopwearmouth, writes in favour of gin and water; indeed, he states that sufferers from the dry spasmodic asthma have, under his own observation, derived a cure from gin and water, when all medicines and every other kind of spirits, had completely failed.—*Dawson's Practice of Physic,* p. 331.

Dr. Bree, the author of an approve work on disordered respiration, advises the following draught to be taken every three hours during the paroxysm. "Many patients", says he, "who had taken the most powerful antispasmodics, have assured me that none had been so useful; and two gentlemen, now under my direction, inform me, that it is the only medicine that has ever given them relief in the fits".

Take of Extract of henbane	3	grains;
Diluted nitric acid	30	drop;
Tincture of squill	15	drops;
Water	1½	ounce.

Mix them together.

Asthma is frequently observed in *middle-aged* and *elderly* persons, to take on much of the character of a slow inflammation and obstruction in the lungs, being attended with a good deal of pain in the chest, feverishness and hard pulse, especially in the winter and spring; and then, says Dr. Bree, seneka is the most certainly useful medicine that I have tried. In such cases, while the feverishness continues, it must be united with a saline, as three drachms of the solution of acetate of ammonia, to an ounce and a half of decoction of seneka, to be taken three or four times a day. When the feverishness gives way, it should be combined with squill and ammonia, which will be found to promote expectoration, perspiration, and urine in a powerful manner.

Take of Decoction of seneka	1½	ounce;
Vinegar of squill		half a drachm;
Solution of acetate of ammonia	1	drachm.

Mix for a draught, to be taken three or four times a day.

The mixture No. 78A, or 78 D, page 180-81 will also be very useful in asthma, complicated with obstruction.

Dr. Copland says *(Dict. of Practical Medicine,* p. 148), " The distilled laurel water or the prussic acid, particularly the latter, is often productive of much benefit in the paroxysm. I have found it of great advantage, when given in from two to four drops at the accession of the paroxysm, and in small doses in the intervals, particularly when the disease is attended with much irritability of the stomach and flatulence. It may be conjoined with camphor, ipecacuanha, etc".

It is a too common practice among some persons to bleed the patient during a severe asthmatic fit, but unless there is great fulness of habit, with a tendency to inflammation, it should never be resorted to; for it greatly augments the subsequent weakness, without mitigating even the present severity of the disease.

During the intervals of the fits, the most valuable medicines are ammoniac, assafoetida, squill, seneka, ipecacuanha, preparations of zinc or steel, mercurial alteratives, and the *lobelia inflata,* combined with such a diet and regimen as are calculated to invigorate the digestive functions, the organs within the chest, and the constitution at large. In some cases, where no inflam-matory symptoms are present, the following pills are very serviceable.

Take of Gum ammoniac, gum assafoetida, of each	1 drachm;
Powder of ipecacuanha	15 grains;

Peruvian balsam, a sufficient quantity to form the whole into a mass, to be divided into thirty pills.

Two or three to be taken twice or thrice a day.

Or these :

Take of Compound squill pill	1	drachm;
Powder of ipecacuanha	12	grains;
Purified Turkey opium	3	grains;
Camphor	1	scruple.

Mix them, and divide into twenty pills. Take two pills three times a day.

When the patient is fully recovered from the fit, either of the stomachic medicines, Nos. 102, 103, 104 or 104 A, pages 196-97 will frequently be found eminently useful. Some persons will derive most advantage from the pills No. 102, and others from the No. 104 or No. 104 A or No. 106 A, page 198. Those patients who are soon heated by tonics, and those in whom they readily excite head-ache, will derive the greatest advantage from the pills 104 A or No. 106. These pills have more of a tonic property than No. 104, and will be more suitable than steel to such persons as have just been described on account of their not being so heating.

The compound tincture of Benjamin, when good, is sometimes a useful medicine, and may be taken to the extent of thirty or forty drops, three times a day, in mucilage.

I have already adverted to the value of occasional emetics, of ipecacuanha powder, in the intervals. They are almost invariably useful, especially in habitual asthma, and may be had recourse to occasionally, provided the patient is strong. Fifteen or twenty grains of ipecacuanha powder is a proper dose. Ipecacuanha and camphor are remedies applicable to all the forms of asthma, and to all conditions of the system at the time of the attack.

There can be no doubt that asthma may frequently be much relieved by the skilful employment of mercurial alteratives, and I believe it possible even to cure some cases of the disease, both in its habitual and spasmodic form, by such means. The most superficial observer, who has seen many cases of asthma, must have often perceived it to be closely connected with a deranged state of the digestive organs, and symptoms of internal obstruction, when the efficacy of mercurial preparations is considerable. Therefore, under such circumstances, I would advise the pill No. 98, page 181, to be taken every night, in addition to any other medicine that may be resorted to during the day. This pill may be advantageously persevered in for several weeks, but after the first week, I recommend its exhibition only every second night.

I have remarked on the use of the *lobelia inflata* at page 81. The American physicians have great confidence in the power of this article in spasmodic asthma. Dr. Eberle, of Philadelphia, says, *(Treatise on the Practice of Physic,* Vol. 2, p. 219, 1831).

> "Of all the remedies we possess, the *lobelia inflata* is, I think, decidedly the most valuable in this affection. Within the last five years, I have had an opportunity of witnessing its good effects in four cases; and I can truly say, that in two of them it acted like a charm. I have known the most violent paroxysm of spasmodic asthma completely subdued in less than thirty minutes by this medicine. It appears to me that ergot does not more certainly act upon the gravid uterus during parturition, than the lobelia upon the pulmonary organs in asthma. I have even found it to mitigate the difficulty of breathing, which occurs in consequence of organic affections of the heart. Since the publication of the first edition of this work, I have had occasion to prescribe this article in a violent, and inveterate case of this malady. The good effects, in this instance, were as prompt and decisive as in any case I had previously witnessed. In one hour after the exhibition of the remedy, the patient's respiration was entirely free from difficulty or oppression."
>
> "The good effects of a full dose of this medicine are often experienced in the course of ten or fifteen minutes after it is taken."

We should commence with a dose not exceeding a tea-spoonful in water.

Occasional blisters are very advisable but a perpetual issue or seton in the side arm or between the shoulders, is of still greater effect, and sometimes proves a powerful remedy. It ought never to be neglected in bad cases, for if it fails to cure, it rarely falls short in relieving.

The inhalation of oxygen gas has been known to prove curative in asthma. It is chiefly in those instances where the face is pale, and the strength reduced, that it is a valuable remedy, since its principal effects are those of a powerful tonic. Dr. Beddoes of Bristol, who has related cases of asthma treated with complete success by this means, observes, "no sooner does the oxygen gas touch the lungs, than the livid colour of the countenance disappears, the laborious respiration ceases, and the functions of all the organs of the chest go on easily and pleasantly again". Dr. Ferriar of Manchester, has spoken in equally high terms of the inhalation of hydrogen gas. It seems to be more particularly applicable to those cases in which the complexion still continues florid, and the general strength is but little impaired, especially in the dry or spasmodic asthma.

Dr. Wilson Philip discovered that, in habitual asthma, the application of galvanism is often of great benefit, and some times effects a complete cure. From eight to sixteen four-inch plates of zinc and copper are sufficient in power, with a fluid composed of a hundred and twenty parts water and one part muriatic acid. The galvanism is applied in the following manner :— Two thin plates of metal, about two or three inches in diameter, dipped in water are applied, one to the nape of the neck, the other to the lower part of the region of the stomach. The wires from the different ends of the trough are brought into contact with these plates, and as great a galvanic power maintained as the patient could bear without complaint. In this way the galvanic influence was sent through the lungs as much as possible in the direction of their nerves. It is proper constantly to move the wires upon the metal plates, particularly the negative wire, otherwise the skin is injured in the places on which they rest. The relief seems much the same, whether the positive wire is applied to the nape of the neck or the pit of the stomach.

The galvanism is to be discontinued as soon as the patient says that the breathing is easy, which varies from five to fifteen minutes. It is remarkable, that in several who had laboured under oppressed breathing from ten to twenty years, it gave relief quite as readily as in mono recent cases.

In all inflammatory cases of asthma, the application of galvanism would be injurious; and in cases arising from dropsy, or any other mechanical impediment, little or nothing, it is evident, is to be expected from it.

Probably the chief immediate cause of habitual asthma is a deficiency of nervous power in the lungs, and experiment droves that galvanism has a greater and more immediate effect in restoring the nervous influence to these organs than any other remedy. It is from this property, therefore, that it is so frequently found of such essential service in this complaint, when no ordinary means are able to reach the case. Mr. Cole, the house-surgeon of Worcester Infirmary, states that no other means there employed have been equally efficacious in relieving this disease; indeed it is asserted, that this remedy has succeeded there in curing and relieving asthma, in the ratio of ninety cases out of a hundred. Mr. La Beaume likewise says, in referring to his own practice, Many instances of habitual as well as spasmodic asthma, recurring in winter or summer, after certain intervals have been perfectly and permanently cured, in patients of different ages, by gal-vanism". In my opinion, this remedy has not gained that confidence and attention in the treatment of asthma, which it merits both from the patient and practitioner.

Among other instances of remarkable recovery in the present malady, from the skilful use of galvanic influence, Mr. La Beaume relates the following very satisfactory case.

> "About seven years ago, a gentleman far advanced in life came to me for relief; his breathing was hurried, and very laborious, and he had been for more than twenty years constantly suffering from

habitual asthma, and a great difficulty in expectorating the tough viscid phlegm, which almost impeded respiration. In a very few minutes after he was subjected to the galvanic current, his breathing became perfectly easy, and he was able to expectorate freely, and to walk up stairs without any difficulty. After a month he obtained perfect and permanent recovery."

Equal success has attended the administration of this means in France.

The warm bath is generally hurtful, but the cold bath often proves extremely useful. It must be used only during the absence of the fit, and seems particularly beneficial to persons of great constitutional vigour. In 1793, a Dr. Ryan published a valuable work on asthma, in which he adduces many instances of successful treatment by the cold bath. I have known the free use of cold water very beneficial.

The smoking of tobacco or stramonium, is frequently of the greatest service, although some physicians object to the practice. *See* p. 126. Like other remidies, it sometimes fails altogether; but in some dases, says Dr. Watson, "it calms the paroxysm like a charm".—*Lectures,* Vol. 2, p. 362. It would seem to be especially applicable to humoral asthma, in which form the patient expectorates rather copiously, and where there is no great fulness of habit.[1] A remedy of great efficacy are the fumes from blotting paper steeped in a strong solution of saltpetre, and afterwards dried. A little of this paper should be burnt before the patient, and the fumes inhaled. I have known it afford considerable relief.

For the flatulency accompanying this disease, the following may be found an appropriate and efficacious medicine. It will also relieve the cough and oppression of the chest.

Take of Distilled vinerar	2 ounces;
Powder of ipecacuanha	4 grains;

1. "*Stramonium* is one of the best remedies that can be prescribed in the spasmodic form of asthma. It is principally used by smoking it as tobacco."—Dr. Copland's *Dictionary of Medicine,* p. 148.

Water .... 3 ounces;

Mix, and take one or two table-spoonfuls every four hours, or as occasion requires.

A distressing pain sometimes affects the integuments of the head, and generally at the back of the head. I have known a blister afford perfect relief in this pain, but in general the most effectual remedies are stomachic and volatile medicines, with diaphoretics, as the draught, No. 32 or the mixture No. 77 or 78, which may be accompanied, if necessary, with a pill containing three grains of the compound ipecacuanha powder, twice or thrice a day.

The diet must uniformly be light, and easy of digestion, consisting chiefly of fresh animal food, eggs, bread, tea, cocoa, etc. That recommended under the head of INDIGESTION is the best that can be resorted to. A waistcoat of wash leather, or flannel, worn constantly next the skin, from September to May, inclusive, is highly to be recommended.

With respect to regimen, the points most worthy of atten. tion are, to keep the bowels regular, by diet and friction; to preserve the surface of the body warm, avoiding damp, wet and the east and north-east winds; and to take daily exercise in the open air, when the weather permits, short of fatigue. Horse and carriage exercise are by far the best. Removal to a mild climate is highly advisable; and what is said on this point under the head of CONSUMPTION is applicable here. The Isle of Wight, Clifton, and the southern parts of Devonshire, are the most eligible situations for asthmatic persons, most of whom live there with far greater comfort and security, than in any other part of Great Britain. Epsom, Dorking, or Reigate, in Surrey, are eligible situations for those who will not, or cannot go far from London.

BARRENNESS

The *causes* of barrenness are various, but the most usual kinds are :

1. Barrenness from impotency or imperfection or abolition of the conceptive power;
2. Barrenness from the monthly discharge being either morbidly retained, or secreted with difficulty or in profusion;
3. Barrenness from personal aversion or want of appetency. And the first kind may be either atonic or organic, that is, proceeding from direct imbecility or want of tone or produced by some structural hindrance or defect, whether natural or accidental.

In the first kind, proceeding from imbecility or want of tone, the proper remedies are, local and general tonics and stimulants, especially cold bathing, preparations of iron with bitters, as No. 102 or 103, page 196, electricity, blisters, issues or setons and ginseng, combined with change of air and scene. Abstinence for a time is likewise very advisable.

If this condition is produced by some hindrance or defect in the structure of the parts concerned, that hindrance must, if possible, be removed, and then the most efficacious course consists of alteratives, as the pill No. 98, page 181, at night, with ten or twelve ounces of the compound decoction of sarsaparilla, in divided doses during the day, (or the powder of sarsaparilla), and an occasional tepid bath, at about 95 degrees, the bowels, being kept regular with a mild aperient pill.

When the barrenness arises from painful menstruation, the cure must depend upon a removal of the particular kind of morbid affection that operates at the time, and lays a foundation for the disease, the proper means for effecting which will be found under the head of *Menstruation, Retention of the Menses,* and *Suppression of the Menses.*

Female sterility from personal aversion is a complaint irremediable by the healing art, and can only be attacked by a kind, assiduous, and very affectionate attention, which will rarely fail of its object.

In my Treatise on the Diseases of Females, I have entered at some length into the several causes and the management of female sterility, and refer the reader to that book; but I take this opportunity of stating, that a Dr. Taylor, who many years since practised at Croydon, when consulted on the point, looking to the probable advantage of a spare diet, used to place both the husband and wife on a diet of milk and vegetables, and by this means he succeeded in several instances, in realizing the hopes of a family.[1] This is an excellent practice where it is not contra-indicated by any peculiar condition of the parties, and especially when conjoined with an active life, in a good country air. The effects of a spare and rather low diet upon the procreative powers are certainly remarkable, and within the sphere of every man's observation; for the married poor almost every where abound with children, while the rich are often childless, and large families among them are comparatively rare. Twins are extremely common in the Highlands of Scotland, and still more so in Ireland, where the diet of the majority of the inhabitants is scanty, and of no very nutritious qualities. In the Lying-in Hospital in London, twins occur once in every 85 births, and three children at a birth, once in every 14,393 ; while in Dublin, the proportions are 1 to 49 for the former, and 1 to 1,462 for the latter.

BILIOUS COMPLAINTS

The disorders of the liver have attracted so great and unrea sonable a degree of attention of late, both from the profession and the public at large, that it is exceedingly common for almost all complaints subsisting within the abdomen (or belly), to be resolved into some

1. "I remember Dr. Taylor, the milk doctor of Croydon, pointing out to me two or three opulent families in his neighbourhood, who, after marriage, had continued several years without posterity, and were extremely solicitous about it; and whom, in two or three years' time, he had brought to have several fine children, by keeping both parents all that time to a total *milk and seed diet.* This he solemnly averred to me, and we know, that even old *Homer* had observed, that the feeders on milk were the *most honest* of Men."— *Cheyne Natural Method of Curing the Diseases of the Body,* 1742, p. 281.

irregularity or deficiency in the secretions of that organ; and as by far the greater number of disorders found among civilized men, whether local or general, originate or centre in the aberrations of the important organs of digestion, and are most readily cured by the employment of remedies which have the power of bringing them again into a healthy state, and improving the quality of the blood, the prevailing opinion of the paramount influence of the bile over the well-being of our whole frame, has appeared so well founded, as to have gained almost universal belief, and the terms *bilious* and *liver* complaints have, cons-equently, become *fashionable,* and are freely employed persons of every rank and condition. But this prevailing opinion has not so good a foundation as it seems to have. The liver is, indeed, a large organ, and it is unquestionably of much consequence that the bile it secretes should be healthy and in proper quantity. But many physicians consider that the state of the biliary system depends on the general state of the health; and that the absence of redundancy of bile is not the cause, but the consequence of disorder or disease.

Unquestionably, if sufficient exercise is not taken, and the diet and general mode of living are bad, all the natural discharges of the body will suffer, the blood will become impure, and the liver will cease to excrete bile in sufficient quantity, and of good quality. Hence arise *sick-headache, indigestion, languor, debility, diarrhoea,* and other accompaniments and indications of biliousness.

By far the greater number of bilious affections, are examples of *Indigestion* and *Impoverished Blood.* They are owing to an unhealthy condition of the digestive tube, and of the blood, and thus the author hopes his readers will constantly view them, knowing that as such they are invariably most safely and successfully treated.

For the symptoms and treatment of bilious complaints, the reader is, therefore, referred to INDIGESTION. Whether these prevailing maladies are considered bilious or stomach complaints, *it is certain* the administration of much mercury is never necessary, and always hurtful. A little calomel, or blue pill, for example, a quarter of a grain of the former, or two, gains of the latter, given every other night, is frequently of great service, but beyond this, they are seldom safe; and now that calomel is so frequently and largely administered to the great injury of those who thus take it, this is a point worthy of serious attention.[1] A nourishing diet should be observed.

Some persons, troubled with bilious affections, are in the habit of taking strong calomel pills for the removal of their disorders; others have frequent recourse to emetics or purges; both these measures are wrong in principle, and bad in practice. They are wrong in principle, because these complaints necessarily imply the existence of weakness and disorder of the stomach and bowels, in other words, of deficient and irregular action, and such means are not calculated to remove the former, nor correct the latter; and they are bad in practice, since both calomel and emetics, when frequently repeated and long continued, cannot fail to aggravate and confirm the evil they were intended to cure. They often afford present relief, I allow, but that very relief is but a prelude to another attack, from the inefficacy of the means employed, and the increase of weakness they have occasioned.

One of the most useful plans of treatment in bilious disorders, which I am acquainted with, consists in carefully regulating the bowels by diet and regimen, or by the pill No. 104, the region of the stomach and bowels being well rubbed twice a day with the flesh-brush, the patient taking the decoction of dandelion, and washing the body well over with cold water once or twice daily. Active exercise also in the open air is essentially necessary. A rigid twelve months course of such *training,* with the use of the pills No. 104, or 104 A, or of the mixture No. 84 A or 84 B, page 184, and the free use of cold water, will perfectly cure six cases out of seven of the most severe bilious disorder; and I have no doubt that an extensive experience of the extraordinary effects of this plan, will uniformly sanction the correctness of the opinion.[2] An entire

1. See my volume on INFANCY AND CHILDHOOD, in which this subject is investigated more at length.
2. For an ample account of the system of *training,* see the "BEST METHODS OF IMPROVING HEALTH", or the Art of Living comfortably, by regulating the Diet and Regimen.

disuse of sugar in tea will often afford material aid towards the cure.

Another very good plan is to take a dose of Dr. Budd's remedy, No. 74 D, page 178, every morning, a pill No. 104, page 197, every day at one o'clock, and to have recourse to free exercise, a spare diet and early hours.

DISEASE OF THE BLADDER

There are two complaints affecting the bladder, which ought not to pass unnoticed in the present volume, as they are sometimes extremely distressing and alarming : they are, an irritable painful state of the organ, and a thick whitish discharge from it.

The Irritable Bladder

Is generally a very painful malady, in which the patient is distressed by a frequent desire to void his urine, accompanied with great pain in the region of the bladder; and in the continuance of the disease, the former symptom becomes at length so urgent, that he cannot pass more than ten or fifteen minutes without feeling the inclination to recur. In this case, the bladder is the subject of chronic or slow inflammation, when the stimulus of the urine is such as to excite excessive pain, and an incontrollable desire to part with it nearly as soon as secreted. This is proved by the degree of pain felt being invariably in proportion to the quantity of urine contained in the bladder, and also by the nature of the means which are found most effectual in curing the disease, which are detailed below. Sometimes in this complaint the urine is mixed with blood; and should it go on to produce ulceration in the organ, there will be a discharge both of blood and mucus, and frequently of matter (pus).

Perhaps the most common cause of the present disease, is retaining the urine for a considerable time after feeling an inclination to part with it. This cause alone has been known, in many instances, to induce the complaint in a most severe degree, and has occasionally even proved fatal. This affection is likewise not unfrequently a consequence of gonorrhoea; and sometimes it accompanies stricture.

It may be *distinguished* from stone in the bladder, by observing, that, in the latter complaint, severe pain is felt after the water is voided, while in irritable bladder its expulsion is always followed by considerable and sometimes perfect relief.

TREATMENT. The objects to be accomplished in this case, are to keep the organ in a state of rest and ease, by constantly wearing a catheter; and to allay pain and irritation by the internal use of alkalise, combined with opium, occasional doses of calomel and opium, cupping on the loins, the warm bath and warm fomentations, etc.

When, therefore, a patient is suffering from irritable bladder, he should immediately have ten or twelve ounces of blood taken from the loins by cupping; a blister should then be placed on the lowest part of the belly over the region of the affected organ, after the part has been shaved, and a grain of opium mixed with a grain of calomel, and made into a pill, be taken directly, and repeated every night, or twice a day if the symptoms are severe. The anodyne enema, No. 9, page 147, may also be injected with considerable advantage, and warm fomentations, with the tepid bath, at 97 or 98 degrees, are proper. Through the whole course of the complaint, the bowels must be preserved free from confinement by the use of castor oil.

To keep the bladder in a state of rest, a short flexible cathe- ter should be introduced without delay, and constantly afforn by the patient until he has perfectly recovered. This instrument affords great ease, by allowing the urine to escape as fast as it is secreted by the kidneys, thus keeping the bladder continually empty. The point of the catheter should only just enter the bladder, to accomplish which it is necessary to pass it to the extent of about nine inches, when, after the remainder has been cut off, its points should be tied to a bandage carried between the thighs and round the loins. As much quietude as possible must be observed.

The foregoing means will afford immediate and sensible relief, and alleviate the acute symptoms, when the patient will act wisely to take twenty drops of the liquor potassoe, or half a tea-spoonful of the *alkaline solution,* (page 2), with four drops of laudanum, three or four times a day, in barley-water; and this medicine, if it agrees, should be continued for a month or more, till the cure is established. As the patient recovers, the quantity of opium, may be gradually lessened to one or two drops in a dose.

Now and then the irritability of the urinary passage, as yell as that of the neck of the bladder, is so great, as to render it impossible to pass the catheter, without occasioning considerable pain, and subsequent increase of the irritation for some days. This is a rare occurrence, but when it does happen, the catheter must be laid aside altogether, and the other means just noticed trusted to alone.

When the case is of an aggravated nature, and the bladder has become ulcerated, the same treatment ought to be adopted, as it is the most effectual one with which we are acquainted. Here the remedies will require a longer perseverance, and instead of the pill of calomel and opium simply, as prescribed above, I should prefer the pill No. 99, page 192, or that marked No. 98, given regularly every night, or twice a day, with the alkali and opium, as just recommended. The powder of bear's whortle-berry is a medicine of great power in ulcerated bladder. See page 17. The power of whortle-berry, combined in equal proportions with the powder of sarsaparilla, will be found very efficacious in most diseases of the bladder. Half a drachm, or a drachm of each may be given, twice or thrice a day, in dill or common water.

The *buchu* leaves, and *pareira brava*, are also of great service in irritable bladder. In some cases they will be found of greater efficacy than either of the medicines previously noticed. The mode of using them is explained at pages 23, 100. If the whortle-berry or sarsaparila powder are not sufficient alone, take them in an infusion of the buchu leaves or a decoction of the pareira brava.

In some severe cases of irritable bladder, the patient is compelled, by the painful symptoms present, to have recourse daily to large doses of opium or some other anodyne. As it is of consequence to avoid the frequent use of large quantities of opium, I would recommend, in such cases, a trial of the compound ipecacuanha powder, combined with extract of hemlock, or henbane, which will be found very valuable. The farm No. 110, page 199, is proper. One or two pills may be taken once, twice, or thrice a day, according to the exigencies of the case. In some instances, the proper use of this combination will have more than a palliative effect.

Of course, attacks of pain in the bladder are met with in medical practice which continue for a longer or a shorter time after making water, or come on without making water. I have lately seen a case in a lady in which the pain continued most severely for four hours. This kind of case, when not inflammatory, is generally the result of great derangement of the digestive functions, and will be most effectually combated by restoring the digestive organs to a state of healthy action.

Mucous Discharge from the Bladder

Now and then we meet with a patient who discharges by the urethra a large quantity of thick ropy mucus of a yellow colour, unmixed with blood, which medical men call the mucous disease of the bladder. In general, this discharge is produced from the internal surface of the kidneys, ureters and bladder.

Its *causes* are various. When there is a disposition in the parts affected to so free a secretion, whatever deranges the general health or directly impairs the energies of the urinary organs, may be productive of this complaint.

TREATMENT.—The best remedies here are the pareira brava (page 100), buchu leaves (page 23-24), balsam of capivi, the bi-chloride of mercury and alkalies. If the patient tries the capivi balsam, he should take *Jozeau's saccharated capsules* of copaiba, as advised at page 12-13. If the disorder resist the use of this medicine, and also of the pareira brava or buchu leaves, which is not often the case, half a tea-spoonful or more, of the solution of bi-chloride of mercury, and half a drachm of sweet spirit of nitre, may be taken in water thrice a day. Whatever medicine be resorted to, Thwaites's soda-water, sparingly used or lime water, will be a useful beverage; and the bowels ought to be preserved free from any accumulation by the mildest measures, as the use of small doses of castor oil or the pill No. 100 or 101D, page 195.

BLEEDING FROM THE NOSE

A considerable discharge of blood from the nose is usually preceded by chilliness, coldness of the limbs, weakness, pains of the back and head, costiveness, frequent, full and sometimes hard pulse, with boat, fulness and tension about the nose, strong beating of the arteries of the head and neck, and flushing of the face; but occasionally bleeding from the nose, like all other bleedings from constitutional causes, makes its appearance without any preceding symptom, especially when it is inconsiderable.

Whatever are the symptoms preceding this flow of blood, the chief cause generally lies in an unhealthy condition of the constitution, or in a confined state of the bowels. The former seems to obtain most frequently in adults, and the latter in children.

It is very seldom dangerous.

TREATMENT.—In the treatment of this discharge of blood, it is necessary we should first consider, whether it be owing to a plethoric or a debilitated state of the body and whether it appears to afford relief from any previous unhealthy symptoms, or is attended with manifest injury. For, in full habits, where there is considerable corporeal vigour, it is generally attended with advantage, and our principal regard should be paid to prevent its continuing too long, or being too profuse; while in weakly persons it is certainly hurtful, and for the most part requires to be checked without delay.

If then a considerable haemorrhage from the nose occurs in a young or middle aged person, in whom no weakness is apparent, but rather a sufficient circulation of blood, the best and most proper remedies will consist in local astringents and emetics. The face may be frequently immersed in the coldest water, and the temples, or even the whole head, be surrounded with a band or napkin moistened with it, and frequently changed. Cold applied to the back by means of cold cloths, or any cold metal, as a bit of tin, will frequently succeed, but it is still more certain if applied to the genitals; or cold water and vinegar may be thrown up the nostrils with a syringe. These means will seldom fail to check the flow of blood, but when they do, an emetic of twenty grains of ipecacuanha powder may be administered in water, which is often a powerful remedy. It may now and then be requisite to give the patient ten drops of the tincture of digitalis three times a day, when the foregoing means are not perfectly successful. The diet in this case should be small in quantity and consist of the simplest articles.

In any large bleeding from the nose, some let blood from the arm, and it may now and then be advisable; but it is by no means so desirable a practice as some medical men think, for if the bleeding takes place in a strong person, particularly if full of blood, it is often a salutary effort of the constitution to relieve itself, which relief ought to be, and will be, much better attained by allowing the blood to flow from the nostrils, than by substituting an artificial abstraction by means of the lancet, our care being to prevent the discharge from being excessive, by the use of astringent applications. Should the hamorrhage, on the contrary, occur in a weakly person, or in those of average health, it has its foundation in debility, when, of course, the employment of the lancet would be highly reprehensible.

When bleeding from the nose occurs in debilitated habits, the arterial action is weak, the blood frequently thin and of a diluted red, and it generally flows without heat or head-ache. Here bleeding must never be had recourse to, but take directly the powder No. 130A, page 209, and repeat it every morning. The general rule is to proceed at once with a tonic plan of treatment, giving ten or fifteen grains of powdered bark or two grains of quinine or a pill composed of five grains of carbonate of iron, and a third of a grain of powdered aloes, with a little extract of gentian, three times a day, applying the cold astringents locally, as above noticed. Twenty drops of tincture of muriat of iron, thrice a day, in a wine-glassful of water, is a valuable remedy. Should the bleeding be obstinate, the following pill may be resorted to, as one of the most efficacious medicines that can be given :

Take of superacetate of lead .... 5 grains;
Powdered opium .... 2 grains.
Mix, and make, with a little conserve of roses, into five pills.
One to be taken three times a day.

The diet should be mild but nourishing; and if the loss of blood has been great, and has occasioned considerable exhaustion, a little port wine may be given immediately or a little quinine.

In all cases, the bowels should be opened by some saline aperient, such as No. 130 A, page 209. Children of a costive habit, who are subject to frequent bleeding at the nose, will find a great advantage from having the mild opening powder, No. 130A, administered every other morning or three times a week, for six or eight weeks, continuing it afterwards occasionally, so as to prevent constipation.

BLOOD DISCHARGED FROM THE BLADDER

The chief causes of this discharge of blood are a stone in the bladder; a violent blow on the kidneys or bladder; or general weakness and indisposition.

The treatment is the same as has just been described in case of bleeding of the nose. It is, however, most frequently dependent upon debility, and the most efficacious remedies are the superacetate of lead, gallic acid, and the tincture of muriate of iron. Twenty or thirty drops of the tincture of muriate of iron may be taken in water every hour or every second hour, till the bleeding stops.

Whatever are the medicines resorted to, the compound powder of ipecacuanha may be given with great advantage at the same time, to allay pain and irritation. Three or four grains made into a pill with extract of hemlock, three times a day, is the proper dose. The use of mucilaginous drinks will likewise be very proper, as a strong solution of gum arabic in water, linseed tea or decoction of marshmallows.

Dr. Golding Bird recommends in the strongest manner galllic acid, (N.B. *not* tannic acid) as a remedy of extraordinary value in the treatment of *hoematuria* or bleeding from the bladder. It should be given in doses of five or six grains in a draught, with an ounce and a half of mucilage of gum arabic, and ten drops of tincture of henbane, which draught is to be repeated at short intervals. He says, he has seen "this drug arrest for many weeks bleeding from an enlarged (and fungoid?) kidney, after all other remedies had failed." *Bird on Urinary Deposits*, 3rd edition, p. 329.

If the blood is discharged mixed with mucus or pus, and is of a slow protracted character, the pareira brava or the buchu leaves may be tried; or twenty grains of fresh whortle-berry powder, taken three times a day, is often of much benefit, and the pill No. 99, page 192, may be taken every night, at the same time. *See* IRRITABLE BLADDER, page 383.

BLOOD DISCHARGED FROM THE BOWELS

Now and then blood is suddenly discharged from the bowels, without the presence of dysentery; in which case the superacetate of lead, as in the preceding page, or the tincture of muriate of iron, internally, with cold applications externally, form the most effectual means of checking it. The cinnamon mixture, No. 82A, is also useful–See BLEEDING FROM THE NOSE. In this disorder, and also in the two preceding affections, attention should be given to improve the state of the blood and constitution, as directed under CHRONIC DISEASE and INDIGESTION.

BOILS

A boil is a small tumour or abscess common to every part of the surface of the body, hard, circumscribed, acutely tender to the touch, and suppurating with a core in the centre. It is chiefly found in persons of a full habit and great vigour, but is sometimes met with also in debilitated patients, who are evidently suffering from ill health.

As a general rule, no application is so useful as adhesive plaster, a piece large enough completely to cover each boil being applied, and renewed about every second day. This preserves the tender part from friction, supports the vessels, and relieves pain, while it does not at all interfere with the discharge of matter, should the boil suppurate. At the same time take an alterative pill, No. 98A, page 193, every night and a quinine pill twice a day.

When it occurs in the strong and vigorous, some cooling opening medicine should be given, as No. 73 or 71, or 74A, page 176, or the saline powder, No. 130A, page 209. A common poultice may sometimes be applied with advantage till the boil suppurates and breaks, when it may be dressed twice a day with the calamine cerate, or Goulard ointment, till it heals; but no plan is generally so good as covering the boil with adhesive plaster. The aperient must be repeated every other day. If the ulcer gets into a chronic state, and wants stimulating in order to its healing, apply an ointment composed of two parts of spermaceti ointment, and one part of the ointment of nitrate of mercury. The composition of these ointments is to be seen at page 188-89.

Boils not unfrequently arise in weakly habits, or where the constitution is evidently in an unhealthy state; in such cases the alterative pill, No. 98A, page 192, given every night, or every other night, with an aperient pill occasionally, and a tonic in the day will be found of great service. The first thing to be done is to take an aperient pill, No. 97, page 191. The powder or compound decoction of sarsaparilla is likewise an excellent medicine, and may be taken at the same time; and sometimes quinine will be serviceable. A table-spoonful or two of yeast, thrice a day, has been found of great efficacy; even where boils have been epidemic. In strong constitutions, mild and systematic purging, as with No. 130A, page 209, is often of the greatest service.

Boils on the Gums

Gum-boils are sometimes limited to the substance of the gums, and sometimes connected with the decay of a tooth or socket. In the first variety, it is a disease only of a few days duration, and ceases almost as soon as it has burst or is opened; in the second, it will often continue troublesome till the carious tooth is extracted, or the carious socket has exfoliated, or the whole of its texture is absorbed.

Gum-boils, when connected with an unhealthy condition of the subjacent teeth, rarely disperse without passing into suppuration, and it is, therefore, generally better to encourage this process by the use of warm fomentations, or cataplasms, than to repel it. If much pain is present, the application of a leech or two to the parts may be of great service. An early opening of the tumour is of importance, as, from the structure of the parts concerned, the walls of the abscess are mostly tough and thick, and the confined matter seldom obtains a natural exit with sufficient freedom. A little mild opening medicine, as No. 73 or 74, page 176, every other day, will be found useful; and after the abscess has burst or been opened, washing the mouth twice or thrice a day, with an astringent lotion will tend materially to make the cure permanent. Twenty grains of sulphate of zinc, dissolved in half a pint of rose-water, will be a suitable lotion for this purpose. Quinine is often a useful medicine in this complaint.

BREAST-PANG

This is an acute constrictive pain about the breast-bone, extending towards the arms, attended with anxiety, difficulty of breathing and a sense of suffocation. It is called by medical men *angina pectoris.*

Those afflicted with this disease are seized while they are walking, (more especially if it be up hill, and soon after eating), with a painful and most disagreeable sensation in the breast, which seems as if it would extinguish life, if it were to increase or continue; but the moment they stand still all this uneasiness vanishes. The pain is sometimes situated in the upper part, sometimes in the middle, and sometimes at the bottom of the breast-bone, and often more inclined to the left than to the right side. In the beginning, it often extends only to the top of the shoulder or middle of the arm, but soon finds its way to the elbow, wrist and fingers' ends. The pulse is, at least sometimes, not disturbed by the pain.

After it has continued a year or two, or more, it will not cease so instantaneously upon standing still, and it will come on not only when the persons are walking, but when they are lying down, especially if they lie on the left side, and oblige them, to rise up out of their beds. In some inveterate cases it is brought on by the motion of a horse or a carriage, and even by swallowing, coughing, going to stool, or speaking, or any disturbance of mind. When the complaint has been of long standing, the pain will sometimes last a considerable time; indeed so long, that I have known it professionally treated, by very active measures, as the pain of inflammation.

The cause very often lies in some kind of positive disease in the structure of the heart, or its larger blood-vessels; but sometimes it is only a spasmodic affection, arising from imperfect digestion, etc. According to my experience, spasmodic breast-pang, occurring in persons below forty, is much more frequent now than formerly, and the reader will find, under *Neuralgia,* some further remarks on this point.

Men are most subject to this malady, especially such as have passed their fortieth year, and those who have short necks, and are of a corpulent habit. Frequent attacks of acute rheumatism or gout seem strongly to dispose to diseases of the heart, and to give rise to this complaint; and it is invariably much aggravated, whatever may have been its original cause, by anxiety, excessive exertion of mind or body, and food of difficult digestion. An indolent or sedentary studious life may cause it, especially if distress of mind be superadded.

Some authors have scarcely witnessed it under fifty years of age, but I have seen an unusually well marked case in a gentleman about thirty. He was a very rheumatic subject, (this was the person referred to under acute rheumatism), and died suddenly of an attack of *angina* at the age of thirty-six.

Perhaps the most common opinion among physicians is, that the disease is a species of *neuralgia* of the nerves of the lungs and heart, affecting the functions of the heart and respiratory organs, and extending, by nervous connection, to other parts; the organic lesions found in fatal cases being either causes, coincidences, or effects of the disease. To this opinion I subscribe.

The acute constrictive pain across the chest running down the left arm, supervening suddenly upon motion, and as quickly relieved by rest, taken in conjunction with the age of the patient, is sufficiently distinctive of this affection.

TREATMENT— During the paroxysm, effectual relief is generally obtained by quiet, rest, opium and cordials. When attacked, the patient should invariably and immediately sit or lie down, and take fifteen drops of laudanum, or ten of Battley's solution, in a glass of lukewarm water. Battley's solution of opium is a valuable palliative in this complaint, and preferable to laudanum. Or a little warm brandy and water, or half a tea-spoonful of ether, in water, may be taken.

Some physicians have recommended a small bleeding, especially if the patient be of a full habit; others prescribe an emetic to carry off the paroxysm. But they appear to me to be at best but very doubtful remedies, except there is a well-marked fulness of habit, and I fully concur in the opinion of Dr. Heberden, who was the first physician who published a full and perspicuous account of the disease, that in general bleeding, vomiting and purging are improper.

The most powerful remedies, in the intervals of the fits, are the metallic tonics, as oxide of bismuth, sulphate of zinc and preparations of iron; sulphate of quinine; ammoniated tincture of guaiacum; blisters or issues; and such a plan of diet and regimen as is calculated to allay irritation in the digestive organs, and to invigorate the general system. When the disease depends upon a faulty state of the organs of digestion, these means will often perfectly succeed in curing the patient; and when it is owing to organic injury of the heart, they will frequently be very useful, and rarely fail of affording relief. In most cases, I should give at the same time a Plummer's pill every second night.

The bismuth pills, No. 103A, page 197, or the sulphate of zinc pills, No. 106A, may be tried with the prospect of advantage. I have found the ammoniated tincture of guaiacum very useful, and it appears to me to be particularly indicated where the disease has followed rheumatic fever. An issue on the breast, or between the shoulders, or a perpetual blister, should be resorted to at the same time. The mezereon issue is a good one; see page 84. In all cases, a local drain of this description is likely to be of much service, and when the disease has followed the sudden suppression of any habitual discharge, it is highly necessary. The eruption effected by the use of the tartar emetic ointment, will often be of more immediate and lasting benefit than what follows either an issue or blister. Whatever other medicine is taken, should the bowels be constipated, they must be kept regular by an occasional use of the pills, No. 100, 101A, or 101B, page 193-94 ; or the powder No. 130A, page 209; and when there is any considerable irritability present, or want of sleep, twenty drops of Battley's solution of opium, or six grains of the extract of henbane, may be administered at bed-time.

The diet should be light and sparing; all spirituous and heating liquors must be given up; the exercise indulged in be of the gentlest kind; and all anxiety and violent emotions of the mind be carefully avoided. The diet and regimen advised under INDIGESTION, and at page 363-64, are the best that can be advised.

The nitrate of silver, and other metallic remedies, besides those above referred to, have been recommended for the cure of this affection; but men now are ever hunting after new remedies, and too seldom satisfied with either the new or old, and we ought to be on our guard against this desire for novelty. The means previously described will always succeed if any will, and our chief business should be to apply them in the most skilful manner, so as to meet the changes and exigencies of every case. Even arsenic has been praised for its effects in *angina pectoris*; but it appears to me to be a particularly ineligible medicine, since it has undoubtedly a strong tendency to produce disease of the heart. I may, however, mentions that prussic acid will sometimes be found very useful to allay the pain and irritability of the heart ; and the *lobelia inflata* also is useful, as a palliative, in certain cases. *See* page 374.

BRIGHT'S DISEASE AND DROPSY ARISING FROM IT

This remarkable disease appears under two forms, *viz.* the *acute* and *chronic.* In the acute form the kidneys are found to be very large and swollen, from an increased quantity of blood. Symptoms of inflammation in them exist; and Dr. Watson thinks, and with good reason, that the change in the structure of the kidneys, "in all its varieties of aspect, may be ultimately traceable to an undue accumulation and stagnation of blood in the blood-vessels of the kidney." *Practice of Physic,* vol. 2, p. 584. The urine is of a smutty appearance, as if soot had been stirred into it, and it is highly albuminous, that is, it contains a considerable quantity of the albuminous matter of the blood. In an advanced stage of this *acute* form, the disease having run on unchecked, the kidney becomes large and white, and the urine of high specific gravity; and then the red particles of the blood being greatly impoverished, the patient's skin acquires a peculiar pallid, doughy, and even waxy aspect, and he becomes dropsical. In the *chronic* form, there is a wasting of the entire kidney, and it is essentially a degeneration of that organ. The urine is of low specific gravity, but it is only slightly albuminous, if at all so, and generally the symptoms of dropsy are few and inconsiderable.

The urine is highly characteristic, but we cannot enter into this subject in a work designed principally for domestic use. For the guidance of junior medical practitioners we may, however, state that a desquamation of renal cells, to be recognized under the microscope, is usually considered a certain sign of the' acute form of Bright's disease.

The pale and watery condition of the blood in the *acute* forms of this disease, at length produces unpleasant and alarming symptoms in the head, such as stupor and coma, owing probably, at least in part, to, the functions of the brain being exercised very irregularly and languidly, and at length not at all. Vomiting and diarrhoea frequently accompany the other symptoms. Disease of the heart is a frequent accompaniment of *Bright's disease* of the kidney; and sooner or later severe bronchitis is apt to be developed.

The *causes* of this malady often lie in obscurity. Scarlet fever is, however, a certain cause in many instances, and so is intemperance. Exposure to cold and damp, and the checked perspiration consequent thereon, appears to have been a frequent cause.

TREATMENT–A remarkable deterioration in the blood exists here, and many uncomfortable feelings are complained of, and yet the only symptom that usually leads us to suspect disease of the kidney is dropsy. General dropsy is commonly a consequence of this disease, the fluid effused not being confined to the lower extremities, or the abdomen, but affecting the upper limbs also, and the face, showing itself particularly beneath the eye. The genitals are always affected by it. The dropsy is most decided where the urine is most albuminous, and the blood most abundant in water; there being then the greatest drain from the blood.

To ascertain whether the urine contains albumen, boil a little in a small glass tube. If it is albuminous, curdy fragments or flakes will appear. Then drop four drops of nitric acid into two tea-spoonfuls of this urine, and if albumen is present, the flaky appearance will remain.

In any stage of dropsy from Bright's disease of the kidney, stimulating diuretics, such as squalls, nitre, turpentine, cantharides, should not be employed; but the most efficacious remedies are Mindererus's spirit (solution of acetate of ammonia) combined with tartarized antimony and water, as No. 87A, to be given during the day, and two scruples of compound jalap powder every night, or every other night. These medicines lower the action of the heart, relieve congestion in the kidneys, and extreme circulation, and promote healthy secretions from the skin. By these means the albumen will cease almost entirely from being found in the urine, and the dropsy disappear. The compound jalap powder, as a purgative here, is far better than calomel and jalap, because the cream of tartar it contains is a good blood medicine, and the calomel a bad one. I advise calomel never to be used in this disease; but digitalis and cream of tartar are very suitable and serviceable. The cream of tartar, sulphate of potash and tartarized antimony —

without the squalls — prescribed under *Dropsy,* is applicable here. The squalls would be too stimulating in this form of general dropsy.

Copping of the loins, when the patient's pulse is strong and hard, is generally a very necessary and beneficial measure; and if it sensibly relieves, it may be repeated two or three times a week. The hot-air bath or the vapour bath, should never be neglected, as it is eminently calculated to relieve the kidneys by acting on the skin.

I am now writing of dropsy from *kidney* disease; not from *heart* disease. These are distinct classes of dropsy. In dropsy from *heart* disease or feebleness, calomel and squalls form an excellent remedy, but not in that which originates from disease of the kidneys. If general dropsy has come on after scarlet fever, or after an attack of other fever, or the urine is of low specific gravity (below 1010) and albuminous, and the dropsical parts do not pit much upon pressure, then we may be almost certain that it arises from *kidney* disease.

The dropsical limbs, etc. may he greatly relieved by *acupuncture,* that is, by perforating the skin here and there, the perforation being two or three inches from one another, with a fine needle. The pent-up liquid trickles rapidly forth, and will often soak through the patient's bed, and run on the floor. If any redness appears after the punctures, strips of linen, wetted with Goulard water, should be laid over the inflamed surface. These incisions should be made in the thighs and scrotum, never in the legs; and great care must be taken to keep the part warm by the use of warm fomentation's and flannel.

In the CHRONIC FORM OF BRIGHT'S DISEASE, that in which there is a wasting of the kidney, and little or no dropsy; probably one of the most distinguishing signs is sub-mucous effusion at times underneath the white of the eye. It looks like a tear resting on the eyelid, but is really an accumulation of fluid beneath the thinnest skin of the *conjunctiva,* or white of the eye. Bronchitis, more or less severe, is apt to come on in winter, and pain in the head is a frequent symptom, with scanty urine. If *heart* disease is also present, which is sometimes the case, there are likewise scanty stools. Owing to the deficient secretion from the kidneys, excretory matter, which ought to have been eliminated by them, accumulates in the blood, and produces cramp in the limbs, and many uncomfortable sensations in the head and elsewhere.

This form of disease often exists for years without being discovered, or even suspected. The patient suffers from flatulence, dry mouth, pain in the back, indigestion, and scanty urine,— or from cramp in the legs, head-ache and general discomfort, and all this is referred generally to dyspepsia, liver complaint, or something else. Little can be done by *treatment,* beyond urging the sufferer to have recourse steadily to all those natural means of invigoration which have so remarkable an influence in promoting the general health; such as a nutritious diet of easy digestion, plenty of pure air and exercise, either on foot or horseback, early retiring to bed and rising, avoiding everything which distresses the mind. Quiet slow travelling or change of air to a very salubrious locality, every year, is of the utmost consequence. Only the mildest medicines can be used with safety. Some physicians recommend aperients to be taken frequently, to keep the bowels regular, but I am decidedly of opinion that this is a bad practice. It irritates both the bowels and kidneys, and therefore, the patient should regulate the bowels daily by sufficient exercise, friction, fruit, and the other natural means recommended under *Costiveness.* By a religious observance of these rules, people may live to a good old age, although they are affected to a considerable degree with the chronic form of this malady. But a neglect of them is sure to shorten life, by inducing bronchitis, complaints of the head or other dangerous affections. Mercury is poison.

Dandelion is a useful medicine in this complaint, particularly if the recent expressed juice can be procured. A wine-glassful twice a day is the proper dose. The skin is likely to become dry and rough, when an occasional warm bath may be beneficial, and the mixture of acetate of ammonia, No. 87A (or No. 73D), may be taken twice a day for ten days, then discontinued for the same period, and afterwards resumed for ten days.

BRONCHITIS

This is an inflammation of the lining membrane of the air passages–the *bronchia,* and their ramifications through the lungs. Its prominent symptom is severe cough, and it is well known to be of frequent occurrence, and may be either *acute* or *chronic.*

The air tubes, or passages, are of vast extent. After repeated divisions and sub-divisions they terminate in small cells, upon the walls of which a minute hair-like network of blood-vesacle is distributed; and through the membranes which constitutes these cells, the atmosphere acts upon the blood, changing it from venous to *arterial.* This membrane is about *thirty times as extensive as the surface of the body,* and the lungs, therefore, constitute one vast excreting surface, pouring out constantly carbonic acid gas and water. In a healthy state, about a pint of water is excreted by it daily. These facts help to explain the cause of the severity of the pain, fever and difficulty of breathing in acute bronchitis, which is an active inflammation of the membrane lining the bronchial cells, the important functions of which membrane is then necessarily so seriously obstructed.

Acute Bronchitis

When a person suffers under an attack of *acute bronchitis,* the principal symptoms are lassitude and pains in the bank and limbs, irritation about the throat, great oppression in the chest, sometimes pain, aggravated by coughing or taking a deep inspiration. The cough is at first sort, frequent and without expecto-ration; and the tongue is furred, the skin hot and dry; there is thirst, headache, difficult breathings and a frequent pulse. Usually in two or three days the cough begins to be attended with the expectoration of a glairy frothy mucus, transparent and adhesive; if poured from one vessel to another it is extremely tenacious and viscid, and the degree of this indicates the degree of existing inflammation. The fever, difficulty of breathing, and oppression are now very great, and the disease may be considered at its height.

After this, if the disease gives way to the treatment employed, the expectoration is looser, and becomes of an opaque white, and is mixed with pellets or portions of a yellow or greenish colour, which is a satisfactory sign of resolution or recovery. The expectoration is now called *ripe,* and the breathing becomes more tranquil, the pulse is more natural, and the fever subsides. Should the expectoration go back at any time to a state of transparency, stickiness and froth, and the fever return, that is an index of a return to, or increase of inflammation.

The most frequent *cause* of *acute bronchitis* is exposure to cold, or cold and damp combined, particularly when in a state of perspiration. This disease is common to children, and teething predisposes to it in infants. Luxurious habits give rise to it.

TREATMENT— Of course the patient should retire to bed, and send for his medical attendant. One of the best plans of treatment is at once to lay ten leeches over the chest, or to cup the patient between the shoulders to six or eight ounces, and to give a dose of the mixture, No. 78B, every tree hours, until the difficulty of breathing and cough are sensibly relieved, when it should be taken every five or six hours. If it produces nausea or sickness at the commencement, that will rather do good than harms and in continuing the mixture the sickness will cease. To clear the bowels, the purgative powder, No. 120, ought to be taken directly—the first thing; and the steam of warm water should be frequently inhaled, by means of an inhaler. It is very soothing and promotes expectoration. The diet should be of the mildest, blandest description, such as bread, gruel, barley water and tea, all of which should be taken lukewarm—certainly not hot; the patient returning to his ordinary diet by degrees. The cough will be relieved by taking a little of the mixture, No. 76, page 178, or 78C page 177, now and then, or by a dose of the linctus, No. 67A, page 173, when the cough is troublesome.

An emetic, as No. 123, page 206, given at the commencement of an attack of bronchitis is generally of uncommon service. It at once relieves the state of congestion of the blood vessels of the mucous membrane of the bronchia, which exists to a great degree in this disease, and it is especially useful in the bronchitis of infants. The best emetic far infants consists of four grains of ipecacuanha powder in a table-spoonful of water.

When the leeches drop off, cover the chest with a warm bran poultice, in a muslin bag, and renew it as often as it grows cold; and at the end of three or four days apply a large blister over the chest on going to bed. A mustard plaster is very proper, but it is not half so efficacious as a blister.

To procure rest at night some recommend opium, but I do not. It checks expectoration, and is here a dangerous medicine, and should *never* be given when the complexion is dusky, and the lips bluish. The best anodyne at night is the pill, No. 112A, page 201. If one of these pills at night is not sufficient to relieve the cough, try one, two or three times a day, until the disease and cough are .decidedly relieved, or try the powder, No. 124A, or No. 129, page 208.

If the pulse becomes exceedingly small, while the impulse of the heart is powerful, it indicates great obstruction to the passage of the blood from the right to the left side of the heart. Then ammonia and a little wine are clearly indicated, and the utmost quietude. Dr. Watson says, (*Practice of Physic*, vol. 2, p. 33) referring to symptoms of debility and sinking, "five or six grains of the carbonate of ammonia, given in solution every four or six hours, are often followed by free expectoration and a marked improvement".

In unfavourable cases the fever and difficulty of breathing increase, the lips, cheeks and fingers assume a purplish colour, a livid paleness is spread over the face, the expression of the countenance becomes more anxious, and the pulse becomes soft, irregular and intermittent. Then ammonia is one of the best remedies, and a dose of the mixtures No. 78D, should be taken every three or four hours.

Ammonia exercises specific influence on the *bronchia,* it is at once sustaining and expectorant; therefore should symptoms of debility and sinking supervene, which they are apt to do in old people suffering from an attack of acute bronchitis, and in intemperate persons, no medicine is equal to the combination of ammonia, prescribed in No. 42 in my book ON FEMALE DISEASES, or in No. 78D, page 181 of this volume, which is similar in composition. It subdues inflammation, without exhausting the patient's strength; facilitates expectoration, without stimulating the bronchia; allays irritation without oppressing the brain; and it relieves the lungs by maintaining a free action of the skin, kidneys and the other excreting organs.

In a state of exhaustion, particularly, in old people, and those who have been much accustomed to wine, a little wine may be allowed to the extent of two glasses a day, provided it does not increase the fever and difficulty of breathing.

Chronic Bronchitis

No complaint is more frequently met with than *chronic bronchitis* or *winter cough.* Its chief symptoms are cough, particularly in the winter, wheezing, sometimes difficulty of breathing, especially on lying down, deficient appetite, and considerable expectoration. If the walls of the bronchial tubes, and air cells, are much thickened and dilated, without great expectoration, there will be considerable wheezing, and the lips and ends of the fingers will be blue, the countenance bloated. In the severest cases, if the patient dies, it will be from suffocation. This arises from obstruction to the oxygenation of the blood in the lungs. But there is another kind of severe *chronic bronchitis,* in which there exists an excessive expectoration of mucus or pus, where the patient is in danger of dying from exhaustion, I mean in extreme cases. In this instance, the lips are pallid, and the patient emaciated.

But these two forms are seldom met with uncomplicated. They are usually more or less connected. When the expectoration its abundant, it is frequently half mucus and half pus, and part of it may be coughed up in round lumps, like coins, owing to the mucus having been for sometime lying in the dilated pouches of the bronchial tubes.

Generally, the expectoration is less glutinous, and more opaque than in the recent cough, and sometimes it is nearly puriform, that is, like pus or matter. Occasionally it is of a dirty greyish or greenish hue, from an admixture of the black pulmonary matter.[1] It is usually inodorous, but sometimes more or less fetid, and now and then assumes the smell as well as the other physical qualities of the different kinds of pus; having at one time the smell of good pus from a recent wound; at another, the strong odour of the contents of a large abscess, and occasionally approaching the gangrenous fetor. The quantity of the expectoration is variable; not unfrequently it amounts to one or two pounds in the course of twenty-four hours. It is increased on every fresh attack of cold.

This disease is very common in old persons, and is indeed, the most frequent infirmity of age. It is not rare in childhood, but seldom begins in the middle period of life. The repulsion of cutaneous eruptions, and the suppression of an habitual discharge, have frequently a decided influence in developing this disorder.

In advanced life, and particularly in those whose constitutions have been debilitated by excess, or by sedentary habits, a chronic cough is found, which is called the *pituitous* cough, from the expectoration being mostly colourless, transparent, ropy, frothy on the surface, and underneath like white of egg diluted with water. This is common in gouty subjects in whom the gout has lost its regular form, and become less strongly marked. It usually comes on by slow degrees, and when this pituitous discharge is once fully established, it becomes frequently intermittent, and sometimes with considerable regularity. There are generally two fits of cough and expectoration in the twenty-four hours, the one on waking from sleep, the other in the evening; but not unfrequently the fits immediately follow the patient's meals. The quantity of fluid

1. There is a black matter deposited in great abundance in particular parts of the cellular membrane of the lungs, and it is from this substance, which is not a diseased secretion, since it is always found in adult lungs, that the small black dots sometimes observed in the pearly sputa of the dry cough are derived; as also the blackish or grey colour of certain kinds of mucous expectoration, and the greyish tint occasionally exhibited by the matter of pulmonary abscess, which resembles a mixture of pus and ashes. This black matter is not found in the lungs of young children. In adults and elderly persons it is more or less abundant; while in very old subjects it, perhaps, is found in less quantity.

expectorated is always very great; some patients discharge in the course of one or two hours from two to three pounds.[1] Difficulty of breathing always accompanies the attack, and when the disease has existed some time, the countenance assumes a pale bluish tint, and the body becomes emaciated. In this state the complaint may exist a great many years, but as age advances, the fits become longer and more frequent, the difficulty of breathing becomes habitual, and the disorder then acquires the name of *Asthma*.

The chief causes of chronic bronchitis are sudden exposure to cold air, especially if associated with dampness; living in highly heated rooms; the constant use of Arnoffs stove; intemperate habits; exposure to cold night air. Arnott's stoves are apt to produce a slight feeling of constriction and distress within the chest. In the lower orders, the manufacture of needles, cutlery, pottery and certain textile fabrics, are provoking causes of bronchitis, by mechanically irritating the air passages, and by diffusing grit, or dust of flax or cotton, which are inhaled during the process of manufacture. Bronchitis often accompanies other diseases, such as measles, continued fevers and affections of the heart and kidneys.

It is the internal or mucous membrane of the *bronchial tubes* which is chiefly, and very often exclusively, affected in cough, whatever may be its distinctive character, a redness and thickening of flat membrane being the chief visible appearances.

TREATMENT—In this complaint the tonicity of the bronchial tubes; and of the constitution generally, is deficient, the habit is relaxed, and the blood impure. Therefore, every thing debilitating is to be avoided, and every thing mildly invigorating to be used. Should the patient be resident in a large town, he ought at once to

---

1. M. Laennec says, (*Treatise on Diseases of the Chest*, page 85), I am acquainted with two old gentlemen, one of whom, upwards of seventy, has expectorated during the last ten or twelve years, in two daily paroxysms, about four pounds of a colourless, ropy, and frothy fluid, The other brings up every morning by gentle spontaneous vomiting, repeated at short intervals, during several hours, from three to six pounds of a liquid exactly like white of egg, mixed with a third part of water. This gentleman is upwards of sixty, enjoys tolerable health, and walks several hours every day. Some patients, however, die of exhaustion within a mach shorter period, and from a much smaller discharge.

remove into the country, to a moderately bracing air, such as Dorking, Reigate, Clifton or Epsom.

I strongly recommend the following plan of treatment. Take the mixture, No. 78A, during the day, and one or two of the pills, No. 104 or 107, every night at bed time. Rub the chest well night and morning with the liniment, No. 46, page 163, and observe the general principles laid down above, together with a diet easy of digestion. To old persons accustomed to wine, two or three glasses a day may be useful. The mixture, No. 78A, is particularly valuable, especially when the expectoration is abundant. One of the pills, No. 112A, page 201, taken every night for a week, or every other night for a fortnight, will relieve feverishness and cough, and assist materially in the recovery of the patient. Should the patient require a tonic, the pills, No. 106 or 106A, may be found serviceable, with which a good deal of exercise should always be conjoined. Horse exercise is particularly to be recommended.

The plaster, No. 131, page 210, or that marked No. 136, will be found useful if applied to the chest.

Make use of those means which have the power of strengthening the general habit as well as the pulmonary organs. Tonics, with the warmer and more pungent expectorants, are chiefly indicated; such are the forms No. 76A, 77, 102, 105, or 106, pages 179, and 196-198. The pills, No. 106A, are particularly useful in cases of some standing. The following are likewise very efficacious.

Take of Carbonate of iron .... 20 grains;
Myrrh, in powder .... 1 drachm;
Ginger, in powder .... 20 grains;

Mucilage of gum arabic, a sufficient quantity to make the whole into a mass, to be divided into twenty pills. Two to be taken twice a day.

Take of Myrrh, in powder .... 2 drachms;
Sesqui-carbonate of ammonia, in powder .... 1½ drachms.

Mix, and with a sufficient quantity of extract of gentian, make into forty pills;— two or three to be taken twice or thrice a day.

As people are very fond of taking laudanum, paregoric, or some other form of opium, for cough, I strongly advise them not to indulge in it when the lips are bluish and the complexion dusky. *See* the *General Principles,* page 345. Many persons are seriously injured by taking opiates for coughs, especially aged people. *Godbold's Balsam* is useful.

It must be admitted that there are many cases, in which the long continuance of the disease, and the age and debility of the patients, afford slight grounds for hope of a cure, even from an appropriate mode of treatment; but there are others, on the contrary, in which the practitioner too soon despairs of success, and consequently renounces the use of means which are really efficacious. Among these means, emetics of ipecacuanha are frequently useful, repeated according to the patient's strength and his power of supporting their action. M. Laennec says, "I have cured, in this way, coughs of long standing in old persons and still more in adults and children. In the case of an old lady of eighty-five, who had laboured under a chronic cough for eighteen months, with an expectoration amounting to two pounds daily, I prescribed fifteen emetics in one month, and with complete success, as the patient lived eight years afterwards free from complaint". After the use of emetics, mild tonics should be administered, especially No. 106A.

Tar water was at one time a famous remedy in old coughs, and is sometimes useful. The tar vapour is also an appropriate means, and seems to be more beneficial here, than in any other kind of cough[1]—that is in *chronic cough, or bronchitis*. But the compound tincture of Benjamin is still more useful. The dose is from half a tea-spoonful to a tea-spoonful, in mucilage of gum arabic, thrice a day, together with a little syrup of tolu. I am partial to the following mixture, which is sustaining :

---

1. Dr. James Forbes states, in the *Medical and Physical Journal for October,* 1822, that he had tried the tar vapour in chronic cough in one of the military hospitals, and that of thirty-two cases, it had produced a cure in eight, an improvement in six, no effect in eighteen, and a bad effect in none; and this, I think, may be considered as a fair average of its probable effects in this complaint.

Take of Compound tincture of benjamin		half an ounce;
Thin mucilage of gum arabic	6½	ounces;
Sesqui-carbonate of ammonia		half a drachm;
Syrup of tolu	1	ounce.

Mix, and take three table-spoonfuls,when the cough is troublesome.

Cough is often only *symptomatic,* originating chiefly in some affection of the stomach, bowels, liver, kidneys or other distant part; hence the terms *stomach* and *liver cough.* It assumes the general symptoms of chronic mucous cough; and it is worthy of particular notice, that it is extremely rare for a symptomatic or sympathetic cough to establish itself without there having previously existed a dry or *latent* cough, that is, a thickening or congestion in the mucous membrane of the bronchia. Under the existence of this congestion, disorder of the digestive organs, etc. is very likely to develope troublesome cough.

In this kind, the patient seldom coughs when he draws in his breath fully; which he commonly does when the cough is owing to a fault in the chest. The symptomatic cough is to be cured only by those means which invigorate and enliven, such as active exercise in the open air, especially on horseback, with frequent changes of scene, regulation of the bowels and tonic medicines. The pills, No. 101D, 102, 103, 104, 105, 106 or 106A, page 198, will be found useful. When the flowers of zinc were in the height of their popularity, some years since, they were supposed to be an unfailing remedy for nervous cough, and Dr. Percival of Manchester, has given numerous examples of their complete success. *The stomach cough* will be known by its being attended with a weak state of that viscus, and many of the usual symptoms of disorder in the digestive organs. Generally there will be a confined state of the bowels, acrid eructations, and a deficient or faulty biliary secretion; and the alterative pill, No. 98 or 98A, or No. 99, page 192, every other night, will be of great service. An occasional emetic of ipecacuanha powder is advisable. The pills of hemlock and ipecacuanha mentioned at the end of HOOPING COUGH, have been in some cases of signal service. I have been informed of one or two persons who were cured by them, having taken the prescription from a former edition of this book, and who appeared to be in an advanced stage of consumption.

Every person should pay attention to a cough, and especially those who are delicate, and have weak lungs, as a neglected cough is frequently followed by troublesome and dangerous consequences. Those who are much subject to coughs ought to avoid the night air, crowded cities, and elevated spots of ground; and they should sponge the whole body every morning with salt and water. The embrocation No. 45, page 163, rubbed on the chest, is an eligible remedy in the coughs of infants.

Suffocative cough is a variety of bronchitis occurring in very young, or in aged persons, and in those of a bad habit of body, with lax fibres and exhausted bodily powers. Very often they have been liable to chronic coughs, and it may be to considerable expectoration. Its chief symptoms are severe fits of coughing, with wheezing and suppressed breathing; fur-loaded tongue; loss of appetite; quick, small, sometimes irregular pulse; cold extremities; pain in the head. In the severest cases, the countenance is pallid and anxious; the oppression of breathing great; a full breath brings on a severe fit of coughing.

Not only are old people subject to this form of *bronchitis,* but it is the most common form in which it is met with in the children of populous cities, and among those of the poor, who are ill-fed, ill-clothed, and those living in cellars, and badly ventilated courts and apartments. It is that form of bronchitis which is so remarkably prevalent during the winter and spring, among the ill-fed, weakly and aged.

The treatment of this *suffocative* cough chiefly consists in giving frequent small doses of tartar emetic, or ipecacuanha, and other expectorants, together with ammonia and demulcents, as the mixture, No. 78D, page 181, and the compound decoction of barley, page 146. Both the chest and spine should be rubbed with a strong liniment, such as No. 46, page 163, and the mixture, No. 78A, page 180, for *chronic bronchitis,* may be given with great success. The ammonia sustains the patient at the same time that the squills promotes an easy and copious expectoration, to the sensible and immediate relief of the patient. The liniment should be well rubbed into the chest and spine three times a day. The bowels should be regulated by an occasional dose of tincture of rhubarb and a little magnesia, or a little Gregory's powder, No. 121A, or by the pill, No. 100 or 101, page 194. And two of the pills, No. 107, page 199, taken every night at bed-time, will be found a valuable adjunct, with the view of tranquillizing the patient for the night, and promoting an easy expectoration on the following morning. The diet should be very sustaining. The children of the poor should be well sustained with arrow-root, isinglass jelly, mutton broth and beef-tea.

Cox's Hive Syrup is a celebrated remedy in this complaint, equally applicable for children and old persons. A full description of it will be found in the author's book *On Infancy and Childhood.*

Bronchocele

On the fore-part of the neck a gland is found, called the *thyroid gland,* which is not perceivable in a healthy state of the body, but which sometimes enlarges to a considerable size, so as to deform the person and impede the breathing. This is called *bronchocele,* or *Derbyshire neck.* It is *endemical* in Switzerland, where it is called *goitre*.

It usually appears as a soft and rather flabby swelling, lying across the fore-part of the neck, extending more or less to each side; and when much increased in size is pendulous. Sometimes it is irregularly swelled, in some parts soft and others hard. It is free from pain and is not discoloured.

It rarely appears in males, and is most commonly found is certain unhealthy districts, especially in the low, moist, and marshy valleys of Derbyshire, Nottinghamshire, Sussex, and Hampshire, in this country; and on the continent, those of Savoy, Switzerland, and Tyrol. The causes of this disease are enveloped in some obscurity, at least as it appears in many healthy parts of this country; yet it is generally found in girls of a delicate and loose fibre, and is not unfrequently connected with some kind of irregularity or disorder in the complaints peculiar to women. The drinking of hard spring water strongly disposes to the disease, if it does not actually cause it. It appears to me to be quite sufficient for its production. Captain Franklin says, that at Edmondstone, a part touched at in his journeys to the Polar sea, bronchocele greatly prevails in those who drink the river water, and that those who use melted snow escape. He asserts, that a residence of a single year at this place is sufficient to give rise to the disease in a whole family, if they drink the common river water.

Occasionally tumours of a different description appear on the fore-part of the throat, but they are easily distinguished from bronchocele, by their more rapid rise,—redness of the surface,—pains and increased temperature.

TREATMENT—Many remedies have been recommended for the cure of this affection, but *burnt sponge, iodine,* and preparations of iron, are those only which can be depended on. I have some confidence, likewise, in mild mercurial alteratives at night, and tonic medicines, with a good air and diet, during the day. It is said that galvanism, with friction over the swelling with the iodine ointment, has completely removed a bronchocele, although neither was successful alone.

The burnt sponge may be taken in doses of ten or twenty grains, three times a day, in a little calf's-foot or currant jelly; or the patient may take the following pills, which is sometimesa more eligible form of administering burnt sponge.:

Take of Burnt sponge .... 2½ drachms;
Carbonate of soda .... half a drachm;
Extract of gentian, a sufficient quantity to make the mass.
Divide it into thirty-six pills, of which take three twice or thrice a day.

But the plan which I particularly recommend is, to take eight or twelve drops of *the solution of iodide of potassium* (made by dissolving half a drachm of *iodide of potassium* in one ounce of distilled water), three times a day in barley-water, augmenting the dose after ten days, to twenty drops, thrice a day; accom-panying it with the use of a mild alterative pill, composed of two grains of carbonate of iron, two grains of rhubarb and one grain of extract of henbane, every night. Or, instead of this pill, should there be disorder of the functions peculiar to women, one or two tea-spoonfuls of the electuary, No. 37, page 160, may be taken every night.

Another plan which I have adopted with success is, to rub a little of the ointment of *iodide of potassium* into the swelling, night and morning, or, (what appears to be still better), a little of the ointment of iodide of lead, or *iodide of cadmium*, giving twenty or thirty drops of the tincture of muriate of iron, twice a day in water.

The diet in all cases must be mild, nourishing, and easy of digestion. If there exists a good deal of debilit or delicacy in the habit of females in whom bronchocele is found, the tepid bath, at 95 degrees, may sometimes be advantageously employed thrice a week, especially if uterine obstructions are present; or during the heat of summer, cold sea-bathing may tried.

The continued use of burnt sponge, or iodine, not unfrequently produces constitutional disturbance, indicated by pains in the limbs or joints, or faintness, trembling, palpitation and other nervous symptoms; its effects must consequently be carefully watched. Considerable emaciation is a common consequence of the efficient use of iodine, but this we need not regard much, provided no other unpleasant symptoms arise; since by the use of quinine or steel or other tonics, with a generous diet and change of air, after the iodine has been discontinued, the patient's original plumpness may be restored.

Those who are able should remove their residence to a more salubrious part of the country, which has better water. I have lately been credibly informed of a case in which the female on removing from Mattock to Deptford, near London, for a time, quite lost her bronchocele, without the use of any other means, and which returned after her return to Matlock.

BRONZED SKIN

This is a disease of a very peculiar nature. The whole surface of the body is discoloured, or bronzed, but particularly the face neck and arms. The shades of colour are various, being dingy, deep amber, chesnut brown or bronze. The pulse is small and feeble, or if large it is extremely soft and compressible; the appetite is impaired or entirely lost; the sufferer is languid weak and incapable of exertion; the whites of the eyes are pearly and the body wastes. The characteristic condition is one of bloodlessness, emaciation and exhaustion.

All these symptoms arise from a peculiar disease of small bodies, called capsules, lying above the kidneys.

TREATMENT—The disease is incurable. Hitherto it has always been fatal; and the sufferer is evidently called upon earnestly to prepare for another world. Here the Holy Scriptures are the best guide.

All strong medicines will do harm. The patient should on no account take mercury in any form, nor iodine, opium or purgatives. The powder of sarsaparilla is the only medicine I think worthy of the least confidence.

But many cases of bloodlessness, emaciation and exhaustion occur in which there is no disease of the capsules of the kidney; and from which the patients perfectly recover. Such a state may follow great loss of blood, exhausting diarrhoea, green-sickness, consumption or glandular obstructions; and it is important to draw a line of distinction, which an able professional man will always be able to do. The peculiar *bronzed* condition of the skin, and the wasting of the body will usually clearly distinguish it from ordinary bloodlessness and exhaustion.

BRUISES AND SPRAINS

The best treatment for the slightest kinds of bruises and sprains, consists in giving rest to the part affected, and using one of the embrocations, Nos. 39, 40 or 45, page 163, three or four times a day.

The severer description of bruises may require the application of six or eight leeches to the part, or even make it desirable that eight or ten ounces of blood should be drawn from the arm, the patient afterwards keeping the parts perfectly at rest, and applying a poultice of linseed meal and vinegar, or crumb of bread and vinegar. This treatment may be required, because of the tendency to inflammation, or actual inflammation resulting from very severe bruises. But in general severe bruises will get well by the use of the bread and vinegar poultice alone. When all consequent inflammation has subsided, one of the above embrocations may be used with daily frictions. It will frequently be necessary at the same time, to attend to the state of the constitution, supporting it by tonic medicines, and proper diet when weak, and correcting it by alteratives and aperients, when disordered.

If a weakness be left behind in consequence of a sprain, cold water may be pumped every morning upon the part, and a calico or laced, or adhesive plaster bandage worn to support it.

BURNS AND SCALDS

Burns may be divided into *three states,* or *conditions,* which division is a natural one, and absolutely necessary to be attended to, in order to their being treated with safety and success.

The first is, where the injury consists in a simple blistering of the outer, or scarf skin, which remains unbroken.

The second is, where the outer, or scarf skin, is extensively separated from the surface of the true skin, so that the minute extremities of the nerves are exposed, which is most frequently the case from the application of fire.

The third is a still deeper injury, in which the life of the true skin is destroyed and where the process of suppuration is absolutely necessary.

TREATMENT–The danger of *the fist state* is but little, provided the vesications or blisters are not disturbed. It is a principal object to keep the blister from breaking, as a considerable discharge would come on, creating great irritation and consequently danger. Cold applications are the best in these cases. The lotion, No. 69, page 173, added to half a pint of water, will be proper, and may be applied cold by means of linen cloths dipped in it, which should be frequently renewed; or cold water, vinegar and water, or scraped potatoes, may be used. When the heat and inflammation have subsided, leave these off, and apply a liniment composed of three ounces of olive or linseed oil added to six ounces of lime water; or dress the parts with the Gonlard ointment, No. 94, page 190, spread on fine lint, or with an ointment consisting of equal parts of the lead and zinc ointment *(unguentum plumbi et unguentum zinci)*.[1] I have found one drachm of Turner's cerate, mixed with three drachms of white cerate, a very soothing application, when the saturnine ceate ceased to agree.

There is one case in which it is not advisable to employ cold water, namely, in cases of extensive scald. It appears that when the scald extends over a considerable part of the body, the system feels the injury so much, and is so much disposed to flag, that the use of cold applications materially depresses the vital powers and prevents a reaction.

Some American practitioners have asserted that the best application for superficial burns is *raw cotton*, thinly spread out, or finely carded and put directly on the injured parts. Many surgeons of our own country have reported of it very favourably. If its application causes pain, it is not suitable.

---

1. "When the hot fluid has been directly applied to any exposed surface, as the hands, the speedy employment of the antidote, cold, will often prevent vesication", (blistering) "and the case will terminate by resolution. It more commonly, however, happens, that the part affected is at the time enveloped in some article of clothing, as the legs and feet with stockings; in which case more or less vesication is likely to occur, from the clothes retaining the hot liquid in contact with the skin. It unfortunately happens too frequently, under these circumstances, that the first thing that is done is to remove the stockings or clothes, which never fails to bring away with it large portions of the *cuticle*", (external skin), "leaving the highly inflamed cubs"; (true skin) "quite denuded. If, instead of this forcible removal of the clothes, such limbs were to be immediately immersed in the coldest water, this most serious result would generally be prevented".—Eanle's *Lectures on* the *Treatment of Burns*. When it is requisite to remove the dress covering the part scalded, it should be very carefully cut away.

The danger attending on the *second state* described, is greater than in the preceding, owing to the increased sensibility of the parts, and the instant suppression of the natural functions of a large portion of the skin, and death may take place soon after such an accident, when extensive. In this case, the pulse is quick and small, the patient frequently chilly, and, if the termination is unfavourable, he ultimately falls a victim to the first impression. The best practice here is to apply lime-water end milk, in equal proportions, as a lotion; or the liniment of olive oil and lime water, which may be frequently spread over the parts with a pencil or feather.

Take of Lime-water, olive or linseed oil, of each, half a pint.
Mix them, for a lotion.

At the same time, it will be right to give the patient a little warm wine and water occasionally, especially if chilliness is complained of, and about ten, fifteen, or twenty drops of laudanum, or of Battley's solution of opium, should be given once or twice in the first fourteen hours. As to the quantity of laudanum to be given, however, we must be guided by the pain, and symptoms of irritation, or of exhaustion present. The stupor with which patients severely burnt are often attacked, receives more relief from opium than anything else. If a good deal of irritation and fever be present, the fever mixture, No. 81, page 183, should be given through the day until it is removed. A little mild aperient medicine will also be advisable; and the diet during the period of the symptomatic fever should be, for the most part, of a mild vegetable and farinaceous description. After a short time, the parts granulate, and throw up small red eminences, which is a necessary process previous to healing, when the following lotion ought to be applied by means of linen rags, and it will promote the formation of a new skin, even over an extensive surface.

Take of Sulphate of zinc .... 12 grains;
Cold water .... half a pint.
Mix them together.

In *the third state,* though there is no immediate danger, yet there is a remote one; for the skin being destroyed, separates and forms an eschar, which must naturally debilitate the living powers, by calling on them beyond their natural capacity. In this condition, we find stimulating applications of the greatest service. The injured parts are to be bathed two or three times with spirit of wine, or spirit of wine with camphor or spirit of turpentine. After this, let a liniment be applied on soft cloth, composed of the common yellow basilicon, softened with spirit of turpentine. This should remain on untouched for fifteen hours. At the second dressing, wash the parts with proof spirit of wine, or tincture of opium made warm, and then dress as before with the common yellow basilicon, softened with camphorated oil instead of turpentine. On the third day milder applications must be employed, and a dressing once in twelve hours, of the Goulard ointment, No. 94, or Turner's cerate, No. 95, will be most proper. Powdered chalk may be used to absorb any great degree of discharge from the ulcer.

It is not in general proper to give strong purgatives in burns. We must be cautious in the administration of this class of medicines, as *diarrhoea* is very apt to follow severe burns. The *diarrhoea* is usually the consequence of inflammation of the mucous or serous membranes of the abdomen. According to Baron Dupuytren, a French surgeon of celebrity of the present day, extensive and deep burns always occasion inflammation of the mucous or serous membranes of the digestive organs; a circumstance supposed to explain those curious instances of deaths which so often occur when the ulcers are on the point of healing.

When burns are produced by gunpowder, some of the grains may be forced into the skin; these should be picked out with the point of a needle, and an emollient poultice applied, which will dissolve and bring away any particles of gunpowder yet remaining.

In this third state, of deep burns which must ulcerate, stimulants internally are likewise advisable, and a dose of laudanum should be administered after the receipt of the injury, proportionate to the age of the patient and the severity of the symptoms. A little wine and water or beer, should follow occasionally, till suppuration takes place, when any stimulant will no longer be required, excepting in a very moderate quantity, to support the strength under any great discharge.

In severe burns and in warm weather, should the discharge be profuse and the fetor considerable, there may be a generation of maggots and a daily change of the dressings be called for; in which case the application of a solution of the chloride of lime is very beneficial. Two grains of the chloride of lime may be dissolved in an ounce of water, and lint moistened with this should be kept laid over the burnt parts, or the solution of chloride of lime or soda, sold in the shops, may be used according to the directions accompanying it.

In deep and extensive burns, Mr. Abernethy warns us, in his Lectures, against continuing the stimulating plan too long (it should seldom be continued beyond the third day). By so doing, the patient will be brought into great danger. He cites the cases of the men burnt at Covent Garden Theatre, all of whom that were in Bartholomew's Hospital, died in a few days of an extraordinary nervous affection, although they were previously apparently doing well. The sudden and fatal alteration he attributes to their friends having privately brought them wine and other cordials, so that they lived too freely.

Houseleek and cream mixed together, and applied to the parts burnt, form a very excellent application, so soothing and efficacious, that it may be used to the tenderest parts with the most gratifying results. Nothing is more healing, and it does not require to be removed, for it will separate of itself when the parts underneath have sufficiently recovered. One layer of houseleek and cream may be laid over another daily, if necessary. The best way is to pound the houseleek well in a mortar, and mix an equal quantity of cream with it; then the burnt parts can be covered with this mixture by means of a feather or camel's hair pencil; and in the most extensive burns in the face and limbs, this has been found sufficient to effect a cure.

Mr. Cleghorn's plan of managing these injuries may frequently be adopted with advantage. This gentleman, who was a brewer at

Edinburgh, was induced to pay great attention to the effects of various modes of treating burns, on account of the frequency of those accidents among his workmen. He preferred the application of vinegar, which was to be continued for some hours, by any of the most convenient means, until the pain abated; and when this returned, the vinegar was repeated. If the burn had been so severe as to have produced a destruction of parts, these, as soon as the pain had ceased, were covered with a poultice, the application of which was continued about six, or at most eight hours, and after its removal, the parts were entirely covered with very finely powdered chalk, so as to take away every appearance of moisture on the surface of the sore. This being done, the whole burnt surface was again covered with the poultice. The same mode was pursued every night and morning, until the cure was complete. If the use of poultices relaxed the ulcers too much, a mild ointment, (as No. 94, page 190), was applied; but the chalk was still sprinkled on the sore.

In cold weather, Mr. Cleghorn sometimes warmed the vinegar a little, placed the patients near the fire, gave them something warm internally, and kept them, in every respect, in a comfortable situation. His object in doing so, was to prevent or lessen the symptoms of trembling or chilliness.

There has been a great difference of opinion among medical men respecting the proper treatment of burns, some recommended cold applications, others hot stimulating ones, and this has arisen from want of attention to the degree and kind of injury inflicted. The above directions may be depended on. They are the result of correct observation and experience, and contain the general practice of Sir Astley Cooper and other eminent surgeons.

It should be remarked that burns occasioned by hydrogen gas, (which are so frequently occurring in the extensive pits and works of the North of England), differ in their nature from those arising from other causes, and require a somewhat different treatment; inasmuch as the former, although rather slight, require a stimulus, even from the beginning, which the others do not. It is in burns from the explosion of hydrogen gas, sometimes called choke damp, that the oil of turpentine is so very beneficial, as advised under the third variety in the preceding page.

CANCER

Cancer is a hard tumour, intersected with firm, whitish, divergent bands, found chiefly in the excretory glands or skin, which is capable of contaminating other parts, either by direct communication or through the medium of the absorbents; is attended with acute and lancinating pains, and generally terminates in a fetid and ichorous ulcer. Its most common seats are the female breast and womb, the lip, tongue and private parts.

When cancer takes place in the breast, it usually commences with a small indolent tumour that excites little attention. In process of time, this tumour is attended with an itching, which is gradually exchanged for a pricking, a shooting, and at length a lancinating pain, a sense of burning, and a livid discoloration of the skin. And however difficult it may be to determine the precise point of time in which the scirrhus first becomes converted into a cancer, where these symptoms are united, there can be no risk in calling the tumour by the latter name. Adhesive bands are now formed in the integuments, which become puckered; while the nipple is drawn inward by suction, and in some instances wholly disappears; the tumour rises higher toward the surface, and feels knotty to the finger; at the same time that the subcutaneous vessels are distended with blood, and show themselves in dark contorted ramifications. The march of this disease may be slow or rapid, for it varies considerably in its pace; but at length the integuments give way in a few points to the ulcerated process, and a small quantity of caustic ichor is thrown forth; the ulceration continues to advance, spreading wider and deeper, till a considerable extent of surface becomes exposed, and a broad excavation is scooped out, with a discharge of a most peculiar and offensive fetor. The ulcer sometimes affords a delusive hope of recovery by its granulating; but the granulations are soft and spongy, and liable to bleed from the loose texture of the new vessels, and frequently while one part is covered with them, another part is sloughing.

When cancer attacks the uterus, it is known by tensive lancinating, pains in this organ, shooting through the region of the pelvis; indurations in the part, sensible to the touch; a preceding and immoderate flow of the whites or menses, or both. As soon as the ulceration has worked to the surface of the organ, there is a sanious or bloody, or mixed discharge, characterized by the peculiar stench of the disease. By degrees, the eternal parts swell, and the swelling sometimes extends along the thigh.

On the tongue, lip, or any outer part of the skin, which is attacked by this disease, it usually commences with a small wart or pimple, which hardens by degrees, grows irritable and malignant, contaminates the neighbouring glands, and finally ulcerates.

Cancerous affections of the lip and skin are more within the control of art than those of the breast or womb; indeed, I have much reason to believe that the former are often curable when properly treated from the beginning.

A cold and variable climate; a deranged state of the general health; the change effected in the constitution of women at the time when the usual monthly discharge altogether ceases; with blows, and other mechanical violence, are the most common *exciting causes* of this complaint. But frequently there is no a parent cause, and when any of the above exist, we must almost invariably consider a disposition in the organ or part affected to take on the diseased actions of cancer, to be necessary to the actual development of this particular malady.

The *distinguishing marks* of this disease are its stony hardness to the feel; its being perfectly circumscribed, so that its whole extent and limits, unconnected with the surrounding parts, may be distinctly felt; its never or very rarely, occurring but in the excretory glands or skin; and especially its power of contaminating other parts in its vicinity, either by direct communication, or through the medium of the absorbents.

TREATMENT–In whatever part the disease may be situated, the treatment resolves itself into that proper when the cancer is unbroken, and that which is required when there is ulceration, or open sore. The former is called occult, and the latter ulcerated cancer.

In the scirrhus, or unbroken cancer, the best local remedies are those which are colling and astringent, being calculated to repress inordinate or irregular action in the blood-vessels of the part, and to promote absorption; with which alterative and tonic medicines must be given internally. The lotion No. 68, page 173, will be found useful, or one of the following. Whatever lotion is used, it must be applied by means of linen rags, four or five double, which are to be kept constantly wet, and closely applied over and around the tumour.

Take of Solution of acetate of ammonia	3	ounces;
Rectified spirit of wine	1	ounce;
Water	2	ounces.

Mix them.

Take of Carbonate of iron	2	drachms;
Distilled vinegar	2	ounces;
Water	12	ounces.

Mix them.

The ointment of iodide of potassium, made by mixing together a drachm of iodide of potassium, and an ounce and a half of recent hog's lard, frequently relieves the pain of cancer, and is sometimes of very signal service in lessening the size and hardness of such tumours. It will not unfrequently disperse very suspicious tumours in the breast and other parts. The size of a nut may be rubbed into the part twice a day, but its use should be discontinued for a week or two occasionally; because from being a very active medicine, it will not be proper to continue it for any length of time, without intermission. This ointment may now and then be advantageously alternated with the application of a warm bread and water poultice, or a poultice made with figs boiled in milk. The latter has been of great service.

The employment of a little camphorated mercurial ointment, rubbed into the tumour twice a day, is another local measure in common use among medical men, and those who wish to try it may use about the size of half a nut, at each time; but it appears to me to be of very doubtful advantage. It is by no means so powerful a discutient as the iodide of potassium.

It is a very usual practice to apply leeches to the swelling, but I have never known any permanent advantage arise from it, and question whether it be not generally hurtful. I am aware the discharge of blood sometimes affords relief, but the benefit is transitory, and when the application of the leeches has been discontinued, it has appeared after a short time to have really tended to increase the rapidity of the subsequent progress of the disease. On this account I could not advise it, and believe that the most eminent surgeons are likewise averse to it.

All cancerous diseases are aggravated by debilitating measures, and relieved by those which strengthen, and which have the power of exciting a new and salutary action in the diseased parts. Therefore, in every case of cancer, every thing which weakens must be studiously avoided, and tonic and alterative medicines internally be conjoined with external applications. The alterative pill, No. 98, page 191, taken every other night, will occasionally be found very useful, and may be accompanied with the strengthening pills, No. 102, through the day, or the following:

Take of Sub-oxy-phosphate of iron . . . . 2 drachms;
Ipecacuanha, in powder . . . . 8 grains;
Aloes, in powder . . . . 3 grains;
Mucilage of gum arabic, a sufficient quantity to form the whole into a mass.
Divide it into thirty pills, and take first one, then two twice a day.

Sir Astley Cooper recommends the following tonic draught to be taken twice or thrice in the day. I advise the soda to be omitted, as it is evidently prescribed here from a mistake respecting its properties and effects.

Take of Compound infusion of gentian . . . . . . 1½ ounce;
Tincture of columba . . . . 1 drachm;

Carbonate of ammonia..................	5	grains;
Carbonate of soda	10	grains.

Mix.

The extract of hemlock, *prepared in vacuo*, is sometimes very serviceable. It has appeared to me to have more power over the cancerous diseases of persons advanced in years than of those who are not aged. Four or five grains of this extract may be made into a pill with a little powder of hemlocks and taken three or four times a day. After a short time the dose may be increased to two, or even three pills thrice daily.

The juice of clivers, taken internally, is said to have been useful in several instances, in removing suspicious enlargements in various parts, and improving the condition of the general health. The compound decoction of sarsaparilla, (or the powder or extract of that substance), is also often a good medicine both in ulcerated and unbroken cancer, and it may be taken together with or without any of the pills above described.

There is reason to consider arsenic a medicine of some value in many cases of cancer, whether in a state of tumour, or open sore. It improves the discharge from open cancer, retards .the progress when unbroken, and in some instances has dispersed the disease completely. The patient may begin with three drops of the arsenical solution, twice or thrice a day, in barley-water, and gradually increase it to six or eight drops; but it is so active a remedy that it will require great caution in its exhibition.—*See Arsenic,* page 7.

The best treatment in ulcerated cancer, consists in administering those medicines which have the power of invigorating and amending the state of the general habit, and in applying to the ulcer articles which are capable of stimulating the sound parts to throw off those that are diseased, and of so altering the diseased condition of action in the vessels of the sounder parts that they may heal. The internal remedies are, therefore, the same as above described for unbroken cancer. The most powerful local applications are arsenic, arseniate of iron, carbonate, phosphate or oxy-phosphate of iron, tar ointment, iodide of potassium, and poultices of mallow leaves, figs or bread and water.

Take of Crow's foot, dog's fennel,		
fresh gathered, of each	1	ounce;
White arsenic	1	drachm;
Flowers of sulphur	5	scruples.

Bruise the crow's foot and dog's fennel together, then add the other ingredients, and beat the whole into a paste; then form this into balls, and dry it in the sun.

When used, they are to be powdered, a sufficient quantity mixed with the yolk of an egg, and applied on a piece of bladder, to the ulcer. In this state the caustic is to remain, till the part which it destroys separates spontaneously; when another plaster may be applied in the same way, till it separates its portion, and so on till the whole of the diseased surface is brought away, when a common healing salve, as No. 94 or 95, page 190, may be used. This is the once famous Plunkett's powder. I am inclined, to think it is not without efficacy in some cases, but its great activity requires it to be used with much caution, and only under surgical advice. It is not so safe as the chloride of zinc.

The arseniate of iron, however, is a milder and more manageable remedy, and perhaps equally efficacious, or more so. A scruple may be mixed with the white of an egg, and applied to the ulcer by means of a camel's hair pencil, and renewed when the slough separates. The chloride of zinc is often still more efficacious than the arseniate of iron. See the author's book *on the Diseases of Females.*

Or the ulceration may be dressed twice a day with carbonate or oxy-phosphate of iron, mixed with a little water, or white of egg. In many cases these are of great advantage.

Tar ointment combined with sulphur has been very useful, and ample directions for its use will be found in the author's book ON FEMALE DISEASES.

Whatever powder is made use of, occasional poultices, to bring away the discharge and separated portions of the ulcer, are proper and beneficial.

The iodide of potassium or cadmium has great effect in mitigating pain, and improving the discharge of cancerous ulcers. A drachm may be mixed with an ounce of simple syrup, and a little of this solution laid over the whole ulcer, twice a day.

Patients afflicted with the present disease are often obliged to have recourse to opium in some form. The best preparations of opium, in such cases, are Battley's *solution of opium* and the *muriate* or *acetate of morphia*, or the *Black Drop.* They are exceedingly valuable in relieving pain, and in regard to the dose proper in such cases see the remarks at page 97.

The diet, in all cases of cancer, should be mild and nourishing. A little animal food should be taken once a day, with eggs, and other light nutritious food. A little mild malt liquor, or white wine, will also be proper in most cases. Some professional men have advised a low diet in this disease; but, in my opinion, it is extremely injurious. Sir Astley Cooper protests strongly against it.

Change of air and scene, with daily exercise, proportioned to the strength, is always advisable.

An operation for the removal of ulcerated cancer in the breast is now never performed by men of judgment; and very rarely recommended by them in scirrhus, or unbroken cancer, except in the earliest stage, and before the occurrence of lancinating pain. After the commencement of pain, the use of the knife serves only to aggravate the patient's suffering, and accelerate her death. Persons at a distance from London will do well to note this, as it is no uncommon thing for a quite different advice to be given in the country, to the great injury and distress of the sufferer. Indeed, I am much disposed to question whether an operation ever succeeds in real cancer of the breast, except in the *very earliest* stage, in elderly people. Even then success is seldom witnessed. This opinion is given as the result of close attention for several years to the progress of cases in which an operation has been performed.

The subject of cancer in the womb is considered at length in the author's Treatise on the Diseases of Females. He has there also treated of the different tumours of the breast and womb, which simulate cancer.

In cancerous affections of the tongue powdered sulphate of copper is of admirable service, as described in my *Treatise on the Diseases of Females.*

CARBUNCLE

A carbuncle is a broad, flat, firm, burning tumour, in which the cellular structure takes on a sloughy or gangrenous state. It is so denominated from the redness and fiery heat of the inflammation. The first appearance it assumes is similar to a boil, and of a bluish colour, rising a little above the skin, having within it commonly a bloody serum.

It occurs mostly in elderly people, and in weakly depraved habits; and we frequently meet with it in those who have debilitated their frames by an excess of good living. It is a very common symptom in the plague.

It can be distinguished from other swellings by pressure, which causes a discharge in several parts of its surface.

TREATMENT—As this disorder usually appears only in bad and irritable constitutions, a treatment which soothes and supports the system is required, and as it easily assumes a gangrenous or mortified aspect, almost the same treatment will be necessary as in gangrene. Warm, aromatic fomentations, as No. 52, page 167, and emollient poultices of linseed meal and oil, are to be made use of. Stimulating lotions are likewise proper; and' one of the following may be employed with advantage.

Take of Spirit of turpentine, olive oil, of each . 3 ounces.
Mix for a lotion.

Take of Tincture of muriate of iron . . . . 2 ounces;
Water . . . . 14 ounces.
Mix.

One of these is to be applied by laying over the tumour soft rags moistened with the lotion, and renew in them frequently.

A free incision should be made early through the whole length of the tumour, and as much of the contents be squeezed out as can possibly be done without giving great pain.

The constitutional treatment consists in the exhibition of bark, aromatic confection, opium, etc., as recommended for mortification; a fresh or salt warm bath at 94° twice a week; allowing a generous and nourishing diet, proportionate to the severity of the symptoms. The food should, however, be such as is very easy of digestion. Porter and wine, are very proper. See *Mortification.*

Take of Peruvian bark, 15 grains, or of sulphate of quinine	2 grains or more;
Tincture of bark	2 drachma;
Tincture of opium	5 drops, or more;
Aromatic confection	10 grains;
Decoction of bark	1½ ounce.

Mix for a draught, to be taken three or four times a day.

A pill composed of from half a grain to a grain of opium, with three grains of James's powder, and half a grain of calomel, is a very useful night pill; and mild purgatives, such as No. 130A, page 209 are of essential service, and should never be neglected.

CATALEPSY OR TRANCE

Catalepsy is a total suspension of sensibility and voluntary motion, and for the most part, of mental power, the pulsation and breathing continuing, the muscles being flexible, and the body yielding to, and retaining any given position.

The complaint is rare, and many of its symptoms so singular, that some physicians, who have never witnessed an example of it, are disposed to regard it in every case as an imposture; but there is now no doubt of its being a real disease.

A highly nervous or irritable temperament is the chief predisposing cause; and the disease is capable of being excite by terror, or other violent emotions of the mind, and by various corporeal irritations, particularly those of the stomach, suppressed menstruation, repelled chronic eruptions and plethora.

Treatment—If it arises from fulness in the brain, a modes rate bleeding, with purging, will probably be the most effectual means of relief; but it is commonly a disease of nervous debility, when there is a necessary disturbance of the balance of the nervous system, and stimulants will. usually be found far more appropriate and serviceable, such as No. 82 or 84, page 184, or No. 102 or 103, page 196. Blisters to the head and breast, or between the shoulders, mustard poultices, and other rubefacients, *see* No. 46, page 163, to the extremities, together with injections into the rectum, may be useful. The body in the meanwhile should be kept warm, with a free influx of pure air; general friction may be often had recourse to, and a little brandy, ether, or ammonia may be introduced into the stomach, if possible. Fifteen drops of strong water of ammonia, in a wine-glassful of water is excellent.

After the paroxysm is over, the patient should enter upon, and steadily pursue, a plan for invigorating the whole constitution, and one of the tonics just recommended, or the stomach pills, No. 104 or 104A, or quinine, with change of air and scene, will be found some of the most powerful means of effecting this object. An entire change of air and scene is usually of the first importance.

CATARACT

The cataract is an opaque state of the *crystalline lens,* by which the rays of light are obstructed in their passage to the retina, or expansion of the optic nerve, on the bottom of the eye. There are three kinds of cataract, the lenticular, in which the opacity exists in the lens itself, and is confined to it; the capsular, where the opacity is confined to the capsule, or membrane of the lens; and the complicated, in which it is common to the lens and its capsule.

At the commencement, there is an indistinctness of vision, as if a cloud hung over the eyes, or the objects were enveloped in a mist; there is a sensation of a mote floating before the eye; it being, for the most part, a single mote and stationery; and the patient sees better in a weak than in a strong light. In the progress of the disease, an opacity becomes sensible, and gradually increases, until nearly a total loss of vision is produced; the crystalline lens by degrees changes from a state of transparency to a perfect white or grey colour; in some rare instances, it has been black, and also red; and in appearance resembles a pearl, or other extraneous body of alike colour, situated immediately behind the pupil

It frequently originates from causes we cannot trace; but it has often followed upon convulsions, chronic head-ache, syphilis, rheumatism, suppressed perspiration, and protracted inflammation of the eye. It is. most commonly met with after forty. If it suddenly forms from a severe injury, the lens frequently recovers its transparency without any operation being necessary.

TREATMENT–The power of medicine is generally very limited in this complaint, and the patient is, therefore, in the majority of instances, obliged to submit to a surgical operation for the recovery of sight. Yet recoveries have been witnessed after the employment of suitable remedial measures, and it is a question whether they would not often occur, if mole hope of success were commonly cherished by professional men. However this may be, a fair trial should in all cases be given to medical treatment, before resorting to an operation.

Perhaps the most powerful remedy here is the oxymuriate of mercury.

Take of Bi-chloride of mercury	2 grains;
Distilled water	3 ounces;
Rectified spirit of wine	3 drachms.
Mix.	

The dose of this mixture is thirty drops, twice or thrice a day in water, gradually increased to a tea-spoonful. It is best taken on a full stomach, and when there is considerable general weakness, it may be advantageously combined with a drachm or two, of compound tincture of bark at each dose.

The alterative pill, No. 98, page 191, has likewise been of service. And whether this, or the oxymuriate be tried, the compound extract or decoction of sarsaparilla will occasionally be found a valuable adjunct, especially when there is a deranged state of the general health, or signs of scrophula in the constitution.

The above remedies will be particularly indicated, if long-continued indolent inflammation has existed in the eyes.

Henbane has been highly extolled. From five to ten grains, or more, of the extract (*prepared in vacuo*) may be taken, two or three times a day, either alone, made into a pill, or with a small quantity of calomel, say, two grains, to a drachm of the extract of henbane.

Electricity, in the form of aura, or weak sparks, has been recommended. Mr. Ware, the well known oculists used to advise a drop or two of ether, to be rubbed into the eye, once or twice a day, occasionally rubbing the aye, over the lid, with the point of the finger dipped in mercurial liniment.

There is on record a remarkable instance of cataract, which was dispersed by general and persevering friction over the eye, the lid being closed. It occurred in the person of Admiral Henry, of Rolvelden, in Kent, who was himself the operator, and has published his own case in a shilling pamphlet.

When it is necessary to have recourse to the needle to remove the cataract from the axis of vision, it may be done by three different operations, each of which has its advocates. The first is by *extraction,* or the removal of the lens, by a semi-circular incision made through the transparent cornea: the second is that of *couching* or *depression of the lens*, in to the vitreous humour : the third is bby *puneturing the capsule* of the lens, so as to allow of the discharge of this crystalline body into the interior chamber of the eye. Mr. Ware, and Baron Wenzel, were attached to the first; Mr. Hey, of leds, and the distinguished Scarpa, practised the second; and Mr. Saunders, of the Eye Infirmary, adopted the last. Mr. Green considers Mr. Saunders's operation "greatly preferable to any other, in those cases which admit of it".—*Lancet,* vol. 1, p. 618. 1823-24. Mr. Tyrrell appears to prefer the operation of depression.—

Lancet, vol. 2, p. 472. 1823-24. Each operation is supported and practised by men of great eminence, and it is extremely difficult to say which is the best. The operation of extraction is much more difficult and complicated than that of couching, and is more liable to be thwarted of sucess by subsequent inflammation;[1] but if it succeed, the recovery of sight is usually more perfect. The operation of puncturing the capsule is as simple as that of couching, and does not expose the patient to a repetition as the latter does. We may also remark, that if couching should not succeed in the first instance, it may be often repeated; whereas in the mode by extraction, if a cure be not accomplished in the first instance, the eye will be inevitably lost. It is reasonable, however, to suppose, that neither extraction, depression, or puncturing the capsule, is alike adapted to every case of cataract; but that the mode of operating ought always to be suited to the exiqeucies of the particular case. This is a point which has been too much overlooked by oculist. Beer, a very able and scientific German surgeon, whose treatise on diseases of the eyes has attracted great attention in this country, ridicules the idea of adhering exclusively to any one plan of operating; and whenever the question is put to him, what is his own plan? he answers that his custom is to operate in the manner which appears to him to be the best adapted to each particular case about which he is consulted.

We have been adverting above to the necessity for operating when both eyes are affected with this disease, but sometimes only one eye is affected, and the other is sound: in regard to the question, whether an operation ought to be done in this latter case, a difference of opinion prevails, though the majority of surgeons seem to answer in the affirmative, and I am disposed to think this is right. When there is a full-formed cataract in one eye, and vision is retained in the other, Mr. Travers thinks the postponement of the operation worng. "I am satisfied", says he, "that the cataractous eye, if it becomes the subject of an accidental inflammation, is strongly disposed to go into amaurosis, and further, that the retina[2] loses

1. Wenzel used to say that a man must poke out a hatful of eyes before he can hope to perform extraction with success.
2. The expansion of the optic nerve on the bottom of the eye.

its vigour by the permanent exclusion of light. I speak from repeated observation of the fact". On the contrary, Mr. Lawrence is averse from operating under these circumstances.

The late Mr. Saunders was very successful in operating upon the eyes of infants and very young children, afflicted with cataract. His greatest success attended the operation between the ages of eighteen months and four years.

CHICKEN-POX

In the chicken-pox, after slight symptoms of fever, as lassitude, loss of sleep, wandering pains, loss of appetite, etc., an eruption appears; first on the back, consisting of small reddish pimples, much resembling the first appearance of small-pox. On the *second* day, the red pimples become small vesicles, containing a colourless fluid, and sometimes a yellowish transparent liquor. On the *third,* the vesicles arrive at their full maturity, and, in some instances, very much resemble the genuine small-pox. Soon after, the fluid escapes from the tender vesicle, and a thin scab is formed at the top of the pock, without pus ever being formed, as in the true small-pox. Generally before the *fifth* day the whole eruption disappears, and no cicatrix or mark is left behind.

It is entirely free from danger, unless the eruption be of the confluent kind, that is, the pimples being numerous and running into each other, when the danger is to be appreciated from the degree of violence of the concomitant fever.

Chicken-pox is more common now than before vaccination was introduced, when small-pox was more prevalent.

It is sufficiently *distinguished* from the small-pox by its fluid, except in a few anomalous cases, being limpid throughout; and by its concreting into crust as early as the third or fourth day from tire eruption: while in small-pox the fluid consists of pus (thick matter) as soon as formed, and does not concrete into crusts till the seventh day, and often much later.

The chicken-pox vesicle is full of watery serum on the top, on the *first* day of the eruption—a distinctive mark from small-pox.

Dr. Willan has well described another characteristic circumstance—That small-pox pustules are, on the first and second day, small, *hard,* globular, red and painful; imparting the sensation when the finger is pressed over them, similar to that which one might conceive would be excited by the pressure of small round seeds under the skin; while in chicken-pox, almost every *vesicle* has, on the first day, a hard inflamed *margin;* but the sensation communicated to the finger is like that from a round seed flattened by pressure.

TREATMENT—In the ordinary course of this complaint, the symptoms are so slight as not to require the aid of medicine. Gentle purges are all that are in general necessary. If the shivering, sickness, head-ache and pains in the limbs, are severe, an active purge, as No. 27, page 155, should be administered, succeeded by some diluting drink; and the patient should be confined to a quiet, spacious, and well ventilated room, with a cool dress, till the febrile symptoms have left him.

CHILBLAINS

The Chilblain is a painful inflammatory swelling, of either a florid, deep purple, or leaden colour, appearing on the fingers, toes, heels, and other extreme parts of the body. The pain is sometimes intermitting and pungent, but the patient is more frequently annoyed by an obstinate itching, and sense of tingling. The part often swells, and ulceration not unfrequntly follows; in which case a simple separation of the skin is first observed, and below this there appears a foul, irregular, painful ulcer.

It is most frequently found in children, and older persons of relaxed fibres; and the common exciting cause is exposure to severe degrees of cold.

TREATMENT—A stimulant mode of treatment is the only one that will answer. When a person is much troubled with chilblains, I advise them to take a tonic, as steel or bark internally.

In the inflamed unbroken state, the topical application of a stimulating liniment, or lotion, is generally sufficient for a cure, if it be used early, and with perseverance, the part being defended, at the same time from the severity of the external air. The liniments, No. 41, 45 and 46, pages 162-63, are the most efficacious. The lotion, No. 68, page 173, is also useful. Sir Astley Cooper is said to have been partial to the following liniment, which I think an admirable application.

Take of Camphorated spirit of wine	1 ounce;
Goulard's extract (pure)..................	half an ounce.

Mix, and apply to the part.

In the ulcerated state, warm and irritating dressings will alone succeed in effecting a cure. Let the ulcer be dressed night and morning with one of the ointments, No. 94, 95 or 96, at page 190. If fungus flesh should appear, apply the citrine, or white precipitate ointment, as No. 89, page 188, till it has been removed, then dress with one of the former ointments till well. The following application is much esteemed in the ulcerated state.

Take of Honey	4 ounces;
Turpentine	4 ounces.

Mix these together, and then stir in a sufficient quantity of the finest wheat flour to give it the consistency of a cerate. Dress the part with it twice daily, in the usual way.

But there are very few applications–few indeed—which are more effectual than *strong brine.* It should be rubbed in two or three times a day; and is applicable both to broken and unbroken chilblains.

Many persons subject to chilblains might prevent their occurrence, or very much lessen their severity, if, upon the approach of winter, they were to defend the parts from external cold, by wearing leather socks, or a warm diachylon or Burgundy pitch plaster, spread upon leather. Dally friction with the flesh brush should also be resorted to, and the liniment, No. 45, be occasionally rubbed in, which will harden the skin, and effectually promote the circulation of the parts.

No person troubled with chilblains ought ever to allow the employment of any means which tend to weaken either the part affected or the general system. Sometimes the chilblain will swell to a considerable size, and appear very red and inflamed, but this inflammation is dependent on weakness, and will never fail to be much increased by poultices, confinement, and every other measure that has not the effect of diving tone and strength to the local and general circulation. Under these circumstances I should order the patient a little quinine thrice daily.

CHOLERA MORBUS

By cholera is meant a vomiting and purging, which is often of an alarming character, especially in hot climates. This disease has been generally considered to be an inordinate secretion of bile of a vitiated quality; but it is now certain that those are the most alarming cases, in which the secretion of bile is wholly suppressed. It appears to me, that an intense irritation of the internal membrane of the stomach and small intestines, and a poisoned state of the blood, has much more to do in producing this complaint, than any diseased affection of the liver, gall ducts or any other organ.

The most frequent symptoms are nausea, pain and distention of the stomach and intestines; quickly succeeded by violent and frequent vomiting, and painful purging of thin and watery, or bilious, or other ill-conditioned fluids; agony of the intestines and abdomen; distressing thirst and heat, followed by cold sweats; a quick, small, and sometimes unequal pulse; great anxiety and extreme restlessness; excruciating spasms of the legs, arms, chest and abdomen; faintings, sometimes universal convulsions.

The attack of this complaint is generally sudden. In this country, the bowels are seized with griping pains, and the stools, which are at first thin and watery, as in common looseness, are passed frequently; then the stomach is attacked with sickness, discharges its contents, and rejects what is swallowed. In the course of a few hours, the matter vomited, as well as that discharged by stool, appears to be of a very bilious nature, and passes off both ways in considerable quantities; or it may be a thin, gruel-like fluid, devoid of smell. The griping pains in the intestines and stomach now become more severe, and are accompanied with spasmodic contractions both in the bowels and limbs.

In India, also, the disease commences nearly in the same manner, but there it often attacks with extreme violence, and proceeds with frightful rapidity. In Ceylon, where it often appears in its most concentrated states it is frequently called *Mort de Chien*,—the death of a dog,—which is nothing more than cholera appearing in its worst form.

The *essential* manifestations of *malignant* cholera, are sudden prostration of strength, collapsed countenance, blue lips and nails, shrunken fingers, the total failure of the animal heat, and the usual secretions, suspension of the pulse, stagnation of the venous circulation, and violent cramps in the legs and bowels. We see from this statement that vomiting and purging may be absent.

The most dangerous signs in the ordinary progress of the disease, are an icy coldness of the surface of the body, extending over the region of the heart and stomach; the skin under the nails becoming incurvated; the tongue icy cold; an universal colliquative sweat breaking forth, with a shrivelling of the palms of the hands and soles of the feet; an absence of vomiting and purging. The violence of the attack may destroy life in three, six, twelve or twenty-four hours or less, but this is not a frequent occurrence in Great Britain.[1]

1. In regard to the epidemic cholera lately raging on the Continent of Europe, it should be observed, that vomiting and purging were often amongst the least important symptoms, though the appearance of the fluid evacuated was highly characteristic. Rice-water strained, and allowed to settle down, is, when shaken up, the best type. The evacuations, both upwards and downwards, either soon ceased, or were easily repressed, while in many cases, and these the very worst, there were either none, or they were very trifling. It was the sudden paralysis and rapidly diminishing action of the heart, of the arteries, and of the organs of respiration, with thickening of the blood, the loss of the power to generate heat, that constituted the real danger of the first–the most fatal stage of the disease.

Dr. Barry says, "It is in the above state, particularly if there be violent spasm, that the *magisterium bismuthi (subnitrate of bismuth)* has been found so serviceable; assisted by cordials, and synapisms covering the whole belly and frictions.

This disease is most frequently *caused,* in our own country, by suppressed perspiration, particularly by cold or damp applied to the feet; cold indigestible fruit, as unripe apples, cucumbers, melons, etc., violent purgatives; sudden fright; and it prevails most at the close of summer, and the beginning of autumn.

But it is to India that we are to look for cholera in its most exquisite forms, where it is frequently epidemic, and from its malignant character, often frightfully destructive of human life. The remote cause of the epidemic cholera of India and Russia seems to be a peculiar poisonous state of the atmosphere, and a specific contagion. Very many medical men do not at all admit its contagious nature, but the facts in proof of this are so many and so strong that many have changed their opinion, (and the present author is one of these), and consider it as decidedly contagious under favourable circumstances.

In respect to the causes which predispose to, or excite the disease in India, the most able practitioners agree that they are rapid atmospherical vicissitudes, in regard either to temperature or moisture; exposure of the body to currents of cold air, particularly the chill of the evening, after being heated by violent exercise of any kind, inducing debility or exhaustion; low marshy situations; flatulent or indigestible food, especially crude and watery vegetables, which compose a large proportion of the diet of the natives; and particularly that gradual undermining of the constitution, which arises in a condensed, dirty and ill-fed mass of population.

It has been usual with medical writers to consider severe affection of the liver, or of the bile ducts, or of the bowels, to be the immediate cause of cholera, (in other words, in what the disease essentially consists), but the present author is convinced that it is not so mach a liver or bowel complaint, as a disease of the Blood, caused by the inhalation of an atmospheric poison acting directly thereon.

When the vomiting and purging are absent, it is distinguished from colic by symptoms of intense anxiety, collapsed countenance, and severe cramps in the legs and muscles of the belly. The body becomes colder than an ordinary corpse, and often as pulseless, and the countenance more cadaverous and ghastly than in ordinary death; the eyes are sunk deep in their sockets, and the voice becomes a tremulous croak or whisper.

TREATMENT–In the slighter cases of cholera, the proper treatment consists in freely administering mild diluting drinks, as weak chicken broth, barley-water, toast-water, made with thoroughly toasted bread, and the like. Dr. Douglas strongly recommends toast-water made with toasted oat-bread boiled in the water, which he declares that he never knew rejected. These may likewise be exhibited by the rectum. After the stomach and bowels are thus cleared, the saline mixture in the act of effervescence should be given, (*see* No. 81, page 183); and repeated doses of laudanum must follow, to subdue the spasmodic action. Forty drops of laudanum may be given every hour, in the saline effervescing draught, or in spearmint water; or a grain and a half of opium be exhibited in a pill. Solid opium generally suits best in all cases of cholera.

A grain of calomel, combined with a grain of opium, is a powerful remedy, and may be given every two hours, or oftener, till the symptoms subside. Give also a dose of the astringent mixture, No. 80B, page 182, after every liquid motion. When the patient can retain nothing swallowed, opium should be rubbed into the pit of the stomach. *See* No. 39, page 161. If the extremities become cold and the pulse feeble, brandy and water, with ten drops of liquid ammonia in each draught, should also be given.

Dr. W. Ainslie has very highly extolled the efficacy of magnesia in cholera. Two drachms and a half, or three drachms, of sub-carbonate of magnesia, may be given in water, and repeated two or three times, if necessary. I think this may prove a very valuable remedy in the milder cases of cholera occurring in Great Britain, but we ought not to trust to it in malignant cholera.

In the cholera of India, however, and even in the severer description of cases in our own country, a more decisive and active plan of treatment is always necessary. *At once endeavour to check the diarrhoea,* by giving astringents and opium, as in No. 80B, page 182, and enjoining confinement to bed. One of the principal indications is to restore the vital functions, and to stimulate the heart into renewed action. For this purpose give the patient large draughts of *cold water,* and let half a drachm of bi-carbonate of potash be dissolved in one of the draughts of water, and repeated every three hours, or as often as either vomiting or purging occurs. This is calculated to produce a complete re-action in the system, and to restore animal heat. In Indian cholera the plan pursued with most success is that just advised, immediately afterwards administering calomel with opium, in very free doses of from eight to ten grains of the former, in a dose, with one or two grains of opium, or fifty or sixty drops of laudanum, and a scruple of columba powder, which is to be repeated, if necessary, every one, two or three hours, till the urgency of the symptoms subsides. To these should be added a liberal use of the most diffusible stimuli, as the sweet spirit of nitre, sesqui-carbonate of ammonia, (No. 79, page 181), tincture of cloves, camphor, hot arrack and water, mixed with camphor mixture, or warm punch. In many cases I believe cold arrack or cold brandy and water, will be more grateful to the patient,and more useful. The hot air or vapour bath is also necessary, and stimulating embrocations to the abdomen and limbs, or friction with hot flannels. *See* No. 41 or 46, pages 161, 163. In short, every means must be tried to determine to the surface of the body, and restore a natural warm perspiration.

When all medicines by the mouth have been ineffectual in allaying the irritability of the stomach and bowels, a hundred or a hundred and twenty drops of laudanum, should be given in an injection, mixed with warm starch or gruel. This has sometimes been successful.

The application of *dry* heat is, on the whole, much to be preferred to any other method of communicating heat to the body in cholera. For this purpose, dry salt or sand may be placed in a pan over the fire, and heated as hot as the skin will bear it, then put into pillow cases, or shirts tied at the ends; the cases should not be full, in order that they might be very pliant, and readily applied to every part of the surface.

A writer on the epidemic cholera of India reports the effects of a fortunate blunder, in one instance, in the following terms: By mistake, twenty grains of calomel and sixty minims" (equal to one hundred and twenty drops) "of laudanum were given at an interval of less than half an hour. The patient was inclined to sleep; nothing more was done; and in two hours and a half he was as well as ever he was in his life".

The following directions for the cure of cholera, I regard as excellent. They were much approved by the Madras Medical Board, and are easily to be understood and practised. Give the patient the following draught

Take of Tincture of opium, sulphuric ether, of each 1 drachm;
Brandy or arrack . . . . half an ounce;
Water . . . . 1 ounce.
Mix.

If this be vomited, let it be repeated, every time, in ten minutes after the vomiting.[1] In half an hour after the vomiting has ceased, give a bolus of this prescription :

Take of Calomel . . . . 12 grains;
Camphor . . . . 3 grains;
Opium . . . . 1 grain;
Oil of peppermint . . . . 3 drops.
Make into a bolus.

If this bolus be vomited, it must be repeated in a similar manner each time, half an hour after the vomiting has ceased.

If the vomiting be violent, give an injection of one drachm and a half of laudanum in four ounces of barley-water : and let it be repeated as often as it is rejected. Half the quantity of this injection should also be administered after every liquid stool.

1. In case of vomiting, I think the addition of a scruple or half a drachm of columba powder an excellent practice. It often most materially assists in allaying vomiting.

When no vomiting occurs at all, give the following draught and a bolus.

Take of Tincture of opium, sulphuric ether,
of each half a drachm; Ipecacuanha wine .... half an ounce;
Water .... 2 ounces.
Mix for a draught.

Take of Calomel .... 12 grains;
Extract of jalap .... 4 grains;
Camphor .... 3 grains;
Opium .... 1 grain;
Oil of peppermint .... 2 drops.
Make : into a bolus.

If these produce no effect, repeat the draught after every forty minutes.

In all cases rub the arms and legs with hot sand, and apply a blister or mustard poultice over the stomach, *immediately* after the first dose of medicine is given.

If the case be lingering and doubtful, after much medicine has been given, then omit all other medicines but this :

Take of Calomel .... 3 grains;
Ipecacuanha .... 2 grains;
Aloes .... 3 grains;
Opium .... half a grain.
Make into a pill; one to be taken every hour.

Take of Barley-water .... 4 ounces;
Brandy, or arrack .... 3 drachms.
Mix to be taken every hour.

The patient, if thirsty, is to be frequently and freely supplied with cold water, or cold water containing a scruple of bi-carbonate of soda or potash in each half pint of water, as already recommended. Mr. Annesley states, that cold water, or cold water acidulated with nitric acid, was the general drink at the Madras hospital, and that it relieves a very distressing symptom, the burning sensation at the pit of the stomach. Placing a small piece of ice in the mouth often checks the sickness, and is a comfort to the patient.

A friend of mine, an old Indian officer, was given over in cholera; his pulse scarcely to be felt; but he was just able to whisper to his medical attendant that he should like some good port wine. It was given, and immediately he began to recover. He had found it a saving remedy several years before in similar circumstances.

If the patient survive there is sometimes a distressing sickness, with vomiting of green bilious matter. Dr. Barlow says, *(Practice of Medicine,* p. 702) " We have found the best remedy to be five grains of calcined magnesia in a table-spoonful of water every hour and a half or two hours. After the sickness has subsided, the chlorate of potass appears to act as a diuretic, and helps to restore the circulation".

Mr. Hope, a surgeon in the Navy, recommends the following medicine for the cure of cholera, and states that for thirty years it has succeeded in his practice in a very satisfactory way. I believe it to be an admirable remedy.

Take of Nitrous acid, (not nitric acid)	1	drachm;
Peppermint water or camphor mixture	1	ounce;
Tincture of opium	40	drops.

Mix them, and give a fourth part every two, three or four hours, in a cupful of thin gruel.

The belly should be covered with a succession of hot cloths, *dry;* bottles of hot water applied to the feet; and the patient should be allowed constant warm sippings of finely strained gruel, sago, or tapioca. No malt liquors can be permitted till restoration is fully established. When recovering, beef-tea, chicken broth, jellies, and sago or arrow-root with wine, may be given the patient.

The wearing of a large flannel belt or waistcoat is of the first importance as a preventive measure, and should be particularly enforced on the poor. It has been found a great preservative in India.

The mode of treating this malady stated in the preceding pages is approved by the most experienced practitioners, but as the following presents some additional points, and is given by Dr. James Johnson, who had many opportunities of treating Indian cholera, I have much pleasure in inserting it in the present edition of this volume. Dr. Johnson says, (*Med. Chirurg. Rev.,* October, 1831,) "We have often been asked, what we ourselves would do, in the event of meeting with a case of malignant cholera", as now appearing on the continent of Europe. "The following contains the treatment which we would wish to be pursued in our own case".

> "The first step which we would advise, would be the placing the patient in a warm bed, where he is to be chafed with hot flannels all over the body, while a hot bath is preparing. The flannels might be impregnated with ardent spirits, and hot water, as soon as procured, substituted for the dry flannel. Meantime, we would administer three grains of opium and ten grains of calomel instantly, followed by moderate potations of warm brandy and water, while the skin is cold, and the circulation concentrated about the internal organs. We would be inclined to repeat three grains of calomel and one of opium every two or three hours, till reaction took place, and the the of the circulation flowed to the surface. As soon as the bath was ready we would place the patient in it, having put a good allowance of salt and mustard in the water. If by these means heat be restored to the skin, and the spasms and vomiting be allayed, the great danger is over, and the management of the feverish re-action requires but very moderate skill. The injection of fifty or one hundred drops of Battley's sedative, or common laudanum, in a small quantity of starch or gruel, into the rectum, might be beneficial. These we conceive, are the main indications of treatment; and if they fail, we apprehend that most of the complicated machinery of practical medicine, recommended by some, more from speculation than experience, will be found to share the same fate".

I am glad to see that the Austrian Government, in their official regulations, issued during the period of the epidemic in 1832, called upon all the clergy to "inspire the people with confidence in Divine Providence"; and a late writer on this disease (Mr. Annesley) has the following remarks in point : "There is a moral courage possessed by some individuals, who are even the weakest, perhaps, as respects physical powers which resists more efficiently the causes of intertropical diseases, than the bodily powers of the strongest, who are not similarly endowed". The highest-style of this courage, which is often so acknowledged a safeguard in pestilential diseases, and which with certainty softens all the calamities of life is not that of the mind, but of the *heart:* it is not a natural courage, but that which is drawn directly from the skies, and inspired by the vital principles of pure christianity and faith in God.

COLD AND COUGH

A cold in the head or chest, is a slight inflammation of the membrane lining the back part of the mouth, and extending to the terminations of the windpipe, (called *bronchia),* and the nose being attended with a stuffing of the nostrils, sneezing, and for the most part, a mucous expectoration, or discharge from the nose.

Its symptoms are well known to be feverishness; weight and pain in the head; oppression of the chest, and impeded respiration; sense of fulness and stopping of the nose; watery inflamed eyes; *cold* shiverings, succeeded by transient flushes of heat; soreness of the fauces and windpipe; cough; pains in the chest; and increased secretion of mucus from the parts affected.

There are *two species* of this complaint, *common cough* or *cold*; and the *epidemic cough,* or *influenza.* The usual cause of the first is cold applied to the body; of the second, contagion, or rather, atmospheric influence.

The epidemic cough or influenza, differs from common cold in the suddenness of its attack, the severity of its symptoms, and very generally in the rapidity of its transition, as well as in the nature of its cause. The middle aged, the strong and the robust, are the soonest affected by it, and suffer most severely, while the young and the old are less susceptible of its influence. The fever is often strikingly depressive. Indeed the influenza may be considered as a catarrhal fever, accompanied with, and followed by, extraordinary depression of the nervous energy for several weeks after the fever has ceased.

TREATMENT—*In the common cold,* a little domestic repose in a very moderately warm atmosphere, diluting drinks, of a temperature not higher than lukewarm, and abstinence from animal food and fermented liquors, with a sudorific posset of treacle and milk, or some warm gruel, or the draught No. 35A, page 158, at night, is usually sufficient to carry off the complaint. If the cold be rather severe, four grains of James's powder alone, taken at bed time, is a useful remedy and a little aperient medicine, as No. 73 or 74, page 176, should be taken in the morning. And the draught No. 35A, if taken two or three times a day, will be found very soothing and refreshing. If the cough be troublesome at night, four grains of compound powder of ipecacuanha in a pill, taken on going to bed, may be advisable, or a dose of No. 78B, page 180.

Dr. Watson's advice is judicious, with the exception of the patient's remaining in bed, which I do not recommend. He says, (*Prac. of Physic*, vol. ii. p. 27).

> Every man, in regard to a cold, thinks himself qualified to be his own doctor. But. if you are consulted, keep your patient in the house, or even in bed; let him live upon slops; give him a gentle apperient, and then some of those medicines which are esteemed to be diaphoretic small doses of James's powder; three drachms of the solution of acetate of ammonia, with a drachm of the sweet spirit of nitre, and an ounce of camphor; or a saline draught (as No. 35A, page 158), with an excess of alkali and a few grains of nitre, or a little antimonial wine; give some such gose three times a day; and let him take four grains of Dover's powder, and put his feet and legs into a warm bath just before he goes to bed. In this way you may conduce to his recovery; and he may be simple enough to suppose that yon have *cured* him".

Should the cough be of a severer description, with extreme oppression of the chest, difficulty of breathing, and considerable fever, it may be necessary to let blood to the extent of six or eight ounces, and the mixture No. 78B, page 180, must be taken; but then the complaint is bronchitis, to which I refer the reader.

It is not a correct practice, after a cold is caught, to make the room the person sits in much warmer than usual, to increase the quantity of bed clothes, wrap up in flannel, and drink a large quantity of hot tea, gruel, or other slops, because it will inevitably increase the feverishness present, and, in the majority of instances, prolong rather than lessen the duration of the cold. It is well known that confining inoculated persons in warm rooms, will make their small pox more violent, by augmenting the general heat and fever, and it is for the same reason that a similar practice, in the present complaint, is attended with analogous results, a cold being in reality a slight fever. Indeed, some professional men recommend a reduced atmosphere, and frequent draughts of cold fluids, as the most efficacious remedies for a recent cold, and when the patient's habit is full and plethoric, I believe it will be found the best treatment, at least in the commencement. In some parts of England, among the lower orders of the people, a large glass or two of cold spring water, taken going to bed, is found to be a successful remedy.

A cold is so common a complaint in our variable climate, and becomes so frequently the parent of more formidable maladies, that the subject of *prevention* is one of considerable moment; and I shall consequently make a few observations respecting it, which, if attended to, cannot fail to be extremely useful to all persons, and more particularly to those who are liable to suffer severely from this disorder.

Colds are sometimes produced in the following manner when a person in cold weather goes into the open air, every time he draws in his breath the cold air passes through his nostrils and windpipe into the lungs, and, consequently, diminishes the heat of these parts. As long as the person continues in the cold air, he feels no bad effects from it; but as soon as he returns home, he approaches the fire to warm himself, and very often takes some warm and comfortable drink to keep out *the cold,* as it is said. The inevitable consequence is, that he will first perceive a glow within his nostrils and breast, as well as over the whole surface of the body. Soon afterwards, a disagreeable dryness and huskiness will be felt in the nostrils and breast. By and by, a short, dry, tickling cough comes on. He feels a shivering, which makes him draw nearer to the fire, but all to no purpose; the more he tries to heat himself the more he becomes chilled. All the mischief is here caused by the violent action of the heat.

Such being a frequent cause of cold, the following rules for avoiding the complaint may be adopted with great advantage.

When you come out of a very cold atmosphere, you should not at first go into a room that has a fire in it, or, if you cannot avoid that, you should keep for a considerable time at as great a distance as possible, and above all, refrain from taking warm or strong liquors when you are cold. This rule is founded upon the same principle as the treatment of any part of the body when frost-bitten. If it were brought to the fire, it would soon mortify, whereas, if rubbed with snow, no bad cnsequences follow from it. Hence, if the following rule were strictly observed, *when the whole body, or any part of it is chilled, bring it to its natural feeling and warmth by degrees,* the frequent colds we experience in winter, would, in a great measure, be prevented.

Some persons labour under what seems like a cold in the head for weeks or months, but this is merely a symptom of general derangement of the system, and must be treated accordingly. It requires the use of the alterative pill, No. 98, page 191, every other night, and a stomachic pill, No. 102 or 104, page 197, or bark and ammonia, No. 84B, page 185, twice a day, together with cold sponging every morning on rising, and a rather generous diet, with plenty of exercise in the open air.

In the INFLUENZA, bleeding is never required, notwithstanding the violence with which this disease often makes its assault, and from the debility so soon induced, should be avoided. If urgent pleuritic pains are present, it will be best to trust to dry cupping simply, a strong liniment, No. 46, page 163, and the mixture, No. 78B, page 180. The most successful treatment is a sustaining one, and consists in repose, diluting drinks, and the employment of the usual means, above noticed, to obtain and preserve a gentle perspiration, the bowels being kept free from confinement. If the chest be much oppressed, an emetic, or a mustard poultice will afford the best relief; and if the cough be troublesome, and the.

breathing laborious, and the mixture, No. 78B, does not relieve it, then give the following :—

Take of Ipecacuanha, in powder	4	grains;
Oxymel of squills........................	2	drachms;
Sweet spirit of nitre	1	drachm;
Spearmint water..........................	2½	ounces;
Syrup of orange peel	1½	drachm.

Mix, and take a table-spoonful four or five times in the twenty four hours.

Unless the inflammatory symptoms run very high, the diet should be nourishing throughout, though mild.

In 1833, an epidemic influenza raged throughout Europe, and it is supposed that in most of the largest cities in this quarter of the globe, almost one-half of the inhabitants were attacked by it. Blood-letting and all depletory measures were found hurtful. But the epidemic influenza of 1837 was far more general, severe and fatal than that of 1833; in all these respects it probably exceeded any epidemic with which Great Britain has been visited within the memory of man. In this awful visitation, with which it pleased Almighty God to visit our land, small blood-lettings and all lowering measures did harm, even in plethoric habits. The most successful treatment in severe influenza is, I believe, that which consists chiefly in the administration of the ammonia mixture, No. 78B, or 78D, page 181, taking care to observe a strict mild diet, and to avoid exposure to the easterly winds. In these mixtures the tartar emetic unloads the chest, keeps the bronchia and skin free, abates fever, and regulates the bowels, while the ammonia is sustaining. They are admirable remedies. A dose of the cordial mixture, No. 79, page 181, may also be taken twice at least in the twenty-four hours. The draught, No. 35A, page 158, now and then is also excellent, should any thing more of a sustaining nature be required. For the hiccup, which now and then occurs with alarming severity in influenza, perhaps the best means of relief is a mustard poultice to the pit of the stomach, and ten drops of liquid ammonia internally in water.

The influenza frequently leaves behind a good deal of weakness, and a troublesome cough. The debility is to be removed by a free use of decoction of bark and ammonia, No. 84B, page 185, gentle exercise, cold bathing, a nutritious diet, and especially by change of air. For the cough, small doses of tartar emetic, or No. 76A, page 179, or No. 78A, will be found the most beneficial.

Some of the most intractable diseases originate in neglected colds; and it is, therefore, highly necessary that this complaint should at all times be attended to, and removed as quickly as possible. It is a vulgar saying, "feed a cold, and starve a fever", but it is not correct; the proper treatment has been pointed out. The weakly and delicate, who are subject to frequent colds, should endeavour by diet, regimen, daily sponging with cold water, and medicine, to invigorate the general habit, remembering that the most effectual way of guarding against cold, is by rendering themselves superior to its influence; which most people may do by constant exposure to the air, and cold bathing, with active exercise, and avoiding enervating indulgencies within doors. It is a very pernicious practice to sleep and dress in a room that has a fire in it, even in winter. The smoke, dust, and heat arising from burning fuel in a bed-room, are highly injurious to health, more especially to the health of the weakly.

Strong and robust persons, liable to frequent colds, will find temperance, plenty of cold water, and attention to the preceding rules, a certain preventive. To all, the daily use of the flesh-brush to the throat, neck and breast, and sponging the whole body with cold water every morning on first getting out of bed, will prove of great service in rendering the party less susceptible to the action of cold. These are means highly deserving of the confidence and attention of the delicate who are much troubled with colds and hoarseness. Sir Astley Cooper attributed his freedom from colds, in a great measure, to the constant practice of sponging the body daily with cold water. He remarks,

> "The methods by which preserve my own health, are temperance, early rising, and sponging the body every morning with cold water,

> immediately after getting out of bed, a practice which I have adopted for thirty years; and though I go from the hot theatre into the squares of the Hospital, in the severest winter nights, with merely silk stockings on my legs, yet I scarcely ever have a cold. Should it happen that I feel indisposed, my never failing remedy is one grain of calomel combined with four grains of cathartic extract, which I take at night with a basin of hot tea about two hours before I rise the following morning, in order to excite a free perspiration, and my indisposition soon subsides."—*Surgical Lect. No. IV.*

Dr. Heberden says, that a patient of his was cured of an habitual cold in the head whilst taking a full dose of Peruvian bark, two or three times a day, for the relief of some other complaint; a circumstance proving the advantage of a suitable tonic in an habitual cold.

COLIC

Colic is a griping pain of the bowels, chiefly about the navel, and often accompanied with a painful distension of the whole of the lower region of the bowels, with vomiting, costiveness, and spasmodic contraction of the muscles of the abdomen.

There are several varieties of this disease, the principal of which are, the stercoraceous colic or iliac passion; the Devonshire or painter's colic; the flatulent colic and the constipative colic. The first is chiefly remarkable, for the vomiting of the faces, or of substances injected by the anus; the second for its attacking painters, plumbers, and other persons exposed to the poison of lead, and being frequently followed by palsy of the wrists and arms; the third, from the existing symptoms of great flatulence, and the relief following the expulsion of wind; and the last, for the obstinate constipation and great tension present, with little flatulence. A remarkable symptom in *lead colic* is a bluish or purplish line along the edges of the gums.

The complaint is produced by various *causes,* such as crude, indigestible fruits; long continued costiveness; cold beverages on a heated stomach; catching cold in the feet or bowels; violent purgatives; worms; calculous, or other concretions formed in the intestines; transferred gout or rheumatism. The cause of the painter's colic is invariably the poison of lead received into the system, from exposure to its fumes, or from taking it internally, as is sometimes done by persons who drink impure cyder or wine.

The colic is to be *distinguished* from inflammation by the spasmodic contraction of the muscles of the abdomen; by the absence or trifling degree of fever; by the pulse being little affected; and by the ease with which the patient submits to pressure, which, indeed, frequently affords relief. Severe colic, however, is sometimes, in its progress, combined with inflam-mation, which will be known by the usual symptoms noticed under that head.

TREATMENT—The indications are to relax the spasm, and to evacuate the bowels; and the most powerful remedies are the warm bath,—warm fomentations,—copious warm clysters, opium, either by the mouth or in clysters,—stimulants to the belly, as turpentine, or volatile alkali rubbed on it;—purgatives,—aromatic stimulants and antispasmodics, internally. The patient may be directly plunged into a warm bath at 98 or 100 degrees, or warm fomentations be applied over the bowels, two table-spoonfuls of castor oil being likewise administered, or one of the purgatives marked No. 27 or 28, pages 155-56. An ounce of castor oil, and a drachm of spirits of turpentine, mixed together, is often a valuable purgative. Frequently it will be advisable to give two or three of the pills No. 97, and to assist their operation by occasional doses of No. 73, page 176. A copious clyster, as No. 8, page 146, is sometimes a valuable remedy; and if the first be insufficient, a second or third may be injected without delay. Often the administration of opium is necessary, and one of the best forms is an injection, a hundred and twenty drops of laudanum may be mixed with four ounces of warm olive oil for this purpose. If the colic continues obstinate, notwithstanding the employment of these means, give a grain of calomel and a grain of opium every three hours; and in case of great irritation of the stomach, with frequent vomiting, the effervescing saline draught, No. 24, page 153, may be taken, with or without ten drops of laudanum or a little brandy.

The colic which is so frequent in the West Indies may be successfully treated in the same way, but here a five or six grain dose of calomel is often of much service, if administered early.

As an outline of the treatment called for according to the particular *causes* of the complaint, we may say, that colic proceeding from cold acid beverages will require antacids, combined with aromatics and anodynes, as No. 79, page 181, to which mixture two drachms of tincture of henbane, or thirty drops of laudanum, may be added; this should be followed by the exhibition of the clyster No. 8, page 146. If it has been caused by acid, indigestible fruit or food, an emetic of thirty grains of ipecacuanha powder in brandy and water, should be the first thing taken, and after it has ceased to operate, the mixture No. 79 may be taken as just advised, and followed by a warm purgative, as No. 25, page 154. If the colic has been produced by eating fish, Cayenne pepper is an almost unfailing antidote. In the flatulent colic, a small quantity of brandy, or an aromatic cordial, as a drachm of aromatic confection, with a table-spoonful of tincture of rhubarb, and a little peppermint water, is often effectual. But here the assafoetida injection is still more useful, and sometimes acts like a charm. *See* No. 10, page 147.

When all the above means fail, cold applications have been resorted to with success, especially the dashing of cold water upon the thighs and abdomen, or the application of ice or snow.

Whenever inflammation supervenes, or a decided tendency towards it, evidenced by shivering or a full pulse, blood should be drawn freely from the arm, whatever may be the cause of the colic.

In the painter's colic, the use of large doses of opium should be the first thing resorted to, as experience has proved it to be the most powerful means of relieving the spasmodic pain in this species of colic, and of preparing the way for the effectual operation of subsequent medicines. The patient should therefore take immediately sixty drops of laudanum in a little cinnamon water, which may be repeated in the course of two hours, if relief be not obtained. When the spasm begins to relax, purgative medicines should be administered, and castor oil, in free closes, is one of the best purgatives that can be employed. If the pain returns, opium should again be exhi bited, and afterwards opening medicine, and so on till the disease is entirely overcome. Should the complaint be particularly obstinate, the opium may be combined with calomel, in the following proportions, purgatives being still occasionally interposed :

Take of Calomel .... 6 grains;
Purified opinm .... 12 grains;
Conserve of roses, a sufficient quantity to make the whole into six pills.
One to he taken three or four times in the twenty-four hours.

The poison of lead frequently occasions a palsied state of the wrists and arms, for the removal of which the nitrate of silver, and iodide of potassium, seem to be the most efficacious medicines. The nitrate of silver may be given in the dose of one or two grains, made into pills with a little bread crumb and mucilage, and repeated two or three times a day. This has performed cures in cases of considerable standing.

Persons subject to colic should be attentive to their diet, and to the regulation of the bowels, and particularly avoid cold, indigestible, or undressed vegetables. Painters, plumbers, and others exposed to the fumes of lead, should observe the greatest cleanliness, and always wash their hands and face before taking a meal, and, if possible, throw off their dirty clothes after leaving work. They should mix a little diluted sulphuric acid with their beer or other drink.

PULMONARY CONSUMPTION

Before I enter on the subject of consumption, it may be of service to many to remark, that it is common to confound diseases of the lungs and heart. Disease of the lungs is indeed, very common, but these maladies are not so frequent as is generally supposed, many of the cases, especially where cough is present, being rather diseases of the heart than the lungs.

Pulmonary consumption is a disease of the blood, a disorder specially affecting the nutritive functions. It is generally regarded as a wasting dependent upon disease of the lungs. It consists in a general emaciation of the body, with debility and cough, for the most part attended with hectic fever, and frequently with purulent expectoration. Most physicians call that disease alone pulmonary consumption, or *phthisis pulmonalis,* which is the consequence of the development in the lungs of a particular species of production or deposit, called *tubercle.*

This is a disease of the first importance, both on account of its frequency and fatality. It has been pretty accurately calculated to carry off prematurely one-fourth of the inhabitants of Europe; and it is supposed that the annual victims to its ravages in Great Britain exceed seventy thousand.

Dr. C.J.B. Williams has the following valuable remarks on the nature of this disease, in his *Lectures before the College of Physicians in* 1862.

> "The more fully we recognise the relations of the disease to the general economy, and the less it is treated as a mere local affection, the more likely are we to make progress."
>
> "There seems to me to be two prominent varieties of phthisis. In the one, as the natural change of tissue goes on, this degenerate material (tubercle) is laid down in its place. Tubercle occurs in the blood, and the blood-cells themselves may be so altered. Thus tubercle may occur as a change of ordinary nutrition; but if the nutrition be altered by inflammation and congestion, an imperfectly formed material being effused as the consequence of the condition of the blood,—that material not being capable of forming proper membrane, nor yet of being absorbed as healthy lymph would be,—it remains a source of irritation, and may undergo further tubercular degeneration. These views, which I first expressed now thirty years ago, have rather been confirmed than altered by the lapse of time and the concurrent progress of science."

The earliest *symptoms* of consumption are often insidious and obscure. The patient is sensible of a deficient appetite, and an unusual languor, perhaps complains of indigestion, and breathes with less freedom than formerly, so that his respirations are shorter and increased in number. He coughs occasionally, but does not complain of its being troublesome, and rarely expectorates at the same time; yet if he make a deep inspiration, he is sensible of slight uneasiness in a particular part of the chest. These symptoms gradually increase, and at length the pulse is found quicker than usual, particularly towards the evening; a more than ordinary perspiration may take place in the course of the night; and if the sleep be not disturbed by coughing, a considerable fit of coughing takes place in the morning, and the patient feels relaxed and enfeebled. This may be said to form the first stage of the disease.

The cough increases in frequency, and, from being dry, is accompanied with a purulent mucus, varying, according to the peculiar modification of the disease, from a watery whey-like sanies, occasionally tinted with blood, to an expectoration of nearly genuine pus; and the malady is now decidedly established. The fluid spit out may be livid, deep-black, light-brown, light-green, or yellowish white; flattened or round; hard or soft; fetid or without smell. In many cases it is very scanty, and it may happen that there is no expectoration at all; for in the apostematious species, the sufferer has now and then died before the abscess has broken. Commonly, what is called a vomica, or abscess in the lungs, is the result of the softening and bursting of a mass of tubercles. The uneasiness in the chest, only perceived at first on making a deep inspiration, is now permanent and attended with a sense of weight; the hectic fever has assumed its full character; and the patient can only lie-with comfort on one side. The strength now fails apace; the pulse varies from about a hundred to hundred and twenty or thirty; the teeth increase in transparency, and the white of the eye is pearly-white; the fingers are shrunk, except at the joints, which become prominent; the nails are bent for want of support, and become painful; the nose is sharp; the cheeks are red; the eyes sunk, but bright; the countenance as if smiling; the spine projects; and the shoulder blades stand out like the wings of birds.

The local pains in this disease are uncertain; most of the patients have some pain; many have none at all, and some have very acute pain. In general, the pains in the chest in cases of phthisis are owing to slight chronic pleurisy, that is, chronic inflammation of the membrane lining the chest.

The *third stage* is melancholy and distressing. It commences with a depressing and colliquative looseness; but till this period, and occasionally, indeed, through it, the patient supports his spirits, and flatters himself with ultimate recovery. The voice becomes hoarse; the mouth beset with small white pustules, or the throat ulcerated. Frequently dropsy, in various forms, now makes its approach; a languid delirium sometimes occurs; but, in general, the faculties are entire, and the senses acute; until the extremities grow cold, and the closing scene arrives.

Though this is the common progress and termination of the disease, yet it varies considerably in the character and combination of its symptoms. We may clearly distinguish : 1. *Regular manifest consumption;* 2. *Irregular manifest consumption;* 3. *Latent consumption;* 4. *Acute consumption;* and 5. *Chronic consumption.*

The *first* is that which observes the regular course described above; the *second,* includes those cases of phthisis, in which the disease seems to begin in some other organ besides the lungs. For example, it is by no means uncommon to find the local and general systems of consumption preceded by chronic diarrhoea or looseness of long standing. Here often ulcers exist in the intestines, and small miliary tubercles. 3. *Latent* consumption is that where the symptoms are masked for a long time, as by nervous disorder, habitual indigestion, or common cough.[1] 4. *Acute* phthisis are those cases

1. These are cases in which previous disorder of some kind has existed for a long time, and which has terminated in consumption, from the previous disorder not having been cured. A case of this description is the following : "A person for several years hypochondriacal, but who still preserved his strength and plumpness, (a pretty sure sign that he would have recovered his health, *Deo volente,* had he used the proper means), was suddenly attacked with an acute catarrh, which was succeeded after five days by an expectoration of *pus* and mucus, mixed with a little blood. These symptoms subsided in the course of a few days; but after six months they were succeeded by symptoms of a decided phthisis, which carried the patient off in six weeks".

which unfold themselves all at once, with acute fever, emaciation; and other symptoms of such severity as to carry off the patient sometimes as early as the end of six weeks, or even a month. 5. *Chronic* phthisis includes those examples which last five or six years, or even longer.

The chief predisposing *causes* appertain to a peculiarity of constitution, marked by a long neck, prominent shoulders, narrow chest, long slender fingers, and symptoms of constitutional irritability that is easily affected by external agents. The occasional causes are very numerous, as frequent and sudden changes of temperature, or imprudent exposure of the body to cold; the dust to which certain artificers are exposed, as needle-pointers, stone-cutters, millers, etc.; over action in speaking, singing, or playing on a wind instrument; the irritation of various other diseases, as measles, small pox, hooping cough asthma, or syphilis; the sudden suppression of a cutaneous disease, or of any habitual discharge; the irritation of a too rapid growth of the body; and the operation of the depressing passions. The disease may also arise from the lodgement of any extraneous substance in the gullet, or in the windpipe; from profuse evacuations; and from continuing to suckle too long under a debilitated state.

Consumption is often said to be caused by spitting of blood; it certainly not unfrequently follows the discharge of blood called *haemoptysis,* but very generally tubercles in the lungs precede or are co-existent with that condition of those organs which give rise to haemoptysis, and we ought consequently to say, that the spitting of blood is rather a sign or symptom of consumption than the cause of it. The particular consumptive constitution most liable to haemoptysis is distinguished by the brilliant whiteness of the skin, the bright redness of the cheeks, the narrowness of the chest, the projecting or winged configuration of the shoulders, and the slenderness of the limbs and trunk.

A French physician (Laennec) who had an uncommon experience in consumption says, "it has appeared to me that almost all those who become phthisical, without being constitutionally predisposed to the disease, might attribute the origin of their complaint to grief, either very deep or of long continuance".[1]

The species of consumption to which artificers are liable who are exposed to much dust, is the catarrhal, called *bronchitis.*

Consumption may be distinguished from *bronchitis* by some expectoration always attending the cough of *bronchitis,* while the cough of consumption is often, for a long while, dry. Bronchitis is not accompanied by spitting of blood. The pain that occurs in bronchitis is felt beneath the breast bone; in consumption pain is most frequently felt in the sides, and between the shoulders.

1. Some people seem to doubt whether consumption, when truly formed, is ever cured, but this is to disregard the evidence of our senses, (which certain persons are not unwilling to do) in a matter of fact. They may with as much propriety deny that indigestion, when fully formed, is curable. Notwithstanding the uncommon fatality of consumption, do we not happily see continually cases recover which had been by every one thought desperate, and that after hectic fever was clearly established ? Can any man long in extensive practice deny this, without disputing the reality of a matter of fact? I think not. Supposing that ulceration has taken place in the lungs, why should it not heal there, under efficient treatment, as well as elsewhere? No good reason can be given why it should not; and, indeed, we know it may. The following sentiment of Mr. Abernethy on this point, may be acceptable to many of my readers. It is oddly expressed, and embraces only a limited view of the subject, but is, nevertheless, valuable. He says, "Can consumption be cured? bless me, that's a question which a man who had lived in a dissecting room would laugh at: how many people do you examine who have lungs tubercular, which are otherwise sound. What is consumption? It is (ulcerated) tubercles of the lungs; then, if those tubercles were healed, and the longs otherwise sound, the patient must get better".—*Anatomical Lectures.*

   M. Laennec has described what he found on the dissection of the body of a woman, aged 52, who died from disease in the chest after she had been "many years cured of consumption". She had many years suffered from disease in the chest, but the dissection proved that an ulcer which she formerly had been perfectly healed. "In the upper and posterior part of the right lung, (he says, *Treatise on Diseases of the Chest,* page 171), there was found an excavation of an oval shape, about two inches in length, above an inch broad in the centre, and the sixth of an inch deep. The inner surface of this cavity was smooth and polished, though somewhat irregular; it was white, but interspersed with red specks, arising from numerous small vessels. This cyst was entirely empty." M. Laennec's work contains several cases equally conclusive, and in M. Andral's *Clinic. Medical,* vol. iii. page 382, eight or ten examples of cicatrization of the lungs after tubercles are given. Laennec says, page 305, " I am convinced, from a great number of facts, that, in some cases, consumption is curable in the latter stages, that is, *after* the softening of the tubercles and the formation of an ulcerous excavation."

The more readily oil is saponified, or formed into an emulsion in the stomach, the more easily it is digested and the more nourishing it proves to the body.

Tubercular consumption, as already remarked, arises from the deposition of tubercles in the air cells, or cell walls, of the lungs, generally commencing in the apex of the lung. Tubercles are small, hard bodies, or cheese-like, either grey, semi-transparent, or of a crude yellow colour, and they are mostly the product of a mild and chronic form of inflammation in the lungs. There are three stages of this disease: first, that of *deposition;* secondly, that of *softening;* and lastly, that of ulceration. The symptoms of *deposition* are cough, and expectoration of a frothy or mucilaginous kind,—sometimes streaked with blood—slight pain in the chest, frequent and small pulse, loss of appetite, and some loss of flesh, and frequently in females a sudden stoppage of their usual monthly relief. A slight flattening is observed under the collar bones, and a diminished expansion of the chest. The symptoms of *softening* are those of considerable suppuration and hectic fever; pearly whiteness of the eyes, red tongue, irregular bowels nocturnal perspiration, hoarseness of voice, and the expectoration of a pus-like mucus. The cough is now more troublesome than it was. There is an increased flattening of the chest, and dulness on percussion. In the last stage of *excavation,* all the symptoms are aggravated; the hectic fever is severe, and the emaciation usually extreme, the pulse extremely small and frequent, there are night sweats and diarrhoea, the cheeks hollow, and the eyes sunken, with a clammy perspiration. Spitting of blood often occurs after softening, and then from the rupture of some vessel opened by ulceration. In the progress of the disease, stitch or pain in the side *(pleuritis)* is frequently present, and at an advanced period ulceration of the larynx.

Tuberculous matter generally occupies chiefly the upper part of the upper lobes of the lungs, but it may remain quiet for a long time, and if no low inflammation supervenes, the patient may be but little, if at all inconvenienced, by it. If the patient can be invigorated,—if the nourishment of the whole system can be increased, he will generally be placed in a state of security. But when, from any cause, an inflamed condition occurs, then a sort of suppuration takes place; the tubercles become soft, break down, and are ultimately expelled by coughing through the bronchia, windpipe, and mouth. The cavities left in the lung after this process of expulsion are called excavations, or *vomicae*. These excavations of course vary in size; they may be as small as a pea, or as large as a man's fist. The lung tissue around such a cavity is condensed and solidified, and if the cavity is single, and it becomes completely emptied of tuberculous matter, it may gradually contract, become obliterated, and the patient recover. Consequently it is a grand object of treatment to promote such an emptying and contraction of the excavation, and to prevent any fresh deposition elsewhere of tuberculous matter.

Dr. T. K. Chambers's remarks on this point are very instructive. He says *(On the Treatment of Consumption,* published in the *Medical Circular,* 1862) :—

> "What the patient has to fear, is not the remaining of the tubercls in the body, but its increase. That which is once there has done its mischief, its path of ruin is past, the portion of lung which it has occupied is gone for ever, and cannot grow again any more than an amputated leg. The *post-mortem* examination of consumptives show almost always the cause of death to be a fresh formation of tubercle at no distant period, which has abridged the remaining organ to a degree inconsistent with life. A single deposit of tubercle to a moderate extent can almost always be recovered from. It is the continuous repetition of the process which is so fatal. I cannot, therefore, too strongly impress upon you, that not so much the tubercle as the tendency to form tubercle, not the morbid matter but the diathesis, is that which should occupy your thoughts."
>
> "When tubercle first takes its place in the pulmonary tissue, the lung feels a good deal inconvenienced by its presence; there is cough, inflammation round it, condensation of the neighbouring substance and from the unaccustomed loss of part of the respiratory function, there is general ill-health. These consequences are directly proportioned to the quantity of lung spoilt. They may be so severe as to cause death by what is called "tuberculous pneumonia", or by "galloping consumption", when a large extent is very quickly

rendered unserviceable. Or, when the injury is slower and slighter, they may be so insignificant as not to have attracted notice at all. The other day, in a patient who died of chores dependent on a tubercle in the spinal cord, you saw scattered tubercles in both lungs which had caused no symptoms at all during life, though they probably had been there longer than the tubercle in the less usual situation which proved fatal. And very often in persons killed by accident, apparently the prime of activity and with no history of any serious illness, you find crude tubercles, scars of former tubercles and the chalk-like *debris* of tubercular matter. And, to come to more agreeable evidence, you find people with very large quantities of tubercle in the lungs so large as to have proved almost fatal, who yet recover to a great extend from the mischief which it has caused. When once the lung has got over the shock of illness produced by the presence of the first crop, the health recovers, and the patient (though imperfect in body of course), has only to fear a fresh development. It is astonishing what enormous ravages may be made in the lung, and yet with the help of what remains people recover the health that has been lost. I dare say you may remember in the summer a poor woman sent to the hospital apparently to die. There was in the left upper lobe a vomica, so large that there was "metallic tinkling" in it; and for some weeks I took the opportunity of teaching you this rare sound. You know that it hardly ever occurs except with air in the cheat and perforation, and indicates a cavity bigger than your fist. So weakened was the patient by the loss of so much lung, that she was at first unable to feed herself even, and quite soaked the bed with colliquative perspiraions. Yet, contrary to all we expected, she lost her perspiraed flesh, walked about the ward, and, finally, walked home during my absence from London, so that I cannot say what was the exact state of her chest on leaving. But I take for granted that the cavity remained unclosed, and probably will remain unclosed for the rest of her life. That it will do so for many years, I know from other cases. For example: R. S., a wine merchant, aged forty-two, was, in 1846, under the care of several of the most experienced in chest complaints of London physicians. He had a large vomica in the left apex, was excessively debilitated by it, and was sent home with the information that he could not live a month. Well, he picked up strength and flesh, was enabled to return to his business, and, when I saw him in 1858, twelve years afterwards, was in fair health, and as able to do a moderate day's work as anybody I know; but

> ascultation left no doubt that the vomica was still open in the lung, and that the small quantity of pus he expectorated came from it. In 1855, I advised a young man, with softening tubercles in the left lung, to accept a chance which he had of settling in the West Indies. Six years and a half afterwards, he returned to England for a temporary purpose, and came to me about some symptoms not entirely connected with his chest. I found that his vomica was still there, and secreting pus; but that he had never permanently lost again the flesh which a course of iron and cod-oil had put upon him. He had even had an attack of haemoptysis and gone through yellow fever, without serious injury."

TREATMENT—The remedies which promise most in tubercular consumption are such as improve the quality of the blood, and the general nutrition of the body—and foremost we may reckon cod-liver oil, rum and milk, preparations of steel combined with ammonia, or myrrh and other tonics, a pure, mild, dry air, a very nutritious diet, plenty of exercise, and a regimen tending to invigorate the whole frame.

For many years I have been convinced that it is to the healthy nutrition of the general system that we are called to direct our attention, and not to the state of the lungs. Our endeavours should be specially directed to the use of those means which invigorate the powers of life and thus allay irritation within the chest; and it is gratifying to find that my views are confirmed by Dr. C. J. B. Williams, a physician of the same age as myself, and also by Dr. T. K. Chambers, an able physician some years younger—both men of high professional standing. It is not so much the *existing* tubercles which we have to fear, as the constitutional *tendency* to tubercles and the increase of them. Dr. Chambers says, *(On Consumption, Medical Circular,* May 28, 1862).

> "There is no question about the future conduct of the war, if only reinforcements"—he means the increase of tubercles—"can be stopped in their march. If the remaining portion of lung has retained life so long, it can retain life longer and the whole attention can be applied to its conservation. In what direction must we turn to aid in

this conservation? To the lungs? But if we look to the histories of those who have lived long with vomicae or tubercles, they are by no means found to have taken special care of their lungs—they have not coddled or lived in-doors in even temperatures, hanging their lives on to their thermometers for fear of coughs; they have gone on with their professions or business or work; they have not 'laid a knife to their throat', but have eaten and drank like other people, and have enjoyed the gratification of their appetites. A patient of mine, over fifty, with copious formation of pus and condensed lungs (probably tubercular) from his youth, has kept hounds, broken his bones like other Nimrods, contested county elections, sat in parliament, enjoyed his champagne and other good things, but *never allows any doctoring of his chest.* An examination of it is a favour as a contribution to science. Leave then the respiratory organs alone, and turn your attention to the stomach and bowels, the true organs of nutrition, which will receive with open arms any care you bestow upon them."

The great object at which we should aim is to get the greatest amount of good food well digested and assimilated. Thus, the whole frame is most certainly and effectually renewed, and nature is assisted to got rid of the morbid product—tuberculous matter—which otherwise might be the death of the sufferer. For this purpose nothing yet discovered is half so suitable and efficacious as cod-liver oil in ginger or orange wine. It is easily assimilated, and the body is so sensibly nourished by it that it seems like a directly life-giving article. But as the appetite is often exceedingly deficient, quinine pills, No.115, page 202, or steel and quinine, as No. 84A, 84B or 85, page 184-85, should be taken alone first, or in conjunction with the oil. If a disgust for food is present, then first give milk in small and frequently repeated doses. Dr. Chambers has given some good advice on this subject. He says:

"If you find milk lie long in the stomach, and produce heartburn or acid eructations add lime-water to it. Food has an illogical habit of arguing in a circle; it creates the desire for food—of course, by strengthening the digestive organs; and thus, after a few days of milk diet, the patients will voluntarily ask for meat, and enjoy as a luxury that which a short time before excited the greatest disgust."

"In the same way cod-liver oil will also act. It will often, like milk, create an appetite. But as a rule, especially in private practice, it is as well not to commence it too soon, as the disagreeableness of the taste and smell is difficult to get over at first, and it is much easier to take it when the appetite has begun to be renewed. Then it is not felt as a hardship even to begin, and in a short time patients will get really to like it; and they will like it, not merely as reasonable men like that which does them good but will, irrespectively of such knowledge, find it nice to the palate. Thus, children who always object to being done good to, will still often take to their oil with gusto."

At the commencement, the best plan is to take a tea-spoonful or two of the oil, twice or thrice a day, floating on a little ginger or orange wine, or on a dose of the mixture, No.84 A or 85. In the course of eight or ten days, the dose may be increased to three tea-spoonfuls, or a table-spoonful at a dose; and it may be taken at any time of the day the patient likes best, but the greatest distance from meals is to be preferred.

One of the most approved forms of administering steel and myrrh in this disease, is that so strongly recommended by Dr. Moses Griffiths.

Take of Myrrh, in powder	1	drachm;
Subcarbonate of potash	25	grains;
Rose water	7½	ounces;
Sulphate of iron	1	scruple;
Spirit of nutmeg	4	drachms;
White sugar	1	drachm.

Mix, and take three or four table-spoonfuls thrice a day.

If the patient prefers it in pills, he may take the following :

Take of Myrrh, in powder	2	drachms;
Sulphate of iron	1	scruple;
Subcarbonate of potash	1	drachm;
Extract of gentian	1½	drachm;

Simple syrup, a sufficient quantity to make the whole into a mass.

Divide into sixty pills, and take two or three twice a day.

Steel and ammonia I think still better, and as already stated, they may be taken as prescribed in No. 84A, page 184. It is an excellent plan to take this medicine first for ten days, then to commence the oil.

Mercury, purgatives and squills ought to be avoided, because they are debilitating. *Blancard's pills of iodine and iron* merit particular confidence, as a tonic, and will often be found superior in their effects to iron and myrrh, or iron and ammonia. They may be procured at Jozeau's, 49, Haymarket.

COD-LIVER OIL, AND NEAT'S-FOOT OIL ALSO DUGONG OIL are remedies now highly and justly extolled in the treatment of consumptive diseases. In these diseases there is a deficient proportion of red globules in the blood, which these oils have the property of restoring and increasing. So efficacious has cod-liver oil been found in the Hospital for Consumption at Brompton that the physicians there use now about 600 gallons annually. At page 36, the reader will find a short description of the virtues of these substances, and likewise the relation of a case of consumption, in which the administration of neat's foot oil was followed by results highly satisfactory. As the improvement of the faulty nutrition which originates and keeps up this disease is of all things most important, our endeavours should be specially directed to cause a larger quantity of fatty matter to be assimilated. All kinds of food rich in fat will frequently produce these effects, and hence the value long attributed to milk, especially asses' milk,—the produce of the dairy, such as cream and milk, fat bacon, etc.; but in many cases, from the impaired state of the powers of the stomach, the patient is unable to digest such fat powers of food, and then the animal oils themselves are indicated, by giving which we save the digestive apparatus the trouble of manufacturing or separating them from the food. By giving considerable quantities of oil directly, a large proportion of it is at once assimilated, and the blood nourished and improved in quality. Such appears to be the *rationale* of the good effects of cod-liver oil. On this subject Dr. C. J. B. Williams says :

> "The proper treatment of consumption seems to be that which is calculated to improve the nutrition, prevent the irregularities of the circulation which tend to promote the tuberculous deposits, and as far as possible to elevate the condition of the health".
>
> "Pure air, nutritive digestible food, regular exercise, and well-arranged Habits of life,—these and their correlative hygienic measures stand in the first place, because they are equal or superior in power to any form of medicine, properly so called, in preventing the development of the disease".
>
> "There is one remedy infinitely superior to any other, and which stands quite in front of the rank of the other remedies. It is cod liver oil: it stands entirely alone as an agent in counteracting the cachectic condition which is characteristic of phthisical disease. It is in my opinion a mistaken view to regard cod-liver oil as a material which only plays the part in the body of a simple nutrient. Twenty years of experience, various in kind and extensive in its range, have convinced me that it has other and directly therapeutic powers. Over and over again I have seen not only an improvement of the system generally under its use, but a diminution in the amount of tubercular deposit. I entertain the conviction that it promotes the dispersion, absorption and removal of tubercle. This is a question too long to discuss here; but it may be observed that the cod-liver oil has a power of pervading the system more thoroughly than any other oil. It is highly assimilable, and peculiarly well tolerated by the stomach. It makes a particularly perfect emulsion. An indication of one of its remarkable properties is, the preference which it has had over other oils for the purpose of currying leather, owing to the penetrative power which it possesses. This divisibility promotes absorption, and the oil being taken into the blood pervades the system; and we have, as it were, a liquid oleaginous bath operating on the tuberculous matter."

Many patients take the oil unmixed, floated on a little ginger wine or milk or coffee. Some say that the addition of creosote occasionally makes the stomach more tolerant of the remedy. An ounce and a half of cod-liver oil, two drops of creosote, two drachms of compound tragacanth powder, and four ounces and a half of aniseed water, form a suitable mixture, of which an ounce or two may be taken thrice daily. Those who take the oil unmixed, on ginger wine, may cover the taste by eating dried orange-peel, or by introducing a little dinner salt into the mouth before and after the oil.

Ozonized cod-liver oil seems sometimes to be more efficacious than the common oil. From a long course of experiments, conducted at the Hospital for Consumption, Brompton, Ozonized cod-liver oil has been found to possess the remarkable property of reducing the rapidity of the pulse to its natural standard, without in any way lowering the power of the system.

This reduction usually takes place in the course of two or three days, and is progressively maintained for a considerable period of time, while the ozonized cod-liver oil is being taken, till it reaches its proper standard. A reduction of twenty beats has in some cases been observed to result in two, three, four or six days; in other instances a reduction of twenty-four has been noted in fourteen days thirty-four in thirteen days, thirty-six in twenty-two days, and forty in eleven days.

Rum and milk in the morning I have found exceedingly useful, not only in this disease, but also in many other complaints of debility. I have known *Godbold's balsam* very useful. Dr. Duncan of Edinburgh, states *(Observations on Pulmonary Consumption)* that in several instances he has known cough, with alarming appearances, removed by the use of this balsam. It may be taken to the extent of a dessert-spoonful three or four times a day, and if it be applicable to the case, it generally works a beneficial change within a fortnight.

Some people have puffed off the *hypo-phosphites of iron,* soda, etc., as a cure for consumption, but they have been tried at the Consumptive Hospital, and proved useless. Arseniate of soda, or iron, has also been highly extolled, and many other things, all equally worthless.

Gass-stoves and every other kind of stove, are extremely prejudicial in all cases of consumption and bronchitis.

The diet should be very nutritious. A certain quantity of the milder kinds of animal food, and even a little wine when the strength is much reduced, are proper, if they are not found to increase the feverishness. A wine called *Catalan* is light and very suitable. It is much used in the Consumptive Hospital at Brompton, and is sold by Messrs. Kinloch and Co., 14, Barge Yard, Bucklersbury. Chocolate and fat bacon or pork for breakfast are much to be recommended. The object here is to nourish without stimulating, and the richest milk and cream, with fresh eggs, are advisable. In every species of consumption a much freer diet is required in the advanced periods of the disease, than can be safely indulged in at the the commencement. Rum and milk, the first thing in the morning or twice a day, I strongly recommend as of the greatest service. It is often almost as efficacious as cod-liver oil. It may be taken with bread and butter, as a meal, at breakfast and tea, if the patient prefers those times. A tumblerful of rich milk, a table-spoonful of old rum and a little sugar is the usual quantity at each period.

In every stage of consumption particular symptoms require palliation; such are pain in the chest, cough and night sweats, and for these certain remedies are generally applicable. For local pain, blisters or issues sometimes afford great relief. The following plaster is strongly recommended by Dr. Paris, and is useful in relieving both the pain and cough :

Take of Hard soap	1 ounce;
Lead plaster	2 drachms;
Muriate of ammonia, in powder	half a drachm.

Mix, and make a plaster. Spread it on leather, apply it to the chest immediately, and renew it once in twenty-four hours.

The following draught is much worthy of attention as a palliative for the cough; but if the cod-liver oil relieves the cough, no other medicine need be taken :

Take of Extract of hemlock	2 grains;
Extract of henbane	2 grains;
Mucilage of gum arabic	2 drachms.

Rub these well together till they are thoroughly incorporated, then add acetated liquor of ammonia, pure water, of each, half an ounce; syrup, one drachm. This makes a draught, to be taken every four hours.

Aniseed has considerable power in allaying the cough. Infuse half an ounce of the bruised seeds in half a pint of distilled water at a temperature not exceeding 120 degrees. Let it stand till it is cold, and try a wine-glassful of this aniseed infusion when the cough is troublesome. It is better than any form of opium, but if it does not succeed, then add half a tea-spoonful of ipecacuanha wine, or paregoric, to each dose.

In general, acids most effectually check the night pera-pirations. Thirty or forty drops of the diluted vitriolic acid may be given at bed-time, in a little water. If this fail, four or five grains of the compound power of ipecacuanha may be taken, and it often perfectly succeeds. Dr. Vatson says he has found the compound kino powder, in doses of ten or twelve grains "an admirable medicine for the nocturnal perspirations.—*Prac. of Physic*, vol. 2; p. 209.

Dr. Barlow says, (*Practice of Physic,* p. 318), "Against night sweats there is no remedy equal to the combination of zinc and henbane".

Take of Sulphate of zinc	6	grains;
Extract of henbane	24	grains.

Mix them, and divide into six pills; one to be taken every night.

Diarrhoea must always be checked, for it is very exhausting, and its continuance increases the tendency to the deposition of tubercles. For this purpose chalk mixture will sometimes be sufficient. The sulphate of copper is very effectual; it should be taken in the dose of a fourth or half of a grain at first, made into a pill with confection of roses, and repeated two or three times a day. Or five grains of extract of logwood may be taken in a draught with a table-spoonful of water, and one of cinnamon water.

Take of Sulphate of copper .... 3 grains;
Extract of logwood .... 2½ scruples.

Mix them, and divide into twelve pills; one to be taken after every liquid motion.

Or the combination, No. 127, page 208, may be employed. Small doses of the superacetate of lead (page 119-20) are often useful in moderating the diarrhoea, and also the night sweats; and the nitrate of bismuth answers well in some instances.[1] In some

---

1. The following is an instructive case of *tuberculous phthisis* cured, and will be interesting to my readers. It occurred at Paris, in the practice of M. Laennec. He says, "An English gentleman, aged thirty-six, detained in Paris as a prisoner of war in September 1813, had an attack of spitting of blood, followed by a cough, at first dry, but in the course of a few weeks, accompanied by purulent sputa", (that is, expectoration of pus or matter). "To these symptoms were added a well-marked hectic, considerable diffculty of breathing, copious night sweats, emaciation, and great debility. The chest sounded well every where, except under the right clavicle and in the arm-pit of the same side. The spitting of blood returned, in a slight degree, now and then, and in December he had diarrhoea, which was with difficulty checked by astringents. In the beginning of January he was so much reduced, that both M. Halle and Bayle agreed with me in opinion, that his death might be daily looked for. On the 15th of January, during a severe fit of coughing and after bringing up some blood, he expectorated a solid mass of the size of a filbert, which, on examination, I found to be evidently a tubercle in the second stage, surrounded, apparently, by a portion of the pulmonary tissue. This patient remained in the same degree of extreme emaciation and debility all January, being expected to die daily; but in the beginning of February, the perspiration and diarrhoea ceased spontaneously, the expectoration sensibly diminished, and the pulse, which had been constantly as high as 120, fell to 90. In a few days the appetite returned, the patient began to move about in his room, his emaciation became less, and against the end of the month, his convalescence was evident. In the beginning of April he was perfectly recovered; and his health has continued good ever since, without even the least cough, and without his being at all guarded in his climate or regimen. In 1818, this patient again consulted me for a different complaint, and I took the opportunity of examining his chest, by means of the stethoscope. The only thing I could detect, was the comparative indistinctness of respiration in the superior portion of the right lung, as low as the third rib. This part, however, sounded as well on peroussion as the opposite side. From these circumstances, I am of opinion that the excavation which contained the expectorated tubercles must have been healed; and as the total absence of cough, difculty of breathing, and expectoration, for so long a period, forbids the supposition of the existence of others in the lungs, I think we have a right to consider this patient as perfectly cured. In 1824, this gentleman was examined at Rome by Dr. James Clarke, who recognized him as the subject

(Contd. next page)

cases of chronic consumption in which distressing diarrhoea is a prominent symptom, the alkaline infusion of sarsaparilla will be found of much service in checking the diarrhoea, and greatly improving the general condition of the patient.

Take of Sarsaparilla root	4 ounces;
Liquorice root	3 drachms;
Lime-water	1 quart.

Let the roots divest in the lime-water eight hours, then strain, and take a quarter of a pint twice a day.

For spitting of blood -*(hoemoptysis)*, a draught of ipecacuanha wine and sulphate of soda is particularly valuable, and so it is for feverishness and the reduction of inordinate vascular action generally.

Take of Ipecacuanha wine	1½ drachm;
Sulphate of soda	1 drachm;
infusion of cascarilla bark	10 drachms.

Mix them for a draught, to be taken thrice a day until the spitting of blood is checked; then about once a day.

It now only remains for me to advert to air and exercise, a subject of importance at all times, and, in the commencement of the disease of the first moment. All consumptive invalids require a dry and equable atmosphere, and the sooner this is resorted to the greater will be the probability of success. A great diversity of opinion has obtained among professional men in respect to the value and efficacy of the climate of different places, in consumptive disorders, but this has arisen from the same source as the interminable differences and contradictions existing on all subjects of knowledge, namely, ignorance of the subjects or at least, insufficient information amongst the majority. Of late years it has

---

(Contd.)

of the case just detailed. I saw him also the same year, and found him precisely in the same state as in 1818."—*Treatise on Diseases of the Chest*, page 326. Sir James Clarke testifies that this gentleman was living in 1827, and in good health.

been fully investigated, and the most valuable *data* have been furnished, whereby we are enabled to form correct opinions, and the sum of what is known on this question will, therefore, I hope, be found in these pages.

It is certain that in Italy, France, Madeira, Lisbon and other southern parts of Europe, consumption is very frequent among the native inhabitants; that in the latter stages of the disease, a change to either of them generally accelerates rather than retards a fatal termination in English patients; that the duration of the disease in Italy often does not exceed three or four months; and that the accommodations in almost all these places are bad. The Italian physicians acknowledge, that in a hundred deaths in that country, there are, on an average, twenty-five by pulmonary consumption; and the distinguished M. Bayle, whose authority cannot be doubted, has asserted, that of five hundred patients who die in the Parisian hospitals, one hundred die of *phthisis* and of the remaining four hundred, at least fifty are complicated with that malady.

Drs. Gourlay, Cordon and Heineker, each of whom resided at Madeira, discourage us from sending persons thither, unless in the very beginning of the malady; the first observing, that whole families have at times been swept off there, by consumption. Several object to the whole of Dauphine, a great part of the South of France and North of Italy, and many of the neighbouring places, as being under the influence of cold winds from the mountains in the vicinity, and as destructive to foreigners labouring under *phthisis*. Drs. Southey, James Johnson, Sinclair, and Hennen, think unfavourably of Malta, Sicily, and other islands in the Mediterranean; and M. Portal has the same feeling with respect to the South of France.[1]

1. Montpelier was formerly a celebrated place for the resort of English patients labouring under consumption. Dr. Hawkins says, 1829, (*Medical Statistics*, page 31). The annual proportion of deaths at Montpelier was greater thirty years ago, and is greater at present, than in London; and although the mortality of great cities is usually much larger than that of provinces or countries, yet the mortality of London is exactly the Same at present as that of the department of the Herault, the southern and fertile, and long supposed most salubrious district of France, of which Montpelier is the capital. Finke, a German writer, who wrote on *Medical Geography*, in 1792, speaks with surprise and reprobation of the custom which then prevailed in England, of sending invalids

(Contd. next page)

The abrupt vicissitudes of the climate of the Mediterranean are extremely productive of pulmonary consumption among the European residents; and several able British practitioners state, that when it does approach, nothing but a retreat from its shores before the autumn sets in, can give a shadow of hope of safety to the patient, as has been proved by the recovery of many. invalids sent home in the autumn, and the death of many who remained behind—*Dr. J. Johnson on tropical Climates*, p. 338. The deaths by consumption among the inhabitants of Malta, constitute nearly one-tenth of the whole mortality.

It is of far greater importance how such patients are managed, how they live in the house and out of the house, than where they live. The general plan of treating such cases is thoroughly unsound; instead of being soothing, sustaining and invigorating, it is ordinarily irritating and debilitating. The system must be changed, and the tissues be strengthened instead of being defended; the patient should, if possible, enjoy a dry air, and *plenty of it*, of course, cautiously taken with free exercise, which will be found a far wiser and better course than to send them to a foreign station. Boating is excellent.

Dr. Renton says, that between the years 1827 and 1830, *nineteen* patients labouring under confirmed consumption arrived at Madeira, the whole of whom died, some speedily and the rest at no distant period. In another statement he remarks that of *forty-seven* such advanced cases sent to Madeira, thirty-two died within six months after their arrival; six died on a second winter's trial of the climate; six died after returning to England: what is the result of the remaining three cases is not known. Dr. Mason says, "Few places will be found where the system is more liable to disorder"; and I am entirely of this opinion.

A trustworthy visitor to Pau says the weather there "is really very variable", and that the "prostration of energies", both mental

---

(Contd.)

to the South of France; and declares that the cutting winds of those quarters annually destroy many of those wanderers in quest of a milder sky". Notwithstanding these facts are so instructive and admonitory, it may be doubted whether the ordinary practice in these cases is even now much improved.

and physical, is felt by all "Sometimes Pau is visited by what is called 'Le vent d'Espagne', a sort of mild sirocco, specially unfavourable for those persons whose lungs are affected". I should think so Egypt, and Mentone, and its neighbourhood, are now the fashionable resorts of the consumptive.

Every consumptive person, indeed—all invalids, should be careful to select a house with a *southern aspect,* wherever they reside. Attention to this point is, in most cases, of considerable moment.

Exercise, and frequent change of air, are of the highest importance in this disease, and will, in some instances, prove a powerful means of cure; for many patients, by constant change, (travelling as much as possible on horseback, or in an open carriage), have perfectly recovered, who always became worse when they remained a few days at a place.—*Dr. Foart Simmons on Pulmonary Consumption.* Where the circumstances of the individual will not allow of this perpetual change, as much exercise as possible, short of fatigue should be substituted at home. Exercise on a spring deal board is one of the most preferable modes within doors, and in a carriage or on horseback abroad. Sydenham, one of the most sensible and discerning of physicians, used to recommend horse exercise as a remedy of great power in the cure of consumption, and when this malady occurs in a cathetic, impoverished habit, it is without doubt often of much service. Cases might easily be brought forward in which it proved an effectual means of recovery, after all hope of such an event had been abandoned. Dr. Baynard, by constant riding in the open air, recovered from a consumption, when every body gave him over as lost; and the author of *"The Best Methods of Preserving Health"*, relates an instance where a patient was cured by riding, after being brought so low, that no recovery could be expected, either from medicine or even exercise. See also the value of exercise, (although of a different kind), illustrated in the case of severe cough and curved spine, which I have related from Captain Clias's observations on Gymnastics, under *Spinal Curvature.*

Ladies suffering from nervous pain in the chest and cough, are constantly to be found under a medical treatment applicable only to true tubercular phthisis. They have lowering febrifuge draughts given them, and antimonials; blisters are ordered, leeches, confinement to the house; and often they are condemned to Madeira ! The consequence is they grow worse and worse. The system is unnatural, debilitating, and the very reverse of what the condition requires. Perhaps it may be of some service to introduce a case in illustration from my own practice, for the families are numerous who are exceedingly distressed by the consequences of not merely so unnecessary, but of so injurious a mode of proceeding.

> A young lady was sent to me from the North of Scotland, suffering from cough, pain in the side, general weakness, quick pulse and loss of appetite. She had been for some time declining in health, and had grown nervous and fearful; did not sleep well at night; and the skin had become harsh and dark coloured. The family physician at Inverness had confined her to the house, ordered blisters to the side, and thought so unfavourably of her case, as at once to declare that she ought to go without delay to Madeira! Her mother had died of consumption about twelve months before, and she had already an elder sister at Madeira for the benefit of her health. It was, however, very inconvenient for the father to send this daughter thither also, and having been recommended to send her to Epsom, she came in the month of December. At that time, in addition to the symptoms enumerated above, she was regularly flushed in the face in the evening, and then suffered from increased pain in the side, and acceleration of the pulse.
>
> What was to be done? On examination I was convinced it was altogether a case of nervous and muscular debility; that the cough, pain, and feverishness had this origin and no other; that there was no present disease in the lungs whatever, and that there was every reason to believe if she was treated on a general plan, which soothed and encouraged the mind at the same time that it gave tone and firmness to the physical frame, she would soon exhibit symptoms of amendment, and by degrees perfectly recover. We were not disappointed in our expectations. She was extremely ill for the first month after her arrival here, and we found every thing of an enervating nature to be immediately and decidedly injurious. An invigorating plan was therefore adopted throughout. She was taken

daily into the air, and enjoined to use regular exercise indoors. Before six weeks had expired she was on horse-back regularly, every day the weather permitted; and in June returned home, blooming in appearance, and in perfect health. Madeira, with its moist climate, and the walls of its habitations streaming continually with moisture[1], not being found to agree with her elder sister, she was requested to return to England, and place herself under our care here, which she did; and by pursuing the same means, she also soon returned home in a very improved state of health.

I think it my duty to warn the heads of families against being easily persuaded either to banish their children to Madeira or Italy, or to shut them up in warm rooms at home. These are generally very unnecessary practices, and worse than useless. There is often extreme cruelty in them. It is of far greater consequence how such patients live out of the house and in the house, than where they live; and if they would only avail themselves of all the advantages they enjoy in this country, they never need think of visiting another.

Sydenham considered horse exercise not only proper in slight indispositions, accompanied with a frequent cough and wasting, but even in confirmed consumption, wherein looseness has supervened, and is succeeded by night sweats, and I have no doubt of its eminent utility in such instances. Exercise, and particularly constant travelling, has a considerable and very sensible effect in restraining inordinate secretions in the body, so that those who have been a long time troubled with looseness, generally become costive in travelling, and such as have been harassed by habitual cough, almost always find it much ameliorated, and often entirely removed by this means.[2] It ought to be observed, however, that riding on horseback, in young persons of a plethoric habit, and high complexion, must be resorted to with caution, as it might otherwise tend to occasion or increase symptoms of inflammation in the lungs.

---

1. This arises from the houses being built with sea sand.
2. Interesting cases of consumption, cured by exercise, will be found in my Best *Methods of Improving Health*, by regulating the diet and regimen.

In the consumption met with in mothers who have suckled their infants too long, and without enjoying sufficient nourishment, the Peruvian bark in free doses, combined with a nutritious diet, will be the best remedy. In emaciated and consumptive habits from a venereal cause, Sir William Fordyce praises the compound decoction of sarsaparilla as the greatest restorer of the appetite, flesh, colour, and strength, which he knew of; and, no doubt, it is in such consumptive cases, a medicine of eminent utility.

Is consumption contagious? Some eminent physicians answer decidedly in the negative; my answer is as decidedly in the affirmative. The human body is extremely sensitive to infection, and therefore no person should for any great length of time sleep with an invalid actually in a consumption, or even strongly disposed to it. Young members of the same family ought not to be constantly with such an invalid.

CONVULSIONS

Convulsions are violent and involuntary contractions of a part, or the whole of the body, accompanied in some cases with rigidity and tension, but more frequently with strong and sudden agitations. There is frequently a gnashing of the teeth, and a forcible clenching of the hands. Differences occur in the character of the disease in different persons, and depend upon the peculiar disposition, habit, or stage of life, in which it makes its appearance.

The symptoms indicating the approach of convulsions are often overlooked; in children especially they will most frequently be found to have been preceded by feverish symptoms, by drowsiness, yawning, sighing, increased irritability, frequent crying and peevishness, impatience of sound and light, or by some derangement of the process of digestion, or some peculiarity of respiration.

The most frequent *causes* of convulsion consist in pressure on the brain, or in irritation situated in some very sensitive organ, as the stomach, bowels, womb or kidneys. It frequently follows severe fright, and the suppression of an accustomed discharge. In adults it may arise from a strong excitement of the passions, and from sympathy; and in infants obscure inflammation of the brain is not an unfrequent cause, as is the case also with inflammation of the *glottis.*

Treatment—Give directly a glass or two of good wine, and the draught of ether and sal. volatile, No. 35B, page 159, and follow it in ten minutes with the aperient draught, No. 28, page 156, and one of the pills, No. 97, page 191. It is a primary object to procure a sufficient motion; and after that, tonics are usually the best remedies, with plenty of exercise. The pills, No. 102, 103, or 115, page 202, are suitable, and so is the mixture, No. 84 B, page 185. The head and face should be freely sponged with cold water. Twelve drops of liquid ammonia in water is excellent for relief in the fit.

The convulsions of infants invariably originate in some irritation in the brain, bowels or stomach, or from teething; and are most successfully treated by aperients or purgatives, and by the immediate use of a warm bath at about 98 or 100 degrees, giving in the intervals, some mild aperient occasionally, with plenty of free air and exercise, great attention being, at the same time, paid to diet. Half a grain of calomel and flve of rhubarb, form one of the best purgatives for exhibition during the fit, and to prevent its recurrence, the powder, No. 121, page 205, will be found very useful. If the stools are of an unhealthy colour, this powder should be given twice or thrice a week, till they recover a healthy appearance and the little patient looks well.

It is not advisable to abstract blood in the convulsions of infants or children, unless there should exist a full habit of body, and signs of an overloaded state of the vessels of the brain, or of inflammation in the brain, the principal of which signs are—warm, tumid scalp and face, flushed countenance, the fore part of the head *(fontanelle)* elevated and tense, eyes suffused with blood, quick, full, hard pulse, or one that is slow and oppressed, the veins of the head and neck large and dark. In this case leeches may be advantageously applied behind the ears; or the jugular vein may be punctured; but in general the means above advised are the most proper, to which we may add the free sprinkling of cold water over the face and head (which is one of the most powerful stimulants known), the application of smelling salts to the nostrils, and the rubbing the hands and feet well with eau de Cologne; or any mild stimulant. Purgatives cannot always be given immediately, from the children not having the power of swallowing, but the clyster No. 8, page 146, should be exhibited as speedily as possible. Should these ingredients not be easily procure the clyster may consist of some warm water, salt and oil or melted butter, which may be thrown up with a common syringe, *if Twinberrow's Syringe* is not at hand.

A great many children die in convulsions, the consequence of excessive feeding, and improper confinement within doors; and it will be well for mothers, whose infants are subject to convulsive fits, to be attentive to the quantity and quality of their food, and to their having sufficient exercise. I know a lady of rank, who lost as many as three or four infants (it may be more), in this way, and from this cause alone. The parents are both healthy, and the children were all full-grown, strong, and healthy at the birth, and appeared so for some months after; but they invariably died at about the age of twelve or sixteen months, evidently from improper treatment, though the too fond mother could never conceive the cause. The nurse and mother joined in stuffing them throughout the day, and thinking that they would perish if left without food during the night, it was a regular practice to take them up and feed them four times during that period![1]

Dr. Underwood correctly remarks, that when infantile convulsions prove suddenly fatal, they are commonly symptomatic, and are occasioned much oftener than is suspected by over-feeding. When, therefore, an infant falls suddenly into a convulsion very soon after sucking or feeding (more especially if on any thing actually improper), and the bowels have been some days in an orderly state, we may reasonably presume the irritation to be in the stomach; and in such instances, the fittest and most expeditious means of recovery consists in the prompt administration

1. I have known some of the largest and finest infants I have ever seen, die suddenly in the month, immediately after the nurse had boasted of their having eaten *three boats full of victuals!"—Dr. Underwood on Children's Diseases,* p. 246.

of an emetic, for as soon as the offending material is discharged, the child almost instantly begins to recover. As an emetic, three or four grains of ipecacuanha powder, or sulphate of zinc, dissolved in water, and given directly, will be found the most speedy in its operation, but as no time is to be lost in bad cases, and it will require some minutes at least to procure this medicine, the nurse ought to endeavour to provoke immediate vomiting, by irritating the back part of the throat with the finger or a feather, the child being, at the same time, supported by a hand placed under the stomach and belly, in which position it will be made to vomit more readily than in any other.

An examination of the state of the gums should always be made when convulsions take place during teething, and if they are even full, they ought to be scarified; but if they are inflamed, the scarification should be very free, so as not only to take away some blood from the part inflamed, but also to remove the whole tension of the gums and of the membrane which covers the tooth.[1]

There is a *peculiar kind of convulsions* found in infants and young children, connected with attacks of sonorous inspiration and a crowing sound, which merits particular attention. It consists in a peculiar mode of inspiration, which it is difficult accurately to describe : the convulsive affection occurs by fits, with longer or shorter intervals between them, and of longer or shorter duration in different cases. The child having had no apparent warning is suddenly seized with a spasmodic inspiration, consisting of distinct

---

1. "This membrane, under inflammation, becomes extremely sensible, to pain, and being stretched upon the tooth, requires to be entirely set at liberty. When convulsions occur in teething, the lenity of the surgeon who omits to destroy the inflamed gum sufficiently with the knife, is ill judged, and is in effect, the greatest cruelty, to the child. The writer has seen many cases in which convulsions have ceased on scarifying the gums extensively, after slight incisions of them have failed to produce any advantage. The late Mr. John Hunter, in his work on the subject of the teeth, mentions that he had scarified the gums of a child ten times, with manifest advantage each time, and a diminution of the symptoms which had arisen from the advancement of the tooth to the surface."—*The John Clarke on the Diseases of Children,* page 104. This is an extract from a very able work of a physician of great discernment, and who is deservedly a high authority in practical medicine.

attempts to fill the chest, between each of which a squeaking noise is often made; the eyes stare, and the child is evidently in great distress; the face and the extremities, if the fit continues long, become purple, the head is thrown backwards, wad the spine is often bent forwards; at length a strong expiration takes place, a fit of crying generally succeeds, and the child, evidently much exhausted, often falls asleep. These paroxysms usually occur many times in the day, and are often brought on by straining, by exercise, and by fretting, and sometimes they come on from no apparent cause. The child may die in one of these attacks. The complaint is often found during teething.

Accompanying the above symptoms, there is sometimes a bending of the toes downwards, clenching of the fists, and the insertion of the thumbs into the palms of the hands, not only during the paroxysm, but at other times.

The attacks commonly take place after a full meal, and often occur immediately upon waking from sleepy though before the time of waking the child had been lying in a most-tranquil state. This affection is sometimes called *chronic croup*, but it is totally different from croup, and seems to be owing to *a spasm and contraction of the glottis,* or top of the windpipe. It is technically called *Laryngismus Stridulus,* and by some *Childcrowing.*

Dr. John Cheyne says, in his work on water in the head, that the distinctive mark of this disease is "*a crowing inspiration with purple complexion, not followed by cough*". In some cases this affection is attended not merely with a permanent clenching of the hand upon the thumb, but also with a very remarkable fixed spasm of the toes, particularly the great toe, which gives a look of swelled deformity to the upper part of the foot.

This disease is unaccompanied by fever, or any material derangement of the general health. When cough attends, which is not always the case, it is not hoarse, and the breathing during the intervals is perfectly free. These circumstances distinguish it from croup.

Treatment—During the fit, the little patient should be instantly plunged into a warm bath at 98 degrees, and be kept in it for fifteen or twenty minutes, and whilst in the bath cold water should be freely sprinkled on the face. An injection of warm water and oil or soap should be instantly thrown up the rectum, and if tincture of assafoetida or oil of turpentine is at hand, one or two tea-spoonfuls may be mixed with the injection. Striking the child well on the back, and applying ammonia to the nostrils, are also advisable.

After recovery from the fits the treatment mainly consists in the administration of warm purgative, as No. 121, page 205, with two or three brains of mercury, with chalk, at bed-time—a well regulated diet,—and pure air. An immediate change into a very pure country air is of eminent service. The room the child inhabits should be large, and freely ventilated; and sometimes a little carbonate of ammonia, as in No. 79, page 181, will be found serviceable. When the head is evidently affected, leeches behind the ears are required; but if the cheeks of the child are cold and flabby, the abstraction of blood must be avoided.[1] I have seen this treatment of the utmost service. In one case the complaint had become chronic, and the catch or spasm on the breath of the infant, which frequently took place, was occasionally very alarming; the apothecary said nothing more could be done; however, the means now advised speedily restored the child, and it continues well.

In Puerperal Convulsions

Or the convulsions occurring in child-bed, the immediate cause is the peculiar irritation of the nervous system, as participating in the irritation of the womb; and hence it seems obvious, that the radical and specific cure is a termination of the labour. The first step is to open a vein and bleed copiously, and from a large orifice, till the patient faints; the hair should be immediately removed from the head, lotions of cold water, or pounded ice, be applied all over it

1. By giving the child the advantage of a pure air, and of a succession of good nurses, during the whole period of dentition, more good has appeared to be done than by all other measures put together. Dr. Marsh remarks, that all his cases occurred in children of a scrofulous constitution; a fact which leads him to insist stilt more strongly on the importance of a pure atmosphere, healthy nutriments and tonics.—*Cyclopaedia of Pract. Medicine,* vol. ii. p. 350.

by wetted napkins, changed for others as soon as they acquire the least degree of warmth. At the same time a purgative injection, (as No. 8, page 146, to which two drachms of assafoetida gum must be added), should be thrown up the rectum, which may be followed by two grains of calomel given by the mouth, with the purgative draught, No. 28, page 156.

If the mouth of the womb should be rigid, and but little dilated at the commencement of the convulsions, this depleting plan generally renders it lax and dilatable, when the midwife should without delay introduce the hand, slowly dilate the mouth of the womb, break the membranes, lay hold of the child's feet, and deliver by turning. This should be done although there be no distinct labour-pains, provided the mouth of the womb is open.

If the convulsions arise from excessive *haemorrhage,* and other sources of exhaustion, blood-letting would be improper. Then give henbane and camphor, as in No. 79, page 181 and No. 124A, page 206. Convulsions may be of an *hysterical* character. Then give brandy, ether, and sal volatile, as in No. 35B, page 159, and a purge.

CORNS

In their first formation, corns are the production of the outer skin alone, but by gradually thickening they come at length to be connected with the true skin beneath, and in some instances, even to proceed to the depth of the subjacent muscles. They are owing to repeated and long continued pressure.

The cure consists in removing pressure from the part, by wearing very easy shoes, and in cutting or paring the excrescence down as close as possible, without giving pain, after soaking them a little in warm water, when some stimulating preparation, as No. 46, p. 163, should be rubbed over it night and morning. The best applications are No. 46, the juice of house-leek, or purslane, or the compound ammoniac plaster, No. 132, page 210. Mr. Samuel Cooper, in his invaluable SURGICAL DICTIONARY, recommends the plaster, No. 139, page 214, as infallible. When the corn is on the sole of the foot, a felt sole should be put in the shoe, wherein a hole has been cut, corresponding to the situation, size and figure of the corn.

I cannot but think that the state of the general health even influences the growth of corns, because there are persons, who for life wear tight shoes, and take no care of their feet, and yet are never incommoded with corns, while others are constantly troubled with them, although they pay much attention to themselves; and because some are for a time vexed with corns, and then become quite free from them, though they continue to wear the same kind of shoes and stockings. Therefore, an attention to the improvement of the general health may sometimes have great effect in assisting us to remove corns.

COSTIVENESS

Habitual constipation is met with in two different descriptions of persons, that is, in those who are of a robust habit, with a hearty appetite and strong digestive powers; and in others who are of infirm or delicate health, with moderate or deficient appetite, and weak digestion. The motions of the former when discharged are compact and voluminous; those of the latter generally hard, slender and sometimes lumpy.

The first kind of costiveness seems to arise from an excess of action in the absorbent, or other vessels of the bowels, and from a free use of heating, astringent food, which such persons generally indulge in; while the other description depends upon weakness of the intestines, and a consequent sluggishness in the peristaltic motion. Both kinds are very much increased by all sorts of astringent food.

Whatever gives rise to an impaired nervous or muscular power in any part of the intestinal canal, may be a *cause* of costiveness. I would direct the reader's attention particularly to the following causes of the complaint, *viz* the use of heavy, adulterated bread; tea and other astringent beverages; spirits and other stimulant drinks; too long indulgence in sleep and too warm beds; excessive perspiration; contraction of the *colon* or *coecum*, or chronic inflammation there; contraction or stricture of the rectum; a deficiency of active exercise, and inattention to the first intimation to motion. Valvular disease of the heart, and affection of the kidneys, are also causes of scanty motions and constipation.

Costiveness in the human subject is now so common an evil, and one which may lead to such serious consequences; it is one so frequently a symptom of considerable disorder and mischief, and sometimes in itself an affection giving rise to the most painful feelings, and requiring so prompt and skilful a treatment, that I shall consult the interests of the public in treating it at some length, and offering here a sketch of the anatomy and physiology of the lower intestines.

The intestines are divided into the *small* and *large* intestines; the former are subdivided into the *duodenum, jejunum* and *ileum*, the latter into the *coecum*, *colon*, and *rectum*. The small intestines are usually thirty feet in length, or about five times the length of the body in the adult, and the large intestines about six feet, or one length of the body.[1] The younger the subject the longer is the intestinal canal. In an infant they have been found to be upwards of eleven times the length of the body.

The intestinal canal has three coats or membranes, *viz*. the peritoneal, the muscular and the mucous. The muscular coat of the *coecum* and *colon* is much paler and thinner, (while the muscular coat of the rectum is thicker), than that of the small intestines. The muscular membrane or coat both in the small and large intestines is composed of longitudinal and circular fibres, but the longitudinal fibres of the large intestines are united into three distinct bands, and are shorter than the intestine itself, so that they cause it to become puckered, shortened, as it were, and to present certain prominencies externally.

---

1. Bell says, about six feet *(Anatomy of the Human Body,* vol. iii. page 305, *sixth edition);* Cloquet says, " the total length of the large intestines is about seven feet in a man of ordinary size. It forms about the fifth of that of the small intestines". — *System of Anatomy*, page 619, *second edition.*

At the termination of the *ileum*, the large intestines begin by the *ileum* entering the *coecum*, which is inserted into it so as to form an acute angle below, and nearly a right angle above. Here a valve is formed, clearly marking the commencement of the large intestines, which valve is designed to prevent the regurgitation of the faeces into the small intestines. The length of the *coecum* is about three or four fingers-breadth; it is a round or slightly conical sac, divided into large cells, presenting on its outer surface large bulgings. Its volume is considerable, being often three times that of the small intestines, and surpasses that of the colon and rectum.

The *colon* is the most considerable and the most important portion of the large intestines. It ascends on the right side of the small intestines, until it gets under the margin of the liver, and in contact with the gall-bladder—then it takes a course across the belly, forming an arch (called the transverse arch of the colon) before or immediately under the stomach, above the small intestines,—then it descends, bending down on the left side, ending in the sigmoid flexure of the colon, which is formed by a narrowing and contraction, and closer adhesion of the gut to the loins below the left kidney, occupying the cup of the ileum on the left side. The colon then terminates in the *rectum,* the lower extremity of which terminates in the anus or fundament.

From this account, it is evident that the colon describes in the belly a circle which measures nearly its whole circumference, and which surrounds the convolutions of the small intestines. An engraving of the course of the larger bowels, and likewise one skewing the different regions of the abdomen, may be seen in the author's TREATISE ON THE DISEASES OF FAMALES. These engravings will materially aid the reader in understanding this subject.

The *rectum,* the last portion of the large intestines, falls into the pelvis, running down betwixt the sacrum, (the broad bone at the bottom of the spine), and bladder of urine. It has a strong muscular coat, and the mouths of many ducts or follicles open on its surface, in part the source of the mucous discharge, sometimes poured out in this gut.[1] It is cylindrical in the greater part of its

1. No intestine receives so many blood-vessels as the rectum in proportion to its volume." *Cloquet's Anatomy*, page 622, *second edition*,

extent; but near the fundament commonly presents a more or less considerable expansion. It is less voluminous than the coecum and colon, yet is susceptible of very great dilatation.

Digestion in the stomach consists chiefly in the solution of the food in the gastric juices, whereby a semi-fluid, opaque, yellowish-white mass is formed, called *chyme;* this after a time passes through the *pyloric*, or lower orifice of the stomach, into the small intestines, where it experiences other new and essential changes. The *chyme* which passes out of the stomach is a slimy homogeneous pulp, consisting of two parts, the smaller portion excrementitious, and the larger portion chylous or nutritive, and the office of the small intestines is the absorption into the blood of the nutritive part of the food, by the lacteal vessels opening on their internal surface.

One obvious use of the large intestines is to be a receptacle and reservoir for the useless part of the food; and especially for the fecal secretion from the blood. They are more capacious, though shorter, than the smaller bowels. The peculiar odour in the large intestines is supposed to proceed from a volatile oil, apparently secreted chiefly in the coecum. The *coecum* is considered a very important part of the large intestines also, because the last act of digestion is performed in it, an acid, albuminous, and solvent fluid being secreted for this purpose, by its large follicular glands,—and because it much retards the descent of the food and faeces.

Professional men have usually regarded the foeces as solely the excrementitious portion of the food, separated in the intestines from the nutritive part; but this is an error. The foeces are mainly a secretion from the blood—a secretion of worn-out material which nature seeks to expel by this channel; and hence we discover the principal cause of the various discomforts and injuries resulting from habitual constipation. It is a direct check on one of the most essential functions of digestion—of one of the most important means of purifying the blood, and aiding in the nutrition of the general frame. Under habitual constipation, the blood cannot be fully purified ; wornout and noxious matter is thrown back again upon the blood, to contaminate and obstruct all the vessels of the body. Hence arise acrid eructations, deficient appetite, nausea, confusion and pains in the head, cramps, giddiness and other painful feelings.[1]

The received opinion among physiologists is, that the faecal matter passes freely from the sigmoid flexure of the colon into the rectum, and gradually distends the latter until, by its pressure, such a sense of uneasiness is communicated to the sphincter muscle of the anus and perineum, as to rouse the diaphragm and abdominal muscles to effect its expulsion from the body. It seems also a general opinion, that an accumulation of the faeces ordinarily takes place in the pouch or lower portion of the rectum.

TREATMENT—In the first place, I warn the constipated not to depend on aperient medicine for their relief, for it never answers. It is a very injurious practice, the refuge of ignorance, always aggravating the evil. They must endeavour to conquer it by diet, exercise, friction, patience, and by resorting daily to the closet, and patiently soliciting nature. Some professional men,—yes, men of the best abilities—recommend to the habitually costive a pill every day before dinner, or every night at bed-time. Nothing can be more false in principle, or more injurious in practice than this. It deserves the severest reprobation, and is a proof how far astray able medical men will sometimes go. I do not believe there is any case of removable costiveness which will not be conquered by the

---

1. The internal surface of the intestinal canal is furnished with a vast number of glands, and Dr. Carpenter makes the following instructive remarks on their important uses (*Physiology*, page 431)— "There is strong reason to believe that the function of the numerous glands which beset the walls of the small intestines, and which are known as Brunner's and Peyer's glands (after the names of their discoverers), is purely excretory; and that they are destined to eliminate putrescent matters from the blood, and to convey them, by the readiest channel, completely out of the body. That the putrescent elements of the faeces are not immediately derived from the food taken in, so much as from the secreting action of the intestinal glands, appears from this consideration— that faecal matter is still discharged, even in considerable quantities, long after the intestinal tube has been completely emptied of its alimentary contents. We see this in the course of many diseases, when food is not taken for many days, during which time the bowels are completely emptied of their previous contents by repeated evacuations; and whatever then passes, must be derived from the intestinal walls themselves".

use of the water-closet every morning, giving plenty of time there for the bowels to act, together with a recourse to a laxative diet, friction, and exercise. The daily use of an aperient pill is apt to produce spasm, flatulence, and many of the worst symptoms of indigestion. Let the patient go to the water-closet regularly after breakfast every morning, and make use of a good deal of friction over the bowels while there, and stay till some movement is effected, and if this habit is acquired, few indeed will complain of want of success. Of course if the stools are scanty from valvular disease of the heart, a large motion can never be expected, but this habit will still be of great service, as assisting in the regular exoneration of the bowels without medicine. Aperient medicine *is peculiarly injurious in constipation from valvular disease of the heart.*

The powder of ipecacuanha is sometimes of service in the present disorder, and scarcely any medicine is so appropriate, since it is peculiarly well calculated to stimulate the digestive organs, and relieve the weakness upon which the constipation is generally dependent, at the same time that it relaxes the bowels and skin. I know no case in which it will fail to be beneficial, while in numerous instances, even when of long standing, it must prove of essential utility. Half a grain of the best ipecacuanha powder may be made into a pill with three grains of Castile soap, and taken before dinner and supper; or, one pill may be taken before dinner, and two every night at bed-time. This remedy has considerable effect in removing a dry, harsh state of the skin, and in curing cutaneous eruptions.

The *alkaline tincture of rhubarb* also is an excellent medicine in costiveness. It is made by infusing an ounce of rhubarb, grossly powdered, in a quart of the alkaline solution, (page 2), which after standing for a day or two, and being well shaken together several times during that period, is fit for use, when filtered or poured off clear. One tea-spoonful of this tincture may be taken every night at bed-time, in a tea-cupful of thin gruel, barley-water or fresh small beer. I found it of eminent utility in regulating the bowels of a gentleman residing in Hampshire, who had long been most severely harassed by costiveness, flatulence, pains in the lower belly, and other painful feelings dependent on a want of proper tone and action in the intestines. He used double the quantity of rhubarb ordered above.

The compound tincture of benjamin is one of the most valuable medicines which can be used in those cases of constipation in which the *coecum* and *colon* are much affected. In chronic inflammation of the mucous membrane of those parts it is of great service, in the dose of half a drachm, twice or thrice a day, rubbed up with a wine-glassful of mucilage of gum arabic and water in equal proportions.

When people will take physic, the aperients employed should be warm, aromatic, and very mild in their operation, but I advise their rejection altogether. The form of pill is generally by far the best for such persons, and if the means previously recommended fail, either No. 97, 100, 100A, or those prescribed at pages 191, 193, may be resorted to with advantage. Of laxative medicines, two of the best are sulphur, and the common Seidlitz powders. About a tea-spoonful of sulphur, and somethingless than half a tea-spoonful of cream of tartar, mixed with a little treacle, is a proper dose. The Seidlitz powders, and the powder, No 130A, page 196, are valuable in this complaint, because they operate in an unusually mild manner, and correct acidity in the stomach, without increasing their tendency to costiveness after their operation is over. The *Beaume de Vie* is a good medicine. Another very mild and valuable medicine is the *Mixture for Constipation and Acidity,* No. 23, in my volume *On Infancy and Childhood.*

In all cases of constipation purgatives must be avoided, for though they relieve the bowels for the time, their irritation invariably induces still greater weakness in the intestinal canal, which occasions more obstinate costiveness, and thus in reality aggravates the evil they were intended to remove.

In point of diet, great attention should be paid in avoiding all articles that are astringent, and in indulging moderately in those which are relaxing. Generally speaking, the patient will find that excess of diet will increase the costive habit, by disordering and still further weakening the bowels. The constant use of brown instead of white bread is a measure that will frequently overcome this habit, when aperient medicine is resorted to with only partial and unsatisfactory, benefit; and if, after a time, it should lose its effect, it may be alternated with bread make of one-third or one-half rye flour, mixed with the wheaten flour. Barley bread also has considerable effect in promoting a soluble state of the bowels, and so has barley-meal porridge. It is easily digested, and very wholesome. The self-acting clyster machine will likewise be a useful instrument in such cases for occasional use, and a little soap dissolved in warm water is, perhaps, the best fluid that can be thrown up. Active exercise in the open air should be freely employed, with daily friction over the region of the stomach and bowels. The hand alone may be used, or with either of the liniments at page 161.

A constipated habit of body is a fruitful source of many complaints, as piles, fistula, strictures of the rectum, general debility, lowness of spirits, head-aches and various other evils. The bowels are organs so sensible and important, that it should never be forgotten, that habitual constipation necessarily produces disorder, and disorder leads to disease; and the correction of this habit, therefore, deserves far more attention from the subjects of it than it commonly obtains. The most pleasant and effectual way of correcting it is by *draughts of cold water,* diet, friction, exercise, and the occasional use of the lavement or clyster machine, if necessary; but I believe it will be seldom requisite. It is an unwise and unsatisfactory plan for the constipated to trust chiefly or altogether to the frequent use of aperient medicine; this now and then interposed is sometimes of great service, but the relief gained by cold water, a vegetable and fruit diet, friction, and the occasional employment of the clyster machine, is more certain, permanent and beneficial. Twinberrow's *Injection Apparatus* is excellent for giving an enema, *see* page 146, and probably to be preferred to all others for all ordinary occasions.

If the state of the stomach does not forbid it, a little wholesome ripe fruit, as strawberries, raspberries, pears, or baked apples or pears, etc., should be taken frequently.

The means above recommended are certainly very useful, but I must do the cold *water system* (See *Appendix)* the justice of saying, that it is far more effectual in curing this habit than any thing else I have ever employed, or known to be used. A wet compress must be worn over the bowels night and day, and the patient should drink one tumbler of cold water before breakfast, and one every night at bed-time. All aperient medicine must be abandoned. I am quite certain the most obstinate cases of constipation may be *cured* in this way, having witnessed such results repeatedly.

Very obstinate attacks of constipation may be successfully treated by the introduction of a large-sized gum elastic tube (called O'Beirne's instrument) through the anus quite up into the sigmoid flexure of the colon—that is, the *gradual, cautious,* and *slow* introduction of this tube through its whole length, (eighteen inches,) up into the bowels, when the syringe in common use in the enema apparatus is adapted to the lower and of the tube, and a quart of tepid gruel being previously prepared, and mixed with two ounces of castor oil, the whole is pumped up. As soon as the surgeon or nurse begins to pump up this injection, the patient will ordinarily express a desire to go to stool, and be very urgent to be allowed to do so after every succeeding one; but the effect will be rendered much more complete by not complying with his entreaties, and persevering until the necessary quantity is thrown up, when the tube is to be slowly withdrawn. The moment this is done, he will rarely fail to hurry to the night-chair, and discharge a copious, and, in many instances, an enormous stool.

An injection composed of extract of colocynth, infusion of senna and gruel, or warm water, or any ordinary purgative injection, may be used when gruel and castor oil alone are insufficient.

O'Beirne's *Enema Machine* may be got at Weiss's, No. 62, or at Watts' No. 68, in the Strand.

When the bowels are so obstinately confined as to resist the action of strong purgatives, and from the long continuance of the constipation, to excite alarm, other means must be immediately resorted to, supposing O'Beirne's *Enema Apparatus* not to be at hand. Dr. Willan, who is justly considered a high authority in practical medicine, has. some valuable remarks on this subject, in his reports on the diseases of London, under the head of Constipatio, which I would here insert.

> By the term constipatio", says he, "is expressed not merely costiveness, but a stoppage of the bowels from some original or local affection, as rupture, scirrhosity, or stricture of some portion of the intestine, narrowing and often obliterating the canal. Tumours and concretions, external to the bowels, have occasionally the same effect. Strictures take place in different situations; but they occur so frequently about the sigmoid flexure of the intestine colon, near its termination in the rectum (or last gut), that this part should be carefully examined in every case of a total obstruction of the bowels. The insertion of an unyielding tallow candle, though often practised, has generally been found painful and inefficacious. It is requisite for the propose to employ a bougie thirteen inches long, and of a proportionate strength; which should also be directed with a nice hand, by a skilful surgeon. I lately saw a lady thus relieved, who had been twenty-six days without any evacuation from the bowels, and who seemed nearly exhausted by violence of pain and distention of the abdomen, incessant vomiting, hiccough, cold sweats, etc. It is remarkable how long patients suffer under these distressing circumstances. In one instance, the time was twenty-nine days; in another patient, thirty-three days. As the latter recovered, after enduring every torture such a disorder could inflict, practitioners may be encouraged to persevere steadily in their attentions, and to retain some hopes even in the greatest extremity".

If O'Beirne's Bougie or Twinberrow's *Injecting Apparatus*, fail in affording relief, cold water should be freely and suddenly dashed over the patient's belly and thighs: and where the habit of body is strong and plethoric, bleeding from the arm will often be advisable. One, two or three drops of croton oil is sometimes a valuable purgative in cases of obstinate costiveness. It may advantageously be mixed with half an ounce of castor oil, and one drachm of spirit of turpentine, and two table-spoonfuls of water, by rubbing the castor oil with the yolk of an egg, then adding the cuoton oil, and lastly the turpentine.

Sometimes constipation is occasioned by a stricture, or narrowing of the rectum, or last intestine, and then it can never be removed but by removing this contraction, in the manner pointed out under STRICTURE. Many persons so circumstanced are harassed for years by costiveness, and its numerous painful consequences, without at any time gaining more than very partial relief, because their chief complaint, which is the contraction now referred to, has been altogether overlooked.

When a total obstruction of the bowels is accompanied with severe pain, and a hard quick pulse, it is generally dependent on inflammation, and must be treated accordingly by copious blood-letting, calomel and opium combined, cold applications, etc. Here the obstinate constipation can be removed only by removing the inflammations and although this is so clear a case, yet I have known, in several instances, respectable physicians dwell so entirely on the obstruction, to the neglect of the inflammation, which was its only cause, that the patients perished for want of recourse to the proper measures. I would, therefore, warn the reader against this fatal, and perhaps not very unfrequent mistake.

COW-POX

The genuine inoculated cow-pox is distinguished by the following signs : the vehicle produced is single and confined to the puncture; cellular; bluish-brown in the middle; fluid, transparent, and colourless to the last; concreting into a hard, dark-coloured scab after the twelfth day. If the fluid be not transparent, it forms a decisive proof either that it is spurious or imperfect.

The general progress of the disease is as follows:—The puncture disappears soon after the insertion of the lancet; but on the third day a minute inflamed spot becomes visible. This gradually increases in size, hardens, and produces a small circular tumour, slightly elevated above the level of the skin. About the sixth day, the centre of the tumour shews a discoloured speck formed by the secretion of a minute quantity of fluid; the speck augments in size, and becomes a manifest vesicle, which continues to fill and to be distended till the tenth day; at which time it displays in perfection the peculiar features that distinguish it from the inoculated small-pox pustule. Its shape is circular, sometimes a little oval; but' the margin is always well turned, and never rough or jagged;

the centre dips instead of pointing, and is less elevated than the circumference.

In inoculating for the vaccine disease, the following circumstances should be carefully attended to.

First that the child to be vaccinated should be free from fever, and any eruption on the skin.

Second that the fluid should be taken between the fifth and ninth day.

Third that it should be perfectly transparent.

Fourth that if not used immediately, it should be dried gradually, and thoroughly, before it is laid by for future use.

Fifth that the punctures should be made as superficially as possible, and three punctures in each arm.

Sixth that any excess of inflammation that may arise should be repressed by the application of rag dipped in cold water or a cold lotion, as No. 68, page 173.

It is of the first consequence that vaccine lymph should be procured from the *National Vaccine Institution.* Pure vaccine lymph, taken at the proper period for vaccination, is amorphous and transparent. Examined by the microscope, it is found to contain no globules resembling those of either blood or pus.

If, in any doubtful case, the lymph, when so examined, is seen to contain any such corpuscles, it should not be used for the purpose of vaccination.

An important circumstance in relation to the mutual influence of the vaccine disease and other cutaneous affections, is the well-established fact that important varieties and modiflcations of the vaccine pustule are caused by herpetie and other eruptive states of the skin. Dr. Jenner, in a paper published in the *sixty-sixth number of the London Medical and Physical Journal*, points out the fact, that a single serous blotch existing upon the skin during the progress of the vaccine vesicle, may occasion such irregularity and deviation from the genuine course and character of the disease, that it cannot be depended on as a prophylactic against the small-pox infection. In a letter addressed by him to the medical profession generally, dated April, 1821, he observes : "I have found abrasions of the skin to produce the same effect—such, for example, as we find in the nurseries of the opulent, as well as in the cottages of the poor, behind the ears, and upon many other parts where the skin is tender. We find irregularity in the vaccine vesicle if the skin is beset with herpetic blotches or even simple serous oozings from an abraded cuticle. A speck behind the ear, which might be covered with a split pea, is capable of disordering the progress of the vaccine vesicle".

An attention to the following circumstances will enable us to distinguish the genuine from the spurious disease :

1. In the genuine cow-pox, little or no inflammation, except what occasionally arises from the mere puncture of the lancet, can be perceived until about the third day, and sometimes several days later. In the spurious affection, on the contrary, considerable inflammation and elevation of the skin at the punctured point, generally appears as early as the second day.

2. In the genuine disease, the small point of inflammation which appears three or four days after the matter is inserted, increases gradually until about the seventh day after its first appearance, at which time it is in its full state of perfection. In the spurious disease, the pustule arrives at maturity and finishes its course in a much shorter time. By the third or fifth day from the first appearance of the inflammation scabbing commences.

3. In genuine cow-pox, a beautiful circular and circumscribed areola almost always surrounds the pustule; and this areola efflorescence is usually in its perfect state about the seventh or eighth day. In spurious affections of this kind, an irregular superficial inflammation occurs on the first or second day after the appearance of the pustule; and the pustule itself appears more like a common festering sore produced by a thorn than a pustule excited by the vaccine virus.

4. The genuine pustule is perfectly circumscribed, with a flattened surface and a slightly depressed centre, and contains a colourless transparent fluid. The spurious pox is more elevated, not depressed in the centre, is irregular or angulated in its circumference, and contains an opaque, purulent matter.

According to Dr. Willan, the vaccine vesicle is to be regarded as imperfect when : 1. though perfect in its form and appearances, it is without an aerola on the ninth or tenth day; 2. when the vesicle is very small, pearl-coloured, flattened, with a hard, inflamed and slightly elevated base, a dark red aerola, and without a rounded or prominent margin; 3. when the vesicle is small, pointed, with a very extensive pale red aerola. The spurious disease may be produced—1. by the genuine vaccine virus acting on a system affected with some cutaneous disease; 2. by vaccinating with matter which has undergone more or less decomposition by long keeping; 3. by vaccinating with matter taken from a spurious pustule; and 4. by the genuine vaccine matter being controlled or in some way diverted from its regular operation by idiosyncrasy or a depraved condition of the system.

It is rase that any medical treatment is necessary. If the constitutional indisposition should be severe or necessary. Troublesome a dose or two of James's powder, and of aperient medicine, as No. 73, page 176, is all that will be required. If serious symptoms arise, no medicine is equal to ammonia, as in No. 78D, page 181.

The value of cow-pox as a prophylactic or safe-guard against small-pox, is now pretty certainly ascertained, and is generally admitted by professional men. Cases of the latter disease occurring after vaccination have unquestionably happened, and will continue to happen, as more or less negligence will always be evinced by some in selecting the genuine virus, and in attending to the regular progress of the vesicle, and the other points of moment above noticed; besides which the vaccine fluid does not prove a permanent preservative in a few articular habits, of the nature of which, however, we know nothing.

It is now generally admitted that the protective power of vaccination in any individual, is impaired by time, and that it is probably still further influenced by the change which takes place in the system at the time of manhood. It is, therefore, expedient to renew it, and to re-vaccinate every person about the age of eighteen.

CRAMP OR SPASM

The cramp is a sudden and rigid contraction of one or more muscles of the body, mostly of the stomach and limbs, which is vehemently painful, but of short duration.

The parts chiefly attacked with cramp are the calves of the legs, the neck and the stomach. When the muscles are affected, they feel as though they were puckered and drawn to a point or seem to be writhed and twisted into a hard knot; the pain is agonizing, and frequently produces a violent perspiration. If the stomach be the affected organ, the midriff associates in the constriction, and the breathing is short and distressing.

The usual *causes* are sudden exposure to cold, drinking cold liquids during great heat and perspiration, eating cold indigestible fruits, overstretching the muscles of the limbs, and the excitement of transferred gout. Impaired health and cold night air are common causes of cramp, and it is still a more frequent attendant upon swimming.

TREATMENT.—When it occurs in the limbs, warm friction with the naked hand or with a stimulating liniment, as No. 45, page 163, will generally be found to succeed in removing it.

Where the stomach is affected, a glass of brandy should be taken directly, and after that either, laudanum or tincture ginger afford the speediest means of cure. The following draught may be taken with great advantage.

Take of Laudanum	40	or 50 drops;
Tinture of ginger	2	drachms;
Syrup of poppies	1	drachm;
Cinnamon or mint water	1	ounce.

Mix, for a draught. To be repeated in an hour if necessary.

In severe cases, it will be advisable, at the same time, to apply hot flannels, either alone or moistened with the liniment, No. 46, page 163 ; and sometimes it may be found necessary to apply mustard poultices to the feet, which is often of great advantage. In the intervals, the patient should be particularly attentive to his diet, and to the regulation of the bowels, instructions for which will be found under the heads of INDIGFESTION AND COSTIVENESS. When the cause is constitutional, warm tonics, as Nos. 102, 104 or 106, pages 196-98, constant exercise, and a free state of the bowels are the best remedies. Those who are frequently attacked with this kind of pain will derive great advantage from the use of the means pointed out under *Pain in the Stomach;* but since in such cases the chief cause exists in a derangement of the general health, the most valuable information will be found under *General Principles*, at page 345, and the best remedies will be those that most effectually tend to enliven, comfort and invigorate the patient.

In spasm of the stomach, bowels or limbs, frequently occurring, I would direct the reader's attention particularly to two things, *viz* : 1. To an enquiry whether there may not be habitually some error in diet, either as it respects quantity or quality; 2. If great costiveness is present, there may be accumulation in the colon, which is frequently the cause of spasms. Should diarrhoea occasionally come on in costive habits, we have an additional reason for suspecting torpor of the colon. Then purgatives of calomel, and extract of colocynth, as in the pill No. 97, page 191, must be given, and O'Beirne's Enema Syringe be used. *See* page 493.

In alarming cramp of the stomach from transferred gout, a large dose of brandy and opium, with mustard poultices to the feet, will frequently save the patient from impending death.

CROUP

The croup is a violent and peculiar inflammation of the membrane lining the windpipe, and especially the *bronchia,* producing a secretion of an uncommon plastic kind, which assumes a concrete and membranous form, and lines the windpipe through a part or even the whole. of its course.[1] It is attended with a peculiar ringing

1. "The false membrane of croup corresponds exactly with the form of the canals which it covers. Its thickness is usually somewhat greater in the larynx and trachea than in the bronchia, and varies from less than half a line to a line. Its consistence is about that of boiled white of egg; but this usually- diminishes

sound of the voice, breathing permanently laborious and suffocative and fever. The essence of the disease consists in the secretion of this viscid and concrete lining, which is perpetually endangering suffocation.

Young children are chiefly subject to its attack, and those who have once had it are more susceptible of it than before, though the susceptibility gradually wears off as they grow older. It scarcely ever occurs after puberty. It sometimes terminates fatally within twenty-four hours, although when death happens, it more commonly occurs on the fourth or fifth day. In many cases the fate of the patient will be determined in twelve hours or even less.

The supervention of severe inflammation of the bronchia is the usual cause of death.

It commences usually with a slight cough, hoarseness, and sneezing, as though the patient had caught cold; to which succeeds, in a day or two, sometimes sooner, a peculiar shrillness and singing of the voice, as if the sound were sent through a brazen tube. In the progress of the disease, there is a sense of pain about the top of the windpipe, and a difficulty of breathing, with a wheezing sound in the inspiration, as if the passage of the air were straightened; the cough which attends is sometimes dry, and if any thing be spit up, it is a matter of purulent appearance, and sometimes films resembling portions of a membrane. There is a frequency of pulse, restlessness, and uneasy sense of heat; frequently a redness and swelling in the back part of the mouth, but sometimes no appearance of inflammation. The countenance exhibits great distress; the head and face are covered with perspiration from the violence of the struggles; and the lips and cheeks are alternately pale and livid. Many of the symptoms enumerated above may exist without much present danger, this being usually to be measured chiefly by the difficulty of breathing, and the state of the pulse. Hoarseness, a hard ringing cough, and a crowing inspiration may exist without

---

towards its extremities, so that it becomes sometimes, in this situation, scarcely more solid than the thick phlegm of catarrh. It is of a white colour, with some times a shade of yellow, and is almost entirely opaque."—*Laeunec on Diseases of the Chest*, p. 124, *third edition*.

danger; but when the breathing is audible and difficult, and the pulse hard and frequent, accompanied with much fever, the case calls for the most vigilant attention, and most active treatment.

The preceding is the *first stage* of the malady; the second is denoted by a husky and suffocative cough, rather than one loud and sonorous; the voice is whispering; the respiration wheezing; the countenance pale; the eye languid; the pupils dilated; the tongue loaded and with purplish edges; the skin much less hot; and the stools dark and fetid. From this *second stage* of croup comparatively few patients recover. Should the disease advance to a fatal termination, the eyes become hollow; the countenance sinks; the extremities grow cold; the breathing becomes frequent, interrupted, and laborious; and great restlessness is manifested.

The power of swallowing is unimpaired.

Whatever tends to weaken the system or produce any degree of irritation in the lungs, may be considered to predispose to this alarming complaint; and it is, therefore, not difficult to account for the greater frequency of the disease in later than in former times, since the modern system of bringing up children is so much more sedentary and luxurious than that formerly pursued, and, therefore, more likely to weaken the organs of the chest, together with the general constitution. General weakness, no doubt, disposes to it; and it is certain, that all diseases originating directly or more remotely, in a delicate and irritable state of body, are greatly multiplied of late years. Cold is the principal exciting cause; and it is most frequent in winter and spring, in marshy situations, and near the sea-coast. It is probable that certain disordered states of the digestive organs materially assist in producing it. Particular families are severely affected by it, at which we cannot be surprised. It is not contagious.

There is a disease which often attacks the superior part of the wind-pipe, and especially of infants and children, which has so near a resemblance to croup, as to be very generally confounded with it : it is called *spasmodic croup* or *child crowing* by some authors, and *the acute asthma of infants* by others; and is described at page 480-81 ; but notwithstanding the resemblance of many of its symptoms, it is essentially different, and may generally be easily distinguished from it. The *acute asthma* comes on suddenly, and generally in the night; it is intermitting, the spasm subsiding in a short time, though it may return in an hour or two or less, but *in the interval the patient enjoys perfect ease,* although the voice is rendered hoarse from the previous straining. On the contrary, *the croup* very rarely commences abruptly, for it has usually the precursive symptoms of a slight cough and hoarseness for a day or two, and it commonly begins in the day-time; it is not intermittent, but when the inflammation has once taken effect, it becomes a permanent cause of excitement, and the anxiety and struggle continue with little, if any abatement, till the inflammation is subdued or death ensues.

Hysterics sometimes mimic croup. A young lady has been known to be attacked with a croupy cough, wheezing, uneasiness at the top of the wind-pipe, etc., which has deceived her medical attendant in the onset, but who on finding that blood letting, etc. was not applicable to the cure, has cured his patient with draughts of camphor and ammonia, with alteratives. The age of the patient is a material assistant here, in ascertaining the nature of the case, croup not occurring in adult age, and hysterics being as rare before puberty.

TREATMENT—The safest, most powerful, and most speedy remedy in croup is the TARTAR EMETIC; all other means are very unsatisfactory when compared to it. Therefore, I advise an *immediate* recourse to the tartar emetic, which should be given to children as young as two or three years, in half-grain doses, (in water,) every half-hour, tull full *vomiting* supervenes. When the vomiting has subsided two hours, the tartar emetic should be recommenced and continued as before, and thus we may continue to treat the patient till the disease is evidently arrested in its progress, when it may be continued in the smaller doses of a quarter of a grain every two, three or four hours.

It is a common practice with medical men to give three, four, and even five grains of calomel at a dose, and to repeat it frequently even to very young children; but this is unnecessary, and is certainly attended with danger; for, in several instances, the inflammation of the wind-pipe has suddenly given way under the employment of such large doses of the mineral, and has been immediately followed by a violent inflammation of the bowels, which has proceeded to a fatal termination, in spite of every remedy that great skill and experience could suggest. In this disease calomel in any quantity cannot be depended on. *Tartar emetic* is worthy of all confidence alone; the addition of calomel, except as a purgative, is altogether unnecessary, and would therefore be bad practice. One powerful efficient remedy is better than many inferior and uncertain ones.

A local warm bath should be instantly applied, and even when the disease is intense, Dr. Graves says:

"The disease may be arrested in its progress by the adoption of the immediate application of hot water in the following manner : A sponge about the size of a large fist, dipped in water as hot as the hand can bear, must be gently squeezed half dry, and instantly applied under the little sufferer's chin over the larynx and wind-pipe," (that is, at the top of the throat); "when the sponge has been thus held fur a few minutes in contact with the skin, its temperature begins to sink; a second sponge heated in the same way should be used alternately with the first. A perseverance in this plan during; ten or twenty minutes, produces a vivid redness of the skin over the whole front of the throat, just as if a strong mustard poultice had been applied; this redness must not be attended or followed by blistering of the skin. In the meantime the whole system feels the influence of the throat treatment; a warm perspiration breaks out, which will be encouraged by warm drinks, as whey; weak tea, etc., and a notable diminution takes place in the frequency and tone of the cough, while the hoarseness almost disappear, and the rough, ringing sound of voice subsides along with the difficulty of breathing and restlessness in short, all danger is over, and the little patient again falls asleep, and awakes in the morning without any appearance of having recently suffered from so dangerous an attack. I have repeatedly treated the disease on this plan, and with the most uniform success. It is, however, only applicable at the very onset of the disease, but it has the advantage of being simple, efficacious, and easily put in practice, and it's effects are not productive of the least injury to the constitution".

Very copious general bleeding at the commencement of the

attack leas occasionally carried off the disease at once, but leeches will usually be found to answer best in infants.

The bowels should be opened early by the exhibition of an active purgative, such as three grains of calomel with ten grains of rhubarb.

Blistering is of doubtful advantage, and I would never torture a child by resorting to it in the active stage of this complaint. After the violence of the symptoms has been subdued by the foregoing means, a blister is likely to be serviceable as an assistant in perfecting the cure, and making it permanent. But it should never be applied on the throat. The best place is on the nape of the neck or the pit of the stomach.

M. Jadelot, whose opportunities of treating this fatal disease have been very numerous, as senior physician to the Hospital for children in Paris, employed most frequently in its treatment bleeding by leeches and emetics. Emetics alone in his practice have often been sufficient to stop the disease, especially in weak, pale or bloated subjects; but in stronger children, he orders the application of leeches, and allows the blood to flow until the child becomes pale, and the pulse loses its strength. After bleeding he causes vomiting several times in succession, as ordered above; and the practice is said to be attended with the greatest success, relief being very apparent after each vomit. This is the course M. Jadelot pursues in almost all cases, whether he is called early or not till the second stage of the malady, and likewise when the disease is very rapid. The emetic he appears to prefer is a combination of infusion of seneka with the emetic tartar and squills. In reality the emetic tartar does the business. Now and then the medicines may fail to excite vomiting, when the back part of the throat (*pharnyx*) should be irritated with a feather.

When the fits are alarmingly severe, with spasm and threatened suffocation, nothing is of so much service as the *tartar emetic.*

After the first and acute symptoms have been conquered, to relieve the febrile symptoms, the mixture No. 81, page 183 or the draught No. 24, page 153, may be given as there directed. The tincture of digitalis, in the close of five or six drops every four hours, has been recommended as being very serviceable, but it is not to be depended upon at the height of the disease; when the patient. is recovering, it may sometimes be a useful assistant. The decoction of seneka will likewise be a valuable medicine in some instances, at the same period. It has seemed powerfully to assist the separation of the membranous concretion within the windpipe. *See* page 112.

If the pulse becomes fuller, more steady, and less frequent, the breathing freer, and less hurried, the peculiar sound of the voice and cough begin to wear off, and the patient appears less anxious and oppressed, the prognostic is good; but we cannot with certainty rely on the favourable change till the remission has lasted a considerable time; for, after the most favourable appearances, the disease has returned with greater violence, and provéd fatal. It is, therefore, of the utmost importance that the means of coure should not be abandoned too early. The practitioner should be particularly on his guard where the patient, though he may have obtained a great freedom in breathing, still remains dejected and oppressed.

When symptoms of dejection and exhaustion supervene, after the disease has been subdued by the preceding means, small doses of ammonia and camphor, as in No. 79, page 181, may be administered with good effect.

Should the disease have been subdued by the use of the means above recommended, the utmost attention to the diet and regimen of the patient is absolutely necessary for many days. Now and then the alarming symptoms will return in full force, and then the medical attendant has to begin again with bleeding and emetic tartar, as if he was treating the malady for the first time.

When all the foregoing means prove unsuccessful, and the difficulty of breathing greatly increases, it has been recommended by some practitioners to make a small opening into the windpipe, in order to prevent suffocation. This operation, which is called *tracheotomy,* is by no means formidable in very skilful hands; it may be done in a few minutes, and in extreme cases it is said to have saved the patient from impending death. I doubt, however, whether it is applicable to croup; it is certainly called for in extreme cases of inflammation of the larynx. Dr. J. Cheyne's remarks *(Pathology of the Larynx and Bronchia,* p. 41, 1809), which are unfavourable to the operation, are undoubtedly just.

The diet during the inflammatory stage should be very spare, and consist only of farinaceous decoctions, as thin gruel, toast-water, etc.

Croup has become a frequent complaint of late years, but is by no means so common as some people suppose, a deep-croaking cough, and the infantile acute asthma, (which is a spasmodic complaint), being often mistaken for it. The best means to prevent a recurrence of this disease in those who have been attacked with it, and to ward off its occurrence in those who appear disposed to it, from family make and constitution or other causes, are *the use of a good air, and plenty of it daily,* tonic medicines, as No. 78A or 78D, pages 180-81, the cold bath or sponging, a nutritious diet of easy digestion, a strict attention to the state of the bowels, active exercise and guarding against taking cold.

Croup now and then assumes a chronic character, and runs on for many days or even weeks. In such cases, the most effectual remedies are an occasional antimonial emetic, blisters on the chest or between the shoulders, a spare though nurtitious diets and *plenty of good country air*—the patient must be taken daily into the air. When the croup fits occasionally return during several weeks or months, and the foregoing means fail in preventing their recurrence, assafoetida will sometimes remove them entirely.

CUTS

Generally speaking, all that is necessary to be done in case of incised wounds or cuts, is to clear away the surrounding blood, with all extraneous substances, and then to bring the lips of the wound neatly and closely together, retaining them in that position by slips of adhesive plaster, spread on linen; and if the cut be deep and extensive, supporting it and the surrounding parts by a bandage.

In large wounds, interstices should be carefully left between each of the slips of plaster, to facilitate the escape of secreted matter or effused blood. The first dressings should remain on untouched for three or four days; and if much pain or inflammation follows the accident, a little of the aperient mixture No. 73, will be advisable, with the pill No. 98, page 191, every night, and a spare diet.

The bleeding consequent upon wounds may generally be stopped by pressure and rest, which is the best mode. The application of cobweb may, however, be resorted to, and is sometimes useful in obstinate bleeding from cuts.

Formerly, it was the common practice of surgeons to sew up long or deep wounds with the needle, but this is now rarely done, and may almost always be avoided. 'The lips of the most severe cuts can generally be retained in contact much better, and with far less irritation, by means of adhesive plaster and a bandage, than by any ligature.

In cuts which nearly separate any particular member of the body, a finger for example, a union by the foregoing means ought to be invariably attempted, and will usually succeed if the attempt be made without delay. It is well known that even the nose, after being nearly or quite separated from the face, has been perfectly united to it again by means of strips of adhesive plaster.

For slight cuts with a knife or any other sharp instrument either the Riga balsam or Friar's balsam is an excellent application. It usually stops the bleeding immediately.

In case of a cut that penetrates to, and divides an artery, the tourniquet must be immediately applied a little above the injury, until the assistance of a skilful surgeon can be obtained. If a tourniquet is not at hand, a hard conical compress should be made, and fixed over the seat of injury, the conical point being placed as near as possible over the mouth of the bleeding vessel. In defect of any thing better, a conical compress may be made with farthings, half-pence, and penny pieces, arranged and bound up in a piece of linen.

DEAFNESS

By deafness is usually meant a total inability of hearing or distinguishing sounds; but in this place that term will also include hardness of hearing, in which this faculty is so diminished, that articulated sounds can be heard only with considerable difficulty or with the assistance of a particular apparatus.

Deafness most commonly originates either from some organic defect or impediment or from local debility or relaxation.

The organic defect may exist in the outer or inner entrance or in the cavity of the ear. The outer entrance has sometimes been closed by a preternatural membrane, which may be situated either superficially or deep in the external cavity of the ear; sometimes it has been blocked up by indurated wax, insects or other extraneous substances. Obstruction of the Eustachian tube is often a cause of a considerable degree of deafness; or it may arise from ulceration or some other affection of the tympanum or drum of the ear; or from an insensible state of the auditory nerve or of the surfaces on which its filaments are spread. If the defect exist in the internal cavity of the ear, its precise nature can seldom be known during life, and if known, would rarely admit of a remedy.

Deafness dependent on local debility or relaxation, may be induced by a cold, a long exposure to loud and deafening noises, various fevers, and inflammations, rheumatism, head-ache and repelled cutaneous eruptions.

TREATMENT—The particular plan of treatment to be pursued will depend on the nature of the cause giving rise to the deafness, and must, therefore, vary considerably in different cases; and the exercise of great attention will frequently be necessary in order to ascertain the real nature of the case. Children are sometimes born with a preternatural membrane, which closes the external opening of the ear, and then this membrane must be carefully divided with a small knife, the flaps be cut away, a tent of a suitable size be introduced into the opening, and the wound be thus kept constantly dilated, until it be completely healed.

If the hardness of hearing be owing to the lodgment of indurated wax, the patient, besides his inability to hear, complains of noises, particularly a clash or confused sound in mastication, and of heavy sounds, like the ponderous strokes of a hammer. The most speedy and effectual way of removing the hardened wax, is by syringing the ear with warm water and soap, three or four times a day, until it is brought away. A large syringe, capable of holding six or eight ounces of water, should be employed for this purpose; and the evening before the syringe is used, a little sweet oil may be dropped into the ear.

Insects, and foreign bodies lodged in the ear, frequently occasion deafness, and sometimes give rise to extraordinary symptoms. Cherry-stones, peas or other small bodies, may generally be extracted by a pair of forceps, a little oil of almonds being first injected; and wormns or other insects are most certainly dislodged by introducing into the ear some bitter oil, which is fetal to these animals. One of the best oils for this purpose is an infusion of tobacco in oil of almonds.

The external passage of the ear is occasionally too narrow for the admission of a due quantity of the sonorous undulations, and the sense of hearing is of course impaired. If this depends upon malformation of the bone, it is manifestly incurable; but if it is owing to a thickening of the soft parts within the passage, great good may in general be gained by gradually dilating the passage with tents, which should be increased in size from time to time; and lastly, making the patient wear, for a considerable period, a tube, adopted to the part in shape. Sometimes it may be advisable to inject into the passage a strong solution of lunar caustic, in order to produce a detachment of the thickened portions of the skin. Mr. Earle of London, cured a patient of hardness of hearing depending on a narrowness of the external passage, by the solution of lunar caustic.

Sulphuric ether has been declared to be very efficacious in the cure of deafness (see *Bulletin de Therapeutique,* 30 April, 1860). From four to eight drops are to be daily dropped into each ear of children, and double the quantity into the ears of adults.

Deafness, depending on an eruption of small ulcers affecting the external passages of the ear, is, for the most part, curable. In such cases, the ichor, which exudes, from the pores of the ulcerated surface, thickens in the passage, and not only obstructs the entrance of sound, but is accompanied with a great degree of fetor. Here the alterative pill No. 98 or 99, page 181, should be given every ether night, and the ear be injected, once or twice a day, with the lotion No. 70, page 174 or with a lotion made by dissolving four grains of bi-chloride of mercury in a pint, of lime-water. The ointment No. 89, page 188, is also a useful application. Sarsaparilla and small doses of bi-chloride of mercury given internally are an admirable remedy. *See* page 15.

I know an old woman who was cured of deafness by having salt, first well dried, blown into her ears.

When deafness originates from disease of the tympanum or cavity directly under the drum of the ear, there is usually a discharge of pus, and the treatment is the same as advised in the last paragraph. In this state blisters or setons behind the ear or between the shoulders, may also be advantageously employed.

Obstruction of the Eustachian tube, which runs from the back part of the mouth into the internal cavity of the ear, is often a cause of a considerable degree of deafness; because it is necessary for perfect hearing, that air should be conveyed from the mouth through this passage into the cavity of the tympanum, which now can no longer happen. When this tube is obstructed, the patient cannot feel the drum crackle, as it were, in his ear, on blowing forcibly with his nose and mouth stopped. Previous ulceration or disease of the throat, will assist us in ascertaining the nature of the case, since it generally arises from ulceration in the superior part of the throat or from a very severe cold. The most effectual remedy for this kind of deafness, consists in making a small puncture in the membrane of the tympanum. Sir Astley Cooper first recommended this operation, and he resorted to it successfully in several instances.

Nervous deafness is accompanied with various complaints in different cases;—noises in the head of sundry kinds, the murmuring of waters, the hissing of a boiling kettle, rustling of leaves, blowing of wind, etc. Other patients speak of a beating noise, corresponding with the pulse, and increased by bodily exertion, in the same degree as the action of the heart. The treatment proper in nervous deafness, consists in administering tonic medicines during the day, as No. 102, 103 or 115, pages 196, 202, together with a mercurial alterative at night, as No. 99, page 192, and occasional aperients. If the patient be of a spare habit, the aperient pill, No. 100, 101, 101A or B, will be most proper; if of a full habit, the draught No. 27 or 28, pages 155-56, should be preferred. A blister should likewise be applied behind the ears, once in eight or ten days, and electricity is in some cases very useful. Electricity is considered hurtful by most writers, when the patient is very irritable, and subject to vertigo, bleeding from the nose, and great determination of blood to the head. The fumes of tobacco have sometimes been perfectly successful in this and other kinds of deafness. They are to be drawn into the mouth, and forcibly pressed against the Eustachian tubes by closing the lips and nostrils, and then urgently sniffing the vapour upwards to the palate. The late Mr. Grosvenor, an eminent surgeon at Oxford, is said to have been cured of severe deafness by the use of tobacco smoke.

Glycerine has been very strongly recommended by Mr. Wakley, surgeon to the Royal Free Hospital, London, for that particular kind of deafness arising from a thickening of the passage *(meatus)* down to the tympanum or drum of the ear. In this case there is a greater or less degree of deafness, corresponding with the amount of thickening; cessation. of the secretion of wax; and frequently singing or hissing in the ears. In applying the *Glycerine*, the *meatus* or external opening of the ear is to be well cleansed with tepid water by means of cotton used with the forceps. Mr. Wakley says—*Lancet*, 15th May, 1852, p. 467.

> "The *Glycerine* is now poured into the ear, and a plug of gutta percha, softened in boiling water, made to fit the external opening; this takes the exact form of the ear, becomes hard, and effectually prevents either the entrance of atmospheric air or the exit of the glycerine. The ear should be examined daily, and the same process repeated. The lining membrane can be examined with a blunt silver probe, passed gently through the speculum auris, to ascertain the effect of

the glycerine upon the articular thickening. The *meatus* or opening; will gradually lose its shining pearly appearance, and softened pieces will fall off, and can be removed either by the forceps or gently syringing. The practitioner should never attempt to tear them away, but allow them to come away by the means just stated. The treatment occupies ordinarily from two to four weeks, and is generally without pain or inconvenience of any kind to the patient, and the results, in some cases, have been very gratifying."

Galvanism is sometimes useful; or the magnet may be tried, as recommended under CHRONIC RHEUMATISM. I have lately heard of a person who derived great benefit from the use of the magnet.

Polypus or fungous excrescences in the ears, will sometimes bear to be remove by ligature or the knife, but great caution is necessary in resorting to these measures.

Mr. Abernethy thought diseases of the ears require a soothing plan of treatment, and he was, therefore, averse to any experimental or irritating measures. He believed deafness might often be relieved by improving the condition of the digestive organs, and relates, that a gentleman applied to him for what he thought a syphilitic affection; Mr. Abernethy assured him it was no such thing, and recommended attention to diet and regimen, with five grains of blue pill, to be taken every other night, and a pint of compound decoction of sarsaparilla, in divided portions, in the course of the day; by these means, besides being freed from his disorder, he was cured of a great portion of habitual deafness. Undoubtedly deafness is often dependent on deranged health, and the remarks made under GENERAL PRINCIPLES, page 338, are worthy of attention.

DELIRIUM TREMENS (*Brain Fever of Drunkards*)

This complaint is characterised by general inquietude, tremor, continued watchfulnas cool moist skin, perspiration, delirious loquacity and illusion. It occurs only in *habitual* drunkards, and in such as are addicted to the inordinate use of opium or other narcotic stimulants. So long as the customary quantity of the stimulus is taken, the disease seldom, if ever, supervenes, but if from necessity or a temporary disgust, the ordinary stimulating potations are suddenly left off; or greatly diminished, then the activity of the brain becomes morbidly increased, and mental disorder, in many instances, speedily ensues.

The principal *symptoms* are want of appetite, nausea, and vomiting, giddiness, a sense of confusion in the head, want of sleep, an anxious expression of the countenance, and tremor of the hands. Then the patient exhibits an expression of alarm and suspicion, the eyes are cast about with quick and scrutinizing glances or apparently fixed upon some particular object; the tremor of the hands increases; the patient becomes irritable, and sometimes irascible; he is extremely restless, walks continually to and fro, and is unable to obtain a moment's sleep. After this follows mental disorder, loquaciousness, and a continued succession of various alarming, disgusting, and ludicrous *apparitions.* He fancies he sees dogs, snakes, cats, mice and other animals in his room or that various persons have entered his room for the purpose of robbing killing or annoying him; and to avoid these he runs to the door to make his escape or to the window to leap out, and sometimes raves violently. He often starts with terror and agitation.

The pulse varies considerably in different cases, being sometimes hard, full and frequent, but much more frequently soft, full and quick, without strength or tension. The tongue and skin are moist, the urine abundant and the pupil dilated. The bowels are usually torpid, with an entire loathing of food throughout the whole course of the disease.

TREATMENT—Tincture of digitalis, tartar emetic, opium and tincture of hops are the sheet, anchors in this disease. They afford a gentle support to the brain, quiet nervous disturbance and favour the return of sleep—the grand desideratum. In many cases, the patient must *sleep or die.* Let a black draught be given immediately, with a pill, composed of two grains of calomel, and four of compound extract of colocynth. Its free operation generally sensibly relieves the patient, particularly if young and of a full strong habit. In weakly subjects, half the above quantity of the purgative will be sufficient or a table-spoonful of castor oil may be given instead.

Should the patient be young and robust, cold cloths to the head, and active purgatives are essential, and perhaps twelve leeches to the head; but in old, debilitated and confirmed drunkards, these means would not be advisable, but digitalis or opium should be given at once, together with a mild aperient. Give two grains of opium every two hours, to be continued until sleep ensues. Should opium induce a contraction of the pupil, it must not be repeated. If opium particularly disagrees with the patient's habit, half an ounce of tincture of hops may be given every two hours, alternately with the opium, when, after one, two or three doses, the patient is found susceptible to the influence of the narcotic, the interval of its administration should be lengthened to four hours or more or the quantity diminished—or tincture of digitalis would probably be better still. Upon his awaking from the first sleep, should the least tendency to wandering or incoherence remain, the medicine is to be given in smaller quantities so as to control this tendency.

Tincture of digitalis has been strongly recommended as having been, in many instances, effectual in sending the patient to sleep, after opium had failed. Half a drachm or a drachm may be given in water, every two hours, till sleep is induced.

Sometimes the debility is so great, that the moderate use of opium alone is not sufficient to counteract it, and there is danger of fatal prostration, unless the patient receive further support. In such cases a little malt liquor or wine must be allowed, such as a quart of ale or porter or four or five glasses of good wine in twenty-four hours. In extreme cases of exhaustion, a little brandy may be necessary to sustain a due strength of pulse.

To obviate excessive tremors and tendency to convulsion, nothing is equal to sesqui-carbonate of ammonia, (No. 79, page 181). Ammonia is a most valuable remedy in this complaint, and should never be neglected. Musk is also recommended, and sal volatile or what is better, two or three drachms of compound spirit of sulphuric ether, and two drachms of assafoetida, in water, every two hours.

Irritability of the stomach may be relieved by lime water and milk, effervescing draughts, soda water, sal volatile, and a mustard plaster or blister to the pit of the stomach; and should opiates be rejected from the stomach, they may be administered in double the quantity by the rectum.

In very obstinate cases of sleeplessness, which resist tire usual measures, and persist for a week or more, a blister over the whole scalp sometimes has a very happy effect or a linen bandage wet with the coldest water may be applied to the head, and be frequently renewed. When the disease has long resisted opium, sleep has repeatedly been induced by inhaling ether. Another *admirable remedy* to procure sleep is Dr. Graves's mixture, No. 87B, page 187, the quantity of laudanum ordered being doubled. *See* also page 370.

The best diet ordinarily is broth, egg and wine, farinaceous substances, milk punch and a little animal food.

I am a decided enemy to blood-letting in this malady. Cupping will be useful if the patient is young and of vigorous constitution, and there exists much vascular turgescence of the head, and a state of delirium approaching the raving of *phrenitis* or inflammation of the brain.

DIABETES

Diabetes is a considerable discharge of urine, for the most part excessive, of a violet smell and sweet taste, and attended with great thirst and general debility.

It often makes its approach insidiously, and may arise to a considerable degree, and exist for some weeks without being particularly noticed. It is attended mostly with a most voracious appetite; an insatiable thirst; a dry harsh skin; a white and foul tongue, sometimes unnaturally clean and red; depraved taste, a sense of weight or even acute pain in the loins; and frequently with a hay-like scent or odour in the breath, and issuing from the body. The kidneys discharge a fluid usually very limped and large in quantity, though sometimes tinged with green, like a diluted mixture of honey and water, and possessing a sweet taste more or less powerful; the pulse is quicker than in health; the flesh wastes rapidly; and in a very advanced stage of the disease, the feet and legs swell, and the skin becomes cold and damp. A troublesome costiveness frequently attends, and often disease of the lungs.

The quantity of urine evacuated by diabetic patients is generally profuse, and in some instances, has amounted to the astonishing increase of sixteen or twenty quarts in twenty-four hours.

This disease is occasionally to be met with in early life, but generally occurs at a more advanced period, especially in constitutions broken down by intemperance. The *predisposing* and *exciting causes* are chiefly such as debilitate the general system, as the abuse of spirituous liquors, cold applied to the body, immoderate evacuations, crude unwholesome diet, and the excessive use of mercury. It is most frequently met with in men, and it seems to prevail in particular families.

Medical men differ respecting the *immediate cause* of diabetes, but the most general opinion is, that it is dependent upon a morbid action of the stomach and other digestive organs, which necessarily, therefore, constitute its real seat. This is the opinion of the present author, who, however, conceives the explanation to be incomplete without admitting the existence of a peculiar condition of the kidneys, and more especially of the blood.

The *distinguishing sign* of diabetes is the presence of sugar in the urine. Every excessive urinal flow unaccompanied by this symptom, belongs to or forms a different complaint, and is very generally the consequence of some nervous disorder or of a simple relaxation of the univerous tubes.

TREATMENT—The objects are *to restore the general health and digestive energies of the frame; and to diminish the quantity, and improve the quality of the secretion from the kidneys.*

The most successful plan of treatment hitherto discovered, consists in a strict adherence, both in regard to quantity and quality, to the most wholesome diet chiefly of animal food, together with regular exercise in the country, and the use of tonic, astringent and narcotic medicines, the most efficacious of which are the mineral acids, particularly the nitric,—lime-water,—bark,— ammonia,—

whortle-berry powder,— preparations of steel and opium. Blood-letting also is sometimes advisable, but requires the exercise of a nice discrimination. In this disease, the animal salts are deficient in the urine, while sugar is secreted in considerable quantity, and these means are calculated to yield the former, and to counteract the latter, at the same time that they are capable of correcting the morbid action of the digestive organs.

Mercury in every form is decidedly injurious. Dr. Watson has known *creosote* useful and Dr. Barlow thinks highly of ammonia, and so does the present author.

The nitric acid is a medicine of great importance, as it is both tonic and astringent, and it has, in several cases of diabetes, been found to succeed alone. Dr. Gilby of Birmingham, relates instances of its success, and Mr. Earnest has given a striking proof of its value in the thirteenth volume of the London Medical Journal. It may be taken in the following way :

Take of Nitric acid........................	1½	drachm;
Barley water............................	9	ounces;
Simple syrup	1	ounce.

Mix, and take two table-spoonfuls in the like quantity of water, three times a day, gradually increasing the dose to four table-spoonfuls.

The late Dr. Ferrier of Manchester, recommended a combination of bark, whortle-berry and opium, after having used it with success, and it is no doubt a useful formula.

Take of Yellow bark, in powder, whortle-berry, in powder, of each.................	1	scruple;
Opium, in powder		half a grain.

Mix. To be taken four times a day, in a glass of lime-water.

He recommends lime-water for the common beverage or distilled water may be used.

Opium is, in many instances, eminently serviceable, and has

been most advantageously employed in large doses. It has the recommendation of many eminent physicians; and where it cannot be trusted to solely for effecting a cure, will often prove a valuable auxiliary to the other means employed to overcome the existing irritation. The purified opium may be administered in doses of from one to three, four or five grains, three times a day, either alone or in conjunction with the nitric acid, lime-water, bark or any other tonic. The opium in the foregoing prescription of Dr. Ferrier, may frequently be increased with advantage, from half a grain, to one, two or three grains.

For allaying the nervous irritability in this disease, Dover's powder is very appropriate. It may often be advantageously combined with a tonic, as a grain of quinine with four or five grains of Dover's powder, made into a pill, and taken thrice daily. Or six grains of the carbonate of iron, may be combined with the same quantity of Dover's powder, -and given in the same way.

I think sarsaparilla and pareira brava to be medicines likely to be of eminent service in some cases of this disease; and the vapour bath is much worthy of notice. The vapour bath often alters, not only the quantity, but likewise the quality of the urine. In one instance, the use of a vapour bath every second day, cured the patient.

Dr. Barlow says, *Practice of Medicine,* p. 537, "Most vegetables are objectionable, except the cruciferous plants; malt liquor is to be shunned, bread sparingly used, and potatoes and turnips not at all. Let the patient have for breakfast tea or coffee, with plenty of milk, a rasher of bacon, and a little toasted bread. For dinner, beef or mutton, game or fish, with greens or spinach, and Italian maccaroni boiled in milk. Let him drink a little brandy and water. He may have some tea, with a little well-toasted bread in the evening; and as he will want some supper, he may have a mutton chop with maccaroni or a mess of maccaroni and milk. Of medicines we know of none that have any certain control over the disease. Some years ago the author recommended the use of ammonia in considerable doses, and the remedy has certainly been found useful by the late Dr. Golding Bird, and others, as well as by the author.

A few months ago the author received a letter from a medical practitioner who has long been suffering from diabetes. He said, "I attribute my recovery, under Providence, to the ammonia, the diabetic biscuits and a tranquil mind".

Whatever medicine is resorted to, daily friction over the region of the kidneys, with either of the liniments at page 163, should be persevered in at the same time; and in obstinate cases it will be advisable to try the effect of an issue made in that part.

Blood-letting has been strongly recommended in this disease by the late Dr. Watt of Glasgow, and is countenanced by other professional men; but it is not applicable to those cases which are the result of advanced years, and of a debilitated constitution. On the contrary, where the pulse is hard, and the pain urgent; where the constitution does not seem seriously affected, and the soundness of the stomach and other assimilating viscera are sufficiently proved, by the perpetual desire for food to supply the waste that is taking place, cupping on the loins may frequently be useful.

Dr. Baillie's sentiments on this disease merit attention.

> "I have in the course of my medical life", says he, "seen a good many instances of this formidable disease. Of late years, a considerable proportion of such cases have got well finder my care or have had the symptoms very much mitigated. The most successful plan of treatment has been to give considerable doses of opium combined with rhubarb or some other bitter; fifty drops of laudanum, for instance, may be given three or four times a day, mixed with some infusion of rhubarb or infusion of columba. The rhubarb may also be given separately, in the form of pills. Under this treatment, the disease will often gradually subside, and at length cease altogether. It is, however, very apt to recur, and therefore this plan of treatment, in more moderate doses, should be continued for some months after the patient is apparently well. Bleeding from the system generally, and topical bleeding from the loins are often useful; for the blood-vessels of the kidneys, in this disease, are generally more or less distended with blood. The diet should be temperate, and should consist chiefly of animal food; and the best kind of drink, is, upon the whole, Bristol water".—Dr. Baillie's *Posthumous Writings,* p. 220.

For an account of the use of the Bristol Hotwell water in diabetes, *see* page 243-44. Malvern water is excellent.

Under the use of either of the preceding remedies, the diet should be almost strictly and perseveringly confined to small quantities of the most digestible animal food, combined with a little farinaceous matter. The Gluten bread made by Messrs. Van Abbott, 148, Fenchurch Street, London, is recommended by eminent physicians as extremely useful, and so is the almond bread and biscuits made by Hill, 61, Bishopsgate Street. Domes of Gower Street North, Euston Square, makes bran biscuits that are useful. Diabetes is generally an obstinate, and too often a dangerous malady; and an attention to this circumstance will be absolutely necessary in all cases, without exception. Distilled water, acidulated with phosphoric acid, appeases the urgent thirst. Claret is an excellent beverage for diabetic patients. Alum-whey or lime-water or animal broths, are useful for the common beverage; and the bowels should be kept regular by the pills No. 100 or 101 or 101D, pages 194-95 or by a little compound powder of jalap.

DIARRHOEA OR LOOSENESS

Diarrhoea is well known to be a complaint in which the evacuations from the bowels are crude, loose and too frequent, with little griping or tenesmus.

There are several species of the complaint, the principal of which are the bilious looseness, in which the faeces are of a bright yellow; the mucous looseness, characterized by a considerable discharge of acrid mucus; the milky looseness, known by the milky appearance of the stools; the lientery, in which the food is passed rapidly and with little change; the serous looseness, in which the motions are almost entirely liquid and limpid; and the yeasty looseness, remarkable for the sour smell, and the frothy, yeasty appearance of the evacuations.

In all the forms of this disease, the chief *immediate cause* of the diarrhoea is an increase of the natural peristaltic action throughout the whole or a great part of the intestinal canal, which may be produced by irritating materials thrown into the bowels by the mouth; by a diseased change in the fluids, which are naturally secreted in them; or by an irritable state of the intestines themselves or the membrane that lines their inner surface.

The principal *exciting causes* are the application of cold to the surface of the body, and especially the transition from a hot climate into a colder region; the sudden change from a cold to a hot climate; suppressed perspiration; acrid indigestible aliment; inertness or turpitude of the glands of the intestines; the abuse of active purgatives; worms; and a diseased condition of some part of the intestinal canal.

The diarrhoea produced by sudden cold is commonly of the acrid mucous character; while that caused by a transition from a cold to a hot climate is in general the bilious looseness; and that remarkable for the yeasty appearance of the motions, is almost invariably the consequence of positive disease in some part of the bowels, particularly the larger bowels.

The disease is *distinguished* from dysentery by being unattended either with inflammation or tenesmus; and by the appearance of the stools, which in diarrhoea are generally composed of some portion of the usual alimentary matter, white in dysentery, they are, for the most part, wholly destitute of it, and bloody.

TREATMENT—Generally speaking, ipecacuanha, both in the form of the simple and compound powder; simarouba bark; tormentil root; and alterative doses of calomel will be applicable, perhaps, to every species of diarrhoea, and will often be eminently serviceable. The following combination of ipecacuanha and simarouba bark will be found a powerful remedy.

Take of Ipecacuanha, in powder .... Three-fourths of a grain;

Infusion of simarouba bark .... 1 ounce.

Mix for a draught to be taken three times a day.

In numerous cases nitric acid and opium, combined with infusion of gentian, will be still more efficacious. Dr. Abercrombie and Dr. Hynes of Nottingham, have strongly recommended this prescription:

Take of Tincture of opium	1½	drachm;
Nitric acid, ...	20	minims or drops;

Compound infusion of gentian, sufficient to fill an eight ounce phial.
Mix, and take two table-spoonfuls after every liquid stool or painful evacuation.

That very skilful physician, Dr. George Fordyce, was partial to a union of ipecacuanha and tormentil root, which is certainly of great value, and applicable to looseness, whether recent or of long standing, and whether the result of simple debility and irritation in the intestines or of positive disease.

Take of Ipecacuanha, in powder	Three-fourths of a
grain or a	grain;
Tormentil root, in powder, ...	half a drachm.

Mix. To be taken in dill or common water, three or four times a day.

Three or four grains of the compound powder of ipecacuanha is also very useful, especially if combined with two or three grains of mercury with chalk, and a warm bath at ninety-seven or ninety-eight degrees, accompanying it with a flannel roller round the abdomen for a few days, which, when laid aside, should be carefully and gradually removed. These medicines may be made into a pill with a sufficient quantity of opiate confection, and repeated three or four times in twenty-four hours. All these medicines determine to the surface of the body, and thus relieve the internal parts; and the above prescriptions are likewise capable of giving tone to the intestinal canal. In obstinate cases of diarrhoea, especially if symptoms appear of any actual disorganization in the parts affected, the compound calomel pill No. 98 or 99, page 192, every night or every other night, will be advisable in conjunction with the above.

In the *bilious* diarrhoea, a little calomel is usually necessary. Two grains, combined with eight grains of powdered rhubarb in jelly, will be a proper form for its exhibition; which should be followed by the administration of diluting and demulcent drinks, as infusion of linseed or quince seed, and decoction of sago, Embden grits or isinglass, with a little good brandy in it. The calomel and rhubarb may here be repeated for two or three days, and be succeeded by the compound powder of ipecacuanha if the looseness continue; or the patient may at once take two grains of mercury with chalk, (*grey powder*) and two grains of compound powder of ipecacuanha, twice or thrice a day, following it on the second day with a little castor oil. This plan will likewise be frequently of great service in the milky diarrhoea.

In the *lientery* or that species of diarrhoea in which the food is passed rapidly, and with little change, the most efficacious medicines are those which are capable of giving energy to the digestive organs, such as the tonics recommended under *Indigestion*, particularly infusion of columba, with nitric acid and opium; and rhubarb with ipecacuanha and ginger. The *alkaline tincture of rhubarb* (page 4) is a very useful medicine.

The first prescriptions above are among the most valuable in the *acrid mucous* diarrhoea, and in that of the serous description. And in that kind remarkable for the yeasty appearance of the stools, alterative doses of mercury at night, as No. 98, 99, pp. 191-92 with the ipecacuanha and tormentil powder in the day, and an occasional tepid bath at ninety-seven or ninety-eight degrees, are certainly some of the means which have been found most beneficial. This last species is of a very unfavourable description; but I am much inclined to think that the nitro-muriatic acid bath (*see* page 92-93), would sometimes be very useful.

A very peculiar kind of diarrhoea is occasionally met with, in which the patient voids, along with the excrement, whitish membrane-like tubes, which give to the unprofessional inspectors the idea of the internal mucous membrane of the bowels coming away. These tubes are a diseased secretion, and show a great degree of irritability in the bowels, and, probably, of slow inflammation.

The faeces are mostly discharged with great pain, and of a small calibre. The balsam of capivi will be found eminently serviceable in this species, with which may be advantageously joined the pill, No. 99, page 192, every or every other night. The balsam may be taken in doses of thirty-forty or fifty drops, three tines a day, mixed with mucilage of gum arabic; and an injection of a pint of warm water, with a tea-spoonful of laudanum, should be thrown up once or twice a day. Emollient injections as No. 9, page 147, are also useful.

Beside the medicines already noticed as beneficial in looseness, the decoction of oak-bark, infusion of quassia, decoction of Iceland moss, alum and lime-water, have all been occasionally found very useful. They have been more especially serviceable in chronic or long standing diarrhoea, which ought to be removed by degrees, and require a strengthening medicine, which is, at the same time, astringent and tonic. In this protracted species, some persons have obtained much benefit from drinking about a pint of lime-water during the day, mixed with an equal quantity of milk, in which an ounce of gum arabic has been dissolved. It is likely to be generally useful in the diarrhoea of old people, and where there is positive disease in the bowels.

Should this complaint occasionally occur in persons of a costive habit, we ought to examine whether it is not owing to torpor or chronic inflammation of the colon or some part of the large interstines, with morbid accumulation there, for this may be a cause of diarrhoea—the bowels being sometimes relaxed, while concretions often remain behind, notwithstanding that the patient is at times harassed with spontaneous purging. In this case, the means pointed out under *Costiveness* will be the most effectual.

For an excellent remedy in the diarrhoea of the consumptive *see* page 472.

When this complaint makes its attack with great foulness of the stomach or follows excess in diet, it is frequently advisable to commence the treatment by administering an emetic of twenty grains of ipecacuanha powder; but the calomel and rhubarb previously noticed will usually remove this foulness of stomach.

Diarrhoea is extremely common in infants and children, especially from the commencement of teething or the time of weaning to the third year. If it occurs at the period of weaning, the stools are usually greenish, watery or slimy; sometimes ash-coloured, and attended by griping pains, often by retchings and vomiting, with symptomatic fever. Sometimes they are pulpy of a clayey colour, and very offensive. Here, in general, the best treatment consists in giving a grain or two of calomel, following it directly with a dose of castor oil, if matters appear accumulated in the bowels; if not, give three grains of mercury with chalk, three grains of calcined magnesia, and one grain and a half of Dover's powder, in jelly. Do not attempt forcibly to check the looseness, but rattler to moderate it, and to improve the stools. If the motions are very slimy or bloody or squirted out forcibly, three or four leeches should be applied to the belly, and followed by fomentations, and a clyster of thin warm starch and olive oil; the medicines just named must likewise be continued in smaller doses, and a flannel bandage applied round the belly.

From whatever cause a diarrhoea proceeds, whenever it is found necessary to check it, the diet ought, at least in elderly people, to consist of rice, boiled with milk or beef-tea with asked flour, together with preparations of sago, pearl-barley, arrow-root, and Embden grits, and the lighter sorts of roast meat, as mutton and lamb. Vegetables should be altogether avoided, and a little weak brandy and water be taken now and then instead of malt liquor. But in children and young persons ripe fruit, such as cherries, strawberries, gooseberries, cooked apples and pears, may be allowed with great advantage. People usually suppose that fruit is a bad thing in diarrhoea, but this is a great mistake as it respects young people.

Those who are liable to frequent returns of this disease, either from peculiar weakness or too great an irritability of the bowels, should live temperately, avoiding crude fruits, unwholesome vegetables, and all food of difficult digestion.[1] They ought likewise to be aware of cold, damp, and all sudden changes; and they should wear flannel next the skin.

In most cases of this complaint, purgatives are found to be injurious, although mild aperients are sometimes very useful, especially if the patient has taken indigestible food or eaten to excess; which forms a grand mark of distinction between the treatment of dysentery and diarrhoea, as in the former, purgatives are almost always more or less necessary and frequently of eminent utility.

It is a common domestic practice to give mulled port wine and spices for the cure of looseness, but it is seldom advisable, and very often injurious. A little brandy and water is a better remedy, especially if it be followed by four or five grains of the compound powder of ipecacuanha. The powder No. 127, page 208, is a valuable remedy in the looseness and disorder of the bowels so frequent in the autumn. For the simple ordinary purging of children, give three grains of rhubarb with the same quantity of magnesia, in cinnamon or spearmint water, and repeat it if necessary, once in two days. The diarrhoea that occurs during teething should never be hastily checked. It ordinarily keeps off feverish irritation; and when violent, should be moderated, but not subdued. It may be lessened by giving the infant a little rice milk or milk and baked flour boiled together. The gums should be lanced. Further valuable information respecting the looseness of children will be found in the author's volume *On Infancy and Childhood.*

DIPHTHERIA OR THROAT DISEASE

This is not, strictly speaking, a new disease in this country, but a new phase of an old disease—scarlet fever, showing itself particularly in a swelled throat, inside and outside, the tonsils and whole of the throat being covered with a thick cream-coloured or ash-coloured exudation. In fact, a plastic, false membrane is formed in the throat (pharynx); tonsils and uvula. It is often seen like patches of chamois leather, coating the inside of the throat. Difficult breathing is present, and a difficulty of swallowing, and the type

1. See the information given respecting diet under INDIGESTION, which is applicable here.

of the disease is evidently asthenic, that is, of a depressing nature. In severe cases, the urine is generally albuminous. After slight symptoms of cough and sore throat, with external swelling of the throat—not at all alarming at first, the child is suddenly seized with difficult breathing and swallowing, and the symptoms become alarming. In some instances, death takes place in a few hours after the difficulty of breathing and swallowing are manifested.

This disease proved very fatal at Haverfordwest in 1849, and at Boulogne in 1855 and 1856, and several years since at Tours in France, and other low unhealthy places. It is infectious, and often frightfully destructive to life, and has been epidemic in certain districts.

The *causes* of this alarming malady are—a specific contagion, and a poison from defective drainage.

TREATMENT—In some cases, the skin of the entire body is covered with a rash resembling scarlatina, and although the rash is not visible in many cases, yet I believe the disease is a dangerous species of scarlet fever with sore throat,—it is essentially scarlet fever, although there may be no eruption; and the best remedy is the sesqui-carbonate of ammonia internally, together with an emetic, and the use of a mixture of strong *liquid ammonia* and water, in the proportion of fifteen drops to a wine-glassful of water, to the throat. About six grains of the ammonia should be given to a child of ten years old, eight times in the twenty-four hours or oftener, in a table-spoonful of water, sweetened with some syrup. No acid drink is to be allowed. This is a far more efficacious remedy than bark, quinine, acids, chlorate of potash or any thing else that can be given.

There always exists a marked depression of the vital powers, and it is an interesting and important question, what is the cause of the sudden death which so frequently takes place in this malady? I believe it to be owing to the deposition of fibrinous clots in the heart or great vessels, at once arresting the circulation, because such clots have been found in dissection, and also because this tendency to fibrinous exudation is characteristic of the disease.

Now ammonia is one of the most powerful blood solvents

known, and by administering it freely, we shall be more likely to succeed in curing the patient than by any other means. In the severest cases, should the sesqui-carbonate of ammonia not relieve, I strongly recommend the *liquor ammoniae* (strong liquid ammonia) to be given every second hour, in the dose of ten drops to an adult, in a wine glassful of water, since it operates more quickly acid sensibly than the sesqui-carbonate of ammonia, although this is usually sufficiently efficacious. But where sudden and alarming prostration occurs, the liquid ammonia is to be preferred, and will be found far more beneficial than wine. Brandy or steel wine, however, should be given at the same time, if symptoms of sinking appear.

At the same time, the solution of liquid ammonia and water, above prescribed, (fifteen drops to a wine-glassful of water), should be well rubbed over the tonsils and inside of the throat, by means of a camel's hair pencil or a pen with a piece of sponge tied securely on the end of it, and dipped into the solution. An emetic of ten or twenty grains of ipecacuanha powder, according to the age, will be useful in relieving the throat, and detaching the plastic membrane there; and the apartments ought to be fumigated with the nitric acid vapour, *see* page 302. Change of air also should be speedily resorted to; and the moment one child is attacked by the disease, the other children of the family ought to be instantly sent miles from home.

Many medical men use a strong solution of nitrate of silver to the throat, but it is painful, and I see no good in it, and believe the weak solution of liquid ammonia is better. Don't caustic the patient's throat, for the disease is in the blood, and the throat must be cured through that.

Chills must be carefully guarded against in diphtheria, the skin being extremely sensitive, and painfully alive to the slightest exposure to cold air. The rooms should be well fumigated with chloride of lime or Condy's fluid or Burnett's disinfecting fluid,. if not by the nitric acid vapour, which I prefer. But the principal remedy is ammonia, which ought to be commenced immediately any symptoms of this disease manifest themselves and steadily repeated.

One of the best medicines next to ammonia is tincture of muriate of iron, which may be given in the dose of ten drops every two or three hours, in two table-spoonfuls of water, to a child of eight years old.

DROPSY

Dropsy is a preternatural collection of serous or watery fluid in the cellular membrane, beneath the skin or in different cavities of the body, and receives different technical appellations, according to the particular situation in which it is lodged. The chief varieties, each of which we shall distinctly notice, are—

1. General dropsy, that is, of the cellular membrane of the body, generally attacking both the upper and lower limbs. Called *Anasarca*.
2. Dropsy of the belly, that is, in the cavity of the abdomen Called *Ascites*. Including Ovarian Dropsy.
3. Dropsy or water in the chest. Called *Hydro-thorax*.
4. Dropsy of the head.
5. Dropsy of the scrotal bag. Called *Hydrocele*.

Dropsy under whatever form it takes place, is, in most instances, a disease of debility. Its general *causes* are those which induce debility, either general or local, such are protracted fevers; long exposure to a cold and moist atmosphere; excessive labour; unkindly child-bearing; excessive use of ardent spirits; habitual indigestion; great loss of blood; drinking cold water when heated; and insufficient or innutritious and indigestible food. Positive disease in some important organ is a frequent cause, particularly disease in the heart, liver or kidneys. Scarlatina, obstruction in the veins, and increased fluidity of the blood produce dropsy.

The *immediate cause* of all kinds of dropsy is, either a profuse exhalation on the part of the small excernent arteries of the dropsical part or a want of action in the absorbing vessels; or both may be united.

General Dropsy

This form generally commences in the lower extremities, and first shows itself towards evening with a swelling of the feet and ankles, which by degrees ascends, and successively occupies the thighs and trunk of the body. When it has become very general, the internal organs are affected in a similar way; the lungs partake of the affection; the breathing becomes difficult; and is accompanied by cough and the expectoration of a watery fluid; the urine is small in quantity, high coloured, and deposits a reddish sediment; sometimes, however, it is of a pale whey colour and more copious. There is costiveness; insatiable thirst; a pale dry skin; sallow complexion; torpor; heaviness; troublesome cough; and slow fever. The water often oozes through the pores of the skin or raises it in the form of small blisters.

Its *causes* have been stated above.

TREATMENT.—The indications of treatment are to palliate or remove the exciting cause of the complaint; then to unload the system of the weight that oppresses it; and lastly, to reesta blish the frame in health and vigour.

If a habit of intemperance, a sedentary life, innutritious food, exposure to a cold or moist atmosphere or similar causes, have originated the dropsy, these must, of course, be corrected, before any medical plan for evacuating the water can be of permanent benefit. And where the cause lies, in obstruction in the heart or liver, alterative doses of mercury offer the greatest probability of removing it, particularly the pill, No. 98, 99, page 191-92 or No. 117, page 203, which may be administered in conjunction with any of the medicines next to be spoken of.

The principal means of evacuating the accumulated fluid in all dropsies, are by the employment of certain purgative and diuretic medicines, and by scarification or other cutaneous drains. Elaterium; cream of tartar; black hellebore; the inner bark of the elder tree; gamboge; and seneka root, are generally considered to be the most efficacious purgatives in this disease; and foxglove; squill; nitre; bi-carbonate of potash; and hedge-hyssop, to be the most valuable diuretics.

The elaterium is a powerful purgative, and will sometimes prove of great service in expelling the water. It seems best adapted to those cases in which the strength is not greatly reduced.

> Take of Elaterium .... 6 grains;
> Calomel .... 6 grains.
>
> Rub them carefully together, and with a sufficient quantity of extract of gentian, form into twelve pills. Of these one should be taken every hour, commencing early in the morning, till they *begin* to operate, when they must be discontinued. During their operation, the patient's strength ought to be supported by strong beef tea and bread, with a little wine.

Cream of tartar has been a favourite medicine in dropsy, and very deservedly so, with many celebrated physicians. An ounce of it, mixed with ten grains of powdered ginger, may be given every three hours till it operates copiously; or half an ounce of it may be combined, with two grains of gamboge, and repeated in the same way. Dr. Home of Edinburgh, has observed that it radically cured fourteen patients out of twenty in whom he tried it. In Dr. Ferriar's practice, out of forty-three cases treated chiefly with this remedy, thirty-three were cured. They were cases of abdominal and anasarcous dropsy. Mixed with a large quantity of water it quenches the thirst very pleasantly, and the patient should, therefore, take this drink as a common beverage.

Elaterium not unfrequently produces violent irritation in the mucous membranes of the bowels, which renders it an unsafe medicine in domestic practice; I would, therefore, recommend the following form of administering cream of tartar always to be tried first—this is a valuable prescription, producing copious watery stools, together with a considerable flow of urine. It is one of peculiar efficacy, well suited to domestic, practice, and has cured dropsy in many instances after a great variety of diuretics and hydragogues had been employed in vain. Perhaps no remedy known is equal to this in dropsy, not originating in disease of the *kidney,* especially when a pill of calomel and squills is given every night at bed-time.

Take of Cream of tartar	1½	ounce;
Sulphate of potash		half an ounce;
Powdered squills	2	drachm;
Tartar emetic	1	grain.

Mix them well together, and take a tea-spoonful in water or barley water, four times a day, if not oftener.

Black hellebore has also been highly praised. The following pill, called Bacher's pill, was once in high reputation, and sold all over Europe, for the cure of dropsy.

Take of Extract of black hellebore		half a drachm;
Myrrh, in powder, carduus benedictus, in powder, of each	11	grains.

Mix and divide the maps into seventy pills, five of which are to be taken every six hours, till they operate well on the bowels.

The expressed juice of the inner bark of the common elder tree may be taken in the dose of from a drachm to half an ounce, and repeated every three or four hours, till it has the desired effect of producing copious evacuations by stool and urine, which it is capable of doing and by which means the illustrious Sydenham observes that he had cured a vast number of cases. The decoction of seneka may be taken in the doses mentioned at page 113; but it is certainly inferior to the foregoing remedies, which may be likewise asserted of gamboge.

Sydenham very wisely remarks that, before administering purgatives, we should ascertain whether the patient be easy or hard to purge, because in the former case, the milder purgatives will generally answer best; while in the latter, the strong drastic cathartics, as elaterium, black hellebore, etc. will be absolutely necessary to produce any good effect. He speaks favourably of the syrup of buckthorn, as an effectual purge to those dropsical patients who are easily moved and relates the case of a woman who had this complaint to a great degree, her belly being swelled to an incredible size. He gave her an ounce of the syrup of buckthorn before dinner, and it brought away an almost inconceivable quantity of water. "Encouraged by this success", says he, "I gave it every day, only interposing a day or two occasionally, when she seemed weaker than ordinary. And the water being by these means carried off by degrees, the swelling of the belly diminished daily, and she recovered".

As diuretic remedies, *squill, foxglove* and *nitre,* are undoubtedly very valuable. The following combinations are esteemed forms for exhibiting squill :

Take of Dried squill, in powder	3	grains;
Opium, in powder		half a rain;
Cinnamon bark, in powder	10	grains.

Mix for a powder to be taken in any agreeable vehicle, three or four times in twenty-four hours.

If there appears to be a diseased obstruction in the heart, liver or lungs, the following formula will be found highly serviceable or that marked No. 116, page 202. I have employed this combination of squills and calomel with perfect success in apparently desperate cases; but it must not be given in dropsy *from disease of the kidneys. See* pages 397-98

Take of Compound squill pills	1	drachm;
Calomel	6	grains

Mix them well together with oil of juniper, and divide into twelve pills. One to be taken twice a day.

Foxglove is rarely applicable to dropsical persons of tense fibres and great natural strength; but in those with a feeble or intermitting pulse, whose dropsical limbs and body are soft and yielding, the complexion pale, and the skin cold, it is sometimes a valuable diuretic.

Take of Infusion of foxglove	4	ounces;
Tincture of foxglove		half a drachm;
Acetate of potash	1	drachm;
Liquid laudanum	10	drops.

Mix and let one table-spoonful bc taken three times a day in water.

The wine of *colchicum* has been recommended, but it is very debilitating, and I cannot advise any trial of it. From a scruple to half a drachm of the powder of hedge-hyssop may be administered twice a day, and is said to be particularly efficacious in those dropsies which are the consequence of obstructions in some of the abdominal organs. *Broom ashes* or the *Broom-seed,* were formerly a famous remedy; but it being supposed that they owe their virtues to the fixed alkali they contain, medical men usually prefer giving ten or twenty grains of the bi-carbonate of potash twice a day, to the exhibition of the ashes or seeds themselves. It is, however, best to take the broom-seeds themselves. It has been said, that a large spoonful of unbruised mustard seed, taken every night and morning, together with the bi-carbonate of potash in the middle of the day, has performed a cure in a very bad case of dropsy.

If general debility has occasioned the disease, the alkali may he advantageously united with a bitter tonic.

Take of Bi-carbonate of potash	10	grains;
Compound infusion of gentian	1½	ounce;
Compound spirit of ether		half of drachm;
Tincture of cinnamon		half a drachm.

Mix for a draught, to be taken twice a day.

Notwithstanding what is said respecting the virtues of *broom-seed* as contained in the fixed alkali to be found in them, I very much prefer giving this remedy as it is presented to us by nature. It is true, and we rejoice in the fact, that the art of the chymist is often turned to great advantage in extracting the essential part of plants, and presenting them to us, as remedies, in a small compass, and even in a more efficient form, of which the invaluable preparation from Peruvian bark, called *quinine,* is an example; but this cannot be done with all vegetable substances, the attempt being in some instances worse than a failure, a valuable remedy being thereby brought into discredit. I think well of the broom-seed, and advise it to be tried in the following manner :

> Take of broom-seed, well powdered and sifted, one drachm; let it stand twelve hours in a glass of good white wine, and take it in the morning fasting, having first shaken it, so that the whole may be swallowed. Walk after it, if able; if not able to walk, use what exercise is possible, for on hour and a half; after which take an ounce of olive oil. Nothing must be eaten or drank for half an hour or an hour, after taking the oil. This is to be repeated every day till cured.

It is considered essential that no blood should be lost during the use of this medicine. Many cases of dropsy cured by these simple means have been related on unexceptionable authority, and that recently, as well as formerly. Sydenham says, *(Works by Swan.* 1769, p. 529,) of a form very similar to the above, "By this remedy- alone I have known this distemper cured, in persons of too weak a constitution to bear purging, when the case was judged desperate".

Dr. Buchan speaks favourably of the efficacy of a drachm of *nitrate of potash,* taken every morning in a draught of ale; and I have known it succeed in more than one case. It is most applicable in the dropsy of young persons, and those who have a good measure of strength remaining.

In those instances in which the dropsy appears to have originated in general weakness, where there is a feeble pulse, and a blanched complexion, without organic injury, the inhalation of *oxygen gas* has sometimes proved the most valuable tonic which experience could suggest. It has immediately invigorated the whole constitution, and thus enabled it to struggle effectually with the disease so as finally to overcome it; and in all such cases as those described, it merits a fair trial. See what is said of it under *Dropsy of the Chest.*

Under the use of either of the preceding remedies, it will frequently be highly proper to scarify the legs at the same time, which is a simple and very safe operation, if it be not left to a late period. The scarification should be made with a lancet on the outside of each knee, a little below the joint; the incision resembling in form the letter T, and just penetrating through the skin. From this cut, which will not easily close, the water will sometimes drain away in a surprising manner, and the benefit arising is often permanent.

I have said nothing respecting blood-letting in dropsy, but it is necessary to advert to it. It is a remedy which has been now and then resorted to from the earliest ages, although very cautiously; of late years several practitioners have strongly recommended it; and some of them much too strongly. In the *acute* form of dropsy, whether general or confined to the abdomen, that is, in cases where it may have appeared suddenly or advanced rapidly, from whatever cause arising, supposing the pulse to be quick, full and strong, and the constitutional powers of the patient unbroken, a single blood-letting from the arm to the extent of sixteen or twenty ounces, will often afford great relief, and pave the way for the more effectual operation of other remedies. This may frequently be followed, if necessary, by local blood-letting, by means of the cupping glasses or the application of leeches; and one of the best medicines which can be prescribed to follow the abstraction of blood is the calomel and squill pill (page 535), twelve grains of *James's powder* being added to the twelve pills.

The diet, in all dropsical cases, ought to be nourishing, that food being selected which is easiest of digestion. Tile pungent aromatic vegetables are also proper, such as garlic, onions, cresses, horse-radish, etc; and the patient's strong desire for drink may be freely gratified, for which purpose, cream of tartar dissolved in a large quantity of water, butter-milk, table-beer, weak cider of cider mired with water, will be among the most useful beverages he can resort to.

After the water has been evacuated, we must endeavour to invigorate the constitution by the use of bitter and metallic tonics, with aromatics, regular exercise, change of air, and the cold bath. The tonics may be taken as recommended under the head of *Indigestion.* The daily use of a little wine will be advisable, particularly Rhenish wine.

In having recourse to active purgatives in this disease, it should never be forgotten that we are treating a disease of debility, and that every purge which does not diminish the general bulk, adds to the complaint by increasing the debility. If, therefore, upon a few trials the plan be not found to answer this salutary purpose, it cannot too soon be desisted from.

Beside the medicines above noticed, a few others have at times been praised for their virtues in dropsy, the chief of which are juniper berries, nitrous ether, the diuretic salt, and the green lettuce; but they are certainly of very inferior value. Emetics, and certain sweating medicines, have also occasionally been employed; but they are uncertain in their operation, and are now rarely resorted to. Mr. Mudge, however, relates the case of a woman about forty years old, who was cured of a dropsy in the belly, of long standing, by taking two scruples of compound ipecacuanha powder at bed time, for three successive nights.

It not unfrequently happens that water accumulates in the legs, thighs, and even in the belly, as a direct consequence of consumption of long standing; from poor weak blood; old ulcers, accompanied with a considerable discharge; great weakness; and an immoderate evacuation of the juices and spirits by a salivation, sweating or purging; or from too slender a diet in the cure of the venereal disease. In such instances, purging, and other violent measures, must be avoided, the cure then depending upon invigorating the general babit by the use of nourishing diet, and tonic medicines, especially steel tonics. Ten grains of tartarized iron, combined with fifteen grains of calumba powder, and given three times a day, prove very serviceable here.

The following is an instructive case of dropsy from pressure on the external iliac vein, especially from the observations of Sir Astley Cooper which it contains, and the skilfulness of the treatment adopted; *see Lancet,* vol. ii. p. 466, 1823-24.

"W. W., aged forty, was admitted into Job's ward, June 30th, with a swelling of the right leg. He says that, about two years since, he was kicked by a horse, whilst at work in the stables at Greenwich; the blow given by one foot of the horse was received just above the crista of the ilium, and the other foot struck the upper part of the right thigh, which produced great inflammation in it; and soon after, the glands in the grain began to swell, and remained very large and hard for a considerable time. He applied leeches and washes to the upper part of the thigh, which reduced the inflammation, but did not remove it; and, about six weeks after, an abscess formed, which burst and discharged, according to the patient's account, a considerable quantity of matter. This kept up the irritation in the gland, and will account for its remaining a long time enlarged. The gland, however, did not suppurate. For the five months preceding his admission, he says, the limb was just as large as when he came in. It was then about twice the size of the other leg. The skin had a brawny feel and appearance. The swelling was rather tense, but yielded to pressure, and, immediately that pressure was removed, it recovered its former figure. The patient complained of its feeling very heavy, and of there being a great numbness in the foot. There was also an enlarged absorbent gland, situated just beneath Poupart's ligament, and near its insertion into the pubes; in size as large as a pigeon's egg, and very hard. His tongue was moist, his pulse regular, his sleep good, his appetite unimpaired, his look florid and his general health not at all disturbed.

"Mr. Morgan being unwell to-day, July 2nd, Sir A. Cooper saw this patient, and at his bed-side made the following remarks : 'Dropsy, it is said, arises from an increased action of the exhalents or from a diminished action in the absorbents, and this, in a general way, is true; but the appearances of the dropsy produced by these causes are very different. In the one you have a tense, shining, semi-transparent skin; and, if you press your finger on it, you will find it will sink into the swelling, as if you were kneading dough, and that depression will continue some time; but, in the other or that which arises from a mechanical impediment on the trunks of the absorbents, you cannot produce any pitting on pressure, and the skin has the appearance which you now see'. He then ordered a grain and a half of calomel twice a day, and the limb to be anointed with the camphorated mercurial ointment every night. The patient was also ordered rest and the horizontal posture, with a low diet. With this treatment the swelling rapidly decreased in a week, and continued to do so, more slowly, for a fortnight. He then left off his mercury, as his mouth had been kept some time very sore, and was ordered some brisk aperient medicine".

"July 26th—The leg now is very little larger than the other; he can use it without any inconvenience, and the glandular enlargement has almost entirely subsided. He takes no other medicine but the house physic every morning, which is necessary to keep his bowels regular. His health continues very good."

Dropsy of the Belly

This variety often comes on with loss of appetite; sluggishness; inactivity; dryness of the akin; oppression of the chest; cough; diminished urine; costiveness; and the other symptoms enumerated under the first variety. Shortly after a protuberance is perceived in the hypogastrium, which gradually extending, at length occupies the whole abdomen, which uniformly becomes swelled and tense, in a small degree elastic and communicates to the hand when struck against it, the sensation of its containing an undulating fluid. The disease seldom continues long without inducing a dropsical state of the lower extremities.

In the dropsy of the belly most commonly met with, the water is contained in the general cavity of the abdomen; but there is another form sometimes occurring, in which the fluid is collected in sacs formed upon, and connected with, one of the abdominal organs : this is called the *encysted* dropsy. It is seldom accompanied, in the first instance, with any disordered state of the system; is distinctly observed to begin in a particular part of the belly, and thence gradually to diffuse itself; the strength of the patient is long unimpaired; and the appetite and respiration continue good, until the bulk and pressure of the fluid bring on those constitutional effects, which usually attend the ordinary forms of abdominal dropsy in its early stages. The *encysted dropsy of the ovaria* is not uncommon, and is treated of in my book ON THE DISEASES OF FEMALES.

In addition to the general *causes* of dropsy described at page

530-31, we may notice disease in the bowels, liver or pancreas; enlargement of the mesenteric glands; and local injury.

It is sometimes difficult to *distinguish* abdominal dropsy from pregnancy, where the latter is wished to be concealed; and the real nature of the case can only be known by a suitable enquiry into the state of the monthly discharge, of the breasts and of the swelling itself.

TREATMENT—The indications and general plan of treatment are precisely the same as have been detailed under the first variety; but here, instead of evacuating the water by scarification, we draw it off at once by tapping. When the fluid lies in the general cavity of the belly we can often afford very great relief by this process, and sometimes an effectual cure. If, therefore, the foregoing remedies fail to evacuate the water, tapping should not be delayed; indeed, it is the opinion of some well-informed professional men, that, under these circumstances, the operation cannot be too soon performed after a fluctuation is directly felt, and the swelling from its bulk has become troublesome to the breathing, and interferes with the night's rest. In this opinion the present author fully concurs, and believes that though the first operation should not succeed, we shall frequently gain great advantage from a repetition of it. Instances have occurred in which a cure has been effected after twelve, sixteen or more tappings; and a foreign author relates a cure after sixty tappings within two years and a half, in conjunction with a steady use of aperients and tonics.

One of the most efficacious remedies in this form of dropsy, is the pill of calomel and squill, prescribed at page 534. Sir Astley Cooper found this medicine very valuable in dropsy of the belly, and I have a repeatedly experienced it to be far superior to any other medicine employed; indeed, how strongly soever other means may be vaunted, it is my fixed belief, drawn from repeated observation, that its efficacy *very far exceeds* that of any other single medicine or combination whatever,[1] if we except the powder described at page 532-33.

1. "Mercurial preparations are not always applicable; for when the dropsy is connected with organic change in the substance of the liver, they should be

(Contd. next page)

> "The medicines which experience has proved to be the most beneficial here, are calomel and squill; one grain of calomel and three of squill in powder may be formed into a pill or two grains of blue pill with three of squill; one of these should be administered every night or every other night, and in the day you should give a mixture, composed of from seven to ten grains of carbonate of ammonia, one drachm of sweet spirit of nitre, twenty drops of tincture of digitalis, and an ounce and a half of camphor mixture. This draught, given once or twice a day, with one of the above pills at night, will often succeed in restoring a person to health whose constitution may be considered so broken and faulty, that it may be deemed impossible for him ever to regain a sound state of body. Should the dropsy have arisen from the irritation caused by hard drinking, this practice must be relinquished or the complaint will not disappear."—*Surgical Lectures,* No. 46.

This eminent practitioner correctly remarks in another part.

> "Medical treatment, when judiciously pursued, is very often successful in the cure of ascites; in the use of medicines, however, you most take care to direct their influence against the cause of the dropsy. Therefore, if the liver is the defective organ, you should endeavour to restore its healthy functions, and in this attempt your efforts will frequently be crowned with success, unless the disease has existed so long a time as completely to have broken up the constitution."

Bright's Dropsical Disease

A few years since Dr. Bright brought under the consideration of the medical profession a peculiar kind of dropsy, *originating in disease of the kidneys,* which is indicated by the coagulability of

---

(Contd.)
given with circumspection. When the obstruction exists chiefly in the venous and lymphatic systems or depend upon disease of the heart; or when the effusion is caused by increased action in the serous membranes; they are valuable medicines. The scrophulous habit and weak; vital energy are not always satisfactory reasons against their use."—Dr. Copland's *Dictionary of Medicine,* vol. ii. p. 619.

the urine. I have already treated of this complaint at page 388, but would make here a few additional remarks.

The disease may have been in existence for months, nay, even for a year or more, without the consciousness, on the part of the patient or any material departure from health. He may have been sensible of a growing weakness, of some derangement of digestion, of an occasional tendency to frequent micturition, of some obscure or fugitive pain in the loins; he may even have observed a diminution in the quantity of his urine or some irregularity in its appearance; but these symptoms were perhaps insufficient to call his serious attention or excite alarm. The first thing which occasions anxiety, and leads to an application for medical aid, is usually the occurrence of edematous or puffy swelling, commencing often in the face, and extending rapidly over the body. The physician is consulted on account of the dropsical symptoms, and the previous existence of the phenomena above mentioned is ascertained upon enquiry.

Dram drinking is a very frequent cause of this peculiar kind of dropsy, but it is certainly not confined to this species of intemperance, as it is frequently found in patients who have suffered from any tedious exhausting disease, such as diarrhoea and consumption, and may arise independently of these complaints. Some disease of the heart is often associated with Bright's disease.

This kind of dropsy is distinguished from others by the urine being coagulated by heat and nitric acid.

TREATMENT—Symptoms of congestion in the head often accompany this form of dropsy, arising probably from an insufficient supply of blood. Dr. B. Jones says he knows no single remedy in this disease which has produced an effect at all equal to that of a blister on the back of the neck. This appears to indicate that there is some local congestion of the brain, as well as some poison in the blood.

The principal indications are to relieve the congested kidneys, and to improve the general health. Dandelion, digitalis, cream of tartar, three times a day, and a little compound jalap powder every other night, and abstinence from stimulants, are the best agents.

To improve the health, proper air, exercise, food, cod-liver oil, and small doses of iron are essential. Mercury should never be employed in this malady.

This is a dangerous form of dropsy, and temporary relief is generally all that is obtained from medical treatment. Life may be prolonged for years. "Even with ascites," says Dr. Bence Jones, *Medical Times and Gazette,* May 8, 1952, "I have known a patient in and out of St. George's Hospital "I have knon a patient in and out of St. George's Hospital for ten years. Usually, although every complication may be removed, the albumen continues in the urine. The patient resumes his work, and considers that he is recovered; but heat and nitric acid she that this is not the case, and it is only by great care that the return of the former symptoms or to gout, can be prevented." Ten drops of tincture of digitalis may be given in conjunction with a drachm of cream of tatar, in barley water, thrice a day.

Dropsy of the Chest

This complaint commences with diffculty of breathing, particularly on exertion or lying down which is usually acompanied with a dry and troublesome cough, and a swelling of the ankles towards the evening. There is a sense of oppression at the chest; increasing diffculty of breating; pale countenance, sometimes, however, it has a livid tinge, and conveys a peculiar and striking expression of anxiety; urine high coloured and spare; pulse irregular, and often intermiting; palpitation of the heat; and dropsical swelling of the arms and legs. The sleep is disturbed by frightful dreams; the patient suddenly starts from his bed with a dreadful sense of suffocation; and through the whole course of the complaint, there is, for the most part, a peculiar posture in which the patient sits constantly upright, with his shoulders raised and fixed,, which he often contrives to effect by fixing his forehead on the back part of a chair, and thus pressing forcibly upon it.

The *causes* are those already noticed at page 530-31, acting more immediately on the organs of the chest.

Treatment—The general plan of treatment is the same as that already laid down at the 40th and following pages; but squill is here sometimes particularly valuable, affording great relief to the teasing cough, besides being a useful diuretic. Either of the prescriptions for the exhibition of squill, given at pages 529-30, may be employed, adding two grains of James's powder to each dose; or the mixture No. 78A, page 180, may be tried; with which frequent blisters to the chest should be combined. Indeed, whatever medicine is resorted to, blisters ought not to be omitted, as they appear to be very serviceable in this variety of dropsy. Five or six grains of the compound powder of ipecacuanha, combined with a grain of calomel, is an eligible night pill to procure rest.

Many physicians have extolled the foxglove in this disease, and the form No. 86, page 186, is an excellent one for its administration, but it requires the superintendence of a professional man.

If there be much debility, myrrh and sweet spirit of nitre have been recommended.

Take of Myrrh, in powder	10	grains;
Sweet spirit. of nitre......................	1	drachm;
Infusion of roses	14	drachms;
Syrup of roses	1	drachm.

Mix for a draught, to be taken three times a day.

If other remedies fail, the inhalation of oxygen gas merits a trial. It has certainly been used with complete success in bad cases, and I would never leave a patient afflicted with dropsy of the chest without resorting to it. Mr. Barr of Birmingham, has related a case cured by it, in which "the patient's face was become pale and emaciated; his eyes stared as if taking a last conscious view of their objects; his legs were swelled to such a degree, that the skin was become much inflamed; ha had a continued tenesmus, and made very little urine; he could not endure a horizontal posture for a moment; he slept little, and frequently started from his sleep, under an impression of immediate suffocation". In four weeks from the patient's beginning to inspire the vital air, not a vestige of the disorder remained, except weakness; and at the age of sixty, he seemed to possess uncommon strength, agility and vivacity.

If there be a palpable fluctuation of the chest, and all other means have been tried without avail, it is usual to evacuate the water by passing a trocar between the fourth and fifth false ribs.

Dropsy of the Head

Dropsy of the head consists in an enlargement of that organ from watery accumulation, the sutures or natural articulations of the skull generally gaping. It is a chronic disease, and not uncommon in children, yet it ought to be carefully distinguished from the acute complaint called water in the head, of which we now hear so much, as this latter is in reality an active inflammation of the brain, and is fully described elsewhere.

It usually commences with a gradual enlargement of the head, from a separation of the natural divisions of the skull, attended with slight fever, heavy pain in the head, and sometimes stupor and disorder in the bowels. But the last symptoms are occasionally very slight.

Its common *cause* is debility, either general or local.

The *marks of distinction* between this complaint and the acute inflammation of the brain, now so generally called "*water in the head*", are clearly pointed out under that article.

TREATMENT—As the present is a chronic disease of debility, no very active medicines are proper. Alterative doses of cacomel, as in the pill No. 98 or 98A, page 192, given every night or every other night, with steel medicines No. 84A, page 184, cold lotions to the head, and an occasional aperient, form the most valuable plan of proceeding hitherto suggested. Blistering the head and neck also is sometimes useful.

When the integuments of the head are much distended, and the articulations gape wide, the skin has been punctured with a lancet, and the water drawn off by degrees. This has occasionally been done with success, but it must always be resorted to with great caution, and the fluid discharged by separate stages; for if the whole were drawn off at once it will produce fainting, and may be followed by a dangerous exhaustion.

Dropsy of the Scrotal Bag or Hydrocele

The hydrocele is a soft, transparent, pearl-shaped, dropsical swelling of the scrotum, which progressively enlarges without pain.

The ordinary treatment consists in puncturing the scrotum, and injecting a slightly stimulating fluid, as wine and water, which excites a moderate degree of inflammation, by which means the two surfaces, between which the dropsical fluid is contained, adhere together, and the cavity being thus destroyed, all future accumulation is prevented. This operation must, of course, be done by a surgeon.

In recent cases, however, an emetic administered every day or every other day, has sometimes succeeded in dispersing the swelling. Alterative doses of mercury are also occasionally useful, with which may be combined the application of a stimulating lotion, (as No. 68, page 173) to the affected part. If there be any pain, leeches should be applied before using the lotion.

DYSENTERY OR BLOODY FLUX

Dysentery is an inflammatory affection of the larger bowels, in which the stools are frequent, and often bloody, attended with griping and tenesmus, the ordinary excrement being seldom discharged, and when it is, the quantity is small, and voided in the form of hard nodules. Fever very frequently attends the acute form of the disease.

It is a disease of vast importance on account of its frequent fatality. It is frequent and dangerous in Europe, especially when large bodies of men are collected together, as in fleets and armies; and in hot climates it is probably the most fatal of all diseases, not excepting fever. It was the most destructive disease in the British army in Holland, in 1748, and in the Peninsula, when the Duke of

Wellington commanded. It has often appeared as a destructive epidemic in various parts of the world. That noble man and distinguished soldier, Sir Henry Havelock, died of it in India.

The disease sometimes comes on with shivering, succeeded by heat and thirst, and other *symptoms* of fever; at others, the affection of the intestines is the first symptom. There exists unusual flatulence in the bowels; severe griping; frequent inclination to go to stool; tenesmus; loss of appetite; nausea; vomiting; frequency of pulse; and a frequent discharge of a peculiarly fetid matter by stool. This matter varies in appearance, being sometimes pure mucus or mucus mixed with blood; pure unmixed blood; matter (pus) or putrid sanies; and often films of a membranous appearance or small fatty masses, floating in a large quantity of liquid matter. Hardened excrement is likewise sometimes passed. There follows great emaciation and debility, a quick and weak pulse, sense of burning heat and intolerable bearing down of the parts. The urine is always scanty and high-coloured, and sometimes of a pungent odour.[1]

The fever accompanying dysentery may be either the simple inflammatory or the typhus fever. In the latter case, the disease is powerfully contagious and of a dangerous nature.

This complaint appears under an *acute* and a chronic form. In the *acute* form, the symptoms are urgent and clearly inflammatory; the natural faces very rarely appearing, the pain and tormina great, and blood often passing in large quantities. It terminates, for the most part, within a month.

The *chronic* species is generally a sequela or consequence of the acute, and is, as its name imports, of a less inflammatory and more protracted character than the latter; here the stools are often

1. In every case of dysentery", says Dr. Johnson, "that has ever come within the range of my observation, two functions were invariably disordered from the very onset, and soon drew other derangements in their grain. These were the functions of the skin and the liver; or perspiration and biliary secretion. I defy any one who has attentively regarded this disease at the bed-side, to produce a single instance, in which these functions were carried on in a natural manner at any period of the disease".—*James Johnson on the Influence of Tropical Climates.*

frequent, loose, and have much the appearance of the natural excrement, but mixed with blood, and passed with severe tenesmus or bearing down of the anus.

It will be seen from these observations, that those who have never before been attacked with dysentery or after a long interval of health, more especially if of a strong or intemperate habit, are most likely to have it in the acute form, at the commencement at least; while those who have repeatedly suffered from it or whose constitutions have been broken down by excessive fatigue, intemperance or other causes, will often be invaded by the chronic species, even from the beginning.

The dissection of those who die of dysentery, has invariably disclosed an inflamed and ulcerated state of the internal membrane of the lower intestines, and especially of the colon and rectum, thus proving that the essence of the disease consists in an inflammation of those parts. The small intestines are likewise often inflamed, although not to so great a degree as the large. The liver is sometimes found diseased, but this is probably only a secondary affection, found chiefly orexclusively, in those who have a previous disposition to liver complaint.

The *principal causes* are, suppressed perspiration; a rich and stimulating or indigestible diet; the immoderate use of fruit; a damp atmosphere, succeeding to a high temperature; exposure to noxious exhalations and vapours; sleeping on damp ground; and especially a specific contagion.

It is most common in summer and autumn, and in weak, ill-fed and intemperate habits.

It is chiefly *distinguished* by the presence of gripings, tenesmus, fever, and more especially by evacuations of blood.—See *Diarrhoea.*

TREATMENT—*The indications of treatment in acute dysentery are, to subdue the local infammation; to allay irritation; and to restore a healthy secretion from the skin;* and these objects are most certainly secured by the use of ipecacuanha, calomel and opium combined,—or nitric acid and opium, by purgatives, and blood-letting. Almost the whole of these remedies are called for in proper succession, according to the symptoms that present themselves, in all very severe cases, more particularly in hot climates.

In Europe, a valuable plan is to give immediately a full dose of salts (No. 73, page 176) to clear the bowels; with six grains of Dover's powder, and half a grain of calomel, made into two pills, thrice a day, the emollient injection No. 9, page 147, twice daily, and the warm bath at ninety-eight degrees in the evening. These salts must be repeated every morning afterwards, at least in the beginning, and until the acute symptoms give way, when their repetition once in two days will generally be sufficient; the Dover's powder and calomel being continued as just advised, with the warm bath, formentations and clysters.

Another excellent plan is to give a scruple of the tartrate of potash and soda, and eight minims of laudanum, in two table-spoonfuls of water, every four hours; the patient being strictly confined to bed, and supported on sago, baked flour, and other fluid nourishment—and the whole belly being enveloped by a large hot poultice of linseed meal.

If severe bilious symptoms are present, a dose of calomel and rhubarb, as two grains of the former with fifteen of the latter, may sometimes be advantageously employed as a purgative in the morning, instead of the salts above described. The calomel and rhubarb might be given twice or thrice a week, and the salts on the remaining days, when purgatives are required.

Blood-letting is rarely required in this country; but in tropical climates, if no typhoid symptoms exist, and if the pulse be full and hard, and the patient strong, sixteen or twenty ounces of blood should be drawn from the arm directly, and it may be quickly repeated, if these symptoms denoting inflammation continue but little abated by the first bleeding. In the majority of severe cases, the application of leeches to the lower part of the belly will be very useful, whether general blood-letting be resorted to or not. In many instances, a large blister or a linseed-meal poultice, may be laid over the abdomen with much advantage, after leeching; and the bowels should be invariably encircled by a broad roll of warm flannel.

A combination of calomel, ipecacuanha, and opium will often be found of inestimable service in this complaint; indeed, there are perhaps few physicians who do not consider it the most powerful medicine in dysentery we possess. Therefore, it ought never to be overlooked in hot climates. A grain of calomel, three grains of ipecacuanha powder, with the third of a grain of powdered opium, may be made into a pill with aromatic confection, and given three times a day; or half a grain of calomel and six grains of Dover's powder, (for Dover's powder contains both opium and ipecacuanha), made into a pill in the same manner, may be administered thrice daily, as already advised.

Ipecacuanha is justly considered one of the most valuable medicines in dysentery, both in Europe and sultry climates, being sometimes found more efficacious in procuring a discharge of the natural stools than any other remedy. This property it owes to its well-known power of gently stimulating the mucous membrane of the intestinal canal, and thereby lessening irritation and preternatural contraction there, at the same time that it determines to the surface of the body. It has been regarded by some even as a specific in this complaint, and I know no respectable writer who denies its usefulness. The usual mode of exhibiting it here, is to give it in such small doses as will act moderately on the bowels, without proving, emetic, for example, two grains three or four times a day. In these dose, as I have above remarked, it may be advantageously united with calomel, and may also be added to each aperient draught of salts. But larger doses of ipecacuanha may be used with perfect safety and great benefit in severe cases, in hot climates. The following is very sound practice in India, Africa and other hot countries—give half a drachm of ipecacuanha powder directly, fasting. Let the patient lie in bed quietly, and not drink anything to excite vomiting. Repeat the ipecacuanha every morning fasting, until it produces copious bilious stools, and the patient is sensibly relieved. At the same time, administer night and morning the following ipecacuanha injection :—

Pour a pint and a half of hot water on one drachm of bruised ipecacuanha root. After standing an hour, strain it, and add an ounce of syrup of morphia.

This treatment soon relieves the dysentery, and on the third or fourth morning give a full dose of castor oil, that is, three table-spoonfuls. After relief obtained in this wax, though no blood should appear in the stools, yet a mucous diarrhoea, with tenesmus, tray harass the patient. If so, give the pomegranate bark mixture, No. 85B, page 186.

In the *commencement* of acute attach of dysentery, more especially if the inflammatory symptoms run very high, opium should not be given alone, either in a liquid or a solid state. In such a condition, our chief regard must be directed to lessen the existing inflammation by ipecacuanha, aperients, the warm bath, and emollient clysters. As an anodyne in this complaint, there appears none so suitable and efficacious for general use, as Dover's powder, that is, the compound ipecacuanha powder. If, therefore, it is not exhibited through the day, as one of the principal remedies, a dose of eight or ten grains may be given in pills, every night. No 124A, page 206, is also good.

In the aggravated cases of bloody flue so often witnessed in India, and other hot climates, the following will be found a safe and efficacious mode of proceeding. Let half a drachm of calomel, two scruples of ipecacuanha powder, and eight grains of powdered opium, be made with aromatic confection into twenty-four pills, of which two are to be taken, two, three or four times in the twenty-four hours, according to the urgency of the symptoms; a full dose of the mixture No. 73 or an ounce of castor oil, being given every day to clear the bowels, with the warm bath and fomentations, emollient clysters, and a flannel bandage, as already advised. At the same time, if the inflammatory symptoms are considerable or blood appears alarmingly in the stools, bleeding may be immediately resorted to, and be soon repeated, if the inflammation does not give way. Should the symptoms of local uneasiness and tenesmus be great, a ten-grain dose of Dover's powder may be taken at night.

In cases of great urgency occurring in India, calomel administered in the dose of a scruple, twice or thrice a day, with the use of the other means just noticed, has been often found of signal service.

Nitric acid and opium, mixed with water, sometimes produces the most excellent effects, both in dysentery and diarrhoea, and it may always be tried with safety, in the following form. It has plucked many from the jaws of death.

Take of nitric acid..................... 2 drachms;
Solid opium......................... 2 gains;
Water .... 3 ounces.
Mix, and take a tea-spoonful three or four times a day, in common or barley-water.

The object is to support the strength with as little irritation as possible. The diet, therefore, ought to be mucilaginous and diluting, consisting chiefly of preparations of sago, rice, arrow-root, gruel, baked-flour and such like. At the commencement of the disease, it will generally be best to confine the patient to these; but in a more advanced stage, and when the weakness is considerable, jellies and broths, taken with bread, may be allowed. Should the debility be extreme, without any tendency to acute inflammation, the complaint having lasted some time, a little wine diluted with water and mucilage will sometimes be advisable. The drink should be always lukewarm.

When the patient begins to recover, his appetite sometimes outstrips his digestion, and care moust, consequently, be exercised not to exceed a very moderate quantity of food, even where the appetite is keen, for if too much indulged in the weakest organ suffers increased irritation, and a severe relapse invariably follows.

The horizontal posture and perfect rest must be constantly observed, and the greater the irritation the more requisite they are. The patient ought not to give way to the frequent inclination to stool, but stifle it as much as possible. The stools must be immediately removed from the patient's chamber, which should be freely ventilated at all times, and frequently sprinkled with vinegar. In malignant dysentery, the patient should void his motions into a vessel half full of water, to which a tea-spoonful or two of the concentrated chloride of lime has been added: this removes all smell instantly, and destroys infection. In such bad cases, the diluted chloride must he sprinkled over the apartment twice a day, (*see* page 305). It is advisable also to bury the motions when the disease is malignant, as the effluvia arising from them has been known to give the disease both to men and animals, even after they have been deposited in the usual receptacle.

During convalescence, flannel should be constantly worn next the skin, and the most scrupulous attention be paid to avoid dews, damp night air, and sudden atmospherical vicissitudes, more especially in hot or unhealthy climates; and no article of diet difficult of digestion must be touched.

After leaving off other medicines, the patient should take an infusion of calumba or quassia, with or without a little nitrous acid and opium, to give tone to the bowels, which should be continued till they have recovered their vigour. This combination of the quassia infusion and nitrous acid is often of great utility as a restorative in the decline of the disease.

Take of nitrous acid	1 drachm;
Infusion of quassia	8 ounces;
Tincture of opium	40 drops.

Mix, and let one fourth part be taken three times a day.

It must be the *nitrous* acid, and not the *nitric*, which has not he same effect.

If pain and irritation are still occasionally felt, four or five grains of the compound ipecacuanha powder may be taken when the pain calls for it.

In Chronic Dysentery (that is, the protracted species of the disease, in which the acute inflammatory symptoms have subsided or been subdued), our objects are nearly the same as in the acute variety, only we are called upon constantly to remember, that debility is invariably associated with this form of the complaint, and therefore every proper means of preserving and increasing the general strength must be employed. Of all the remedies yet discovered for chronic flux, calomel, opium, and ipecacuanha in combination are, undoubtedly, the safest and the best. Many patients, tormented for a long time by this painful malady, have been speedily relieved, and ultimately completely cured by this invaluable medicine. It is equally adapted to the protracted dysentery so often met with in hot climates, and to that of colder regions. An old medical aquaintance of mine, who had this disease dreadfully severe, while attached to the British army of occupation in France, was perfectly cured in a short time by this medicine alone, after the numerous expedients previously resorted to by almost the whole medical staff had entirely failed. The following is an eligible form of exhibiting this combination :

Take of Calomel	10	grains;
Turkey opium, in powder	5	grains;
Ipecacuanha powder	20	grains.

Rub them well together, then form them into a mass with aromatic confection, and divide it into ten pills. One should be taken directly, and repeated every night and morning till the severity of the symptoms is overcome, when its repetition every night will be sufficient.

If the exhibition of the preceding pills should not be followed by satisfactory results, the union of Dover's powder and calomel may be very serviceable. A grain of calomel and three or four grains of Dover's powder may be made into a pill, with a little aromatic or opiate confection, and taken twice or thrice a day.

The mixture of nitrous acid and quassia bark, noticed above, is likewise often useful. This medicine may be given with great advantage after leaving off the mercurial remedy, to give tone to the bowels, and perfect the cure.

Some physicians say they have found a combination of charcoal powder and Dover's powder very useful in the chronic form, and others speak favourably of the sulphate of copper. The latter medicine is given in doses of half a grain, gradually increased, if necessary, to one or two grains, with half a grain of opium, thricc daily.

The diet in chronic dysentery must, of course, be mild, unirritating, and chiefly farinaceous, consisting mutton broth, rice, sago, arrow-root, oatmeal gruel and boiled milk. A very excellent diet here is flour and milk, well boiled together, which, with a very little sugar and spice, is highly relished by the debilitated patient.

The patient, must constantly wear a flannel bandage round the bowels, and keep the feet and legs warm by wearing woollen stockings and drawers.

If, after the subsidence of the dysentery, there remains a sallow hue of the complexion, tenderness on pressure in the right side, and a clayey appearance of the excrement, take the pill No. 117, page 203 or No. 99, page 192, every night, a tea-cupful of lime-water thrice a day, and be very attentive to daily exercises, and to friction over the region of the liver and bowels, with the liniment No. 45, page 163.

EAR-ACHE

Some persons are much troubled with ear-ache on exposure to cold, which usually depends on a natural weakness of the organ or an unnatural susceptibility imparted to it by disorder of the digestive organs. In such a state, a little cotton should be loosely worn in the ear to defend it from the external air, and every appropriate means be taken to strengthen both the part and the general constitution, by means of frequent washing with cold water, cold bathing, and the employment of those measures calculated to amend the general health.

Treatment.—Sometimes ear-ache is connected with chronic ulceration in the internal or external part of the ear, when injections of warm water and soap are advisable. In this case, there is sometimes a constant fetid discharge, for which in union of Peruvian balsam with ox-gall has been recommended by Dr. Hugh Smith :

Take of Ox-gall	3 drachms;
Balsam of Peru.	1 drachm.

Mix. A drop or two to be put into the ear with a little cotton.

For the treatment of an accumulation or deficiency of wax, see the article DEAFNESS.

In all chronic affections of the ear, a soothing plan of treatment is the best; and it should be particularly remarked, that this organ will not bear tampering with, as from its vicinity to the membranes of the brain, improper or irritating applications are frequently dangerous.

But pain in the ear may be so severe as to indicate the presence of inflammation, which will be known by the accompanying frequency and hardness of the pulse, and the presence of fever. An acute disease will then demand our attention, and will require bleeding, by means of leeches applied near the part affected or by the use of the lancet, followed by warm formentations, blisters behind the ears, and the saline purgative No. 73, page 176. The employment of leeches will generally be sufficient, and the diet should be confined to simple farinaceous decoctions of barley, grits, etc.

But one of the best modes of treating this disease is by exhibiting an emetic, combined with a purgative medicine. This will often cure ear-ache far more certainly and more speedily than blood-letting, blisters, fomentations or any other means; and the reason is, that this complaint generally originates in congestion of the liver, and derangement of the other digestive organs, which the emetico-purgative medicine is eminently calculated to remove. For this purpose, thirty grains of ipecacuanha powder, one grain of tartrate of antimony, and three grains of calomel, may be taken together in a little treacle, and followed by a free draught of lukewarm water. This may be repeated twice or thrice, if necessary. Dr. James Kennedy affirms, that he has treated twenty-five cases of this disease in this manner, with uniform, rapid and complete success.

If the patient thinks the preceding too severe a course, let him take the pill No. 98, page 191, every night, with the draught No. 27, page 155, the first thing on awaking, and the pills No. 104 or 104A, page 197, during the day. After the ear-ache has been removed, let a dose of the fluid extract of sarsaparilla be taken in water twice a day or the mixture of bark and muriatic acid No. 84, page 184.

Ear-ache is sometimes connected with carious teeth or stumps, and if the disorder resists the means used, we may suspect this to be its origin. Creosote may then be of great service, if extraction be not resorted to. For the mode of using it see TOOTH-ACHE.

Now and then the pain spreads from the ear over the whole or a greater part of the head, attended with high fever, giving us reason to suspect that the inflammation has extended to the brain; delirium not unfrequently follows, and the disease becomes dangerous. The most powerful local and general means must now be combined, and the proper course to be pursued will be found under the head of *Inflammation of the Brain.* It is a happy circumstance, however, that the most violent forms of inflammation of the ear more frequently terminate in suppuration than in death; and if the brain has partaken of the inflammation, the suppuration in the ear generally relieves it.

Should suppuration occur, matter will be discharged for some time, when the simplest and mildest injections only ought to be employed to keep the parts clean, and promote the healing of the ulcer, as soap and warm water or from five to ten grains of sulphate of zinc dissolved in a pint of rose water, to be used lukewarm.

EPILEPSY OR FALLING FITS

This is a disease consisting of paroxysms of convulsions, returning at uncertain periods, accompanied by an abolition of sense and voluntary motion, and ending in somnolency or complete sleep.

Its attacks are sometimes sudden, when the patient falls at once to the ground in a state of utter insensibility; sometimes they are preceded by certain premonitory symptoms, such as languor, pain or giddiness in the head, drowsiness, dimness of sight, and ringing in the ears, etc. In the fit, the involuntary muscular power is often excessive; the body is bent forwards or drawn backwards with great force; the eyes roll furiously; the lips are convulsed, and covered with a frothy saliva; the tongue is thrust violently from the mouth, and is sometimes shockingly lacerated; the pulse is irregular; the breathing oppressed and occasionally highly laborious; and in some cases, bilious matter in large quantities is erected from the stomach. These *symptoms* sooner or later gradually give way, and the unhappy patient falls into a profound sleep.

The paroxysms vary greatly in degree, duration and period of return, in different cases.

The most frequent *causes* are irritation in the stomach and intestines; a diseased state of the spinal marrow; sudden fright; excessive grief; great loss of blood; the suppression of accustomed discharges or cutaneous eruptions; the action of mineral poisons; excess in drinking; and the imprudent use of calomel.

On the dissection of those who have died epileptic, various diseased appearances have been observable, chiefly within the head, such as tumours, effusions, indurations and marks of disorganization in some part of the brain. M. Wenzel, Professor of Anatomy in the College of Mayence, who has had great opportunities of instituting anatomical examinations in this disease, says, "that in a very great proportion of the heads he examined he found the cerebrum[1] in a healthy state, but the cerebellum[2] uniformly, and in a very extraordinary degree and manner, diseased.[3] But after the most careful examination, the inquiry perpetually recurs, whether we are to consider

---

1. The large and upper portion of the brain.
2. The small portion of the brain, situated at the base of the head.
3. According, to Flourens, a French physiologist, it will be found that in slicing the cerebrum the intellect is affected, while in slicing the cerebellum the motion will be affected; from which we may fairly draw the inference, that the cerebrum is most connected with the intellect, and the cerebellum with the locomotive and muscular powers of man. Thus, it will be seen what great support the experiments of Flourens affords to the inference naturally drawn from Wenzell's examinations, that the *immediate cause* of Epileptic Convulsions is some alteration in the structure or functions of the cerebellum.

the diseased appearances present, as the cause or consequence of the disease?

The involuntary laughing or weeping, and the sensation of a globe rising in the throat, which accompany hysterics, will sufficiently *distinguish* this disease from epilepsy. For the signs distinguishing it from Apoplexy, see that article.

TREATMENT—The most powerful remedies in epilepsy are, the ammoniate of copper; flowers of zinc; leaves of the orange tree; misseltoe; lady's smock; setons or issues; and a strict regard to the diet and regimen proper for the case. Dr. Cullen, the celebrated Professor at Edinburgh, was very partial to the ammoniate of copper, and numerous cases are on record in which it was successfully employed. Dr. Beattie says, " it seldom fails to cure epilepsy; never, if the disease be idiopathic[1] and the patient not exhausted".

Take of Ammoniate of copper .... 20 grains;

Bread crumb and mucilage of gum arabic, a sufficient quantity to form it into a mass : which is to be divided into forty pills.

In the beginning, one of these is to be taken three times a day, and gradually increased to two or even three pills, thrice a day.

The flowers of zinc were once in high repute in epilepsy, and in all other spasmodic complaints; but they have suffered of late, like every other medicine, from druggists having frequently sold a bad article. The dose is three grains, made into a pill with extract of gentian, twice or thrice a day, which may be increased to six or seven grains. These preparations of copper and zinc may be given alone, as now directed or each dose of either medicine may be combined with three grains of camphor, which Dr. Cullen thought capable of increasing their virtues.

The leaves of the orange tree have been little used in this country, but have been an esteemed remedy on the continent, having been used at the Hague, and in the hospitals of Vienna, with evident advantage. M. Locker administered this medicine in the hospital of St. Mark to a great many epileptic persons, and found it superior,

1. A primary disease, not depending on another.

he says, to the most celebrated remedies, all of which he had tried. The dose is from a scruple to a drachm of the powder, three times a day. The powder of misseltoe is an ancient anti-epileptic, and is frequently of great service. Boerhaave Van Swieten, Dr. Willan, and other celebrated physicians, have employed it with success. The dose is the same as that of the last article.

The lady's smock enjoyed the confidence of Sir George Baker and Ray mentions it in his letters with approbation. A Cornish clergyman, of the name of Gregor, has observed, that the flowering tops of the lady's smock had been used by his family for some generations in the cure of epilepsies. They should be gathered in June or July; and the dose is a scruple twice a day, which should be increased by decrees to a drachm or a drachm and a half.

A seton or issue, in the neighbourhood of the spine, should seldom be neglected in this disease. It is frequently a valuable adjunct to the internal medicine made use if, and is sometimes effectual alone. It seems particularly indicated where there is a preternatural fulness in the blood-vessels of the head.

Beside the above remedies, the nitrate of silver, valerian, nux vomica, thorn apple, the oil of turpentine, and some other medicines, have been occasionally useful; but they are, in my opinion, inferior to the preceding. The nitrate of silver owes the reputation it has lately gained, as a remedy for epilepsy, principally to the support given it by Dr. Baillie. It certainly has been employed with success; and may be administered in doses of from one to six grains, three times a day, made into pills with crumb of bread, and mucilage of gum arabic. Of all the forms of giving valerian, that of the oil would seem to be the most eligible, which is a favourite medicine for this complaint in Germany.

The tincture of nux vomica is strongly recommended in that species of epilepsy which appears on the cessation of the menses. Sixteen drops may be given every three hours, increasing it gradually to twenty-five drops or more in water.

Many of the ancient authors had great faith in the virtues of cinnabar, hence it acquired the name of *magnes epilepsioe.* Some German physicians of the present day regard it almost as a divine remedy, and in a recent number of *Hulfeland's Journal* it is much praised in the following form :

Take of Factitious cinnabar, oxide of bismuth, and herb tobacco, of each	1 scruple;
Extract of aloes	5 grains.

Mix them well, and divide the mass into twenty pills; one of which is to be taken twice a day.

The external application of opium is sometimes worthy of trial. A young lady was brought to M. Portal, an eminent Parisian physician, who was every day attacked by violent epileptic fits, which began in one of her toes; this circumstance suggested to him the idea of cutting the nerve, for the purpose of interrupting the communication, but he began by the application of opium to the nerve, and that alone proved sufficient to effect a complete cure. The use of the opiate liniment No. 39, page 161, is very useful in that furious state, which sometimes supervenes a fit in strong robust habits. It soon effects a calm and induces sleep. A combination of genuine musk with opium, as an internal medicine is likely to prove very valuable in some cases of epilepsy.

Electricity and galvanism are reported to have been resorted to with considerable benefit in some bad cases of epilepsy.

A new remedy for epilepsy has lately been tried on the continent, by Dr. Burdach of Triebal and Professor Hufeland of Berlin, consisting of the roots of the common mug-wort, *(artemisia vulgaris),* dried in the shade, and a short time before it is used, powdered. The dose is from fifty to seventy grains or a large tea-spoonful, of the powder, in a little warm beer, about half an hour before the expected attack. The patient should then be placed in a bed, well covered and drink warm beer. The first dose, it is said, generally gives some relief, and sometimes performs a complete cure; but the dose should be repeated every other day. Out of ten cases treated by Professor Hufeland, three were perfectly cured, and three greatly relieved. The other four did not experience much benefit. One of this physician's cases is very striking; a girl aged seventeen, had had a fit every day for ten or twelve years, in consequence of a blow on the head she was quite cured by a single dose. A man, aged twenty-nine, who had had fits for years, was quite cured by two doses. Since the publication of the second edition of this book, it is said that Dr. Boire, the physician of the hospital at Versailles, has for some time been very successfully exhibiting mug-wort in cases of epilepsy. A drachm was given four times a day, by Dr. Home of Edinburgh, to a woman who had been affected with *hysteric* fits for many years, the fits ceased in a few days. In this patient, assafoetida and ether had been given to no purpose.

The following prescription has perfectly succeeded in a very severe case of epilepsy occurring in a strong young man in the author's connexion, and it has also been effectual in the last two or three instances reported to him.

Take of Oxide of zinc		half a drachm;
Powder of squills	1	drachm;
Gum assafoetida	1½	drachm.

Mix, and divide into thirty-six pills, of which take one pill three times a day in the beginning, and gradually increase the dose to two pills thrice daily.

The *bromide of potassium* has been used with success, and the reader will find some valuable remarks on the subject in the author's book *On Female Diseases,* seventh edition, under Painful Menstruation.

In debilitated habits, the cold bath is an advisable assistant. The cold affusion to the head is more generally applicable, and frequently more beneficial. When the disease is the consequence of onanism or excessive indulgence of the venereal appetite, the affusion of cold water on the head, and organs of generation, should not be neglected.

When the disease appears to have been occasioned by excessive evacuations, we should endeavour to restrain them; when by suppressed discharges, they ought, if possible, to be restored. In the latter case, blisters, issues, the warm bath, and diaphoretics, are among the best remedies. If the piles are suppressed, leeches should be applied to the anus, and aloetic purgatives administered.

Blood-letting is a frequent resource among professional men in the present complaint; but I very much disapprove of it. The plethora sometimes associated with the disease is much more safely and effectually reduced by a spare diet, purgatives, etc., than by bleeding. *See* page 284.

Attention to diet and exercise is of great consequence. If the malady be connected with or dependent upon, debility, the diet should be generous and nutritious; but to avoid irritation, the quantity must be small. For instructions as to the quantity and quality of the food, see *Indigestion.* In strong robust constitutions, the diet should be spare; and if the habit be very plethoric, a total abstinence from animal food and strong drink will be highly necessary. Such a course has proved of great service to plethoric epileptics.

The observance of early hours is valuable, and horse exercise is much to be recommended. It has been wisely suggested that the patient should make an entire change in his habits, which is a practice worthy of general adoption. I have known several epileptics in whom the disease has ceased spontaneously, after an ineffectual trial of various medicines, which occurrence has probably followed some unobserved, though to them important, change in their general mode of living.

When the fit is actually present, the patient should be placed on a bed or sofa, the head somewhat raised, and those parts of the dress removed that are likely to press upon the vessels of the neck. In order to prevent the tongue being injured by the spasmodic action of the muscles of the jaws, a piece of soft wood or a napkin properly rolled up, should be introduced between the teeth. It was formerly the practice to apply acrid stimulants to the mouth and nose, but these are now generally condemned.

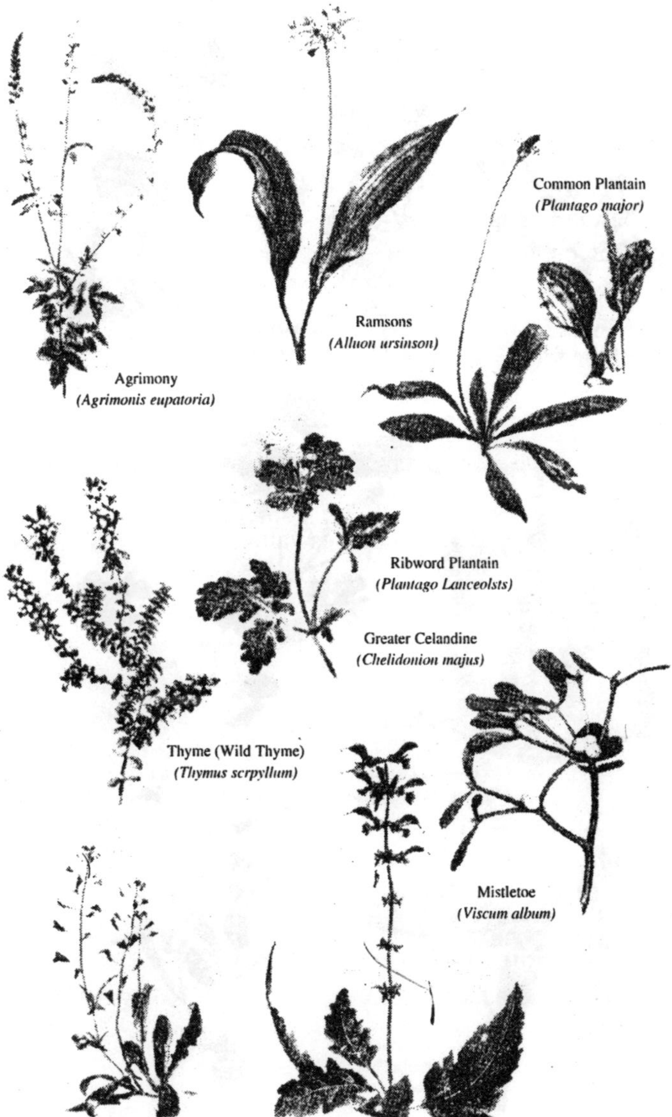
Agrimony
(Agrimonis eupatoria)
Ramsons
(Alluon ursinson)
Common Plantain
(Plantago major)
Ribword Plantain
(Plantago Lanceolsts)
Greater Celandine
(Chelidonion majus)
Thyme (Wild Thyme)
(Thymus scrpyllum)
Mistletoe
(Viscum album)
Shepherd's Pursc
(Capsells bursa-pastoris)
Sage
(Salvia officinalis)

Dandelion
(Taraxacion officnale)

Bedstraw
(Galiom)

Coltsfoot
(Tussilago farfara)

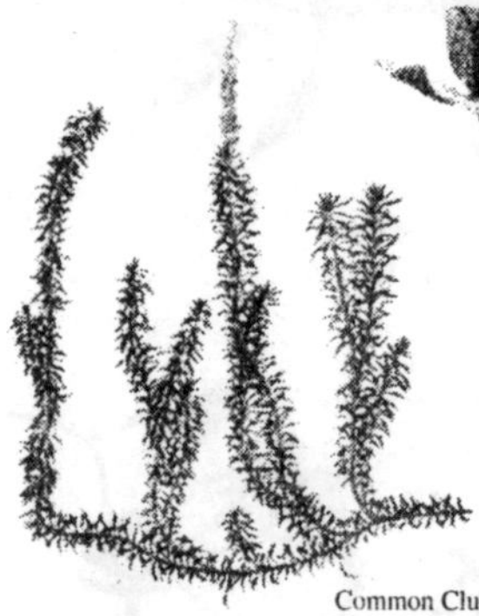

Common Club Moss
(Lycopodion clavattum)

Mallow
(Malus valgaris)

Butterbur,
Umbrella Plant
(Petasites officinalis)

Calendula, Marigold
(Calendula officinalis)

Lady's Mantle
(Alchenills tulgaris)

Indian Corn
(Zea Mays)

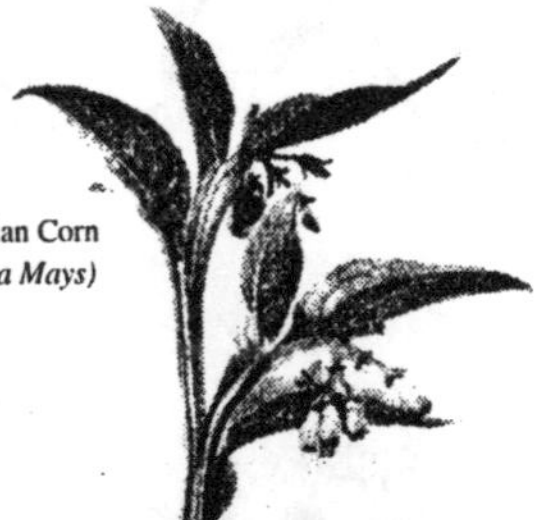

Comfrey
(Symphyton officinale)

Walnut
(Juglans regia)

Stinging Nettle
(Urtica dioica)

Cowslip
(Primula officinalis)

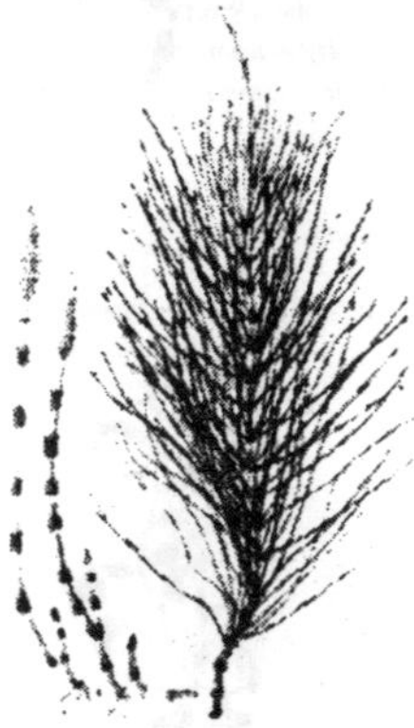

Horsetail
(Equisetum arvense)

Yellow Dead Nettle
(Lamium galeobdolon)
Wood Sorrel
(Oxalis acetosella)
Camomile
(Matricaria chamomilla)
St. John's Wort
(Hypericum perforation)
Small Flowered Willow-herd
(Epilobium parvflorum)
Golden Rod
(Solidago virga-arrea)
Speedwell
(Veronica officmalis)
Calamus, Sweet Flag
(Acorus calamus)

Ayurvedic Materia Medica
for
Domestic Use

VOLUME - TWO

Ayurvedic Materia Medica
for
Domestic Use

A Guide for Every Home

VOLUME - TWO

By

Thomas J. Graham

LOGOS PRESS, NEW DELHI-110002

Cataloging in Publication Data—DK
Courtesy: D.K. Agencies (P) Ltd. <docinfo@dkagencies.com>
Graham, Thomas J.

Ayurvedic materia medica for domestic use : a guide for every home/ by Thomas J. Graham.

2 v. cm.

Includes index.

ISBN 8172680848 (set)
ISBN 8172680856 (v. 1)
ISBN 8172680864 (v. 2)

1. Materia medica, Vegetable. 2. Medicine, Ayurvedic. I. Title.

DDC 615.53 21

ISBN : 81-7268-085-6....(Vol. I)
ISBN : 81-7268-086-4.......(Vol. II)
ISBN : 81-7268-084-8....(Set)

Edition : Published in this form 2006

Printed & Published by
LOGOS PRESS
Building No. 4788-90, Street No. 23, Ansari Road,
Darya Ganj, New Delhi-110 002 (India)
Phone : 23272187

PREFACE

My object in the composition of the following Treatise has been to present the unprofessional reader with a clear and correct description of the nature, symptoms, causes, distinction, and most approved treatment of the diseases to which the human frame is liable; knowing that such a work is in constant requisition by clergymen in their endeavours to help their poor parishioners, and also by the heads of families in the absence of their medical friend; and that to travellers, emigrants, and persons proceeding to a foreign climate, it must prove of frequent, and sometimes of signal, service. The chief design of the writer of a work of this description should be, I conceive, to lay before his readers a just and clear view of the nature of the different maladies treated of, and the best and most manageable remedies for the relief of pain and irritation, and the cure of disease; and these are the objects which I have constantly kept in view throughout the volume, and to the accomplishment of which every consideration of minor importance has been sacrificed. In every instance, the HEAD OF TREATMENT has received the greatest attention, because it is the most important; and under this division the plan or plans of management which are generally applicable to the particular malady treated of, and which are the most certain of success, in the majority of cases, have in general been first laid down, and afterwards almost every other useful remedy has been described separately. So that the reader will, I hope, find a determinate mode of treatment, of general and superior efficacy, detailed under each complaint for which he may be desirous of prescribing, and thus be preserved from doubt and anxiety as to those remedies which merit his first and chief regard.

So far as my experience and observation extend, the soothing plan of treating diseases will be found almost invariably the best and most successful, and this conviction has constantly influenced me in the advice and instructions now offered. On this point, no higher general principles can be presented for the reader's consideration and guidance than these,—THE FORMATION OF HEALTHY BLOOD AND THE RELIEF OF IRRITATION ARE THE GREAT OBJECTS OF MEDICINE. These truths it is of immense importance he should bear in mind, whenever he wishes to alleviate bodily sufferings in himself of others; for he will uniformly find, that those means which are the most powerful in promoting the life and purity of the blood, and in allaying irritation, are the most speedy and effectual in the relief and cure of disease. These facts have stimulated me to oppose, to the best of my ability, in these volumes, as well as in my other publications, the frequent and excessive use of mercury, and all other debilitating means,—a practice far more general and destructive than is commonly apprehended. Mercurial preparations, especially calomel, are of inestimable value; but it must never be overlooked, that the quentity administered ought to be very small. Mercury, taken in minute doses, soothes and tranquillizes the disordered system, and sometimes proves the most certain and powerful means of recovery; but when given in large doses it breaks down the integrity of the blood, becomes highly irritating to all the organs, and, for the most part, permanently deleterious.

The human body often falls quickly into a state of debility and disease, but from such a condition, the progress towards recovery is generally slow, (although it may be certain), even under the use of the most efficient means of cure; consequently, when any advantage is gained in the beginning, from the administration of medicine, together with a good diet and regimen, we have much reason to be satisfied, and both our wisdom and strength will lie in following up this advantage by perseverance in nearly the same measures. In the practice of medicine, small beginnings frequently ripen into grand results, and it is too often from a disregard of this truth, and a foolish desire to try new plans of treatment, that persons afflicted with severe diseases fail to get well.

In the original composition of these volumes, and in its subsequent revision, I have uniformly and earnestly endeavoured to exhibit the real value of different professional opinions and modes of medical practice; being desirous throughout to divest myself of all undue partiality, either to the one side or the other, so that my readers may be enabled to recognize here a fair statement, and an unbiassed opinion of the real value, both of prevailing and conflicting sentiments, so far as my ability enables me to exhibit them. In all the affairs of human life, it is, unhappily, too frequently found that prepossession, prejudice, of interested motives, exert a powerful sway, as well over the judgment as the affections of mankind; and hence partly have arisen the error, misrepresentation, and conflict, so remarkably conspicuous in medical writings and opinion. Of course, I cannot hope that the present sheets will be found free from imperfection and error; but if I have erred, I enjoy the sweet satisfaction of knowing that it has not only not been wilful, but also that it has not been without a most sincere and resolute endeavour to state the *real truth*. In no case, to my knowledge, have I delivered an opinion, more especially if relating to practical matters, which has not been verified by personsl experience, or sanctioned by the authority of distinguished professional men, whose veracity and ability are undoubted.

I do not desire or expect to make unprofessional people skilful physicians, but the diseases to which flesh is heir are so many, so painful, and so complicated; the circumstances of the sufferers are so various and changeable; the difficulty of procuring immediately efficient medical assistance is sometimes so great, and the influence of medicines and other means, that may always be safely used, is so salutary, —that we possess herein multiplied and sufficient reasons for diffusing among the public minute descriptions of diseases, and the most precise directions, that can be embodied in a moderate space, for the use of efficient medical means of relief and cure. Accordingly, from medical men in the army and navy, from retired professional men, and also from some of high standing in active practice, the author has received the most flattering testimonies to the value and usefulness of this work. I shall only add in the words of one of the most illustrious of physicians : — "I have always thought it a greater happiness to discover a certain method of curing even the slightest disease, than to accumulate the largest fortune; and whoever compasses the former, I esteem not only happier, but also better and wiser. For can a person give a stronger proof of his benevolence and wisdom than by endeavouring always to promote the public good, rather than his private interest, as he makes so small and inconsiderable a part of the whole? and, in reality, as it is the part of a wicked man to destroy his fellow-creatures, so it is the duty of a good man to preserve them, and instruct others how to save them from death, even after his own decease. Nor can anything be more inhuman and detestable than to insinuate a disregard and unconcern for whatever misfortunes may happen to mankind after our death." — *Sydenham's Works*, vol.ii. p. 384.

I beg leave to recommend to the female part of my readers my TREATISE OR THE DISEASES OF FEMALES, and to the clergh and heads of families my volume. ON INFANCY AND CHILDHOOD.The first describes the proper management of women before and after delivery, with an ample consideration of their peculiar maladies, and of many points of uncommon consequence, especially to persons living in the country, or embarking for foreign lands. It contains also engravings of the different regions of the body and the situation of the viscera, with a Glassary of Medical terms, additional prescriptions, etc.. The volume on *Infancy and childhood* embraces the subjects of nursing, food, weaning, choice of wet nurses, exercises of children, bathing, clothing, moral management of children, hints for the mother's management of herself, approved prescriptions in children's disorders, and a consideration of the complaints peculiar to Infants and Children, etc. Both these works should invariably accompany the *Domestic Medicine*, to which they are designed to be supplementary and companions.

N.B. The reader's attention is requested to the following remarks, and also to those on the anatomy and physiology of the intestines at page 696.

1. By the term *disorder of function* is here meant, a derangement of the natural of healthy functions of the organ or part affected. For example, a disordered liver, or a disorder of the stomach, indicates a derangement of the biliary secretion, or a derangement in the secretions and general functions of the stomach.

2. By *organic disease* or *organic injury* is meant, actual disease in the structure of the part affected. A diseased liver or stomach, therefore, means an actual alteration in the structure of the liver or stomach; which, for the most part, is incurable, except in the incipient stage, but commonly admits of great relief. Persons with organic disease may live and enjoy a large measure of comfort for many years, provided their method of living is well regulated.

3. As disorders or diseases of the lungs form so large a proportion of our bodily maladies, the reader will find it necessary to have some clear ideas of the structure of the lungs, in order to understand what is said of the nature and causes of *asthma, cough*, etc. I would, therefore, remark, that the most accurate investigations seem to prove that the pulmonary organs are principally composed of the windpipe, and its terminations called *bronchia*, which, at their extremities, are subdivided into a multitude of small canals, terminated by culs-de-sac of a globular form, grouped somewhat in the manner of the terminal branchlets of the cauliflower. So that we may say, that the parenchyma, or substance of the lungs, is formed by the aggregation of a multitude of small vesicles (called air cells), of an irregularly spheroid or ovoid figure, full of air, and separated from each other by opaque white partitions.

Thomas J. Graham

CONTENTS

VOLUME - TWO

VOLUME - TWO

ERUPTIONS ON THE SKIN

The red, hard, distinct, stationary pimples, so frequently seen in the face of different individuals, are the consequence of a sympathy of the small excreting vessels of the part affected, with a disordered condition of the stomach, bowels and liver. If they will yield to medical treatment, suborifics and alteratives internally, with some local stimulant at the same time, are the most efficient remedies. Dr. Mason Good recommends *(Study of Medicine)* ten or fifteen grains of the compound powder of ipecacuanha, to be taken at bed-time for several nights in succession, the part affected being at the same time wrapped in flannel; I think a grain of calomel should be added to it, and the whole made into three pills with extract of gentian. If this is not effectual, the pill No. 117, page 203, taken twice a day, with ten grains of camphor, may be tried, the pimples being anointed twice or thrice a day, with the strong liniment of ammonia, No. 45 or with the Prussic acid lotion below. The lotion of bi-chloride of mercury No. 72A, at page 175, is a most efficacious application when great itching is present. Dr. Darwin, in the *second volume of his Zoonomia,* has a copious collection of cases of this complaint, with the means employed for their cure, which it may be worth the while of the afflicted reader to turn to. Among the rest, is that of "Miss L., a young lady about eighteen, who had tried a variety of advice for pimples over the greatest part of her face, in vain. She took rhubarb, five grains, and emetic tartar, a quarter of a grain, every night for many weeks, and blistered, her face by degrees all over, and became quite beautiful". These red, stationary pimples in the face, form a complaint called by professional men *gutta rosea,* and are often a source of much disgust to the female part of society. *Gowland's lotion* is a favourite remedy for their removal; but, as it is a strong solution of corrosive sublimate, it is by no means safe; the above means will be found more permanently beneficial without being dangerous. Glycerine may be tried with every prospect of advantage.

Cutaneous eruptions are divided chiefly into *vesicular, pustular* or *scaly* eruptions. *Eczema* or *running scall*, and *herpes* or *tetter* are the principal vesicular eruptions. They are small, round, pointed elevations of the skin, containing a transparent or colourless or pearly fluid; they break, and are succeeded by scurf, scales or open sores.

Eczema is an eruption of small slightly-raised elevations, crowded together on broad irregular patches of bright red skin, accompanied by severe tingling or smarting. Then the vesicles burst, and the fluid dries into thin yellowish-green scabs or shining crusts.

In *herpes* or *tetter* the rash soon coalesces, and their contents become yellowish-white or yellow and form a scab. The shingles belong to this class.

One of the best modes of treating this class is to wash the parts affected very frequently or keep them constantly wet, by means of lint, with au alkaline wash—a drachm of carbonate of soda to half a pint of water; and to take fifteen or twenty drops of tincture of muriate of iron, in a wine-glassful of water, thrice a day. Or, instead of the iron, ammonia will be found very efficacious.

In all cutaneous eruptions, the ammonia mixture No. 78D, page 181, will be found very useful, and the alkaline wash is applicable to every kind, whether of *vesicles, pustules or scales.*

The *grog blossoms* of hard drinkers can be readily cured only by a return to habits of temperance, with the persevering employment of the means just noticed.

The red discharging pimples occurring on the chin, and about the mouth, are a symptom of some internal disorder or of impurity of the blood, and may almost invariably be removed by the use of the sarsaparilla decoction in the day, and the alterative pill No. 98, every other night. The solution of bi-chloride of mercury, *(liquor hydrargyri bi-chloridi),* in doses of from half a tea-spoonful to a tea-spoonful twice a day in water is likewise very beneficial it may be taken in water or in the decoction of sarsaparilla. This is both tonic and alterative, and is a suitable remedy for almost all kinds of skin disease. For these, and, indeed, most other kinds of pimples, sulphur internally is an admirable medicine, and the following lotion may be used externally with great advantage : *see* page 121.

Take of Prussic acid, ...	2	drachms;
Oxymuriate of mercury	6	grains;
Emulsion of bitter almonds		half a pint.

Mix for a lotion, to be used twice a day.

This lotion is particularly useful in allaying the trouble some itching, so often attending eruptions of this description.

For chronic affections of the skin which appear in distinct patches on the hands, arms, neck, face or any other part of the body, and which generally show more or less of a scaly appearance, glycerine may be spread over the parts or the following ointment will be found useful as a topical application, while some alterative medicine should be taken internally.

Take of Ointment of nitrate of mercury......	2	drachms;
Saturnine ointment (page 179)	6	or 8 drachms.

Mix, and apply night and morning on a piece of linen rag.

One of the very best applications to allay the itching of cutaneous eruptions is made by mixing together bees' wax and olive oil, in tire proportion of one part wax to two or three of oil; with which every irritated part may be anointed nighg and morning. I lave known this succeed in a case of unusual suffering, after from twelve to twenty different lotions and ointments had been tried in vain. The benzoated ointment of oxide of zinc, (to be procured at Bell's, in Oxford Street), is said to be a valuable application. Two ounces should be mined with two drachms of rectified spirit of wine, and then smeared on the part night and morning.

Not only the warm, but also the vapour bath is sometimes an effectual remedy in cutaneous eruptions of every kind, and should be tried in all obstinate cases. It may be used about once a week. See *Appendix.*

The red gum, and other eruptions on the skin of infants and young children, are usually the effects of acidity or other disorders in the stomach, and are best treated with absorbents, and gentle aperients occasionally. An absorbent powder of magnesia and gum tragacanth in powder, and the aperient No. 121, page 205, will be proper. The whole surface of the body should be kept clean and be frequently washed with lukewarm water. If any imprudent exposure to cold should suddenly drive in the eruption, the child must be immediately plunged into a warm bath at about one hundred degrees, which is generally sufficient to reproduce it. See the author's volume *On Infancy and Childhood.*

This must be remembered as A PRINCIIPLE OF GREAT MOMENT—that almost all cutaneous eruptions,—all foulness of the skin—depend upon a vitiated condition of the blood and digestive orans or derangement of the general health, and, therefore, the most efficient remedies for them are those which tend to improve this condition, and have, at the same time, the power of relaxing the skin such as preparations of antimony and calomel of ipecacuanha, sarsaparilla root, dandelion, nitric acid, and the other means above recommended. The solution of iodide of potassium is sometimes efficacious; and in all cases an exact diet of easily-digested food, and regular active exercise is of great importance. In females, if their female health is irregular, and debility is present, the pills of steel and aloes recommended under GREEN SICKNESS will be advisable.

ERYSIPELAS

ERYSIPELAS or Saint Anthony's fire, is an inflammatory, cutaneous, and trivially elevated swelling, attended with a redness, which disappears, and leaves a white spot for a short time, after being touched with the end of the finger. It is, in fact, an inflammation of an unhealthy character, which is mostly superficial.

This eruption appears in the form of a red blotch or stain, which spreads with more or less rapidity; the part is generally of a bright red colour, clear and shining, the tumour being not accompanied by throbbing, but by a burning heat and tingling rather than acute pain. After the redness has continued for an uncertain time, blisters of various sizes sometimes rise on the skin, generally containing a thin, sometimes limped, sometimes yellowish fluid. The red colour changes to a yellow as the eruption goes off, and the parts which were not occupied by the blister often suffer a desquamation or peeling off of the skin. In mild cases, the eruption often gradually disappears or is carried off by a spontaneous sweating in a day or two. In others, it continues, without beginning to decline, for twelve or fourteen days or longer.

When this disease attacks the face and head, it is most dangerous, because of the inflammation being apt to spread to the brain. It has there the same appearance as on other parts of the body. A red spot appears on some part of the face, generally of no great extent, which spreads till it sometimes covers, not only the whole face, but the scalp also, now and then descending a considerable way down the neck. The face, and frequently the whole head swell, the fever is considerable, and the tumid eyelids sometimes suppurate.

The prognosis is particularly influenced by the seat of the inflammation; in the limbs it is safer than in the trunk, in the trunk than in the face, and all other things being equal, the more extensive the inflammation the greater the danger.

Whatever part the erysipelas attacks, it is generally preceded by chilliness, succeeded by heat, anxiety, quick pulse, thirst and other febrile symptoms. It is likewise frequently attended with what are called bilious symptoms, as a bitter taste in the mouth, foul tongue, pain in the stomach, head-ache, giddiness, nausea, and even vomiting and purging, frequently of bile.

The *chief causes* are violent passions, such as anger, acute grief, etc.; exposure to the heat of the sun or that of the fire; cold, combined with damp, especially in variable weather; too full a diet, particularly the abuse of fermented liquors; the action of various vegetable, mineral and animal poisons. Wounds, contusions and fractures are frequent causes. Whatever renders the holy irritable predisposes to erysipelas; and it is most frequent in spring and autumn. It is unquestionably contagious.

In most cases, it would seem to be intimately dependent on an enervated state of the constitution, and poor blood. Thus persons in the habit of drunkenness and other kinds of intemperance, and who, in a state of intoxication, meet with local injuries, often hang an inflammation of an erysipelatous character; while other subjects, who lead more regular lives, experience, when they meet with similar injuries, healthy inflammation. It is an ancient opinion, that this disease commonly originates in disorder of the liver, and other digestive organs; Hippocrates and Galen entertained this opinion; and the celebrated foreign physician, Tissot, with others of great eminence, have written at length in favour of this view of the subject. But the blood also is in a very unhealthy state, that is, erysipelas is a constitutional complaint.[1]

Its characteristic appearances are a florid skin, with vesicles or small bladders, containing an amber-coloured secretion under the raised skin.

TREATMENT—Almost all cases of erysipelas are so connected with a deranged state of the stomach and bowels, as to make a free evacuation from the intestinal canal, by the exhibition of mercurial and saline aperients, of primary importance; with which an emetic may be conjoined. In severe cases of the disease, the emetic No. 29, page 156, should be given immediately; and after it has operated, a purgative powder, composed of a grain of calomel and ten grains of rhubarb or compound jalap powder, which may be washed down with the draught, No. 27 or 28. This purgative may afterwards be repeated every morning or every second morning, according to the state of the bowels, and the disease; and the cordial mixture No. 79, page 181, should be given every four hours during the day. A

---

1. The occurrence of erysipelas shows something very wrong about a man's health".—"It is always the result of a disordered state of the digestive organs I never see it come on if the digestive organs be right, and it goes away as soon as they are pat right".—*Adbernethy's Surgical Lectures.* In Abernethy's opinion, disorder of the digestive organs was the sole and sufficient source of all maladies; he had no idea whatever of impoverished blood being frequently at the root of particular complaints, erysipelas for example; and herein his views were defective and erroneous. Still he saw clearly an important part of the truth.

cooling vegetable diet is likewise necessary for the first day or two, and afterwards mild nourishing food should be taken, with a little animal food once a day.

After this give bark and ammonia, as in the mixture No. 84B, page 185. The most skilful physicians consider that ammonia is peculiarly efficacious in this disease. Blood-letting is now almost universally condemned in erysipelas, and in no case is the application of leeches or cupping advisable. In very acute cases of erysipelas, the frequent administration of mild purgatives, as No. 120, page 205 or No. 73 or 74, page 176-77, are particularly indicated. The powder No. 120, may, therefore, be given at night, and a dose of the mixture No. 74, on the following morning, and they may be repeated every day or according to the severity of the symptoms; the ammonia mixture No. 84B, page 185, being taken at the same time, three or four times, during the day. An occasional draught of soda water is also proper, if the thirst be urgent. Should the patient be affected with great and heavy sleep, what medical men call *coma*, the feet must be frequently bathed with warm water, a mustard poultice applied to them afterwards, and ammonia given internally.[1]

The diet in these cases should be mild and diluting, consisting, for the first few days, solely of vegetable food, and animal broths, with frequent draughts of weak lemonade, barley-water or toast-water.

Severe erysipelas is most frequently met with in delicate and irritable constitutions or in persons debilitated by age, intemperance, poor living or other causes, and then we find universally, that a strengthening mode of treatment is far the best, and often absolutely necessary to the preservation of life. In such examples, especially if the patient inhabit a crowded and populous city or the inflammation change to a purple or livid hue, our chief dependence must be upon a liberal use of bark and ammonia, and wine, as advised under MORTIFICATION. In the first place, the powder

---

1. Free incsion with a scapel, ontheinflamed surface, have been recommended, but I calive they are now generally condomned

No. 120, page 205, should be given in order to empty the bowels, and restore the secretions, and then the sulphate of quinine in doses of three or five grains every four hours, with four, six or eight ounces of food Sherry or Madeira wine. The sulphate of quinine is a superior preparation of bark, and is sometimes a remedy of great value in the present complaint. The bark and ammonia mixture No. 84B, is, in my opinion, still more to be depended on, as I have already remarked, because ammonia is, in eryspelas, of peculiar efficacy, and it is suitable however hard the pulse may be. The diet also must be generous. A little of the most digestible animal food may be allowed once or twice a day, with fresh eggs, sago, panada, etc.; and if the patient has lived intemperately, and indulged much in fermented or spirituous liquors, it will generally be necessary to allow him a little of his favourite drink; under such circumstances even gin has been allowed with advantage. In illustration of the correctness of this remark, I would quote the observations of Sir Astley Cooper on a case in point : A "man", says this distinguished and very able surgeon, who had weakened his constitution by the excessive use of ardent spirits, and who belonged to the lower orders of London, had erysipelas dreadfully severe; his head was swollen to an enormous size, and his recovery, by every person, thought impossible. It was discovered one day, that his wife brought him some gin. He declared that he was better from having drank it, was consequently permitted its continuance, and, to the astonishment of all, rapidly got well".—*Lectures on Surgery by Sir A. Cooper,* No. xv.

The *tincture of muriate of iron* (sometimes called sesqui-chloride of iron) is, next to bark and ammonia, probably the most efficacious remedy for erysipelas, both in adults and children, and the profession generally place great confidence in it. It is now much employed in the London hospitals. Mr. Paget has great confidence in iron, and has said, "iron is not useful in all cases; but no one can be more convinced that there ace certain cases in which iron is a direct and distinct cure for erysipelas".—*Address in Surgery to the Medical Association.* Fifteen or twenty drops of the tincture of muriate of iron may be given to an adult, three or four times a day, in a wine-glassful of water or camphor mixture, and ten drops to a child of ten years old. Mr. Hamilton Bell, of Edinburgh, was one of the first to call attention to this valuable medicine, and I have introduced a large extract from his observations in my volume on INFANCY AND CHILDHOOD.

Our most experienced physicians altogether condemn bleeding and other evacuations in this disease, and declare that bark, ammonia, and wine are the most powerful remedies in all cases, without exception; an opinion in which I entirely concur. Wine is in many cases of far greater service than bark or quinine; indeed, so much so, that patients with sometimes die or have *a very protracted convalescence,* who are treated with bark or quinine alone, but will quickly recover if allowed six or eight ounces of good wine a day. Should the patient be delirious, that will be an additional reason for the immediate use of wine.

As a local application, it is very common to make use of flour, starch, and similar powdery substances, but the best plan in the early stage of the complaint is, to wash the inflamed parts three or four times a day with lukewarm water or with a lotion made by mixing together an ounce of the solution of acetate of ammonia and six ounces of tepid water. When the blisters break, and the fluid they contain oozes out, the attendants cannot do better than wash the parts, from time to time, with a decoction of elder flowers and poppy-heads. An excellent ointment is composed of equal parts of calamine cerate, soap cerate and the ointment of acetate of lead. It has been found very useful in St. George's Hospital in erysipelas from a wound in the head.

Blisters applied over the inflamed surface, will often promptly arrest the progress of the inflammation. It is a favourite remedy with many practitioners in America and France. It is said to be most useful when there is but a moderate degree of feverish reaction, with a moist and slightly red tongue, and somewhat hot and tense skin.

When this complaint arises from a wound or bruise, a warm bread and water poultice should be applied over the part, and be frequently renewed, the general treatment being such as is recommended above.

A slow chronic kind of erysipelas is frequently seen, which hangs about the sufferer for many weeks or months or is often off and on. This always indicates deranged general health, and if the bowels are constipated, requires a saline aperient every morning, such as No. 130B or 130A, with bark and ammonia, twice or thrice a day, as No. 84B— a generous diet, and plenty of country air and exercise.

Before this article is closed, the erysipelas of infants must be noticed, on account of its dangerous nature. It attacks children soon after birth, begins about the navel, and often spreads over the whole belly. The inflamed skin is hard and very painful to the touch; and it appears to seize the most robust as well as delicate children. Sometimes it is seated on the fingers and hands or the feet and uncles, when it is always less dangerous than when it seizes on the belly or any other part of the trunk of the body. This species of erysipelas is most apt to terminate in gangrene. The belly often becomes uniformly tense, and mortified spots make their appearance.

In the treatment of the infantile erysipelas, bark and ammonia or bark with the muriated tincture of iron, have been found of all medicines the most useful. The best form of giving the bark to infants and children, as I have frequently observed in the course of this work, is the sulphate of amorphous quinine. A quarter of a grain may be mixed with a little cinnamon water, and given every two or three hours. The little patient should likewise be nourished from a breast of good milk; and linen compresses, wrung out of camphorated spirit of wine, be applied over the inflamed parts.

EXCORIATIONS

The best treatment of common excoriations consists in dressing them with the Goulard ointment No. 94, page 190 or with the simple ointment, No. 88 or with Turner's cerate No. 95. If there is much inflammation present, the cooling lotion No. 68 or 69, page 173, may be first used, and afterwards the ointment or the bees' wax and olive oil mentioned in page 538-39. Should the excoriation to depend upon constitutional causes, internal medicine likewise will be necessary; when the sarsaparilla powder or the compound extract of sarsaparilla, dandelion or the quinine pills No. 115, page 202, in the day, and the alterative pill No. 99, every other night, will be found a valuable plan.

The excoriations of infants are effectually treated with Goulard water, No. 69 or by dusting a little flour or calamine powder, over them twice a day. Washing with cold water is also a good practice.

FAINTING OR SYNCOPE

In fainting, the motion of the heart and lungs becomes feeble and imperfect, the sensibility. and perception are diminished, the pulse is small and weak, the voice uniformly lost, and the face pale. It may occur suddenly and accidentally, ceasing without any tendency to recurrence; or it may occur at periods more or less regular, with occasional palpitation of the heart during the intervals, and impeded respiration during the fit.

The usual *causes* are fatigue; long fasting; sudden loss of blood; acute pain; overwhelming emotions of the mind, and excess in diet. It may arise also from some structural disease of the heart or the large arteries issuing from it; and where the returns are frequent, and the breathing during the paroxysm, though feeble, is anxious and obstructed; the face livid, with a tendency to restlessness, and without any ordinary exciting cause, as unusual exertion or emotion, being evident, we may with propriety suspect some such lurking mischief.

TREATMENT—In common cases it is only necessary to place the patient in a recumbent position, to apply ammonia, strong vinegar or any other pungent odour to the nostrils, and to use friction to the arms and legs. When the patient is capable of swallowing, a little wine or brandy and water, should be administered; and the occasional causes should be sedulously avoided in future. If the syncope frequently returns, we may be sure the patient requires proper medical attention, and one of the aperient pills No. 100, 101 or 101B, pages 194-95 should be given every other night, with some tonic medicine in the day, such as the pills No. 102, 103 or 104 or the mixture No. 79, 82 or 83. Cold or tepid bathing may also he resorted to, with exercise, regular hours, and light meals; in short the patient ought to attend to the advice given under *Indigestion.*

When we have reason to suspect some organic impediment about the heart, the pill No. 106A, page 198, may be useful or No. 103A, page 197 or a full dose of sarsaparilla, twice a day; and the alterative pill No. 98A, page 192, every other night, at the same time, will correct any bilious derangement.

Tranquillity of mind and body, exercise an abstinence from all stimulating food, and a regular state of the bowels, should be constantly observed.

FEVER

Under the term fever is comprehended a very important class of diseases, one very liable to be misunderstood, especially by unprofessional persons, and in which the patient is often indifferently or improperly treated. There are no cases in which a clear insight into the *nature* of the malady, may be of more essential service to the patient, and none in which unprofessional persons at a distance from an able medical practitioner, feel more sensibly the want of a skilful guide.

TREATMENT—Fever cannot be cured instantaneously, but it may be moderated; it may be gradually subdued; from being violent and dangerous it may be rendered mild and safe. The physician may be favoured to bring it to this condition; and he can rarely accomplish more than this. Under *typhous fever* I have stated my opinion that fever is not a disease of the solid parts of the frame, but of THE BLOOD, and to that article I refer my readers.

The particular remedies of the greatest service in fever are pointed out under the respective titles, but it is certain that cold drinks, sponging with cold water, Seidlitz powders, and James's powder at night, are grand remedies in the early stages; and in the second or depressive stage, muriatic acid, decoction of bark and wine. For pains in the head, chest or abdomen, local bleeding may *in the very beginning,* be had recourse to. It is worthy of remark that smaller bleedings will subdue fever than pure inflammation. In all kinds of fever, when the pulse is quick, and the patient extremely hot, and the skin dry, nothing is of greater and more sensible benefit than wrapping the whole body in a wet sheet; let the patient lay in it for half an hour, then take him out, dip the sheet again in cold water, and wrap it again round the patient. This may be renewed to the third or fourth time, if the fever is not quite subdued before. *See* the Appendix, page 965. When the skin is hot and dry, the wet sheet is far more efficacious than any medicine, and far safer than most medicines prescribed.

Observe: a moderate spontaneous looseness is frequently a salutary crisis of fever, and if it do not prove exhausting, should by no means be interfered with.

The following remarks of Sydenham, in reference to the great diversity in the causes and symptoms of fevers, tire necessity of caution in the use of remedies, and the folly of adhering to exclusive systematic views, are admirably instructive :

> "This, however, I am convinced of, from numerous careful observations, that the same method which cures in the middle of the year, may possibly prove destructive at the conclusion of it; and when I had once happily fallen upon a genuine method of treating any species of fever suitably to its nature, I always proved successful, (proper regard being had to the constitution, age, and other particular circumstances of the patient), till that species became extinct, and a new one arose, when I was again doubtful how to proceed, and notwithstanding the utmost caution, could scarce ever preserve my first patients from danger, till I had thoroughly investigated the nature of the distemper, and then I proceeded in a direct and safer way to the cure."

There is a fever, not uncommonly met with, sometimes called *bilious,* but now more frequently *gastric* fever, as originating in stomachic and intestinal irritation, and which I have noticed under the head of GASTRIC FEVER. This often begins in an unusual manner, and also follows an unusual course. Sometimes patents will be for weeks under the influence of this fever, without knowing it, although they are very sensible they are not well. Its most remarkable *symptoms* are—general uneasiness and restlessness or as the patient expresses it, a state of complete wretchedness,—a very unpleasant state of the mouth, with an extremely bad taste,—heat, tenderness or pain in the pit of the stomach, and redness of tire back part of the mouth.

This fever is sometimes epidemic; it was so in 1826-27. The treatment of this fever must be cautiously pursued, and mainly consists in giving mild aperients, as No. 120 or 121, page 205 or clysters,with saline medicines, as No. 24, page 153 or No. 35A, page 158, moderating the heat of the surface by washing it frequently with tepid or cold water,—by attention to a fluid, easily digested diet, and comforting the patient in every possible point of view.

FILMS OR SPECKS ON THE FYE

By films or specks on the eye, is meant the opaque spots which are frequently seen on the anterior transparent convey part of that organ, and which are almost universally the consequence of active or slow inflammation. The opacity may be confined to a point or tray extend over the whole or the greeter part of the tunic, which is in technical language, called *cornea.*

The ophthalmic ointment No. 92, page 189, will remove these specks when recent. The ointment No. 89, page 188, is likewise of great utility, and will remove both the specks and the slow inflammation on which they depend. If the films are of long standing, and obstinate, the following eye-water is recommended by Scarps, the able and celebrated Italian surgeon.

Take of Muriate of ammonia	2 scruples;
Acetate of copper	4 grains;
Lime-water	8 ounces.

Mix. The fluid is to be filtered, after standing twenty-four hours. To be used with an eye-glass, twice or thrice a day.

After this has been employed for two or three weeks, it should be changed for a stimulating ointment, which may be applied in the same way as the above ointments.

Take of Prepared tutty	1	drachm;
Socotorine aloes, in powder.	2	grains;
Calomel	2	grains;
Prepared hog's lard		half an ounce.

Mix.

This ointment is praised by the judicious Scarps. When the eyes are very irritable, and cannot bear these applications, the oil of walnuts may be tried or the ointment—a most efficacious one No. 89 or 92 pages 188-89. Thirty drops or even a drachm, of the solution of the bi-chloride of mercury, (page 17), taken morning and evening, is a powerful assistant to these remedies.

It is generally necessary to persevere with one or other of these applications for many weeks, and in obstinate cases, it will frequently require many months to eradicate the opacity. The general health should be improved by every proper means. Occasionally some of the small vessels ramifying on the external surface of the eye, become turgid and prominent, and connect themselves with the films, when, if the foregoing remedies are not of themselves effectual in correcting this appearance, the assistance of an oculist will be necessary.

FLATULENCY

Flatulency is, for the most part, a symptom of indigestion, colic, hysterics, hypochondriasis, and other complaints which originate in or are connected with, a weakened state of the stomach and intestinal canal. When the energies of these organs are impaired, they lose the corrective power which they possess in a healthy condition over the materials they contain and, as a consequence, a rapid fermentation takes place, and the digestive canal is distended and overloaded with the air disengaged; relief being only obtained by frequent rejection upwards or downwards. In a highly debilitated state of this canal, the quantity of gas separated in this manner is sometimes prodigious, and may amount to an eructation of many hogsheads in an hour; a circumstance not unfrequent where weakness of stomach and imprudence in diet are co-existent. Nor need we be surprised at this, since a single apple, during fermentation, will give out, according to the experiments of Dr. Hales, about six hundred times its bulk of common air; and many of the vegetables introduced iota the stomach possess as much or more ventosity than apples.

But flatulency occasionally exists without any other symptom of indigestion; occurring, for example, in healthy persons after the enjoyment of a full meal, in which case it is plainly at once the effect and indication of excess, by which the stomach is oppressed and enfeebled in its functions, and rendered incapable of exerting its full control over all the food it contains, part of which therefore, ferments and extricates gas. And from this explanation it will be easily understood how a frequent, unrestricted indulgence of the appetite, may convert a temporary weakness of the stomach, and an occasional flatulency into a permanent disorder.

Generally speaking, the *immediate cause is* owing to a delicate or weakened condition of the stomach and bowels, which explains why infants are so subject to flatulency, from the natural delicacy of these organs in them. It will be seen, from what has been said above, that whatever tends to weaken the digestive organs, may act as an exciting cause; such as drinking a large quantity of cold fluid when the body is heated, a poor vegetable diet, violent purgatives, worms, and lingering chronic complaints. An immoderate indulgence of the appetite, as an exciting cause, has already been alluded to.

It is generally supposed, that air is occasionally separated from the mouths of the secreting vessels into the digestive organs; but in the present instance, there can be little or no doubt, that it is merely given out by the materials introduced into the stomach in the form of food, and tending towards fermentation.

TREATMENT—The cure depends upon giving tone to the digestive canal, and improving the health, which will be most certainly accomplished by carefully regulating the bowels by means of diet and exercise, and by taking tonics and aromatics, together with nourishing food of the most easy digestion. The plan of cure laid down under the head of *Indigestion,* will probably be the best which the patient can resort to. Constant active exercise in the open air, with regular friction over the bowels, twice a day, is of the greatest consequence. The pills No. 102 or 104, pages 196-97 or the mixture No. 82, page 183, are among the best tonics which can be taken. Daily exercise to the extent of a free perspiration will cure nineteen cases out of twenty.

Dry biscuit is a useful article of diet in this complaint.

In those flatulencies which come on about the time the menstrual discharge ceases, a daily use of the saline powder No. 130A, page 209, often gives more relief than any other remedy, if' we page the pill No. 98, page 191.

As a palliative, to give quick relief when the patient is greatly oppressed with wind, a tea-spoonful of ether or of tincture of ginger, may be taken in a little water or brandy and water; or twelve drops of water of ammonia in a wine-glassful of water.

FLOODING

It is only of the haemorrhage or flooding after delivery that I intend to treat here. For a small discharge of blood to continue for some time after childbirth is a circumstance neither uncommon or alarming, but when it is excessive it is called a flooding, and then becomes dangerous, requiring a prompt and decisive treatment for its suppression.

It is sometimes produced by pulling too forcibly at the umbilical chord, and separating the after-bird from the walls of the womb before its blood-vessels have sufficiently contracted. It may also arise from clots of blood remaining in the womb, and preventing its due contraction; but the most common cause seems to be an exhausted state of the vessels themselves, and a consequent inability to contract their mouths, so that the blood flows through them without resistance.

TREATMENT—In the treatment of this affection, we must ever bear in mind the principle, *that contraction of the womb is the only remedy for hoemorrhage from that organ,* and, therefore, our efforts should be directed to secure this contraction as speedily as possible. One of the most effectual means to obtain this is, by friction and pressure of the surface of the abdomen over the seat of the womb. This part should be courageously but cautiously grasped, and well rubbed, until it is found to contract under the hand, when the bleeding will be arrested *See* my TREATISE ON THE DISEASE OF FEMALES. Another of the most powerful means of checking flooding, is dashing cold water on the naked abdomen *from on high.* This, if I am not mistaken, was first pointed out by the late Dr. Gooch, a midwifery practitioner in London, who has remarked on its instantaneous effect in putting a stop to the bleeding, after the coldest water has been used in vain, in the common way of applying it to the part by means of cloths. After dashing the cold water on the abdomen *from on high,* it will be proper to continue the application of cold, by means of wet cloths kept constantly applied to the parts, till all haelmorrhage has ceased; the windows should be at the same time thrown open, and the patient covered only with a sheet, and kept perfectly quiet.

Should this plan fail or there is reason to suspect the retention of clots of blood in the womb, the accoucheur's hand should be directly introduced and the clots be withdrawn, when the bleeding will often immediately cease. It is probable, that the gentle stimulus or irritation conveyed to the womb, by the simple introduction of the hand into its cavity, has some effect in every instance where benefit has followed the practice; therefore, we may calculate upon a frequent advantage from this stimulus alone, even where there are no clots to bring away.

Should the rush of blood be so prodigious as to produce so great and sudden exhaustion as to threaten the immediate extinction of life, the warmest and most active cordials must be given. Wine or brandy, in an undiluted state, should be administered; and if we succeed in rousing the patient, they should be dropped by degrees or exchanged for food of a rich and nutritive, but less stimulant description. Opium also is, in this condition of the female, of the greatest value, especially in irritable, delicate constitutions; and it must be given in the extremity of danger in large quantities, as one or two tea-spoonfuls of the tincture for a dose, (in water or brandy and water), to be frequently repeated. Opium restores the lost energy of the arterial system, and in the nervous agitation which follows flooding, is sometimes capable of saving persons apparently in the jaws of death.

For the giddiness, noises in the ears and pains in the bead, which are apt to follow great loss of blood in lying-in women, the best remedies are a saline aperient (No. 27, page 155) every other morning, with about fifteen or twenty drops of tincture of opium, once or twice a day.

GALL-STONES

Gall-stones or *Biliary Calculi,* are concretions formed in the passages through which the bile passes from the liver into the gall-bladder or into the first intestine.

They occasion, in manv instances, some disturbance, with paroxysms of pain, commonly referred to the pit of the stomach, and right side, darting through to the back, and sometimes give rise, whilst passing into the bowels, to sickness or vomiting, to jaundice or to severe attacks of colic. In their passing along the *ducts*, the pain is often very acute, and attended with nausea, flatulence, a bitter taste in the mouth, acid or bitter eructations, colic, distention of the belly, and perhaps vomiting, and either complete jaundice or a slight yellow tint over the eyes or lips. *The pulse is usually unaffected, and there is no fever,* unless the symptoms are particularly violent or of long duration. In the severest examples, there is commonly present a furred, dark-yellowish tongue, great restlessness, anxiety, loss of flesh and strength, and considerable tenderness at the pit of the stomach. The bowels are mostly confined, and the motions devoid of bile. The attacks vary much in regard to their duration and recurrence.

Persons rarely, if ever, pass gall-stones, who have not been previously suffering for months or years from indigestion and bilious affection. It is a previous state of deranged digestion, and affection of the liver, which originates the formation and passage of these concretions; and, consequently, whatever occasions weakness and disorder of the digestive organs, preventing the perfect assimilation of the food (*see* INDIGESTION) may be *causes* of this disease. They occur most frequently in the female sex, probably from their more sedentary habits, and in the decline of life, and are commonly met with in fat persons.

TREATMENT—During the paroxysm of pain, etc. endured while the concretions are passing, our object should be entirely to empty the bowels by the use of purgative clysters as No. 8, page 146, and the use of two of the purgative pills No. 97, followed by a draught No. 27 or 28, pages 155-56 or by an ounce of castor oil, rubbed together in a mortar with the yolk of an egg, and a little water; to which may be added warm fomentations, bladders of hot water being applied over the pit of the stomach or friction with the liniment No. 39. In order to procure a speedy evacuation of the bowels, O'Beirne's or Twinberrow's Clyster Machine will be found of the most essential service.

When the bowels are freely evacuated, relief in general speedily follows, but if the continued pain or uneasiness demands an anodyne, a pill containing half a grain of the muriate of morphia may be taken directly and repeated in half au hour, and that once, twice or thrice, should the severity of the pain require it; or fifty drops of laudanum may be taken in water. Almost incredible quantities of opium have been taken, in a very short period, in this distance.

If considerable swelling and tenderness exist at the pit of the stomach, especially if the pulse should be full and hard, we may suspect inflammation of the gall-bladder and ducts, and twelve leeches should be applied over the swelling; or in case the patient is of full habit, twelve or sixteen ounces of blood may be drawn from the arm.

In the intervals of the attacks, our object should be to improve the secretions from the liver and stomach, to promote their regular discharge, and to invigorate those organs; and in order to accomplish these objects, the patient should be very attentive to his diet, (see INDIGESTION), and to walking exercise or riding on horseback daily and freely, while he regulates his bowels by the pill No. 100, 101 or 101C or 101D, pages 194-95, and takes a tea-cupful of the decoction of dandelion, twice a day or half a tea-spoonful of the alkaline *solution* or the *alkaline tincture* of *rhubarb* (page 4), twice or thrice a day. The pill No. 99, page 192, taken at the same time every night, is a valuable remedy. Daily friction over the pit of the stomach should not be omitted, and a course of the Cheltenham or Leamington waters is likely to prove very serviceable.

The following prescription may be tried should the preceding medicine not have a satisfactory effect. It is called the remedy of Durande, and is much recommended on the continent. It is, no doubt, a useful remedy,[1] especially with the addition of tincture of henbane, but is not equal in my opinion to the remedies above named.

Take of The compound spirit of sulphuric ether. . 6 drachms;
Rectified spirit of turpentine . . . . 4 drachms.

Mix them together, and, as I advise, add of tincture of henbane, three drachms. The dose is a tea-spoonful in water, twice or thrice daily.

Fatty substances should be carefully avoided in diet, and country air, with very active exercise, is of the first importance.

GASTRIC OR REMITTENT FEVER

Gastric, Bilious or Remittent fever is not uncommon in this country, but is most frequent in the Mediterranean, the East Indies, Africa and America. It is the jungle and hill fever of the East Indies, and the mild kind of yellow fever of the West Indies. Our soldiers and sailors are much subject to it in various parts of the world; and in no place, probably, more severely and dangerously than in Africa.

1. I have prescribed the remedy of Durande in somewhat larger doses, and combined with it tincture of henbane, and certainly with marked benefit." Dr. Copland's *Dictionary of Medicine*, p. 396.

It is sometimes epidemic; especially in autumn when the summer has been hot, after great falls of rain or after inundations. It is observed chiefly in persons of a bilious and sanguine temperament, and who live freely or take insufficient exercise.

Its chief *causes* are over feeding, and deficient exercise, associated with the heat of summer or the depressing influences of the atmosphere of autumn, when fetid exhalations from the soil are apt to prevail, particularly in certain districts, such as low shots lying near the coast, and in jungles. Anxiety of mind is sometimes a powerful cause; and one of the principal symptoms is *extreme prostration of strength.*

The *symptoms* are yellowness of the skin, and bilious vomiting; in some cases constipation, in others diarrhoea; the tongue is white, and red at the tip and edges; the pulse is from 90 to 120; intense thirst, great heat of skin, delirium and prostration.

TREATMENT—The principal indications are to evacuate the morbid secretions in the first passages—the stomach and intestines; and to invigorate the system, and moderate the fever attendant upon the period of excitement which soon appears. For these purposes nothing is so effectual as a couple of calomel pills No. 97, page 191 or the calomel powder No. 120, page 205, taken directly, and followed by a seidlitz powder or three drachms of Epsom salts, in water; after which, give quinine in five grain doses every four hours, and the fever mixture No. 81, page 183, should be given frequently.

This should be followed by the cold ablution or sponging of the whole body, as recommended under FEVER at page 580. A free sponging of the whole body; or even the front of it, with cold water, *when the skin is hot and dry,* is attended with great and immediate relief. It not only enables that extensive and important organ the skin to resume its duties of arterializing the blood, but it tends, at the same time, most efficiently to support the nervous and vital powers. By these means it relieves internal organs, and wards off inflammatory attacks of the liver, intestines or chest. A part of the body may be sponged at each time, if preferred, and it is always safe and highly refreshing when *the skin is hot and dry.*

Quinine is a principal remedy. Mr. Durrant, of St. Ives,

Cornwall, had considerable experience in the treatment of African fever, and says :—

> "The treatment was as follows :—Twenty grains of quinine, and the same of powdered ginger, were administered in hot wine and a little sugar immediately. This generally stopped the severe shivering fit, and five grains of quinine were administered every three or four hours in the same manner. Nearly the whole of the ship's crew had symptoms of fever during the two years we were in the river and on the coast, and the majority were at the customary duties on the third day after the attack. Other treatment was of a subsidiary character, consisting of warm and tepid bathings in the hot stage, according to circumstances, with light and nutritious diet. Wine and brandy were indispensable aids on account of the extreme prostration, and in one case brandy was administered to the extent of a bottle in the forty-eight hours. In no case was calomel exhibited more than once, and thrat at the commencement, in combination with rhubarb, with the sole view of clearing the first passage. Not a single death from African fever occurred. I myself had three distinct attacks, the last being the remittent type. Our sojourn in the Delta, and for six hundred miles up the river, and continually visiting the towns, occupied nearly two years. The fevers of Africa being essentially those of debility, the administration of calomel and blood-letting should be avoided."—*Lancet*, August 15th, 1863.

Should head symptoms supervene, and the patient grow incoherent and very violent, *Dr. Grave's Fever* Mixture No. 87B, page 187, is excellent. It soothes the whole system; and after this, when the patient begins to recover, give a tonic, such as quinine or the bark mixture No. 84B, page 185. These means, with change of air, will usually be sufficient to restore the patient. As a tonic, the mixture, No. 84, page 184, is likewise most suitable, but I prefer No. 84B. *See* Mr. Annesley's valuable remark on the use of quinine in Indian remittent fever at page 108.

Decoction and tincture of bark will often do more good than quinine. *See* recipe, No. 84, page 184.

As soon as possible the patient should be taken into the air, on the hills surrounding his residence, and the cold or tepid sponging should be practised every morning.

If *diarrhoea* of a mild character comes on, it should not be interfered with; but if the stools are watery and very offensive or otherwise morbid, then small doses, such as two grains; of each, of grey powder and Dover's powder, should be given about every six hours or as the diarrhoea may render necessary.

GOUT

Great difference of opinion has prevailed respecting the *nature, causes,* and *treatment of gout,* but it is now generally admitted to be, in whatever way it shows itself, a disease of the constitution; and, when appearing in a regular form, it must be looked upon as a salutary re-action and evacuation of the system, whereby the equilibrium of the circulation, and a comparatively healthy state of the various functions are, for a time at least, restored. This is the view taken of it by very many, if not the majority, of the ablest physicians.

It is correctly divided into three varieties *viz*., ACUTE, CHRONIC AND RETROCEDENT gout.

The gout sometimes comes on very suddenly, particularly in its first attacks. In general, however, the inflammation of the joint is preceded by *various symptoms* indicating a want of vigour in different parts of the body. The patient is incapable of his usual exertions, either of mind or body; becomes languid, listless, and subject to slight feverish attacks, especially in the evening; he complains of pains in tire head, coldness of the feet and hands, impaired appetite, flatulency, heart-burn, spasms of the stomach, and the usual symptoms of indigestion. He is oppressed with heaviness after meals, and a disturbed unrefreshing sleep ensues. The bowels are seldom regular, being either constipated or too much relaxed; the mind at this period, being generally irritable, anxious, and alarmed at the least appearance of danger. A deficiency of perspiration in the feet also, with a distended state of their veins, cramps, and numbness of the feet and legs, and other strange sensations, often presage the approaching fit. The duration of these symptoms previous to the fit, is various; sometimes only a day or two, at other times, many weeks.

The fit sometimes makes its attack in the evening, more commonly, about two or three o'clock in the morning. The patient goes to bed free from pain, and is awakened about this time by a very acute pain, generally in the first joint of the great toe, the pain often resembling that of a dislocated bone, with a sensation as if hot water were poured on the part. It sometimes extends itself over all the bones of the toes, and fore part of the foot, resembling the pain occasioned by the tension or laceration of a membrane. Cold shivering is felt at the commencement of the pain, which is succeeded by heat and other symptoms of fever. The pain and fever increase, with much restlessness, till about the middle of the succeeding night; after which they gradually abate, and in the most favourable cases, there is little either of pain or fever for twenty-four hours after their first appearance. The patient, as soon as he obtains some relief from pain, generally falls asleep, a gentle sweat comes on, and the part which the pain occupied becomes red and swelled. In most cases, however, the fit is not over, for the pain and fever return on the succeeding night with less violence, and continue to do so for several nights, becoming less severe till they cease.

Such is a simple fit of Acute gout. But it often happens, that after the pain has abated in one foot, it attacks the other, where it runs the same course; and in dose who have laboured under repeated attacks of the disease, the foot first attached is often seized a second time, as the pain in the other subsides, which is again attacked in its turn, and they are thus alternately affected for a considerable length of time. In other cases, it seizes on both feet at the same time. After frequent returns, it begins to seize upon the joints of the hand, and at length the larger joints. When the gouty tendency is very great, almost every joint of the body suffers; the pain when it leaves one, immediately fixing in another.

In strong people, the whole fit is generally finished in about fourteen days. In the aged, and those who have been long subject to gout, it generally lasts about two months; and in those who are much debilitated, either by age or the long continuance of the disease, till the summer heats set in. In the first attacks, the joints soon recover their strength and suppleness; but after the disease has recurred frequently, and the fits are long protracted, they remain weak and stiff, and at length lose all motion.

The above are the *symptoms* of *acute* or *regular* gout.

CHRONIC Gout, (which is by some physicians called *irregular* gout), is the disease of a weakly or debilitated constitution. Here the inflammation and pain are more slight, irregular, and wandering than in the acute; there is only faint redness of the affected joint or no change at all of the natural appearance of the surface; much permanent distension of parts or continued swelling, with unpaired moving power; and no critical indications of the disease terminating. The symptoms are always associated with a disordered state of the digestive organs, a languid or oppressed circulation, and much nervous irritation in the system. The patient is distressed with various uneasy sensations in the stomach, as flatulent distensions, craving or deficient appetite, heart-burn, etc., the bowels are either costive or too much relaxed; fluttering sensations are often felt about the heart; the painful sensations felt in the affected part are rather those of heat and coldness alternately, than of the more continued *burnings* which take place in the acute form of the disease; the spirits are depressed, and the mind very irritable.

The subjects of chronic gout are generally such as have for a considerable time laboured under regular attacks of the acute form of this disease; this, however, is not universally the case, for in some weakly or enfeebled constitutions the gout soon begins to assume the chronic form.

RETROCEDENT gout is that form of the disease in which the gouty action is suddenly transferred from the joint or other external part affected, to some internal organ, as the stomach, intestines, head etc.

Whatever tends to produce an unhealthy fulness of the blood-vessels, hurts the digestive organs, and impairs the vigour of the system, may be ranked among the *causes* of gout. Perhaps the *principal causes* are an indolent and luxurious life or a sedentary and studious one; hereditary predisposition; anxiety or vexation of mind; excessive evacuations of any kind; cold, flatulent diet or immoderate indulgence in acid and vinous liquors;[1] the suppression of any accustomed discharge; sudden exposure to cold, when the body is heated; wet applied to the feet; costiveness; a variable climate. These may act both as predisposing and exciting causes.

It seems indisputable, that the more violent the fit, and the longer its continuance, the more the gouty disposition is confirmed, and the oftener the attack is renewed.

A continued imprudence or excess in diet, disposes the gout to become chronic, and at last retrocedent, and to attack the stomach in the enervated, and the head in the corpulent.

One of the most frequent and powerful causes of chronic gout in the present day, is the excessive, unskilful use of Wilson's tincture, Reynolds's specific, and other preparations of meadow saffron. They are poisons.

This disease is *distinguished* from rheumatism by the previous symptoms of indigestion above noticed, which do not occur in rheumatism; by the pains attacking particularly the smaller joints, while rheumatism occupies the larger; by the deeper redness and greater swelling of the parts affected in gout than in rheumatism; and by the age of the patient, his habit of body, and mode of living. Gout has a sort of elective affinity for the big-toe or the fingers, while these are seldom or never attacked with rheumatism. In gout the skin is more affected, it presents a deep dusky mahogany colour, shining with the veins much enlarged; there is also more of oedema or puffy swelling and effusion about the joints; we seldom or ever see this in rheumatism. In out the swelling of the hand makes it like a boning-glove. Gout chiefly attacks men, seldom so young as twenty-seven or thirty; rheumatism is very common at this age, both in men and women.

---

1. It seems that Champagne, Claret and Port, have a considerably stronger tendency to produce Gout than Madeira, Lisbon, and Sherry, because in addition to their equal or greater heating effects, they give rise to more acidity in the blood and first passages.

TREATMENT—The treatment of *acute* gout naturally resolves itself into that proper while the fit is on, and that required during the intervals.

When a patient is warned of the probable approach of a gouty paroxysm, by the occurrence of drowsiness, heart-burn, flatulence, costiveness, pain or pricking and numbness in the lower extremities, coldness of the legs and feet, general chilliness, and other premonitory symptoms which the subjects of the disease are well acquainted with, it will be invariably advisable to attend to these signs, and to administer suitable medicines without delay, since by proper management the threatened attack may frequently, be averted; and even if this object should not be accomplished, the paroxysms will be thereby rendered milder, and probably shorter. One of the best plans for a person to adopt who is threatened with an attack of gout, is to take the following pills at eight, and the draught No. 27, 27 A or 28, pages 155-56, early on the following morning:

Take of Calomel	1 grain;
James's powder	3 grains;
Compound extract of colocynth	4 grains;

Oil of juniper or cloves, sufficient to form the whole into two pills.

These pills should afterwards be repeated every night or every other night, with the draught, No. 27A, in the morning or a seidlitz powder; and if the pain should be sharp, let him take one of White's pill No. 114A, page 202, every night, till the pain is relieved. He should be careful to keep the bowels in a lax state, and to join with the use of these medicines great moderation in diet, repose of mind and early hours. When the patient is of a full habit, it will in general be necessary for him to observe a rigid course of abstinence for a few days; and, if the tongue be much furred, and attended with heart-burn and nausea, an emetic of fifteen grains of ipecacuanha powder will also be proper, and often afford very sensible relief. By these means an apprehended fit of the gout is frequently warded off.

During the fit, the most rational and efficacious treatment is that which clears the stomach and bowels, and aims at the restoration of healthy secretions from all the digestive organs; and the most effectual way of accomplishing these purposes, is by the administration of purgatives and diuretics, combined with mild mercurial alteratives, as in White's pill No. 114A, page 202, and a spare diluting diet.

Many of the phenomena of gout justify the opinion that this disease is often dependent upon the circulation of a poisonous matter in the blood, and that it is of an *acid nature,* hence the beneficial operation of alkaline medicines. The condition of the kidneys, liver and skin should always be closely, investigated in gouty affections. To restore the due actions of these organs is, in numerors cases, the principal indication, and, when fulfilled, paves the way most certainly to the cure. Colchicum has the effect of increasing the amount of lithic acid, when its excretion is suppressed, but then it is a deleterious article, if taken in more than a small quantity.

Professional men are now fully agreed as to the propriety and necessity of endeavouring, by an immediate recourse to the foregoing means, to correct the disorder of the blood and digestive functions, on which gout in all cases depends. As soon, therefore, as a patient is attacked with a gouty fit, he should take the pills of calomel, James's powder, and extract of colocynth, advised in the preceding page, washing them down with a purgative draught, combined with a suitable diuretic medicine, as in either of the following forms. In the beginning, these pills must be repeated every night or every second night, according to the severity of the symptoms, and the state of the secretions, as evinced by the appearance of the motions and urine. As a general rule, these pills ought to be thus repeated so long as the stools are particularly offensive or discoloured, and the urine deposits a sediment.

Take of Calcined magnesia	15	grains;
Epsom salts	1½	drachm;
Vinegar of colchicum		half a drachm;

Spearmint water . . . . 1½ ounce;
Syrup of orange peel . . . . 1 drachm.
Mix them together for a draught.

Take Epsom salt, Glauber's salt, of each, ... 1 drachm;
Vinegar of colchicum . . . . ½ drachm;
Spearmint water . . . . 1½ ounce;
Tincture of senna . . . . 2 drachms.
Mix for a drought.

One of these draughts must he repeated every four or six hours, according to the urgency of the symptoms, and the extent of its operation on the bowels; since the principal objects to be accomplished by its use are, to clear thoroughly the intestinal canal, and to relieve the painful symptoms present, and these indications are, in every instance, most certainly fulfilled by maintaining a free discharge from the intestines, throughout the whole course of the fit. After this medicine has operated copiously three or four times, a sufficient action may in general be kept up by administering it once in the twenty-four hours, say every morning, which repetition will be necessary until all inflammation is removed, the stools and urine acquire a healthy appearance, and the tongue is nearly free from fur. Should it be preferred, either of these draughts may be taken in the act of effervescence; if so, twenty-five grains of carbonate of potash should be added to the draught, when it is taken, and a table-spoonful of lemon juice. This addition will make it more agreeable to many persons, and when much fever is present, is to be preferred.

After the above pills and draught have been so taken as to act freely on the bowels, if severe pain continue, some anodyne may be necessary. If so, give one of Anthony White's pills at bed time, (No. 114A, page 202) or ten grains of the diaphoretic powder No. 124A, page 206.

Blood-letting and the use of leeches are now properly prescribed in gout; they are considered injurious.

One of the most efficacious and best local means of relief, consists in the use of a warm evaporating lotion, as that advised by

Sir Astley Cooper in common inflammation, consisting of two ounces of spirit of wine mixed with eight ounces of water; or that strongly recommended by Sir C. Scudamore, which is made by mixing together four ounces of spirit of wine, and eight ounces of camphor mixture. After having rendered the lotion selected agreeably lukewarm, by immersing a thin cup containing it in a bason of very hot water, it is to be applied to the affected part by means of rags of fine linen, which are to be renewed as often as they become dry. It would be improper to use either of these lotions hot or cold, because when hot, they are found too stimulating, and when cold, there is a risk of checking the gouty action too suddenly. During the night when the lotion cannot be used, the part may be covered with a piece of oil silk, just the size of the linen rags.

Hot poultices to the inflamed part are injurious. But a poultice made by wetting a sufficient quantity of fine bread crumb, with one of the above lotions hot, and applying it to the inflamed joint when it has become just comfortably lukewarm, is often of considerable service in relieving the pain and inflammation, and sometimes agrees remarkably well. This poultice may be repeated twice in the twenty-four hours.

Under symptoms of very severe suffering, it may frequently be advisable to apply some anodyne directly to the part affected, and the extract of belladonna appears to be a very appropriate and efficacious application for this purpose. A drachm of this extract may be mixed with an ounce of spermaceti ointment, and a sufficient quantity of this mixture to cover the affected part, spread on lint, and applied over the seat of pain. In urgent cases, it may be repeated twice or thrice in the twenty-four hours, if necessary, and sometimes its tranquillizing effects will be augmented by covering it with the bread poultice, made with spirit of wine and camphor mixture, as just described.

Warm fomentations do not appear to me to be by any means well adapted to alleviate the pain or remove the inflammation of gout, and their ultimate effects are those of weakness and relaxation. Hot bathing of the feet is, for the most part, highly objectionable during the fit. Neither should the inflamed joint be kept very warm by the use of flannel or other means, since this practice invariably aggravates the severity, and prolongs the duration of the paroxysm. The proper practice is to keep the affected part in such a moderately cool state as is comfortable to the patient's feelings without being so great as to check the insensible perspiration. By this means we repress inflammation, allay pain and do not increase the subsequent debility of the joint.

Sydenham long ago pronounced a fluid, diluting diet, the proper one in a fit of the gout, and such a diet is still recommended by the best informed of the profession. Under very acute symptoms, the nourishment must be wholly fluid, unstimulating, and rather small in quantity, until the severity of the inflammation, etc. has been subdued, and the patient is beginning to recover. The best food for the patient in this stage is bread and milk, light bread puddings, mutton or chicken broth, gruel, barley-water and rennet-whey. Roasted apples, grapes and oranges, are likewise generally admissible; and when the patient begins to recover, an egg may be added to the above, and sometimes a little bit of chicken or roast mutton for dinner. It should be particularly noticed, that even a small excess or impropriety in diet during a gouty paroxysm, always materially aggravates and prolongs the attendant sufferings, and sometimes gives rise to severe erysipclas, either in conjunction with the disease or as an immediate sequel to it.

It may be safely assumed as a general rule, which is rarely liable to exceptions, that when the patient is strong and full of blood, and the inflammatory symptoms run high, a spare diet, wholly fluid, is highly necessary. When, on the other hand, he has lived freely; when he has long been subject to attacks of gout; especially when these have shewn a tendency to become irregular; when the system has fallen into a state of debility, and the inflammatory symptoms do not run high, the diet ought not to be so low, although great caution is still necessary in taking care to increase a little its nourishing qualities without rendering it stimulating. Therefore, in the case of a debilitated stomach, with weak constitutional powers, accompanied with extreme languor and depression, a small quantity of animal food, daily, may be added to the articles above specified. In such instances, if a little wine does not injure, it should be mixed with sago, gruel or panada, instead of giving it pure or diluted with water.

Ripe oranges and grapes are usually admissible during the fit, but acidulated drinks do not generally agree at that period and acid matter must be always avoided, in every shape, during the operation of the calomel purgative pill.

The patient should take a little *lithia water* or *potash water,* once or twice a day. They lessen the red deposit in the urine, relieve fever, diminish the frequency of the attacks, and improve the quality of the blood. They are also useful in *chronic* gout, and may be obtained pure from Messrs. Blake and Co., 47, Piccadilly, London.

In a severe fit of the gout, and during the height of it, the patient is of necessity confined to his bed in a helpless state, and then the affected limp must be carefully placed on small pillows, in the most easy position; but except under such extreme circumstances, the patient ought not to indulge in bed beyond what is unavoidable. When able, he should every morning leave the bed for the couch or the chair, having his legs raised and supported in the most easy position; and, in proportion as pain and inflammation abate, should gradually employ such further exertion as relieves rather than produces irritation. Subsequent stiffness and debility of the limbs are invariably to be counteracted, in a great degree, by moderate and early efforts of exercise, carefully attempted.

When the patient is convalescents he must, notwithstanding, continue the use of the proper operative and aperient medicine for some time, indeed, until all the secretions assume healthy characters. Therefore, in a state of convalescence from a fit of the gout, discontinue colchicum altogether, and take one of Plumner's pills No. 117, page 203 or one of the pills No. 98 or 99, every second or third night, with half a pint of compound decoction of sarsaparilla, in divided doses, through the day; the bowels being carefully regulated by the occasional use of a mild aperient pill, as No. 100 or 101A; 101 or 101C pages 193-95; or by the use of a seidlitz powder or one of the powders No. 130A, page 209. Sometimes the pill composed of calomel, James's powder and extract of colocynth, mentioned at page 595-96, will answer still better as an aperient; it is certainly a useful form, and will be of much service to many gouty individuals. The proper object at this period, in the employment of opening medicine, is gently to clear the bowels, and excite healthy secretions from them, without inducing a direct purgative effect.

It is a common practice, in the state of convalescence, to recommend a stomachic and strengthening medicine to be taken during the day, and either a vegetable bitter or some preparation of steel, is usually selected by medical men. It will generally be best to commence with a bitter infusion combined with an alkali, and from that to proceed to the use of some preparation of steel. If, therefore, the sarsaparilla above referred to, be not taken, the mixture No. 83, page 184, may be resorted to or the following, which sometimes agrees remarkably well.

Take of Compound decoction of aloes	2 ounces;
Compound infusion of gentian	3 ounces;
Camphor mixture......................	6 drachms;
Compound spirit of ammonia	2 drachms.

Mix, and take two or three table-spoonfuls twice a day.

After the pain and inflammation have subsided, some physicians recommend small doses, what they call alterative doses of colchicum, to be taken thrice a day; but this is very bad practice. Colchicum, in combination with aperients, should be taken *only during* pain and inflammation. When they have been relieved, never take colchicum; and never take it in the intervals.

As a separate mineral tonic, the tincture of muriated iron or the tincture of ammoniated iron, are eligible forms. Twenty drops of the former or thirty of the latter, may be taken twice or thrice daily, in an ounce and a half of infusion of columba or cascarilla. The pills No. 102, page 196, are also very proper.

The diet during the state of convalescence, should consist of a moderate quantity of the most digestible animal food, once a day, with eggs, bread and vegetables; and change of air and scene, with suitable exercise, will always be very serviceable.

The limbs and especially the affected parts, should now be regularly sponged with cold salt and water, every morning; and after the skin has been wiped quite dry, they should be well rubbed with the band or flesh brush, till a comfortable glow in the parts is produced. This practice, if persevered in, will generally be very effectual in removing debility and stiffness of the joints. Should any particular feebleness exist, in addition to the morning sponging, a stimulating liniment as No. 40, page 161 or the following, may be freely rubbed over the joints, twice a day.

Take of Compound camphor liniment, and
compound soap liniment, of each .... 1½ ounce;
Tincture of Spanish fly .... 3 drachms.
Mix for a liniment.

If the lower limbs are affected with swelling, the use of a calico or flannel roller will be found useful.

During the intervals, strict attention should be given to observe a suitable and moderate diet, active exercise in a salubrious air, and early rising, united with a proper use of aperient, alterative, and stomachic medicine.[1]

A PROPER DIET AND REGIMEN HAVE LONG BEEN REGARDED, AS AMONG THE MOST ESSENTIAL PARTS OF THE TREATMENT OF GOUT as well in the intervals as during the fit; indeed, they are of such pre-eminent utility, that they will alone often display a remarkable power in bettering the condition of the patient, and sometimes even nearly approach to a curative effect, yea to an effect perfectly curative,

1. "Amongst the remarks, (says the illustrious Sydenham) I proceed to communicate, on the cure of *Gout*, this is primarily and chiefly to be attended to namely, that all *stomachic* or *digestive* remedies, whether they consist of a course of medicines; regimen or exercise, are not to be entered upon in a heedless manner, but to be persisted in daily with great exactness. For since the cause in this and most other chronic distempers, is become habitual, and in a manner changed into, a second nature, it cannot reasonably be imagined, that the cure can be accomplished by means of some slight and momentary change made in the blood and juices by any kind of medicine or regimen, but the whole constitution is to be altered and the body to be in a manner formed anew."—*Bydenham's Works by Swan*. p. 486.

while without them, no other means will be attended with any great or lasting benefit. If the patient be of a full habit, especially if young, and not long afflicted with the disease, his diet should constantly be very mild, and rather small in quantity, consisting chiefly of vegetable food; but if he has been long harassed by the disease, and is deficient in strength, his diet, although mild, and moderate in quantity, ought to be nourishing, and should therefore, consist of a suitable proportion of animal and vegetable food, to which, in some cases, may be added a glass of Marsala, Sherry or Madeira wine daily, diluted with water. Ardent spirits are altogether inadmissible in every case, and the strong and plethoric should avoid wine.[1] Ale and all the stronger malt liquors must also be forsaken. "In inflammatory gout, above everything malt liquors should be given up; I have known two or three patients. make marvellous recoveries by this simple expedient alone". —*Dr. Budd.*

In the intervals, the condition of the stomach and bowels should claim constant and especial attention, as it is of the utmost consequence that they should be preserved free from any accumulation or irregularity in their action. A principal point is, to keep the bowels clear, and if this cannot be done without medicine, a little of the aperient mixture No. 74, page 176 or the powder, No. 130A, page 209, taken occasionally in the morning or one or two of the pills No. 100 or 101, pages 193-94, at night, will be found useful. If at any time, the secretions are unhealthy, the means pointed out in the commencement of this article, as proper to be resorted to when the patient is threatened with a fit, should be used and persevered in till they become healthy. The compound decoction of sarsaparilla is a good medicine here in numerous instances. Sir Halford's *Gout Cordial* is useful as a stomachic to gouty people.

Take of Tincture of rhubarb .... 1½ ounce;

1. I think there are very few cases, even among those where debility is present, in which a total abstinence from wine will not be advisable and useful. Sir Wm. Temple's remark well expresses my opinion.—"I have known so great cures, and so many, done by obstinate resolutions of drinking no wine at all, that I put more weight upon the part of temperance, than any other".

Compound infusion of gentian .... 4½ ounces;
Bi-carbonate of potash .... 1 drachm.

Mix. Take a fourth part every day at noon, for a fortnight; then discontinue it for the same period, and then resume it.

The above observations I believe to present the reader with a correct view of the proper treatment of *acute* gout, and it now remains for me to speak of that which is applicable to *chronic* gout; but before I proceed to this subject, it will be proper to notice a few of those medicines which are at this time so highly extolled by some persons as valuable remedies in this disease, particularly *colchicum, eau medicinale, Wilson's tincture,* and *Reynolds's specific.*

There is no doubt that *colchicum* possesses specific powers in relieving the pain of this disease, and that, under judicious management, it becomes a remedy of some value; but if used frequently and in large doses, as a principal means of removing the malady it can never fail of proving highly and permanently injurious. Its good and bad effects may be stated in a few words. When it is used in small doses, occasionally repeated, in conjunction with suitable purgatives and alteratives, it frequently materially assists the full and efficient operation of those medicines, and is certainly of great service in relieving the pain of the disease, without being followed by any subsequent injury. But if, on the other hand, it be employed in considerable doses, freely repeated, as a chief means of cure, the practice is as destructive in effect as it is bad in principle; for although in first using it the patient finds its operation to be most pleasing and soothing, yet, in this way of employing it, it soon grows less and less effectual in relieving the fits, while, from its injurious influence on the stomach and nerves, it engenders so great a degree of debility in them, as leads to a more speedy return of subsequent paroxysms, which also become of a more severe and intractable character. Thus the unhappy victim of an apparently valuable but delusive remedy, finds, often when too late, that he has been trusting to that which, in giving him present relief, has robbed him of future comfort, by entailing on him excessive and permanent debility of the stomach, nerves, and general system, and by inducing a state of chronic gout from which he is scarcely ever free. This is a true statement of the ordinary and inevitable consequences of an injudicious use of colchicum; and I, therefore, earnestly recommend the gouty patient never to employ that article, except in small doses, as an auxiliary to purgative medicine. Woe be to the man when

> *"Pain compels his impatient soul to seize*
> *On promised hope of instantaneous ease"—*

and be flies to a large dose of colchicum as his remedy.

Eau medicinale, Wilson's tincture, and *Reynolds's specific* are, undoubtedly preparations of colchicum. The man who uses either of these "*specifics*" freely will repent it, perhaps as long as he lives.

The Bath waters are by no means so useful to gouty persons as many individuals suppose. They are not beneficial in the fit, nor during the intervals, when any inflammatory disposition exists; and when gout is, as it is expressed, flying about a patient's constitution, they are highly dangerous. This is the opinion of the late Dr. Parry, an eminent physician at Bath. and also Sir George Gibbs, who lately resided there. These waters are, however, sometimes very serviceable in removing the indigestion, and general debility, left after a fit of this disease, but the Cheltenham or Leamington waters are a still better, and a more certain remedy.

CHRONIC GOUT, see page 594. The principal indications of treatment in *chronic* gout, are to lessen irritation in the stomach and intestines, and restore the healthy secretions of the system; to strengthen the constitution at large, and to apply mild applications. of a soothing, cooling quality, to the affected joints.

The best means of nourishing the blood, and imparting increased strength to the system generally, is by perseverance in the proper use of alterative, and strengthening medicine, combined with a mild; moderate, and nutritious diet, a correct regimen, and daily active exercise in an open salubrious air; with which the occasional use of alkaline medicine should be united. The due regulation of the bowels is of the first consequence but from the local as well as general debility present, purgatives must be avoided. If the bowels can be regulated by diet and exercise so much the better, but if not, mild aperients, chiefly of a warm, aromatic quality should be resorted to, once, twice or thrice a week or as occasion requires. For occasional use, the mixture No. 74 or 74A, page 176, will be proper, and sometimes prove particularly beneficial; but for ordinary use, a warm laxative pill, as No. 100, 101 or 101A or 101C, pages 193-95 is preferable. Generally speaking, calomel should not make any part of the aperient administered, unless the secretions are in a vitiated condition, as evidenced by the unhealthy appearance of the stools, urine and tongue, when small doses of calomel, given every second or third night, either with the aperient ingredient, as in No. 97 or separately, as in No. 98 or 99 will be of great service. The Seidlitz powders and the powder No. 130A, page 209 are often useful aperients for the gouty. It must be particularly noticed, that the proper object in the employment of aperients in this form of gout is to keep the bowels clear without irritating them or weakening the general system; and that, in resorting to mercurial alteratives, care should be exercised not to allow it sensibly to affect the constitution by its specific operation, as whenever it affects the mouth or renders the pulse quick and hard, its injurious effects are certain. The alterative pill No. 98 or 99, page 191, taken twice or thrice a week regularly, is frequently very beneficial, and sometimes six ounces of the compound decoction of sarsaparilla or a little of the compound extract, may be advantageously taken twice a day, at the same time.

As tonics, the alkaline solution (page 2) or carbonate of potash, with infusion of cascarilla, gentian, and columba, and *lithia* or *potash water,* preparations of steel, merit the most confidence. Alkalies have always been favourite medicines with physicians in the treatment of chronic gout. The patient should take half a tea-spoonful of the alkaline solution, twice a day, in water, infusion of cascarilla or decoction of sarsaparilla. In its continuance, it almost always favours the natural action of the bowels,—a circumstance of no small moment to the gouty. The tonic draught, No. 35, page 158 or the mixture of compound decoction of aloes, etc., given at page 610 or the pill No. 102 or 103, will sometimes agree very well.

In most cases, the warm bath is a useful auxiliary, and the Buxton waters are worthy of still greater confidence. The purging waters of Cheltenham, Leamington or Harrowgate, are frequently of the highest value, and where they agree; will frequently have a greater effect in giving tone to the stomach, and strength to the whole frame, than any kind of tonic.

The local treatment of chronic gout is similar to flat recommended far the acute form, at page 594. The lotion of spirit of wine and camphor mixture, prescribed at page 598, should be applied whenever there is any tenderness or inflammation in the parts affected or if there be much pain, the belladonna ointment. No leeches, blisters or fomentations should be tried. When the inflammatory symptoms of the joints have been removed by the above lotion, the system of sponging the joints and lower extremities with cold or lukewarm salt water in the morning, and active friction afterwards, twice in the day, with a stimulating liniment, as No. 39 or 45, will be found highly useful.

The Bath and Burton waters are a valuable local as well as general remedy in chronic gout. I think very highly of the effecacy of the Buxton water, particularly in aggravated cases; it is in the highest degree soothing and invigorating.

To relieve the pains of the chronic form of the present disease, the milder form of anodynes should be given, such as Dover's powder in small doses, in conjunction with the saline effervescing. draught or with the draught No. 24, page 153, the extract of garden lettuce, (*lactucarium*), Battley's sedative liquor of opium or the muriate of morphia. Four grains of Dover's powder may be taken at bed-time or three grains twice or thrice a day, in conjunction with the saline draught, which augments its good effects. Or five grains of the extract of garden lettuce may be taken when the pain calls for it. A quarter of a grain of the muriate of morphia is likewise a valuable anodyne in these cases and so is the powder No. 124A, page 206.

But the patient ought not to place too great a dependence on medicine, since a proper diet and regimen, sufficient active exercise, and change of air and scene, will sometimes be of more service than all the drugs of the apothecary, and are invariably of considerable use. The diet should consist of mild nourishing food, of a moderate quantity, and chiefly solid food, with a small quantity of *lithia* water daily; his hours of rising and retiring to rest, should be early, and habitually observed; all anxiety of mind, and severe studious habits, must be avoided; and he should be as much in the open air as possible. The advice given on these points under *Indigestion* will be applicable here. Temperance and exercise judiciously resorted to, and persevered in, have often wrought great and salutary changes in the gouty man's constitution.[1]

The Cold Water System is of great service in gout, but will not work those wonders which some assert. It is chiefly useful in persons of good constitutions, and operates beneficially by freeing the secretions and improving the general health.—*See Appendix* p. 965.

Friction, as a mode of exercise, and means of invigorating both locally and generally, is of the highest value, and is particularly worthy of attention in this complaint, because. the patient is so frequently rendered incapable, for a long period, of resorting to the usual modes of exercise with much advantage. Under such circumstances, friction may be employed as an agreeable and certain means of restoring energy, at first to the limbs, and ultimately to the whole frame. It promotes the circulation and perspiration, resolves obstructions, reduces swellings, and thickenings, and when persisted in daily, has an amazing effect in

---

1. Sydenham, who is justly considered, by the physicians of this and every other civilized country, as one of the highest authorities in practical medicine, and who suffered severely from gout in his own person, says, "Exercise, unless it be used freely and daily, will do no service. A person may think this hard, who, besides age, inability to motion, and indolence, which is in a manner natural in this disease, is likewise tormented with pain; yet, if exercise be omitted, all the remedies which have been hitherto discovered will not at all avail".—*Sydenham's Works,* p. 497. For illustrations of the remarkable power of exercise in the cure of this disease, see the small work entitled, *"Best Methods of Improving Health and Prolonging Life,* etc."

strengthening weak parts. Dr. Cadogan has observed, that when a gouty patient is unable to walk or ride at all, he may, by degrees, be brought to do both, by means of friction. This I firmly believe. Dr. Stukeley, (a Fellow of the London College of Physicians), affirms that he could produce about five hundred cases of gout, in which friction had been resorted to with the most signal and permanent benefit. It is applicable to the state of convalescence both from acute and chronic gout, and should be used twice or thrice a day, for ten, fifteen or twenty minutes or more, at each time. If the patient is not able to do it himself, an active servant must be employed until he is able, which will soon occur. It may be performed with flannels, flannel gloves or a flesh brush. The latter is in general the best instrument. In resorting to this remedy, the limbs and parts principally affected by the disease should claim the chief attention, but it may be carried over every part of the body with great effect. Next to the limbs, the reason of the stomach and bowels ought to be attended to, as it is of very considerable service in promoting digestion and increasing the appetite.

When the gout suddenly quits the limbs, and fixes on some internal organ, as the stomach, bowels, lungs or head for example, it is called *retrocedent* gout. It is generally *spasmodic*, and if any indigestible food has been taken, an emetic No. 123, page 206, is the best remedy. If that fail, a glass of brandy will sometimes relieve the pain completely. Error in diet is the most frequent cause of gout attacking the stomach or head, and then an emetic and purge are most efficacious. The parts most commonly attacked in such cases are, the stomach and intestines, and the symptoms present are exquisite pain and spasm, and usually sickness. If the attack be purely spasmodic, the muscles of the belly are rigidly contracted, pressure affords relief, and the pulse is not much affected. In very delicate nervous subjects, the attack is spasmodic; in the corpulent or vigorous, it is generally inflammatory, especially when it has followed imprudent exposure to cold.

The treatment of retrocedent gout will, therefore, differ, according as the attack is spasmodic or inflammatory. If we have reason, from the above considerations, to consider it spasmodic, give an emetic, and five or ten brains of calomel, which may be immediately followed by an injection, as No. 8, page 146, and when the stomach will retain a purgative medicine, by the draught, No. 28, page 156. Hot fomentation of the bowels may likewise be employed at the same time, and if speedy relief is not gained by these means, fifty or sixty drops of laudanum or a third of a grain of muriate of morphia, must be given in any warm drink, as brandy and water, etc. and repeated, if necessary, every half hour, till the pain abates.

If the attack occur in a person of a full vigorous habit, and there is reason to regard it as inflammatory, the usual means for checking inflammation must be resorted to with promptness and decision. If the emetic and purge do not relieve, sixteen or twenty ounces of blood must be taken from the arm; leeches may also be applied over the bowels; warm fomentations to the abdomen; and a mustard poultice be applied to the feet, in order to solicit back the gout to the extremities. After bleeding has been resorted to, a large blister should be immediately applied near the part affected.

When gout attacks the head, it is generally of an inflammatory nature, and will require cupping, blisters, purgatives, mustard poultices to the feet, etc.

GRAVEL AND STONE

The urine, in a state of health, is one of the most compound fluids of the animal system, consisting of various acids, alkalies, calcareous earth, and other materials; and it is, therefore, not surprising that, under the injurious, and often contrary, influence of the many deteriorating causes to which man is incessantly exposed, the natural affinity between these various elements should frequently be subverted and give rise to a deposition of one or other of them, thus producing the complaint called gravel.

The urinary sand or gravel deposited on the side or bottom of a receiving vessel is of two kinds, *red* and *white;* and it is of great importance to distinguish the one from the other, as they proceed from different causes, and require a different mode of treatment.

The *symptoms* of red gravel are well known. The shade of colour may vary from a reddish-brown or pink, to a perfect red. Here the urinary secretion is generally small in quantity, and high coloured, and the disease inflammatory the nearer the deposit approaches to a perfect *red,* the more severe in general are the symptoms.

The *pink* sediment usually indicates uncommon irritability in the system. The most perfect specimens of this kind of deposit are obtained from the urine of dropsical persons, those labouring under hectic fever, and those suffering from chronic disease of important internal organs, as the liver, bowels, etc.

White gravel is less common, but has long been observed to be attended by very distressing symptoms. They consist in great irritability of the system, and derangement of the digestive organs in general. There is often a sallow, haggard expression of countenance; and as the disease proceeds, symptoms somewhat analogous to those of diabetes begin to appear, such as great languor and depression of spirits, coldness of the legs, and other symptoms of extreme debility. The urine is invariably pale, and voided in greater quantity than usual; and after standing, for a greater or less time, always deposits a most copious precipitate of white impalpable powder. In all such cases, the urine is extremely prone to decomposition, and emits a most disgusting smell.

Those persons who habitually secrete urine that deposits a white sediment are generally pale and sallow; incapable of much bodily and mental exertion, and complain of lassitude and weariness.

In many persons there is an hereditary tendency to this complaint; general indolence or a sedentary life or an excessive indulgence in fermented liquors, and the luxuries of the table, become *predisposing causes* in others. But the chief cause seems to be a want of constitutional vigour, and especially in the digestive organs; and hence the periods of life in which this disease occurs most frequently are from infancy to the age of puberty, and in declining years; while it is rarely found during the busy and restless term of the prime of life. A cold and variable climate often becomes a cause, calculous complaints being seldom met with in warm climates; and the drinking of hard water often influences very sensibly the state of the complaint. White gravel may often be very distinctly traced to an injury of the back.

The urine in a healthy state is always an acid secretion, and it is the excess of its acid *(the uric or lithic acid)* that holds the earthy salts in solution. If, from any cause, it be deprived of this excess, or, in other words, the secretion of its acid be unduly diminished, the earthy parts are no longer held in solution, and a tendency to form *white* sand or gravel immediately commences. If, on the contrary, the acid be in greater excess than usual, instead of in deficiency or the natural secretion of earth be deficient while the acid retains its usual measure, the acid itself has a tendency to form a deposit, and hence the modification of *red* sand or gravel, (which is pure *lithic acid)* that is so frequently found coating the bottom of chamber-utensils.

TREATMENT—*The red gravel* is by far the most frequent kind of deposit, and the most effectual remedies for it are the alkalies, and the alkaline carbonates, such as lime-water, Brandish's alkaline solution, the bi-carbonate of potash or soda, magnesia, and *lithia* or *potash* water. But to be really useful, as Dr. Prout[1] has very correctly remarked, they must be conjoined with alteratives and aperients; for it ought never to be forgotten, in the treatment of gravel and stone, that they owe their formation chiefly to a weakened and vitiated action of the digestive organs, which will invariably require this conjunction, in order to the accomplishment of a permanently beneficial effect .

Half a drachm of bi-carbonate of potash or soda, may be taken in infusion of casearilla or water, once or twice a day, with one of the alterative pills No. 99 or 98 page 191-93 or four grains of the compound calomel pill No. 117, page 203 or three grains of blue pill, every other night; the following draught being taken every morning or every other morning, as a gentle and suitable aperient :

1. Dr. Prout has written one of the most valuable books on *Disorders of the Urinary Organs* that has ever appeared in this country, and I have much pleasure in recommending it to the notice of my afflicted readers. *Brodie's Observations on Disorders of the Urinary Organs* are likewise valuable.

Take of Rochelle salts	2 drachms;
Carbonate of soda	1 scruple;
Water 3	table-spoonfuls

Mix, and after adding a table-spoonful of lemon juice or thirty grains of tartaric acid, let it be drank directly.

Instead of the carbonate of potash, half a tea-spoonful of the alkaline solution, page 2, many be taken twice a day; and as it is tonic, as well as antacid, it will often be found a valuable remedy in all red deposits from the urine. It is particularly useful when red gravel is connected with gout, and the two diseases show a disposition to alternate. *See* what is said of it at page 2.

If the deposition of *red* gravel is accompanied with diarrhoea, lime water will be an appropriate remedy.

Sir Everard Home and Mr. Brande have strongly recommended the use of magnesia in this species of gravel, and it is of considerable use. Mr. Brande has related a case which yielded to it, after the alkalies previously given had failed. It may be taken either alone, in doses of ten grains once or twice a day or combined with the carbonate of soda, in the proportion of six or eight grains of the former to ten grains of the latter, twice or thrice a day. Or ten grains of magnesia may be dissolved in a draught of soda water, which is an excellent way of administering it.

Alkalies should not usually be taken in the morning. The time when the urine is most acid, and alkalies principally required, is after dinner; they should be given three or four hours afterwards, for if sooner, they sometimes interfere with digestion. Often it is better for the patient to take his magnesia or alkali when he wakes accidentally in the middle of the night. In many cases only a single dose of magnesia at bed-time is required; but in others it will be found necessary in the middle of the day also.

Ten grains of the sesqui-carbonate of ammonia or twelve drops of the water of ammonia, in water, twice a day, is likewise a useful medicine, especially in cases where great languor or weakness and coldness of the stomach is present. It is a powerful corrector of acidity, and a most valuable cordial.

Care is necessary in apportioning the dose of alkali in each individual case. If too little alkali is given, red sand is still deposited, though in smaller quantity; if too much, the urine is rendered alkaline, and a white sediment may follow.

A very convenient and valuable mode of combining an alkali with an aperient, and gentle bitter tonic, is as follows : it is worthy of particular regard when weakness of the stomach, costiveness, and red gravel are combined.

Take of Carbonate of soda	10	grains;
Epsom salt	½	or 1 drachm;
Compound infusion of gentian	3	table-spoonfuls;
Compound tincture of cardamoms		a tea-spoonful.

Mix for a draught, to be taken once or twice a day, according to its action on the bowels, which should be gentle.

The bowels should be kept gently open by it, and, therefore, the Epsom salt may be either increased or diminished, according to circumstances.

The powder of bear's whortle-berry is both tonic and astringent, and has been well spoken of, for its virtues in gravel and stone, by physicians of high authority. It may be alternated with the alkalies; and where general debility exists or there is a discharge of pus-like matter from the bladder, denoting ulceration or a very faulty condition of its secreting vessels, it is at once an appropriate and excellent medicine. The dose is from a scruple to a drachm of the powder, twice or thrice a day; or a strong tea may be made by pouring hot water upon the leaves of the plant, to three table spoonfuls of which may be added ten grains of carbonate of soda or a tea-spoonful of Brandish's alkaline solution, and drank twice or thrice a day.

In *white* gravel the whortle-berry may be given with the nitric or muriatic acid.

A decoction of coltsfoot and wormwood, in equal proportions, is said to have wrought wonders in some calculous cases. I think think very highly of them. A tea-cupful of the above decoction may be taken twice a day.

The diet of persons troubled with *red* gravel should be moderate in quantity, and of a nutritious and wholesome quality, consisting principally of fresh animal food, and farinaceous vegetables. All acids, and acescent food, must be carefully avoided, and likewise heavy bread, fat and hard-boiled puddings, and soups. Red wine is altogether objectionable, but a small quantity of white wine should be allowed. Toast or barley-water should be the common beverage. Jelly or jam made of the common bramble-berry will be found useful, taken as an article of diet, spread on bread instead of butter. This appears to have been highly esteemed by Mr. Pott, a surgeon of great and deserved ability in the last century.

Constant active exercise is of the first importance in all gravelly disorders; and flannel should be constantly worn.[1] Sailors and other persons accustomed to constant and laborious exercise in the open air, are very rarely affected with these complaints. M. Magendie, a celebrated Parisian physician, has given a striking example of the advantages to be derived from exercise and abstinence, and the mischievous effects of luxury, in the case of a merchant of one of the Hanseatic towns. "In the year 1814, this gentleman", says he, "was possessed of a considerable fortune, lived in an appropriate style, and kept a very good table, of which he himself made no very sparing use. He was at this time troubled with the gravel. Some political measures unexpectedly took place, which caused him the loss of his whole fortune, and obliged him to take refuge in England, where he passed nearly a year in a state bordering upon extreme distress, which obliged him to submit to numberless

1. "But more, after all, is to be effected by attention to diet and mode of living, than by medicine"—"*Brodi on Disorders of the Urinary Organs*, p. 156. He adds, (p. 149) "Persons who lead a sedentary life, and who never take exercise so as to produce perspiration, are especially liable to the formation of red sand. It seems as if, during perspiration, something was carried off from the blood in the cutaneous vessels, which would otherwise cause the urine to be loaded with acid."

privations, but his gravel disappeared. By degrees he succeeded in re-establishing his affairs; he resumed his old habits, and the gravel very shortly began to return. A second reverse occasioned him once more the loss of all he had acquired. He went to France almost without the means of subsistence, when his diet being in proportion to his exhausted resources, the gravel again a second time vanished. Again his industry restored him to comfortable circumstances; again he indulged in the pleasures of the table, and had to pay the tax of his old complaint".

In cases of *white sand* or *gravel,* an acid is the best medicine, and all the acids seem to answer the purpose, though the muriatic; nitric, and citric acids, have been in the greatest repute. The citric acid or lemon juice, is preferable for children, as being the pleasantest, and that which may be persevered in for a considerable time, it may be mixed with water in any proportion that is agreeable. The muriatic acid may be given in doses of from five to twenty drops, twice or thrice a day, in four table-spoonfuls of water; and the nitric acid in doses of from five to twelve drops, in the same proportion of fluid. Tonics also, as quinine, bitter infusions, and decoction of *pareira brava* (page 107), and steel are suitable and useful. All mercurial preparations are likely to be injurious.

The general diet should be nutritious, easy of digestion, and moderate in quantity, and, if they sit easy on the stomach, it should be intermixed with acids, salads, fruits and especially oranges and lemons. Malt liquor must be abstained from; and if the habit of the patient require that he should continue the use of wine, Champagne, Claret or Hock will be preferable to Madeira or Port. Water, saturated with carbonic acid, is the best common beverage in this kind of gravel, and attention being paid to diet and exercise, will sometimes be alone a sufficient remedy.

If pain attend the gravel, opium or extract of henbane should be occasionally administered, according to the urgency of that symptom. Thirty or forty drops of laudanum or from five to ten grains of the extract of henbane, may be given alone or in any draught which the patient may be taking, and repeated until the pain is relieved. Opium seems generally preferable in the *white* gravel; and henbane in the *red.* In *white* gravel, the solution of acetate of morphia (Dr. Porter's formula) is particularly indicated as an anodyne, since the acid it contains is an appropriate and efficient remedy for the complaint, and, at the same time, counteracts the injurious effects likely to result from the frequent use of opium, when taken in any of its common forms. Dr. Prout has judiciously remarked, that there is in all severe urinary diseases more or less of such irritability in the system, as is immediately and permanently relieved by the use of anodynes, especially opium. In case of great pain and irritation about the urinary organs, an opiate injection will be proper, and often of much service or two or three grains of opium may be made into a pill and inserted within the rectum, as a suppository.

A Burgundy pitch or a galbanum plaster may be applied over the loins with advantage. If the symptoms are unusually severe, and connected with manifest injury of the bladder or kidneys, a seton or issue should be instituted in the back.

Sometimes there is a secretion of a ropy mucus from the internal membrane of the bladder accompanying white gravel, when the exhibition of the decoction of the root of the *pareira brava* is, in many instances, productive of excellent effects.

Whether the gravel be white or red, when a small stone passes from the kidneys into the bladder, there is generally a fit of pain and irritation; to relieve which, the warm bath or hot fomentations, together with forty or fifty drops of laudanum every three hours, will be the most proper and effectual remedies. The passing of a small stone from the kidneys to the bladder, is denoted by a flxed pain in the region of the affected kidney, with a numbness of the thigh on the same side. The pain is sometimes very acute, and accompanied with nausea and fainting, but the pulse is rarely accelerated. During the whole of the passage from the kidneys, the urine is usually high coloured, and frequently mixed with blood.

Before I conclude this article, it will be necessary to say a few words respecting stones or calculi in the bladder. They differ greatly in their composition, form, size, and colour; but by for the most frequent is the uric acid calculus; while the mulberry calculus is productive of the greatest suffering. Their magnitude is generally in an inverse ratio to their number, the average size may be compared with that of the chesnut, walnut or small hen's egg. The largest stone met with in this country is that which was taken from the bladder of the late Sir David Ogilvie. It weighed forty-four ounces, and was of an oval shape, its long axis measuring sixteen inches, and the shorter fourteen.

The symptoms of a stone in the bladder are, a sort of itching along the urethra, particularly at the extremity of the glans, from which the patient often acquires a habit of pulling the prepuce, which becomes very much elongated; frequent propensities to make water, and go to stool; great pain in voiding the urine, and difficulty in retaining it; the stream of urine, being liable to stop suddenly, while flowing in a full current, although the bladder is not empty, so that the fluid is expelled by fits as it were; and the pain being greatest towards the end of, and just after the evacuation. There is a dull pain about the neck of the bladder, together with a sense of weight or pressure, at the lower part of the belly; and a large quantity of mucus is mixed with the urine, and sometimes the latter is tinged with blood, especially after exercise. But all these symptoms are so equivocal, and bear so great a resemblance to the effects of several other disorders, that they cannot be depended upon, and consequently, no well informed surgeon will venture to pronounce positively that there is a stone in the bladder, unless he can distinctly feel it with a sound.

The causes of calculi are the same as those which give rise to gravel. They are much more frequent in Norfolk than in any other county in England or than in the whole of Ireland or Scotland. It has been conjectured that women are less liable to the stone than men, but it is a question not yet completely settled. Infants and children to the age of twelve or fourteen, are particularly subject to it.

The treatment of stone is precisely the some as that of gravel, both in regard to medicines and diet; if the urine deposits a *red* sand, the alkalies, and other remedies just mentioned, must be taken; if *white* sand, the acids. There is this difference between gravel and stone, that, in the former, active exercise is highly advisable; whereas, during the presence of an actual stone in the bladder, the patient's exercise ought, for obvious reasons, to be less active and constant.

Dr. Morris of Canada, has lately found that an injection of castor oil has great effect in relieving the sufferings occasioned by a stone in the bladder, and, as the pain and irritation arising from this cause are often very great, I have much pleasure in recommending it to the notice of those who are labouring under so severe an affliction, hoping that they may find it of inestimable advantage. Different considerations had inclined Dr. Morris to the opinion, that the introduction of a lubricating fluid into the bladder would, under such circumstances, be productive of ease and advantage, and, being afflicted with the stone, he soon had an opportunity of trying the experiment on his own person.

> "I first took care", says he "to rid myself of the contents of my bladder; this I had no sooner accomplished than, with a large syringe, I injected, through a small leaden tube reaching to the sphincter, about two ounces of cold-drawn castor oil, and I cannot express to you my feelings occasioned by the change which took place upon the moment of its introduction, for it seemed as a new lower half had been given me. The absence of former painful symptoms still continuing, I went to bed, and can safely say, that I had not known, for some time previous, the pleasure of a sound and uninterrupted sleep. Latterly, I never awoke without a wish to make water, and the morning following was the first exception to it. When I did obey the call, I first took care, finding that the oil came last, to leave as much within the bladder as I could. This I had little difficulty in effecting, as it does not dispose the bladder to contract as other fluids do".

After this, the bladder was constantly supplied with two or three ounces of castor oil, and under this treatment every symptom of irritation vanished, and during two months no one symptom reappeared to remind him of the existence of the calculous concretions.

When all the foregoing means of relief fail, and the general health is worn out by a long succession of pain and anxiety, nothing remains but the operation of extraction. In females, stones, even of a large size, may frequently, perhaps generally, be extracted by dilating the urethra, by means of sponge tents, to a size sufficient to allow the calculus to pass, without the use of the knife at all.

The decoction of coltsfoot and wormwood, mentioned at page 616, should be made by gently boiling three or four ounces of each in two quarts of water down to a quart.

GREEN-SICKNESS OR RETENTION OF THE MENSES

Chlorosis or green-sickness, is a complaint which occurs chiefly in girls about the age of puberty, and is characterized by a pale blanched complexion, languor, listlessness, and depraved appetite and digestion; the several secretions being faulty or inert, especially at the commencement. It is called green-sickness from the pale, livid, and greenish cast of the skin, so commonly present in advanced cases.

The *symptoms* consist chiefly in a general sense of oppression, languor and indigestion. The languor extends over the whole system, and affects the mind as well as the body; and hence, while the appetite is feeble and capricious, and shows a desire for the most unaccountable and innutrient substances; as lime, chalk, etc., the mind is capricious and variable, often pleased with trifles, and incapable of fixing on any serious pursuit. The heat of the system is diffused irregularly, and is almost always below the point of health; there is, consequently, great general inactivity, and particularly in the small vessels, and extreme parts of the body. In advanced cases, the pulse is quick and low, the breathing attended with labour, the sleep disturbed, the face pale, the feet cold and swelled, the nostrils dry, the bowels irregularly confined, and the urine colourless. There is, also, sometimes an irritable and distressing cough; and the patient is thought to be on the verge of a decline; or perhaps to be running rapidly through its stages. Such severe instances of Chlorosis are not without danger. In general it is easily cured, but when swelling of the feet and legs, and other symptoms of dropsy are present, there is a proportionate degree of danger attending the complaint, and great attention must be given to it. In advanced cases there exists such an impaired condition of the blood, such a remarkable deficiency of this vital fluid, as calls for watchful attention.

All the symptoms indicate it to be a disease of debility. The functions of digestion, assimilation, sanguification, nutrition and generation, are inadequately performed.

The *principal causes* are indigestion and constipation occurring at the age of puberty, poverty of the blood, combined with a want of energy in the organic nervous system, and in the excernent vessels of the womb, etc., which prevents them from fulfilling their office. Constitutional weakness and relaxation frequently dispose to green-sickness; and whatever enervates the general habit or the stomach in particular, such as indulgence in heated rooms and late hours, long residence in crowded cities, insufficient or innutritious diet and constipation, may be ranked among its causes.

TREATMENT—The great object of treatment is, to get the system into a state of good general health, and to improve the quality of the blood, by the use of tonics, alteratives, and aperients; in conjunction with horse exercise, change of air and scene, a moderate but very nutritious diet, and cheerful society. Perhaps one of the best plans which can be laid down is, to give the patient one of the pills No. 100 directly or 101A, commencing immediately after with the steel pills, according to the directions subjoined to the prescription below, a warm bath at ninety-four degrees, being interposed twice a week. One of the warm aperient pills No. 100, 101 or 101B, pages 193-94, may be taken occasionally, if necessary, so as to prevent constipation. The *aperient electuary*, No. 37, page 160, is often a valuable aperient in this disorder, especially when eruptions on the skin appear in its coarse. At the same time the patient should take daily exercise in the open air, particularly on horseback, resorting to change of air and scene as often as circumstances will permit, and making use of the most nutritive food of easy digestion, with a small quantity of good home-brewed beer or Bass or Allsopp's ale or should it agree well, one or two glasses of sound wine daily. The rules to be observed with respect to diet and regimen, are fully detailed at pages 245-254, and under INDIGESTION; and active friction twice a day, with the flesh-brush or strong liniment of ammonia, over the region of the stomach and bowels, is highly advisable. Sometimes friction over the region of the loins with a strong liniment is useful. Friction is often of considerable service here, and as it is a remedy within the reach of every female, should never be disregarded. It should be performed by the patient herself, at least night and morning, for fifteen minutes at each time.

Take of Sulphate of iron 20grains;
Socotorine aloes 3grains;
Ipecacuanha, in powder 3grains;
Aromatic powder 6grains;
Extract of gentian . . . . 2scruples.
Mix, and with a little syrup, make the whole into a mass, to be divided into twenty pills. Two to be taken three times a day, after every meal.

Steel has a peculiar power of increasing the richness and redness of the blood, although by an operation not well understood, and therefore, it has always been found one of the most valuable tonics in green-sickness; and the sulphate, above ordered, may be gradually increased to thirty or thirty-five grains in the twenty pills. But if it does not suit or fails in producing the desired effect, the following form may be used :

Take of Steel pill with myrrh (both as ordered in the Pharmacopoeia) 2 drachms; . . . .
Aloes pill with myrrh . . . . 1 drachm;
Powder of capsicum . . . . 12 grains;
Oil of cloves a sufficient quantity to make a mass.
Divide it into forty pills, and take two pills twice or thrice a day.

A simpler form of pills is as follows, and one which in most instances will be found equal, if not superior, in their efficacy to any that can be prescribed.

Take of Sulphate of iron .... 11½ drachm;
Socotorine aloes........................ 1 scruple;
Gum mastic .... 15 grains;
Syrup, a sufficient quantity to make the mass into thirty pills.

The dose is one pill in the morning and afternoon, unless it purges too much; when they may be omitted for a day, and then resumed as before.[1]

The Tunbridge water is a strong chalybeate, and very serviceable; so that Tunbridge Wells is among the best places to which chlorotic girls, in the higher ranks of society, can resort. If the stomach be weak, and irritable, the fresh-drawn water is apt to prove too cold, and to occasion nausea and sickness which inconvenience may be prevented by putting it into a bottle, which should be closely corked, and then immersed in hot water.—*See* pages 227-28.

Should the disorder commence with considerable swelling of the glands of the neck, small doses of *iodine,* (page 78), given thrice a day, with five grains of the myrrh and aloes pill every night, may be advantageously tried, if the foregoing means have not proved effectual; or the iodide of iron may be taken—two or three grains, twice a day, is the dose.

For the pain in the head and side, when severe, friction with eau de Cologne is one of the best remedies. No blood-letting must

---

1. The effect of iron upon the constitution of the blood is astonishing. The proportion of the solid constituents, and especially of the red globules, is rapidly increased;—the only exception is the fibrin, which appears to be somewhat diminished, and which may be consequent upon its conversion into the substance of the red globules. The blood of a chlorotic female of twenty years old was carefully examined, and the following results were obtained. The first column contains the result before she had taken iron, the second, after a course of chaly beats which continued about ten weeks.

Water	868.340.	....	807.080.
Solid Constituents......	131.660.	....	192.290.
Fibrin	3.609.	....	1.950.
Fat	2.310.	....	2.470.
Albumen	78.200.	....	81.509.
Red Globules	38.060.	....	98.319.
Extractive Matter and Salts	8.921.	....	8.236

be attempted; it would be highly injurious. Ten drops of tincture of henbane in water may be given for the relief of palpitation.

Some physicians have employed cold bathing, but I decidedly prefer the tepid bath. Dr. Saunders used to say that, according to his observation, the cold bath is injurious in this complaint, but warm bathing often of essential service.

Electricity, in the form of sparks drawn from the lower belly or of slight shocks passed through it, may be resorted to in obstinate cases, and frequently with a prospect of advantage. In some cases, I should place much confidence also in Lavagna's injection, as described under *Suppression of the Menses;* and is the volatile tincture of guaiacum. From thirty drops to a tea-spoonful of this tincture may be administered in milk, three times a day. It is a valuable and appropriate stimulant and alterative.

Electricity is often of great use in those cases of this disorder, which are uncomplicated with a bloodless condition; but nothing can be more ridiculous than applying electricity or any other local stimulant, when in that state. In chlorotic retention, indeed, in the large majority of cases of menstrual retention, the complaint depends upon an anaemic or bloodless condition of the system, and the patient does not menstruate, simply because of existing debility, and that she has no blood to spare. After the general health has been improved by the use of iron, and small doses of Epsom salts, if the patient does not menstruate, then a few electrical shocks transmitted through the pelvis, seldom fail to effect a cure.

Now and then it happens, that symptoms of green-sickness appear in florid, full-bosomed girls, who have no mean share of general vigour, in which case the pulse is full and tense, and the pains in the head and loins very severe. The ordinary cause of this species, is catching cold in the feet at the period of the menstrual discharge; and the plethoric condition of the patient will bear and require *at the commencement* small bleedings by leeches, from the abdomen or loins, and cooling purgatives, as No.7: 3, 74 or 74A, pages 176-177. The warm bath also should be steadily used, with a plain diet and regular exercise.

GUTTA SERENA

Gutta serena or amaurosis, is that diminution or total loss of sight, which immediately depends upon a diseased state of the optic nerve, and its expansion on the bottom of the eye. It is a blindness in which the pupil is generally dilated and immovable, but without any other apparent defect. When vision is completely destroyed, it is called *perfect* gutta serena, when only diminished, *imperfect*.

One of the most common *symptoms* of a beginning amaurosis, is an appearance, in the patient's fancy, as if gnats, flies or serpentine diminutive bodies were flying before his eyes; or there appears an immovable black speck; or all objects seem covered with a dense mist. Sometimes objects appear indistinct, but double; or the patient seems to see through a network or gauze; and occasionally object are seen in the beginning pretty distinctly, but appear of a different colour from the real ones. Frequently a defective, interrupted sight is present, a greater or less portion of objects being undistinguishable. The generality of patients who have a beginning imperfect amaurosis, can always see objects, laterally situated, better than those which are immediately before them; and a degree of squinting is a very common symptom, particularly when only one eye is affected.

This disease may attach both eyes at once or only one. It may take place quickly, so as to be complete in a few days or weeks or what is most frequently the case, may be produced gradually, several years elapsing before it attains its utmost degree. It may, likewise, be either permanent or temporary.

As the accompanying symptoms are liable to great variation, so are the *causes* to much obscurity. The principal causes appear to be, a diseased condition of the digestive organs; general or local debility of the nerves; an extraordinary fulness of the blood-vessels of the brain or of those of the optic nerve,—or other sources of compression; the suppression of habitual discharges; external injuries of the head; violent gusts of passion; immoderate salivations; a fixed attention to minute objects too long continued; sudden fright and the excessive use of tobacco.

According to Richter, the periodical gutta serena commonly depends upon irritation affecting the digestive organs, the stimulus of worms or irregularity in the menstrual discharge.

It is *distinguished* from cataract by the blackness and dilated state of the pupil, and by the absence of any other apparent defect.

TREATMENT—As in all other complaints, the treatment must be regulated, in a great measure, by the age, habits and condition of the patient, and by the nature of the causes which have given rise to the amaurosis. If it seem to arise from a preternatural fulness of the blood-vessels of the brain or eye, the quantity of blood must be diminished by bleeding from the arm or by the use of leeches. Twelve or sixteen ounces of blood may be taken from the arm, and afterwards ten or twelve leeches applied to the temples and neck; a dose of the aperient mixture No. 73, page 176, being given every other morning, and the alterative pill No. 99, page 192, every night. This plan is clearly not applicable to debilitated nervous patients, but to the plethoric and strong it is sometimes of much service. Richter, a celebrated German surgeon, informs us of a woman, who, on leaving off having children, lost her sight; but recovered it again by being only once bled in the foot. Schmucker, another German surgeon of reputation, relates, that by means of bleeding, and an emetic, he has often restored the eye-sight of soldiers, who had lost it by making forced marches, with heavy burdens. If this disease follow violent anger, the same treatment is indicated. A clergyman (unhappy man!) became completely blind, after being in a furious passion, but his eye-sight was restored the very next day, by means of an emetic, which was given him with a view of relieving some obvious marks of indigestion in the stomach.

In gutta serena, arising from the suppression of the menses, leeches should be applied to the external sexual parts, the feet be bathed once or twice a day in warm water, the emetic No. 29, page 156, being also administered, and afterwards Richter's resolvent pills, noticed on the other side (page 629); or the pills of steel and aloes at page 623, which appear to me still more valuable. If these means fail in re-establishing the discharge, great confidence may be placed in a stream of electricity, conducted from the loins across the pelvis, in every direction, and thence repeatedly to the thighs and feet. This plan has frequently succeeded after a trial of several weeks.

In amaurosis from general nervous debility, excessive loss of blood, convulsions from want of food, and long continued intense study, especially by candle-light, the alimentary canal should be regulated by one of the aperient pills, No. 100, 101 or 101B, 101C or 101D, pages 193-94, given every other night, with tonic cordial medicines in the day, as cascarilla, columba or bark infusion, with tincture of the same, and carbonate of ammonia. *See* No. 79, 82 or 83, 84A, 84B, pages 184-85. At the same time, the vapour of the water of ammonia should be applied to the eyes, night and morning, by the patient's holding a cup, containing that liquid, sufficiently near the eyes to make them feel a smarting, occasioned by the very penetrating vapours with which they are enveloped. Every thing which has a tendency to weaken the nervous system must be sedulously avoided; the diet should be nourishing, and of easy digestion; and the exercise, in fair weather, should be constant, especially on horseback. Gold bathing may likewise be resorted to.

But it is highly probable, that the curable species of this disease commonly depends on some disease or irritation, existing in the stomach and bowels, which is occasionally complicated with general nervous debility, in which the eyes participate. Here the most efficient mode of treatment, is to exhibit mercurial alteratives, as the pill No. 98, page 191, every other night, with tonics and aperients during the day, the tonics being such as No. 102, 104, 106 or 115 or a course of sarsaparilla powder; the diet and regimen being the same as described under *Indigestion.* Mr. Travers is partial to a course of the blue pill, gentle saline purgatives, and bitter tonics, such as No. 74C or 130A, page 209, and No. 125. Mr. Lawrence *(Lectures in the Lancet, vol. ii. p.* 714, 1829-30), considers the antiphlogistic treatment in general the most proper, and consequently his chief remedies appear to be blood-letting, "and afterwards the use of mercury, so as to affect the system". He is an enemy to tonics and stimulants. I cannot think the disorder so frequently calls for the use of so much blood-letting or so active a use of mercury, as he advocates; but believe that a slight affection of the gums, by the employment of mercury, as in the pill No. 99, is often of signal service.

Richter recommends a vomit of tartar emetic at the commencement, which is to be repeated to the third or fourth time, at intervals of a day or two, according to the state of the tongue, and the bitter taste in the mouth. After this, three of the following pills are to be given twice a day, for a month or six weeks.

Take of ammoniac bum, assafoetida gum,
Castile soap, of each .... 1 drachm;
Rhubarb, in powder .... 1½ drachms;
Tartarised antimony .... 16 grains
Syrup of buckthorn, a sufcient quantity to form the whole into a mass, to be divided into sixty pills.

After using these pills, as ordered, he prescribes that an ounce of bark, and half an ounce of valerian powder, should be divided into six equal parts, one of which is to be taken in the morning, and another in the evening, in any convenient vehicle, for at least five or six weeks. The patient's food ought to be nourishing, and of easy digestion, with a moderate quantity of white wine, and proper exercise should be taken in a salubrious air. For exciting the action of the nerves of the eye, the vapour of water of ammonia, already spoken of, is of the greatest service; these vapours may be employed directly after the emetic has operated, and should not be discontinued till long after the eyes have been cured. Frequent blisters may also be applied to the temples, and nape of the neck; and likewise friction on the eye-brow, with eau de Cologne or Hoffman's anodyne liquor; the irritation of the nerves of the nostrils by the sternutative powder of Mr. Ware; and electric sparks or streams.

If an unusual dryness of the internal membrane of the nose is perceived, it will be right to make use of a mercurial snuff. Mr. Ware's snuff, in which he sometimes placed much reliance, is composed of ten grains of turbith mineral, and a drachm of liquorice powder or common sugar. A small pinch of this snuff, taken up the nose, generally occasions a very large discharge of mucus. Both Mr. Ware and Mr. Hey of Leeds, relate several cases of the present disease which were cured by electricity; and I am inclined to consider it as often a valuable remedy, and one which ought never to be left untried, unless there are circumstances in the case which contra-indicate its employment. It has been particularly useful in amaurosis originating from lightning; and, in general, the pupil has been dilated in the cases benefited by it.

But sometimes the pupil is contracted in gutta, serena, when the bi-chloride of mercury may often be resorted to with great advantage. It is especially indicated when an internal inflammation of the eye is the original cause of the disease. From thirty to fifty drops of the solution of oxymuriate of mercury, may be taken at breakfast and tea-blue, and should be continued uninterruptedly for many weeks. I have just left a patient afflicted with amaurosis in both eyes, who has used this medicine with excellent effect in subduing the excruciating pain in the eye-ball and forehead, under which she has laboured, and in strengthening the stomach and general habit. It is an appropriate medicine when the complaint is connected with syphilis.

A very short time since a Wesleyan-methodist minister, of the name of Stanley, was perfectly cured of amaurosis in both eyes, by the single use of a large blister applied down the spine. The blister was nine inches long and three broad, and reached from the nape of the neck downwards. He had some time before consulted several able oculists and surgeons to little or no purpose; and further relates, that a patient to whom he has since recommended the same means, has been completely cured by it.

It is said, that an infusion of Cayenne pepper has been successfully employed in the Liverpool Infirmary.

Take of Cayenne pepper, in powder .... 2 grains;
Hot water .... 2 drachms.

Macerate for an lour, and then strain for use. A drop or two is to be dropped into the eye, night and morning.

Many eminent surgeons consider the frequent smoking of tobacco to be a cause of blindness; they assert that its effects on boys and young men are terrible, and that it should be abandoned by all who wish for an heir.

INJURIES OF THE HEAD

Injuries of the head from blows, falls or other external violence, may be divided into the two states of *concussion* of the brain (commonly called stunning) and *compression.*

The *symptoms of severe concussion* are, total insensibility, the patient scarcely feeling any injury that may be inflicted upon him—loss of voluntary motion,—difficult breathing, but in general without the stertorous noise,—intermitting pulse, cold extremities,—contracted pupil; after a longer or shorter time, there is sickness,—the pulse and breathing become better, and though not regularly performed, are sufficient to maintain life, and to diffuse a little warmth over the extreme parts of the body,—the feeling of the patient is now so far restored, that he is sensible if his skin be pinched, but lies stupid and inattentive to slight external impressions. As the stupor goes off, inflammation very frequently arises.

If the injury to the head be such that a portion of bone is driven inwards or blood is poured out on the surface of the brain, symptoms often occur *denoting compression;* they are insensibility and loss of voluntary motion,—laborious breathing, with a stertorous noise,—slow laboring pulse, but not generally intermitting,— cold extremities,—pupil of the eye much dilated, but no sickness, at least till the compression is removed by the use of the proper instrument or other means. There is no return of feeling, so that the patient is insensible to pinching or other injuries inflicted, until the pressure is taken off from the brain.

TREATMENT—The best treatment at the commencement of a violent stunning, is to place the patient in a warm bed, to apply bladders of hot water over the region of the heart and stomach, and to employ gentle friction to the limbs. When he begins to recover, a little warm slop may be given, but no brandy, wine or other stimulants, for all severe injuries of the head are liable to be followed by inflammation, and we should have our eye to this probable consequence for many days after the receipt of such an injury. It was formerly a common practice in cases of concussion to apply strong stimulants to the rose, anti to administer them internally, but these are now abandoned by all good surgeons, for the reasons just given. The patient must be kept quiet, and have a black draught to empty the bowels. If, as he recovers sense and the power of motion, he grows irritable, and has pain in the head, and flushing of the face, and the patient is decidedly strong, we should anticipate inflammation by taking a pint of blood from the arm, and giving some more purging physic; but if there is a delicacy of constitution or want of vigour, then it is best to wait before bleeding. Should active inflammation of the brain supervene, the means noticed under that head must be rigorously enforced.

In *compression,* it will sometimes be necessary to employ an instrument called a trephine, in order to raise the depressed portion of bone or to remove blood which may have been poured out and be pressing down the brain, which operation falls, of course, to the province of the surgeon; and a full consultation should always be had previous to resorting to it. It frequently happens, however, that a man will fracture his skull without any decided symptoms of compression taking place, at least immediately; men have walked to a public hospital after such accident. In this case, I am certain that the soundest practice is not to trephine, unless symptoms of compression of the brain should subsequently appear; for this is a very severe operation, and patients who have been trephined under these circumstances, without evident signs of compression existing, have generally died, while those upon whom no operation has been performed, have as frequently recovered. Much meddling makes great mischief here. By all means be patient, and give nature time to recover herself.

In all wounds and lacerations of the scalp, it is now the universal practice of well informed surgeons to free the torn piece from dirt or foreign bodies, and restore it as quickly, and as perfectly as possible to its natural situation. No cutting away any part of the scalp is, at this time, ever advised; and it is very rarely that sewing is necessary, the application of slips of adhesive plaster being almost invariably sufficient to insure the union.

HEAD-ACHE

Head-ache is a very common complaint, and is of different kinds. The chief species are the sick head-ache, the nervous head-ache, the rheumatic or chronic head-ache, and the hemicrania or head-ache affecting only one side of the head.

The *bilious* or *sick head-ache* is by far the most frequent. It sometimes commences in the after part of the day, but more commonly in the morning, affecting only some particular part of the head, most frequently the forehead, and extending over one or both eyes. There is some degree of nausea or sickness usually connected with it; and the duration of the pain varies from two or three hours to twenty-four hours or longer. Its returns are very irregular; but those who use but little exercise, are inattentive to their diet, and are confined in their bowels, suffer most frequently and severely.

The *nervous head-ache* generally occurs in persons with a peculiar irritability of the nervous system. It is particularly apt to arise after any unusual exertion of mind or body or any sudden emotion of the mind, whether pleasing or painful; and is, I think, most frequent in the afternoon or evening, being always very much or entirely relieved by sleep.

The *rheumatic* or *chronic head-ache* is often connected with rheumatism, and frequently arises from the same causes. It is not unfrequently periodical, the pain is very acute, and motion of the head highly irksome.

Hemicrania is distinguished by its being confined to one side of the head. Its seat seems to be chiefly in the integuments of the head, and its principal symptoms are, tenderness on pressure, an obscure redness of the skin, and a suffusion of the eyes.

All these species of head-ache are closely connected, and are apt to run into each other. The most *common cause* of head-ache is debility and an unhealthy condition of the digestive organs, especially of the stomach and bowels; constipation is a fruitful source of these pains. The other chief causes are local irritation, suddenly checked perspiration, exposure to cold and damp, weakness or irritability of the nervous system, and the suppression of some accustomed discharge. All debilitating causes may be considered as giving rise to these pains. Several of my patients have been afflicted with a violent rheumatic head-ache from suckling their children too long; it ceased immediately the child was weaned. One patient has been tormented with a violent hemicrania, apparently the effect of an attempt to dye the hair of her head, by the use of some nostrum sold for that purpose.

TREATMENT—Head-ache is most frequently found in persons who are delicate, and who make poor blood; a fact which clearly indicates that an invigorating blood-restoring treatment is usually called for. It is in general a symptom of indigestion or congested liver or a consequence of a confined state of the bowels. One of the most efficacious plans of treatment is to administer a mercurial alterative, No. 98A, page 192, every other night, with a bitter or metallic tonic in the day, as No. 102 or 106A, page 198; and to keep the bowels regular by the means advised under *Costiveness.* pages 485-495. Attention should at the same time be paid to diet, exercise, and regimen, as directed under INDIGESTION. The pills No. 102, page 196 or No. 104, I have known of the greatest use. Some will find the mixture No. 84A or No. 85 page 185, more useful than the pills above described.

These are the means which are more or less applicable to all head-aches, as they are calculated to correct internal disorder of whatever kind, and to strengthen the general constitution. In many cases they will prove of immediate and striking utility; but they should never be dropped under three months, and in obstinate or long continued instances, will require a perseverance of double this time, in order to their full and permanent effect. When quick relief is sought, the temples may be bathed with eau de Cologne or with a mixture composed of equal parts of rose-water and spirit of mindererus or a bandage dipped in the coldest water may be bound round the head and removed as soon as it becomes warm; or ten drops of water of ammonia, may be taken in water, strong coffee or any other agreeable vehicle. But one of the most effectual means of quickly relieving head-ache is a sitz or hip-bath. Let the sufferer sit in it for fifteen or twenty minutes, and rarely indeed will it fail to remove the pain.

If the habit be plethoric and gross, with a well-marked preternatural fulness in the blood-vessels of the head, a few leeches may be useful; but the principal dependence ought to be on the above treatment. I would warn my readers against the abstraction of blood, in any quantity, in the majority of cases of head-ache. It is only in very full strong habits that it is indicated in almost all other examples it will do harm, and if the person is nervous and irritable—of a very susceptible frame—it may do such injury that it will require months to repair. I very much disapprove of the ordinary practice of letting blood in cases of head-ache.[1]

A similar plan will be advisable in *nervous* head-ache, with which should be combined horse-exercise and the cold bath or *cold water system*—avoiding fatigue. The assafoetida aperient pills will be most useful here; and the ammoniate of copper, as a tonic, is particularly indicated. If the pain be periodical, bark should be tried or the solution of arsenic, which Dr. Fowler of York, has found very beneficial. Four or five drops of this solution may be given twice or thrice a day.

---

1. The medical writings of the late Dr. Baillie, although he was a man of great reputation and of equal practice, are not at all remarkable either for sagacity or information, but the following remarks, in his *Posthumous Observations,* page 165, are valuable. He did not approve of blood-letting ordinarily in head-ache, and says, "In the accounts which patients have given me of the effect of this remedy, they have said that they have either received from it no benefit at all or that it has lasted but a few hours; or that the head-aches have been worse after cupping or the application of leeches". His neat remark is equally correct and valuable. "I have generally found such head-aches to be most benefited by temperate living, great attention to avoid improper diet, and purgative medicines, and by giving bitters. .The best common medicine is rhubarb and soap, in such doses as to give two motions daily",—one is better.

In the *rheumatic* species, three or four grains of the compound powder of ipecacuanha taken two or three times daily, with the aperient pills above recommended, every other night, will be found of eminent services or thirty drops of the volatile tincture of guaiacum may be taken in milk twice a day, with the following pill at bed-time :

Take of Aloes pills, with myrrh .... 5 grains;
True James's powder .... 4 grains;
Syrup of buckthorn, a sufficient quantity to make the ingredients into two pills.
To be taken nightly or every other night.

Sometimes the chronic head-ache is connected with a caries of some bone within the head, when the compound decoction of sarsaparilla or the compound extract in pills, should be taken with the pill No. 117, page 203. If such a head-ache follow syphilis or the free use of mercury, the compound decoction of sarsaparilla should be trusted to without the alterative pill; but the patient may take four grains of compound ipecacuanha powder at bed-time instead of that pill.

Chronic head-ache frequently arises from a syphilitic taint, when a peculiar treatment is absolutely necessary; then take iodide of potassium and diluted nitric acid No. 87 E.F., *Appendix.*

One of my plans for the cure of head-ache is this:—The patient should have not less than four hours exercise in the open air daily, two hours in the morning and two in the afternoon, and regulate the bowels by means of friction, and a regular solicitation of nature, depending chiefly on a very strict diet of bread, meat, gruel, biscuit, cocoa and tea. They should take one mutton chop or an equal quantity of roast meat, with a thick piece of bread, and a little potatoe or French bean, for dinner; an egg and one cupful of cocoa or tea or gruel, with one slice of bread and butter, for breakfast, and also at tea; and a small basin full of gruel at supper or a little bread and butter with wine and water. This is the whole quantity which is allowable; and no veal, pork, bacon, pastry, pudding or fruit can be permitted. Nothing is to be drank at dinner, but one hour after, a tumbler full of barley water or home-brewed beer, may be tried. This plan has wrought unexpected changes for the better. Sometimes a glass and a half of good wine, with water, may be allowed after dinner instead of the beer or any other liquid.

But this plan will not succeed with many. They require, together with a good deal of exercise and pure air, a very generous diet of the most easily digested food, with home-brewed malt-liquor and wine, but all moderate in point of quantity. Two things with them are essential,—to nourish the blood, and to avoid everything in diet which is found by experience to disagree with the stomach. In such cases, take steel and ammonia or No. 74C or 84A, page 184, take animal food twice a day, avoid all slops, take a glass or two of wine at dinner and supper, and always let fatigue be avoided. With many persons fatigue alone will bring on violent head-ache, and then rest is essential to relief. If such persons will work themselves hard, they cannot avoid head-ache.

The *hemicrania* may be treated in the same way as the sick head-ache. In addition to the remedies already recommended for that species, the patient must here try five or ten grains of the extract of henbane or eight grains of carbonate of ammonia, twice or thrice daily, which are sometimes valuable medicines in head-ache.

The external use of opium is at times worthy of much regard, and therefore, the patient may rub in warm laudanum over that part of the head affected with pain or apply the following plaister to the shaved scalp :

Take of Powdered opium.................	2	scruples;
Camphor,............................		half a drachm;

Burgundy pitch and lead plaister, of each, an equal quantity, and sufficient to form a plaister, to be spread on leather.

When this complaint appears as a sequel upon any suppressed evacuation or repelled eruption, the best means of obtaining relief will always be found in restoring the system to its former state, by the frequent employment of the warm bath, leeches, and stimulating poultices; and where this restoration cannot be effected, we must furnish the best substitute we can by some temporary irritation or drain, by means of the tartar emetic ointment rubbed on the back or other parts of the body or by an issue. An issue or a seton will often prove of the greatest advantage in obstinate and severe head-aches. In the *Transactions of National Curiosities* is a case of ten years' duration, completely cured by the last application.

Ray, the botanist, relates a remarkable cure of Mr. Oldacre, who by snuffing up the juice of ground ivy was cured of an inveterate head-ache.

In many severe head-aches, I should place much confidence in electricity, in the form of aura or gentle sparks drawn from the head, in conjunction with the general remedies advised at the commencement of this article. The use of a strong snuff is likewise often of material service, by promoting a discharge from the vessels of the nose and head. In very obstinate cases, a snuff composed of turbith mineral mixed with a little sugar, should always be tried—ten grains to a drachm of sugar.

In strong persons, who leave a great deal of blood flowing to the head, I have known the use of a wet night cap cure, the head-ache. The common night cap was dipped in cold water, wrung out, and then slept in till the morning, far two or three nights, in succession, if necessary. The *cold water system* is eminently efficacious in the cure of head-ache.

A palliative remedy of mach service in most cases of head-ache is smelling to horse-radish fresh-scraped. It is applicable to almost every kind of this affection.

It is worthy of especial notice, that whatsoever remedy is resorted to in this complaint, the regulation of the bowels, and attention to diet and exercise, should never be neglected.

HEARTBURN

Heartburn is a burning or gnawing uneasiness at the pit or upper orifice of the stomach, mostly attended with offensive eructations and other symptoms of acidity, and frequently with nausea. Sometimes vomiting occurs, with anxiety and tendency to faint.

The upper orifice of the stomach, called *cardia*, is particularly sensible, and therefore liable to evince symptoms of irritation from the presence of acidity or other irritating causes in that organ, whence the present complaint is denominated, in technical language, *cardialgia*. But irritability of the whole or any other part of the stomach, and perhaps of the adjoining organs, as the first intestines, pancreas, and liver, will often produce the same local pain. In a few instances, it has been ascertained after death to have been occasioned by some positive disease of the lower orifice of the stomach.

The most frequent cause of heartburn is the presence of acidity in the stomach, from too great, an indulgence in oily indigestible food or other articles of diet which disagree with the individual, and tend to weaken the stomach. Indeed, whatever debilitates this organ may be considered as a cause, and therefore it arises from a habitual and copious use of very cold or very hot beverages; indulgence in spirituous liquors; worms; violent purges; obstructed perspiration; and swallowing stones or kernels of fruit. Cheese eaten in excess has produced a heartburn that continued for three years. To so great a degree does the acrimony from acidity sometimes arise, that the contents of the stomach when rejected on a marble hearth, has been seen to produce an effervescence on it.

Treatment—One of the most powerful remedies for heartburn is the *alkaline solution* (page 2). Half a tea-spoonful should be taken twice a day in linseed tea, beer or milk and water. The alkalies have always been resorted to as the most efficient medicines in this complaint; and the alkaline solution exerts a decided superiority over many others, inasmuch as it at once neutralizes the offending acid exhilarates the spirits, and strengthens the stomach and whole constitution.

Another excellent medicine is Jephson's mixture No. 74C, 168—another is No. 84B, page 185, and a combination soap and ipecacuanha with rhubarb forms a fourth valuable remedy.

Take of Castile soap	3	drachms;
Ipecacuanha, in powder, ...	10	grains;

Extract of gentian, a sufficient quantity to form the ingredients into a mass.

To be divided into forty pills, two of which are to be taken twice a day.

Dr. Cullen of Edinburgh, was partial to the use of soap, and the following is another very useful form for its exhibition. It forms a bitter alterative and tonic, which is likely to prove in many instances of durable advantage.

Take of Castile soap	2	drachms;
Ipecacuanha, in powder	8	grains;
Extract of chamomile	1	drachm.

Mix, and divide into forty pills. Two to be taken twice a day.

Magnesia is a valuable medicine here, and so is the carbonate of ammonia. Ten grains of ether may be taken in a glassful of soda water or be united with the same quantity of columba powder, and repeated twice daily.

Sometimes, however, the mineral acids will check fermentation in the stomach more effectually, and be more permanently beneficial, than any alkali. Six or seven drops of diluted nitric or sulphuric acid should be taken, either in a large wine-glassful of water or infusion of cascarilla bark, and repeated three times in the twenty-four hours. If sickness attend heartburn, the nitric acid is often eminently serviceable.

But now and then acidity and heartburn will be incorrigible, either by alkalies or acids, even though the patient confines himself almost entirely to a diet of animal food alone. In such cases, ox-gall has been found completely successful; and is by some professional men considered to be infallible.

Take of Fresh ox-gall	30	grains;
Assafoetida gum	20	grains.

Mix and divide into twelve pills. Three to be taken thrice a day.

The diet should consist of articles least disposed to ferment, and most easy of digestion, as fresh animal food, eggs, biscuit, and bread; and for drink, good malt-liquor, weak brandy and water, lime-water or toast-water. Home-brewed malt liquor, well-hopped, is the best of all fermented liquors in this complaint. Friction over the region of the stomach will likewise be advisable, with the other resources in point of regimen and diet described under INDIGESTION.

In all cases of heartburn, the bowels should be kept regular by the use of the aperient pill No. 100, 101 or 101B or C, pages 194-95, if it cannot be done by diet and exercise. The present complaint is most commonly a symptom of Indigestion, and all the means noticed under that head are applicable here, a constant regard to the quantity and quality of the food, and to exercise in the open air, being in the majority of instances, absolutely necessary to a perfect cure.

HICCOUGH OR HICCUP

Hiccough is a convulsive catch of the muscles of respiration, attended with a sonorous inspiration, and returning at short intervals.

Though the spasmodic action in this affection exists chiefly in the midriff, the principal seat of the disease is the stomach. Debility, from whatever cause arising, is the ordinary predisposing, and some accidental stimulus the exciting, cause; excess of food, and especially in a weak stomach, is often a sufficient stimulus; and hence the frequency of the complaint among infants. It is likewise produced by acidity, worms, external pressure on the stomach and eating too fast.

TREATMENT—This affection cures itself in ordinary cases; and if not, it usually yields to a simple antispasmodic, as a draught of cold water or thirty drops of spirit of hartshorn or sal volatile or ten drops of water of ammonia, in any agreeable vehicle. Holding the breath will frequently succeed. But where this does not prove sufficient, fifteen or twenty drops of laudanum may be given in a little mint water; and should the complaint show a disposition to a frequent return, the means recommended under *Indigestion,* for strengthening the stomach and system in general, must be resorted to in the intervals. A warm bitter, as No. 104A or 106, page 197 or No. 130, page 208, with pure air, exercise, and cold bathing, will be found of great service in obstinate cases, the bowels being regulated by the occasional use of the aperient pill No. 100 or 101, page 194. The pill No. 104 is simple, but very efficacious, especially if the pill No. 99 be also taken every second night. In the hiccough attending asthma, and in some other instances, a little common or distilled vinegar is sometimes an effectual remedy.

One of the best medicines for this disorder in infants, is a little magnesia given in mint water, about once a day, for a week or two; or the magnesia may be combined with a small proportion of rhubarb. Six or eight drops of sal volatile, in water, is likewise a useful remedy for infants; or the pit of the stomach may be frequently rubbed with a little soap liniment.

All persons subject to frequent hiccough should be attentive to their diet, and the regulation of their bowels, and resort to the usual means for strengthening their digestive organs.

A French physician, (Laennec), of acknowledged judgment and high authority, recommends the magnet. He says, "By means of these plates I stopped, at once, an hiccup which had lasted three years. At the end of six months the patient having one morning neglected to put on the plates, the hiccup returned but was removed, upon their being replaced."[1]

HOOPING COUGH

This is a convulsive cough, accompanied with a shrill hoop, and returning in fits that are frequently terminated by vomiting. The

1. Magnetism was too much cried up by some medical men and others in the last century, but it appears to be too much neglected at present. That it acts on the animal system is sufficiently proved by the fact of its giving rise not only to very obvious general effects, but even to local ones. After a certain time, it commonly produces an eruption of small pimples, which are sometimes so painful as to oblige us to interrupt the process for some days. This effect cannot be attributed to the action of the oxidized plates on the skin, as the eruption almost always takes place under. the anterior one. See the remarks on this subject under CHRONIC RHEUMATISM.

Greeks called it the "wild or untameable cough", from its violence; and in the north of Europe, it is called chin-cough or kin-cough.

The disease comes on with a slight difficulty of breathing, thirst, quick pulse, hoarseness, cough and all the symptoms of a common cold. In the second or third week after the attack, it puts on its particular and characteristic symptoms: the expiratory motions, peculiar to coughing, are made with more rapidity and violence than usual; and after several of these expirations thus convulsively made, a sadden and full inspiration succeeds, in which, by the air rushing through the top of the windpipe with unusual velocity, a peculiar sound is caused, which has obtained the name of hoop. When this sonorous inspiration has happened, the convulsive coughing is again renewed, and continues in the same manner as before, tell a quantity of mucus is thrown up from the lungs or the contents of the stomach are evacuated by vomiting, which generally terminates the fit; the patient is then most frequently enabled to return to the amusements he was employed in before its accession, and often expresses a desire for food; but when the attack has been severe, it is succeeded by much fatigue, hurried breathing, and general languor and debility. After a longer or shorter continuance of the disease, the paroxysms become less severe, and at length entirely cease. In some instances, it has, however, been protracted for several months, and even for a year.

Although the hooping cough often proves tedious, and is liable to return with violence on any fresh exposure to cold, when not entirely removed, it nevertheless is seldom fatal, except to very young children, who are always likely to suffer more from it than those of a more advanced age. The danger seems always to be in proportion to the youth of the patient, to the degree of fever and difficulty of breathing which accompany the disease, and to the state of debility which prevails.

Children are most commonly the subjects of this disease, and it appears to depend on a specific contagion, which affects them but once in their life. The disease being produced, the fits of coughing are often repeated without any evident cause; but, in many cases, the contagion may be considered as only giving the predisposition, and the frequency of the fits may depend upon various exciting causes, such as too full a meal, the having taken food of difficult digestion, and irritation of the lungs by dust, smoke or disagreeable odours. Emotions of the mind may likewise act as an exciting cause.

Its immediate cause seems to be an irritation and inflammation (in the majority of instances moderate) of the windpipe, and its termination called *bronchia.* When death occurs, it seems owing to the supervention of *acute bronchitis,* that is, inflammation of the bronchia.

It is clearly *distinguished* from other coughs by the peculiar hoop; and it may very often be recognized before this sonorous inspiration occurs, by an evident swelling of all or most of the features.

TREATMENT—According to Dr. Cullen, (the celebrated medical professor at Edinburgh) the indications of treatment in hooping-cough are two-fold: *viz.* in the early stage of the disease, to moderate its violence, and to palliate urgent symptoms; and in the advanced period, to interrupt its course, and to oppose the spasmodic habit by antispasmodic remedies.

The disease will run a certain course, but we ought to endeavour to diminish its violence, to promote a healthy perspiration, and toward off inflammation in the chest. For this purpose few things are more useful than the pills No. 119A, page 204. If the child is under two years of age, half a pill or powder, will be sufficient. If that is not given, Sir William Watson's prescription may be tried; it is an excellent one:

Take of Tartarized antimony	1	grain;
Laudanum	20	drops;
Water 1		ounce.

Mix them, and give one or two tea-spoonfuls every evening, according to the age of the child—one for a child above two years, and two if above four years. To children under two years, let three grains of ipecacuanha be substituted in this mixture for the tartarized antimony.

Dr. Gooch used to say that his mother became famous as a village doctress by the help of this prescription. If the child is restless at night, few medicines are better than a quarter or half a grain of ipecacuanha powder, two of Dover's powder, and two of carbonate of soda in jelly, for children above three years old.

At the same time, rub the chest and spine with the embrocation No. 41, page 161; and the diet should consist of the mildest nourishment, such as milk, light puddings, baked fruit, barley water and eggs; and the rooms should be of the temperature of 60 degrees. In the summer, let the children go out daily; in the winter they are better in the house, and their bedroom should be kept at a temperature of 60 degrees. The preceding treatment will be sufficient in all ordinary cases.

In severe cases, one of the most dangerous attendants of hooping cough is an inflammation of the *bronchia—bronchitis,* and should the child have permanent difficulty of breathing between the fits, we may be almost certain of the existence of inflammation, when the use of leeches is necessary. Apply four or five leeches either to the temples or chest. Then give directly the mixture for bronchitis, No. 78B. This is an invaluable mixture in severe cases of hooping cough, and is far better than calomel. When the symptoms of difficult respiration are severe, threatening suffocation, leeches applied to the upper part of the throat, the top of the windpipe, are often of signal benefit. There is often serious affection of the brain in the worst cases of hooping cough, (denoted by severe pain in the head after each fit of coughing). and, therefore, leeches applied to the temples or behind the ears, are sometimes found of uncommon service.

An occasional emetic of ipecacuanha or antimonial wine is an excellent remedy in the beginning, and will generally supersede the necessity of blood-letting; it clears the stomach, relaxes the skin, moderates the fever, and tends to keep the bowels open. A tea-spoonful or two of either of these wines may be given every other morning, according to the age of the child.

In very acute examples, *where the inflammation is great,* if we do not bleed and administer the mixture, No. 78B, directly, the inflammation cannot subsequently be so well controlled. We would therefore say, that in very severe attacks, *the grand indication in the beginning is, to subdue inflammation.*

In this disease, unless the child is under two years old, antimonial wine is preferred to ipecacuanha.

The pills for hooping cough No. 119A, are very valuable at all stages of the disease.

Should the paroxysms be violent, and the patient's friends object to the employment of leeches, of have applied them without much benefit, the tartar emetic ointment ought to be rubbed on the chest three times in the twenty-four hours, till an eruption appears, when it should be discontinued. It is made by rubbing together, in a mortar, a drachm of tartar emetic and an ounce of hog's lard; about the size of a common nut being rubbed on the chest at each application. Its effects are much superior to those arising from the use of blisters, and it is far more eligible in infants and young children. At the same time the valour from a quantity of boiling water may be inhaled several times during the day, and the feet bathed in warm water in the evening.

The first or inflammatory stage possibly includes about the first two or three weeks, during which time anti-inflammatory measures, as we have already stated, should alone be employed. But in the second stage, when the disease begins to drop the symptoms of inflammation, and to assume more of a spasmodic or simply nervous character, antispasmodics, tonics, and alteratives ought to be tried, and will often succeed in curing the complaint, which, without them, would often run on to a great length, and by its continuance induce so much debility and disorder, both in the lungs and whole constitution, as to pave the way for consumption or some other fatal malady. The sulphate of zinc, extract of hemlock or bark, are, in my opinion, the best internal remedies at this period, and stimulating embrocations to the spine or the tartar emetic ointment to the chest, the most efficacious external applications.

In the second stage, half a grain of the sulphate of zinc, made into a pill with extract of hemlock, may be given to children of ten years old two or three times a day. Or, a grain or two of extract of hemlock, and one of rhubarb powder, may be administered in the same way, to children of the same age. *See* No. 119A, page 204.

The extract of night-shade has been praised beyond any other remedy in the *second stage* of hooping cough by the skilful and discerning Dr. Golis, physician to the hospital for sick children at Vienna. He says, that during a period of eighteen years he has found it to be a most valuable remedy in this complaint. It is a powerful sedative and antispasmodic, and, under medical superintendence, worthy of attention in obstinate cases of this species of cough. The experienced French physician Laennec considered it very useful here, and superior to all other narcotics. Children of six years old may take it according to the following prescription, the dose of the extract being either diminished or increased for patients of a more tender or advanced age.

Take of good extract of night-shade	6	grains;
Acetated liquor of ammonia	1	ounce;
Spearmint or simple water	21	ounces;
Simple syrup		half a n ounce.

Mix. Dose, a table-spoonful three times a day.

The wine or tincture of meadow-saffron has been well spoken of by some physicians on the continent, but I am not partial to it. It is not half so efficacious as the mixture No. 78B, page 180 or an occasional emetic of ipecacuanha.

Dr. Cullen was wont to rely almost exclusively on bark, in *the second stage* of the complaint. As children are with great difficulty prevailed upon to take a moderate quantity of this medicine in powder, quinine (*see* page 129) will be found an excellent mode of administering it. From half a grain to three or four grains of quinine, made into a pill with extract of gentian, may be given twice or thrice a day. Quinine is particularly indicated when the paroxysms assume a periodical type.

Beside the above remedies, both the acetate of lead and prussic acid have been employed with success, and recommended by respectable practitioners for the cure of chronic hooping-cough. They are very active remedies, and ought not to be used till other means have failed; when this is the case, the acetate of lead is the safer medicine.

Take of acetate of lead (plumbi super-acetas).	2 grains;
Opium	1 grain;
Extract of hemlock	10 grains.

Mix, and divide into eight pills. Dose for a child of ten years old, one pill three times a day.

At the same time that we give suitable medicine internally, some stimulating ointment or embrocation should be rubbed on the chest or spine, and I know none superior to the tartar emetic ointment or lotion. The ointment has already been described, and the lotion is as follows :

Take of tartarized antimony, one drachm. Dissolve it in two ounces of water, and add tincture of Spanish flies, one ounce. Mix for a lotion, a little of which is to be rubbed over the pit of the stomach, three or four times a day, till relief is obtained.

This was once a famous *nostrum,* called Struve's lotion for the looping-cough, and is often very efficacious. Roche's embrocation is made by mixing an ounce of oil of amber, with two ounces of olive oil, which is scented strongly with oil of cloves; a tea-spoonful or two may be rubbed on the chest or down the spine, frequently through the day, but it is not so effectual as the above lotion. Either No. 41, page 161 or No. 46, page 163, is an excellent stimulating embrocation for the purpose, and superior to Roche's.

Mr. Ward, of Manchester, spears of several violent cases of this cough, cured by opiate friction alone, after many other things lead failed. The liniment, No. 39, page 161, may be employed.

In the latter periods, the diet should be nourishing, but mild and easy of digestion; and where it is practicable, change of air especially at the sea-coast, is of the first importance in severe cases. cold bathing or sponging is often of immediate and permanent advantage.

HYPOCHONDRIASIS OR LOW SPIRITS

Hypochondriasis, low spirits or vapours, is a certain state of the mind accompanied with indigestion, wherein tile greatest evils are apprehended upon the slightest grounds, and the worst consequences imagined from any unusual feeling even of the slightest kind; and in respect to such apprehensions and feelings, there is always the most obstinate belief and persuasion.

Ancient medical writers supposed this disease to be confined to those particular regions of the abdomen technically called *hypochondria,* which are situated on the right and left side of that cavity, whence comes the name of hypochondriasis. See the engraving of the different regions of the body in my book On The Diseases of Females.

The *common corporeal symptoms* are, a troublesome flatulency in the stomach or bowels, acrid eructations, costiveness, a copious discharge of pale urine, spasmodic pains in the head and other parts of the body, giddiness, dimness of sight, palpitations, general sleeplessness, and often an utter inability of fixing the attention upon any subject of importance or engaging in any thing that demands vigour or courage. The mental feelings, and peculiar train of ideas that haunt the imagination and overwhelm the judgment; exhibit an infinite diversity, sometimes the hypochondriac is tormented with a visionary or exaggerated sense of pains or some concealed disease; a whimsical dislike of particular persons, places or things; a groundless apprehension of personal danger or poverty; a general listlessness and disgust; or an irksomeness and weariness of life; in other instances, the disease is strikingly accompanied with peevishness, and general malevolence;. they are soon tired with all things; discontented; disquieted; upon every light occasion or no occasion object; often tempted to make away with themselves; they cannot die, they will not live; they complain, weep, lament, and think they lead a most miserable life, never was any one so bad.

The whims that are sometimes seriously entertained under this complaint are of the most ludicrous description. A foreign writer makes mention of a baker at Ferrara who thought himself a lump of butter, and durst not sit in the sun or comp near the fire, for fear of being melted. The wisest and best of mankind are as open to this affliction as the weakest. The excellent Pascal was at one time so hallucinated with hypochondriacism, as to believe that he was always on the verge of an abyss, into which he was in danger of falling; and under the influence of this terror, he would never sit down till a chair was placed on that side of him on which he thought he saw it, and thus proved the floor to be substantial. Rousseau was a perfect hypochondriac, and morally one of the worst description.

The *chief cause* may be a strong constitutional predisposition or the disease may be the consequence of a sedentary life of any kind, especially severe study protracted to a late hour in the night, and rarely relieved by social intercourse or exercise; a debauched and dissolute habit; great excess in eating and drinking; the immoderate use of mercury; violent purgatives; the suppression of some habitual discharge or long continued eruption. Our excellent poet, Cowper, who was deeply depressed by hypochon-driacism for the greater part of his life, was thus afflicted after having had a cutaneous eruption repelled, to which he had been for some time subject.

Congestion or some peculiar affection (by whatever cause produced) of one or more of the important organs within the abdomen, is a frequent cause. M. Pinel, a French writer on this disease of considerable reputation, regards a displacement of the transverse arch of the colon[1] as a powerful and ready cause of hypochondriasis; and M. Esquirol, another distinguished French physician of the present day, has found it as frequently as M. Pinel. This displacement sometimes consists in an oblique, and sometimes in a perpendicular direction of the intestine; but no disease of the organization has been found in any instance, and hence the change of place seems to proceed from relaxation and debility alone.

---

1. The *colon* is one of the large intestines, next above the *rectum* or last gut. It is an organ of uncommon importance, as may be seen by referring to what we have said at pages 476-479.

TREATMENT—The principal objects of treatment are, to remove the indigestion, to strengthen the body, and to enliven the spirits; and one of the best plans with which I am acquainted, for the fulfilment of these intentions, is, constant exercise and change of place, with a warm bath about thrice a week, early hours, regular meals, and pleasant conversation; the bowels being at the same time carefully regulated by the mildest means (pages 489-90), and the stomach strengthened by some appropriate tonic medicine. The exercise should be very considerable daily, and of all common modes, that on horseback or in an open carriage, is the best, which should be combined, if possible, with constant change of air and scene. Indeed, travelling alone is a most powerful remedy in this disease, since it is often one of the most efficient means in removing indigestion, of strengthening the body, and exhi-larating the spirits; and where the patient's circumstances will permit, it ought invariably to be one of the first measures resorted to, as it will undoubtedly be found one of the best. If displacement of the colon is a frequent cause of this malady, as I believe, adopting the views of Pinel and Esquirol, we have therein strong reasons for recommending travelling to the hypochondriac. At the same time, a warm bath at ninety-five or ninety-six degrees should be taken every other morning; the patient accustoming himself to early using, and regular meals of nourishing and easily digested food. The bowels are almost always torpid in hypochondriacs, and will, therefore, require constant attention in selecting articles of diet which are of an opening quality, with the occasional employment of a warm pill. The aperient pills, No. 97, 100, 101 or 101A or C, pages 194-95, are very suitable, one or two of which may be taken thrice a week. The bitter and metallic tonics advised under *Indigestion,* are generally prescribed in this complaint, and all of them are sometimes of great service; but I question whether any other article is here of such eminent utility, as a tonic, as ipecacuanha. It at once invigorates the stomach, relaxes the skin, and favours the natural action of the bowels. It may be taken according to the following formula :

Take of Ipecacuanha, in powder	20 grains;
Castile soap	1 drachm;
Extract of chamomile....................	1 drachm.

Mix, and divide into forty pills. Take one or two twice or thrice a day.

Regular daily friction over the limbs and bowels with the flesh brush, is very advisable; and the general diet and regimen should be governed by the principles laid down for treating indigestion.

The sulphate of quinine, in doses of two or three grains, two or three times a day, may prove a useful tonic medicine in some instances. It is certainly the best way in which bark can be administered.

The waters of Tunbridge, and other chalybeate springs are proper; and the Harrowgate water has appeared to have been of eminent service in many cases.

Some physicians have recommended a free use of mercury, but it is a measure which, in my opinion, should never be resorted to in hypochondriasis, without a strict investigation into the causes which may have given rise to it in the particular instance to be treated, and a careful consideration of the present and past state of the health and strength; fuor should the patient's habit be weakly, and the complaint have been brought on by sedentary occupation, violent purgatives or other direct causes of debility, the active employment of mercurials will rarely fail to augment both the local and general relaxation, and to give strength to the disease. If, however, the patient possesses a good share of general vigour, and the low spirits seem to have arisen from a very confined state of the bowels or other source of internal congestion or from a repelled eruption, the cautious use of mercurial alteratives may some times prove of the greatest benefit. In such cases the pill No. 98 or 99, page 191 or No. 117 may be given every other night, in conjunction with the general plan above noticed.

For local pain in the head or stomach, the most efficacious means are blisters, applied to the neighbourhood of the part affected or friction with an anodyne liniment as No. 39, page 161; or five or ten grains of extract of hemlock, with two grains of true James's powder, may be administered as occasion requires or a few drops of Battley's opiate drops.

In regard to the *moral management,* assiduous kindness and consoling conversation produce a deeper effect than they seem to do. The patient should rarely be opposed in the expression of his sentiments, and never with ridicule. A very grand object is to gain the patient's confidence, and in order to effect this, we must humour his foibles, and seem to fall in with his views. When he is dwelling upon some imaginary disease, it must be prescribed for, and should his anxiety pass in succession from one complaint to another, they ought all to be prescribed for in their turn, for there is seldom any other way of removing the groundless fears associated with hypochondriacism. To show the effect of judicious moral management in the present disorder, I have transcribed the following case, which is to be found in one of Dr. Cox's publications:

> "Mr. aged forty, of a spare and melancholic temperament, remarkable for general and almost universal acquired knowledge, and always possessing singular equanimity, had injured his health by too close an attention to extensive mercantile concerns. At length he was observed to be very attentive to every feeling, of which he made minute descriptions to his family: this increasing, he became a prey to empiricism, red several ridiculous popular pamphlets, and was soon worked up to a belief that his body was the common receptacle of diseases : pills, potions, powders, auctions, lotions, and mercurial girdles, were employed and dismissed in succession. The metallic tractors for a time amused him, till it was proved to the patient, and to his friends who witnessed the experiments, that these expensive baubles possessed no more properties than a rusty nail. All the fears of the patient became at length concentrated in one, from the contemplation of, and conversation on which, no arguments could divert him, he believed all his sufferings arose from repelled itch; a formal consultation of medical men was, therefore, determincd on, who having previously agreed on the propriety of humouring the patient, were unanimously of opinion that his conjecture was just. A medical plan was laid down some stimulating applications to different

parts of the body occasioned crops of eruptions from time to time, which were washed with some simple preparation. This farce continued a few weeks, and the patient at length was perfectly restored to health and reason."

HYSTERICS

Hysterics consist in a convulsive struggling, alternately remitting and increasing, with a sense of a suffocating ball in the throat, drowsiness, copious discharge of pale urine. rumbling in the bowels and fickleness of temper.

The hysteric fit often takes place without any previous, warning, though generally there are some precursive signs, as yawning, stretching, dejection of spirits, anxiety of mind, sickness at the stomach, palpitation of the heart, and a sudden burst of tears without any assignable cause. The paroxysm soon succeeds, with a coldness and shivering over the whole body, and frequently with an acute pain on the left side, and a sense of distention, giving the idea of a ball or globe rolling about in the abdomen, and gradually advancing upwards till it gets into the stomach; thence removing to the throat, it occasions the sensation of an extraneous body lodged there, which is called *globus hysterious*. The disease having arrived at its height, the patient appears threatened with suffocation, she becomes faint, and is affected with stupor and insensibility; whilst, at the same time, the trunk of the body is twisted backward and forward, the limbs are variously agitated, and the fists are closed so firmly, that it is difficult, if not impossible, to open the fingers, wild and irregular actions follow, in alternate fits of laughter, crying, and screaming, incoherent expressions are uttered, and sometimes a most obstinate and distressing fit of hiccough takes place. The spasms at length abating, a quantity of wind is evacuated upwards, with frequent sighing and sobbing; and the patient, after appearing for some time quite spent, recovers the exercise of sense and motion, without any other feeling than a general soreness and a pain in the head. It is rarely that a hysteric fit has become dangerous; though it has, in a few instances, terminated in epilepsy or insanity.

Hysteric affections occur much more frequently in the unmarried than in the married, and most commonly between the age of puberty and that of thirty-five years and they make their attack oftener about the period of menstruation than at any other time. Women of a delicate habit, and whose nervous system is extremely sensitive, are those most subject to hysterics; and the habit which predisposes to their attacks is acquired by inactivity and a sedentary life, grief, anxiety of mind, late hours, dissipation, a suppression or obstruction of the menstrual flux, excessive evacuations and the constant use of an innutritious diet. They are readily excited in those who are subject to them by passions of the mind, and by every considerable emotion, especially when the erect of surprise; hence sudden joy, grief or fear, are very apt to occasion them. They have also been known to arise from irritation and sympathy.

They frequently assume the character of hip-joint or knee disease, great spinal irritation, peculiar uterine pain, and other complaints; so that even able practitioners have been mistaken, and attributed to real disease in the hip or knee or back, what was merely a hysterical affection.

Constipation, and severe disorder of the bowels, will sometimes give rise to very painful hysteric fits.

This complaint is easily *distinguished* from hypochondriasis by its convulsive struggling fits making their onset suddenly and violently; by its being accompanied with the sensation of a ball rising upwards in the throat; by the copious discharge of pale urine; and by its occurring at an early period of life. Hypochon-driasis, on the contrary, is gradual in its accession, and tedious in its progress; it comes on about the middle age; the dejection of spirits is constant and very great; and there is no convulsive paroxysm.

Hysterics are sufflciently *distinguished* from epilepsy by the greater degree of insensibility during the paroxysms of the latter, by the profound sleep which follows it, and by the absence of laughing, crying, moaning and other symptoms above detailed.

Treatment—During the fit, it will be the safest practice to rouse the patient by applying burnt feathers, assafoetida or smelling salts to the nose; by rubbing the temples with ammonia, and by putting the feet into warm water. In obstinate cases, cold water may be dashed over the limbs, and the laxative clyster No. 8, page 146, should be exhibited. A clyster of cold water alone has been effectual in putting an end to the fit.

Blood-letting is now never prescribed in hysterics.

In the intervals of the paroxysms, the object is to obviate costiveness and indigestion, and to strengthen the whole constitution; every remote or exciting cause being sedulously avoided. The use of mild aperients and tonics, with active exercise in the open air; regular meals of nourishing food, early rising, and cheerful company, are the principal means of invigorating the body and mind, and thus effecting a radical cure of hysterics. The warm aperient pill Nos. 100, 101 or 101A, B or C, pages 194-95, may be proper for occasional use; and the ammoniate of copper, sulphate or flowers of zinc, sulphate or carbonate of iron, guaiacum, quassia, and bark, are the most celebrated and valuable tonics. The bark may be taken as advised in No. 115, page 190; the preparations of copper and zinc may be administered as recommended under EPILEPSY, and the sulphate or carbonate of iron according to the forms given under INDIGESTION. The ammoniated tincture of guaiacum, in doses of thirty drops, twice or thrice a day, in milk and water, is sometimes an excellent medicine; it may be given in conjunction with the tincture of muriate of iron, if it does not succeeds alone.

Dr. Paris writes in favour of the virtues of quassia. "It has been observed", says he, "that in hysterical debility, to which the female sex is so prone, the quassia affords more vigour and relief to the system, than the Peruvian bark, especially when combined with a small proportion of sulphate of zinc".

Take of sulphate of zinc, four grains, gradually increased to six or eight; infusion of quassia, five and a half ounces; tincture of columba, half an ounce.—Mix, and take two table-spoonfuls three times a day.

The preparation of bark called the sulphate of quinine is a useful remedy. In hysterics returning periodically, it has not unfrequently effected a cure after other tonics had failed. The cold bath is useful; and Vichy or other mineral waters may be drank with the prospect of great benefit.

When hysteric affections arise from a suppression or obstruction of the menses, these evacuations must be fully restored by adopting the means recommended under those particular heads.

Anodynes and antispasmodics, as opium, musk, castor and valerian, are often had recourse to in this complaint, but are, in, my opinion, of very doubtful advantage. Dr. Buchan remarks, that all the extraordinary cures he ever witnessed in hysteric cases were performed by means of tonic and corroborating medicines, which entirely agrees with my own experience. Mugwort has been useful. *See* EPILEPSY, pages 558-60.

The tincture of colchicum has completely succeeded in curing an obstinate case of hysterics; and from its acknowledged power of allaying pain and nervous irritation, I am disposed to consider it worthy of notice in some instances of this disorder; but it must be used with great caution. Used as a palliative to put an end to the actual fit, half a tea-spoonful may be given, in water, and repeated to the second time, if necessary; and when employed, in the intervals, with the view of obtaining a radical cure, ten drops may be given, twice a day, in any agreeabte vehicle. In its power of affording present relief, it may sometimes be superior to assafoetida or any of the antispasmodics in common use. But it is a powerful medicine, and should not be continued for any length of time; in general, not longer than a week at one time.

Regular exercise on horseback, with variety of scene, and early rising, are particularly desirable. The diet should be nourishing, and such as is recommended in indigestion.

Cramp and local pain may be relieved by the means pointed out under hypochondriasis. Dry cupping is an excellent means of relieving pain. A full account of it is given in my TREATISE ON THE DISEASE OF FEMALES. In that publication will likewise be found some instructive cases of *hysterical hip* and *knee-joint affection,* and *hysterical spinal affection,* to which I beg to direct the serious attention of the reader, for they are full of interest and importance.

The late Dr. Good has correctly observed, that where the disease occurs in the bloom of life, and there is reason to apprehend the ordinary orgasm of this age to be in excess, the surest remedy is a happy marriage.

INCONTINENCE OF URINE

Incontinence of urine is a frequent or perpetual discharge of that fluid, with difficulty of retaining it.

This disease usually proceeds from relaxation or palsy of the sphincter muscle of the bladder, induced by debility, the abuse of spirituous liquors, excess in venery, etc. or it arises from a peculiar acrimony in the fluid itself; from a diseased state of the organ, injury done to the parts, either by accident, by the process of ulceration or by the performance of the operation of lithotomy; irritation produced by stones in the bladder or the pressure of the womb in a state of pregnancy.

TREATMENT—As the complaint commonly proceeds from debility, tonics, and stimulants are generally found to be the most efficacious remedies; such as bark, steel, turpentine, tincture of Spanish fly, capivi balsam, lime-water, and bear's whortle-berry. The following prescriptions are sometimes very serviceable, and should one fail, the patient can try another.

Take of Sulphate of zinc	1 drachm;
Common turpentine	3 drachms,
Rhubarb, in powder	half a drachm.

Mix, and make into sixty pills; one to be taken thrice a day.

Take of Tincture of Spanish fly	16, 20 or 30 drops;

Decoction of bear's whortle-berry, 4 table-spoonfuls.

Mix for a draught, to be taken three times a day.

Take of Balsam of capivi	half an ounce;
Frankincense, in powder	2 drachms;

Mucilage of gum arabic	1½	ounce;
Simple syrup		half an ounce;
Cinnamon water	5	ounces.

Mix, and take three table-spoonfuls twice a day.

Should there be a discharge of white mucous fluid from the bladder, Mr. Cline recommended two drachms of common turpentine, and one drachm of best rhubarb powder, to be mixed together, and made into thirty-six pills, two or three of which are to be taken three times a day, with a wine-glassful of decoction of bear's whortle-berry. Should this fail, I advise a trial of the *pareira brava* or the buchu leaves.

At the same time that one of the above remedies are taken internally, cold water should be freely applied locally; and an occasional blister to the *sacrum* or broad bone at the bottom of the spine, is frequently of material service. Blisters applied to the *sacrum* of boys who are apt to wet their beds, have often completely cured them of this incontinence without the use of any other remedy.

Pressure is also of great service in many instances. A case of nine years' standing was cured in three days by passing a of bougie through the whole course of the urethra, and binding it tightly in that direction by means of adhesive plaster. In obstinate cases, electricity is worthy of a trial.

If these means are ineffectual, it will be advisable for the male patient to wear a *jugum*, and the female a *pessary*, which will mechanically prevent the urine being evacuated involuntarily. They are to be bought of any surgeons' instrument maker—Weiss, 62, Strand, is a clever maker of these instruments. Or males may wear a small bag of oiled silk, with a small piece of sponge placed in it as an absorbent; and females a large piece of soft sponge loosely attached externally.

When this complaint arises from the irritation of stones in the bladder, small doses of opium, taken in the decoction of whortle-berry,—diluting mucilaginous drinks, as solutions of gum arabic, linseed, and isinglass,-lime-water, and other alkalies, will be the most proper and useful remedies.

In pregnant women, the complaint may be relieved by the patient's confining herself as much as possible to an horizontal posture.[1]

Incontinence of urine is now and then met with from laceration of the parts during a difficult labour, when the constitution is to be invigorated by tonics, and the usual surgical means should be employed, under the direction of a surgeon, for procuring a union of the divided parts. Even in this distressing case, much may often be done by careful attention, and perseverance on the part of the medical attendant. The bear's whortle-berry, buchu leaves, and the balsam of capivi, seem particularly worthy of regard in this variety of the complaint.

INDIGESTION OR DYSPEPSIA

Indigestion is a disorder of the stomach and first intestines, the most striking symptoms of which are, difficult digestion of the food, sense of oppression or uneasiness after eating, capricious and deficient appetite, and costiveness. It is essentially a debility of the stomach and smaller bowels, though the weakness, and disorder of function, frequently extends to the liver, pancreas, and other organs associated in the perfect digestion of the food.

A sense of distension or oppression after eating; acrid eructations ; constipation and uneasiness of the bowels, sometimes looseness; furred tongue; impaired appetite and strength; flatulency; discoloured stools, they being either green, black or much too light; nausea; head-ache; sometimes bilious vomiting; palpitation of the heart; pain in the pit of the stomach, and towards the right side; sallowness of complexion; and depression of spirits, are the chief *symptoms* of this complaint. The whole of these *symptoms*, however, are not always present in indigestion, but under whatever form, and from whatever cause the disease occurs, there is a considerable degree of general languor and debility; exercise or exertion of any kind soon fatigues; the pulse is weak; the sleep disturbed; the limbs

1. Some further remarks and directions may be seen in my TREATISE ON THE DISEASES OF FEMALES.

are cold or rendered so on slight occasions; and a sense of distension .and oppression, of acrid eructations, nausea, head-ache, constipation, pain in the pit of the stomach, and sallowness of complexion, are pretty constantly present.

Frequently there is a good deal of general feverish heat, flushing of the face, dryness in the mouth, weakness of the knees, and a dry scurfy state of the general surface of the body.

These symptoms are now very commonly called *bilious*, and when they assume a severe and obstinate character, are often referred to disease of the liver, and denominated a liver complaint; but, generally speaking, these are very incorrect names for the disorder, for though the biliary secretion is here often faulty in quality or deficient in quantity, it is, for the most part, a secondary and sympathetic affection, dependant upon the debility and disorder of the stomach and bowels, which are the primary and chief seat of the malady. Besides, indigestion may continue for a great length of time, and be of a very severe description, without any disorganization existing in the liver or any other of the digestive organs, and since an active use of mercury is, at the present time, so commonly considered as absolutely necessary to the recovery of the patient, indeed, as "the fit and only remedy", it is of considerable moment that these remarks should have close attention from the reader; for such an employment of mercurial preparations in dyspepsia, seldom fails to be attended with great and permanent injury. The real fact is, that indigestion is a frequent disorder, liver complaints comparatively rare.

For a peculiar inflammatory form of indigestion very often misunderstood and ill treated, the reader must refer to *chronic gastritis*, under INFLAMMATION OF THE STOMACH; and to BRIGHT'S DISEASE, page 396.

Every thing which weakens the system in general or the stomach in particular, may be a *cause*; such are an excessive indulgence in warm relaxing fluids, as tea, coffee and soups; an equal indulgence in stimulant and acrid materials, as ardent spirits, tobacco, acids and snuff; a daily habit of distending the stomach by hard eating and drinking; rigid abstemiousness, and very protracted periods of fasting; Imperfect mastication and eating too fast; an indolent or sedentary life; habitual exhaustion from intense study. Grief and anxiety are frequent and powerful causes.

The foundation of this complaint is often laid in infancy and youth by the excessive employment of calomel, a practice totally wrong in principle, but which has been very much *in fashion* of late years. And where the patient has fortunately escaped its frequent use in very early life, it has often proved a direct cause of indigestion at a later period. Calomel is a strong and peculiar stimulant to the digestive organs, and when used in large doses, it impairs their natural enemies, breaks down the blood, and exerts a very depressing and distressing effect upon the whole nervous system.[1]

But, perhaps, the *principal cause* of the very great prevalence of indigestion which has been witnessed in this kingdom within the last thirty years, is our present anxious fast and sedentary mode of living. The general mode of living in England now differs greatly from what was practised by our forefathers; indeed, there is a striking difference within the last fifty years.[2] Our hours of rest and rising are later; the floors of our houses universally are covered with thick warm carpeting, and the windows and doors are made air tight; cities and large towns have multiplied, and surprisingly increased in population, while the country has been comparatively

1. PUBLIC HOUSE BEER AND SPIRITS. There are men who go round to public houses to prepare the stock for retail axle. To the beer they not only add "water" or "liquor," as it is technically termed, but tire *coculus indices* berry, as a substitute for malt and bops, *fubia amara* (*nux vomica*), sulphate of iron, and other, dangerous poisons. Alcoholic liquors are "doctored" with subacetate of lead, oil of almonds, oil of vitriol, oil of turpentine, sulphuric acid, sulphate of zinc or white vitriol. The use of such deleterious compounds is the cause of indigestion, and of many other maladies which puzzle medical men. These strong pungent substances admit of large quantities of water being added to the original spirit us delivered from the distillery. The depraved taste and diseased palates of dram-drinkers do not perceive the adulterations, and rather desire the stimulus of these diluted poisons. No wonder that publicans, by help of these adulterations, can in a short time make large fortunes.
2. In the time of Queen Elizabeth the nobility and gentry were accustomed to dine at eleven, to sup between five and six, and go to rest at ten;—a maid of honour in the Queen's court, breakfasted upon beef, and drank ale after it; while the sportsman, the mechanic, and even the day-labourer, now breakfast on tea or coffee.

forsaken. As a necessary consequence of this, sedentary occupations in crowded places have augmented beyond all former example, to the neglect of those engagements which carry men abroad into fields and open country, and impose a necessity for active an continued bodily exertion. The healthful employments of the farmer and country gentleman, have been, in a great measure, relinquished for the more lucrative pursuits of trade and commerce, which have necessarily brought men in large bodies into a narrow space, in which they breathe a deteriorated and unwholesome atmosphere, and by which they are deprived of the means of adhering to the regular hours and sober habits of a country life, whilst they are exposed to much greater toil, care and anxiety. Even country families of sufficient property consider it now absolutely necessary to have a town house, where it is common for them to reside for a great part of the year; and thus they sacrifice their health and strength to their desire of mixing with the fashionable world, and indulging in the vanities of novelty and splendour. By these means, a great degree of general chronic debility has been silently, but certainly engendered in the constitution, in which the stomach and intestines sympathize, and of which they largely partake.

The *immediate cause* seems to be a debility of the nervous influence and muscular fibres of the stomach and bowels.

TREATMENT—The indications of treatment are, first, to relinquish whatever cause has laid a foundation for the complaint; and then to endeavour to promote healthy secretions, and to restore the debilitated organs, and whole system, to their proper tone.

The first and most important step to be taken in the cure of indigestion is, to remove such habits and pursuits as may have tended to give rise to the disease, and continue to aggravate it : until this has been effected, remedies will be found of little avail. If the patient leads a fashionable life, it will be necessary for him to forsake the haunts and habits of dissipation; to leave the crowded city; to shun luxurious tables, indolence, and late hours; and to retrace the footsteps by which he has deviated from simple nature, and to court the country, pure air, active exercise, early rising, simple diet, the society of a few select friends and pleasing occupations. The man of severe study must in a great measure lay aside his books; the fagging tradesman or merchant will find it indispensably necessary to enjoy relaxation; the hard drinker must greatly diminish his potations, especially of ardent spirits; and all dyspeptics must take exercise in the open air freely, rise early, seek cheerful society, and carefully observe a moderate and correct diet.

Smoking and chewing tobacco, and even constant snuffing, have often produced indigestion. "I have found", says Dr. Cullen, of Edinburgh, "all the symptoms of dyspepsia produced by snuffing, and particularly pains in the stomach occurring every day. The dependence of these upon the use of snuff became very evident from hence, that upon an accidental interruption of snuffing for some days, these pains did not occur; but upon a return to snuffing the pains also recurred; and this alternation of pains of the stomach, and of snuffing, having occurred again, the snuff was entirely laid aside, and the pains did not occur for many months afterwards, nor, so far as I know, for the rest of life". In another place, he relates a singular case of a lady to whom this practice became injurious. This lady had been for more than twenty years accustomed to take snuff, and that at every time of the day; but she came at length to observe, that snuffing a good deal before dinner took away her appetite and that even a single pinch, taken at any time in the morning, destroyed almost entirely her relish for that meal. When, however, she abstained entirely from snuff before dinner, her appetite continued as usual; and after dinner for the rest of the day she took snuff' pretty freely without any inconvenience.

There are few points of greater importance than the proper regulation of the bowels, more especially without medicine. They ought to be comfortably exonerated once a day or once in two days. *Purging should be avoided;* indeed all aperient medicine should be laid aside. It is a wretched system to depend in any degree on physic. Refer to the article on COSTIVENESS. In many cases of indigestion the bowels are very irritable, and the operation of even a slight purgative is inexpressibly distressing; in such examples no aperient whatever should be taken. Where the bowels are so unusually weak and irritable, the union of a tonic with the aperient, as in No. 101B or C, page 195, is worthy of much notice, if aperient medicine should be at all used for that purpose, which I doubt.

To palliate flatulency, the means recommended under that head may be resorted to. Half a tea-spoonful of tincture of ginger or cardamoms, in a glass of peppermint or cinnamon water, will be found a useful medicine for this purpose; but should acidity prevail, ten grains of magnesia or ten drops of water of ammonia in water is preferable. The mineral acids are sometimes very efficacious correctors of the latter symptom.

For nausea and vomiting one of the most effectual remedies is an effervescent draught, made either with bi-carbonate of potash or ammonia—*see Citric Acid,* page 34. Should this fail to allay the sickness, a blister or wet bandage may be applied over the pit of the stomach. Dr. Barlow (*Practice of Physic*, p. 398) says that strychnine is a very efficacious remedy for the sickness of dyspepsia, "in doses of from a 32nd to a 24th part of a grain", and the following is his form of administering it :

Take of Strychnine	1/4	of a grain;
Diluted acetic acid	2	drachms;
Distilled water, sufficient to complete	4	ounces.

Mix them, and take one table-spoonful every four hours.

Indigestion—dyspepsia—a feeble and imperfect action of the digestive organs, is a complaint of the very first consideration, because the state of the digestive functions are all-important in the cure of disease, and in the well-being of the system at large. To an unhealthy state of these organs, we are enabled to trace many disordered conditions which are not only manifested in particular organs, but which affect the whole body. If food is imperfectly assimilated, and therefore *not converted into good blood,* that bad blood cannot sufficiently supply the necessary vitality; and the various changes in the muscles, nerves, arteries, veins, absorbents, and the other parts of the frame, cannot possibly take place in a healthy and perfect manner. Deranged digestion affects more or less all the functions of the body, and necessarily reduces the vigour of life. My experience entirely accords with that of Dr. Chambers. "I The more I see of disease", he says, "the more convinced I become that the most important function for us to pay attention to, in all cases, is the digestion. In chronic cases, it outweighs all the other functions put together".—*Clinical Lectures,* p. 351. The chief thing is to allay irritability in the stomach, to free the secretions, and to nourish the blood; and one of the most excellent plans of treatment is to begin by taking one of the powders No. 130A, page 209, before breakfast, and the next day to take the pills No. 104, page 197, twice a day, and to continue them for three weeks. At the end of that time, lay them aside, and take some suitable tonic, such as No. 84A, page 184 or No. 87C, in the *Appendix.* If these should not suit, try a quinine pill, twice a day, No. 115, page 202. At the same time the patient must take exercise twice a day, by riding on horseback or walking, two or three hours at each time, and sponge himself all over with cold water every morning on rising, following it with a good deal of friction with a flesh brush or hair gloves. The diet must be plain and moderate in quantity for breakfast, a breakfast-cupful of *good* black tea (not the stuff usually sold) without sugar, but with plenty of milk, and not hot; with bread and butter, dry toast or plain biscuit. For dinner, mutton, beef or chicken, with a little vegetable and bread, but no pastry or pudding. He may take one glass of wine and water or one glassful of Bass's, Allsopp's or home-brewed beer, whichever agrees best. For tea, the same as breakfast; then, probably, cocoa will suit better than tea. For supper, cocoa or oatmeal gruel with salt, may be taken with bread and butter or biscuit. Some persons find that a glass of wine and water or ale, suits them at supper time better than gruel. If the patient dines late, then he should take for luncheon a slice of cold meat and bread, and either a glass of Allsopp's ale or wine. Slow careful mastication is important, and the bowels should be regulated without recourse to aperient medicine.

The best brown ipecacuanha powder is a valuable astringent tonic, and is a remedy of great value in the present complaint. It may be given either alone, made into pills with a little soap or in combination with iron, extract of chamomile or gentian or any other bitter extract. The celebrated French physician, Daubenton, recommended it for the indigestion of elderly persons especially, but it is, perhaps, equally efficacious in younger patients; and it possesses a great advantage over many other remedies, inasmuch as it is applicable to the early as well as the later stages of the complaint, and may often be administered with evident benefit when there is a good deal of pain, and slow inflammatory action going on, in the region of the stomach; a state in which the metallic tonics, and even the vegetable bitters, are frequently altogether inadmissible. The following are excellent forms of exhibiting it :

Take of Ipecacuanha, in powder	20	grains;
Carbonate of iron	2	drachms,
Extract of chamomile.....................	1	drachm.

Mix, and divide into sixty pills; one or two to be taken twice or thrice a day.

Or,

Take of Ipecacuanha, in powder	15 or 20	grains ;
White oxyde of bismuth	2	drachms;
Extract of gentian	1	drachm.

Mix, and divide into sixty pills; two to be taken two or three times a day.

The most efficacious bitters are chamomile, bitter orange-peel gentian, cascarilla, serpenteria, columba, wormwood, and Peruvian bark. All these possess a power of invigorating the digestive organs, and are particularly serviceable in the earlier stages of indigestion. But in the advanced periods they become less useful, and sometimes cannot be borne at all, since almost all of them possess a stimulant as well as a tonic quality, which does not agree with the irritable and inflamed state of the stomach at this period, denoted by pain in the region of that organ. The stimulant quality of the bitters in common use nearly accords with the order in which they here stand, the chamomile possessing the least, and the bark the most of this power; so that in taking them for the relief and cure of the present disorder, we must make our selection accordingly. Generally speaking, the bark is inferior to the other bitters as a remedy in dyspepsia; yet, in the earlier periods of the disease, when it follows debilitated states of the constitution, and the stomach still retains considerable comparative vigour, a cold infusion of the bark is often the most beneficial of all bitters.

Columba is considered, by some superior writers, to be peculiarly calculated for dyspepsia in all its forms.

Some of the most approved modes of prescribing bitters may be seen at pages 157 and 170-71.

Diluted nitric, muriatic and sulphuric acid or diluted nitro-muriatic acid, are appropriate tonics in indigestion. The first of these acids appear to me to be the most valuable; and it may often be given with great advantage in long standing cases, and where the patient complains of a great deal of pain at the pit of the stomach. In those severe examples which are so frequently but erroneously denominated *liver complaints*, it will be found of the greatest service; the appetite and strength sensibly increasing under its continued use, and the sallow hue of the complexion as quickly disappearing. Two drachms of it may be mixed with two ounces of water, and from a tea-spoonful to a tea-spoonful and a half of this mixture to be taken, three times a day, in water. From five to twenty drops of diluted muriatic acid, and from ten to twenty drops of the diluted sulphuric acid, taken in some agreeable vehicle, twice a day, are the proper doses of these articles. These acids may be administered as in the form of No. 85A. The muriatic acid should always be administered in some bland fluid, as barley-water, gruel, etc. To prevent these acids from injuring the enamel of the teeth, they may be sucked through a quill, and the mouth should be carefully washed after each dose.

The mineral acids are efficacious correctors of morbid acidity as well as being highly tonic, and, therefore, when acidity in the stomach is a troublesome symptom of the present disorder, they will often be found among the most eligible remedies.

It is in those forms of dyspepsia, where the urine is free from a red deposit–where there is a disposition to the formation of oxalate of lime in the urine in which case there is not unfrequently a tendency to white deposit, that the nitro-muriatic acid, and the other mineral acids, are especially of service. From eight to fifteen drops of the dilute nitric acid, and the same dose of diluted muriatic acid, may be given twice a day, in a wine-glassful of barley-water or infusion of calumba, half an hour before breakfast and dinner.

In some instances of indigestion, however, the acids have but little effect, and appear too cold for the stomach, when the *alkaline solution of Brandish* (see page 2), is often particularly useful as an alterative. It is in those cases in which coldness of the feet, chilliness of the general surface, languor, fluttering at the pit of the stomach, and morbid acidity, are the most prominent symptoms, that it displays its full powers. The dose is half a tea-spoonful three times a day, in milk and water; or it may be taken in a bitter infusion.

In this complaint, soda is more generally useful than potash, probably from its more direct effect upon the liver. When it occurs in persons who take little exercise and live freely, fifteen grains of bi-carbonate of soda in infusion of calumba, twice a day, with one or two of the pills No. 97, page 191, at night, to increase the secretions of the liver and bowels, will be found very useful.

When the urine from the first has a deposit of lithic acid or lithate of ammonia (brickdust colour), the mineral acids should not be given; then the best remedy is eitht or ten grains of sesqui-carbonate of ammonia in water or half a tea-spoonful of sal volatile, twice a day. Lithic acid deposits are most frequent in the members of gouty families, and in people of middle age who lead the kind of life that conduces to gout—that is, eat largely of animal food, and drink freely of malt liquors.

Dr. Belcombe of York, states, that for some years he has been in the habit of prescribing in cases of severe dyspepsia, frequently attended with water-brush, the following pill :

Take of Camphor . . . . 1 drachm;
Strychnia . . . . 1 grain.

Mix them, and divide into thirty pills, one to be taken twice a day.

Dr. Chambers recommends a minute quantity of strychnine as very valuable in relieving the sense of *oppression* at the stomach.

Iron has always been considered of much service. The carbonate, sulphates or citrate of iron; are the preparations most commonly resorted to, and they may be taken either alone, made into pills with mucilage of gum arabic or combined with extract of chamomile or with ipecaeuanha.

Take of Carbonate of iron	2 drachms;
Myrrh, in powder	1 scruple;
Extract of chamomile	1 drachm;
Socotrine aloes in powder	4 or E grains.

Mix, and divide into forty pills, two or three to be taken twice a day.

Take of Sulphate of iron	2 drachms;
Extract of gentian	1 drachm;
Socotrine aloes, in powder	4 grains.

Mix, and divide into forty pills; two to be taken twice a day.

The recipe No. 84A is also an eligible one.

All the preparations of iron, however, are much less serviceable in the advanced periods than in the early stages. They are frequently found too heating, when they should be changed for the mineral acids, ipecacuanha or the alkaline solution.

When the pain in the stomach, of a chronic description, and apparently depending rather upon deficient energy of the organ, than upon slow inflammation, is a troublesome symptom, the white oxyde of bismuth is very efficacious in removing it. Four grains of it may be made into a pill with a little extract of gentian, and given three times a day; the dose being gradually increased, if necessary, to six or eight grains; at the same time apply a wet bandage round the stomach.

The sulphate of zinc has been praised for its virtues as a tonic in this disorder, and being less heating than preparations of iron, may generally be taken when they are found too oppressive; but it must not be given beyond the extent of a grain at a dose.

Take of Sulphate of zinc	25 grains;
Myrrh, in powder........................	15 grains;
Extract of chamomile.....................	1 drachm.

Mix, and divide into thirty pills; one of which should be taken three times a day, and gradually increased to two.

Rhubarb is an excellent corrector of vitiated biliary secretion, and in small doses becomes a valuable stimulant and tonic to the stomach and bowels. A grain or two may be given two or three times a day, united with soap or with ipecacuanha and soap. It is particularly indicated when the complexion is sallow, and the stools much discoloured, the use of mercury being at the same time, very limited or altogether objectionable. In my practice, the rhubarb pills No. 104, page 197, have proved of the most essential service to numerous persons afflicted with indigestion and bilious symptoms.

In many cases of protracted indigestion, tartarized antimony (emetic tartar) in small doses, is found of essential service, more especially when the long continuance of the complaint has induced a determination of blood to the head or severe nervous irritation. *See* what is said at pages 48-49.

Calomel, blue pill, and other mercurial medicines, are often employed in the treatment of indigestion, and though by no means of so much consequence as the generality of medical men suppose, they are sometimes of eminent utility. But if the complaint originates in, and is very nearly or altogether confined to the stomach, they are of inferior value, and often of no use whatever; while in those cases of disease which centre principally in the bowels or liver, they are generally of the greatest service, by promoting healthy secretion, and removing obstruction.[1] The only

1. Mr. Abernethy, in his Lectures, has a useful remark in point. " If", says he, "the fault lie principally in the stomach, no blue pill will avail; if in the liver, bitters will be of little service".

safe, and, indeed, the most efficient mode of taking them, is in small doses, every other night, with a quinine pill or a draught of some bitter infusion, as No. 35, page 158, once a day. Calomel should never be given alone in indigestion, and in combination only in small doses. It ought not to be employed here as a purgative, but only as an alterative, as in No. 98A, page 192. Those cases are most benefited by mercurial medicines, in which the stools are remarkably discoloured and offensive, the appetite and strength not greatly impaired, and where there is a tendency to the formation of some obstinate or severe local disease. In all delicate constitutions, in which the appetite has habitually been somewhat capricious, and the general strength inconsiderable, mercury will be a doubtful remedy, and require great caution in its use. Whatever is the state of the disorder and constitution, the patient will do well to remember, that it is only by a skilful employment of minute doses of thus mineral that he can reasonably hope to derive great and lasting benefit. For general use, I know no mercurial combination equal to the pill No. 98A or three grains of grey powder and one of extract of henbane.

Ablution with diluted mineral acids has been recommended as a valuable substitute for mercury, in protracted and severe cases of indigestion, and disease within the abdomen, and the practice is one worthy of much confidence; but as these acid baths and ablutions are more particularly applicable to cases of long standing or where there is positive disease in the alimentary canal and liver, I shall defer any description of their properties and mode of preparation, till I shall in course treat of *liver complaint.*

It now and then happens, that both the bitter and metallic tonics are found to be of very little or no service in indigestion, the most sensible benefit arising from the cautious use of mild aperient medicine, and especially the saline aperients, as combinations of Epsom and Glauber's salt, etc. In such examples, the seat of the complaint is chiefly the internal surface of the bowels, and the liver, and the symptoms are, for the most part, those which are generally considered to point out a high degree of bilious disorder; such are sallowness of complexion, dryness of skin, shooting pains about the pit of the stomach, and either whitish or very dark coloured motions. Here the Cheltenham, Leamington or Epsom waters, are often of eminent utility; and when these cannot be resorted to, the following draught may be substituted with much advantage.

Take of sulphate of magnesia	1	drachm;
Sulphate of soda		half a drachm;
Sulphate of iron	1	grain.

Mix, and dissolve in half a pint of cold or lukewarm water; to be taken every morning or three or four times a week, before breakfast.

This is a mild, pleasant, and very efficacious saline aperient, and is very nearly, if not quite, as effectual as the Cheltenham, Leamington and Gloucester waters. Or, a soothing powder, No. 130A, page 209 or the mixture No. 74C, page 177, may be tried for ten days, and followed by a steel tonic No. 84A, page 184.

Mr. Abernethy found the tincture of rhubarb or senna to be sometimes more effectual in exciting healthy secretions from the bowels than any other aperient. This seems to occur where there is a great deal of direct debility of the stomach, with coldness, and that general state of feeling which is relieved by some mild aromatic cordial. In such examples, about one drachm of each of these compound tinctures may be taken, in a little water, and repeated three, four or five times a week.

Having now, in a great measure, concluded what I have to say respecting the use of medicine in this malady, it is material to observe, that, *in protracted cases*, whatever plan is adopted, much depends on the gentleness of the effect produced, the morbid condition in such instances being only to be removed by a slight effect, regularly kept up for a considerable length of time. All powerful means, which are necessarily transitory, because they would, soon destroy the patient if they were continued, not only fail to cure, but very often aggravate the disease. It is, therefore, of the greatest importance that the patient should remember, it is by the most gentle and frequently repeated impressions, that the organs are solicited to resume their healthy action in all protracted cases, more especially if considerable hardness of the pulse be present.

Those cases of indigestion in which there is a permanent tenderness extending across the stomach quite to the left side, and those in which the skin, instead of being obstinately dry, is constantly moist or apt to become so on every slight occasion, without any relief to the disease, (the pulse being hard), are very generally obstinate, and will require particular attention to the preceding hints.

As an auxiliary remedy, the cold bath merits much attention, or, if preferred, cold sponging may be substituted for the cold bath. The whole surface of the body should be sponged regularly every morning with cold water, the patient rubbing himself dry after it with a coarse towel. This is a very refreshing and salutary practice, and one which Sir Astley Cooper considered to have very materially contributed to insure the excellent health which he so long enjoyed. He uniformly resorted to it immediately on rising, and speaks of it as an effectual preventive against taking cold.

The internal use of the warm waters of Buxton and Bath are occasionally of great service. They relieve pain and uneasiness in the stomach, and often promote digestion. The late Dr. Saunders of London, thought highly of tepid water as a remedy in this complaint, and questioned whether drinking the water at the celebrated springs at Buxton, would, upon trials be found more efficacious in these complaints, than the regular use of the same quantity of any pure water heated to the same temperature. Those who wish to try it may take a small tumbler-full after dinner and supper. For pain or uneasiness in the stomach, occurring after dinner or any other solid meal, the addition of half a tea-spoonful of tincture of ginger to the tepid water may prove of great benefit.

Whenever there is a great deal of tenderness on pressure or pain at the pit of the stomach, which does not yield to the general treatment, the application of leeches may be useful. Four or six leeches may be applied once a week, for three or four weeks, if this symptom is not removed in a shorter time; but we must be careful not to induce debility by the use of this means. It will frequently be proper to apply a blister after the leeches have been removed; but probably a wet bandage round the stomach, if renewed thrice a day, will be equally serviceable without any risk of inducing debility. See the remarks on *chronic gastritis,* at the end of the article on INFLAMMATION OF THE STOMACH.

A correct regimen is of the utmost consequence, and a strict and constant attention to it is absolutely necessary, in order to obtain a perfect cure. All sedentary occupations must be for-saken as much as possible, and if they can be entirely given up, the prospect of complete relief will be far greater. Indeed, considerable and permanent advantage can only be obtained, in the majority of instances, by relinquishing in a very great measure all such engagements, and quitting the confined atmosphere and late hours of the crowded city, for the pure, dry, bracing air of the country, with its early rising, and active exercise.[1] It is the common neglect of such a regimen that makes indigestion so rarely and imperfectly cured; for where a high state of chronic debility and nervous irritability, has been induced by long continued exposure to the depressing effects of confinement, and intense application to business, literary pursuits or pleasure; no medicine nor even diet. can be employed with much effect as a substitute for country air, daily active exercise, cheerful company and early rising. The patient should quit his bed by six O'clock in the morning in the summer, and by seven in the winter; and after partaking of a light breakfast, take exercise freely for two or three hours before dinner. After dinner, gentle exercise should he again taken for an hour or two. Of all exercises, those of walking and riding on horseback are the most beneficial and where the patient's means and strength allow, they should be used alternately; but when the strength is much reduced, horse exercise is almost invariably to be preferred.

The power of daily active exercise in the open air in curing indigestion is very great, indeed such as would appear to the majority of persons almost incredible, and therefore, it cannot be

1. Large towns have been emphatically called the *graves of the human species.* Constant residence in a populous city has certainly a very considerable influence in producing disease, and abridging the term of human life. The constitution of the generality of citizens is weak, irritable, and easily susceptible of diseased actions, a fact, to the truth of which the experience of every medical man who has practised much in such places bears ample testimony. The Roman poet most justly exclaims against Pericula mille Saevac Aurbis.

too much insisted upon by the physician, as an indispensable requisite to insure perfect freedom from this complaint. Many medical men lay great stress upon attention to diet, as necessary in the treatment of this and other chronic disease, and so it is; no one acquainted with my writings will suspect me of undervaluing it, but I am fully persuaded that regimen is of still greater moment, and experience proves, that exercise and cold water are the most essential branches of the athletic regimen. Exercise is not so strenuously recommended as it ought to be or its virtues so fully known as they deserve.[1]

Cheerful company and lively conversation, with proper clothing, are also subjects of importance. The feet and chest should be kept warm, and, if the debility be great, with a considerable reduction of the natural heat of the body, a flannel waistcoat worn next the skin during the colder months will be very proper. The bed clothes should be no more than sufficient to keep the patient comfortably warm, and a mattress is always preferable to a feather bed.

Diet has always been considered a subject of no small moment in the treatment of the present complaint. The grand maxim with regard to it is, to eat and drink sparingly, at stated intervals, and of food the most digestible, and that agrees best with the individual. No bilious or dyspeptic persons should eat more than three or four times a day, and those periods ought to be, as near as possible, at regular intervals of five hours, say eight, one, six, and half-past nine o'clock. It is a common, but very erroneous and injurious supposition, that such patients ought to eat little and often; because by taking food in this way, scarcely two hours elapse throughout the whole day without something being swallowed, by which means the stomach has no time for the perfect digestion of the previous meal, and is kept in a constant state of irritation and disorder. No

1. The system called *training* merits most particular regard from every dyspeptic, and more especially from these who are suffering under the present malady in its aggravated and protracted forms, on account of its surprising influence in giving tone to the digestive organs, and every part of the frame, and the marked effect it has in improving and equalizing all the secretions. See the note at page 382. *Also Appendix.*

rest is given to it, and therefore, instead of gaining strength, it loses it. It may be safely received as a general rule, that food should not be taken in the intervals of meals, and a want of this kind will seldom be felt by those who adhere to the hours just mentioned.

Where a considerable degree of hardness exists in the pulse, with much feverish heat generally, an inflammatory tendency exists in the system, when a diet wholly vegetable, and even a total abstinence from wine, must for the most part be observed, and is strikingly beneficial. The best vegetables are, young cabbage, brocoli, French beans, asparagus and potatoes; no other should be taken. In this state of the complaint, light, plain puddings are allowable, but pastry is altogether inadmissible in every description of case.

In the greater number of instances, however, the hardness of pulse just noticed is not present, and then an animal diet is the best. Mutton, venison, partridge and pheasant, are the most wholesome and digestible of meats; and next to these come fowl, chicken, tender beef and lamb. Of either of these, a small quantity roasted and little done may be taken at dinner, it being seldom proper for a dyspeptic to eat animal food more than once a day. The flesh of full-grown animals is to be preferred to that of young ones, and I know no exception to this rule. Some medical men, however, have gone so far, and erred so widely, as to assert the reverse of this to be the truth; but they are blind leaders. Preference has, indeed, been given to veal over beef, by some physicians of judgment who agree as to the superior digestibility of the flesh of full-grown animals in general; but, according to my experience, it is a preference that ought not to be maintained, for certainly few articles of diet are more indigestible and irritating than veal and, therefore, in my practice, it is universally forbidden to those of weak digestive powers. Full-grown tender mutton and venison are, unquestionably, the most digestible and best of all meats. All salted and dried meat is inadmissible, and boiled fresh meat of any kind is not quite free from objection in severe indigestion. Excepting oysters in their natural state, every sort of fish is bad in the present disorder, and must be altogether avoided, at least in the beginning.

In common language, fish is called a *light* article of diet, but it is an error to suppose it to be easy of digestion. It is given to patients convalescent from acute diseases, in preference to flesh, not because it admits of a more ready solution in the stomach, but on account of its exciting less heat and fever. Both vegetable and animal food cooked a second time is very objectionable; and, therefore, hashes, harricoes, stews and the like, must make no part of the dyspeptic's cookery. In all cases, plain biscuit is preferable to white bread, but well-made brown bread is better than either, when the bowels are confined, and there is strength of stomach sufficient to digest it.

Generally speaking, all slop fluids are much more difficult of digestion than solids, and a weakened stomach is quite incapable of digesting even the ordinary quantity of slops which is taken in health with satisfaction and benefit. It is for this reason that broths and soups are injurious to most dyspeptics, and that drinking too freely of soups, tea and the like, will sometimes throw such persons almost into agonies. They should, therefore, be abstained from as much as possible.

Port wine is almost invariably hurtful, but a little foreign white wine taken after dinner, is sometimes useful. The best wine is old sherry, but with some patients good claret answers very well. Mild home-brewed beer (such as Bass's or Allsopp's draught beer) generally agrees better than wine or brandy. It ought not to be strong ale, which is at all times difficult of digestion; neither should it be poor weak beer, but that of a moderate strength and body. There exists a general prejudice against the use of beer in indigestion and bilious complaints, but I am fully persuaded it is, in the majority of instances, without substantial foundation. If patients are properly treated, they will, in general, find *good home-brewed* beer—and Bass's and Allsopp's–to agree very well. Barley-water is useful to quench thirst; well-made toast and water is likewise a proper drink, and so is lemon or orange tea, that is, lemon or orange-peel infused in boiling water. The latter possesses a stimulus which is very useful to some disordered stomachs.

Tea, cocoa or thin chocolate, made with water, may be taken for breakfast, and at tea-time; with biscuit, bread and butter or dry toast. Rolls, and all other spongy bread are bad; and coffee must be wholly forsaken. One fresh lightly-boiled egg may be taken at breakfast, if it agrees. Whatever liquid is taken in the morning and evening, the patient should not exceed a common breakfast-cupful at each time.

The supper should be very light and small in quantity, consisting of a roasted apple or potatoe (if they agree) or an egg lightly boiled, with a biscuit or some bread and butter. In summer, a little good ripe fruit in season will make a very wholesome supper. A small tumbler-full of mild beer may likewise be allowed if it agrees, and the portion of food then taken be solid. Some dyspeptics find well-made grit or oatmeal gruel, with or without milk, to form an agreeable and wholesome supper. Further information respecting diet will be found under that article at page 229.

The food should be well masticated, and quietness, with rest, observed for at least an hour after each meal. Digestion almost invariably proceeds much better in a sitting, than in a recumbent position.

There are, however, not a few cases of indigestion in which a different mode of proceeding must be observed with regard to diet, on account of the very excited, irritable state of the nerves of the stomach and intestines. This mode I have detailed in my BEST METHODS OF IMPROVING HEALTH, under the head of *Quantity of Food.* The cases I refer to are those of irritative dyspepsia, in which great uneasiness or pain occurs in the *stomach* after eating or uncommon restlessness and nervousness *generally,* etc.

There are two determinate principles of superior importance, which we have to guide us in the treatment of the present complaint, both as it respects diet and medicine, a notice of which shall form the conclusion of what I have to say, on this important subject. These principles are highly valuable, because they lead us directly to an acquaintance with two opposite states of the constitution, with which indigestion is continually found to be associated, and which demand a different treatment, pointing out to us when a direct tonic plan will generally answer, and, also, when the comfort and even safety of our patient requires a mild, unstimulating, although not a lowering mode of procedure.

These principles are, first, That when the pulse is hard, as in *irritative dyspepsia,* all the secreting surfaces are in a measure bound up, the skin being dry and harsh, and the extreme vessels on the surface of the alimentary canal also suffering constriction, as evinced by the dry condition of the mouth and nose,—when the more permanent stimulants and tonics, as iron, bark, strong alkalies and bitters, etc., are in the beginning totally inadmissible; second, That when there is no perceptible hardness in the pulse, the secreting surfaces are more or less free, and the skilful use of permanent tonics or *cold water will* be generally a certain means of recovery, which, indeed, cannot then be insured by any other kind of remedies.

The hardness of pulse here alluded to, is not the striking contraction felt in acute-inflammation, but a slighter hardness, which is readily felt on lightly pressing the artery with the finger, although the pulse is often feeble at the same time. United with this state of the pulse, there is commonly a good deal of permanent tenderness, on pressure, in the pit of the stomach, with much feverish irritation generally, and in some instances there may be also some symptoms of determination of blood to the head or other indications of an inflammatory tendency in the system.

In this state, the great object of treatment at the commen-cement should be to relax the blood-vessels and secreting surfaces, in other words, to produce a soft skin and natural pulse, by the cautious use of the mildest medicines, as nitrate of potash, tartarized antimony, ipecacuanha or small doses of carbonate of ammonia. The compound decoction of sarsaparilla or the alkaline solution of this root (page 145) or the powder, is sometimes of remarkable service in these cases, as a tonic and alterative.

INFLAMMATION

By the term *inflammation* is generally understood the state of a part in which it is painful, hotter, redder and somewhat more turgid than natural; which topical symptoms when present in any considerable degree or when they affect very sensible parts, are attended with fever or a general disturbance of the system.

All parts of the body, except the skin, nails, hardest part of the teeth, and hair, are subject to inflammation. Healthy, inflammation is of a pale red; when less healthy, it is of a darker colour; but in every constitution, the inflamed parts will partake more of the healthy red, the nearer they are to the source of the circulation. Speaking of inflammation in general, it may be observed, that when situated in highly organized and very vascular parts, it is generally more disposed to take a prosperous course, and is more governable by art than in parts of an opposite texture. The nearer also such vascular parts are to the heart, the greater will be their tendency to do well. Hence inflammation of the skin, cellular substance and muscles, more frequently ends favourably, than the same affection of bones, tendons and ligaments. It is also more manageable by surgery; for those parts of the body which are not what anatomists term vascular, seem to enjoy only inferior powers of life, and, consequently, when excited in a preternatural degree frequently mortify.

But inflammation of vital parts, though they may be exceedingly, vascular, cannot go on so favourably as in other parts of resembling structure, but of different functions because the natural operations of universal health depend so much upon the sound condition of such organs. The truth of this observation is illustrated in cases of inflammation of the stomach, lungs, etc.

Too full a diet, particularly too free a use of fermented liquors, may be regarded as the chief *predisposing cause.* All causes which check habitual discharges, whether artificial or natural, especially the secretion by the skin, and all causes which considerably increase the force of the circulation, predispose to inflammation; and, if applied suddenly and to a great degree, may act as *exciting causes.* Whatever increases the impetus of the blood towards the part may become a cause, and all mechanical and chemical irritants are well known frequently to produce it; such are heat, sudden changes of temperature, the action of strong acids, alkalies, metallic salts, acrid vapours, acrid vegetable oils, bruises, wounds, etc. The strong, vigorous and plethoric are most liable to inflammation.

TREATMENT—In the present article we intend to advert only to the treatment of external inflammation, such, for example, as occurs in the limbs, trunk or any part of the surface of the body; as the inflammatory affections of internal organs, and particular parts which are more deeply seated, will be treated of under their respective heads.

Inflammation is of two kinds, *acute* and *chronic,* and it will be necessary to notice the treatment of these modifications separately.

Acute or Active, inflammation is that which is, for the most part, attended with considerable heat, redness, and pain in the part affected, and with more or less fever in the general system, and a hard, quick pulse. Its characters and progress are in general clearly marked, although its symptoms of course differ, in respect to intensity, in different instances.

In all cases of acute inflammation situated externally, the first circumstance to be attended to, is the removal of all such exciting causes as may happen to present themselves. If the irritation of a splinter oı wood, bone, etc. for example, were to excite inflammation, every one would immediately see the propriety of removing it, and such a course must be adopted with every kind of mechanical or chemical irritant present. After this is done, it will be necessary to moderate the increased action of the arterial vessels, thus lessening the velocity of the blood's motion towards the inflamed part, and to increase the secretions, by means of blood-letting, purgatives, antimonial and cooling diaphoretic medicines, cold lotions, a spare diet, rest, and a relaxed easy position of the part inflamed.

If the patient be young, robust, and full of blood, and the inflammation run high, he should lose fourteen or sixteen ounces of blood from the arm; but, in general, the application of leeches, at a short distance from the affected part, will be sufficient and preferable, more especially in feeble or elderly persons, and where the inflammation appears to be connected with a deranged state of the digestive functions. After this, we must endeavour to restore free and healthy secretions from the bowels, liver and skin, by administering purgatives and antimonials. The employment of calomel and saline purgatives in almost every case of acute inflammation, whether situated externally or internally, is of the first importance. Two of the pills No. 98, page 191, should be given directly, and followed by a black draught in the morning or after three or four hours, and these pills must subsequently be continued every day, until the inflammation is much relieved, when they can be employed once in two or three days or as occasion may require. At the same time, the following cold lotion ought to be constantly applied by means of linen rags.

Take of Sal ammoniac	1	ounce;
Common or distilled vinegar	3	ounces;
Cold water	12	ounces.

Mix for a lotion.

Or either of the lotions No. 68 or 69, page 173, will be proper. Sir Astley Cooper thinks that one of the best lotions that can be applied to inflamed parts, for the purpose of producing cold, is a mixture of one ounce of rectified spirit of wine, and five of water. In applying these lotions, the linen ought to be fine, and put lightly on the inflamed part, in order that evaporation may go on with facility, this being the grand object in view.

Tartarized antimony is likewise an invaluable remedy in all acute inflammations, and it may be given as recommended under INFLAMMATION OF THE LUNGS, provided the calomel and saline purgatives do not speedily produce the desired effect.

The saline effervescing draught, No. 24, page 153, may be given thrice a day, if the heat and fever are considerable; and should the pain be very severe, an opiate ought to be occasionally administered, after evacuations have been procured. Solid opium or the compound ipecacuanha powder, combined with calomel, forms the best opiate in these cases. Five grains of the compound ipecacuanha powder, and one grain of calomel, made into a pill with confection of opium, and given at night or when the pain is violent, will be found very useful.

The whole body, but more especially the inflamed part must be preserved in as complete a state of rest as possible; and in inflammation of the limbs a proper position is highly necessary. They ought not to be allowed to remain in a dependent position, but be constantly supported in one that is elevated and easy, so long as the inflammation is at all violent. Sir Astley Cooper gives us the following example of the use of position in inflammation of the leg, which merits a record in this place.

> "I was sent for (says he) to see a gentleman farmer in the neighbourhood of Rayleigh, in Essex, who for a long time had been subject to a very severe inflammation in both his legs; they were exceedingly red, and very much swollen, in a state threatening gangrene; the constitutional irritation was very great, and the tongue covered with a brown fur. I found him with his legs in a tub of water; I took out one of them, and it smoked excessively; I saw there was no time to be lost, had him immediately placed on a sofa, and contrived to rest his legs upon the end of the sofa; consequently they were raised considerably higher than his body; the vessels soon began to unload themselves, and the skin, in a short time, was evidently less red than when taken out of the water. I then applied flannels wrung out of warm water; these soon produced a very considerable perspiration, by which the cellular membranes became unloaded, the swelling much less, and the pain materially abated. He gradually recovered, and in six weeks was enabled to ride a considerable distance to market."[1]—*Surgical Lectures*, No. 6.

The diet must be spare and low, all spirituous and fermented liquors, and animal food, being avoided for the first two or three days or until the acute symptoms have passed away. Watery, cooling, mucilaginous drinks are highly proper and useful, and the best of such fluids are whey, butter-milk, barley-water, water-gruel, and decoctions of dried fruits, as figs etc.

Inflammation often terminates in suppuration or abscess, and now and then in gangrene or mortification; when the treatment

---

1. We are not to suppose that the mere altered position of the limbs cured the patient, but this extract shows the value of even slight changes in many cases. No doubt the farmer was constitutionally indisposed, and saline with alterative medicines were given him.

will be the same as that laid down for those diseases. *See* ABSCESS AND MORTIFICATION.

When suppuration takes place, the pain and redness, for the most part, abate, the temperature falls nearer to the healthy degree, and the throbbing becomes more sensible. A conical eminence or *pointing,* as it is termed, takes place at some part of the tumour, generally near its middle. In this situation, a whitish or yellowish appearance is generally observable, instead of a deep red, which is previously apparent, and fluctuation of a fluid underneath may be discovered, on a careful examination with the fingers.

On the approach of gangrene, the part, which was of a bright red, becomes of a livid hue; small vesicles, filled with a thin foetid serum, arise on its surface, and air is plainly felt within the cellular membrane. The pain is suddenly diminished, but the pulse sinks, while the tumour is gradually changed into a black-fibrous mass.

BY CHRONIC INFLAMMATION surgeons mean an inflammatory affection of a subdued and imperfect character, in which the part affected often appears redder than usual, but there are also present evident marks of languor and debility in the local circulation. Indeed the essence of the disease is debility, and the languor often extends, in a greater or less deree, through the whole system. There is seldom much hardness in the pulse here; sometimes it participates in the general weakness, and is small and feeble. A good example of visible chronic inflammation is seen in the eye, when this organ appears permanently red, somewhat painful, and more sensible to light than usual, although not so much so as to prevent the patient going about and transacting business. In delicate habits, this affection generally arises unpreceded by acute inflammation of the part, but in robust frames and those who are less delicate, it is often a mere sequel or consequence of the latter. But frequently chronic inflammatory action occurs, in internal organs and parts not to be seen, when it is detected by the presence of pain, uneasiness, and weakness of the part affected, generally associated with a furred tongue, impaired appetite and strength, nervousness or other indications of derangement of the general health. Of such a case, that disease of the knee joint forms an instance, which, in its advanced stage, is commonly called a white swelling. In the beginning, this is simply a chronic or slow indolent inflammation of the internal part of the joint. The enlargement of the glands of the neck or other parts of the body in scrophulous subjects; the formation of tumours of various kinds, and of strictures in the urinary canal, are but so many additional examples of chronic inflammation, giving rise to determinate maladies. This subject is an extensive and very interesting one, and if I were writing for the profession, it would be necessary to enlarge upon it; but my present purpose being to convey to the public a little of the most valuable information relating to the various points connected with the preservation of health, and the cure of diseases, I must pass on to notice the treatment of chronic inflammation in general. The reader is referred to page 338 for valuable GENERAL PRINCIPLES. Chronic inflammation of the eye, of the glands of the neck, and of the knee, are examples of chronic disease, and what is said in the article at page 338, in reference to the principles of management, is strictly applicable to them.

As already remarked, the essence of this disease is debility, and this must never be lost sight of in its treatment, because all very active or violent measures, which inevitably disturb and weaken the constitution, will very rarely fail to aggravate the complaint, and will sometimes do so much injury as no subsequent means can repair. Imperfect nutrition lies at the basis of most chronic maladies. If, therefore, chronic inflammation occur in the eye, glands of the neck, knee or hip joint, liver or elsewhere, we must have recourse to mild unirritating measures, which are capable of increasing the appetite and vigour of the stomach, and gradually altering the condition of action in the blood-vessels of the affected part, whereby strength to the whole constitution and healthy secretions will be restored, both locally and generally. These are the grand objects to be kept in view, and for the accomplishment of them the use of a little steel and quinine or cod-liver oil, with the pill No. 98A, a nourishing diet, and plenty of exercise, will be found the most efficacious means. I think very highly of sarsaparilla and dandelion as internal remedies, and cold water as an external remedy. Rest must also be given to the affected organ, with as easy a position as possible. The diet must be nourishing, but rather small in quantity, so as to prevent the possibility of exciting irritation.

The principles laid down at page 345 will be found of universal application in chronic inflammation wheresoever situated, and an adherence to them will not only preserve us from doing injury, but will enable us very generally to effect much good. I cannot but again advert to these fundamental principles of practical medicine, which ought ever to be impressed upon the mind of the bodily sufferer, and the consideration of which is of vast importance in the present affection, particularly to these, that THE RELIEF OF IRRITATION AND THE IMPROVEMENT OF THE QUALITY OF THE BLOOD, ARE THE GREAT OBJECTS OF MEDICINE. Now they are to be effected only by soothing, strengthening and slightly stimulant measures; and in proportion as we succeed, by the employment of such means, in accomplishing these objects, so do we free our patient from the symptoms of pain and uneasiness, both local and general, and aid in bringing the diseased organ, and the whole constitution, into a state of healthy and vigorous action. Large and frequently repeated doses of any active medicine will, consequently, hardly ever fail in defeating this object, and it is on these grounds that I oppose the employment of mercury and aperients in *large* quantities, and particularly if used with the intention of producing salivation; because salivation invariably irritates the whole system (and therefore the organ diseased), rendering it weaker, and generally yielding it an easy prey to the most uncomfortable and painful sensations. I repeat, mercury used in small doses, and in combination with antimonials, is invaluable, but in large quantities it is, for the most part destructive.

Inflammation of the Brain

The characteristics of this disease, are severe pain in the head, redness of the face and eyes, intolerance of light and sound, watchfulness, and ferocious delirium.

It often comes on with a sense of fulness in the head, flushing of the countenance, redness of the eyes, and fulness of the pulse;

followed by restlessness and disturbed pulse. Or it may make its attack with pain or a peculiar sense of uneasiness of the head, back, loins, and joints or tremors of the limbs, and intolerable pains of the hands, feet and legs :—or with anxiety, and a sense of tension referred to the breast, with palpitation of the heart. As the disease advances, the pain greatly increases, and with it the redness of the face and eyes; the countenance acquires a peculiar fierceness, the patient talks incoherently, and delirium follows, and often arrives at a state of frenzy. The face becomes turgid, the eyes stare, and seem as if starting from their sockets, tears, and sometimes blood flow from them, the patient resembling a furious maniac, from whom it is often impossible to distinguish him, except by the shorter duration of the disease. The eyes are incapable of bearing the light, and the least noise is intolerable; respiration is deep and stow, and swallowing difficult, the pulse being generally remarkably hard and small.

The stomach is often oppressed with bile, which is an unfavourable symptom. Sometimes there is a deficiency of bile, which, for the most part, affords a still worse prognostic. The stools being of a white colour, and a black cloud in the urine, are regarded by Dr. Lobb as fatal symptoms.

An injury immediately applied to the brain, such as violent exercise, intoxication, rage or the head being exposed long to a powerful sun; long and intense study; cold; fatigue; excessive venery; indigestible and poisonous substances received into the stomach; and the suppression of habitual discharges, are the *most frequent causes.*

It occurs most commonly during the progress of general fevers, particularly inflammatory and typhus fevers.

Inflammation of the brain is to be *distinguished* from inflammatory fever, by there being a mach greater derangement in the mental functions and in all the organs of sense, in the former than in the latter. In inflammation of the brain, the symptoms (as pain and heat of the head, etc.) denoting the local affection, are often well marked before the pulse is much disturbed; in inflammatory fever, the pulse from the commencement is frequent, strong and rapid.

TREATMENT—The most vigorous depleting measures are requisite in this disease. It should be commenced by a copious blood-letting from the temporal artery, jugular vein or arm, through a large orifice, so that the blood may be rapidly extracted. Its extent and repetition must be regulated by the age and constitution of the patient, and by the severity of the symptoms, but the first bleeding should rarely be less than twenty ounces. This should be followed by the application of a dozen leeches to the temples; after which the head should be shaved, and cloths dipped in vinegar and water or iced water, be freely applied over it, and renewed as often as they show a tendency to become warm. The application of ice to the shaven head is here often of striking advantage.[1] At the same time some active purgative medicine, as No. 120, page 205 or No. 27, page 155, must be administered, and repeated every morning. If a looseness comes on, care must be taken not to check it; and the same care should be exercised in preventing a suppression of a bleeding from the nose, since these evacuations often act as the most efficient remedies in this disease.

Give directly Dr. Graves's mixture No. 87B, page 187. It is one of the most efficacious remedies; and at the same time active purging with the draught No. 27, page 155, should be kept up.

On the subject of bleeding in active inflammation, Sir Astley Cooper instructively remarks, in his lectures,—

---

1. Sometimes the pain and heat in the head in this disease is so extremely great as even to cause cloths dipped in iced water to dry with astonishing rapidity; and then the *cold dash* should be had recourse to immediately. It consists in pouring a column of cold water upon the head, in a continued stream, from a height of from six to nine feet. The patient is to be seated in a large tub; a table is placed at the side of the tub, upon which a man stands, and at as great an elevation as his arms can reach, pours upon the naked head of the patient a steady but continued stream of cold or iced water, from a watering pot without the rose. The stream should fall as nearly as possible upon one and the same spot; but at first the elevation must be slight, otherwise the shock will be too violent. There is no degree of burning heat which the animal economy is capable of producing, and no violence of pain that can resist its continued application. It usually exerts its full effect in fifteen or twenty minutes. After it, the patient should be wiped dry quickly, and be put to bed. If the pain and heat return, recourse should again be had to this remedy.

> "In our endeavours to reduce inflammation, we shall rarely find local means sufficient. Our chief means are constitutional, particularly in the inflammation of vital organs, and the first of these is blood-letting. It diminishes the momentum of blood, and weakens the nervous power, by lessening the quantity of blood going to the head; and as the effect of blood-letting depends upon the quickness with which the blood is drawn away, it is necessary, in employing the lancet, to make a large orifice in the blood-vessels selected for the operation. When considering the propriety of a repetition of the bleeding, little or no dependence is to be placed on the buffy appearance of the blood, since this is often accidental. This buffiness depends on the rapidity of the circulation, and you will witness a cupped state of the blood when the circulation is rapid, although no inflammation is present. A repetition of the bleeding is indicated by a continuance of the hard pulse, that is, by the rapid, contracted pulse. After taking away blood, you will sometimes have a full, throbbing, irritable pulse—it is worthy of particular notice, that this is not the pulse which indicates a second bleeding, but will be relieved by an opiate at night, and a purgative in the morning."

All stimulating liniments applied to the head or legs, with warm bathing of the feet, are of very doubtful advantage, and, in my opinion, ought not to be employed. Neither does blistering, on account of its stimulating operation, appear to me advisable at the commencement; but after the general excitement has been reduced by the foregoing evacuations, a large blister may be applied to the nape of the neck or between the shoulders, and often with much benefit.

Should the disease lave followed a suppression of some habitual discharge, attempts to restore it must make part of the treatment.

During the whole course of the disease, the patient ought to be kept cool, and as quiet and undisturbed as possible, light being almost totally excluded. The diet should be the same as that recommended for inflammatory fever, it being absolutely necessary that it should be very spare, and consist merely of toast and water, and such like. Cold acidulated liquors, as lemon or orange juice, mixed with water, should be allowed with freedom.

A little tincture of digitalis, given thrice daily, is valuable, after the violence of the disease has been subdued by the preceding remedies, to which the alterative pill No. 99, may be added every night, if bilious symptoms are present.

Acute Inflammation of the Eye or Ophthalmia

The *symptoms* are piercing pains confined to a point, as if occasioned by the presence of extraneous matter; great heat and redness; the parts swell, and the vessels of the eye not only increase in size, and become turgid, but appear more numerous than in their natural state. With these symptoms there are likewise great pain upon the least motion of the eye-ball; morbid sensibility to light; effusion of tears of an excoriating quality; and should the inflammation run high, fever attends.

After a longer or shorter continuance these appearances gradually abate or entirely cease; but in some cases, although the patient is left free from pain, tumour and symptomatic fever, yet the suffused redness of the eye, and the external marks of inflammation still remain, and long continue to exist after every other symptom has subsided, thereby showing that the *acute* inflammation has terminated in one that is *chronic,* that is, possessing a slow and subdued character in which weakness is apparent.

When the inflammation continues unrestrained in its force, small ulcers, and little collections of matter, are sometimes formed.

In general, the eye appears very red in this disease, but occasionally the inflammation is very deeply seated, when it may be making a quick and dangerous progress without any external redness being apparent, a fact that demands very serious attention. For it has happened that a surgeon on visiting a patient in such a condition, has thought his disease of no moment from there being little or no visible inflammation, and has only prescribed a common was, and five or six leeches on visiting him next day, he has been found with high fever, confined to his chamber, and unable to bear the admission of a ray of light. In this state the eye-lids have been opened to inspect the eyc more attentively, it has burst and discharged its contents, with a great quantity of matter! The deep-seated inflammation of the eye may be known by the patient's complaining of acute pain, and being altogether incapable of bearing the least pressure on the ball of the organ.

The *most usual causes* are external injuries, such as blows, contusions, and wounds of the eyes; extraneous bodies of an irritating nature, introduced under the eye-lids; exposure to bleak winds and cold; too free a use of vinous and spirituous liquors; suppression of accustomed discharges; long exposure to strong light; a fixed attention to some minute object, and inversion of the eye-lids.

It must be remembered that the inflammation now treated of is of an active character, acutely painful, rapid in its progress, and in which the eye cannot bear the light. It is also generally attended with fever, and is of short duration, for though the redness of the eyes may continue for a considerable time after the pain has greatly abated, and the fever wholly subsided, yet the disease has then become *chronic* or in other words, of a slow indolent character, the essence of which is weakness. This is a point worthy of attention, for by mistaking a chronic inflammation of the eyes for one of an active kind, and, in consequence, having recourse to the abstraction of blood, purging, and other debilitating measures, the eyes have been frequently irretrievably injured. The slow, indolent inflammation of the eyes, so, often witnessed, is known either by its having followed,—and become a termination of an acute inflammation or from its having arisen slowly; its being in both instances of some continuance, and unattended by that acute pain which denotes the present disease.

Treatment—The remedies for an acute inflammation of the eyes are the same as in other inflammations, and consist in bleeding, purging, the mixture No. 87B, page 187, calomel and opium, the use of cooling febrifuge medicines, and the employment of blisters. If the inflammation runs very high, a pint of blood should be taken from the arm; but, in general, the application of eight or nine leeches to the temples will be sufficient, they being re-applied after a short time, if the symptoms require it.

In very severe cases, however, it will be necessary to bleed from the arm a second, third or fourth time, and that within a short period, in order to prevent the total destruction of the eye. Some surgeons have advised, that the inflamed vessels should be scarified at the same time, but this, in my opinion, is improper in the early stage of the disease, as likely to create irritation and maintain the inflammation.

After this, calomel and opium, with a portion of tartar emetic, should be given as advised under *Infammation of the Intestines,* and the purgative medicine prescribed in No. 73, page 176, may be administered, and repeated every morning; and a large blister be applied to the nape of the neck or a small one behind each ear.

The cooling febrifuge draught No. 24, page 153, ought to be taken every three hours; and the following lotion be applied to the inflamed eye constantly :

Take of Solution of acetate of ammonia	half an ounce;
Hot distilled water	6 ounces;
Soft extract of opium	10 grains.

Dissolve the soft extract of opium in the boiling water; strain through linen, and add the acetated liquor of ammonia. Let it be applied over the eyes by means of linen rags, kept constantly wet with it, occasionally insinuating a little, between the eye-lids, by the use of an eye-glass.

No cold lotion should be used in the first stage, but when the violence of the complaint has in some measure abated, either of those marked No. 11 and 12, pages 147, may be employed, instead of the warm collyrium.

Acute inflammation of the eye is sometimes epidemic; and now and then is contracted from washing the face with foul linen or urine. Matter (pus) may be poured out abundantly. Dr. Mackenzie of the Infirmary, Glasgow, treats this disease with a wash, made by dissolving four grains of lunar caustic in one ounce of distilled water, and it is an excellent remedy. It should be dropped into the eyes two or three times a day. It has often been found superior to all ordinary eye-waters.

When our endeavours to check the acute inflammation are unsuccessful, and we are threatened with a rupture of the cornea or anterior membrane of the eye, which is known by the membrane losing its transparency, and a white ring forming round its circumference, it has been found highly advantageous to puncture the aqueous humour, by inserting the point of a common lancet into the anterior chamber of the eye. So much relief has always followed this operation, as to make it one of great moment when violent inflammation threatens to terminate in a rupture of the organ. It has been successfully used by Mr. Wardrop, and Mr. Ware, and appears to operate by the sudden removal of tension.

Every thing must be avoided which would occasion irritation. The patient should be kept quiet, and in a chamber where the light is partly excluded. At the commencement of very acute cases, the light ought to be wholly excluded; but when the patient is recovering it must only be moderated, and the eyes gradually brought to bear it in its usual strength. In the worst cases, the diet must be very spare, such as rusks, tea and barley-water; but in less acute examples, mild diet of vegetable food should be observed, animal food and all spirituous and fermented liquors, being avoided.

A moderate inflammation of the eye is often seen in persons who are, notwithstanding, able to go abroad, and transact their usual business, and which may continue for many weeks, months or years. In this case the eyes look red, and are occasionally painful, though not often acutely so; but there is little or no feverishness present, and the complaint seems wholly to be a disease of debility, since it is met with, for the most part, in persons of delicate health, and weakly habits, and is invariably most effectually removed by slight astringents, stimulants and tonics. This is what surgeons call a *chronic* or indolent inflammation of the eye, and requires the administration of some strengthening medicine, as the pills No. 102 or 103, page 196, during the day, with the pill No. 99, every other night, and the application of a stimulant lotion or ointment to the eyes. The eye water No. 15, page 148, is very useful; but, in general, there is no external application equal to the nitrated ointment of quicksilver, No. 89, page 188 or No. 92, page 189.

This should be applied night and morning, the pills being taken at the same time, and the general diet and regimen being such as tends to invigorate the constitution. No leeches should be applied here, as they would certainly aggravate the disease, though such treatment is sometimes pursued from not distinguishing chronic inflammation of the eyes from that which is acute.

Sometimes an acute inflammation of the eyes leaves behind so great a degree of weakness in those organs, that their vessels remain enlarged, and full of red blood, and, are altogether very weak and irritable. In such a case, the active inflammation has terminated in one that is *chronic* or passive, which will be most speedily removed by the use of mildly astringent and tonic medicines, combined with mercurial alteratives, as just recommended.

A drop of the wine of opium, dropped into the eye night and morning, is also a valuable remedy in indolent inflammation of the organ, especially, if there be a great deal of soreness and irritation present. This medicine made a great noise when first brought into notice, but it has of late unjustly lost much of its reputation from having been used in acute inflammation of the eyes, to which state it is not applicable.

Sore eyes or rather sore and inflamed eye-lids, are often very troublesome. One of the best modes of treatment is to wash the eyes thrice daily with an eye-water made by mixing together twelve grains of acetate of lead, one drachm of wine of opium, and six ounces of water; the following ointment being applied by means of the end of a straw, to the eye-lid night and morning:

Take of Ointment of nitric oxyde of mercury,. half a scruple;
Spermaceti ointment .... 1 drachm.
Mix them.

Intestines

This disease is denoted by acute pain in the belly, increased upon pressure, and shooting in a twisting manner around the navel; by obstinate costiveness; tension of the abdomen; tenesmus or vomiting, etc., as the inflammation happens to be in the inferior or superior portion of the intestines; the vomiting being generally bilious, dark coloured or fetid. Fever likewise attends, with a quick, hard, contracted pulse, great prostration of strength, and high coloured urine.

The disease either gradually abates and goes off or terminates in ulceration or gangrene. It is often attended with considerable danger, and may terminate in gangrene in the space of a few days, and sometimes of a few hours, from its commencement. This event is marked by a sudden remission of the pain, sinking of the pulse, shrinking of the features, suppression of urine, hiccup, and distension of the belly. If the symptoms appear to yield to the means employed, the pain abating gradually, natural stools being passed, and the pulse becoming firm and equal, a favourable termination may be expected. A copious discharge of loaded urine, and an universal perspiration, are favourable symptoms.

The suppression of perspiration, by the application of cold to the feet or exposing the body to cold when over heated, etc.; acrid or irritating substances introduced by the mouth; obstinate costiveness; and violent passions of the mind, are the *most frequent causes*. It is most apt to occur at an advanced period of life, and is very liable to a relapse.

It is *distinguished* from colic by its being accompanied with fever, and a quick, hard, small pulse, and by the pain being increased on pressure, symptoms which do not occur in colic.

In inflammation of the stomach, the pain is seated higher in the region of the abdomen, and is of a peculiarly burning kind; the vomiting and hiccup are more severe; and the dejection of mind, and prostration of strength, much greater.

TREATMENT—Blood-letting is one of the chief remedies in this disease, and should never be neglected. It ought to be employed early and freely, according to the stage of the complaint, and the strength and age of the patient. In the commencement, blood should be drawn from the arm, and the operation be repeated to the second, third or fourth time, at intervals of a few hours, according to the severity of the symptoms; it being always remembered that the abstraction of a certain quantity of blood within a short period is invariably to be preferred to withdrawing the same quantity at a long period. Indeed, two pints of blood drawn within twelve hours will frequently be of much greater service in acute inflammations, than three or four pints taken in three days. The application of fourteen or twenty leeches to the abdomen, should immediately follow the general bleeding, and be repeated as the symptoms may require. Purgative medicine must not be administered, since it is of importance to keep the bowels in a quiet state, until the inflammation is subdued. It is worthy of special attention, that in inflammation of the bowels, and other organs within the abdomen, the strongest purgatives will often fail of any effect until the inflammation is in some measure subdued by the other remedies employed. In such cases, obstinate constipation generally attends, and there is a danger lest the attention of the medical attendant, and the patient's friends should be too exclusively directed to the importance and removal of this symptom. I have known even physicians lay the entire stress of the case upon the unconquerable constipation, and direct all or a very principal part of their treatment to its removal, by the use of purgatives and clysters, to the neglect of free and continued blood-letting, and the other means herein recommended. In consequence of which the patients died, and when opened, extensive ulceration and mortification presented themselves. The fact is, that the constipated state of the bowels depends upon the inflammation, which must be subdued by the use of the lancet, and of calomel and opium, before it can be overcome; and, therefore, to treat a patient in this constipated state, complaining of great pain within the abdomen, chiefly or entirely with purgatives, clysters, the warm bath, and quicksilver, would be a very bad and dangerous practice.

Should the vomiting be continued and severe, it may often be allayed, so as to admit of the effectual administration of internal medicines, by giving the effervescing saline draught No. 24, page 153, occasionally or by the employment of the means pointed out under the article on inflammation of the stomach.

The purgative clyster No. 8, pages 146, may be injected; and the warm bath, together with warm fomentations, are very proper. Bladders filled with warm water should be hid over the whole surface of the abdomen; and when the general excitement has subsided, and the disease seems to be giving way, a large blister should be applied to that region.

But there are few remedies more powerful in subduing acute inflammation, within the abdomen, than calomel combined with opium, especially after the free employment of blood-letting. Indeed, this composition is a remedy of great power, in most acute inflammations of internal organs, and membranes of importance. It is of the first consequence in inflammation of the lungs, stomach, and liver, and in what is erroneously called, water in the head. Dr. Hamilton of Lynn Regis, in Norfolk, was one of the first physicians who made known its remarkable power in such diseases; and the late Dr. Armstrong of London, has well observed, that so great is its efficacy in many such cases, that it deserves to be written in *letters* of gold, and always to be borne in mind by medical practitioners. Sir Astley Cooper, in speaking of inflammation generally, says, "the treatment of inflammation has been improved of late, by exhibiting calomel and opium". I should, therefore, never trust to blood-letting, as the chief remedy in the active inflammations just noticed, but invariably combine with it the administration of tartar emetic, calomel and opium.

Take of Calomel	10	grains;.
Purified opium	10	grains;
Tartar emetic	2½	grains;

Opiate confection, a sufficient quantity to form the ingredients into a mass, to be divided into ten pills.

One may be taken directly, after a full bleeding, and repeated every second, third, fourth or fifth hour, according to the urgency of the symptoms.

In the less severe cases of inflammation of the bowels, the use of these pills, together with a few leeches to the abdomen, a blister, and a low diet (the patient returning to his ordinary diet slowly and carefully), will usually be quite sufficient to remove all complaint.

Should the calomel show its action by producing, swelling of the gums, it must then be withdrawn, and the pills be continued of opium and tartar emetic alone.

Quicksilver was formerly a favourite medicine in this disease, no doubt from its supposed superior power of finding a passage through the bowels, when nothing else would pass; but as the inflammation is the cause of the constipation, and the latter symptom is only effectually to be overcome by subduing the former, this mineral can be of no use, and no physician of judgment now trusts to it.

The diet should be the same as directed for inflammation of the eyes, consisting of barley-water, tea and thin gruel.

Kidneys

The most prominent symptom of this disease is a deep-seated pain in the small of the back, increased on pressure; sometimes sharp and severe, sometimes heavy, obtuse or burning; often extending downwards, and attended with a retraction of the testicle, and perhaps numbness of the thigh. When both kidneys are affected, the urine is sometimes almost suppressed; and then comatose symptoms are apt to supervene. Generally the fever is high; and the stomach is usually very irritable; the urine scanty and high coloured. Pain is produced by pressure on the region of the kidneys.

TREATMENT—Blood-letting is indispensable in this disease, and the best mode of effecting it is by freely cupping over the loins. Give at the same time tartarized antimony and Mindererus's spirit, thrice a day, as in No. 78B, page 180; with which should be combined the use of compound powder of jalap. The bowels should be kept freely opened by the use of compound powder of jalap, half a drachm of which should be taken in water, and repeated every evening or oftener.

The effervescing saline draught No. 24, page 153, given occasionally, will be found an excellent assistant. The diet should be the same as for *Inflammation of the Intestines.*

Larynx

The *larynx* is the head or figured part of the wind-pipe, and is the organ of voice. It is formed of cartilage, that it may stand firm and uncompressed, either by the passage of the food or by the weight of the outward air.

This part is subject both to acute and chronic inflammation. The chronic inflammation sometimes forms a variety of consumption (*See* pages 458-60), and the acute inflammation of this organ is of a most dangerous character. Happily it is not a common complaint, and rarely occurs before puberty.

The disease sometimes commences like an ordinary sore throat attended with hoarseness. Its chief *symptoms* are, pain in the upper and forepart of the throat, increased on pressure; a sense of stricture in the same part; harsh cough; difficult rather than painful swallowing; voice at first acute, then thick, hoarse and whispering, and at last completely suppressed; fever and quick, laborious respiration.

The difficult respiration and the inadequate supply of air do not long continue without very visibly affecting the appearance of the patient; great anxiety is depicted upon a pallid countenance; the lips become of a leaden hue; the eyes protruding and watery; the pulse quick and feeble, and the heat of the surface of the body diminishes. The patient is restless and apprehensive, and often feels on the point of suffocation. If he begins to dose, he soon starts up in a state of the greatest agitation, gasping for breath.

Paleness and a lividity of the complexion, and lethargy or stupor, are symptoms indicative of great danger.

An advancing period of life is a frequent cause in those who have suffered much from indigestion or from intemperance or anxiety. Exposure to cold or wet is often the exciting cause of the malady.[1] It affects chiefly those who are liable to ordinary sore-throats.

1. The illustrious American, General Washington,—a man of rare virtue,–died of this complaint, which came on in the night of a day in which he had been exposed to rain. It proved fatal within twenty-four hours.

The age of the patients ordinarily attacked with this complaint, which is much beyond that of puberty, with the severity and rapidity of the symptoms, especially the laborious respiration, extreme anxiety, and sense of suffocation, clearly *distinguist* the disease from all others.

TREATMENT—Give directly the emetic powder No. 123, page 206, the operation of which will sometimes arrest at the outset attacks of a very threatening character. *See* pages 419-20. This powder should be followed by the use of the mixture No. 78B, page 180, in such doses as will not occasion vomiting or nausea, but will promote expectoration, and give relief to the breathing.

At the same time, if the symptoms of laborious respiration and pain are severe, let the patient be freely cupped at the back of the neck: This is better than bleeding from the arm or applying leeches to the throat.

A remarkable result of this inflammation, is a serous effusion into the cellular tissue beneath the mucous membrane of the larynx, which greatly augments the danger, and the difficulty of cure or relief. Hereby the opening of the windpipe may be so contracted as speedily to cause death; from strangulation; but death much more commonly occurs from the blood becoming gradually depraved, in consequence of the extreme difficulty of inspiring air.

Blisters are of doubtful efficacy, but the application of hot water to the throat, as advised at pages 504-05, is often of marked advantage.

The operation of *bronchotomy,* that is, making an opening into the windpipe, promises to be of eminent service in this malady, and should not be delayed beyond a few hours, if the laborious respiration is extreme, and the symptoms of prostration of strength, quickness of pulse, and suffocating cough, do not yield to the general remedies.

Liver

An inflammation of the liver is denoted by tension, soreness and pain in the region of that organ, with pain about the right shoulder, difficulty of lying on the left side and a short dry cough.

If the disease is very acute, it commences with the ordinary *symptoms* of chilliness, succeeded by heat, frequent, hard pulse and a furred tongue; the bowels are irregular, mostly costive; the evacuations little tinged with bile; the urine often saffron-coloured; the skin dry; the thirst extreme, with occasional sickness.

When the symptoms are most severe, and we have reason to suspect that the disease is confined to the membranes, the duration is often short, and the termination is in most cases favourable. But when less active, and seated in the substance of the liver, it generally tends to suppuration; and if the convex side of the liver be the part affected, a tumour is visible externally, the cough becomes aggravated, and there is a difficulty of breathing. If adhesions have preceded the suppuration, the pus points to the skin, and the abscess opens on the surface; but if it break internally, it generally proves fatal by inducing a hectic fever, though sometimes, in consequence of fortunate adhesions, the abscess discharges itself into the hepatic duct, which terminates in the first intestines, and the pus (matter) is carried off by this channel.

This disease is usually divided into the *acute* and *chronic* inflammation of the liver, but as the second variety is what is popularly called *a liver complaint,* it will be treated of under that head, the affection now considered being the acute inflammation.

It is excited by all the usual *causes* of inflammation. People of a choleric and melancholic temperament are most liable to it; and it is far more frequent in hot than in cold or temperate climates. Exposure to the rays of the vertical sun, and to the damps of the night in sultry climates, are two of its most frequent causes.

TREATMENT—The treatment proper is very similar to that laid down under the next article. Blood-letting is generally found serviceable at the commencement, and should be repeated as the violence of the symptoms requires, and the strength of the constitution allows. Purgatives of Epsom and Glauber salt, and of calomel, as No. 120, page 205, should follow, and are considered particularly efficacious.

After these remedies have been employed, the calomel and opium pills prescribed under inflammation of the intestines, should be given every three hours till the disease gives way, when they may be administered at longer intervals of four or six hours. In sultry climates, where the disease is met with in its most acute forms, and where it often runs on with an astonishing rapidity, much larger doses of calomel than are contained in those pills, must be given. Here four, five or six grains, with a quarter or half a grain of opium or three grains of Dover's powder, will frequently be required every second or third hour, until the symptoms are relieved, when it should be continued in smaller quantities. Professional men practising in hot countries, place more dependence on the powers of calomel in this complaint than any other means whatever.

Hot fomentations, the warm bath, and blisters, are proper; and the cooling febrifuge medicine recommended at page 183, No. 81, may likewise be employed with advantage.

The diet should be mild and small in quantity, the same as advised for the two preceding inflammations.

So long as pain on pressure on the right side continues, we must be on our guard, for chronic inflammation of the liver often remains after the acute symptoms have subsided.

Lungs

This inflammation is denoted by pain in the chest; constant and anxious difficulty of breathing, alleviated by an erect position; tumid, purple face or lips; distressing cough; a strong, hard and frequent pulse; pungent heat of skin and fever. These symptoms vary considerably in different cases. The difficulty of breathing is the most constant symptom, and becomes considerable in all cases as the disease advances. The pain is sometimes peculiarly acute and at other times heavy and dull, and it may be either in the right or left side or under the breast-bone, collar-bone, spine or shoulder-blades. The cough is often very distressing, being in some cases dry, in others attended with spitting. The pulse is very hard and strong; the thirst considerable; the tongue often dry, white and rough; the urine scanty and high coloured, and there is an anxious expression and dusky hue of complexion.

When the determination of blood to the head is very great, and marked by stupor in the commencement of the disease, the symptom is extremely unfavourable. Delirium is likewise a very dangerous symptom.

Inflammation of the lungs may exist with little or no pain, when the real nature of the case may be known by the constant difficulty of breathing, painful cough, presence of fever, and sometimes by the nature of the expectoration. In many cases this has an appearance quite characteristic, it is remarkably *glutinous,* and when received into a flat and open vessel, unites into so viscous and tenacious a mass, that we may turn it upside down without the expectorated matter being detached; and if we shake the vessel its contents vibrate like jelly, though in a less degree.

When inflammation of the lungs terminates favourably by a distinct crisis, the most common is a red or white sediment in the urine; and we should distrust any other, unless this also occurs at the same time. Next to this disposition, a sweat and moderate diarrhoea are the most common forms of crisis. A copious expectoration of mucus is also sometimes critical.

The most *common causes* are, exposure to cold; violent exercise; violent coughing; acrid vapours and dust received with the breath; to which may be added every thing which conduces to a full habit, as luxurious living, indolence, repelled eruptions, suppressed excretions.

The strong and plethoric, who use much exercise, and readily digest their food, are most subject to it; and it is generally most frequent in the colder, moister and more changeable weather. It is, however, common and fatal in old persons; and children are very subject to it. It is said that about three-fifths of the children that die in the hospitals between birth and the conclusion of the first teething, die of this disease, and chiefly in a latent or concealed state.

No inflammation is more easily renewed in those who have formerly laboured under it.

It is usual in systems of physic, to lay down the rules for *distinguishing* inflammation of the lungs from that of the pleura, heart, and membrane covering the heart, called *pericardium*; but the symptoms, causes and treatment, are so nearly alike in all, as to snake it unnecessary to treat of them distinctly in a popular work.

Pleurisy or inflammation of the pleura, is, perhaps, generally attended with more acute pain than inflammation of the lungs; and in an inflamed state of the heart, all the symptoms are commonly more severe.

TREATMENT—The first remedy had recourse to in this disease should be blood-letting, both by the use of the lancet and cupping or the application of leeches, provided the patient is young and strong, and the attack has lasted only a day or two, and the skin is hot, the tongue white, and the Tube *hard and not compressible.* If the pulse is soft and easily compressed, bleeding is not advisable. In London and other large cities, physicians now generally recommend a little wine and ammonia to be given immediately, even in those cases in which it is advisable to bleed. In large cities, half an ounce of good port or sherry wine may be given every three hours, especially where the nervous system is prostrated by the disease, so as to produce tremor of the hands, quivering of the tongue or dry brown tongue or delirium. In old persons, and those who have indulged too freely in wine, it is particularly indicated. In children it is not required nor in healthy localities in the country. As in inflammation of other vital organs, the bleeding at the commencement should be prompt and copious, the quantity -first drawn being rarely less than eighteen or twenty ounces, provided the patient is in good health, and not old. Immediately after the general bleeding, the cupping glasses or ten leeches, must be applied over the chest. The laxative draught No. 28, page 156, should likewise be given once a day, but, purging is here of no advantage. The cooling febrifuge mixture No. 81, page 183, may be advantageously employed, every three or four hours. In case of debility, the ammonia mixture No. 78D, page 181, is still better. Blisters to the chest are useful after the fever has been subdued by the above means.

Directly blood has been drawn envelope the whole chest in a large warm bath-like poultice. The warmth and moisture tend directly to relieve the difficulty of breathing,—the hot fevered skin becomes moist and active, and the patient is sensibly relieved. Make the poultice of bruised meal, if it can be got; if not, of bread. Spread it half an inch thick at least, on a cloth or flannel, as broad as the circumference of the chest; and let it be deep enough to cover the whole chest from the collar bones to the sides below the ribs. Keep it in its place by means of a tape stitched on in front, and one behind, to tie over each shoulder. Renew it as often as it becomes at all cold, but never remove the poultice till another hot one is ready to go on. I have peculiar pleasure in urging the immediate use of this bath-like poultice, because it can at once be used at all ages, and in all conditions, with the greatest safety and prospect of benefit, by the mother of the family. Of course, an able medical man should be immediately sent for in so acute a disease as this, but the head of the family ought not to delay a moment in applying this poultice, it being in every case so suitable and soothing. The poultice must be kept on hot and hot till all pain is gone, and the breath can be drawn quite freely and easily.

When the fever, pungent heat of skin, pain, and difficulty of breathing are urgent, especially in patients in the country, and tolerably strong, blood-letting should be instantly had recourse to, and will prove a remedy of great power. But if the patient's constitution is weak and exhausted, and low fever is present, then blood-letting will do no good. If inflammation of the lungs has come on after extreme domestic anxiety and distress, whereby the general powers of the system have been prostrated or in a weakly habit or in old age, blood-letting should not be employed; then I much prefer an entire dependence on tartar emetic, and a little calomel and opium, together with the bath-like poultice.

The administration of tartar emetic is of great service in all inflammations occurring within the chest. It is trusted to alone in these complaints, by many French and Italian physicians, indeed, by many English practitioners also.[1] M. Peschier, of the Canton de

1. Its value as a powerful anti-inflammatory remedy "is now established by the united experience of the most distinguished British and continental practitioners. In our own hands, we have seen the most surprising effects produced by it". *Cyclopaedia of Practical Medicine,* vol. ii. p. 806–1833.

Vaud, has trusted entirely to large does of this substance in such cases for many years pest, and, according to his report, with admirable success. He does not bleed or blister, but immediately commences with giving the patient a table-spoonful of the following mixture, every two hours, in a tea-cupful of barley-water or tamarind tea.

Take of Emetic tartar	14	grains.
Water	6	ounces;
Syrup of saffron	2	drachms.
Mix.		

In general, the quantity of emetic tartar ordered in this mixture should be increased three grains a day, till the patient takes twelve, fifteen or twenty grains during the twenty-four hours; the dose of the mixture being still a table-spoonful every two hours. If much tendency to sweating occurs, three or four drachms of the sweet spirit of nitre may be added to the mixture; and should there be much uneasiness and sleeplessness, a drachm of tincture of opium may be mixed with it. The following are the usual effects of the medicine; the patient generally vomits after the second or third dose of the first mixture, and afterwards it either acts on the bowels or produces no other sensible effect than that of mitigating quickly the symptoms of the disease. M. Peschier remarks, that large doses of this article produce much less vomiting than small ones, which always give rise to great distress without beneficial results. I am very favourable to this plan. When we consider that a free expectoration is the means which nature often adopts for carrying off inflammation within the chest, and that the tartar emetic is a powerful expectorant; as well as corrector of inordinate vascular action, the plan appears evidently rational and well founded. I should, however, in general, prefer combining the tartar emetic with the calomel and opium above recommended, more especially in the severer cases.

As soon as we have obtained, by the use of emetic tartar, some amelioration of the symptoms, although but slight, we may in general be assured that the continuation of the remedy will effect complete resolution of the disease, without any relapse; and it is in regard to this point more particularly, that the greatest practical difference between the emetic; tartar and blood-letting consists. By the latter measure, we often obtain a diminution of the fever, of the oppression, and the bloody expectoration, so as to lead both the patient and the attendants to believe that recovery is about to take place; frequently after a few hours, however, the unfavourable symptoms return with fresh vigour; and the same scene is not uncommonly renewed, often five or six times, after as many successive and large bleedings. On the other hand, these renewed attacks, under the use of the emetic tartar, are not witnessed.

The vapour of warm water should be inhaled frequently.

During the whole course of the complaint, the patient should be strictly confined to bed, and the room be kept quiet, and moderately warm. All kinds of animal food must be avoided, and the diet consist of light vegetables, with diluting drinks, as barley-water, tamarind tea, wine, etc. On recovering, constant care must be taken to guard against cold, and any irregularity likely to occasion a relapse, a circumstance very apt to take place.

Elderly persons, and those who have greatly weakened their constitutions by excesses, are sometimes attacked with a spurious *inflammation of the lungs,* which will not bear blood-letting or any other means of active depletion. The patient, in this case, is hot and cold alternately, feels giddy, and complaints of an acute pain in the head, especially when there is a teazing cough. He rejects all fluids, sometimes from paroxysms of coughing, and sometimes without; the urine is turbid, and of a deep red. The patient breathes quick and with difficulty; complains of a general pain throughout the entire breast, and as he coughs, discovers a *wheezing* to the attendants. The cheeks and eyes appear slightly inflamed; the pulse is small, often intermitting; and lying low or on one side, is peculiarly distressing.

The *treatment* of this spurious inflammation of debilitate subjects, consists in administering tartar emetic, and a mixture of sesqui-carbonate of ammonia and the tincture of squills in camphor mixture, as in No. 78A, page 180. When the inflam-matory symptoms appear somewhat severe, the mixture No. 78D, page 181, should be given instead of 78A.

The mixture of tartar emetic No. 78D, as above recom-mended, is likely to prove of great benefit here, from its tendency to promote spitting, and occasional vomiting, which greatly relieves the lungs, and often cuts short the complaint. The treatment is very similar to that recommended for *suffocative* cough at page 409.

Blistering the chest is often of great advantage, but bleeding should never be employed; for this complaint consists rather in congestion within the chest than in positive inflammation. It is the *suffocative* cough of some authors, and, as was before remarked, is found only in the old or infirm.

The food must be mild, but somewhat more nutritious than can be allowed in true inflammation of the lungs.

Peritoneum

The bowels, and other organs of the belly are invested by a serous membrane called *peritoneum,* which lines the sides of the belly, and is sometimes inflamed, giving rise to the disease called *peritonitis.*

The chief *symptoms* of acute inflammation of the peritoneum are severe pain and tenderness of the abdomen, a contracted hard pulse, and costiveness. The legs are drawn up in order to relax the muscles, the breathing is hurried, and the least pressure of the bed-clothes is scarcely to be endured. Coughing induces agonizing pain. There may be a remission of pain, but the tenderness is constant. In the commencement, the urine is commonly scanty and high coloured. If it is *albuminous*, we may suspect disease of the kidneys; if it is pale and in large quantities, then we may suspect hysteria or neuralgic pain simulating inflammation of the peritoneum.

The usual *causes* of this inflammation are exposure to cold and excessive fatigue; sitting on damp ground; perforation of the stomach or of the intestines; irritation of the ovaries, and the use of drastic purgatives.

The inflammation of the peritoneum occurring in lying in women, called *puerperal peritonitis,* is an alarming species of this disease. The child-bed fever usually arises from this cause.

TREATMENT—The first thing to be done in grown persons is to have fourteen or sixteen ounces of blood taken from the arm, and then to cover the surface of the belly with fifteen or twenty leeches. After the leeches have fallen off, spread a light bread and water poultice over the belly, and renew it as frequently as it becomes cold. At the same time give the following pills of calomel and opium every four hours :

Take of Calomel	8	grains;
Purified opium	15	grains.

Mix, and, with mucilage of gum arabic, divide them into ten pills.

The patient is not to be allowed to raise himself, on any account, into a sitting position; and the diet must be of the simplest description, such as gruel, barley-water, and tea.

In CHRONIC INFLAMMATION of the peritoneum, there is tenderness of the belly on pressures occasional or frequent pain, a sensation of fulness and tension of the belly, and very often an irregular state of the bowels, with unnatural evacuations from them. Throughout there is some fever, quickness of pulse, and progressive emaciation and debility. The face is pale, and there is an expression of languor and disease.

In these mild cases, a few leeches should be applied to the belly, and followed by a soft bread poultice; and the calomel and opium pills should be given about three times in the twenty-four hours—or three grains of grey powder and half a grain of opium, made into a pill with extract of henbane, may be given three times in the twenty-four hours.

If these means are not effectual, give the patient one drachm of sarsaparilla powder, in a wine-glass of tepid water, three times a day. Bihloride of mercury also is sometimes very effectual. *See* page 15.

Stomach

Burning pain at the pit of the stomach, increased on swallowing; rejection of every thing swallowed; hiccup; with oppression and dejection of mind, and high fever, are the *symptoms* denoting this disease. The pain is extremely acute, but is not always confined exactly to the region of the stomach, for it sometimes extends as low as the false ribs, and often shoots to the back. It is always much increased by even the slightest external pressure, and the vomiting is a more constant symptom than the hiccup. The pulse is frequent, small, contracted, hard, and sometimes intermitting. The thirst is urgent, and the bowels costive.

The depression of strength is more sudden and general than in any other inflammation. The patient complains of anxiety and anguish referred to the pit of the stomach, and actual fainting sometimes occurs.

The *causes* are the same as those that give rise to inflammar tion of the bowels, which have already been described. There is, perhaps, no cause of this disease so common as suddenly checking the perspiration by drinking cold fluids.

Spasm of the stomach is *distinguished* from inflammation by its being unattended with the sudden sinking of strength above noticed, by the pulse being natural, and by there being little or no increase of pain on receiving any thing into the stomach or on pressure.

TREATMENT—The treatment so nearly resembles that laid down for inflammation of the bowels, as to make it unnecessary to say much more here than what has already been said under that head. Blood-letting, calomel and opium, blisters, the warm bath, and clisters, are the chief remedies.

There is no case of inflammation in which bleeding is carried to a greater extent than in that of the stomach. Recourse must be had to it immediately the disease shows itself, and if the symptoms do not yield, it must be carried as far as the habit will bear. And so far from only letting blood when the pulse is full and strong, the smaller and weaker it is, generally speaking, the more necessary does copious and early bloodletting become. After a large quantity of blood has been taken away, the inflammation will often suddenly disappear, but we must be prepared for a recurrence of the disease, which, to a greater or less extent, almost always happens. One of the calomel and opium pills (page 698) must be taken, at the same time, every three hours.

Purgative medicines are not applicable in the present case, but purgative clysters, as No. 8, page 146, may be frequently injected with advantage. When, however, the inflammation arises from over-distension of the stomach, the patient is often tormented with ineffectual efforts to vomit, in which case, endeavours should be made to relieve the stomach by the exhibition of purging medicine, since emetics are invariably inadmissible.

The warm bath and warm fomentations should be used freely; and after the excitement has been reduced by bleeding, etc., a large blister should be laid over the region of the affected organ, and repeated to the third or fourth time, if necessary.

The patient may, with advantage, drink freely of marshmallow tea, barley-water or gum water; and sometimes orange juice, diluted with water, forms an excellent drink in this disease.

There is a CHRONIC INFLAMMATION of the stomach *(chronic gastritis)* which merits serious attention, since it is a frequent complaint in this country, and is often mistaken for ordinary indigestion. In many instances the first *symptoms* are—acidity, flatulence, a sense of heaviness and oppression after eating, eructations, and transient slight pains in the region of the stomach. As the disorder advances, the pit of the stomach becomes somewhat tense, and sore to the touch, the distress becomes more and more troublesome after eating, and nausea or vomiting may occur an hour or two after taking food. The pain in the stomach is generally confined to one spot, and a sensation of pressure against the diaphragm or midriff; as if by a large ball, is occasionally experienced by some patients, whilst others complain of a feeling, as if a bar were fixed across the stomach, preventing the passage of food or drink into the stomach. In some instances, a fluid resembling the white of egg is copiously thrown up from the stomach, and many suffer much from water-brash. The pulse is generally quick and tense; there is much muscular prostration, and great indisposition both to bodily and mental exertion.

All the usual causes of indigestion will give rise to it or it may be the consequence of the acute form.

It requires in many instances a discerning eye to distinguish this complaint from indigestion, thc symptoms of the two affections so nearly resemble each other. When, however, the patient feels considerable pain *in a particular spot* in the region of the stomach, followed by vomiting soon after eating, and a severe feeling of *pyrosis* or water-brash, attended with a vermillion redness and tenderness of the tongue, especially of the sides and tip, and throat, and the individual becomes much weakened and emaciated, we may reasonably suspect the existence of *chronic* inflammation of the stomach.

TREATMENT—The proper treatment of this affection demands a very strict attention to diet, scarcely any thing being allowed, but the blandest, and certainly nothing but the most digestible, articles of diet, such as good cold black tea, barley or gum water, thin gruel, cold water, fluid preparations of sago, arrowroot, tapioca, boiled milk, and animal jellies. Good plain biscuit and rusks soaked in water or in milk and water, are excellent, but no solid articles of food, at least in the beginning, excepting the mildest and most easily digested vegetables (well boiled), such as asparagus, spinach, and brocoli. Sometimes a slice of roast mutton may be allowed at dinner. *See* the remarks at pages 345-49.

Leeching the pit of the stomach may be tried or a wet bandage; also the application of a blister over that part or friction with the tartar emetic ointment. I think very favourably of the powder of sarsaparilla, in the dose of a drachm, two or three times a day, in a wine-glassful of cold water. If this does not succeed, try the oxide of bismuth, taken united with ipecacuanha powder and extract of hop, henbane or hemlock, as in No. 103A, page 197. Ipecacuanha is a particularly appropriate and valuable medicine in this disorder, and it may generally be given very early, if simply combined with soap. Sometimes the patient will derive considerable benefit from a pill, composed of a grain of blue pill, combined with three or our grains of extract of henbane or hemlock, which may be given every night, and repeated in the day, if the pain or general irritability calls for it.

If that does not answer, take the following pill of grey powder and extract of henbane :

Take of Grey powder....................	half a drachm;
Extract of henbane......................	half a drachm.

Mix, and divide into twelve pills. Take one every night or night and morning.

Should it slightly affect the gums, this is an event which is usually coincident with a marked improvement in all the symptoms.

Dr. Eberle, of Philadelphia, recommends *(Treatise on the Practice of Medicine,* vol. 1, p. 97, 1831), a trial of "a weak emulsion of the balsam of copaiva," an article which (he says) I have used in a few well-marked cases of this disease with considerable benefit :

Take of Balsam of copaiva	1½	drachm;
Gum arabic powder	2	drachma ;
Syrup of lemon.........................		half an ounce;
Water	8	ounces;
Laudanum	30	drops.

Mix, and take a table-spoonful twice daily.

But I do not think this half so efficacious as sarsaparilla powder in the day, and a grey powder pill at night.

The bowels should be kept regular by means of clysters of oil and warm water or minute doses of castor oil or draughts of cold water. The case of *chronic gastritis* cured by cold water, introduced in the *Appendix*; is worthy of much notice. I am certain the cold water system is of eminent service in this painful and frequent complaint.

THROAT OR QUINSY

The *Quinsy* is an inflammatory affection of the throat, denoted by swelling and florid redness of the back part of the throat, with difficulty of swallowing and fever.

The disease generally begins with an uneasy sense of tightness about the throat, and difficulty and pain in swallowing. On inspecting the back part of the mouth, the parts, as far as the inflammation extends, appear swelled, and of a more florid red than natural; and here and there, particularly on the tonsils, small white or yellow specks are often observed. While these remain of a light colour, and the pulse continues sufficiently strong and full, they never indicate danger. As the disease advances, the difficulty of swallowing and breathing becomes greater, the speech grows indistinct, the dryness of the throat, and the thirst increase; the tongue swells and is much furred, and the pulse is full, hard, and frequent. When the *symptoms* are considerable, the whole face partakes of it, the eyes are inflamed, the cheeks florid and swelled, the breathing is performed with difficulty, and the patient is obliged to be supported in nearly an erect position to prevent suffocation. Even delirium sometimes comes on.

The inflammation is generally confined to the parts which can be brought into view by opening the mouth; it sometimes, however, extends along the oesophagus or gullet, and occasionally to the windpipe. In the former case, the difficulty and pain of swallowing is very great; in the latter, the breathing becomes peculiarly difficult and distressing. In both, the danger is very great. Moderate fever, free respiration, swallowing not much impeded, the inflammation being of a vivid red colour, universal but gentle sweat, and a copious spitting or moderate looseness, coming on about the fifth day, are very favourable symptoms.

It is most apt to attack the young, robust, and plethoric; and is most frequent in spring and autumn. Cold, particularly if alternating with a high temperature or partially applied, especially if applied to the seat of the disease, is the *chief exciting cause*.

It is usually a mild disease. It is only in the highly predisposed that it assumes its more alarming forms.

It is readily *distinguished* from the putrid sore throat, since, in the latter disease, the redness of the tonsils is of a darker crimson colour, and covered with spreading alterations, and sloughs of an ash colour, while the fever is of a low typhous character.

An acute inflammation of the *larynx* or top of the windpipe, is sometimes met with, which may, by ignorant persons, be confounded with inflammation of the throat. *See* page 699-700.

TREATMENT—The first thing to be done in this disease, is to administer an emetic of tartarized antimony, as No. 29, page 156; and it may be repeated to the second or third time, in the course of twenty-four or thirty-six hours, should the symptoms require it. Emetics given early often put a stop to the disease more speedily and effectually than any other remedy, and seldom fail to bring considerable relief. Patients labouring under severe attacks of this disease have been snatched apparently from the jaws of death by an emetic. It is sometimes employed with advantage even after the formation of an abscess; for should the surgeon be unable to reach it, the exhibition of an emetic, if it is ripe, will almost always occasion its bursting. No one now need delay to take an emetic in sore throat.

After this, cooling purgatives should be given, as No. 73, page 176, and leeches be applied to the external surface of the throat. If the fever runs very high, it will be proper to take blood from the jugular vein or arm. Under all circumstances, the vapour of warm water should be freely inhaled several times a day. It may be drawn in through the spout of a tea-kettle or more effectually by the instrument termed an inhaler. The use of gargles is likewise proper. A very good gargle may be made by mixing three drachms of tincture of myrrh with seven ounces of infusion of roses; or by adding half a drachm of muriatic acid to seven ounces of barley-water. *See* also No. 57, page 169. If suppuration is unavoidable, the gargle should be mild, and used warm, and in large quantity, as the object in such a case is to promote a favourable suppuration. A very good gargle, for this purpose, may be made by boiling a few figs and linseed together in water, to which may be added a little mucilage of gum arabic.

A stimulant embrocation should likewise be rubbed on the neck and throat, as No. 45, page 163; and a large blister be applied near the seat of the disease. When the first blister fails, a second often succeeds. But should the quinsy be very severe, and the fever run high, with a hard, quick pulse, the blisters and embrocations ought to be delayed till the fever is reduced by the employment of emetics and purgatives; or otherwise the irritation occasioned by these remedies would be more likely to increase than diminish the inflammation.

Febrifuge medicines which determine to the surface of the body are also proper. One of the best of these is James's powder. Four grains of it may be taken twice or thrice a day, made into a pill with conserve of hips. Or the diaphoretic draught, No. 26, page 155, may be used in its stead.

When the swelling in the throat is so great as to threaten suffocation, the enlarged tonsils should be scarified by the surgeon, and if this fails to afford relief, the operation of making on opening in the windpipe (called tracheotomy) ought not to be delayed. In such cases, the most alarming symptoms are often the consequence of impeded respiration, and will disappear when a free passage is given to the air. This operation is not severe or dangerous.

In very severe cases, all kinds of animal food and fermented liquors must be avoided, and the diet be mild, spare and diluting, as recommended for inflammation. Plentiful dilution, by drinking of warm barley-water, thin gruel, and the like, is in all cases advisable. Should swallowing be wholly interrupted, the patient must be nourished by nutritive clysters of mutton broth and bread or decoctions of barley, oatmeal, and arrow-root, till by the most active means the inflammation of the throat is reduced.

When the quinsy has been severe, it is often succeeded by a considerable degree of debility. Nourishing food, and the moderate use of wine, are generally sufficient to restore the strength; but if the tendency to the disease has wholly subsided, a cold infusion of bark will be very useful. The relaxation of the throat left after the attack has gone off, may be removed by the use of one of the astringent gargles above mentioned.

In the slight cases of quinsy so often met with, the use of the volatile liniment, No. 45, page 163, with an astringent gargle, No. 56 or 57, page 169, a little purgative medicine every other day, as No. 74, page 176, and five grains of James's powder at night, will be sufficient to carry off all complaint. Should the disease be growing severe, a vomit of tartar emetic ought to be taken immediately.

I think I cannot close this part of the present article better, than with an extract from the observations of the late Dr. Baillie on this disease.

> "I have but one observation," says he, "to make with regard to this disease, which is of some little importance. It is usual to endeavour throughout the course of it to prevent suppuration from taking place, by the repeated application of leeches under the angles of the lower jaw. It is certainly very desirable that suppuration should be prevented, and that inflammation of the tonsils should gradually subside by resolution; I have found, however, by experience, that suppuration is by such means very often not prevented, but only that inflammation proceeds more slowly to this issue. Hence the patient suffers for a considerably longer time; and the suffering in this disease is often very great. If, therefore, one or two applications of leeches do not lessen materially the inflammation of the tonsils and palate, I should recommend the progress of the inflammation to be encouraged by the inhaling of warm vapour into the mouth, and the application of poultices to the external fauces. In this way the disease will go through its progress more quickly, and the patient will suffer much less."—Dr. Bailie's *Posthumous Writings*, p. 175.

INSANITY OR MENTAL DERANGEMENT

Insanity is well known to mean unsoundness of mind. In referring to a general division, for the sake of perspicuity, we may remark, that there are two states of insanity; the one state is characterized by an unrestrained behaviour; by an irritability which urges on the patient in an extravagant pursuit of something real or imaginary, to the ruin of himself or annoyance to his friends; and ultimately leads him, if opposed in his disordered wishes, to acts of extreme violence. This is what many physicians call MANIA or MADNESS; and others, the HIGH or STHENIC form of insanity.

The other state is marked by an unusual lowness, sometimes amounting to despair, a loathing of life, and every thing connected with it, accompanied too often by an uncontrollable effort of the patient to rescue himself, by his own hand, from his real or imaginary distresses. This is the MELANCHOLY of some authors, and the LOW OR ASTHENIC form of insanity of others.

Mental derangement is generally divided by medical men into MADNESS and MELANCHOLY, and I shall say a little on each of these heads separately. But first it will be advisable to make a few remarks upon certain points which are equally applicable to both these forms of insanity.

It is very commonly supposed that the intellect or reasoning faculty is chiefly or even solely, disordered in persons afflicted with mental derangement, but this is a great mistake, for many cases are to be met with in which it consists in a morbid perversion of the moral affections, without, at least, any perceptible lesion of the intellectual faculties. Pinel, the late able physician of the Bicêtre, a large lunatic asylum in Paris, was the first person who distinctly noticed this fact; and Esquirol, a Parisian physician who at the present day practises extensively in lunatic cases, and who possesses a superior judgment, says *(Diction. des Sciences Medicales,* tom. xvi). "This moral alienation is so constant, that it appears to me to be the proper characteristic of mental derangement. There are mad men in whom it is difficult to discover any trace of hallucination, but there are none in whom the passions and moral affections are not disordered, perverted or destroyed. I have in this particular met with no exceptions."[1]

1. "A return to the proper and natural state of the moral affections, the desire of seeing once more children or friends; the tears of sensibility; the wish manifested by the individual to open his heart and return into the bosom of his family, to resume his former habits, afford *a certain indication* of cure, while the contrary dispositions have been marked by approaching insanity or the symptoms of a threatened relapse. This is not the case where there is merely a disappearance of the hallucination, which then only is a certain sign of convalescence, when the patients return to their natural and original affections."—*Esquirol, in Diction. des Sciences Medicales,* tom. xvi.

In conformity with this view of the subject, the following divisions of insanity (extracted from the *Cyclopaedia of Practical Medicine,* vol. ii. p. 826, 1833) appear to me peculiarly just and valuable.

"1. *Moral insanity* or madness consisting in a morbid perversion of the natural feelings, affections, inclinations, temper, habits, and moral disposition, without any notable lesion of the intellect or knowing or reasoning faculties, and particularly without any maniacal hallucination.

"2. *Intellectual insanity* or madness attended with hallucination; in which the insane person is impressed with the belief of some unreal event as of a thing which has actually taken place or in which he has taken up some notion repugnant to his own experience and to common sense, as if it were true and indisputable, and acts under the influence of this erroneous conviction."

3. *Incoherent madness.* This is another well marked division, "in which the whole mind, if we may use the expression, seems to be equally deranged. The most striking phenomena in this form of the disease are the rapidity and disorder with which the ideas follow each other, almost without any discoverable connexion or association, in a state of complete incoherence and confusion. It is impossible to fix the attention of the patient long enough to obtain a reply to the most simple question. His understanding is wholly lost in the constant hurry, of ideas which crowd upon him, and which appear to exceed the power of distinct utterance, while his habits betray a corresponding degree of restless activity and extravagance."

The *causes* of this disease are a changeable climate, subject to great atmospherical vicissitudes; extremes of heat and cold; intense study, especially where the efforts of the mind are directed more exclusively in one channel; intoxication; prostitution (a twentieth part of the insane females admitted into the Salpetriêre Hospital, at Paris, are previously prostitutes); the excessive ascendancy of the factitious passions, as self-interest, ambition, pride, avarice; the struggle between the principles of religion, morality and education, on the one side, and the passions on the other; hereditary disposition; child-birth; menstrual irregularities; epilepsy, a fruitful source; the abuse of mercury, etc.

The passions and emotions most productive of this complaint are love, fear, fright, rage, ambition, reverse of fortune, and the greatest of all, domestic chagrin or family dissension. The combination of moral and physical causes is much more commonly the origin of insanity, than either of them singly. Some medical men consider the moral causes to predominate far, in number and force, over the physical; others look upon bodily disease as the chief foundation of the complaint in the generality of instances. In the great majority of instances that I have seen, considerable bodily disorder has been not only coincident with the mental malady, but its precursor.

Whether the derangement assume the form of madness or melancholy, is owing rather to the constitutional disposition of the individual affected, than to the nature of the exciting cause; for the causes above noticed are alike applicable to both forms of the diseases, sometimes giving rise to one modification and sometimes to the other.

It is undoubted, that the more tranquil a country is, and the less agitated by "the pride of life", the inordinate desires, and the many wants of civilization and refinement, the less frequent we find the present malady. Therefore in Turkey, Egypt, Russia, etc., the number of the insane is very small and in France and England very large.

Insanity on the increase in England. Nervous affections, including, of course, among them insanity, have alarmingly increased of late years in this country. The fact must be obvious to those whose situation and avocations give them an opportunity of obtaining an insight into the present conditions of society. The medical profession appears conscious of the evil, and yet are fearful of admitting its existence. In hesitating to grapple with the common enemy, we allow it to obtain possession of the citadel. We are like soldiers sleeping at our posts, instead of being actively employed in watching for the first appearance of the foe. The stream is allowed to flow until it swells into a torrent, sweeping everything away that attempts to impede its progress. It is painful to contemplate the encroachments that this the most terrible of human afflictions is making among the ranks of the British aristocracy. It may be said that there is no public record of this fact, that the general and medical press are silent on the point. This may be the case, but it should be recollected that it is not in such channels that information relating to the increase of mental disease in the upper walks of life is to be obtained. Sufficient sources of information enable me to state as a fact, that the public is but little aware of the awful extent to which insanity has increased in England. Many causes operate in keeping the public mind ignorant of this fact. Insanity is supposed to cast a stigma, and leave a stain, on any noble or aristocratic family in which it may make its appearance; consequently, they are most desirous of concealing the existence of any such ailment when it unfortunately develops itself. The origin of the evil is to be sought for in that artificial state of society which grows necessarily out of constant advancement and civilization. We multiply our comforts, and by consequence our cares and crosses. We beat out and expand our minds as it were, and thus create a more extended surface for impression.

The *causes* of insanity do not always act directly on the brain; more frequently, on the contrary, they are preying on some organ at a distance; the nervous, sanguiferous or lymphatic systems, the digestive organs or the organs of generation, being the primary seats of the evil. M. Pinel the distinguished French physician and writer on this disease, before mentioned, refers the *immediate cause,* in almost every instance, to a deranged condition of the stomach, and other digestive organs. It is here he supposes the disease to commence, and contends that the affection of the brain, and of the mental faculties, is subsequent to the symptoms of internal irritation, and dependent upon them. This opinion in some degree corresponds with the results of my experience; we must not, however, lose sight of the influence of the congenital size of particular organs of the brain, and the augmentation of that size, in the production of insanity.

In order to render my opinion on this important point quite clear, I would add, that there appears to me the most substantial reason to believe, that mental derangement is mostly a symptom of disease in the brain, either slight or severe; but then that cerebral disease will be always much influenced by the patient's general health, so that if the person in whom there is cerebral disease pursues a proper course of living, and can have his digestive functions, and the secretions of other organs, brought into and kept in a healthy state, he will usually escape insanity. It is a fundamental principle, that the brain is the organ of the mind,—the mind never manifests itself in this world except through the instrumentality of this corporeal organ, and therefore the condition of this organ must always influence the quality of the mental manifestations; mental derangement is, therefore, a disordered state of the functions of the brain, arising from some existing diseased action in that organ, and also from considerable derangement in the functions of digestion.[1]

The disease is either continued, intermittent or remittent. A certain change in the countenance, with a sense of general lassitude; sleep; natural appetite; softness of skin; freedom of the secretions and excretions; and a return of moral feeling, are indicative of approaching recovery. This will be perfect, if, with the return of reason, the patient resumes his usual affections, habits, and general character. But if, on the other hand, the sleep, the appetite, the secretions and excretions, come back to their usual healthy standard, without a corresponding sanity of mind, the disease is likely to pass into a chronic state or fatuity itself.

Cures are affected in about one in three cases. It is in the first month that there is the greatest probability of success. It would appear that in the first two years of insanity, the greatest number of cures are performed. That the medium curable period is somewhat less than a year. That after the third year there is not above one in thirty cured. The most favourable epoch of life for

1. Dr. A. Combs's *Obser : on Mental Derangement* is a very able work, in which the reader will find this point, and many others of equal moment, treated in a masterly manner. At the same time I ought not to fail remarking, that this author is far too much disposed in his writings to magnify the weight and importance of *physical causes* in the production of certain effects, to the exclusion of *moral causes*. This is a very great error.

the cure of the disease is between the age of twenty and thirty. After fifty there is little chance. Madness is more frequently cured than melancholy.

In all mental aberrations, if bodily indisposition is not apparent, the chance of cure is hereby diminished.

It has long been a current opinion, that insanity is a disease more common to our own country than to any other, but it appears to have no solid foundation. Dr. Burrows, of London, has collected a great deal of information on this point, and he considers that the disease is not more frequent in England than in several of the neighbouring continental nations. From the table collected by Dr. Burrows it appears, that suicide is much more frequent in Paris, Berlin, and Copenhagen, than in London.

Madness

The *principal symptoms* are an altered and peculiar appearance of the eyes, protruding and wild; rapid and successive change of features; unusual vigour and uncommon agitation of the whole muscular powers; insusceptibility to extremes of heat and cold, and to the influence of contagious diseases; insensibility of the skin, stomach, and bowels, hence obstinate costiveness; absence of sleep; high bounding spirits; erroneous imagination, incessant talking, singing, shouting, etc.; obscene language and gestures; sometimes excruciating pain, denoted by frequent change of posture, heating the forehead, breasts, stomach, sides or belly; eructations of wind from the stomach of a very peculiar fetor; high coloured urine; delirium. The skin is dry, harsh and cold, sometimes with partial, cold, and clammy perspirations; breath hot and offensive; hurried respiration.

The most common period of attack is between the ages of eighteen and forty.

Madness very frequently terminates in the opposite form or melancholy. Chronic incurable derangement or fatuity, embraces a large proportion of its subjects.

The *causes* are detailed above and the distinction between this form of insanity and melancholy, may be readily perceived by comparing the symptoms of the one with those of the other.

TREATMENT—One of the first things to be done in all cases of insanity, under whatever form it may appear, is to separate the patient from his friends and home, as this separation is invariably conducive to recovery. Foreigners are more certainly cured in England than the natives; and strangers sent to Paris for treatment are more readily restored to reason than the inhabitants of that city.

The judicious exercise of the faculties conduces much to recovery. This must be done by exciting the patients' attention—by presenting new objects to their contemplation—by giving way, in some measure, to their hallucinations. If by these means their confidence can be gained, the probability of cure is much increased. The passions also must be carefully managed. The proud and rebellious passions and emotions must be tamed and kept in subjection, while the timid and melancholy are to be dissipated by encouragement. It is sometimes proper to substitute a real for an imaginary grievance. Suppose a melancholic is devoured with *ennui* in the midst of the pleasures and enjoyments of life—if we withdraw him from his usual habits, and impose on him real privations, he will then suffer real *ennui,* which will prove a powerful means of cure.

Travelling is often of extraordinary benefit; and so is active corporeal exercise. A farmer, at a distance from London, gained great repute for the cure of insanity, by taking his patients into the fields, and compelling them to draw the plough, a practice drat proved of much service. Every maniac should have constant employment, especially in gardening or agriculture.

The clothing should be warm and comfortable; and the food prevented from being devoured with voracity. In the majority of cases, a plain and regular course of living is essential. Patients accustomed to wine ought not to be wholly debarred from it. When the symptoms of indigestion exist, a suitable diet must be enforced. When exhaustion is apprehended from a long continuance of high excitement, the most nutritious food should be given.

A principal object in the medical treatment is to procure for the patient sound and refreshing sleep, and the endeavours should be directed towards insuring it for many nights consecutively. If it can be insured by exercise and regimen, they will be the best means, but if not, soporific medicines should be given, but no opium, except in the form of muriate of morphia. Camphor, extract of henbane, and James's powder, combined in large doses, is frequently a valuable form for the purpose.

> Take of camphor, from a scruple to half a drachm; spirit of wine, a few drops to dissolve the camphor; James's powder, six or eight grains; extract of henbane, twenty grains.—Mix and divide into five or six pills, to be taken about seven or eight o'clock. Or the whole may be put into wafer paper and swallowed.

Camphor alone, in large doses, has been highly extolled as a remedy in this disease; but it is still more efficacious in combination with henbane and hop, as in the following draught, to be taken at bed-time:

Take of Tincture of henbane	30	drops;
Tincture of hop	2	drachms;
Camphor	10	grains;
Syrup of orange peel	2	drachms;
Camphor mixture	1	ounce.

Mix for a draught.

The employment of soporifics is frequently called for in all mental affections, and is often found to be of the greatest service in relieving and curing the patient. If sleep can be artificially induced, the threatened affection may be sometimes retarded and even altogether prevented; and when it has actually established itself, the judicious application of a narcotic will frequently act as a charm. The muriate or hydrochlorate of morphia or the acetate of morphia, are the most valuable remedies we possess for calming excitement. The usual dose of either of these preparations is half a grain, mixed with extract of liquorice and given at bed-time. Dr. Seymour says, that he has had the opportunity of testing the efficiency of the acetate of morphia in numerous cases of insanity, characterized by a gloomy despon-dency, and a strong disposition to suicide. In suicidal cases, it seems to exercise an irresistible influence over the patients in preventing them from doing mischief, when fairly brought under its power.

When kept steadily under the influence of opium or other soporifics, the brain is rendered in some measure insensible to those morbid impressions, which have a constant tendency to disturb it. Though the patient may not be restored to reason, yet the irregular mental movements are much repressed and the proverbially cheering influence of the drug restrains the tumult of the feelings, and induces a better condition of the brain.

The following testimony to the value of chloroform in insanity is given by Dr. Henry Thompson, Visiting Physician to the Omagh District Lunatic Asylum :

> "I wish to add to the information already acquired on the subject of the internal administration of chloroform, as a narcotic and tranquilliser of the nervous system, that it has been used with marked advantage in the Omagh District Lunatic Asylum, in cases of insanity complicated with sleeplessness or rather noisy wakefulness, at night. In such cases we have been in the habit of giving it in dram doses, repeated if requisite and it has proved so much more efficacious than any of the other narcotics, that it has almost entirely superseded them. No unpleasant effects of any kind have been observed to follow its use. I was led to recommend it in these cases by experience of its value in delirium tremens, as suggested by Dar. Butcher some time ago, and I have now no hesitation in saying, that it is a perfectly safe and powerful remedy for conditions of the nervous system such as I allude to."

When the patient falls into convulsions, ammonia should be held near his nose, that he may inhale it, as it has considerable effect in removing the convulsions. It possesses another excellent power also, that of inducing patients to take their food.

Purgatives are of considerable use, especially those which act on the liver, and those which tend to produce the piles; such are combinations of calomel and jalap, and calomel with aloes. Four grains of calomel may be united with a scruple of extract of jalap or with eight or ten grains of aloes. Maniacs require large doses of purgatives. and sometimes more than what is now ordered will be necessary. The warm bath, at about ninety-six degrees, every other day; is likewise sometimes very useful, but the cold bath rarely so. When, however, the patient is young, robust, and complaining of internal heat, the cold bath may sometimes be beneficial. The cold shower-bath is often a very useful remedy.

Strong and repeated emetics are often very efficacious, especially when the sensibility is greatly diminished, and torpor prevails. Setons, issues or frequent blisters, are useful where there has been a sudden disappearance of some local disease, the head directly becoming affected. They are also indicated when there is apparent disease in the stomach, bowels, womb, etc. The extraction of a little blood occasionally, from the seat of pain, by means of leeches or cupping, may be useful; but the lancet should never be employed. The most experienced physicians strongly condemn it.

In insanity following child-bed or typhous fever, excessive bleeding or great fatigue, if great irritability is present, the bark will often be of the greatest service; but the bowels must be kept open at the same time, with small doses of the mixture, No. 74, page 176.

Swinging has been recommended by Dr. Cox, of Bristol and other practitioners. It appears more particularly useful in cases accompanied with high excitement, and after proper evacuation, by purging, etc. ; and in those which are fast verging to a chronic state.

Melancholy

The chief *symptoms* in a strongly marked case of melancholy are great apathy; obstinate disposition to dwell upon some mournful topic; sleeplessness; pertinacious silence, and other symptoms of morbid intensity of thought; the pupils of the eye dilated, with a peculiar dull muddy look, often employed in a fixed, unmeaning state or vacancy; general slight nervous thrilling of the muscular powers; anxious solicitude, and importance attached to frivolous inconveniences, especially regarding the sufferer's health; love of solitude; dread of death, and fear of eternal punishment. In general, there are well-marked symptoms of indigestion, such as pallid complexion, dull eye, languid circulation, loss of appetite, furred tongue, disturbed and restless nights, sometimes attended with fever, debility, frequent sighing. Frequently there is a relaxation of the scalp.

Melancholy rarely attacks young athletic persons. It is most common after forty.

The general *causes* have already been pointed out. Debility, with disorder of some important abdominal organ, as the stomach or intestinal canal or womb, is the usual foundation of this form of mental aberration.

For the symptoms *distinguishing* melancholy from hypochondriasis, see the latter article.

TREATMENT—The place of retreat and security should be light, airy, pleasant, and cheerful; and the same attention should be paid to the patient's cleanliness, and to the procuring of regular stools, and discharge of urine, as in the first form or madness.

The cure is to be attempted by enforcing regular and active exercise, and by the exhibition of mercurial alteratives, as the pill No. 99, page 192, every night, gentle emetics, purgatives, tonics, and soporifics; by morphia and proper moral management.[1] Gentle emetics of emetic tartar and ipecacuanha are particularly indicated,

---

1. "Drs. Duncan, Perfect, and Osiander, have strongly recommended the use of camphor in that form of melancholy and mental disturbance, which not unfrequently occurs during the period when the sexual feelings are developed. A more important remedy is the application of cold to the occiput and nape of the neck. Frequent ablutions with cold water is the simplest and most effectual method; occasionally, too, the local detraction of blood by leeches or the cupping-glasses, may be of great service."—*Johnson's Medico- Chirurgical Review,* No. xii, p. 213. A bladder of ice applied to the back part of the head and nape of the neck, is still more efficacious than cold water. If ice cannot be procured, the coldest water and vinegar mixed together, in the proportion of one-third vinegar and two-thirds water, should be used.

where there is such torpor of the abdominal viscera as shows oppression, rather than exhaustion of the vital powers. Constipation must be removed by a suitable aperient of colocynth, calomel, and James's powder, etc., as No. 97, page 191; and the aperients mast be so managed as simply to act as such from day to day, and not to debilitate. Sometimes, however, active purging with No. 74D, page 178, is more useful, as when the strength is little impaired. If there is an obstruction to the usual monthly discharge in women, a combination of aloes, assafoetida and James's powder, is particularly useful :

Take of Socotorine aloes, in powder	10	grains;
Assafoetida gum	10	grains;
James's powder	5	grains;

Mucilage of gum arabic, a sufficient quantity to form the whole into five pills.

Take three or four every night or every other night, so as to preserve the bowels in a regular state.

Tonic remedies will generally be required. Among the most useful tonics here are ipecacuanha, cascarilla bark, gentian, columba, and Peruvian bark. Cordials are also indicated, especially the aromatic spirit of ammonia. For prescriptions, see No. 79, 82 or 85, pages 181-85 or No. 104, 106, pages 197-98.

Soporofics are very beneficial, as it is of much consequence to ensure beneficial sleep; but opium must not be employed. Now and then we may with great advantage give a third or half of a grain of muriate of morphia. The best soporifics are camphor, extract of henbane and James's powder, and the tepid shower bath used just before going to bed.

Mild purgatives, and the extract of henbane, combined with camphor and sometimes with James's powder, are the most efficacious remedies in insanity following child-birth. As soon as they can be commenced, tonics are often of great service; one of the best is the carbonate of ammonia, given in an infusion of columba or cascarilla. Exercise should not be neglected.[1]

Local pain, and disturbance in the stomach, sides, belly or head, must be combated by frictions with the flesh-brush, by repeated blisters upon spots at a moderate distance and by the administration of the extract of hemlock.

The warm bath is sometimes a useful remedy. I believe it is said, that in the Retreat, near York, more benefit has been derived from the employment of this remedy than from any other.

The exercise should be of an active kind, and gestation in new bad roads is excellent. All employment should be as opposite as possible to former occupation and diametrically opposed to the ruling topic of conversation or of thought. All hurtful instruments must be removed. The diet should be the same as directed for madness, only in general somewhat more nutritious.

Travelling and constant employment are equally applicable in melancholy and in madness, and are worthy of the highest confidence.[2] It is remarkable how much the subject of travelling is disregarded in professed Treatises on Insanity. In one of the latest and most popular books on the subject no mention whatever is made of travelling; yet in point of fact it is generally of far more value than all other remedies put together. Even an entire change of place and society will frequently cure the patient, without travelling.

---

1. Dr. William Hunter, a very able midwifery practitioner of the last century, says, in referring to the insanity of women in childbed, " Mania is not an uncommon appearance in the course of the month, but of that species from which they generally recover. *When out of their senses, attended with fever, like paraphrenitis, they will is all probability die*; but when without fever, it is not fatal, though it (that is fever) generally takes place before they get well. I have had several private patients and have been called in when a great number of stimulating medicines and blisters have been administered, but they have gone on as at another time, talking nonsense, till the disease has gone off, and they have become sensible. It is a species of madness they generally recover from, but I know of nothing of any singular service in it." The meaning of Dr. Hunter is, that there are *two forms* of puerperal or child-bed insanity : one of them is attended by fever or rather by a rapid pulse; the other is accompanied by a very moderate disturbance of the circulation or no fever. Cases of the latter kind, which happily are by far the most frequent, terminate in recovery; the former are generally fatal, do what we will :—and this seems to be supported by the general observation of practitioners.
2. Boswell states, that Dr. Samuel Johnson observed to him, "employment and hardship prevent melancholy," an opinion in which he was perfectly correct.

Firmness on the part of the attendant, with conciliatory manners, has done wonders, but a sense of authority must be maintained; though occasional severity should be necessary for this purpose; yet it will rarely be needful to exceed the coercion of the strait waistcoat. The immediate attendant must learn to govern by wisdom rather than subdue by terror. Judicious conversation and cheering advice are also of great importance. In many cases, the cure mainly depends upon withdrawing the patient's mind as much as possible from every former scene and every former companion, in setting before him a new world and giving an entire change to the current of his recollections and ideas.

What is said at the end of the article on *Epilepsy* is applicable to the present afflictive malady, in whatever form it may manifest itself, and I would, therefore, direct the reader's attention to it, and especially to the recorded cases of cure from a recourse to the extraordinary means there alluded to.

ITCH

The itch is an eruption of minute pimples, attended with an intolerable itching, and terminating in scabs. The pimples may contain either a white or yellow matter (pus) or a thin watery fluid and these are frequently intermixed. The eruption is found chiefly between the fingers or in the flexures of the joints and is contagious.

As a *primary* disease, itch is, in every instance, the result of personal uncleanliness and an accumulation of sordes upon the skin, though the most cleanly are capable of receiving it by contact; and it always appears most readily where close air, meagre diet, and little exercise, are companions of personal filth. In camps and prisons, where the constitution has been debilitated by confined air and innutritious diet, the eruption has sometimes been known to assume a malignant character.

Some very able physicians have considered the presence of insects to be the sole cause of itch, but I believe them to be the effect and not the cause of the disease, as all stagnant fluids sometimes generate microscopic animals; and this is the general opinion among medical men. Such insects are not always to be traced in this complaint, but are undoubtedly to be seen occasionally.

Treatment—The remedy which has been employed with the greatest success in the cure of this disease is sulphur, which is made into an ointment with hog's lard, and rubbed over the infected part every night. The sulphur ointment sold by the druggists may be used in this way and washed off in the morning; a few such applications being, in general, sufficient to cure the disease. The following is a very efficacious ointment, which may be employed in the same way as the simple sulphur ointment.

Take of Sulphur, bay-berries, in powder	
sulphate of zinc, of each	2 drachms;
Essence of bergamot	10 or 20 drops;

Olive oil, a sufficient quantity to make an ointment.

These are the safest and most effectual applications. But when it is impracticable to employ them, the following lotion is recommended.

Take of Muriated quicksilver	half a drachm;
Water	1 pint;
Sal ammoniac	2 drachms;
Purified nitre	half an ounce.

Mix. The hands are to be washed with this solution night and morning and a little of it is to be applied with a clean sponge to the pustules and other parts.

If it be practicable, a warm bath may be advantageously taken every other day till the patient is well. And when the constitution has been influenced, aperient medicines, as No. 73 or 74, will also be necessary and ought not to be neglected. Sulphur taken internally is often highly advisable.

JAUNDICE

Jaundice is characterized by yellowness of the eyes and skin, whitish or clay-coloured stools, and dark saffron-coloured urine, which communicates a saffron dye.

It comes on with languor, inactivity, loss of appetite, bitter taste in the mouth, lowness of spirits, and costiveness or looseness. As it advances in its progress, the skin and eyes become tinged of a deep yellow; there is a sense of heat and pricking in the skin; nausea; vomiting; sense of uneasiness or pain in the bowels and towards the right side and other symptoms of indigestion. The stools are of a clay-colour or white or very dark; the pulse is generally slow, yet sometimes, especially where the pain is acute, it becomes quick and hard and there is a feverish heat and dryness of the skin. It may be distinguished from disease of the renal capsules by the means pointed out under *Bronzed Skin.*

The disease, when of long continuance and proceeding from a chronic affection of the liver or other neighbouring abdominal organs, is often attended with dropsical swellings and sometimes with dropsy of the belly.

Jaundice is of two kinds, *viz.,* the yellow and the green. In the first kind, the skin and the white of the eyes are more or less tinged of a yellow colour; in the second kind, the skin and the white of the eyes are tinged of a green colour, more or less mixed with yellow, but the green colour is very predominant. In some parts of the skin the green colour is very deep, so as to have some blackness in its hue· aid this circumstance has given rise to the name of black jaundice, by which this form of the disease has been often distinguished.

The green jaundice by no means occurs so frequently as the yellow jaundice. It is most common at the middle and more advanced periods of life, and appears more frequent in men than in women. It is in general more difficult of cure than the yellow jaundice.

The *most frequent causes* are, the pressure of biliary calculi, (or stones) in the gall-bladder, and its ducts; spasmodic constriction of the ducts themselves; pressure upon the ducts; either by collections of hardened excrement or by tumours of the neighbouring organs or swelling of the glands; redundant secretion of bile; general and severe disorder of the intestines and other digestive organs. Costiveness and loaded bowels is a frequent cause and disease of the right kidney or even of the right lung, may give rise to it. The complaint is often closely connected with irritation in the internal surface of the intestines and the liver may be but inconsiderably affected. Diminished circulation of blood in the liver, arising in some cases from disease in the lungs or heart, is a cause.

An irregular or sedentary mode of living will produce it, especially continued indulgence in spirituous liquors. Great mental agitation will cause it in those disposed to it.

The *immediate cause* is the absorption of bile into the vascular system, by which means it is mixed with the blood and circulates with it.

TREATMENT—The principal objects of treatment are, to allay irritation in the intestinal canal, and to remove the obstruction existing to the free passage of the bile through the biliary ducts and along the intestines. It will be frequently found that the best means of allaying irritation in these parts will be the most effectual in removing the jaundice. The most powerful means for this purpose consists in the use of a warm bath., with purgatives occasionally, as No. 73, 74 or 74A or 74C, page 176-77 or mild aperients regularly, soap and other alkaline medicines, stomachic bitters, very mild mercurial alteratives and the Cheltenham or Bath waters, particularly the former.

The patient should take a warm bath at ninety-six or seven degrees, every other morning about eleven o'clock, with the following pills during the day.

Take of Castile soap	1½	drachm;
Rhubarb, in powder	8	grains;
Ipecacuanha, in powder	10	grains

Oil of juniper .... 10 drops;

Syrup of orange peel, a sufficient quantity to make the whole into twenty-four pills, three to be taken, twice or thrice a day.

At the same time the warm stomachic pill, No. 100 or 101, pages 193-94, should be taken every other night or as frequently as is necessary, to preserve the bowels in a free laxative state, without their being purged. Or when there is a good deal of pain in the bowels, the following opening pill may be used instead.

Take of Compound extract of colocynth, ... 1 drachm;

Extract of henbane, ... 1 drachm.

Mix, and divide into twenty-four pills, one, two or three to be taken as above directed.

Gentle purging with the neutral salts is often most beneficial; and the aperient waters of Cheltenham or Leamington, are of singular service. If they cannot be obtained, one drachm of both the Epsom and Glauber's salt (or even half a drachm of each) may be dissolved in half a pint of lukewarm water, and taken every morning for a fortnight; and resumed for another fortnight or three weeks, after being laid aside for a week. The mild relaxation occasioned by these small doses of salts and by the Cheltenham waters, does not generally produce debility; on the contrary, they are sensibly invigorating, for they have a blood-restoring power. Dr. Baillie states, that he has found the practice of keeping up the gentle action on the bowels, by means of the neutral salts, to be very useful in green jaundice. Dr. Budd recommends the mixture No. 74D, page 178, and it is an excellent prescription; but in cases where the patient is not robust, with a strong pulse, I believe that one dose a day, that is, before breakfast, will be better than twice a day. The patient should feel his way in this.

The infusion of columba or compound infusion of gentian, are sometimes beneficial stomachics, for use during the day.

Many have a notion that mercury is always necessary for the cure of jaundice, which is a great and pernicious error. If it increase the secretion without removing the obstruction, it must injure the liver; and in all cases, I object to it except in small doses, as an alterative, as in No. 98 or 98A.

Where there appears a good deal of obstinate obstruction about the organs affected, the compound calomel pill, No. 98 or 117, page 203, should be taken every night, in conjunction with the above remedies. It ought to be cautiously taken when the liver is evidently indurated or enlarged. And when the local pain is not acute, a gentle emetic of ipecacuanha powder, about once a week, will be advisable.

The preceding means will generally succeed in curing jaundice, and are very safe; but I have some confidence in raw eggs, and if the patient prefers trying this simple remedy first, he cannot be said to act unwisely. The late Charles White, a surgeon of eminence and ability, at Manchester, held the use of raw eggs in great estimation, and makes the following sensible remarks on the subject, in his *Treatise on the Management of Lying-in-Women,* p.74, third editions, 1785.

> "It is not improbable that the temporary jaundice to which women with child, new-born infants, and even adults of both sexes are frequently subject, owes its origin to the stoppage of the mouth of the *ductus communis choledochus,*[1] (the duct which carries the bile into the intestines), by some tenacious gluten obstructing either totally or in part, the passage of the bile into the duodenum, and thereby occasioning its return into the blood. The attention I have paid to jaundiced patients of both sexes and of every age, who have been cured by frequently taking raw eggs in cold spring water, has inclined me much to this opinion. My supposition is, that eggs act as a dissolvent of the gluten which obstructs the mouth of the duct, thereby opening a free passage for the bile into the duodenum. We know that yolks of eggs will destroy the tenacity of gums and resins, and render not only them, but also oils and natural balsams, miscible with water.
>
> "The first trial I had of this remedy, was upon myself about fourteen years ago, when I had been afflicted with the jaundice for many

1. An engraving in the Author's publication On The Diseases of Women displays this duct very clearly.

weeks and was much reduced, no bile having for a long time passed into the intestines, when my skin was almost black, and after I had in vain taken large quantities of soap, madder, steel, rhubarb and aloetic medicines. An officer of marines told me that if he might be allowed to prescribe, he would immediately cure me. I laughed at his proposal; when he informed me that some years before, in the Mediterranean, he was troubled with the same disorder, to as great a degree as myself and that after he had ineffectually tried all the remedies the surgeon of the ship could think of, a Spanish physician at Minorca, had assured him he could cure him in a few days, by this simple prescription only—two raw eggs, the whites as well as yolks, to be taken every morning in a glass of water, fasting, with the addition of an egg every four hours during the day. That in three days after following this advice, he began to perceive the bile in his stools, though none had appeared in them for many weeks before; that he immediately began to recover, and was very soon effectually cured. Upon considering the dissolvent property of yolks of eggs, and that eggs must, at least, afford a nourishment totally void of acrimony, I began to entertain a more favourable opinion of the recipe."

"I tried it, and found it had exactly the same effect which he had promised me. Though I was certain no bile had passed through me for six weeks before, upon taking the eggs only three days,.it began to flow, and in only one day more, in as great plenty as I could wish. I continued, however, to take them several months and have never since had any return of the disorder."

"I have recommended the use of them to many persons under the same complaint and have always had the satisfaction of finding their success, except in cases where the disorder was occasioned by a diseased liver or by stones in the gall bladder."

In two instances of the most obstinate and long protracted jaundice, where the patients were reduced to skeletons, and the skin for many months the colour of mahogany, inspisated ox-gall produced the best effects. It tinged the motions, lessened the irritability of the stomach, increased the peristaltic action of the bowels, and in both instances recovery ultimately took place, after all hopes had been abandoned both by physicians and friends.

The Bath waters have been much recommended, and will be sometimes very serviceable, especially where the disease has originated from too free an indulgence in spirituous liquors or a residence in a tropical climate.

Where there is a great deal of torpidity about the biliary ducts, which is unaffected by other remedies, electricity promises to be of much service. A few slight shocks may be passed daily in the coarse of these ducts.

When the disease originates in positive disease of the liver or other abdominal organ, only the means recommended under the head of LIVER COMPLAINT can succeed. Should obstinate costiveness, and accumulated excrement, be the cause, the purgative clyster, No. 8, page 146, must be frequently admi-nistered, with purgatives by the mouth, warm fomentations, and the warm bath.

For the relief of acute pain in the pit of the stomach and bowels, the most efficient remedies are hot fomentations, warm emollient clysters of gruel and oil, and pills of opium and hemlock or dry cupping. A gain of opium may be united with six or eight grains of extract of hemlock, and given every three or four hours, if the pain be owing to spasm which it commonly is. If inflammation be present, bleeding, of course, must be resorted to.

The warm bath, warm fomentations to the abdomen and gentle aperient medicine, are means applicable to every case of jaundice, from whatever cause it may arise.

The bitter-sweet (*dulcamara*) has been praised for its excellent effects in this disease and as it is, without doubt, a powerful medicine in many cases, I think it worthy of some confidence in jaundice. If the foregoing means fail in affording satisfactory relief, it may be tried with much propriety in the following manner : Infuse a pound and a half of bitter-sweet in two bottles of white mountain wine, over a very slow fire, for seven or eight hours, then, after removing it from the fire and allowing it to become cold, press the bitter-sweet as dry as possible and strain it for use. The plant should, if possible, be of the last year's growth, and fresh gathered; and it should be cut into pieces of four or five inches long, and every piece beat flat, before it is infused in the wine. The dose is a quarter of a pint every morning, fasting. During the use of this medicine, the urine of the patient should be examined daily and when it ceases to deposit a sediment, the dose of the infusion should be decreased to one-third and in a few. days left off. This is said to have been employed, in numerous instances of severe jaundice, with complete success.

The nitro-muriatic acid bath has been recommended as a valuable remedy for jaundice, as well as for all other severe diseases in which the biliary organs are principally concerned. It certainly has great power in allaying irritation in the digestive organs, and is, therefore, deserving a trial, where the preceding means fail. It may be used in the way directed at page 107.

Should the disease assume a scorbutic form, the administration of the vegetable and mineral acids, as advised under scurvy, must make a part of the general treatment.

In all cases, daily exercise is useful, and should be used freely, but short of much fatigue. Horse exercise is particularly advisable. The diet should be mild, but sufficiently nutritious, being regulated by the principles laid down under INDIGESTION.

Occasionally, infants are attacked with- jaundice soon after birth, which will generally yield to a dose of castor oil or any other active purgative. When a purge is not sufficient to remove it, an emetic of ipecacuanha wine will be advisable and effectual.—*See* my book ON INFANCY AND CHILDHOOD.

Many persons who have resided long in a hot climate, contract a sallow, yellowish complexion, which hue often pervades the whole skin; this is generally regarded as a mild sort of jaundice or as arising from the absorption of bile, but it is usually of a different nature. In most instances, it is not owing to this cause, but to a peculiar alteration in the capillary[1] circulation on the external surface of the body, in consequence of the skin's sympathizing with a weakened and irritated condition of the digestive organs, more especially of the stomach and bowels. "These organs, at all times, exert a marked and powerful influence on the skin;—when

1. The capillaries are the minute blood vessels acid absorbents.

they are in health and performing their functions with energy, we find the skin soft and smooth; when they are disordered and weakened, it is uniformly harsh, dry and unpleasant :—and as the exhausting effects of sultry climates greatly enervate the digestive canal, in this we see a sufficient reason for the sallow, rough and unhealthy condition of the skin, so often witnessed in persons lately returned from a tropical region. Such a state of the skin and liver is most safely and effectually removed by a strong decoction of dandelion or by sarsaparilla powders, with a mercurial alterative twice a week, as No. 98A, page 192, and a warm bath at ninety-six degrees occasionally. The saline waters of Cheltenham, Leamington and Harrowgate, are frequently of the greatest service.

LEPROSY

Leprosy is a scaly disease of the skin, which is rare in this country, but not unfrequent in sultry climates. It is frequently met with in Egypt and the countries bordering upon it. There are three or four varieties of it, the mild sort being incapable of communication, while the most severe are certainly contagious.

The leprosy appears in the form of white scales, of a circular form, preceded by reddish and glossy elevations of the skin and encircled with a red border. The scales may be either dull-white, dusky or livid or glossy-white.

It is produced chiefly by cold; moisture; great heat and uncleanliness combined; excessive fatigue, combined with a low and precarious diet.

Treatment—Warm bathing is useful in all cases of leprosy, and in general, the Harrowgate waters, whether applied externally or internally, are of much service. The hemlock dropwort has likewise been highly spoken of, and the tincture of cantharides; but the most active and salutary medicine is arsenic : it will, however, require great caution in its use. As external applications, either the tar ointment or the ointment of nitrated mercury undiluted or equal harts of tar ointment and diluted ointment of nitrated mercury, (No. 89, page 188), may be rubbed into the parts affected every night and carefully washed off the next morning with warm water. Kreosote may, in some cases, be still more useful as a lotion, mixed with water. Glycerine may be tried.

In mild cases, the cure may be safely trusted to the external use of one of these ointments and the warm bath, with the administration internally of the Harrowgate or any other sulphureous mineral water, the bowels being kept regular by a mild pill, (No. 100, 100A or 101, pages 193-94,) and the diet such as is calculated to nourish and strengthen.

In the severer examples, two or three tea-spoonfuls of the juice of the hemlock drop-wort or one or two table-spoonfuls of a strong infusion of the leaves, may be taken every morning. Or from five to six drops of the arsenical solution may be tried twice or thrice a day. It is best borne on a full stomach; but both these medicines must be very cautiously used. The warm bath, and one of the ointments just notice must be employed at the same time.

LIVER COMPLAINT

By liver complaint I mean congestion, slow inflammation or some other more or less positive disease, of a chronic character, in the structure of that viscus.

The most frequent *symptoms* are, a sense of weight or uneasiness in the right side; pain at the top of the shoulder; sallow complexion; impaired or capricious appetite; irregular bowels and discoloured offensive motions; progressive emaciation and debility; a quick, regular pulse, and a dusky yellowish complexion. The pain is generally much increased on pressure below the ribs of the side affected; a sudden jerk, from a false step or other accident, occasions acute pain in the right side; there is, for the most part, some degree of cough with expectoration; the breading is sometimes difficult and oppressed; the urine is high coloured and scanty; and the patient cannot, in general, lie on the left side. Sometimes there is an enlargement to be felt on manual examination, under the false ribs on the right side.

Whatever greatly weakens and disorders the stomach and liver or impairs the general health, may lay the foundation of disease in the liver. It is most frequently induced by the exhausting and deleterious influence of a sultry climate; combined with the excesses so commonly indulged in by European residents, in such regions; by anxiety of mind; excessive use of mercury or of ardent spirits; insufficient exercise and sedentary occupations. It is not unfrequently met with as a sequel of acute inflammation in the organ. A frequent immediate cause of congestion of the liver is obstruction to a free passage of the blood through the right side of the heart.

The term *liver complaint* is far too indiscriminately employed. It is properly applied to designate some kind of disease in the texture of the liver; but the majority of the maladies called by, that name are in reality severe disorders of the digestive canal, that is, chronic derangement of the stomach or intestines.

Liver complaints may generally be *distinguished* from severe disorder of the functions of the stomach or intestinal canal, by the slow but progressive emaciation and loss of muscular strength present, by the fixed character of the malady,—the quick, but regular pulse—the scanty urine—and the continued pain or uneasiness in the right side and shoulder. In functional disorder of the digestive canal, on the contrary, the loss of flesh is not often so great and never progressive; the complaint frequently varies; the pulse is generally irregular, slow and sometimes intermitting; and the uneasiness felt in the abdomen is chiefly about the pit of the stomach or in the bowels.

TREATMENT—The unthinking and less skilful, part of the profession almost universally agree, that mercury, is here the "fit and only remedy," and in general they scruple not to prescribe it very freely; but those whose experience and judgment are to be depended on, are very cautious in the employment of that mineral, and place little reliance on it in the treatment of this disease, when uncombined with other medicines, and a correct diet and regimen. Notwithstanding, mercury, when judiciously prescribed as an alterative, in small doses, and in conjunction with antimony and now and then opium, is sometimes very beneficial and seldom hurtful; but salivation is invariably to be avoided, at least in this country. In tropical climates, this remedy may be carried to a greater extent in treating the present disease, not only without injury, but with advantage; yet even in such a situation I think much mischief is often produced by its incautious employment, in consequence of practitioners considering its utility to be nearly proportionate to the quantity speedily introduced into the system and from their forgetting that diseases of a chronic character which are slow in their progress, can never be cured quickly or by violent measures. When calomel or any other mercurial preparation, is employed in liver complaints, it should be admi–stered in such small doses as relieve pain and irritation, without very sensibly affecting the constitution in any other way.[1] With thin view, the pill, No. 98, or 99, or Plummer's pill, No. 117, page 203, may be taken every other night, with a saline aperient, as No. 74C, page 177, every morning, and a stomachic or the dandelion, in the day. Half a drachm of both Epsom and Glauber's salts in chilled water, every morning, is an admirable aperient and alterative. The stomachic mixture, No. 82, page 183, will sometimes prove useful. As auxiliaries to this plan, a warm bath at ninety-five degrees twice a week, an occasional blister over the region of the liver or a seton in the side, with change of air and scene; and the diet and regimen recommended for Indigestion, will be very proper and beneficial. Frequently, the alkaline solution (page 2) may be taken in the day as a tonic, with much advantage.

The dandelion (*see* page 54) is a more useful medicine here than mercury. A man aged about 46, living at Wallington, in this neighbourhood, had felt uneasiness in the right side for several years; about two years since it increased to actual pain, which being

1. Some persons are extremely sensible to the influence of mercury on their system, and when we do not know the constitution of the individual, we should always commence with the smallest doses. The extreme sensibility of some persons under the action of mercury is forcibly illustrated by the following fact :— A patient has been known to regulate his hepatic system, whenever there was a deficiency of bile in his motions, by taking, asses, milk medicated by giving the animal a certain quantity of the nitrate of mercury. The effect was very marked and he could bear no mercury in any other shape.

accompanied with a quick hard pulse, loss of flesh and considerable debility, caused him to relinquish his employment. All the symptoms concurred in proving this disease to be a severe liver complaint. Many means were tried for many months; as bleeding, cupping, mercurial alteratives, blistering, mild aperients, stomachics, etc., but they proved no remedies to him; at length we advised him to take a teacupful of a strong decoction of dandelion, twice a day, and to lay aside all other medicines. He did so, and I saw him no more as a patient; it succeeded to admiration in relieving and restoring him.[1]

The mineral acids, particularly the nitric acid, are sometimes of great benefit in this disease. After the above plan has been persevered in for two or three months, or more, if necessary and the mercurial pill has been laid aside, twenty, thirty or forty drops of the diluted nitric acid may be taken, three times a day, in water or infusion of cascarilla and whether the preceding remedies have been useful or not, these drops will be proper and often serviceable.

As aperients, the saline water of Cheltenham and Leamington are, undoubtedly, employed with superior advantage and often with striking benefit. Therefore, when it is convenient for the patient to resort to them, they should be substituted for the draught, No. 27, noticed above. The Chelenham and Leamington salts are no better than Glauber's salt.—*See* page 38.

The waters of Buxton or Malvern Wells are also valuable in this disease, and when the patient's means allow, he may, frequently go from Cheltenham or Leamington to the waters of Buxton or Malvern Wells with increasing benefit. The Harrowgate water is likewise deserving of confidence.

The late Dr. Scott, of Russell Square, who practised many years in India, has recommended the nitro-muriatic acid bath as a valuable remedy in liver complaints ; and although it has met with a good deal of opposition in some quarters, I am persuaded from personal experience that, in some cases of this disease, it will produce very

1. Dr. James Johnson says, (Medico-Chirurgical Review, Jan., 1829). "The more the dandelion is employed, the more certain proofs will it afford of its utility." But I do not approve of its being united with soda, a too common practice.

beneficial effects, and be more useful than mercury in any form and than almost any other remedy.—*See* page 107.

In the present case, leeches are frequently applied to the region of the liver, but I think, without satisfactory results, unless the tension and pain are very considerable and the other remedies fail to remove these symptoms.

One of the most important diseases of the liver is the *bees'-wax liver,* in which it is yellowish, pale and puckered, technically called *cirrhosis.* It is frequently produced by spirit drinking and is the effect of deep-seated adhesive inflammation in the substance of the organ, and involving the branches of the great veins of the liver. The principal *symptoms* are, considerable sallowness, yellowness of the white of the eyes, feverishness, dull pain in the right side, scanty urine, indigestion, dark or clay-coloured stools and symptoms of dropsy. It is essentially of slow growth, a chronic affection, in the first instance induced by the effusion of lymph in the substance of the organ, which ultimately contracts. Whatever stimulates the liver in an extreme degree tends to produce it, such as long continued exposure to heat, a very stimulating diet, confined air, and want of exercise. It is likely to be followed by the known results of obstructed circulation through the liver, such as scanty urine, bleeding piles, bleeding from the nose, and dropsy of the belly and lower limbs.

The best *remedies* are, a quiet country life, sufficient daily exercise (page 345-49), a carefully regulated diet, dandelion and an occasional dose *of Dr. Budd's remedy for jaundice,* No. 74D. The nitro-muriatic acid internally or employed externally as a bath, is also clearly indicated. If dropsy supervenes, the means recommended under that head ought to be employed.

LUMBAGO

Lumbago means rheumatism of the loins. Its causes and general treatment are laid down under the article *Rheumatism;* but as it is necessary, in a popular work, to be as clear and explicit as possible in giving directions for the cure of every form of this disease, I shall say a little here on those remedies which seem more especially applicable to this variety of rheumatic affection.

One of the most efficacious plans for the cure of severe lumbago, is to take the *guaiacum mixture*, No. 72C, page 175, or fifty or sixty drops of the ammoniated tincture of guaiacum, in milk and water, three times a day; to rub the liniment, No. 45, page 163, into the parts affected, morning, noon, and night and to take one or two of the aperient pills, No. 100 or 101, pages 194-95, every other evening, so as to keep the bowels regular without purging them. A warm bath at ninety-six degrees should likewise be taken every other morning; and the diet should be nutritious and easy of digestion, as directed for INDIGESTION.

Should this plan fail, from a scruple to half a drachm of Peruvian bark, in powder, or two grains of sulphate of quinine made into a pill, may be taken thrice a day and one of the alterative pills, No. 98, or 99, page 192, every other night; the bowels being kept free from confinement by the above aperient pills and the liniment and warm bath employed as just directed. If the bark disagree, it may be changed for a strong bitter infusion, as No. 82 or 83, pages 183-84 the pills No. 104.

Now and then lumbago is particularly obstinate and severe. In such instances, the external use of the warm waters of Buxton are frequently an admirable remedy, with which may be conjoined the alterative pill, No. 98, or 99 or the opiate pill, No. 109 and constant friction over the loins, either with the flesh brush or the liniment, No. 39 or 41, page 161.

In such examples, I advise a trial of *blue, flannel*, several times dyed. It is worn round the loins like other flannel. It is sometimes perfectly curative, and may be had at W. Hamper's, 116, Newgate Street, London.

Should the pain be urgent, one of the best and most efficacious medicines for its relief is the compound powder of ipecacuanha, and camphor, three or four grains of each of which, made into two pills, may be taken occasionally. It will not interfere with the effects of any other medicine. Or a dose of the powder, No. 124 A, page 206, may be taken. The pills of calomel, tartar emetic, and guaiacum, prescribed in No. 98, page 191, are likewise excellent.

Some persons are too apt to let blood in severe lumbago; but it rarely fails to render the disease still more intractable.

MEASLES

The measles is an infectious fever attended with an eruption on the skin, which very rarely attacks the same person a second time.

The patient for the first day generally complains of alternate heats and chills, and the other feelings usually preceding an attack of fever; on the second day, though sometimes not till the third, the fever is completely formed. Much thirst is now complained of, often accompanied with nausea and sometimes with vomiting; the tongue is generally white and moist; there are pains of the head, back and loins; the face is flushed; the pulse frequent and hard and the breathing hurried. The patient is early attacked with a dry cough and hoarseness; the eyes are red, swelled, itchy, very sensible to light and watery : the nose is inflamed and often discharges a copious thin secretion. There is generally some remission of the *symptoms* in the morning, but they return in the evening with increased severity. In the more alarming cases, there are spasms of the limbs, sometimes delirium, but more frequently a lethargic stupor.

The eruption generally shows itself towards the end of the third or the beginning of the fourth day; sometimes not till the fifth. It comes out on the forehead in small points, which are generally distinct at first, but here and there increasing in number and size, are soon formed into small clusters, so that the face seems marked with red stars of various size and figure. The parts occupied by the points are rough to the touch. From the face the eruption gradually spreads to the neck, breast, trunk and limbs, generally appearing on the limbs the day after it shews itself on the face. The stains on the face continue red for two days, on the third they assume a brownish colour, and, in the course of the fifth or at most the sixth, that is about the eighth or ninth day of the disease, the redness on the face nearly disappears, although traces of it often remain for four or five days longer.

There is generally a considerable tendency to inflammation throughout the whole course of the measles and those parts are most subject to it which are most apt to be inflamed in common cold, the eyes, the nose, throat, and lungs. The inflammation of the eyes, nose, and throat is usually of little consequence; it seldom becomes very troublesome and declines with the other symptoms. The inflammation of the lungs may come on at any period, but is most frequent after the eruption is gone off.

Its consequences are often troublesome. Most frequently they are, the various forms of scrophula, as glandular tumours, wasting from obstruction in the mesenteric glands of the belly, obstinate sores, a weak and inflamed state of the eyes and pulmonary consumption. A moisture of the skin at the appearance of the eruption; early and free expectoration; moderate looseness, and mild fever, are favourable symptoms.

The *grand cause,* in every instance, is a specific contagion.[1]

The symptoms by which the eruptive fever of measles is *distinguished* from small pox and other diseases, are the dry cough and hoarseness; the sneezing and discharge from the nose; and the appearance of the eyes, which are red, swelled, itchy, very sensible to light, and frequently loaded with tears; but now and then the symptoms of scarlet fever and measles so run one into the other, that it is impossible to say to which disease the case belongs. As it regards treatment this is of no consequence, ammonia being the best remedy in both complaints.

---

1. When a number of children are living in the same house where the measles is present, as in boarding schools, poor houses, etc., it is of much moment to be acquainted with the means of preventing the spread of the contagion, and I would here recommend the free use of the chloride of soda or lime, or Condy's Fluid, as a safe and effectual antidote. The manner of using them at page 282. M. Labarraque, of Paris, says that he witnessed a satisfactory instance in which the infection arising from measles, which had occurred in a boarding school, had been perfectly arrested without the removal of any of the pupils, by the employment of these chlorides. And M. Lisfrarñc, surgeon in chief of the hospital la Piéty, in Paris, has fully ascertained that the air of wards where small-pox patients are confined, no longer communicates the disease, whilst daily sprinklings with these solutions are employed. But it must not be forgotten, that the use of these chlorides ought never to supersede free ventilation.

TREATMENT—In mild cases, the object of treatment is, to promote a gentle perspiration, and a free expectoration, which is most certainly secured by ammonia, with diluting drinks, and a spare low diet. In simple cases, it is a great point not to do much, but to leave the main work to the natural efforts of the system, aided by the ordinary doses of the sesqui-carbonate of ammonia every four hours. It should always be given, even in the mildest cases. Give three grains, in water, every four hours, to a child of eight years old. The best medicine in measles is *sesqui-carbonate of ammonia,* and under its use I question if we ever see great difficulty of breathing supervene or any other symptoms of inflammation of the lungs. Ammonia, from its power to neutralize poisonous matter in the blood and to promote healthy cutaneous secretions, attacks this disease at its root and thus prevents the accession of the worst symptoms, as I have fully explained under *Scarlet Fever.* I believe this volatile alkali to be more efficacious, even in the worst cases of measles, than all other means united; and no one need hesitate in domestic practice to resort to it. It is as safe as it is successful.

Some physicians of great ability recommend an emetic, No. 29, page 156, as always useful on the incursion of the disease, and it is worthy of attention. After it has operated, the purgative medicine, No. 28, page 156, may be given and repeated every day, if necessary, so as to preserve the bowels in a lax state. The diluting drinks recommended in inflammation, such as barley-water, tamarind tea, and the like, should be taken freely; and all animal food and fermented liquors must be avoided. All the drink should be tepid, and the patient confined to a warm chamber.

We must bear in mind this principle—*that in cases of a mild and regular character, the less we interfere with the operations of nature the better.* Even when the general fever is considerable, during the period of eruption, purgatives and bloodletting are not only generally unnecessary, but often decidedly injurious, provided no local inflammation be present. The eruption is a sort of critical deposition on the surface, by which the animal economy endeavours to relieve itself from some internal morbid irritation.

But when the symptoms are severe, and there is a good deal of pain in the chest, and difficulty of breathing, blood-letting must be resorted to, as, in addition to the object to be fulfilled in mild cases, we have here to prevent or remove inflammation in the chest. It is seldom, however, that these symptoms come on till the eruption is gone off, and the abstraction of blood should never be resorted to early in the disease, unless it be clearly necessary.[1] Under the circumstances just stated, of great difficulty of breathing and an unusually hard pulse, in a child of ten years old, from four to six ounces of blood should be taken from the arm and if these symptoms continue little or not at all relieved by the first evacuation, cupping between the shoulders should be had recourse to the same extent. The application of leeches to the chest is often advisable in addition to the general bleeding. And after the loss of blood a blister should be applied over the chest; the purgative and saline medicines (No. 78B), with diluting drinks, and a low diet, being resorted to as just advised. In the severer forms the diet, of course, must be very spare and low, and the purgative medicine may be administered a little more freely than is necessary under the milder attacks. In such acute cases as we now advert to, in which inflammation of the lungs is to be suspected, I am partial to the use of the mixture No. 78B, page 180, believing it to be most efficacious.

With regard to exercise, if the patient finds himself inclined from the commencement to remain in bed, he should not be prevented; at the same time, there is no occasion to confine him to it against his inclination. In all cases, towards the period of the eruption he feels fatigued, and averse to motion. Whether he be in bed or not, extremes of heat and cold are equally to be avoided. In every case, the room in which the patient is confined should be large and airy, and free from currents of cold. Free exposure to cold is highly serviceable in small-pox, and therefore, some medical men have recommended it in measles; but the testimony of a great majority of the medical profession is decidedly against it. On

1. "As this fever," Dr. Cullen remarks, "is sometimes violent before the eruption, though a sufficiently mild disease be to follow, so bleeding is seldom very necessary during the eruptive fever, and may often be reserved for the periods of greater danger, which are, perhaps, to ensue."

account of the cough always present in this disease and there being a great tendency to inflammation of the lungs, cold must in all cases be carefully guarded against. If the cough be troublesome, it will be useful to breathe the steam of warm water, not through an inhaler, but over a large basin, with the head covered with a flannel large enough to hang over its edges; and by this means the inflamed eyes will also have the benefit of the relaxing vapour.

If the oppression of the chest, pain, and hard pulse, should return, as they are apt to do, on the disappearance of the eruption, blood-letting or cupping must again be had recourse to, however freely they may have been employed antecedently.

Opium should never be given to relieve the cough, as it generally fails in effecting this object, and always increases the fever and restlessness. One of the best cough medicines is a little of the mixture, No. 78D, page 181, or No. 78C.

A spontaneous looseness proves the most favourable crisis. When moderate, it should not be interfered with and even when it appears excessive, only the mildest astringents should be given in small doses, so as to lessen, but not altogether remove it. A few grains of tormentil powder, with or without ipecacuanha, is perhaps the best medicine for this purpose. *See* pages 522-23. The abstraction of a little blood, however, in severe diarrhoea is sometimes of immediate and great utility.

In case the measles should suddenly disappear, endeavours should be immediately resorted to in order to restore the eruption to the skin. The patient must be placed in a warm bath and four or five grains of sesqui-carbonate of ammonia, in water, given every hour. If this is not sufficient, blisters may be applied to the inside of the thighs or legs, and to the chest, and a little warm wine diluted with water be given frequently.

Now and then the progress of the measles is irregular, and the symptoms malignant, the fever terminating early in typhus. In such instances, the best medicines are ammonia and wine. If the oppression of the chest be considerable, blisters should be applied. The tartar emetic ointment, rubbed on the chest, may be sometimes still more beneficial; or a mustard poultice, quickened with oil of turpentine, and applied to the chest, may prove of the greatest service when there are symptoms denoting inflammation within the chest, and the debility at the same time to great too admit of bleeding.

Some of the most troublesome consequences of measles is a hoarseness, cough, shortness of the breath, and inflammation of the ayes. They are all best removed by ammonia, as in No. 78D, page 181. A gentle purgative frequently relieves the shortness and difficulty of breathing, and if that fails, a blister to the breast bone and frequently repeated or the tartar emetic lotion, (No. 44, page 162) rubbed freely into the same part, are the best means. To moderate and remove the inflamed state of the eyes, exposure to light should be avoided, and the eyes be frequently washed with the lotion, No. 13, page 148. After the inflammation has been subdued by means of quietude, low diet, and exclusion from the light, and the complaint assumes an indolent character, one of the most efficacious remedies is the diluted ointment of nitrated quicksilver, No. 89, page 188.

It is, however, remarkable that blood-letting sometimes removes certain symptoms remaining after measles, for the removal of which, under other circumstances, very little is to be expected from it. Thus it has removed cough, although unaccompanied by fever, or the other symptoms denoting inflammation. It may, therefore be tried to a small extent when the previous means fail to remove the cough, difficulty of breathing and other symptoms above mentioned.

It will be necessary cautiously to avoid exposure to cold for some time after the patient has recovered.

Tonics are almost always injurious during convalescence from measles. When the system is left exhausted, being free from irritation, if any strengthening medicine is likely to be of service, it is the serpentaria in infusion, *See* page 120 ; but I do not think that will be required if ammonia has been given during the attack.

The following interesting and valuable observations of Dr. Armstrong are worthy of record here:

"It is a remarkable fact, that when any cutaneous affections arise after measles, the internal organs generally remain free from disease; and even where some internal disorder has existed, I have not unfrequently seen it disappear on the occurrence of some spontaneous eruption of the skin. Indeed, there are many cases of this nature already on record. At all times we should, therefore, be most wary in meddling with vesicles, pustules, boils, and the like, when they come out after the measles; for although they may be temporary blemishes on the surface, they are often the occasion of saving the vital walls within."

MENSTRUATION

The time at which the menstrual discharge commences varies from many circumstances, chiefly, however, from those of climate, and of peculiarity of constitution. In warm climates, menstruation appears often as early as at eight or nine years of age; for here the general growth of the body advances more rapidly than in colder quarters, and the atmosphere is more stimulant. In temperate climates it is usually postponed till the thirteenth or fourteenth year; and in the arctic regions till the nineteenth or twentieth. In all climates, however, when the constitution has acquired the age in which it is prepared for the discharge, various causes may accelerate its appearance. The chief of these are, preternatural degrees of heat or feverishness, or any other stimulus that quickens the circulation; anger, or any other violent emotion of the mind; inordinate exercise; fear, and severe grief.

The discharge usually lasts from three to five days, and the quantity lost upon an average is about six ounces; but with many women it continues longer, and they lose more than this, while with some both the period and quantity are less. The monthly return continues till the fortieth or fiftieth year. Women of a delicate habit and lax fibre, have a more copious and longer continued discharge than those of a robust constitution.

For the two or three first times of its appearing, it is apt to be somewhat irregular, both as to the quantity of blood which is discharged, and the period of its return; but after these, it usually observes stated times, and nearly the same quantity is lost at each visitation, unless some irregularity takes place.

About the first appearance of this discharge, the constitution undergoes a very considerable change, generally indeed for the better, though sometimes for the worse. The greater care is then necessary, as the future health and happiness of the female depends in a great measure upon her conduct at that period.

She should be careful to take exercise daily in the open air, to partake of a wholesome nutritious diet, and not to indulge in tight clothes. The exercise should be free and active, which will be found to promote digestion, to enliven the spirits, and to insure a proper discharge. It is worthy of the especial attention of young women, that one seldom meets, at this period, with complaints from obstructions amongst the more active and industrious part of the sex, whereas the indolent, inactive, and luxurious, are seldom free from them.

After the *menses* have begun to flow, great care should be taken to avoid every thing that may tend to obstruct them. Females ought to be exceedingly cautious not to stand long or suffer any excessive fatigue, and they should be careful in what they eat and drink at the time they are out of order. Everything that is cold or apt to sour on tile stomach, and all things which are found by experience to disagree, ought to be avoided.

Exposure to cold is extremely hurtful at this period.[1] More females date their diseases from cold caught while they are in this situation than from all other causes. A degree of cold that will not

1. "Frank mentions the case of a young lady, who put her feet several times into cold water, during this period, because she expected her lover, which produced a suppression; an inflammation of the womb followed, and she was brought dying into the hospital at Vienna. He also states, on the authority of a celebrated surgeon of Helmstadt, that a young lady was attacked with amaurosis of one eye, in consequence of the sudden suppression of the menses, from putting her feet in cold water—and when this discharge was recalled, she fortunately recovered the sight of her eye."—*Dewees on the Diseases of Females*, p. 116.

in the least hurt them at another time, will at this period often be sufficient entirely to ruin their health and constitution. It is not meant that they should then confine themselves wholly in the house and warm rooms, but that imprudent exposures should be warded against, and the clothing be somewhat warmer than usual. I have lately heard of a young lady, in my neighbourhood, who was suddenly seized with mental derangement after the improper use of cold water at this particular time; and all the means hitherto employed to restore her health and reason have altogether failed.

The final cessation of the menstrual discharge is likewise a critical period with all women, and therefore, I shall here say a little on the treatment necessary at this time; and also of painful menstruation. The retention and suppression of this discharge are distinct diseases, which are treated of under those heads respectively.

The Final Cessation of the Menses

This discharge seldom ceases all at once, but for some time before its stoppage becomes somewhat irregular both as to the periods and the quantity. The time of this final cessation is always a critical one, because the constitution then undergoes a consi-derable change, and there is often a strong tendency to the formation of obstinate and painful chronic complaints.

The brand object of treatment at this period should be to quiet irregular local irritation wherever necessary, by gentle laxatives, as No. 73 or 74, page 176, and moderate opiates or anodynes, as No. 112, page 200, and to prevent any incidental stimulus or painful mental emotion. The diet should be nutritious and plain: the exercise moderate; and costiveness carefully prevented by attention to diet, and by lenient warm aperients, as No. 100, 101, or 101C or 101D, pages 194-195.

When the discharge happens to disappear suddenly in women of a full plethoric habit, the diet should be more spare than usual, regular exercise be taken, and every other day the opening draught, No. 28, page 156. As a gentle purgative, the *hiera picra* is often very useful in such instances. *See* page 70, and also the author's book On The Diseases of Females. When the patient is sensible of a seeming fulness of the vessels of the head, with a giddiness and pain, a small bleeding or two may be advisable.

If ulcers break out in the legs, or any other part of the body, at this period, they ought to be regarded as critical discharges, and the wisest practice is not to interfere with them further than is necessary to keep them clean and prevent them from spreading; but in such cases I would advise the pill, No. 98 or 98A, page 192, to be taken every other night.

Painful Menstruation

Sometimes this discharge recurs every month with little or no irregularity in this respect, but it is accompanied with great local pain, which is occasionally very severe and forcing, especially about the loins, hips, and region of the womb. The quantity thrown forth may or may not be too small; but what chiefly demands our attention here, is the great pain accompanying the flow. It is most frequent in young women soon after marriage.

The pain is chiefly owing to a deranged state of the general health, accompanied with a chronic inflammation of the vessels of the womb itself. In unhealthy or delicate females, painful menstruation is the consequence of strong and imperfect efforts to expel a sort of nidus or secretion of coagulable lymph in the womb. And one of the most efficacious plans of treatment with which I am acquainted, is to administer from thirty to forty or even fifty drops of the volatile tincture of guaiacum in milk and water, three times a day; with an aperient pill, No. 97 or 100, page 193, every other night, so that the bowels may be kept regular without being purged: or, instead of the guaiacum, the patient may take a drachm of the powder of sarsaparilla, twice a day. I have known this of great service. At the same time, the patient ought to take much exercise daily in the open air, either on horseback or an foot; to be attentive to the rules of diet laid down under Indigestion; and to mingle with cheerful society : A hip bath of cold water—when not unwell—every morning at twelve o'clock, will likewise be advisable; and change of air and scene will much conduce to recovery. This plan ought, to be persevered in for a considerable time, until the patient is sensibly restored to the full enjoyment of health and strength, for this is the object to be attained by it, the accomplishment of which will very rarely fail to prevent the recurrence of pain at the future return of this discharge.

It affords me satisfaction to perceive that the volatile tincture of guaiacum has lately been very highly extolled in this complaint by several physicians, and by none more than by the experienced American physican Dewees. He says, *(Treatise on the Diseases of Women,* p. 139) "We could furnish very many instances of success from the use of the guaiacum,—indeed, more than a hundred." The guaiacum was many years since recommended in this volume. In my TREATISE ON THE DISEASES OF FEMALES, a case is related from Dewees, in which a lady who had been married nineteen years, without issue, had a fine girl in about twelve months after having gone through a course of guaiacum.

As a local means, perhaps the most useful palliative is the application of warmth to the region of the womb and over the whole surface of the abdomen, by means of bottles filled with hot water. Warmth may also be applied at the same time to the feet. And the injection of warm water into the womb is sometimes useful.

If the tincture of guaiacum fail to produce any decided effect, then try the following plan : Take the mixture No. 78D, page 181, twice a day regularly, and the alterative pill, No. 98A, page 192, every other night, with the pills, No. 110, page 199, when in pain. Three grains of sulphate of iron, and ten grains of Epsom salts, in water, twice a day or No. 74C, may be tried, if the previous means fail.

When the pain is severe, take also the anodyne pills, No. 110, page 199, or the powder, No. 129, page 208. The anodyne clyster, No. 9, page 147, may also be administered.

Profuse Menstruation

This disorder may arise where there is too great a fulness of habit, and too irritable a state of the vessels of the uterus; or where both general and local debility are present. It is almost always attended with pain in the back and loins, and often with a feeling of weight or bearing down, and a sense of fulness and heat. The repeated recurrence of this complaint seldom fails to break down a strong constitution, engendering great feebleness, and thus *menorrhagia,* as it is technically called, which was in the beginning of an acute character, may soon assume the appearance of a passive or indolent nature.

The chief causes are luxurious living, without sufficient exercise; or general debility, and uncommon irritability of the uterine system; or it may arise from organic mischief, or from polypus.

TREATMENT—*In the ,first variety,* where the symptoms are those of too great fulness, oppression of the chest, together with heat and thirst, we must prohibit the use of animal food, and prescribe a very mild and spare diet for several days, and regulate the bowels by the use of mild saline aperients, as No. 73 or 74, page 176. At the same time, the free application of cold to the belly, loins, and back, will materially assist in checking the discharge; and the patient should take the acetate of lead pills, page 128.

In the second variety, where debility is clearly marked in the constitution, we are called upon to try invigorating means, both locally and generally. Cold hip-bathing is here indicated, with change of air and an invigorating diet. The diet should consist of articles the most easy of digestion, and a little good Sherry or Port wine may be allowed in all cases, where it sits easy on the stomach, and does not prove heating. Friction over the loins and lower extremities will be found soothing and beneficial, and the exercise must be of the gentlest description.

The best internal medicines are rhatany, cream of tartar, zinc, steel, or quinine, combined with rhubarb, and extract of hop, hemlock, or henbane, as in the pills, No. 106, 102, or 115. The mixture, No. 82A, is also efficacious.

Opium is of great value in cases of severe *menorrhagia,* to allay that peculiar irritability and restlessness so frequently present, and black drop may be given in doses of ten drops, or more, in a saline draught. In my TREATISE ON THE DISEASES OF FEMALES painful menstruation is more fully considered, and I think every female may derive considerable benefit from the possession of that publication.

MISCARRIAGE

The usual term of pregnancy is forty weeks or nine calendar months, but the fetus (as the child in the womb is called) may be expelled at any time previous to the expiration of this period. If the expulsion takes place at any time before the commencement of the seventh month, it is considered a miscarriage; for should the fetus have completed its seventh month and be expelled, it will often live, but very rarely survives when the exclusion occurs before that month.

Miscarriage is an accident of frequent occurrence, which is always attended with disagreeable circumstances, and which, although it seldom proves immediately fatal, may still be productive of much mischief at a future period. It may happen at any period of pregnancy, but it is most frequent about the third month, proving that there is then a greater susceptibility in the womb to have its action interrupted, than either before or afterwards.

It is often preceded by a general sense of coldness, flaccidity of the breasts, slight pains in the loins, and lower regions of the belly, sometimes accompanied with fever. In full habits, and where the miscarriage proceeds from excessive action in the blood- vessels of the womb, the fever is original, and precedes the discharge. After a short continuance of these *symptoms*, a slight flow of blood ensues, coming away sometimes in clots, and at others, gushing out in a florid stream, then stopping, perhaps for a short time, and again returning violently. Not unfrequently coagula only can be perceived. When the whole contents of the womb are expelled, a bloody discharge continues for a few hours and is then succeeded by a thin serous fluid.

Should the pregnancy have advanced beyond the third month, and miscarriage be likely to occur, there is much bearing down, together with a derangement of the stomach, causing sickness and faintness, and sometimes there is a very quick and profuse discharge of blood. In this stage; the membranes enveloping the fetus often give way, the fetus escaping with the contained water, whilst the membranes are retained for some hours, or even days. In some instances, the whole comes away entire, which is generally far better than its being excluded in parts; because in the latter case, some portion is apt to lodge in the passage; and keep up the irritation and discharge.

But in the symptoms and duration of miscarriage, there is a great diversity in different instances. In some cases, the pains are severe and long continued; in others, short and trifling. Sometimes the bleeding is profuse and alarming; at other times, although circumstances may not be apparently very different, it is moderate or inconsiderable. A few hours in many, and not above three days in the majority of cases, is sufficient to complete the process; but we occasionally meet with instances in which it is threatened for a long time, and possibly some weeks elapse before the expulsion takes place.

Miscarriages are more or less dangerous according to the stage of pregnancy in which they happen. The farther a woman is advanced therein, the greater will be the risk, but the are seldom attended with immediate danger before the fifth month; but should they form a habit of recurrence in subsequent pregnancies, the blood, from such frequent discharges, loses its proper strength; the vigour of the constitution is broken down; all the functions of the system are in consequence performed with a considerable degree of languor; and a foundation is often laid for some obstinate chronic disease.

The *causes* which give rise to abortions, are violent exertions of strength, lifting heavy weights, severe exercise, the fatiguing dissipations of fashionable life, sudden surprises and frights, violent fits of passion, great anxiety of mind, aloetic purges, too free a use of warm pediluvia, and profuse evacuations. Whatever else tends to disturb or check the circulation suddenly, and thereby to produce fainting, will often prove a cause of miscarriage : and when once this affection has been produced, the organs with difficulty recover their elasticity, and it is extremely apt to recur upon the slightest causes.

Fulness of blood (what medical men call plethora) is a very frequent cause, and this plethora may occur either in delicate women who live luxuriously, and use little exercise, or in those of a robust and vigorous constitution.

TREATMENT—Should the miscarriage be only threatened, and we are called upon to prevent it, the first step to be taken is a recumbent position;—the patient should be wholly confined to a couch or bed, being very lightly covered, and kept quite quiet. Should the female be strong, and full of blood, from eight to ten ounces of blood may be taken from the arm; but in very delicate irritable habits, it must not be thought of. The bowels ought to be immediately emptied by a mild purgative, as No. 27, page 155, or a laxative injection, as No. 8, page 146; after which, thirty or forty drops of laudanum may be taken in some cold liquid, and repeated, if necessary, every four or five hours. All the drink should be cold, and the patient be kept as cool as possible. And if the constitution be very feeble or emaciated, six or eight drops of the aromatic sulphuric acid should be taken in water, three or four times in the twenty-four hours. "Opiates," says Dr. Burns, with his usual discrimination, *(Principles of Midwifery,* p. 356), "are very useful in cases of *threatened* abortion; more especially in accidental separation of the membranes and consequent discharge. They do not directly preserve the action of gestation, but they prevent the tendency to muscular contraction, and thus do good. In weakly or emaciated habits, opiates alone, if given upon the first appearance of mischief, are often sufficient to prevent abortion; and in opposite conditions, when preceded by venesection, they are of great service. Opiates are likewise useful for allaying those sympathetic pains about the bowels, and many of the nervous affections which precede, or accompany abortion. They are also of much benefit in cases where we have considerable and protracted discharge, with trifling pains, as the uterus is then not contracting sufficiently to expel the ovum, but merely to separate vessels and excite hemorrhage. They either at once render the pain brisker, or by suspending, for a time, the action, it returns afterwards with more vigour and perfection and finishes the process."

By this plan the pains from incidental causes are often checked, arid the miscarriage prevented. But the remedial process is thus far merely begun: the patient for some weeks, must be peculiarly, attentive to her diet, which should be light and sparing; and if exercise of any kind be allowed, it should be that of swinging, or of an easy carriage. Cold bathing is of great impor-tance; and if there should be the slightest issue of blood from the parts, injections of the coldest water may be thrown up the passage two or three times a day. If the constituation be delicate, a glass or two of wine may be allowed daily, and eight grains of powdered chlorate of potash, in water, be taken thrice daily. But if the habit be vigorous and robust, no wine ought to be permitted, and the soft bed should be exchanged for a hard mattress.

But if the pains are regular, and accompanied with strong expulsatory efforts, with a considerable discharge of blood, it is not likely that the abortion can be prevented, and, in ordinary cases, all that is necessary to be done, is, to confine the patient to a bed lightly covered with clothing, and to give her thirty or forty drops of laudanum, in a saline draught, No. 24, page 153. The chlorate of potash should be taken as prescribed above. Should this discharge continue but in small quantity it is best to let it take its course. Bleeding is often had recourse to under such circumstances as the present, but is never necessary, and may do harm; for an actual miscarriage must be attended with some loss of blood, and to add to this loss by the use of the lancet, is uncalled for in strong women, and clearly improper in delicate subjects.

This discharge may, however, be in great abundance, and amount to a flooding; and the patient be faint and sinking, and in appearance ready to expire. To the inexperienced these symptoms are truly alarming; but it rarely happens that the patient does not recover in an hour or two from the fainting. Cold, both external and internal, is here of the utmost importance; the bed curtains should be undrawn, the windows thrown open, and a sheet alone flung over the patient; while linen wrung in cold water should be applied to the lower parts of the body, and renewed as its temperature becomes warm; withholding the application, however, as soon as the bleeding ceases. Cold injections should, in this case, be desisted from; but the parts may be tightly plugged with folds of linen, or a silk handkerchief, smeared over with oil. Laudanum is the most powerful cordial in the present instance, and is capable of even saving life when it is threatened by a very sudden and profuse discharge of blood. Dr. Hamilton, professor of midwifery in the University of Edinburgh, recommended large doses is be given; but it is seldom necessary to go beyond a drachm at a dose, which may be repeated, in cases of great exhaustion, every ones two, or three hours.—*See* FLOODING, page 585-86.

Should the flooding occur after the sixth or seventh month, no time should be lost in gaining the assistance of an able medical practitioner; for it will then frequently be necessary gently to dilate the mouth of the womb to turn the child, and to bring it away by the hand.

It has of late been very much the custom to confine women of a delicate frame, who have once miscarried, to a recumbent position, from the first symptom of conception through the whole term of pregnancy. In a few cases this may be right; but is not, in my opinion, generally advisable, being, in the majority of instances, much more likely to hurry on miscarriage than to prevent it. A better plan is to observe great moderation in the exercise of body and mind, with a plain diet, and regular hours, the position being generally recumbent when within doors, and strictly so for a fortnight about the time in which a miscarriage might be expected. Gentle exercise daily in the open air ought not to be neglected; and if the habit be delicate, a course of such tonic medicines as are found best to agree with the system may be entered upon, as No. 82, 83, 84, or 85, pages 183-85.

But the best of all resources for those subject to miscarriage is, directly pregnancy commences to take *eight grains* of *powdered chlorate of potash* in water, thrice a day, and to continue it for four or five months. This so improves the quality of the blood as to prevent miscarriage, and insure healthy children. Many ladies have taken the chlorate of Potash for seven or eight months and should there be any fear of miscarriage so late as that, the Potash should not be discontinued till all ground for fear has been removed.

MORTIFICATION

By mortification is meant the death of a portion of the body, while the rest continues alive, often in a sound state.

When mortification is the consequence of inflammation, there is excessive, acute and constant pain; great anxiety; often delirium, followed by a sudden cessation of every inflammatory sympitom—the part before tense now becomes flaccid, of a livid colour and loses its heat and sensibility; small bladders are formed, under which are perceived. spots of a brownish hue; the part, acquire a fetid smell, and become black. If the event prove favourable, the mortified portion becomes completely circumscribed; a proces of ulceration is set up in the contiguous living substance, by which the dead matter is separated, and at length cast off ill sloughs. If, on the contrary, the termination be fatal, the mortification rapidly extends, great constitutional irritation arises, the pulse becomes small, rapid and irregular, there is great anxiety and prostration of strength and death soon ensue. Such are the symptoms of mortification arising from violent inflammation.

But this affection is frequently the effect of a debilitated state of the constitution, where there is no sensible degree of inflamatory action present; and then there is often considerable irritation in the system, but not generally the excessive pain above mentioned, and much lea fever. Sometimes little or no pain or fever attends, especially when gangrene occurs in elderly perons.

The *most usual causes* of the first variety of mortification are excessive inflamation induced by whatever cause, severe external injury, as constusion, fracture, etc.; a high degree of erysipelas. A peculiar condition of the constitution often disposes to it.

The second variety generally originates in debility from age, habits of life, disorder of the digestive organs, fever, poor living, foul air, improper food, scurvy, depressing remedies, cold, etc.

Gangrene and mortification are frequently used synonymously; but, correctly speaking, the former is an incipient mortification, in which the affected part becomes soft, of a brown livid colour, and loses more or less of its natural warmth and sensibility; the latter is a perfect *sphacelus*, or death, when the part becomes a cold, black, fibrous, insensible substance.

Treatment—When ganwrene seems to the threatened from the violence of inflammation, soothing remedies are the best; and those which tend to allay irritation in general system and arrest the inflammatory action that may still exist in the part. A mild mercurial purge, as two grains of calomel, combined with three grains of compound extract of colocynth, should, therefore, be given at night, to improve the deranged secretions of the intestinal canal, and the cooling draught, No. 26, page 155, with the addition of fifteen drops of laudanum, through the day. Or, instead of this, the effervescing saline draught, No. 24, with three grains of Dover's powder, may be taken every four hours during the day. In addition to these remedies, soothing applications must, at the same time, be made to the affected part, such as poppy fomentations and poppy poultices, applied *moderately warm.* Leeches are also proper, and a small bleeding from the arm, when the inflammation occurs in strong healthy subjects living in the country. Such are the means proper when inflammation threatens to terminate in gangrene.

But if the gangrene has actually commenced, a mild antiseptic poultice must be immediately laid over the part; and one of the best that can be used, is made by stirring a sufficient quantity of oatmeal or linseed-meal, into stale beer grounds; or the yeast poultice, No. 3, page 143, may be resorted to. A port wine poultice, made by stirring oatmeal into good port wine, is also sometimes of eminent utility in these cases : I think a little yeast mixed with this poultice improves it greatly. The poultice should be applied moderately warm and renewed every six or eight hours and every time it is removed, the parts may be fomented with a warm spirituous fomentation, made by boiling four ounces of oak bark in three pints of water, for fifteen minutes, and just before using it, adding to it three ounces of camphorated spirit of wine. At the same time; medicines to support the living powers of the constitution must be given, and the best are ammonia, united with opium, or musk, and sulphate of quinine. Sir Astley Cooper says, that the exhibition of ammonia with opium is the best means of supporting the constitution in these circumstances and recommends from seven to ten grains of the sesqui-carbornate of ammonia, with twenty drops of laudanum, to be taken, in camphor mixture, every four hours. Another excellent medicine is six or eight grains of the sesqui-carbonate of ammonia, and ten grains of musk; made into a bolus with conserve of hips and given every three or four hours. This has been much praised in cases of gangrene from local injury. Bitters were also formerly much employed, but modern practitioners have little confidence in them, and consider them to be sometimes even injurious. The sulphate of quinine, however, is frequently of service, especially when symptoms of considerable debility are present. It is sometimes employed with marked advantage in mortification following erysipelas, provided suitable evacuations from the bowels have been premised at a proper period. A two-grain pill of this substance may be taken every four hours. Serpentaria also often proves very useful.—*See* page 120.

The diet in all cases of mortification must be nourishing, but care must be taken not to overload the stomach. A certain quantity of good wine, proportioned to the patient's strength and habits, and the symptoms of the complaint, is proper. Broiled mutton or lamb-chops, and fresh eggs, lightly boiled, are very suitable; and water, impregnated with carbonic acid gas, must be taken as the common drink. This acid gas is sometimes of the highest efficacy in mortification.

After great want of circulation in any part, from the course of the blood having been arrested, sloughing sores are very apt to occur. On this kind of gangrene, Sir Astley Cooper remarks:

> "Thus, after the operation of tying the great artery of the thigh, if the limb be suffered to rest in the same position for a considerable time, a small gangrenous spot frequently appears. In such cases the spirit of turpentine is the best application. Yeast is often applied with the same view. A lotion much used in the other hospital, for this purpose, is made by mixing together an ounce of confection of roses, two

> drachms of honey of roses, two drachms of tincture of opium, and the same quantity of extract of lead, (*liquor plumbi subacetatis*). This is an application which accords extremely well with limbs in a state of gangrene, when the dead are separating from the living parts. During the sloughing process, the nitric acid lotion is the best application that can be used; therefore, when the gangrene stops and the line of demarcation is drawn, and the sloughing process is commencing, the nitric acid lotion may be employed in the proportion of fifty drops to a pint of water."—*Lectures on Surgery by Sir Astley Cooper, No. xv.*

In the mortification of the toes or other extreme parts of the body, occurring in old people, antiseptics are required locally, and internally, cordials and tonics. The port wine poultice, mentioned above, should be laid over the part affected, the part being first well rubbed with the liniment, No. 45, page 163, and opium and ammonia, given internally, with which must be combined a generous diet as already advised. Mr. Pott used to give a grain of crude opium every three or four hours, in the mortification of the toes of elderly people. From the languid powers of circulation in advanced life, these cases frequently prove fatal, especially in those who are tall and who have lived luxuriously.

Mortification arising from poor living, improper food and depressing remedies, will require the same treatment as now recommended when it occurs in old persons.

In gangrene following exposure to extreme cold, the parts should be very gently rubbed with snow, or the coldest water, for some time, and then with camphorated spirit of wine. When the first effects of cold are removed by these means, cold poultices of stale beer grounds, yeast, or port wine, should be applied; and opium and ammonia may be given internally. In these cases, great care must be taken not to bring the patient into a warm room until the parts affected have recovered themselves a little. For a remedy in mortification occurring in tropical climates, *see* page 12.

MUMPS

The mumps is a painful tumour of the parotid glands of the neck, which often extends to the maxillary glands, and is conspicuous externally.

The tumour, though sometimes confined to one side of the neck, more usually appears on both; it is at first moveable, but soon becomes diffused to a considerable extent. It increases till the fourth day, and often involves the maxillary glands in the inflammation, is evidently contagious, and often epidemic. After the fourth day it gradually declines; and for the most part, there is but little fever, or need for medical aid. As the swelling of the throat subsides, it not unfrequently happens, that a swelling takes place in the testes of males, and in the breasts of females; which is by no means an unfavourable sign; for it has occasionally been found, that where this sympathy has not been manifested or the glandular swelling has been suddenly repelled, the symptomatic fever has been greatly increased and delirium has ensued.

The cause has just been stated to be a specific contagion.

TREATMENT—I have already remarked that the mumps do not often require the assistance of medicine. All that is in general requisite is, to keep the head and face moderately warm, to avoid taking cold, to observe a mild diet, and to open the bowels by a very gentle aperient, as No. 74, page 176.

In cases of mild fever, eight or ten grains of compound contrayerva powder, with two or three grains of nitre, may be given in water every night. On the other hand, should uncommon languor supervene without much fever, give five grains of sesqui-carbonate of ammonia, in water, thrice a day. It is not necessary to keep the patient in bed, unless the fever is considerable.

When the testes and breasts simply enlarge, they ought to be interfered with very cautiously; should they be very painful, and tend to suppurate or break, cooling purgative medicine, as No. 73 or 74, should lie given, a few leeches be applied, and afterwards a warm poultice.

"In the treatment of this complaint under a change of seat," (he means, to the purse in boys and the breasts in girls) "regard should always be paid to the part originally affected. With this view we have always blistered the parts immediately over the parotids and we think with decided adavntage. If the change has taken place in the male, we also) exhibit an emetic, and apply warm vinegar by means of flannel to the scrotum, and this is to be repeated from time to time. A brisk purging should instantly instituted after the operation of the emetic is entirely over, provided neither the blistering nor the vomiting has been successful in recalling the morbid action to the original seat of the disease."—Dewees' *Practice of Physic*, vol. i., p. 344.

In case of high fever occurring, with outer alarming symptoms, the usual means of reducing inordinate vascular action by bleeding, purging, etc., must ho resorted to.

Should any hardness be left in the glands after recovery, they ought to be anointed freely with tile liniment, No. 42, page 162.

GENERAL NERVOUS DISORDER

Weakness and irregular action of the greater part or whole of the nervous system is now so common, that I am desirous of impressing my readers with the fact that no treatment is half so efficacious in such complaints as the free use of cold water, plenty of active exercise, and a little steel and carbonate of ammonia; and sometimes a drachm of Epsom salts every morning, in chilled water. No blood-letting or aperient medicine should be bad recourse to. *See* the OBSERVATIONS ON THE COLD IT WATER, CURE at the end of this volume.

So valuable is constant exercise and pure air in the cure of general nervous disorder, that a celebrated foreign physician accumulated a large property from his success in the treatment of such affections by these means.[1] He was in the habit of imposing long rides or walks every day, with early rising, so that his patients

1. If my memory is correct, this was Dr. Tronchin, of Geneva, whom the miserable, daring infidel Voltaire sent for in his last illness, and whom he be sought with extreme earnestness and anxiety to prolong his existence, if possible.

were fully exercised, but short of any particular fatigue; by which practice he ensured a keen appetite, perfect digestion, refreshing sleep, and regular bowels, and by degrees gave an abiding tone to the nerves and muscles of every part. This was similar to Dr. Jephson's excellent practice, and to that imposed by the water system.

NETTLE-RASH

This is an eruption resembling that produced by the stinging of nettles; whence its name. The rash often appears instantaneously, especially if the skin be rubbed or scratched, and seldom stays many hours in the same place, but vanishes; and again makes its appearance in another part of the skin. The parts affected with the eruption are often considerably swelled, and a troublesome itching is invariably present.

The cause may be either mechanical irritation or acidity and other disorder in the stomach.

It is usually a very mild disease and rarely requires any medicine beyond a cooling purgative, as No. 27 or 28, pages 155-56. Should the feverishness at night be considerable, the draught, No. 24, page 153, may be taken, or five grains of James's powder in a pill; and if the rash frequently returns, particular attention should be paid to regulate the bowels, and allay irritation in the stomach, and the ammonia mixture, No. 78D, page 181, should be given. Keep the bowels free from confinement by an occasional use of the saline powder, No. 130A, page 209.

NEURALGIA

This is a class of affections which consist chiefly in acute pain in some part of the body, and have their site in the *nerves,* since the pains present follow the course of these, but of the precise nature of which we are ignorant. There are many species or varieties of *neuralgia,* for example, *tic douloureux, sciatica,* or hip gout, etc., are varieties of this affection; but I have introduce the present article, chiefly for the purpose of noticing *neuralgia* of the *lungs* and of *the heart.* In neuralgia we cannot discover any constant lesion of the solids nor evident alteration in the fluids, and must therefore consider the disorder to be one of the nervous influence. In these cases, dissection has afforded variable results: frequently no diseased condition of the nerve affected has been found; sometimes it has been found smaller, at other times larger than natural; and in some rare instances, the sheath or envelope of the nerve has appeared red from injection of its vessels.

It cannot be doubted, that there are two sorts of *neuralgia,* very different from each other in almost every respect, and yet too apt to be confounded. The one proceeds or arises from a local and circumscribed cause, which may, in some cases, be removed by a surgical operation, or by magnetism. The other appears to, depend upon a constitutional cause, that is, upon great deran-gement of the general health, and is treated successfully only by attention to this derangement. The latter species is usually seated in some of the most superficial nerves, returns at irregular intervals, induces little or no change in the appearance of the part affected, either during life, or when examined after death, and may, therefore, be supposed to have a constitutional or systematic origin, and not merely a local and circumscribed one. Some persons consider neuralgia to be dependent upon an inflammatory state of some portion of the nervous system, but I do not consider this correct.

1. *Neuralgia, or nervous pains in the lungs.* It is by no means rare to meet with individuals who, without any physical or rational sign of organic disease and sometimes even while enjoying the most perfect health in other respects, suffer acute pain, occasionally even extremely acute pain, in the interior of the chest. This pain may be momentary or of long duration, intermittent or continued, confined to one spot or diffused, fixed or moveable; and sometimes it shoots by fits along the walls of the chest and the neighbouring parts, in the course of the intercostal and anterior nerve of the chest or the congeries of nerves in the arm-pit. It is frequently deep-seated between the spine and shoulder-blade.

It is worthy of notice here, that many young women are very

subject to pain in the side, about the middle of the false ribs. This is commonly connected with some derangement in the health, poor blood and sometimes with more or less lateral curvature of the spine. Bleeding is by no means proper in this affection, which is most certainly removed by those measures which tend to invigorate the system, and establish the general health. There is a pain in the left side of peculiar origin, which is fully treated of in my DISEASES OF FEMALES.

2. *Neuralgia, or nervous pains in the heart.* Sometimes these pains are confined to the region of the heart, but frequently they extend at the same time, or vicariously, over a greater or less portion of the lungs and stomach. Sometimes they exist simultaneously in the superficial nerves of the neck and extend along the tract of the branches supplied by these to the anterior parts of the chest; still more frequently at the very time they are felt most severely in the heart, they shoot with corresponding violence along the nerve of the arm-pit, and more particularly along the nerve of the arm to the elbow; and sometimes as far as the fingers, simulating the organic affection, called *breast-pany* or *angina pectoris.*

It is of consequence to observe, that this affection sometimes so strongly resembles the organic disease called *angina pectoris,* as to require the aid and exercise of considerable judgment to distinguish one from the other. This fact should inspire the patient with hope, and induce calmness and composure, and it should lead the medical practitioner to offer his opinion cautiously and with some reservation in the majority of instances. Neuralgia is met with much more frequently in some years than others and it seems that the prevalent type of disease influences its development.

TREATMENT—Whatever has the greatest effect in invigorating the system, and restoring all the functions of the body to a state of healthy action, will be almost uniformly of the greatest service in the treatment; so that we should be guided therein by the principles laid down at pages 345-49, and employ the remedies referred to under INDIGESTION. Cod-liver oil, and the mixture of iron and ammonia, No. 84A are excellent remedies. Of local remedies, either magnetism,[1] galvanism or electricity, will be found the most useful. " When the pains are fixed (says the late able French physician, M. Laennec), I have frequently relieved them by the long-continued application of two magnetised steel plates, disposed in such a manner as to throw the magnetic current existing between them, through the affected part." *See* it the case mentioned under HICCUP.

In nervous pains of the limbs, as well as the heart and lungs, the mixture, No. 74C, page 177, twice daily, or half a drachm of Epsom and Glauber's salts, every morning, in chilled water, is an admirable remedy.

NIGHT-MARE

This is certainly a nervous affection, in which there is a violent struggle and tremor, with a severe pressure on the chest. The sensation is frequently preceded by some fearful dream, as that of an implacable enemy, known or unknown, in close pursuit of the dreamer, from whose grasp he feels incapable of escaping; or of exposure to some overwhelming danger.

It appears most frequently in persons of an irritable or nervous temperament, and of a weakly constitution; particularly amongst those who are predisposed to low spirits. Others, indeed, are occasionally affected by it, but more rarely, and perhaps in a less degree. The most usual exciting causes, are great fatigue of body and mind; indigestible food; and long continued disorder of the stomach and bowels. It may often be looked upon as a certain indication of deranged health.

TREATMENT—The treatment is very similar to that directed for indigestion. The mind and body should be kept free from all undue fatigue and commotion; the diet be light, and especially towards evening; and the bowels be preserved regular, by the occasional use of the pills, No. 100, page 193. I recommend two grains of

1. Although magnetism has fallen into contempt in England, it is well known that the Commission appointed by the Royal Society of Medicine in Paris, in 1776 to investigate its effects, published a very favourable report of them.

quinine and two of sulphate of iron in a pill, twice a day, as a valuable remedy.

If the stomach and general habit are weak, the appetite deficient, and the pill of quinine and sulphate of iron is not tried, then the patient should take the carbonate of iron pills, No. 102, recommended for nervous disorders or the quinine pills, No. 115, or the mixture, No. 74C; with very considerable daily exercise on foot or horseback. The pills, No. 104, are often useful. In all cases, the supper must be very simple, and small in quantity, animal food being then altogether avoided.

PAIN IN THE STOMACH

The pain of the stomach here adverted to is often of frequent though uncertain occurrence. It is quite unconnected with inflam-mation, being purely of a slow chronic character. In some persons, the pain is moderate; in others excruciating, and of a very depres-sing nature. The stomach may feel empty, or distended, and sometimes there are bitter or saltish eructations. The more excruciating sort of pain scarcely ever exists with pain in the head; and in such cases the moment it ceases, the patient is often as well as he could wish. This is not the case in CHRONIC GASTRITIS, noticed at pages 710-12.

The causes of this complaint are sometimes obscure, but it is generally owing to a peculiar weakness and disorder of the stomach; and indigestible food, anxiety of mind, great fatigue of body, costiveness, and exposure to wet, are the most frequent exciting causes of the pain.

When neither vomiting nor emaciation prevails, it is very seldom a dangerous complaint.

TREATMENT—A very good plan of treatment is to take the following draught of volatile alkali, magnesia, mint water and tincture of henbane, about twice a day; with moderate exercise in the open air, avoiding excessive fatigue, and injurious exposure to damp and wet.

Take of pure water of ammonia	10	drops;
Calcined magnesia	5	grains;
Peppermint water	1½	ounces,
Tincture of henbane		half a drachm.

Mix, for a draught, to be taken two or three times a day.

A rigid animal food diet should, at the same time, be adhered to in bad cases, little vegetable food whatever being taken, except a little plain biscuit, and bread. All slop fluids, as coffee soup, etc., must be avoided, but a little good white wine or very weak brandy and water, may be taken every day, if they do not disagree. In very severe cases, it will be absolutely necessary to be exact in following this plan, in order to obtain a cure.

If the preceding draught does not produce all the effect desired, it may be changed for *the sulphate of quinine,* or *the oxide of bismuth,* No. 103A, page 197, which are sometimes of excellent use.

Take of sulphate of quinine	20	grains;

Extract of gentian, a sufficient quantity to make fifteen pills.

One to be taken three times a day.

When the pain is so severe as to demand immediate relief, opium will often be found of inestimable advantage; but it should not be forgotten, that it is only a palliative, and that we must look to the above plan for effecting a cure. To procure a speedy relief, from thirty to forty drops of laudanum may be given in a little peppermint water, and repeated in an hours if necessary. Or, from ten to fourteen drops of the black drop may be taken in the same way; or a quarter of a grain of muriate of morphia; these are less likely to affect the head than laudanum, especially the muriate of morphia.

The oxide of bismuth is justly considered one of the moat efficacious medicines in this complaint, and the pill No. 103A, is very effectual. I have found the following pills persevered in for three or four weeks of superior service :

Take of powdered rhubarb, ...	25	grains;
Powdered ipecacuanha, ...	6	grains;
Castile soap, ...		half a drachm;

Extract of gentian, a sufficient quantity to form the mass, which is to be divided into twenty pills.

One to be taken twice a day, with one of the pills, No. 99; every other night.

Sometimes what people call pain in the stomach is a pain in the bowels, and it is material to observe that this pain may arise from chronic inflammation, or a highly irritated state, of the mucous membrane of some part of the intestinal canal, similar to the *chronic gastritis* mentioned at page 710-12. This we call *chronic enteritis,* and the treatment well be similar to that described at page 696 : the compound tincture of Benjamin will be found useful here.

PALPITATION OF THE HEART

Palpitation is a vehement and irregular motion of the heart. It is sometimes sharp and strong, in which case it is called a *throbbing* of the heart; and sometimes soft and feeble, when it is called a *fluttering* of this organ. The rebound of the heart against the inside of the chest is sometimes so very strong as to be distinctly heard, and to agitate the bed of the patient so violently, that his pulse has been counted by looking at the motions of the curtain of the bed.

Palpitation is frequently found at the pit of the stomach, (which professional men call the *epigastric regions),* when it appears to proceed from some particular excitement of one of the large arteries passing through that part, the heart being unconcerned in its presence.

Palpitations of the nervous kind are frequently much more troublesome than those connected with organic lesion. The former, far from being removed by the most complete repose, are in general felt to be most distressing during the first part of the night. It frequently happens that they prevent sleep for several hours, while a moderate degree of exercise proportioned to the patient's strength, removes or at least alleviates, the distressing feeling of them.

Its *causes* cannot always be satisfactorily ascertained, but it may be simply a nervous affection, dependent upon an excessive irritability of the muscular fibres of the heart, or large arteries; or the effect of positive disease in those or other parts. Pope Urban the Eighth was troubled with this complaint, and after death his heart was found ossified in its general substance. Great disorder of the digestive functions is a very frequent cause of this complaint, especially in excitable patients, and they quite recover.

Its *exciting causes* are violent emotions of the mind, constiveness, and other disorders of the digestive organs, and excessive exercise of body or mind. It not unfrequently follows acute rheumatism.

I have known a disease in the rectum, or last gut, accompanied with stricture, produce a severe and long continued palpitation. Great weakness and disorder of the stomach and bowels is a frequent cause in those cases which are curable.

TREATMENT—People with diseased valves, and with other affections of the heart, live for years and years, and generally enjoy tolerable health if they are attentive to diet and exercise, and to observe tranquillity of mind. Palpitation is by no means a dangerous complaint. *It is of primary importance to guard against a bad state of blood (anaemia), and degeneration of the muscular fibres of the heart.* To do this, the patient should take a two or three weeks course of iron, three or four times a year, such as No. 84A, page 184, No. 102, No. 103A or No. 106A, and observe a generous diet, eating a good deal of salt with the food. Our first object should be to endeavour to ascertain whether the palpitation be owing to general debility, a peculiar irritability of the nervous system, and indigestion; or to an enlarged, or otherwise diseased state, of the heart, or its vessels. In the first cases tonics and antispasmodics, with quietude of mind, regular hours, light meals, pure air, and such daily exercise as agrees with the individual, will almost always produce much relief and sometimes effect a radical cure. The best tonics are the carbonate and sulphate of iron, or of zinc, sulphate of quinine and ipecacuanha, as above referred to. The most useful sedatives and antispasmodics are the extracts of henbane and hemlock sarsaparilla and digitalis.

If the preceding means fail, an efficacious plan is to- take the steel mixture, No. 87C.Y. *in the Appendix* p. 961; still maintaining a generous diet. The exercise should be of the gentlest kind in the beginning, but be gradually increased. Sponging the whole body daily with cold water will be found a useful auxiliary.

If we have reason to apprehend some positive affection of the structure of the heart, or larger blood-vessels, the probability of cure is much lessened, and the great dependence must be upon iron, with or without digitalis, with the warm bath at ninety-five degrees, an issue, rest of mind, and proper exercise of body, food of the easiest digestion, and pure air. Sometimes a little *strychnine* is serviceable, and perhaps no form can be found better than one-twentieth of a grain in two or three table-spoonfuls of the compound steel mixture of the pharmacopaeia, taken twice a day.

Whatever may be the cause of the disease, if the palpitation is more than ordinarily troublesome, some mild narcotic should be taken to allay the irritation. From ten to twenty drops of Batley's sedative liquor of opium or the solution of acetate of morphia, may be taken in a little mint-water, every second hour, till relief is obtained; or from five to six grains either of the extract of henbane or of hemlock, may be administered in the same manner. Quiet is indispensable.

If the palpitation is connected with a very full habit of body, some recommend the loss of a small quantity of blood; but this fulness of. blood is almost invariably much more safely and effectually removed by a cautious diet and exercise, with sarsaparilla powder, twice a day.

Even should the complaint be severe and obstinate, we ought never to be hasty in deciding upon any positive disease of the heart, or any of the larger organs closely associated with it nor upon any incurable cause whatever; for it has frequently happened, that a palpitation of long standing, and which has been regarded as of a dangerous kind, has gradually subsided. Dr. Cullen, of Edinburgh, has given a striking case in confirmation of this remark, in the eighth chapter of the second part of his Materia Medica;—"A gentleman," says he, "pretty well advanced in life, was frequently attacked with palpitation of his heart, which, by degrees, increased both in frequency and violence, and thus continued for two or three years. As the patient was a man of the profession, he was visited by many physicians, who were very unanimously of opinion, that the disease depended upon an organic affection of the heart, and considered it as absolutely incurable. The disease, however, after some years, gradually abated, both in its frequency and violence, and at length ceased altogether; and since that time, for the space of seven, or eight years, the gentleman has remained in perfect health, without the slightest symptom of his former complaint."

The palpitation in the *epigastric region,* that is, in the pit of the stomach, at the end of the breast bone, is in fact a strong pulsation of the aorta, or some other large artery in that part, and is by no means of unfrequent occurrence. As the late Dr. Baillie's remarks on this subject contain my own sentiments, both as to the symptoms, progress, and treatment of the affection, I cannot do better than transcribe a part of them into this page, especially as his observations thereon are very generally approved by the best informed in the profession.

> " I have been frequently consulted," he says, "within the last fifteen years, respecting a pulsation which is distinctly felt in the epigastric region. When the patient first discovers this pulsation he is generally greatly alarmed, and he has seldom found much comfort from the opinion given him by his medical attendant concerning its nature. From a good deal of experience, in cases of this kind, I am enabled to state that the increased pulsation of the aorta in the epigastric region, very rarefy depends on any disease of the aorta itself, or of its large branches in that place; and that this occurrence is almost constantly of very little importance. In the course of my experience, I recollect but one instance in which such a pulsation depended on a diseased swelling of the artery."
>
> "In many instances, it is, perhaps, difficult to ascertain the causes of the pulsation; but, in most cases, it will be found to be connected with an imperfect digestion, and are irritable constitution. When it has once taken place, I believe it seldom subsides entirely. However, it does not produce much inconvenience, more especially when the

> mind has ceased being anxious about it; and a person may continue to live with this symptom or complaint, just as long as if it did not exist."

In regard to the treatment of this complaint, Dr. Baillie has observed, that whatever improves the digestion, and renders the constitution less irritable, will be of use in mitigating the increased pulsation; and that it is useful to remove the patient's anxiety respecting this disease, where it can fairly be done. Therefore, the best treatment in such cases is that advised for INDIGESTION.

PALSY

Palsy is a diminution or total loss of the power of motion and sensibility in certain parts of the body, but without that oppressive sleep witnessed in apoplexy. Sometimes the powers of voluntary motion alone are affected in any considerable degree, while those of sensation are only rendered a little more obtuse; at other times, however, both kinds are equally torpid and sometimes several of the faculties of the mind participated in the debility, though they are never so completely lost as in apoplexy.

There are three varieties of this disease, the hemiplegic palsy, the paraplegic palsy; and the local palsy. In the first, the disease affects only one side of the body; in the second, it is confined to the lower part of the body on both sides; and in the third, to particular limbs.

Palsy usually comes on with a sudden, though slight, loss of the power of motion in the parts affected, which is frequently preceded by a numbness, coldness, and paleness, and sometimes by convulsive twitches. In some cases, this loss of motive power continues to increase till it becomes complete; in others, it is stationary and partial. When the head is much affected, the eye and mouth are drawn on one side, the memory and judgment are impaired, and the speech is indistinct and incoherent. If the disease affects the limbs, and has been of long duration, it not only produces a loss of motion and sensibiltiy, but likewise a considerable flacidity and wasting away in the muscles of the parts affected.

The progress of the disease is uncertain; and depends very much upon the state of the nervous system at the time of the attack. If there be no chronic debility or other morbid condition of the brain, the patient will sometimes recover entirely in a week, or even less; but if this system or some particular part of it, be in an infirm state, he recovers only imperfectly; and obtains, perhaps, a thorough or a limited use of the lower limb, while the upper remains immovable; or he is compelled to pass through the remainder of a painful existence with only one half of his body subservient to his will.

The paralytic state of the lower limbs generally depends upon a diseased affection of the spine, in its bones, ligaments or interior. In such examples, there is at first nothing more than a slight numbness in the lower limbs, with an appearance of stiffness or awkwardness in the motion of the muscles; these symptoms increase by degrees; there is a great difficulty in walking, and an inability in preserving a balance; the aid of a staff, or the arm of an assistant, is next demanded; and the urine is often found to flow in a feeble stream, or perhaps involuntarily. The bowels are at fist always costive; but as the sphincter of the anus loses its power of contraction, the motions at length pass off involuntarily. The disease may continue for years, and either terminate in recovery or the patient may, at last, sink from general exhaustion.

Palsy is frequently the consequence of fit of apoplexy; and all the *causes* of apoplexy may give rise to this disease, though no apoplectic fit actually precedes it. The causes are compression on the brain from the effusion of blood, tumours or induration of the membranes; the circumstances predisposing to this disease being advanced age, corpulency, fulness and grossness of habit, an inordinate indulgence in wines, and heavy fermented liquors, eγcessive heat and whatever tends to relax and enervate the system.

All its varieties more generally appear in the aged and infirm, than in the young and robust; and the left side is, perhaps, more frequently affected than the right.

It will be easily *distinguished* from apoplexy by contrasting the symptoms of the two diseases.

TREATMENT—As in all other complaints, the treatment proper

for this disease will depend on the age of the patient and the healthy or unhealthy state of the constitution. If the patient is young and strong, and the habit full, bleeding and purging are generally proper in the commencement, and they are then particularly indicated when the head is much affected. In such a state, fourteen or sixteen ounces of blood should be directly taken from the jugular vein, or temporal artery; the saline purgative, No. 28, page 156, being given so as to act freely on the bowels; then quietness should be enjoined; and as little exercise of body as possible. Plain food should be given, and but little of it.

But if the age be considerable, the habit debilitated, and the pulse feeble and intermitting, we shall do better to abstain from the use of the lancet, and give the purgative, No. 28, as above advised. If the constitution be very weak, a warmer purgative than this will be advisable, as No. 97, page 191. The purgative should be repeated about once a day, according to its effects, for the first day or two.

After the skin has become cool and moist, take small doses of bi-chloride of mercury in decoction of sarsaparilla, (page 20). We are called upon to endeavour to re-invigorate the brain and nervous system in general, by means of bi-chloride of mercury and stimulants, both external and internal. Electricity and galvanism, warm bathing, leopard's-bane, iodine, vomic nut, and moxa, are the most powerful stimulant remedies in palsy.

Numerous cases have been cured, or greatly benefited, by the judicious use of electricity or galvanism and unless there are symptoms which contra-indicate their employment, they should never be neglected, when other remedies fail. They are more likely to be useful in palsy connected with general debility, than when it occurs in full habits. Physicians generally recommend galvanism as superior to electricity in palsy. Dr. Bardsley, of Manchester, says, that he has found to succeed, when the latter has failed.

In weakly habits, warm bathing is sometimes useful, especially the natural warm waters of Buxton; but in persons who are full of blood, they are not so useful, and should be used with caution. Buxton water is, however, even then of more value than any medicine.

The leopard's-bane *(arnica montana)* has been a good deal praised by some continental physicians, and is worthy of trial. It is said to be particularly useful in palsy of the bladder, and in local palsies of the organs of sense. But the sumach *(rhus toxicodendron)* is, perhaps, much more beneficial. Dr. Alderson, of Hull, employed it with success in twenty-four cases. He began with half a grain, or a grain of the powdered leaves, three times a day, and gradually increased it to five or six grains or till he found a sense of tingling produced in the paralytic part, accompanied with some degree of twitching or convulsive motion.

The vomic nut (*nux vomica*) and *strychnine* is another medicine which has been useful in some instances. Dr. Fouquir, of Paris, and other French physicians, speak well of it. Four grains of the powder may be taken three or four times a day, and increased to sixteen or twenty grains, its effects being carefully watched;—or it may be taken as advised at pages 125-26. It seems of most service in sanguine habits, where there has been a good deal of general strength and energetic health, after irritation has been allayed and the pulse brought down to a subdued and temperate state, by means of blood-letting, purgatives and a mild spare diet. When the head is soon affected by small doses, it is rarely of much use.

The leopard's-bane, iodine and vomic nut, are very active medicines and therefore, must be employed under the superintendence of a careful medical man.

Turpentine, guaiacum, camphor, mustard, horse-radish, garlic and other stimulating medicines of the same kind, have commonly been employed in palsy, but are only applicable to those instances in which debility prevails, and then they are occasionally beneficial. Under such circumstances, the guaiacum mixture or the volatile tincture of guaiacum may be taken to the extent of fifty or sixty drops, three or four times a day, in milk and water; or two, three or four tea-spoonfuls of mustard seed may be swallowed twice a day. Either of the stimulating liniments, No. 39 or 45, pages 161, 163, may be rubbed freely over the parts affected, at the same time. The application of moxa is worthy of a trial in severe cases. *See* page 96.

In palsy of the lower limbs arising from a disease in the spine, a very useful remedy is a large issue, made as near as possible to the diseased part of the spine, which must be kept open for a great length of time.—*See Spinal Curvature.*

If the palsy arises from the use of lead or exposure to its fumes, the means pointed out under DEVONSHIRE COLIC must be resorted to and the palsied arms supported in splints and a sling.

Both *palsy of one side of the body,* and *palsy of the lower limbs,* is sometimes met with, as originating in a venereal affection of the membranes of the brain. Patients have perfectly recovered from such formidable attacks; and mercury in mild doses is the best remedy. A Plummer's pill, or a pill No, 99, page 192, twice a day, with a dose of sarsaparilla in the morning, will be found effectual, if persevered in for a sufficient length of time, such as six or eight weeks or more.

In debilitated subjects, especially after the disease has lasted some time, the diet should be nutritious, but mild and moderate in quantity.

The preceding directions for the treatment of palsy are those authorised by the best informed physicians of this country, but we ought, I think, to regard palsy commonly, if not universally, as a loss of the power of motion, and of sensibility in certain parts, depending on impoverished blood and deranged general health. We should, therefore, consider what are the best means of re-establishing the general health and strength, rather than to search after medicines or means of a supposed specific character, which is a practice far too commonly indulged in, both in this and other chronic maladies. My experience leads me to believe that a treatment founded on this view is not only the most efficacious, but the only one which will succeed well in the majority of instances.—*See* GENERAL PRINCIPLES, page 345.

SHAKING PALSY is noticed as a distinct complaint.

PERIOSTEAL DISEASE OF BONES

The periosteum is the membrane covering the bones under the skin; it is subject to inflammation, thickening, swelling and in some cases there is ulceration, usually denoted by pain, more or less acute, referred to the surface of the bone affected. The shin bone is particularly subject to it.

The *treatment* is very similar to that recommended for *chronic rheumatism.* A Plummer's pill every night, No. 117, page 203, with a dose or two of the guaiacum mixture every day, are excellent remedies. The iodide of potassium (page 76), is one of the chief remedies in *hard* periosteal nodes; but if the node has become soft, that is, if suppuration has commenced, sarsaparilla is the remedy, iodine then being useless. Then take a drachm of sarsaparilla powder, in a wine-glassful of watery two or three times a day.

PILES

The piles consist in a distension of what are technically called the haemorrhoidal veins; or in a relaxation of the surrounding skin and cellular substance, with an effusion of blood into it, forming small tumours, either within the anus or its verge or sometimes producing one tumid ring, by which it is surrounded.

In some cases, they are attended with a discharge of blood, particularly when the patient goes to stool, called the bleeding or open piles; in others, there is no discharge, when they are denominated the *blind piles.* Sometimes they are situated within the gut, and obtain the name of *internal piles;* but more frequently they proturde beyond the anus (or fundament), and are called *external piles.*

They are sometimes preceded by a sense of weight in the back, loins, and bottom of the belly, together with uneasiness of the stomach, and flatulency in the bowels; on going to stool, a pungent pain is felt in the fundament, and small tumours are found to project beyond its verge. If these break, a quantity of blood is voided, and considerable relief from pain is obtained; if they continue unbroken, the patient experiences great torture every time he goes to stool and feels an inconvenience when sitting down on any hard seat. Sometimes incontinence of urine accompanies the complaint.

Frequently, however, the *symptoms* are not so severe as this, but are, notwithstanding, very troublesome, as the patient is, from time to time, annoyed by a relaxation of the skin about the anus, and the formation of a small tumour, which is apt to increase and be very painful, when the patient is walking or standing long. The tumour will sometimes bleed, at other times it will not.

Piles which bleed but little are not of much consequence; but those which bleed profusely, cause violent pain, or induce inflammation and its effects, demand the greatest attention.

In some instances, there is a considerable protrusion externally, forming *prolapsus of the gut*, and constituting a combination of piles with prolapsus. In these cases the patient is greatly annoyed in walking or riding on horseback, indeed, in any situation in which he cannot, by the use of the fingers, put the protruded part up above the grasp of the sphincter muscle.

General debility and habitual costiveness are the *most frequent causes* of piles. They may likewise be produced by hard riding; fulness of blood; excessive indulgence in heating liquors; the use of aloes; the suppression of long accustomed discharges; and the pressure of the pregnant womb.

Persons who lead sedentary lives are those most subject to this complaint, as such a mode of living renders the bowels sluggish in their action, weakens the whole intestinal canal, produces internal obstruction, and enervates the general habit.

TREATMENT—As the piles are generally owing to costiveness, and weakness of the bowels, particularly relaxation of the rectum, one of the best plans of treatment consists in keeping the bowels in a lax condition, by means of some very mild aperient, such as sulphur combined with lenitive electuary and after this has been used for two or three weeks and any accumulation of excrement removed, a suitable warm aromatic or stimulant, as black pepper, or balsam of capivi, should follow. The brimstone and lenitive electuary is one of the most proper aperients in this complaint, for it clears the bowels without. irritating them; and the aromatics recommended gently stimulate the bowel, and give it tone.

Take of Flower of brimstone .... 2 drachms;
Lenitive electuary .... 1 ounce;
Cream of tartar .... 2 drachms;
Syrup of ginger, a sufficient quantity to make 'the whole into an electuary.
A tea-spoonful should be taken once, twice or thrice a day, so as to keep the bowels gently open.

After using this for a short time, take cubebs and confection of black pepper, as here directed, still constantly preserving the bowels free from confinement, by the brimstone electuary, if it cannot be effected by diet and regular solicitation. Cubebs and black pepper I have known of eminent service in piles and painful relaxation in the last bowel.

Take of Cubebs, in powder .... half a drachm.
Confection of black pepper .... half a drachm.
Mix them, and take this twice a day.

Another remedy is thirty or forty drops of balsam of capivi, twice or thrice a day, either on sugar or in water or what is still better, in capsules. *See* page 16. This balsam is of much service in piles which occur in delicate persons, and depend upon relaxation of the parts.

Together with the use of the above internal medicines, the patient may apply locally, twice or thrice a day, the ointment No. 94 or the lotion No. 72. In many cases, they will be found very efficacious. If any inflammation exist in the part, the patient should apply cold salt and water freely before using an ointment. Cold salt and water is an admirable lotion for piles.

It is very important to bathe and cleanse the fundament every night and morning with hard yellow soap and water and then to introduce a little of the pile wort ointment into the rectum with the finger. In the case of internal piles, I usually recommend the use of a metallic rectum bougie or a wax bougie well covered with the ointment and allowed to remain for half an hour or an hour, in the bowel. Only thin brown paper should be used and cold salt and water freely employed after every evacuation of the bowels.

In almost all cases of piles, whether occurring in strong or weakly habits, the pain or irritation present are mach relieved by the free application of cold water; and also by gently pushing the piles up within the grasp of the sphincter muscle, with the fore finger, when they are situated externally. If the heat and irritation are very severe, the immersion of the parts in a bidet or hip bath of cold water should be resorted to, and will afford the most grateful relief. Generally speaking, the use of cold water is far more beneficial than warm fomentations; but now and then the latter are found of most service, when, of course, they should be preferred.

If the above plan of treatment is not attended with satisfactory relief, the sulphate of quinine pills, No. 115, page 202, may be taken, twice or thrice a day, at the same time. In weakly persons this medicine is sometimes of considerable service as an auxiliary to the foregoing measures.

But should the piles occur in strong persons from hard riding, excess in heating liquors, or other causes, the black pepper paste would not be proper, in consequence of its heating qualities, nor will the balsam of capivi be often of service. In such instances, the objects are, to preserve the bowels in a lax condition by the occasional use of the brimstone electuary, or the mixture, No. 73 or 74, page 176, and to allay the inflammation locally by the liberal use of cold salt and water, after applying eight or ten leeches to the parts. Rest, and the horizontal position, should be observed, together with a mild vegetable diet, until the inflammation has subsided. Here leeches are sometimes very beneficially employed, but they are seldom proper when the complaint occurs in weakly habits.

Now and then persons of a strong constitution are frequently troubled with the present complaint, although they are temperate in their habits; in which case, the best remedies are, the brimstone electuary, with a dose of the mixture, No. 74, occasionally, cold water being applied to the parts as often as occasion requires, and once a day, or once in two days, the cooling ointment, No. 95, page 190. In point of diet, every thing heating and constipating must be avoided. It is in habits of this description, that the piles are sometimes salutary from the discharge attending them, and when this is the case, that discharge must be moderated, but not altogether checked.

In the open piles, should the bleeding be profuse, the coldest water must be constantly applied to the parts, with pressure by means of cloths dipped in cold water. But there is, perhaps, nothing which so directly stops the bleeding, as putting the piles up within the grasp of the sphincter muscle, which may almost always be readily done by gentle pressure with the finger, smeared with cold cream.

Sometimes patients mistake some other disease about the last gut for the piles, and whenever there is any doubt upon the subject, the advice of an attentive and well-informed surgeon should be taken without delay. I recommend Mr. Skey, of Lower Grosvenor Street, or Mr. Henry Smith, 16, Caroline Street, Bedford Square.—*See* STRICTURE OF THE RECTUM.

It is quite possible, by means of nitric acid, perfectly to cure piles, a discovery made by Mr. Henry Smith, of King's College Hospital. The piles having been brought into view the piles to which the acid is to be applied, should be very carefully wiped with lint. The surgeon then dips the end of a small flat piece of wood, or a glass rod into pure strong nitric acid and touches the whole of the piles carefully with it. The part touched, and the neighbouring mucous membrane, must now be well smeared with oil, and then the whole of the exposed parts should be returned within the anus.[1] Mr. Smith says it produces little pain, and may be applied, if necessary, a second and third time at intervals of a week; but, of course, if there is any ulcer present, that must first be cured. No one suffering from piles or prolapsus, within reach of Mr. Smith, should fail to consult him.

The most efficacious means of preventing a recurrence of the piles is, to keep the bowels free from confinement by some mild opening medicine, and attention to diet and exercise, now and then resorting to a little black pepper paste, or the balsam of capivi. Strong persons, who have a great deal of blood flowing in their

---

1. Smith, *On Piles,* p. 43.

veins, may take with advantage a little Epsom and Glauber's salt occasionally, as No. 27, page 155, or the powder No. 130, page 208. The excision of these excrescences is, however, the most certainly radical cure. It may be performed either by ligature, the knife, or scissors. Some surgeons advise the use of the ligature; others recommend the knife. The opinion of the majority of the most able surgeons is in favour of excision by the knife, but they are sometimes led to prefer the ligature, that is, when the piles are too large safely to admit of the use of the knife. Cutting off these excrescences, by means of the scissors, is a very simple and safe operation, provided they are small and is a mode of relief which well merits the attention of every one suffering much from this complaint.

An opinion has commonly prevailed that the bleeding from piles is of a salutary or critical nature, but this is more frequently false than true. In weakly persons; of a confined habit of body, they are very generally a symptom of unsound health, and ought to be cured in the way advised. In robust patients, however, and those who are full of blood, the bleeding piles are sometimes useful; and clearly so, when any complaint, to which the patient may have been previously subject, is either removed or lessened in severity, on their appearance. In such instances, as I have just remarked, they should be moderated, but not altogether checked, which is likewise to be observed when they appear in the place of some other and long-accustomed discharge, as bleeding from the nose, etc.

When there is *a prolapsus of the gut*, as referred to at pages 787-788, an operation may frequently be performed with complete and permanent relief; but should the patient be beyond fifty years of age and have suffered long from the complaint, or should other causes exist indicating the propriety of not risking the event of an operation, I would strongly recommend a spring truss for supporting the part when walking or riding, made by Mr. Atkinson, 3, Hemming's Row, St. Martin's Lane. He has shewn a great deal of ingenuity in the construction of this truss, and if it generally answers so well as he says it does, the comfort derived from it will be great indeed. Bell and Moody, of Bath, have also a truss which is spoken well of.

PLEURISY

The chief symptom of pleurisy is a catching pain in the side on drawing in the breath.

The symptoms and treatment of pleurisy or inflammation of the membrane lining the chest and which is called the pleura, are so much like those noticed under inflammation of the lungs, as to render it quite unnecessary for me to treat of the former affection separately, and I, therefore, refer the reader to the article on inflammation of the lungs for the usual symptoms and correct treatment of pleurisy. Indeed, many of the most able physicians assert that the two diseases cannot ordinarily be distinguished with certainty from each other during the life of the patient and all agree that they do not materially differ in their treatment. Leeches applied to the side, followed by a large and hot poultice, are the principal means of cure.

But there is a Bastard or Spurous Pleurisy which might be mistaken, by inexperienced persons, for the true acute pleurisy, and which I think it proper briefly to notice. This bastard pleurisy is an inflammatory affection of the muscles covering and passing between the ribs, which produces an acute pain of the side, increased on inspiration. It is distinguished from the true pleurisy, which is an internal affection, by being attended with little or no fever, and scarcely with any cough; and by the increase of pain which always takes place on movement of the chest or any exertion causing the contraction of the inflamed muscles.

The bastard pleurisy seems to be a sort of rheumatism; yet it sometimes spreads internally, occasioning the true pleurisy.

The most effectual means of removing it is, to foment the part affected with hot water, and to take a pill, composed of a grain of calomel, a grain of opium, and three grains of James's powder, or a quarter of a grain of tartarized antimony, at bed time, which may be repeated every night, or even twice in the twenty-four hours, till the complaint is cured. At the same time the bowels should be opened by some mild aperient, as No. 74, page 176 or No. 100 or 101, pages 193-94, and the feet kept warm and dry. If these means fail, a blister may be applied to the chest; and the above calomel pill continued.

POLYPUS

Polypus of the womb is an important, and not an unfrequent complaint, and is considered at length in a place more suitable than the present publication, *viz.*, in my *Treatise on the Diseases of Females.* I shall here make a few remarks respecting *Polypus of the Nose.*

There are different kinds of polypus : the principal are the *fleshy polypus,* a red, soft, and sensible swelling, free from pain, like a piece of healthy flesh; the *gelatinous polypus,* a softer, semi-transparent tumour, of a pale yellowish colour; and the *hydatid polypus*, which generally occurs in young people, and the cysts of which may be burst by pressure and the fluid in them discharged. These are *benign polypi.* The *malignant polypi* are hard, scirrhous, and painful; the *cancerous polypus* is a disease of old age, and there is a malignant polypus called *fungoid,* that is, of a *fungous* character.

The *causes* of this disease are involved in some obscurity. My opinion is, that there must be supposed to exist in the constitution a disposition to some local malady, and the nasal membrane being in such instances peculiarly disposed to assume a deranged action, extraneous matter is thrown out, or an extraneous growth is seen, which constitutes the disease called polypus; or should there be no disorder of the constitution, there must still be a local disposition to this form of affection and local agents may give rise to it, or at least strengthen the disposition, so as to bring it fully into action.

Treatment—This disease when *benign,* is usually treated either by extracting it with *forceps,* which is the most common and proper method, or extirpating it by means of a *ligature.*

Of course the most able surgeons should be consulted in such a case. It requires. sometimes strong powers of discrimination to distinguish whether a polypus is fit for an operation.

In most cases, the patient will find advantage from an alterative course of medicine, in which I would recommend particularly the sarsaparilla, or dandelion; with the pill, No. 98 or 99, pages 191-92, every or every other night; following, at the same time, the rules in regard to diet and regimen, recommended under INDIGESTION, and trying change of air. The air should be dry and bracing.

Under TUMOURS, the patient may read a valuable case of swelling in the left nostril cured by sarsaparilla, taken in large doses.

PUTRID SORE THROAT

There is a fashion in medicine, as well as every thing else in this world, and we never now hear of putrid sore throat, but it is all *diphtheria;* and therefore what I have stated with respect to the symptoms, causes and treatment of *diphtheria,* is applicable to putrid sore throat. Diphtheria is nothing but the old ulcerated or putrid sore throat.

The chief *symptoms* are those of frequent pulse, stiffness in the neck, and sore throat. The whole internal part of the throat appears of a fiery red colour, changing into large whitish-coloured stains, patches of chamois leather appearance and extensive sloughs.

In the worst cases, the sloughs corrode deeper and deeper, and spread throughout the whole alimentary tube,[1] or to the windpipe; the symptoms of irritation continue to increase; incipient mortification supervenes; a severe purging comes on; and the patient expires. Death usually takes place before the seventh, often as early as the third or fourth day.

TREATMENT—What I have said under *Scarlet Fever* and *Diphtheria,* is strictly applicable to the treatment of the present disease, of which, indeed, it is only a particular phase. Therefore I

1. The alimentary tube, or canal, includes the internal surface of the gullet, stomach and intestines, that is, the whole space from the beginning of the gullet to the anus.

strongly recommend five or six grains of *sesqui carbonate* of ammonia to be given in water, every two or three hours, to a child of twelve years old, until the patient is evidently relieved, when its repetition every four or five hours will be sufficient, or the prescription for ammonia given under Scarlet Fever may be used. Ammonia possesses specific powers in this terrible malady, and may be trusted to with the utmost confidence in the very worst cases. Some medical men will not trust to it, but that should not deter others.

If the patient can gargle, he should make use frequently of a gargle composed of fifteen drops of liquid ammonia in a wine glass of water; and if he cannot gargle, then the whole of the throat should be mopped with a very soft piece of sponge dipped in that solution of ammonia and water. Wine should be given freely. Women, unaccustomed to wine, have taken it successfully under this disease in the proportion of two bottles a day, for more than a fortnight.

If the patient will not trust to ammonia, the next best thing is muriatic acid, or the tincture of muriate of iron. The muriatic acid may be taken as recommended under Typhus Fever, but I do not think it here by any means so *efficacious* as ammonia.

Dr. Willan recommended the oxygenated muriatic acid as a tonic of very superior value in this disease, and there can be no doubt of its being an efficacious antiseptic. It may always be got pure at Mr. Garden's, Chemist, Oxford Street. The dose is half a drachm, three times a day, in cinnamon water.

The patient's linen must be frequently changed, the windows and doors opened, and pure air freely admitted and fumigation with the nitrous acid vapour often resorted to. This vapour is disengaged by putting half an ounce of sulphuric acid into a china saucer, or any other suitable vehicle, and sprinkling into it, from time to time, a little nitre, the china saucer containing the acid being warmed over a lamp, or put into heated sand. Several of these vessels may be placed in the apartment, and the passages leading to it, at twenty or thirty feet distance from each other. Dr. Willan has remarked, that the refreshing antiseptic vapour detached by this process, and circulated through the room, presently clears the patient's throat and at the same time removes the fetor both of the breath and perspiration.

The putrid sore throat being highly contagious, especially among children, it will be prudent on the first appearance of the disease, to separate the sick from the rest of the family; and it is absolutely necessary that the excrement and urine, together with the discharge from the patient's mouth, should be removed from the house directly they are voided.

RECTUM—DISEASES OF THE

Excoriations and slight ulcerations are sometimes met with at the orifice of the rectum, causing disproportionate suffering and anxiety. The present work being already sufficiently voluminous, I cannot introduce here more than a passing remark respecting the nature and treatment of this painful affection and must refer my readers for an ample account of the disease to my Treatise ON THE MANAGEMENT AND DISORDERS OF INFANCY AND CHILDHOOD.

In the treatment it is of importance to keep the bowels open by dietetic management, and the occasional use of confection of senna. The ulceration should be touched with the point of a little piece of sulphate of copper, morning and evening, and after the bowels have been opened, apply hot water with a sponge for a few minutes; and then an ointment consisting of half a drachm of grey powder mixed with an ounce of spermaceti cerate. If this does not cure the patient, the disease may require that a probe pointed bistoury should be passed through the ulcer, fairly dividing it longitudinally down to the subjacent tissue. The reader will find the details of an interesting and instructive case or two, successfully treated, in the volume above mentioned.

In all complaints of the rectum frequent washing with cold salt and water will be found of eminent service.

RHEUMATISM

This complaint naturally divides itself into two species, *Rheumatic*

Fever and *Chronic Rheumatism,* which, as they differ, both in their symptoms and treatment, I shall treat of separately.

Rheumatic Fever

Acute rheumatism, or rheumatic fever, consists in pain, inflammation, and fulness, usually about the larger joints and surrounding muscles,—symptoms which often wander from one part to another; the urine depositing a red sediment and the accompanying fever being inflammatory.

It is usually called *rheumatic fever,* but some people very erroneously denominate it *rheumatic gout.* I have known even medical men of respectability, call it by the latter name, a convincing proof that sufficient attention was not paid to the pathology of the complaint.

Acute rheumatism usually commences with languor, chilliness succeeded by heat, thirst, restlessness and a quick pulse; there is also a sense of weight, coldness of the limbs, and confined bowels. In the course of a day or two, inflammation, with acute pain, tumour, and tension, makes it appearance in one or more, of the larger joints of the body. The pain is frequently transitory and apt to shift from joint to joint, leaving the part previously occupied, swollen, red and extremely tender to the touch. The pulse now becomes full and hard, usually 120 or 130 in a minute; the blood, when drawn from a vein, is cupped, exhibiting the inflammatory surface; the tongue is much furred; the bowels are commonly, very costive; the urine high-coloured and loaded; and there is a profuse sour-smelling perspiration, unattended by relief.

Sometimes, however, the pain is the first symptom and the fever follows. When the pain is not very severe and confined to a few parts, the fever is slight, and the disease is *sub-acute;* when it is severe and felt in many parts, the fever is more considerable, and it is most so when the pains extend over the whole body. Both the pain and fever generally suffer an increase in the evening, and a remission towards morning. The pains are much increased on the slightest motion requiring the action of the muscles affected, and are most severe, as well as most apt to shift their place, in the night-time. The fever abates sooner than the local symptoms and is rarely protracted beyond a fortnight or three weeks. The pains, for the most part, are the last symptom which leaves the patient. They often begin to abate about the eighth or tenth day, but generally continue, with more or less severity, to the thirtieth or fortieth. Sometimes they continue for months, and even years; and it is very uncommon for them to disappear before the twentieth day.

Cold or damp applied when the body is heated, is the most usual cause; and the young and vigorous and those between the age of puberty and thirty-five, are most subject to it. It is more frequent m the beginning and towards the end of winter, than at any other season. Both rheumatism and gout are now regarded as diseases of the blood. In the former disease the morbific matter is supposed to be *lactic* acid; in the latter, *lithic* acid.

Persons who are full of blood are frequently attacked by it, and whatever occasions a sudden fulness of habit may be ranked among its exciting causes.

The only disease with which it is liable to be confounded is gout, which see. The gout is preceded by more evident symptoms of indigestion; comes on more suddenly; attacks the small joints; and has not so strongly marked an increase of the fever and other symptoms at night, as we witness in acute rheumatism.

TREATMENT—Many different modes of treatment have been recommended in this disease, but the *alkaline* treatment is unquestionably the best; and one of the most successful modes of proceeding is to take the draught, No. 27B, page 156, every four hours, with two of the pills, No. 97, page 191, at bed time. This draught should be taken every four hours until the patient is sensibly relieved, and the urine is no longer acid, but has become *alkaline;* then every six hours will be often enough to repeat the draught. As long as the bowels do not act freely and comfortably, the purgative pills, No. 97, should be taken at bed time; and if the pain in the joints is severe, the calomel, opium and James's powder pill, recommended at pages 801-02, may also be taken in the evening. In the commencement of this disease the diet should consist only of slops, such as gruel, bread and butter, tea and such like; and oranges or lemons may be freely sucked.

The preceding means will generally very greatly and sensibly relieve the patient in the course of two or three days, but it will not cure him so soon. At the end of these three days, should the urine continue alkaline, and the pulse be less frequent, then is the time to discontinue the draught No. 27B, and to take a draught composed of a wine-glassful of decoction of bark and one scruple of bi-carbonate of potash, thrice a day. Bark now sustains the patient's strength without heating or exciting him; on the contrary, it relieves the fever and perspiration, and even if the tongue is furred, bark should be given, provided the urine has become *alkaline,* and a free action of the bowels is kept up by Seidlitz powders, or the pills, No. 97. As soon as the improvement of the patient admits of the use of bark, the diet should be more generous, such as a little rice or bread pudding, porridge, asparagus, mashed potatoes, and mutton broth, for dinner, and an egg for breakfast. The best drink throughout are saline draughts, thin barley water, or *Thwaits's soda water.* Meat is apt to disagree and produce a relapse if taken too early and this occurs even in rheumatic attacks not attended with a bounding pulse or profuse perspiration.

Throughout this disease, it is a grand point to keep the bowels acting freely, and as long as they are loaded with unhealthy, dark-coloured, offensive secretions, a grain or two of calomel should be given at night, combined with four grains of compound colocynth pill; or the pills, No. 97, may be taken; or a Seidlitz powder is a very suitable aperient, and that may be taken at any time of the day.

Another good plan of treatment is, instead of the draught, No. 27B, to give a dose of the following mixture every second hour, night and day, when awake.

Take of bi-carbonate of potash	4	drachms;
Camphor mixture	12	ounces.

Mix them, and take three table-spoonfuls for a dose.

After about four or five days, when the patient is decidedly better, then lay this medicine aside, and give instead the bark and carbonate of potash as already advised or bark and ammonia.

In all cases of this disease a danger exists that the heart may become affected, to prevent which the alkaline medicine, No. 27B, or potash should be given in free and repeated doses so as to render the urine alkaline, when the heart may be considered safe. This affection of the heart is the greatest peril to which rheumatic fever exposes the patient, and nothing serves so certainly to ward it off as the alkaline treatment. The state of the urine, whether acid or alkaline, may always be easily ascertained by inserting into it a little test or litmus paper, sold by all druggists. Of course in acute rheumatism. a skilful medical man should be immediately called in; but such cannot be found in every place and therefore the most precise directions are here given for the public benefit.

The affected joints should be carefully wrapped in cotton wool; or five drachms of the carbonate of potash may be dissolved in half a pint of hot water and five fluid drachms of Battley's sedative liquor of opium added to it; thin flannel, soaked in this warm lotion, may be applied to the inflamed joint; and the whole be wrapped in a covering of thin gutta percha or oiled silk.

Shortness of breath, or a complaint of pain in the chest, when suffering from rheumatic fever, especially when accompanied with irregularity in the pulse, indicates that the heart is affected; and then eight leeches should be applied at once, followed by a blister over the region of the heart and the pill of calomel, opium and James's powder, prescribed on the other side, taken thrice a day, until the pain in the chest is removed; the alkaline draught, No. 27B, being also taken as previously advised.

In the first instance, while perspiring freely, the patient should be encircled with flannel. The sheets should be removed from the bed, while the patient lies in good warm blankets. The night dress must be either of calico, flannel or merino. No exposure to cold whatever should be made of the body. We cannot exaggerate the importance of repose and a warm temperature to the skin in this disease. They will powerfully contribute to preserve the heart from being attacked; and the patient should return cautiously to the use of linen.

When rheumatism attacks people of a weakly constitution, and the tongue is tolerably clean, the urine not muddy, the skin not perspiring profusely with a sour smell, but only warm and moist, a tonic method of treatment should be at once commenced. Here the vital powers are low, and the most effectual remedies are bark and ammonia, as No. 84B, or bark and potash, that is, half a drachm of bi-carbonate of potash in a wine-glassful of decoction of bark, thrice a day. When bark is given, give a Seidlitz powder every morning as a mild aperient.

Dr. Fuller says, in his *Treatise on Rheumatism,* p. 107, "The alkaline treatment has now been pursued in a large number of cases, and in almost every instance has produced the most astonishingly favourable results." Dr. Golding Bird himself suffered from acute rheumatism, and was deeply impressed with the superiority of the alkaline treatment. He was partial to the acetate of potash. Dr. Vaston says, *(Lect.* vol. ii. p. 748), "Alkalies, or the alkaline salts, are always, in my opinion, fit remedies to be employed in acute rheumatism." Many physicians recommend an addition of colchicum, but it is not suitable for domestic practice, nor for that of the young practitioner; beides, it is a very dangerous medicine, and I protest against its use. It certainly relieves pain, but so does opium and opium is a more manageable and less dangerous article; so do the neutral salts, and effervescing draughts and they never produce unpleasant consequences.

Blood-letting is now seldom employed by physicians in rheumatism, and certainly must not be employed for the purpose of efficiently relieving pain. It is the state of the fever only which is to direct us in the use of the lancet, the abstraction of the blood, if ever proper in acute rheumatism, being so only because of the violence of the fever. It must also be regulated, in a great measure, by the age, strength, and habits of the patient; and his residence, whether in town or country, ought likewise to be considered. If the patient be young and vigorous, and leading an active country life, a single bleeding will sometimes be followed by much relief, but the repetition of the blood-letting is seldom necessary. Patients who enjoy the advantages of a healthful country residence, will bear bleeding in this disease, when those who inhabit populous cities, or marshy districts, will not bear it at all. Upon the whole, the employment of the lancet is seldom proper in any but the young and plethoric. It is not allowable after the fifth day, and at no time when the fever is abating, although the pains should become worse.[1]

The sheet anchor of the practitioner here, in the relief of acute pain, is half a grain of calomel, combined with a grain or two of opium, and two grains of James's powder, or the eighth of a grain of emetic tartar and made into a pill with a little conserve of roses, which is to be given every night, at bed Time.[2] This pill may be called for night and morning, or even thrice in the twenty-four hours, by the severity of the pain. It relieves pain and inflammation and sometimes has uncommon influence in shortening the term of the disease. If the patient should be peculiarly susceptible to the action of opium, it will often be better to give a quarter of a grain of the acetate of morphia instead of the opium. But opium is generally of eminent service here by relieving the pain and promoting sleep.

The Peruvian bark has been praised by physicians of the highest authority, among whom are Sir Edward Hulse, Dr. Fothergill and Dr. Fordyce, as being capable alone of curing the severest cases. It is, no doubt, often an admirable medicine after the first week or two, the hardness of pulse and fever having been reduced by alkaline remedies, and an abatement of the symptoms begun to be perceived. In such cases, twenty grains of powdered bark may be taken, in water, every three hours, or the mixture, No. 84B, page 185. One

1. "We have long been convinced," says Dr. James Johnson, "from attentive observation, that the system of detracting large quantities of blood, in cases of acute rheumatism, is productive of more frequent metastasis from the extremities to internal organs than a more moderate treatment."—*Medico-Chirurgical Review,* June 1823, p. 215.
2. "In acute rheumatism, in which my experience has led me to discard bleeding, unless the patient be of a very strong, sanguine temperament, I know nothing that proves more serviceable than a combination of one grain of calomel, a quarter of a grain of emetic tartar, and from one to two grains of opium."—Dr. A. T. Thomson's *Elements of Materia Medica,* vol. ii. p. 495.

of the most striking cases of quick recovery, clearly obtained by medical treatment in an acute disease, which I ever witnessed, was the cure of a very violent attack of the present complaint by the Peruvian bark, but then the violence of the disease had abated. The patient was a young man, about thirty years of age, who, when I first saw him, had been confined to his room by inflammatory rheumatism for about ten weeks. He had improperly been largely bled and purged and had sweated profusely, yet the symptoms, at the end of ten weeks, seemed to be almost as severe as ever, although he had occasional remissions of two, three or four days' duration. The night I commenced my attendance he was in a great deal of pain, confined to his bed, sweating profusely and through every covering, with a pulse full, quick and throbbing, but not hard and his friends were much alarmed for his safety. His physician had seen him two or three hours before and wished to have him bled again; but the family having wisely objected to that, he ordered a large dose of a sweating powder, which, however, was not given. On visiting him, I ordered the bark, in doses of fifteen grains of the powder every four hours, which was immediately commenced and continued in the same quantities for near a fortnight. The next day he was sensibly much better, the pains were greatly relieved, the perspiration was removed and never again returned, and by degrees his appetite and sleep became good; in short, he grew evidently better and better every day, and in less than a fortnight too a journey of nearly one hundred miles without sustaining the least injury.

Some order the sulphate of quinine in preference to any other form of giving the bark, supposing it is likely to be still more beneficial; but I prefer the powder, as being snore febrifuge. The proper dose of quinine here is two or three grains, three times a day.

Some American physicians look upon the black snake root *(tincture of actea)* as their most valuable remedy in acute rheumatism, but I believe the preceding treatment is far better. They give the tincture in doses of fifty drops, thrice a day, in water.

In December, 1831, I met with a very severe case of subacute rheumatism in a man of about forty-five years of age, with the following symptoms; considerable difficulty of breathing and great pain and oppression in the chest, so that sometimes in endeavouring to expectorate he seemed in danger of suffocation; great pain and stiffness in many other parts of the body, but especially in the left elbow, wrist and hand, which are much inflamed and so swollen as not to permit the least motion; tongue furred; pulse hard, full and not less than one hundred and twenty in a minute; very restless nights; no appetite; urine very high-coloured, and depositing considerable sediment. He had been confined to his bed for a fortnight. The following pills were prescribed with the most sensible and striking advantage; in a few hours he lost the oppression and pain in the chest, and his pains generally were greatly mitigated; the perspiration diminished, and in a week he was able to rise from his bed. In a former attack, having had only parish attendance, he was confined to the house five months. I introduce the prescription here as it is an invaluable one, both for acute and chronic rheumatism. The case being very urgent, this man took one pill every six hours, night and day, for two days and a night; the next three days he took one pill thrice a day, and afterwards for five days, one night and morning. He had no other medicine. In chronic rheumatism, one pill regularly night and morning for a week, and afterwards every night for a fortnight, will usually be quite sufficient.

Take of Calomel	10	
grains; Tartar emetic	½	grains;
Powder of gum guaiacum	20	grains;
Compound powder of ipecacuanha	20	grains.

Mix, and by means of conserve of hips, make them into a mass and divide them into ten pills.

Lemon or lime juice has recently been strongly recommended as an efficacious remedy in *acute* rheumatism, in doses of two or three ounces, three times a clay, in tepid water. Some have ordered not less than four or five ounces taken in a draught, without any admixture, three times a day. The only unequivocal effect that uniformly takes place from its use, is a diminution in the number and power of the pulse, and of the heart's action. It may sometimes be used with advantage in chronic rheumatism; but it is of less use in cachectic subjects—patients in the lower orders, with poor blood, weak and rapid pulse, and whose history is one of long mental and physical suffering. In these cases, the exhibition of muriate of morphia, in full doses, is a far better remedy, but the best remedy is cod-liver oil. The action of lemon juice in acute rheumatism is sometimes so remarkable that it will quickly produce cessation of pain, and decrease of swelling and redness, in a way far superior to what can be obtained from colchicum, even when administered in the best manner.

I do not think the lemon juice is by any means so efficacious as the alkaline medicines referred to at pages 798-99.

For any stiffness or chronic pains left in the joints after the disease has been removed, bathing the parts twice a day, with lukewarm salt and water and then rubbing them once a day with a stimulating liniment, as advised under Gout, will generally be the most effectual means of removing those symptoms. When convalescent, the patient should likewise resort to moderate exercise, both within doors and in the open air; and if his strength will permit, a walk of several miles every other day, will be found of eminent service in restoring use to the limbs, and perfecting the recovery.

The temperature of the patient's room should be as uniform as possible and of moderate warmth.

Should bark not have been used in the active stages of the disease, it will be found in its decline a useful tonic in expediting and perfecting a return to the patient's former health and strength. *See* the prescriptions, No. 35, No. 125.

Chronic Rueumatism

Chronic rheumatism differs from the *acute,* or *rheumatic fever,* in being attended with little or no fever or inflammation, the chief symptoms being pain and swelling in the large joints, and in the course of certain muscles. The former is clearly a disease of debility; the latter is an inflammatory complaint.

The chronic species becomes fixed most frequently in the loins, hip, knee and ankles, but every large joint is liable to its attacks. The general heat of the body seldom exceeds its natural temperature and the pulse is rarely quicker than eighty strokes in a minute; the joints are swollen, but not to so great a degree as in the acute species, being of a pale hue, cold and stiff, roused with difficulty to perspiration and always comforted by the application of warmth.

The same causes give rise to this and to the acute species; and violent strains and spasms will cause chronic rheumatism where the constitution is peculiarly disposed to the malady.

TREATMENT.—It is a disease of debility and the mode of treatment must be founded on this fact. Bleeding and purging, therefore, ought not to be thought of here; the most efficacious remedies being those which are of a warm balsamic nature, and which nourish the blood, and promote the insensible perspiration; such as cod-liver oil, guaiacum, sulphur, Dover's powder, turpentine, camphor, cajeput oil, mustard and the compound ipecacuanha powder. Local stimulants are likewise often of great service, more especially the stimulus of Galvanism or Electricity.

The compound ipecacuanha powder, (especially if sulphur be taken in the day), is eminently serviceable in relieving the pains, disposing to sleep, and keeping up a gentle and salutary discharge from the skin, which of all others is the evacuation affording most benefit in cases of this description. Three grains of this powder may be made into a pill with a little extract of gentian and given three or four times a day; about a quarter of a grain of aloes being added to each pill, to prevent costiveness. At the same time the affected parts may be rubbed, thrice a day, for a quarter of an hour, with one of the liniments, No. 41, 45, or 46, pages 161, 163 ; the painful joints being always wrapped in flannel. If the pains are very severe and the patient's general health appears deranged, a grain of calomel, two grains of James's powder and a grain of opium, may be made into a pill with a little conserve and taken every night at bed-time. This pill will sometimes be found of great value. In addition to these means, a tepid bath at ninety-five degrees should be used every other morning, for about half an hour or forty minutes; or a trial be given to the air-pump vapour bath, if within the patient's reach.

Next in efficacy to the above ipecacuanha powder is, I think, either the hydrochlorate of ammonia or the guaiacum mixture, noticed at page 176, or the volatile or ammoniated tincture of guaiacum, which may be tried in (doses of thirty, forty or fifty ops, every four hours, taken in milk and water.—The liniment being applied locally, and the calomel pill taken at night, with the warm bath occasionally, as just advised. The guaiacum mixture sometimes acts better than the tincture. But in my experience no remedy has been half so efficacious as cod-liver oil, in the close of a table-spoonful, twice or thrice a day. It so improves the nutritive functions, as in a remarkable manner to impart new life to the blood and all the joints; and effectually cure the patient.

Dr. Fuller says, *Treatise on Rheumatism and Gout,* p. 373, Hydrochlorate of ammonia sometimes produces marvellous results, in the dose of a scruple, in three table-spoonfuls of decoction of bark, thrice a day.

A very good plan of treatment is to give a scruple of sublimed sulphur in milk and water, thrice a day, unless the bowels become much affected by it, when it should be taken less frequently, with a Dover's powder pill to relieve pain as often as may be required, and the pill of calomel, James's powder and opium, just noticed, every night. In some cases of this disease, the pain is so extremely severe as to require the free use of opium, and then we should not be afraid of its liberal employment and instead of one grain of powdered opium being used in the night pill just recommended, we may give two grains.

I have been told that lime juice has been taken, in water, sweetened with sugar, with complete success, in very bad cases.

If these fail, the oil of turpentine may be taken internally, said is sometimes very useful.[1] Half an ounce of this oil may be mixed

1. "In chronic rheumatic pains of the hips (*sciatica*), and muscles of the loins (*lumbago*), the *spirit of turpentine* is among our most efficacious remedies. Home states, (in his *Clinical Observations* and *Experiments*) that he cured five out of seven cases of sciatica with this article. Within the present year, I

(Contd. on next page)

with an equal quantity of sweet spirit of nitre, of which mixture a tea-spoonful, three times a day, in the infusion of cloves, is the proper dose.

Should the complaint prove particularly obstinate, which is not uncommon, I would recommend a trial of the following pills, instead of those made with the compound ipecacuanha powder alone; but this is not equal to cod-liver oil.

Take of Compound ipecacuanha powder	36 grains;
Extract of hemlock, prepared in vacuo	1 drachm;
Best gum guaiacum, in powder	24 grains;
Socotorine aloes, in powder...............	4 grains.

Mix, and divide into twenty-four pills. Two or three to be taken three times a day.

Of course the liniments before recommended, with the pill, No. 89A, at night, and the warm bath, must not be neglected while taking these pills.

The arsenical solution is a medicine which has been highly praised by Dr. Bardsley, of Manchester, and others; but, from its activity, it ought not to be used till the foregoing remedies have failed of success. It is, in general, of no use in recent cases and in young persons; but in the long-standing attacks of old subjects, it will sometimes perfectly succeed after every previous expedient has failed. *See* what is said of this medicine at page 12.

Colchicum has been much extolled of late years by some respectable practitioners. It is not, however, well adapted to the *chronic* species; and what has been said of it under the article on GOUT, is likewise true of its use in the present disease. If it be used

(Contd.)

succeeded completely in removing a violent and protracted case of this affection by the turpentine, given in doses of twenty drops, with a scruple of *lac sulphuric* three times daily." *Eberles' Practice of Medicine;* vol. i. p. 385. The able author of these remarks seems to have forgotten for the moment, that the *milk of sulphur* is in itself an invaluable remedy for chronic rheumatism, and we may well be at a loss to determine which had most to do with this cure,—the milk of sulphur or the turpentine ? I think the sulphur is the most powerful remedy.

very moderately, and in conjunction with the other approved remedies here noticed, it may be of service; but if trusted to alone, and incautiously employed in large quantities, it will not fail to be extremely injurious. In such large quantities it may mitigate the patient's sufferings, but it will also weaken his stomach, debilitate his whole frame and shorten his life. I cannot recommend it.

Iodide of potassium is almost a specific in certain suspicious pains of the bones and joints and therefore, if other means fail, it should be tried in doses of three or four grains, thrice a day. In violent pains of the elbow and other joints, aggravated at night, I have known it attended with the most complete and gratifying success. Dr. Barlow thinks highly of it.—*Practice of Medicine*, p. 148.

The local stimulants of most service here, are the strong liniments mentioned at pages 165-68, the burning of moxa and Electricity or Galvanism. Whatever liniment is applied to the affected parts, it should be rubbed in frequently, and with active friction, by the patient himself. The friction can hardly be too long continued at one time, or too frequently resorted to, for it alone wrought wonders in desperate cases. Dr. Balfour, of Edinburgh, has published a useful book on the good effects of friction and compression in rheumatism, in which he relates numerous examples of its efficacy in the worst cases. Admiral Henry, of Rolvenden, in Kent, was almost a cripple from a very protracted attack of chronic rheumatism, and he cured himself by the steady use of friction alone. Besides the hand, he employed small pieces of wood, rounded at the top, with which he used to rub and compress the stiff and painful parts. In severe and obstinate instances, I would strongly urge a trial of moxa, which has sometimes been very successful in removing stiffness and pain in inveterate forms of this malady. For the manner of using it, *see* the directions at page 98.

Electricity, in the form of aura or sparks, or in slight shocks, is worthy of much confidence; and the same may be said of Galvanism.

The operation of Galvanism is more soothing and agreeable to most persons than that of Electricity, and, perhaps, is commonly more efficacious here. It has, undoubtedly, effected great and salutary changes in this painful complaint and ought not to be neglected if the more common plans of treatment fail.

The vapour bath is also of eminent service in many cases. It may be used at about one hundred and ten degrees, once or twice a week. By promoting a free perspiration, it greatly relieves the internal parts.—*See Appendix.*

The air pump vapour bath has been found of remarkable service in many extreme cases of chronic rheumatism, even when accompanied with stiffness and contraction of the joints and muscles, and after the vapour bath, applied in the usual manner, had failed to produce any beneficial effects. The air pump bath is a local application to the parts immediately affected and combines the powers of the most effectual fomentations with those of dry cupping; so that by removing the weight of the atmosphere from the injured parts and promoting a free perspiration at the same time, it resolves obstruction, imparts a freedom to the local circulation and effectually assists nature in her efforts to change the diseased condition of action present, for one that is healthy. If the case requires it, it may be used alternately with Galvanism, and these remedies united, are, in some obstinate cases, much more efficacious than either of them employed alone. See what is said of the air-pump vapour bath at page 234, and in M. La Beaume's Essay on this bath.

The Bath and Buxton warm waters are well known to be of exceeding efficacy in the present complaint. A course of warm bathing at Buxton is one of the best means which can be resorted to, for a cure of the stiffness and chronic pains left after an attack of acute rheumatism. The Duke of Devonshire lately requested Dr. Playfair to make an analysis of the thermal springs of Buxton, which has resulted in a discovery of great consequence to the reputation of these celebrated waters. It was found that every imperial gallon of the waters contained 206 *cubic inches of nitrogen;* and upon this gaseous element Dr. Playfair considers the medicinal properties of the Buxton waters entirely to depend. Hitherto only 5.57 cubic inches per gallon were supposed to be the proportion in which this important element was contained in these waters. The great and singularly lasting effects of these baths, and of the internal use of this water, are unquestioned and indisputable. Their use is almost specific for the relief or alleviation of most cases of chronic rheumatism and of many cases of gout, for which the use of other means and appliances has been sought and tried in vain. Large numbers of poor handicraftsmen, who have proved the effect of this water on their suffering and imperfectly usable limbs, are known to undergo great privations, in order to secure its use at stated intervals, from finding that no other means within their reach enables them to maintain such a state of their joints as is needful to enable them to follow their employment. The yearly reports of the Buxton Bath Charity certify, that of 15,497 patients, for the most part sufferers from rheumatism, admitted to the benefit of the institution, from the year 1838 to 1851, only 613 had to be sent home as being "no better," the large proportion of 11,740 having been discharged as "cured or much relieved." These are grand results, and may *vie* with any of the vaunts of the thermalists of Germany. They should send our invalids to this beautiful locality, in preference to the continental watering-places.

The tartar emetic ointment rubbed near the seat of any fixed and severe rheumatic pain, will bring out a large crop of pustules, and sometimes afford essential relief.

Acupuncturation has lately been recommended in this disease, and may be tried in severe examples, where the preceding remedies fail. It consists in making a small puncture in or near the part of the body affected, with a long needle. The puncture produces little or no pain, and should be followed by no bleeding. A single puncture is sometimes found sufficient to remove the pain; and if it shoots to another part, that is punctured in the same way as the original seat of the irritation. Now and then, acupuncturation appears to have been followed by very striking advantages; but the improvement of the general health must be attended to at the same time.

The best remedies for chronic rheumatism originating in a syphilitic affection, or accompanying secondary symptoms, are a quarter of a pint of compound decoction of sarsaparilla, twice or thrice a day, with half a tea-spoonful of solution of bichloride of mercury, gradually increased to a tea-spoonful.

Chronic rheumatism originating in a disreputable source, and accompanied with swelling in the bones of the leg, arm or head, is often peculiarly obstinate; and nothing is usually, I believe, so efficacious in this peculiar case as the bi-chloride of mercury, taken in the manner just advised. Dr. Fuller, of St. George's Hospital, recommends in such cases the following draught, which, he says, has succeeded after almost every thing else has failed; but I question whether it is more efficacious than the combination of bi-chloride of mercury and decoction of sarsaparilla alone.

Take of iodide of potassium	6	grains;
Solution of bi-chloride of mercury	½	or 1 drachm;
Decoction of bark	10	drachms.

Mix them for a draught, to be taken thrice a day, after a meal.

The gums should be watched while taking this medicine and if any swelling and soreness are felt there, salivation may ensue, and of course the mercury should at once be omitted, and the bark and iodide of potassium taken alone.

The clothing should be warm, and the diet generous and stimulating, but moderate in quantity, so that the stomach may never be overloaded. As an article of clothing for the rheumatic, an under waistcoat of chamois leather is, generally, of very great service and sometimes proves of the most striking advantage. If the lower extremities of the body are much affected, drawers also, made of the same material, should be worn. This leather washes like linen, only it must not be washed in hot water. For the first day or two, it usually feels cold and uncomfortable, but soon becomes more comfortable than flannel. It is proper to have several sets, and to change them frequently. The price is about sixteen shillings a set.

Before concluding this article it is necessary to apprize the reader, that we frequently meet in practice with flying or fixed chronic pains, attended by stiffness, which imitate rheumatic pains, but are owing to a disordered state of the stomach and bowels and poor blood; indeed, some of these cases may be correctly called rheumatic. In such instances, the symptoms of indigestion will generally present themselves more or less clearly marked and the most effectual remedies will be those pointed out under that complaint, especially the alterative pill, No. 98 or 99, every other night, with a little, bitter infusion and carbonate of soda, as No. 83, page 184—or cod-liver oil through the day, the bowels being preserved regular by the aperient pill, No. 100 or 101, pages 193-94. Another valuable plan in these particular instances is, to take half a pint of the compound decoction of sarsaparilla, twice a day, with two grains of blue pill and five of extract of hemlock, made into two pills, every night. If the pains are severe, the patient may increase the quantity of hemlock here ordered, and take ten grains of it once or twice a day, with two grains of the blue pill in the whole, daily. Whatever medicine be resorted to, the diet and regimen laid down under INDIGESTION must be attentively pursued; considerable exercise on foot or horse back being taken every day, if possible, with friction, early rising, etc. *Rheumatic Gout* is a combination of rheumatism and gout, in which some of both the larger and smaller joints are, more or less, affected with pain, swelling and stiffness. In its treatment, special regard must be given to those means which improve the quality of the blood and restore the health—the chief of which are bark, quinine, cod-liver oil, strychnine and sarsaparilla, with nourishing diet.

Dr. Fuller, physician to St. George's Hospital, strongly recommends small doses of *strychnine* for the nervous depression met with in rheumatic gout. It may be given in decoction of bark. He says:

> "In the whole catalogue of the pharmacopaeia I know of no remedy equal to *strychnia* as a tonic when the nervous system is unduly depressed and the patient is nervous and low spirited. Its value in cases of rheumatic gout, in which these symptoms are often very distressing, can scarcely be over-estimated, for it certainly produces effects which you may seek in vain from quinine and other vegetable

bitters. It seems to rouse and invigorate the patient by stimulating the nervous system and thus indirectly promoting increased activity of the various functions of the body."—*Lancet,* 26th Sept., 1863.

RICKETS

This disease consists in a want of due firmness in the bones, in consequence of a deficiency of the phosphate of lime in their structure.

It often comes on slowly, the first appearance being a flaccidity of the flesh, emaciation of the body and paleness of the complexion. The head, at the same time, appears large with respect to the body and the sutures are preternaturally open. The head continues to increase in size; the forehead becomes unusually prominent; the neck is short; the teething is very slow and much later than usual and the teeth that do appear soon spoil and are apt to fall out. The ribs lose their convexity; the breast bone protrudes; the spine is incurvated; the extremities of the bones of the limbs enlarge, while the other part of the bones appear more slender than natural; in their whole length they become soft and flexible, unable to support the weight of the body and at last much distorted.

The child's strength is also diminished, he is averse to making exertion and is unable to walk; the appetite is sometimes good, but often capricious and deficient; the motions are offensive and of a bad colour; and the belly often much swelled and hard. In the beginning there is no fever, but in the advanced stage a frequent pulse, with thirst, heat and other symptoms of a hectic nature attend.

A deficient formation of bony earth constitutes the *immediate cause* of rickets; but the *remote* and *predisposing causes* are often involved in much obsecurity. In general, however, they are the same as those which give rise to scrophula, though there must exist in the child's constitution a disposition to this particular form of disease rather than to any other.

Parents of a weakly habit of body, whether natural or acquired by an irregular and injurious mode of living, are most liable to have their offspring afflicted with this disease. A damp and cold residence, impure air, inattention to cleanliness, deficient exercise, innutritious food and severe disorder of the digestive organs, will favour, in a powerful manner, the action of the exciting causes.

The disease seldom appears before the ninth month and rarely slows itself after the second or third year. It seems to be almost solely confined to cold and variable climates.

TREATMENT—As this complaint is strictly one of general debility, the great object is to afford strength to the system by the use of strengthening medicines, combined with a nutritious diet, pure bracing air, daily exercise, friction and the tepid bath.

The tonic medicines of most service here, are cod-oil, carbonate and sulphate of iron, and sulphate or tincture of quinine. The preparations of iron and quinine may be taken as advised under INDIGESTION OR SCROPHULA. Alkalies have been highly praised for their efficacy in this malady; but they should ever be combined with tonics, as in No. 84B, page 185 or No. 87C, in *the Appendix.*

The sulphate of quinine may be given in doses of half a grain or a grain, mixed with extract of gentian, three times a day; the dose being proportioned to the patient's age.

But the state of the bowels will always require close attention at the same time. If costive, they should be regulated by a small quantity of rhubarb and sal polychrest, given every other night or by the use of a little manna or the following, liquid—

Take of decoction of bar, ...	1 ounce;
Infusion of rhubarb	1 ounce;
Camphor mixture	1 ounce.

This is to be taken, at once or twice, during the day.

Dr. Trousseau, physician to the Children's Hospital at Paris, speaks very highly of the different fish-oils, *viz.*, cod, ray, shark, whale, etc. for the treatment of rickets; but cod-liver oil is the variety which Dr. Trousseau prescribes most frequently. Rapidly increasing doses, never exceeding one ounce and a half, taken for two or three months, have cured children of one and two years, who could not walk, and whose limbs were bending under them. Cod-liver oil has been for a long period of time a common remedy on the coasts of the Baltic for rickety children. It is said that a Dutch gentleman went to settle at Tours, in France, in 1826, when one of his children began to suffer from rickets. M. Bretonneau, who was consulted, gave the child salt-water baths, without good results. The father then stated that he had cured other children of his with fish-oil in his native country; it was again tried in this case; the child recovered and hence the introduction of the remedy.

In addition to these medicines, the patient should have a nourishing diet, consisting of the most digestible animal food and vegetables, eggs, good malt liquor, and wine; but the quantity of food allowed ought to be moderate and no more than can be digested with ease. The air should be salubrious, dry and bracing; and the exercise be considerable and as active as the strength, of the patient will permit. Friction, likewise, is of no mean service in this complaint. It should be carried alternately over the limbs, and every other part of the body, being resorted to for a quarter of an hour, three times a day at least; and the hand may be defended with a little flour or olive oil. The patient should lie on a hard mattress and rise early in the morning.

There is commonly too great a degree of weakness to admit of the use of the cold bath, but the tepid bath at from ninety to ninety-five degrees, three or four times a week, may sometimes be a useful auxiliary to the foregoing measures.

Perseverance in the above plans will often be rewarded with great success; but little is to be accomplished here without the exercise of considerable patience and attention.

It is the practice of some persons to endeavour to give support to the limbs and promote the restoration of their proper figure by the use of bandages and other mechanical instruments, but they are now very seldom employed by enlightened and judicious practitioners. They generally agree that it is far best to leave to nature alone, assisted by good medical treatment, the duty of rectifying bones deformed by the rickets. It has been wisely said by an eminent physician, (Dr. Good) that the best mechanical instruments are a hard incompressible couch, and a level floor, on which the infant may lie at full length and stretch his limbs as he pleases. The couch should be made light and moveable, so that he may be carried upon it into the open air for exercise.[1]

When a rickety state of the constitution in young girls gives rise to a crooked spine, and growing out of the shoulder, it must be treated in the manner described under *Spinal Curvature.*

RINGWORM OF THE SCALP

Ringworm of the scalp and scald-head, are generally considered by unprofessional persons to be synonymous terms, and they are so nearly alike as to make it unnecessary to draw a distinction between them in a popular treatise on medicine. There are several varieties of ringworm or porrigo as medical men call it; but as the treatment is very similar in all, we shall not now attempt to describe them separately.

The ringworm of the scalp is well-known to make its appearance in separate patches, of an irregular circular shape, upon the scalp, forehead and neck. It commences with clusters of small light yellow pustules, which soon break and form thin scabs, which, if neglected, become thick and hard. If the scabs are removed, however, the surface underneath is left red and shining, but studded with slightly elevated points or pustules. When the disorder is neglected, the patches run together and the whole head becomes affected. Where the disease is situated the hair becomes lighter in its colour, it falls off, and its roots are destroyed. It generally occurs in children and frequently proves exceedingly obstinate.

Sometimes it seems to originate spontaneously in children of a feeble and flabby habit and who are ill-fed, uncleanly and not sufficiently exercised. But it is chiefly propagated by contagion, that is, by the actual conveyance of the matter from the diseased to

---

1. "In rickety affections of the knees, horse exercise is of great advantage; if the patient is very young, he may be allowed to ride the rocking horse as long as he likes. The position on horseback throws the knees outwards, while the exercise is beneficial to the general health of the patient."—*Sir Astley Cooper, Lancet,* vol. ii, p. 464, 1823-24.

the healthy, as may happen in the frequent contact of the heads of children, the use of the same towels, combs, caps and hats.

TREATMENT.—There are few applications equal to the citrine ointment, No. 89, page 188, which will often cure very bad cases of this disease. In the beginning, it must be mixed with an equal quantity of simple cerate, with which every affected part ought to be anointed night and morning; the strength of the ointment being gradually increased till it is used undiluted. Take the mixture, No. 87C, in *the Appendix*.

The hair is first to be cut off as close as may be, or the head shaved; the scalp is than to be slowly and carefully washed with soap and water night and morning and well dried afterwards. The ointment is to be applied after the washing every night and is to be well rubbed all over the head. It may be washed off in the morning and when the scalp is made dry, instead of applying it through the day, the head may be thoroughly powdered with the finest starch contained in a fine linen or cambric bag. The scabs and incrustations will hereby become dried or often brittle and in this state they should be gently picked or combed off one after another, as they grow loose and become detached at the edges.

The following composition has been much praised, and should the citrine ointment fail, it is worthy of a trial.

Take of calomel	2	drachms;
Dried alum	1	ounce;
Acetate of lead	1	ounce;
Venice turpentine	6	drachms;
Spermaceti cerate	1½	ounces.

Mix.

One drachm of sulphuret of potash, dissolved in a pint of lime water, is an excellent lotion, and so is from six to ten grains of nitrate of silver, dissolved in an ounce of distilled water. These lotions may be tried with the prospect of success even after the foregoing ointments have failed. It is only necessary to wash the diseased parts with them twice a day.

Warm white wine vinegar has been sometimes effectually used as a lotion night and morning.

Whatever remedy is resorted to, the scalp must be shaved every eight or ten days, and where that is not practicable, the hair should be cut very close, and kept so; nothing but a light linen or oil skin cap being worn, which ought to be often changed.

In general, no local applications agree well if long continued, and it is often necessary to have recourse alternately to several of those just noticed.

The mode of treatment that I would recommend from experience in this disease, as decidedly the most effectual, is, after shaving the head, to wash every affected part with a saturated solution of sulphate of copper, every night for five or six nights, or longer, washing well with soap and water in the morning. At the end of the six days the ringworm should be anointed every morning with a little of the best castor oil, and this must be continued till the cure is established. This is a most efficacious method of treatment and in conjunction with constitutional management, will, I hope, be found almost infallible. Only the parts affected should be touched with the solution of copper, as it is rather caustic. At the same time, pay great attention to improve the general health. For this purpose give the tonic, No. 87C, in *the Appendix*, or tincture of muriate of iron, No. 87 C.Y. in *the Appendix*. The mixture, No. 84B, is also excellent;[1] and let the patient have plenty of air and exercise.

Should the complaint be of long standing, and have become chronic, the irritation must be lessened gradually, by using the local applications in a weaker state and by a steady use of the alterative pill, No. 96 or 98A, thrice a week.

---

1. A useful book has lately been published by *Mr. Macilwain on Porrigo* or *Scald Head*, in which he states his conviction, that the constitutional treatment of this affection has been too generally neglected and that it can seldom be cured without much attention to this point, as advised above. Dr. Ross, of 11, Hart Street, Bloomsbury Square, is worthy of much confidence by sufferers from this complaint.

If, after having employed different remedies for a considerable time for the cure of ringworm, the disease seems nearly well, the head being, however, not quite clear and the disorder now stationary, under the use of all the means tried, I would advise every application to be laid aside (the head being kept very clean); as, frequently, under such circumstances, the skin seems only to require a respites and nature herself completes the cure.

RUPTURE

By the term rupture is understood a tumour, formed by the protrusion of some portion of intestine out of the cavity of the belly, into a kind of sac, composed of that part of the membrane called peritoneum, which is pushed before the bowel.

The parts of the body where ruptures most frequently make their appearance, are the groin, the navel and the upper and fore part of the thigh; they do also occur at every point of the anterior part of the abdomen; and less commonly at a few other particular points, which it is not necessary particularly to describe in this work. The small intestine is more frequently protruded than the large, especially the last portion of the small intestines. A part only of the diameter of the tube is sometimes included in a rupture; any larger quantity may descend, from a single fold to the whole moveable portion of the canal.

When the protruded bowels lie quietly in the sac and admit of being readily put back into the abdomen, the case is termed a *reducible rupture;* and when they suffer no constriction, yet cannot be put back, owing to adhesions or their large size in relation to the aperture through which they have to pass, the rupture is termed *irreducible.* A *strangulated rupture* signifies one, which not only cannot be reduced, but suffers constriction; so that if a piece of intestine be protruded, the pressure to which it is subjected stops the passage of its contents towards the anus, excites inflammation of the bowels, and brings on a train of alarming and often fatal consequences.

The *general symptoms* of a rupture which is reducible and free from strangulation, are an indolent tumour at some point of the belly, most frequently descending out of the abdominal ring, or from just below what is called Poupart's ligament, that is, in or near the groin, or else out of the navel; but occasionally from various other situations. The swelling often originates suddenly, and is subject to a change of size, being smaller when the patient lies down on his back, and larger when he stands up or holds his breath. It frequently diminishes when pressed and grows large again when the pressure is removed. Its size and tension often increase after a meal or when the patient is flatulent.

In consequence of the unnatural situation of the bowels, many patients with rupture are occasionally troubled with colic, costiveness, and vomiting. Sometimes, however, the functions of the viscera seem to suffer little or no interruption.

The *chief symptoms* of a *strangulated rupture* are, tumour in the groin or scrotum, attended with pain, not only in the part, but all over the belly and creating sickness and inclination to vomit, suppression of stools and fever;—symptoms which grow quickly more and more severe, until the strangulation is overcome or death ensues.

The *causes predisposing* to rupture are, a preternaturally large size of the openings at which the bowels are liable to protrude; a weakness and relaxation of the margins of these apertures; a preternatural laxity of the membrane covering and supporting the bowels, and which is called peritoneum, etc.

The chief *exciting cause* is the powerful action of the abdominal muscles and diaphragm on the bowels and other viscera, which takes place under great bodily exertion, such as jumping, running, lifting and carrying heavy weights, vomiting, straining at stool, playing on wind instruments, etc. In such exertions, the pressure which the contents of the abdomen must often encounter, sufficiently accounts for their protruding at any part, where the abdominal sides do not make adequate resistance.

Ruptures are more frequent on the right than on the left side of the body.

TREATMENT—I shall separately notice the leading parts of the treatment proper for *reducible, irreducible* and *strangulated rupture.*

A person who has a *reducible rupture* should constantly wear a truss. Without this he is never safe; for, from the rupture being unsupported by this instrument, the quantity of intestine in the rupture is always liable to be increased and when down, to be bound by a stricture. In this unsupported condition, it is also liable to be seriously injured by any accidental blow or fall or an inflammation may occur in the parts from other causes, which may put the life of the patient in imminent danger. Therefore, no person should ever be careless respecting keeping a reducible rupture well supported by the use of a proper truss. It is a mistaken notion to suppose that because a rupture is small, it is of little or no consequence, since the smaller these tumours are, the greater in general is the danger and, therefore, the more necessary it is that a truss should be worn. Some surgeons recommend the truss to be worn only during the day but I think it should be worn constantly night and day and this was also the opinion of Sir Astley Cooper. By wearing the truss constantly night and day, the ruptured patient, if young, is frequently cured in two, three, four or more years, in consequence of the pressure gradually closing the opening in the belly through which the bowel descends; but by removing the instrument at night, the sides of the abdominal opening are relaxed and liable to enlarge again, which protracts the period of cure, where a cure is practicable and in all cases renders it less certain. Even adults are sometimes perfectly cured of this complaint by unremittingly wearing a truss. However, before applying a truss, the parts must be completely reduced by the patient's lying down on his back and gently pushing them up with the fingers. If at any time the rupture should descend, and a difficulty be found in reducing it again, the patient should lie down on his back for some time, and apply cold water to the parts, which will enable him to effect his purpose, unless strangulation or adhesion has taken place. The application of cold water will be particularly useful if any inflammation or great irritation is present.

Infants and very young children, are not unfrequently troubled with the present complaint, and they should wear a truss as well as older persons. Infants of two or three months old may and ought to wear a truss with springs. In their case the pressure should be extremely light and when the infant is afflicted with the rupture soon after birth, it may, at first, wear a truss made in the form of the common springtruss, without any spring. There is, however, one exception to these rules, that is, when a male child is afflicted with a rupture, the testicle is situated above the abdominal ring (or in the groin); in this case a truss must not be worn until the testicle has descended into the scrotum or bag, its proper receptacle.

When children have a protrusion of some part of the intestines at the navel, instead of the groin, it is called by surgeons an umbilical rupture. The proper treatment in this kind of case is, to apply one half of an ivory ball or a small pad, on the naval, fastening it down with straps of adhesive plaster, over which a belt must be put which encircles the whole trunk for some space both above and below the navel. This belt must have straps attached to it, which are to come round the lower part of the belly and thighs. A little waistcoat fastened by two strings may also be worn over the whole.

Trusses are of various kinds, but in general the common kind of truss is a very good one, and quite equal to the patient's want. The goodness of a truss is known by its making effectual and equal pressure on the parts, without causing pain or inconvenience to the patient and by not slipping out of its right situation, in the varying motions and positions of the body. That truss is objectionable which cannot be worn night and day. Very good trusses are made by Huxley, 12, Old Cavendish Street; White, 112, Piccadilly; Salmon and Ody, in the Strand; Pinden and Gawan, in Fleet Street and other persons. Cases of rupture occasionally occur, which, after being reduced, cannot be kept up with any of the trusses commonly employed; under such circumstances, the patient must seek for a truss of a different description; and it appears that a person in London, of the name of Goldfinch, makes a truss of a peculiar construction, which often succeeds in keeping up ruptures that cannot be properly supported by other trusses. Mr. Coles, of Charing Cross, is also said to have a truss that is effectually worn in such particular instances.

Irreducible ruptures, as I have before said, are those in which the tumour cannot he made to disappear by putting the protruded parts back again into the abdomen. In these cases a truss should rarely, if ever, be worn, as it would press upon the parts and occasion pain, inflammation and perhaps strangulation. The only thing that can be done, in the generality of these instances, is for the patient to wear a simple suspensory bandage, so as to afford a gentle support to the parts, and to prevent the increase of the tumour. If a reducible rupture has lately become irreducible, the patient may sometimes gain considerable advantage from lying in a recumbent position for a few days and applying ice or very cold water to the parts frequently. These means, combined with rather a spare diet, will occasionally effect so great a reduction in the size of the tumour, in ruptures recently become irreducible, that it may be returned into the abdomen and allow a truss to be worn as before. Persons affliced with irreducible rupture should be particularly careful not to exert themselves beyond their strength and to beware of pressure on the parts, bruises, etc. The bowels also should be preserved free from confinement.

The symptoms of *strangulated* rupture have been pointed out above. In this case the assistance of an able surgeon should be obtained as soon as possible. A little delay is here often fatal.[1] The principal means of reducing a strangulated rupture are, the application of ice, or a freezing mixture, bleeding from the arm, the *taxis*, and an injection of an infusion of tobacco. These may be tried nearly in the order in which they here stand. The *taxis* means a particular kind of gentle pressure on the tumour with the fingers,

1. Sir Astley Cooper says, (*Lancet*, vol. i. 1823-4, p. 464), he would not wait more than twelve hours without performing the operation, if the tobacco enema and the other means above advised, had been employed. He adds a case :— "Now let me allude to the case of a late illustrious nobleman, (Francis, Duke of Bedford), who died of this disease; be was in the county and during his stay there had strangulated rupture. He was attended by a person of strong mind, and who had studied his profession with industry; he offered to perform the operation, but it was delayed, on the ground that London skill and advice should be obtained; but before this could be had the nobleman died. I do not mean to undervalue London skill, but it is certainly great folly to delay in this complaint.

by which the surgeon endeavours to return the parts into the abdomen. The previous application of ice to the tumour and of bleeding from the arm, often greatly facilitates the operator's object in making this attempt with the hand. If the above means fail, recourse should be immediately had to the operation. It is seldom safe to spend more than twelve hours in the employment of these means.

SAINT VITUS'S DANCE

This disease attacks boys and girls indiscriminately; and those chiefly who are of a weak constitution or whose natural good health and vigour has been impaired by confinement or by the use of scanty or improper nourishment. It appears most commonly from the eighth to the fourteenth year. Its approaches are often slow. A variable and frequently a ravenous appetite, loss of usual vivacity and playfulness, a swelling and hardness of the lower belly, and in general, a constipated state of the bowels, aggravated as the disease advances and slight, irregular, involuntary motions of different muscles, particularly those of the face, which are thought to be the effect of irritation, precede the more violent convulsive motions, which now attract the attention of the patient's friends.

These convulsive motions vary. The muscles of the limbs and of the face, those moving the lower jaw, the head and the trunk of the body, are, at different times and in different instances, affected by it. In this state the patient does not walk steadily; his gait resembles a jumping or starting, he sometimes cannot walk at all and seems palsied; he cannot perform the common and necessary motions with the affected arms. This convulsive motion is more or less violent; and is constant except during sleep, when, in most instances, it ceases altogether. Articulation is very frequently impeded and swallowing is also occasionally performed with difficulty. In very bad cases, the eye loses its lustre and intelligence, the complexion is pale and the countenance expressive of vacancy and languor.

General weakness and irritability of the nervous system during childhood; sudden fright; and the suppression of eruptions on the skin, have proved causes of this disease; but there is no cause so frequent as debility and irritation in the stomach and bowels.

TREATMENT—There are no medicines so generally and decidedly useful in this malady, as the sulphate of zinc and purgatives, the purgatives being repeated every other morning, with the promise of great advantage every way and without danger of inducing debility. Either of the purgatives, No. 27 or 28, page 155 or No. 74, page 176, may be employed in the morning or the pill, No. 98, page 191, at night; and this plan should be persevered in for many weeks. The mixture, No. 74C, page 177, is also worthy of confidence. For a knowledge of the superior value of purgatives in this disease, we are principally indebted to Dr. Hamilton, Senior, of Edinburgh. The late Dr. Parr, of Exeter, says, that he pursued the purgative plan with great activity through sixty cases of the disease which occurred to him in the course of twenty years' practice and was successful in the whole of these cases except one. After it has been adopted for a week, give the following zinc pills :

Take of sulphate of zinc.................. 20 grains;
Extract of gentian .... half a drachm.
Mix, and divide into twenty pills.

Begin with one pill thrice a day, and when the twenty pills have been taken, let the sulphate of zinc be doubled in the twenty pills, and give still one thrice a day. Thus by gradually increasing the dose of zinc, as much as six grams may be taken thrice a day with advantage.

If this plan does not greatly benefit, try No. 87C, in the *Appendix,* and let the bowels be regularly acted upon by small doses of *Beaume de Vie* taken every second morning.

Arsenic has been recommended by some respectable practitioners as having been perfectly successful in several cases, and when we remember how effectually and speedily it allays the irritation of the stomach and bowels, which gives rise to ague, and thus cures the complaint, we cannot be surprised at its good effects in St. Vitus's dance, a disease which, in the majority of instances, certainly has its origin in irritation and debility of the stomach and the remaining portion of the alimentary canal. Still it is so violent a medicine that I cannot recommend its being tried. The arsenical solution, as ordered by the London College of Physicians, may be given in doses of from three to five drops to a youth of twelve or fourteen years of age, three times a day; the dose being cautiously increased, if necessary.

Black snake-root *(tincture of actea) is* often given with excellent effect. Dr. Simpson, of Edinburgh, has found it succeed after zinc, iron, arsenic and all the usual remedies had failed.

Should there be reason to suppose that the disease is caused by worms, the oil of turpentine will be a suitable and often a valuable remedy. It should be given in large doses, as from half an ounce to an ounce, even to a child of ten years old, which may be repeated twice or thrice in the course of a week. The most agreeable way of taking it, is to rub this quantity in a mortar with half an ounce of mucilage of gum arabic, a part of the yolk of an egg, and an ounce or two of water; or it may be taken simply suspended in a little water.

In some instances, electricity has been very useful. Dr. Addison found the tincture of colchicum effectual in a case following rheumatic fever. It should be limited to such cases. The dose is ten or twenty drops twice a day. But *gymnastic exercises* and sulphur baths are far more effectual. An ample account of their beneficial effects will be found in my volume, on *Infancy and Childhood.*

SCARLET FEVER

This disease is divided by medical writers into two varieties, that is, scarlet fever without sore throat, called also simply scarlet fever; and scarlet fever with sore throat. But it is not necessary to treat of each of these distinctly, for they differ only in the severity of their symptoms. Scarlet fever without sore throat is usually a mild disease, which terminates favourably within a short period; but when attended with an affection of the throat, it is generally more or less sever and dangerous, the intensity of its symptoms and its danger being, for the most part, proportioned to the degree in which the throat is affected. Indeed, when the ulcerations in this part are deep, foul and corroding, it does not differ in its nature and treatment from putrid sore throat, to which disease I refer the reader, for the proper treatment to be pursued in such cases.

The disease is ushered in by the usual *incipient symptoms* of common inflammatory fever, such as chilliness, succeeded by heat, quick pulse, languor, thirst, etc., about the second day from which, in simple variety, numerous specks or minute patches of a vivid red colour appear about the face and neck; and within twenty-four hours, a like efflorescence is diffused over the surface of the body, and occasionally even tinges the inside of the lips, cheeks, palate and fauces. Sometimes the scarlet eruption is continuous and universal; but more generally on the trunk of the body, there are intervals of a natural hue between the patches, with papulous dots scattered over them. There is an increase of the fever in the evening, at which time the rash is most florid. On the fifth day, the eruption begins to decline; the interstices widen and the florid hue fades; on the sixth, it is very, indistinct and is wholly gone on the seventh. The pulse, while the rash is coming out, is commonly very quick and feeble; the tongue is covered with a whitish for in the middle, its sides being of a dark red; the face is considerably swelled; and there is great anxiety and restlessness, with a sense of tingling or itching in the skin, and sometimes at night a slight delirium. Though the fever is in most cases moderate, it now and then runs high, but in the simple variety of the disease is rarely alarming. In many cases, indeed, the eruption appears and passes through its course with little inconvenience of any kind from fever, itching and restlessness.

In scarlet fever attended with sore throat, all the symptoms are more violent; the fever is more severe, accompanied with nausea, vomiting of bile, great heat and languor; considerable anxiety, head-ache and delirium. The pulse is feeble, the breathing quick; the throat is inflamed and becomes excoriated, throws off a large quantity of minute superficial whitish sloughs, which intermix with the increased flow of mucus and augment the difficulty of swallowing. The sloughs generally separate about the fifth, sixth or seventh day.

This is the ordinary course; but in many cases, the symptoms run still higher; and the disease, so far at least as regards the proper treatment, is identified with putrid sore throat.

Children are by far the most frequent subjects of both these varieties, and communicate it readily to each other. When unaccompanied by sore throat, it is only slightly contagious; when sore throat is present, it is highly so. They are both occasionally epidemic and in this form occur most usually at the close of the summer.

Scarlet fever may generally be easily *distinguished* from measles by the eruption usually coming out within the first forty-eight hours of the fever; whereas in measles the rash rarely appears until the third and most commonly not until the fourth day. The eruption in scarlet fever appears like a diffused superficial blush of the skin, with innumerable points intermixed with small minute pimples, dispersed over the outer skin. The rash of measles, on the contrary, consists of small circular dots like flea-bites, of a deeper red in the centre than at the circumference, so that in running into each other, the skin presents a less uniform blush than in scarlatina. These red and slightly elevated dots generally appear in clusters or patches, assuming an irregular *crescent shape;* hence Bateman observes, "The *crescent-like form* of the patches of measles and the more diffuse and irregular shape of those of scarlet fever, will be a material diagnostic guide"—he means a distinctive mark.

It may be distinguished from miliary fever by the miliary eruption being almost universally attended with considerable perspiration, which is not the case on the appearance of the efflorescence of scarlatina. The coming out of the miliary eruption is likewise attended with great anxiety at the pit of the stomach *(proecordia)*.

A specific contagion is the *grand cause;* though particular states of the atmosphere and of the body, dispose to the reception of this contagion, as is proved by persons frequently escaping when exposed to its operation under aggravated circumstances, and afterwards becoming affected by it from comparatively slight sources. But in what this particular state of the atmosphere and body consists, we are almost totally ignorant.

TREATMENT—All that will in general he requisite in the treatment of simple scarlet fever, that is, without any affection of the throat, is to keep the patient in a moderate and equable temperature, (about sixty degrees of Fahrenheit's thermometer); to preserve the apartments clean, open, and well ventilated; to enforce a light spare diet, without animal food; to direct cooling liquors, such as barley water toast and water, or tea for common drink; and to administer ammonia daily, and gentle aperients, as No. 120, page 205, occasionally, more particularly towards the decline of the eruption. The emetic. No. 29, ought likewise to be given at the commencement and four or five grains of sesqui-carbonate of ammonia, in water, taken three or four times a day, by a child of twelve years old.

Scarlet fever is at all times a disease of debility, which prostrates both the body and mind and always calls for the use of *ammonia*. Even in the mildest cases, ammonia should be given, thrice a day, because they are often the most troublesome in their consequences, which the use of ammonia mitigates or wholly prevents. Physicians generally trust alone to the ordinary saline medicines, but ammonia is the only medicine to be relied on.

In treating the second variety or scarlet fever with an affection of the throat, however severe the throat may be attacked, ammonia ought to be given at once and trusted to as the principal remedy.

Dr. Peart, a physician in considerable practice at Gainsborough, was one of the first discoverers of the value of sesquicarbonate of ammonia in scarlet fever and putrid sore throat. He dissolved two drachms of the sesqui-carbonate of ammonia in five ounces of water and directed the patient to take half a table-spoonful, or two tea-spoonfuls every two, three or four hours, according to the urgency of the symptoms. If the difficulty of swallowing abate and the patient wish for it, a little cold water may be added to each dose. Cold water or toast and water, may be drunk at pleasure. The above remedy was given in every form, and in every stage of scarlatina. " Some," he says, "were glowing with universal efflorescence; in some, the extremities were swelled; in others, foetid ulcers appeared; in most, the throat was swelled and inflamed, often ulcerated; and respiration almost prevented; but, in the most alarming cases, a scorching fever and raging delirium, rendered the patient's situation horribly distressing : yet, in all these variations of the disease, the volatile alkali was my specific, which I administered to between two and three hundred patients successively and successfully." The immediate effects of the remedy are stated to be "a diminution of heat, fever and delirium and a disposition to sleep."

The eruption is well known to be a critical deposition on the surface, by which the animal economy endeavours to relieve itself from some internal morbific irritation. The appearance of the rash is essential to the perfect and safe resolution of the disease and a remedy like ammonia, which at the same time moderates the precursory and attendant fever, softens the dry and burning skin, and sustains the vital and nervous power, is of eminent service in insuring the regular appearance and character of the eruption. Indeed, it is found to be far more efficacious in this than the warm bath, hot friction, warn drink or anything else and for this reason, that it is at once carried into the circulation and in a striking manner improves the quality of the blood and expels the offending matter from the system. Hence scarlet fever and measles when treated with ammonia are not found complicated with visceral inflammation, oppressive internal congestions or other irregular and dangerous symptoms, as they are when subjected to other kinds of treatment.

In scarlet fever and measles the natural secretion from the skin is checked and the kidneys are very liable to assume a congested state, which causes the accumulation of excrementitious and poisonous matter in the blood and tends to the aggravation of the disorder. It must, therefore, always be a principal indication to eliminate this matter and ammonia, from its known influence as a diaphoretic and wild diuretic, by its evident salutary action on the skin and kidneys, sets free these grand emunctories through which the morbid matter is expelled. The patient should be put into the best ventilated apartment at command, where an abundant supply of pure air can be secured, *free from all draughts and the possibility of chills.*

Dr. Witt, of Spring Gardens, has recently published a valuable pamphlet, in which he states that he has "from long and varied experience found ammonia to be a sure remedy for the cure of scarlet fever and measles." He was a pupil and private friend of the late Mr. Wilkinson, and writes with equal confidence of the efficacy of this medicine; adding (p. 8), "My own medical friends, to whom this practice was before unknown, have shown the greatest readiness, after due explanation had been given, to afford it a fair trial; and I can add, that they all, without a single exception, have since expressed their conviction of its surprising efficacy."

Mild aperients are likewise necessary and a combination of calomel and rhubarb is generally the most useful. A grain of calomel and eight grains of powdered rhubarb, may be given to a child of ten years old, every other morning, should the bowels be confined.

At the commencement of the disease, cold effusion or ablution is strongly advised by the most eminent physicians. It must not be resorted to except where the heat of the skin is great and without perspiration and then it is often of signal service in moderating the subsequent symptoms. The patient may be stripped naked and cold water be dashed over him every evening for the first three or four days; or the whole body may be quickly sponged with cold water. The refreshment is often instantaneous and operates like a charm.[1] See what is said of this valuable remedy under TYPHOUS FEVER.

1. Bateman's remarks on this point are worthy of record here and more especially since he was a physician of careful observation, considerable discernment and superior integrity. It would be delightful to see physicians generally copying his example. See *Memoirs of Dr. Bateman.* He says in regard to the employment of cold water in this disease, " We are possessed of no physical agent, as far as my experience has taught me (not excepting the use of blood-letting in acute inflammation), by which the functions of the animal economy are controlled with so much certainty, safety and promptitude, as by the application of cold water to the skin, under the augmented heat of scarlatina and of some other fevers. This expedient combines in itself all the

(Contd. on next page)

Antiseptic gargles or sponging should be employed and the room be often and freely fumigated with the nitrous acid vapour, as advised under PUTRID SORE THROAT, or be sprinkled with the chloride of lime or Condy's fluid, as recommended at pages 299-300. The gargles noticed in that article are proper here; or a very useful gargle may be made by mixing a drachm of muriatic acid with seven ounces of barley water, and an ounce of honey of roses. When the state of the throat is bad, these applications should be made strong and be frequently used. If the patient is unable to use a gargle, then sponge the throat with a little of the gargle. In boarding schools and large families, the nitrous acid fumigation, or the use of chloride of lime, is of great moment.

Towards the decline of the disease, it will generally be advisable to administer mild strengthening medicines, of which a decoction of bark with ammonia, as No. 84B, is the most appropriate and effectual.

In the beginning the diet should be spare and mild, because the inflammatory symptoms then run high; but afterwards those of debility prevail, when the food should be nutritious, but moderate in quantity, consisting of jellies, preparations of arrow-root sago, Embden grits and a little wine. If the symptoms are malignant towards the decline of the disease, the throat being deeply affected with spreading foul ulcerations, wine and ammonia must be given more frequently and the fumigation with nitrous acid vapour strictly attended to.

Next to ammonia, I believe the *tincture of muriate of iron* will

---

(Contd.)

medicinal properties which are indicated in this state of disease, and which we should scarcely *á priori* expect it to possess; for it is not only the most effectual *febrifuge* (the *febrifugum magnum*, as a reverend author, Dr. Hancock, long ago called it), but it is in fact, the only *sudorific* or *anodyne* which will not disappoint the expectations of the practitioner, under these circumstances. I have had the satisfaction in numerous instances, of witnessing the immediate improvement of the symptoms and the rapid change in the countenance of the patient produced by washing the skin. Invariably in the course of a few minutes, the pulse has been diminished in frequency, the thirst abated, the tongue has become moist, a general free perspiration has broken forth, the skin has become soft and cool, and the eyes have brightened; and these indications of relief have been speedily followed by a calm and refreshing sleep."

be found the most efficacious medicine. It may be given as in No. 87C.Y. in the *Appendix.*

Scarlet fever has a great tendency to weaken the absorbent system and incapacitate it for carrying off the fluids that are exhaled into the internal cavities of the body and hence to produce dropsy. This consequence is, however, in general prevented by ammonia or very easily removed by giving five or ten drops of the tincture of foxglove, according to the age of the patient, three times a day, in a little wine and water or infusion of bark, with an occasional dose of compound jalap powder.

PREVENTION.—Dr. Hannemann, of Leipsic, the founder of homoeopathy, has asserted nightshade to be a preventive of scarlet fever, but it is, like many of his other assertions, utterly worthless.

It will be highly advisable to sprinkle the rooms of the house where this fever prevails, with either the chloride of lime or of soda, which have a striking effect in destroying the infection of this disease.—*See* pages 299-300.

SCIATICA

Sciatica is a technical term for chronic rheumatism fixed in the hip joint, in which situation it frequently proves particularly obstinate. It is of the nature of *neuralgia* or painful affection of nerve. Its symptoms and causes are, for the most part, the same as those detailed under CHRONIC RHEUMATISM; and in respect to the treatment little can be added to what is there said. In treating it, I should place the greatest dependance upon the use of the compound ipecacuanha powder or the ammoniated tincture of guaiacum,—or the guaiacum mixture of the pharmacopoeia,—or turpentine and sulphur combined, (as advised under CHRONIC RHEUMATISM) in the day, with a pill composed of a grain of calomel, four grains of James's powder and a grain or two of opium, at night; the tepid bath at ninety-five degrees being taken every other morning or night or the vapour bath once or twice a week. The air-pump vapour bath is in general the most efficacious mode of applying vapour and the power of galvanism or electricity is often very considerable;

it should never be neglected in bad cases. The diet and regimen advised under INDIGESTION must be strictly adhered to. In some instances, it will be very advisable to rub the tartar emetic ointment on the external surface of the joint, so as to bring out a large crop of pustules, which should be kept discharging for a month or two. —*See* CHRONIC RHEUMATISM..

In severe cases of this malady which resist the use of the preceding means, I would always try the Veratria ointment, made by mixing together fifteen grains of Veratria and an ounce of lard, the size of a nut being rubbed into the part night and morning, until it produces a pricking sensation. Should it occasion vomiting, it must be laid aside for a few days; at the end of which time it may be tried again, if the degree of pain calls for it.

Sciatica is generally so entirely dependent on the state of the health, that I would advise the patient to try *a spare diet.* Nothing but meat and bread should be taken at dinner; with a little wine and water; and a cupful of tea or cocoa (with good bread), morning and evening, should not be exceeded.

SCROPHULA OR KING'S EVIL

Scrophula (from *scrofa,* a sow), is so called because swine are said to be subject to it. It is also called *King's Evil*, from Edward the Confessor and other succeeding kings, both of England and France, pretending to cure it by the touch.

It is a disease, one of the chief or most palpable symptoms of which is a chronic swelling of the glands, in various parts of the body, which glands generally tend very slowly to imperfect suppuration. The first appearances, however, sometimes consist of spots on different parts of the body and of eruptions and ulcerations behind the ears; but the glands seldom or never fail to become affected in the course of the complaint.

The diseases, for the most part, shows itself early in life, though rarely before the second, and commonly not till the third year of infancy; from which period it continues to prey on the system till the seventh, tenth, fifteenth year or longer, when, in ordinary cases, it gradually subsides. The attack is sometimes postponed till after the twelfth or fifteenth year. The first tumours are usually upon the sides of the neck, below the ears, or under the chin; they are, in general, two, three or four in number, but often still more numerous and are moveable, soft and slightly elastic, of a globular or oval figure, without pain or discolouration of the skin. In this state they continue for some time, when they grow larger, become more fixed, and acquire a purplish redness. They then give a feeling of greater softness and should they ulcerate, the skin, in one or more of them, becomes paler and a peculiar thin liquid is poured forth at several small apertures, which soon becomes of a curd-like form. The tumour or tumours then subside, but frequently others arise in their neighbourhood and in this manner the disease proceeds, the same process being continued for several years; after which the ulcers heal with punctured and indelible indentations, provided the complaint terminates favourably; but if not, other parts of the body become tainted with the morbid influence, especially the eyelids, cheek, groin, joints, and limbs.

In the worst and severest stages of the disease, the entire system appears to be contaminated; hectic fever ensues and sometimes tubercular consumption, which gradually puts an end to the contest.

In infants and young children, the belly often swells and becomes hard, proving that the mesenteric glands are affected.

It has been said above, that there is little or no pain in scrophulous tumours, which is generally true, but sometimes the pain is severe, especially when the disease arrives at its worst stage.

The scrophulous ulcer has a pallid and indolent appearance, the surface being covered with a transparent shining fluid giving it a glassy look. The discharge is generally a whitish curdled matter; the surrounding skin of a deep brown or livid colour; the edges are thick, retorted and insensible. Sometimes, however, the edges are inverted and exquisitely painful.

It most commonly affects children of soft and flaccid flesh; of fair hair and blue eyes; smooth skins and rosy cheeks; and such children have frequently a tumid upper lip, with a chap in the middle of it. It is not, however, exclusively confined to such habits, for it is not unfrequently met with in individuals of a dark complexion, with dark eyes and hair.

The *remote* and *exciting causes* are almost invariably such as debilitate and which reduce the tone of the living fibre. And hence we find the common debilitating powers of cold, damp, deficiency of active exercise in an open salubrious air, excessive use of mercurial medicines, meagre or unwholesome food and the close atmosphere of populous towns, to he the most usual incidental sources of scrophula. It is very frequent in large manufacturing towns, and often follows other diseases which enervate the constitution, such as measles, small-pox and hooping-cough. A variable climate is the most favourable for its appearance, it being much less common in regions uniformly cold or hot.[1]

TREATMENT.—The general idea of scrophula is, that it is a disease of debility; and therefore, the great object is to invigorate the habit by every possible means. The most celebrated and efficacious remedies here are strengthening and alterative medicines, as cod-liver oil, preparations of iodine and iron, coltsfoot juice, the compound calomel pill, burnt sponge, extract of hemlock and oxygen gas; warm and cold bathing; together with a nourishing diet of animal food and ale and constant exercise in a salubrious atmosphere.

Cod-liver oil is now regarded as one of the best remedies in scrophula; and one of the best modes of taking it is that described at page 44, a little ginger wine being added thereto. The tumours

---

1. "Among the *causes* which appear to give rise to scrophula in children, are the practices of rearing them by the hand and suckling them too long—two extremes both of which often lead to the same result, the imperfect nourishment of the child." —A similar injurious effect will be produced by allowing the same wet-nurse to suckle several children in succession, which we have known to be pursued as far as three, when debility and symptomatic amaurosis forced the woman to resign her charge. Imperfect nourishment of the child and consequent tendency to scrophula, is also likely to be induced in those cases where the wet-nurse menstruates regularly during lactation. It is an opinion professed by Wiseman, and other writers of great ability and experience, that a scrophulous *wet-nurse* may occasion the disease to appear in the child to whom she gives the breast,"— *Cyclopaedia of Practical Medicine*, vol. iii, p. 716. To the correctness of these opinions I entirely subscribe.

should be frequently washed with a strong solution of common salt and water or vinegar and water. A poultice of sea tang, bruised, is likewise a very valuable application to scrophulous tumours. Together with the use of these means, the patient, when it is practicable, should make use of a tepid bath of about eighty-five or ninety degrees, three or four times a week. Cold sea-bathing is much resorted to, but many very able professional men prefer the tepid bath as just recommended, among whom is Sir Astley Cooper. Where, however, there is a good deal of remaining strength, the cold bath may be useful if the patient feels a glow after coming out; but as a general resource, I think the tepid bath, especially of salt water, is decidedly to be preferred, and the sweating bath more than all. Regular friction with the hand or flesh brush, should likewise be resorted to, and I would recommend it to be employed constantly night and morning, for ten or fifteen minutes, over the weakest parts, and, in change, over every part of the frame. When the swellings will bear it, the friction may be carried over the surface. Some respectable surgeons have made very favourable reports of the use of this means in indolent scrophulous tumours.

Dr. Cullen, of Edinburgh, was partial to the use of the juice of coltsfoot, and it is certainly worthy of confidence, particularly when a cough is present, with feverishness towards night. From two to four table-spoonfuls of the expressed juice of this herb may be taken, twice or thrice a day. I have a good deal of confidence in the decoction of coltsfoot and wormwood, prescribed under *Gravel* and *Stone.*

The mild alterative pill, No. 98A, page 192, given every other night, will sometimes be useful. When the belly is enlarged, or there is evident obstruction internally, it ought always to accompany the other remedies employed; but in no case should it be given in such doses as will be likely to affect the mouth and occasion salivation. The only correct use of calomel in this complaint is in small doses, united with some antimonial preparation and employed with a view to its alterative effects.

Sir Astley Cooper has recommended the oxymuriate or bichloride of quicksilver combined with bark. He says that, in every case, much benefit may be derived from this medicine. He advises it to be given in small doses, when it has not the specific effect of mercury, but acts merely as a tonic.

Take of Solution of bi-chloride of mercury, made according to the London Pharmacopoeia,....	1	ounce;
Compound tincture of bark,...............	2	ounces.

Mix, and take a tea-spoonful and a half, three times a day, in water and after three weeks increase it two tea-spoonfuls. It is best taken directly after a meal, as after breakfast, tea or supper.

Sir Astley Cooper further says, respecting the treatment of this disease :—

"Air, exercise and nourishment, are the three great points to be kept in view in the treatment of scrophulous affections. The state of the atmosphere to be chosen, is that in which the air is dry and warm; a bleak wind is not advisable. It is a mistake to suppose that the air of the coast in the wet and cold season is of any advantage to scrophulous children; it is only in warm and dry weather that any benefit will be obtained. In cold weather the sea coast is not desirable. Children with scrophulous affections, or even those predisposed to them, should take a great deal of exercise in the open air."—"I will now mention what are the best medicines; once a week, or every ten days, two grains of calomel and eight grains of rhubarb, should he given, in order to restore the secretions. A good medicine to be given daily, for a short time, is the rhubarb and steel—two grains of rhubarb and from three to five grains of the carbonate of iron. This is a very good tonic. Another good tonic consists of two grains of rhubarb and from four to six grains of dried subcarbonate of soda, with ten grains of columba, which may be taken mixed with sugar twice or thrice a day."—"It is right to recommend sea-bathing; the bath should be taken about three times a week, at eleven in the morning. The temperature of the bath should be ninety-four degrees; the patient should remain from sixteen to twenty minutes in it and walk afterwards."—*Lectures on Surgery, by Sir Astley Cooper, No. 66.*

Sir Astley's two grains of calomel and eight of rhubarb is making too free with calomel in scrophulous habits; half a grain of calomel with the eight of rhubarb will answer much better.

Burnt sponge has considerable effect in reducing the size of scrophulous glands, but citrate of iron, or some other tonic, should be given at the same time, since the sponge has a debilitating influence on the general habit when continued for a long period. One or two drachms may be taken thrice a day.

In irritable and painful scrophulous ulcerations, the extract of hemlock, in doses of five or ten grains, thrice a day, is often very useful. Dr. Fothergill thought highly of it in such instances, and, in my opinion, it is entitled tc all the confidence he placed in it. It relieves pain, allays irritability and disposes the ulcer to heal. Dr. Baillie states, in his posthumous writings, that in scro-phulous swellings of the glands of the neck, he had experienced good effects from sarsaparilla and soda, with some preparation of steel—but more powerful effects from sea-air and sea-bathing—and most of all from the air and waters of Malvern. EPSOM, OR MALVERN WELLS, I strongly recommend, with abundance of exercise.

Scrophula is remarkable for the presence of great debility, with little or no irritability, in the general habit, and when this is the case, the inhalation of oxygen gas may be of great utility. It has been strongly recommended in this disease, and from being a powerful tonic and stimulant, will, no doubt, be found serviceable in many instances. Sometimes there is so great a degree of torpor or in-irritability in the constitution, that the most valuable tonic medicines have little or no effect; in which case I should expect much advantage from the use of this gas, as it has often had a very sensible effect in giving tone to the system after almost all other means had failed. The same may be said of cod-liver oil.

Iodine is under careful and judicious management, a remedy of great value in certain cases of scrophulous swellings and indurations. I do not mean that it will cure the disease, but that it will be found of much use as an auxiliary. The best way of taking it is in small doses, combined with a vegetable bitter; for example, ten drops of the solution of iodide of potassium may be taken twice a day, in two ounces of compound infusion of gentian, or in double the quantity of compound decoction of sarsaparilla. I think it should rarely be carried beyond this quantity, for when administered to any great extent, it invariably enfeebles the consti-tution and produces fainting, trembling and other unpleasant effects. The ointment of iodide of potassium may be used as directed under CANCER. Its power in alleviating the pain in scrophulous swellings and induration, is greater than anything I am acquainted with.

Iron is now combined with iodine, forming an *iodide of iron,* which promises to be much more beneficial in scrophula than iodine in any other form: it may he taken as recommended under WHITE SWELLING. Davenport's *Syrup iodide of quinine and iron* is a ternary compound of marked efficacy in cases of scropbula, and bloodlessness *(anaemia).* It is borne well by the stomach and not possessing the nauseous qualities of its constituents, is admirably adapted for children. The dose is one or two tea-spoonfuls, thrice a day, in water.

The best ointments for dressing the ulcers with, are the red precipitate, nitrate of mercury, (No. 89, page 188,) and zinc. Either of these may be used, and when one begins to lose its effect, a second may be tried. The carbonate of iron sprinkled on the surface of the ulcer is likewise a good application. The late Dr. Beddoes, of Bristol, recommended the following plan of treating scrophulous ulcerations, which he learnt from an old farmer in Ireland, who had practised it for many yearn with remarkable success. A sufficient quantity of the leaves and stalks of wood sorrel is prepared by wrapping them in a cabbage leaf and macerating them by their own juices in warm peat ashes. This pulp is applied as a poultice to the ulcer and left on twenty-four hours; it is then to be renewed in the same way to the fourth time, the poultice, at each dressing, being left on for twenty-four hours. After the removal of the fourth poultice, a sufficient quantity of the roots of the meadow-sweet is to be bruised and mixed with the sour head that appears on butter-milk, left in the churn, which is to be applied as a poultice, in the same manner, till the sore heals. Dr. Beddoes remarks, that he was told the healing always took place speedily and often in two or three weeks; and the whole statement is corroborated by an extract of a letter from Mr. Edgeworth. The leaves of the wood-sorrel are the most efficient articles in this treatment.

In every instance, the diet should be very nutritious, consisting of the most digestible animal food, eggs, good home-brewed or Allsopp's beer, wine and the usual articles of a wholesome and nourishing diet. A growing girl of seventeen has taken four or five glasses of port wine daily, with the utmost benefit. No pork or salt meat should be taken. Constant exercise in an open dry atmosphere is of the last importance. I will venture to assert, that no medicine will succeed here, without much daily exercise in a salubrious air. The influence which deficient exercise has in producing scrophula, is proved to a demonstration by the fact, that for one boy afflicted with this complaint we meet with at least four girls. Now boys will have exercise, they cannot be kept within doors, but girls are too often deprived of it, and thus mothers and governesses make them scrophulous, rickety and hump-backed, that they might excel in music, drawing and other accomplishments. It is an indisputable fact, that five cases out of six of curved spine and growing out of the shoulder, occurring in young girls, are entirely owing to the deficiency of exercise in the open air; and we find there is no cure for this spinal curvature, in the majority of instances, but in a skilful use of exercise. Friction is a species of exercise and is worthy of much confidence in the management of scrophula.

SCURVY

Scurvy is a disease of great debility, in which there are livid spots on the skin, from blood which has escaped out of its proper vessels; languor and loss of muscular strength; and pains in the limbs. The cutaneous eruptions, so commonly called scurvy by unprofessional persons, is of a very different nature, being simply some foulness of the skin depending upon internal disorder, the treatment of which has been described at page 843-44.

This disease is frequently divided into the land and sea scurvy; but as they differ very little in their symptoms, and not at all in their treatment, I think it unnecessary to perpetuate the distinction.

Its first appearances are a pales bloated countenance, lassitude, disinclination to motion and diminished strength. If the gums be examined, they will be found spongy and apt to bleed on being touched, while the teeth are loosened in their sockets. The skin is sometimes rough, but more, generally smooth and shining, covered with bluish or livid spots, which do not rise above it; and these spots often coalesce in large blotches, particularly in the legs and thighs. About the same period, old ulcers often break out again, and the slightest mercurial preparation quickly produces salivation. The ulcers often discharge a thin fetid fluid, and the edges are livid, with irregular granulations, which sometimes run into a bloody fungus. The stools are usually frequent and offensive, but there is sometimes an obstinate costiveness; the urine is commonly high coloured and stinking; the pulse feeble; and the joints very weak. A shrinking of the flexor muscles soon takes place and renders the limbs useless; the calves of the legs fall away, with sometimes an irregular hardness; and even those bones which have been formerly broken and re-united, become again separate at the line of re-union.

In the worst stage, blood is frequently discharged from the bowels, bladder, and other organs; the slightest motion brings on faintness, and sometimes immediate death; and catchings of the breath are frequent and dangerous.

A diet of salt provisions, with a deficiency of vegetables; want of cleanliness; cold united with moisture; and neglect of exercise, are the *most common causes*. In certain habits, it may be excited from poor living, and a neglect of cleanliness and exercise, when salted provisions have made no part of the patient's diet.

The *immediate cause is* an impoverished and putrescent state of the blood and a diminution of the vital power.

It may be readily *distinguished* from malignant fever by the absence of heat, quick pulse, and the other symptoms denoting severe fever; by the intellectual faculties being little or not at all impaired; and by its coming on more gradually and continuing a much longer time than putrid fever.

TREATMENT—The object is to restore to the body its wonted

energy and strength, which is here most effectually accomplished by observing great cleanliness and free ventilation and resorting to a dry air, with the use of fresh provisions of a nutritious quality, fermented liquors, as ale, cider and spruce beer, vegetable acids, acid fruits and such vegetables as scurvygrass, water-cress, brook lime and garlic. If these are employed in time, the disease will be found to yield easily; but when the prostration of strength is great, the patient must be positively forbidden to use the least bodily exertion, as it is very apt to induce faintness and even death. In cases of extreme weakness, the external air alone, and especially when sharp or in a current, is sufficient from its pressure and stimulus to destroy the small degree of vitality remaining; a fact long ago observed and recently confirmed by five men dying in the boat belonging to the Prince of Wales ship of war, between the Downs and Deal Hospital.

Lemon juice is of the greatest service in this disease. It should be mixed with water and sugar and drunk freely. Where it cannot be got, the juice of limes, oranges or the shaddock, may be substituted and used in the same way.

Captain Cook thought very highly of malt sweet wort or infusion of malt; and Dr. Silvester's antiscorbutic drink is also valuable. It is made by boiling three ounces of cream of tartar, four ounces of juniper berries, two drachms of ginger, in powder and five pounds of coarse sugar, in six gallons of water. After boiling half an hour, the whole is poured into a tub and allowed to ferment. It may be drunk, in the quantity of from one to three pints daily, as soon as the fermentation commences. Sowens, an article of diet well known in Scotland, was also considered by Captain Cook of great efficacy.

Exercise and amusement are of consequence the prevention of scurvy. From the narrative of Sir E. Parry's voyage to the Polar Seas, it appears that he was fully impressed with the expediency of amusement as well as of exercise, for the preservation of the health of his men; and this point should not be overlooked in the treatment of scurvy.

Costiveness must be prevented by dissolving a little cream of tartar in a decoction of tamarinds and prunes, a little of which may be taken occasionally, so as to keep the bowels free from confinement without their being purged. It is of much moment that the bowels should not in any degree be purged.

Ulceration of the gums requires the daily use of an astringent gargle, as No. 56 or 57, page 169. For the relief of acute pain, there is, perhaps, nothing so suitable and efficient as the compound powder of ipecacuanha, which may be taken in doses of three or four grains, three times a day, made into a pill with conserve of roses. Contractions of the muscles of the legs should be treated with warm fomentations of vinegar and water, and gentle friction.

Scorbutic ulcers on the legs are best treated by sprinkling on them a little carbonate of iron, once or twice a day or touching them with tincture of myrrh; a carrot poultice or one of bread and water, into which a table spoonful of yeast has been stirred, being applied occasionally at night. These ulcers are most benefited by stimulating applications.[1]

SHAKING PALSY

The shaking palsy is a permanent agitation of the head or limbs without any exertion of the will, the body being generally bent forward, often with a propensity to run or fall headlong. It commonly appears after mature age.

The approach of this malady is so imperceptible, that the precise period of its commencement is seldom recollected by the patient. A slight sense of weakness, with a proneness to tumbling, sometimes in the head, but more commonly in the hands or arms, are the first symptoms noticed. These affections gradually increase, the patient bends himself forward, and, by degrees, the legs suffer similar agitations, and there is a loss of power with the hands and arms. As the disease advances, the limbs become less and less capable of executing the dictates of the will, while the sufferer

1. Dr. Ross, of 11, Hart Street, Bloomsbury Square, has closely studied the varieties and treatment of *Cutaneous Diseases* and is worthy of all confidence by those suffering from any such complaint.

seldom experiences even a few minutes suspension of the tremulous agitation; and should it be stopped in one limb by a sudden change of posture, it soon makes its appearance in another.

In the more advanced stage, the tremulous motions of the limbs occur during sleep and augment in violence till they awaken the patient in much agitation and alarm; the power of conveying the food to the mouth is impeded; the bowels are exceedingly torpid; the trunk of the body is permanently bowed; muscular power diminished; mastication and swallowing difficult; and the saliva constantly dribbles from the mouth.

The disease, however, often continues a long time before it arrives at this extreme state.

Long exposure to damp vapour, by lying from night to night on the bare earth, has produced it, as well as other *causes* of chronic rheumatism; and it has frequently followed chronic rheumatism itself, and long indulgence in spirituous liquors. Indeed, any thing that greatly debilitates the vital power may prove a cause, as the daily exhalation of metallic and other injurious vapours, etc. But sometimes the *remote causes* are involved in obscurity.

The part of the nervous system more immediately affected seems to be the spinal marrow, and, perhaps, a peculiar affection of this sensitive and important substance is, in the majority of instances, the immediate cause of shaking palsy.

It is to be *distinguished* from St. Vitus's Dance, by its attacking those in mature and advanced life, and by- the peculiar symptoms above described. St. Vitus's Dance almost invariably attacks the young.

TREATMENT—Those remedies which have the power of promoting a healthy state and action of the spinal marrow are the most useful. Large blisters frequently applied down the spine, setons and issues cut near it, and stimulating embrocations, as No. 39, page 161, freely rubbed over it, promise benefit. The burning of moxa (see page 103) on the same part may prove of great service in many instances; and the skilful use of galvanism or the magnet, is worthy of much regard.

Some respectable physicians have recommended an active purgative plan as very efficacious. It may be pursued in the way advised under St. Vitus's Dance. The arsenical solution has likewise been well spoken of—*See* page 825.

When the disease is suspected to be of rheumatic origin, the means noticed under chronic rheumatism are proper, especially the use of the compound decoction or extract of sarsaparilla, with the compound ipecacuanha powder and an alterative pill of calomel, James's powder and opium or No. 99, page 192. The dandelion may in some cases be useful. Bathing in the Buxton and Bath springs is very advisable.

The *nux vomica* appears to possess a specific influence over the spinal marrow, and in those cases which resist the employment of the preceding remedies, I would strongly advise it to be tried. It may be taken as directed at page 137; and see what is said of cupping along the spine under Tetanus.

SHINGLES

Shingles *(herpes) is* an eruption of vesicles in small distinct clusters, with a red margin, which spread round the body like a girdle; in short, it is a variety of ringworm, or tetter, occupying the trunk of the body.

Frequently it occasions little inconvenience beyond what arises from the heat and itching; but sometimes it is preceded and accompanied with considerable constitutional affection, as sickness, head-ache, thirst, sleeplessness, and feverishness and the pain is considerable. The first symptoms of the local disease are those of heat, itching and tingling, in some parts of the trunk, which, when examined, is found to be studded with small red patches of an irregular shape, upon each of which, numerous minute elevations are seen clustering together. In the course of twenty-four hours, these vesicles enlarge to the size of small pearls, are perfectly transparent, and filled with a limpid fluid. During three or four days, other clusters arise in succession and with considerable regularity, that is, nearly in a line with the first, extending always towards the spine at one extremity and towards the breast bone at the other; most commonly passing round the waist like half a sash, but sometimes like a sword belt, across the shoulder. The vesicles terminate in thin dark scabs, which fall off about the twelfth or fourteenth day.

It is most frequent in summer and autumn, when slight causes will often excite it, and especially exposure to cold after violent exercise and the use of cold vegetables. It is sometimes connected with considerable disorder of the digestive organs and mental anxiety.

TREATMENT—The complaint is generally of little importance, and rarely requires any thing beyond the exhibition of a mild purge, No. 28, page 156, every other day and a little of the ointment, No. 94, page 190, spread on linen, applied to the eruption. The diet should be simple and small in quantity. If the feverish symptoms and irritation are considerable, which is sometimes the case, then give four grains of James's powder, every night, the mixture, No. 78D, page 181, being taken thrice a day. Ammonia is the principal remedy in this complaint. The cordial mixture, No. 79, page 181, may be found of great service. A Plummer's pill every night is a very useful medicine in most cases. Powdered starch, either alone or mixed with white oxide of zinc, in the proportion of two drachms of oxide of zinc to four ounces of powdered starch, forms an excellent application to the shingles, and, indeed, to all irritating skin diseases.

Now and then it happens, on the decline of the eruption, that the patient is affected with an intense deep-seated pain in the chest, and if the pulse should then be frequent and hard and the patient of a very full habit, it will generally be necessary to give the mixture, No. 78D, page 181, every second hour, until relief is obtained and to direct the observance of a mild diet, with a little opening medicine occasionally, such as No. 120, page 205. This will be the best plan for relieving the pain.

SMALL-POX

Small-pox is divided by medical writers into two species; the *distinct* or *benign,* and the *confluent* or *malignant.* In the former, the pustules are perfectly distinct and separate from each other; in the latter, they coalesce, and the eruption is continuous.

The nature of this disease is best known and consequently its species may be determined, from observing the state of the face, the danger being better estimated by the number and appearance of the pustules there than on any other part of the body. If they be distinct and few in number on the face, even although in some degree confluent elsewhere, the disease is termed the distinct small-pox and the danger is inconsiderable. If, on the other hand, there be a load of pustules on the face, if they run into each other so that it appears uniformly of a whitish colour, as if, to use Sydenham's expression, it were covered with parchment, whatever appearance the eruption may have on other parts of the body, the disease is termed confluent, and the danger is considerable.

Of the benign or distinct kind. This form is usually ushered in by a fever of the inflammatory type, characterised by considerable pains in the back and loins, nausea, vomiting, pain in the pit of the stomach on pressure and disposition to drowsiness; the skin and throat are parched, the bowels costive, the urine at first pale, afterwards more scanty and high-coloured and in infants there is sometimes one or more epileptic fits.

Towards the end of the third day from its commencement, the eruption makes its appearance, first on the face and hairy scalp, then on the neck, and at length over the whole body. The patient is often affected by sneezing as soon as the pustules show themselves, which continue to recur while they are coming out. About the fifth or sixth day, counting from the commencement of the fever, that is, the second or third of the eruption, a little vesicle, which appears depressed in the middle, is seen on the top of each pustule, containing a matter nearly colourless. The eruptive fever now disappears. For two or three days the vesicles increase in breadth, the matter gradually assuming the purulent appearance. About the eighth day of the disease they become spherical and the pustules are completely formed; being then very itchy, hard and prominent and also terminated by a point. At this time, when the pustules are pretty numerous, the face swells and is often affected with acute pain; the swelling sometimes extends to the whole head; the eyelids seem as if distended with a fluid and are often so much enlarged as entirely to close the eyes. When the eyes are much affected from the beginning, the sight is sometimes lost, generally in consequence of one or more pustules forming on the cornea.

About the eleventh or twelfth day from the commencement of the fever, the pustules have gained their full size,—which differs a little in different epidemics, but is generally about that of a pea,—a dark spot appears on each, and from being soft and smooth, they become rough and throw out a yellow matter. They now begin to shrink and the matter drying forms a small crust. Sometimes only part is thrown out, which, together with what remains, hardens and in a few days falls off, leaving the skin in the places which it covered of a dark brown colour, that often continues for a long time after the patient is well; and in cases where the pustules have been large or late in becoming dry, deep indentations of the skin remain. At this time, the swelling of the face and other parts gradually subsides.

On the coming out of the pustules, the fever suffers a remission, and in the mildest cases disappears entirely about the fifth day, at which time the eruption is completed; but when the pustules are numerous, a return of fever usually happens about the eleventh day. This is called the secondary fever and is much to be dreaded in the severe form of the disease; but in the distinct small-pox, it is for the most part slight, and disappears in a few days.

The later the eruption is in appearing, and the sooner the pustules become dry and fall off, the better in general is the prognosis.

Of the confluent or malignant form. The sensation of cold, anxiety, pains in the back and loins, nausea, vomiting, pain in the pit of the stomach on pressure, etc., are present in this as well as in the mild form of the disease, but are here experienced in a greater degree. In the distinct small-pox, the eruptive fever is inflammatory and never shows a tendency to typhus, while in the confluent, although in the beginning inflammatory, it generally soon shows this tendeney. In the most alarming cases, indeed, the fever is a typhus almost from the first. The tendeney to sweat is uncommon in this form; but a looseness often precedes the eruption, and continues for a day or two after its appearance. In adults, a salivation often attends instead of a looseness.

Small-pox appearing in a regular and mild form is seldom fatal, if properly managed; but it often induces an irritable and debilitated state of some important organs, as the lungs, bowels, or eyes and thus leaves behind a disposition to cough, inflammatory affection of the chest or bowels, and an inflamed condition of the eyes. Sometimes the whole system is so enervated by it, as easily to fall a prey to scrophula in its worst forms.

Confluent small-pox must always be considered a dangerous disease. The chief symptoms indicating danger are, great prostration of strength, the pustules becoming flttened or brown and black, great anxiety, oppression at the chest, delirium and the appearance of small purple spots in the skin. If the stools are unusually fetid, the prognostic is bad.

The eleventh day is the most fatal in small-pox.

The disease is well known to be the effect of a specific contagion.[1]

The marks of *distinction* between this disease and measles, and between it and chicken-pox, may be readily seen by referring to what has been said of those complaints, at pages 433 and 748.

TREATMENT—Small-pox is an eruptive fever, which, in the commencement, is almost always attended with marks of high excitement in the system and the principal objects of attention in every case are, to moderate the fever and to obviate any unfavourable symptom that may arise in the course of the disease. The most appropriate and effectual means of keeping under the fever and promoting a happy recovery, are, the use of the following mixture of cream of tartar, rhubarb and cold air, with mild purgatives, combined with a spare diet in the beginning, succeeded by one that is nutritive.

1. For the means of arresting the progress of this contagion in any particular situation, *see* page 310, and the note at page 749.

Bitartrate of potash (cream of tartar) exerts a very salutary influence on the blood, and I believe the following prescription will be found of eminent service in all cases of small-pox.

Take of Cream of tartar	¾ of an ounce;
Powdered rhubarb	12 grains;
Water	1 pint.

Mix, and give the patient half of this mixture directly, and repeat it in six hours.

Afterwards, if one half of the mixture is given once a day, I think it will be found equal to conduct even severe cases to a favourable issue. It subdues the fever and sensibly relieves the patient in every way.

If the bowels are confined, give the powder, No. 120, page 205, which will mostly operate two or three times, and every day afterwards the bowels must be kept in a soluble state, by the occasional use of the mixture, No. 74, page 176, if necessary, and the higher the fever rises the more freely must it be employed. When the fever runs high, no fear of subsequent debility should deter us from administering purgative medicine freely, since, so far from producing this effect, it is the most certain means of preventing it, under such circumstances, by moderating the excessive action present; which if allowed to go on unchecked, would undoubtedly induce great prostration of strength, and, perhaps, a putrid state of the humours. I do not mean to recommend very active *purging,* but the regular administration of the *milder kinds* of purgatives. But if a dose of the preceding mixture of cream of tartar and rhubarb is given daily, probably aperient medicine will not be required.

The patient must, at the same time, be exposed to fresh and cold air, and at no period should he be confined to the house, whatever be the season, unless the fever be such as confines him to bed. He should lie with a few bed clothes and on a mattress; his room should be cool; and a free use of cold drink and frequent changes of cold linen, are highly proper and useful. The cooling *regimen* has great effect in moderating the eruptive fever.

So long as the fever continues considerable, the diet should be mild and rather spare, consisting chiefly of decoctions on barley, grits and such like, with bread. Toast and water lemonade, or cream of tartar and water, may be taken for common drink; but it is now the usual plan to allow a libera diet.

These means are usually sufficient to conduct the benig disease to a favourable issue but if any unusual and sever symptoms arise in the progress of the disease, they will require to be combated by the usual measures. For example, if great irritability and restlessness occur, ammonia should be given, as in No. 78D, page 181, the purgatives, cold air and cooling diet, as above advised, being still continued.

When obstinate vomiting occurs, it must be restrained by exhibiting the effervescing draught, No. 24, or the pill of camphor and opium advised under VOMITING. Should a looseness come on early and be moderate, it must never be interfered with; it is only when it proves excessive and debilitating that it should be checked, by the employment of mild astringents, as a powder composed of two grains of compound powder of ipecacuanha and ten grains of tormentil powder, which may be repeated after every liquid stool or by the other mild measures recommended under DIARRHOEA.

Blood-letting is rarely advisable in small-pox, even when the fever is very considerable, since the excitement is much better reduced by the use of purgatives and a cold regimen. If, however, the inflammation of the eyes, or the heaviness and stupor, what medical men call coma, are considerable, six leeches may be advantageously applied to the temples and a blister put behind the ears.

To prevent the pustules from affecting the globe of the eye and inuring the sight, pieces of folded linen wet with cold water should be kept applied to the eyes during the eruptive fever and the cream of tartar mixture be given.

In the confluent or malignant small-pox, the same plan of treatment, by the exhibition of cream of tartar, purgatives and a cooling regimen, is necessary in the beginning, as above recommended for the miler variety; and the higher the symptoms of general excitement rise at the commencement, the more assiduous must we be in the use of these means and in enforcing the employment of cold air and drink. Here, after the first few days, symptoms of debility generally appear and on their appearance ammonia and a supporting system must be entered upon directly, the patient still being kept cool and every source of irritation avoided. When signs of debility appear, the fever for the most part changes from inflammatory to typhus and the means detailed under the latter article are the most proper. But of all the tonics employed in malignant small-pox, there appears none so well adapted to the support of the system as sulphuric or muriatic acid, especially for the first few days of debility. For there is then a great deal of heat and feverishness still continuing, although accompanied with symptoms of debility, and these acids prove powerfully tonic at the same time that they are cooling. Muriatic acid is the best and may be taken as prescribed under Typhus.[1] Ammonia is also a valuable medicine in this state of the disease. If the symptoms of debility increase and especially if the pulse sinks, the pustules flatten and the surface of the body turns pallid, wine must be added to the other remedies, blisters and mustard poultices applied to the feet; and the other means advised under typhus should he resorted to.

SPITTING OF BLOOD

Haemoptysis or spitting of blood, is a discharge of blood from the lungs, or windpipe and its terminations, called bronchia.

It is generally preceded by a sense of weight, anxiety and pains about the breast, with some degree of difficulty of breathing, often of a sense of heat, sometimes under the breast-bone, and sometimes moving from place to place; and a little before the blood appears, there is frequently a saltish taste in the mouth. At length a tickling at the top of the windpipe occasions hawking, which brings up a

1. "The sulphuric acid (or muriatic acid) is the only remedy, in conjunction with wine, on which we can rely in the confluent small-pox, when the pustules are filled with a bloody sanies. and the urine is coloured by broken-down particles of blood."—Dr. Anthony Thomson's *Elements of Materia Medica.* vol. i. p. 704.

little blood of a florid colour and more or less frothy. Frequently there is a cough attended by much irritation of the larynx, and sometimes by very acute pain in the chest. As the quantity of blood increases, there is a rattling noise in the windpipe before it is brought up and then it comes less by hawking than by coughing, which is sometimes the ease from the first.

These *local symptoms* are often preceded by general chilliness, with weariness of the limbs, pains of the back and head, costiveness, frequent, full pulse, and other symptoms of fever. The pulse has usually a particular kind of vibration, which may continue for many days after the haemoptysis has ceased.

The slighter cases of *haemoptysis* depend on a similar extravasation of blood from the mucous membrane of the *bronchia.* It is rather by exhalation or secretion that the over-loaded vessels relieve themselves, than by laceration or rupture. It is usually an evidence of further disease of an active character, and calling for careful attention. Those cases, however, of violent and extreme haemorrhage, which sometimes resist all medical treatment, arise from a very different and more dangerous cause. In these, some part of the substance of the lungs has undergone organic changes being indurated to a very great degree. The ordinary extent of this induration, is from one to four cubic inches; it is almost always very exactly circumscribed, being as considerable at the very point of termination as in the centre. In this induration, the diseased part appears quite homogeneous being altogether black or of a very deep brown, and disclosing nothing of the natural texture of the part, except, perhaps, the bronchial tubes and the larger blood vessels.

In advanced cases of pulmonary consumption we sometimes meet with considerable losses of blood from the lungs, which may result from the rupture of a vessel traversing an excavation formed by the ulceration and discharge of a tubercle.

This disease is often of an alarming character, from its indicating a tendency to ulceration of the lungs, especially when it occurs in persons of a narrow chest, and of a consumptive appearance. If it be followed by cough, pain or difficulty of breathing, the danger is considerable.

Those of a sanguine habit, slender make, and delicate constitution, are most subject to it, and it occurs most frequently at from fifteen to thirty-five years of age, and in spring or autumn. Fulness of blood disposes to it, and so does great sensibility and irritability, combined with a narrow conformation of the chest.

The *occasional causes* of this affection are, external heat,—a considerable and sudden diminution of the weight of the atmosphere,—whatever increases the force of the circulation, violent exercise or straining,—the external application of cold.

The spitting of blood which is met with in consumptive patients, and accompanies the formation of tubercles, is most frequently of the bronchial species,—the blood proceeds from the windpipe or its terminations; while that which occurs in subjects affected with disease of the heart, is commonly owing to an induration in the substance of the lungs.

When blood is discharged from the stomach, it is called vomiting of blood, and is usually in much more considerable quantity than when it takes place from the lungs,—of a darker colour,—more grumous,—often mixed with other contents of the stomach, and commonly unattended with cough. In the present disease, it is brought up by hawking or coughing, is of a florid red colour, and mixed with a little frothy mucus.

TREATMENT—A discharge of blood from the lungs may appear either in the sanguine and florid, or in the debilitated and pale. In the former case, it is accompanied with increased vascular action, and the blood is florid and tenacious; in the latter it is attended with general laxity or debility, weak vascular action, and the blood is thin and of a diluted red.

In all cases, the best remedies are, ipecacuanha and Glauber's salt united; nitre; superacetate of lead; common salt; and a mild spare diet of vegetable food.

Ipecacuanha wine, or powder, and Glauber's salt, combined in such small doses as operate mildly on the bowels, and produce slight nausea, prove of the utmost service in this complaint, and are applicable to almost every case. They have frequently succeeded after many other powerful remedies have failed. Therefore give the following draught immediately, and should the nausea excited by it be insufficient or the bowels be too much acted upon, the dose of ipecacuanha may be increased, or that of the salts lessened, accordingly, and vice versa, since the proper manner of using this form is, to combine the medicines in such proportions as will act mildly, yet sufficiently, in the way just now described.

Take of Ipecacuanha wine.	1	or 2 drachms,
(Or ipecacuanha powder.	1	or 2 grains;)
Glauber's salt	1	drachm;
Infusion of cascarilla bark, ...	10	drachms.

Mix for a draught; to be taken in the beginning, every second hour, and after it has checked the bleeding, twice or thrice a day, so as to keep up a gentle action on the bowels.

In cases of emergency, where no other remedy is at hand, give a tea-spoonful of common salt, and repeat it frequently.

Nitre has been strongly recommended, and is often of great value, more especially in full habits. The Italian physicians have unlimited confidence in it, and employ it in large doses, as half a drachm dissolved in cold water, repeated three or four times a day. It should not be continued longer than two or three days at a time.

If the foregoing means fail of success, which they rarely will, the superacetate of lead should be tried. It is a most powerful astringent, and may be given in this form :—

Take of Acetate of lead	3	grains;
Distilled vinegar		half a drachm;
Laudanum	10	drops;
water	1½	ounces.

Mix for a draught, to be taken every two or three hours, until relief is obtained, giving every morning the powder, No. 130A, page 209.

Should the bleeding occur in a full habit, where the strength is considerable, and the pulse full and hard, bleeding from the arm, to the extent of twelve ounces, has been recommended, but I think it a bad practice. In all cases, it is far better to trust to the draught of ipecacuanha and Glauber's salt, to nitre, or superacetate of lead, than to blood-letting, or anything else. Great injury is often done by bleeding in this disorder. In by far the greater number of cases, if not in all, I am convinced that blood-letting is decidedly improper.[1]

Fainting is often serviceable in checking bleeding from the lungs, and it is, therefore, improper to use means to prevent it, where the bleeding is considerable. On this account, cordials, strong odours, and every other means of rousing the patient, should be avoided, in every case of active haemoptysis, occurring in full habits. When the complaint occurs in a debilitated or delicate habit, and is the consequence of weakness, the course of proceeding should clearly be different, and every proper means of preventing fainting must be employed.

At the same time that the above remedies are resorted to, the temperature of the patient's room should be kept as low as possible,

---

1. It is a singular fact, that in a person threatened with haemorrhage, either from the lungs, brain, or elsewhere, the application of leeches, and other methods of drawing blood, frequently decide the very occurrence of the disease it was intended to prevent. M. Laennec, a late French physician of great experience, says (*Treatise on Diseases of the Chest,* page 197), "It occasionally happens that both local and general bleeding, in place of proving derivative, seems, on the contrary, to excite haemorrhage. I have noticed the return of the menses, and aggravation of the monthly discharge, during the application of leeches to the pit of the stomach. General bleedings appear sometimes to have alike effect on haemoptysis." Sir James Clark also says, " I have more than once seen slight haemoptysis follow the application of leeches round the anus, (and have warned patients not to be alarmed at it), when applied to obviate pulmonary hemorrhage. In one case, a severe attack of haemoptysis took place a few hours after the application of leeches." The inference I draw from this fact is, that debility being commonly one of the chief causes of haemorrhage, we might reasonably expect that since the artificial abstraction of blood tends still more to augment the weakness, it would in manyinstances really increase the evil it was ignorantly designed to remove. I think this fact affords great support to the opinion, that we are not justified in the artificial abstraction of blood. Invigorating measures will be of more immediate and manifest service.

by the usual means, as cold externally applied is sometimes of great service. Do not apply cold water to the chest, for it is dangerous.

In the *haemoptysis* of weakly habits, if ipecacuanha and Glauber's salt, and nitre, or acetate of lead, fail, the oil of turpentine is often serviceable, and so are the vegetable and metallic tonics. Fifteen drops of the oil of turpentine, in cold water, may be given every second hour, till the bleeding stops, and afterwards the tonics.

In all cases of *haemoptysis*, in which the strength of the patient is exhausted, the use of invigorating medicines is necessary; but it generally requires a good judgment to adapt them to the excitable state of the system. The tonic selected must be given in small doses. Bark, or the bitter infusions, as No. 63, 65, or 85, page 171-72, 185, or diluted sulphuric acid, may be prescribed. The pills of sulphate of quinine, No. 115, page 202, are very proper; or twenty drops of diluted sulphuric acid may be given in a wine-glassful of infusion of gentian, thrice a day. In these instances, a blister applied to the chest or between the shoulders, is sometimes serviceable.

In the *haemoptysis* of young females from menstrual irregularities, we must resort to the means advised here, under *Suppression of the Menses* or in the author's book ON THE DISEASES OF FEMALES.

When this complaint arises in persons of a sanguine habit or florid complexion, whose strength is little or not at all impaired, the diet should be scanty, and of a mild vegetable description; all kinds of animal food, and fermented liquors, must be forbidden, and the quantity of drink should be small. The use of acidulous fruits, as oranges, lemons, etc., and vebetable acids, are proper, and whatever food is taken should be cold. All muscular exertion, and even great exertion of mind, is hurtful. If, however, this malady occurs in an enfeebled constitution, the diet must be nourishing, though very mild, consisting of milk, eggs, the most digestible kinds of animal food, and a little white wine. Here change of air and very gentle exercise, are advisable.

After the bleeding has stopped altogether, the patient must resort to means to prevent its recurrence in future, and, for this purpose, those who are of a full habit should constantly observe a mild and chiefly vegetable diet, and moderate exercise, with the occasional use of the saline aperient, No. 130A, page 209; while those who are weakly and delicate, at the same time that they take the powder, No. 130A; occasionally, must endeavour to strengthen the chest and constitution at large, by a cautious but continued use of the tonics above prescribed, with cold sponging, daily exercise on horseback proportionate to their strength and change of air and scene.

Those who are subject to a spitting of blood should carefully avoid elevated, cold and bleak situations, and choose a flat or low country where the air is heavy. If the place is, at the same time, sheltered, it will be still more desirable. This advice is of great importance, as the most valuable remedies will generally fail of any good effect in this complaint, so long as the patient continues in an unfavourable situation.

SPINAL CURVATURE

Distortion of the spine has of late years become very frequent, especially in young females. Correctly speaking, it is of two kinds : 1. Lateral distortion, arising from weakness or rickets; 2. Distortion forwards, arising from caries of the bones of the spine, or ulceration of the intervertebral substance.

The *lateral distortion* is usually to the right side, and is the kind of curvature now most commonly met with. The first circumstance that attracts attention in a beginning curvature of the spine, is one breast appearing larger than the other, or so unequal as to lead to a suspicion that it is growing out of its place; or the patient's friends are struck by the right shoulder appearing enlarged, and farther removed from the spine than the left. At the same time there is generally an apparent enlargement of the left hip; so that the ordinary visible effects of the lateral distortion are, such a change in the appearance of the right shoulder and hip on the opposite side, that mothers, in describing the state of their child, when the spine begins to be distorted, explain it as a *growing out of the right shoulder and of the left hip.* In this condition, the patient, when in certain positions, appears to have one leg shorter than the other; and in walking, there is a constrained position of the head and neck, and inclination to one side and also an inequality in the step.

If, when these appearances present themselves, the spine be examined, it will be found nearly in the form of an italic *ʃ*, and perhaps with a slight bend outwards; and the whole of the right side will be of a rounded or barrel-like form, while the left is diminished and contracted, the ribs being closer together than is natural.

In the distortion forwards, the spine is bent forwards, that is, from within outwards, (not laterally), so as to form an angle posteriorly. In most cases of this kind of disease in the spine, the lower limbs are sooner or later affected with some loss of the power of voluntary motion, and ultimately with complete paralysis. Indeed, on minute inquiry, it is found that languor, listlessness, unwillingness to move, and unsteadiness in motion, have preceded the visible disease of the spine, in a greater or less degree.

The *immediate cause* of the lateral curvature is debility, however induced, and affecting more especially the muscles and ligaments of the back. This debility may be induced by the want of sufficient general exercise, and especially of that which acts more immediately on the muscles of the back,—by sitting long at work, or in practising on a musical instrument without artificial support,—by a habit of lounging on one leg, —by indulging much in sleep on a soft bed with a high pillow,—by the fashionable but pernicious attempts that are made to correct the figure, or to model it into a certain form.

The lateral curvature is one among the many disorders of debility which have grown out of the errors of our present refinement; it is a part of the mischief resulting from the evils of moral and physical education.[1] But very frequently it is not really

1. It is surprising and sometimes amusing, to witness the various forms which this disorder assumes, (some of them anomalous nervous affections), that arise from the evil of our present moral and physical education. Sir B. Brodie talks of hysterical White-Swellings (*see it* WHITE-SWELLING) no doubt arising chiefly from this source; but there is a remark of his relative to the present

(Contd. on next page)

so serious an evil as it seems to be. I mean, it is more certainly and readily cured than the public suppose, or than the ill judged course pursued by many of the profession will lead them to believe. The skilful and successful treatment of Mr. Harrup, of Brighton, has fully proved this.

The true cause of the distortion forwards, is a morbid state of the spine, or of some of the soft parts connected with it. This diseased state of parts will, upon careful inquiry, be always found to have preceded the deformity some length of time. The majority of those who labour under this kind of distortion are young children, and particularly those of a scrophulous habit; while the lateral curvature occurs most commonly in young females of from fifteen to one-and-twenty years of age.

TREATMENT—*The lateral curvature,* arising from weakness, is almost always curable if attended to in time. The indications of treatment are, to give due strength to the back, and whole constitution, by a proper and continued use of exercise and rest, nutritious food, and strengthening medicine. Gymnastic exercises are found to be of the highest value in this complaint, which I shall presently illustrate by an example. The exercise must be of a kind which will restore tone to a debilitated frame, and, therefore, it must be resorted to daily, the modes and degrees of it being varied and gradually increased, and it being always short of any particular fatigue. Friction and shampooing are species of exercise well adapted to this disease, since they have the power of giving tone to the back, and general system, without occasioning fatigue to the patient. Therefore, in addition to the gymnastic exercises, friction

(Contd.)

complaint, which is of uncommon value *(Medico-Chirurgical Review,* Nov. 1828. p. 58), viz., that nine out of ten of "those unfortunate young women who have been *doctored* of late years, for '*spinal diseases,*' have really laboured under nothing but *hysterical pains* in the back. The friends of young ladies are often shamefully imposed on in this affection, from a much longer time being taken in the cure than is necessary and their being put to great and needless expense. London is the worst place in the kingdom for their treatment, and those who advice such patients to be sent up to them there, are the most to be shunned. The treatment should always be carried on in a dry bracing country air.

over the chest, spine, and limbs, should be regularly practised once or twice a day, and that *very freely*. The friction commonly employed is not sufficiently energetic. The *patent portable gymnastic apparatus* of Mons. Huguenin will be found very useful. It may be procured from him, at No. 17, Lord Street, Liverpool.

Proper rest is of much consequence, because the patient being weak and easily fatigued, if a state of comfortable rest were not observed at those times when the necessary exercise is not resorted to, the weakest part would be likely to suffer from the effects of exhaustion and languor, and the spine, in consequence, to become more distorted. Occasional ease and rest should, consequently, be given to the muscles of the spine by the patient's lying down, either on an inclined plane, or on a couch, and this she should do whenever she feels fatigued, or a want of such rest. It has been a very common practice of late years to confine young ladies to the inclined plane, or to the couch for months together, often without their being allowed to rise during any part of the day, and this wearisome rest alone has been considered sufficient to cure the distortion; but the practice is extremely irrational and injurious, and should never be followed in lateral curvature. It invariably injures the general health, and by augmenting the debility of the muscles of the back, and whole constitution, increases the curvature, and sometimes induces additional complaints of a serious nature.—See my volume ON THE DISEASES OF FEMALES. Sir Astley Cooper relates the case of a lady who submitted to this vile practice for many months, and in the end rose without any favourable alteration in the state of the spine, but with a disease in the bladder, which afterwards spread to the womb, and proved fatal.—*Lancet,* vol. ii. p. 464, 1823-24. Mr. Abernethy also objected to a state of constant recumbency, and to lying down in any constrained attitude. He says, "I would by no means deprive the patient from taking that degree of active exercise which is conducive to health." Patients afflicted with the present complaints should have rest, but it should be only occasional rest, taken at any time in the day that they find a need of it, and not continued so long as to interfere with the necessary exercises, or to injure the general health. The best thing for the patient to repose upon is a moderately hard hair mattress, which may be placed on an inclined plane, if preferred.[1]

The food should be of a mild nutritive quality, consisting chiefly of broiled mutton or lamb chops, tender roast beef; fowl, venison, eggs, biscuit, tea, cocoa, or thin chocolate, the most digestible vegetables, and a little wine or malt liquor. The advice given on this subject under INDIGESTION, is applicable here. Salubrious country air is highly advisable.

The administration of cod-liver oil, steel, or vegetable bitters, will assist the foregoing means. The pills, No. 102, 103, 104A, pages 193-96 or No. 115, page 202, may be taken, or the mixture, No. 82 or 83. The bowels must be carefully regulated by diet and exercise. Whenever there is an appearance of scrophula or rickets in the constitution, cod-liver oil will be clearly indicated, and cold water sponging.

In illustration of the good effects of gymnastic exercises, in cases of distorted spine, arising from debility, I transcribe the following case from Captain Clias's observations thereon.

> "Miss A. B., aged sixteen years, had been affected for several years with a distortion of the spine, from the right to the left side, with general weakness, particularly of the arms and chest; she was extremely pale and thin; her sleep much disturbed, and her appetite nearly gone; she had an obstinate cough; her voice was weak, and nearly inaudible. She had a continued pain in the left side, resulting from the pressure of stays, which she had worn for some months, with the expectation of re-establishing the straight position of her back. Her head reclined upon her chest; and what are a called the false ribs of the left side, were bent one over the other, and forced inwards. In this condition the young lady was confided to my care, on the 22nd of October, by a physician who had seen and visited her

1. Mr. Minter, 33, Gerrard Street, Soho, is very ingenious in the construction of chairs, couches, and spinal carriages, and all persons suffering from any spinal disease will consult their ease and relief, and probably aid in their own restoration, by inspecting his manufactory, and availing themselves of his valuable assistance in this way.

for some years. I may be allowed to say, that it was almost with repugnance that I engaged to employ my system of exercise in the case of a person who appeared to be nearly in a dying condition, but the entreaties of the relations, and the solicitations of the medical attendant, were so urgent, that I could not forbear making the trial. The table of exercises which I employed in this case, will give a just idea to those persons who interest themselves in this practice, how far I deserved the confidence reposed in me.

Table of Gymnastic Exercises resorted to in this case, by which the reader will perceive the slow but gradual manner in which, patients, in such cases, proceed from slight exercise to those which require greater strength and exertion.

"1. To make prolonged inspirations, sitting. 2. Prolonged inspirations, the patient standing, the arms fixed. 3. The same exercise, the arms hanging down. 4. The same, the arms extending horizontally. 5. The same, the arms fixed to a horizontal pole. 6. Deep inspiration, and counting a certain number without drawing the breath. 7. Movement of the feet on the ground, the patient sitting. 8. Deep inspiration, the patient lying on the left side, and leaning on the elbow. 9. In the same position to raise and to lower the body. 10. Walking slowly, and making deep inspirations. 11. Walking a little faster, and counting several steps without drawing breath. 12. Bending without rising, the weak hand fixed above. 13. Beating time with both hands fined to the horizontal pole. 14-15. Beating time, bearing a weight in the weak hand. 16-17. Lifting up a Small box from the ground with both hands, and then with the weak hand. 18-19-20. To declaim without moving, and to sing without drawing breath. 21-22-23. Movements of balance simple, in front and on one side. 25-26-27-28. Develop other motions of the arms and to imitate the motion of sawing. 29-30. These exercises with the weak hand only. 31-32. To draw upon a spring with the weak hand only, and then with the arms, and body fixed. 33. Seated on the ground, to rise with the assistance of the arms, the feet fixed. 34. Lying down horizontally, to raise the body without the assistance of the arms. Other exertions of a similar kind, which it is not necessary to describe, follow these."

"On the 27th of November, the cough having entirely ceased, and the progress of the patient giving me reason to expect the happiest results, I began to employ friction during the exercise on the diseased parts. At this time, I also took with her the first promenade, the weak arm supported, and afterwards in a carriage. On the 12th of January, she was so much recovered, that she could without inconvenience resume her lessons in singing, playing and drawing, and walk several miles without fatigue. The cough and pain in the side had entirely ceased; she had an appearance of health, and her spirits were good. All the animal functions were perfectly restored."

In the distortion forwards, arising from disease in the bones of the spine; or in the intervertabral substance, the most effectual means of cure, are perfect rest, and a large issue in the neighbourhood of the disease. The burning of moxa (*see it* page 96) on the affected part is sometimes likewise of great service in such cases. Disease is apt to occur near the *sacrum* and last *Lumbar Vertebra,* and pressure on that part causes pain. When this is the case, the patient must lie down constantly. Mr. Hilton, of Guy's Hospital, is a desirable person to consult in such cases.

Good stays are sometimes of use here, and I recommend Mrs. Rogers, 6, Trinity Square, Borough, to the notice of the sufferer. *Invisible* crutches are made by a Mrs. Strickland, of Bristol, which are said to be very useful. I have not myself tried them.

This kind of distortion forwards is very different in its nature and in the means required for its cure, from the lateral curvature. I have described its symptoms in my book on the DISEASES OF FEMALES, and have there detailed at length a remarkably interesting case, in which the patient had lost all power of motion in the lower limbs, his motions passing involuntarily and unconsciously, and which was nevertheless conducted to a successful issue. Sir Astley Cooper, and Mr. Mayo, gave the case up as hopeless.

STRANGURY OR RETENTION OF URINE

Strangury is an inability of properly expelling the urine contained in the bladder, the efforts to do so being attended with pain, and the urine passing by drops, sometimes not at all.

In this complaint, the distended bladder generally forms a hard and circumscribed tumour in the front of the lower part of the belly, giving pain to the patient when pressed with the hand; and if it be not speedily relieved, usually excites some degree of fever. There is a great differēnce in different cases, with regard to the quantity of urine passed in this complaint. In some instances violent efforts to make water are excited at intervals, and, during the strainings, small quantities of urine are expelled, mostly in drops; in others, the patient may make water in a stream, for once, or twice, or more and discharge a quantity equal to that which is commonly discharged by a person in health, yet still pain and distension of the bladder continue, till the pain is relieved by the introduction of a proper instrument, called a *catheter,* by which the accumulated water is drawn off. It also now and then happens, that after a good deal of pain and suffering, when the bladder has suffered its utmost distension, the urine runs off or dribbles away by the natural channel, as fast as it is excreted by the kidneys, but without lessening the quantity originally distending the bladder; and this circumstance has caused a serious misapprehension, on the part of the uninformed, of the true nature of the case.

It arises from many different *causes,* the chief of which are, strictures in the urethra; eniargement of the prostate gland; inflammation of the bladder; stones, or other foreign bodies, in the urethra; inflammation of the urethra; a want of tone in the bladder, induced by retaining its contents too long.

It is necessary to *distinguish* RETENTION FROM SUPPRESSION of urine. In the former complaint the urine is merely retained in the bladder from an inability to expel it by the natural afforts; in the latter, there is a partial or total defect in the secretion of this fluid by the kidneys.

TREATMENT—Every case of retention of urine demands prom assistance, but where the disorder presents itself in its complete form, the mischief of delay is of the most serious nature; for if the bladder remains preternaturally distended, it not only loses its contractile power, but is quickly attacked with inflammation and sloughing; the bladder at last bursts, the urine is extravasated in the surroupding parts, and death is the consequence. An able surgeon should be sent for instantly.

In general, the first step in the treatment of retention of urine should be an attempt to draw off the collected urine, by the introduction of a catheter into the bladder. Where the complaint depends on inflammation, blood-letting, the warm bath, and a warm purgative clyster, No. 8, page 146, must be resorted to before attempting the introduction of the instrument. A discharge of the urine through the natural passage is effected more frequently by the use of the catheter than any other means, but whether it be successfully used or not, the proper means of lessening existing irritation in the parts affected must be employed, such are warm fomentations, the warm bath, bleeding, mucilaginous drinks, and opium combined with calomel, followed by cooling medicines; for it must never be forgotten, that irritation of some kind or other is the common cause of the present malady, and the great object is to allay it by the above means and this practice will be necessary whether the catheter be used or not.

The retention of urine to which persons of advanced age are liable, is generally owing to an enlargement of the prostate gland, and here the use of the catheter is of great service. If symptoms of inflammation exist, the patient should be immediately placed in a warm bath, warm fomentations should be used, with the other means just described. A grain of calomel, united with an equal quantity of opium and James's powder, and made into a pill, may also be given every four or five hours, if the symptoms of irritation are severe. This pill is sometimes of eminent service in the present complaint, and may be given in every variety of it. It is, particularly indicated when great pain exists. Sir Astley Cooper says, that the catheter will always overcome the obstruction arising from an enlargement of the prostate, and that it is never necessary to puncture the bladder under such circumstances. He also cautions young surgeons from puncturing the bladder from the rectum in elderly persons, in consequence of this operation being frequently followed by troublesome consequences at an advanced age.

When the disease is produced by a stricture in the urethra, the means recommended under that head must first be tried, such as the application of leeches to the neighbouring part, the warm bath, bleeding from the arm, and an opiate clyster, as No. 9, page 147. *Graves's mixture,* No.87B, page 177, is also proper; and when there is much spasmodic action. present, Mr. Cline has recommended twenty drops of the muriated tincture of iron to be iven in water every ten minutes. If these means fail to afford relief, the exhibition of a tobacco clyster may be resorted to, but only under the directions of a professional man. Sometimes, in this case, a fine bougie will admit of being passed into the bladder when a catheter will not, and ten being withdrawn, the urine follows, and is discharged; and an attempt should, therefore, be made accordingly. —*See* STRICTURE.

Retention of urine from inflammation of the bladder is known by its sudden attack; the frequent desire to make water; the acute pain in the region of the bladder,—pain, which is increased by the efforts to make water, and which shoot up to the loins and along the urinary canal to the end of the glands; the frequency and hardness of the pulse; the aggravation of pain when pressure is made on the region of the bladder; and by the red inflammatory colour of the urine. When the complaint arises from inflammation of the urinary canal (called urethra), the symptoms are those of inflammation in general, as just described, but affecting more particularly the parts in the course of that canal; the private parts are swollen and tender; there is a scalding sensation in the passage; and when the .patient makes a little water, he experiences a great deal of smarting, which is sometimes insupportable. In this case, give directly *Graves's mixture,* No. 87B, page 187. If that does not succeed, then let the patient be bled, have the warm bath, and calomel and opium, etc. (as one grain of calomel, two of James's powder, and half a grain of opium), every third hour. I recommend also a tea-cupful of strong decoction of linseed to be drank thrice a day. When inflammation of the bladder gives rise to this disorder, the catheter should be directly introduced, so as to free that organ from the irritation which the pressure of the urine must occasion; but when the strangury is the consequence of inflammation in the urinary canal, (or urethra), the employment of the catheter must be delayed until this inflammatory state has been reduced by the use of the foregoing measures, since the passing of instruments in this diseased condition of the canal cannot fail to increase irritation.

When strangury is the effect of want of tone in the bladder, as an accompaniment of old age, or induced by retaining its contents, too long, it will be necessary to introduce the catheter directly, and to repeat it twice or thrice a day, until the organ recovers itself, which it usually does in a short time, without further assistance. The tincture of cantharides, in doses of twenty or thirty drops in water, twice or thrice a day, is an excellent remedy in this case. As soon as this medicine occasions smarting in making water, it must be laid aside. Richter, an able German surgeon, states that in some cases of retention from paralysis of the bladder (that is, loss of tone), almost immediate and very considerable relief was obtained by pouring cold water from the spout of a pitcher, in a stream descending several yards, upon the front and lower part of the belly—this appears to me to be a valuable remedy.

If the complaint arise from the free use of blisters, or other sources of simple irritation, the patient should drink very freely of warm dilating fluids, as barley-water (No. 20, page 151), or linseed tea, and a clyster of starch and opium, as No. 9, page 147, should be injected into, the rectum, and repeated occasionally, if necessary. Fomentations to the region of the bladder are also proper.

When all the foregoing means fail of relieving the bladder from the accumulation of urine, that organ must, of course, be punctured.

STITCH OR PAIN IN THE SIDE

Stitch or pain in the side, is generally symptomatic of some disorder in the lungs or digestive organs, when it is to be removed by the means usually employed to restore those viscera to a healthy state; but sometimes it is not clearly connected with any primary affection of those parts, and arises from neglect of exercise.—See NEURALGIA. Sometimes this pain is owing to an affection of the womb, and I have treated of this full in my book on the DISEASES OF WOMEN. When women suffer much from *whites,* bearing down, and severe pain in the side, especially if it be the left side, they may expect prolapsus of the womb.

When it does not occur as symptomatic of a disorder in the lungs or stomach, it is usually occasioned by chronic inflammation of the pleura, that is, the membrane lining the cavity of the chest; by habitually forcing the chest, in writing, against the hard edge of a desk, or by the use of tight stays. If the patient has reason to consider it to be owing to either of the last two causes, he may generally regard it as depending on this inflamed state of the pleura, especially if the pain is increased on pressure, and on taking a deep inspiration. In such a case, one of the best plans of treatment consists in giving a pill composed of a quarter of a grain of calomel, with a gain of James's powder and a grain of Dover's powder, every night, with one of the pills, No. 104, page 197, twice a day; the bowels being, at the same time, properly regulated, and a blister applied to the chest or between the shoulders. Sometimes, the application of a few leeches may be advisable, but I would recommend the preceding remedies to be fairly tried first. If the, patient is of a very full habit, ten or twelve ounces of blood may be taken from the arm, and leeches be afterwards applied to the chest, should the preceding means have failed to cure. Exercise is of great consequence in these cases : it should be taken daily and freely. But let the patient read attentively the observations at the end of this volume, in the *Appendix on Cold Water.*

Should close application to writing or the use of tight stays, have given rise to this pain, it will of course be absolutely necessary that these causes are avoided in future. Without this, no great or permanent benefit can be gained from the prescriptions of the physician, but with it, the use of the means just noticed will seldom fail to remove the complaint.

When pain in the side is associated with a deranged state of the stomach and general health, and there is a good deal of general languor and debility, the above pill of calomel and opium, at night, will, for the most part, be found very useful, with which some mild tonic medicine ought to be given during the day, such as the pill, No. 102 or 103 or the mixture, No. 74C or 82, 83 or 84. The bowels must be kept free from confinement, by diet and regular solicitation; and exercise, thrice a day, is important. The powder or compound decoction of sarsaparilla is a very useful medicine in this complaint. And if the pain resists the action of the preceding means, the veratria ointment may be tried.

STRICTURE

The word stricture, in medical language, is intended to signify a contraction of some canal in the body, by which a part of the canal becomes narrower than the rest. Strictures most frequently occur in the *urethra* of men, and in the *rectum :* and I shall notice each of these maladies separately. This is a disorder never requiring any active treatment, but rather the exercise of *tact*, and mild appropriate measures.

Stricture in the Urethra[1]

This disease is so common, and often so alarming, as to demand the first and chief notice under the present head. There is no part of the urethra which may not be narrowed by a stricture; but the most common seats of this contraction appear to be about six inches and a half, and four inches, or four and a half, from the external orifice. It may occupy only a very small extent of the passage, being such a constriction as. would arise from the application of a piece of packthread round it, or it may extend to a considerable distance.

The *first symptoms* of which a patient affected with this disease most frequently complains, are an inability to retain his water so long as usual; an obscure uneasiness about the seat; and an alteration in the stream of urine, which, instead of being full and equal, is smaller than usual, and is forked, spiral, or scattered. The first symptom, just noticed, compels the patient to rise once or twice in the night, to void his urine, and he also generally finds that a greater force is necessary to its complete expulsion than he has been in the habit of exerting, in consequence of the resistance made to the free

1. The canal leading into the bladder.

passage of the water by the stricture. Nocturnal emissions are a common symptom of this complaint; and sometimes there is a mucous discharge from the urethra, which is seen adhering to the bottom of the receiving vessels. When the disease is of a very aggravated nature, the urine will often become quite white, and be mixed with matter (pus), or blood, there will be great difficulty and pain in voiding the urine, and likewise much general debility.

The *immediate cause* of stricture is a slow inflammation in the part affected, which occasions a thickening of the canal, and a deposition of adhesive matter around that thickening, so as to produce a diminution of the diameter of the canal; and I conceive, that whatever gives rise to considerable irritation in the urethra, may prove a cause of stricture there. Hence the disease very frequently follows gonorrhoea; or it may be induced by drinking or riding hard, and by direct injury of the parts. When a patient, labouring under gonorrhoea, is so imprudent as to indulge in hard riding, and free drinking, he exposes himself to the most powerful causes of the present malady, and such as rarely fail to produce it in its worst forms.

Sometimes, however, it is merely a spasmodic affection. Deranged health produces spasm of various degrees of intensity, in many structures, indeed, it may induce it in any structure; and we cannot be surprised that spasm is frequently induced in the urethra by disorder of the general system. This is a case which of course yields more readily to medical treatment than the fixed stricture, and a curious example is referred to at page 128.

TREATMENT—When a surgeon suspects the existence of urethral stricture in any patient, the first thing he does is to pass a full sized bougie [1] down the canal, in order to ascertain whether his conjecture be well founded or not. For it is clear that if there be any contraction in the tube, the bougie will stop when it arrives at the part in which it is situated, and thus place the reality of the complaint beyond all doubt; but if there be no contraction, the instrument will slide

---

1. A bougie is a long smooth flexible instrument, usually made of linen or lint rolled into a proper shape, and then dipped into a mixture of wax and lard, etc.

completely into the bladder. When the patient is able to procure the assistance of an able medical practitioner, he should immediately avail himself of it, and implicitly adhere to the instructions given; but, unhappily, ignorance and inattention are much more common than their opposites, and it is an indisputable fact, that a vast number of persons afflicted with the present complaint, find it a difficult matter to obtain judicious and efficient aid, and even some who enjoy ample pecuniary means attain to it only after a long and damaging search.

The dilatation of the strictured parts is to be accomplished chiefly by a frequent use of the bougie, or by Holt's dilator; and it is to a skilful use of these instruments that the most able surgeons of the present day trust for the cure of the disease. A small-sized bougie must be introduced through the stricture once a day, or once in two days, and allowed to remain at first for five or ten minutes, the time being afterwards gradually lengthened to half an hour, or an hour, or longer. If possible, no pain should be produced in passing the instrument and the moment any particular uneasiness is felt from its presence, it should be withdrawn. In the beginning, one of the smallest size bougies will in general be necessary, in order to succeed in passing the stricture; and in increasing the size, we must be regulated by the facility with which the stricture becomes dilated, and the ease with which the patient bears the dilatation. If the size of this instrument can be gradually augmented, it should satisfy us, and this advantage ought to be followed up till a bougie of a large size can pass freely.

Bougies are of various kinds, but those made of wax or silver are the best. The common wax bougie appears to me decidedly the best for all ordinary occasions. When the stricture is particularly small, it is sometimes necessary to employ a catgut bougie, in the first instance. Sir Astley Cooper generally used a conical silver bougie.

The great art in using this instrument well, consists in passing it down the canal with as much gentleness, and, therefore, so as to occasion as little irritation as possible. It should be introduced slowly and when it arrives at the stricture, *allowed to rest there for a few seconds; then the operator must press it forward very gently,* and if it be still obstructed in its passage; a longer rest ought to be observed, and thus by humouring the part, the bougie will often at length pass, when a less gentle mode of proceeding would entirely fail in carrying it into the bladder. A late eminent surgeon in London, (Abernethy), remarkable for his eccentricity, and, I am happy to add, no less so for his mild and soothing plan of treating all diseases, remarked to me, that not one surgeon in a thousand should pass a bougie for him. He conceived the usual mode of its introduction to be much too irritating. Wax bougies should always be warmed a little, curved and smeared with olive oil, before being used. Mr. Liston said that the passing a catheter is one of the most difficult operations in surgery. He had the greatest possible objection to cutting instruments and caustics in the treatment of stricture, and with the best reason; and I earnestly warn every sufferer against consulting those advertising unprin-cipled fellows who are always found in London, and other large cities. Only such respectable surgeons as Mr. Henry Smith or Mr. Holt, surgeon to the Westminster Hospital, should be consulted. And let me here say, that there is no such disease as *Spermatorrhoea.* People are frightened only with the view of being eased of their money.

At the same time that we use the bougie, great attention ought to be paid to improve the state of the general health. The bowels should be carefully regulated by diet and mild medicine, as No. 74D, page 178, every morning; the condition of the stomach be improved by the use of alkalies, bitter, or steel, as the circumstances of the case point out. Sarsaparilla is often a very good medicine here, especially if taken with one of the pills, No. 98A, page 192, every night.

As a local means of relief, I would strongly recommend the iodide of potassium, or of cadmium. A drachm of this salt mixed with an ounce and a half of hog's lard, forms an ointment, of which the size of a nut may be rubbed along the course of the urethra once or twice a day, for a fortnight, with great advantage. This preparation has unquestionably a remarkable power in promoting absorption, and I know from experience, that it will often succeed effectually in allaying irritation in this canal, so as to render the introduction of a bougie easy, which before its use was impossible. It is worthy the attention of all medical practitioners, more especially in the severer forms of this malady.

Some time since it was much the fashion to use bougies armed with caustic, with the view of gradually destroying the stricture; the injuries committed by it were incalculable in number, and almost inconceivable in severity. It is a vile and dangerous practice, which no considerate surgeon will now ever resort to, except in cases of extremity, and then very seldom. Sir Astley Cooper's opinion is that it ought never to be employed, unless the stricture be accompanied with fistula in *perinoeo*, and that fistula behind the stricture. Mr. Wakley, surgeon to the Free Hospital, recommends silver tubes in the treatment of stricture, as a vast improvement on the old method. Mr. Skey, of Lower Grosvenor Street, is worthy of confidence in the treatment of stricture; and so is Mr. Henry Smith, of Caroline Street, Bedford Square, whose cautious and mild treatment I greatly admire. Mr. Holt, of the Westminster Hospital, is also very skilful in his excellent method of treatment by direct dilatation.

The preceding remarks refer to cases of established or *permanent* stricture, but sometimes a patient is suddenly seized with a difficulty or impossibility of making water, although a few hours before he may have passed it in a full stream, and with great ease—this is called *spasmodic* stricture. To relieve this sudden or spasmodic stricture, let the ointment of iodide of potassium, or of cadmium, above described, be rubbed freely along the surface of the canal, the patient taking, at the same time, fifteen or twenty drops of muriated tincture of iron, in water, every half hour, or hour, till relief is obtained. Lime-water is also occasionally of much service; and the warm bath is proper. Whatever medicine is taken, it is generally advisable to endeavour to introduce a bougie or catheter into the bladder; but it must be done very slowly, and with as much gentleness as possible. The point of the bougie may be smeared with extract of belladonna. In general, I think it far better to use the iodine ointment, and the muriated tincture of iron, before attempting to pass the catheter. At page 128 (as before noticed) the reader will find the relation of a case of spasmodic stricture cured by quinine.

In concluding this article, I would earnestly recommend the strictured patient ever to bear in mind this truth—THE RELIEF OF IRRITATION IS THE GREAT OBJECT OF MEDICINE. Throughout this volume I have endeavoured to impress the minds of my readers with the value and importance of this axiom, because in all cases of severe protracted disease, an adherence to it will be found of immediate and lasting benefit, and in no complaint is it capable of conferring greater advantages than in that now under consideration. In stricture, indeed, it is worthy of particular attention, since both patient and surgeon are too often eager to effect a great change in a short time, and evince such impatience when obstacles occur to its accomplishment, as very frequently leads to the aggravation of the malady. If the means made use of are mild, soothing, and appropriate, as those noticed above, no strictured patient need fear any evil consequences from his complaint, but let him bear in mind that he has everything to dread from harsh and violent measures.

Stricture in the Rectum[1]

This is a disease of precisely the same nature as that last treated of, differing in general only in its seat, which, instead of being the urethral tube, is the last intestine. It is of frequent occurrence, and often exists a long time without being discovered.[2]

Its chief *symptoms* are habitual costiveness; considerable irritation about the anus, the patient being generally troubled with piles, uneasiness on going to stool, discharge of blood, and

1. The rectum is the last intestine.
2. Talma, the well-known French tragic actor, died from the effects of an undis. covered stricture in the rectum. He had experienced for some years before his death, a difficulty in evacuating the bowels; and would frequently go in great haste to the water closet, thinking there was a copious motion to come away, and yet when the attempt was made, nothing but air, or a minute quantity of liquid faeces, would escape. The body was examined after death, and, from the appearances that presented themselves, it seems probable, that a timely use of the bougie would have saved his life.

prolapsus ani; flatulence; frequent pain in the *sacrum*, sometimes extending down the thigh, in the course of the large nerves. Very frequently there is a great deal of difficulty in passing the motions, which are of small size and figured.

Whatever produces great disorder or weakness in the bowels may prove a cause of strictured rectum.

TREATMENT—This disease is generally to be cured by passing very carefully a rectum bougie through the stricture daily, or once in two or three days, which must remain at first for ten or twenty minutes, the time being afterwards increased to two, three, or four hours, or longer. The directions given under stricture of the urethra respecting the use of bougies are strictly applicable here, excepting that the size of the instrument must of course be larger. A rectum bougie of a small size must be gently passed first, and the size gradually augmented. Surgeons in general do not observe so much care and gentleness in the introduction of rectum bougies as they ought. It should not cause pain. The common rectum bougies I decidedly object to, on account of their irritating quality, and advise them never to be employed. The best sort are made by rolling a long piece of lint very carefully and closely together, which after it is stitched neatly up on one side, and tied with a piece of string at one end, must be dipped twice in a mixture of lard and yellow wax melted together :—the proportions should be one part of wax to two of lard. Very good rectum bougies, and at a reasonable price, may be procured from Watts, Chemist, 68, Strand, and from all the best instrument makers. During the employment of the bougie, the bowels should be kept very gently open by an occasional use of a little castor oil or decoction of aloes, or the pill, No. 100, or 101, pages 193-94.

Most persons afflicted with this malady are distressed by frequent fits of severe nervous agitation and irritability, which are found to come on whenever the bowels are more disordered than ordinary. Such patients, if properly treated when the stricture is discovered, always gain much relief, and are often restored to a state of good health, and comfortable feeling, to which they might have been perfect strangers for years. I am superintending a case of this description at the time (1830) this sheet is going through the press. I would, however, caution my readers against the practices of some people who think, or affect to think, almost every one has a strictured rectum, an interested conceit, which they fail not to turn to their own profit,—at least, if that money can be considered profitable which is ill-gotten. Mr. Henry Smith, surgeon to King's College Hospital, is worthy of all confidence.

STYE

The stye is strictly only a little boil, which projects from the edge of the eyelid. It is of a dark red colour, much inflamed, and occasionally a great deal more painful than might be expected, considering its small size. It usually disappears of itself, after a little time, especially if some purgative medicine be taken. If, however, it should be very painful and inflamed, a small warm poultice of linseed meal, or bread and milk, must be laid over it, and renewed every five or six hours, and the bowels be freely acted upon by a purgative draught, as No. 74, page 176 or No. 28, page 156. When the stye appears ripe, an opening should be made into it with the point of a lancet, or large needle, and afterwards a little of the ointment, No. 88, page 188, may be smeared over it once or twice a day. Those who are much troubled with this complaint should attend to the directions at page 345-49.

SUN-STROKE

Blood-letting should never be resorted to in sun-stroke, unless the patient is of a full habit, and has not been previously exhausted by fatigue. Soldiers and sailors are most exposed to it, and the best remedies are quiet, cool air, dashing cold water on the head and face, and the use of tonics, particularly quinine and wine, and drinking cold wine and water.

SUPPRESSION OF THE MENSES

I have already treated of chlorosis or *retention* of the menses, which is the complaint of young girls, in whom this discharge has never properly appeared; and have now to advert to a *suppression* of the menses, which signifies an interruption to the discharge, occurring at any time of life after it has become habitual. It may, therefore, occur in women of any age, previous to forty-five or fifty.

Of course, the chief symptom is the disappearance of the usual monthly discharge, with which various strange and unusual feelings are associated, and varying in different indiv'duals, such are, a feverish heat and dryness of the skin, flushing of the face, head-ache, pains in the loins and back, costiveness, difficulty of breading, palpitation of the heart and sometimes bleeding from the nose, stomach or lungs.

The most frequent *causes* of this suppression are, great anxiety of mind; suddenly suppressed perspiration from cold, especially if occurring while the discharge was flowing; sudden alarm or terror; protracted fever; scanty and poor living; or some very considerable disorder in the constitution.

TREATMENT—It demands especial attention that there are two states of the system in which *suppression* may be found, viz. *the first* where there is a morbid fulness, with a quick tense, or full pulse, severe head-ache, and perhaps flushings of the face; *the second,* where debility evidently exists, the pulse being feeble.

In the ,first case, it will be advisable for the patient to have the bowels fully relieved by the mixture, No. 73, page 176, and for the first days of treatment to observe a vegetable diet. Let a dose of No. 73 be taken every morning for a week. After this, take a drachm of madder thrice a day, and if this is taken near the period at which the menses should appear, the more likely it is to be successful. If the madder fails, the tincture of cantharides may be tried, in doses of thirty-five or forty drops, thrice a day in water. This is a more effectual remedy than the madder, but not generally so much so as the volatile tincture of guaiacum, or the guaiacum mixture, No. 72C, page 175. A tea-spoonful of the tincture may be taken every morning, noon and evening, in a wine-glassful of milk or water. A tumbler full of cold water should be drank after each dose. The tincture of guaiacum is a strong stimulant and will, therefore, require particular attention to the preparatory treatment above advised, in respect to purgatives, low diet, etc. in those females who are of full habit, with an irritable pulse. Indeed, in such cases, the guaiacum mixture, No. 72C, page 175, is a more suitable remedy than the tincture.

In the second case, the pills prescribed at page 623-24 are the best remedy; with which we must combine a very nutritious diet. In all cases, daily friction over the loins and lower part of the abdomen will be necessary, and the bowels must be kept in a lax state. If the above pills are not sufficient to act on the bowels, take five or six grains of the compound powder of aloes, in a pill, every other night. The warm bath, at ninety-six degrees, should also be used thrice a week. Daily gentle exercise, on foot and on horseback alternately, is invariably of consequence.

Beside the foregoing remedies, the application of electricity may be tried in obstinate cases. The electric fluid passed through the pelvis, is sometimes very effectual in restoring the discharge;[1] and so is the iron mixture, No. 84A.

If the suspension should have suddenly occurred during the flow of the menses, blood-letting will be absolutely necessary. The present complaint is fully treated of in my TREATISE ON THE DISEASES OF FEMALES.

TENESMUS OR STRAINING

Tenesmus is a painful and frequent desire to go to stool, attended with straining, and a discharge of little else than mucus, in small quantities. Sometimes it is intolerably severe, and accompanied with a protrusion of the gut and the mucous discharge is tinged with blood.

This complaint is generally a symptom of dysentery or bloody flux, but is now and then met with as an original affection, when it usually arises from an injudicious use of acrid purgatives, especially

1. *Twinberrow's female syringe* is an excellent instrument for injecting mild liquids.

of aloes, from the passage of acrid humours, local exposure to cold or severe costiveness.

In general, the best means of relief are, to take five grains of the compound powder of ipecacuanha, twice or thrice a day or as occasion requires, and to throw into the rectum the opiate injection, No. 9, page 147, or a pill, composed of a grain or more, of blue pill, a grain of extract of henbane and three grains, or more, of compound ipecacuanha powder, will be found sometimes still more serviceable. Take also, every morning and evening, a tea-cupfull of compound decoction of linseed. If, however, the complaint originates in a confined state of the bowels, they must be first cleared by the use of a mild purgative clyster, as No. 8, or by taking some aperient medicine as No. 74, page 176; or No. 74C ; and after they have operated, the above means should be had recourse to. When the straining is very severe, and has induced a degree of inflammation in the parts, a few leeches may also be applied in the neighbourhood of the anus and the parts afterwards washed with the lotion, No. 69 or 72, or with cold salt and water.

When the gut is protruded, it must be carefully replaced directly, by the patient gently pressing it upwards with his two fore-fingers, bathing with cold water being previously resorted to, if necessary, and followed by the use of cold water.

TETANUS

Tetanus is a violent and extensive contraction of the muscles, attended with tension and rigidity of the parts affected. The excessive contraction of the muscles is kept up, without any intervals of complete relaxation, mostly without any relaxation whatever; but the powers of sensation and intellect are unimpaired.

Either the whole, or a part, of the body may be attacked with this malady. Sometimes only the flexor muscles are affected, when the body is rigidly bent forwards; sometimes only the extensor muscles, when it is as rigidly bent backwards; at other times both sets of muscles are involved, and the body is rigidly erect. When its effects are confined to the muscles of the jaw or throat, it is called lock jaw.

This disease differs greatly, in different cases, in the intensity of its *symptoms*, and in the mode in which it makes its attack. Generally speaking, the commencement of the disorder is announced by a sensation of stiffness about the neck, which increasing, the motion of the head becomes painful and there is a difficulty and pain in swallowing; there is also a severe pain at the bottom of the breast-bone, darting backwards to the spine; the spasms of all the muscles of the neck become exceedingly violent, and together with the spasm at the pit of the stomach, recur every ten, fifteen or twenty minutes ; at the same time that the spasms increase, the retraction and rigidity of the muscles affected become stronger, the belly feels as hard and tense as a board, and the body is drawn forward, backward or to one side, according to the muscles chiefly affected. The muscular contractions are always accompanied with the most excruciating pain and when the disease arrives at its height, a violent convulsion usually puts an end to the patient's misery.

The most *common causes* are, scratches, punctures, lacerations, or other mechanical injuries. Considerable irritation in the digestive organs seems also sometimes to give rise to this disease. It is much more frequent in warm than in temperate climates and especially in the hot seasons of those climates and in marshy situations. The male sex more frequently suffer than the female; and the robust and vigorous more frequently than the weak.

TREATMENT—Tetanus is a dangerous malady and medical men are not yet agreed respecting the most effectual remedies for it. It is clear, however, that a principal point is to remove all sources of irritation: and the exhibition of tobacco, calomel, and opium,—opium, camphor, and nitre,—opium and ipecacuanha, as in Dover's powder,—and mild purgatives of calomel, jalap, and rhubarb, seem to have been the most useful means, when used in conjunction with the warm or cold bath, as the circumstances of the case pointed out.

A proper plan in most cases is, to give two grains of opium, and a grain of calomel, made into a bill with a little mucilage of gum arabic, every three or four hours, with a mild purgative, as castor oil, or No. 120, page 205, or No. 74, page 176, every morning, or every other morning, allowing a generous diet, with a few glasses of good wine daily. In addition to these means, the cold bath is generally safe when the disease occurs in a hot climate, and is sometimes of great service, especially when it arises from other causes than a wound. It has not appeared applicable to tetanus arising from wounds, and in all cases is most proper when the heat of the body is not below the natural standard. It may be repeated, if necessary, every three or four hours. The cold bath has been strongly recommended in this disease by many physicians, and appears to be preferred at the present time throughout the West Indies.

Recent investigations authorize the opinion, that of all things hitherto tried for the cure of this formidable malady, an injection into the rectum of an infusion of tobacco is the most successful; but then it must be carefully and skilfully done by means of O'Beirne's Clyster Machine (*see* pages 493-94). It is to Dr. O'Beirne, of Dublin, we are indebted for this discovery.

The French surgeon-general, Larrey, states, that he found a combination of extract of opium, camphor, nitre and almond emulsion, the most useful medicine in this disease; and it may, therefore, be taken, if preferred, instead of the calomel and opium, recommended above. A grain of extract of opium, ten grains of camphor, and five grains of nitre, may be mixed in a mortar, with an ounce and a half of almond emulsion (page 166), and given four or five times a day. The compound powder of ipecacuanha (Dover's powder) is also said to have been useful. It is, no doubt, a valuable medicine, in allaying general irritation, and may be taken in this complaint in doses of ten grains, every three or four hours. Instead of the calomel and opium above advised, some practitioners recommend large doses of opium alone, for example, five or ten grains of this substance in its crude state, every three or four hours, and this practice appears to have been attended with success; but in general I should place much greater dependence upon free doses of Dover's powder, in conjunction with a small proportion of calomel, or moderate doses of calomel combined with opium.

If the patient be of full habit, especially if he has a wound which is inflamed, swelled and painful, twelve or fourteen ounces of blood may be advantageously taken from the arm.[1]

When tetanus occurs in a debilitated subject, the tonic plan of treatment recommended by Dr. Rush, of America, should be employed and ether, carbonate of ammonia, in doses of ten grains, bark, and a liberal quantity of wine, may be taken. The sulphate of quinine may probably be useful in such instances.

But frequently the patient is unable to swallow and then the medicines used must be injected into the rectum.

If tetanus originates from a puncture or any other kind of wound, it is advisable to soothe the irritation existing in it by the use of mild anodyne applications, and, perhaps, there is nothing superior, if equal to a watery solution of opium. A sufficient quantity of solid opium to cover the wound should be liquefied with a little water, and laid over the surface with a feather or camel's hair pencil. This is the application made use of by Sir Astley Cooper. In some cases, lunar caustic might be useful.

The treatment proper for *locked-jaw* is the same as above described, and mild aperients, with Dover's powder, or calomel and opium, with a generous diet, and the cold bath, will be found the best remedies. The locked-jaw of infants and very young children almost invariably arises from irritation in the stomach

---

1. I cannot avoid taking this opportunity of making public my experience of the powerful influence of cupping along *the spine,* in relieving the spasmodic rigidity of the muscles in tetanus, in conjunction with the exhibition of cathartic glysters, as long as the pain remains fixed; and purgatives combined with opium, on the first moment that any relaxation of the spasm permits their introduction into the stomach. I have had an opportunity of witnessing the successful effects of this plan of treatment in two cases; one of which was a case of *traumatic tetanus.* Blood was drawn from the cervical (neck) portion only of the spine, but dry cupping was employed throughout the whole length of the spine three times a day. The patient informed me that each time the cups were applied, the acute pain under the apex of the sternum was always relieved, and did not return for sometime afterwards." Dr. A. Thomson's *Elements of Materia Medica,* vol. ii, p. 372. The cupping along the spine is a means I very much approve in this disease: even dry cupping is a valuable remedy, and it is easily performed. Cases showing its efficacy in painful affections, together with the mode of its application, may be seen in my publication *on the Diseases of Women.*

and bowels, and is most successfully treated by the frequent exhibition of mild aperients, as castor oil, or No. 120, page 205, with an occasional purgative clyster, as No. 8, page 146. A mixture of small doses of camphor, ipecacuanha wine, and the almond emulsion, may also be given. Some physicians advise opium to be given, but this medicine so generally and so greatly disagrees with infants, that if ever I employed it, it would be in combination with ipecacuanba, as in Dover's powder a grain or two of which might be administered to a very young child, every three hours, in extreme cases.

THRUSH

This is the term employed (technically termed *Aphthae)* to denote those numerous white specks or vesicles that sometimes appear on the tongue and palate, and gradually diffuse themselves over the inside of the mouth. They are apt to fall off and re-appear alternately in successive crops, when we find the cuticle or scarf skin abraded underneath, and the parts excessively sore and smarting.

It is chiefly a disease of *infancy,* and owing to the large size of this volume, I am obliged to refer the reader to my volume ON INFANCY AND CHILDHOOD, for a full account of this complaint. Being symptomatic of constitutional disorder, and especially of a very irritable condition of the alimentary canal, the *treatment* must be directed rather to the disease that is at the foundation, than to the thrush in the mouth and throat. Therefore, give six grains of *Gregory's powder,* No. 121A, page 205, twice a day. But local applications are often useful in imparting temporary relief, and for this purpose nothing probably can be found more efficacious, than a gargle composed of three drachms of borate of soda, six ounces of water, and one ounce of tincture of myrrh. These are to be mixed together, and frequent sips taken and held in the mouth for four or five minutes, and afterwards discharged. Sipping a little raspberry vinegar is useful.

TIC DOULOUREUX

This is a dreadfully painful affection of the nerves of the face; at least, it occurs most frequently in the face, although other parts of the body are now and then attacked with it.

The pain experienced by those afflicted with this malady is of the most acute, distressing, and indescribable kind; it is not continual, but occurs in violent paroxysms, which often make their attack like the sudden and painful shocks of electricity, and vary in duration in different instances.

When tic douloureux occurs in the face, its most common seats are the forehead and temple, or the fore part of the cheek. In the former case, the agonizing pain darts into the inner angle and ball of the eye, and in its progress affects the whole side of the head; in the latter, it strikes towards the mouth and angles of the nose, then backwards to the ear, and sometimes spreads upward to the forehead.

Its *causes* are sometimes involved in obscurity; but frequently they are sufficiently clear, and are found to consist in great derangement of the digestive organs and general health. I am persuaded this derangement is by far the most frequent cause of tic douloureux; no man will deny that it is equal to the effect, and the evidences of its existence are very often, perhaps generally, equally apparent.

The disease is *distinguished* from rheumatism and tooth ache, by the agonizing violence of the pain, the shortness of its duration, and the absence of all swelling or inflammation; it is also sometimes excited by the slightest touch.

Treatment—As I believe the majority of cases of tic douloureux to originate in severe disorder of the general health, that state of general derangement of the system, in which nervousness and bloodlessness are prominent symptoms, I have no doubt that the best and most successful plan of treatment consists in correcting that derangement, and invigorating the general habit, by the administration of suitable aperients, alteratives, and tonics, combined with the topical use of aconitine, change of air and scene, and a correct diet and regimen. From the accounts which have been published of cases of the disease successfully treated, it clearly appears, that a very considerable majority of them were cured by the preceding means alone.

Aconitine mixed with simple cerate, and applied to the seat of pain, is probably one of the most efficacious remedies known. It has perfectly succeeded after almost every other means had been tried in vain. One grain of aconitine (procured from *Morson's, Southampton Row*), should be well mixed with one drachm of simple cerate, and a small portion of this is to be smeared over the track of the painful nerve, once or twice a day, for six days. This cured Mr. Spry, a surgeon, of Charter House Square, who had suffered greatly from tic douloureux in the face, for eight years.—Watson's *Practice of Physic*), vol. i. p. 695.

Costiveness, or an irregular and disordered condition of the bowels, with furred tongue, and other symptoms of abdominal derangement, have very generally prevailed in cases of this disease, which I have seen or heard of; and I would recommend particular attention being paid to the regulation of the bowels, by means of attention to diet, and the occasional use of mild aperients, and to the restoration of healthy secretions from all the digestive viscera, by having recourse to mercurial and other alteratives, in conjunction with tonics, daily active exercise, etc. The patient should take the aperient pill No. 100 or 101, pages 193-94, at first every other night, or the powder, No. 130A, page 209, every other morning, with the pill No. 98A, on the alternate night, and two grains of sulphate of quinine, and quarter of a grain of ipecacuanha powder, made into a pill with extract of gentian, three times a day. On this plan, the dose of sulphate of quinine may be gradually increased to three grains, or more, thrice a day, if it be found to agree. Together with the preceding remedies, a warm bath at ninetyfive degrees may be advantageously taken thrice a week, and the painful part freely rubbed occasionally with the embrocation, No. 46, page 163. In some cases, the *cold water system* is of great efficacy. In most instances, a perpetual blister, or an issue, between the shoulders, or a seton in the nape of the neck, will be found a valuable auxiliary;

and if the stools are much discoloured, I would advise the pill, No. 98A or 127, to be taken every night.

The carbonate of iron has been strongly recommended as a tonic in this complaint, and if the sulphate of quinine fail to afford the patient satisfactory relief, it may be changed for the iron, eight or ten grains of which may be taken thrice a day, and gradually increased to one, two, or even three scruples at a dose. It will sit better on the stomach when two or three grains of aromatic powder are taken with each quantity; and, if it confine the bowels, a very small proportion of powdered aloes should also be added. The mixture, No. 74C, is likewise worthy of confidence.

The arsenical solution appears to have been useful in some cases, and may be tried under medical superintendence. It certainly has sometimes a considerable power of allaying internal irritation. (The mode of taking it is described at page 12). The extract of belladonna is also another article which has occasionally succeeded, but it must not be taken except under medical supervision.

But I am desirous of impressing the sufferer with the necessity of constant attention to a correct diet, abundant exercise, and to the regulation of the bowels, whatever medicine be resorted to. Whether, therefore, he takes the carbonate of iron, sulphate of quinine, etc., he should resort to active daily exercise in the country, on foot, or horseback; he should retire and rise early; should, if practicable, change the air and scene, and regulate his diet and regimen by the principles laid down under INDIGESTION, and at pages 345-49. The more I see of the nature and treatment of tic douloureux, the more entirely am I convinced of the absolute necessity of attention to these means, in order to obtain much permanent relief in the majority of cases. Every medical man of observation, who has seen this disease frequently, must acknowledge, that instances continually occur in which steel, quinine, kreosote, and arsenic, fail of any curative, or even satisfactory effect, if the patient trusts to either of them alone. Pure air, a great deal of active exercise, and rather a spare diet of nutritious food of easy digestion, are essential to a cure in the majority of cases.

The operation of dividing the trunk of the affected nerve is sometimes resorted to, and if the complaint originate in local causes, as from some source of irritation fixed in or near the affected part, and directly irritating the nerve, may frequently be effectual, and the best mode of treatment. But if it arise from deteriorated blood, and derangement of the digestive functions, the operation will generally fall short of affording much relief, and the little advantage gained will not be permanent; sometimes, under such circumstances, it fails altogether.

Some professional men have advised the liberal use of mercury, but I warn the patient against the practice; it usually augments the general irritability without influencing the pain.

TOOTH-ACHE

Tooth-ache proves sometimes a very troublesome and distressing malady, from its attacking the sufferer frequently, and proving uncommonly severe and obstinate in its character. In this case, I have found it almost constantly to arise from constitutional causes, and chiefly from an impaired state of the blood and digestive functions, accompanied with costiveness. This is the most frequent cause of a caries or decay in, the substance of the teeth, although not the only one, since we sometimes meet with carious teeth in robust persons, enjoying apparently high health. Yet, even in persons of the latter description, suffering from tooth-ache, I have generally found a costive habit of body, or other symptom of internal disorder. This pain may also be induced by cold,—the excessive use of mercury,—rheumatism,—or pre-gnancy.

TREATMENT—The more I become conversant with disease, and the effect of various remedies, the more strongly am I convinced of the dependence of local affections, in whatever form appearing, upon constitutional derangement. By many the teeth are considered not to be so much within the influence of the disorders of the general system as the soft parts, and hence the usual indifference to constitutional treatment in this complaint, and the entire dependence on local management. But in reality the teeth are not less influenced by the state of the constitution than the soft parts of the body, and it will, therefore, be found that the most rational and successful treatment of toothache is that which best succeeds in carrying off vitiated humours, improving the blood and secretions, and augmenting the strength.

In a fit of tooth-ache, I, consequently, advise the patient immediately to take some active aperient, which will operate speedily, as one of the pills, No. 97, with the draught, No. 28, assisting their operation by sipping frequently a little warm slop. So soon as the bowels are freely opened, the patient usually experiences much relief; and after this, one of the best plans of treatment that can be adopted is to preserve a regular state of the bowels by attention to diet, and the occasional use of the clyster machine, or the pills, No. 100, 101 or 101A or 101B, page 194, and, at the same time, to endeavour to improve the condition of the digestive functions by resorting to daily active exercise, friction over the region of the stomach and bowels, and the use of some mild stomachic or tonic. As a tonic, the pills, No. 102, 103 or 104, will be found useful, particularly the first and last number. This is a rational plan when the pain originates in internal irritation, and is certainly the most successful means of curing the affection, when it admits of cure and when it does not, of lessening its frequency and severity.

Should the pain appear to be of a rheumatic character, the means pointed out under chronic rheumatism or lumbago should be used. Here,[1] a scruple of sulphur every morning and four grains of compound ipecacuanha powder and a twelfth of a grain of calomel at night are excellent remedies. Let the part be rubbed with a stimulating embrocation, as No. 45, or 46, page 163.

Local means of relief are generally serviceable. If the tooth be carious, a grain of opium, and a grain of camphor, may be made into a pill, and inserted into the hollow; or a small piece of lint, dipped in strong compound tincture of Benjamin, may be put into it, and another piece placed along the gum. This tincture I have found very useful. Filling the cavity with collodion is an excellent

1. In tooth-ache from pregnancy, the tooth should never be drawn.—See the reasons in my publication *on the Diseases of Females.*

practice. Another very beneficial application is formed of two drachms of camphor dissolved in an ounce of oil of turpentine, which is to be applied by means of lint, as just advised. It is said that the insertion of a piece of gall nut into a decayed tooth, is an effectual remedy for the pain. Rubbing the gum and side of the face with oil of cajeput, or of cloves, will also sometimes be very useful. Dr. Blake says he has been enabled to cure the most desperate cases of tooth-ache, (unless the disease were connected with rheumatism), by the application of the following remedy to the diseased tooth by means of lint :—take of alum, in impalpable powder, two drachms; sweet spirit of nitre, seven drachms :—Mix them.

Nitric acid has been applied with much success. The effect of its use is often immediate, and no pain whatever is induced. The best mode of applying it is by means of lint wrapped round a probe and moistened with the acid, which is then to be slowly applied to the cavity of the tooth; care being taken not to touch the other teeth, the gums or the cheek. The mouth is next to be washed with tepid water. The acid should thus be applied to the whole cavity of the tooth, or otherwise a second application will be required before complete relief will be obtained.

This acid may be used when the gum and cheek are inflamed, so as to preclude the possibility of extraction. In cases where the diseased fang remains and when the caries faces the adjacent tooth, it obviates the necessity of extraction in all cases of hollow teeth.

Kreosote has lately been praised as specific in tooth-ache. One drop may be placed in the hollow of a decayed tooth; if the tooth is not decayed, a drop or two may be mixed with one drachm of water and applied to the tooth by means of a camels hair pencil. It does not prevent the return of the pain, nor the progress of the caries.

One of the best local applications for tooth-ache that I am acquainted with, is warm salt and water. It should be made as strong as possible, a little taken into the mouth, and held for some minutes on and around the painful tooth, when it may be rejected, and a little more taken into the mouth; two or three of such applications generally succeed in affording relief.

When the above medicines are not at hand, or have been tried in vain, the mastication of pungent, aromatic, and stimulating plants, will sometimes succeed in relieving the pain, such as ginger, horse-radish, common hartwort, or pellitory root.

Those who are subject to tooth-ache, ought to be particular in keeping the teeth clean by the frequent use of a soft brush and water, and the occasional use of a suitable dentrifrice.

Flowers of sulphur, and charcoal powder, are among the best dentifrices : the former may be used every clay, and the latter twice a week. The best common charcoal powder should be employed, not the *prepared charcoal,* which is too often a combination of hurtful ingredients. When the gums are loose or spongy, a powder composed of equal parts of Peruvian bark, powder of catechu, and armenian bole, will be found a valuable dentifrice, and may be used three or four times a week. I have known this to be of essential service in preventing the return of tooth-ache.

Stopping, filling the hollows of carious teeth, with gum-lac and other substances, is now practised by the most skilful dentists, and is often of great service, both in delivering from present pain, and in arresting the further progress of decay.

In conclusion, I would strongly advise the patient never to have a tooth extracted, till he certainly finds he cannot retain it any longer with safety or satisfaction ; for the practice of drawing teeth immediately a patient complains of a severe pain in them, and there is a slight caries or decay, is far too common, and is attended with many disadvantages. Celsus, an ancient writer on surgery of great celebrity, warns us against this practice, and it is reprobated by many of the most able dentists of the present day.

TUMOURS

By the term *tumour* is understood a swelling possessing some solidity. Tumours in general are considered to be formed by the effusion of coagulated lymph, like the white of an egg, in the part, either accidentally, or in consequence of disease, which is afterwards converted into a living part, by the growth of the adjacent vessels and nerves into it.

I have considered at some length the subject of tumours in the breast and womb, in my TREATISE ON THE DISEASES OF FEMALES.

Two of the best treatises *on Tumours* ever published in this country is that by the late Mr. Abernethy, and one by Mr. Macilwain. The tumours most frequently met with, are the *common vascular,* the *fatty,* the *pancreatic,* and the *schirrous* or *cancerous.* All these vary much in size, the two first remarkably so. An enormous mass of the kind first-named, weighing forty-four pounds, was removed by an operation some years since at Edinburgh (see *Edinburgh. Medical and Surgical Journal*, No. 77); and Sir Astley Cooper not long since removed a fatty swelling, which weighed, independently of the blood in it, thirty-seven pounds ten ounces and was situated on the abdomen of a man, aged fifty-seven, (see *Medico-Chirurgical Transactions, vol. II.* p. 440).

TREATMENT—These diseases often require removal by the knife of the surgeon. But in some cases the most powerful alterative medicines and a strong solution of salt and water, will be beneficial. The most powerful alterative medicines here are sarsaparilla, the alkaline solution, liquor *potassce,* preparations of iodine and iron, and salt and water.

I have seen most satisfactory changes wrought by sarsaparilla, and in illustration of its admirable effects in a tumour dependent on a derangement of the general health, the following case will be read with interest :—

> "A lady, about thirty years of age, had a tumour arising from the cavity of the left nostril, of so large a size as to enlarge the nose considerabl. It was firm to the touch, painful, and attended with throbbing, with head-ache. A large consultation, consisting of Mr. Cline, Mr. Cooper, Mr. Abernethy, and the author, was summoned, and it was determined that the tumour should be touched with *kali purum* frequently, and that small quantities of blue pill should be given occasionally, great attention being paid to the digestive organs. This plan was pursued for some time. The part of the tumour to which the *kali purum* was applied, was destroyed by it, but the old surface regenerated a new tumour. Another consultation was held; the plan was altered, but, notwithstanding, the disease increased,

and the patient's health gave way. She was then desired to take powder of sarsaparilla, in the quantity of an ounce daily" (a very large quantity). "In less than a month the tumour lessened, it was eventually absorbed, an adhesion formed between the surfaces of the ulcerated nostril, leaving a small opening only; and no return of the complaint has taken place, although it is now two years since the commencement of the plan; during nearly the whole of which time the lady has continued to take the remedy in smaller doses, habit having so far familiarised her to it that she has no dislike to it."—*Sir Charles M. Clarke on the Diseases of Women, Part I, second edit.* p. 238.

Small tumours are often effectually greatly controlled and reduced by the free application of salt and water thrice a day.

Iodine is sometimes employed in the reduction and cure of tumours : two remarkable cases in which it was very serviceable may be seen in *Dr. J. Johnson's Medico-Chirurgical Review,* No. 24, pp. 429-30. *Blancard's pills* of iodine and iron are worthy of notice.

TYPHUS AND TYPHOID FEVER

Typhus and typhoid fevers are continued fevers, which are characterised by being contagious, by the pulse being small, weak, and frequent, the mind much disturbed, and the strength greatly reduced, and by the presence of either rose-coloured, or mulberry-coloured spots on the body. They are fevers which usually, run a lengthened course, generally not less than one-and-twenty days, and which are attended with evident symptoms of depressed nervous power, and depraved secretions.

The symptoms of typhus and typhoid fever vary considerably in their first appearance, and in their progress and severity, in different instances, owing to the difference of cause, constitution, age, situation, or other circumstances; but, in the generality of cases, the following are the chief symptoms. There is an uneasy and peculiar sensation in the stomach, nausea, and giddiness, languor, lassitude, anxiety about the pit of the stomach, and region of the heart, alternate heats and chills, or a sense of creeping, in different parts of the body; confusion, uneasiness, and pain in the head, redness and dulness about the eyes, dejection of mind, tremulous motion of the lips and tongue, and restlessness; short anxious breathing, acute pains in the back and other parts of the body, much thirst, nausea, vertigo, great prostration of strength, clammy, profuse perspiration, sometimes preceded by a hot, dry skin; stupor, or low muttering delirium. Sometimes the pulse is not much affected in the beginning, but as the disease advances, it usually becomes small, weak, frequent, and often irregular; and the tongue at fist only covered with a little white mucus, afterwards becomes coated with a thick, brown or black dry and firm fur.

Such are the most prominent symptoms of mild typhus, or what is sometimes called *low nervous fever.* If it proceed to a fatal termination, the symptoms of debility increase, and become extreme; the patient lies prostrate on the back, with extended arms, and insensibly glides down to the bottom of the bed; there is a continued state of insensibility; a low muttering delirium; a peculiar yet indescribable expression of anguish in the countenance; twitching of the tendons; picking at the bed-clothes; involuntary evacuations and hiccup.

If the disease appear under the form of the severer or *malignant typhus,* frequently called *putrid fewer,* its attack is more sudden and violent, its progress more rapid, and all the symptoms of debility and putridity appear earlier, and in an aggravated form. Here the rigors are extremely severe,— the heat of the skin often peculiarly acrid and burning,—the head-ache intensely painful,—the expression of anguish indescribably acute, the pulse tense, hard, quick, and fluttering. The prostration of strength appears early, and is extreme; the fever sensibly increases every evening; the delirium is high and ferocious; the complexion is brownish, or of a slight pink hue; the eyes are heavy and much inflamed; the breath hot and offensive; the tongue dry, dark, livid, or black; and the teeth and lips affected with brown sordes; vomiting of black, bilious matter is present; and the stools are blackish and very fetid. In the advanced period of putrid fever, cold clammy sweats occur with red spots called *petechiae,* under the skin, bleeding from various parts of the body, and a black gangrenous thrush appears about the mouth and throat; the guise sinks and intermits, the extremities grow cold and death ensues.

A moderate degree of deafness; the respiration returning to a natural state; moderate looseness at an early period; the urine natural in quantity, and depositing a red sediment; a thin and universal sweat, not profuse; the pulse becoming fuller and slower; light-coloured thrush, particularly if accompanied with an increased secretion of mucus from the fauces, or of saliva; and swelling and suppuration of the glands of the neck, are favourable symptoms. If the breathing and swallowing be free, the prognostic is often favourable, although the other symptoms appear alarming.

The following are very unfavourable appearances, viz., convulsions, a depravation of sight, the eyes appearing as if covered with a film, especially if blood flow from them; the voice being very much affected in an unnatural manner; a thin watery looseness at a late period; the urine being pale and limpid, or appearing brown, and depositing a matter like coffee grounds, or being suppressed without pain or distension of the bladder; no complaint of thirst, when the mouth and fauces are very dry; extreme and increasing debility. All bleedings, at an advanced period of the disease, are unfavourable, especially from the pores of the skin; and the danger of *petechiae* (little blackish-red points, appearing under the skin), is in proportion to the darkness of their colour.

Whatever debilitates the living powers of the human system, may become a cause of typhus or typhoid fever; and among the most frequent and powerful sources are, poor living,—a confined stagnant. atmosphere,—bad drainage,—grief, and other depressing passions of the mind,—sedentary living,—intemperance,—excessive indulgence in the use of intoxicating liquors,—profuse evacuations, and exposure to cold, united with moisture. Any of the ordinary causes of fever may be the cause of typhus, if the season of the year, the state of the atmosphere or the constitution of the patient, disposes to this form of the disease.

Typhus is often propagated by contagion, that is, by the

effluvium issuing from a living body labouring under the disease; and when a patient afflicted with typhus is confined in a damp, close, and stagnant atmosphere, deprived of free ventilation, and exposed to the noxious exhalations of accumulated dirt and filth, he is in a condition to communicate the disease in its worst form, and it is from such a source that the severer or putrid form of typhus commonly arises. Indeed, this fever frequently arises in crowded places, among persons previously healthy, when due attention has not been paid to ventilation; and in this way it often appears in jails, transport ships, hospitals, and the crowded and filthy habitations of the poor.

We are indebted to Dr. Jenner, physician to the (queen, for pointing out the two kinds of low fever now generally recognized, namely, *typhus* and *typhoid.*

Typhus fever attacks people of the mean age of nearly fortytwo years; *typhoid* fever of the mean age of twenty-two years. Under twenty years of age, typhus is rarely fatal; above fifty, the mortality may be sixty per cent. In typhus relapses rarely occur; in typhoid fever they are frequent. In typhus there is an eruption on the body and limbs, of *dusky pink* or *mulberry-coloured spots,* not removed by pressure, and passing into *petechiae.* In typhoid fever the spots are *bright rose coloured,* disappearing entirely on pressure, and re-appearing when the pressure is removed. In typhus the glands of the intestinal canal, called *Peyer's glands*, are not ulcerated; in typhoid fever they are almost always diseased, which accounts for the greater frequency and obstinacy of *diarrhoea,* and *haemorrhage* from the bowels, which occur in *typhoid* fever.

The rash in *typhus is* never papular, or pimply, but consists of very slightly elevated spots of a *mulberry* colour; each spot is flattened on its surface, and irregular in outline. After the third day of the eruption no fresh spots appear. The *typhoid* eruption is popular, or pimply, consisting of little-circular spots of a *bright rose* colour. Fresh spots come out every day or two, till the third week.

"The small dry tongue, with red tip and edges, smooth, furred of a pale brownish yellow, and fissured, the surface seen between the fissures being of a deep red," Dr. Jenner considers distinctive of *typhoid* fever.

While *typhus* fever arises from the effluvia of living bodies, in close unventilated places, *typhoid* fever often appears in country places, and in well-aired houses. These fevers do not prevail together, and one does not communicate the other. *Typhoid* is the endemic fever of Britain, France, and America, and frequently appears when typhus is unknown. The "Croydon fever," and the "Westminster fever," was *typhoid. Typhus* and *relapsing* fever prevails only in crowded localities, *typhoid* in all paces. The former invariably commences among the poor and ill-fed; the latter among the well-to-do, and the rich suffer greatly.

Typhoid fever (sometimes called *intestinal* or *enteric),* was that which proved fatal to Count Cavour and the Prince Consort. It is always more prevalent in autumn. In America they call it the "*autumnal,*" or "*fall fever.*" Bad drainage is a fruitful source of it. Fever arising from the offensive effluvia of drains, sewers, and cesspools, appears to be always of the *typhoid* type.

Constipation is usually present in *typhus* and diarrhoea in *typhoid* fever. The stools in the latter are peculiar, being liquid, and of the colour of yellow-ochre, the odour very offensive—or they may resemble mud or bird lime, and are alkaline. The stools in *typhus* are either of a natural consistence and colour, or they are of a dark-greenish brown, and are usually acid. Haemorrhage from the bowels is extremely rare in *typhus,* but is often met with in *typhoid* fever. Delirium and impairment of the mental faculties are common in *typhus,* but not so in *typhoid* fever; and debility and prostration are earlier and greater in the former than the latter. The pupil of the eye is usually contracted in *typhus* and dilated in *typhoid* fever.

TREATMENT—In the treatment of this fever, we must ever be guided, in some measure, by the nature of the symptoms, the age of the patient, his habits, and constitution; but as it is in its later stages a disease of debility, a mild tonic plan of treatment is the most proper and successful, and the means that have been found of the greatest service, are an emetic at the commencement, free ventilation and fumigation, the affusion or ablution of cold and tepid water, and the exhibition of mineral acids, and wine, with suitable nourishment.

The first points to be attended to in the management of patients afflicted with typhus, whether it appear under the milder form of a low nervous fever, or the more severe and aggravated character of a putrid, jail, or hospital fever, are free and sufficient ventilation and fumigation. These means are too often neglected, but are universally called for, and will frequently prove of more service than any other cordial. The windows and doors must be freely and constantly opened, and the apartments fumigated with the nitrous acid vapour, in the manner described under putrid sore throat, or with, what is still better, the chloride of lime (p. 282). It should never be forgotten, that a contagious atmosphere is injurious to the patient, as well as dangerous to the attendants, and, therefore, every proper means of purifying the air surrounding him must be resorted to, and steadily persevered in. The bed-clothes covering him should be few and light; his chamber should be freed from all unnecessary furniture and attendants; his sheets and body linen should be frequently changed, and instantly removed from the room; as should also his stools and urine. He must also be kept quiet, and every mental exertion avoided.

No doubt fever is not a disease of the solid parts of the frame, but of THE BLOOD. The blood is the part of the system which feels first and chiefly the effect of the remote cause, whatever that may be. It is the blood which imbibes the poisonous effluvia, when the disease arises from infection; it is likewise this vital fluid which is early, most certainly, and most deeply implicated in all the morbid changes consequent on exhausting fatigue, and on deficient and innutritious food. All the secretions and excretions suffer, in consequence, a morbid change; and thus it is that fever disturbs every function of the body and deranges every faculty of the mind. An obstinate disregard of the state of the BLOOD—the pabulum of life— "the life of all flesh"—lies at the root of the frightful havoc which has followed from the common methods of treating fever.

In the treatment, the grand aim of the practitioner should be to IMPROVE THE QUALITY OF THE BLOOD, and to nourish the patient; and if this can be done, in most cases *(Deo volente)* the safety of the sufferer is secured.

In the commencement of typhus, a seidlitz powder should be given, in cold water, in the morning of the first three days. If it does not operate, it should be quickly repeated with one drachm of Epsom salts added to it; a dose of the common saline mixture in a state of effervescence, with eight grains of nitrate of potash in each dose, should be given, twice a day, in half a tumbler of cold water,— the first dose at three o'clock in the afternoon, and the second at ten o'clock at night; eight grains of James's powder being given every evening at seven o'clock. This treatment will be sufficient to carry the patient through the first stage of the disease.

The symptoms of high excitement usually pass off in about a week; at the end of which period the tongue begins to assume a brown appearance, denoting the accession of *the second stage.* Immediately that a brown streak is observed down the middle of the tongue, extending to the sides, give muriatic acid. In typhus, and all diseases of the typhoid type, the mineral acids are admirable remedies. Twenty drops, or minims, of the diluted acid, should be given in a wine-glassful of barley water, or sugar and water, every two hours.

In typhus, and all diseases of the typhoid type, the mineral acids, particularly the muriatic, are of signal service, because the blood-globules are partly dissolved and there is a feeble power of coagulation, conditions of the blood effectually removed by the muriatic acid. Dr. Richardson's opinions on this point are very valuable. *On Coagulation of the Blood,* p. 446, he says, "In, true typhus and typhoid, the mineral acids are the remedies. The muriatic, from its less fixed character, holds the first place. Of late, I have given the acid from the first, and with the best success." Dr. Murchison, physician to the Fever Hospital, is of the same opinion.

Dr. Chambers, physician to St. Mary's Hospital, truly considers that low fever shows diminished vitality of the blood, and system generally, and that it should be treated on the *restorative* principle. Therefore his plan is to give muriatic acid, milk and lime water, beef tea, chicken broth, and wine. Two or three ounces of milk with half the quantity of lime water, or the same quantity of beef tea, should be given every two hours, and if a little powdered biscuit can be dissolved in it, so much the better. Barley water and good butter milk also are useful. "If there is very complete prostration and delirium of a low muttering character, wine is required. A tremulous state or quivering of the hands and fingers is a good test of the necessity for wine; and so is a sharp, weak, unequal beat of the heart."—*Clinical Lectures,* p. 61. I think highly of muriatic acid, and Dr. Chambers recommends it to be given in the following agreeable form :

Take of Diluted muriatic acid	20	minims;
Simple Syrup		a tea-spoonful or two;
Barley water or water	2	or 3 table-spoonfuls.

Mix, and give this draught every two hours.

It usually diminishes the repugnance to food and lessens thirst and diarrhoea.

If the patient gets a superficial sore on the back, by saturating his sheets with urine and stools, then paint the parts directly they get red with gutta percha, softened in chloroform. Keep plenty of the gutta percha in the chloroform bottle, so that it may be of the consistence of paint.

A gentle diarrhoea is a favourable symptom, and should by no means be interfered with; but if the bowels are acted on more than three times in the twenty-four hours, then give half a drachm of the compound powder of chalk in cinnamon water, gruel, as often as requisite, or the acetate of lead draught prescribed at page 857. If, on the contrary, the bowels become confined, , no aperient is so suitable and useful as a seidlitz powder, with one drachm of Epsom salts. To relieve vomiting or burning heat at the pit of the stomach, at any period of the complaint (symptoms which are sometimes very distressing), give half a drachm of carbonate of soda in a little water.[1]

Blood-letting has been of late years strongly advised in typhus fever, but I cannot recommend it, being persuaded it is rarely required, and that it is often very injurious. An emetic at the commencement of all fevers, is always a safe and useful means, such as No. 123, page 206. "It is astonishing," says Sydenham, "how it happens that a vomit, which does not produce either a large or a morbid discharge from the stomach, should so materially relieve the nausea, restlessness, anxiety and furred tongue of the patient." That it is followed by these good effects is certain, and when we consider that tartar emetic and ipecacuanha clear the stomach of acrid contents, powerfully relax the skin and excite a new action throughout the system, we cannot be at a loss to account for their beneficial effects.

The affusion or ablution of cold water is a remedy of mighty power in the early periods of these fevers. It enables that extensive and important organ the skin to resume its duties of arterializing the blood, circulating it through the minutest vessels, and evacuating the sweat. The sooner it is employed the better, if all chilliness has disappeared, and the skin is hot and dry. It must never be employed when any degree of perspiration is present, and rarely after the first three or four days from the commen-cement of the fever. If, therefore, on the first, second or early on the third day, the skin be unusually hot and dry, the patient should be stripped naked, supported on a stool in a low wide tub, and two or three gallons of cold water briskly thrown over him from the head downwards. It may be repeated twice a day, at noon, and in the evening, about seven or eight o'clock; and so great is the value of this remedy, that, in most instances, it proves extremely grateful and refreshing to the patient, directly diminishing the general heat of the body, and the frequency of the pulse, and disposing to sleep, while it mitigates the subsequent violence of the symptoms; and sometimes

1. So efficacious is the carbonate of soda that fever of a malignant type is successfully treated by its use alone, in some of the most swampy and pestilential districts of America. The common fever of Western Africa is the Marsh Fever, a nd the carbonate of soda will be found of signal service in it.

it suddenly cuts short the fever. But after the third day, the cold affusion would be improper and dangerous, and we must then substitute cold ablution, which, although it fails to cut short the progress of the disease, is often attended with manifest advantage, since it cools and refreshes the patient, lowers the pulse, and tends to alleviate all the symptoms of inordinate excitement, without endangering any subsequent debility. Consequently, from the third to the eighth day, the patient may be washed all over quickly with a sponge, dipped in cold water, and immediately rubbed dry after it. This may be repeated twice daily, at those times when the skin is most affected with extreme heat and dryness. From the eighth to the thirteenth day the washing should be performed with lukewarm water or luke warm vinegar and water which at that period answers better than cold water.

Camphor has been highly praised by some eminent authors, as a cordial in this fever, and when a great degree of restlessness and debility comes on early, it may be a very suitable anodyne, and should be cautiously tried.

If the symptoms of debility are considerable, a little wine may be given in conjunction with muriatic acid, and the greater the debility the more clearly is this cordial indicated. But small quantities only should be given in the beginning, with great caution, they being gradually increased or diminished according to their effects. If, by giving a small quantity of wine, for example, a glass of old Port, Sherry, or Madeira, three times in twenty-four hours, we find that we gain an advantage, the symptoms of debility being permanently relieved without its occasioning any great degree of heat and general excitement, we ought in general to be satisfied, and not to augment the dose. And when its administration is not attended with this desirable effect, caution must be exercised in increasing the quantity. If it quickly, and to any considerable degree raise the pulse, we may be assured that we are giving too much. If the symptoms of sinking and debility return soon after the cordial effects of each dose, the proper practice is, not to in crease the dose, but to lessen it, and give it more frequently. Those cases of typhus which are accompanied with petechioe, or small red spots under the skin, and with a strong tendency to gangrene, call most for the use of wine; and those in which the skin is soft and inclined to be damp, bear it best. The tongue being tremulous, moist or not very dry and the delirium consisting of low muttering incoherence, are symptoms which afford additional reasons to hope that it will prove useful. It may be given also more freely, and with less risk, to old persons, and weakly habits, to those accustomed to the free use of fermented liquors, and those inhabiting low crowded situations and large towns, than in the opposite circumstances. The late Dr. Todd introduced a plan of giving large quantities of wine in typhus and typhoid fever, which was extremely injurious. I believe; with Dr. Gairdner, of Glasgow Infirmary, that in children and young people wine in these fevers is very often "poisonous and destructive."—*Lancet*, 12th March, 1864. It is in elderly people, and those who have been much accustomed to wine, that it sometimes proves very useful. These fevers occurring in autumn, shew a greater tendency to debility than when they appear in spring, and, therefore, call for more wine. *See* also what is said of the use of wine in typhus, at page 140.[1]

Experienced physicians recommend opium to be given to procure sleep and that in a full dose; but its use requires caution. It is a ticklish medicine in fever, for it may do either serious injury, or much good; and probably we possess a far better remedy for sleeplessness and delirium in tartarized antimony, as prescribed in Dr. Graves's fever mixture, No. 87B, page 187. This will never do harm, and it will rarely fail to soothe and dispose to sleep. No opium should ever be given where *the pupils are contracted,* or the urine scanty and loaded, or where there is much difficulty of breathing, and a livid countenance. It is true that two or three nights spent in restless delirium are followed by the worst consequences; and patients who pass *three* nights in succession in that way very

1. The action of the heart will frequently guide us in the use of wine and other stimulants, even better than the state of the pulse. If its impulse is weaker, and its sounds are fainter and less distinct than in health, we may with confidence, administer wine; or rather when the first sound of the heart is nearly lost, and becomes much more feeble than the second, wine is indicated. Dr. Murchison is of this opinion.

often die. One third of a grain of acetate of morphia, in the evening, will often produce sleep, followed by striking amendment on the following day; but no opiate should ever be given *if the pupil of the eye is contracted;* and, as I have already remarked, we have a more certain remedy in Dr. Graves's mixture.

For the relief of tremors, startings, spasms, delirium and other symptoms of great irritation, cobweb is frequently found of remarkable service. It will sometimes calm the patient more effectually than opium, wine, or camphor, and may be given in the dose of eight or ten grains, which may be repeated to the second time in the space of twenty-four hours, if necessary.

Yeast was at one time in high repute as an antiseptic in this disease, and is worthy of some confidence. It is well suited to domestic practice, since it is a simple remedy, and easily procured. It is said, that a son of the Earl of Essex was given over by Dr. John Willis in typhus fever, and afterwards restored by sponging the body with vinegar, and using yeast internally by mouth and clysters. One of the best modes of giving this article, is in an infusion of malt,—a combination from which Dr. Haygarth, of Chester, says, that he has derived great advantage in the treatment of putrid fever. A teaspoonful of yeast is mixed with a pint of strong wort, and the vessel then covered close, and placed near a fire. In less than an hour, it is covered with a white cap of yeast, and should be drank in that state. One or two pints of this mixture must be taken in divided doses during the day. If good wort cannot be got from the brewer, the patient's friends may make it by pouring a little more than two pints of hot water on two pints of malt, which, after it has stood close covered for two hours, should be strained off for use. The water should not be poured on the malt boiling, but be allowed to cool for a few minutes.[1]

1. I am glad to see that recent testimonies are much in favour of the efficacy of yeast in typhus fever. " Dr. Stokes (of Dublin), who seems to have used it more extensively than any other physician of the present day, speaks highly of its efficacy, after a trial of its powers for upwards of thirty years, both in public and private practice. He has administered it in cases where purple extremities or gangrenous sloughing took place, accompanied with symptoms of inflammation. The result of his experience is, that balm or yeast is well suited to every stage of typhus fever in which it can be borne by the stomach.

(Contd. on next page)

In low nervous fever, that is, the milder sort of typhus, blisters to the nape of the neck, or between the shoulders, will often afford considerable relief from head-ache and delirium. The kind of delirium most benefited by these means is, that accompanied by a suffused redness of the eyes; and whenever they are employed, it is seldom proper to allow more than one to be applied to the body at one time. Blisters are rarely advisable in the severer or malignant typhus, on account of the existing tendency to gangrene, which they are very apt to increase. The tartarized antimony is, however, a still more efficacious remedy in delirium.

Sometimes raving comes on at night (or in the day) with a quick pulse, suffused eyes, and hot head. The patient makes violent efforts to rise from bed, may become almost unmanageable, imagining that he sees frightful apparitions, he may shout or scream, and, look extremely wild. The indication here is to relieve the brain and the mildest and most efficacious remedy is tartarized antimony. Leeches and blisters are rarely of much service, but the mixture of tartarized antimony and laudanum, No. 87B, page 187; is always a safe medicine and generally remarkably soothing and effectual. It produces perspiration when the skin is dry, a moist tongue, a soft pulse, and general quietude. After a time, it induces sleep, and great relief. From the use of this admirable remedy alone, many

---

(Contd.)

It is in general easily taken alone, or with any medicine that it may be deemed advisable to join with it; but in the worst forms of typhous fever, when it is most needed, it not only is seldom rejected by the stomach, when any other medicine can be retained, but the patient in such cases often expresses a liking for it. According to this author, yeast, being moderately laxative, often supersedes the necessity of repeated doses of purgatives; but, if required, an aperient tincture may be added to it. Should, however the bowels be purged, a few drops of tincture of opium should be added occasionally. He ascribes its efficacy to its power of correcting the morbid contents of the alimentary canal, and consequently the symptoms of putrescence, and asserts that in his idea, petechiae and a black loaded tongue will be found more effectually remedied by it than by other medicine. In adverting to the objection to this remedy, that it may be likely, by promoting fermentation, to increase the tendency to tympanitic distension, Dr. Stokes states, that in some of the most obstinate cases of tympanitis, clysters of yeast and assafoetida have proved the most efficacious remedies."—*Cyclopoedia of Practical Medicine*, vol. ii, p. 210, 1833.

will recover from a state of stupor and coma, or from a raving unmanageable sleepless condition, who otherwise would soon die. Nothing calms the nervous agitation so well, and so certainly produces sleep. Whenever there is undoubted evidence of determination of blood to the head, this medicine is indicated, and its effects will sometimes appear to be magical. Graves's *Clinical Medicine,* p. 143. Typhus and typhoid fever are apt to be complicated with congestion and inflammation of the chest, as well as the head, for which also Dr. Graves's mixture is peculiarly adapted.

Delirium and sleeplessness in fever are alarming symptoms, and hoping that the relation of the following case, cured by emetic tartar and opium *(Dr. Graves's mixture,* No. 87B, page 187), may be very useful, I have transcribed it here at length from Graves's *Clinical Medicine,* p. 156.

> "The case of Mr. William Murphy is well worthy of notice. The father of this gentleman, a practitioner of well known reputation at Fermoy, where he has been physician to the Fever Hospital for many years, arrived in Dublin the very day his son's state appeared to be hopeless, soon after the consultation, when Dr. Stokes and I agreed to use the tartar emetic and opium. Dr. Murphy admitted afterwards that he never felt so much surprised as he was at this treatment, but having intrusted the care of his son to us, he very properly expressed no opinion on the subject, a mode of proceeding he has never since ceased to congratulate himself on, for had he opposed us, the case was apparently so desperate, that it may be doubted whether we would have ventured to put the plan into execution.
>
> "On the tenth day, I had the benefit of Dr. Stokes' advice. We found our patient in a state truly appalling. He lay panting on his back, restless, and without sleep ; every muscular fibre in his face and limbs was agitated with spasmodic twitches, giving rise to the greatest possible degree of jerking, which distorted his face, caused him to bite his under lip every instant, rendered him quite unable to put out his tongue, although he endeavoured to do so. The jerkings prevented us from being able to feel the pulse, now weak and rapid, at the wrist. In the meantime, though he often moaned and raved, he muttered indistinctly; he evidently understood what was said to him,

and as far as we could collect, he seemed to suffer much less from pain in his head. Still, the temporal arteries were turgid, and his eyes suffused. He had retention of urine, and since yesterday it was drawn off with the catheter. What was now to be done? Under these circumstances, we resolved to try tartar emetic, and we ordered the following mixture :

Take of Tartar emetic	2	grains;
Musk	30	grains;
Mucilage and syrup, of each	1	ounce;
Water	10	ounces.

Mix, and take a table-spoonful every hour.

After he had taken about six doses of this medicine, he seemed rather better, and the symptoms of determination to the head appeared less marked; we therefore, added *fifteen minims of patent black drop* to the remaining nine ounces of the mixture, and directed small quantities of porter and chicken broth to be given repeatedly during the night.

"On the eleventh day we found a change for the better truly surprising, the pulse had diminished remarkably infrequency and had become softer and fuller; a warm sweat had broken out, he had raved but little, and had slept tranquilly. We ordered a continuance of the same nourishment and medicines, the latter at much longer intervals. The case need not be further detailed, as Mr. Murphy rapidly recovered, and enjoyed a speedy convalescence. Here, then, is a case which would assuredly have been lost, but for the well-tried application of the new method of treatment. I say this emphatically, for Mr. Glyssan, Mr. Boyton, Mr. Clarke and Dr. Murphy, all anxious and competent observers, assured us that from the moment he began the bottle its good effects were apparent and increased after each dose."

If much affection of the head exists, the hair should be cut off, and a cold lotion of spirit of wine and water, or cold water alone, must be applied by means of rags wet with it, and frequently renewed. The feather pillow should be removed and a hard horse hair pillow substituted, or, what is still better, a water pillow. Nothing is better to apply to the head than the coldest water.

When the extremities become cold, bottles of hot water, or a mustard poultice, may be applied to the feet. A mild looseness should rarely be interfered with, but if more than two motions occur in twenty-four hours, give a starch enema, with fifteen drops of laudanum in it, and repeat it every evening. If that is not sufficient, give the acetate of lead draught, here recommended for haemorrhage. Should bleeding arise during the course of the fever, and the mineral acids not check it, give a draught, every four hours, composed of three grains of acetate of lead, and the eighth of a grain of acetate of morphia, in spearmint water. If there is pain in the right side of the belly, with diarrhoea and bearing down (tenesmus), a few leeches applied to the seat of pain will do great good.

If the bowels are constipated in typhoid fever, only the mildest aperients should be employed, such as a tea-spoonful of castor oil, or a gruel enema, every second or third day. And whenever there is *diarrhoea,* or pain in the bowels, let flannel wrung out of hot water, covered with oiled silk, be applied over the bowels frequently.

The food, in all cases of typhus, should be nutritious, but the stomach must never be overloaded. It should be easy of digestion and given frequently,—that is, every two or three hours, and in small quantity. This precept to feed frequently is as necessary in any low fever as that of feeding well. The best kinds of food are, cooked fruits, farinaceous vegetables, as sago, panada, decoction of barley, grits, etc., jellies, bread and animal broths. Tea and coffee are useful both in typhus and typhoid fever, and salt should be freely mixed with the broth, beef-tea, and gruel. The liquid food given should, if possible, be always mixed with some portion of that which is solid, and especially with bread; and when the debility is considerable the stomach ought not to be permitted to remain long empty. No kind of animal food is proper while a tendency to exacerbation or feverish increase continues; but when convalescent, animal food is of great service, and a little pepsine with it will make it digest better. In the worst cases of typhus, the powers of digestion are wholly suspended, and as the state of the stomach does not then admit of any kind of solid food, our great dependence must be upon the use of milk, beef-tea, and arrowroot, and. wine must be given frequently, but in small quantities. Dr. Murchison's advice is *(Treatise on Fever,* p. 354):

> "In the morning at nine, a cup of coffee and milk, with dry toast, or milk alone may be given; and at noon a basin of strong beef-tea or chicken-tea, to which may be added arrowroot, vermicelli, or gelatine. At three o'clock, the beef-tea or chicken-tea may be repeated, or arrowroot made with water, milk, or port wine, substituted. At six, another cup of coffee, with toast, may be given; and at nine o'clock, a tumbler of wine-whey, or of wine-whey beaten tip with egg. Beef-tea, arrowroot, and wine-whey are to be given three or four times in the course of the night, while wine and mild drinks are to be administered along with, and in the intervals of the meals, according to circumstances. As soon as the appetite returns, or if the tongue is moist, calf's-feet jelly, chicken panada, port wine jel custard, sago, tapioca, or arrowroot puddings, or stewed apples may be allowed. It is well to prohibit uncooked fruits of all sorts, during an attack of typhus, as they often produce tormina, flatulence, or troublesome diarrhoea. When the tongue is dry and brown, all solids must be prohibited."

The patient should be allowed to quench his thirst, by drinking as freely as he pleases of mild diluting drinks, as barleywater, tamarind tea, lemonade, etc. Soda-water is, for the most part very proper, especially that prepared by Thwaites of Regent Street.

ULCERS

An ulcer is a breach of continuity in any of the soft parts of the body, attended with a secretion of matter, or some kind of discharge.

Ulcers are of different kinds, varying in their appearance, and the symptoms, whether local or constitutional, by which they are accompanied; and in order to treat them with success, it is essential to attend to these symptoms and appearances. Ulcers are chiefly of the following kind, viz. : THE HEALTHY, THE IRRITABLE, THE INDOLENT, THE INFLAMED THE SLOUGHING or GANGRENOUS, and THE SINUOUS

Healthy Ulcer

The Healthy Ulcer has a florid appearance; the little red eminences, called granulations, are small and pointed at the top; the surface of the sore is even with the surrounding skin, or only a little above it; it secretes a bland, whitish, opaque matter, and its edges are thin, and even with the surface. Here the healing process goes gradually on until a cure is effected; and all that is necessary to be done in the generality of cases; is, to avoid every source of irritation, and to apply the cold water dressing. Dip some rag in cold water, wringing it gently, lay it over the ulcer and inflamed parts, and then cover the whole with a piece of oiled silk. Renew this water dressing five or six times a day; and wind over the whole a small linen bandage.

This is a mode of treating of the highest value in almost all ulcers, as thereby the inflammation is reduced, the vessels are strengthened, and the ulcer disposed to heal. It is very soothing in *inflamed* and *irritable* ulcers, and invigorating in *indolent* ulcer. If proud flesh appears, or discoloration, dip a small piece of lint just the size of the ulcer—in a little *black-wash,* (page 190) apply that night and morning; then cover with the simple cold water dressing, as before advised.

At the same time, take every other morning before breakfast, the powder, No. 130A, page 209, and a drachm of sarsaparilla powder, twice a day; or a dose of the nitric acid mixture, No. 83A, in *the Appendix,* twice daily. If that does not answer, try bark and ammonia, as in No. 84B, page 185.

If the ulcer should be large, and especially if it has followed an abscess, it will generally be advisable for the patient to rest, and to keep the part supported in an horizontal position. The food should be easy of digestion and nutritious.

It is not unusual for proud flesh to appear in these ulcers; when it does, a small piece of lint should be laid in the middle of the sore, and the surrounding part close to the edges touched every day with lunar caustic, strips of adhesive plaster being. afterwards applied rather tightly, so as to keep the luxuriant growth down.

Irritable Ulcer

The Irritable Ulcer is exquisitely tender and painful, although it may be but slightly inflamed; its surface is unequal, being in some parts high, in others very low, and without the florid appearance of a healthy ulcer; and the discharge is either matter mixed with blood, or of a thin irritating nature. Often the margin of the surrounding skin is jagged and sharp. No dressing is in general half so efficacious in it as the cold water dressing; the constitutional treatment being the same as above advised.

This kind of ulcer is frequently very difficult to manage, and compels us often to change and vary our remedies. If, therefore, it be found necessary to use other means than those just recommended, the nitric acid lotion, in the proportion of fifty drops of the acid to a quart of water, will sometimes prove very beneficial; to be used twice a day instead of the cold water dressing. Or a piece of lint dipped in the tincture of opium, or in a solution of lunar caustic, in the proportion of half a drachm of the caustic to an ounce of distilled water, may be laid over the ulcer and covered with a pledget of lint spread with spermaceti ointment. Bandages do not generally agree with irritable ulcers. Whatever applications are made to the sore, internal medicines must not be neglected, since the constitution is, in these cases, almost invariably in an irritable unhealthy state. Change of air and attention to diet are of the first importance.

Indolent or Chronic Ulcer

The Indolent or Chronic Ulcer is characterized by the glassy and semi-transparent appearance of the surface, in which there is little or no attempt towards healing, the sore remaining nearly in the same state for a considerable time. The languid indolent ulcer requires stimulating applications locally, in conjunction with a nutritious diet and strengthening medicines. It may be dressed, once or twice a day, with the ointment of nitric oxide of mercury, or with that marked No. 89, or 92, pages 188-89 or with tar ointment mixed with an equal quantity of sublimed sulphur. Sometimes a stimulating lotion will answer better, as the solution of lunar caustic above mentioned, or a solution made by mixing together eight grains of oxymuriate of quicksilver, and six ounces of lime water, either of which may be applied twice daily;—or kreosote may be tried, as advised under TOOTH-ACHE. The part must be constantly bandaged after being dressed, and the patient should take gentle exercise. As a strengthening medicine, the pills, No. 102, 103, pages 184-85, or No. 115, or No. 74C, may be taken at the same time.

Generally speaking, scrophulous ulcers are of an indolent nature. A very good plan of treating these ulcers consists in applying to them, once or twice a day, a poultice composed of sea-weed, or sea-tang, bruised and taking at the same time, thrice a day, a grain or two of the best sulphate of quinine, made into a pill with three grains of extract of hemlock, prepared in vacuo. The patient should, if possible, have the benefit also of a nutritious diet and pure air. If the sea-weed cannot be got, dress the ulcers, twice a day, with cerate of carbonate of ammonia, made by mixing together a drachm of this salt and an ounce of simple cerate; or wash them as frequently with a lotion formed of equal quantities of tincture of myrrh and lime water.

Inflamed Ulcer

The Inflamed Ulcer is painful and accompanied with fiery redness and other appearances of inflammation oil the surface, and in surrounding parts. The discharge is of a thin bloody nature; the surface is often covered with a brown incrustation and sometimes there is a disposition in the sore to slough. The best manner of treating these ulcers is by the cold water dressing, as advised at pages 911-12.

Sloughing and Gangrenous Ulcers

Sloughing and Gangrenous Ulcers occur mostly in intemperate and debilitated subjects. Their surface is free from any discharge; the surrounding edges are of a livid appearance, with small blistered spots on them; and the patient suffers from a good deal of irritative fever. Sometimes the greater part of the ulcer looks livid or black. The treatment is precisely the same as we have recommended for MORTIFICATION. The patient should cover the part with a poultice of Port wine and linseed meal, or of stale beer grounds and meal, renewing it every eight or ten hours; he should take the draught of carbonate of ammonia and bark, No. 84B, page 185, every four hours; and make use of a generous diet. Wine and porter may be allowed, and even brandy, if the patient has been much used to it. The nitric acid lotion, (forty or fifty drops of the acid to a quart of water), is also an excellent application to the ulcer. It is highly praised by Sir Astley Cooper, and may be applied, if required, instead of the above poultice, twice or thrice a day, by means of a camel's hair pencil or lint.

Sinuous Ulcers

The SINUOUS ULCER is one that occupies a sinus, or long narrow opening. When a sore extends to any considerable depth, so that the discharge has to travel through a channel before it arrives at the surface, such an ulceration is called sinuous. A fistula, for example, is a sinuous ulcer. The discharge from such ulcers is generally of a thin or otherwise unhealthy kind, the external opening is usually small, and there is a want of energy in the sore, which requires the use of stimulating applications. When, therefore, an ulcer of this description exists in any part, (running under the skin and muscles), the patient should inject into it a little tincture of Spanish fly once or twice a day, and be careful in keeping the sides of the ulcer in contact, by compressing them, through their whole extent, by means of a compress of linen, sheet-lead, or any other convenient substance, bound down over the tract of the sore, with a roller, or adhesive plaster. Two grains of corrosive sublimate, mixed with an ounce of distilled water, forms a solution which is injected into such ulcers with great advantage; and if the tincture of Spanish fly fail to be beneficial, it should be tried. A mild nutritious diet is necessary, and in general the pill, No. 99, taken at night, with half a drachm of the powder of sarsaparilla and three grains of hemlock powder, twice or thrice a day, will improve the condition of the general health, and assist in curing the ulcer.

A Fistula in Ano is to be treated precisely in the same way; but a sinuous ulcer in this situation is rarely cured without an operation, which is very simple, and consists in dividing the intestine rectum from the verge of the anus, up as high as the top of the hollow in which the matter was formed; thereby laying the two cavities of the gut and abscess into one. By this means the hollow sinuous sore is converted into an open one, which contracts and heals from the bottom upwards, and a firm and permanent cure is thus obtained. Persons troubled with a fistula should be careful in regulating their bowels, by the use of some mild medicine, as No. 100, or the laxative electuary recommended for piles, at page 164, and should avoid everything that irritates the lower bowels. Fistula in Ano is so commonly dependent on a disordered condition of distant parts, that the operation seldom succeeds unless great attention be paid, at the same time, to improve the state of the constitution. The best means of invigorating the system I have pointed out above, and at pages 340-42, and 663-64. The quinine pills, No. 181, or the sarsaparilla decoction given during the day, with the pill, No. 99, page 192, every night, and a mild nutritive diet, will be found of great service. Ward's paste, and cubebs powder combined, (pages 788-89), are often given with much advantage in stimulating the fistulous ulcer to a healthy action. Now and then it happens, that a fistulous ulcer occurs near the anus in habits to which the accompanying discharge proves advantageous, and relieves complaints with which they were previously troubled; in this case, great judgment is necessary to determining on the propriety of an operation; and the advice of a skilful surgeon must be procured.

Sometimes women are afflicted with ulcers, which have a close connection with a partial or total stoppage of the natural monthly discharge. In such cases, the ulcer is often covered with blood, especially about the period at which the menses should appear. The saturnine ointment, No. 94, may be applied to the ulcer, or it may be washed with a lotion composed of ten grains of calomel, and half a pint of lime water; and medicines must be given internally, to invigorate the constitution, and restore the natural discharge. The patient should take Dr. Griffith's steel mixture, according to the directions at pages 465-67, during the day, together with the pill, No. 98, or 99, pages 191-92, every night. The tepid hip bath, at ninety-five degrees, will also be useful at the same time, taken daily for twenty minutes, and active friction over the loins and abdomen, with the flesh brush, should be resorted to. If this plan fail, the other means of re-establishing; this flux, pointed out under RETENTION, or SUPPRESSION OF THE MENSES, must be employed.

Ulcers on the nose and face are sometimes of a very troublesome description and difficult to cure. They now and then assume a malignant aspect. In this kind of ulcer, preparations of iron, are the most efficacious applications. The ulcer may be dressed night and morning with the carbonate of iron, moistened with a little water. No. 84A, page 184, or No. 87C.Y. in *the Appendix,* should be taken thrice a day.

In ulcers that form on the fingers and toes, near or under a nail, the principal object of treatment is to obviate the irritation arising from the pressure of the nail, which, as long as it is suffered to act on the ulcer, will prevent its healing, and will sometimes cause it to be very painful and troublesome. The nail should be paired down as thin as possible, without producing bleeding, then raised a little, and a small piece of lint introduced under it, so as to keep it from irritating the ulcer. The lint may be applied dry, or spread with Turner's cerate, or the ointment, No. 94, page 190. By this simple means, the ulcer will, in general, be effectually assisted in its attempts to heal. In a bad case of this description that lately occurred in my practice, I found the application of a small blister, over the ulcer and nail of much service, the above means being afterwards employed.

It is absolutely necessary that in every case of obstinate or severe ulceration, the patient should endeavour to amend the state of the general health, by means of a nutritious diet, recourse to pure air, and the use of alterative and strengthening medicines; for if an ulcer be not healthy, it will always be much assisted in healing by this attention, and when unusually obstinate and painful, will be quite intractable without it. In addition, therefore, to any local application made use of, let the patient take iodine and nitric acid, as in No. 83A, in *the Appendix* or iron and quinine, as in No. 87C—and the pill, No. 98A, page 192, every other night. If that does not answer, try the decoction or powder of sarsaparilla, twice or thrice a day, the bowels being kept regular by the occasional use of the pill, No. 100. The proper diet is described under INDIGESTION. It must be such as will invigorate, as will rectify impaired vital power. Therefore, take plenty of good meat, wine, and ale. These are the best means of improving the state of the constitution. Whenever severe pain attends, a pill composed of a quarter of a grain of acetate or muriate of morphia and a grain of calomel will afford the most effectual relief.

Ulcers often follow ABSCESSES, but here the consideration of Abscess must follow that of Ulcers. Having omitted to notice the subject of abscesses in alphabetical order, I shall make a few remarks in this place respecting their nature and treatment.

An ABSCESSES is a tumour containing matter produced by inflammation; and there is heat, pain, redness, swelling. When an inflammation in any part of the body terminates in the actual formation of an abscess, there is a remission of all the painful and inflammatory symptoms. The throbbing, severe pain present, goes off, and is succeeded by a dull, heavy, pain; and the swelling becomes gradually more elevated above the surface of the surrounding skin, acquiring a softness to the feel, and showing a tendency to point in one particular place, in which situation a whitish or yellowish appearance is generally observable, instead of a deep red, which was previously apparent. If the process be suffered to go on without interruption, the skin becomes thinner every day, and at last gives way, when the matter is discharged at the opening.

Do not attempt to check or cure abscesses by leeches, purging, antimony or any other weakening means; especially in elderly or delicate people, or among the poor. The time for such treatment is gone by. A wet rag kept constantly wet with cold water, bark, a little wine, and such like, are the proper remedies. Let the treatment be soothing and sustaining, decidedly sustaining.

When an abscess is formed in a healthy person, the matter is thick, and of a white or yellowish white colour, and the application of warm poultices and fomentations is all that is requisite, in conjunction with a little cooling opening medicine. The fomentation should consist of a decoction of mallows, chamomile flowers, poppy heads, or hemlock leaves; the poultice, of bread and water, or linseed meal. If the abscess has not burst, or been opened, both these must be used freely, particularly in the beginning of its formation, and while any inflammation continues; but after the discharge of matter, the fomentations may, for the most part, be laid aside, and a warm bread and water or linseed meal poultice be continued until all tenderness has left the part, and there is a free outlet for the discharge of matter, when the poultice may be discontinued, and a piece of dry lint applied to the opening, and over it a pledget, made by spreading a little spermaceti ointment on another piece of lint. To keep these simple dressings on, and to give support to the sides of the abscess, the part may be lightly bandaged with a linen roller, taking care that a free opening is left for the discharge of matter. If no particular pain be present, any common cooling physic will answer, as the draught No. 27, or 28, page 155-56, which may be repeated every morning; but when the pain and general irritation are considerable, which sometimes is the case, especially if the abscess be large, or situated near a part of great importance, opium must be added to the purgative medicine, and the patient may have recourse to the following mixture :

Take of Epsom salt	1	ounce;
Solution of acetate of ammonia	3	ounces;
Water	3	ounces;
Laudanum, or solution of acetate of morphia .	1	drachm.

Mix, and take three or four table-spoonfuls twice a day.

If the abscess has become ripe, and does not quickly burst spontaneously, it should be opened with the point of a lancet. When these tumours are of a favourable description, and come forward kindly, it is not usually a matter of much consequence whether they burst of themselves, or are opened by the lancet; but when they are situated under a thick expansion of skin, or of ligamentous or other unyielding substance, they must invariably be opened early, that is, as soon as matter is formed. Abscesses in the palm of the hand and sole of the foot, and those which form close upon any bone, are of this kind; indeed, such a practice is highly advisable in any part, when the abscess appears bound down by any unyielding substance situated above it.

Such is the proper treatment of healthy acute abscesses occurring in sound constitutions. If the abscess degenerate into an ulcer, it must be treated according to the directions laid down in the pages immediately preceding.

But it not unfrequently happens, that abscesses are of an indolent character, and occur in debilitated constitutions, when they, for the most part, require local applications of a stimulating nature, and cordial strengthening medicines to be taken internally. In these cases, matter is a long time in forming, and when formed is not healthy: it is often thin, curd-like, sometimes bloody and generally small in quantity. Here, a stimulating poultice, made by wetting oatmeal with a strong solution of salt and water, should be applied cold, night and morning; or the poultice may be made of oatmeal, water and yeast, mixed together to a proper consistence. After one of these has been used, for a short time, the part may be covered with compound galbanum plaster, or the plaster of ammonia with quicksilver, spread on leather. Pressure, by means of plasters, is of great service in these cases, and is too much neglected. See what is said of it in my DISEASES OF FEMALES, under the head of *flammation of the Breasts*. At the same time, the sulphate of quinine pills, No. 115, page 202, or the mixture of carbonate of ammonia, recommended at page 182, must be taken thrice a day, and the patient should have the advantage of a generous diet, but moderate in quantity, with pure air, and daily exercise. The bowels must be kept regular by the occasional use of the pills, No. 100, page 193.

The abscess in the female breast, called the MAMMARY or MILK ABSCESSES, should not, I think, be treated with warm but with cold applications; at least, the latter appears to me to be generally the best plan. Milk abscess appears in weakly consti-tutions, and we should soothe and invigorate. Nothing is more soothing than cold wet linen laid over the abscess. Dr. John Clarke (*Essays on the Diseases of Lying in Women)* strongly advises against the employment of warm applications; and Dr. Dewees, of Philadelphia, (a physician of extensive practice, and considerable judgment), remarks *(Treatise on the Diseases of Females, fourth edition,* p. 504), "It should be a never failing rule to treat a mammary inflammation as if it were not to suppurate." He likewise says, he has "never found any application so successful in the very early stage of this disease, as the frequent use of warm vinegar to the part. Its efficacy appears to us so certain, when sufficiently soon employed, that we need not in many instances look for any other remedy. It is particularly prompt in that condition of the breast, in which a want of proper drawing leaves them; or where they become greatly and painfully distended by the sudden secretion of milk, but which cannot be extracted with ease, or in sufficient quantity to relieve the tension." In my TREATISE ON THE DISEASES OF FEMALES, I have noticed, with much approbation, a plan of treating milk abscess by bandaging the whole breast with broad strips of adhesive plaster. This plan is peculiarly valuable from its having an extraordinary influence in relieving pain and being applicable to every stage of the abscess.

VOMITING

Vomiting, or sickness, is a very distressing affection, and when it proves obstinate or severe, calls for the immediate assistance of art, in order to its being removed.

Its causes are various; but it is much oftener a secondary and sympathetic affection, depending upon the existence of some other severe disease in the system, than an original complaint. When it appears in the latter form, it is generally dependent upon a peculiar state of chronic debility in the stomach, or first intestine.

TREATMENT—Try at once the following excellent prescription :—

Take of Epsom salts..........................	1 drachm;
Water	half a pint.

Mix, and take half of it directly, and repeat the dose in an hour.

This quarter of a pint may be taken with advantage every morning for a week, or more, and will be found very useful. If this does not answer, then add half a drachm of Epsom salts to a small tumbler of soda water, made with the soda powders.

Another efficacious remedy for vomiting is a strong infusion of cloves, given to the patient by table-spoonfuls. This is very efficacious.

Curds and whey, carefully made, are very useful in allaying violent vomiting, and will succeed in extreme cases. The curds must be quite light, and scarcely separated from the whey.

For the vomiting or nausea which occur in weakly habits from some primary complaint of the stomach, the most efficacious remedies are, bismuth, iron, and the pills, No. 104, page 197. The nitric acid is also a useful remedy :—

Take of Diluted nitric acid................	20 drops;
Infusion of quassia, or columba............	1½ ounces.

Mix, and take this draught twice a day.

Perhaps, the most generally useful medicine here, is the white oxide of bismuth, which may be taken in the dose of two grains and a half, made into a pill with extract of gentian, and repeated thrice daily; the dose being gradually increased to four or five grains in each pill. The pills, No. 102, 103, 104 or 105, page 196-98, may likewise be tried. In this chronic state of the complaint, great attention must be paid to diet and regimen, as advised under INDIGESTION, and at pages 345-49; also to the regulation of the bowels by the occasional use of the pill No. 100, or 101 or the mixture, No. 74C.

For the sickness which so frequently harasses pregnant women, either of the means just noticed may be had recourse to. In their case, two or three ounces of infusion of columba is often an efficacious remedy. It may be frequently repeated. A draught composed of twenty drops of diluted nitric acid, and two ounces of water, is also very serviceable. Women in this situation, who are much troubled with nausea and vomiting, should be a great part of the day in the open air, and be careful to keep the bowels regular by the occasional use of the brimstone electuary, No. 37, or 38, page 160, or the mixture, No. 74, page 176. In a very severe case of vomiting of this kind, that had resisted all the usual means of relief and which continued so incessantly as to become alarming, a blister applied over the pit of the stomach succeeded in removing it.

The reader should refer to the article on INFLAMMATION OF THE STOMACH, at pages 711-12, and should the vomiting proceed from extreme pain in the stomach, increased by pressure, with quick hard pulse and other symptoms of inflammation, then opium must not be given, excepting in conjunction with calomel, as at page 200, No. 112.

There is a peculiar affection of the stomach, called *water-brash* or *black water,* in which the patient brings up frequently a considerable quantity of thin watery liquor. This complaint attacks mostly persons past the middle age, particularly females and the fit comes on generally in the morning and forenoon. It usually begins with a pain at the pit of the stomach, attended with a sense of constriction, and soon after a quantity of thin, watery fluid is thrown up, which is sometimes insipid, at other times of an acrid taste. The causes of this complaint are various, but whatever debilitates the stomach may give rise to it in those so disposed. It appears to be owing to a peculiar state of stomachic debility and irritation; and is most certainly relieved by the use of the white oxide of bismuth, as No. 103A, page 197. This medicine will often perfectly cure *water-brasha;* but attention to the diet and regimen laid down at pages 196 and 345, is of much consequence, and will be absolutely necessary in order to render the cure permanent. A diet chiefly of animal food is the best here, with which may be united the use of biscuits, home-made bread, tea, cocoa, and lime-water; and if it can be procured, mild home-brewed beer. Daily exercise abroad must also be taken, and friction with the flesh brush; over the region of the stomach and bowels, is of no small service. If the bismuth is not effectual, either of the pills, No. 102, 103, or 104, page 196-97, may be used as there directed and are often of great service. They may be taken alone or each pill be washed down with three table-spoonfuls of infusion of quassia, or columba.

VOMITING OF BLOOD

Vomiting of blood is a discharge of blood from the stomach, and is generally preceded by affections of that organ and of structures in its neighbourhood. There is often pain or uneasiness of the left side, with anxiety and a sense of tightness in the chest. The blood discharged is generally dark-coloured, grumous and often mixed with some of the contents of the stomach. It may occur in persons of a full habit and robust constitution, but is most common in those who are weakly or who labour under a faulty condition of the blood and obstruction in the liver.

Whatever greatly deranges the functions of the stomach or produces bad blood and internal obstruction, may give rise to it; and the *most frequent causes* appear to be grief, or other depressing or violent passions; costiveness, especially if occurring in a constitution in which the stomach is peculiarly irritable; blows on the region of the organ affected; fulness of habit combined with an intemperate mode of life. It is generally a symptom of something wrong in the general system.

It is, in general, easily *distinguished* from spitting of blood, by the blood being here brought up by vomiting, and by its being of a deep modena colour. It is also generally mixed with some of the contents of the stomach. In spitting of blood, on the contrary, the fluid discharged from the lungs is brought up by hawking, or coughing and is of a bright red colour.

TREATMENT—Give directly the powder, No. 130A, page 209, and repeat it in the course of a couple of hours, two or three times, until it acts on the bowels, which it will do mildly and effectually. This powder should be continued about twice a day for the first three or four days, and after that every morning, taken in cold water. In all discharges of blood, *saline remedies* are of the first importance, as I have already stated at page 341. They relieve congestion in the circulation of the liver, unload the bowels, promote healthy secretions, and improve the quality of the blood.

If this powder is not effectual, give the patient the draught of ipecacuanha and Epsom salts, recommended at pages 857-58, twice or thrice a day, so as to keep the bowels gently open,[1] and observe the diet and regimen laid down at, pages 675-76. After the discharge of blood has been checked by these means, the tonic pills of sulphate of quinine, No. 115, page 202, or the iron mixture, No. 84A, page 184, should be entered upon, and taken thrice a days until the blood is improved, and the stomach and general system have recovered that degree of tone, which will pretty certainly secure the patient against the recurrence of the vomiting. During the time that these medicines are taken, and indeed for ever after, the bowels must be kept regular by the use of some gentle aperient, as No. 130A, page 209, or the Seidlitz powders. Persons of a costive habit, attacked with this complaint, must pay particular attention to this point. If the sulphate of quinine does not agree, it may be changed for the pills, No. 105, or for the steel mixture, No. 87C.Y. in *the Appendix*.

In cases of *emergency,* when nothing better is at hand, give half a tea-spoonful of common kitchen salt, and a quarter of a tea-spoonful of nitre, in cold water, and repeat it in half an hour.

If it be necessary, from the great discharge of blood, effectually to put a stop to the vomiting immediately, an emetic of twenty-five

1. "British practitioners, especially since the publication of Dr. Hamilton's Treatise (on purgative medicines), have placed great confidence in active purging, as the best mode of treatment in many cases of this disorder, more particularly in that form which occurs in young and middle-aged females, and is connected with uterine torpor, and a sluggish action of the bowels. In such cases, Dr. Bateman states *(Reports on the Diseases of London,* p. 150), as the result of his experience, that the success of this treatment is more decidedly conspicuous than in any other disease, in which Dr. Hamilton has recommended it."—*Dr. Godie, in Cyclopaedia of Practical Medicine,* vol. ii. p. 399, 1833.

grains of ipecacuanha powder should be taken, and if the first emetic fail to stop it, a second may be administered after an interval of two or three hours. This emetic is frequently of great service in the present complaint; but in order to render the benefit obtained from its exhibition permanent, in delicate subjects, the tonic plan just described must be entered upon without delay, and persevered in. This powder is applicable to the case of strong as well as weakly persons.

The superacetate or sugar of lead, also, is a powerful medicine here, as well as in all other profuse bleedings. If the circumstances of the case are particularly urgent, it may be the first remedy resorted to, and should be taken as described at pages 857-58.

Change of air and scene should be had recourse to, when practicable. The diet recommended under INDIGESTION will, in general, be the most proper, and an attention to the rules there laid down, and at page 345, for the improvement of the general health and strength, can seldom fail to be followed by satisfactory results.

WARTS

Warts are well known to be firm hard excrescences, growing from the skin. As they are adventitious substances, their powers of life are weak, and they may, consequently, be easily removed by the application of some strong stimulant to their surface. The best applications of this description are, the juice of cellandine, or of houseleek, concentrated acetic acid, and Goulard's extract undiluted (the solution of acetate of lead). If warts are touched with either of these liquids, once or twice a day, they will in general disappear in a short time. I rather prefer Goulard's extract.

WATER IN THE HEAD

Water in the head, as it usually appears, is an acute disease, and is unquestionably an inflammation of the membranes or vessels of the brain, mostly a deep seated inflammation. The effusion of water into the ventricles of the brain is merely a consequence of the inflammation, and is, therefore, rather an effect of the disease than the disease itself.

The *chief symptoms* are, those of great constitutional irritation and inflammation of the brain, arising nearly in the following order. There is giddiness; momentary confusion from quick movement of the head; pains in the hands, feet, and nape of the neck; disturbed unrefreshing sleep, accompanied by talking or mumbling; impaired appetite and thirst; a scanty discharge by urine and stool; momentary changes in the colour of the complexion, and a disappearance of its natural bloom; heaviness of the head, a stumbling gait, without equilibrium and firmness; indifference to former amusements; peevishness; a natural pulse, only with a few pulsations weaker or omitted; fits of musing; sighing; dry skin.

In the second stage, when inflammation supervenes, the most remarkable symptoms are, a distressing pain in the forehead, pressing on the eyes, and continuing during sleep, which often alternates with pains in the belly and stomach, with little fever; retreating of the eye backward into the socket, and aversion to light; in sleep it is only half covered, with contracted pupil; great restlessness; increased heat of the head; a pale and otherwise altered countenance; dry nose; hard cracked lips a perfect absence of appetite and thirst; repeated vomiting; always increased by moving the patient; a peculiar foul smell in what is rejected; frequent sighing, and a peculiar foetor of the breath; obstinate costiveness; scanty turbid urine, with a white heavy sediment; acute bearing; pulse generally slow, sometimes quick, but almost invariably intermitting, irregular, and with weak, intervening strokes; a great falling in of the belly, without any increased discharge by stool; little or no flatulence; general and rapid emaciation.—I have said above, that there is rarely any fever in this stage, and these are the most common cases; but sometimes there is a vehement attack of fever, with convulsions, and other alarming symptoms of affection of the head.

These inflammatory symptoms may last from a few hours to two, four or six days, and even longer; and when not overcome by the remedies made use of, are followed by those which indicate the effusion of water into the ventricles of the brain. When the effusion takes place, the restless desire for a frequent change of posture ceases, the patient lies on the side in an oblique posture, or on the back, and is observed to indulge in frequent movements of the legs, stamping against the bed clothes with one or both feet ; there is a gloomy earnestness of countenance; all the external senses, except hearing, are dull or annihilated; the glance of the eye is oblique or squinting, and the pupil dilated; the tones uttered are through the nose; the urine is passed unconsciously, but a stool can scarcely be procured; the pulse increases m irregularity and weakness; the breathing is more and more interrupted by sighs and deep moanings; the emaciation is extreme; and the heavy sleepy state in which the patient lies passes into a complete stupor. This state usually lasts for several days, and sometimes the little sufferer will regain his consciousness for a short period, and even take food and ask for playthings. But this momentary change is deceitful, and soon the fourth stage is ushered in by general convulsions, spinal cramps, palsy on one side, and violent fever, followed by hectic redness of the cheeks, blindness, efforts to vomit without effect, pulse extremely quick, weak and inter-mitting, difficult swallowing and death sweats.

The whole duration of this disease is, in general, from twelve to twenty-one days. Death seldom takes place earlier than the fourth stage. It is a very dangerous complaint, and the prognostic is always unfavourable. The disease being detected early and the proper remedies promptly applied; the symptoms having been subdued on the first or second day and not returning for two or three days during a perseverance in them; and a general steaming perspiration breaking out during quiet sleep, and continuing several hours, after the employment of the necessary remedies, are favourable circumstances.

Late interference, and ignorance of the nature of the disease, are the grand causes of the great fatality of water on the brain.

This disease chiefly attacks children under seven years of age. Injuries of the head in the birth,—the hooping cough, small-pox, and scarlet fever,—strong and continued excitement of the brain, from severe application to learning,[1] or other causes,—great terror and anxiety in the mother during the last months of pregnancy,—and a scrophulous habit, dispose to it. And continued irritation from teething, or severe disorder in the stomach and bowels,—excessive cold applied to the head violent agitation of the brain from fall or blows,—violent vomiting, and suddenly suppressed discharges from ulcers, moist eruptions on the head, etc. are, perhaps, the most frequent causes which directly excite the disease. Almost any highly irritating cause may induce it in those disposed to it, but by far the most frequent source is a deranged state of the digestive organs. Most physicians suppose five cases out of six to originate from stomachic and intestinal irritation.[2]

Water in the head may in general be *distinguished* from worm fever, and other complaints resembling it, by strict attention to the symptoms above laid down, many of which do not occur in those complaints. In the irritation produced by worms, or severe disorder of the bowels, the patient sometimes eats greedily, generally drinks thirstily, and often passes large stools, either spontaneously, or from the operation of medicines, and also a great quantity of urine; the pulse is quick throughout; and there are other symptoms of considerable fever; perspiration is frequent after eating and drinking, and usual on every increase of fever; the hearing is dull; sleep is often sound; there is little wasting of the body for many days; the belly does not shrink, and flatus passes audibly; symptoms which are not found in the present disease.

---

1. "The parents and instructors of children of a peculiarly precocious intellect should be made aware of the danger of early and protracted application. In such individuals it should be our object, if possible, rather to retard than to accelerate the development of the brain and of the mental faculties connected with it; and it is only by postponing the interests of their intellectual to those of their physical education, till the constitution has become established and the period of danger is passed, that this object can be obtained."—*Cyclopoedia of Practical Medicine,* vol. ii. p. 453, 1833.
2. It is certain that in children the brain is the part most liable to suffer from the general irritation kept up by a deranged state of the digestive organs; for once that water in the head arises from other causes, it arises twenty times from affections of these organs, the pathological reason of which I have explained in my volume *On Infancy and Childhood.*

We frequently meet with children out of health, who look pale, have large bellies and large heads, appear stupid at times, have confined or irregular bowels, discoloured and offensive motions, and fall down occasionally almost senseless, and such children are often, but very erroneously, said to have water in the brain, although they may continue in this state, sometimes better and sometimes worse, for many weeks, and are able to walk abroad. It should be recollected, that water in the head, properly so called, is a highly acute disease, consisting of distinct stages, and almost necessarily confining the patient to the sick-room.

TREATMENT—As the immediate cause of this complaint is an inflammation of the brain, and obstructed liver, and the patient can rarely be cured but in the earlier stages of its progress, a vigorous purgative plan is clearly indicated in all cases and must be carried into effect without the least delay. The most effectual remedies next to purgatives are, calomel, cold applications to the head, leeches, blisters, and medicines which have a cooling effect, and determine to the surface of the body.

"The value of purgatives in its treatment can scarcely be over-rated," an opinion of Dr. West *(Diseases of Children,* p. 100), in which I fully concur. Therefore give directly two grains of calomel and six of jalap, in currant jelly, and follow it up with a dose of the following mixture, every hour, until the bowels operate freely :

Take of Epsom salts	2 drachms;
Syrup of orange peel	2 drachms;
Carraway water	6 drachms.

Mix, and give two tea-spoonfuls every hour to a child three years old, until the bowels act freely.

After the bowels have been effectually opened by the preceding means, they must be kept so by giving through the succeeding days the following mixture, and every night two grains of grey powder and three of rhubarb, in jelly.

Take of Nitrate of potash	10 grains;
Epsom salts	1 drachm;
Syrup of lemons.........................	3 drachms;
Distilled water	9 drachms.

Mix, and give three tea-spoonfuls, thrice a day, to a child two years old.

By these means a free action on the bowels and kidneys may be secured, day by day, which is of the first consequence.

Physicians now are fully convinced of the great value and necessity of active purging in this malady, more especially in the early stages. "While the disease is forming, there is generally," says Dr. John Cheyne (*On Dropsy of the Brain,* p. 47), "a defect in the functions of the liver. It seems to admit of only a scanty and imperfect formation of the bile, insufficient to stimulate the intestinal canal, which becomes torpid, and is sometimes loaded with foetid clay-coloured excrement. This state of the canal, in conjunction with the disordered condition of the liver, is, perhaps, one cause of the dyspeptic symptoms which are almost invariably present in the beginning,"[1] He adds, "The increased arterial action on the surface of the liver, the remains of which I have observed in my dissections, to every appearance, had been of some standing, and in two or three instances, from the extent of the adhesions, it evidently had been of great intensity." Therefore, the preceding purgative medicines demand the first attention, but don't give more calomel.[2]

---

1. "Purges have generally been given in this disease; but, when called early, what I recommend is the exhibition of the largest dose, which can with safety be prescribed, of some powerfully cathartic medicine, two, three, or four times a day, and this continued for several days, or until natural stools are procured. The advantage of keeping the intestinal canal under the continued influence of stimulus, I have, in various instances, found to be so great, I am induced to repeat the declaration of my belief, that the happiest result may be expected from this measure."—*Dr. John Cheyne on Dropsy in the Brain,* p. 96, 1808.
2. "Purging actively seemed to Abercrombie" (of Edinburgh), "to be the remedy which is of the most importance in all the forms of the disease; and though he sets a due value on the aid of venesection, he believes that more recoveries from head affections take place, under the use of very strong purgatives, that a under any other mode of treatment whatever. He has found the croton oil one of the most convenient and effectual cathartics in diseases of this kind,

(Contd. on next page)

The patient should be placed in a roomy airy chamber, screened from strong day-light, with the head and shoulders slightly raised, and every kind of noise be avoided. Blood must be immediately and freely drawn from the temples, nape of the neck, and arm, by the application of leeches, and the use of the lancet, the quantity of blood drawn being in proportion to the age and strength of the patient and the severity of the symptoms. In very young children, a sufficient quantity of blood may be drawn from the top of the head by the free application of leeches; and it must be particularly noticed, that in all cases strongly marked, the abstraction of blood must be free and immediate, as this is a disease which will not admit of delay, and which cannot be overcome but by the employment of very active measures. As soon as the leeches have bled freely, the head should be shaven and be kept constantly covered with cloths wet with ice-water or vinegar and water. The coldest water should be chosen, and ice-water, when it can be procured, is much to be preferred. The cloths must be repeatedly renewed, directly they contract any warmth. The use of blisters is also advisable, but the head is not a proper place for them in any case of this malady, on account of their irritating qualities being likely to increase the irritation and inflammation existing within the head, if they are placed on, or very near it. They may be applied to the pit of the stomach, between the shoulders, or to the inside of the thighs, with the prospect of much advantage, especially after the painful symptoms about the head have been relieved by leeches, and the use of cold applications.

The continued application of cold water to the shaven scalp, is very likely to help us materially in arresting the increased activity of the circulation, provided it be used in the first stage. A cold lotion of spirit of wine and water (consisting of three table-spoonfuls of spirit of wine, and ten of cold water), may be freely applied to

---

(Contd.)

which are so often accompanied by great obstinacy of the bowels. Whytt" (the author of one of the first and most able publications on Water in the Head) "never saw even temporary relief of the symptoms produced by any other means than those which increased the evacuations; and Rush was likewise a strenuous advocate for the employment of medicines of this kind."—Dr. Joy, *in Cyclopaedia of Practical Medicine,* vol. ii. p. 468, 1833.

the head, or a bladder, filled with pounded ice, placed over it, and renewed as often as appears necessary. It is said, that the late Dr. Darwell, of Birmingham, had known cases which seemed utterly hopeless, recover by letting water drop in a small stream upon the scalp, and continuing it till the head no longer recovered its high temperature on intermitting the stream. This is a remedy more particularly applicable to well-marked cases, in which there is uncommon heat in the head, and it is similar in its nature and effects to the *cold-dash,* so strongly advised under INFLAMMATION OF THE BRAIN, at pages 687-88. Dr. Abercrombie, of Edinburgh, was a strenuous advocate for its utility in this disease.

In addition to the above measures, a mustard poultice may sometimes be advantageously applied to the feet, but bathing them with warm water is rarely advisable.

The diet must be very simple, light, and cooling, consisting chiefly of barley water, toast and water, and thin gruel. In raising the patient to take food, medicine; etc., all quick, rough movements must be carefully avoided. It is of no small importance that the patient should be kept perfectly quiet, and be seen by none but the few persons necessarily required to attend him, and that for some days after the disease has been subdued. In recovering, a return to his ordinary food must be made slowly and very cautiously.

The above I believe to be the best and most likely means of conducting the disease to a favourable issue. Some physicians have recommended foxglove to be given at the same time, and others have placed much dependence upon the free use of mercury externally, in the form of ointment rubbed into the arms and thighs. Foxglove is a doubtful remedy in well marked cases of this disease, and not worthy of any dependence; and rubbing in mercurial ointment cannot be relied on.

Should the practitioner be favoured to succeed in arresting the progress of the disease in its earliest stages, and the patient is evidently recovering, it is highly advisable that the blisters should be kept open for a few days; and in some instances, where the constitutional tendency to the disease seems very strong, it will be proper to make an issue, or pass a seton, in order to insure a perfect cure.

If the remedies employed in the above stages have occasioned a great deal of debility, the after treatment consists in giving small doses of infusion of bark, calumba, or gentian, with change of air. Half the draught, No. 35, page 158, may be given to a child, mixed with an equal quantity of water, and repeated twice a day, or small doses of the mixture, No. 82, page 183, may be administered in the same way. If great irritability of the arterial system, evidenced by a quick irritable pulse, etc. exist, foxglove may now be taken with great advantage in conjunction with the tonic. A child may take four or six drops of the tincture, in each tonic draught, for a few days.

Those cases of indolent affection of the head, noticed at page 547, which are so often, but erroneously, called water in the brain, and supposed to be the same with the present complaint; must be treated with purgatives, alterative doses of calomel, change of air, a very careful diet, etc., as advised under DROPSY OF THE HEAD; and thus they will generally be treated successfully.

WEN

A wen is a tumour contained in a cyst or small bag. It is moveable, and has a pulpy feel. There are several sorts of wen, the difference between them being occasioned by the difference of the matter contained in the cyst, which differs chiefly in regard to its consistence.

In regard to the treatment, it is not often any advantage arises from the use of local applications, and wens are therefore to be removed in general only by the knife. Sometimes, however, a strong stimulant frequently applied to their surface, will disperse them when small and recently formed; and of all stimulants electricity appears to be the most efficacious. Those who wish to try it, may have sparks drawn from the tumour, and slight shocks passed through it daily. A very strong solution of salt and water is likewise a powerful stimulant in some cases of wens, and has been known to bring them away by causing the cyst to open and discharge its contents. The surface of the wen must be bathed with this solution very frequently every day. No benefit can be expected in less than a fortnight, and sometimes not sooner than a month or two. I am disposed to think this remedy worthy of more attention in those cases, than it has yet obtained. A great advantage attending it is, that it gives no pain or inconvenience of any kind.

The operation of removing wens by the knife is attended with much less pain than is generally supposed; and sometimes a large tumour of this description may be opened and turned out, with its cyst, with a very inconsiderable degree of pain.

For the swellings sometimes found in the front of the throat, see BRONCHOCELE.

WHITES

The complaint is technically called *Leucorrhoea;*[1] and consists in a discharge of a colourless, yellowish-white or greenish fluid from the womb and its passage. Frequently, the discharge proceeds from the mouth or neck of the womb, and not from its cavity. In the mildest cases, the discharge is mostly of a whitish colour, sometimes almost colourless, small in quantity, and unaccompanied with any irritation in the parts; but in the severer examples, it is yellow, greenish, or dark coloured, thin, sometimes very acrid, and highly offensive, and occasioning itching, smarting, and other local symptoms of a very irritating nature. In most cases there is pain and weakness in the back, and a sense of general languor; and when the disease is severe and of long standing, it is generally associated with an unhealthy countenance, weak stomach, general debility, and a dry, hot skin.

Sir Charles M. Clarke considers those cases where the discharge is whitish and opaque, becoming creamy when rubbed between the fingers, and rendering water turbid, to be owing chiefly to an inflamed condition of the *cervix uteri,* or neck of the womb. In these instances, there is rarely an abundant discharge, but much disorder of health and local pain are present.

1. There are numerous uterine diseases which give rise to discharges, and this should ever be borne in mind, for very often the term whites is applied to very dissimilar complaints.

It occurs most frequently in women of delicate constitutions, or in those whose strength has been greatly impaired by profuse evacuations, poor diet, sedentary living, grief, or other *causes* of exhaustion. It sometimes, however, arises chiefly from debility and relaxation of the parts themselves, in consequence of lard labours, frequent miscarriages, or other causes. Women of all ages are subject to it.

TREATMENT—It is not by local applications, but by internal constitutional remedies that this disease can be cured. The cure is generally difficult, and one principal source of this difficulty is an extreme inattention to the nature of the discharge, and more especially from neglect of perseverance in the use of remedies. *See* PROLAPSUS OF THE WOMB in the author's DISEASES OF FEMALES, for proofs of this. When a cure is practicable, we arrive at it only by slow degrees; and it is, therefore, highly necessary, when a patient experiences advantage from adopting any plan of treatment, that she should persevere with it.

Generally speaking, the principal object to be aimed at is to give firmness to the general habit, and strength to the weakened and relaxed membranes of the womb and its passage, by the employment of vegetable and metallic tonics, or stimulants, vegetable alteratives, cold bathing, astringent injections, pure air, and sufficient exercise, aided by a mild but nutritious diet.

The first thing to be done is to take one of the pills, No. 98, page 191, at bed time, and on the following morning a double dose of the mixture, No. 74C, page 177. Take this for three nights and mornings in succession; then begin with the acid mixture, No. 85A, page 185, twice or thrice a day. By these means, the liver will be roused to active secretion, and the bowels effectually cleared; and then the acid and bitter tonics will improve the general health, and diminish the discharge.

Dr. Rigby *(On Female Diseases,* page 101), says, "I know of no astringent tonic so powerful as the recent infusion of red bark *(cinchona oblongifolia)*;" and he recommends the nitromuriatic acid to be taken in three table-spoonfuls of that infusion, twice or thrice a day, as in No. 84, page 184.

The cold hip bath should be used twice or thrice a week. Some very delicate women will find the most advantage from the tepid bath at about eighty-six degrees. Lime-water should be taken as common drink, or in the quantity of a pint a day, in divided doses; and a blister may be applied to the sacrum, or broad bone at, the bottom of the spine, and occasionally repeated. Whatever the general plan of treatment may bc, the lime-water, bitters, and blisters are almost always applicable, and more or less serviceable.

Injections into the womb are seldom of service. If the patient wishes to try one, the simplest is the best—one drachm of extract of lead, added to one pint of cold water. A little of this may be injected, twice a day, by means of *Twinberrow's female syringe.*

If the above means fail, I would advise a trial of the following pills during the day, instead of the above bitter draughts, the other parts of the preceding plan being still strictly adhered to. These hemlock pills have been of eminent utility in many cases, and are particularly worthy of attention when great pain attends this disorder, and in cases where, from the irritation, tension, and heat present in the parts, we have reason to suspect an inflammatory condition to exist.

Take of Extract of hemlock, prepared in vacuo,	2	drachms;
Guaiacum, in powder....................	1	drachm.

Mix them, and divide the mass into thirty-six pills. Take one pill three times a day, for eight or ten days, then increase the dose to two pills.

The alterative pill, No. 98A, page 192, should also be taken every other night, at the same time, especially if the disease be obstinate, or there appears to be internal obstruction, or chronic inflammation. This pill is a valuable alterative, and will frequently be of great service in correcting the diseased action of the womb. It is applicable to most instances of the complaint, whether occurring in the young or old.

Of the tincture of Spanish-fly I think very highly : it is one of the most efficacious remedies, and may be taken in doses of thirty or fifty drops, or more, thrice daily, in water. It should be increased in dose until it produces either scalding in making water, or a sense of heat in the parts, when it may be laid aside for a few days, and then resumed. *See* my TREATISE OF THE DISEASES OF FEMALES.

Preparations of steel or zinc are sometimes useful when the patient is weakly, and if the foregoing means are not found to be productive of satisfactory advantage, the pills, No. 102, 103, or 105, pages 196-98 or the mixture, No. 84A, page 184, may be tried. The chalybeate water of Tunbridge, Brighton, and other places, is proper in those cases, with which the steel pills agree. The muriated tincture of iron is an excellent form of taking steel in this malady. The dose is from twenty to forty drops, twice daily, in pimento water. *See* No. 87C.Y. in *the Appendix.*

The balsam of capivi will sometimes be a useful auxiliary to the preceding means. When the disease depends upon debility and relaxation of the general system, it can hardly be expected to succeed alone; but from its power of stimulating the uterine passages, it may sometimes materially assist in the general plan. It appears to be often useful when the whites follow the final cessation of the monthly courses, and are attended with a bearing down, and other painful symptoms in the parts. The manner of taking it may be learnt by referring to page 15.[1]

When the discharge is of an acrid nature, and long standing, it will not be proper to attempt the suppression very quickly. In such a case, it will be advisable for the patient to take a purging draught, as No. 27 or 28, pages 155-56, every other morning, or three times

---

1. The efficacy of the Balsam of Copaiba in various affections, particularly of mucous surfaces, is well established; but hitherto the disgust created by its odour and its consequent operation on the stomach and bowels, has prevented its free employment. This seems now obviated by Jozeau's *Capsules,* or by *Howard's Aromatic Balsam of Copaiba,* that preparation being, it is said without injury to its properties, deprived of all unpleasant taste or smell. The proprietor states that it produces no disagreeable action on the digestive organs, and may be taken by those who have been unable to use Copaiba in any of its ordinary forms, neither can its presence be detected in the breath of those who are employing it. It is sold by Savory and Moore, Chemists, 143, New Bond-Street, and 220, Regent Street, London.

a week with the alterative pill, No. 98, every second night, for three or four weeks, and to use one of the astringent infections above noticed, reduced in strength by the addition of an equal quantity of water. These mild cooling measures are particularly eligible if the patient be of a full or gross habit, as a soluble state of the bowels is then found to afford very sensible relief, and opens the way for the more effectual operation of other remedies. If, in a case of long standing, the patient be reduced in strength, and of a feeble habit, the pills No. 100, or 101, may be substituted for the draught, No. 28, or the latter taken a little weaker than ordered at page 162, and she may take also the tonic draught of nitric acid and infusion of quassia once or twice a day. After the use of the opening medicine for the time now specified, the patient should have recourse to the hemlock pills, the balsam of capivi, preparations of steel, or the other means previously advised.

When the pain and irritation are considerable in this disorder, and these symptoms are not relieved by the foregoing measures, a pill composed of half a grain of opium, and a grain of calomel, will frequently give great ease. If necessary, it may be repeated every night, instead of the pill, No. 99; or instead of this pill, the compound powder of ipecacuanha may be taken in doses of three or four grains, and sometimes will be of the greatest use in mitigating the severity of these symptoms.

In some cases, which occur in debilitated persons, the application of a strengthening plaster to the loins, as No. 131 or 138, page 214, will be useful; or, when the discharge appears to depend on local relaxation, cold water may be pumped on that part every morning.

In the majority of instances, the diet should be nutritious, and in all it must be easy of digestion, and moderate in quantity. The general regimen advised under INDIGESTION, and GENERAL PRINCIPLES, page 345, is the most proper; and it is of much consequence the patient should never forget that a principal object in the treatment of her case is to restore firmness and health to the whole frame, by perseverance in the use of suitable diet, exercise, and change of air, in conjunction with internal medicine and local applications.

When the constitution is much disordered, it is in vain to endeavour to restore it to health by the employment of strengthening medicines alone; the diet and regimen must be strictly attended to at the same time, and it is too often from a neglect of these means, that women fail to gain much relief in the present disorder. If the patient be of a costive habit, the removal of that state should be accomplished by the use of the measures advised under *Costiveness.*

In my TREATISE ON THE DISEASES OF FEMALES, the reader will find more ample information on the difference subsisting in the various kinds of discharges which simulate *whites*, and also with respect to the treatment. Warm water is often useful as an injection, and advice on this point is given in that volume.

It has become a common medical practice in female complaints to institute ocular examinations, and to apply iodine, or some caustic to the mouth of the womb. This is a *very unnecessary* and objectionable practice. It may answer in a pecuniary point of view to the practitioner, but *it serves only to distress and injure the patient.* It never does any good, and I advise my fair readers to refuse both the examination and the application to the neck or mouth of the womb, or any other part. If the disease, whatever it may be, is not curable by *constitutional* remedies, and *outward* local applications, it will not be cured by such abominably bad practice as I have above referred to. Many physicians and sureons, even in London, are in the habit of making applications directly to the womb for the *cure* of *whites*!—a most scandalous practice, of which they ought to be ashamed. I must refer the reader to my volume On *Female Diseases,* for further information on this point. Dr. Rig by used justly to denounce these practices as *dishonest—thoroughly dishonest.* To patients in London I recommend Dr. Ross, 11, Hart Street, Bloomsbury Squares or Dr. Waterworth, 6, Bengal Place, New Kent Road.

WHITE-SWELLING

This is a disease of one of the larger joints. It is mostly of a slow or chronic character, and occurs chiefly in the knee joint, although the elbow-joint, hip-joint, and even the ankle joint, are not unfrequently the seat of it. In the present observations I refer principally to the disease of the knee-joint.

The *first symptom* is often a deep-seated, dull, heavy pain in the joint, which is not constant nor severe, but is usually much increased in using the joint. It is generally seated in one particular part of the joint. In white-swelling of the knee joint, the patient keeps the knee bent, and from the pain occasioned by extension, gets into the habit of only touching the ground with his toes. At first there is no external swelling or inflammation, but in the progress of the disease the knee swells, and gradually increases in size, but the skin is not at all altered in colour, and the swelling is generally so firm as to yield very little to pressure. In the slowness or rapidity of its progress, and in the severity of the pain, the disease differs much in different cases. Sometimes, the pain is very acute, and the swelling gradually attains to a very large size. In the end, collections of matter often form about the joint, and at length burst, and discharge a thin curd-like matter. But it is not unusual for the disease to continue for several years without the formation of any abscess, particularly if the patient has been under correct treatment.

When the disease goes on to a fatal termination, hectic fever arises, and destroys the patient, unless the limb be removed.

This disease mostly occurs in scrophulous subjects, and rarely after five-and-twenty, or thirty years of age. It is, however, not unfrequently met with in young persons whose constitutions are delicate, but who have never given any decided proof of a scrophulous habit.

When there is a constitutional disposition to the disease, a blow, fall, or any other kind of mechanical injury, may excite it into action. With such a predisposition, it is also not unfrequently induced by long continued disorder of the digestive organs, or whatever greatly deranges the general health.

There is a rheumatic affection of the large-joints, particularly of the keen joint, which in some of its symptoms resembles white-swelling, but which, although it is for the present, perhaps, quite as painful, is essentially different from the latter, and proves ultimately much more tractable. This rheumatic affection appears mostly in young persons of a full plethoric habit who are disposed to other forms of rheumatism; and is induced by imprudent exposure to cold, or other accidental causes of that malady.

There are likewise other diseases of the joints, which differ widely from white-swelling, properly so called, but it would occupy so large a space in the present article for me to enter into a particular description of them, that I can only advise an immediate application to some professional man of superior judgment, such as Mr. Henry Smith, of Icing's College Hospital, whenever there appears any doubt respecting the real nature of the case. The chief of these diseases differing from white-swelling, are a thickened and otherwise diseased state of the internal membrane of the joint, called synovial membrane, which secretes the lubricating fluid of the joint,—an inflammation of this membrane, of a peculiar character,—a state of chronic disease in the joint, supervening an attack of healthy acute inflammation, which, from neglect, or improper treatment, has degenerated into an unhealthy indolent complaint,—and a *neuralgic* affection of the knee, in which there is very severe pain, but no swelling. *See* NEURALGIA.

TREATMENT—This disease is universally acknowledged to be of a serious nature, often difficult of cure, and always requiring great attention and perseverance. Here trifling is certainly followed by the loss of the limb, or the destruction of life; and the use of half-measures, or a want of perseverance in the employment of the most effectual remedies, never fail to disappoint the patient, and aggravate the disease. In treating white-swelling, it must not be forgotten that it is a disease of debility and poor blood, occurring mostly in delicate constitutions, and will, therefore, require the persevering use of those means which are capable of restoring firmness and health to the general system, as well as of those which are more directly calculated to arrest the progress of the local injury. I am desirous of impressing this view of the treatment on the mind of the sufferer, from being fully persuaded of its correctness and importance, and because it is too often overlooked. Local measures are of the utmost consequence, but general means, of an invigorating nature, must be resorted to at the same time, and it is from this union, and from this alone in the majority of instances, that we can reasonably hope to conduct the complaint to a favourable issue.

In my opinion, one of the best plans of treatment that can be suggested is, to cover the knee with a poultice made of seatang, or the common sea-weed containing small bladders filled with a glutinous matter, bruised; to take rum and milk the first thing in the morning, and cod-liver oil, as prescribed at page 40, twice a day; and to allow a generous mild diet, consisting chiefly of animal food, eggs, biscuit, and good malt liquor—sometimes a little wine also. Sometimes the union of cod-liver oil and. quinine will be better. At the same time, the patient must have the advantage of a pure country air, and as much of it as can possibly be taken without exercising the affected limb; and he must retire and rise early, and sleep on the mattress. This poultice should be renewed twice a day, and, *at each removal, the joint should be well washed with a strong solution of salt and water, used cold.* A generous diet is highly proper, but care must be exercised never to load the stomach, or to take any indigestible food, however small in quantity, since excess or imprudence in these respects, will rarely fail materially and immediately to injure the joint. The generous diet ordered under INDIGESTION is the most suitable. The joint must be kept perfectly quiet, and the straight position of the limb is in general the best. In most instances, I would also give one of the pills, No. 98A, page 192, every other night. This pill has great power in relieving pain, and sometimes in arresting the progress of organic mischief; and is applicable to most cases of the present disease.

The sea-weed cataplasm, (or rags constantly wet with salt water), is, I think, one of the most efficacious local applications; but if it does not answer, a vinegar poultice, (made by stirring oatmeal into the best vinegar), may be applied in the same way. This will in a few days bring out some pimples on the surface of the joint, when it must be laid aside, and the pimples anointed, once or twice a day, with a stimulating; ointment, as No. 89, page 188, or washed with the lotion, No. 44, which will heat them and occasion a discharge. This discharge should be kept up as long as possible; but when the pimples disappear, cover the joint with a piece of soap plaster. After the pimples have disappeared, it will often be advisable to renew the application of the vinegar poultice, and to proceed in the same course again, and that repeatedly. This poultice was highly thought of by Sir Astley Cooper.

The tartar emetic ointment, (page 56), is likewise a very useful application, and is much approved at the present day. It acts in the same way as the vinegar captaplasm, and the object in using it is, to produce and maintain a discharge from the external surface of the joint, and thus to relieve the internal parts; but it has not appeared to me to be in any degree so useful as the sea-weed, or as rags wet with salt and water, kept constantly applied to the joint. Blistering is sometimes recommended, but it is not so useful as salt and water.

Iodine (page 70) has great power over some cases of the present disease, and is worthy of trial when other means fail. Indeed, it will often be advisable for the patient to commence with this medicine, particularly if the sea-weed cannot be procured. A drachm of the iodide of potassium, or of cadmium, or of lead, may be mixed with an ounce and a half of hogs lard, and about the size of a nut rubbed gently over the joint, night and morning, for ten days, when it must be discontinued for five or six days, and then resumed, and laid aside again for the same period, and so on as long as it is employed. I have lately found this ointment of very great service, as a local remedy in this disease. A solution of iodine may also be taken inwardly at the same time, if the symptoms are urgent; but it is a very active medicine, and must be used cautiously. The solution is formed by dissolving half a drachm of the iodide of potassium in an ounce and a-half of rose-water, of which a child of ten years old may take six drops twice a day, in infusion of chamomile, or decoction of sarsaparilla, or with the alkaline solution already advised. *See* the directions at page 70.

Should the cod-liver oil be refused, then preparations of steel may be tried, and are often of considerable service. The muriated tincture of iron is an excellent tonic, and may be taken in doses of twenty, thirty or forty drops, thrice a day, in an infusion of chamomiles. Or the pills No. 102, or 103, may be tried. Besides this class of remedies, the mineral acids, sulphate of quinine, and carbonate of soda, are sometimes taken with much advantage. When the formation of abscesses excite fever in the system, the sulphuric or nitric acid is peculiarly eligible as a tonic and refrigerant. For the doses, *see* pages 129, 98. The sulphate of quinine pills No. 115, are proper; or, if there be much general irritation present, a grain or two of quinine may be made into a pill with three or four grains of the extract of hemlock, prepared in vacuo, and given thrice daily. If the hemlock is useful, which it frequently will be, the quantity now ordered may be combined, with great advantage, with a grain of sulphate of zinc.

The *iodide of iron* will often agree better, and be more beneficial, than either iodine or iron given alone. It combines these two valuable medicines, and may be given as a tonic, having a salutary influence over the capillary system, in doses of from twenty to forty or sixty drops of the solution, thrice a day, in water. This solution is well made by Mr. Squires, Chemist, Oxford Street, corner of Duke Street, but it may also be obtained from Allen's, Plough Court, and most able chemists. Davenport's *Syrup of iodide of quinine and iron* is still more efficacious in many instances. The reader may turn with advantage to my remarks respecting this preparation under the head of Scrophula. The dose is from half a tea-spoonful to a tea-spoonful, two or three times a day, for an adult.

Unless considerable inflammation is actually present, never apply leeches. Rags dipped in the coldest water, or salt and water, and frequently renewed, will be the best means to reduce all ordinary inflammation. They will do it without weakening the joint.

Sea-air and sea-bathing have long been regarded as valuable auxiliaries to the foregoing plans,—certainly they sometimes prove of material service; but particular parts of the coast do not agree with certain individuals, and, therefore, if on making a removal of this kind, the patient grow worse, I would by all means advise a removal to Malvern without a moment's delay;—indeed, it is better to go thither first. Malvern Wells and Epsom are very eligible situations for such patients, on account of the purity of their water, and the uncommon salubrity of the air.

I have said above, that perfect rest should be observed, and it is material that the patient should attend to this advice.[1] If by keeping the joint constantly at rest, it should become stiff, this stiffness may often be entirely removed by active friction for an hour or two every day, after the patient has perfectly recovered. Of course it must not be attempted till the disease has been entirely subdued.

In Disease of the Hip Joint, the leg and thigh of the affected side appear lessened in circumference, and the limb is elongated, in the commencement, but afterwards it becomes shorter than the sound limb; all the motions of the joints are impeded and painful; if the surgeon attempts to turn the limb inwards, it occasions particular pain; and great uneasiness is felt when, after laying the patient on his back, pressure is made on the front of the joint, near the groin, or if he lies on his face, and the pressure is made on the back part of the joint.

The treatment of the disease is similar to that just recommended for white-swelling of the knee joint. Caustic issues, or a perpetual blister, with perfect rest, are the remedies most frequently used, particularly if the disease be of some weeks standing; but surgeons have not so much confidence in them now as formerly. In the very commencement, leeches are useful if much pain or uneasiness attend; but I am disposed to think *perfect rest,* and cod-liver oil, are the best means of cure.

WHITLOW

Whitlow is an inflamed and exceedingly painful swelling, terminating in an abscess by the side of a nail. The excessive pain and irritation produced by this little swelling, arise chiefly in consequence of its situation under the nail, and thickened skin at

1. To obtain rest for an inflamed joint is one of our grand principles in the treatment, and no good can be done without it : it is curious to observe how nature herself directs this; for where a joint is diseased, the muscles which act upon that joint have lost their power : thus, if a man has an inflammation of the wrist, and you put your hand into his, and desire him to squeeze it, you find that he cannot do so, or that the attempt is exceedingly feeble. In inflammation of the joints of the lower extremities, the muscles of the part in like manner lose their vigour." —*Astley Cooper's Lectures,* No. 6.

the end of the finger or toe, which from their unyielding nature, confine the inflamed part, and prevent its coming properly forward, and discharging the matter formed.

Whitlows so frequently trouble some persons as to prove, that they are produced by constitutional indisposition; but the most usual causes are of a local nature, especially bruises, pricks with a sharp-pointed instrument, and other, ordinary sources of inflammation.

TREATMENT—A principal point in the treatment of this complaint is, to soothe and soften the part affected by the free use of warm fomentations and poultices, which render the nail and skin supple, and thus assist in the formation of healthy matter, and its free discharge. If the inflammation be considerable, it will sometimes be advisable also to apply a leech or two to the part; and when the pain and irritation continue severe, notwithstanding the employment of these measures, a grain of opium and a grain of calomel should be made into a pill, and taken directly. It is very proper for the patient to take this pill at bed-time, if the pain be so great as to threaten him with the loss of rest. In most cases it will be useful to take a little opening medicine, as No. 28, or 74, pages 156, 176, as soon as the whitlow is detected.

After fomenting and poulticing well, an early opening should in general be made, by putting the point of a lancet into the most prominent part of the swelling, if the abscess does not burst spontaneously; and the nail ought to be paired away as thin as possible, and if there be any portion of it loose, it should be removed. In this way, pressure on the part will be much lessened, and a free outlet be afforded for the escape of matter. When the abscess has burst, or been opened, it is proper to continue the warm poultice for a day or two, or longer, renewing it every eight hours; and after that time, if the ulcer goes on well towards heating, it may be dressed with Turner's cerate, (No. 95, page 190,) or the saturnine ointment, No. 94, twice daily. But should it prove troublesome after bursting, and the poultice appear to have very little effect upon it, I would advise the patient to lay a small blister over the whole of the affected part. This occasions an increased discharge from the ulcer, gives a new and salutary stimulus to the diseased parts, and is attended with immediate and manifest benefit. After the blister has been on twelve hours, it may be removed and the surface dressed with spermaceti cerate, or the ointment, No. 94, until it is well. If the complaint be obstinate, it may require the application of two or three blisters before it will heal effectually.

One kind of Whitlow is to be met with in which, notwithstanding the most excruciating pain, there is little swelling in the affected finger, but a vast deal in the hand and wrist, and even over the whole fore-arm. Here the disease is situated in the tendons and their sheaths, and a free incision must be made into the affected parts very early—not later than the third day; otherwise the tendons will be destroyed. This will afford speedy relief.

Fungus, or proud flesh, sometimes arises in these cases, but it is not advisable to apply caustic to it. If the patient proceed in the manner above described, this fungus will disappear.

Those who are frequently troubled with Whitlow, should enter on a course of the pill, No. 98A, every other night, with the pill, No. 104, or No. 115, or 103, twice a day; or, if that course does not satisfactorily improve the general condition the sarsaparilla powder may be tried, or No. 84A, page 184. Cold bathing also is excellent, and so is a tumbler full of rum and milk the first thing in the morning, with a nutritious diet daily.

WORMS

There are several kinds of worms which infest the intestinal canal of man, but the chief are the *ascarides,* or small white thread worms (varying from the eighth of an inch to an inch and a half in length), mostly found in the rectum, or last gut; the lumbrici, or long round worms, usually found in the small intestines; and the *toenia,* or tape-worm, which occupies the upper part of the intestinal tube, and is occasionally found in every part of it. The *lumbrici* are from two or three to ten or twelve inches in length, round, of a yellowish-white or brownish-red colour. The *toenia* are of two sorts; one, the common tape-worm, which frequently acquires a length from thirty to forty feet, and more; the other is passed off in pieces of a greater or less number of joints, or in single joints, bearing a considerable resemblance to the seeds of gourds.

Worms can hardly exist in so sensible and highly organized a part as the intestines, without producing some degree of irritation there, and we are certain that irritation cannot take place in that canal without producing, sooner or later, and in a greater or less degree, disagreeable effects in various parts of the system, and especially in the stomach and head. Hence these animals frequently occasion a variable appetite, which is sometimes deficient, at other times voracious; pains in the stomach; fetid breath; nausea; head-ache; vertigo and giddiness; cough; irritation about the nose and anus; disturbed sleep; and a disordered state of the bowels. In children, hardness and fulness of the belly frequently occur, with frequent slimy stools, and sometimes convulsive fits. In adults, as well as in children, worms not unfrequently give rise to severe epileptic fits; and sometimes occasion great emaciation.

Worms most frequently appear in those of a relaxed habit, especially in those whose digestive organs are weak; and an excessive use of vegetable food, of fruits, of sugar, or any other. saccharine or highly nutritive substance, very strongly favours their generation. The reason why children are more infested with them than adults, appears to be chiefly because they are allowed to indulge in eating sweet things, to the partial or total neglect of salt. (*See* page 45). That worms are vastly more common in some countries or districts than in others is unquestionable. It is said that in Savoy and Chambray, also in Holland and Switzerland, they are remarkably common in every class of society. In Switzerland, the abundant use of milk and cheese is supposed to be the principal cause of this condition.

Simple disorder of the stomach and bowels will often produce all the symptoms above described, and, in some cases, it is difficult to ascertain whether worms do or do not exist in the bowels, when none have ever been discharged. In such instances, we can determine the real nature of the case only by an attentive consideration of all the symptoms, and the patient's habits, more particularly with respect to the use of food.

TREATMENT—The fundamental principle in the treatment of worms is, to strengthen the system generally, and the stomach and intestines in particular, and thus not only to dislodge them, but to render them incapable of reproduction. On this principle, it will be found almost invariably, that those medicines and plans of treatment are the most eligible, which tend directly to invigorate the whole constitution, at the same time that they expel the worms; and the principal remedies of this kind are, salt, preparations of iron, sulphur, and camphor, employed in conjunction with a suitable diet and regimen.

A great deal has, at different times, been said about the efficacy of certain medicines in the cure of worms, which I have not now named, but I believe that there are few cases which will resist the proper use of salt, more especially if the usual means of strengthening a weakly constitution be resorted to, and saccharine substances be avoided as much as possible. Salt is a natural and necessary stimulant to the digestive organs; it excites them to a healthy and vigorous action, and is particularly obnoxious to all kinds of worms. I would, therefore, advise persons troubled with these animals to increase their quantity of salt at each meal; to lessen that of every kind of sweet food; to avoid partaking much of vegetables; to regulate the bowels by the occasional employment of a mild pill as No. 100 or 101, pages 193-94, and to avail themselves of the usual means of strengthening the general habit, by having recourse to active exercise daily, early rising, the use of the cold or tepid bath, etc. These measures are highly advisable and useful, whatever kind of medicine be employed, and this is a point which I wish the reader to bear in mind. At the same time a dose of salt and water, for example, an ounce of common salt dissolved in nearly half a pint of water, should be taken in the morning fasting, and repeated at the end of three or four days. This will generally act as a purgative, and will certainly bring away almost every kind of worm. If necessary, the repetition may be extended to the third or fourth time, and in very severe cases, the quantity of salt used at each dose may be increased to three ounces.

This plan is applicable to the cases of children, as well as to those of adults, and, from what I have before said, it will be perceived how necessary it is for them to be restricted in the use of sweet things, and be taught to make a free use of salt at almost every meal. As a purging portion for young children, half an ounce of salt dissolved in a quarter of a pint of water, will usually be sufficient :[1]—or the flowers of sulphur may be tried. Some medical men have recommended sulphur as a very efficacious remedy for the destruction of the small thread worm, and I have confidence in it.

Preparations of iron are sometimes very useful in expelling these animals, and in strengthening the alimentary canal so as to preclude their reproduction. They are, in general, very appropriate remedies when considerable debility has been induced from the irritation excited by the worms. Therefore, if the patient be averse to using the salt and water purgative, he may take the pills No. 102, page 196, not forgetting to attend, at the same time, to the advice given above respecting diet and regimen. In taking these pills; the quantity of carbonate of iron should be gradually increased to double what is ordered at page 196.

Camphor has been highly praised for its virtues in cases of worms, by many eminent physicians. An Italian physician of the name of Brera, who has lately published an approved work on

1. In 1832 I met with an extraordinary case of indigestion, in which surprising and satisfactory effects followed the use of salt as a medicine. The gentleman who was the subject of this case, was led by what is said of salt in the first part of this book, to take a small tea-spoonful of it twice or thrice a day, with a view to give tone to the stomach, and to excite a new action in it, he having for fifteen years suffered more than words can express, from uneasiness in that organ, depraved digestion, and nervousness. After he had taken the salt a few days, he began in the morning to feel as if something wanted to come away, and calling for a hand-basin he threw up a small clot of dark-brown stuff, composed of salt and secretion from the stomach : this was repeated for several mornings, and at length he brought up a living creature in the middle of one of these dark masses, which, on inspection, was found to be a live spider of a peculiar shape and character : it lived several days, and is now preserved in spirit. In a day or two after, he threw up what appears to have been the nest or defence of the spider, presenting the appearance of a long cone of tough coagulated albuminous matter. His general feelings since, be describes to be as different from what they were formerly as can well be conceived.

verminous diseases, has great confidence in it, and asserts that he has always employed it with marked success. Eight or ten grains of this substance may be dissolved, by means of a few drops of rectified spirit of wine, in an ounce and a half of water, and taken twice or thrice a day. This may be tried alone, or taken in the intervals between the use of the salt, and water purgative. It appears to be particularly efficacious in the destruction of the long round worms *(lumbrici)*.

For tape-worm, the oil of turpentine is an effectual remedy. An ounce may be given to an adult, or half an ounce to a child, and may be repeated to the second or third time in the course of a fortnight. It may be swallowed simply suspended on water. It is seldom advisable to repeat it more than three times, unless under the direction of a medical practitioner.

Lately the pomegranate bark has been found very useful in obstinate cases of tape-worm. Although it is only lately that it has been much recommended in this complaint, yet it is a very ancient remedy, and was highly extolled by Celsus, *De Re Medic. lib.* iv, *cap.* xvii. It appears to have advantages over the oil of turpentine, from its being quite harmless, not nearly so disgusting, producing its effects with great rapidity, and in not requiring any preparative treatment. The mode of administering it is, by boiling two ounces of the bark in a pint and a half of water down to a wine pint, the whole of which is to be taken in the course of the morning, fasting, in four draughts, with an interval of half an hour between each. Sometimes it will bring away the worm on the first day; in other cases it is necessary to repeat the medicine to the second, third, or even fourth tune, precisely as above directed.

In the small white thread worm, so often infesting the last gut in children, half a pint or a pint of lime-water should be injected once a day, and the purgative, No. 120, page 205, or a dose of castor oil, be given once a week for three or four weeks. Or, instead of tile lime-water, a strong decoction of worm-seed, or a solution of salt and water, may be injected after the same manner. This plan is generally successful.

The bristly down of the pods of cowhage is also a powerful remedy for worms. It may be taken as directed at page 45.

A great number of other medicines have been recommended, as tin-filings, male-fern, tansy, rue, tobacco, etc., and several of them are effectual; but the preceding remedies are, perhaps, the most powerful and the best, and so very rarely fail in affording satisfactory relief, that it does not appear to me advisable to take further notice of any other. The male-fern is very efficacious. The mode of administering it is described in my TREATISE ON DISORDERS OF CHILDREN. The employment of kousso is described at page 77.

Ching's Worm Cakes, and other patent medicines sold for the cure of worms, are composed chiefly of calomel or some other active purgative. They are, no doubt, sometimes beneficial, but the foregoing measures are far more eligible, and those who adopt them will find no need of resorting to any secret preparation.

The best diet for persons troubled with worms is that recommended for INDIGESTION, at pages 660-65. Although I have so high an opinion of the virtues of salt in killing these animals, I would not be understood to advise the use of salted meat. Plenty of salt eaten with fresh animal food is good, but salt meat is very objectionable.

WOUNDS

When large, they of course require the attention of a surgeon. When small, the best treatment is as follows : Bring the lips of the wound as closely together as is practicable, then with strips of adhesive plaister keep them united, and lay, over the whole a rag dipped in cold water. This should be renewed five or six times a day, or oftener, so as to repress the inflammation and keep the wound as cool as possible. The strips of plaister, probably, need not be removed oftener than three or four days. The patient should take the draught, No. 27, page 155, two or three mornings in succession.

Wounds from fish-hooks. Mr. South gives the following sensible advice : "Persons unskilled in such matters, think it proper to wriggle the hook about, and then pull it out, as they would from a fish's mouth. This is an unfitting and painful mode of treatment, for the barb of the hook cannot be freed from the flesh without dragging away some of the soft parts in which it is entangled. The readiest and least painful mode of managing this accident is, first, to grasp the hook tightly, and with a sharp knife rip off the line and clear the stem of the binding silk; then press the blunt end downwards, so that the point should be made to travel onwards till it penetrates the skin and frees the barbed point, which is then to be taken hold of, and the hook drawn out through the last made wound. Rarely any inconvenience beyond a few hours smarting follows the accident, if thus managed. A poultice should be applied to the part if painful."

YELLOW FEVER

The disease called yellow fever is a remittent fever, of a very severe character, occurring in the West India Islands, and other hot climates, and is so termed from the yellowish suffusion of the skin with which it is accompanied. By remittent fever is meant, one in which evident remissions in the severity of the symptoms can, at certain times, be perceived, although there is no complete interval from fever.

It has been called by various names, chiefly according to the places at which it has raged, and proved particularly destructive, and, therefore, we have, at different times, heard a great deal of the Saint Domingo, Philadelphia, Cadiz, Vera Cruz, Barbadoes, and Jamaica fever; but these are all essentially the same disease, originating in similar causes, displaying like symptoms, and requiring nearly the same plan of treatment. This is the fever which proves so frightfully destructive of human life at Sierra Leone, and other points on the African Coast, at Batavia, and all the other unhealthy islands of the East.

Physicians are generally of opinion, that there exists no difference whatever in kind, but merely a difference in degree, between yellow fever and the common remittent fever of the climate.

In taking a brief view of the *symptoms*, we may state them to be nearly as follows, viz., weariness and languor; faintness, giddiness, and pain in the head; chilliness, succeeded by a general heat, flushings of the face, and strong beating of the arteries of the neck and temples; excessive thirst, redness, heaviness, and burning in the eyes; frequent, small, oppressed pulse; nausea; the skin dry, or covered with a clammy moisture; great restlessness and anxiety; and a peculiar expression in the countenance of inward suffering. To these symptoms succeed a quick, hard, tense, pulse; burning fiery heat of the general surface; the countenance is highly flushed; the eye muddy and inflamed; the urine scanty; frequent sighing, and indescribable fidgetting; burning heat in the stomach, and violent retching; a yellowish tinge appears about the neck and angles of the mouth, and by degrees spreads itself over the whole surface of the body; the tongue is clean and red on the edges, but furred in the middle; the mind is confused, and sometimes delirium arises. After this the animal heat falls below the natural standard, the pulse abates in frequency and force, and a general torpor of body, and indifference of mind, become conspicuous. The vomiting is copious and not to be restrained, the matter brought up being either like muddy coffee, of a faint brown with a tinge of green, or quite black; the delirium often rises high at this period, and the patient is outrageous; bleeding from the nose, ears, gums, and bowels generally occurs, and is followed by faltering speech, stupor and death.

In the abatement which takes place towards the close of the first fourteen or twenty-four hours, the appearances are often flattering, but unless the disease has been previously treated with effect, the symptoms return with increased violence and destroy the patient.

Undoubtedly the *chief cause* of this fever, in whatever part of the world it appears, is *marsh effluvia,* or the noxious exhalations arising from marshes and swamps; it may also be excited by the exhalations from masses of any vegetable matter in a state of putrefactive decomposition, although there are no swamps near. It appears to be principally owing to the extent and number of the swamps round and on the Coast of Africa, of Java, Mexico, and other places within the tropics, that this fever proves there so frequent and so fatal.

The documents sent home from abroad prove two points of great practical importance, viz., first. That even within the limited range of the marsh poison, its power is nearly inert during the day; secondly. That when nocturnal exposure has given rise to the disease, it is not contagious.

It is not contagious under ordinary circumstances, but may become so if a number of the sick be crowded together, and especially if free ventilation be not resorted to, and the accumulation of filth be permitted.

TREATMENT—Generally speaking, yellow fever commences with symptoms of high excitement in the system; in other words, it is of a highly inflammatory type, and then the most efficacious remedies are purgatives, especially saline purgatives, (as a Seidlitz powder, with two tea-spoonfuls of Epsom salts, in cold water), the effusion or ablution of cold water, free ventilation, and salines with quinine.

When, therefore, a patient, more especially if young and strong, is attacked with head-ache, giddiness, flushings of the face, full strong pulse, and other symptoms denoting an invasion of yellow fever, he should take a dose of the purging physic just mentioned; a large blister should be applied between the shoulders or down the spine,[1] and his drink should be *small quantities* of mild diluting drinks, as gum-water, barley-water, toast-water, tea., or lime-water and milk. James's powder is an excellent medicine, which may be given in doses of five grains, three times a day. If, by the use of these means, the symptoms are greatly relieved, and the attack appears likely to be overcome, the Seidlitz powder must be repeated once a day, or once in two days, and the same plan, of dilution, by drinking freely of some simple drink, be continued till recovery is insured. At the same time the whole surface of the body should be washed, twice a day, with cold water, or the patient stripped naked,

---

1. "Mr. Linton of the Royal Navy, states in a report from Jamaica, dated Sept. 1830, that having placed a blister the whole length of the spine in a certain number of cases, the irritability of the stomach was relieved in all except one. Their application to the head is sometimes found beneficial in protracted cases accompanied by affection of the brain"—Dr. Gillkrest in *Cyclopoedia of Practical Medicine*, Vol. ii. p. 280, 1833.

and the coldest water thrown over him, in the manner, and at the times, advised under Typhus; his apartments should be well ventilated; his bed clothes and attendants few, and every other source of irritation avoided.

We must be cautious in the use of purgatives, from the high grade of inflammation certainly existing in the stomach; and therefore the *Seidlitz powders* will be found one of the very best aperients, for they neutralize the acid in the stomach at the same time that they open the bowels. If the Seidlitz powders cannot be procured, take a tea-spoonful or two of Epsom salts every morning in water. Sea-water is likewise a valuable medicine taken daily, if the Epsom salts or Seidlitz powders are not taken. This state of inflammation leads us to advise the application of leeches to the region of the stomach, as a likely means of allaying the vomiting, and otherwise benefiting the patient. Six grains of nitre, thrice a day, in water, is an admirable medicine. It reddens the colour of the blood, and augments its power of stimulating the heart.

Dr. Stevens, who practised for many years in the West Indies, says the best treatment is to give the following salines :

Take of Carbonate of soda	1	scruple;
Common salt	15	grains;
Chlorate of potash	7	grains.

Mix, and give this in barley-water, every three or four hours.

Do not give calomel; it is an abominably bad practice. Let the patient have the Seidlitz powder and the salines, as already advised, and as soon as a remission of the fever occurs, give quinine, or a decoction of bark, thrice a day. *See* pages 591-92.

In the yellow fever which raged so virulently at Carthagena some years since, and which carried off thousands of the inhabitants, it is a well ascertained fact that the rich and more respectable inhabitants, who were largely dosed by the physicians, died almost to a man, while the poor, who had little or no physic given them. beyond a little sea-water daily, as commonly recovered. The simplest and most sustaining treatment of the fever is the best.

If *diarrhoea* supervene during the convalescence, give the pills of calomel and Dover's powder ordered under DYSENTERY.

For vomiting and burning heat at the pit of the stomach, give half a drachm of carbonate of soda occasionally in water. Carbonate of soda is an excellent medicine in yellow fever.

The most grateful drinks are spruce or ginger beer, and Hock or Claret wine and water, made weak.

If, by the use of the preceding remedies, we are favoured to check the progress of the disease, great care will still be requisite to restore the patient from the state of extreme debility to which he is reduced. In this period, quinine, bark and wine must be given, the washing with cold or lukewarm water be continued, and the patient freely exposed to an open pure air. In the use of bark and wine, we must be regulated by the principles laid down under GASTRIC FEVER. In the state of extreme weakness induced by yellow fever, it seems that stimulants may be more freely taken than would be proper or safe in typhus or typhoid fever.

A free exposure to the purest air attainable is of great moment in every case and stage of the present fever, and in the advanced periods is, perhaps, more to be relied on than any other resource. It is, consequently, highly advisable, that when a patient is attacked with the disease in a low unhealthy situation, he should, if possible, be directly removed to a higher and more healthy spot, and there have the advantage of as much of the air of the day as can be given. In general, no danger need be apprehended from removing a patient labouring under yellow fever through the open air; on the contrary, such an exposure is very generally more or less beneficial.

In some situations in sultry climates, as in the Gulf of Persia, and at Cape Coast Castle, and perhaps other places on the African Coast, yellow fever sometimes commences and proceeds with the symptoms of great general depression and debility, the high inflammatory symptoms being nearly or altogether absents and in this case our great dependence must be upon the free use of Seidlitz powders, carbonate of soda, quinine, and bark, frequent washing with cold water, change of air, and the use of wine. *See* page 578. Cold drinks are also proper. If it can possibly be done, remove the patient at once from the place he is attacked in, to one possessing a better air—an air dry, bracing, and free from swampy exhalations. This will frequently prove the means of saving life.

SPLEEN, UVULA AND TONSILS

These being complaints especially troublesome in childhood, and my space not permitting me to notice them in this volume, the reader will find them taken into ample consideration in my publication ON INFANCY AND CHILDHOOD, to which, I am, therefore, constrained to make reference. But I avail myself of this opportunity to recommend those who suffer severely from throat affections, to consult Dr. Yearsley, of Savile Rows who has ably written *On Throat Ailments*. He has certainly paid great attention to this class of complaints, and I believe him to be much experienced in their management.

At the same time, I would warn my readers against certain men who for consumption and cough are fond of *mopping* the windpipe and larynx, pushing down a probang into the windpipe and cauterizing its internal membrane—a horrible practice, that cannot be too severely condemned. Such men are among the pests of society.

DISEASES OF THE HEART

The subject of Diseases of the HEART was overlooked in the former editions of this volume, and it is thought advisable from its large size, not to introduce the subject here, but to append it to the Author's book on the DISEASES OF FEMALES, where the reader will find it treated of at length; indeed, my readers will derive this advantage at least from its being introduced into that volume, that they will find it occupying much more space than could be allotted to it here, a quantity of matter more than double what is ordinary being there introduced, with a notice also of the *sympathetic affections* of the heart. Sympathetic disorders of the heart are now so frequent, as to make it a subject of considerable interest and importance. Exercise and quietness are the grand remedies.

CORPULENCE

A sure way to reduce corpulence is to abstain from bread, butter, milk, sugar, beer and potatoes. These articles contain starch and saccharine matter, which tend to create fat. The following diet may be taken with great advantage, viz.

For Breakfast—4 or 5 oz. of beef, mutton, kidneys, broiled fish, bacon or cold meat of any kind except pork, a large cup of tea (without milk or sugar), a little biscuit or an ounce of dry toast.

For Dinner—5 or 6 oz. of any fish except salmon, any meat except pork, any kind of poultry or game, any vegetable except potatoe, one ounce of dry toast, fruit out of a pudding and two or three glasses of good claret, sherry or madeira—champagne, port and beer must not be touched.

For Tea—2 or 3 oz. of fruit, a rusk or two and a cup of tea without milk or sugar.

For Supper—3 or 4 oz. of meat or fish, similar to dinner, with a glass or two of claret or sherry.

N.B. Heavy quilts and counterpanes I disapprove of as coverings for beds; but have pleasure in recommending the DOWN QUILTS made by Booth and Foxe, 80, Hatton Garden, as light, warm, elegant and inexpensive.

In order fully to understand what is said under COSTIVENESS, and in other parts of this volume, in regard to the situation and functions of the stomach and liver, and the course and functions of the large intestines, engravings are necessary and they will be found in the author's book ON THE DISEASES OF FEMALES. An Engraving will also be found there, showing the different regions of the abdomen; and an explanation or glossary of Medical Terms.

MEDICINES COMMONLY USED IN DOMESTIC PRACTICE

WITH THEIR PROPER DOSES FOR ADULTS AND CHILDREN

In proportioning the dose of any medicine to the age of a child, it may be assumed, as a general rule, that a patient of fourteen years of age will require about two thirds of the quantity proper for an adult; if seven years old, one half; if three years, one fourth, and if twelve months, one eighth.

About sixty drops make a tea-spoonful—one drachm is equal to a tea-spoonful—and half an ounce to a table-spoonful.

MEDICINES	DOSES		
	Children from Adults.	Proper vehicle, etc. 2 to 4 Years	
Alkaline solution	½ to 1 drachm	5 to 10 drops	in water
Aloes	10 to 20 grains	not suitable	in pills
—compound tincture of	1 to 5 drachms	10 to 40 drops	in water
— etherial tincture of	3 to 5 drachms	ditto	ditto
Alum	10 to 20 grains		ditto
Ammonia, sesqui-carbonate of	4 to 10 grains	2 to 4 grains	in almond emulsion
Antimonial powder	5 to 10 grains	1 to 2 grains	honey or jam
Antimony, precipitated sulphuret of	1 to 3 grains	½ to 1 grain	conserve or jam
Antimonial wine (as an emetic)	3 to 6 drachms	1 to 2 drachms	in water
————(as an alterative)	15 to 25 drops	4 to 6 drops	in barley water
Aromatic confection	10 to 40 grains	2 to 10 grains	in cinnamon water
——— powder	5 to 10 grains	1 to 6 grains	in water
——— tincture	½ to 3 drachms	¼ to 1 drachm	ditto
Assafoetida gum	8 to 30 grains	2 to 5 grains	in pills
——— tincture	1 to 2 drachms	10 to 40 drops	in water
Balsam of capivi	10 to 60 drops	2 to 6 drops	in mucilage
——— Peru	10 to 30 grams	2 to 5 grains	ditto
——— Tolu	ditto	ditto	ditto
Bark, in powder	10 gr. or to 1 ½ dr.	2 to 10 grains	in water
——— decoction of	1 to 4 ounces	2 to 4 drachms	
——— compound tincture of	ditto	20 to 30 drops	ditto
——— infusion of	ditto	2 to 6 drachms	
Calomel (as a purgative)	2 to 6 grains	¼ to ½ grain	in jam
——— (as an alterative)	$^1/_{10}$ to ¼ grain ,	not suitable	ditto, daily
Camphor	3 to 20 grains	1 to 4 grains	in a pill
——— julep	1 to 2 ounces	2 to 3 drachms	
Canella Albs, powder of	10 to 30 grains	2 to 4 grains	in water
Cardamoms, compound tincture of	½ to 2 drachma	10 to 20 drops	ditto
Cantor, powder of	5 to 20 grains	2 to 4 grains	in pills
——— tincture of	½ to 4 drachms	10 to 20 drops	in water

MEDICINES	DOSES		Proper vehicle, etc.
	Adults.	Children from 2 to 4 Years,	
Castor oil	½ to 2 ounces	1 to 3 drachms	in mucilage
Cascarilla, infusion of	1 to 4 ounces	½ to 1 ounce	
——— tincture of	½ to 4 drachma	20 to 50 drops	in water
Catechu, extract of	10 to 40 grains	3 to 8 grains	ditto
——— tincture of	½ to 4 drachms	12 to 20 drops	ditto
Chalk, prepared	½ to 2 drachms	8 to 30 grains	ditto
——— powder, compound	½ to 1 drachm	10 to 20 grains	ditto
———— with opium	20 to 40 grains	5 to 6 grains	ditto
Chamomile flowers	10 to 20 grains	2 to 5 grains	in pills
————infusion of	1 to 4 ounces	2 to 4 drachms	
Columba, powder of	10 to 20 grains	2 to 5 grains	in water
——— tincture of	½ to 4 drachms	20 to 50 drops	ditto
——— infusion of	1 to 4 ounces	2 to 6 drachms	
Cheltenham salt	1 to 6 drachms	½ to 1 drachms	in water
Crab's claws, prepared	20 to 60 grains	5 to 20 grains	ditto
Contrayerva powder, compound	15 to 30 grains	1 to 8 grains	ditto
Cream of tartar	1 to 4 drachms	10 to 20 grains	ditto
Colocynth pill, compound	4 to 20 grains	1 to 2 grains	in pills
————extract, compound	3 to 20 grains	ditto	ditto
Dover's powder (to sweat)	8 to 15 grains	not suitable	in jelly
—(as a mild anodyne & diaphoretic	3 to 4 grains	1 to 1½ grain	in pill
Electuary (lenitive)	1 to 8 drachms	½ to 2 drachms	alone
Elixir of vitriol	10 to 60 drops	5 to 6 drops	in water
Emetic tartar (as an emetic)	1 to 3 grains	¼ to ½ grain	ditto
———(as an alterative, etc.)	1/10 to 1/6 grain	1/18 to 1/26 grain	ditto
Epsom salt	1 dr. to ½ ounce	½ to 1 drachm	ditto
Foxglove, powder of	½ to 3 grains	not suitable	in pill
————tincture of	10 to 40 drops	3 drops	in water
———— infusion of	¼ to 1 ounce	½ to 1 drachm	twice a day
Gentian, extract of	5 to 20 grains	1 to 6 grains	in pill
compound infusion of	1 to 4 ounces	2 to 3 drachms	
compound tincture of	1 to 2 drachms	10 to 20 drops	in water
Ginger, powder of	4 to 25 grains	1 to 3 grains	ditto
————tincture of	½ to 2 drachms	5 to 10 drops	ditto
Glauber's salt	2 dr. to 1 ounce	½ to 1 drachm	ditto
Grey powder	3 to 8 grains	2 to 3 grains	in pills
Gnaiacum gum	10 to 30 grains	ditto	ditto
———ammoniated tincture of	40 dps. to 2 drs.	6 to 12 drops	in pills
Hartshorn, spirit of	15 to 50 drops	3 to 6 drops	in water
Hoffman's anodyne liquor	½ to 1½ drachm	10 to 20 drops	ditto
Hemlock, powder of	2 to 20 grains	1 to 2 grains	in pills
————extract of	ditto	ditto	ditto
Hiera piers	½ 2 drachms	2 to 4 grains	in water
Jalap, powder of	10 to 30 grains	2 to 10 grains	ditto
————tincture of	1 to 4 drachma	½ to 1½ drachm	ditto
Ipecacuanha, powd. (as an emetic)	20 to 30 grains	3 to 6 grains	in water
——— powd. (as an alterative)	1 to 2 grains	¼ of a grain	in pills
——— wine (as an emetic)	2 to 8 grains	1 to 2 drachma	in water, or alone
——wine (as an alterative)	30 to 50 drops	10 drops	in almond emulsion
—comp.powd.—See Dover's powd.			
Iron, carbonate of	2 to 30 grains	1 to 3 grains	in pills

MEDICINES	DOSES		Proper vehicle, etc.
	Adults.	Children from 2 to 4 Years,	
——— sulphate of	1 to 6 grains	½ to 1 grain	ditto
———of muriate of	10 dps. to 1 dr.	4 to 10 drops	in water
Laudanum	10 dps. to 2 drs.	drs. not suitable	
Lavender drops	1 to 4 drachma	10 to 20 drops	ditto
Logwood, decoction of	2 to 3 ounces	½ to 1 ounce	
——— extract of	12 to 20 grains	2 to 6 grains	in chalk mixture
Magnesia, carbonate of	20 to 60 grains	3 to 8 grains	in water
calcined	10 to 30 grains	2 to 6 grains	ditto
Manna	¼ to 2 ounces	1 to 4 drachms	ditto
Mercurial, or blue pill	3 to 6 grains	1 to 2 grains	in pills
Mercury, with clalk	3 to 8 grains	2 to 4 grains	ditto
Mistletoe powder	20 to 60 grains	10 to 40 grains	in water
Musk	4 to 20 grains	2 to 5 grains	in pills
Muriatic acid	8 to 20 drops, or more	2 to 4 drops	in water
Myrrh, in powder	10 to 60 grains	1 to 6 grains	in pills
—tincture of	½ to 1 drachm	10 to 15 drops	on sugar
Nitre, purified	8 to 30 grains	2 to 3 grains	in water
——— sweet spirit of	½ to 2 drachms	10 to 40 drops	ditto
Nitric acid, diluted	15 to 35 drops	3 to 6 drops	ditto
Nutmeg, spirit of	1 to 4 drachms	20 to 40 drops	ditto
Opiate confection .	10 to'30 grains	2 to 6 grains	
Opium, powder of	1 to 2 grains}	opium is rarely	
——— purified	½ to 3 grains	advisable in dis	
——— tincture of	10 to 60 drops	orders of children	
Paregoric elixir	½ to 2 drachms	5 to 10 drops	in water
Peppermint, essence of	1 to 4 drachms	5 to 20 drops	ditto
Poppies, extract of	2 to 20 grains	1 to 3 grains	in pill
——— syrup of	½ to 2 ounces	½ to 1 drachm	alone
Qiassoa, infusion of	2 to 4 ounces	2 to 4 drachms	
1 to 2 drachma	10 to 20 drops	10 to 20 drops	in water
Rhubarb powder	4 to 30 grains	2 to 8 grains	ditto
——— infusion of	2 to 4 ounces	½ to I ounce	
——— tincture of.	2 to 8 drachms	1 to 2 drachms	ditto
Rochelle salt	1 to 8 drachms	½ to 1 drachm	ditto
Roses, infusion of	2 to 4 ounces	½ ounce	
——— conserve of	1 to 8 drachms	20 to 60 grains	in bolus
Saffron	10 to 60 grains	2 to 6 grains	in pill
Salt of tartar	10 to 30 grains	3 to 6 grains	in water
——— of wormwood	ditto	ditto	ditto
Sarsaparilla, compound decoction of	4 to 8 ounces		
Scammony, compound powder of	10 to 20 grains	2 to 10 grains	in jelly
——— ——— with calomel	ditto	ditto	ditto
Senna, infusion of	1 to 4 ounces	2 to 6 drachms	
——— tincture of	½ to 1½ ounce	2 to 3 drachms	in water
Soluble tartar	1 to 8 drachms	½ to 2 drachms	ditto
Solution of acetate of morphia	10 to 60 drops	2 to 4 drops	ditto
Spirit of mindererus	1 to 3 drachms	10 to 20 drops	ditto
——— wine	½ to 1 drachm		
——— nitre, sweet	½ to 2 drachms	10 to 12 drops	ditto
——— sal volatile	½ to 1 drachm	5 to 12 drops	ditto
——— ammonia	ditto	5 to 6 drops	ditto

MEDICINES	DOSES		Proper vehicle, etc.
	Adults.	Children from 2 to 4 Years.	
Sponge, burnt	1 to 4 drachms		in jelly
——— lozenges of	1 to 3, thrice dly.		
Squill, powder of	1 to 3 grains	¼ to ½ grain	in pill
——— oxymel of	½ to 2 drachms	10 to 20 drops	in water
——— tincture of	10 to 60 drops	2 to 6 drops	ditto
——— pill	10 to 20 grains	2 to 3 grains	
Steel—See Iron			
Sulphur, flowers of	½ to 2 drachms	10 to 20 grains	in milk
——— milk of	ditto	ditto	ditto
Syrup of poppies, or opium	1 to 6 or 8 drs	¼ to 1 drachm	
——— buckthorn	1 to 2 drachms	½ drachm	in water
——— ginger	1 to 4 drachms	½ to 1 drachm	ditto
Tincture of aloes, compound	½ to 2 drachms	20 to 30 drops	ditto
——— ethereal	½ to 3 drachms	ditto	ditto
——— assafoetida	½ to 2 drachms	10 to 40 drops	ditto
——— bark, compound	1 to 4 drachms	20 to 30 drops	ditto
——— benjamin, compound	¼ to 2 drachms	10 to 30 drops	on sugar
——— cantharides	10 to 60 drops		in water
——— cardamoms, compound	½ to 2 drachms	10 to 20 drops	ditto
——— cascarilla	½ to 4 drachms	20 to 50 drops	ditto
——— catechu	ditto	ditto	ditto
——— columba	ditto	ditto	ditto
——— gentian, compound	1 to 2 drachms	20 to 30 drops	ditto
——— guaiacum, ammoniated	ditto	ditto	on sugar
——— jalap	1 to 4 drachms	½ to 1 drachm	in water
——— lavender, compound	1 to 2 drachms	15 to 20 drops	ditto
——— myrrh	½ to 1 drachm	10 to 15 drops	in mucilage
——— valerian, ammoniated	1 to 2 drachms	15 to 20 drops	in water
Turpentine, Venice	20 to 60 grains	4 to 6 grains	in pills
——— oil of	10 to 60 or 100dp	5 to 10 drops	in water
Valerian powder	1 to 3 scruples	5 to 10 grains	ditto
Vitriol, elixir of .	15 to 40 drops	2 to 6 drops	ditto
Vitriolic acid, diluted	ditto	ditto	ditto
Wine of steel	1 to 4 drachms	20 to 50 drops	ditto
——— meadow saffron	10 to 20 drops,	2 to 4 drops	ditto
Wormwood, salt of	10 to 30 grains	3 to 6 grains	in beer

APPENDIX OF PRESCRIPTIONS

Soothing Injection **No. 67B.**

Take of Acetate of morphia	9	grains;
Water	2	ounces.

Mix for an injection. From twenty to thirty drops of this morphia solution may be injected into the womb, to relieve pain in that organ.

This is a useful remedy in severe pain in the womb, arising from painful menstruation, or arrested menstruation. It relieves the pain without being followed by any of that distress and discomfort which ordinarily succeeds opium taken by the mouth. Laudanum and water has not the same effect.

Mixture for Acute Bronchitis. **No. 78 E. Y.**

Take of Almond emulsion	11	ounces;
Nitrate of potash	2	drachms;
Tartarized antimony, ...	2	grains;
Syrup of tolu, ...	1	ounce.

Mix and give a table-spoonful every hour, or every second hour, until the cough and difficulty of breathing are much relieved.

This is very efficacious in subduing inflammation in the chest, and in cough with fever and pain. It is similar in its effects to No. 78B, but in certain cases of an acute form, is still more effectual. Nitrate of potash and tartarized antimony are among the most efficient means we possess of reducing inflammation.

Mixture for Ulcers and Eruptions

Take of Iodide of potassium		half a drachm;
Dilute nitric acid	1½	or 2 drachms;
Water, or infusion of orange peel	8	ounces.

Dose, two table-spoonfuls, three times a day.

This is an excellent remedy for ulcerations and foul sores, and therefore will be found useful in various kinds of swellings, ulcers, and eruptions, whether suspicious or not.

Iron and Quinine Tonic **No. 87C.**

Take of Citrate of iron and quinine	1½	drachm;
Sesqui-carbonate of ammonia	2	drachms;
Tincture of orange peel	1½	ounce;
Water	1½	ounce.

Mix, and take a tea-spoonful, twice or three times a day, in a wineglassful of water.

This is an agreeable and useful combination of steel, quinine and ammonia, and is very efficacious in most cases of debility and poverty of blood.

Muriate of Iron Mixture **No. 87C.Y.**

Take of Tincture of muriate of iron	3	drachms;
Pimento water	5	ounces;
Syrup of orange peel	5	drachms.

Mix. The dose is a table-spoonful, thrice a day, in a wine-glassful of water.

This is a very decided steel tonic, useful in most cases of debility—useful in scrophula, ulcerations and wherever tone is required in the general system.

Dutch Drops **No. 87D.**

Take of Oil of turpentine		half an ounce;

Sweet spirit of nitre	half an ounce;
Tincture of guaiacum	1 ounce;
Oil of amber	half an ounce;
Oil of cloves	half an ounce.

Mix them, and take a tea-spoonful, twice or thrice a day, in a wine-glassful of water.

This is an old and efficacious remedy for lumbago and other forms of chronic rheumatism and is also useful in chronic pains in the bladder.

Nitric Acid Mixture **No. 87E.F.**

Take of Dilute nitric acid	2 drachms;
Tincture of orange peel	2 drachms;
Compound infusion of orange peel	5½ ounces.

Mix, and take a table-spoonful, or two, in a wine-glassful of water.

This is good for the stomach and liver—a tonic and an alterative. It is also a useful vehicle for cod-liver oil, in cough and consumption.

Grey Powder Pill. **No. 119B.**

Take of Grey powder	half a drachm;
Extract of hemlock	half a drachm.

Mix them and divide into twelve pills.

This is a valuable mild alterative and soothing pill, of great use among professional men, to improve the secretions of the liver and soothe the general frame and many disordered states—such as diarrhoea and bronchitis. One pill may be taken every night, for four or five nights; or night and morning for two or three days.

Soothing Lotion **No. 28A.**

Mix together one pint of water and two handfuls of common kitchen salt.

Many more costly lotions than this may be formed, but few that are so good. It is of the utmost service in strengthening weak parts and in reducing swellings, congestions and slight inflammations. Wash the parts affected with it thrice a day.

APPENDIX

THE COLD-WATER SYSTEM

It cannot excite wonder that a medical author who has for many years strenuously urged on public attention, the immense advantages to be derived from free ablutions of cold water daily, constant exposure to the air and much active exercise, should think favorably of *the Cold-Water System.* This system is now attracting considerable attention in this kingdom, and since I regard it as a valuable auxiliary to medical practice, it is a pleasure to describe its principal baths and manipulations; and to introduce from my own practice an account of some cases benefited by them, hoping that my afflicted readers may gather from it such hints as will be very serviceable in relieving their disorders and augmenting their strength. Probably no situation in England is better adapted for a trial of this system than Epsom Downs and Malvern; but while I would recommend it as sometimes highly beneficial, it is, at the same time, a duty to warn the public against its excess, and the unprincipled adventurers who on all hands have vaunted it to the skies.

The principal remedial means employed in the "*water cure*" are the *Sudorific Process;* the *Cold Bath;* the *Shallow Bath;* the *Wet-Sheet;* the *Sitz Bath*; the *Wet Bandage;* the *Douche;* and the *Foot Bath.*

Sweating is thus effected:—The patient, being undressed, is enveloped in a large coarse blanket; the legs extended, and the arms kept close to the body; the blanket is then wound round it, as tight as possible, and turned well under at the feet: over this is placed, and well tucked in, another blanket or two, and then a small feather bed; finally, a counterpane, and a sheet are spread over all. Perspiration appearing, the windows are opened, and the patient is allowed, if he wishes it, a wine-glassful of cold water, every half hour. If head-ache be induced, a damp cloth is applied. The duration of the sweating depends on the nature of the disease, and the constitution of the individual.

The Cold Bath—It is generally taken after sweating, by those patients who have sufficient vigour for re-action. Strange as it may appear to many, the determination towards the skin induced by the perspiring blankets is a great advantage, prior to the use of the cold bath; because the internal organs are thereby relieved, and the shock has quite a different effect on them from what it would have if they were not first thus soothed and the skin relieved.

The Shallow Bath—This is a bath long enough for a man to sit or lie down in, containing six ox eight inches of water, or more. Either tepid or cold water is used, according to the circumstances of the patient. It is a bath of great service in numerous cases. The patient is rubbed well, all over, while in the bath. With cold water it is very serviceable in general debility; and with tepid water in local inflammations and fever.

Patients sit in this bath, and have cold water poured over them, and are also rubbed well with wet towels. In my opinion, this kind of bath is not so frequently employed in the German mode of practice as it ought to be. It is a most valuable remedy, and there are few cases of debility in which it is not indicated, and in which it will fail to prove invigorating and either to relieve or cure chronic inflammatory action.

The Sitz-Bath—This is a sitting bath, in fact, a hip bath. We use it in this country made of tin; but at Graifenberg the sitz-bath is a small common flat tub, of about eighteen inches in diameter, containing about two gallons of water. The patient sits in this, with the feet resting on the ground, from eight to forty minutes, or more, according as the case indicates; generally every day, and sometimes twice a day; in severe cases, perhaps, thrice a day. It is, unquestionably, a remedy of great power in all disorders of the abdomen and head. It draws the bad humours from the head, strengthens the whole of the digestive organs, and improves their secretions. Only a small quantity of water is used, with the view of securing a re-action, and thus the water soon becomes warm.

The action of the sitz-bath (and also of the foot-bath) is derivative, if employed for a short time without changing the water;—that is, it draws the blood from the upper regions of the body, by the consecutive re-action of the system, which accelerates the circulation in the smaller vessels of the parts immersed. Thus heat in the head is lessened, congestions there are removed, and the pulse is softened and moderated.

The Foot-Bath—The tub used for this bath is oblong and shallow. It is usually ordered to contain only about two inches of water,—sometimes only an inch; and to be used for six or ten minutes at each sitting; either the servant, or the patient, rubbing the feet the whole of the time. The patient must walk out briskly, for half an hour or hour, immediately after it.

This bath is, likewise, employed as a derivative from the superior parts of the body, and I have found it of striking benefit in affections of the head. Its powerful effects in deriving from the head and in warming cold feet, will be credited by few until they have either felt them in their own persons or witnessed them in others. In the whole of the Hydropathic practice there is no means more strikingly powerful than the foot-bath in certain instances. I can recommend it with confidence in determination of blood to the head, in headache, in affections of the eyes, and in habitual coldness of the feet.

The Douche—The douche is a fall of water from a considerable height, usually from 15 to 18 feet, of about the thickness of a man's wrist. The patient goes into the douche-room undressed, and then exposes one member and part of the body after another to this tremendous fall of water,—taking care of the chest and head. It is used for one, two, or more minutes. It is prescribed with a view to invigorate weak parts; to strengthen the whole muscular structure; and, when a crisis is thought necessary, to stir up all the humours, and bring the bad ones to the surface.

The Wet-Sheet—This is one of the principal means employed in the *hydriatic* treatment and is often called packing. Very few patients submit themselves to it without being enveloped, at least occasionally, either in a whole, or half a wet sheet. All that is necessary is to put a sheet into a tub of cold water, wring it out, spread it out on the bed, let the patient lay along in it—then wrap it well close all round him, after which cover him with three or four blankets close tucked in all round. It softens the skin, and reduces or lowers the pulse, relieves fever and is an admirable remedy in almost all fevers and inflammations.

The Umschlags or wet Bandages—The wet bandages are very useful applications in most local complaints and in constipation. They are made of coarse linen, of any convenient width, and are uniformly employed in gout, rheumatism, ulcerations, swellings, sprains and weakness of the limbs; being worn for several hours in the day and sometimes all night. The immediate effect of a wet bandage is to reduce inflammation, allay irritation, and impart tone to the nerves and vessels of the part to which it is applied. If active inflammation be present, the linen is dipped in the coldest water, wrung out, placed over the part inflamed, and renewed as often as it becomes warm. But in ordinary cases, and where no acute inflammatory action is to be encountered, the bandage, after being dipped in cold water, wrung out, and wound round the part, is to be covered with a dry bandage, which is to be drawn closely and tightly over that which is wet, so as to promote perspiration from the surface it covers.

There is no part to which a bandage is so frequently applied as round the body; over the stomach and bowel :—for this purpose, it should be at least three or four yards long, and 12 or 13 inches broad; of which about one yard is to be dipped in cold water, wrung out, and then laid over the stomach and bowels; the remaining two yards being wound tightly over it, and tied on one side.

The hydriatic system naturally divides itself into two parts; viz., the *internal* and *external* use of cold water. These are not equally appropriate to all persons. Some persons I have known cured of disorder by the *internal* use of this fluid; others have been either cured of their complaint, or at least very much relieved, by its external employment alone. Others require its full employment both internally and externally.

CASE 1—A retired medical gentleman of this town—a healthy

octogenarian, the clear red and white of whose complexion shamed that of half of our young people has lately become a decided convert to the efficacy of cold water as an *internal* remedy, from having been cured of a very troublesome, tormenting eruption on the lower part of the stomach. He had tried frequent ablution with cold water in vain, and his own account of the matter is this :—On reflecting on the subject, he enquired, what is the cause of this? and he answered himself—certainly the salts in the blood, which are too strong, and require dilution by means of frequent draughts of pure water. He accordingly drank twelve or thirteen tumblers full of water daily for as many consecutive days; the eruption and itching vanished, and has not returned.

The ingestion of good cold water acts principally, I believe, by cooling the internal membranes, and by diluting and improving the condition of the blood. On being received into the stomach and intestines it cools their surface, constringes the vessels, invigorates them, and represses inordinate vascular action; and by mixing with the circulating fluid, it improves it, and promotes an easy and healthy secretion—a condition of the utmost importance to health. It thus becomes a valuable remedy in the treatment of all maladies in which the pulse is full, strong and quick; or where, in less vigorous habits, a remedial agent is required which will both soothe and strengthen. Hence its utility in unhealthy states of the mucous membranes, whether of the digestive canal or lungs.

Nevertheless, some delicate persons cannot bear the drinking of much water; it renders them wretchedly cold, puts them into a universal shaking, and a proper degree of heat is with difficulty restored. Here we must be cautions and sparing.

Ignorant and over zealous people write and talk as if every one could drink and use cold water freely, if they please; and those who believe them will do a great deal of injury. Cold water is a powerful agent ; and there is as much good sense in talking thus, as there is in declaring, that peoples' being injured by mercury is a fancy, and that everyone may use mercury freely with advantage if they like it. The same difference is to be seen in the use of water as of every thing else in nature—it produces very different effects in different constitutions and circumstances, and great judgment is often required to adapt its quantity to the capabilities and requirements of individual systems.

Claridge has done good by calling the attention of the British Public to this method of practice; but its real value and correct use cannot be understood from such empirical books as his; they are written *ad captandum,* and are not to be depended on. Priessnitz and the other ignorant German practitioners direct it at random, and are wholly destitute of fixed and enlightened principles in its employment. Certainly Priessnitz effected cures, but he very often failed to benefit patients because of his violent and extreme measures and sometimes the consequences were fatal.

CASE 2—A clergyman, who labours hard in his spiritual vocation, felt very unwell; so weakened by what seemed to himself to be a threatened attack of severe illness, that he became somewhat alarmed, and, having a very favourable opinion of the new system, he drank directly two or three tumblers full of cold water, and in the course of the evening of the same day two or three more. He suffered very much from hoarseness and uneasiness about the chest. Feeling himself better, from the use of the water, on the following day he drank it still more plentifully, to the extent of twelve tumblers full. That night he slept well, found himself in a perspiration in the morning and from that hour all symptoms of illness vanished.

I could relate several other instances of benefit equally satisfactory, arising solely from the *internal* use of cold water; particularly that of a clergyman who had been long afflicted with a very painful chronic inflammation of the eyes, in whom the diluting influence of the water was of so great service, that he speedily recovered better health then he had had for three years.

But in many eases the *external* employment of cold water is far more useful. The good effects of cold thus applied are, in my opinion, to be primarily and mainly attributed to its operation in augmenting *the tone or Vitality of* the organic system of *nerves*—that all important system of the great sympathetics, whose fibrilae supply all the organs of digestion, assimilation, circulation, and secretion—and upon whose action all the manifestations essentially vital very much depend. To say that the vital manifestations are much dependant on the action of these nerves, is to assert that the phenomena of health will always be most conspicuous whenever those actions are invigorated and well directed.

We have read of the blind recovering their sight, and the deaf their hearing, in other countries, by means of the *Cold-Water Cure,* but it is for more satisfactory to witness such things in our own land; and it is a high gratification to me to be able to lay before my readers the following case which occurred in my own vicinity—not, indeed, a case of blindness or deafness, but, what is almost equally striking, one of the recovery of speech, etc.

CASE 3—Anne Bright, aged 21. Five years ago she was suddenly attacked with pain in her head, accompanied with fainting fits. At the end of a year hysterical fits commenced (immediately after losing her father) she continued to suffer exceedingly for the following year, at the end of which period her voice failed, and she was soon totally deprived of speech. At the same time her general strength declined, till at length she could not walk more than a hundred yards, and that with much assistance from others.

While in this helpless and deplorable condition, a gentleman and lady residing in the neighbourhood, compassionately took her under their roof, where she continued for two and twenty weeks. She then returned home, but the watchfulness of these kind friends was still extended towards her. This lady an one occasion, when on her way to visit her, was met by the clergyman, who said—"I expect you will be too late, for I thought she would have died while I was with her. During the whole of her illness she was attended by various medical men; she had become so emaciated as to have scarcely anything, but skin to cover her bones; and her last professional man left her as one whose recovery was utterly hopeless. She was thought to be so near death, that her sister sent clothes necessary for a decent interment. In this state a trial of the Cold-Water System was recommended to her and her friends; and they having consented, the treatment was commenced by using the sudorific blankets every morning for an hour and a half, a sitting bath twice a day, and a wet bandage at night. The feet were also rubbed with cold water in the evening, and she drank seven tumblers full of water in the course of the day. On the sixteenth day of treatment similar to this, a kind of hysteric fit came on while she was in the blanket; her sister put a question to her, expecting a reply, as usual, by the movement of her lips, when, to her astonishment, she audibly replied "Yes." The lady, her benevolent friend, then came to her and said, "Is it true that you can speak?" The girl then began laughing hysterically; she was taken out of the blankets, and the usual cold ablutions made use of, during which time her voice fully returned; she spoke as she had formerly done when in health, after a silence of two years and ten months.

From that period she rapidly gained health and strength; she has lately walked nine miles without much fatigue, and has fully recovered her appetite.

CASE 4—A patient of the author's from Van Dieman's Land, is so highly gratified with the treatment he has undergone, as voluntarily to offer to answer any enquiries respecting it. He suffers from paralysis, arising principally from obstruction in the liver, and accompanied with obstinate constipation of the bowels, general languor and debility. He was three months at Epsom, and the Cold-water process has conquered the disorder of the liver and constipation, refreshed and invigorated his whole system, lessened his paralysis, and freed him entirely from an habitual cold.

We have at Epsom a practice of tucking up, in his warm bed, the patient undergoing the *sudorific* process, and then heaping thick blankets on him, which answers much better, in most cases, than the lamp, or the plan of Priessnitz, and is far more agreeable.

CASE 5—Very lately I have witnessed a cough of the most terrific character subdued by cold ablations, cold wet compresses applied to the chest daily, and the use of the shallow bath occasionally. This case had batteled the skill of several eminent medical men of the metropolis. The patient was bled nearly every month for the last year,—she lost in consequence an almost incredible quantity of blood,—and her medical men considered themselves compelled to adopt this course, although against their will, so formidable were the paroxysms of coughing, spasm, and pain. The patient says—"In my own case the Cold-water treatment has done what neither medicine or anything else could; viz., subdued the cough without blood-letting." Some correct idea of the sufferings of this lady, and the extreme severity of her disorder, may be gained from her own account. Referring to her state a few months back, she says—"The palpitation of the heart had increased to a dreadful degree; at times it was so bad, that it appeared impossible to live many hours, and I was frequently obliged to be held by some person, or even two persons, to enable me to endure it."—"During one year I was cupped ninety-seven times, besides frequent bleedings at the arm."

In cases of tender chests-cases which every one has so many opportunities of seeing in this variable climate—the mere washing the chest twice a day with cold water, and rubbing well dry after it, will be of immense benefit. But in actual disease of the lungs; more especially if advanced, the hydriatic method is usually very injurious. It is in consumptive habits, and in the previous stage of debility which so often threatens *pthisis pulmonalis,* that a mild bracing employment of this system is so highly beneficial.

If we can prevail on those who suffer from nervous complaints, or from weakness of stomach, to abstain from hot slops and to drink a little cold water daily, it will be attended with great benefit. A benefited clergyman, in addressing the author, expressed himself to the following effect :—"No medical man I consulted ever before pointed out to me the importance of cold beverages to nervous people. If I had only learnt this in connexion with the water cure, I should thank God." This gentleman states that he derived more benefit from the *hydriatic* treatment, in a protracted nervous complaint, than from all the prescriptions he had tried, drugs and baths, whether English or Continental, put together. And yet I am bound in truth to say, that this clergyman carried his views with respect to cold water, and abstinence from wine, too far, and therefore suffered exceedingly from in enfeebled circulation.

In sore throats the wet bandage put round the throat, and covered with a dry one doubled, is very efficacious; and as sprains, bruises, wounds, and ulcerations, are very frequently met with in the cottages of the poor, I can confidently recommend the Clergy to advise the use of the wet bandage, and ablutions of cold water for their cure. If much inflammation be present, a long bandage should be dipped in cold water, wrung out, and then wound around the sprain or sore, being renewed through the day as often as it becomes warm; if there is little inflammation, or the case is one of long standing, then the smaller wet bandage should be covered with a thick dry one.

The following is an interesting case of costiveness cured by the new method :

CASE 6—"A gentleman, about thirty-four years of age, had suffered from boyhood, but more especially for the last *ten* years, from extreme constipation, and, without the aid of drastic purgatives, the action of the bowels was entirely suspended. However, this mode of obtaining relief at last failed, and nothing but the daily administration of enemas could produce any decided effect. Under these circumstances, so unnatural and unhealthy, functional derangement of the chest soon presented itself. The lungs became symptomatically affected, and the breathing laborious, more especially on ascending a hill. Haemoptisis, or spitting of blood, accompanied with an irritable cough and mucous expectoration, supervened; and his general health became much impaired. Feeling alarmed at the recurrence of those symptoms, and finding his physical strength evidently declining, he resolved upon trying the effect of Hydropathy. At the end of eight or ten weeks' trial, his, bowels had become natural in their action and his evacuations healthy in their character; the cough with the spitting of blood had entirely ceased his physical and mental energies had become fully restored. He has continued the treatment for some time, with the same marked improvement, and feels now altogether well and free from any of his former symptoms. This gentleman regularly walks several miles every morning before the hour of breakfast, and climbs some of the highest mountains with perfect ease and freedom."

This system is truly admirable in that frequent, and too often ill-treated, complaint—

1. Determination of Blood to The Head—The patient should drink from two to four tumblers full of water daily; take a sitz bath for half an hour or an hour, once a day; have the cold ablution on rising; a foot bath for eight or ten minutes once a clay, or oftener; be sparing in diet, and in mental exertion, and unsparing in his exercises. This will effect more good than all the purgatives that can be given, and all the bleedings and blisterings which can be prescribed. These bleedings and blisterings form a very bad practice in such cases, and yet are daily indulged in. Too many are *physicked* into a fixed confirmed weakness of the brain, who might have been cured by the Cold-water method. The patient must not drink any spirituous or fermented liquors.

2. In Constipation and Indigestion—The sufferer must wear the wet bandage round the abdomen for three hours in the middle of the day, and all night; drink two tumblers full of water daily,— of them before breakfast; have the wet sheet, or else a free perspiration by the sudatory or blankets, once a week; have a sitz bath for thirty or forty minutes once a day; the cold ablution every morning, and use energetic friction over the bowels while in the sitz bath. In constipation this treatment is ordinarily completely victorious. I have thus cured persons who have been obstinately costive for many years.

3. In Skin Disease—I have not space to dwell on these. Let it suffice to say, that a patient of mine was cured by daily sweating, the cold bath, umschlags, and drinking cold water, who had previously consulted in vain some of the most eminent of the faculty in London, and had tried unsuccessfully a course of warm and vapour baths. Sir B. Brodie called his obstinate complaint pityriasis ; it was also called psoriasis. Mr. Gaskoyne denominated it *eczema.* His general health has been very much improved under the treatment, and he has been also cured of incipient deafness.

4. In Scarlet Fever—Clergymen are, unhappily, too frequently called to witness the sufferings of poor children under this dangerous disease; and if they will attend to the following directions, they cannot fail to be messengers of mercy, to dry many a poor mother's tears, relieve many a child's agonies, and lessen

materially the spread of virulent infection. Give five grains of sesqui-carbonate of ammonia, in water, every three hours; and sponge the whole body once a day with cold water. Nothing more is necessary to cure scarlet fever—all cases, both mild and severe. *The sponging should be performed only when the Skin is* HOT *and* DRY. The more ardent the fever, the freer should be the sponging. Whenever scarlet fever prevails in a parish, it is almost incredible the amount of good a clergyman may do, who goes amongst the sick armed simply with one ounce of sesqui-carbonate of ammonia and a large sponge. *See* page 808. Indeed, he may leave his sponge at home, if he is afraid of it, and trust to ammonia alone.

5. IN ASTHMA—Some time since a gentleman came from Ireland to Epsom seeking relief in a state of great debility and nervousness, accompanied with asthma. He had been reduced thereby to a very deplorable condition. He could just crawl oat, his pace and distance being one mile in four hours. I put him cautiously under the use of this system, prescribing for him an asthmatic pill at the same time, and enjoining a strict diet. Within a month his pace and distance was four miles an hour. One day he walked on hilly ground ten miles without resting. He had no attack of asthma while at Epsom.

The following quotation is from a letter I have lately received from a general officer, an old patient. It refers to the case of a gentleman of unusual opulence, and a well known sporting character in Hampshire. "Mr.— whom I am hunting with, and have had great sport with, was dying with asthma—could not lay down for fear of suffocation, propped up in his chair day and night;—the cold water system saved his life, made a man of him again, and, although sixty-seven years of age, he can undergo more fatigue than men not half his years;—he is a wonderful man;—hunts his own hounds *himself* four days a week, and the huntsman the other two, though he is never absent from them."

6. IN SCROPHULA AND IN GOUT AND RHEUMATISM : This treatment is often useful. But the public ought not to believe the glowing statements found in books of Hydropathy, which commonly puff' it up as infallible. I know from ample experience that, like all other human means, it is very fallible, and those who make assertions to

the contrary are not worthy of the least confidence or credit. But it is, nevertheless, a valuable auxiliary to medical practice, and as such I sanction it when carefully employed by professional men. The person who introduced Hydropathy into this kingdom, (R. Claridge), was (after his return from Grafenberg) constrained to ask my advice for the cure of a very troublesome complaint, from which his favourite "*Cold-water Cure*," could not deliver him! He was sadly annoyed by an eruption and ulceration about the corners of his mouth, together with a huskiness and uneasiness every morning in his throat and bronchia, causing a sensation as if he had taken cold. His acquaintance rallied him on the extraordinary powers of his "*Cold-water Cure,*" and cried out— "*Hydropath, cure thyself;*" but this he could not do, notwithstanding the very liberal use of the fluid he extolled as a panacea and caustic to boot. He was unwillingly, but not unavailingly, driven into the arms of the physician. We were convinced that the same medical means would probably deliver him at once both from the disorder of the skin and that of the bronchia; and sarsaparilla accordingly cured him perfectly within six weeks. So much for the efficacy of physic.

N.B. The lamp bath so often employed at certain Water-cure Establishments is extremely debilitating. It is often very injurious, and I warn my readers to beware of it. Sweating by exercise followed by packing in blankets is far better.

INDEX